THE ROUGH GUIDE TO

Andalucía

written and researched by

Geoff Garvey and Mark Ellingham

with additional contributions by

Pam Lalonde, Pau Sandham, Hanneke Sanou and Chris Stewart

ROUGH GUIDES

roughguides.com

Contents

OPPOSITE MATADOR POSTER, SEVILLE **PREVIOUS PAGE** FARMER DRINKING WINE, OLVERA

Introduction to
Andalucía

Andalucía is the southernmost territory of Spain and the part of the Iberian peninsula that is most quintessentially Spanish. The popular image of Spain as a land of bullfights, flamenco, sherry and ruined castles derives from this spectacularly beautiful region. The influences that have washed over Andalucía since the first paintings were etched on cave walls here more than 25,000 years ago are many – Phoenicians, Carthaginians, Greeks, Romans, Visigoths and Vandals all came and left their mark. And the most influential invaders of all, the Moors, who ruled the region for seven centuries and named it *al-Andalus*, have left an enduring imprint on Andalucian culture and customs.

The heartland of Andalucía is the fertile valley of the mighty **Río Guadalquivir**, flowing across the region from its source in the Cazorla mountains in the northeast through the magnificent cities of Córdoba and Seville, before draining into the marshes and wetlands of the Doñana National Park and the Gulf of Cádiz. North of this great artery rise the undulating hills of the **Sierra Morena**, from where was gouged the mineral wealth – silver, lead and tin – sought by successive waves of invaders from Phoenicians to Romans. The **Moors**, who arrived in the eighth century, were more interested in harvesting Andalucía's natural wealth and turned the region into an orchard rich in olives, citrus fruits, almonds, saffron, figs and vines – still the major products of the land today. In 1492 the Christian reconquest, after centuries of struggle, finally succeeded in wresting Spain from its Moorish occupiers, the victors symbolically planting their flags on the towers of the Alhambra, the emblematic monument of Andalucía.

The **Moorish legacy** is the most striking feature of Andalucía today, not only in the dazzling historical monuments such as those of Seville, Córdoba and Granada but also in the whitewashed houses of many of its smaller medieval towns such as Ronda or the flat-roofed villages of Las Alpujarras. The Moorish love of water is to be seen in the pleasure gardens of the Alhambra, and the typical Andalucian patio – tiled

ABOVE PUENTE NUEVO, RONDA **RIGHT** ALMONASTER LA REAL

plant-bedecked courtyards often with a central fountain – is another Arab legacy, as are the ubiquitous wrought-iron window grilles which lend character to any village street. The dances and music of **flamenco**, whilst probably not of Moorish origin, display the soul of Andalucía and can be an electrifying spectacle when dancers in brilliantly coloured dresses drill their heels into the floorboards in a frenzy of emotion or, in *cante jondo* (deep song), turn the art form into a blues-style lament. The Muslim influence on speech and vocabulary, a stoical fatalism in the face of adversity, and an obsession with the drama of death – publicly displayed in the spectacle of the bullfight – are also facets of the modern Andalucian character. Contrastingly, the *andaluzes* also love nothing more than a party, and the colour and sheer energy of the region's countless and legendary **fiestas** – always in traditional flamenco costume worn with pride – make them among the most exciting in the world. The **romerías**, wild and semi-religious pilgrimages to honour local saints at country shrines, are yet another excuse for a jamboree.

Despite the region's abundant natural wealth, poverty is widespread, a legacy of the repressive **latifundia** landholding system of large estates with absentee landlords. The Christian monarchs who ousted the Moorish farmers doled out the conquered land to the Church, the military orders and individual nobles. These new proprietors often had little interest in the land nor personal contact with those who worked their estates, often leaving an overseer in charge, and an atmosphere of resentment built up towards the wretched pay and miserable conditions that this system entailed.

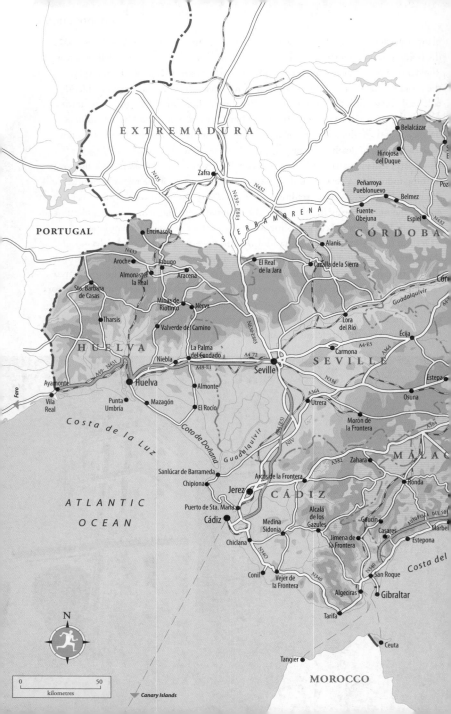

FACT FILE

• Andalucía's **land area** of 90,000 square kilometres is about the size of Ireland or Indiana. With a population of seven million, it is the second largest of Spain's seventeen autonomous regions, with its own administration and parliament based in the regional capital, Seville.

• Physically, Andalucía is a land of stark contrasts. To the west the **dunes** and **wetlands** of the Coto de Doñana National Park comprise the largest roadless area in western Europe, whilst in the east the province of Almería has Europe's only **desert**. The province of Granada has the Iberian peninsula's **highest peak**, the 3483m Mulhacén.

• Andalucía's **economy** is based on tourism and agriculture, the main products of which – sherry, olive oil and *jamón serrano* (cured ham) – are prized throughout Spain.

• Despite its sunny image Andalucía contains an area with the **highest rainfall** on the Spanish peninsula, the natural park of **Grazalema**.

• Love it or hate it, Andalucía is devoted to the **bullfight**. This multi-billion euro business employs thousands of workers both in the rings and on the ranches where the fearsome *toro bravo*, a beast descended from an ancient species of fighting bull, is raised. In the poverty-ridden backstreets of Seville and Málaga, the route to fame in the *corrida* is a fabulous temptation for young men (and sometimes women) and big name *toreros* are idolized and wealthy.

It is perhaps not surprising that many inhabitants emigrated to find work in northern Spain or abroad, or that anarchism found many converts among the desperate *braceros* (farmhands) of Andalucía before the Spanish Civil War. Two percent of the landowners still possess fifty percent of the land today, and in the 1960s alone a million Andalucians left their native region to seek a better life elsewhere.

Whilst life for many in the countryside remains hard, new industries, particularly tourism, have had a major impact on the region's **economy**. Apart from the petrochemical industry around Algeciras, mining in Huelva and aircraft manufacture in Sevilla, Andalucía has little heavy industry and those not employed in agriculture are usually working in fishing or tourism. One growth industry of recent years is servicing the population of mainly northern European emigrants who have come to the south of Spain to live, retire or do business. Now numbering close to half of a million, these expatriates have funded much building and development particularly along the coastal strip of the Costa del Sol.

Where to go

Andalucía's manageable size makes it easy to take in something of each of its elements – inland cities, extensive coastline and mountainous sierras – even on a brief visit. The region's eight provinces take their names from the **provincial capitals**, which are both compellingly individual cultural centres and vibrant cosmopolitan beehives in their own right. The most important is **Seville**, Andalucía's stylishly exuberant capital city, home of *Carmen* and all the clichés of the Spanish south with beautiful *barrios* (quarters), major Christian and Moorish monuments, fine museums and extraordinary **festivals** at Easter and at the April *feria*. Close behind comes **Granada** whose Alhambra palace has a fair claim to being the most sensual building

in Europe, whilst at **Córdoba**, the exquisite Mezquita, a former mosque, is another breathtakingly beautiful building left behind by the Moors. Coastal **Málaga** boasts a fine Moorish fort and a good museum stuffed with artworks by its most famous son, **Picasso**, and further down the coast sea-locked **Cádiz** is one of the most atmospheric cities of the south and Andalucía's seafood capital. Whilst they do not always attract the attention lavished on their more immediately appealing neighbours, the cities of **Huelva**, **Jaén** and **Almería** also all have sights well worthy of a visit. Inland, small-scale towns and villages, once grand, now hardly significant, are an Andalucian speciality. **Baeza** and **Úbeda** in Jaén are remarkable treasure-houses of Renaissance architecture, while **Ronda** and the **Pueblos Blancos** (White Towns) to the west are among the most picturesque hill villages in Spain.

Not that Andalucía is predominantly about cities and monuments. Few places in the world can boast such a wealth of **natural wonders** in so compact an area. The 400km-long Río Guadalquivir, which crosses and irrigates the region, reaches the sea at the dune-fringed beaches and *marismas* (wetlands/marshes) of the **Coto de Doñana National Park**, Europe's largest and most important wildlife sanctuary. To the east and towering above Granada are the peaks of the **Sierra Nevada National Park**, snowcapped for most of the year, and only thirty or so kilometres from the sweltering coastal beaches. Nestling in the folds of the same mountains are the valleys of the **Alpujarras**, a wildly picturesque region dotted with dozens of mountain villages,

Author picks

Our hard-travelling authors have visited every corner of Andalucia – from the cool mountains of the Sierra Nevada and the lush Doñana National Park to the sweltering deserts of Almería – to bring you some unique travel experiences. These are some of their own, personal favourites.

Scrumptious seafood Feasting on fish and crustaceans in sight of the sea is a tip-top treat. Three of the best places to do it are *La Ola* (p.547), *El Bigote* (p.213) and *La Escollera* (p.122).

Delightful villages They may not be famous, but they're perfectly picturesque – don't miss Zahara de la Sierra (p.231), Zuheros (p.404), Alhama de Granada (p.491) and Segura de la Sierra (p.446).

Brilliant beaches Among scores of candidates our votes go to the Playa Cuesta de Maneli (p.335), the Playa Camarinal (p.172) and Agua Amarga (p.548).

Classic hikes Put those boots to work on bracing mountain hikes in the Sierra Nevada, setting off from Capileira (p.506), Trevélez (p.507) and Pitres (p.507).

Aladdin's caves Among Andalucía's spectacular caves, standouts include the Gruta de las Maravillas (p.345), the Cueva de los Murciélagos (p.404), the Cueva de la Pileta (p.140) and the magnificent cave at Sorbas (p.560).

Tops for tapas Andalucía's tapas bars are the best in the Spain. Four tip-top bars include *Casa Balbino* (p.214), *Bar Maestro* (p.138), *Sociedad Plateros* (p.389) and *Casa Puga* (p.535).

¡Feria! Every city, town and village lets its hair down with an annual *feria* – Cádiz's *Carnaval* (p.184), Seville's *Feria de Abril* (p.301) and the *Feria de Málaga* (p.66) are all worth going out of your way for.

Fantastic forts If castles are your thing these won't disappoint – La Calahorra (p.379), Velez Blanco (p.555), Almería (p.527) and Baños de la Encina (p.416).

Our author recommendations don't end here. We've flagged up our favourite places – a perfectly sited hotel, an atmospheric café, a special restaurant – throughout the guide, highlighted with the ★ symbol.

LEFT WHITE STORKS **FROM TOP** LA OLA; PLAYA CUESTA DE MANELI; CÁDIZ CARNAVAL

ANCIENT ANDALUCÍA

Andalucía's rich and varied history has resulted in a great number of ancient sites, many unique in Europe. The dolmens at **Antequera** and the third-millenium BC settlement at **Los Millares** in Almería are remarkable vestiges from the prehistoric age. Roman sites are scattered across the region, but the excavated towns at **Baelo Claudia** near Tarifa and **Itálica** near Seville plus a fascinating necropolis at **Carmona** are worth making a special effort to get to. Two sites in superb locations are the newly unearthed Roman town of **Turobriga** near Aroche in the Sierra de Aracena, and **Ocuri**, another township atop a bluff to the north of Ubrique in Cádiz, while one sensational discovery of recent years is the Roman villa at **Almedinilla**, complete with a spectacular cascade feature in its dining room.

many of them little changed since Moorish times. Further east come the gulch-ridden badlands and lunar landscapes of Almería's **deserts**, sought out by film-makers and astronomers for the clearest skies in Europe.

Andalucía's rural areas are a paradise for hikers and naturalists and the Sierra Nevada and Las Alpujarras are excellent places for **trekking**, as are the densely wooded hills of the **Sierra de Cazorla** and the **Sierra de Morena** – including the latter's less well-known offshoot, the **Sierra de Aracena**, to the north of Huelva. The region also has a score of other *parques naturales* (natural parks), all located in areas of great natural beauty and detailed throughout the Guide.

On **the coast** it's often easy to despair. Extending to the west of **Málaga** is the **Costa del Sol**, Europe's most developed coastline, with its beaches hidden behind a remorseless density of concrete hotels and apartment complexes. This is Andalucía's summer playground, famous for its in-your-face brashness and the unlimited nightlife on offer at every resort. Despite the fact that many places such as **Torremolinos** have

ABOVE BAELO CLAUDIA RUINS, CÁDIZ PROVINCE

given themselves a thorough makeover with new theme parks and improved facilities, the Costa del Sol's appeal is not to everyone's taste. Thankfully though, even here the other Andalucía is still to be found if you're prepared to seek it out: go merely a few kilometres inland and you'll encounter the timeless Spain of high sierras, white villages and wholehearted country fiestas. Alternatively, travel further both east and west along the coast and you'll find some of the best beaches in all Spain: the **Costa de la Luz** to the west, where Atlantic breakers wash the white-sand strands of **Tarifa**, **Conil de la Frontera** and **Isla Cristina**; in the centre at the less frenzied resorts of **Nerja** and **Almuñecar** on the **Costa Tropical**; and to the east along the **Costa de Almería** where appealing resorts like **San José**, **Agua Amarga** and **Mojacár** all hark back to pre-Costa del Sol tranquillity.

Wherever you go in Andalucía you can't fail to notice the *andaluzes'* infectious enthusiasm for life. This is always ebulliently evident in the countless celebrations, **ferias** and **fiestas** that happen almost daily at one town or village or another throughout the summer months. But at other times too, and even in the smallest towns, there will always be good food, drink and a surprising range of nightlife and entertainment to be enjoyed. And there are few greater pleasures than joining the regulars at a local bar to wind down over a glass of **fino** (dry sherry from Jerez) while nibbling **tapas** – Andalucía's great titbit invention.

When to go

In terms of climate the question is mainly one of how much heat you can take. During the **summer** months of July and August temperatures of over 40°C (104°F) on the coast are normal and inland they can rise even higher in cities such as Seville, generally reckoned to be the hottest in Spain. The solution here is to follow the natives and get about in the relative cool of the mornings and late afternoons, finding somewhere shady to rest up as the city roasts in the midday furnace. The major resorts are busy in July and packed in August (the Spanish holiday month) when prices also are at their highest.

Better times to visit are the **spring** months of April, May and early June when lower temperatures combine with a greener landscape awash with wild flowers. **Autumn** is good, too, although by late October much of the coastal landscape looks parched and the resorts have begun to wind down; in hilly and mountainous areas, however, such as the sierras of Cazorla, Nevada and Aracena and the high valleys of Las Alpujarras, the splendours of autumn can be especially scenic. The **winter** months – particularly December and January – can often be dismal and wet as well as cold at high altitude, although the past decade, when the extended drought of the 1990s was followed by some unusually wet winters, has tended to throw the normal weather patterns into confusion. The winter, of course, is a good time to visit the museums and monuments of Seville, Málaga, Córdoba and Granada when they are far less crowded and – should you be lucky with the weather – the cities themselves can look wonderful, too. The desert province of Almería sees only one day of rain a year on average and in winter has many days of perfect crystal visibility.

27

things not to miss

It's not possible to see everything Andalucía has to offer in one trip – and we don't suggest you try. What follows, in no particular order, is a selection of the region's highlights, including outstanding buildings and natural wonders, vibrant festivals and delicious food. Each entry has a page reference to take you straight into the Guide, where you can find out more.

1 SEVILLE CATHEDRAL
Page 256

The world's largest Gothic church is a treasure house full of artistic riches. Its astonishingly beautiful Moorish minaret, the Giralda, is now its bell-tower, and can be climbed for a stunning view.

2 RONDA
Page 129

Ringed by mountains and perched astride the yawning El Tajo gorge, irresistible Ronda is one of the most dramatically sited towns in Andalucía.

3 HIKING
Pages 495 & 542

Andalucía is prime hiking territory. There are great walks to be had in the Sierra Nevada National Park and in the region's 24 natural parks, including the Cabo de Gata in Almería.

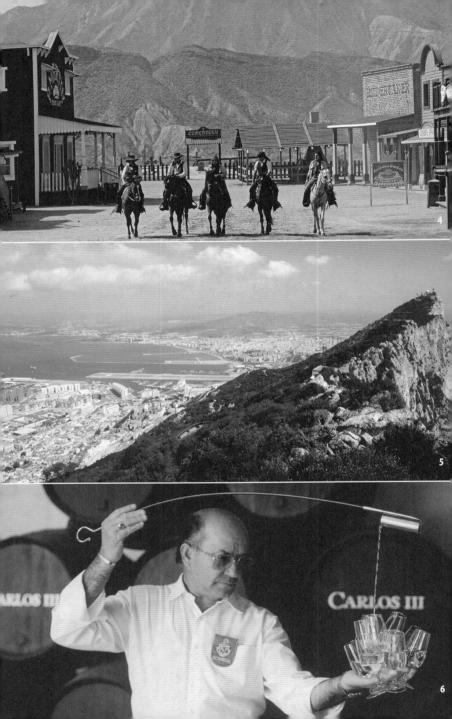

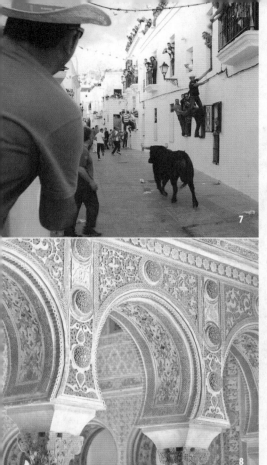

4 MINI HOLLYWOOD
Page 557

Clint Eastwood, Yul Brynner and Steve McQueen all faced gunfighters on the streets of Mini Hollywood in the Almerian desert, where the film sets of many famous westerns are preserved.

5 GIBRALTAR
Page 151

Beneath a towering rock, this colonial hangover with its pubs, sterling currency and Barbary apes makes a bizarre contrast with the rest of Andalucía.

6 SHERRY
Page 196

Andalucía's great wine comes from the "sherry triangle" towns of Jerez, El Puerto de Santa María and Sanlúcar de Barrameda, each with plenty of *bodegas* to visit.

7 ENCIERRO
Page 229

No village fiesta is complete without an *encierro*, when a fierce *toro bravo* roams the streets looking for an encounter with anyone who thinks they're brave enough.

8 ALCÁZAR, SEVILLE
Page 263

This fabulous Mudéjar palace, with enchanting gardens and dazzling artesonado ceilings, tiles and stuccowork, is one of the glories of the city.

9 ALHAMBRA, GRANADA
Page 460

One of the most sensual palaces ever built, the magical Alhambra is the pinnacle of Moorish architectural splendour in Spain.

10 MEZQUITA, CÓRDOBA
Page 371

Nothing can prepare you for the beauty of Córdoba's medieval mosque, one of the greatest Islamic buildings of all time.

 11 PARQUE NACIONAL DE COTO DE DOÑANA
Page 330

The vast wilderness of Spain's biggest wildlife reserve is home to exotic flamingos, imperial eagles and the endangered Spanish lynx.

 12 CABO DE GATA, ALMERÍA
Page 542

The Cabo de Gata natural park is famous for its rugged coastline, salt marshes and birdlife including storks, egrets and magnificent pink flamingos.

 13 FLAMENCO
Page 582

The soul of Andalucía, flamenco dance, music and song express the *alegría y dolor* (happiness and pain) of *andaluz* life.

14 THE ALBAICÍN, GRANADA
Page 470

Granada's atmospheric old Moorish quarter stands on the Sacromonte hill. Its sinuous alleys and cobblestoned streets are a delight to explore.

15 LAS ALPUJARRAS
Page 497

Ancient cobble-streeted villages are situated in a dramatically beautiful area of woodland and gushing mountain streams.

10

11

16 TAPAS BARS
Page 37

Dine Andalucían style, sampling plates of delicious tapas in a variety of atmospheric bars.

17 SIERRA DE GRAZALEMA
Page 227

The pretty white village of Grazalema lends its name to the surrounding *parque natural*, where soaring limestone peaks are swathed in forests of oak and fir.

18 MUSEO BELLAS ARTES, SEVILLE
Page 273

An eighteenth-century former convent provides a magnificent setting for Seville's fine arts museum, filled with major works.

19 PARQUE NATURAL SIERRA DE CAZORLA
Page 442

Andalucía's largest natural park is a vast area of soaring peaks and forested valleys inhabited by a feast of wildlife. Hilltop Segura de la Sierra is its most dramatically sited village.

20 CÁDIZ
Page 181

Steeped in history, sealocked Cádiz is one of the great cities of the Spanish south and serves up the best seafood in Andalucía.

21 EL ROCÍO
Page 333

On the edge of the Doñana National Park and surrounded by wetlands, this village's church holds a venerated image of the Virgin, the focus for one of the most extraordinary pilgrimages in Spain.

22 MEDINA AZAHARA
Page 390

The ruins of Caliph Abd ar-Rahman III's palace-city, named after his favourite wife, az-Zahra, evoke the splendour of the Cordoban caliphate.

24

25

26

27

Itineraries

Whether you want to take in a few of the major high points, feast on Andalucía's best culinary treats or focus your trip on some truly special places to stay, these itineraries – each of which also leads you through some of the region's most dramatic scenery – will lead the way. You'll need a couple of weeks to cover each route in detail, but it's possible to cover part of one in a week or so, perhaps mixing and matching it with sections of the others.

THE BEST OF ANDALUCÍA

❶ Málaga As a major transport hub, Málaga is the obvious place to start, but it's also worth lingering for a day to enjoy this vibrant coastal city. **See p.60**

❷ Ronda Sited astride a towering gorge is the queen of Andalucía's white towns. **See p.129**

❸ Seville The essence of all things *andaluz*, with a stunning cathedral, Moorish Alcázar and atmospheric old quarter. **See p.252**

❹ Córdoba A must-see destination, featuring one of the world's greatest Moorish buildings, the Mezquita, at its heart. **See p.370**

❺ Baeza and Úbeda These twin Renaissance architectural jewels are filled with a wealth of monuments in honey-tinted stone. **See p.426 & 431**

❻ Cazorla Natural Park A stunning array of wildlife inhabits the rugged mountains, gorges and forested valleys of Cazorla. **See p.442**

❼ Granada Overlooked by the seductive Alhambra, the historic city of Granada is one of Spain's most compelling attractions. **See p.456**

❽ Almuñécar The Costa Tropical's main resort has great beaches and plenty of places to eat, drink and dance the night away. **See p.538**

A TASTE OF ANDALUCÍA

❶ Villaluenga del Rosario This Cádiz mountain village is famous for its prize-winning goat's milk cheeses. **See p.234**

❷ Jerez The home of fino and brandy, where you can stop off to visit a bodega, taste their blends and buy some to take home. **See p.214**

❸ Jabugo The sensational and incomparable taste of *jamón de bellota* can be sampled at producers' outlets in the village. **See p.357**

❹ Rute This pleasant country town is famed throughout Spain for its anís (aniseed liqueur); sample it at *Bodega Machequita*. **See p.399**

❺ Baena Córdoba province's olive oil has been prized since Roman times – you can taste why at the Núñez de Prado mill. **See p.402**

❻ Segura de la Sierra The Sierra de Cazorla's most stunningly sited village, clinging to a hilltop, produces another famed olive oil with its own *denominación de origen*. **See p.446**

❼ Trevélez Tucked away in the mountains, the highest village in Spain is the home of Granada province's famed *jamón de Trevélez*. **See p.507**

❽ Lanjarón The mineral springs here have attracted cure seekers since ancient times – at the village's spa you can taste the waters straight from the mountain. **See p.500**

ABOVE THE ALHAMBRA, GRANADA

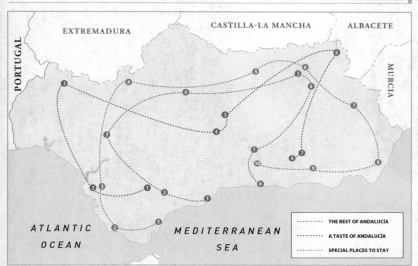

SPECIAL PLACES TO STAY

❶ Convento la Almoraima, Castellar de la Frontera. Just above the Bay of Algeciras, this is a magical hotel housed inside a seventeenth-century convent with a stunning patio and imposing Florentine tower. **See p.126**

❷ La Casa del Califa, Vejer de la Frontera. Reflecting the town's Moorish origins, the enchanting *Califa* occupies a partly Moorish house and has magnificent views towards the coast far below. **See p.176**

❸ La Casa Grande, Arcos de la Frontera. Perched on a clifftop, this former *casa señorial* has a spectacular columned patio and sensational views across the *vega* from a terrace bar. **See p.244**

❹ Hospedería La Cartuja, Cazalla de la Sierra. The gatehouse of a former Carthusian monastery has been transformed into a charming hotel, while the evocative ruin of the fifteenth-century monastery behind contains an art gallery. **See p.361**

❺ Los Pinos Andújar. Secreted away in the densely wooded Parque Natural Sierra de Andújar – home to the threatened Iberian lynx – this is a very pleasant *hotel rural* with villas

arranged around a pool and plenty of good hiking nearby. **See p.416**

❻ Palacio de la Rambla, Ubeda. This elegant Renaissance *casa palacio* is the last word in understated taste, furnished with artworks and featuring a dreamy patio. **See p.436**

❼ Cuevas de Orce, Orce. A wonderful cave-hotel where you can live the troglodyte life for a night or two. **See p.557**

❽ Hotel Rodalquilar, Rodalquilar. In a former gold mining village in Almería's desert, this modern spa-inn is focused on a sunken courtyard with lofty palms and makes a great base to explore a dramatic gulch-riven landscape. **See p.547**

❾ Alquería de Morayma, Cadiar. The *cortijo* (farmhouse) of an extensive estate is now a superb hotel. Watch its organic farm in action, producing the wine, cheese and olive oil served in its restaurant. **See p.512**

❿ La Seguiriya, Alhama de Granada. The amiable proprietors – he a former flamenco singer, she a wonderful chef – make a stay in this charming hotel-restaurant very special – the perfect end to any Andalucía trip. **See p.494**

SEMANA SANTA

Basics

Getting there

Flying is the quickest way of getting to Andalucía, with by far the widest choice of routes being from the UK and Ireland. Málaga – which now has direct flights from New York – is Andalucía's busiest airport, though the summer holiday trade to the areas beyond the costas, and the rapid growth of European budget airlines, has opened up regional airports right across the region from Seville and Jerez in the west to Granada and Almería in the east. It's also possible to take the train from the UK to Andalucía, and should you want to drive (a bit more of an adventure) there are several routes.

Air, train and ferry fares are seasonal, at their highest in summer (June to end Sept) and around Christmas/New Year and Easter week. You should always book as far in advance as possible to get the best deals.

Flights from the UK and Ireland

Flight time to Andalucía is two to three hours, depending on the route, and usually the cheapest flights are with the no-frills **budget airlines** such as bmibaby (W bmibaby.com), easyJet (W easyjet.com) and Ryanair (W ryanair.com), who between them fly from over twenty regional UK and Irish airports direct to destinations all over Andalucía. London flights tend to depart from Stansted or Luton; other budget airlines, including Jet2 (from Leeds/Bradford, Manchester, Newcastle, Blackpool and Edinburgh; W jet2.com) or flybe (from Manchester, Southampton, Belfast, Glasgow, Dublin and six other UK airports; W flybe.com), concentrate on flights out of particular British regions, while easyJet also flies out of Belfast. **Fares** for flights on all routes start at around £9.99 each way, or sometimes (depending on the airline) even free with just the (not inconsiderable) taxes to pay. However, book last minute in the summer and you can expect to pay considerably more, up to £100 each way depending on the route.

For flights to the **Costa del Sol**, you can also check the websites of holiday and charter companies such as Monarch (W flymonarch.com), First Choice (W firstchoice.co.uk), Thomas Cook (W flythomascook.com) and Thomson (W thomson fly.com). You might not get the rock-bottom deals of the budget airlines, as schedules and prices are geared towards the summer holiday season, but flights depart from regional airports right around the UK.

The widest range of **scheduled flights** is with the now-merged Iberia (W iberia.com) and British Airways (W ba.com), with direct services from London Gatwick or Heathrow to Málaga and Seville. You'll also be able to arrange add-on connections to London from regional UK airports such as Manchester or Newcastle or from Scotland. Special offers mean prices start at around £100 return, though again a typical late-booking summer rate will be far higher.

From Ireland, you can fly with Iberia from Dublin to Madrid, or with Aer Lingus (W aerlingus.com) from Dublin or Cork to up to eight Spanish airports (including Málaga). Ryanair also connects Dublin and Shannon with Málaga, plus Seville and Almería. Prices are highly flexible, starting at around €40 each way, though these rise sharply for last-minute bookings or to popular summer destinations.

Flights from the US and Canada

The widest choice of scheduled flights **from the United States** to Spain is with Iberia (W iberia.com), which flies direct, non-stop from New York to Madrid or Barcelona, and from Miami and Chicago to Madrid. Journey time (typically overnight) is between 7hr 10min and 8hr 30min, depending on the route. Fares start at around $1000 return. The advantage of flying with Iberia is that it offers connecting flights to six airports throughout Andalucía, which can be very good value if booked with your transatlantic flight. Other airlines offering

---

A BETTER KIND OF TRAVEL

At Rough Guides we are passionately committed to travel. We feel that travelling is the best way to understand the world we live in and the people we share it with – plus tourism has brought a great deal of benefit to developing economies around the world over the last few decades. But the growth in tourism has also damaged some places irreparably, and climate change is exacerbated by most forms of transport, especially flying. All Rough Guides' trips are carbon-offset, and every year we donate money to a variety of charities devoted to combating the effects of climate change.

Spanish routes (some on a code-share basis with Iberia or other airlines), include American Airlines (@aa.com), Continental (@continental.com), Spanair (@spanair.com) and United (@united.com). Delta (@delta.com) also offers a **direct flight to Málaga** from New York four days a week.

You can also fly to Spain with airlines such as Air France, KLM, Lufthansa, TAP or British Airways, which tend to fly via their respective European hubs – in which case, you can add 3 to 4 hours to your total travel time, depending on the connection.

From Canada, there's a direct, non-stop route from Toronto to Madrid with Air Canada (@air canada.com), with onward connections across Spain with their partner Spanair. Or fly with one of the major European airlines via their respective hubs – fares in all cases start from Can\$1100 return.

Flights from Australia, New Zealand and South Africa

There are no direct flights to Spain **from Australia or New Zealand**, but many airlines offer through-tickets with their partners via their European or Asian hubs. Flights via Asia are generally the cheaper option, but fares don't vary as much between airlines as you might think, and in the end you'll be basing your choice on things like flight timings, routes and possible stop-offs on the way. If you're seeing Spain as part of a wider European trip, you might want to aim first for the UK, since there's a wide choice of cheap flights to Spain once there. Or consider a Round-the-World fare, with most basic options able to offer Madrid or Barcelona as standard stopovers.

From **South Africa**, there are direct flights with Iberia (@iberia.com) from Johannesburg to Madrid, which take around 10 hours.

Package holidays, tours and city breaks

The basic, mass-market **package holidays** to the traditional resorts on the Costa del Sol and elsewhere are not to everyone's taste, but bargains can be found online or at any UK high-street travel agent, from as little as £99 for a seven-night flight-and-hotel package. There are often really good deals for families, either in hotels or in self-catering apartments, though the time of year you visit can increase prices significantly (school holidays are always most expensive).

A huge number of **specialist tour operators** offer a wider range of **activity holidays** or tours,

from hiking in the Alpujarras to touring the artistic highlights of Andalucía. We've given a flavour of what's available in the reviews at the end of this section, but the options are almost endless. Prices vary wildly depending on the quality of accommodation offered and whether the tours are fully inclusive or not. Many cycle or hiking tours, for example, can either be guided or done on a more independent (and cheaper) self-guided basis. Spanish-based tour operators offer some of the more interesting, off-the-beaten-track options (but for these you'll usually have to arrange your own flights to Spain), while some foreign-based operators also tend to quote for their holidays exclusive of airfares.

Popular **city break** destinations include Seville, Córdoba and Granada. UK prices start at around £200 for three-day (two-night) breaks, including return flights, airport transfer and B&B in a centrally located one-, two- or three-star hotel. Adding extra nights or upgrading your hotel is possible, too, usually at a fairly reasonable cost. The bigger US operators, such as American Express and Delta Vacations, can also easily organize short city breaks to Spain on a flight-and-hotel basis, while from Australia Iberian specialist Ibertours (@ibertours .com.au) can arrange two- or three-night packages in most Spanish cities.

Other package deals worth considering are **fly-drive** offers, where you'll get a flight, accommodation and car rental arranged through your tour operator. Some companies specialize in villas and apartments, or off-the-beaten-track farmhouses and the like, while on other holiday packages you can tour the country's historic *paradores*, with car rental included.

Specialist tour operators

BACKPACKER TRAVEL

Busabout UK ☎ 0845 0267 514, @ busabout.com. The European backpacker bus service also offers a seven-day Spain/Portugal bus tour (basically Andalucía and the Portuguese Algarve; from £449); prices include hostel accommodation, guides, transport, surf lessons and the like, all aimed at a young, party crowd.

BIRDWATCHING

Andalucian Guides Spain @ andalucianguides.com. Guided birdwatching trips in Cádiz by the week or the day. Day-trips (8hr) cost around €175 for two or less depending on the number of people.
Limosa Holidays UK ☎ 01263 578 143, @ limosaholidays .co.uk. Birdwatching tours to the Straits of Gibraltar. See the great spring and autumn migrations accompanied by knowledgeable guides.

CYCLING

Bravobike Spain ☎ 917 582 945, ⓦ www.bravobike.com.
A variety of cycle tours across the region. Prices range from €30 for a
short day trip to €840 per week self-guided, and from €1000 guided.

Easy Rider Tours US ☎ 1 800 488 8332, ⓦ easyridertours.com.
Guided cycling and sightseeing tours in Andalucía (and elsewhere). One
week-long trip takes in the White Towns. Tours are all-inclusive and fully
supported, and cost from around $3000 for a week, airfares extra.

Explore! UK ☎ 0845 013 0537, ⓦ explore.co.uk. Walking and
cycling holidays in Axarquía and Alpujarras.

Iberocycle Spain ☎ 942 581 085, ⓦ iberocycle.com. An
English-run, Spain-based company specializing in supported or
self-guided cycling tours, offering White Towns, Moorish villages and
Sierra de Aracena tours. Seven-night trips from around €940.

DANCE

Club Dance Holidays UK ☎ 020 7099 4816, ⓦ clubdance
holidays.com. Flamenco, salsa and Argentinian tango holiday courses in
Seville, Córdoba and Granada. From £500 per week including tuition but
excluding flights.

FOOD AND DRINK

Arblaster & Clarke UK ☎ 01730 263 111, ⓦ arblasterandclarke
.com. The most notable wine-tour specialist, with quality trips to all of
Spain's wine-producing regions, including a tour of bodegas in the sherry
triangle. Around £1500 for a five-night all-included trip.

A Taste of Spain Spain ☎ 856 079 626, ⓦ atasteofspain.com.
Gourmet Iberian culinary tours focusing on fino in Jerez, *jamón serrano*
in Jabugo and olive oil in the provinces of Córdoba and Jaén, with
tastings, meals and cookery lessons. Prices for six nights, all-inclusive,
start at €2300.

Winetrails UK ☎ 01306 712 111, ⓦ winetrails.co.uk. Wine-based
tours of Andalucía.

HISTORY, ART AND CULTURE

Abercrombie and Kent UK ☎ 0845 618 2203, ⓦ abercrombie
andkent.co.uk; US ☎ 1 800 554 7016, ⓦ abercrombiekent.com.
Pricey, upmarket independent or fully escorted tours, taking in cities
like Córdoba, Granada and Seville, including a private guide for
monument visits.

Kirker Travel UK ☎ 020 7593 1899, ⓦ kirkerholidays.com. Short
breaks and holiday packages in Andalucían towns and cities. A six-night
tour of Moorish Seville, Córdoba and Granada costs £1448 per person
including flights.

Martin Randall Travel UK ☎ 020 8742 3355, ⓦ martinrandall
.com. Small-group cultural tours to Seville, Granada, Córdoba and
elsewhere, led by experts on art, archeology or music. Several departures
a year on various trips and themes. From around £1800 for seven nights.

HORSERIDING

Fantasia Adventure Holidays Spain ☎ 610 943 685,
ⓦ fantasiaadventureholidays.com. British-run company offering
riding breaks on the Costa de la Luz, from full-board weekends to
week-long holidays (from £795 excluding flights).

Rustic Blue Spain ☎ 958 763 381, ⓦ rusticblue.com.
Alpujarras-based company (see p.510) specializing in rural and activity
holidays including horse trekking.

PAINTING

Andalucian Painting Holidays UK ☎ 01382 553 736,
ⓦ langeart.co.uk. Painting holidays led by a Scottish artist based in the
pretty Málaga hill village of Ojén.

SURFING

Nomadsurfers Spain ☎ 911 895 146, ⓦ nomadsurfers.com.
Tarifa-based kitesurf courses costing from €505 a week (including
tuition and accommodation) or from €290 for a five-day course
(tuition only).

Surf Spain UK ☎ 01691 648 514, ⓦ surfspain.co.uk. Surf
camps, short-break surfing-course holidays based at El Palmar on
the Costa de la Luz, with a typical seven-night break costing from
£399 per person (including accommodation and tuition but
excluding flights).

WALKING, CYCLING AND ADVENTURE

Adventure Center US ☎ 1 800 228 8747, ⓦ adventurecenter
.com. Active vacations in Andalucía and the Sierra Nevada.

Exodus Travels UK ☎ 020 8675 5550, ⓦ exodus.co.uk. Walking
and cycling in Andalucía, as well as cultural and sightseeing trips. There's
a wide range of options, at all prices, but a typical week's walking or
cycling will cost around £890 including flights.

Inntravel UK ☎ 01653 617 945, ⓦ inntravel.co.uk. Experienced and
reliable company offering self-guided cycling tours (Sierra de Grazalema
and Ronda) and walking tours (Sierras de Aracena and Grazalema, Las
Alpujarras, Cabo de Gata and more) on which your baggage is moved to
the next destination. A week's walking in the Alpujarras starts at £598
(excluding airfares).

Olé Spain US ☎ 1 888 869 7156, ⓦ olespain.com. Small-group
cultural walking tours in Seville, Córdoba and Granada provinces with a
mixture of city sightseeing and open-country trekking. Prices start at
$3300 for an eight-day tour (excluding airfares).

Ramblers Worldwide Holidays UK ☎ 01707 331 133,
ⓦ ramblersholidays.co.uk. Long-established walking tour operator,
offering walking and hiking holidays throughout Spain including tours of
classical Andalucía. From around £760 for an all-inclusive week in the
Sierra Nevada.

Sherpa Expeditions UK ☎ 020 8577 2717, ⓦ sherpa-walking
-holidays.co.uk. Trekking in the Sierra Nevada and the Alpujarras.

Spirit of Adventure UK ☎ 01822 880 277, ⓦ spirit-of
-adventure.com. Multi-activity holidays throughout Spain, including a
week's trekking based in the Sierra de Grazalema. From £450 per person,
excluding flights.

WalkAlpujarra Spain Spain ☎ 958 858 580, ⓦ walkalpujarra
.com. Founded by Alpujarras-based writer and walking guide Jeremy
Rabjohns, this company offers guided or self-led hikes (from one day
upwards) with maps and information provided and baggage moved to
next day's destination. Seven nights from €420 based on two sharing
(excluding flights). Also offers painting holidays.

Trains

Travelling **by train from the UK to Andalucía** is a viable – and fun – option, with a total journey time from London of around 20 hours. You take the afternoon **Eurostar** (W eurostar.com) from London St Pancras International to Paris and change there for the comfortable overnight "train-hotel" for Madrid, followed by a lightning-fast trip to Seville or Málaga on the superlative new AVE high-speed train in a little over two hours. **Fares** start at £69 return for the Eurostar to Paris (through-tickets are available from UK towns and cities), plus £130 return for the cheapest sleeper accommodation on the overnight train. The cheapest pre-booked one-way ticket for the AVE high-speed train from Madrid to Seville or Málaga costs around €85 (no discount for return). You'll have to book well in advance on all services to get the lowest prices. There are alternative daytime services through France and Spain, though they don't save you any money.

The best first stop for information about train travel to Spain is the excellent **W seat61.com**, which provides full route, ticket, timetable and contact information. You can book the whole journey **online** with Rail Europe (W raileurope. co.uk) or contact a specialist **rail agent** such as Ffestiniog Travel (W ffestiniogtravel.co.uk) or the Spanish Rail Service (W spanish-rail.co.uk). If you live outside the UK, you can book Eurostar and "train-hotel" tickets through the websites W raileurope.com, W raileurope.ca and W rail europe.com.au. These agencies can also advise about **rail passes** (principally InterRail and Eurail), which have to be bought before leaving home (see opposite).

Buses

You can reach most major cities in Andalucía by bus from the UK with **Eurolines** services (W eurolines.co.uk). The main routes are from London (though add-on fares are available from any British city) to Barcelona (25hr), Madrid (27hr) and Valencia (30hr), with connections to Andalucía adding an additional 5 to 6 hours, but it's a long time to spend cooped up in a bus. Standard return fares are around £145–192 to Málaga, and £122–160 to Seville, depending upon season and when booked. There are advance deals and special offers and it's always cheapest to book online.

Driving to Spain

Provided you're not in a hurry, **driving to Spain** from the UK is an interesting way to get there, but with fuel, toll and overnight costs it doesn't compare in terms of price with flying or taking the train. It's about 2500km from London to Málaga, for example, which, not including stops, takes almost two full days to drive.

Many people use the conventional **cross-Channel ferry links**, principally Dover–Calais, though services to Brittany or Normandy might be more convenient depending on where you live (and they cut out the trek around Paris). However, the quickest way of crossing the Channel is to use the **Eurotunnel** (W eurotunnel.com), which operates drive-on-drive-off shuttle trains between Folkestone and Calais/Coquelles. The 24-hour service runs every 20 minutes throughout the day; though you can just turn up, booking is advised, especially at weekends and in the summer holidays, or if you want the best deals (from £53 one way).

The best way to cut driving time is to use either of the direct **UK–Spain ferry crossings**. Brittany Ferries (W brittany-ferries.co.uk) operates a car and passenger ferry from Portsmouth and **Plymouth to Santander** in Cantabria (3 weekly; 20–24hr), or **Bilbao** in the Basque country (2 weekly; 24hr). Fares start at around £200 return per person (includes the car), but it costs significantly more in summer, particularly August – it's cheaper for foot-passengers, though everyone has to book some form of seating or cabin accommodation. From the Basque country to the northern border of Andalucía is a journey of around 650km or a day's drive.

Any ferry company or travel agent can supply up-to-date schedules and ticket information, or you can consult the encyclopedic W directferries .com, which has details about, and links to, every European ferry service.

Getting around

Most of Andalucía is well covered by public transport. The rail network reaches all the provincial capitals and the main towns along the inter-city lines and high-speed trains connect the cities of Málaga and Seville with Madrid. Inter-city bus services are often more frequent, cheaper and just as fast as the regular trains, and will usually take you closer to your destination, as some train stations

are a few kilometres from the town or village they serve. Driving, meanwhile, will give you the freedom to head away from the major tourist routes and take in some of the spectacular scenery at your own pace.

One important point to remember is that all public transport, and the bus service especially, is drastically reduced on **Sundays and public holidays** – don't even consider travelling to out-of-the-way places on these days. The words to look out for on timetables are *diario* (daily), *laborables* (workdays, including Sat), and *domingos y festivos* (Sun and public holidays).

By train

Andalucía's trains, operated by **RENFE** (☎902 320 320, ⓦrenfe.es), tend to be efficient and comfortable, and nearly always run on time. There's a confusing array of services, though the website has a useful English-language version on which you can check timetables and buy tickets with a credit card (printing them out at home before you travel).

Cercanías are local commuter trains in and around the major cities, while **media distancia** (regional) and **larga distancia** (long-distance) trains go under a bewildering number of names, including Intercity (IC), Regionales and Talgo services. These differ in terms of speed, service and number of stops, and you'll always pay more on the quickest routes (sometimes quite a lot more). The premier services are the high-speed trains, such as the expanding **AVE** (Alta Velocidad Española) network from Madrid to Seville and Málaga. The AVE trains have cut travelling times dramatically, with Madrid to Seville, for example, taking 2 hours 30 minutes compared with 6 to 9 hours on the slower trains. One great feature of Andalucía's train network is that it still takes in a wide variety of inviting rural destinations including the Sierra de Aracena, the Sierra Norte, the Serranía de Ronda, and the Parque Natural de los Alcornocales with many small rural stations set in the midst of scenic countryside.

Tickets and fares

Although you can just turn up at the station for short hops, **advance booking** is advisable for longer journeys between say, Seville and Granada or Almería and especially at weekends in summer or Spanish public holidays. Advance tickets can be bought at the stations between sixty days and five minutes before departure, but don't leave it to the last minute, as there are usually long queues (and often separate windows for the different types of train). Automatic **ticket machines** at main stations take some of the hassle out of queueing, or you can buy tickets at **travel agents** that display the RENFE sign – the cost is the same as at the station.

The best deals are always available **online** on the RENFE website, where "Web" and "Estrella" fares offer discounts of up to sixty percent on the full fares. Otherwise, **return fares** (*ida y vuelta*) are discounted by ten to twenty percent, depending on the service – you can buy a single, and so long as you show it when you buy the return, you'll still get the discount. There's also a whole range of other **discounted fares** of between 25 and 40 percent for those over 60 or under 26, the disabled, and children aged 4 to 11 years.

Actual fares vary wildly, but as an example, you'll pay around €20 one-way (10–20 percent discount for a return) on the regional service from Seville to Málaga (2hr 30min), while on the high-speed AVE service between Córdoba and Málaga (50min) you'll pay around €45 one-way with no discount for a return.

Rail passes

The major pan-European **rail passes** (InterRail and Eurail) are only worth considering if you're visiting Spain as part of a wider European tour. Both schemes also have single-country rail passes available, which might be better value depending on your Spanish itinerary. The **InterRail Spain Pass** (ⓦwww.interrailnet.com) is only available to European residents and allows three, four, six or eight days' train travel within one month, with under-26, second- and first-class versions available. Again, these really only become cost-effective if you're combining your stay in Andalucía with journeys to other parts of Spain. For anyone else, **Eurail** (ⓦraileurope.com) has various Spain passes available, typically offering three days' travel in two months, again in various classes. You can check current prices on the websites, but bear in mind that it often works out cheaper to buy individual tickets in Spain as you need them, and it's certainly more convenient to be free to choose long-distance buses on some routes. All passes have to be bought before you leave home, and you'll still be liable for supplements and seat reservations on long-distance and high-speed trains.

By bus

Buses will probably meet most of your transport needs, especially if you're venturing away from the larger towns and cities. Many smaller villages and rural areas are only accessible by bus, almost always originating in the capital of their province. Services are pretty reliable, whether it's the two-buses-a-day school or market run or the regular services between major cities (the latter often far more conveniently scheduled than the equivalent train services). **Fares** are very reasonable, too; Seville to Granada (2hr 45min) for example, costs around €20 or Málaga to Ronda (1hr 45min) €12. On inter-city runs, you'll usually be assigned a seat when you buy your ticket. Some destinations are served by more than one **bus company**, but main bus stations have posted timetables for all services and you can check timetables on the company websites; Alsa (Ⓦalsa.es) is one of the main companies with nationwide services, and has an English-language version of its website.

There are only a few cities in Andalucía (Seville and Granada, for example) where you'll need to use the **local bus** network. You'll also sometimes need to take a local bus out to a campsite or distant museum or monastery. Fares are very cheap – rarely more than €1.50.

By car

Andalucía's roads and highways are generally toll free but exceptions are the toll **autopista** (motorway) between Seville and Cádiz and the *Autopista del Sol* which passes all the major Costa del Sol resorts between Málaga and Estepona. The second-grade roads, **autovías**, often follow similar routes and in many respects resemble motorways, but their speed limits are lower. Locals tend to shy away from the toll routes, which are relatively expensive by local standards, but the lighter traffic encountered perhaps makes it a price worth paying for the visitor. You can usually pay with a credit card, although it would be wise to carry enough cash just in case. Toll roads are usually designated by an "AP" or "R" or the word "*peaje*".

You can pay by credit card (with proof of identity) at most petrol stations for **fuel** (*gasolina*), the main companies being Cepsa and Repsol. Unleaded petrol (*sin plomo*) comes in normal (95 octane) and super (98 octane) grades and diesel is referred to as *diesel* or *gasóleo*. Pumps are colour coded to avoid error: green for unleaded; red for leaded; yellow and black for diesel.

Rules and regulations

An EU **driver's licence** is sufficient if you want to drive in Spain. US, Canadian, Australian and New Zealand licences should also be enough, though you may want to get an International Driver's Licence as well, just to be on the safe side. If you are bringing your own car, you will need your vehicle registration and insurance papers – and check with your insurers that you are covered to drive the car abroad. It's also **compulsory** to carry two hazard triangles, reflective jackets in case of accident or breakdown, an official first-aid kit and a set of spare bulbs. Rear seatbelts are also compulsory, as are child seats for infants.

THE SPANISH DRIVING EXPERIENCE

If it's your first time out on a Spanish road, especially in one of the bigger cities, you could be forgiven for thinking you've stumbled upon the local chapter of Mad Max devotees, out for a burn-up. In fact, those wild-eyed, dangerously speeding, non-signalling, bumper-hogging, mobile-talking, horn-sounding road warriors are normal law-abiding Spanish citizens on their way to work. **Traffic lights** and **pedestrian crossings** in particular present a difficult conceptual challenge – if you are going to stop at either, make sure you give plenty of warning to avoid another vehicle running into the back of you, and keep an eye out for cars crossing your path who have jumped the lights. **Signposting** is universally poor (yes, *that* was the turn you wanted), even on main roads and highways, while joining and exiting **autopistas/autovías** can be particularly dangerous, as it's almost a point of honour not to let anyone in or out. Many of the worst **accidents** are on the N roads, which have only a single carriageway in each direction, so take particular care on these. Major roads are generally in good **condition**, though some minor and mountain roads can be rather hairy and are little more than dirt tracks in the more remote regions. Sheep, goats and cattle are also regular hazards. Having said all this, things are (slowly) improving and drivers are a bit more careful these days because of increased use of radar and speed controls and the introduction of a points system for infractions which (if you accumulate too many) can lead to a driving ban. The police are also setting up more **drink-driving** controls than before, though you have to remember that this is a country where it's considered a good idea to have bars in motorway service stations.

ANDALUCÍA'S FIVE BEST DRIVES

Colmenar to Málaga This 35km/45min drive from the Axarquía village of Colmenar (see p.97), known for its honey, descends through the Montes de Málaga natural park offering, in its latter stages, magnificent views over the Costa del Sol. Route: A7000.

Grazalema to Vejer A dramatic 130km/3hr drive from the gorgeous White Town of Grazalema (see p.226) through the spectacular Sierra de Grazalema and Alocornocales natural parks, the latter with Europe's largest cork oak forest, to the atmospheric Moorish hill-top town of Vejer (see p.174). Route: A2304 & A2228.

Valverde del Camino to Aracena One of the most striking drives in Andalucía is this 77km/1hr 15min journey from the small town of Valverde del Camino (see p.339) along the N435, turning off along the A461 to traverse the strange, forbidding landscape of the Río Tinto mining zone. This mineral-rich

panorama with fissured crags and glinting rivulets of ochre, rust and cadmium has been mined for five millennia. Route: N435 & A461.

Cazorla to Segura de la Sierra Starting out in the charming town of Cazorla (see p.438), this 90km/2hr 30min route through the densely forested Cazorla natural park – Andalucía's biggest – takes in the source of the Río Guadalquivir and finally climbs dizzily to the hilltop village of Segura de la Sierra (see p.446) with an impressive Moorish fort. Route: A319 & JA9118.

Lanjarón to Yegen Traversing the delightful wooded foothills of the Sierra Nevada mountain range, this 75km/2hr route visits many of the rustic villages of Las Alpujarras, starting at Lanjarón (see p.500) and ending up at the most famous of them all, Yegen (see p.514), the inspiration for Gerald Brenan's *South from Granada*. Route: A4132 & A4130.

The Spanish **drive on the right**, and **speed limits** are enforced throughout the country. On most *autopistas* it is 120kph, on the *autovia* 90kph, on minor roads 80kph or 90kph, and in towns and villages 50kph. Police have the power to fine drivers on the spot for speeding or any other transgressions (such as using a hand-held mobile phone while driving), and if you don't have any cash, they will escort you to the nearest cash machine and issue you with a receipt there and then. Failure to pay will result in your car being impounded until you do.

Parking

Parking can be a major pain in the neck, especially in big cities and old-town areas. Finding on-street parking spaces is often impossible, although if you can time your arrival with the start of the siesta (around 2pm, when everyone rushes home for lunch) you stand a better chance. Metered parking zones usually have stays limited to a couple of hours, though parking between 8pm and 8am, on Saturday afternoons and all day Sundays tends to be free. It's always worth double-checking street signs, or asking the locals, that you're allowed to park where you've just left your car, as any illegally parked vehicle will be promptly removed. If your car disappears off the street it is best to assume that it has been towed to the local pound, and enquiries in any hotel, government office or police station should produce the address. In cities it's probably best to pay extra for a hotel with parking or use a pay car

park, for which you'll need to budget anything from €12 to €20 a day. There's usually no problem finding on-street parking in villages, although even here things are more difficult than they used to be.

Car rental

Car rental is often cheapest arranged in advance through one of the large multinational agencies (Avis, Budget, Europcar, Hertz, for example), who charge from around £130/$200 a week for a two-door Ford Ka or Ford Fiesta, more for larger vehicles and in peak holiday periods. Local Spanish companies (such as Atesa; Ⓦ atesa.es) can sometimes offer better value for money, as can the online rental outfits easyCar (Ⓦ easycar.com) and Skycars (Ⓦ skycars.com), with high-season prices starting from around €25 per day for renting a small car in Andalucía. Reliable and competitive **Andalucía-based companies** include Málaga Car Hire (with pick-up and drop-off points throughout the region; Ⓦ malagacarhire.com), Malagacar (Ⓦ malagacar.com) and Need2Rent-a-Car (Ⓦ need torentacar.com) all offering a three-door small car for around €150 per week in high season. Naturally, out of high season rates fall substantially.

You'll need to be 21 or over (and have been driving for at least a year) to rent a car in Spain. It's essential to check that you have adequate **insurance cover** for your rental car, and that all visible damage on a car you're picking up is duly marked on the rental sheet. It's definitely worth considering paying the extra charge to reduce the "excess" payment levied for any damage, but these waiver charges (by the day) soon add up. However, you can avoid all **excess charges** in the event of damage by taking out an annual insurance policy (from around £38) with ⓦinsurance4carhire.com, which also covers windscreen and tyre damage.

By bike

Cycling is a great way to see parts of the region that might otherwise pass you by, though bear in mind that peninsular Spain is one of the most mountainous countries in Europe and Andalucía contains its two highest peaks. Added to punishing climbs, there are often searing high-summer temperatures with which to contend. However, don't be put off; pacing yourself and using the cooler hours of the day (after dawn and before dusk) can make for a highly enjoyable trip.

For serious cycle touring, you'll need your own bike and to be properly equipped. **Bike rental** is not common, save in resort areas or in tourist-oriented cities such as Seville, Córdoba or Granada, where you can expect to pay up to €20 a day – or around €25 for a half-day bike tour. In Seville tourists can also use the excellent Sevici bike hire scheme run by the city government. Although the Spanish themselves are keen sport cyclists, other facilities are practically nonexistent. Cycle paths, for example, are rare (again, Seville and Córdoba are exceptions), and cycling around most major Andalucian cities is a hair-raising, if not downright dangerous business.

Most airlines are happy to take bikes as ordinary **baggage**, though it's essential to check first, especially if you're flying with a budget airline, when extra charges may apply. Spanish bus drivers are reasonably amenable, and (space permitting) should let you throw your bicycle in with the baggage. Trains are more problematic, as there are specific trains, times and routes on which bikes are not allowed. As a rule, local trains are fine but high-speed trains are out, unless your bike is boxed up or you're travelling by overnight sleeper.

You should have no trouble finding bike shops in larger towns, and parts can often be found at auto repair shops or garages. On the road, cars tend to hoot before they pass, which can be alarming at first but is useful once you're used to it. On busier roads it's better not to ride two abreast as Spanish drivers (unused to cyclists) have frequently caused accidents and even fatalities when colliding with the cyclist on the outside. Finally, try not to leave your bike on the street overnight (especially in cities), even with a secure lock, as thieves view them as easy pickings.

Accommodation

There's a great variety of accommodation in Andalucía, ranging from humble family-run pensiones to five-star luxury hotels, often in dramatic historic buildings. The mainstay of the coastal resort is the typical beachfront holiday hotel, though renting an apartment or a villa gives you more freedom, while farm stays, village guesthouses and mountain inns are all increasingly popular possibilities.

In almost any town, you'll be able to get a no-frills double room in a *pensión* or *hostal* (both words describe small hotels) for around €40, sometimes even less, especially out in the sticks. As a rule, you can expect to pay upwards of €90 for a three-star city hotel in high season (less in small towns and country areas), around €120 for four-star and boutique places, and €150–200 for five-star hotels and historic *paradores*. However, the trend is bucked by Seville and Granada, in particular, and some coastal and resort areas, where hotel (but not *hostal*) rooms are often appreciably more expensive.

If you want to guarantee a room at a particular place, **advance reservations** are essential in major cities and resort areas at peak holiday, festival or convention times. Local festivals and annual events also tend to fill all available accommodation weeks in advance. Unlike most countries, you don't always pay more for a central location; indeed, the newer three- and four-star properties tend to be located more on the outskirts. **Families** will find that most places have rooms with three or even four beds at not a great deal more than the price for a double room; also extra beds for children can often be added to double rooms for little extra cost. However, **single travellers** often get a comparatively bad deal, and can end up paying sixty to eighty percent of the price of a double room. Accommodation prices are **seasonal**, but minimum and maximum rates should be displayed at reception. In high season on the coast (usually the month of Aug), some hotels only take bookings for a minimum of a week, while others also require at least a half-board stay. Note, however that high season isn't always summer – in the ski resorts of

ACCOMMODATION PRICES

We give a room price for all establishments reviewed in this guide. Unless otherwise stated, this represents the price for the **cheapest available double or twin room in high season** (ie Christmas/New Year, Easter, and June–Sept, though some local variations apply). Consequently, at other times of the year, or during special promotions, you'll often find a room for a lower price than that suggested. For **youth hostels** and anywhere else with **dorm beds**, we also give the per-person overnight rate. Note that **eight percent tax** (IVA) is added to all accommodation bills, which might not be specifically stated until it is time to pay, so always ask if you're uncertain.

the Sierra Nevada for example – and that inland cities such as Seville, Córdoba and Granada tend to have cheaper prices in August, when everyone heads for the coast. Be aware, too, that the Spanish love to build *puentes* (bridges) between a national or regional holiday that occurs on say, a Thursday or a Tuesday, and the weekend that follows or precedes it. The hotel trade treats these dates as "high-season" and not only are prices higher but accommodation in many places becomes tight.

Where possible, **website bookings** nearly always offer the best deals, especially with the larger hotel groups that have made big inroads into Spain – it's always worth checking *NH Hoteles* (Ⓦnh-hotels .com), *Accor/Ibis* (Ⓦaccorhotels.com) and *Sol Meliá* (Ⓦsolmelia.com) for current deals. Many hotels also use **specialist sites** to fill their rooms, especially in low season, and often you can find some real bargains: two of the best, Ⓦatrapalo.com and Ⓦrumbo.es, are in Spanish only but fairly easy to use.

Rooms

The cheapest beds are usually in **private rooms**, in someone's house or above a bar or restaurant. The signs to look for are *habitaciones* (rooms) or *camas* (beds), both becoming less obvious in Andalucía, or they might be touted at resort bus and train stations in summer as you arrive. The rooms should be clean, but might well be very simple and timeworn; you'll probably share a communal bathroom.

Pensiones, hostales and hotels

Official places to stay are generally classified as **pensiones**, **hostales** or **hotels**, though that's just the start of it, as several other names are used to describe accommodation throughout the region.

Pensiones

Of the official guesthouses and hotels, at the budget end of the scale are **pensiones** (marked P,

classified by a two-star system), where straight-forward rooms often have shared bathroom facilities (there's usually a washbasin in the room). Other variants are **fondas** (F), which traditionally had a restaurant or dining room attached, and **casas de huéspedes** (CH), literally an old-fashioned "guesthouse". In some such *pensiones*, facilities are likely to be minimal and comforts rationed; things like heating, furniture (other than bed, chair and desk) and even external windows might be too much to hope for. On the other hand, some *pensiones* are lovingly cared for and very good value.

Hostales

Next step up from the *pensiones*, and far more common, are **hostales** (Hs) and **hostal-residencias** (HsR), classified from one to three stars. These are not hostels, in any sense, but budget hotels, generally offering good, if functional, rooms, usually with private bathrooms, TV and – in the better places – probably heating and air-conditioning. Many also have cheaper rooms available without private bathrooms. Some *hostales* really are excellent, with good service and up-to-date furnishings and facilities, including wi-fi or internet access.

Hotels

Fully fledged **hotels** are graded from one to five stars, with star-rating dependent on things like room size, staffing levels and whether or not there's a lift rather than any intrinsic attraction. There's often not much difference in price between a one-star hotel and a three-star *hostal*, for example, and the *hostal* might be nicer. At three and four stars, prices start to increase and you can expect soundproofing, a lift, an English-language channel on the TV and a buffet breakfast spread. At five stars, you're in the luxury class, with pools, gyms, jacuzzis, and prices to match.

The excellent Rusticae (Ⓦrusticae.es) highlights stylish **rural and urban hotels** across the country, while the Asociación de Hoteles Rurales de

Andalucía (Ⓦahra.es) has information on some of the region's most charming **country hotels**.

Paradores

Spain has over ninety superior hotels in a class of their own, called **paradores** (Ⓦparador.es), spectacular lodgings often converted from castles, monasteries and other Spanish monuments (although some are purpose-built). They can be really special places to stay, sited in the most beautiful parts of the country, and in some of the most historic cities, and prices are very good when compared with the five-star hotels with which they often compete.

Paradores are banded into five categories, depending on location and popularity, with high season rates starting at around €120 a night, though €150–180 is more typical. That said, a whole host of special offers and web deals (through the official website) offer rooms from as little as €60, and deals for the over 60s, the 20s to 30s or for multi-night stays. Three-night packages, where you stay in a different *parador* every night, start at around €150 per person (based on two sharing, car rental not included). All the details are on the website, or contact the official *parador* **agents**, Keytel in the UK (Ⓦkeytel.co.uk) or Petrabax in the US (Ⓦpetrabax.com).

Villas, apartments and rural tourism

Most UK and European tour operators can find you a self-catering **villa** or **apartment**, usually (but not exclusively) on the coast or in one of the many sierras. They are rented by the week, and range from simple town-centre apartments to luxury coastal villas with private pools, and prices vary wildly. The best deals are often packages, including flights and car rental, with endless companies like First Choice (Ⓦfirst choice.co.uk/villas) and Iglu Villas (Ⓦigluvillas.com).

Casas rurales (rural houses) are where many Spanish holidaymakers stay. These cover a broad range, from cave dwellings to restored manor houses, many with pools and gardens, plus all mod cons. You can rent by the room, or by the property, sometimes on a B&B basis and sometimes self-catering. Many of the *casas* also come with opportunities to take part in outdoor activities such as horseriding, walking, fishing and cycling. They offer excellent value for money, starting at around €30 per person, even cheaper if you're in a group or staying for longer than a night or two.

ASETUR (Ⓦecoturismorural.com), the association for rural tourism in Spain, has an excellent website where you can search thousands of properties by region, while many of Andalucía's tourist-office websites also carry information on *casas rurales*. You could also contact **agencies** like Top Rural (Ⓦtoprural.com), which has many properties in Andalucía, and Andalucía-based **agencies** such as the Red Andaluza de Alojamientos Rurales (Ⓦraar .es) or Rustic Blue (Ⓦrusticblue.com).

Youth hostels

There are twenty official youth hostels (*albergues juveniles*) in Andalucía under the umbrella of the **Red Española de Albergues Juveniles** (REAJ; Ⓦreaj .com), the Spanish youth hostel association that is affiliated to the international organization, Hostelling International (HI; Ⓦhihostels.com). Partly funded by the Junta de Andalucía, the network in Andalucía is administered by **Inturjoven** (Ⓦinturjoven.com). There are full details of each hostel on the Inturjoven website (English-language version available), and we've included some of the best in the *Guide*.

Andalucía has some of the most modern youth hostels in the country (including a stunning new one in **Jaén**), many with two- or four-bed en-suite rooms, and a handful of options in stunning **rural**

ANDALUCÍA'S TOP FIVE PARADORES

Mazagón A modern *parador* made very special by its isolated location on one of the best beaches in Andalucía, reached via steps from the hotel's extensive gardens. See p.335

Jaén Housed in a Moorish fortress atop a crag high above the city of Jaén, this is the most spectacularly sited *parador* in Andalucía, if not Spain. See p.425.

Úbeda On arguably the most beautiful square in Andalucía, this *parador* occupies a stunning sixteenth-century Renaissance mansion. See p.436.

Cazorla Another modern *parador*, but a setting deep inside the lushly wooded Sierra de Cazorla natural park makes for a memorable hotel. See p.447.

Granada One of the world's top hotels, in a fifteenth-century monastery inside the Alhambra grounds, this offers a heady combination of opulence and history. See p.483.

locations. Bear in mind, though, that in some cities hostels may be inconveniently located and at school holiday periods can be block-booked by school/youth groups. You'll also need an HI membership card, though you can buy one at most hostels on your first night. And at €21–27 per person a night in high season (less for under 26s, and out of season), they can end up no cheaper than a basic double room in a *hostal* or *pensión*. That said, hostels are also good places for cheap meals and meeting other travellers.

Camping

There are hundreds of authorized **campsites** in Spain, mostly on the coast and in holiday areas. They work out at about €4.50–6 per person plus the same again for a tent, and a similar amount for each car or caravan. The best-located sites, or the ones with top-range facilities (restaurant, swimming pool, bar, supermarket), are significantly more expensive. If you plan to camp extensively, buy the annual *Guía de Campings*, which you can find in large bookshops, or visit Ⓦ vayacamping.net.

In most cases, **camping outside campsites** is legal – but there are certain restrictions. You're not allowed to camp "in urban areas, areas prohibited for military or touristic reasons, or within 1km of an official campsite". What this means in practice is that you can't camp on the beach, while in national parks, camping is only allowed in officially designated areas. Aside from these restrictions, however, and with a little sensitivity, you can set up a tent for a short period almost anywhere in the countryside. Whenever possible, ask locally first.

Food and drink

The rich and varied cuisine of Andalucía is a reflection of its dramatic history. One of its signature dishes, gazpacho, was introduced by the Romans in the first millennium BC, and didn't reach its final version until peppers and tomatoes arrived in Spain following the voyages of Columbus. Another great influence came from the Moors who changed the face of southern Spain forever with the planting of orange, olive and almond trees. They also introduced spices such as cumin, cinnamon, nutmeg and saffron plus vegetables and fruits like aubergine, spinach, quince and pomegranate.

The cooking of modern Andalucía falls into mountain and coastal food. Five of Andalucía's eight provinces have access to a coastline, and here **fish** and **seafood** is king. Inland, rich stews, **jamones** (cured hams) and game are preferred. In recent years there has been a revival of interest in developing the region's cuisine in a more creative direction, and a reflection of this is a number of very good restaurants with numerous chefs sporting one or even two Michelin stars. Of course, not every restaurant is a gourmet experience and not every dish is a classic of its kind. Tourist resorts can be disappointing, especially those aimed at a foreign clientele, and a week on the Costa del Sol can just as easily convince you that the Spanish national diet is egg and chips, sangria, pizza and Guinness. However, even here you'll always find good restaurants and tapas bars where the locals eat, and few places in Europe are still as good value, especially if you have the **menú del día**, the bargain fixed-price lunch (and often dinner) that's a fixture across the region. There's a **menu reader** in our Language section (see p.597).

Breakfast, snacks and sandwiches

The traditional *andaluz* **breakfast** (*desayuno*) is *chocolate con churros* – long, extruded tubular doughnuts served with thick drinking chocolate or coffee. Some places specialize in these but many city bars and cafés also serve cakes and pastries (*bollos* or *pasteles*), croissants (*cruasán*) and toast (*pan tostada*), or crusty sandwiches (*bocadillos*) with a choice of fillings (try one with omelette, *tortilla*). A "sandwich", incidentally, is usually a less appetizing ham or cheese sandwich in white processed bread. Other good places for snacks are **cake shops** (*pastelerías* or *confiterías*) or the local bakery (*panadería*), where they might also have savoury pasties and turnovers.

Bars, tapas and raciónes

One of Spain's and Andalucía's glories is the phenomenon of **tapas** – the little portions of food that traditionally used to be served up free with a drink in a bar. The origins are disputed but the word is from *tapar*, "to cover", suggesting a cover for drinks' glasses, perhaps to keep the flies off in the baking sun. Tapas can be anything – a handful of olives, a slice or two of cured ham, a little dish of meatballs or chorizo, spicy fried potatoes or battered squid. They will often be laid out in a glass-fronted chill-cabinet on the counter, so you can see what's available, or there might be a blackboard menu. Occasionally the *dueño* (boss) or barman carries the list around in his head to be verbally rattled off to each new customer – an exacting test of your Spanish. Most bars have a speciality; indeed, Spaniards will commonly move from bar to bar, having just the one dish that they consider each bar does well. Conversely, if you're in a bar with just some pre-fried potatoes and day-old Russian salad on display, and a prominent microwave, go somewhere else to eat.

Aside from a few olives or crisps sometimes handed out with a drink, you pay for tapas these days (the eastern end of Andalucía, particularly the city of Granada, is an honourable exception here) – usually around €1–3 a portion. **Raciónes** (around €6–12) are simply bigger plates of tapas, perfect for sharing or enough for a meal – you're sometimes asked if you want a *tapa* or a *ración* of whatever it is you've chosen. And in the evenings many bars give up serving the cheaper tapas, and serve only the more profitable *raciones* when you'll be told "*solo hay raciones.*" Seville, as the city that claims to have invented tapas, is one of the best places to sample this culinary art, but you'll find many other outstanding bars throughout Andalucía.

Most cafés and bars have some kind of tapas available, while you'll also find a decent display in **bodegas**, **tabernas**, **mesónes** (various kinds of taverns) and **cervecerías** (beer-houses). It's always cheapest to stand at the bar to eat; you'll pay more to sit at tables and more again to sit outside on a terrace.

Restaurants

The simplest kind of restaurant is the **comedor** (dining room), fast disappearing from the *andaluz* townscape. Often a room at the back of a bar or the dining room of a *hostal* or *pensión*, it now survives only in rural areas. Traditionally, these are family-run places aimed at lunching workers, usually offering a straightforward set meal at budget prices. The highway equivalent are known as **ventas**, or inns, dotted along the main roads between towns and cities. These have been serving Spanish wayfarers for centuries – some of them quite literally – and the best places are immediately picked out by the line of cars and trucks outside. Proper restaurants, **restaurantes**, come in a myriad of guises, from rustic village restaurants to stylish Michelin-starred eateries; **asadores** specialize in grilled meats, **marisquerías** in shellfish and seafood.

Almost every *venta* and *restaurante* serves a weekday, fixed-price lunchtime meal, the **menú del día**. For this you generally get three courses including a beer or glass of wine for €7–12, occasionally even less, depending on where you are (you might also see the words *menú de la casa*); this is obviously a terrific deal. The *menú del día* is only sporadically available at night, and in Andalucía it's generally not available at all at weekends, the time traditionally when families eat out together. The very cheapest places are unlikely to have a written menu, and the waiter will tell you what the day's dishes are. In smarter restaurants in bigger cities and resorts, there will still be a *menú del día*, though it might be a shadow of the usual à la carte menu, and drinks may be excluded. Even so, it's a way of eating at a restaurant that might normally cost you three or four times as much. Top city restaurants often also feature an upmarket *menú* called a **menú de degustación** (tasting menu), which again can be excellent value, allowing you to try out some of the country's finest cooking for anything from €30 to €60 a head; some even throw in a bottle of decent wine.

Otherwise, in bars and so-called *cafeterías*, meals often come in the form of a **plato combinado** – literally a combined dish – which will be a one-plate

---

ANDALUCÍA'S TOP TEN RESTAURANTS

Andalucía has some of the best restaurants in Spain, and quite a few places where you could blow a pretty big hole in your credit card account. While many recommended restaurants in the Guide may score higher in terms of cuisine alone, at any of the places below we feel the welcome, ambience, location and excellent food all contribute to creating a truly memorable experience.

El Almejero Garrucha. See p.551
El Bigote Sanlúcar de Barrameda. See p.213
El Chaleco Almuñécar. See p.540
El Faro de El Puerto El Puerto de Santa
 María. See p.201
José Vicente Aracena. See p.347

La Escollera Estepona. See p.122
Las Candelas Huelva. See p.324
Parador de Málaga-Gibralfaro Málaga.
 See p.77
Santiago Marbella. See p.117
Taberna El Alabardero Seville. See p.293

meal of something like steak, egg and chips, or *calamares* and salad, occasionally with bread and a drink included. This will generally cost in the region of €5–10.

If you want a menu in a restaurant, ask for **la carta**; *menú* refers only to the fixed-price meal. In all but the most rock-bottom establishments it is customary to leave a small **tip** (*propina*), though five percent of the bill is considered sufficient and service is normally included in a *menú del día*. IVA, the eight-percent **tax**, is also charged, but it should say on the menu if this included in the price or not.

Spaniards generally eat very late and *andaluzes* eat later still, with **lunch** served from around 1pm (you'll generally be the first person there at this time) until 4pm, and **dinner** from 8.30pm or 9pm to midnight. Obviously, in rural areas people dine slightly earlier, but making a dinner reservation for 10.30pm or even later is considered perfectly normal in Andalucía and it's not uncommon to see a group of diners being ushered to a table with midnight approaching. Most restaurants **close one day a week**, usually Sunday or Monday.

What to eat

If you like **fish and seafood** you'll be in heaven in Andalucía, as it forms the basis of a vast variety of tapas and is fresh and excellent everywhere. It's not cheap, unfortunately, so rarely forms part of the lowest priced *menús* (though they might feature the most common fish – cod, often salted, and hake – or squid) but you really should make the most of what's on offer. Fish **stews** (*zarzuelas*) and rice-based paellas (which also contain meat, usually rabbit or chicken) are often memorable in seafood restaurants. Paella comes originally from Valencia and is still best there, but you'll find **arroz marinero**, the Andalucian version, to be very good. The coastal strip is great for seafood, of course, although Cádiz and the nearby "sherry triangle" of Sanlúcar, El Puerto de Santa María and Jerez deserve top billing for sheer volume and variety. Be aware when ordering fish in restaurants that often the price quoted is per kilo or per 100g, and an average white-fish portion will be around 200–300g (don't be afraid to ask the waiter for a price quote when ordering).

Meat is most often grilled and served with a few fried potatoes and a couple of salad leaves, or cured or dried and served as a starter or in sandwiches. **Jamón serrano** is superb, makes a wonderful starter and is consumed with a passion in Andalucía. The finest varieties, though, produced from *cerdos ibéricos* (Iberian black pigs) at Jabugo in the Sierra de Aracena (see p.357) and Trevélez in the Sierra Nevada (see p.507), are extremely expensive. If you're tempted, they are best appreciated with a glass of fino (see p.42). More meat is eaten in inland provinces than on the coast and Córdoba's **rabo de toro** (stewed bull's tail) is renowned. The Sierra de Aracena is also a good place for *setas* (mushrooms) and cooked pork dishes, with **solomillo de cerdo** (pork loin) usually outstanding. In country areas bordering the slopes of the Sierra Morena and in the province of Jaén, game is very much a speciality – venison, partridge, hare and wild boar all feature on menus in these parts, as well as fresh trout.

Vegetables

Vegetables rarely amount to more than a few fries or boiled potatoes with the main dish (though you can often order a side dish à la carte). The provinces of Córdoba and Jaén are again the exceptions, and the latter's **pipirrana jaenera** (salad with green peppers and hard-boiled eggs) is just one of a number of hearty vegetable-based dishes to be found in these parts. It's more usual, though, to start your meal with a simple salad or with Andalucía's most famous dish, chilled **gazpacho**. Made from puréed bread and garlic with added peppers, cucumbers and tomatoes, regional variations of gazpacho include Córdoba's *salmorejo*, Málaga's *ajo blanco* and Cádiz's *sopa de picadillo*.

Desserts

Dessert (*postre*) in Andalucía tends to be sweet and sticky – another hangover from the region's long Moorish period. The cheaper places will usually offer little variety: nearly always fresh fruit or *flan*, the Spanish crème caramel, often replaced on Andalucian menus by the similar *tocino de cielo* ("heavenly lard") or *natillas* (custard). *Arroz con leche* (cold rice pudding), *crema catalana* (crème brûlée) and *helado* (ice cream) often make an appearance in the more mundane places. Keep an eye out in upmarket restaurants for delicious **regional specialities** such as *peras al vino* (pears baked in wine with cinnamon) from Málaga, *piononos* (liqueur-soaked cakes) from Granada and *crema de Jerez* (sherry pudding) from Cádiz, as well as *brazo de gitano* (rolled pastry filled with cream), an Andalucía-wide dessert. In smarter places the desserts will always be made in house or by a reputable local artisan (or even convent) but in cheaper and out-of-the-way places they often cut corners by offering factory-produced desserts, anathema to most *andaluz* diners; "*es casero?*" ("is it homemade?") is the question to ask.

Cheese

Cheese (*queso*) is always eaten as a *tapa* rather than after a meal in Andalucía. The cheeses of the region don't usually travel beyond their immediate area of production, which offers you the chance to make some interesting discoveries, especially in areas such as Las Alpujarras. The best-known region-wide brand is Córdoba Province's sheep's-milk cheese from Pedroches, although the hard, salty *Manchego* from neighbouring La Mancha is also common. One cheese worth knowing about from the Sierra de Grazalema is cured goats'- and sheep's-milk cheeses made by prizewinning cheesemaker Payoyo.

Vegetarians

Vegetarians generally have a fairly hard time of it in Andalucía, though there's an increasing number of veggie and veggie-friendly restaurants in the bigger cities. In more rural areas, there's usually something to eat, but you may get weary of eggs and omelettes. It's worth noting that many **tapas** favourites are vegetarian dishes: *espinacas con garbanzos* (spinach with chick-peas), *tortilla* (potato omelette), *berenjenas fritas* (fried aubergine) and *patatas bravas* (potatoes in spicy sauce) are to be found throughout Andalucía. Otherwise, superb fresh fruit and veg, and excellent cheese, is always available in the markets and shops.

In restaurants, you're faced with the extra problem that pieces of meat – especially ham, which the Spanish don't regard as real meat – and tuna are often added to vegetable dishes and salads to "spice them up". You'll also find chunks of chorizo and sausage turning up in otherwise veg-friendly soups or bean stews. The phrases to get to know are "*Soy vegetariano/a. Como sólo verduras. Hay algo sin carne?*" ("I'm a vegetarian. I only eat vegetables. Is there anything without meat?"); you may have to add "*y sin marisco*" ("and without seafood") and "*y sin jamón*" ("and without ham") to be really safe.

Some salads and vegetable dishes are strictly **vegan**, but they're few and far between. Fruit and nuts are widely available; nuts are sold by street vendors everywhere and stocked in larger supermarkets.

Coffee, tea and soft drinks

Café (coffee) is invariably an espresso (*café solo*); for a large cup of weaker, black coffee, ask for an *americano*. A *café cortado* is a *café solo* with a drop of milk; a *café con leche* is made with lots of hot milk. Coffee is also frequently mixed with brandy (*coñac*) or whisky (pronounced "whicky"), all such concoctions being called a *carajillo*. Iced coffee is *café con hielo* (you'll be served a coffee and a separate glass of ice cubes – you pour the former over the latter to make a great summer refresher). **Chocolate** (hot chocolate) is a popular breakfast drink, or for after a long night on the town, but it's usually incredibly thick and sweet. For a thinner, cocoa-style drink, ask for a brand name, like Cola Cao.

Spaniards usually drink **té** (tea) black, so if you want milk it's safest to ask for it afterwards, since ordering *té con leche* might well get you a glass of warm milk with a tea bag floating on top. Herbal teas (*infusiones*) are widely available, like *manzanilla* (camomile), *poleo* (mint tea) and *hierba luisa* (lemon verbena).

Local soft drinks include **granizado** (slush) or **horchata** (a milky drink made from tiger nuts or almonds), available from summer street stalls, and from milk bars and ice-cream parlours (*heladerías*). Although you can drink the **water** almost everywhere, it tastes revolting in some cities and coastal areas – inexpensive *agua mineral* comes either sparkling (*con gas*) or still (*sin gas*).

Wine, beer and spirits

Wine (*vino*), either *tinto* (red), *blanco* (white) or *rosado/clarete* (rosé), is the invariable accompaniment to every meal and is, as a rule, extremely inexpensive. Andalucía's wine-making genius lies elsewhere (see p.42) and so most table wines are imported from outside the region (see box opposite). One thing worth knowing about Spanish wine is the terms related to the **ageing process** which defines the best wines: *crianza* wines must have a minimum of two years ageing before sale; red *reserva* wines at least two years (of which one must be in oak barrels); red *gran reserva* must have at least two years in oak and three in the bottle. *Vino de Mesa* and *Vino de la Tierra* are the equivalent of France's Vin de Table, and DO (*Denominación de Origen*) is Spain's version of the French Appellation Contrôlée regulating grape varieties and region of origin.

Dining out away from the larger towns and cities your choice of wine (especially in remote *ventas*) will be severely limited. Busier *ventas* and restaurants with a healthy reputation, however, usually have well-stocked cellars and will only be too pleased to let you peruse their *carta de vinos*.

WINING AND DINING

One of the great pleasures of eating out in Andalucía is the chance to sample some of Spain's excellent wines. Restaurant **wine prices** compare very favourably with other parts of Europe and in most restaurants and *ventas* you'll often be able to find a decent bottle for under €12. Most establishments usually have an economical house wine too for around half this price or less (ask for *caserío* or *vino de la casa*) and sometimes this will be served straight from the barrel in a half-litre or litre carafe (*jarra*). This can be great, it can be lousy, but at least it will be distinctively local.

The most common bottled red wine in Andalucía is **Valdepeñas**, a good standard wine from the central plains of New Castile (Los Llanos, Viña Albali and Señorío de Guadianeja are good labels). **Rioja**, from the area round Logroño in the north, is one of Spain's classic wines but a lot more expensive (Cune, Faustino I & V, Muga, Beronia, Marqués de Cáceres, Bordón, Viña Ardanza, Marqués de Riscal and Izadi are some names to look out for). Another top-drawer, and currently fashionable, region is **Ribera del Duero** in Castilla-León. This produces Spain's most expensive wine, Vega Sicilia, along with other outstanding whites (Belondrade y Lurtón) and reds (Pesquera, Viña Pedrosa, Protos and Señorío de Nava). There are also scores of other excellent wines from regions such as Catalunya (Bach, Raimat, Torres) which also produces the champagne-like Cava (Codorníu, Freixenet) and the new and pricey Priorat reds which have taken the wine world by storm (Clos Mogador, Alvaro Palacios). Galicia, known for its fragrant whites (Fefiñanes, Fin de Siglo and San Trocado); Navarra (Gran Feudo, Señorío de Sarría, Ochoa); and Valencia (Murviedro, Gandía) are others, and even the once unpromising La Mancha (Santa Rita, Casa Gualda, Estola) is now making a name for itself as a producer of quality wines.

Andalucía's solitary table-wine area of any volume is the **Condado de Huelva**, which turns out reasonable dry whites, which go well with seafood. Red wines have also made some headway in a region long thought to be too hot to produce quality vintages: in 2007 US wine guru Robert Parker caused a sensation when he awarded 95 points (out of a hundred) to Arcos de la Frontera bodega Huerta de Albalá's Taberner no. 1, comparing it to "the best of the northern Rhones". There are also many local wines made in the country districts, with some, such as the **costa** wine of the western Alpujarras, and the **Laujar de Andarax** wines of the eastern Alpujarras, always worth trying.

In Andalucía you will often be asked in restaurants – especially at lunchtime in summer – if you would like your wine "con Casera". La Casera is a brand of lemonade that many *andaluzes* use to dilute the wine, turning it into a "spritzer". This combination also forms a legitimate bar drink called *tinto de verano* where red wine is mixed with soda or lemonade and makes a great summer refresher. Equally refreshing, though often deceptively strong, is **sangría**, a wine-and-fruit punch that you'll come across at fiestas and in tourist bars.

In a bar, a small glass of wine will generally cost around €0.50–2 depending on location (rural bars are usually much cheaper than city places); in a restaurant, if wine is not included in the *menú*, prices start at around €7 a bottle in basic establishments but at anywhere with pretensions you're looking at paying at least €10–12 for a decent bottle and significantly more if you start fancying the vintage stuff. These days, in times of paring costs to the bone, many establishments are now tending to cut the "free" wine from their *menús*, or offering at best a single glass.

Beer

Beer (*cerveza*) is nearly always lager-style, though some Spanish breweries also now make stout-style brews, wheat beers and other types. It comes in 300ml bottles (*botellines*) or, for about the same price, on tap – a *caña* of draught beer is a small glass, a *caña doble* larger, and asking for *un tubo* (a tubular glass) gets you about half a pint. Mahou, Cruz Campo, San Miguel, Damm, Estrella de Galicia and Alhambra are all decent beers. A **shandy** is a *clara*, either with fizzy lemon (*con limón*) or lemonade (*con casera*).

Spirits

In mid-afternoon – or, let's face it, even at breakfast – Spaniards take a *copa* of liqueur with their coffee, such as *anís* (similar to Pernod) or *coñac*, the local **brandy**, which has a distinct vanilla flavour. Most brandies are produced by the great sherry houses in Jerez and the best – such as Carlos 1 or Lepanto – compare favourably with any top Cognac. Other classy non-*jerezano* brands include the Armagnac-like Mascaró and Torres, both from Catalunya. Instead of brandy, at the end of a meal many places serve **chupitos** – little shot glasses of flavoured schnapps or local firewater, such as *pacharán* (a sloes and anis combination).

You should order **spirits** by brand name, since there are generally less expensive Spanish equivalents for standard imports, or simply specify *nacional*. Larios gin from Málaga, for instance, is about half the price of Gordon's. Measures are staggeringly generous – bar staff generally pour from the bottle until you suggest they stop. Long drinks include the universal *Gin-Tónic* and *Cuba Libre* (rum and Coke), and there are often Spanish Caribbean rums (*ron*) such as Cacique from Venezuela or Havana Club from Cuba.

Sherry

The classic Andalucian wine is **sherry** – *vino de jerez* or *fino* as it's popularly known – which is excellent, widely available and consumed with gusto by *andaluzes*. Served chilled or at bodega temperature – a perfect drink to wash down tapas – like everything Spanish, it comes in a perplexing variety of forms. The main distinctions are between *fino* or *jerez seco* (dry sherry), *amontillado* (medium), and *oloroso* (full-bodied) or *jerez dulce* (sweet), and these are the terms you should use to order. Similar in the way they are made – though not identical in flavour – are *Montilla* and *manzanilla*, which are not fortified with alcohol as is the case with other finos. The first of these dry, sherry-like wines comes from the province of Córdoba, and the latter from Sanlúcar de Barrameda, part of the "sherry triangle" along with Jerez and El Puerto de Santa María.

The media

The ubiquitous Spanish newspaper kiosk is your first stop for regional and national newspapers and magazines, though hotels and bars nearly always have a few lying around for customers. The bigger cities, tourist towns and resorts will also have foreign newspapers available (some of which are actually published in Spain), generally on the day of issue or perhaps a day late. Television is all-pervasive in bars, cafés and restaurants; most pensión and hotel rooms have a TV, too, though only in the fancier places will you get any English-language programming, and then probably only BBC World, CNN or Eurosport satellite channels.

Newspapers and magazines

Andalucians, in line with the Spanish generally, are not great devourers of newsprint and none of the Spanish **national newspapers** has a circulation above 400,000. The best of these are the Madrid-based centre-left *El País* (𝕎elpais.es) and the centre-right *El Mundo* (𝕎elmundo.es), both of which have good arts and foreign news coverage, and include daily comprehensive Andalucía **regional supplements** with news and "what's on" listings. Other national papers include the solidly old-order *ABC* with a hard moral line against divorce and abortion, and Barcelona's centrist *La Vanguardia* (also available in Andalucía). Andalucía's **regional press** is generally run by local magnates and predominantly right-of-centre, but often provides an entertaining read. The best of Andalucía's regional **dailies** are Málaga's *Sur*, *Diario de Cádiz*, *Córdoba*, and Granada's *Ideal*. The paper with the highest circulation is *Marca* (𝕎marca.com), the country's top **sports daily**, mainly football-dominated; there's also *As* (𝕎as .com), *El Mundo Deportivo* (𝕎elmundodeportivo .es) and *Sport* (𝕎sport.es). The main cities such as Seville, Málaga and Granada are also awash with **free newspapers**, which are handed out at bus stops and train stations.

There's a bewildering variety of **magazines** specializing in celebrity gossip (known collectively as *la prensa rosa*), ranging from the more traditional *Hola* to the sensationalist *QMD!* (*Que me Dices*). *El Jueves* is the Spanish equivalent to the British comic *Viz*, while the online daily *El Confidencial* (𝕎elconfidencial.com) gives the inside track on serious economic and political stories. There are also various **English-language magazines** and papers produced by or for the huge expatriate community now resident in Andalucía. Málaga's *Sur* newspaper produces the free weekly *Sur in English* (𝕎surinenglish.com) which has a news digest and popular classified columns. Another decent production is the monthly **online** 𝕎andalucia.com, but the best of the bunch is the *Olive Press* (𝕎the olivepress.es), a fortnightly paper which frequently campaigns on local and regional issues.

Radio

There are hundreds of local radio channels (almost every major town in Andalucía has its local radio station), broadcasting alongside a handful of national ones. The state-run **RNE** (𝕎rtve.es/radio) network covers five stations: RNE 1, a general news and information channel; Radio Clásica, broadcasting mainly classical music and related programmes; the popular music channel RNE 3; RNE 4, in Catalan; and the rolling news and sports channel RNE 5. Radio Exterior is RNE's international shortwave service. Other **popular channels** include Cadena Ser and Onda Cero (news, talk, sports and culture), the rightist Catholic church-run COPE, 40 Principales (for the latest hits, Spanish and otherwise) and Cadena 100 (music and cultural programming). Radio Marca (dedicated sports radio) is also very popular. Full listings, local stations and frequencies can be found in *El País*, and the local press, or bring a shortwave radio to tune in to the BBC World Service (W bbc.co.uk/worldservice) or Voice of America (W voa.gov).

Television

RTV (W rtve.es/television) provides the main, state-run channels, namely TVE1, a general entertainment and news channel, and its sister La 2 (ie "Dos"), given over to sports and culture. Although the state channels no longer carry advertising following a change in the law in 2009, they still compete aggressively (particularly TVE 1) for audience share with the private stations which largely results in a tedious mix of game, reality and celebrity scandal shows, sport, films and *telenovelas* (soaps) across the board. **Private national stations** are Antena 3, Cuatro (ie Four), Telecinco (Five) and La Sexta (Sixth) while Andalucía's Canal Sur has local programming. The main **satellite** channel is Canal+.

Festivals

The fiesta or feria is a crucial part of Spanish life. Even the smallest village or most modern city suburb devotes at least a couple of days a year to partying, and coinciding with such an event can be huge fun, propelling you right into the heart of Spanish culture. It's hard to beat the experience of arriving in some tiny hamlet, expecting no more than a bed for the night, to discover the streets decked out with flags and streamers, spectacular fireworks lighting up the sky, a band playing in the plaza and the entire population out celebrating the local fiesta.

Festivals usually mark the local saint's day, but there are celebrations, too, of harvests, of deliverance from the Moors, of safe return from the sea – any excuse will do.

Each festival has its own particular characteristics but there are facets common to them all. Horses, **flamenco**, fireworks and the guitar are essential parts of any celebration, usually accompanied by the downing of oceans of **fino** – which is probably why the sherry companies seem to provide most of the bunting. And along with the music there is always **dancing** – usually *sevillanas* (see box, p.584) in traditional flamenco costume and an immense spirit of enjoyment. The main event of most fiestas is a **parade**, either behind a revered holy image, or a more celebratory affair with fancy costumes and *gigantones*, grotesque giant carnival figures which terrorize children.

Although these festivals take place throughout the year – and it is often the obscure and unexpected event that proves to be most fun – there are certain occasions that stand out. Easter Week (**Semana Santa**) and **Corpus Christi** (in early June) are celebrated throughout Andalucía with magnificent religious processions. Easter, particularly, is worth trying to coincide with – head for Seville, Málaga, Granada or Córdoba, where huge *pasos*, floats of wildly theatrical religious scenes, are carried down the streets, accompanied by weirdly hooded penitents atoning for the year's misdeeds. And just as moving in their own more intimate way are the countless small town and village observances of Semana Santa with smaller processions, traditional customs and sometimes a Passion play. Outsiders are always welcome, the one problem being that during any of the most popular (though usually not at the small town and village affairs) you'll find it difficult and expensive to find a bed. If you're planning to coincide with a major festival, try and book your accommodation well in advance.

Among the biggest and best-known of Andalucía's **other popular festivals** are the Cádiz Carnaval (mid-Feb); Seville's enormous April Feria (a week at the end of the month); Jerez's Feria del Caballo (Horse Fair, April/May); the Romería del Rocío, an extraordinary pilgrimage to El Rocío near Huelva (arriving there on Whit Sunday); and Málaga's boisterous and good-humoured Feria (mid-Aug).

Listed below are some of Andalucía's main fiestas, all worth trying to get to if you're going to be in the area around the time; more are described with the relevant locations covered in the Guide section. Note that saints' day festivals – indeed all Spanish celebrations – can vary in date, and are often observed over the weekend closest to the dates given here.

The list is potentially endless. In addition to our selection (below), check the Junta de Andalucía's annual **Ferias y Fiestas de Andalucía** guide, available from local tourist offices, and see ⓦ fiestasdeandalucia.com.

A festival calendar

JANUARY

1–2: Día de la Toma. Celebration of the 1492 entry of the Reyes Católicos into the city – at Granada.

5: Cabalgata de los Reyes Magon. Epiphany parade at Málaga.

6: Romería de la Virgen del Mar. Pilgrimage procession from Almería.

17: Romería del Ermita del Santo. Pilgrimage procession at Guadix.

FEBRUARY

1: San Cecilio. Fiesta in Granada's traditionally *gitano* (gypsy) quarter of Sacromonte.

Mid-month: Carnaval. Extravagant week-long event (leading up to Lent) in all the Andalucian cities. Cádiz, above all, celebrates with fancy dress, flamenco, spectacular parades and street-singers' competitions.

MARCH

5–15: El Puerto de Santa María Carnaval in Cádiz.

March/April: Semana Santa (Holy Week). Following Palm Sunday, this has its most elaborate and dramatic celebrations in Andalucía. You'll find moving and memorable processions of floats and penitents at (in descending order of importance) Seville, Málaga, Granada and Córdoba, and to a lesser extent in smaller towns such as Jerez, Arcos, Baeza and Úbeda. All culminate with the full drama of the Passion on Good Friday, with Easter Day itself more of a family occasion.

APRIL

Last week: Feria de Abril (2 weeks after Easter, usually in April, occasionally May; check with the tourist office). Week-long Feria de Abril at Seville: the largest fair in Spain, a little refined in the way of the city, but an extraordinary event nonetheless. A small April fair – featuring bull-running – is held in Vejer.

Last Sunday: Romería de Nuestra Señora de la Cabeza. Three days of celebrations in Andújar (Jaén) culminate in a huge procession to the sanctuary of the Virgin in the Sierra Morena.

MAY

1–2: Romería de Nuestra Señora de la Estrella at Navas de San Juan. Jaén Province's most important pilgrimage.

3: "Moors and Christians" Carnival at Pampaneira (Alpujarras).

First two weeks: Cruces de Mayo (Festival of the Patios). Córdoba celebrates the Holy Cross; includes a competition for the prettiest patio and numerous events and concerts organized by the local city council.

Early May (usually the week after Seville's fair): Horse Fair Somewhat aristocratic Horse Fair at Jerez de la Frontera.

17: San Isidro Romería at Setenil (Cádiz).

Pentecost (7 weeks after Easter): Romería del Rocío. Spain's biggest *romería*: a million often inebriated pilgrims in horse-drawn carriages and processions converge on El Rocío (Huelva) from all over the south.

Variable – Thurs after Trinity: Corpus Christi. Bullfights and festivities at Granada, Seville, Ronda, Vejer and Zahara de la Sierra. At Seville, Los Seises (Six Choirboys) perform a dance before the altar of the cathedral.

Third weekend: Romería de Santa Eulalia. Pilgrimage, fireworks, parades and fandangos at Almonaster La Real in the Sierra de Aracena in honour of the village's patron saint.

Last week: Feria de la Manzanilla. Prolonged binge in Sanlúcar de Barrameda to celebrate the town's major product. The sherry is used to wash down huge quantities of seafood while watching flamenco and sporting events from beachfront *casetas* (party tents).

JUNE

Second week: Feria de San Bernabé. Marbella's fair is often spectacular, since this is the richest town in Andalucía.

13–14: Fiestas Patronales de San Antonio. At Trevélez (Alpujarras); includes mock battles between Moors and Christians.

23–24: Candelas de San Juan. Bonfires and effigies at Vejer and all along the coast as crowds party all night while waiting to celebrate the dawn.

23–26: Feria de Alhaurín de la Torre. Processions, giants and an important flamenco competition in Málaga.

30: Conil (Cádiz) feria.

End June/early July: International Festival of Music and Dance. Major dance groups, chamber orchestras and flamenco artistes perform in Granada's Alhambra palace, Generalife and Carlos V palace.

JULY

Early July: International Guitar Festival. Brings together top international acts in Córdoba from classical, flamenco and Latin American music.

9–14: Feast of San Francisco Solano. Montilla (Córdoba) celebrates its annual feria.

End of July: Virgen del Mar summer fiesta. Parades, horseriding events and usually a handful of major jazz and rock concerts in Almería's Plaza Vieja.

AUGUST

First week: Berja fiesta. Annual fiesta in Almería in honour of the Virgin of Gádor.

3: Huelva fiesta. Colombinas celebrate Columbus's voyages of discovery with a fiesta.

5: Trevélez (Granadan Alpujarras) romería. A midnight *romería* to Mulhacén.

13–21: Feria de Málaga. One of Andalucía's most enjoyable fiestas for visitors, who are heartily welcomed by the ebullient *malagueños*.

15: Ascension of the Virgin. Fair with *casetas* at Vejer and throughout Andalucía.

15: Noche del Vino. A riotous wine festival at Competa (Málaga) with dancing, singing and endless drinking.

17–20: The first cycle of horse races along Sanlúcar de Barrameda's beach. Heavy official and unofficial betting; the second tournament takes place exactly a week later.

19–21: Vendimia. Grape harvest fiesta at Montilla (Córdoba).

Third week: Algeciras fair and fiesta.

Third weekend: Fiesta de San Mamés. At Aroche (Huelva) in the extremities of the Sierra de Aracena, this is unpretentious and great fun, everything a village fiesta should be.

22–25: Feria de Grazalema (Cádiz).

23–25: Guadalquivir festival. Bullfights and an important flamenco competition at Sanlúcar de Barrameda.

25–30: Fiestas Patronales. In honour of San Agustín at Mojácar (Almería).

SEPTEMBER

6: Fiesta de Cascamorras. Annual feria at Baza (Granada) where the Cascamorras or interloper from nearby Guadix attempts to make off with their Virgen and is doused in dirty oil for his pains.

7: Romería del Cristo de la Yedra. Singing and dancing in the streets at Baeza (Jaén).

7–14: Feria de la Moscatel/Feria de Nuestra Señora de Regla. At Chipiona (Cádiz): includes bull-running, flamenco tournaments and much wine-swilling to acclaim the sweet sherry grape grown hereabouts.

8: Romería de Nuestra Señora de los Ángeles. Colourful event at Alajar (Huelva), with horse-races to the peak sanctuary of Arias Montano.

8–9: Fiesta de la Virgen de la Luz. At Almuñécar (Granada).

First/second week: Vendimia. Celebration of the vintage at Jerez. Starts with the blessing of the new grapes, after which everyone gets sozzled on the old.

6–13: Celebration of the Virgen de la Luz. Street processions and horseriding in Tarifa.

First two weeks: Ronda feria. Ronda bursts into life with a feria, flamenco contests and the Corrida Goyesca, bullfights in eighteenth-century dress.

24–25: Día del Señor (Lord's Day). Celebrated at Orgiva (Granada) with impressive fireworks and processions.

29: Fiesta de San Miguel. A fair and *casetas* at Úbeda (Jaén).

OCTOBER

1: Fiesta de San Miguel. Held in Granada's Albaicín quarter and dozens of other towns, including Torremolinos.

6–12: Feria del Rosario. Fuengirola horseriding events and flamenco.

15–23: Feria de San Lucas. Jaén's major fiesta, dating back to the fifteenth century.

NOVEMBER

1: Todos Los Santos (All Saints Day). Celebrated throughout Andalucía with church services and processions to graveyards.

DECEMBER

28: Fiesta de los Verdiales/Santos Inocentes. Various towns and villages of Málaga's mountain districts celebrate Spain's equivalent of April Fool's Day with dances, pulsating Moorish-inspired music and outlandish headdress. Good places to see it include Comares, Almogía, Casabermeja in the Axarquía to the east of Málaga and the Venta de San Cayetano, Puerto de la Torre, slightly to the northwest.

Bullfighting

Bullfights are an integral part of many Spanish festivals. In Andalucía especially, any village that can afford it will put on a corrida for an afternoon, while in big cities like Seville, the main festivals are accompanied by a week-long (or more) season of prestige fights attended by a veritable who's who of the great and the good. It is no coincidence that the fighting bull is the country's national symbol or that provinces like Cádiz – where many bulls are bred – is devoted to the whole culture of taurinismo and treats its matadores like gods.

Los Toros (or **La Lidia**, as Spaniards refer to bullfighting, is big business. Each year an estimated 24,000 bulls are killed before a live audience of over thirty million (with many more watching on television). It is said that 150,000 people are involved, in some way, in the industry, and the top performers, the *matadores*, are major earners, on a par with the country's biggest pop stars. There is some **opposition** to the activity from animal welfare groups but it is not widespread: if Spaniards tell you that bullfighting is controversial, they are likely to be referring to practices in the trade That said, the city of Barcelona recently outlawed bullfighting as did the Canary Islands. In recent years, bullfighting critics (whom you will find on the arts pages of the newspapers) have been expressing their perennial outrage at the widespread but illegal shaving of bulls' horns prior to the *corrida*. Bulls' horns are as sensitive as fingernails, and shaving just a few millimetres deters the animal from charging; they affect the creature's balance, too, reducing the danger for the *matador* still further.

Notwithstanding such abuse (and there is plenty more), Los Toros maintains its loyal aficionados throughout the country. Indeed, in some areas they are on the rise, with the elaborate language of the *corrida* quite a cult among the young, as the days of Franco's patronage of bullfighting are forgotten, and TV stations pay big money for major events. To **aficionados** (a word that implies more knowledge and appreciation than "fan"), the events are a culture and a ritual – one in which the emphasis is on the way man and bull "perform" together – in which the *arte* (art) is at issue rather than the cruelty. If pressed on the issue of the slaughter of an animal, they generally fail to understand. Fighting bulls are, they will tell you, bred for the industry;

ANTI-BULLFIGHT ORGANIZATIONS

ADDA (Asociación para la Defensa de los Derechos del Animal) C/Bailén 164, Local 2 interior, 08037 Barcelona ☎ 934 591 601, ⓦ addaong.org. Co-ordinates Spain's national opposition to bullfighting.

ASANDA (Asociación Andaluza para la Defensa de los Animales) C/Gracia Fernández Palacios 4, 41001 Seville

☎ 954 561 058, ⓦ asanda.org. Andalucía's anti-bullfighting pressure group.

World Society for the Protection of Animals 89 Albert Embankment, London SE1 2TP ☎ 0800 316 9966, ⓦ wspa .org.uk. The website has links to affiliates in Australia, Canada and the USA.

---

compared to beasts bred for the abattoir they live a pampered and idyllic life before they are killed; and, if the bullfight went, so too would the bulls.

Whether you attend a *corrida*, obviously, is down to your own feelings and ethics. If you spend any time at all in Spain during the **season** (which runs from March to Oct), you will encounter Los Toros, at least on a bar TV, and that will as likely as not make up your mind. If you decide to go, try to attend the biggest and most prestigious that is on, in a major city, where star performers are likely to dispatch the bulls with "*arte*" and a successful, "clean" kill. This happens much less frequently than many aficionados would have you believe and the beginners' fights, or *novilladas*, are often little more than a gruesome repetition of botched jobs. Even in the senior *corridas*, there are few sights worse than a *matador* making a prolonged and messy kill, while the audience whistles its disgust.

The matadores

Top **matadores** include the current idol of the rings, the moody, quixotic and media-shy José Tomás, who nearly died after a goring in Mexico in 2010 only to return in triumph to the *corrida* a year later; the world's top-paid *matador*, he earns a minimum of €150,000 to dispatch each bull. Other established and popular *matadores* include the veteran Enrique Ponce, El Fandi, Finito de Córdoba, El Cid and Julian "El Juli" López who learned his trade in Mexico as an under-age teenager before he was legally able to fight in Spain. Since the eighteenth century women have also fought bulls and the recently retired Cristina Sánchez became the first woman to have been carried shoulder-high through the *puerta grande* of Las Ventas, the prestigious Madrid ring – a distinction awarded to few of her male peers. Currently the top female *matador* is Mari Paz Vegá from Málaga.

Perhaps the most exciting and skilful performances of all are by mounted *matadores*, or **rejoneadores** as they are known (from *rejón*, "lance"); this is the oldest form of *corrida*, developed at

Ronda in the seventeenth century and the way these supremely skilful horsemen (and women) manoeuvre their steeds away from the bull's lethal horns to plant the *banderillas* and then make the kill – all the while mounted – can be breathtaking.

The corrida

The **corrida** begins with a procession, to the accompaniment of a *paso doble* by the band. Leading the procession are two *alguacilillos* or "constables", on horseback and in traditional costume, followed by the three *matadores*, who will each fight two bulls, and their *cuadrillas*, their personal "team", each comprising two mounted *picadores* and three *banderilleros*. At the back are the mule teams who will drag off the dead bulls. The ensuing *corrida* takes the form of a drama in three acts or stages (called **suertes**) presided over by a **presidente** who is there to see that a multitude of regulations are adhered to, and award trophies if a *matador's* performance has merited them.

Suerte de picar

Once the ring is empty, at the president's signal the **alguacilillo** opens the *toril* (the bulls' enclosure) and the first bull (weighing 500–600kg) appears – a moment of great physical beauty – to be "tested" by the *matador* or his *banderilleros* using pink and gold capes. These preliminaries conducted (and they can be short, if the bull is ferocious), the **suerte de picar** ensues, in which the **picadores** ride out and take up positions at opposite sides of the ring, while the bull is distracted by other *toreros*. Once they are in place, the bull is made to charge one of the horses, at which moment the *picador* drives his short-pointed lance into the bull's neck, while it tries to toss his padded and blindfolded (on the right eye) mount. The whole purpose here is to tire and weaken the bull's powerful neck and shoulder muscles, thus forcing him to lower his head – without which it would be impossibly dangerous to fight and kill on foot. This is repeated up to three times, until the horn sounds for the *picadores* to leave. For most neutral spectators, it is the least acceptable and most squalid stage of the proceedings, and it is clearly not a pleasant experience for the horses, their ears stuffed with rags to shut out the noise of the bull and spectators, and their vocal cords cut to prevent any terrified cries from alarming the crowd.

Suerte de bandilleras

The next stage, the **suerte de banderillas**, involves the placing of three sets of *banderillas* (barbed darts mounted on coloured shafts) into the bull's shoulders. Each of the three **banderilleros** delivers these in turn, attracting the bull's attention with the movement of his own body rather than a cape, and deftly placing the *banderillas* whilst both he and the bull are running towards each other. He then runs to safety out of the bull's vision, sometimes with the assistance of his colleagues, but occasionally a canny animal will set off in pursuit of his tormentor, often resulting in an undignified leap over the *barrera* to escape the charging horns.

Suerte de matar

Once the *banderillas* have been placed, the **suerte de matar** begins, and the **matador** enters the ring alone, having exchanged his pink and gold cape for the red *muleta*. He (or she) salutes the president and then dedicates the bull either to an individual, to whom he gives his hat, or to the audience, by placing his hat in the centre of the ring. It is in this part of the *corrida* that judgements are made and the performance is focused, as the *matador* displays his skills on the (by now exhausted) bull. He uses the movements of the cape to attract the bull, while his body remains still. If he does well, the band will start to play, while the crowd "olé" each pass. This stage lasts around ten minutes and ends with the kill. The *matador* attempts to get the bull into a position where he can drive a sword between its shoulders and through to the heart for a *coup de grâce*. In practice, they rarely succeed in this, instead taking a second sword, the *descabello*, crossed at the end, to cut the bull's spinal cord; this causes instant death. If things get really bad and he can't finish the job with this, then he will instruct one of his *cuadrilla* to end the business with a *puntilla*, a dagger stabbed into the base of the beast's skull. By this time the crowd will be whistling their derision whilst "the whole spectacle of theatre, courage and art is reduced to the level of a knacker's yard", as one commentator vividly described it.

Alternatively, if the audience are impressed by the *matador*'s performance, they will wave their handkerchiefs and shout for an award to be made by the president. He can award one or both ears, and a tail – the better the display, the more pieces the *matador* gets – while if he has excelled himself, he will be carried shoulder high out of the ring by the crowd, through the *puerta grande*, the main door, which is normally kept locked. The bull, too, may be applauded for its performance, as it is dragged out by the mule team.

Tickets

Tickets for *corridas* in the major city *plazas de toros* start at around €20 for a *sol* seat (see below) rising to €100 and above for the prime seats at prestigious fights in rings such as Seville's Maestranza. The cheapest seats are *gradas*, the highest rows at the back, from where you can see everything that happens without too much of the detail; the front rows are known as the *barreras*. Seats are also divided into *sol* (sun), *sombra* (shade), and *sol y sombra* (shaded after a while), though these distinctions have become less relevant as more bullfights start later in the day, at 6pm or 7pm, rather than the traditional 5pm. The *sombra* seats are more expensive – not so much for the spectators' personal comfort but because most of the action takes place in the shade. Tickets for *novilladas* (novice fights with young bulls) are much cheaper, costing €10–40, and are often given away free by bars or agents outside the bullring prior to the *corrida* if there hasn't been much demand (which is often the case).

On the way in, you can rent cushions – two hours sitting on concrete is not much fun. They also count as something to toss in the ring when there's an especially awful performance – as frequently happens. Beer and soft drinks are sold inside.

Football

The nation threw a huge party when finally, at the 2008 European Championships, the Spanish national football team shook off decades of habitual underperformance and actually won something, beating Germany to become European champions in some style. They threw an even bigger party when this football-crazy nation added the World Cup to the trophy cabinet in 2010.

It's been a good while coming – although **fútbol** has long been the most popular sport in Spain, it's only recently that Spanish football has made much of an international splash, possibly because many of Spain's better players went abroad to hone their skills. In the English Premier League alone there are more than thirty Spanish professionals of whom Pepe Reina, Fernando Torres, David de Gea and David Silva are the best known. The Spanish domestic top flight has been weakened as a result, but still remains one of the most competitive in Europe. Certainly, if you want the excitement of a genuinely Spanish event, watching a Sunday-evening game in La Liga (ⓦ lfp.es) usually produces as much passion as anything you'll find in the Plaza de Toros.

For decades, the country's two dominant teams have been Real Madrid and F.C. Barcelona. In the early years of the new millennium the big two faced a bit more opposition than usual from clubs like Valencia, Villareal and Sevilla, but the Madrid-Barcelona power axis has since reasserted itself – any weekend, the big football story will be if either of the two giants fails to win by a convincing score.

Andaluz teams

Sevilla are the main team in Andalucía, followed in recent seasons by their fierce city rivals **Real Betis**. Other *andaluz* clubs in the top flight include yo-yo team **Málaga** who achieved promotion back to the First Division yet again in 2007–08 after a couple of seasons in Division Two. Two others of note are **Recreativo Huelva**, Spain's oldest club, and the remarkable **Almería** who reached the First Division less than twenty years after being founded in 1989. The most amazing *andaluz* story, though, belongs to plucky little CF Granada who nearly went out of business due to financial difficulties in July 2009 when in the Third Division; they dramatically turned things around and following successive promotions attained the dizzy heights of the First Division where they last played in the 1970s.

Seeing a game

The league **season** runs from late August until mid-May or early June, and most games kick off at 5pm or 7pm on Sundays, though live TV demands that one key game kicks off at 9pm or 10pm on Saturday and Sunday.

With the exception of a few important games – such as when either of the big two plays Sevilla or the two Seville teams play their derbys – match tickets are pretty easy to get; they start at around €30 for average First Division games but get close to double this when *Real* or *Barca* are in town. Trouble is very rare: English fans, in particular, will be amazed at the easy-going family atmosphere and mixed-sex crowds. August is a surprisingly good time to catch games since there's a glut of warm-up matches for the new season, often involving top foreign clubs.

If you don't go to a game, the atmosphere can be pretty good watching on TV in a local bar, especially in a city whose team is playing away. Many bars advertise the matches they screen, which, if they have satellite connections, can include Sunday afternoon English League and Cup games. ⓦ soccer-spain.com is a very good English-language website where you'll find comprehensive news and articles.

Travelling with children

Spain is a good country to travel with children of any age; they will be well received everywhere, and babies and toddlers, in particular, will be the centre of attention. You will probably have to change your usual routine, since young children stay up late in Spain, especially in the summer. It's very common for them to be running around pavement cafés and public squares after 10pm or 11pm, and yours will no doubt enjoy joining in. It's expected that families dine out with their children, too, and it's not unusual to see up to four generations of the same family eating tapas in a bar.

Holidays

Many holiday hotels and self-contained club-style resorts offer things like kids' clubs, babysitting, sports and entertainment. The only caveat is that, of course, you're unlikely to see much of Spain on these family-oriented holidays. The two best cities to take children, hands down, are **Seville** and **Granada**, which have loads of child-friendly attractions. Otherwise, The region also has various theme parks and leisure activities specifically aimed at kids, most notably the **Isla Mágica** in Seville (see p.280), **Tivoli World** near Benalmádena on the Costa del Sol (see p.110) and the Western film set of **Mini**

Hollywood in Almería (see p.557), while Andalucía's long coastline has a bunch of popular **water parks.**

Museums, galleries and sights throughout Andalucía either offer **discounts** or **free entry** for children (places are often free for under-4s or even under-7s), and it's the same on trains, sightseeing tours, boat trips and most other usual tourist attractions.

Accommodation

If you're travelling independently, finding **child-friendly accommodation** shouldn't be a problem, as *hostales* and *pensiones* generally offer rooms with three or four beds. Bear in mind, though, that much budget accommodation in towns and cities is located on the upper floors of buildings, often without lifts. It's also worth noting that some older-style *pensiones* don't have heating systems – and it can get very cold in winter. If you want a cot provided, or baby-listening or **baby-sitting** services, you'll usually have to stay in a more expensive hotel – and even then, never assume that these facilities are provided, and always check in advance. **Self-catering accommodation** offers the most flexibility, and there's plenty of it throughout the region, from seaside apartments to country houses; even in major cities, it's easy to rent an apartment by the night or week and enjoy living like a local with your family.

Products, clothes and services

Baby food, **disposable nappies**, **formula milk** and other standard items are widely available in pharmacies and supermarkets, though not necessarily with the same range or brands that you will be used to at home. Organic baby food, for example, is hard to come by away from the big-city supermarkets and most Spanish non-organic baby foods contain small amounts of sugar or salt. Fresh milk, too, is not always available; UHT is more commonly drunk by small children. If you require anything specific, it's best to bring it with you or check with the manufacturer about equivalent brands.

Families might eat out a lot, but things like **high chairs and special children's menus** are rare although many more restaurants are now making an effort in this area. Most bars and cafés will be happy to heat milk bottles for you. **Baby-changing areas** are also relatively rare, except in department stores and shopping centres, and even where they do exist they are not always up to scratch.

Travel essentials

Addresses

Addresses are written as: C/Picasso 2, 4° izda. – which means Picasso Street (*calle*) no. 2, fourth floor, left- (*izquierda*) hand flat or office; dcha. (*derecha*) is right; cto. (*centro*) centre; s/n (*sin número*) means the building has no number; *bajo* signifies ground floor.

Climate

Overall, spring, early summer and autumn are ideal times for a trip to Andalucía – though the weather does vary significantly from region to region: the Sierra de Grazalema records Spain's highest **rainfall**, while the province of Almería has the most hours of **sun**. Note that our chart (see p.50) shows average temperatures – and while Seville, the hottest city in Spain, can soar high into the high 30s at midday in summer, it is a fairly comfortable 23–27°C (75–80°F) through much of the morning and late afternoon. Temperatures in mountain regions, in the Sierra Nevada or the Sierra de Cazorla for example, can approach freezing at night in winter, but remain refreshingly cool throughout the hottest summers – a boon for hikers and anyone uncomfortable with blistering heat.

Complaints

By law, all establishments (including hotels and restaurants) must keep a *libro de reclamaciones* (**complaints book**) and bring it out for regular inspection by the authorities. If you think you've been overcharged, or have any other problems, you can usually produce an immediate resolution by asking for the book. Most establishments prefer to keep them empty, thus attracting no unwelcome attention from officialdom, which, of course, works in your favour. If you do make an entry, English is acceptable but write clearly and simply; add your home address, too, as you are entitled to be informed of any action, including – but don't count on it – compensation. You can also take your complaint to any local Turismo, which should attempt to resolve the matter while you wait.

Costs

Prices in Andalucía and Spain have increased considerably over the last ten years or so, but there are still few places in Europe where you'll get a

AVERAGE DAILY TEMPERATURES

	Feb	Apr	Jun	Aug	Oct	Dec
ALMERÍA						
Max/min (°C)	16/8	20/12	26/18	29/22	23/16	17/9
Max/min (°F)	61/46	68/54	79/64	84/72	73/61	63/48
CÁDIZ						
Max/min (°C)	16/9	21/12	27/18	30/20	23/16	16/9
Max/min (°F)	61/48	70/54	80/64	86/68	73/61	61/48
CÓRDOBA						
Max/min (°C)	16/5	23/10	32/17	36/20	24/13	14/5
Max/min (°F)	61/41	73/50	90/63	97/68	75/55	57/41
GRANADA						
Max/min (°C)	14/2	20/7	30/14	34/17	22/9	12/2
Max/min (°F)	57/36	68/45	86/57	93/63	72/48	54/36
HUELVA						
Max/min (°C)	18/7	22/11	29/16	32/18	25/14	17/7
Max/min (°F)	64/45	72/52	84/61	90/64	77/57	63/45
JAÉN						
Max/min (°C)	14/5	20/10	30/17	34/21	22/13	12/5
Max/min (°F)	57/41	68/50	86/63	93/70	72/55	54/41
MÁLAGA						
Max/min (°C)	17/8	21/11	28/17	30/20	24/15	17/9
Max/min (°F)	63/46	70/52	82/63	86/68	75/59	63/48
SEVILLE						
Max/min (°C)	17/6	23/11	32/17	36/20	26/14	16/7
Max/min (°F)	63/43	73/52	90/63	97/68	79/57	61/45
TARIFA						
Max/min (°C)	17/11	20/13	24/17	27/20	23/17	17/11
Max/min (°F)	63/52	68/55	75/63	80/68	73/63	63/52

better deal on the cost of simple meals and drinks. Public transport, too, remains very good value. Big cities and tourist resorts are invariably more expensive than remoter areas, and prices are hiked to take advantage of special events, so for example you'd be lucky to find a room in Seville during Semana Santa (Holy Week) or the Feria de Abril at less than a third above the usual rate.

It's difficult to come up with a **daily budget** for the region, as your €0.60 glass of wine and €30 *pensión* room in rural Andalucía might be €1.50 and €50, respectively, in Seville or Granada. However, as a very rough guide, if you always share a room in the cheapest *pensiones* and hotels, use public transport and stick to local restaurants and bars, you could get by on between €50 and €80 a day. Stay somewhere a bit more stylish or comfortable, eat in fancier restaurants, and go out on the town, and you'll need more like €80–120 a day. And if you're holidaying in Spain's magnificent *paradores* or five-star hotels, that figure will hardly cover your room. There's more detailed information about prices in the "Accommodation" (see p.35), "Getting around" (see p.31) and "Food and drink" (see p.37) sections.

Visiting museums, galleries, churches and monasteries soon adds up – if you visited every sight we cover in Granada alone, for example, you'd be out of pocket by €40 or so. Accordingly, it pays to take along any **student/youth** or **senior citizen cards** you may be entitled to, such as the International Student ID Card (ISIC; ⓦisiccard.com), as most attractions offer discounts (and make sure you carry your passport or ID card, although most places will accept a reasonably clear photocopy of these). Some museums and attractions are **free** on a certain day of the week or month (though note that this is sometimes limited to EU citizens only; you'll need to show your passport). Any **entrance fees** noted in the Guide are for the full adult price; children (as well as seniors) usually get a discount, and younger kids are often free.

Crime and personal safety

The **Guardia Civil**, in green uniforms, is a national police force, formerly a military organization, and has responsibility for national crime, as well as roads, borders and guarding public buildings. There's also the blue-uniformed **Policía Nacional**, mainly seen in cities, who deal with crime, drugs, crowd control, identity and immigration matters, and the like. Locally, most policing is carried out by the **Policía Local** or **Municipal**, who wear blue-and-white uniforms, and these tend to be the most approachable in the first instance if you're reporting a crime. There's obviously a certain overlap between regional and municipal forces, and you may be passed from one to another, depending on what you're reporting.

In the unlikely event that you're mugged or otherwise robbed, go straight to the police, where you'll need to make an official statement known as a **denuncia**, not least because your insurance company will require a police report. Expect it to be a time-consuming and laborious business – you can do the bulk of it by phone, or even online (ⓦpolicia.es), but you'll still have to go into the station to sign it. If you have your passport stolen, contact your nearest embassy or consulate; to find this visit a site such as ⓦprojectvisa.com, ⓦembassiesabroad.com or ⓦspainexpat.com who have complete lists with contact numbers. Alternatively, see the "Directory" sections in Málaga (p.79) and Seville (p.303) for consulates in Andalucía.

Avoiding trouble

Petty crime – pickpocketing and bag-snatching – is, unfortunately, a fact of life in Spanish cities and tourist resorts, though no more so than anywhere else in Europe. The usual sensible **precautions** include: carrying bags slung across your neck, not

over your shoulder; not putting wallets in your back pocket; leaving passport and tickets in the hotel safe; and keeping a photocopy of your passport, plus notes of your credit card number helplines and so on. Take special care on public transport, and don't leave **bags** unattended anywhere, even if you're looking at rooms upstairs in a *hostal*; know where your belongings are at all times.

Drivers shouldn't leave anything in view in a **parked car** particularly in Málaga or Seville; take the SatNav, iPod and (if detachable) radio/CD player with you. **On the road**, be cautious about accepting help from anyone other than a uniformed police officer – some roadside thieves pose as "good Samaritans" to people experiencing car and tyre problems, some of which, such as slashed tyres, may have been inflicted at rest stops or service stations in advance. The thieves typically attempt to divert your attention by pointing out a problem and then steal items from the vehicle while you are looking elsewhere.

Incidentally, if you are stopped by a proper police officer for a **driving offence**, being foreign just won't wash as an excuse. They'll fine you on the spot, cash or card.

Sexual harassment

Spain's macho image has faded dramatically, and these days there are relatively few parts of the country where foreign **women travelling alone** are likely to feel intimidated or attract unwanted attention. There is little of the pestering that you have to contend with in, say, the larger Italian cities, and the outdoor culture of *terrazas* (terrace bars) and the tendency of Spaniards to move around in large, mixed crowds, help to make you feel less exposed. "*Déjame en paz*" ("leave me in peace") is a fairly standard rebuff and if you are in any doubt, take a taxi, always the safest way to travel late at night.

The major **resorts** of the *costas* have their own artificial holiday culture, where any problems are most likely to be caused by other alcohol-fuelled holidaymakers. You are actually more vulnerable in isolated, **rural regions**, where you can walk for hours without coming across an inhabited farm or house, though it's rare that this poses a threat –

EMERGENCY NUMBERS

❶ **112** All emergency services
❶ **061** Ambulance
❶ **080** Fire service
❶ **062** Guardia Civil
❶ **091** Policía Nacional

help and hospitality are much more the norm. Many single women happily tramp the long-distance footpaths, from Tarifa to the Sierra Nevada, though you are always best advised to stay in rooms and *pensiones* rather than camping wild.

Electricity

The current in most of Spain is 220v – bring an adaptor (and transformer) to use UK and US laptops, cellphone chargers and the like.

Entry requirements

EU citizens (and those of Norway, Iceland, Liechtenstein and Switzerland) need only a valid national-identity card or passport to enter Spain. Other Europeans, and citizens of the **United States**, **Canada**, **Australia**, **New Zealand** require a passport but no visa, and can stay as a tourist for up to ninety days. Other nationalities (including South Africans) will need to get a visa from a Spanish embassy or consulate before departure. Visa requirements do change, and it's always advisable to check the current situation before leaving home.

Most EU citizens who want to stay in Spain for longer than three months, rather than just visit as a tourist, need to register at a provincial **Oficina de Extranjeros** (Foreigners' Office), where they'll be issued with a residence certificate; you'll find a list of offices (eventually) on the Ministry of Interior website (Ⓦ mir.es). You don't need the certificate if you're an EU citizen living and working legally in Spain, or if you're legally self-employed or a student (on an exchange programme or otherwise). US citizens can apply for one ninety-day extension, showing proof of funds, but this must be done from outside Spain. Other nationalities wishing to extend their stay will need to get a special visa from a Spanish embassy or consulate before departure.

Gay and lesbian travellers

Same-sex marriages were made legal in Spain in 2005, giving same-sex couples the same rights as heterosexual couples, including the right to adopt, and the age of consent is sixteen – the same as for heterosexual couples.

There's a thriving **gay scene** in most of Andalucía's main cities, most notably, of course, in Seville and Cádiz. The latter is long famous for its liberal traditions and its **Carnaval** is a wonderfully hedonistic time to visit, while **Torremolinos** (voted

best Spanish gay destination by one gay website) is another popular holiday location. The Spanish term for the gay scene is *"el ambiente"* ("the atmosphere"), while another useful expression is *"entiendo"*, literally, "I understand", but meaning "I'm gay".

USEFUL CONTACTS

Ⓦ fundacióntriangulo.org
Ⓦ andalucia.com/living/gay.htm
Ⓦ gayinfospain.com

Health

The **European Health Insurance Card** (EHIC) gives EU citizens access to Spanish state public-health services under reciprocal agreements. While this will provide free or reduced-cost medical care in the event of minor injuries and emergencies, it won't cover every eventuality – and it only applies to EU citizens in possession of the card – so travel insurance (see below) is essential.

No **inoculations** are required for Spain, and the worst that's likely to happen to you is that you might fall victim to an upset stomach. To be safe, wash fruit and avoid tapas dishes that look as if they were prepared last week. Water at public fountains is fine, unless there's a sign saying *"agua no potable"*, in which case don't drink it.

For minor complaints, go to a **farmacia** – they're easy to find, and pharmacists are highly trained, willing to give advice (often in English) and able to dispense many drugs that would be available only on prescription in other countries. They keep usual shop hours (Mon–Fri 9am–1.30pm & 5–8pm), but some open late and at weekends, while a rota system keeps at least one open 24 hours in every town. The rota is displayed in the window of every pharmacy, or you can check the list in the local newspaper.

If you have special medical or dietary requirements, it is advisable to carry a letter from your doctor, translated into Spanish, indicating the nature of your condition and necessary treatments. With luck, you'll get the address of an English-speaking **doctor** from the nearest *farmacia*, police station or tourist office – it's obviously more likely in resorts and big cities. Treatment at **hospitals** for EU citizens in possession of the EHIC card is free; otherwise, you'll be charged at private-hospital rates, which can be very expensive.

Insurance

You should take out a comprehensive **insurance policy** before travelling to Spain, to cover against

ROUGH GUIDES TRAVEL INSURANCE

Rough Guides has teamed up with WorldNomads.com to offer great travel insurance deals. Policies are available to residents of over 150 countries, with cover for a wide range of adventure sports, 24hr emergency assistance, high levels of medical and evacuation cover and a stream of travel safety information. Roughguides.com users can take advantage of their policies online 24/7, from anywhere in the world – even if you're already travelling. And since plans often change when you're on the road, you can extend your policy and even claim online. Roughguides.com users who buy travel insurance with WorldNomads.com can also leave a positive footprint and donate to a community development project. For more information go to ⓦ roughguides.com/shop.

loss, theft, illness or injury. A typical policy will provide cover for loss of baggage, tickets and – up to a certain limit – cash or travellers' cheques, as well as cancellation or curtailment of your journey. When securing baggage cover, make sure that the per-article limit will cover your most valuable possession. Most policies exclude so-called **dangerous sports** unless an extra premium is paid: in Spain, this can mean most watersports are excluded (plus rafting, canyoning, horseriding etc), though probably not things like bike tours or hiking.

If you need to make a claim, you should keep receipts for medicines and medical treatment, and in the event you have anything stolen, you must obtain an official statement from the police (see p.51).

Internet

Wireless internet access (wi-fi, pronounced "wee-fee" in Spain) is now widespread in cafés, bars, hotels and other public "hotspots" – such as certain central areas in major cities. Ask at any tourist office and they should be able to help you locate these and provide any password necessary to get online. Internet access is also widely available at cafés (often referred to as *cibercafés*), computer shops and phone offices (*locutorios*). You'll pay as little as €1 an hour in many places, though it can cost two or three times as much. Many backpacker hostels and small *pensiones* provide cheap or free internet access for guests, but hotel business centres or hotel bedrooms wired for access tend to be far more expensive than going out on the street to an internet place.

Laundry

You'll find a few coin-op self-service laundries (*lavanderías automáticas*) in most provincial capitals, but you normally have to leave your clothes for a service wash and dry at a *lavandería*. A dry cleaner

is a *tintorería*. Note that by law you're not allowed to leave laundry hanging out of windows over a street, and many *pensiones* and *hostales* expressly forbid washing clothes in the sink. To avoid an international incident, ask first if there's somewhere you can wash your clothes.

Mail

Post offices (Correos; ⓦ correos.es) are normally open weekdays from 8am to 2pm and again from 5pm to 7.30pm, though branches in bigger places may have longer hours, may not close at noon and may open on Saturday mornings. Correspondingly in smaller towns and villages the economic downturn has led to many offices cutting out the Saturday service altogether, and some the evening service too. The office-finder on the website gives exact opening hours and contact details for each post office in Spain. As you can also pay bills and buy phonecards in post offices, queues can be long – it's often easier to buy **stamps** at tobacconists (look for the brown and yellow *estanco* sign).

Outbound mail is reasonably reliable, with letters or cards taking around three days to a week to the UK and the rest of Europe, a week to ten days to North America, New Zealand and Australia, although it can be more erratic in the summer. There's also a whole host of express-mail services (ask for *urgente* or *exprés*).

Maps

In addition to the maps in this guide, you'll probably want a reasonable **road map**. This can be bought in Spain from most bookshops (*librerías*), and at street kiosks and petrol stations. The best single map for Andalucía is the regularly updated *Michelin Andalucía* (1:400,000), which includes a plan to get you in and out of Seville, the region's only serious traffic headache. It's widely available from bookshops in Spain and abroad. This has recently been complemented by the equally excellent larger scale *Michelin Costa del Sol* (1:200,000) covering not only the coast between Algeciras and Almería but a considerable way inland too, taking in significant chunks of the provinces of Cádiz, Málaga, Granada and Almería. An alternative is the rip-proof/waterproof *Rough Guide Andalucía Map* (1:650,000/1:150,000).

Any good book or travel shop in your own country should be able to provide a decent range of maps, or buy online from specialist stores such as Ⓦstanfords.co.uk or Ⓦrandmcnally.com. For hiking and trekking maps, specialist map/travel shops – and the **CNIG** (National Geographical Information Centre, Ⓦcnig.es) in each of Andalucía's provincial capitals – will stock the **topographical maps** issued by two government agencies, the Instituto Geográfico Nacional and the Servicio Geográfico del Ejército. These are available at scales of 1:200,000, 1:100,000, 1:50,000 and even occasionally 1:25,000. The various SGE series are considered to be more up to date, although neither agency is hugely reliable.

A Catalunya-based company, Editorial Alpina (Ⓦeditorialalpina.com) produces useful 1:40,000 or 1:25,000 map/booklet sets for many of the **mountain and foothill hiking areas** in Andalucía, and these are also on sale in many bookshops.

Money

Spain's currency is the **euro** (€), with notes issued in denominations of 5, 10, 20, 50, 100, 200 and 500 euros, and coins in denominations of 1, 2, 5, 10, 20 and 50 cents, and 1 and 2 euros. It's worth noting that many shops and businesses refuse to accept the larger €500 and even €200 notes, due to counterfeiting incidents in recent years. Up-to-the-minute currency **exchange rates** are posted on Ⓦoanda.com.

By far the easiest way to get money is to use your bank debit card to withdraw cash from an **ATM**, found in villages, towns and cities all over Spain, as well as on arrival at the airports and major train stations. You can usually withdraw up to €300 a day, and instructions are offered in English once you insert your card. Make sure you have a personal identification number (PIN) that's designed to work overseas, and take a note of your bank's emergency contact number in case the machine swallows your card. This can be a major hassle and it's worth drawing money from the ATM while the bank is open; should you lose your card there's then a reasonable chance the bank can retrieve it for you.

Some European debit cards can also be used directly in shops to pay for purchases; you'll need to check first with your bank.

All major **credit cards** are accepted in hotels, restaurants and shops, and for tours, tickets and transport, though don't count on being able to use them in every small *pensión* or village café. You can also use your credit card in an ATM to withdraw cash, though remember that these advances will be treated as loans, with interest accruing daily from the date of withdrawal. If you use a foreign credit card in some shops, you may also be asked for photo ID, so be prepared to show a driving licence or passport. Make sure you make a note of the number for reporting lost or stolen cards to your credit card company.

Spanish **bancos** (banks) and **cajas de ahorros** (savings banks) have branches in all but the smallest villages. **Banking hours** are usually Monday to Friday 8.30am–2pm, with some city branches open Saturday 8.30am–1pm (except June–Sept when all banks close on Sat), although times can vary from bank to bank. Outside these times, it's usually possible to change cash at larger hotels (generally with bad rates and low commission) or with travel agents – useful for small amounts in a hurry. One place that doesn't charge a hefty commission on exchange is the department store El Corte Inglés, with branches in all Andalucía's provincial capitals and many large towns.

In tourist areas, you'll also find specialist **casas de cambio**, with more convenient hours (though rates vary), while some major tourist offices and larger train stations also have exchange facilities open throughout business hours.

Opening hours

Almost everything in Andalucía – shops, museums, churches, tourist offices – closes for a **siesta** of at least three hours in the middle part of the day. There's a lot of variation, with many major supermarkets now tending to stay open all day, but you'll get far less aggravated if you accept that the early afternoon is best spent asleep, or in a bar, or both.

Basic **working hours** are Monday to Friday 9.30am to 2pm and 5 to 8pm. Many **shops** open slightly later on a Saturday (at 10am) and close for the day at 2pm, though you'll still find plenty of places open in cities, and there are regional variations. Moreover, department and chain stores and shopping malls tend to open a straight Monday to Saturday 10am to 9 or 10pm.

Museums and galleries, with very few exceptions (Granada's Alhambra is one), also take a break between 1pm or 2pm and 4pm. On Sundays, most open mornings only, and on Mondays the majority close all day. Opening hours vary from year to year, though normally not by more than half an hour or so. Some are also seasonal, and usually in Andalucía "summer" means from Easter until September and "winter" from October until Easter. However, some museums and tourist offices regard summer as referring to the high summer months of July and August.

The most important **cathedrals, churches and monasteries** operate in much the same way as museums, with regular visiting hours and admission charges. Other churches, though, are kept locked, opening only for worship in the early morning and/or the evening (usually between 6pm and 9pm).

Phones

Spanish **telephone numbers** have nine digits; mobile numbers begin with a "6", freephone numbers begin "900", while other "90 +" and "80 +" numbers are nationwide standard-rate or special-rate services. To **call Spain from abroad**, you dial your country's international access code + 34 (Spain's country code) + the nine-digit Spanish number.

Public telephones have instructions in English, and accept coins, credit cards and phonecards. **Phonecards** (*tarjetas*) with discounted rates for calls are available in tobacconists, newsagents and post offices, issued in various denominations either by Telefónica (the dominant operator) or one of its rivals. Credit cards are not recommended for local and national calls, since most have a minimum charge that is far more than a normal call is likely to cost. It's also best to avoid making calls from the phone in your hotel room, as even local calls will be slapped with a heavy surcharge.

You can make international calls from any public pay phone, but it's cheaper to go to one of the ubiquitous phone centres, or **locutorios**, which specialize in discounted overseas connections. **Calling home from Spain**, you dial ☎00 (Spain's international access code) + your country code + city/area code minus initial zero + number. For **reverse-charge calls,** dial the international operator (☎1008 Europe, ☎1005 rest of the world).

Most European **mobile phones** will work in Spain, though it's worth checking with your provider whether you need to get international access switched on and whether there are any extra charges involved. Even though prices are coming down, it's still expensive to use your own mobile extensively while abroad, and you will pay for receiving incoming calls, for example. You could always simply buy a local **SIM card** instead for your mobile, from operators such as Vodafone (Ⓦvodafone.es) or Movistar (Ⓦmovistar.es). Or if you plan to spend some time in Spain, it's almost certainly better to buy a Spanish mobile, as the cheapest non-contract, **pay-as-you-go phones** cost from around €29. You can buy top-up cards, or have them recharged for you, in phone shops, *estancos* (tobacconists), newsstands, supermarkets and post offices, and from ATMs.

Public holidays

Alongside the Spanish **national public holidays** (see box below) there are scores of regional holidays and local fiestas (often marking the local saint's day), any of which will mean that everything except hotels, bars and restaurants locks its doors.

In addition, **August** is traditionally Spain's holiday month, when many of the big cities – especially Seville and Cordoba – are semi-deserted, with many of the shops and restaurants closed for the duration. In contrast, it can prove nearly impossible to find a room in the more popular coastal and mountain resorts at these times; similarly, seats on planes, trains and buses in August should if possible be booked in advance.

Shopping

Shopping in Andalucía can range from digging around in local **flea markets** to browsing the **designer boutiques** in Seville and Granada. In the

---

SPANISH NATIONAL PUBLIC HOLIDAYS

January 1 *Año Nuevo* New Year's Day
January 6 *Epifanía* Epiphany
March/April *Viernes Santo* Good Friday
May 1 *Fiesta del Trabajo* May Day
August 15 *La Asunción* Assumption of the Virgin
October 12 *Día de la Hispanidad* National Day
November 1 *Todos los Santos* All Saints'
December 6 *Día de la Constitución* Constitution Day
December 8 *Inmaculada Concepción*
December 25 *Navidad* Christmas Day

larger towns and cities, most high streets will feature Spanish clothing favourites such as Mango and Zara, along with Camper, the country's most famous shoe brand. For food, **supermarkets** are easy to locate, while **street markets** (*mercadillos*) are held virtually everywhere, and are a great place to pick up fresh produce. The main department store found in most major towns and cities is El Corte Inglés, where you can buy almost anything.

The region is also well known for its local crafts. **Leatherwork**, such as belts, bags, purses and even saddles are best sought out in Córdoba or the medieval leather town of Ubrique (Cádiz), while Seville is where you'll be able to pick up the most authentic **flamenco** accessories such as dresses, fans, shawls and lace. Córdoba is also the place for stylish handmade **hats**, which are sold at bargain prices. **Ceramics** are widely available, but are especially good in Úbeda (where there's a thriving ancient pottery tradition), Níjar and Sorbas (both in Almería). Handwoven **carpets** and **ponchos** are to be found in Las Alpujarras and the Sierra de Grazalema, and Níjar is also famed for its *jarapas* (carpets made from rags). Jerez is, of course the place for buying **sherry**, and nearby Sanlúcar de Barrameda's *manzanilla* variety shouldn't be overlooked either. **Olive oil** makes a great gift to take home and Andalucía has some of the finest producers in the world in places like Baena and Zuheros (Córdoba) and Segura de la Sierra (Jaén). The region is also, of course, the home of the **guitar** and some of the finest (and most beautiful) instruments are made by the craftsmen in Granada.

Smoking

Since 2006 **smoking in public places** in Spain has been regulated by law, and tougher restrictions introduced in 2011 mean that it's now forbidden to smoke in all public buildings and transport facilities, plus bars, restaurants, clubs and cafés. Compared to other countries with smoking restrictions in force, you'll find there's still an awful lot of puffing going on, though the ban is generally observed.

Taxes

Sales tax – **IVA** (pronounced "eeba") – often comes as an unexpected surprise when you pay the bill for food or accommodation. It's not always specified, and is eight percent for hotels and restaurants and eighteen percent for other goods and services (though most other prices are quoted inclusive of IVA). **Non-EU residents** are able to

claim back the sales tax on purchases that come to over €90. To do this, make sure the shop you're buying from fills out the correct paperwork, and present this to customs before you check in at the airport for your return flight.

Time

Spain is one hour ahead of the UK, six hours ahead of Eastern Standard Time, nine hours ahead of Pacific Standard Time, eight hours behind Australia, ten hours behind New Zealand, and the same time as South Africa. Clocks go forward in the last week in March and back again in the last week in October. It's worth noting, if you're planning to cross the border, that Portugal is an hour behind Spain throughout the year.

Tipping

Tipping is common in Spain, although not always expected. Locals are small tippers and twenty cents on a bar table or five percent in a restaurant is usually enough. It is also common practice to tip taxi drivers, hotel porters and the like in small change.

Toilets

Public toilets are generally reasonably clean but don't always have paper. They can very occasionally, in rural locations, still be squat-style. They are most commonly referred to and labelled *Los Servicios* (which is what you should ask for), though signs may point you to *baños* or *aseos*. *Damas* (Ladies) or *Señoras* (often signed with a "D" or "S") and *Caballeros* (Gentlemen, often marked simply "C") are the usual distinguishing signs for gender, though you may also see the potentially confusing combination of *Señoras* (Women) and *Señores* (Men).

Tourist information

The Spanish national tourist office, **Turespaña** (Ⓦ spain.info), is an excellent source of information when planning your trip. The website is full of ideas, information and searchable databases, and there are links to similar websites of Turespaña offices in your own country. In Andalucía, you'll find Junta de Andalucía (regional government) **Turismos** (tourist offices) in every provincial capital and many reasonably sized towns. These are typically open Monday to Friday 9am–2pm & 4–7pm, Saturday and Sunday 9am to 2pm, but hours do vary from place to place.

In major cities and coastal resorts the offices tend to remain open all day Saturday and on Sunday morning between April and September. In addition to the Junta's offices many towns and cities also provide their own **municipal tourist offices** which are frequently excellent and usually less busy than the Junta's outlets.

Travellers with disabilities

The classic tourist images of Andalucía – the medieval old towns, winding lanes, the castles and monasteries – don't exactly fill you with confidence if you're in a wheelchair. However, Spain is changing and facilities are improving rapidly, especially in the more go-ahead, contemporary cities. There are accessible rooms and hotels in all major Spanish cities and resorts and, by law, all new public buildings (including revamped museums and galleries) are required to be fully accessible. Public transport is the main problem, since most local buses and trains are virtually impossible for wheelchairs, though again there are pockets of excellence throughout the region. The AVE high-speed train service, for example, is fully accessible, as is every city bus in Málaga. In many towns and cities, acoustic traffic-light signals and dropped kerbs are common.

Some organizations at home may be able to advise you further about travel to Spain, like the very useful UK-based **Tourism For All** (Ⓦtourism forall.org.uk). **Access Travel** (Ⓦaccess-travel.co.uk) can arrange flights, transfers and accommodation in Andalucía, and at the very least, local tourist offices in Spain should also be able to recommend a suitable hotel or taxi company.

Málaga province

RONDA

1

Málaga province

The Andalucian sun starts singing a fire song, and all creation trembles at the sound.   Federico García Lorca

The smallest of Andalucía's eight provinces, Málaga is also its most populous, swelling to bursting point with the sheer weight of visitors in high summer. Although primarily known as the gateway to the Costa del Sol and its unashamedly commercial resorts such as Torremolinos and Marbella, the province has much more to offer than just its coastline. To most incoming tourists the provincial capital of Málaga is merely "the place by the airport", but it's also a vibrant city in its own right, with a revamped centre and plenty of exciting nightlife and places to eat, as well as a trio of outstanding art galleries.

In the west of Málaga's provincial heartland lies the **Serranía de Ronda**, a series of small mountain ranges sprinkled with gleaming, whitewashed *pueblos blancos* (White Towns), of which **Ronda**, located astride the stunningly beautiful El Tajo gorge, is justly the most famous. To the north lies the appealing market town of **Antequera** with its remarkable prehistoric dolmens and sumptuous Baroque churches, and from here it's a quick hop south to the natural wonders of **El Torcal**, where vast limestone outcrops have been eroded into a landscape of weird natural sculptures. Another possible trip from Antequera is to the spectacular **El Chorro Gorge**, which, along with the Embalse de Guadalhorce, has become a major climbing and camping centre. Nearby, the saline **Laguna de Fuente de Piedra** is Europe's only inland breeding ground for the greater flamingo, whose flying flocks make a spectacular sight in summer.

The far eastern section of Málaga province is the largely unknown and little-visited **Axarquía** region, an area of rugged natural beauty and once the haunt of mountain bandits. Now the domain of the *cabra hispánica*, a distinctive Iberian long-horned goat, the area's magnificent scenery and earthy villages contrast starkly with the crowded **beaches** to the south.

Málaga

First impressions of **MÁLAGA** are not encouraging. A large and bustling seaport with a population passing half a million, it's the second city of Andalucía (after Seville) and also one of the poorest, with unemployment numbers persistently among the highest in the region. Yet, though many visitors get no further than the train or bus stations, put off by the grim clusters of high-rises on the fringes, if you penetrate beyond these you will find yourself in one of the most atmospheric and historic cities in Spain. Lorca described Málaga as his favourite town and, given a chance, it can be a surprisingly attractive place, an impression boosted by the ebullient and big-hearted *malagueños*, among the friendliest people in Andalucía.

Overlooking the town and port, the wonderfully preserved fourteenth-century citadels of the **Alcazaba** and **Gibralfaro** bear remarkable witness to the city's Moorish past, while

Festivals in Málaga p.66
Convento dulces p.76
Walking the Camino del Rey p.80
Ibn Hafsun p.81

A walk near Frigiliana p.105
Pedro Romero: father of the corrida p.133
A walk from Benaoján to Jimera de Libar p.142

FOUNTAIN IN FRONT OF THE GIBRALFARO, MÁLAGA

Highlights

❶ Málaga A vibrant city crammed with bars, cafés, museums and a fabulous Moorish fortress. **See p.60**

❷ Museo Picasso With over 280 artworks by Málaga's most famous son, this remarkable museum shouldn't be missed. **See p.68**

❸ Ronda Beautiful hill town set astride a yawning gorge with sensational views over the Serranía de Ronda. **See p.129**

❹ Serranía de Ronda This mountainous country south of Ronda is some of the wildest and most spectacular in Andalucía. **See p.141**

❺ Costa del Sol Despite its downmarket image, there are individual resorts – Nerja, Marbella and Estepona – with plenty of style. **See p.106**

❻ Marbella Lively resort with bags of glitz and glamour, plus a vibrant nightlife and great tapas bars and restaurants. **See p.113**

❼ Parque Natural El Torcal El Torcal is famous for its almost lunar landscape and surreal limestone formations. **See p.90**

❽ Laguna de Fuente de Piedra The largest natural lake in Andalucía and one of Europe's major breeding grounds for the greater flamingo. **See p.91**

HIGHLIGHTS ARE MARKED ON THE MAP ON P.62

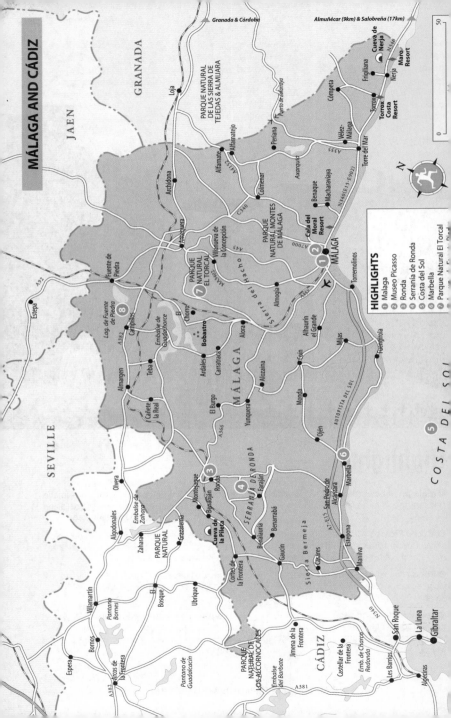

a **Roman theatre** below predates them by a over a millenium. The city also has a trio of outstanding art galleries, including the spectacular **Museo Picasso Málaga**, housing a major collection of work by Picasso (who was born in Málaga). And if on sultrier days you want to escape from the crowds and heat, the nineteenth-century **Jardín Botánico de la Concepción** (botanical garden) is tailor-made, with a fine collection of plants and trees from all over the world. Further afield, the traditional fishing villages of **El Palo** and **Pedregalejo**, now absorbed into the suburbs, are home to a series of small beaches and a *paseo* lined with some of the best fish and seafood cafés in the province.

Málaga is bisected by the seasonal **Guadalmedina river**, which was unsuccessfully landscaped in the 1990s at colossal cost, with dismal walkways and reluctant grass. All the major sights lie to the east of this and below the Alcazaba. From the **Alameda**, the city's main thoroughfare, the cathedral, Museo Picasso, Carmen Thyssen and modern art museums, and a clutch of interesting churches all lie within a few minutes' walk. The city government has done an impressive job over the last decade in tidying up the monumental zone and the *casco antiguo* (old quarter), making it a wonderful place to wander through streets and squares filled with animated bars and cafés as well as craft and fashion shops. The centrepiece of this scheme has been the pedestrianizing and laying with marble of the whole of Calle Marqués de Larios – the city's most fashionable shopping street – and the focal Plaza de la Constitución.

Brief history

The **Phoenicians** founded the settlement they called Malaka in the eighth century BC, building a fortress on the summit of the hill that is today dominated by the Alcazaba. Later incorporated into the Roman province of Baetica in the wake of Rome's victory over Carthage, Málaga prospered as a **trading port** exporting iron, copper and lead from mines in the hills near Ronda, as well as olive oil, wine and *garum*, a relish made from pickled fish to which the Romans were particularly partial. After falling to the **Moors** early in the eighth century, Málaga was soon flourishing again as the main port for the city of Granada. Although in the fourteenth century the ruler Yusuf I constructed the Gibralfaro as defence, in 1487 Málaga was taken by Christian forces following a bitter siege, after which the large Moorish population was persecuted and its property confiscated on a grand scale; the city's main mosque was also transformed into a cathedral, and a further twenty into churches. Málaga then entered a period of decline only exacerbated by a revolt of the Moors in 1568 that resulted in their complete expulsion. It was not until the nineteenth century that real prosperity returned – and then only briefly. Middle-class families arriving from the north invested in textile factories, sugar refineries and shipyards, and gave their names to city streets such as Larios and Heredia, while Málaga **dessert wine** became the favourite tipple of Victorian ladies. Then, in the early part of the twentieth century, the bottom fell out of the boom as the new industries succumbed to foreign competition and the phylloxera bug got to work wiping out the vines. A number of radical revolts leading up to the Civil War also brought the city an unhealthy reputation.

The Civil War to today

Given its volatile nature it was inevitable that Málaga would be staunchly Republican during the **Civil War**. In the turbulent years leading up to the war and during the conflict itself churches and convents were burned, while in 1937 Italian planes bombed the city, destroying much of its ancient central core, and mass executions of "reds and anarchists" by the conquering Franco forces left enduring emotional scars. This period is vividly described in a contemporaneous account, *Malaga Burning*, by Gamel Woolsey (see p.591).

The 1960s finally brought an economic lifeline in the form of **mass tourism** and the exploitation of the Costa del Sol, though the coastal nightmares barely touch the heart of Málaga. The opening of the **AVE** high-speed train line connecting Málaga with Madrid in two-and-a-half hours has also had an impact on raising the town's profile. In recent years

1

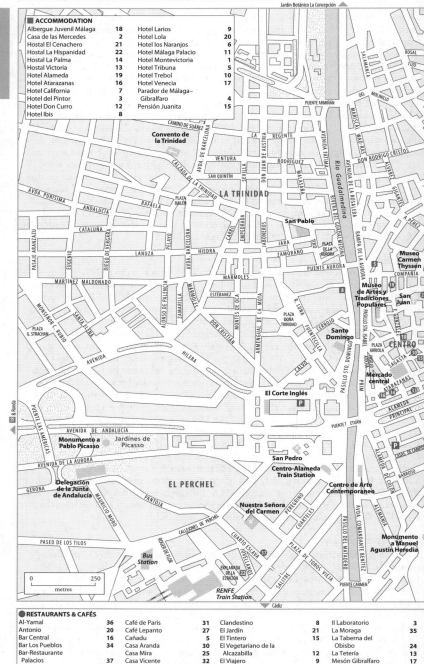

Jardín Botánico La Concepción

ACCOMMODATION

Albergue Juvenil Málaga	18	Hotel Larios	9
Casa de las Mercedes	2	Hotel Lola	20
Hostal El Cenachero	21	Hotel los Naranjos	6
Hostal La Hispanidad	22	Hotel Málaga Palacio	11
Hostal La Palma	14	Hotel Montevictoria	1
Hostal Victoria	13	Hotel Tribuna	5
Hotel Alameda	19	Hotel Trebol	10
Hotel Atarazanas	16	Hotel Venecia	17
Hotel California	7	Parador de Málaga–	
Hotel del Pintor	3	Gibralfaro	4
Hotel Don Curro	12	Pensión Juanita	15
Hotel Ibis	8		

● RESTAURANTS & CAFÉS

Al-Yamal	36	Café de Paris	31	Clandestino	8	Il Laboratorio	3
Antonio	20	Café Lepanto	27	El Jardín	21	La Moraga	35
Bar Central	16	Cañadu	5	El Tintero	15	La Taberna del	
Bar Los Pueblos	34	Casa Aranda	30	El Vegetariano de la		Obisbo	24
Bar-Restaurante		Casa Mira	25	Alcazabilla	12	La Tetería	13
Palacios	37	Casa Vicente	32	El Viajero	9	Mesón Gibralfaro	17

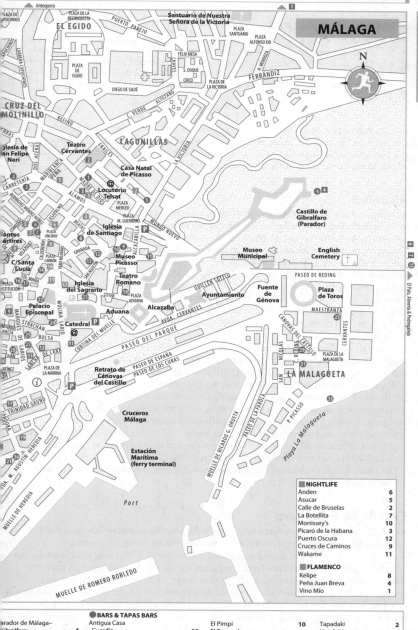

MÁLAGA

Antequera

Santuario de Nuestra Señora de la Victoria

PLAZA DEL PUCHINOS
PLAZA DE LA RECONQUISTA
PUERTO PAREJO
EL EGIDO
PLAZA SANTUARIO
PLAZA ALFONSO XIII
CARRERA APICHINOS
APICHINOS
PLAZA DE EGIDO
FÉLIX MESA
S. DUQUE
CIRCO
CHAVES
DIEGO DE SILOÉ
PLAZA DE LA VICTORIA
FERRÁNDIZ
M. MENDOZA
CRUZ DEL MOLINILLO
REFINO
C. VERDE
ALOZANO
LAGUNILLAS
LA VICTORIA
Iglesia de an Felipe Neri
Teatro Cervantes
FRAILES
Casa Natal de Pícasso
Locutorio Telsat
PLAZA MERCED
PLAZA M. GUERRERO
MUNGO NUEVO
Castillo de Gibralfaro (Parador)
CARRETERÍA
MADRE DE DIOS
ÁLAMOS
BEATAS
Iglesia de Santiago
ALCAZABILLA
ártos rtires
PLAZA UNCIBAY
GRANADA
Museo Picasso
Museo Municipal
English Cemetery
C/Santa Lucía
STA. MARÍA
Teatro Romano
PLAZA CONSTITUCIÓN
Iglesia del Sagrario
PLAZA ADUANA
GUILLEN SOTELO
Ayuntamiento
Fuente de Génova
PASEO DE REDING
Plaza de Toros
Palacio Episcopal
MOLINA LARIO
Aduana
Alcazaba
AVDA. CERVANTES
MAESTRANZA
CERVANTES
MARQUÉS
STRACHAN
BOLSA
Catedral
CORTINA DEL MUELLE
PASEO DEL PARQUE
CÁNOVAS DEL CASTILLO
SAN NICOLÁS
C. REDING
PLAZA DE LA MALAGUETA
LARIOS
PLAZA DE LA MARINA
Retrato de Cánovas del Castillo
PASEO DE ESPAÑA
PASEO DE LOS CURAS
LA MALAGUETA
SAN
PASEO DE LA FAROLA
P. PICASSO
TRINIDAD GRUND
Cruceros Málaga
MUELLE DE RICARDO G. ORUETA
Playa La Malagueta
M. AGUSTÍN HEREDIA
Estación Marítima (ferry terminal)
MUELLE DE HEREDIA
Port
MUELLE DE ROMERO ROBLEDO

El Palo, Almería & Pedregalejo

NIGHTLIFE

Anden	6
Asucar	5
Calle de Bruselas	2
La Botellita	7
Morrissey's	10
Picaro de la Habana	3
Puerto Oscura	12
Cruces de Caminos	9
Wakame	11

FLAMENCO

Kelipe	8
Peña Juan Breva	4
Vino Mío	1

arador de Málaga–ibralfaro	4	**BARS & TAPAS BARS**		El Pimpi	10	Tapadaki	2
efectorium	23	Antigua Casa Guardia	33	El Tapeo de Cervantes	1	Uvedoble	19
estaurante Tormes	11	Antigua Reja	7	Kobe	18		
al Gorda	29	Bar Lo Güeno	26	La Quesería	14		
		Bar Orellana	22	Mesón Las Garrafas	6		
		Bodegas Quitapeñas	28				

1

FESTIVALS IN MÁLAGA

While *sevillanos* loudly proclaim that there is only one **Semana Santa** worthy of the name, *malagueños* furiously disagree. The processions are celebrated here with great fervour and with much larger floats (*tronos*, or "thrones" as they're called here) than those in Seville, carried by up to two hundred sober-suited males or robed penitents. In mid-August, at the peak of the tourist season, the town lets rip in its **Feria de Málaga** – one of the wildest and most spectacular in Andalucía.

---

the city has tried to muscle in on the Costa del Sol tourist boom by projecting itself as a beach resort as well as a cultural centre, and work has been carried out to landscape the beaches and promenades to the west of the harbour as far as El Palo. So far, however, all this seems to have had little adverse impact on the city's unique character.

Alcazaba

Main entrance at Plaza de la Aduana; alternatively, a lift on C/Guillen Sotelo, directly behind the Ayuntamiento, transports you effortlessly up to the heart of the palace, saving you the climb • Tues–Sun: April–Sept 9.30am–8pm; Oct–March 8.30am–5.45pm • €2.10, or €3.40 combined ticket with Gibralfaro; free entry Sun after 2pm

Málaga's magnificent **Alcazaba** – along with the Gibralfaro (see below) – is an exuberant contrast to the dour fortresses of Castile. At the Alcazaba's entrance stands a **Teatro Romano**, unearthed in 1951 during building works. The theatre, constructed in the second century BC, is now used as an auditorium for various outdoor entertainments. From here a path winds upwards, lined by the cypresses and flower-encircled arbours so loved by the sybaritic Moors. The citadel too is Roman in origin, with recycled blocks and columns of classical marble interspersed among the Moorish brick of the double- and triple-arched gateways.

Although the Moors began building on the hill in the 700s, the Alcazaba with its palace as we see it today dates from the early decades of the eleventh century and was substantially restored and rebuilt in 1930. It was the residence of the Arab emirs of Málaga, who carved out an independent kingdom for themselves following the break-up of the Western Caliphate during the same period. Their independence lasted a mere thirty years, but for a while the kingdom grew to include Granada, Carmona and Jaén. Strolling among the restored patios and terraces lined with cypresses, aromatic plants and ornamental pools the impression is of a smaller-scale Alhambra, and traces of stucco decoration surviving on the arches are similar to the artistry to be seen at Medina Azahara near Córdoba (see p.390).

The recently refurbished small **palace** houses displays of ceramics found during archeological excavations.

Castillo de Gibralfaro

Monte de Gibralfaro • Bus #35 from the Alameda in the city centre will drop you by the castle entrance • Tues–Sun: April–Sept 9.30am–8pm; Oct–March 8.30am–5.45pm • €2.10, or €3.40 combined ticket with Alcazaba; free entry Sun after 2pm

Rrising to the northeast of the Alcazaba (and connected to it by a long double wall – the *coracha*), is the **Castillo de Gibralfaro**. It's reached by climbing a twisting path from the Alcazaba that skirts the southern walls, passing bougainvillea-draped ramparts and sentry-box-shaped Moorish wells. You can also approach from the town side, as the tourist coaches do, using the Subida al Gibralfaro (accessed from Calle Mundo Nuevo), but this is a lengthy, rather unattractive walk and not one to be done alone after sundown.

Built by Yusuf I of Granada in the fourteenth century and last used in 1936 during the Civil War, the castle, with its formidable walls and turrets, has, like the Alcazaba, been wonderfully restored and now houses an interesting **museum** dealing with the Gibralfaro's history. Among a collection of military exhibits from all periods there is a splendid scale

1

model letting you see how the city and Alcazaba complex would have looked in Moorish times. There's also a display of seventeenth-century playing cards that were made in the factory in nearby Macharaviaya (see p.92). A walk around the castle's **ramparts** affords terrific views over the city, the *coracha*, and the complex fortifications of the Alcazaba.

The Gibralfaro has its own **bar**, but while you're up here, a pleasant place for a **meal** or a **drink** is the nearby *Parador de Málaga Gibralfaro* (see p.77), with its terrace overlooking the city. It's reached by following the road leading out of the castle's car park for 100m and turning right into the parador's grounds. Next to the parador's entrance is a **mirador** with a stunning **view** over the harbour, city and Plaza de Toros.

The Catedral and Iglesia del Sagrario

C/Molino Lario • Both Mon–Fri 10am–6pm, Sat 10am–5pm, closed Sun except for services • €5

Dominating the views from the Gibralfaro is Málaga's peculiar, unfinished **Catedral**. It lacks a tower on the west front, the result of a radical *malagueño* bishop having donated the earmarked money to the American War of Independence against the British. Despite this curiosity, which has resulted in the building's popular nickname La Manquita ("the one-armed lady"), the cathedral lacks much else of interest. The soaring interior is distinguished only by an intricately carved and naturalistic seventeenth-century *sillería* (choir stall) with outstanding sculptural work – in particular *St Francis* and *John the Baptist* – by Pedro de Mena.

The **Iglesia del Sagrario**, on the cathedral's northern flank, is worth a look, if only for its fine Gothic **portal**, dating from an earlier, uncompleted Isabelline church. Inside is a restored and magnificent gilded **Plateresque retablo** by Juan Balmaseda, brilliantly illuminated during services.

Paseo del Parque

South of the cathedral, the **Paseo del Parque** is an elegant, palm-shaded avenue laid out at the beginning of the twentieth century on land reclaimed from the sea – an ideal place for a stroll, especially on summer evenings when the air has cooled. Along its length are a number of architectural delights as well as a remarkable **botanical garden** containing hundreds of exotic plants and flowers and many varieties of fig, bamboo, jacaranda and yucca trees. Discreet plaques placed at intervals along the esplanade identify the different species.

Among the buildings of note are the Neoclassical **Aduana**, the former customs house, soon to house the city's Museo de Bellas Artes (see p.69), started in 1788, with an austerely impressive patio. Further west lies **El Correo**, the old post office, followed a little further on by the paseo's star turn, the exuberant **Ayuntamiento**, a delightful cream and brown Art Nouveau pile, constructed to coincide with the opening of the esplanade.

Almost opposite the Correo in the gardens stand the first two of *malagueño* Jaime Pimentel's trio of evocative bronzes, which are among Málaga's best-loved sculptures: **El Jazminero** (*The Jasmine Seller*) celebrates the men who once sold trays of their blooms throughout the city while the nearby **El Verdialero** pays tribute to the colourful and frenetic Verdiales musicians from the mountains of Málaga to the northeast of the city. The third bronze, **El Cenachero** (*The Fish Seller*), commemorating men who, with their baskets of fish dangling from a yoke, used to be a common sight on the city's streets, is sited behind the municipal tourist office on Plaza de la Marina.

Fuente de Genova

Plaza del General Torrijos

At the paseo's eastern end you'll come to the **Fuente de Genova**, or Genoa Fountain, on a roundabout almost constantly encircled by traffic and difficult to appreciate. An

1

extremely fine Italian Renaissance work, it was captured by pirates during the reign of Carlos V while being transported to its Spanish buyer; when it was finally retrieved, the king awarded it to the city by royal edict.

The English Cemetery

Avda. de Pries 1 • Tues–Sun 9am–2.30pm • Free, but donations welcome

Flanked by carved stone rampant lions, the **English Cemetery** dates from an era when gunboats flying Union Jacks held the world in awe. This did not, however, disturb the Spanish authorities from their post-*Reconquista* custom of denying Christian burial to all "infidels" unlucky enough to die on Iberian turf. British Protestants – who were included in this grouping – suffered the indignity after death of "burial upright in the sand till their necks, below the tide line". Málaga's expatriate population, which increased during the early nineteenth century, was, understandably, not amused when some of these "shore burials" were washed up on the beach or even seen bobbing on the waves. Thus in 1830 the British consul, William Mark, finally persuaded the authorities to let him found the English Cemetery. In the early days, and to get the place established, it seems that Mark pursued corpses with the zeal of a body-snatcher, hardly waiting for the deceased to expire before carting them off to the new graveyard. Traveller Richard Ford, whose wife's frailty was his original reason for coming to Spain, became alarmed when Mark began to make overtures. "Hearing of my wife's ill health, he tried all in his power to get me to Málaga to have a pretty female specimen in his sepulchral museum," he wrote to a friend.

The cemetery

The cemetery itself, once an isolated site overlooking the sea but now enveloped by urban sprawl, is still nevertheless a leafy and tranquil oasis. Follow the path from the Paseo de Reding up to the modest red stone **church of St George** where, just before it, stands the sepulchre of William Mark. Further up the hill you'll see the original **walled cemetery** containing the oldest graves, among them a number studded with seashells (an ancient symbol of immortality), marking the passing of child victims of fever and consumption, the scourge of that age.

Alongside the old cemetery's eastern wall the tombstone of **Gamel Woolsey**, poet and wife of Gerald Brenan, and author of *Malaga Burning* (see p.591) is inscribed with a poignant message from Shakespeare's *Cymbeline*: "Fear no more the heat o' the sun." In 2001 the remains of her husband (who died in 1987) were finally placed in a grave alongside hers. The writer's epitaph is eloquently laconic: "RIP Gerald Brenan, Escritor Inglés, Amigo de España." Many of the other tombstones dotted around the cemetery with their dedications to wives, loyal servants and men of military zeal, most of them in English, make fascinating reading.

Due to funding problems in recent years the cemetery's future has been been thrown into doubt and burials are no longer allowed. In 2010 Málaga city council finally accepted some responsibility for its upkeep and gave a small grant from public funds. A booklet, *The English Cemetery at Malaga* by Marjorie Grice-Hutchinson (herself buried here in 2003) gives a detailed history and is on sale at the gatehouse, with proceeds going to the cemetery's upkeep.

The Museo Picasso

C/San Agustín • Tues–Sun 10am–8pm (also open some Sat evenings during summer, with live music in the garden and other events; €2) • Permanent collection €6, temporary collection €4.50, combined ticket for both €8 • ⓦ museopicassomalaga.org

Located just round the corner from the cathedral is the **Museo Picasso Málaga**, housed in the impressive sixteenth-century Palacio de Buenavista – the former residence of the counts of Buenavista – with an elegant patio. A source of enormous pride for the city, the museum was opened by the king and queen in 2003, one hundred and twelve years after

Picasso left Málaga at the age of ten and to where he returned only once for an unhappy, fleeting visit in 1901. In later life he toyed with the idea of sending "two lorries full of paintings" to set up a museum in Málaga but vowed never to visit Spain while General Franco was still alive – Picasso died in 1973 and was outlived by the dictator by two years.

The museum's **permanent collection** consists of 285 works donated by Christine and Bernard Ruiz-Picasso, the artist's daughter-in-law and grandson, while the **temporary collection** comprises loaned works and special exhibitions (not necessarily connected with Picasso). Whilst not on a par with the Picasso museums in Paris and Barcelona, it does allow you to see some of the lesser-known works that Picasso kept for himself or gave away to his lovers, family and friends – rather harshly described as "the less saleable stuff" by one critic.

The collection

It's worth noting that the collection is rotated and thus not all the works mentioned below may be on show at any one time. Highlights include, in Room 2, *Olga Koklova con Mantilla* (a portrait of his first wife, draped in a hotel tablecloth) and a moving portrait of his son Paul, *Paulo con Gorro Blanco*, painted in 1923. Other rooms have canvases spanning the breadth of Picasso's career including his Blue, Pink and Cubist periods, as well as sculptures in wood, metal and stone and a few ceramics. Two other influential women who figured prominently in the artist's long and turbulent love life are also the subject of powerful images: in Room 5, *Cabeza de Mujer 1939* is a portrait of the beguiling yet tragic Dora Maar, and in Room 8, *Jacqueline Sentada* is a seated representation of Picasso's second wife, Jacqueline Roque. An interesting newly acquired work in the same room is *Desnudo acostado* ("Reclining nude") which Picasso explores a whole range of body positions in a single image.

The museum's basement houses an unexpected collection of **archeological remains** revealed during its construction. Substantial chunks of a Phoenician city wall and tower dating from the seventh century BC survive, while from later periods you can view the remains of a Roman *salazones* factory used to produce the famous *garum*, a fish-based sauce and Roman delicacy, and also the remains of the cellar of the Palacio de Buenavista. A case nearby displays some of the finds unearthed in the excavations including Phoenician, Greek and Roman pottery fragments and a sixth-century BC Egyptian scarab.

The museum also has a good, if cramped, bookshop and an equally cramped **cafetería**, although this spills out onto a pleasant garden terrace in fine weather.

The **Museo de Bellas Artes** that was formerly housed here is due to be relocated to the Aduana (the old customs building on the Paseo del Parque). The refurbishment of this elegant eighteenth-century palace is nearing completion at the time of writing and the new museum (also housing the city's important archeological collection) is expected to open sometime in 2012. Either of the tourist offices should have the latest news on this. The collection includes significant works by Murillo and Zurbarán among others.

Casa Natal de Picasso

Plaza de la Merced 15 • Daily 9.30am–8pm • €1 • ⓦ fundacionpicasso.malaga.eu

Picasso's birthplace and family home during his early years, the **Casa Natal de Picasso** is now the headquarters and museum of the Picasso Foundation. It was during his formative years in Málaga that Picasso's prodigious talent for drawing was first noticed – "When I was a child I could draw like Raphael," he later wrote. "It took me all my life to learn to draw like a child." It was in the cafés around the square that the boy saw the first solid shape that he wanted to commit to paper: *churros*, those oil-steeped fritters that Spaniards dip into their breakfast chocolate.

The recently revamped exhibition space now displays lithographs, etchings and washes by Picasso – mainly with women as the subject matter – while on the stairs are displayed photos of the artist at various stages in his long life. The stairs lead to a reconstructed

1

reception room which has been furnished in the style of the late nineteenth century when Picasso was growing up here. Among the items on display are some embroidered bed linen by the artist's mother, a canvas by his art teacher father and the infant Picasso's christening robe, used in the ceremony at the nearby Iglesia de Santiago.

Pasaje de Chinitas

Tucked behind the Plaza de la Constitución, and on the Turismo's doorstep, is one of Málaga's most evocative corners, the **Pasaje de Chinitas**. In the first half of the last century, when Málaga was a thriving industrial town, this narrow white-walled street was filled with *tascas*, or bars, where businessmen would meet to discuss deals over fine wines before slinking off to the *Café de Chinitas* to hear some of the best flamenco in town. In the 1920s and 1930s the fame of this flamenco shrine, now a mundane textile store, grew as it became a noted meeting place of artists and writers, bullfighters and singers. Lorca loved the place and composed a poem in its honour, part of which appears on a plaque fixed to the former café, at the junction with Calle Sánchez Pastor:

In the Café de Chinitas
Said Paquiro to his brother:
"I'm more valiant than you,
more brave and more gitano."

Museo Carmen Thyssen

C/Compañia 10 • Tues–Sun 10am–8pm • €6 • ⓦ carmenthyssenmalaga.org

Housed in the refurbished sixteenth-century Palacio de Villalón is the **Museo Carmen Thyssen**, named after the spouse of the late baron whose collection forms the core of the Thyssen-Bornemisza museum in Madrid. Opened in 2011, the museum comprises 230 loaned works from Thyssen's collection of Spanish nineteenth-century art. Displayed on three floors (the fourth floor houses temporary exhibitions which have so far featured Monet, Picasso, Matisse and Miró) and divided into sections titled "Romantic", "Naturalist Landscape" and "Fin-de-siècle", most of the works are perhaps more interesting for the glimpses they give of Spanish and *andaluz* life and times rather than intrinsic artistic merit or originality.

The exceptions to this are mainly in the third floor's fin-de-siècle collection, where five paintings by nineteenth-century Valencian Impressionist **Joaquín Sorolla y Bastida** are fine examples of his hallmark high-keyed colouring and vigorous brushwork. The evocative *Lavanderas de Galicia* is perhaps the best of the bunch and demonstrates a deft understanding of light and colour. Other interesting works here include *Julia* by Ramón Casas i Carbó, a rather arrogantly posed image of the lottery seller who was to become his wife, Gustavo Bacarisas's *Feria*, and paintings by *cordobés* artist Julio Romero de Torres (see p.380).

The first floor has a somewhat incongruously titled "Old Masters" room displaying a handful of older works including *San Marina* by Zurbarán and a moving polychrome wood sculpture, *The Dead Christ*, an anonymous Italian work from the thirteenth century. The museum also has a *cafetería* as well as a shop selling books on, and reproductions of, the artworks on display.

Museo de Artes y Tradiciones Populares

C/Pasillo Santa Isabel 10 • Mon–Fri 10am–1.30pm & 4–7pm, Sat 10am–1.30pm • €2 • ⓦ www.museoartespopulares.com

Just east of the Guadalmedina riverbed and housed in a seventeenth-century inn, the entertaining **Museo de Artes y Tradiciones Populares** uses the former stables and stores

1

on the lower floor as well as the lodging rooms above to mount displays of arts, crafts and furniture from previous eras. These include a collection of *barros malagueños* – traditional painted clay figurines – as well as boats, carriages, farming and wine-making implements and rooms furnished in period style.

Mercado Central

C/Atarazanas, just north of the Alameda

Lying at the heart of an area that bustles with life, the nineteenth-century wrought-iron, Mudéjar-style **Mercado Central** (officially the Mercado Central de Atarazanas) incorporates a little-known architectural gem, largely unnoticed by the daily shoppers: a remarkable fourteenth-century **Moorish arch** on its southern facade built for Yusuf I of Granada – the ruler also responsible for that other great gateway, the Puerta de la Justicia in the Alhambra – when Málaga was part of the Nasrid kingdom. In those days it formed the entrance to the Moorish arsenal, and the original building's purpose is preserved in the market's present name: Atarazanas in Arabic translates as "the house that guards the arsenal". Note the two coats of arms in the upper corners inscribed in Arabic with the confident proclamation, "There is no Conqueror but Allah. All Praise to Him." A recently completed major refurbishment has restored the market to its former glory.

Centro de Arte Contemporaneo

C/Alemania s/n • Sept–June Tues–Sun 10am-8pm • July & Aug 10am–2pm & 5–9pm • Free • ⓦ cacmalaga.org

South of the market down the Río Guadalmedina is the **Centro de Arte Contemporaneo**, an excellent modern art museum housed in a converted former market building. The permanent collection displays works by international artists Louis Bourgeois, Cindy Sherman and Damien Hirst, while Spain is represented by Juan Muñoz, Miguel Barcelo and Juan Uslé among others. Check out the website for information on frequent temporary exhibitions. The **cafetería** has a pleasant river-view terrace.

Jardines de Picasso

Avda. de Andalucía • Open access • Free

To the west of the Río Guadalmedina across the Puente Tetuán, around 200m beyond the El Corte Inglés department store, stands a modern garden, the **Jardines de Picasso**. A memorial garden dedicated to the city's favourite son, it is the site of Spain's first monument to the artist, which was erected here in 1978 – a curiously restrained and abstract work by Ramón Calderón. Second thoughts – to celebrate the centenary of Picasso's birth in 1981 – were, however, in a much more monumental vein and *malagueño* sculptor Miguel Ortiz Berrocal was commissioned to produce something of the size required: a wonderfully intestinal bronze flanked by two magnificent dragon trees that are fairly remarkable natural sculptures in their own right. Don't hang around here after dark, however, as the area has a dubious reputation.

Nuestra Señora de la Victoria

Plaza Santuario s/n • Mon–Fri 10am–1pm • €2

Sited on the spot where Fernando and Isabel pitched their tent during the 1487 siege of Málaga, **Nuestra Señora de la Victoria** is, after the cathedral, Málaga's most prestigious church, where the city's Virgin patron is venerated. The fifteenth-century building was substantially rebuilt in the seventeenth century by the Count of Buenavista, whose remains, along with those of his descendants, lie in an eerie **crypt** decorated with symbolic stucco skeletons and skulls. Above, the main altar's centrepiece is an image of the Virgin in a *camarín* attributed to Pedro de Mena.

Jardín Botánico La Concepción

1

Ctra de las Pedrizas, km216, 3km out of Málaga • Guided tours Tues–Sat: April–Sept 9.30am–8.30pm; Oct–March 9.30am–5.30pm; last visit 90min before closing • €4.20; Tues free after 4.30pm in summer and 1.30pm in winter • By car, take the A45 north out of Málaga, turn off at km166, and follow signs for the Jardín Botánico; bus #61 from the north side of Alameda will drop you at the gates on Sat & Sun, but on weekdays it will drop you at its terminus, a 10min walk; alternatively take the Malagatour sightseeing bus (see p.74), or a taxi will cost about €12 from the centre.

A pleasant trip out of town if you want to escape the centre for a few hours is to the remarkable **Jardín Botánico La Concepción**, the city's botanical garden. Among the finest in Spain, the gardens were originally designed in the 1850s by Amalia Loring, granddaughter of the British consul, and only purchased in 1990 by Málaga city council, since when they have been converted into the present tropical gardens. Beneath the thirty species of soaring palms, waving pines and lofty eucalyptus, you'll find yellow-flowering acacia, violet-blooming jacaranda and all kinds of exotic shrubs and grasses. There are trees of all shapes and continents, such as the Australian banyan with its serpentine aerial roots, giant sequoias, and a variety of bamboos, all to be seen on any one of the five guided itineraries.

ARRIVAL AND DEPARTURE

MÁLAGA

By plane From Málaga Airport (☎ 902 404 704) the electric train (Ferrocarril; every 30min 7am–11.45pm; €1.40) provides the easiest and cheapest way into town. The station is beneath the new Terminal 3. Stay on the train right to the end of the line – the Centro-Alameda stop (12min). Exiting Centro-Alameda station, cross the Puente Tetuán over the Río Guadalmedina riverbed to the western end of the tree-lined Alameda, effectively the town centre. Taxis leave from the rank in front of the nearby El Corte Inglés department store just north of Centro-Alameda station. Alternatively, city bus Linea A leaves from outside the Terminal 3 arrivals hall (every 30min 7am–midnight; €1.20), stopping at the train and bus stations en route to the centre and the Paseo del Parque near the port, from where you can also pick it up in the opposite direction when you're returning to the airport. A taxi into town from the rank outside the arrivals hall costs around €20 depending on traffic and time of day and takes roughly fifteen minutes.

By train The city's impressive RENFE train station is southwest of the centre and is now linked by the high-speed AVE with Córdoba and Madrid. Bus #3 runs from here to the centre every 10min or so. For current timetables and ticket information, consult RENFE ☎ 902 240 202, ⓦ www.renfe.es.

Destinations: Algeciras (3 daily; change at Bobadilla; 4hr 30min); Antequera (6 daily; 25min); Córdoba (1 daily; 2hr 20min; AVE 10 daily; 1hr); El Chorro (1 daily; 50min); Fuengirola (every 30min; 45min); Granada (4 daily; change at Antequera; 3hr 30min); Ronda (1 daily direct; 2hr; 6 daily changing at Bobadilla; 3hr); Seville (6 daily; 2hr 30min); Torremolinos (every 30min; 25min).

By bus All buses from and to destinations outside Málaga (run by a number of different companies) operate from the bus station on Paseo de los Tilos (☎ 952 350 061), a little northwest of the RENFE station.

Destinations: Málaga to: Algeciras (8 daily; 3hr); Almería (7 daily; 4 hr 45min); Antequera (Mon–Fri 3 daily, Sat & Sun 1 daily; 50min); Cádiz (7 daily; 4hr); Conil (4 daily; 3 hr); Córdoba (4 daily; 3hr 30min); Estepona (11 daily; 2hr); Fuengirola (8 daily; 45min); Granada (hourly; 2hr); Jerez (3 daily; 4hr 30min); La Linea (5 daily; 3hr); Marbella (up to 20 daily; 1hr 25min); Motril-Lanjarón (6 daily; 2hr); Nerja (24 daily; 1hr); Riogordo (3 daily; 2hr 30min); Osuna (2 daily; 2hr 25min); Ronda (5 daily; 2hr 45min); Seville (5 daily; 2hr 45min); Tarifa (1 daily; 4 hr); Torremolinos (14 daily; 35min); Vejer (4 daily; 4hr).

By ferry The city's only ferry service, with Trasmediterranea, departs from the Estación Marítima to the Spanish enclave of Melilla in Morocco (3hr 45min or 7hr; ☎ 902 454 645, ⓦ trasmediterranea.es). If you're heading for Fes and eastern Morocco, this is a useful connection – particularly so for taking a car over – though most people go for the quicker services at Algeciras and Tarifa to the west. For latest timetables see ⓦ www.directferries.co.uk.

By car There's very little street parking available in Málaga, and the many signed car parks around the centre are extremely expensive; it's best to use a garage connected to your accommodation (for which you will still need to pay, although many hotels offer discounts). Theft from cars is rampant; never leave anything valuable on view in a street-parked vehicle, especially overnight.

INFORMATION

Turismo Pasaje de Chinitas 4 (Mon–Fri 9am–7.30pm, Sat & Sun 9.30am–3pm; ☎ 952 308 911). This central office can provide information on cultural events and accommodation, and sells a detailed map of the city.

There's also a turismo municipal on Plaza de la Marina (daily 9am–6pm, April–Sept closes 8pm; ☎ 951 926 020), with other branches at the bus station and in the airport arrivals hall.

1

Listings *¿Que Hacer?* ("What's On?"). A monthly publication covering events and entertainment throughout Andalucía stocked by both tourist offices. *Sur in English* is a weekly version of Málaga's main daily *Sur* with lots of gen on nightlife, concerts and other events.

Online information ⓦ malagaturismo.com, ⓦ andalucía .org.

TOURS

Bus tour A hop-on hop-off service is operated by Malagatour (☎ 902 101 081, ⓦ city-ss.com; €17, kids half-price, tickets valid 24hr), with services leaving the bus station every half-hour from 9.15am to 7pm; its many stops include the cathedral, Alcazaba, Plaza de la Merced and the Alameda.

iPod city-tours The municipal tourist office lends out iPods loaded with self-guided themed walks ("Picasso's Málaga", "Romantic Málaga", "Historic Málaga", etc). The service is free, although a credit card is required to cover a deposit against the return of the iPod.

ACCOMMODATION

Málaga boasts scores of hotels together with plenty of *pensiones* and *hostales*, so budget rooms are rarely hard to come by except during Semana Santa and the August *feria* (when prices are also hiked). Málaga's **high season** is July and August (the prices quoted here); outside this period there are some real bargains to be had. Numerous possibilities are to be found in the grid of streets just north and south of the Alameda, which is probably the best place to start looking. The cheapest option is the **youth hostel** (*albergue juvenil*), though this isn't particularly convenient for the centre. The town's central **hotels** are generally poorer value than the **hostales**, but for those who want a little more luxury, we've listed a handful of places slightly further out. Málaga has no campsite: the nearest facilities are at Torremolinos heading west (see p.109), and Torre del Mar (see p.93) to the east. All hotels and many hostales have garages or **parking** facilities for cars; these are always charged extra – expect to pay €12–20 per day.

SOUTH OF THE ALAMEDA

Hostal El Cenachero C/Barroso 5 ☎ 952 224 088. Clean, third-floor *hostal* in a quiet street with friendly proprietors just off the seafront end of C/Córdoba. Most rooms are en suite – the four with terrace or balcony are the ones to go for. €58

Hotel Alameda C/Casas de Campos 3 ☎ 952 222 099, ⓦ hotelalamedamalaga.com. Pleasant small hotel in a high-rise block (which lessens traffic noise). Rooms are adequately furnished and come with a/c and TV. Free wi-fi. €58

Hotel Lola C/Casas de Campos 17 ☎ 952 579 300, ⓦ room-matehotels.com. Newish designer-chic boutique hotel where rooms come with flat-screen TV, free internet, DVD player, minibar and safe. Also has own bar-restaurant and garage. €125

Hotel Venecia Alameda Principal 9 ☎ 952 213 636, ⓦ hotelveneciamalaga.com. Overlooking the south side of the Alameda, with good facilities including a/c, balconies, satellite TV and free wi-fi. Own garage with special rates for guests. €120

NORTH OF THE ALAMEDA

Casa de las Mercedes C/Hinestrosa 18 ☎ 952 060 152, ⓦ casadelasmercedes.com. Charming small hotel in a refurbished eighteenth-century *casa-palacio* near the Teatro Cervantes. Beamed rooms retain many of their original features in addition to TV, minibar and free wi-fi. Parking nearby. Breakfast included. €82

Hostal La Palma C/Martínez 7 ☎ 952 226 772, ⓦ hostallapalma.es. One of the best budget places in town, with a/c en-suite doubles in addition to simpler rooms sharing bath; frequent discounts online. Free wi-fi. €40

Hostal Victoria C/Sancha de Lara 3 ☎ 952 224 224, ⓔ pq@hostalvictoria.net. Comfortable *hostal* near the cathedral with good en-suite doubles and singles, all with a/c and satellite TV. Free wi-fi. €50

Hotel Atarazanas C/Atarazanas 19 ☎ 952 121 910, ⓦ balboahoteles.com. Pleasant three-star hotel near the market with well-appointed a/c rooms and free wi-fi throughout. Frequent special offers on website. €150

Hotel del Pintor C/Alamos 27 ☎ 952 060 980, ⓦ hoteldelpintor.com. Small, arty hotel with decor and furnishings designed by *malagueño* painter Pepe Bornoy. The hotel's colour scheme is red and white and each of the soundproofed minimalist rooms is decorated with a Bornoy artwork. Features include TV, safe and free wi-fi. €55

Hotel Don Curro C/Sancha de Lara 7 ☎ 952 227 200, ⓦ hoteldoncurro.com. Central and comfortable, if rather featureless, hotel with a/c rooms and its own car park. Some views from top-floor rooms. €121

Hotel Ibis Paseo Guimbarda 5 ☎ 952 070 741, ⓦ ibis hotel.com. On the west bank of the Guadalmedina, this is part of the international chain, offering functional rooms at attractive prices with frequent website special offers. Can arrange parking. Free wi-fi. €69

Hotel Tribuna C/Carretería 6 ☎ 952 122 230, ⓦ hotel tribunamalaga.com. Elegant hotel offering rooms with satellite TV, in-room safe, minibar and free wi-fi. Most rooms non-smoking. Has its own café-bar next door and can arrange parking. €70

Hotel Larios C/Marqués de Larios 2 ☎ 952 222 200, ⓦ hotel-larios.com. Modern, upmarket hotel on this elegant pedestrianized shopping street. The hotel has been reconstructed inside the shell of an original Art Deco edifice; satellite TV, in-room safes and a panoramic rooftop bar are among the features. Frequent special offers online. €6 with breakfast. **€175**

Hotel Málaga Palacio Cortina del Muelle 1 ☎ 952 215 185, ⓦ ac-hotels.com. This four-star luxury option near the Paseo del Parque has sea-view rooms and pampers its guests with free minibar and bathrobes. Facilities include rooftop pool and gym. See website for special offers. **€200**

Hotel Trebol C/Moreno Carbonero 3 ☎ 952 608 702, ⓦ hoteltrebol.com. Pleasant new small hotel in the atmospheric market area with modern a/c rooms. Features include flat-screen TV, internet connections and a wi-fi zone. **€55**

Pensión Juanita C/Alarcón Luján 8 ☎ 952 213 586. Friendly *pensión* on the fourth floor (there's a lift) near the market, offering clean and tidy en-suite rooms, and others sharing bath. Large, multi-bed family rooms also available. Free wi-fi. **€49**

OUT OF THE CENTRE

Albergue Juvenil Málaga Plaza de Pío XII 6 ☎ 952 308 500. The city's youth hostel has pleasantly modern double rooms complete with a shared sun-terrace. The #18 bus (heading west across the river) from the Alameda will drop you nearby on request. Under-26 **€21**, over-26 **€27**.

Hostal La Hispanidad Explanada de la Estación 5 ☎ 952 311 135, ⓦ hostallahispanidad.com. Facing the train station, this is a useful option if you've got an early train (or bus) to catch. The labyrinthine interior has refurbished en-suite rooms with a/c and TV named after different countries of the Americas, and there are plenty of eating places nearby. **€72**

Hotel Los Naranjos Paseo de Sancha 35 ☎ 952 224 316, ⓦ hotel-losnaranjos.com. Very pleasant small hotel east of the bullring near the beach. Rooms come with terrace and there are spectacular sea views from front-facing rooms on highest floors; features include a/c, safe, free wi-fi and garage. Buses #11, #34 and #35 from the Alameda will drop you outside. **€160**

Hotel California Paseo de Sancha 17, 500m east of the bullring ☎ 952 215 164, ⓦ hotelcalifornianet.com. Charming small hotel near the beach with a flower-bedecked entrance. The well-appointed rooms come with a/c and safes, and the hotel has its own garage. Minimum stay 5 nights in Aug. Buses #11, #34 and #35 from the Alameda will drop you outside on request. **€91**

★ **Hotel Montevictoria** C/Conde de Ureña 58 ☎ 952 656 525, ⓦ hotelmontevictoria.com. Sweet little hotel with friendly proprietors in an elegant villa in the hills above Málaga with great views over the city. Slightly pricier rooms #104 & #105 have their own terrace. Bus #36 from the Alameda (ask for the C/Conde de Ureña stop) will drop you almost outside. **€84**

★ **Parador de Málaga–Gibralfaro** Monte de Gibralfaro ☎ 952 221 902, ⓦ parador.es. You won't get a better panoramic view of the coast than from this eagle's nest on top of the Gibralfaro hill. Rooms come with a/c and satellite TV and, although it's quite small for a *parador*, it does have a pool. Well worth calling in for a drink or a meal (see p.77). **€180**

EATING

Málaga has a justified reputation for its splendid signature seafood platter, **fritura malagueña** (fried mixed fish). You'll find many fish restaurants grouped around the Alameda, and some of the town's big names cluster near the bullring and on La Malagueta seafront. Some of the earthier, more typically *malagueño* places are in the eastern seafront suburbs of Pedrogalejo and El Palo, served by bus #11 from the Paseo del Parque. On the seafront paseo at Pedregalejo, almost all of the cafés and restaurants serve terrific fish. Further on, El Palo is an even better place to eat, with a beach and fishing huts. Most of Málaga's non-seafood restaurants are hardly in the same league, but we've listed some places where the food is well above average for the price. Be aware that some tapas bars have also added a restaurant and these are listed in the "tapas bars" section below.

PLAZA MERCED AND CATHEDRAL AREA

Antonio Fernando Lesseps 7. Popular small restaurant serving well-prepared *malagueño* dishes such as *pepitorio de pollo* (chicken with almonds) with an outdoor terrace in an atmospheric cul-de-sac off the north end of C/Nueva; *menú* for around €12. Daily 1–4pm & 8–11pm.

Cañadu Plaza de la Merced 21. A vegetarian option with a creative touch serving a good selection of salads, couscous and pasta-based dishes accompanied by organic wines and beers. They also serve a wide range of teas and there's a lunch *menú* for around €10. Daily 9am–midnight.

Clandestino C/Niño de Guevara 3. Popular café-diner serving a variety of tapas and *raciones* as well as salads, pasta and other dishes with an Italian slant. Main dishes €7–15. Daily 1pm–1am.

El Vegetariano de la Alcazabilla C/Pozo del Rey 5, off C/Alcazabilla. Good vegetarian and vegan restaurant serving soup, cheese, salads and pasta-based dishes in a cosy atmosphere. Mains €9–12; *menú* €7.50. Mon–Sat 1–4pm & 9–11.30pm; closed Sun.

Il Laboratorio Plaza San Pedro de Alcántara, off C/Carretería. Great little Italian-style pizzeria-trattoria

1

CONVENTO DULCES

Many convents throughout Andalucía and Spain are in the business of supporting their orders by making **dulces de convento**: cakes and pastries that they can sell to the community. Many recipes date back to the Arabs, who used rich combinations of eggs, almonds, sugar and honey to concoct their Moorish goodies. Each convent guards its recipes jealously, and many are so good that they supply local restaurants. The **sherry manufacturers** also had an influence on the development of *convento dulces*, since they traditionally used egg whites to clarify their wines and donated the leftover yolks to the nuns. This is the origin of many egg yolk-based creations such as *tocino de cielo* (Andalucía's richest flan) and *yemas* (sweet cakes), two of the region's most popular pastries.

In most convents you pay your money and are served with the sweets of your choice through a *torno* – a kind of revolving dumb waiter – which means you never see the nun who serves you. In Málaga the nuns at the Abadía (Abbey) of Santa Ana, C/Cister 11 (near the entrance to the Alcazaba), sell their dulces between 9am and 1pm. Specialities are coconut (*pasta de coco*) and quince cakes (*pasta de membrillo*).

serving (besides pizzas) salads and daily specials. They also do breakfasts (try their *revueltos* – scrambled eggs) and there's a small outdoor terrace under the trees in this charming plazuela. Also serves cocktails after sundown. Main dishes €7–16. Daily 10am–midnight.

La Taberna del Obisbo Plaza del Obispo 1. Here the location upstages the food and drink – this little square is a delight on a summer's evening where the imposing cathedral frontage soars above terrace diners. Decent salads and snacks or you could try their seafood paella for two for €20. Main dishes €8–15. Daily 9am–2pm & 8pm–midnight.

Mesón Gibralfaro Pasaje Chinitas 6. Central and inexpensive restaurant serving *platos combinados*, salads and variety of *jamones* until after midnight. Also has a few outdoor tables on this atmospheric alley. Main dishes €8–15. Daily 1–4pm & 8pm–1am.

Restaurante Tormes C/San Agustín 13. Decent meat and fish restaurant with terrace close to the Museo Picasso. They offer a tasty paella (for two) for €22 and also do a veggie version; mains €8–15. Daily 1–4.30pm & 8.30pm–midnight.

ALAMEDA PRINCIPAL AND RÍO GUADALMEDINA

Al-Yamal C/Blasco de Garay 3 ☏ 952 212 046. Long-established Moroccan restaurant serving up pricey but authentic meat in spicy sauces – *cordero* (lamb) couscous is a house special. Also has a decent selection of Moroccan wines. Main dishes €12–17. Mon–Sat 12.30–5pm & 7.30pm–midnight, Sun 12.30–5pm.

Bar Los Pueblos C/Atarazanas 15, almost opposite the mercado. Simple workers' place, serving satisfying food all day – bean soups and *estofados* are their speciality, while the gazpacho is served in half-pint glasses. *Menú* for €7. Daily 8am–10pm.

Casa Vicente C/Comisario 2. Lively *marisquería* in a narrow alley on the northern side of the Alameda. The

similar *Bar El Puerto* next door is also good. Daily 12.30pm–midnight.

PLAZA DE TOROS AND LA MALAGUETA

La Moraga Plaza Malagueta 4 ☏ 952 224 153, ⊛ lamoraga.com. One of Michelin-starred chef Dani García's chain of stylish tapas and *raciones* bars, with seating either on the sea-view terrace or inside the "seventies boutique"-style interior. Portions are small if creatively edged: you could try the mini "bull burgers" – a new take on the US's national dish – or a whole fried *lubina* (sea bass) for €25 per person. The staff are young and enthusiastic but although Sr García designed the menu he is rarely around. Tapas €3–7, main dishes €10–20. Daily 1.30–4pm & 8–11.30pm.

Café de Paris C/Vélez Málaga 8 ☏ 952 225 043, ⊛ www .rcafedeparis.com. Málaga's top restaurant for sampling *la cocina malagueña* at its creative best, under the direction of Michelin-starred chef José Carlos García. Dining à la carte doesn't come cheap with a *menú de degustación* for about €100, but there's a weekday *menú de mercado* lunch menu for €40. House specialities include *bacalao garrapiñado con polvo de almendras* (cod in almond sauce). Main dishes €18–30. Tues–Sat 1.30–3.30pm & 8.30–11pm.

Refectorium C/Cervantes 8, near the Plaza de Toros ☏ 952 218 990. Stylish, medium-priced, mainly fish restaurant where the *ajo blanco*, *fritura malagueña*, *urta* (sea bream) and *pez espada* (swordfish) are mouthwatering tasty. A small bar also serves outstanding tapas. Main dishes €12–20. Daily 12.30–5pm & 8pm–midnight.

★ **Sal Gorda Avda.** Canovas de Castillo 12. Excellent little *raciones* (and *media raciones*) bar-restaurant serving up a mouthwatering range of seafood and shellfish. Their *arroz marinero* at around €30 (for two – and sometimes even cheaper as one of their special offers) is recommended, as is the outstanding draught Asturian *sidra* (cider). Daily 1–4.30pm & 8pm–midnight.

OUT OF THE CENTRE

Bar-Restaurante Palacios C/Eslava 4. Plain, honest food at bargain prices (*menú* €8.50) in a vibrant *comedor* with friendly service; specialities include *jamón ibérico*, fish *surtido* and a mean *paella*. Mon–Sat 8am–11pm, closed Sat eve & all day Sun.

El Tintero El Palo. Right at the far eastern end of the seafront, just before the Club Náutico (bus #11; ask for "Tintero"), this is a huge beach restaurant where the waiters charge round with plates of fish (around €7.50 each) and you shout for, or grab, anything you like. Beware of the larger platters or *bandejas* which can cost significantly more. The fish to go for are, above all, *mero* (a kind of gastronomically evolved cod) and *rosada* (dogfish and catfish), along with Andalucian regulars such as *boquerones* (fresh anchovies), *gambas* (prawns) and *sepia* (cuttlefish). Haute cuisine it certainly isn't, but for sheer entertainment it's a must. Daily 1.30–4.30pm & 8.30–11.30pm.

★ **Parador de Málaga–Gibralfaro** Monte de Gibralfaro ☎952 221 902. Superior terrace dining with spectacular views over the coast and town from this *parador* restaurant next to Gibralfaro (see p.75), specializing in *malagueño* fish and meat dishes. The à la carte is affordable (main dishes €10–20) and wine prices are reasonable, or you could also try the excellent value *menú* (€33 dinner, €23.50 lunch). Book ahead if you want a table with a view. If you can't face the climb, take a taxi or bus #35 east along Paseo del Parque. Daily 1–4pm & 7.30–10.30pm.

DRINKING

Málaga has a variety of places to drink, from bustling breakfast cafés for *churros* and coffee to atmospheric bars where you can while away an evening. The best of the breakfast places are clustered around the Mercado Central, where the daily bustle starts at dawn. Bars for more serious drinking – usually with tapas thrown in – are concentrated north of the Alameda and around the cathedral. A number of traditional bars serve the sweet Málaga wine (*vino dulce*), made from muscatel grapes and dispensed from huge barrels; other options include the new, incredibly sweet wine, Pedriot, and the much more palatable Seco Añejo, which has matured for a year.

CAFÉS

Bar Central East side of Plaza de la Constitución. This venerable institution has been one of the city's favourite meeting places for generations and has the best terrace for people-watching on this focal pedestrianized square. Serves tapas and also has an enticing cake counter. A recent refurb has (thankfully) preserved its unique character and there's a fascinating photo history on the walls inside. Daily 8.30am–11pm.

Café Lepanto C/Larios 7. This smart central café with an outdoor terrace is the perfect place for afternoon tea or coffee and they cook up a magnificent array of tempting *pasteles* to accompany the beverages. Daily 9am–11pm

★ **Casa Aranda** C/Herrería del Rey. One of the best of the market cafés, renowned for its excellent *churros*, served at outside tables. There are actually two bars here, one each side of the alley, but owned by the same family and operating as one. Daily 8am–1pm & 5–9pm.

Casa Mira C/Larios 5. This is the place where *malagueños* flock on summer nights for the best ice creams in town. Daily 11am–11pm.

El Jardín C/Canon s/n, directly behind the cathedral. Nice place for breakfast café and *pasteles*, with a fountain, garden and cathedral view fronting outdoor tables. Does *platos combinados* later in the day, and in the evening transforms into a piano bar with a vaguely Viennese ambience. Mon–Sat 9am–midnight.

El Viajero C/Santiago 8, near the Iglesia de Santiago. Relaxed café with a travelling theme, hosting exhibitions of work by travel photographers; serves a wide range of teas and cafés, plus cocktails after sundown. Daily 3pm–midnight.

La Tetería C/San Agustín 21. Cosy Moroccan tearoom with terrace almost opposite the Museo Picasso, serving a wide range of herbal and Oriental teas. Daily 3–10pm, Fri & Sat until 1am.

BARS AND TAPAS BARS

★ **Antigua Casa Guardia** Corner of C/Pastora, on the Alameda. Great old nineteenth-century spit-and-sawdust bar. Picasso was a devotee of their wines, and a photo on the wall shows him toting one of the bar's *jarras*. Try the house *mejillones* (mussels) or *cola de langosto* (lobster's tail) with Málaga wine. Daily 9am–10pm.

Antigua Reja (aka Casa Barcenas) Plaza de Uncibay. Lively bar at the northern end of this popular square serving various *raciónes* and *tablas* ("boards" of cheese or cured meats). Daily 12.30–11pm.

Bar Lo Güeno C/Marín García 9, off C/Larios. Excellent and atmospheric tapas place; *pincho* (spicy shrimp) and *habas* (broad beans with black sausage) are specials. They also have a very good small restaurant sited immediately opposite. Daily 12.30pm–midnight.

★ **Bar Orellana** Moreno Monroy 5. Down a small side street off the east side of C/Marqués de Larios close to Plaza Constitución, this is one of Málaga's very best and friendliest tapas bars. Tasty house specials include *atún mechada* (tuna), *calamaritos* (squid in batter) and *tortillita de camarones* (shrimp fritters). Daily except Wed 8am–11pm.

1

Bodegas Quitapeñas (aka La Manchega) C/Marín García 4. Another fine old drinking den with its own off-site bodega (which can be visited). Many tapas for under €2 – *jibias guisadas* (stewed cuttlefish) is a speciality – and you can wash them down with Málaga's traditional Moscatel and Sierras de Málaga wines. Daily 12.30–4pm & 7.30pm–midnight.

★ **El Pimpi** C/Granada 62. Cavernous and hugely popular bodega-style bar serving up (among other concoctions) tasty *vino dulce* by the glass or bottle. There are tapas to go with the drinks and you can do a bit of celebrity-spotting on their wall of photos (including a young Antonio Banderas). Don't miss a superb terrace (with Alcazaba view) out the back. A great place to start – or end – the evening. Daily 11am–2am.

★ **El Tapeo de Cervantes** C/Carcer 8 ☎ 952 609 458. Excellent, if Lilliputian, tapas bar with a cosy and welcoming ambience and some creative tapas (€3–5). Try the *atún rojo en salsa coliflor* (tuna in a cauliflower sauce) or *envuelta de jamón* with cheese and rocket. Also has excellent wine sold by the glass. Book if you want to get one of a handful of tables. Noon–4pm & 8pm–midnight.

★ **Kobe** C/Fajardo 6 ☎ 952 221 295. This *tapería gastronómica* is the brainchild of chef Bea Hernandez using skills gained at the renowned *La Consula* hotel and catering school and in the kitchen at *El Bulli* to create this gourmet tapas restaurant. Quality rather than quantity is the mission: *bogovante con alubias verdina* (lobster with beans) and *deconstrucción de la tortilla de papatas* (an egg, onion and foamed-potato concoction once voted plate of the year at *El Bulli*) are typical of what's on offer. With only a dozen tables (half on a terrace), booking is recommended. Expect to pay €20–30pp including drinks. Mon–Sat 1–4pm & 8pm–midnight.

La Quesería C/Sanchez Pastor 2. Some meat dishes are served but, as its name tells you, cheese is king here – a *tabla* (cheeseboard) for two costs €7. Try the prize-winning Payoyo goat cheese from the mountains of Cádiz. Mon–Sat noon–4pm & 8pm–midnight.

Mesón Las Garrafas C/Mendez Núñez 5. Fine and atmospheric century-old bar-bodega with tiled walls, stacked barrels and good fino, plus tasty fish and meat tapas and *raciones*. Daily noon–4.30pm & 8pm–midnight.

Tapadaki C/Carretería 69. A stylish new tapas and *raciones* bar serving a fusion of Asian and Spanish tapas; try their *solomillo de cerdo y shitake* (pork loin with mushrooms). Does special offers on bottled wines. Daily 1–4pm & 8pm–midnight.

Uvedoble C/Cister 15. Modernistic bar offering "designer" tapas in a minimalist setting with a small but interesting tapas and *raciones* menu. Try their *croquetas caseras ibéricos* (croquettes with *jamón*) or *ensalada de membrillo* (quince salad). Also does tasty desserts. Mon–Sat noon–4pm & 8pm–midnight.

NIGHTLIFE

You'll find most of Málaga's nightlife north of the cathedral around Plaza de Uncibay and calles Granada and Beatas, and Plaza de la Merced. In the summer months there's also a scene in Malagueta, south of the bullring. At weekends and holidays dozens of youth-oriented disco-bars fill the crowded streets in these areas, and over the summer – though it's dead out of season – the scene spreads out along the seafront to the suburb of Pedregalejo. Here the streets just behind the beach host most of the action, and dozens of discos and smaller music bars lie along and off the main street, Juan Sebastián Elcano.

Anden Plaza de Uncibay. Disco-bar with a wild crowd and a playlist featuring Spanish pop, house and reggae; the two big dance rooms are serviced by four bars and there are often queues to get in. Fri & Sat only; 11pm–late.

Asúcar Junction of C/Juan de Padilla & C/Lazcano west of Plaza de Uncibay. The place to come for salsa in Málaga (classes also on offer) and they claim to serve the best mojitos in town. Daily 8pm–late.

Calle de Bruselas Plaza de la Merced 16. A laid-back, mainly gay, Belgian-style bar serving breakfasts (until 1pm) and bar food during the day and *copas* after dark. Also stages frequent live music and events and has a lively terrace that stays open into the small hours. Daily 9am–2am, Fri–Sun until 3am.

La Botellita Pasaje Mitjana, slightly west of Plaza Uncibay. Wild place packed to the rafters with local young revellers dancing to the tunes of the Spanish Top 40. At the end of this alley, the tiny Plaza Marqués Vado del Maestre is filled with drinking bars and plenty of night-time action. Thurs–Sat 11pm–4am.

Morrissey's Irish Pub Plaza del Siglo 3. Irish-style pub – and a pretty good imitation of a varnished Dublin bar – that occasionally stages live gigs. Popular with a foreign crowd, and the Guinness isn't bad. Daily 3pm–2am.

Picaro de la Habana C/Madre de Dios 11, off the north end of Plaza de la Merced. Drinking and dancing to salsa and other Latin sounds; popular with an over-30s crowd. Daily 9pm–late.

Puerta Oscura C/Molina Lario 5, near the cathedral. Surrounded by rave clubs, this slightly incongruous classical music bar – sometimes with live performers – serves cocktails, ices and baguettes, and also mounts art exhibitions. T-shirts are definitely a no-no here. Mon–Sat 7pm till 3am.

Cruces de Caminos C/Convalecientes, north of Plaza Uncibay. Late-opening bar serving a wide range of shots and specializing in Spanish rock and techno. Thurs–Sat 11pm–3.30am.

Wakame C/Correo Viejo 4, near the cathedral. Diminutive dance club with a variety of DJs playing reggae, soul, funk, Latin and R&B sounds until the early hours and a bar serving a wide selection of shots. Wed–Sat 8pm–late.

FLAMENCO

Genuine flamenco in Málaga is hard to come by, and the few shows there are aren't up to much – although you could try the venues below for something approaching the real thing. Many flamenco events (generally free) happen in and around the town throughout the year and in the city's annual festival in August. The Turismo Municipal (see p.73) is the best source of information on these.

Kelipe Galerías Goya, Plaza de Uncibay ⓦ www.kelipe .net. This flamenco centre puts on shows at 9.15pm &

10.30pm on Fridays and Saturdays. There's a good atmosphere and the price includes a drink. Tickets should be reserved by phone (ⓣ 692 829 885; €15) in advance.

Peña Juan Breva C/Ramón Franquelo 4 ⓣ 952 221 380, ⓦ www.museodeflamencojuanbreva.com. Founded in 1958, this is one of Málaga's most authentic and welcoming *peñas*, with free concerts each Friday (except in August) at 10pm. Their excellent museum (Tues–Sat 10am–2pm; free but contributions welcome) showcases a fascinating collection of flamenco costumes, posters, antique phonographs plus a range of musical instruments and guitars including one that belonged to Federico García Lorca.

Vino Mío C/Alamos 11. Friendly bar-restaurant serving creative tapas and fusion food (Moroccan/Asian/Spanish) with some veggie options and a free flamenco show (Mon–Sat) at 8.30pm. Daily 1.30pm–1am.

SHOPPING

Bookshops Librerías Prometeo y Proteo, C/Puerta Buenaventura 3, at the eastern end of C/Carretería, is the city's biggest bookshop; alternatively, try the more central Librería Luces, Alameda Principal 16 (north side). Málaga's best travel and outdoor bookshop is Mapas y Compañia, C/Compañia 33, west of Plaza de la Constitución. El Corte Inglés department store, Avda. de Andalucía 4, stocks most foreign newspapers and periodicals.

Fashion The main shopping area for designer labels and shoes is C/Marqués de Larios and the surrounding streets.

Food and drink The supermarket at the El Corte Inglés department store, Avda. de Andalucía 4, has a terrific selection of wines and spirits. La Mallorquina, Plaza Felix Saenz (near the market), is also a good place to pick up *malagueño* cheeses, wines, almonds and dried fruit.

Maps IGN walking maps and 1:50,000 Mapas Cartografía Militar (military maps) are sold by Indice (Mon–Fri 9am–2pm; ⓦ ine.es), C/Panaderos 2, just north of the Alameda, and at Mapas y Compañia (see p.78).

DIRECTORY

Banks and exchange There are numerous ATMS all over town, especially along C/Marqués de Larios and on the Plaza de la Constitución. El Corte Inglés (see above) will also change currency free of charge.

Consulates Ireland, Galería Santa Monica, Fuengirola ⓣ 952 475 108; UK, Edificio Eurocom, C/Mauricio Moro Pareto 2 ⓣ 952 352 300; USA, Avda. Juan Goméz 8, Fuengirola ⓣ 952 474 891.

Football After their promotion back to La Liga in 2008, C.F. Málaga seem to be establishing themselves under ex-Real Madrid manager Manuel Pellegrini. Games are at La Rosaleda stadium, Paseo de Martiricos s/n, at the northern end of the Río Guadalmedina. Tickets can be purchased from the stadium (ⓣ 952 614 210, ⓦ malagacf.es).

Hospital Hospital Carlos Haya, Avda. Carlos Haya, 2km west of the city centre ⓣ 951 290 000.

Internet Free wi-fi is available in the vicinity of the Teatro Cervantes and along the central C/Marqués de Larios. Conventional cybercafés near the centre include Locutorio Telsat, C/Gómez Pallete 7, near the Teatro Cervantes (daily 10am–midnight).

Pharmacy The handy 24hr Farmacia Caffarena (ⓣ 952 212 858) is located at Alameda 2, near the junction with C/Marqués de Larios.

Police Policía Local, Avda. de la Rosaleda 19 (ⓣ 952 126 500); in emergencies dial ⓣ 092 (local police) or ⓣ 091 (national).

Post office C/Santa Lucía 7, slightly north of Plaza de la Constitución. Mon–Fri 8.30am–8pm, Sat 8.30am–2pm.

El Chorro Gorge and around

Some 50km northwest of Málaga is the **Garganta del Chorro** (El Chorro Gorge): an immense cleft cut through a vast limestone massif by the Río Guadalhorce, with daunting walls of rock as high as 400m along its three-kilometre length. But the real attraction is a concrete catwalk, **El Camino del Rey**, which threads the length of the gorge hanging precipitously halfway up its side. Built in the 1920s as part of a

1

WALKING THE CAMINO DEL REY

Walking the **Camino del Rey** catwalk is a risky proposition whichever way you decide to do it, and should not be attempted if you are of a nervous disposition or are without a very good head for heights. Due to the obvious dangers involved, the safest way (and the one we strongly recommend) to do the Camino is on an **organized trip** with expert Swiss climber Jean Hofer at *Finca La Campana* (see p.81), who uses ropes to ensure maximum safety. Repeated accidents and even deaths led Endesa, the electricity company who are proprietors of the structure, to cut access to the catwalk from the El Chorro (southern) and Embalse (northern) ends. This was intended to prevent hikers from using it. The middle section, however, is still roughly intact – though in a terrible state of repair – and this can be accessed from the central part of the gorge, although you will have to return the way you came due to the demolition of each end of the catwalk mentioned above.

A safer way to view the Camino on your own – and easily accessed by car or a fine **walk** in itself – is to follow the road from El Chorro train station, signposted "Pantano de Guadalhorce", reached by crossing over the dam and turning right, then following the road north along the lake towards the hydroelectric plant. After 8km turn right at a junction to reach – after 2km – the bar-restaurant *El Mirador*, poised above a road tunnel and overlooking the various lakes and reservoirs of the Guadalhorce scheme. From the bar (where you should leave any transport), a dirt track on the right, just south of the tunnel entrance, heads towards the gorge. Follow this and take the first track on the right after about 700m. This climbs for some 2km to where it splits into two small trails. The trail to the left leads you to a magnificent viewpoint over the gorge from where you can see the Camino del Rey clinging to the rock face. The right-hand track climbs to an obvious peak, the Pico de Almochon, with more spectacular views, this time over the lakes of the Embalse del Guadalhorce (see below). On both walks you'll need to return the way you came.

burgeoning hydroelectric scheme, the Camino was opened by King Alfonso XIII, who walked its whole length and gave it its name, and used to figure in all the guidebooks as one of the wonders of Spain. However, despite proposals by local and regional governments to renovate the catwalk and make it safe as a tourist attraction, the Camino has largely fallen into disrepair and since 2000 has been officially closed. It's still possible to walk much of its length (see box above), however, despite a few wobbly – and decidedly dangerous – sections (one tourist fell to her death in 1998), with random holes in the concrete through which you can see the gorge hundreds of feet below. If you are not an experienced climber you are strongly advised to go with someone who is, and you will still need a head for heights and at least a full day starting from Málaga. If you've neither, it's possible to get a glimpse of both gorge and Camino from any of the trains going north from Málaga – the line, slipping in and out of tunnels, follows the river for quite a distance along the gorge, before plunging into a last long tunnel just before its head.

El Chorro and the Embalse del Guadalhorce

If you want to explore the gorge, head for **EL CHORRO**, which is reachable by train from Málaga. Not much more than a cluster of houses, bars and hotels around the railway station, it has nevertheless turned itself into one of Spain's major centres for rock climbing.

From the train station it's about 12km to some attractive lakes and reservoirs, such as the **Embalse del Guadalhorce,** part of the huge Embalse Guadalhorce–Guadalteba reservoir and hydroelectric scheme constructed in the early decades of the last century. Recent years of prolonged drought have dramatically lowered the water levels, making this area a great deal less attractive than in the past, but the lakes often sport sufficient water to swim in, and there are also kayaks for hire (see p.81). You can camp along the rocky shores; alternatively, the village of Ardales (see p.82), 4km beyond the lake, has shops, bars, a *hostal* and two daily buses to and from Ronda. Just beyond the *El Mirador* restaurant (see box opposite) you are able to view the impressive dam at the junction of the two great Guadalteba and Guadalhorce reservoirs, with the marble table and throne where Alfonso XIII signed off the completed works on May 21, 1921.

ARRIVAL AND DEPARTURE   EL CHORRO

By train A single daily direct train from Málaga (currently running at 6.19pm) with two daily trains in the opposite direction (8.19am & 3.02pm).

By bus There are no buses from Málaga, but there is a bus from nearby Álora at 12.30pm (Mon & Fri only), which is served by train from Málaga (ten daily).

By taxi A taxi from Álora to El Chorro costs about €20.

ACCOMMODATION

Bar Isabel Train station ☎ 952 495 004. Actually on the station platform, this bar-cum-grocery store offers a few basic rooms sharing bath. **€30**

Bar-Restaurante Garganta del Chorro Off the south end of the station platform ☎ 952 497 219, ⓦ lagarganta.com. Restaurant-and-rooms complex with pleasant rooms, apartments and suites, many with terraces and views inside a converted mill and overlooking a pool. The restaurant (mains €9–20) is the best place to eat in the village. **€81**

Camping El Chorro 400m from the station ☎ 952 495 244, ⓦ alberguecampingelchorro.com. Excellent campsite with a pool and restaurant, reached by heading downhill to your right for 400m after getting off the train. They also rent out wood cabins sleeping up to six. Two people plus car **€20,** cabins **€55**

★ **Finca La Campana** 2km from the station ☎ 626 963 942, ⓦ el-chorro.com. Signs from the station will direct you to this farmhouse set in rural surroundings with a bunkhouse (€12/bunk), double rooms sharing bath and a cluster of pleasant cottages sharing a pool. There's also a small shop selling provisions and hiring out climbing equipment. It's run by Swiss climber Jean Hofer, who also offers courses in rock climbing and caving, rents out mountain bikes and kayaks, and can arrange hiking excursions, as well as guided trips along the Camino del Rey (see box opposite). Doubles **€29**, cottages **€42**

La Posada del Conde Pantano del Chorro 16 ☎ 952 112 411, ⓦ hoteldelconde.com. Attractive small hotel close to the *El Mirador* restaurant (see box opposite). Rooms come with TV and a/c and some have balcony views over the "lake". Also has its own bar and very good restaurant next door. **€75**

Bobastro

A few kilometres southwest of El Chorro, amid some of the wildest scenery in the whole peninsula, lies **BOBASTRO**, the mountain-top remains of a Mozarabic fortified settlement. Famous as the isolated eyrie of colourful ninth-century rebel **Ibn Hafsun** (see box below), the castle was said to be the most impregnable in all Andalucía, but only a ruined **church**, carved into an enormous boulder, remains of the once-great fortress. Situated outside the original fortified area, and below some cave dwellings of

---

IBN HAFSUN

Born near Ronda around 860, **Ibn Hafsun** was a *muwallad* (of mixed Christian–Arab parentage) who, after killing a man, fell out with the Umayyad caliphate at Córdoba and resorted to a life of brigandage. Gathering around him a formidable army, he built his stronghold at Bobastro, and from 880–917 scored a number of spectacular victories over the many Umayyad forces sent to defeat him. At the height of his power Hafsun controlled an area between the straits of Gibraltar in the west and Jaén in the east. His defence of the poor against excessive Umayyad taxation and forced labour further served to increase the popularity of this Robin Hood-style figure, especially among his fellow *muwalladin* who believed they were getting a raw deal from their pure-blooded Arab rulers. After he converted to Christianity in 899, the church at Bobastro was constructed to receive his remains, which were duly interred there upon his death in 917. When Abd ar-Rahman III finally conquered Bobastro in 927, he exhumed the body of Hafsun and hung it on a gibbet outside the Alcázar in Córdoba as a "salutary warning to imitators and a pleasant spectacle to believers (true Muslims)".

1

uncertain date, the church is typically Mozarabic in style, its nave and two aisles separated by horseshoe-arched arcades. The transept, and a deep apse chapel flanked by two side chapels, can clearly be seen, making the edifice one of the few identifiable traces of building from the period. Nearby and to the west is the **Cueva de Doña Trinidad** with paleolithic cave paintings; guided visits to see them are organized by the museum at Ardales (see below).

ARRIVAL AND INFORMATION   BOBASTRO

From El Chorro You can get to Bobastro from El Chorro by crossing the dam from the train station and turning right along the road to *El Mirador* (see box, p.80). After 4km a signed turn-off for the site indicates a twisting 3km route to a ticket booth, where you should leave any vehicle.

Guided tours Visits to the site are by hourly guided tours (leaving on the hour Tues–Sun 10am–5pm; €3) conducted by the guardian. At the start of the visit he will open the entry gate and lead you along a path for 400m through the pinewoods to the site of the church and other remains.

Ardales

At the southern point of the reservoirs that comprise the Guadalteba–Guadalhorce scheme, the compact farming village of **ARDALES** tumbles down the hill below La Peña, a rocky outcrop topped by remains of the Iberian settlement of Turóbriga as well as a Roman fort and ruined Moorish *alcázar*. From the main square, the wide and animated Plaza San Isidro around which most of the activity in Ardales revolves, a steep street climbs to the summit.

Iglesia de la Virgen de los Remedios

On the way up, look out for the fifteenth-century Mudéjar **Iglesia de la Virgen de los Remedios** with its distinctive, partly tiled, tower. When you get closer, it becomes clear that the tower was once the minaret of the former mosque it replaced. To see the church's interior – plus the remains of the Roman fort and Alcázar accessed via the church – call at Calle Iglesia 48, slightly uphill from its main portal. The interior also has Moorish arches dividing the nave and side aisles, the right of which has the mosque's original *mihrab* oriented towards Mecca.

Museo de la Prehistoria

June–Sept Tues–Sat 9am–2pm; Oct–May Tues–Sat 10am–2.30pm & 4–6.30pm (if the museum is closed during official opening hours enquire at the Ayuntamiento on Plaza San Isidro) • ☎ 952 458 046 • €3

The **Museo de la Prehistoria**, facing the bridge as you enter the village, has Roman and Moorish archeological finds as well as copies of the rock paintings in the nearby paleolithic Cueva de Doña Trinidad.

The Cueva de Doña Trinidad

Guided tours Tues–Sun 10am • 1hr 30min • €8 • Book tours advance with Señor Anaya on ☎ 952 458 046 or ✉ prehistoriaardales @guadalteba.com

The curator of the Museo de la Prehistoria, Señor Geraldo Anaya, can provide information on visits to see the **Cueva de Doña Trinidad**. The cave, 1.5km deep, was discovered in 1918 and is one of the most important in Andalucía – traces were found of human occupation dating back to the later Stone Ages making it contemporaneous with the Cueva de las Piletas near Ronda (see p.129). Among some remarkable paintings and engravings dating from between ten and thirty thousand years ago are images of deer, horses, goats, bulls, fish, snakes and what is thought to be the first artistic representation of a human hand. The discovery of human remains in the cave suggests also that it may have had some form of funerary purpose in its latter period. The museum curator can also advise on visiting other caves in the area as well as some recently discovered trenches from the Civil War.

ACCOMMODATION

ARDALES

Camping Parque Ardales 6km east of Ardales along the MA5403 ☎952 112 401, ⓦparqueardales.com. Scenic "lakeside" (although it's actually the reservoir) campsite, which also rents out apartments sleeping up to four (€70) and offers a variety of activities including canoeing on the lake. There's no bus to the campsite but a taxi from Ardales will cost about €20 (any of the bars should be able to arrange this for you). Two people plus car €19

Hostal-Restaurante El Cruce ☎952 459 012, ⓔhostalelcruce@hotmail.com. Sited at the junction before the bridge across the Río Turón, this is a decent

option, with simple en-suite rooms above a restaurant (*menú* €8). There's also a pool. €40

★ **Apartamentos Ardales** C/El Burgo 7, just off the main square ☎952 459 466, ⓦapartamentosardales .com. The best accommodation option, this charming new apart-hotel has 17 apartments ranged around a tranquil patio. All the modern and distinctively decorated a/c apartments come with a small kitchen and balcony or terrace, while the communal rooftop terrace has fine views plus a plunge pool and Jacuzzi. Cycles are available for rent and the owners can provide information on a number of great walks in the surrounding sierra. See webpage for special offers. €78

EATING AND DRINKING

La Alternativa C/Real 4 (effectively the main square). The best restaurant in the village, with tapas, *raciones* and a €12 *menú*. Specialities include *solomillo* (pork loin) and *gambas rebozadas* (battered shrimps), and there's a pleasant terrace fronting the Ayuntamiento.

Bar Millan Plaza San Isidro. This, along with *Bar El Mellizo* opposite, is one of the two popular bars on the main square. Traditional places with no pretensions, both

offer a range of tapas including *boquerones en vinagre* (anchovies) at the former and *patatas bravas* (sautéed potatoes in spicy sauce) at the latter.

Casa Marcos C/San Isidro 31. Just along the tree-lined main street from Plaza San Isidro, this *pastelería is* renowned for its tasty *roscos de almendras* (almond cakes) made from a traditional family recipe. Also has a range of other tasty delicacies including *mantecados* (crumbly shortbreads).

Carratraca

Five kilometres south of Ardales, and reached via a turn-off from the A357 Málaga road, lies the village of **CARRATRACA**, once famous throughout Europe for its **sulphur spa**, now extensively refurbished as part of the *Villa Padierna* hotel (see p.84). Although the baths date back to the days of the Greeks and Romans, it wasn't until the nineteenth century that Carratraca became one of the foremost spas in Europe, and a gathering point for the continent's aristocracy. During its heyday the *balneario* (spa) attracted kings, princesses and literary bigwigs such as Lord Byron, Alexandre Dumas and Rainer Maria Rilke. The three *casinos*, where these socialites used to while away their time between plunges in the stinking, sulphurous waters which gush from the rocks, are long gone. However, two wonderfully elegant, eighteenth-century open-air (now glassed-in) pools circled by classical Tuscan columns have survived intact, forming the refurbished spa's centrepiece. You can use the spa without staying at the hotel. A basic twenty-minute soak will set you back about €15, although other treatments (including various types of massage, detox and thermal circuits) are much pricier.

The Ayuntamiento and the bullring

Carratraca's other sights include a Regency-style **Ayuntamiento**, on the edge of the village, formerly the residence of Doña Trinidad Grund, a local benefactor who donated funds for the excavation of the cave near Bobastro that bears her name. She also provided the backing for the curious **bullring** nearby, hacked out of solid rock and scene of the village Passion play during Semana Santa.

ACCOMMODATION

CARRATRACA

Casa Pepa C/Los Baños 18 ☎952 458 049. Just along from the spa, this friendly *fonda* – run by its eponymous proprietor – offers clean and simple rooms with or

without bath. Pepa also makes meals (*menú* €8) – the aromas emerging from the kitchen are usually very tempting. €35

Villa Padierna C/Antonio Rioboó 9 ☎952 489 542, ⓦthermasdecarratraca.com. Opulent hotel and spa complex with its own restaurant incorporating the royal palace built by the tyrannical King Fernando VII early in the nineteenth century to accommodate himself and his retinue while visiting the spa (although he probably never used it). Minimum two-night stay. **€160**

EATING AND DRINKING

Venta El Trillo C/Álora-Carratraca s/n. One in a line of three *ventas* on the road into the village from Ardales offering tapas, *raciones*, *platos combinados* and a weekday *menú* (under €10). The nearby Bar Venta Martillo and Venta El Punto are both very similar.

Antequera and around

Sitting on two low hills in the valley of the Río Guadalhorce, **ANTEQUERA** is an attractive market town with some important ancient monuments and a clutch of fine churches. On the main train line from Málaga to Granada and Seville, at the junction of roads heading inland to Córdoba, Granada and Seville, it's easy to get to, and makes a good day-trip from Málaga, which lies 40km to the south. Travelling from Málaga, the bus takes you along the fast but largely uninteresting A45 *autovía*. If you're driving, it's far nicer to take the older, more picturesque road (MA3402) that meanders through Almogía, a small hill-town with tortuously narrow streets.

● RESTAURANTS	
El Angelote	7
Hospedería Coso San Francisco	2
La Espuela	9
Plaza de Toros	3

● TAPAS BARS	
Bar-Cafetería A La Fuerza	5
Bar Chicón	8
Bar La Mandragora	6
Bar Numero Uno	1
Café del Centro	4

■ ACCOMMODATION	
Hospedería Coso San Francisco	4
Hostal Reyes	6
Hotel Colón	7
Hotel Coso Viejo	5
Hotel Plaza San Sebastián	8
Número Uno	3
Parador de Antequera	1
Pensión Toril	2

ANTEQUERA

Antequera has a modern appearance that belies its history. In Roman times Anticaria ("ancient city") is thought to have had a substantial population; much later, in 1410, the town was the first in Andalucía to fall to the Christian forces in the *Reconquista*. It's now a bustling agricultural centre where farmers from the surrounding *vega* come to stock up on everything from tractor tyres to seeding attachments.

The town divides into two zones: a **monumental quarter** situated at the foot of the hill dominated by the Alcazaba, and the mainly nineteenth-century **commercial sector** concentrated around the Alameda de Andalucía. This end of town is where modern Antequera works and plays, and there's not much in the way of sights, though the nineteenth-century bullring is worth a look. Probably the most famous sights, however, are the prehistoric **dolmen caves**, on the northern edge of town.

From Antequera a couple of enjoyable trips are to the vast **Parque Natural El Torcal**, with its marvellous weathered limestone rock formations, and the important flamingo breeding grounds of **Fuente de Piedra**.

Museo Municipal

C/Coso Viejo s/n • Tues–Fri 10am–1.30pm & 4.30–6.30pm, Sat 10am–1.30pm, Sun 11am–1.30pm • Hourly guided tours • €3

At the heart of the monumental quarter, the **Museo Municipal** is located in a striking eighteenth-century ducal palace. It's just as well that the palace is worth visiting for itself, because the exhibits do little justice to the setting. Largely a hotchpotch of church vestments, silver plate and indifferent paintings, the collection is, however, distinguished by two works of sculpture: a fine first-century AD **Roman bronze** of a youth known as the *Efebo de Antequera*, and an eerily lifelike carving in wood of **St Francis of Assisi** by the seventeenth-century *andaluz* sculptor Pedro de Mena. More fragments of ancient statuary and tombstones are dotted around the courtyard, and a room on the ground floor devotes itself to the artwork of a modern painter born in Antequera, Cristóbal Toral.

Convento de la Carmelitas Descalzas

Plaza de las Descalzas

To the northeast of the museum, the eighteenth-century **Convento de la Carmelitas Descalzas** (Carmelite nunnery of San José) on has a good selection of *dulces* (see box, p.76), sold via a *torno* in the mornings only. The entrance is behind the small fountain. Inside, asking for a *surtido* (sampler) gets you a bit of everything. You won't see the nun who serves you, but, in a sign of changing times, she may ask you to pay first.

Nuestra Señora del Carmen

Plaza del Carmen • Mon–Sat 10.30am–1.30pm & 4.30–5.45pm, Sun 11am–2pm • €2

The nearby Cuesta de las Rojas climbs steeply to the Postigo de la Estrella, an old postern gate. To the east of this – and not to be missed – lies the seventeenth-century Mudéjar church of **Nuestra Señora del Carmen**, whose plain facade little prepares you for the eighteenth-century interior, painstakingly restored to its former glory. The main altar's sensational thirteen-metre-high **retablo** – one of the finest in Andalucía – is a masterly late-Baroque extravaganza of carved wood by Antonio Primo and Diego Márquez, its centrepiece a Virgin in a *camarín* flanked by a bevy of polychrome saints and soaring angels.

The Alcazaba

Plaza Alta • Tues–Fri 10.30am–2pm & 4–6pm, Sat & Sun 10am–2pm • Free

Further up Cuesta de las Rojas lies the refurbished medieval **Alcazaba**, with its thirteenth-century Islamic fortification, the **Torre del Homenaje**. The first fortress to

1

fall to the Christians during the Reconquest of the kingdom of Granada, the ruined Alcazaba now encloses a municipal garden, giving fine views over the town towards the curiously anthropoid **Peña de los Enamorados** (Lovers' Rock), resembling the profiled head of a sleeping giant. The outcrop acquired its name from two lovers (a Christian girl and a Muslim youth) during the Moorish period, who are said to have thrown themselves from the top when their parents forbade their marriage.

Adjoining the Alcazaba, the sixteenth-century **Arco de los Gigantes** preserves stones and inscriptions embedded in its walls that were rescued by antiquaries from the destruction of the Roman town in the same period.

Colegiata de Santa María la Mayor

Plaza Alta • Tues–Fri 10.30am–2pm & 4–6pm, Sat & Sun 10am–2pm • Free

East of the Alcazaba, the sixteenth-century collegiate church of **Santa María** boasts a great Plateresque facade inspired by a Roman triumphal arch. Inside, the triple-naved church – which now serves as a concert hall – you'll also see a superb Mudéjar coffered ceiling.

San Sebastián

Plaza San Sebastián • Daily 8.30am–1pm & 6–8pm • Free

The seventeenth-century **San Sebastián**, in the elegant plaza of the same name, possesses a striking brick steeple that dominates the town. Note the carved angels and the tower's weather vane, El Angelote, which has the remains of Antequera's patron saint, Santa Euphemia, in a reliquary hung around its neck. The interior contains some beautifully carved choir stalls, as does the nearby eighteenth-century **San Agustín**, at the start of Calle Infante Fernando.

San Juan de Dios

C/Infante Fernando • Wed–Fri 6–9pm, Sun noon–2pm • Free

At the western end of Calle Infante Fernando lies the Renaissance church of **San Juan de Dios**, constructed (or so Richard Ford maintained) in the late sixteenth and early seventeenth centuries almost entirely with stone taken from the demolition of what was a perfectly preserved Roman theatre. Close by lies the Palacio Consistorial – a stylish seventeenth-century mansion now functioning as the **Ayuntamiento** (access to view patio during working hours).

Capilla de la Virgen del Socorro and Santa María de Jesús

Up a steep climb at the southern end of the town lies the flamboyant Baroque-Mudéjar **Capilla de la Virgen del Socorro** (only open during services: Mon–Sat 7–9pm, Sun 10.30am–1.30pm; free), with a double tier of triple arches built to house Antequera's most revered image, Nuestra Señora del Socorro (Our Lady of Succour).

The nearby white-walled Baroque chapel of **Santa María de Jesús** (Tues–Sun 11am–1pm; free), with storks' nests in its belfry, is also worth a look. From a *mirador* behind the churches there are great views towards the Alcazaba and the surrounding hills.

Plaza de Toros

Plaza de la Constitución s/n • Museum Tues–Fri 10am–2pm & 4–6pm; Sat 10am–2pm; Sun 11.30am–2pm • Free

The western end of town has little in the way of sights, though the nineteenth-century **Plaza de Toros**, on the Alameda de Andalucía, is well worth a look – access is usually available to the ring when the restaurant (see p.90) is open. This bullring staged its first *corrida* on August 20, 1848, and whatever your views on bullfighting, it's difficult not to pick up on the atmosphere that the old place generates, especially when you view the amphitheatre from the matador's position in the centre of the arena. The museum has the usual collection of bullfighting posters, photos and memorabilia.

The dolmen caves

Ctra. Antequera–Archidona s/n • Tues–Sat 9am–6pm, Sun 9.30am–2.30pm • Free

On the town's northern outskirts – an easy 1km walk along the Granada road – lies a group of three **prehistoric dolmens**, which rank among the most important in Spain, now enclosed in a futuristic "dolmen park" with visitor centre, car park and a *centro de interpretación*. The two major dolmens are remarkable constructions, while the third lies further away and is best reached with your own transport or a taxi.

Cueva de Menga

The grandest of these megalithic monuments is the **Cueva de Menga**, its roof formed by massive stone slabs, among them a 180-ton monolith. Dating from around 2500 BC, the columned gallery leading to an oval burial chamber was probably the final resting place of an important chieftain. On the last stone slab of the left wall (nearest the entrance) you'll see some engraved – and probably symbolic – forms; the star, however, is a later addition. A recently discovered **well** in the rear of the chamber probably dates from the Roman period. If you stand just inside the entrance to the Menga dolmen you will be able to see the Lovers' Rock, precisely framed in the portal – something that cannot have been accidental and suggests that the rock may have had some religious or ritual significance. This is underlined by the fact that the sun rises behind the "head" of the rock at the summer solstice and penetrates the burial chamber.

Cueva de Viera

The **Cueva de Viera**, dating from a century or two later, has better-cut stones, forming a long, narrow tunnel leading to a smaller burial chamber. The roof consisted of seven stones of which only four remain. To the west it's possible to make out the quarry on the peak of a nearby hill (topped by a rather incongruous school) from where the stone used to construct the dolmens was hewn before being hauled across the intervening valley.

El Romeral

The third dolmen, **El Romeral**, is a further 2km down the road on the left behind an old sugar factory (easily identified by its chimney), reached by following signs from a roundabout (direction Córdoba). Built more than half a millennium later than the other two dolmens and containing dual chambers roofed with splendid corbel vaulting, El Romeral has something of an eastern Mediterranean feel, and bears an uncanny resemblance to the *tholos* tombs constructed in Crete at around the same time.

ARRIVAL AND DEPARTURE	**ANTEQUERA**
By train Antequera's RENFE station (☎ 952 843 226) is 1km north from the centre of town (no bus service) on Avda. Estacion. **By bus** Buses from Málaga terminate at the bus station	(☎ 952 841 957) near the bullring. From here the Alameda de Andalucía and its continuation the C/Infante Don Fernando – the effective centre of town – are within easy walking distance.

INFORMATION

Turismo Municipal Plaza San Sebastián, alongside the church of the same name (June–Sept Mon–Sat 11am–2pm & 5–8pm, Sun 11am–2pm; Oct–May

Mon–Sat 10.30am–1.30pm & 4–7pm, Sun 11am–2pm; ☎ 952 702 505, ⌨ turismoantequera.com).
Private tourist office Plaza Coso Viejo s/n, next door

1

to the *El Angelote* restaurant (Mon–Sat 9am–2pm; ☎952 700 005. This is also a good source of information for the town and surrounding area.

Festival Antequera's annual *feria* happens during the third week in August, taking the form of a harvest fiesta (*recolección*) with *corridas*, dancing and parades.

Internet Veronika's, C/Picadero 4, south of the bullring (daily 9.30am–2pm & 4–11pm).

ACCOMMODATION

You shouldn't have a problem finding a place to stay, as demand tends to be low and the generally good-value room prices reflect this. Most hotels have either their own garage (for which you usually pay extra) or can advise on street parking. The nearest campsite is at El Torcal (see p.90).

★ **Hospedería Coso San Francisco** C/Calzada 25 ☎952 840 014, ⓦcososanfrancisco.com. Comfortable and reasonably priced a/c en-suite rooms with TV plus a friendly welcome make this a winner. Also has a very good restaurant and a tapas bar next door. **€40**

Hostal Reyes C/Tercia 4 ☎952 841 028. Pleasant and central en-suite rooms with a/c, TV and welcoming proprietors. **€30**

Hotel Colón C/Infante Don Fernando 31 ☎952 840 010, ⓦcastelcolon.com. This pleasant central hotel is another reliable choice for competitively priced rooms with balcony and fridge (some), a/c and satellite TV. There's also free internet and wi-fi, and own parking for €5 per day. **€35**

Hotel Coso Viejo C/Encarnación 9 ☎952 705 045, ⓦhotelcosoviejo.com. New three-star hotel housed in a striking eighteenth-century *casa-palacio* with a beautiful patio. Rooms are elegantly furnished and some have views towards the Alcazaba. **€66**

Hotel Plaza San Sebastián Plaza San Sebastián 4 ☎952 844 239, ⓦwww.hotelplazasansebastian.com. Attractive two-star hotel facing the church of San Sebastián offering well-equipped a/c balcony rooms with satellite TV. Own car park. **€45**

Número Uno C/Lucena 40 ☎952 843 134, ⓦhotel numerouno.com. Small hotel with welcoming proprietors and pleasant if sparsely furnished a/c en-suite rooms with TV. There's a roof terrace solarium above and a popular and very good bar-restaurant below, and parking can be arranged. **€35**

Parador de Antequera Paseo García del Olmo s/n ☎952 840 261, ⓦparador.es. A recently refurbished modern *parador*, to the north of the Plaza de Toros, with well-appointed and -equipped rooms plus pleasant gardens and pool. **€138**

Pensión Toril C/Toril 3 ☎952 843 184, ⓦpensiontoril .com. Tranquil and pleasant *pensión* with simple but adequate en-suite rooms with TV arranged around two charming patios. Free parking. **€35**

EATING AND DRINKING

TAPAS BARS

Bar-Cafetería A La Fuerza C/Alameda de Andalucía 32. This excellent bar near the bullring makes a good breakfast stop and is noted for its *churros*. A lengthy tapas menu features *boquerones fritos* (fried anchovies) and *jamón ibérico*, and there's also a tapas *menú de degustación* for €10. Daily 9am–11.30pm.

Bar Chicón C/Infante Don Fernando 1, near the Plaza de San Sebastián. This traditional bar serves breakfasts and, later in the day, tapas and *raciones*, specializing in *montaditos* (*tapa* served on bread). Daily 9.30am–midnight.

Bar La Mandragora Plaza Descalzas 1. A popular tapas bar with a penchant for modern art and a younger ambiente. A wide range of background music includes jazz, blues, rock and reggae and there's a pleasant terrace on this picturesque square. Daily except Tues 9am–midnight.

Bar Numero Uno C/Lucena 40. Attached to the hotel of the same name (see above), this bar is noted for its fish and does a wide range of tapas and *raciones* – try their delicious *gambas a la plancha* (fried shrimps). It also does a *menú* for €8 and there's a restaurant at the back if you want to make a meal of it. Daily 7.30am–11.30pm.

Café del Centro C/Cantareros 3, slightly north of the main street. This is another good breakfast bar where the walls are decorated with photos from Antequera's past. Later in the day it gets into its stride with a good tapas and *raciones* selection – try the paella. Daily 9am–11.30pm.

RESTAURANTS

El Angelote C/Encarnación s/n ☎952 703 465. On the same square as the museum, this is one the town's top restaurants, with an elegant dining room or a pleasant terrace outside. The menu is based on traditional *antequerana* fare with a weekday *menú* for €8.50. Main dishes €10–20. Tues–Sun noon–4pm & 8–11.30pm.

Restaurante Coso San Francisco C/Calzada 25 ☎952 705 045. Located inside the hotel of the same name this is a very good restaurant offering typical dishes of the region – try the *revuelto de bacalao* (cod), *gazpacho de espárragos*, *croquetas* (croquettes) or any of the mouth-watering desserts. The new *Coso de Tapas* tapas bar next door is also excellent and has a range of tasty tapas including *berenjenas con miel* (fried aubergine with honey)

1

and *albondiguilla marinera* (fish balls). Main dishes (restaurant) €9–18. Daily 1pm–midnight.

La Espuela (aka La Reina) C/San Agustin 1, a small cul-de-sac off C/Infante Don Fernando ☎952 703 031. Andalucía's hotel schools are turning out many award-winning chefs these days and restaurants such as this, belonging to Antequera's hotel and catering school, is where they earn their stripes. The bonus is that prices are far from elevated and the cuisine – a combination of *andaluz* and *antequerana* in this case – is frequently excellent with a creative edge. They offer *menús* for €14

and €16 but the best bargain has to be a *menú de degustación* for €30. There's also a small terrace. The restaurant has its own tapas bar which is also very good. Mon–Sat 1–4.30pm & 8–11.30pm, Sun 1–4.30pm.

Restaurante Plaza de Toros Plaza de la Constitución. The bullring's very own restaurant next to the ring itself is worth a try, with a mid-priced *menú* for around €20 as well as more expensive options including a range of *carnes asados* (charcoal-grilled meats). And yes, on fight days *rabo de toro* (stewed bull's tail) is one of the house specials. Main dishes €12–20. Mon–Sat 1–11.30pm, Sun 1–5pm.

Parque Natural El Torcal

EL TORCAL, 13km south of Antequera and 32km north of Málaga, is the most geologically arresting of Andalucía's natural parks. A massive high plateau of eroded grey limestone dating from the Jurassic period, tempered by a lush growth of hawthorn, ivy, wild rose and thirty species of orchid, it's quite easily explored using the **walking routes** that radiate from the centre of the park where the road ends. Try to leave your explorations until the more peaceful late afternoon, when the setting sun throws the natural rock sculptures into sharp relief.

The trails

The best-designed and most exciting **trails** are the yellow and red routes, the former climaxing with suitable drama on a cliff edge with magnificent views over a valley. The latter gives fantastic vantage points of the looming limestone outcrops, eroded into vast, surreal sculptures. Because of the need to protect flora and fauna the red route is in a restricted zone and can only be visited with a **guide** (information on this available from the Centro de Recepción). The **green** and **yellow routes** (waymarked) can be walked without a guide. The green route is the shortest at 1.5km (about 40min if you don't dawdle) while the yellow route takes about two hours. In early summer on the popular green route you may find yourself competing with gangs of schoolkids, who arrive en masse on vaguely educational trips, excitedly trying to spot La Copa (the wineglass), El Lagarto (the lizard) and La Loba (the she-wolf) as well as other celebrated rock sculptures. Keep an eye on the skies while you're here for Griffon vultures, frequent visitors whose huge wingspans make a spectacular sight as they glide overhead.

ARRIVAL AND INFORMATION
PARQUE NATURAL EL TORCAL

There's no public transport to El Torcal. From Antequera it's a 16km hike; the park is reached by following the A7075 towards Villanueva de la Concepción and heading down the second signed turning on the right to El Torcal.

By taxi A taxi costs about €20 one-way for up to four. You can arrange this through the Turismo or by ringing ☎608 951 926 (Spanish only). You can also use this number for your return journey. Make sure to agree a price with the *taxista* before starting out.

Centro de Recepción (April–Sept daily 10am–7pm; Oct–March 10am–5pm; ☎605 787 919) gives out maps and general information on the park and its walks, and has audiovisual presentations covering geology, flora and fauna.

ACCOMMODATION

Camping rough is not allowed inside the park. The Turismo at Antequera can provide information regarding some attractive *casas rurales* to rent in the area.

Camping Torcal Just off the A7975, 6km south of Antequera ☎952 111 608, ⓦwww.campingeltorcal .com. Rural campsite with plenty of shade, plus a restaurant, supermarket and pool. Two people plus car **€17**

Laguna de Fuente de Piedra

About 20km northwest of Antequera lies **Laguna de Fuente de Piedra**, the largest natural lake in Andalucía and a celebrated site for observing birdlife. The shallow water-level and high saline content of the lake, and the crustaceans that these conditions encourage, attract a glorious flock of **greater flamingo** each spring, making this Europe's only inland breeding ground for the species. Unfortunately the droughts of recent years and the demands for more water by local farmers cashing in on an asparagus boom in the nearby Sierra de Yeguas have led to the lake almost drying up completely in the summer months, thus placing many of the young flamingo in peril. This resulted in rescue missions being mounted by teams from the Coto Doñana (see p.330) who transferred many young birds back to the wetlands of Huelva. Andalucía's environmental agency has put in place a system to prevent this happening again. However, even this has not been sufficient and the drought of 2005 resulted in low water-levels surrounding the nesting sites and a reluctance by the birds to breed.

Besides supporting a variety of waders at all times of the year, in winter the lake is often a haven for **cranes**, and the surrounding marshes provide a habitat for numerous amphibians and reptiles. Remember that because this is a sanctuary, the beaches are strictly out of bounds (ruling out swimming) and because many sections are privately owned, limiting access, it's not possible to make a complete circuit of the lake. You're also at a distinct advantage with your own transport, as species such as flamingo often gather at the far end of the lake, up to 7km away, although **mountain bikes** can now be rented from the visitor centre (see below).

ARRIVAL AND DEPARTURE

By bus Four daily from Antequera or Málaga (changing at Antequera).

By train Fuente de Piedra station is on the line between Málaga and Córdoba, a ten-minute walk east from the lake.

By car Take the A45 north from Antequera/Málaga to join the A92 *autovía* (direction Sevilla), and continue along this for 14km until the signed turn-off.

INFORMATION

Centro de Visitantes Over the bridge beyond the train station, the lakeside Centro de Visitantes (daily: April–Oct 10am–2pm & 6–8pm; Nov–March 10am–2pm & 4–6pm; ☏ 952 111 715) has displays on the flora and fauna of the lake, and rents out binoculars and mountain bikes (both €1.50/hr).

ACCOMMODATION

Camping Fuente Piedra C/Campillos 88 ☏ 952 735 294, ⓦ camping-rural.com. The most attractive place to stay is the campsite, close to the village and overlooking the lake. Accommodation is in a/c double rooms or fully equipped wood cabins, sleeping up to four persons. There's also a swimming pool and a decent restaurant with an economical *menú*. The site also offers a variety of activities including guided walks, mountain biking, caving, canoeing and archery. Rooms €50, cabins €85.

Málaga to Torre del Mar

The dreary eastern stretch of the **Costa del Sol** – the beaches within easy distance of Málaga – is a largely unbroken landscape of urbanization and unlovely holiday towns, packed to the gunwales in summer with day-tripping *malagueños*. There are enough places of interest, however, to warrant stopping off en route, before arriving at the unremarkable resort of **Torre del Mar**. With your own transport it's possible to avoid the Málaga suburbs by using the N340 *circunvalación* (ring road) – picked up on the northern edge of town – which eventually becomes the *autovía* linking Málaga with Nerja. To follow the coastal route described below, leave the *autovía* at the Rincón de la Victoria exit (see p.92). Otherwise, the road heading out of Málaga along the Paseo de Reding (passing the north side of the bullring) traverses the suburbs of Pedragalejo and

1

El Palo, where for most of the summer the beaches are covered with a forest of parasols, before arriving at the small resort of Cala de Moral.

Cueva del Tesoro

Guided visits daily: April–Sept 10.45am–1pm & 4.45–7pm; Oct–March 10am–1pm & 3.45–5.15pm • €4.25 • Ⓦ cuevasturisticas.com

Just beyond Cala del Moral, a signed road on the left indicates the **CUEVA DEL TESORO**, a spectacular network of underground marine caves less commercialized than those at Nerja (see p.101). A series of seven chambers leads to the eighth, the **sala de los lagos**, a Gaudí-esque rock cathedral with natural underground pools. Paleolithic cave paintings were discovered here in 1918 (presently not on view) as well as other prehistoric remains indicating almost continual human habitation. The cave's name (*tesoro* means treasure) derives from the legend that five fleeing Moorish kings took refuge in its depths and stashed a large quantity of gold here (now long gone).

Macharaviaya

Beyond the Cueva del Tesoro, **Rincón de la Victoria** is a no-nonsense, untidy sort of place, and a popular resort for *malagueño* families. A seafood speciality here is *coquinas*, tasty small clams. To break the monotony along this strip of coast you could follow a small road heading inland at the featureless suburb of Torre de Benagalbón that winds up into the hills and approaches the hamlet of **MACHARAVIAYA** (from the Moorish Arabic Machar Ibn Yahya, or "lands of the son of Yahya"). Surrounded by slopes covered with olive and almond trees, the village was expanded in the eighteenth century by the Galvéz family, one of Andalucía's great imperial dynasties. Count Bernardo de Galvéz became governor general of Spanish North America and gave his name to Galveston in Texas after laying siege to the town in 1777. Today, even taking into account its impressive Baroque church (a Galvéz construction), it's hard to believe that this tiny, cobble-paved village was once known as "little Madrid". It was a wealthy place, benefiting from the extensive Galvéz family vineyards as well as a playing-card factory that had a monopoly for supplying cards to the Americas. This was all to end, however, when the phylloxera plague of the 1870s wiped out the vines, the card monopoly lapsed and the Galvéz line died out. The family title died with them, and the last Vizconde de Galveston is buried in the church crypt among the tombs and alabaster statues of his ancestors.

San Jacinto

Guided visits, which include the museum and house of Salvador Rueda in Benaque (see opposite) Sat & Sun 10am–3pm • Free • Visits to the church can also be arranged outside official opening hours by calling the Ayuntamiento on ☎ 952 400 042 (English spoken); the church (but not the crypt) is also open for services on Saturdays at 7pm (or 6pm Oct–March)

At the entrance to the village is a rather proprietorial whitewashed brick temple erected by the Galvéz family in 1786 and, at its centre, the once crumbling exterior of the outsize church of **San Jacinto**, somewhat over-restored as part of the Expo '92 celebrations. Inside the single-nave church, altars dedicated to various Galvéz family members are decorated with fine marble, and inscriptions express the ultimately vain hope that Mass would be said on certain days for their souls *in perpetuum*. Don't miss the eerie crypt behind the church, where a remarkable collection of sombre **alabaster family busts** face each other around an alcove and seem about to start up a gloomy conversation. The great marble tomb of Don José Galvéz, marquis of Sonora and minister for the Indias during the eighteenth-century reign of Carlos III, stands nearby.

EATING	MACHARAVIAYA

Taberna El Candil C/Elvira. From the church head uphill along C/Elvira, a short alleyway, to reach this simple and friendly place, which serves tapas, *raciones* and even full meals, if pushed. Snacks include tasty *pitufos de lomo* (rolls filled with grilled pork).

Benaque

Two kilometres north of Macharaviaya – and approached via a side road to the left at the entrance to the village – the village of **BENAQUE** has a Mudéjar church, **Nuestra Señora del Rosario**, its tower formed out of the minaret of the mosque it replaced. The building has recently been sensitively restored.

House of Salvador Rueda

Just before the church a house on the right was the birthplace of Benaque's most famous son, the modernist poet **Salvador Rueda** (1857–1933). Now converted into a **museum** (free, but donations welcome), the disarmingly simple interior has been preserved more or less as it was when the poet lived here. If you want to visit, the key is available from Señor José (Pepe) Cabrera, Calle Salvador Rueda 19, just before the bus shelter to the left as you arrive. The museum can also be seen on guided visits from Macharaviaya – see the San Jacinto section above.

Torre del Mar

Back on the main coast road, the chain of localities with "torre" in their names refers to the numerous *atalayas*, or watchtowers, which have been used to guard this coast since Roman and Moorish times, many strikingly visible on the headlands. There's little to detain you between Torre de Benagalbón and Almayate, from where it's only a couple of kilometres to **TORRE DEL MAR**. A line of concrete tower blocks on a grey, pebble beach, this is Torremolinos without the money or bluster. Nevertheless, it's a fairly easy-going place and the central pedestrianized street, **Paseo de Larios**, which runs from the tram terminal down to the seafront, provides a focus for numerous bars – including some excellent tapas bars – restaurants and cafés. Adjacent to the Paseo de Larios is a small parade of bars with a rather tame nightlife scene, named El Copo.

INFORMATION
TORRE DEL MAR

Turismo Casa Recreo, C/Poniente 2, a couple of blocks in from the seafront (June–Sept daily 10am–2pm; Oct–May Mon–Fri 10am–2pm; ☎952 541 104, ⊛velezmalaga.es). Housed in an elegant early twentieth-century restored seaside villa this helpful office has lots of info on places to stay and can supply a town map.

Internet Free internet access is available at the Biblioteca Publica (public library; Mon–Fri 9am–2pm & 5–8pm), Avda. Andalucía 92, close to the Turismo.
Bookshop Pasa Tiempo, C/Infantes 30 (☎952 543 703), facing Plaza de la Paz, sells new and used books in English as well as the British press and hiking maps.

ACCOMMODATION

Camping Almayate-Costa 2km west of town along the N340 at km267 ☎952 556 289, ⊛camping almayatecosta.com). Close to Torre del Mar, this isn't a bad site with plenty of shade – although it tends to get packed in high summer. Two people plus car €30
Camping Laguna Playa Paseo Maritimo s/n ☎952 540 224, ⊛lagunaplaya.com. West of the centre of Torre del Mar and close to the sea, this is a reasonable site with shade; although it fills to the gunwales in high season. Two people plus car €22

Hostal Don Juan C/Patrón Veneno 14 ☎952 545 870, ⊛hostaldonjuantorredelmar.es. Just 30m from the beach, this renovated and central *hostal* has en-suite a/c rooms with TV, some with terraces and sea views. €60
Hotel Miraya C/Patrón Veneno 6 ☎952 545 969, ⊛hotelmiraya.com. A few doors away from the *Hostal Don Juan*, this pleasant seafront hotel offers a few more creature comforts than its neighbour. Rooms are a/c and come with satellite TV, safe and free wi-fi. €75

EATING

Bar Fernando C/Saladero Viejo S/N. With a lively terrace most nights this is a classic Torre del Mar *marisquería* where the fried fish is fresh and the crustaceans are excellent. The bar's special is *fritura de pescado*, and there's

also a wide range of salads to go with the fish. The neighbouring Bar *Toné* and *Bar El Yate*, both with their own terraces, are also excellent and make good next stops on your tapas trail. Daily noon–4pm & 7.30pm–midnight.

1

Bar-Marisquería Radar Paseo Marítimo 13. Just around the corner from the *Bar Fernando* and with a sea-view terrace this is another excellent *marisquería* and *freiduría*. Try the *gambas rebozadas* (battered shrimps). Daily 12.30–4.30pm & 7.30–11.30pm.

The Central Axarquía

The Axarquía makes a refreshing change from the sun-bed culture of the Costa del Sol. Bounded by the coast, the Sierra de Alhama to the north and, on its eastern flank, the mountainous edge of the province of Granada, this rugged, ham-shaped wedge of territory offers excellent walking country and abundant wildlife, as well as a host of attractive mountain villages. Long a breeding ground for *bandoleros* who preyed on traders carrying produce from the coast to Granada, during the Civil War the Axarquía was also a notorious guerrilla encampment whose members fought on against Franco's Guardia Civil until the early 1950s: it is only in relatively recent times that the area has become safe for travellers.

The main villages of the **Eastern Axarquía** – Cómpeta, Archez and Salares – are covered in the "Torre del Mar to Nerja" section (see p.91).

Vélez-Málaga

Frequent buses and a tram service head 4km inland from Torre del Mar to **VÉLEZ-MÁLAGA**, capital of the Axarquía and a bustling market town and supply centre for the region's farmers. In the fertile valley of the Río Vélez, Vélez-Málaga (often simply referred to as Vélez) was important in both Roman times – under the name of Menoba – and Moorish, when as Ballix-Malaca ("Fortress of Málaga") it had an important role in subduing what has always been a turbulent zone. A number of Phoenician cemeteries and tombs discovered nearby testify to an older pedigree still. Fernando's conquest of the town in 1487 drove a wedge through the kingdom of Granada, dividing it in two and paving the way for the fall of the Nasrid city five years later.

The Castillo

C/de la Fortaleza • Daily during daylight hours • Free

The town climbs up a slope from the main streets, Calle Canalejas and its continuation Calle Cristo – towards the **castillo**, as good a place as any to start a tour of the sights. Founded by the Moors and successively rebuilt and restored after the *Reconquista*, what's left of it clings to a rocky outcrop, which from its dominant position above the white-walled *barrio* of San Sebastián gives good views out over the coast. The castle suffered badly during the War of the Spanish Succession, when the English lost to the French here after a bitter struggle in 1704.

Santa María de la Encarnación and San Juan Bautista

Visible from the castle is the sixteenth-century Mudéjar church of **Santa María de la Encarnación** (Tues–Sat 10am–2pm & 5–8pm; free) whose beautiful tower incorporates the minaret of the mosque that preceded it. Inside, Moorish arches separate a triple nave, and there's a fine Mudéjar ceiling.

East of Santa María de la Encarnación, the late-Gothic **San Juan Bautista** (Tues–Sat 6–8pm; free), on Plaza Constitución, is also worth a look, featuring an elegant tower and, inside, a superbly naturalistic sculpture, *Cristo Crucificado,* by Pedro de Mena.

Palacio del Marqués de Beniel

Plaza Palacio 1 • Mon–Fri 8am–3pm • Free

The restored **Palacio del Marqués de Beniel** is an elegant sixteenth-century mansion – formerly the town hall –with a delightful patio. The building now hosts the

International Summer School of the Axarquía covering all aspects of culture, including poetry and theatre as well as flamenco and classical guitar.

ARRIVAL AND DEPARTURE VÉLEZ-MÁLAGA

By bus Vélez-Málaga's bus station is next to the Parque de Andalucía, south of the centre.

By tram Coming in by tram from Torre del Mar you'll be dropped at the Parque Juan Jurado Lorca, from where the centre is a five-minute walk.

INFORMATION

Tourist office The office in Torre del Mar (see p.99) serves both communities; the Ayuntamiento (Mon–Fri 8.30am–2pm), on the central Plaza de las Carmelitas, can supply a town map.

Festival A prestigious annual guitar competition is held in Vélez Malaga every July, with free concerts held in the delightful patio of the Palacio del Marqués de Beniel. The Ayuntamiento has details of these and other cultural activities taking place throughout the summer.

Walking The Axarquía is a great place to do some hiking:

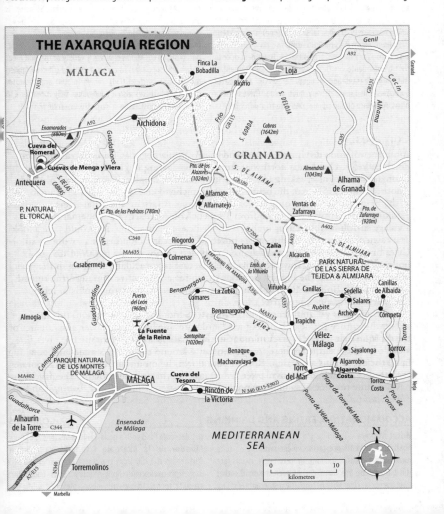

THE AXARQUÍA REGION

1

Walk! the Axarquía by Charles Davis is devoted to hikes in the region; alternatively, *Walking in Andalucía* by Guy Hunter-Watts (see p.593) has half a dozen hikes to follow in the western Axarquía.

ACCOMMODATION

Dila Hotel Avda. Vivar Téllez 3, 200m east of the centre ☎952 503 900, ⌨hoteldila.com. Decent small hotel with a/c rooms with satellite TV, free wi-fi and own car park. €65

Palacio Blanco C/Feliz Lomas 4, below the Castillo ☎952 549 174, ⌨palacioblanco.com. Stunningly attractive boutique hotel in a restored *casa-palacio* with a delightful patio. The beautifully furnished rooms are equipped with shower rooms and there's free internet, wi-fi and a rooftop pool and bar. €102

EATING AND DRINKING

Capri C/Alcalde Juan Barranquero 4, south of Plaza Reyes Católicos. Nice place for a snack or a meal, with a good tapas and *raciones* bar downstairs and restaurant above. There's a good selection of fish and meat options, or try their *tortilla de camarones* (shrimp fritters) or *salchichas caseras al vino* (sausage in wine). Daily except Wed noon–4pm & 8pm–midnight.

Bar Toto Plaza de las Carmelitas 13. Bang next door to the Ayuntamiento on the busy Plaza de las Carmelitas, this very pleasant and tranquil bar serves a range of *bocadillos* and tapas, all very good value. There's also a pleasant terrace on the square. Daily 9am–midnight.

El Caserío de las Monjas C/Félix Lomas 31. On the same street as the *Palacio Blanco* hotel (see above) this is an excellent small tapas and *raciones* bar where a free *tapa* (of your choice) arrives with every drink. Stone walls and beams give it a "lived in" feel. Tues–Sat 1–5pm & 8pm–midnight, Sun 1–5pm.

Mesón Los Migueles Avda. Vivar Tellez 83. The medium-priced *Mesón Los Migueles* serves a variety of fish and meat dishes and specializes in *carnes a la brasa* (charcoal-grilled meats) such as *choto* (kid), *conejo* (rabbit) and *churrasco* (pork steak). There's also a good-value daily *menú* for €10 (€12 at weekends). Daily 1–4pm & 8pm–midnight.

Comares

A number of good driving **routes** around the Axarquía begin at **Trapiche**, about 3km north of Vélez. One heads northwest from Trapiche along the MA3113 towards Benmargosa and, after taking in a detour to Comares, climbs eventually to Colmenar. Another (the A335) takes the other fork at Trapiche to end up, by way of Alcaucín, at the twin northernmost outposts of the Axarquía, Alfarnate and Alfarnatejo.

Taking the northwesterly route from Trapiche you soon arrive at **Benamargosa**, a village surrounded by citrus orchards and avocado plantations. You could take a look at its sixteenth-century Gothic-style church of La Encarnación before moving on to La Zubía, where a winding road signed on the left climbs dizzily to **COMARES**, an impeccably tidy White Town (or village in this case) spectacularly clinging to the peak of its conical hill. At the highest point of all, beside an attractive cemetery, the ruined Moorish fort – built on Roman foundations – was one of the strongholds of rebel leader Ibn Hafsun (see box, p.81).

In the village is yet another church of **Nuestra Señora de la Encarnación**, this time a sixteenth-century Mudéjar building with a picturesque hexagonal tower, the minaret of the mosque that preceded it. A **mirador** in the focal Plaza del Ayuntamiento gives fine views over the Axarquía. There's a **walking route** around the village's major sights taking in all the above plus an ancient Roman path down the mountain and various Moorish architectural remains; it's waymarked by ceramic footprints embedded in the pavement.

A welcome municipal **swimming pool** is sited between *Mirador de la Axarquía* and the *Hotel Atalaya*.

ACCOMMODATION, EATING AND DRINKING   COMARES

Hotel Atalaya C/Encinilla s/n ☎952 509 208. Decent hotel near the entrance to the village with a/c en-suite rooms above a bar-restaurant. Unfortunately, rooms face the barracks of the Guardia Civil over the road rather than the spectacular vista behind. The restaurant serves up regular *venta* food with a good-value *menú* for €7. €50

Mirador de la Axarquía C/Encinilla s/n, slightly further up the hill from the Hotel Atalaya ☎952 509 209. This welcoming *hotel-restaurant* has good-value en-suite rooms, many with views, plus free wi-fi. The restaurant has a pleasant terrace with stunning views, serves up regional dishes and specializes in *carnes a la braza* (charcoal-grilled meat). There's also a weekday *menú* for €7. **€40**

El Molino de los Abuelos Plaza Balcón de la Axarquía 2 ☎ 952 509 309, ⊛ hotelmolinodelosabuelos.com. The village's most luxurious accommodation option offers rooms with and without bath (and no TV) plus suites in an enchantingly refurbished eighteenth-century former olive-oil mill on the main square. Free wi-fi. The hotel also has its own good mid-priced restaurant (mains €10–19; closed Wed) located in the former oil-pressing room with the ancient equipment still on view. A house special is *cordero a la miel* (lamb in honey) and the menu also offers a range of salads and at least two vegetarian options. B&B **€45**

Riogordo

Continuing north along the MA3107, beyond La Zubía the road follows the course of the Río Cueva, finally ascending to **RIOGORDO**, a village with Phoenician and Roman origins that was a fortified stronghold during the Moorish period. After the *Reconquista* the Moors were replaced by settlers from Castile. The Semana Santa celebrated here is a particularly vivid affair, when local people – dressed for the part – act out the scenes from the Passion, often with bloodcurdling gusto. The village also boasts an attractive municipal swimming pool.

Colmenar

From Riogordo, you have a choice of routes: east to Alfarnate (see p.98) or west, following a stiff climb, to **COLMENAR**, another brilliant-white hill town and the Axarquía's most westerly outpost. A centre of honey production thanks to the rich variety of flowering plants and shrubs growing in the surrounding hills, the village takes its name from *colmena*, Spanish for "beehive".

There's a wonderful route from here via the Puerto del Léon down to Málaga, twisting through the forests of cork oaks and pines forming the **Parque Natural de los Montes de Málaga** and offering stunning views over Málaga and the Costa del Sol during its latter stages.

ACCOMMODATION   **COLMENAR**

Hotel El Belén Near the Málaga road ☎ 952 730 578, ⊛ hotel-belen.com. Among a clutch of places to stay in Colmenar, this friendly hotel is a good bet, offering en-suite a/c rooms with TV above a good restaurant with an economical *menú*. **€46**

Viñuela

Another route out of Vélez heads north from Trapiche. At a second fork 8km beyond Trapiche the fast A356 heads west towards Casabermeja, skirting the flanks of the Embalse de Viñuela. Ignoring this route and continuing north along the A402 leads you past a turn-off to **VIÑUELA**, 3km beyond this. Originally a *venta* stop for the traffic heading north and south between Málaga and Granada, the atmospheric old **inn** here, *La Viña*, dates from the eighteenth century and stands opposite the fountain in the narrow main street. A spit-and-sawdust place today, on midsummer afternoons it's usually full of old men arguing around domino tables and farmhands sheltering from the burning sun.

Just down the street, the simple sixteenth-century **Iglesia de San José** (get the key from the neighbour opposite) has a finely worked *pietà*.

ACCOMMODATION   **VIÑUELA**

Hotel Viñuela Ctra. Velez Málaga–Alhama s/n ☎ 952 519 193, ⊛ hotelvinuela.com. Luxurious four-star, situated in attractive palm-filled gardens and with a pool on the shores of the nearby Embalse de Viñuela reservoir. Rooms come with satellite TV, minibar, safe and free wi-fi, and the hotel also has its own restaurant, *cafetería* and bar. B&B **€120**

1

Alcaucín

Still following the old road, at the Puente de Don Manuel, a bridge 3km beyond Viñuela, a road cuts off on the right and ascends to the village of **ALCAUCÍN**. On the way up keep an eye to your left where, across a valley, you will be able to make out the ruins of the deserted medieval village of Zalía (see below) and, beyond, the Puerto de Zafarraya, a great U-shaped cleavage in the Sierra de Alhama through which the ancient route to Granada passes.

Alcaucín itself, perched on the slopes of the Sierra de Tejeda, is a beautiful little village with wrought-iron balconies ablaze with flowering geraniums and a web of narrow white-walled streets reflecting its Moorish origins. As befits a mountain village, there are numerous spring-fed fountains, among which the five-spouted Fuente San Sebastián has been restored very much in the Moorish style, complete with *azulejos*.

Zalía

Continuing north from the Puente de Don Manuel, the A402 heads on towards Granada, passing en route the dauntingly impressive **Zafarraya Pass**, where 30,000-year-old remains found in a nearby cave in 1983 have now been confirmed as the last-known site in Europe inhabited by Neanderthal man. On the way, the road passes the ruins of the fort and the deserted medieval village of **ZALÍA**. Local legend has it that the Moorish village was attacked by a plague of vipers after Patricio, a *malagueño* church minister, arrived in an attempt to convert the inhabitants to Christianity and they spurned him. The more likely explanation is that the population was put to the sword during the uprisings that followed the *Reconquista*. Throughout most of the Moorish period Zalía's fortress, together with those at Comares and Bentomiz (near Arenas to the south), formed a defensive triangle to control this central sector of the Axarquía region.

Taking a left fork along the A7204 heading northwest from the junction just beyond Viñuela leads to **Periana**, a noted centre of peach-growing and *anís* production. Some 3km beyond here, heading into the Axarquía's more remote extremities, you'll reach a fork; if you don't want to face a tortuous switchback secondary road, ignore the sign labelled "Alfarnate 15km" and continue along the road signed to Riogordo and Colmenar. A further 4km will bring you to a right turn and an easier route to the village of Alfarnatejo and its neighbour Alfarnate.

Alfarnatejo and Alfarnate

The Axarquía's most northerly settlements, **ALFARNATEJO** and **ALFARNATE** lie a mere couple of kilometres apart, but it would be difficult to find two places in Andalucía with less in common. Alfarnatejo, the smaller of the two, is staunchly right-wing, while Alfarnate has always been on the left, and, unable to agree or cooperate on anything, they have built up a strong mutual animosity, which even discourages marriages between the two communities. In truth, neither village would win any beauty prizes, though Alfarnate, set on a plain covered with wheatfields, is worth a visit for its attractive church of **Santa Ana**, a sixteenth-century edifice with a graceful Mudéjar tower.

Alfarnate's real claim to fame is the thirteenth-century **Venta de Alfarnate** on the village's western edge, which maintains – with some justification – that it is the oldest **inn** in Andalucía. Situated in an isolated spot in the midst of brooding hills, it's not hard to see what attracted the various brigands and highwaymen to the place. Indeed, the interior, as well as being a bar-restaurant, is also a **museum** dedicated to keeping alive the memory of such outlaws as Luís Candelas, who spent a night in the *venta's* well-preserved prison cell en route to justice in Málaga. By far the most terrifying *bandolero* of all, however, was El Tempranillo, who arrived unannounced one hot day in the 1820s, and, when there were no spoons for him to eat with, ordered the dining clients to eat their wooden ones at gunpoint, cracking their teeth in the process. The place is more civilized these days and its mid-priced restaurant serves a hearty mountain speciality, *huevos a la bestia* (fried eggs with local sausage, ham and black pudding).

Keep your eyes peeled in this area for the amazingly agile **cabra hispánica**, the rare Spanish goat; the long-horned male is a spectacular sight as he effortlessly scales almost vertical cliff faces.

Torre del Mar to Nerja

The coast east from Torre del Mar is a nondescript stretch of faceless towns and the occasional concrete resort, dotted with more ancient *atalayas* (watchtowers). Inland lie more tempting villages in the **eastern Axarquía** but along the coast the first town of any real interest is **Nerja**, with some fine beaches and a relatively slow pace.

Algarrobo and the Phoenician tombs

East of Torre del Mar the coast road climbs slightly to **Algarrobo-Costa**, an unappealing high-rise beach resort. With your own transport it's worth ignoring this – and the bleak stretch of coast that follows – to head inland for some delightful villages in the **eastern Axarquía**, finally rejoining the coastal road 10km east at Torrox Costa.

From Algarrobo-Costa the A7206 climbs inland towards the village of Algarrobo proper. Look out for for some well-conserved **Phoenician tombs** (signposted on the right) dating from the eighth century BC. Originally these tombs formed part of an extensive cemetery, built of stone blocks and roofed in wood.

The older village of **Algarrobo**, 3km inland, which lent its name to the coastal settlement, is a pleasant enough place, though rapidly being enveloped by urban sprawl as the developers move inland from the coast.

Cómpeta and around

Beyond Algarrobo, the road toils on upwards as the fruit orchards of the coastal strip give way to the olive groves and vineyards of the higher slopes. The road then passes **Sayalonga** 5km further on, a pretty village nestling in the valley of the Río Algarrobo, and then ascends again, twisting and turning for a further 8km until it reaches **CÓMPETA**, a huddle of brilliant-white cubes tumbling down a hillside and surrounded by vineyards. A Moorish settlement in origin, and now discovered by expats from northern Europe, Cómpeta retains a relaxed atmosphere, and the easy-going villagers don't seem too worried about being swamped by foreigners. The sweet – and potent – **wine** made from the area's muscatel grapes is renowned as the best in the whole province. You can try it for yourself at the **Museo del Vino** on Avenida de la Constitución close to the charming main square, Plaza de la Almijara (the Jarel brand is recommended).

Each August 15 beneath the lofty bell tower (a later addition) of the sixteenth-century church of La Asunción, Cómpeta rolls out the barrels – scores of them – during its annual **fiesta**, the Noche del Vino. This is when the square fills with revellers determined to sink as much of the free *vino* as they can hold. Above the plaza to the left, Calle San Antonio leads to a shrine with a superb **view** over the valley to the west and the sea beyond.

The road continues for a further 4km north of Cómpeta where it comes to a dead end at the village of **CANILLAS DE ALBAIDA**, something of a mini-Cómpeta, with a place to stay and a couple of decent restaurants.

INFORMATION   **CÓMPETA**

Tourist office Plaza de la Constitución, close to the where buses terminate (daily 10am–2pm; ☎ 952 553 685,

ⓦ www.competa.es).
Bookshop Marco Polo at C/José Antonio 3 (☎ 952

1

516 423). This friendly, English-run bookshop just off the main square stocks walking books, maps and equipment. Copies of a local magazine, *Market Place*, are also stocked here; the magazine includes a useful map of Cómpeta (and many other towns and resorts along the coast to the south).

Internet Dynos Informatica, C/San Antonio 9, near the *Hotel Balcón de Cómpeta* (Mon–Sat 10am–2pm & 5–9pm).

ACCOMMODATION

For a place to stay, the only budget possibilities are the unofficial rooms in places dotted around the village – the best way of contacting them is via the tourist office (or their website).

Hotel Balcón de Cómpeta C/San Antonio s/n ☏ 952 553 535, ⊛ hotel-competa.com. Central and comfortable hotel with balcony rooms overlooking a pool with mountain views beyond. Facilities include a tennis court, boules pitch and free wi-fi zone. They also rent fully equipped wooden bungalows sleeping 2–6 persons. B&B rooms **€76**, bungalows **€76**

Posada La Plaza La Plaza, Canillas de Albaida ☏ 952 554 807, ⊛ posada-laplaza.eu. In neighbouring Canillas de Albaida, on the main square, this is a pleasant *hotel rural* with en-suite balcony rooms with views and a roof terrace. Can advise on walking and birdwatching in the area and arranges horseriding excursions. **€65**

EATING AND DRINKING

Bar-Restaurante Perico Plaza Almijara s/n. This economical bar-restaurant on Cómpeta's main square has a pleasant terrace and makes a good place to eat after the sun has set. Their *pollo al vino de Cómpeta* (chicken cooked in the local wine) is recommended, and there's also a *menú* for €8. Daily except Weds 1–4pm & 9–11pm.

Museo del Vino Avda. La Constitución s/n, downhill from the main square. The restaurant of the Museo del Vino is also good for charcoal-grilled meat and fish and also does *raciones* and *medias* – try the *chorizo ibérico* or *lomo al ajillo* (pork in garlic). Daily 9.30am–11.30pm.

El Pilón C/Laberinto s/n, down steps slightly southwest of the main square. A pleasant small restaurant with eclectic international cuisine including vegetarian options and salads. Main dishes €9–18. Daily 7–11pm.

Restaurante María C/San Antonio 75. The restaurant of the *Hotel Balcón de Cómpeta* is another mid-priced possibility. A speciality here is *solomillo en vino de Cómpeta* (pork loin in wine). Main dishes €10–20. Daily 1–4pm & 8–11pm.

Archez

To penetrate further into the Axarquía from Cómpeta you'll need to double back for 2km to the turning north to **ARCHEZ**. Nestling in the foothills of the Sierra Almijara, it's an attractive village with strong Moorish roots.

This influence is vividly in evidence at the church of **Nuestra Señora de La Encarnación** (open during service times), whose remarkable fourteenth-century tower is the minaret of an earlier mosque, one of the best examples from this period – the *sebka* brickwork and blind arches above are particularly fine.

Salares

From Archez, the road climbs for another 5km to the brilliant white village of **SALARES**, a centre of olive oil and wine production and one of the most picturesque villages of the Axarquía. Its charms are enhanced by the banning of traffic from its narrow streets, where colourful potted geraniums line the walls and dogs lie prostrate in the afternoon heat. There's a car park at the top of the village. From here head downhill along Calle Iglesias and the the church of Santa Ana. Just as the church at Archez, this one retains a fine **minaret** from the mosque it replaced. Inside, a simple interior holds the image of Santa Ana, *patrona* of the village.

INFORMATION

Tourist information In the Ayuntamiento, C/Iglesia 2, next door to the church of Santa Ana (Mon–Fri 9am–1pm), where you can pick up a small map.

Nerja

Although **NERJA**, 20km along the coast from Torre del Mar, cannot claim to have been bypassed by the tidal wave of post-1960s tourist development, this attractive resort has, nevertheless, held out against Torremolinos-type tower blocks, and its mainly villa and *urbanizaciones* construction has been more in keeping with its origins. Its setting, too, is spectacular, nestling among the foothills of the Almijara range and flanked by some good beaches including the attractive **Playa Burriana**, an easily walkable kilometre east of the centre – while there's also a series of coves within walking distance if you want to escape the crowds.

Nerja's **old town** fans out to the north of the **Balcón de Europa**, a striking, palm-lined seafront **belvedere** which offers magnificent views over the rocky coastline. The tangle of pretty, narrow streets is crowded with visitors all summer long, but the brash shops that service them have yet to suffocate the town's easy-going tranquillity. Nerja's obvious charm has attracted the inevitable colony of migrants – in this case the English – who make their presence felt in the numerous foreign-owned shops and bars. Sights, as such, are few, and once you have strolled along the Balcón and taken a look at the nearby seventeenth-century whitewashed **El Salvador** church (open service times) – which has a fine *dolorosa* – you should head for the beach or make a short excursion out of town.

An entertaining **market** takes place on Tuesday (main market) and Sunday (flea market) mornings and spreads along Calle Antonio Ferrándiz (Chanquete), to the east of the centre.

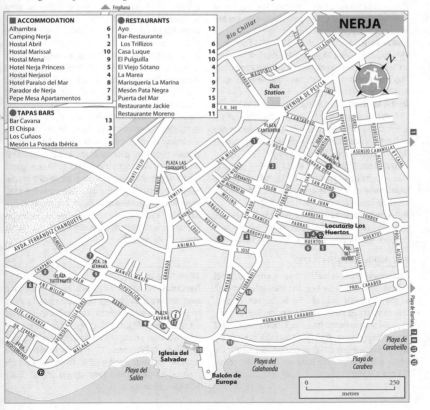

■ ACCOMMODATION		● RESTAURANTS	
Alhambra	6	Ayo	12
Camping Nerja	1	Bar-Restaurante	
Hostal Abril	2	Los Trillizos	6
Hostal Marissal	10	Casa Luque	14
Hostal Mena	9	El Pulguilla	10
Hotel Nerja Princess	5	El Viejo Sótano	4
Hostal Nerjasol	4	La Marea	1
Hotel Paraíso del Mar	8	Marisquería La Marina	9
Parador de Nerja	7	Mesón Pata Negra	7
Pepe Mesa Apartamentos	3	Puerta del Mar	15
		Restaurante Jackie	8
● TAPAS BARS		Restaurante Moreno	11
Bar Cavana	13		
El Chispa	3		
Los Cuñaos	2		
Mesón La Posada Ibérica	5		

ARRIVAL AND INFORMATION   NERJA

By bus The bus station is on Avda. Pescia s/n, at the north end of town close to Plaza Cantarero.

Tourist information Turismo, C/Carmen 1, 50m west of the church of El Salvador and next door to the Ayuntamiento (July–Sept daily 10am–2pm & 6–10pm; Oct–June Mon–Fri 10am–2pm & 5–8pm, Sat 10am–1pm; ☎952 521 531, Ⓦwww.nerja.org). Their free *Guía del Ocio* magazine lists nightlife venues and upcoming special events.

Walking The Turismo has its own leaflets (in English) while the English bookshop WH Smiffs, a few doors along from the post office on C/Almirante Ferrandiz, sells individual leaflets detailing walks in the area by local resident and hiker Elma Thompson, a chirpy Mancunian who also offers guided walks from November to May (☎952 530 782).

ACCOMMODATION

There's usually no problem finding rooms in Nerja except in August, when you should book in advance. The lowest-priced possibilities are in the streets south of the bus station heading towards the sea. If everything's full, one solution is to stay inland at Frigiliana (see p.105), or try renting an apartment. The Turismo can help with information on apartments, and many of the *hostales* listed below have arrangements with *casas particulares* to soak up the overflow.

Alhambra C/Antonio Millón s/n ☎952 522 174, Ⓦhostalalhambra.es. Pleasant *hostal* a little west of the centre offering a friendly welcome and immaculate en-suite rooms, some with sea-facing balcony. Own garage. **€48**

Camping Nerja Ctra N-340, km296, ☎952 529 714, Ⓦnerjacamping.com. Nerja's campsite lies 4km east of the town close to Maro, with good shade, pool, bar and restaurant. Two people plus car **€22**

Hostal Abril C/Pintada 124 ☎952 526 167, Ⓦhostal abril.com. Sparkling *hostal* with excellent en-suite a/c rooms, lots of cool marble and a friendly proprietor. Also has apartments and studios (€80) sleeping up to four. Free internet access. **€50**

Hostal Marissal Paseo Balcón de Europa 3 ☎952 520 199, Ⓦhostalmarissal.com. Bang in the centre of the action, this *hostal* offers a/c en-suite rooms, many with sea view (try for rooms 102–5 or 204–5). Also rents apartments (€100) in same location. Free wi-fi. **€60**

Hostal Mena C/El Barrio 15 ☎952 520 541, Ⓦhostal mena.es. Welcoming hostal with central a/c en-suite rooms, some with terrace and sea views. There's also a delightful garden at the rear. Wi-fi zone. **€43**

Hotel Nerja Princess C/Los Huertos 46 ☎952 528 986, Ⓦhotelnp.com. Excellent small hotel where well-equipped a/c balcony rooms come with satellite TV,

minibar and safe. There's a terrace and pool at the rear and the best beaches are nearby. B&B **€92**

Hostal Nerjasol C/Pintada 54 ☎952 522 121, Ⓦhostal nerjasol.com. On a quiet street, with spotless a/c en-suite rooms equipped with safe, fridge and TV. There's also a rooftop solarium, mini-gym and free wi-fi. They can direct you to a *casa particular* if full. **€50**

Hotel Paraíso del Mar C/Prolongación de Carabeo 22, almost next door to the parador ☎952 521 621, Ⓦhotelparaisodelmar.es. Pleasant upmarket alternative to the *Parador de Nerja*, All rooms come with jacuzzi and many (slightly pricier) come with sea-view balcony; there's also a pool, gardens, sauna dug out of the cliff face, and stairway access to the beach below. B&B **€135**

Parador de Nerja C/Almuñécar 8 ☎952 520 050, Ⓦparador.es. Modern parador which, despite an exterior resembling an open prison, has comfortable rooms, a pleasant, plant-filled garden and patio, a small park with bar (worth a visit) overlooking the sea, plus an elevator (guests only) down the cliff to Burriana, one of Nerja's most popular beaches. The restaurant serves a good-value *menú*. B&B **€180**

Pepe Mesa Apartamentos C/Los Huertos 33 ☎952 524 138, Ⓦpepemesa.com. Good-value apartments and studios with kitchenette and satellite TV, plus rooftop pool and wi-fi zone. **€90**

EATING AND NIGHTLIFE

Restaurant prices in the old town – with a couple of exceptions – tend to be high and standards indifferent so you'll do better to head a bit further out for good, reasonably priced places. On the western side of town, there are many authentic Spanish restaurants concentrated around Plaza Marina. **Nightlife** tends to happen in the numerous music bars and clubs concentrated west of the centre around Plaza Tutti Frutti and along the nearby C/Antonio Millón.

TAPAS BARS

Bar Cavana Plaza Cavana 12. This is one of the oldest and most comfortable bars in Nerja and just the place for a lazy breakfast on its outdoor terrace. Later in the day it serves a limited range of tapas and it's also a nice place in the evening to share a bottle of wine. Daily 9am–midnight.

El Chispa C/San Pedro 12. Friendly neighbourhood tapas bar specializing in fried fish. Try the *jibia con ajo y peregil* (cuttlefish) or superb *almejas* (clams). Daily 8.30am–midnight.

1

Los Cuñaos C/Herrera Oria 19, northeast of the centre. A spacious tapas bar with an outside terrace in warmer weather. All the tapas are excellent – a couple worth trying are *habas con jamón* (beans and serrano ham) and *carne con tomate* (pork in tomato sauce). Daily 10am–11pm.

Mesón La Posada Ibérica C/Nueva 1. Pleasantly cosy and rustic little bar serving a range of tapas. The house special is a fine jamón ibérico and the fish tapas such as *boquerones en vinagre* aren't bad either. Daily 1–4pm & 7.30pm–midnight.

RESTAURANTS

Ayo Burriana beach. Very reasonably priced (for this location), with good seafood. Their giant open-air paella fry-up on Sunday lunchtimes (big plate for around €6) is a Burriana institution. Reasonable wine and fish prices. Daily 10am–midnight.

Bar-Restaurante Los Trillizos C/Los Huertos 38. Cheap and cheerful budget restaurant offering well-prepared fish and meat standards and *platos combinados*, with an attractive terrace at the back. Their €8.50 *menú* is probably the best value in town. Daily 9am–11.30pm.

Casa Luque Plaza Cavana 2. Good but expensive nouvelle cuisine served up in stylish if rather pretentious surroundings, with a panoramic terrace at the rear. Main dishes €9–16. Mon, Tues & Thurs–Sun 12.30–3pm & 7.30–11pm.

★ **El Pulguilla** C/Almirante Ferrandiz 26. Outstanding, long-established seafood tapas and *raciones* bar-restaurant. Everything sold is straight from the sea – *cangrejo* (crab), *calamares*, *sardinas*, you name it – and beyond the bar lies a huge and superb terrace restaurant with more of the same. *Raciones* of grilled fresh fish are on offer here including superb *rosada* (rockfish) and *dorada* (sea bream), plus a weekday *menú*. Daily except Tues 10am–midnight.

El Viejo Sótano C/Los Huertos 33. Good mid-priced restaurant with a range of meat and fish dishes as well as some vegetarian options including pastas and salads. Main dishes €8–18. Daily 6.30–11pm.

La Marea Plaza Cantarero s/n. Good and modestly priced fish restaurant with terrace, owned by the same proprietors as *La Marina* (see below); all the fish and mariscos are ultra-fresh – try the *calamares fritos* or a *frito variada* (fried fish selection). Daily 1–4pm & 8–11.30pm.

★ **Marisquería La Marina** Plaza la Marina s/n. *Marisquerías* don't come any better than this, which is why *La Marina* is so popular. Enjoy superb tapas at the bar or mouthwateringly fresh fish (with some great wines) at their restaurant tables or outdoor terrace. Tapas cost a reasonable €1–3 and a meal for two with wine is possible for under €30. Daily except Weds 1–4pm & 7.30–midnight.

Mesón Pata Negra Plaza La Marina ☎ 952 520 222. Authentic regional dishes, served in formal surroundings, albeit a little more expensive than the other restaurants on this square. *Cordero al horno* (oven-roasted lamb) is a house special. Has a small terrace outside. Main dishes €10–20. Daily 1–5pm & 9–11.30pm.

Puerta del Mar C/Puerta del Mar 2. Almost next door to the Turismo, this upmarket *marisquería* – owned by *La Marina* above – serves excellent fish and seafood, but you pay for the stylish surroundings – €10–20 per *ración*. Daily except Weds 1–4pm & 7.30–midnight.

Restaurante Jackie C/Chaparil, Edificio Corona ☎ 952 521 138. One-time striker for Standard Liège, Jacques "Jackie" Vanhoren built his reputation as a chef in nearby Almuñécar. He's now transferred his stoves west and this is arguably the most serious restaurant in Nerja. The dining room is intimate and the menu classic French with typical dishes like Burgundy snails, lobster thermidor and châteaubriand, although *lubina en salsa de almendras* (sea bass) makes an appearance on the fish menu. *Menú de degustación* for €19. Main dishes €16–23. Daily 7.30–11pm.

Restaurante Moreno Burriana beach. Nicest out of a cluster of economical eating places at the back of the beach; one of the chefs cooks barbecue-style (in an old boat) outside on the terrace. The fried *sardinas* and paella are excellent. Main dishes €8–18. Daily 10am–11.30pm.

DIRECTORY

Bookshop The Book Centre, C/Granada 32, is one of the best secondhand bookshops on the coast. They also take books in part exchange.

Festival The resort's major summer event is the annual Festival de Flamenco (Sept–Oct), with many big names. The Turismo can provide details. Nerja's International Festival of Music and Dance takes place in the first half of July inside the Cuevas de Nerja and features Spanish and international performers and orchestras.

Internet Locutorio Los Huertos, C/Huertos 45 (daily 10am–midnight).

Frigiliana

A popular excursion from Nerja is the six-kilometre trip north to **FRIGILIANA**, a pretty Moorish hill village clinging to the lower slopes of Monte El Fuerte. After the *Reconquista*, Frigiliana became a Morisco settlement where only those Moors who had converted to Christianity were allowed to live. Although a little of the atmosphere of this period survives in the steep, narrow streets, the place is prettified today by the addition of geranium pots and historical plaques.

ARRIVAL AND INFORMATION
FRIGILIANA

By bus Buses (Mon–Fri at least 9 daily; Sat 6 daily) leave for Frigiliana from the bus station in Nerja, the earliest of which gives you enough time to take a walk in the surrounding hills and catch the last bus back at 9pm.

Turismo Cuesta de Apero 10, 50m from the bus terminus (Mon–Fri 10am–5pm, Sat–Sun 10am–2pm & 5–7.30pm;

952 534 261, frigiliana.es). The tourist office also houses a small archeological museum and can provide lists of apartments to rent around the village as well as a useful map. They also stock more of Elma Thompson's walks pamphlets (see p.102) for this area.

ACCOMMODATION

Hospedería El Caravansar Callejón de la Ermita s/n 952 533 586, info@hospederíacaravansar.com. This recently opened *casa rural* has nine compact but comfortable a/c en-suite rooms in a charming village house. **€50**

Hotel Las Chinas Plaza Doña Amparo Guerrero 14 952 533 073. This hospitable hotel is a good bet for a/c balcony rooms with bath (ask for a room at the rear to avoid

street noise). They also have a decent restaurant next door, plus free wi-fi and own garage. **€55**

Hotel Villa Frigiliana C/San Sebastián s/n, near the bus halt 952 534 221, www.ihmhotels.com. The village's luxury option offers pleasant rooms with balcony views (although lacking wi-fi) and manages to squeeze in a small pool. B&B **€72**

EATING AND DRINKING

★ **La Bodeguilla** C/Chorruelo s/n, just above the Plaza de la Iglesia (main square). An excellent and economical village restaurant now into its third decade, this is an all-female operation run by the founder Rosario and her four daughters. The food is honest and simple and *malagueño* specialities such as *ajo blanco* and *fritura* (fried fish) are all competently done. There's a wonderful terrace with vistas at the back and a daily *menú* for under €10. Daily noon–3pm & 7–9pm.

Taberna del Sacristán Plaza de la Iglesia 12. On the main square, fronting the church of San Antonio, with an attractive terrace, this is the upmarket place to eat in the

village. The cooking is good and *chuletas de cordero con tomillo y ajo* (lamb chops with thyme and garlic) is a house special; there are also some vegetarian options. Main dishes €9.50–15. Daily except Tues 10am–3pm & 7–11pm.

Restaurante Las Chinas Plaza Doña Amparo Guerrero 14. The restaurant of the hotel (above) is another quality place and very reasonably priced, with a *menú* for €13 (or *menú vegetariano* €8.50). The *rape en salsa de tomate* (monkfish) is a house special and the *sopa de pescados* (fish soup) is a meal in itself. Small street terrace outside. Main dishes €10–18. Daily noon–4pm & 7.30–11pm.

A WALK NEAR FRIGILIANA

A circular 8km walk covers the **hill country** to the northwest of Frigiliana. Follow the road north out of the village towards the pleasant refreshment stop of *Venta de Frigiliana* (summer: daily 11am–4pm), which you'll reach after 3km. Turn left down the dirt track just beyond the entrance, which leads down the ridge, passing some old cottages and villas.

Ten minutes or so further on you'll pass the gates of the Peñones and the Cortijo del Peñon farmhouses on the right. Continue down this track between pine woods and crags until you reach a crossroads, with a walled villa on the far side. Fork sharply left at this point, passing some more old cottages on the right. One of these has a single palm tree, the ancient Moorish sign of welcome. At the first fork, below a large villa, continue left, uphill. The road winds round the villa wall, swings right and crosses the lower Pedregal valley, from where it climbs up the hill to the col on the Loma de la Cruz. Just below the crest of the ridge, where a *carril* (track) comes up from the right, keep straight on up, passing a villa.

In front of this villa, a water-cover stamped "SAT no. 7196 Monte Ariza" will confirm that you're on the right road. At the col, go straight across at the cross-tracks marked with red paint and follow the track down and round, keeping left of the fork on the next ridge. This will bring you down past the Casa del Valle, on the left. A little further on, round the bend, you'll see some tumbledown houses on the right; the first of these contains an old olive or wine press which is worth a look. The *carril* now passes through open country, then through *huertas*, rejoining the Torrox road at Casa Fernando. A right and then a left turn will take you to the upper car park on the edge of Frigiliana.

1

Cuevas de Nerja

Ctra. de Maro s/n • July & Aug daily 10am–7.30pm; Sept–June 10am–2pm & 4–6.30pm • €8.50 • For more serious explorations (the standard visit allows access to only one-third of the caves), there are fully equipped speleological tours in English and Spanish lasting seven hours (€90; call ☎ 952 529 520 for details) • ⓦ cuevadenerja.es

Cynics might find the "accidental" discovery in 1957 of the **CUEVAS DE NERJA** – neatly coinciding with the arrival of mass tourism – a little suspect. Immediately they were revealed, the series of enormous caverns, scattered with Paleolithic and Neolithic tools, pottery and cave paintings stretching back 30,000 years, became a local, then national, sensation. Nowadays, however, the fairy lights, piped muzak and cave theatre – which hosts various shows from rock to ballet and flamenco as well as serving as the venue for Nerja's International Festival of Music and Dance (see p.104) – can't help but detract from the appreciation of a spectacular natural wonder. Still, if you can block out the razzmatazz the cave is astonishingly huge and the dangling limestone stalactites and soaring stalagmites are pretty awesome. The prehistoric cave paintings are currently not on public view (and possibly never will be). However, you might want to seek out the world's longest known **stalactite** – all 32m of it, and verified by the *Guinness Book of Records* – while you're probing the depths.

A **Centro de Interpretación** (same hours as cave; free) lies close to the cave entrance and uses dioramas to document the history of the cave and its geology.

ARRIVAL AND DEPARTURE   CUEVAS DE NERJA

By public transport Taking a taxi (roughly €10 one-way) or a bus (running approximately hourly) from Nerja bus station is a better alternative to the easy but not particularly pleasant 3km walk east along the main coast road.

EATING AND DRINKING

Restaurants The restaurant at the cave entrance serves buffets but can get very busy in high season; the restaurant of the *Hotel Al Andalus*, down the hill, with economical *menú* and pleasant terrace, is a good alternative.

Maro

Further east of Nerja, the coastal road zigzags around the foothills of the Sierra Almijara, climbing above a number of tiny coves. The first settlement, the coastal hamlet and former fishing village of **MARO**, is a sparkling cluster of white-walled houses set above an attractive cove beach. Lying close to the ancient Roman settlement of Detunda, the town was revitalized in the eighteenth century by the construction of a sugar factory, now a ruin behind the simple church of Nuestra Señora de las Maravillas, which dates from the same period.

ACCOMMODATION AND EATING   MARO

Balcón de Maro Plaza de las Maravillas, near the church ☎ 952 529 523. Inexpensive sea-view balcony studios – sleeping up to four and some with sea views – in a central location. The bar below serves breakfasts and tapas. **€50**

Casa Maro ☎ 952 529 690, ⓦ hotel-casa-maro.com. An attractive option, this German-run apartment hotel offers elegant rooms, most with sea-view balcony and kitchenette; they also have some apartments. **€60**

Hotel Playa Maro C/San Miguel 28 ☎ 952 529 582, ⓦ hotelplayamaro.com. Formal hotel at the entrance to the village with well-equipped rooms (check the website for frequent special offers) and free wi-fi. Also has a good mid-priced terraced restaurant offering a paella for two for €23. B&B **€100**

The Costa del Sol

West of Málaga, the real **Costa del Sol** gets going. If you've never seen this level of touristic development before, it can be quite a shock, not least when you see how grit-grey the sands are; you have to keep going, around the corner to Tarifa (see p.162), before you reach the golden sands of the tourist brochures. With their faceless 1960s' and 1970s' concrete tower blocks, these are certainly not the kind of resorts you find in Greece or even Portugal. Since the 1980s' boom in time-share apartments and leisure complexes, it's estimated that 300,000 foreigners live on the Costa del Sol, the majority of them retired and British. On the other hand, the cheap package-tour industry – largely responsible for the transformation of the string of poverty-stricken fishing villages that dotted this coast until the 1950s – no longer brings in the numbers it once did, placing the future of purpose-built resorts such as Torremolinos in peril.

Approached in the right kind of spirit, it *is* possible to have fun in **Torremolinos** and, at a price, in **Marbella**. The sea, at least, is reasonably clean, the resorts tend not to be plagued with rampaging foreign drunks in high season (as happens in other parts of Spain) and there's a much stronger family feel to it all. However, if you're looking for a more authentic version of Spain your best bet is to keep going until at least Estepona.

Torremolinos

The approach to **TORREMOLINOS** – easiest on the electric railway from Málaga or the airport – is a depressing trawl through a drab, soulless landscape of kitchenette apartments and half-finished developments. The town itself, rechristened "Torrie" by English package tourists, is certainly an experience: a vast, grotesque parody of a seaside resort with its own kitsch fascination. This bizarre place, lined with sweeping (but crowded) beaches and infinite shopping arcades, crammed with Irish pubs and estate agents, has a large permanent expat population of Britons, Germans and Scandinavians. It's a weird mix, which, in addition to thousands of retired people, has attracted – due to a previous lack of extradition arrangements between Britain and Spain – a notorious concentration of British crooks.

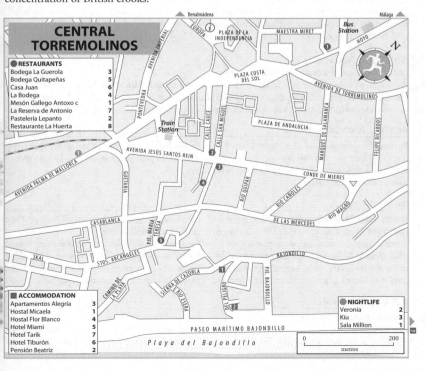

CENTRAL TORREMOLINOS

● **RESTAURANTS**
Bodega La Guerola	3
Bodega Quitapeñas	5
Casa Juan	6
La Bodega	4
Mesón Gallego Antoxo c	1
La Reserva de Antonio	7
Pastelería Lepanto	2
Restaurante La Huerta	8

■ **ACCOMMODATION**
Apartamentos Alegría	3
Hostal Micaela	1
Hostal Flor Blanco	4
Hotel Miami	5
Hotel Tarik	7
Hotel Tiburón	6
Pensión Beatriz	2

● **NIGHTLIFE**
Veronia	2
Kiu	3
Sala Million	1

Playa del Bajondillo

PASEO MARÍTIMO BAJONDILLO

0   200
metres

1

In recent years a dynamic town council has been moving heaven and earth to rid the resort of its "Terrible Torrie" image, and whilst they've stopped short of flattening the concrete monsters overlooking the beach they have made a few commendable improvements. The seafront promenade, which runs all the way to La Carihuela, can be quite scenic in parts and the maze of alleys in the old town – now largely cleared of their tawdry souvenir shops and tacky stalls – also have some charm.

Torremolinos will never be Marbella; its whole purpose is geared to giving people a roaring good time, and if that's what you're looking for, there are few places on the coast with as many bars and clubs. Throughout the summer the municipality puts on an infinite variety of free events, including festivals of music, dance and jazz, as well as beach volleyball and football competitions and children's theatre.

Calle San Miguel and around

To get the flavour of Torremolinos, from the focal Plaza Costa del Sol take a stroll along **Calle San Miguel**, the main pedestrian mall east of the train station. Cutting through the old quarter (which even has a fourteenth-century Moorish tower), the street is lined with garish illuminated signs, tatty amusement arcades and boutiques, and even tattier restaurants serving steak and kidney pie and all its variations.

Unlike the street itself, the maze of alleys **around Calle San Miguel** give you a flavour of the old town prior to the tourist invasion and are dotted with bars and shops used by locals.

The promenade and La Carihuela

The seafront promenade – the **Paseo Marítimo** – is probably the resort's most attractive asset, particularly so at the western end. From here it's a pleasant 1km stroll to the village of **La Carihuela**, a former fishing village and now the more elegant (and slightly saner) part of the resort, with a decent beach and a number of good fish restaurants on and behind the seafront.

Aqualand Aquapark

C/Cuba 10 • May–Sept 10am–5pm • €19.50, children €14.50

A couple of kilometres inland from the centre, **Aqualand Aquapark** boasts assorted chutes, slides, rapids and other watery attractions including the Black Hole, a scarey dinghy ride which twists through a darkened tunnel before emerging into a sunlit pool.

ARRIVAL AND DEPARTURE

TORREMOLINOS

By train The station is on Avda. Jesús Santos Rein (✆ 902 240 202). The train from Málaga drops you right in the centre of the action, a couple of blocks west of the town's main artery, C/San Miguel.

By bus The bus station is at C/Hoyo 10 (✆ 95 238 24 19), a five-minute walk away from the centre. All out-of-town buses arrive here.

INFORMATION

Tourist office The Turismo on Plaza de la Independencia (Mon–Fri 9.30am–1.30pm; ✆ 952 379 512, ⌘ ayto -torremolinos.org), is supported by a number of other sub offices (open April–Sept); the most convenient are located on the seafront at Plaza de las Comunidades Autónomas (daily 10am–2pm & 6–8pm) southeast of the centre, and

in La Carihuela on the seafront just off Plaza del Remo (daily 10am–2pm & 6–8pm).

Bookshop Book Market, just behind C/San Miguel, reached via C/Virgen del Carmen. A haven of tranquillity, this British-run bookshop is an excellent source of used paperbacks and they'll let you trade in your old ones.

ACCOMMODATION

CENTRAL TORREMOLINOS

Hostal Micaela C/Bajondillo 4 ✆ 952 383 310, ⌘ hostal micaela.es. Serviceable rooms with bath, close to the beach, some with sea view. Also has a communal kitchen for use by

guests and a wi-fi zone. €38

Hotel Tarik Paseo Marítimo 49 ✆ 952 382 300, ⌘ hotel tarik.com. Attractive beachfront hotel offering well-equipped a/c rooms with TV and safe, half with sea-view terrace balconies. Public areas include a garden pool, solarium and café-restaurant. Free wi-fi. B&B **€86**

Pensión Beatriz C/del Peligro 4, Playa Bajondillo ☎ 952 385 110, **✉** hostalbeatriz@hotmail.com. Small and good-value *hostal* offering en-suite rooms with a/c, TV and sea view, 20m from the beach. Also has some superior rooms adding a fridge, microwave and kitchenette for a few euros extra. **€45**

LA CARIHUELA

Apartamentos Alegría C/Carmen 23, La Carihuela ☎ 952 380 273 **♁** lacarihuela.com. Charming, two-person a/c seafront studios with modern kitchens and fittings; minimum stay two nights. The friendly owners have similar apartments nearby when this one is full. **€60**

Hostal Flor Blanco Pasaje de la Carihuela 4 ☎ 952 382 071, **✉** hostalflorblanco@hotmail.com. Friendly *hostal* with clean en-suite rooms, some with partial sea views and terraces for the same price (ring ahead to reserve); 50m from the beach in La Carihuela. **€59**

★ Hotel Miami C/Aladino 14 ☎ 952 385 255, **♁** residencia-miami.com. One of the most charming hotels on the whole Costa del Sol, this enchanting villa was built by a cousin of Picasso in the late 1940s and contains many of the original designer furnishings like the stone-built *chimenea* (hearth) and carved wood fittings and beams, along with a walled garden sporting palms and oleanders, and a swimming pool. The simple but comfortable rooms – many with balconies overlooking the garden – come with TV and free wi-fi. **€64**

Hotel Tiburón C/Los Nidos 7, La Carihuela ☎ 952 381 320, **♁** hoteltiburon.com. Attractive small hotel 50m from the beach with pool. All rooms come with bath, TV, ceiling fans and sea views, and there's also internet access and a wi-fi zone. **€60**

CAMPSITE

Camping Torremolinos Loma del Paraíso 2 ☎ 952 382 602, **♁** campingtorremolinos.com. Some 3km east of the centre on the main N340 Málaga–Cádiz highway, near *Hotel Los Alamos* and 500m from the sea, with plenty of shade and good facilities. To get here, take the *cercanía* train (get off at Los Alamos) or go by bus (Línea B) from the central Plaza Costa del Sol. Two people plus car **€26**

EATING AND DRINKING

Hidden away among the many culinary disasters of Torremolinos are a surprising number of excellent bars and restaurants offering good value for money. At the cheaper end of the scale the sheer competition between outlets is so intense that if you're prepared to walk round, checking a few prices, you can have a decent night out for remarkably little money.

CENTRAL TORREMOLINOS

Bodega La Guerola C/Las Mercedes 2, at junction with C/San Miguel. A real beehive of a place that's everything a tapas bar should be. It manages to squeeze in a few tables but serious *tapeadores* rest one elbow on the bar. Daily 9.30am–midnight.

Bodega Quitapeñas C/San Miguel s/n. Delicious fish tapas and *raciones* as well as *ahumados* (smoked fish) served in a bustling bar with a terrace by the steps at the beach end of C/San Miguel. Mon–Sat noon–4pm & 7.30pm–midnight.

La Bodega C/San Miguel 40. Good central and lively tapas bar with small *comedor* and efficient service. Specials include *boquerones en vinagre* (anchovies), *ensalada de pulpo* (octopus), *gambas a la plancha* (grilled prawns) and *calamares fritos*. Daily 10am–midnight.

Goyesca C/San Miguel 42. Long-established and pleasant *pastelería* and café. The *tartas de almendras* (almond cakes) are a house speciality and the *tarta de manzana* (apple pie) is pretty good too. Daily 9am–9pm.

Mesón Gallego Antoxo C/Hoyo 5 ☎ 952 384 533. Oozing class, this is an excellent if seriously expensive Galician restaurant offering dishes and wines from northwestern Spain, including the mandatory *tarta de Santiago* dessert. Fish is shipped in from Galicia daily, including *merluza a la gallega* (hake) and memorable *zamburriñas* (baby scallops). Main dishes €17–25. Mon–Sat 1–4pm & 8pm–midnight, Sun 1–4pm.

Pastelería Lepanto C/San Miguel 54. For afternoon tea or an after-dinner coffee with scrumptious *pasteles* (cakes), this is the place to head for. They also offer a wide range of teas and coffees. Daily 9.30am–9pm.

LA CARIHUELA

Casa Juan Plaza San Ginés, off the eastern end of C/Carmen, La Carihuela. Very good fish restaurant and ma*risquería* now filling this *plazuela* on all sides as the empire grows. *Bacalao al azafrán* (cod cooked with saffron) is a house special, and there are a range of fish and *marisco menús* (€29–84 including wine). Tues–Sun 1–4pm & 8pm–midnight.

La Reserva de Antonio Plaza del Remo 6, La Carihuela, near the Hotel Tropicana ☎ 952 050 735. A change of proprietor has swept one of La Carihuela's favourites upmarket and a complete makeover has resulted in a new kitchen, chef and sky-blue-and-white colour scheme. The fish and *mariscos* are fresh, complemented by a variety of salads and *arrozes* (rice-based dishes). Main dishes €12–26. Tues–Sun 12.30–4pm & 8pm–midnight.

1

Restaurante La Huerta C/Decano Higueras del Castillo 1, La Carihuela, near the Hotel Miami. Great little mid-priced restaurant festooned with plants and vines outside, serving up well-prepared fish and meat dishes, and especially tasty desserts. Daily except Weds 1–4pm & 9pm–midnight.

NIGHTLIFE

When night falls, Torremolinos comes into its own, with a vibrant nightlife lifting off in high summer at about 10pm and continuing well beyond dawn, though it's not as wild as in recent years due to the competition from nearby Benalmádena's Puerto Deportivo nightlife zone. Torrie does, however, maintain its thriving gay scene, with C/Casablanca, running west from C/San Miguel, the centre of gay nightlife with bars and clubs dotted along here and the streets off it.

Veronia Avda. Salvador Allende s/n, opposite the Hotel Pez Espada, La Carihuela. Salsa and Latin venue with two dancefloors and a real party atmosphere after midnight. Five bars keep dancers fuelled with shots and and mojitos until dawn.

Kiu Plaza Sol y Mar, Benalmádena. Massive club consisting of ten bars and four rooms that pulls in the crowds from Torremolinos and Málaga, and manages to fill four dancefloors for most of the summer with a mixture of chart, dance and latin sounds. Fri & Sat stays open until dawn.

Sala Million Avda. Palma de Mallorca 36. Wild place with three dancefloors on two levels playing salsa, pop and house with top DJs and a reputation as one of the hottest venues in town. Open March–Oct only.

Benalmádena

Beyond Carihuela to the west of Torremolinos, the built-up coastline merges imperceptibly – after 4km – into the neighbouring resort of **BENALMÁDENA COSTA**, with its Puerto Deportivo, a pseudo-Moorish harbour complex and a seafront lined with bars, restaurants and *chiringuitos*. Some 3km inland lies the hilltop **BENALMÁDENA PUEBLO**, the original Benalmádena, although this too is fighting a losing battle to preserve its identity as it is gradually engulfed by the unremitting spread of coastal development.

Museo Arqueológico

Avda. Peralta • Mon–Fri 10am–2pm & 4–6pm • Free

The interesting **Museo Arqueológico**, in Benalmádena Pueblo, displays finds from around this area including a beautiful one-and-a-half-metre-high statue of Artemis retrieved from a Roman coastal wreck. There's also a section devoted to the Pre-Columbian peoples of South America.

Tivoli World

Avda. del Tivoli • Daily noon–midnight (July–Aug opens 6pm until the early hours) • €10 • ⓦ tivoli.es

A greater attraction by far for most visitors to Benalmádena is **Tivoli World**, the Costa del Sol's biggest amusement park, sited between Benalmádena Pueblo and Benalmádena Costa and easily reached by train from Fuengirola or Torremolinos (Arroyo de Miel stop). The park has the usual cocktail of rides – including Tower Drop, which plummets riders from sixy metres – as well as restaurants and shows featuring flamenco and assorted tribute bands.

Teleférico

Opposite Tivoli World • Daily July–Aug 11am–midnight, Sept–June 11am–7pm • €7.30 (one-way), €13 (return)

Opposite the Tivoli World entrance the **Teleférico** (cable car) ascends to the peak of Monte Calamorro, from where there are panoramic **views** over the Costa del Sol and – in summer – daily falconry displays. If you choose the one-way fare you have the option of a scenic **walk** back down the mountain along a signed path (a 60–90min trek).

Sea-Life

Puerto Marina s/n • Daily 10am–midnight • €13.95, children €10.95

On the seafront and close to the Puerto Deportivo, **Sea-Life** is the resort's well-presented aquarium, home to a vast array of sea creatures including rays, crabs, octopuses, jellyfish, tropical exotics and turtles. The highlight is a walk-through glass tunnel devoted to sharks who glide eerily a metre above your head; if you coincide your visit with feeding time (Tues, Thurs & Sun at 12.30pm) you'll see just what those molars are capable of.

Fuengirola

FUENGIROLA, a thirty-minute train journey from Torremolinos, or a rapid 21km along the old N340 or the toll *autopista*, is very slightly less developed and infinitely more staid, middle-aged and family-oriented than "Torrie". You wouldn't think it today, but Fuengirola has a distinguished Phoenician (the town started out as a colony), Roman and Moorish past. A number of sights from these eras remain, although most people are here for the **beach**, a huge strand, 7km long, divided into restaurant-beach strips, each renting out lounge chairs and pedal-boats.

Castillo de Sohail

C/Tartesios • Daily: Sept–June 10am–6.30pm; July–Aug 10am–9pm • €3

On the road west out of town is the restored but still impressive **Castillo de Sohail**, a tenth-century fortress built by Abd ar-Rahman III of Córdoba as the hub of a string of towers along the coast to defend against piracy. There are fine views from the battlements over the town and out to sea.

Finca El Secretario

Avda. Padre Jesús Cautivo s/n • Daily July–Aug 10am–2pm & 3–10pm; Sept–June 10am–2pm & 3–7pm • Free

A recently excavated Roman villa, the extensive **Finca El Secretario** lies at the eastern end of town close to the Los Boliches train station on the Fuengirola–Málaga line (whose construction in 1970 first brought the villa to light). It was in use from the first to the fifth century, and excavations have revealed mosaic floors as well as part of the hypocaust system that would have heated the villa's bathhouse. The excavations also unearthed a statue of the Roman goddess Venus, later dubbed the "Venus de Fuengirola", now on display in the Museo de la Historia (see below). Adjoining the villa a fish-salting factory was also discovered, no doubt used to make garum, a pungent fish sauce.

At the eastern end of the seafront Paseo Marítimo there's another vestige from antiquity in the form of the scanty remains of a **Roman temple** comprising four re-erected Doric columns and part of a pediment which are believed to have once formed part of the temple's entrance.

Museo de la Historia

C/María Josefa Larrucea • Mon–Fri 10am–2pm • €2

Northwest of the centre, the **Museo de la Historia** in the Parque de España near the bullring holds a mildly interesting collection documenting the town's development from Phoenician colony and Roman town to the present day. The Roman section features the "Venus de Fuengirola" statue unearthed in a Roman villa (see above), while the modern era has exhibits relating to the town's agricultural and maritime traditions.

Parque Acuático de Mijas

N340, northwest edge of town • Daily May–Sept 10am–7pm • €19, reductions for kids and family groups

A popular summer feature is the **Parque Acuático de Mijas**, a waterpark with all the usual water tubes and chutes. Taking its name from the nearby hill village of Mijas, it is in fact only a few minutes' ride from the Fuengirola bus station (frequent buses throughout the summer).

ARRIVAL AND INFORMATION   FUENGIROLA

By bus The bus station is on Avda. Matías Saenz de Tejada s/n, lightly west of the Turismo ☎ 952 475 066.

By train The train station is on Avda. Juan Gómez Juanito s/n, a couple of blocks north of the bus station ☎ 952 128 080.

1

Tourist information The new and efficient Turismo on Avda. Jesús S. Rein 6 (Mon–Fri 9.30am–2pm & 5–7pm, Sat 9.30am–1.30pm; ☎952 467 457, ⓦfuengirola.org) can supply a town map, help with accommodation problems and hands out copies of a free tapas route leaflet.

Internet There are many internet cafés; Sunny Comunicación, C/Marbella 18 (daily 10am–midnight), slightly west of the focal Plaza Constitución, is one of the most central.

ACCOMMODATION

Hostal Cuevas C/Capitan 7 ☎952 460 606. Pleasant and central hostal offering spotless a/c en-suite rooms with TV, some with balconies overlooking a garden. Free wi-fi, and can assist with parking. **€60**

Hostal Italia C/de la Cruz 1 ☎952 474 193, ⓦhostal-italia.com. This friendy *hostal* is the nicest option around the Plaza de la Constitución for a/c en-suite terrace balcony rooms. Free wi-fi zone. Can arrange parking. **€75**

Hostal Marbella C/Marbella 34 ☎952 664 503, ⓦhostalmarbella.info. Off the west side of the Plaza

Constitución, this is another possibility for light and airy a/c en-suite rooms on a street with other *hostales*. Roof terrace and free wi-fi. Can arrange parking. **€69**

Hotel Las Piramides Paseo Marítimo s/n ☎952 470 600, ⓦhotellaspiramides.com. A luxury option at the western end of the seafront with sea-view rooms, indoor and outdoor pools, gym, sauna and plenty more four-star frills. Check website for special offers. Wi-fi zone and own garage. **€200**

EATING

The streets to the south of the main square (Plaza Constitución) are lined with restaurants of a rather depressing similarity. The following places lie slightly outside the normal tourist beat.

★ **Bar La Paz Garrido** Avda. de Mijas 1, just north of the Plaza de la Constitución. This outstanding and hugely popular bar-restaurant serves up some of the best-value seafood in town – the *gazpacho, boquerones a la plancha* (fried anchovies) and *patatas bravas* (spicy sautéed potatoes) are highly recommended. It's worth trying to grab a table and making a meal of it. Daily 12.30–11pm.

La Plaza Plaza de la Constitución. This pleasant bar with a popular terrace on the square opens for breakfast and does snacks and salads throughout the day. In the evening it serves *copas* (late night drinks). Daily 9am–11pm.

Mesón Don Pé C/de la Cruz s/n. One of the few restaurants worth recommending in the zone south of

the Plaza de la Constitución, specializing in mid-price meat dishes and *cochinillo asado* (suckling pig). Daily 7.30–11.30pm.

Monopol C/Palangreros 7, west of Plaza de la Constitución. This is an excellent little French-style bistro with a good value *menú gourmet* for €19.80 (excluding wine). Besides meat and fish dishes also does salads and pasta. Mon–Sat 7.30–10.30pm.

Old Swiss House C/Marina 28, one block in from the sea and close to the Hotel Las Piramides. Small mid-priced restaurant where the Swiss-influenced cooking has a dash of panache – including the *crêpes suzette* dessert. Mon & Weds–Sun 1–3.30pm & 6–11pm.

Mijas

Often grouped with the more famous White Towns further north (see p.125), the once tranquil hill town of **MIJAS**, a winding eight-kilometre climb into the hills above Fuengirola, is a little too close to the Costa del Sol for its own good, making it an obvious target for bus tours in search of the "typical" Andalucian village. However, despite a host of tacky gift shops and the numbered *burro* (donkey) taxis that transport visitors around the main square (Plaza Virgen de la Peña), the village retains some of its original character, and there are fine views towards the coast.

Plaza de Toros and the church of the Inmaculada Concepción

Southeast of the main square the century-old – and curiously rectangular – **Plaza de Toros**, with a museum (daily 10am–7pm; €3), is worth a look, as is the nearby sixteenth-century **church of the Inmaculada Concepción** (free) with a Mudéjar tower, and the adjacent ruins of a Moorish fort and a **mirador** with a spectacular view over the coast far below.

Casa Museo Etnográfico

Plaza de la Libertad • Daily 10am–2pm & 4–7pm • Free

West of the main square, the **Casa Museo Etnográfico** holds an interesting collection of artefacts from Mijas's past as well as a recreation of the room where Mijas's last socialist mayor, Manuel Cortés Quero, went into hiding in 1936 to avoid the Franco purge. With the aid of his family he stayed hidden in the same underground room for 33 years to emerge in 1969 when the government announced an amnesty.

Carromato de Max

Avda. de Compás s/n • Daily 10am–7pm • €3

Above the main square, the ludicrous **Carromato de Max** is a railway wagon full of junk and claims to house "the smallest curiosities in the world". If items such as Churchill's head sculpted from a stick of chalk, a copy of Leonardo's *Last Supper* painted on a grain of rice, or the shrunken head of a white man retrieved from South American Indians and "certified genuine by the FBI" grab you, then it's well worth the entry fee.

ARRIVAL AND INFORMATION — MIJAS

By bus Frequent buses run between Fuengirola and Mijas stopping on the focal Plaza Virgen de la Peña, the main square.

Tourist information The helpful Turismo, on Plaza Virgen de la Peña s/n (Mon–Fri 9am–7pm, Sat 9am–2pm; T 952 589 034, W mijas.es), can provide a useful village map and gives out a free leaflet detailing a number of walks (2–3hr) in the surrounding hills. They can also provide information on free, twice-weekly guided treks.

Internet Locutorio Mijas Pueblo (daily 10.30am–10pm), Pasaje Salvador Cantos Jiménez s/n, just off the main square.

ACCOMMODATION

★ **Casa El Escudo** C/Trocha de los Pescadores 7 T 952 591 100, W el-escudo.com. Off Plaza de la Constitución, the village's second largest square, this is a delightful small hotel with charming a/c rooms equipped with TV, DVD player, minibar and – in rooms 8, 9 and 10 – a terrace with fine views. Can arrange parking. **€60**

Hostal La Posada C/Coín 47 T 952 485 310. A friendly and good-value *hostal* with a range of room and apartment options. To get here, find your way to Plaza de la Constitución, a small square below the bullring, and ask for directions. **€36–45**

Hotel Mijas C/Tamisa 2 T 952 485 800, W trhhoteles.com. The village's upmarket option is signed to the left on the road into the village. Comfortable rooms are complemented by pool, gardens, tennis court and gymnasium. Wi-fi zone and own car park. **€100**

EATING AND DRINKING

Bar La Gamba c/San Sebastián 19, near the museum. A good bar-restaurant serving *platos combinados* as well as *mariscos*, paellas and their house special *conejo sierra mijas* (rabbit with herbs). 10am–11.30pm.

Bar González Plaza Virgen de la Peña s/n. Another good bar for tapas and *raciones* served inside or on a terrace on the square. There's also a menú for €8.50. 10am–11pm.

★ **Bar-Restaurante Alarcón** c/Lasta 1 T 95 248 52 45. Located near the church of Santa Ana in the Barrio Santana in the older part of the village, this is an excellent-value little place, worth seeking out for its superb traditional cooking (including tapas in the bar), friendly service and a pleasant roof terrace with fine views. Try their costillas (ribs), sardines or morcilla (blood sausage). 9am–11.30pm, closed Sun.

El Castillo Pasaje los Pescadores 2, off Plaza de la Constitución. Modestly priced restaurant for tapas, pizzas and pasta dishes. Also offers a variety of salads and there's a tapas *menú* for €7.50 and a normal *menú* for €9. 12.30–4pm & 8–11pm.

El Mirlo Blanco Plaza Constitución 13 T 952 485 700. Elaborate meals are on offer at this very good if pricey Basque restaurant. House specialities include *bacalao a la vizcaína* (salted cod), *txangurro* (spider crab baked in shell). Main dishes €12–25. 1–3.45pm & 8–11pm.

Marbella

Undisputedly the "quality resort" of the Costa del Sol, **MARBELLA** stands in considerable contrast to most of what's come before. Sheltered from the winds by the hills of the Sierra Blanca, it has a couple of excellent **beaches** which first brought it to the attention of the 1960s' smart set. However, don't strain your eyes for celebrities nowadays; the only time

1

the mega-rich motor down from their villas in the hills is to attend a private club or put in an appearance at glitzy places like the *Puente Romano Hotel* on the way to San Pedro, where a beluga caviar starter in the restaurant will cost you the price of a good hotel room.

Spared the worst excesses of concrete architecture that have been inflicted upon Torremolinos, Marbella is decidedly tasteful, retaining the greater part of its old town or **casco antiguo**. Slowly, this original quarter is being bought up and turned over to "quaint" clothes boutiques and restaurants, but you can still sit in an ordinary bar in a small old square and look up beyond the whitewashed alleyways to the mountains of Ronda.

Brief history

Marbella's image took a nose dive in the 1970s when British crooks and drug barons began setting up home here, bringing their feuds and rivalries with them. In the late 1980s the authorities became even more exercised by the arrival of Russian and Italian

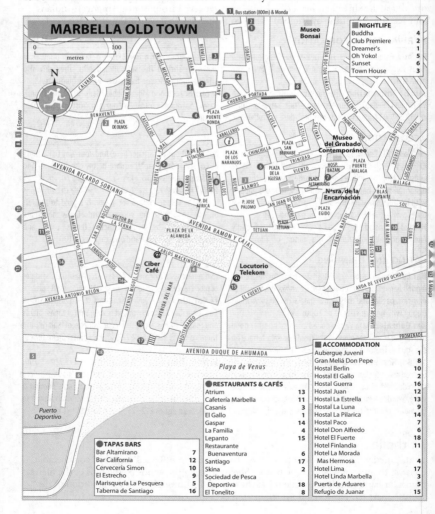

MARBELLA OLD TOWN

■ NIGHTLIFE	
Buddha	4
Club Premiere	2
Dreamer's	1
Oh Yoko!	5
Sunset	6
Town House	3

● RESTAURANTS & CAFÉS	
Atrium	13
Cafetería Marbella	11
Casanis	3
El Gallo	1
Gaspar	14
La Familia	4
Lepanto	15
Restaurante Buenaventura	6
Santiago	17
Skina	2
Sociedad de Pesca Deportiva	18
El Tonelito	8

● TAPAS BARS	
Bar Altamirano	7
Bar California	12
Cervecería Simon	10
El Estrecho	9
Marisquería La Pesquera	5
Taberna de Santiago	16

■ ACCOMMODATION	
Aubergue Juvenil	1
Gran Meliá Don Pepe	8
Hostal Berlin	10
Hostal El Gallo	2
Hostal Guerra	16
Hostal Juan	12
Hostal La Estrella	13
Hostal La Luna	9
Hostal La Pilarica	14
Hostal Paco	7
Hotel Don Alfredo	6
Hotel El Fuerte	18
Hotel Finlandia	11
Hotel La Morada Mas Hermosa	4
Hotel Lima	17
Hotel Linda Marbella	3
Puerta de Aduares	5
Refugio de Juanar	15

mafia bosses, who controlled their empires from luxury villas and yach
in nearby Puerto Banús. Marbella's notoriety continued throughout th
the period of rule by the corrupt mayor Jesús Gil y Gil (who avoided a
term by dying in 2004) and his GIL political party. A host of unsavour
businesses moved into town and in 2005 Spanish police uncovered Euro
ever money-laundering operation, channelling billions of euros from cri
across Europe through Marbella companies into anonymous "trusts". In ......ic twist
of history, there's also been a massive return of Arabs to the area, especially since the
late King Fahd of Saudi Arabia built a White House lookalike, complete with adjacent
mosque, on the town's western outskirts.

The Plaza de los Naranjos

The *casco antiguo*, partially walled, is set back from the sea and hidden from the main
road – the Avenida Ramón y Cajal – that slices through the town. The main sights
are clustered in the web of streets surrounding the picturesque **Plaza de los Naranjos**,
whose charms are somewhat marred by the invasive terraces of the surrounding
restaurants that use it as an open-air dining room. On the plaza (next to the Turismo)
is the striking sixteenth-century Ayuntamiento, still functioning as such and actually
built by Fernando and Isabel following their conquest of the town in 1485. The area
now occupied by the plaza was formerly a warren of narrow streets in the Moorish
town of Marbil-la, but the monarchs cleared this area of housing to create the open
space that Spanish civic life required. Towards the middle of the square – and not easy
to see for the surrounding clutter – lies a fountain constructed in 1504 by Marbella's
first Christian mayor.

Just off the square in the nearby Plaza de la Iglesia is the church of **Nuestra Señora de
la Encarnación**. Also built in the sixteenth century, it was later remodelled in the
Baroque style and has a fine tower as well as a striking retablo inside.

Museo del Grabado Contemporáneo

C/Hospital Bazán s/n • Mon 10am–2pm, Tues–Fri 9am–9pm • €3

This fine Renaissance hospital – founded in the sixteenth century by Alonso Bazán,
then mayor of Marbella – now hosts a mildly interesting **Museo del Grabado
Contemporáneo**, an engraving museum with works by Miró, Dalí and Picasso.

Museo Bonsai

Arroyo de la Represa s/n; daily 10am–1.30pm & 5–8pm; €4

Northeast of the Plaza de los Naranjos you'll find Spain's one and only Bonsai tree
museum, the **Museo Bonsai**, with 150 examples of this arboraceous curiosity.

The beaches

The resort has three main **beaches** stretching from the easternmost Playa de la Bajadilla
and Playa de Venus, both located between its twin harbours, and the Playa de la
Fontanilla to the west, which gets progressively less crowded the further west you go.

ARRIVAL AND DEPARTURE MARBELLA

By bus The bus station is at the northern of Avda.
Trapiche (☏ 902 143 144), a twenty-minute walk from
the centre. Buses from Estepona and San Pedro de
Alcántara (heading east) and Fuengirola (heading west)
also stop in the centre. Otherwise take buses #2 or #7
from the bus station, which will drop you near to the
centre of the old town.

By car There are signed pay car parks around the centre
and all accommodation (if they don't have their own
garage) will advise on possible on-street parking places.

INFORMATION

Tourist information The Turismo, on the north side of
Plaza de los Naranjos (Mon–Fri 9am–9pm, Sat 10am–2pm;
☏ 952 823 550, ⓦ marbellaexclusive.com), has detailed
town maps and produces a leaflet, *Verano Cultural*,

...ne many events held in town throughout the ..., which often star big names. A second office (same ...urs) is sited on Glorieta Fontanilla, a roundabout at the eastern end of the seafront.

Internet Cibercafé, Travesía Carlos Mackintosh, on the south side of the Alameda (Mon–Sat 9am–10pm), and the nearby *Locutorio Telekom*, Avda. Puerta del Mar 1, effectively the same square (daily 10am–midnight).

ACCOMMODATION

All Marbella's budget accommodation is in the old town, on or around C/Luna or, a couple of blocks west, along the pretty C/San Cristóbal, the street of a thousand plants all carefully tended by its residents. In-town accommodation ranges between *hostal* and four-star luxury, with precious little in between. Pressure on rooms is tight in July and extremely so in August, when you should book ahead.

BUDGET AND MODERATE

Albergue Juvenil C/Trapiche 2 ☎ 951 270 301. A very good hostel, if a little removed from the action (5-10min walk to the centre), with double rooms (some with bath), a pool and tennis court plus plenty of activities such as sea angling, mountain biking and watersports. Under 26 **€21**, over 26 **€27**.

Hostal Berlin C/San Ramón 21 ☎ 952 821 310, ⓦ hostalberlin.com. Sparkling and very friendly *hostal*; all rooms come with bath, a/c and satellite TV, and free internet access is available (plus wi-fi throughout). Bargain rates outside July & Aug. **€60**

Hostal El Gallo C/Lobatos 44 ☎ 952 827 998, ⓦ hostal elgallo.es. Extremely welcoming *hostal* with good-value, spotless en-suite a/c rooms with fridge and TV. There's also a roof terrace and the bonus of a great *barrio* restaurant below. Free wi-fi. **€60**

Hostal Guerra Llanos de San Ramón 2 ☎ 952 774 220. Clean, simple and economical rooms with bath, some with balcony, on the eastern flank of the old town near the beach. Free wi-fi zone. **€40**

Hostal Juan C/Luna 18 ☎ 952 779 475, ⓔ pensionjuan @hotmail.com. This *hostal*, located on a tranquil street, comes with friendly proprietor and good-value, well-maintained a/c en-suite rooms with TV and fridge. Free wi-fi. **€45**

Hostal La Estrella C/San Cristóbal 36 ☎ 952 779 472. Nicely located and welcoming option on a pleasant street, offering a/c rooms with bath, fridge, TV and some with balcony. **€45**

Hostal La Luna C/Luna 7 ☎ 952 825 778. Delightful, friendly and spotless *pensión* with balconied rooms around a renovated old patio at the rear; all rooms have bath, fridge, a/c and TV. Can assist with parking. **€55**

Hostal La Pilarica C/San Cristóbal 31 ☎ 952 774 252. Pretty and good-value *hostal* in lovely location. En-suite rooms with TV and fridge. **€55**

Hostal Paco C/Peral 16 ☎ 952 771 200, ⓦ hostal pacomarbella.com. Central and refurbished *hostal* in a traditional town house; all rooms are en suite and come with and TV and free wi-fi. Can advise on parking. **€65**

Hotel Don Alfredo C/Portada 11 ☎ 952 766 978, ⓦ hoteldonalfredo.com. Very pleasant small two-star hotel facing the walls of a ruined castillo. All rooms have a/c, satellite TV and balcony. Free wi-fi. Street parking is often available nearby – the hotel can advise. **€68**

Hotel Finlandia C/Notario Luis Oliver 12 ☎ 952 770 700, ⓦ hotelfinlandia.es. Welcoming and comfortable little one-star hotel on a quiet street. Rooms – some with balcony – come with TV. Fans are available on request and there's a wi-fi zone. **€65**

Hotel Linda Marbella C/Ancha 21 ☎ 952 857 171, ⓦ hotel-lindamarbella.com. Attractive small hotel in a central location with well-appointed a/c rooms (some with balcony) and a roof terrace. Free wi-fi. Can advise on parking nearby. **€80**

EXPENSIVE

Gran Meliá Don Pepe C/José Meliá s/n ☎ 902 144 440, ⓦ solmelia.es. Five-star luxury hotel and part of the Meliá chain, with sea-view balcony rooms plus many facilities including extensive gardens, three pools (one indoor), gym, sauna, tennis courts and Michelin-starred restaurant. **€340**

Hotel El Fuerte Avda. Severo Ochoa 10 ☎ 952 861 500, ⓦ hotel-elfuerte.es. The older and more charming of two four-star hotels with the same name fronting the Playa de Venus. Amenities include beach access, gardens, pool, gym, tennis courts and sauna. **€200**

★ **Hotel La Morada Más Hermosa** C/Montenebros 16 ☎ 952 924 467, ⓦ lamoradamashermosa.com. Taking its name from the first words of Columbus on sighting the New World ("beautiful place"), this is an enchanting small hotel in a refurbished eighteenth-century townhouse with elegant, individually styled a/c rooms (most with terraces). Free wi-fi. **€108**

Hotel Lima Avda. Antonio Belón 2 ☎ 952 770 500, ⓦ hotellimamarbella.com. Efficient and central two-star hotel near the harbour. The light and spacious rooms come with a/c, safe and sea views, while higher rooms have a balcony terrace. Free wi-fi. **€96**

Puerta de Aduares C/Aduar 18 ☎ 952 821 312, ⓦ puertadeaduares.com. Reasonably priced, stylishly decorated and fully serviced a/c apartments (sleeping two or four) with either outdoor terrace or patio. **€99**

★ Refugio de Juanar 12km north of Marbella and signed off the A355 ☎ 952 881 000, ⓦ juanar.com. Tucked away in the pine forests of the Sierra Blanca, this former hunting lodge of the once-powerful *malagueño* Larios family (and where General de Gaulle holed up to write his memoirs – Room 3 if you're curious, complete with framed copy of his payment cheque on the wall) is now a wonderfully tranquil three-star hotel complete with attractive pool and restaurant. Make sure you do the 3km walk to the Mirador de Juanar with spectacular views over the coast. €98

EATING AND DRINKING

When it comes to food and drink you're better off heading for Marbella's numerous and excellent **tapas bars**, rather than the many touristy and overpriced **restaurants** around the Plaza de los Naranjos. There are, however, a fair number of good-value eating places within a five-minute walk of the square, and following the Avda. del Mar – lined with Dalí bronzes – towards the sea will lead you to the Puerto Deportivo and another zone filled with bars and restaurants.

RESTAURANTS

Casanis C/Ancha 8 ☎ 952 900 450. Mid-priced bistro with a French–Belgian kitchen and plenty of ambience and style. *Confit de pato con lentejas* (duck confit with lentils) and *pierno de cordero* (leg of lamb) are house specials and there are also pasta-based dishes and some veggie options. Main dishes €18–22. Daily 9.30am–11.30pm, closed Sun.

El Gallo C/Lobatas 44. Good and popular little neighbourhood restaurant serving up traditional *andaluz* dishes such as *langostinos al pil pil* (prawns with chilli), *conejo al ajillo* (rabbit) and paella. There's a good-value *menú* for €10. Daily 12.30–4pm & 8–11pm.

★ Gaspar C/Notario Luis Oliver 19 ☎ 952 779 098. A gem of a restaurant run by a family from Rioja – which explains the comprehensive wine list. Besides their standard dishes – including *tortilla, cordero asado* (charcoal grilled lamb) and *pastel de berenjenas* (aubergine terrine) you can also order a few plates of *raciones* to share. If you have to wait for a table you can peruse the books in the restaurant's library, and impromptu flamenco sometimes happens when *cantantes* (singers) drop in for a meal. Expect to pay around €25pp. Daily 2–5pm & 9pm–1am.

La Familia C/Cruz 5, off the Plaza Puente de Ronda. Authentic mid-priced Italian cuisine served up in a pleasant atrium dining room. There are excellent home-made pasta dishes – try the *rigatoni alla amatriciana* – while starters include imported Parma ham served on tomato-laced bruschetta. Main dishes €12–29. Daily 7.30–11.30pm.

Restaurante Buenaventura Plaza de la Iglesia 5 ☎ 952 858 069. High-class *andaluz* cuisine served on an elegant courtyard terrace. Main dishes €15–30; *menú de degustación* for €35 (excluding wine). Daily 12.30–4pm & 7pm–midnight; closed Nov.

★ Santiago Avda. Duque de Ahumada s/n ☎ 952 770 078, ⓦ restaurantesantiago.com. For a splurge, head for *Santiago*, near the Puerto Deportivo, one of Marbella's swankiest and oldest restaurants, founded in the 1950s by Santiago Domínguez – who started out with a *chiringuito* on the beach opposite. Over fifty years later Santiago is still overseeing his restaurant and bars and is famous throughout Spain as one of the great restaurateurs. The restaurant serves excellent traditional fare (both fish and meat) with a creative touch. Signature dishes include *ensalada de bogovante* (lobster salad) and *fritura del Mediterráneo* (fried fish). A "value for money" philosophy is typified by a recommended *menú de degustación* (€50 including wine). The restaurant has an attractive seafront terrace. Main dishes €15–27. Daily 1–4.30pm & 8–11pm.

Skina C/Aduar 12 ☎ 952 765 277. Excellent, small (12 covers), if expensive, Michelin-starred restaurant run by *vanguardista* chef Daniel Rosado. *Chivo lechal malagueño* (suckling kid) stands out on a short but highly creative – some say excessively so – meat and fish menu and there's a *menú de degustación* for around €70. Has a small outdoor terrace. Mon–Sat 7.30pm–midnight.

Sociedad de Pesca Deportiva Puerto Deportivo, Local 5, to the left as you enter the port. The Marbella fishermen's club should know a thing or two about seafood and they serve up delicious, reasonably priced fish and *mariscos* at their restaurant with a terrace in the port. Try their *almejas a la marinera* (clams in wine) or *boquerones fritos* (anchovies). Tues–Sun noon–4pm & 7.30–11pm.

TAPAS BARS

Bar Altamirano Plaza de Altamirano 4, southeast of Plaza Naranjos. Great place for some of the freshest seafood *raciones* and *medias* in town; try their *boquerones en vinagre* (anchovies). Eat in their bright bar inside or on a terrace with tables spread across a small square. Daily 10.30am–4pm & 6pm–midnight.

Bar California Junction of C/Málaga & Avda. Severo Ochoa, east of the casco antiguo. Excellent bar where the fino (as proclaimed above the entrance) is as good as the seafood tapas, *pescado frito* and *raciones*. Daily noon–4pm & 6.30–11.30pm.

Cervecería Simon C/Pablo Casals 1, near the seafront at the western end. Fine tapas at low prices and a pleasant terrace on which to enjoy them. Specials include *chopitos fritas* (cuttlefish), *gambas con gabardinas* (shrimps) and *almejas* (clams).

El Estrecho C/San Lázaro 12. Founded in 1954, this is an excellent and atmospheric little tapas bar with a wide range of possibilities. Try their *carne mechada* (larded meat) or *mejillones tigres* (stuffed mussels). Cool jazz and

1

blues sounds permeate the place and there's a cosy dining room off to the side should you want to make a meal of it. In the same alley, *Tierr Aranda* (opposite) and the nearby *Casa Bar Bartolo* – with a *menú* and roof terrace – are also worth a visit. Daily noon–midnight.

Marisquería La Pesquera Plaza de la Victoria s/n, west of Plaza de los Naranjos. More restaurant than *raciones* bar these days, this remains a town favourite, with first-class *fino* too. House specials include *cigalitas cocidas* (Dublin Bay prawns), *almejas marinera* (clams in wine) and a variety of salads. Daily 12.30pm–midnight.

★ **Taberna de Santiago** Avda. del Mar 20. Sited on an avenue dotted with Dalí bronzes leading to the sea, this is the tapas and *raciones* bar of the famous nearby *Santiago* restaurant (see p.117). Everything is top quality and the prices are very reasonable: an *ensalada mixta*, *ración* of *bacalao con tomate* (cod in tomato sauce) and half-litre *jarra* of house wine is easily enough for two and weighs in

at under €30. Or try a paella at €18 for two. Has a pleasant sea-view terrace. If you're feeling expansive you could also try *Santiago's* oyster bar next door. Daily noon–11pm.

CAFÉS AND BARS

Atrium C/Gregorio Marañón 11, west of the centre. One of several fashionable outdoor terrace bars in this area frequented by Marbella's well-heeled set.

Cafetería Marbella Alameda Gardens, Avda. Ramón y Cajal. Nice place for breakfast, in the gardens overlooking the main drag with two shady terraces.

El Tonelito C/Pantaleón 4. Popular *cervecería* with a "no music" policy, making it just the place to recover from the night before.

Lepanto Avda. Puerta del Mar s/n, southeast corner of the Alameda. Stylish café and *pastelería* just south of the old quarter, which excels in chocolate confectionery creations.

NIGHTLIFE

Marbella has one of the liveliest nightlife scenes on the *Costa*, with action centred around Plaza Puente de Ronda, C/Pantaleón and Plaza de Africa, all in the old town, and Plaza de Olivos to the west of here. The once riotous Puerto Deportivo, the seafront yacht harbour, also has a scene, although due to years of complaints from residents about noise it has now transmuted into a laid-back *copas* and cocktails zone with low decibel levels. Nearby Puerto Banús is another nightlife hotspot.

Buddha Avda. del Mar 3. Popular club often featuring themed nights of Latin, Cuban, Salsa and 60s sounds.

Club Premiere Plaza de Olivos 2. One of a clutch of clubs hereabouts, this lively music venue often stages live gigs ranging from pop to electronica and acid-jazz.

Dreamer's Ctra de Cádiz 175, Río Verde. One of the bigger – holds up to 1400 –and better clubs on the outskirts of Puerto Banús, playing a range of garage, house and techno sounds. Only hits its stride in the small hours.

Oh Yoko! Puerto Deportivo. One of the few clubs in this area, this soundproofed dance venue specializes in house and goes on until dawn.

Sunset Puerto Deportivo. Harbourfront bar for lounging with a cool drink on sofas and loungers while the sun goes down in the west. After dark the cocktails fill the tables. One of many similar places along the waterfront.

Town House C/Alamo 1. Long-established *bar de copas* with rock/electronica sounds, and they light a roaring fire in winter.

Puerto Banús

Around 7km west of Marbella the N340 coastal road passes the marina and casino complex of **PUERTO BANÚS**, where the jet set park up their yachts. An utterly modern resort devoid of any architectural charms, in summer the place presents a bizarre spectacle as crowds of Costa del Sol gawpers come to celebrity-spot, while the bronzed plutocrats attempt to steer their Bentleys and Ferraris through the crush to their vessels.

If you're determined to see what the fuss is about – or fancy window-shopping at the numerous designer clothes and jewellery emporia – a useful tip coming in by car is to use the economical car park of the El Corte Inglés department store in the *centro comercial* and walk the five minutes to the gated harbour zone which only vehicles with permits may enter.

San Pedro de Alcántara

Six kilometres west of Puerto Banús, and about the only place on the Costa del Sol that isn't purely a holiday resort, is the small town of **SAN PEDRO DE ALCÁNTARA**, a none-too-inspiring place striving to go the way of its neighbour but hindered by the fact that its centre is set back over a kilometre from the sea, which lies at the end of the Avenida del Mar Mediterráneo.

In the town proper what activity there is centres on the tranquil, palm-fringed **Plaza de la Iglesia** – at its most lively during the Thursday morning **flea market** – but there's not much else to disturb the calm.

The beach

The seafront area behind the beach has been landscaped with the almost obligatory palm-lined promenade and some holiday *urbanizaciones* have been constructed, but this has done little to raise San Pedro's profile. Despite this lack of seafront pizazz, the **beach** itself is top-quality blue flag and five kilometres long, so you'll never have a problem finding somewhere to lay your towel.

INFORMATION **SAN PEDRO DE ALCÁNTARA**

Turismo The helpful Turismo on Avda. Marqués del Duero 69, the main street you turn in to when leaving the N340 (Mon–Fri 9am–9pm, Sat 10am–2pm; ☎ 952 785 252), can supply a map of the town and provide latest information on visiting the three ancient monuments (see below).

Bookshop Shakespeare, C/Lagasca 69, one block west from the Turismo. Useful secondhand bookshop; they will also take any books you wish to offload in part exchange.

ACCOMMODATION

Hostal Acemar C/19 Octubre 17 ☎ 952 783 041. Not far from Turismo, this is a budget possibility for basic but clean a/c en-suite rooms with TV. Can assist with finding on-street parking. €40

Hostal Galea Centro Plaza de la Iglesia s/n ☎ 952 786 864. Facing the church, this upmarket *hostal* offers a/c en-suite rooms with TV, plus wi-fi and free parking. €58

Hotel Doña Catalina Avda. Oriental 14 ☎ 952 853 120, ⓦ hoteldonacatalina.com. Three-star hotel southeast of the church, with a/c balcony rooms with safe, satellite TV and free wi-fi. €80

EATING

For food the place to head for is Avda. Andalucía, to the west of the Turismo and just north of the N340, which is home to a number of restaurants.

Restaurante Alfredo Avda. Andalucía 8. Smoothly professional traditional restaurant offering a good selection of *andaluz* dishes served up in a cool and comfortable dining room. Everything on the menu – both fish and meat – is carefully prepared and the service is excellent. Try their baked fish or *solomillo ibérico* (pork loin). Daily 10am–1am.

Restaurante Casa Fernando Avda. Mediterraneo s/n, about halfway down this avenue leading to the sea. This is nearest decent place to eat near the seafront. It specializes in seafood and there's a leafy garden terrace to enjoy on summer nights. Tues–Sat 1–4.30 & 7–11pm, Sun 1–4.30pm.

Sitar Avda. Andalucía 3. This is a long-standing Indian restaurant for a change of cuisine. All the traditional favourites are served such as tandoori chicken and biryani and the service is good. Mon–Fri 7pm–midnight, Sun 1–3pm, closed Sat.

Ancient ruins around San Pedro

There are three remarkable **ancient ruins** in the vicinity of San Pedro, although to gain entry to the sites you'll need to book a visit with the Delegación de Cultura in Marbella (see p.120). Outside guided visits you can get a partial sight of the Roman villa and Visigothic basilica from behind their fences. The Roman baths – which can be seen from the beach – now lie inside a gated *urbanización* and are inaccessible without a guide.

The Roman villa

Four kilometres back along the road east to Marbella are the remains of a **Roman villa** at Río Verde. To get here from San Pedro, pass the turn-off for Puerto Banús and, after crossing the river, take a right before the *Puente Romano Hotel* and follow the signs. Constructed in the late first or early second century, the rooms are decorated with an unusual series of black and white **mosaics** depicting not classical themes or intricate designs as elsewhere, but everyday kitchen equipment. The kitchen utensils are a delight, and the shoes portrayed by the door are evidence of the Roman custom of leaving one's footwear outside the *triclinium*, or dining room. One of the mosaic's amphorae is so accurately portrayed that its style has helped to date the villa almost precisely. Note also the hanging fowl and fish, ready for the pot.

Visigothic Christian basilica

The sixth-century **Visigothic Christian basilica** of Vega del Mar lies close to the sea at the bottom of the Avenida del Mediterráneo, the main road from San Pedro towards the coast. Take the last road on the right before the beach and you'll come to the railed-off site in the midst of a stand of eucalyptus trees. It's one of the most important Visigothic monuments on the peninsula; the remains enable you to clearly make out a rectangular basilica with a double apse, unique in Spain. Large boulders cemented with lime-mortar were used in its construction along with still-visible brickwork at the corners. A wonderful **baptismal font** is especially well preserved and was deep enough for total immersion, the custom of the time.

In and around the basilica is a cemetery of some two hundred tombs (which yielded a wealth of artefacts now in Marbella and Madrid museums), most with the head to the north, the orientation of the church. Note the graves lined with marble, evidence of social stratification even in death.

The Roman bathhouse

The third site, the **Roman bathhouse** of Las Bovedas, lies a little way west of here, almost on the beach. Leave any transport at the *chiringuito* and walk the fifty metres along the beach to the site where you will be able to glimpse the upper part of the structure. The substantial remains belong to an octagonal third-century Roman baths. Seven chambers, which would have served as a series of heated steam rooms, surround the well-preserved central bath (parts of the underfloor hypocaust system are visible). Above the central pool was a skylight surrounded by a roof terrace. Because the complex was constructed with a special lime – which, when mixed with sand and pebbles from the beach, set to a granite-like hardness – the building has defied the elements impressively.

INFORMATION	AROUND SAN PEDRO
Tours Tours (Mon–Fri at noon) must be booked at least one day in advance with the Delegación de Cultura in Marbella on ☏952 825 035 (English spoken). If the English-speaking personnel are not available, visits can be booked with a phone call to the tourist offices of San Pedro (see p.119) or Marbella (see p.115). Once the	booking is confirmed you will be informed of the time and meeting point (usually the Arco de Marbella, a huge arch astride the N340 between San Pedro and Marbella) at which to rendezvous with the guide. The visit is free and lasts approximately two hours, although you'll need your own transport to get between the sites.

Estepona

West of San Pedro the *autopista* heads inland before turning west, while the coast road is littered with more depressing *urbanizaciones* bearing names such as Picasso or – taking irony to the limit – Paraíso (paradise). Should you feel the urge to stop, **ESTEPONA**, 17km beyond San Pedro, is about the only good bet, a more or less Spanish resort with much of its identity still intact. Lacking the enclosed hills that give Marbella character, it is at least developed on a human scale, while the hotel and apartment blocks which sprawl along the front are restrained in size and free of garish clutter. The seafront too is attractive, with a promenade studded with flowers and palms and an expansive EU blue-flagged stretch of sand which is also home to the **Costa Natura**, the Costa del Sol's oldest nudist beach.

The town behind the seafront has plenty of character, while the **old**
charming corners with cobbled alleyways and two delightful squares,
Flores and Plaza Arce. Calle Terraza bisects the centre; around here yo
the town's eating and drinking options, especially along the pedestrian

To the west of the centre, the modern **Plaza de Toros** is home to four in
museums, while on the coast the **Puerto Deportivo** is a daintier version o
nightlife hotspot, with its few bars and clubs only becoming really anima

The museums of the Plaza de Toros

C/Matías Prats s/n (take a taxi or walk 2km west along the seafront to the Puerto Deportivo and then turn inland) • Daily 10am–2pm &
4–6pm • Free

From May onwards, the town's **bullfighting** season gets under way in the modern
Plaza de Toros on the west side of town, reminiscent of a Henry Moore sculpture.
The building is also home to four museums: the **Museo Etnográfico** (folk museum),
Museo Arqueológico, **Museo Paleontológico** and the **Museo Taurino** (bullfighting). The
folk museum showcases many artefacts from Estepona's agricultural and maritime past;
the archeological museum has local finds from the Phoenician, Roman and Moorish
periods; the paleontology museum houses a collection of fossils and seashells millions
of years old; while the Taurino museum – whatever your position on bullfighting
– gives you some idea of the importance of *taurinismo* in Andalucian culture. There are
the usual trophies and photos of past big names as well as (in the centre of the museum
itself) the actual *toril* (bull-pen) from where the raging bulls are released into the
adjoining ring during *corridas*.

Selwo Adventure Park

6km east from Estepona (signed from N340 and the Autopista del Sol and served by regular buses from all the major Costa del Sol resorts)
• March–Oct daily 10am–6pm (July & Aug until 8pm) • €24.50 adults, €17 kids. Discount vouchers offering 25 percent off are available
from the Estepona Turismo • W selwo.es

East of town, the **Selwo Adventure Park** is a landscaped zoo, home to some two
thousand-plus resident animals who are are allowed to roam around in semi-liberty,
complete with recreations of African Zulu and Masai villages (you can even stay
overnight here in an expensive "African-style" hut with all mod cons – see the website
for details).

Costa Natura

4km west of town • ☎ 952 808 065, W costanatura.com

Estepona's nudist beach and naturist holiday village, the **Costa Natura**, is located a short
bus ride from the centre and rents out apartments (around €100 for the cheapest two
person studio) in a complex with bars, restaurant, pool and gardens.

ARRIVAL AND INFORMATION   ESTEPONA

By bus The bus station (☎ 902 450 550) is on Avda. de
España, west of the centre behind the seafront. Frequent
services to Cádiz, Málaga, Marbella and Torremolinos.

Turismo Town maps and help finding a room are available
at the Turismo (Mon–Fri 9am–8pm, Sat 10am–1.30pm;

☎ 952 802 002) on Avda. San Lorenzo, 1.2km west of the
focal C/Terraza.

Internet Locutorio Estambul (daily 10am–11pm), Avda.
Juan Carlos 1, 50m northwest of the Turismo. The whole of
Plaza Las Flores is a free wi-fi zone.

ACCOMMODATION

Camping Parque Tropical 6km east of town on the
N340 (km162) ☎ 952 793 618. The nearest campsite to
Estepona, set a few hundred metres back from the beach
in a former tropical garden with plenty of shade, plus a
spectacular conservatory-pool and restaurant. Two people
plus car €18

Hostal El Pilar Plaza Las Flores 10 ☎ 952 800 018,
@ hostalpilar@telefonica.net. Friendly *hostal* on a
charming plaza offering en-suite balcony rooms with a/c
and TV. Free wi-fi zone. €55

Hotel Altamarina Avda. San Lorenzo 32, near the
Turismo ☎ 952 806 155, W hotelaltamarina.com.

...est town hotel, with comfortable a/c rooms
...sea views. It also imposes a silly rule during August
...ing you to take lunch or dinner in the hotel restaurant
(€12.50/person added to room price). Wi-fi zone. **€70**

Hotel Buenavista Paseo Marítimo 180 ☎ 952 800 137, ⓦ buenavistaestepona.com. Reasonable-value hotel with plain but clean en-suite sea-view balcony rooms with a/c and TV. Has own car park. **€65**

Hotel Mediterráneo Avda. de España 68, on the seafront to the east of C/Terraza ☎ 952 793 393, ⓦ mediterraneo-estepona.com. Functional but good-value seafront hotel, where a/c en-suite rooms come with

TV and (most) sea views. Own (pay) car park or can advise on street parking nearby. **€65**

Hostal La Malagueña C/Castillo s/n, close to Plaza Las Flores ☎ 952 800 011, ⓦ hlmestepona.com. Comfortable, welcoming and reliable *pensión*, offering a/c en-suite rooms with TV, plus a roof terrace solarium. Free wi-fi zone and parking for €6. **€40**

Hostal San Miguel C/Terraza 16 ☎ 952 802 616. Friendly establishment with its own bar, a little west of Plaza Las Flores. All rooms are en suite and come with a/c, TV and free wi-fi. **€50**

EATING AND DRINKING

Aguilar C/Real 54, off the east side of C/Terraza. An atmospheric tapas and *raciones* bar with an outdoor terrace. Also does pizzas and has a *menú* for €10. Daily noon–midnight.

La Casa de mi Abuela C/Caridad 54, east of C/Terraza. Mid-priced restaurant with a varnished wood interior specializing in *carnes asados* (charcoal-grilled meats) – including Argentine steak – plus fish and *jamón*. Daily 1–4pm & 7pm–midnight.

Casa Típico Andaluz C/Caridad 55. Another good bet for tapas, with a distinctly *andaluz* flavour as its name implies. The speciality *plaza de toros* gets you a little of everything on one plate for around €8. Daily 1–4pm & 8–11pm.

★ **La Escollera** Puerto Pesquero ☎ 952 806 354. Beneath the lighthouse in the fishing harbour adjoining the Puerto Deportivo, this is a vibrant, very reasonably priced place for excellent sea-fresh fish and *mariscos* – now into its eighth decade, in addition to a great tapas bar there's also a wonderful sea-view terrace restaurant. It's best to book at weekends. Tues–Sun 8am–midnight; closed Sun eve & Mon.

El Palangre C/Cristóbal Colón 20, slightly east of the Plaza de Toros ☎ 952 805 857. Another top-notch, Michelin-starred fish restaurant. A house special is arroz a la marinera con cigalas (seafood paella with king prawns) – a bargain at €20 for two. Other dishes include a wide range of fish and *mariscos* plus octopus from Galicia. There's

also a pleasant sea-view terrace for warmer days. Mon, Tues & Thurs–Sun 1–4pm & 7.30pm–midnight.

Heladería Vitin Plaza Las Flores. For an after-dinner ice cream, this place has the edge, if only for location. Daily noon–11pm.

La Palma C/Terraza 57. Busy tapas and *raciones* bar specializing in fish and *mariscos*, though some meat is served too. Try the *gambas pil-pil* (prawns with chilli and garlic) or *boquerones fritos* (fried anchovies). Daily 11am–11pm.

La Rada Avda. España 4, at the extreme northern end of the seafront. This is a lively and excellent fish restaurant and *marisquería*, if somewhat pricier than its competitors. It also serves *raciones* and *medias* but no tapas. Try their *aguacata con gambas* (avocado with prawns) starter or *pulpo de estepona a la gallega* (octopus). Daily 1–4pm & 7pm–midnight.

Restaurante El Gavilán del Mar Plaza Arce. One of the town's oldest restaurants serving a wide range of fish and *mariscos* as well as meat dishes. It's noted for a *zarzuela* (fish and shellfish terrine), one serving of which is enough for two. Try also their *sardinas asadas* (grilled sardines). Daily 11am–midnight.

Simonito Avda. San Lorenzo 6, near the Turismo. Decent tapas bar restaurant specializing in fried fish with an economical *menú*. Try their *ensalada de patata con bacalao* (potato and cod salad) or the *mejillones al vapor* (mussels). Also has an outdoor terrace. Daily 1–4pm and 7.30–11pm.

NIGHTLIFE

When it comes to nightlife, Estepona has a range of possibilities. There are the usual flamenco burlesques which are best avoided, though Peña Flamenca (see below) is the obvious exception. Near the centre, most night-time action takes place along and in the streets around C/Real, where terrace bars, music places and clubs compete for the custom of a mainly local clientele. *Discotecas* and music bars proper are mostly grouped around the Puerto Deportivo.

Peña Flamenca C/Fuerzas Armadas s/n. In the north of town, this place puts on the genuine stuff on Saturday nights at 10pm (except Aug) with both dance and song; the sessions are free and open to all. The Turismo can provide more information.

Plato 68 Avda. Juan Carlos, 1.3km beyond the Turismo on the left. Huge and glitzy dance club with go-go dancers, live acts and international DJs pulling in crowds from miles around.

FROM TOP MARBELLA (P.113); CASARES (P.124) >

1

DIRECTORY

Festival The town's Feria Anual is held the first week of July and is one of the best on this stretch of coast. Events continue day and night for a week, when whole families of *esteponeros* parade in their flamenco-style finery.

Markets The daily market – a good place for picnic supplies – is located in Plaza Cañada, to the west of C/Terraza. A street market is held in the Puerto Deportivo each Sunday morning.

Casares and around

The greyish coast west of Estepona is punctuated with watchtowers used by peoples as diverse as the Phoenicians, Romans and Arabs to protect themselves from pirate attacks. There's little reason to stop along here, although it's worth detouring to **CASARES**, 18km inland from Estepona. One of the lesser-known of Andalucía's White Towns, it's a beautiful place, clinging tenaciously – and spectacularly – to a steep hillside below a castle and attracting its fair share of arty types and expatriates. The village is reputed to take its name from Julius Caesar, who is said to have used the still-functioning sulphurous springs at nearby Manilva (see below) to cure a liver complaint. There are also the ruins of an impressive Moorish **Alcázar** (built on Roman foundations) offering spectacular views as far as Gibraltar on clear days. Most *andaluzes* know of Casares today as the birthplace of **Blas Infante Pérez de Vargas** (1885–1936), the father of "Andalucian nationalism" and designer of Andalucía's green and white flag, based on historical examples. When Franco's forces took this area early in the Civil War he was summarily executed as a regional autonomist and libertarian socialist, both anathema to the new order. His birthplace now houses the tourist office.

Apart from an excellent museum there's little in the way of sights, but it's satisfying enough simply to wander around, losing yourself in the twisting, narrow white-walled streets – another vestige of the Moorish period. Flanked by an eighteenth-century church, the central plaza is a good place to sit and have a drink, cooled by breezes off the sierra. In addition, the surrounding hill country, richly wooded with cork oaks and pine as well as stands of *pinsapo*, the rare Spanish fir, offers a verdant contrast with the arid plains below and is fine **walking** terrain, with plenty of dirt-tracks to follow winding through the folds of the Sierra Bermeja. The tourist office (see p.125) gives out a free hiking booklet describing a number of routes (in English and Spanish) between 2km and 14km.

Museo de Etnohistoria

C/Villa s/n, to the south of the central Plaza de España • Mon–Fri 11am–2.30pm & 4–6.30pm • €2

At the top of a punishing hill, in one of the gates of the ancient *alcázar* that once stood here, the delightful **Museo de Etnohistoria** (history and folk museum) showcases fascinating displays of Roman artefacts and jewellery found on the site. The folk section of the museum has lots of interesting paraphernalia relating to Casares's agricultural past and cultural traditions, the highlight being a wonderful room dedicated to the role of the cinema in Casares, including the cinema's original projector along with various photos relating to the cinema and its history.

The Roman Sulphur Baths of Manilva

Continuing through the village brings you to a junction on the A377. If you've got your own transport you can turn right here to make the 16km detour to the pretty white town of Gaucín (see p.127). Alternatively, turning left (south) along the same road takes you to the remarkably well-preserved **Roman sulphur baths** (open access). To get here, follow the signs for 3km from Manilva where the road passes beneath a spectacular viaduct carrying the latest extension of the Autopista del Sol.

Park your vehicle here and take the path under the viaduct signed "Zona Verde Publica – Charca de la Mina." Following this path, on your right you'll soon pass

Venta Los Alamos (open for food and drinks Tues–Sun noon until late), reached by a bridge over the river. Continuing along the same path for a further 150m, at the top of a rise, the small chapel of San Adolfo comes into view. It's normally locked so you'll need to keep ahead to where, some 300m beyond, the path descends right to the baths – now under a whitewashed concrete canopy. Here you'll need to don a bathing suit – or perhaps not if there's no one around – and plunge inside to see the original Roman stonework. One dubious souvenir you'll take away from the place is a sulphurous stench, which is guaranteed to cling to your swimwear for weeks.

ARRIVAL AND INFORMATION CASARES

By bus Twice-daily buses (Mon–Sat) leave for Casares from Estepona (currently at 1pm & 7pm; return 8am & 4pm; 45min), meaning, if you're without transport, a very brief visit or an overnight stay.

Turismo The Turismo, downhill from Plaza de España at C/Carrera 51 (Mon–Fri 11am–2.30pm & 4–6.30pm; ☎ 952 895 521), can provide information about activities such as walking and horseriding, and has a list of *casas rurales* to rent for longer stays.

ACCOMMODATION

Hostal Plaza Plaza de España s/n ☎ 952 894 030. Budget-priced hostal with simple but clean rooms with shared bath – some overlooking the picturesque square – above a bar. **€30**

Hotel Casares C/Copera 52 ☎ 952 895 211, ⊛ hotel casares.com. A more upmarket choice, signed from the main square, Plaza de España, and offering pleasant a/c rooms with TV, balcony and views. B&B **€60**

EATING AND DRINKING

La Bodeguita de en Medio Plaza de España s/n. Sited on the main square this is the village's most serious restaurant, offering a combination of *andaluz* and Mediterranean cuisine as well as *casareño* specialities. They have a delightful roof terrace overlooking the square. Daily noon–4pm & 8–11pm.

Mesón Los Claveles C/Arrabal 1, by the church. Very friendly, family-run inn offering economical *platos*

combinados, *tortilla*, salads and (in summer) a delicious gazpacho *casareño* soup. There's also a *menú* for €6. Daily noon–4pm & 7.30–10.30pm.

Venta La Terraza On the exit road in the direction of Estepona. Very good *venta*, with plenty of choice and a pleasant location with great views. House specials are gazpacho casareño (hot gazpacho) and *conejo a la montañesa* (rabbit). Noon–4pm & 7.30–11pm.

The White Towns

Though Andalucía boasts many pretty *pueblos blancos*, the best known are the group of **White Towns** – unfeasibly picturesque places, each with its own plaza, church and tavern – set in the roughly triangular area between Málaga, Algeciras and Seville. At their centre, in a region of wild mountainous beauty, is spectacular **Ronda**, very much the transportation hub and a great attraction in its own right. From Ronda, almost any route north or west is rewarding, taking you past a whole series of lovely little villages, among cherry orchards and vines, many of them fortified since the days of the Reconquest – hence the mass of "de la Frontera" suffixes. Of these, **Arcos de la Frontera**, a truly spectacular White Town perched on a high limestone spur, comes close to Ronda as the best place to spend a few days in the region.

There are several possible approaches to Ronda from the coast. **From Málaga**, most of the buses to Ronda follow a rather bleak route, heading along the coast to San Pedro de Alcántara before turning into the mountains along the A376. The train ride up from Málaga is better, with three connecting services daily.

Easily the most rewarding approach, however, is the route up **from Algeciras via Gaucín**, served by both bus or train or, if you've time and energy, do-able as a four- or five-day walk – worth going out of your way to experience. En route, you're always

1

within reach of a river and there's a series of hill towns, each one visible from the next, to provide targets for the day.

Castellar de la Frontera

Heading north out of Algeciras along the A405, after 24km a signed turn-off on the left leads to **CASTELLAR DE LA FRONTERA**, a bizarre hill village within a thirteenth-century Moorish castle, whose population was moved downriver in 1971 to a "new" town on the edge of nearby La Almoraima. A few locals subsequently moved back to their houses in the old village, but many of the vacated dwellings were taken over by retired hippies (mainly affluent Germans). Perhaps not surprisingly, the result wasn't totally successful, and the two groups didn't gel – reflecting this tension, the place today has a brooding, claustrophobic atmosphere.

ACCOMMODATION AND EATING
CASTELLAR DE LA FRONTERA

Apart from the *Restaurante Aljibe* (see below), the only other places for eating and drinking are a *venta* at the start of the road up to Castellar and the bar near the entrance to the castle.

★ **Convento La Almoraima** Ctra Algeciras–Ronda s/n, just before the turn-off for Castellar ☎ 956 693 002, ⦿ la-almoraima.com. Following the turning on the left signed "Casa Convento" leads through expansive woodlands to this enchanting hotel located inside a renovated seventeenth-century convent with a fine Florentine tower and a restaurant in the former cloister. The rooms are elegantly furnished to four-star standard and there's a pool and tennis court. The hotel is surrounded by vast tracts of wooded walking country in the Parque Natural de los Alcornocales (see below), making it hard to imagine a more serene stopover. **€81**

Hotel-Casas Rurales de Castellar C/Rosario 3 ☎ 956 236 620, ⦿ tugasa.com. Well-equipped rooms (some with outstanding views) built into the castle walls, along with further *casas rurales* accommodation in a number of renovated and well-equipped dwellings. The hotel also runs the decent adjacent *Restaurante Aljibe*, with a *menú* for around €18. Hotel B&B **€70**, casa rural **€68**

Jimena de la Frontera

JIMENA DE LA FRONTERA, 20km further north along the A405, is another hill town, far larger and more open than Castellar, rising to a grand if ruined thirteenth-century Moorish **castle** with a triple-gateway entrance and round keep. In recent years the town has become home to a considerable contingent of British expats, attracted by its proximity to Gibraltar.

Parque Natural de los Alcornocales

Jimena is also a gateway to the **Parque Natural de los Alcornocales**, a vast expanse of verdant hill country stretching south to the sea and north to El Bosque and covered with cork oaks (*alcornocales*) – a haven for large numbers of birds and insects. It's also a paradise for walkers. Tourist offices in this area should stock a *Junta de Andalucía* booklet in straightforward Spanish detailing eight walks of between 2km and 7km in various parts of the park, the first of which takes in the Tajo de las Figuras Neolithic cave paintings near Benalup-Casas Viejas (see p.239). *Walking in Andalucía* by Guy Hunter-Watts (see p.593) also describes half a dozen walks in the park, two starting in Jimena.

ACCOMMODATION
JIMENA DE LA FRONTERA

Camping Los Alcornocales On the north side of town (follow C/Sevilla to its end) ☎ 956 640 060. In a superb location with great views; also rents out en-suite wood cabins and has its own restaurant. Two people plus car. **€18**

Hostal El Anon C/Consuelo 34 ☎ 956 640 113, ⦿ hostalanon.com. The best place to stay in the centre of the village, this charming and welcoming *hostal* offers accommodation in a series of tastefully renovated houses and converted stables, with patio, bar, restaurant and rooftop pool. Rooms come with a/c and TV and free wi-fi. B&B **€65**

Hostal Los Arcos Avda. Reina de los Angeles 8 ☎ 956 640 328. A little way out at the train station, this place has decent rooms with bath, as well as its own restaurant. **€40**

EATING

Bar Ventorrillero C/Sevilla s/n. At the foot of C/Sevilla, this friendly bar-restaurant serves good value tapas and *raciones* with a lunchtime *menú* for around €8. They have a twin and equally rustic bar-restaurant *El Pastor*, on nearby Plaza de la Constitución.

Restaurante Bar Cuenca Avda. de los Deportes 31. A decent bar-restaurant for the usual meat and fish dishes. Competent, if slightly pricier than *Bar Ventorrillero*, the ambience is more refined, which is what you're paying for, and it also has a pretty terrace patio at the rear.

Gaucín

Beyond Jimena the A369 climbs for 23km through cork oak woods and olive groves to reach **GAUCÍN**, just beyond the Málaga border. Almost a mountain village and perched on a ridge below yet another Moorish fort, Gaucín commands tremendous views and makes a fine place to stay. The village has a prosperous air sustained by a long-standing community of British and other European emigrants.

The station serving Gaucín is actually at **El Colmenar** on the Algeciras–Ronda line. The village – in reality a hamlet – consists of little more than a couple of rows of houses, bars and restaurants each side of the railway line and station.

Castillo del Aguila

C/de Gaucín s/n • Tues–Sun 11am–1pm & 4–6pm • Free

The village's only attraction of any note is the **Castillo del Aguila**, a Moorish castle reached by a track at the eastern end of the village. From the battlements there are great views across terrain studded with olive, oak and chestnut trees to Gibraltar and even the Moroccan coast beyond on a very clear day. Easter Sunday is always celebrated here with a fiesta and *encierro* (bull run), when beefy fighting bulls career through the streets looking for partying inebriates to get their horns into.

ARRIVAL AND DEPARTURE

GAUCÍN

By bus You can reach Gaucín by bus on weekdays with Transportes Comes (☎ 952 871 992, ⌨ www.tgcomes.es) from Algeciras (currently Mon–Fri 6.15am) and from Ronda with the same company (currently Mon–Fri 1.45pm).

By train The nearest train station is at El Colmenar, 13km

distant, on the line between Algeciras and Ronda (3–4 trains daily in each direction). It's a two- to three-hour uphill walk from here to Gaucín (there's no bus service). Alternatively, a taxi can be arranged outside the station at Bar Flores for around €20 one way.

ACCOMMODATION

GAUCÍN

Hostal Santa Isabel ☎ 952 151 324. Decent en-suite rooms above a restaurant next to the petrol station (where you should enquire about rooms) as you come into the village from Jimena; get a room at the back for a view of the Serranía de Ronda – now somewhat obscured by a recent housing development. **€40**

Hotel Rural Fructuosa C/Convento 67 ☎ 952 151 595, ⌨ lafructuosa.com. Near the centre, this is a charming upmarket option owned by the restaurant of the same name (see p.128). All the lovely rooms come with a/c and most enjoy spectacular views. They produce their own walks leaflets and also rent out a couple of equally attractive houses in the village for longer stays (see website). B&B **€98**

EL COLMENAR

Hacienda la Herriza Ctra Gaucín–El Colmenar ☎ 951 068 200, ⌨ laherriza.com. An inviting *hotel rural* halfway between El Colmenar and Gaucín comprising seventeen one- or two-bedroom suites in woodland with a pool and restaurant. Horseriding is one of numerous activities on offer. B&B **€107**

Hotel Buitreras Pista Forestal s/n ☎ 952 153 070, ⌨ www.serraniaronda.org/html/hotelbuitreras.htm. Across the tracks, this is an attractive hotel with comfortable a/c rooms and dorm beds. It's also a walker-friendly place and can provide copious information about some great hiking in the area, as well as advice on rock-climbing, canyoning and horseriding. Dorms **€15**, rooms **€60**

EATING AND DRINKING

GAUCÍN

Bar Paco-Pepe C/de los Bancos 3, off C/San Juan de Díos. Excellent tapas and *platos combinados* are served at this

homely bar with a pleasant outdoor terrace on a plazuela with spluttering fountain. Try the *croquetas* (croquettes) or equally tasty *jamón serrano*. Daily 9am–11pm.

1

Bonissim C/Luís Armiñán 54, opposite the Hotel Rural Fructuosa. Superb English-run delicatessen/shop/café that bakes breads, pastries and pies and squeezes its own juices. Tapas are on offer too, as well as lasagne, pasta, tagines and a range of salads, all to eat in or take away.

La Fructuosa C/Convento. In the same building as the *Hotel Rural Fructuosa*, this mid-priced restaurant offers delicious traditional cooking with a Mediterranean slant. *Rabo de toro* (bull's tail stew) is a house special and the kitchen uses local *setas* (wild mushrooms) and goat's cheese in many of its dishes. Main dishes €12–19. Mon–Wed 1–4pm, Thurs–Sat 1–4pm & 8–11pm; only opens Thurs–Sat out of high season (July & Aug).

La Fuente C/Toledillo 13, above the fountain on Plaza del Santo Miño (the main plaza) ☎952 151 368. A pleasant mid-priced restaurant with an eclectic menu ranging from Thai coconut prawns to Indian curry and Argentinian steaks. Also has some has vegetarian options, and there's a roof terrace. Main dishes €14.50–20. Mon–Sat 7.30pm–midnight.

Venta Pilar Down the steps across from the petrol station at the entrance to the village. Reliable *venta* serving the usual standards and *platos combinados*; there's also a terrace. Daily noon–4pm & 7–11pm.

Venta Socorro Ronda road. Probably wouldn't win any beauty prizes for its exterior but the kitchen is good and produces a range of tapas and *platos combinados* and is noted for its *chorizo*. Daily 9am–11pm.

EL COLMENAR

Café-Bar España Avda. de Santiago 44 (the main street fronting the station). A friendly and good place to eat, with tapas, *raciones* and a *menú* for €7.50. Daily 9am–11pm.

Rincón del Cani C/Ruiz Zorrilla 2, behind Bar Las Flores. Very good bar-restaurant, popular with locals and serving up a range of local specialities including – in season – *setas* (wild mushrooms), *alcachofas aliñadas* (marinaded artichokes) and a mean gazpacho. Daily 10am–11pm.

Bar-Restaurante Las Flores Opposite the station. Colmenar's main bar-restaurant is a lively place specializing in *venado* (venison) and *jabalí* (wild boar), and offering a weekday *menú* for €7. Daily 8.30am–11pm.

Benarrabá, Algatocín and Jubrique

Five kilometres beyond Gaucín a turn-off from the Ronda road leads to the village of **BENARRABÁ** sited amidst glorious wooded hill country. If you are using this as a staging post on a hiking route to Ronda, there's useful accommodation at La Jimera de Libar (see box, p.142), from where you're within striking distance of Ronda.

A couple of kilometres from Benarrabá, the village of **ALGATOCÍN** (take the road on the left – the A373 – a couple of kilometres along the A369 beyond the Benarrabá turn-off) offers another possible base, while 2km further along the A369 and then right along the MA8301, **JUBRIQUE** is another attractive hill village sited in the midst of more picturesque *serranía* walking country.

INFORMATION

BENARRABÁ, ALGATOCÍN AND JUBRIQUE

Walking Guy Hunter-Watts's book *Walking in Andalucía* (see p.593) has an 11km circular walk from the *Hotel Rural* *Banu Rabbah* (see below), which takes in the picturesque hill village of Genalguacil.

ACCOMMODATION AND EATING

BENARRABÁ

Bar Barroso C/Posito 16, near the Ayuntamiento. In the village proper, which is a nice way to stretch your legs if you're staying at the hotel, this cosy bar is noted for its tapas and in particular the *salchichón* and locally cured *jamón serrano*.

Hotel Rural Banu Rabbah C/Sierra Bermeja s/n ☎952 150 288, ⓦhbenarraba.es. Adopting the village's original Moorish name, this very pleasant hotel has comfortable a/c balcony rooms with TV and stunning views, pool and a good restaurant and bar. €60

ALGATOCÍN

Hotel-Camping Salitre ☎952 117 005, ⓦturismo salitre.com. Attractive complex of hotel, cabins and campsite in wooded surroundings, offering all kinds of outdoor activities as well as a full-blown observatory for use by guests. Almost next door, the *Venta Valdivia* is renowned for its *conejo asado* (grilled rabbit) and is a hugely popular Sunday lunch venue. Cabins €60, hotel B&B €75

JUBRIQUE

Hotel Taha Baja Calle Algatocín ☎952 152 376. This inviting and inexpensive hotel, with its own restaurant, offers another good potential base for exploring the area. €30

Ronda

Rising amid a ring of dark, angular mountains, the full natural drama of **RONDA** appreciated as you enter the town. Built on an isolated ridge of the sierra, it's spl half by a gaping river gorge (El Tajo, though the river itself is the Guadalvín) that sheer for 130m on three sides. Still more spectacular, the gorge is spanned by a stupendous eighteenth-century arched bridge, the **Puente Nuevo**, while tall white-washed houses lean perilously from its precipitous edges.

This extraordinary setting was bound to be a magnet when mass tourism hit the nearby Costa del Sol, but the town has taken this in its stride, sacrificing little of its enchanting character to the flow of day-trippers that frequently fills the central areas to bursting point. And to escape the crowds (who anyway tend to return to the coast at sundown) there are always quieter corners to be found throughout the old Moorish quarter or, expending a little more energy, simply walking down by the river, following one of the donkey tracks through the rich green valley.

The town divides into three parts: on the northwest side of the gorge is the largely modern **Mercadillo** quarter, while across the bridge is the old, maze-like Moorish town, **La Ciudad**, and the **Barrio de San Francisco** quarter. The astonishing El Tajo and its magnificent bridge apart, Ronda has a wealth of other sights and museums that can easily fill a couple of days. In the Mercadillo quarter stands the eighteenth-century **Plaza de Toros** that played a major role in the development of bullfighting, while in the *barrio* of La Ciudad stands the **Iglesia de Santa María La Mayor**, built on the site of a former mosque. Nearby, the **Palacio de Mondragón** contains some impressive remnants of Islamic artistry. From the same epoch date the remarkable **Baños Arabes**, a Moorish *hammam* or public bathhouse, one of the best preserved in Spain. Among a clutch of galleries and museums the pick is perhaps the **Museo Lara**, a fascinating and eclectic collection put together by its eponymous owner, while the **Museo del Bandolero** chronicles the history of the brigands who once roamed the surrounding sierra.

Brief history

Not surprisingly, this dramatic and dominant location attracted not only the early Celts, who named it Arunda, but Phoenicians and Greeks as well. Under Rome it became an important military bastion referred to by Pliny the Elder as Arunda Laus ("the glorious"). When the Moors later came to rule the roost here, Medina Runda was transformed and enlarged into the provincial capital of the Tarakuna district. Embellished with lavish mosques and palaces, the town ruled an independent and isolated **Moorish kingdom** until annexed by Seville in the mid-eleventh century. It then passed successively through the hands of the Almoravids, Almohads and Merinid Emirate of Morocco before ending up as a fief of Nasrid Granada in 1349. Only after a long and bitter struggle did the town finally fall to Fernando and Isabel in 1485.

Ronda is also notable for having been the birthplace of the **Maestranza**, an order of knights who laid down the rules for early bullfights performed on horseback. During the nineteenth century the town became an increasingly popular destination for Romantic travellers, epitomized by author Richard Ford, who describes being awestruck when gazing down from the bridge into El Tajo, able only to proclaim: "Well done, rock and water, by Heavens!"

La Ciudad

Ronda's oldest quarter, **La Ciudad** retains much of its Moorish street plan and a great many of its original houses, interspersed with a number of fine Renaissance mansions – an intricate maze tumbling down to the eighteenth-century **Puente Nuevo**, suspended between walls of limestone rock high above the yawning El Tajo and the Río Guadalvín far below.

RONDA

▲ Marbella

▲ **16**, Algeciras & campsite

■ **ACCOMMODATION**

Alavera de los Baños	5
En Frente Arte	3
El Paso	4
Hostal Andalucía	2
Hostal Doña Carmen	7
Hostal Ronda Sol	8
Hotel Arunda I	1
Hotel Arunda II	6
Hotel Colón	18
Hotel Morales	11
Hotel Don Miguel	13
Hotel El Tajo	15

Hotel Montelirio	17
Hotel Polo	9
Hotel Reina Victoria	20
Hotel Ronda	12
Hotel San Gabriel	14
Hotel Virgen de	
los Reyes	10
Jardín de la Muralla	11
Los Pastores	16
Parador de Ronda	19

■ **NIGHTLIFE**

Dulcinea	1
El Grifo	2
El Paso	4
El Templo	5
Pub Baco	3

● **RESTAURANTS**

Almocabar	8
Atrium	22
Bodega San Francisco	16
Casa María	17
Casa Santa Pola	9
Don Miguel	14
Doña Pepa	11
Parador de Ronda	21
Restaurante del Escudero	23
Restaurante Pedro Romero	18
Tragabuches	19

● **CAFÉS & TAPAS BARS**

Bar Faustino	1
Bar Maestro	12
Bodeguita el Coto	5
Café Alba	2
Casa Mateos	20
Chocolat	10

El Portón	15
La Farola	3
Pastelería Daver	6
Patatín Patatán	7
Rico	4
Tragatapas	13

BARRIO
PADRE
JESÚS

BARRIO
PEÑAS

BARRIO
DE SAN
FRANCISCO

LA
CIUDAD

EL
MERCADILLO

Baños
Árabes

Palacio del Marqués
de Salvatierra

Puente de San
Miguel

Puente
Viejo

Ntro.
Padre
Jesús

Fuente de
los 8 Caños

Arco de
Felipe V

Casa del
Rey Moro

Cvto. Madre
de Dios

Posada de
las Ánimas

Virgen de
los Dolores

Círculo
de Artistas

Convento de
la Merced

Ciber
Mundial

Walid Telecom

Bus
Station

Train
Station

Plaza de
Toros

Puente
Nuevo

Minarete de
S. Sebastián

Museo del
Bandolero

Museo
Lara

Museo
Peinado

Ayuntamiento

Alcázar

Iglesia del
Espíritu
Santo

Puerta
Almocábar

Sta. María
la Mayor

Palacio de
Mondragón

Casa Juan
Bosco

Municipal
Turismo

Plaza
de España

Arroyo de las Culebras

Río Guadalevín

N

200
metres

Málaga & Arriate

▲ Seville

▼ Seville

Puente Nuevo

Centro de Información Mon–Fri 10am–7pm, Sat & Sun 10am–3pm • €2

The late eighteenth-century **Puente Nuevo** bridge spans the gorge between the Mercadillo quarter and La Ciudad, allowing you the chance to peer down the walls of limestone rock into the gorge, with the river – a mere brown sliver – far away in its depths. The bridge has its own **Centro de Información**, housed in a former prison above the central arch, with exhibits documenting the story of its construction and history. Hemingway, in *For Whom the Bell Tolls*, recorded how prisoners were thrown from the bridge to their deaths. Today the bridge and the gorge provide a habitat for a large flock of choughs (members of the crow family) who glide around the rock cliffs seeking perches. Birdwatchers should look out for the lesser kestrels, nesting in and launching themselves from beneath the bridge and the nearby Alameda park, while, lower down, crag martins can be spotted.

Casa del Rey Moro

C/Marqués de Parada (aka C/Santo Domingo) • Daily 10am–7pm • €4

Crossing the Puente Nuevo into La Ciudad brings you to the somewhat arbitrarily named **Casa del Rey Moro** (House of the Moorish King), an early eighteenth-century mansion built on Moorish foundations. Local legend has it that this was the palace of the Moorish emir Badis, an Arabian Bluebeard, who was reputed to drink his wine from the skulls of the victims he had beheaded. From the house a remarkable underground stairway (the Mina) descends to the river at the foot of the Tajo; these 365 steps, guaranteeing a water supply in times of siege, were cut by Christian slaves in the fourteenth century. There's a viewing balcony at the bottom where you can admire the towering walls of rock and the gorge's birdlife, but the long climb back up will probably make you wonder if it was worth the stiff entry fee. Take care on the way back up as the steps tend to be slippery and there have been a number of falls.

Palacio del Marqués de Salvatierra

C/Marqués de Parada

Further down the same street is the **Palacio del Marqués de Salvatierra**, a splendid Renaissance mansion with an oddly primitive, half-grotesque frieze of Adam and Eve on its portal together with the colonial images of four Peruvian Indians; the house is still used by the family and so isn't open to the public.

The Baños Árabes

Cuesta de Santo Domingo s/n • Mon–Fri 10am–7pm, Sat & Sun 10am–3pm • €3, free on Mon.

Just down the hill you reach the two old town bridges – the **Puente Viejo** of 1616 and the fourteenth-century single-span Moorish **Puente de San Miguel**. Nearby, on the southeast bank of the river, are the distinctive hump-shaped cupolas and bizarre glass roof-windows of the wonderfully preserved thirteenth-century **Baños Árabes** (public bathhouse), with remarkable star-shaped windows set in a barrel-vaulted ceiling and beautiful octagonal brick columns supporting horseshoe arches. An aqueduct carried water from the nearby river to the bathhouse complex which was formerly surrounded by plant-filled gardens. One room shows a film on the history of the baths every fifteen minutes.

Minarete de San Sebastián

Uphill from the Baños Arabes, following Calle Marqués de Salvatierra, stands the **Minarete de San Sebastián**, a surviving tower from a fourteenth-century mosque which was razed to make way for the church of San Sebastián. This also fell into disrepair and was demolished, leaving the minaret standing alone.

1

Museo del Bandolero

C/Armiñán 65 • Daily 10.45am–7.30pm • €3.50

The **Museo del Bandolero** is largely devoted to celebrating the Serranía's illustrious, mainly nineteenth-century bandits who preyed on richer travellers and merchants and were greatly feared. The museum includes displays of their weapons and possessions as well as tableaux and audiovisual presentations.

The Alcázar

A little further along the same street, near the southern end of La Ciudad, are the ruins of the **Alcázar**, once impregnable until razed by the French in 1809 and now partially occupied by a school.

Museo Lara

C/Armiñán 29 • Daily 11am–8pm • €4

On the main street which bisects La Ciudad, this interesting museum contains the eclectic lifetime collection of *rondeño* Juan Antonio Lara, a member of the family who own and run the local bus company of the same name. An avid collector since childhood, Señor Lara has filled the extensive museum with a fascinating collection of antique clocks, scientific instruments, pistols and armaments, musical instruments and archeological finds, as well as early cameras and cinematographic equipment, all superbly displayed.

Santa María La Mayor

Plaza Duquesa de Parcent • Daily 10am–7pm, Sun 10am–12.30pm & 2–8pm • €3

At the centre of La Ciudad in Ronda's most picturesque square stands the cathedral church of **Santa María La Mayor**, originally the town's Friday Mosque. Externally it's a graceful combination of Moorish, Gothic and Renaissance styles, with a double gallery overlooking the square and the belfry built on top of the old minaret. Inside, the church itself is sombre and dull but you can see an arch covered with Arabic calligraphy, and, in front of the current street door, a part of the old Arab *mihrab*, or prayer niche.

Museo Joaquín Peinado

Plaza del Gigante • Mon–Fri 10am–6pm, Sat & Sun 10am–3pm • €4

Close by, to the rear of the cathedral, the **Museo Joaquín Peinado** displays the works – influenced by Cézanne and Picasso – of *rondeño* artist Joaquín Peinado (1898–1975), a Paris contemporary and close friend of Picasso in the 1920. The museum's seven rooms display a varied selection of his output, with room 6 ("Nudes and Erotica") featuring paintings in a similar style to Picasso, particularly the ink wash entitled *Desnudo acostado*. The museum is housed in the Palacio de Moctezuma, a former aristocratic mansion with two fine patios.

Palacio de Mondragón

Plaza de Mondragón • Mon–Fri 10am–7pm, Sat & Sun 10am–3pm • €3

A short distance west from Santa María La Mayor is the most important of Ronda's palaces, the fourteenth-century **Palacio de Mondragón**. Probably the royal palace of the Moorish kings, following the *Reconquista* it was much altered in order to accommodate Fernando and Isabel. Inside, three of the patios preserve original stuccowork and mosaics and there's a magnificent carved wood ceiling; the palace also houses a **museum** covering local archeology and aspects of Moorish Ronda, in particular burial practices relating to the recently discovered cemetery outside the walls (see p.133). From a restored Mudéjar courtyard there's a fine **view** over the Tajo towards the Serranía de Ronda.

Casa de San Juan Bosco

C/Tenorio 20 • Daily 9am–6pm • €1.50

Close to the Puente Nuevo bridge lies the **Casa de San Juan Bosco**, a nineteenth-century mansion stuffed full of heavy mahogany furniture. The house itself is dull and oppressive, but the reconstructed Mudéjar gardens with fountain and mosaics are a delight, offering more great views over the Tajo.

Iglesia del Espíritu Santo

Tues–Sat 10am–2pm • €1

Moving downhill along Calle Armiñán, close to the Barrio de San Francisco you'll pass the sixteenth-century **Iglesia del Espíritu Santo**, a fine sandstone church with an elegant vaulted interior, constructed at the behest of King Fernando (see below) in 1485 and finished twenty years later.

Puerta de Almocábar

Continuing beyond the Iglesia del Espíritu Santo leads to the town's principal Moorish gate, the magnificent **Puerta de Almocábar** leading into the Barrio San Francisco. Deriving from the Arabic *al maqabir* (cemetery) it would have led to the burial grounds which – following the Roman practice – were always located outside the walls. In 1485, the Christian conquerors, led by Fernando, passed through this gate to claim the town. The adjoining arch of **Puerta de Carlos V** was constructed during the reign of Fernando's successor, the Habsburg emperor.

El Mercadillo

When Ronda was retaken from the Moors in 1485, the impoverished governors imposed such heavy taxes on all goods and foodstuffs entering it that the merchants set up their own quarter outside La Ciudad to avoid paying them. This area, **El Mercadillo**, has effectively become the centre of the modern town, and is currently undergoing a prolonged face-lift after years of neglect. Many buildings in and around the focal Plaza de España have undergone renovation, among which is a stylish *parador* (see p.137) – the former Ayuntamiento – overlooking the Tajo. A recently constructed path, the **Paseo Blas Infante** (and its continuations the Paseo O Welles and Paseo E Hemingway) at the rear of the *parador*, can be followed along the edge of the Tajo northwards to the Alameda and the *Hotel Reina Victoria* and offers fine **views** towards the Serranía de Ronda.

Plaza de Toros

Daily 10am–8pm • €6

The *barrio's* major monument is the **Plaza de Toros**, the oldest, one of the largest and certainly the most venerated bullring in Spain. Opened in 1785, it became the stage

---

PEDRO ROMERO: FATHER OF THE CORRIDA

Born in Ronda in 1754, Pedro Romero is the father of the modern **bullfight**; previously bulls had been killed only on horseback with a *rejón* or spear, as a patrician pastime. However, Romero was not the first to fight bulls on foot: legend has it that this accolade goes to his grandfather Francisco Romero, who leapt into the ring when an aristocrat had been dismounted by a bull and began to distract it with his hat, delighting the crowd in the process. The hat was changed for the red *muleta*, or cape, and the bullfight was born. Once the *corrida* had been created, however, it was Pedro Romero who laid down the pattern for all future contests with his passes and moves, many still in use today, along with the invention of the almost mystical *arte* – the union of animal and man in a form of ballet. In the newly constructed Ronda ring, Romero killed over five thousand bulls and fought into his eighties, passing on to his students his soberly classical Ronda style, which is markedly different from the more flamboyant styles of Seville and Córdoba. A statue honouring Romero stands in the Alameda del Tajo.

1

upon which the father of the modern bullfight, Pedro Romero, laid down the rules of fighting bulls on foot (see box, p.133). Once you've passed through the elaborate Baroque doorway, it's possible to wander around the arena with its unusual stone barriers and an elegant double tier of seats supported by stone columns.

The **museum** gives an illuminating history of the *corrida* (bullfight); besides posters advertising the first *corrida* held here on May 19, 1785, and Pedro Romero's *traje de luces* ("suit of lights"), there are photos of Hemingway and Orson Welles, two regular visitors. Welles's last wish was to have his ashes buried in Ronda and they are now interred on the nearby estate of his friend and one of Spain's greatest *toreros*, the *rondeño* Antonio Ordóñez, whose bronze statue (alongside that of his father) stands near the bullring's Puerta Grande. The artist Goya made a number of paintings here of the *matadores* in action, and each September in a tribute to Goya and Romero the *corrida goyesca* is staged, with fighters garbed in eighteenth-century-style gear similar to those in the paintings.

La Bola and Plaza del Socorro

A short distance along the pedestrianized **Carrera Espinel** (known colloquially as "La Bola" by *rondeños*), the Mercadillo *barrio*'s main thoroughfare and shopping street, the picturesque **Plaza del Socorro** opens to the left. Also recently pedestrianized, the square has become a favourite spot with *rondeños*, especially on summer nights, when they gather to chat on the terraces of the numerous bars and restaurants. The northern end is overlooked by the **Círculo de Artistas**, a fine eighteenth-century *casa señorial* mansion, now superbly restored as the town's casino. The doorman usually won't object to you stepping inside to have at look at the building's delightful patio.

Alameda del Tajo

Open 24hr • Free

To the north of the Plaza de Toros lies the **Alameda del Tajo**, a pleasant park completed in the early nineteenth century with views towards the Serranía de Ronda. The garden – filled with mature plane trees offering welcome shade in summer – is said to have been laid out at no cost to the local council, the funds raised by fines on those using "obscene language in public, thereby causing a scandal".

Convento de la Merced

Plaza de la Merced • Church: daily 10.15am–1.15pm & 4.45–6.45pm; the hand of Santa Teresa can be viewed on request between 5pm and 6.45pm (when an English-speaking nun will be on duty) by ringing ☎ 952 872 965.

Slightly north of the Alameda lies the elegant Renaissance Carmelite **Convento de la Merced**, its main door flanked by two great palms. Beyond lies an impressively large triple-naved church built in sandstone. The convent (closed to visitors) is home to the **hand of Santa Teresa**, one of Spain's most venerated saints. When Teresa died her incorrupt remains (confirming sainthood) were distributed among the Carmelite order (which she had reformed) and Ronda got the left hand. At the end of the Civil War, General Franco, a devoted admirer of the saint, seized the hand and slept with it by his bedside until he died in 1975, after which it was returned to the convent in 1976.

Beyond a doorway at the end of the short street to the left of the church, the nuns sell their *dulces* (10am–1.15pm and 5–6.45pm) via a *turno* (dumb waiter): *pan rondeño* and *magdalenas* are specialities. British chef Jamie Oliver visited the shop in one of his TV programmes in 2010 and raved about the quality of the convent's cakes and buns, which he described as "little drops of heaven."

Hotel Reina Victoria

Avda. Fleming (aka C/Jerez)

From here, it's a short walk to the **Hotel Reina Victoria**, built by an English company in the first decade of the last century to house British visitors, many of whom came from the military base at Gibraltar. The Austrian poet Rainer Maria Rilke put up here in

1913, and his room (no. 208) – complete with his fascinating framed hotel bill – has been preserved as a museum which the management will allow you to view on request (after 2pm). The hotel's bar has a terrace with stunning views down the Guadiaro river valley to the distant Serranía.

Virgen de los Dolores

C/Virgen de los Dolores s/n

A couple of minutes east from the Plaza de España lies the eighteenth-century **Virgen de los Dolores**. This chapel has a curious porch projecting into the street. Carved on the porch's pillars are some weird, bird-like creatures, as well as others that are part beast and part human, with ropes fastened around their necks. The site of the church was formerly a gallows for condemned prisoners and this strange imagery may be a representation of these unfortunates.

ARRIVAL AND DEPARTURE   RONDA

By bus The bus station is on Plaza Concepción García Redondo s/n, to the north of the centre (☎ 952 872 260).
Destinations: Algeciras (1 daily; 2hr 45min); Antequera (1 daily; 1hr 45min); Arcos (2 daily; 2hr 30min); Cádiz (2 daily; 3hr 15min); Jerez (2 daily; 3hr 30min); Málaga (9 daily; 1hr 45min); Marbella (4 daily; 1hr); Olvera (1 daily; 1hr 30min); San Pedro de Alcántara (5 daily; 1hr 5min); Setenil (1 daily; 1 hr 15min); Seville (5 daily; 2hr 30min); Ubrique (2 daily; 1 hr 30min); Zahara de la Sierra (1 daily Mon–Fri; 55min).

By train The train station is at Avda. de la Victoria 31, off Avda. de Andalucía (☎ 952 871 673). There's a RENFE office for tickets and timetables at C/Infante 20, near the Plaza del Socorro.
Destinations: Algeciras (5 daily; 2hr 15min); Bobadilla (3–4 daily; 55min).

By car For street parking your best bet is to park as far out as possible (near the train station is usually feasible) and walk to the centre, or head straight for one of the pay car parks (clearly signed).

INFORMATION

Turismo The helpful Turismo at Plaza de España 9 (Mon–Fri 9am–7.30pm, Sat & Sun 9.30am–3pm; ☎ 952 871 272) has detailed town maps and walking information on the Serranía de Ronda (see p.141), plus details of organizations offering guided walks.
Turismo Municipal Paseo Blas Infante s/n, facing the south side of the Plaza de Toros opposite the south side of the bullring (Mon–Fri 10am–7pm, Sat 10am–2pm & 3–5pm, Sun 10am–2.30pm ☎ 952 187 119, ⊛ turismo deronda.es). Another good office with copious information on Ronda and the Serranía.

Internet Ciber Ronda Telecom C/Jerez 4 (daily 11am–2pm & 4–11pm), Mundial, C/Cruz Verde 21 (Mon–Sat 10am–2pm & 4–10pm, Sun 4–10pm) and Ciber Walid Telecom, C/Jerez 4 (daily 10.30am–3pm & 4.30–11.30pm) are reasonably central options.
Post office Virgen de la Paz 20, near the Plaza de Toros (Mon–Sat 9am–2pm). The town has no post boxes.
Festivals The Feria Goyesca takes place in the first week in September when *corridas* take place in the bullring with matadors wearing eighteenth-century costumes. Semana Santa (Holy Week) is also a wonderful spectacle in Ronda.

ACTIVITIES

Outdoor activities Sierraventura Ronda, C/Sevilla 16 (☎ 636 291 714, ⊛ sierraventuraronda.es) offers all kinds of outdoor activities in and around Ronda including guided hiking, climbing, mountain biking, canoeing, canyoning and caving. Horseriding is available with Picadero La Granja, Camino de los Molinos del Tajo 27 (☎ 952 875 956). Birdwatching trips in the Serranía for beginners and

experienced birders are offered by Spanish Nature (☎ 616 891 359, ⊛ spanishnature.com).
Maps and equipment Hiking maps of the Serranía de Ronda and Grazalema are available from Librería Dumas, C/Jerez 8, near the Plaza de la Merced. Intersport, C/Molino 8 (opposite the *Hotel Polo*), stocks a range of outdoor clothing and walking boots.

ACCOMMODATION

Many of the best places to stay are in the heart of the Mercadillo quarter, and to the east of the Plaza del Socorro off C/Borrego and its continuations, C/Cristo and then C/Almendra. Upmarket accommodation was once concentrated around the Plaza de Toros, but a number of excellent small hotels have recently sprung up in other parts of the Mercadillo quarter as well as La Ciudad quarter, across the Tajo bridge. Prices increase sharply during Semana Santa and the Feria Goyesca bullfight festival (usually the first week in Sept) but are otherwise reasonable.

1

BUDGET

Camping El Sur Ctra. Ronda–Algeciras km 2.8 ☎ 952 875 939, ⓦ campingelsur.com. Sited a couple of kilometres out of town along the road to Algeciras, Ronda's campsite is well equipped with swimming pool, bar and a decent restaurant. You can rent bungalows here, too. It's not served by bus, so if you don't fancy the walk, take a taxi (approximately €10). Two people plus car **€18**

Hostal Andalucía C/Martínez Astein 19 ☎ 952 875 450, ⓦ hostalandalucia.net. Functional but comfortable a/c en-suite rooms (some more spacious than others) in leafy surroundings opposite the train station. Free wi-fi, plus parking for €5 per day. **€42**

Hostal Doña Carmen C/Naranja 28 ☎ 952 871 994, ✉ mturrillo@yahoo.es. Pleasant, friendly family-run *hostal* for a/c rooms with bath and TV. Also has some simpler rooms sharing bath. En suite **€55**, shared bath **€35**

Hostal Ronda Sol C/Cristo 11 ☎ 952 874 497. Good-value budget *hostal* for rooms with shared bath, but check what you're offered as the two interior rooms (lacking windows) are a bit claustrophobic. Free wi-fi. **€25**

Hotel Arunda I Carrera Espinel 120 ☎ 952 190 102, ⓦ hotelesarunda.com. Small and good-value hotel with a/c rooms (including singles). Some rooms come with balcony, and there's also a garage (€8 per day) and free wi-fi. **€39**

Hotel Arunda II C/José María Castelló Madrid 10 ☎ 952 872 519, ⓦ hotelesarunda.com. Slightly more expensive offshoot of the above near the train and bus stations, this is equally good for a/c rooms with satellite TV. Computer with internet access plus free wi-fi and plenty of parking space in own garage (€8). **€39**

Hotel Colón C/Pozo 1 ☎ 952 870 218, ⓦ hcolon.es. Charming and friendly small hotel with sparkling a/c en-suite facilities and – in rooms 301 & 302 – your own spacious roof terrace. Free wi-fi zone. **€48**

Hotel Morales C/Sevilla 51 ☎ 952 871 538, ⓦ hotelmorales.es. Welcoming small hotel where en-suite rooms come with TV and a/c and there's free internet access and wi-fi for guests. **€45**

Hotel Virgen de los Reyes C/Borrego 13 ☎ 952 871 140. Congenial two-star hotel offering bright, airy and reasonably priced en-suite rooms with a/c and TV. Free wi-fi. Can assist with parking. **€80**

MODERATE TO EXPENSIVE

★ **Alavera de los Baños** C/San Miguel s/n ☎ 952 879 143, ⓦ alaveradelosbanos.com. Enchanting small hotel next to the Moorish baths with compact but elegant a/c rooms, garden and pool. Rooms at the rear have fine views towards grazing sheep on the hill across the river. B&B **€95**

★ **En Frente Arte** C/Real 40 ☎ 952 879 088, ⓦ enfrentearte.com. Stylish hotel inside a restored mansion with distinctive and elegant a/c rooms. Breakfast-brunch is included in the price as are self-service soft drinks and

self-serve beer from a pump in the bar. Additional luxuries include a delightful garden pool and games room plus free sauna and Internet and wi-fi access. B&B **€86**

Hotel Don Miguel C/Villanueva 8 ☎ 952 877 722, ⓦ dmiguel.com. Pleasant hotel with comfortable rooms overlooking the Tajo and a decent restaurant (see p.137). Garage. B&B **€108**

Hotel El Tajo C/Cruz Verde 7 ☎ 952 874 040, ⓦ hotel eltajo.com. Pleasant traditional hotel with refurbished a/c rooms with satellite TVplus own café-restaurant. Garage for €10 per day. **€65**

Hotel Montelirio C/Tenorio 8 ☎ 952 873 855, ⓦ hotel montelirio.com. Spectacularly sited on the edge of the Tajo, this luxury four-star hotel occupies a tastefully renovated *casa palacio* where most of the well-equipped a/c rooms have stunning views. It also manages to squeeze in a small pool and a very good restaurant, the *Albacara*. **€162**

Hotel Polo C/Mariano Soubirón (C/Benitez on some maps) 8 ☎ 952 872 447, ⓦ hotelpolo.net. This long-established hotel has stylishly renovated a/c rooms with sparkling bathrooms and elegant fittings. Wi-fi zone. B&B **€110**

★ **Hotel Reina Victoria** C/Jerez 25 ☎ 952 871 240, ⓦ husa.es. Nineteenth-century retreat for British military visitors from Gibraltar which, although refurbished (and now part of the Husa chain), has a lingering air of decaying grandeur. Ask for one of the corner rooms with a stunning view over the Serranía de Ronda. Facilities include a pool, gardens and parking. Website special offers can make this a real bargain. B&B **€85**

Hotel Ronda Ruedo Doña Elvira 12 ☎ 952 872 232, ⓦ hotelronda.net. Charming flower-bedecked five-room hotel in a quiet street only minutes from the Tajo bridge. Rooms are light and airy, with a/c and free wi-fi. **€77**

★ **Hotel San Gabriel** C/José Holgado 19 ☎ 952 190 392, ⓦ hotelsangabriel.com. Stunning restoration of an eighteenth-century mansion, with beautifully furnished a/c rooms, plus a wonderful five-seater cinema with tip-up seats (for guests) with a collection of classic films on DVD. Friendly proprietors and free wi-fi. **€92**

Jardín de la Muralla C/Espíritu Santo 13 ☎ 952 872 764, ⓦ jardindelamuralla.com. Charming hotel in La Ciudad situated in a wonderful eighteenth-century *casa palacio* with classically furnished rooms, many overlooking a delightful leafy garden with pool. Ten percent discount for *Rough Guide* readers with this guide. **€91**

Los Pastores 4km outside town along the Algeciras road (A369); take right turn 400m after 4km sign ☎ 952 114 464, ⓦ www.fincalospastores.com. Very pleasant rural option in a remodelled former farmhouse surrounded by fine walking country and offering stylish and attractively furnished a/c rooms and apartment-rooms, many with terraces, and all with DVD & CD player. Activities include horseriding lessons and hiking; breakfast available. Rooms **€75**, apartments **€89**

Parador de Ronda Plaza de España ☎952 877 500, ⓦparadores.es. This imposing and relatively new *parador* teetering on the edge of the Tajo is Ronda's flagship hotel, a superb and tasteful building (the former *ayuntamiento*) with luxurious accommodation, pool, terrace bar, restaurant and garage. Free wi-fi. **€180**

EATING, DRINKING AND NIGHTLIFE

Many of Ronda's best eating and drinking options are to be found on or around the pedestrianized Plaza del Socorro, the area to the south of Plaza de Toros and in the Barrio de San Francisco, which has recently acquired some very good bars and restaurants. There are numerous good places for breakfast along Carrera Espinel, and a couple of good restaurants in La Ciudad. For tapas aficionados there are plenty of quality places to try out. Nightlife tends to be provincial and low-key, but with a little persistence and luck you may catch some memorable flamenco.

RESTAURANTS

★ **Almocabar** C/Ruedo Alameda 27, Barrio San Francisco ☎952 875 977. Excellent tapas bar with an equally good restaurant behind. Creative variations on regional dishes are served in the restaurant along with a range of salads such as the *ensalada almocobar*, including figs, cheese, pear and honey. Reservations advised. Main dishes €12–20. Mon & Wed–Sun 1.30–4.30pm & 8–11.30pm.

Atrium C/Blas Infante s/n. Pleasant all-day cafeteria 50m from the Plaza de Toros serving a range of interesting salads, pizzas and meat and fish dishes as well as a €20 paella (for two). Reasonable wine prices and an attractive terrace. Daily 12.30–11pm.

Bodega San Francisco C/Ruedo Alameda 32, close to the Puerta de Carlos V in the Barrio San Francisco. This highly popular tapas bar has opened an equally good restaurant just opposite in this atmospheric *barrio*. The tapas are excellent and the restaurant specializes in *carnes a la brasa* (charcoal-grilled meats). Main dishes €9–13. Mon–Wed & Fri–Sun 11am–1am.

Café-Bar Faustino C/Santa Cecilia 4. Excellent, economical and atmospheric café-bar serving up meals, tapas, *raciones* and *platos combinados* right up until the small hours. Tues–Sun noon–1am.

Casa María C/Ruedo Alameda 27, Barrio San Francisco ☎952 876 212. Chef Elías Vega's little restaurant doesn't have a menu – he cooks whatever inspires him on the day. Excellent fish and meat dishes and – as he's a wine aficionado – one of the best cellars in Ronda. Reckon on about €30–40 per person upwards. Mon, Tues & Thurs–Sun 12.30–4.30pm & 7.30–11.30pm.

Casa Santa Pola C/Santo Domingo 3 ☎952 879 208. Impressive, expensive restaurant in a former *casa palacio* containing bits of the ninth-century house that preceded it. Spread over three floors, with views over the Tajo, it offers a wide range of local dishes – the house speciality is *carnes asados* (charcoal-roasted meats). Main dishes €14–19. Daily 12.30–4.30pm & 7.30–10.30pm.

Don Miguel Hotel Don Miguel, Plaza de España ☎952 877 722. One of the town's leading restaurants, with *rondeño* specialities such as *solomillo de venado* (venison) on the à la carte menu; their unimaginative *menú del día* for €18 is less exciting. The main attraction, though, is the terrace, offering a marvellous view of the Tajo. Main dishes €11–18. Daily 12.30–4pm & 7.30–10.30pm.

Doña Pepa Plaza del Socorro. Decent, family-run restaurant with a shaded terrace. offering a variety of *menús del día* priced between €13–17 which often include paella and *calamares*. Daily 10am–2pm & 9–11pm.

★ **Parador de Ronda** Plaza de España ☎952 877 500. The *parador*'s restaurant has an excellent choice of local and regional dishes such as *cochinillo asado* (suckling pig), many of them appearing on a good-value *menú gastronómico* for €45. Their lunch (€23) and dinner (€33) *menús* are also good value. Main dishes €19–27. Daily 1–4pm & 8–11pm.

Restaurante Albacara Hotel Montelirio, C/Tenorio 8 ☎952 873 855. Excellent, albeit expensive, restaurant with one of the best terraces in town enjoying a stupendous view towards the Serranía de Ronda. The kitchen is top-notch and turns out a variety of *rondeño* specialities among which the *rabo de toro* (stewed bull's tail) and *solomillo de ciervo* (venison loin) are standouts. *Menú de degustación* for €64 (including wine). Main dishes €17–22. Daily 1–4pm & 7.30–11pm.

Restaurante del Escudero Paseo de Blas Infante 1 ☎952 871 367. Very good restaurant specialising in carnes asados (grilled meats), although it also serves fish. It's housed in an elegant mansion with one of Ronda's best garden terraces offering views towards the Serranía de Ronda. Main dishes €15–23, plus *menú* for around €12. Daily 12.30–4.30pm & 7.30–11pm.

Restaurante Pedro Romero C/Virgen de la Paz 18 ☎952 871 110. Excellent, mid-priced restaurant with an attractive main room, serving up signature dishes including *rabo de toro* (stewed bull's tail) and *magret de pato al vino de málaga* (duck breast in wine); there's also a *menú* for around €17. In winter months locals dine in the interior room surrounded by bullfighting memorabilia. Daily 12.30–4pm & 7.30–11pm.

Tragabuches C/José Aparicio 1 ☎952 190 291. Ronda's most stylish, acclaimed (Michelin-starred) and seriously expensive restaurant is named after a celebrated eighteenth-century *rondeño* bullfighter-turned-bandit and, with an adventurous menu and minimalist decor, is worth a splurge if you're into taste sensations rather than a filling your stomach. Current head chef Benito Gómez learned his

1

trade at Ferran Adrià's *El Bulli* so there's lots of chemistry, textures, flavours and foam. A signature dish is *cordero lechal* (suckling lamb) with creative cordón bleu trimmings. *Menús de degustación* €60–95, main dishes €25–33. Booking advised. Tues–Sun 1–4pm & 8.30pm–midnight, closed Sun eve & Mon.

TAPAS BARS

★ **Bar Maestro** C/Espinel 7. One of Ronda's oldest tapas venues, this great hole-in-the-wall establishment offers a tempting menu recited verbally by proprietor Rafael Peña. It's also a *bar taurino*, so the photos of past *torero* greats plus Ernest and Orson (all one-time customers) gaze down from the walls. Try their *pinchos de gambas* (prawns) or *costillas* (ribs) or paella. Mon–Sat 7.30am–midnight.

Bodeguita El Coto C/Nueva 6. Excellent and popular new tapas bar with a winning formula: tapas and beers cost €1 each. Try their *carne mechada* (larded pork) or *boquerones en vinagre* (marinaded anchovies). Has some tables outdoors on this pedestrianized street. Mon, Tues & Thurs–Sun noon–4pm & 7pm–midnight.

Casa Mateos C/Jerez 6. Efficient *marisquería* and tapas bar with plenty of seafood possibilities as well as good *jamón* and *queso*. House specials include *alcachofas gratinadas* (artichokes with cheese) and *choricitos al vino* (chorizo in wine). Tues–Sun 11am–11pm.

El Portón C/Pedro Romero 7, off the west side of Plaza del Socorro. Favourite haunt of bullfighting aficionados; their *lomo de cerdo rondeño* (pork) or *cazón* (shark) tapas; also serves an inexpensive *menú*. Daily 1–4pm & 8.30–11pm.

La Farola Plaza Carmen Abela 9. Tapas at the bar or *bocadillos*, *platos combinados* and salads on a pleasant terrace. Try the *merluza a la vasca* (hake). Mon–Sun 8am–11.30pm.

Patatín Patatán C/Borrego 7, off the east side of Plaza del Socorro. Popular tapas bar with a wide range of specials – try their *ensalada de pulpo* (octopus) or *chorizo al vino*. *La Viña*, next door at no.9, is also good. Mon, Tues & Thurs–Sun 11am–4pm & 7–11pm.

Tragatapas C/Nueva 4. An offspring of Ronda's most famous restaurant, *Tragabuches*, this new tapas bar reflects the ultramodern decor of its progenitor and serves up reasonably priced tapas and *pinchos* with a creative slant. Try the *pollo con coco y curry* (chicken with coconut and curry sauce), *tempura de alcachofa* (artichoke) or *salmón en vainilla y limón*. Has a street terrace. Tues–Sat 1–4pm & 8pm–midnight, Sun 1–4pm.

CAFETERÍAS, BREAKFAST BARS AND HELADERÍAS

Café Alba Carrera Espinel 44. Popular place serving up piping hot *churros* and delicious breakfast coffee. If it's full, the nearby *Cafetería La Ibense* is a good alternative.

Chocolat Carrera Espinel 9. This chocoholic's heaven has 32 different flavours of handmade chocolate in addition to dozens of different teas and seven kinds of coffee in its café. Delicious home-made cakes and tarts, too.

Pastelería Daver C/Los Remedios. Great *pastelería* and café with some tempting confections to go with a tea or coffee – try their *mousse de chocolate con turrón* (chocolate mousse cake).

Rico Carrera Espinel 42, south side of the Plaza del Socorro. The nicest *heladería* (ice-cream bar) in town – also good for afternoon tea and, in winter, steaming cups of hot chocolate.

NIGHTLIFE

Flamenco performances by the Escuela de Danza Pilar Becerra are staged in the Círculo de Artistas de Ronda, Plaza del Socorro, on Mon, Tues & Wed at 10pm (€23 including one drink). Reservations and further details on ☎ 952 871 046. A more commercial show "Flamenco Fusion" is offered by the *Restaurante Doña Pepa* on the same square (see p.137) on Thurs, Fri & Sat (May–Aug only) at 8pm (☎ 952 874 777 for reservations). Tickets cost €32 for dinner and the concert that follows.

Dulcinea C/Río Rosas 3. Late-night music and *copas* bar with a more laidback style and less-deafening sound levels than some of the competition. Daily 4pm–3am.

El Grifo C/Virgen de los Remedios 2, near Plaza del Socorro. Stylish late-night drinking bar for cocktails and long drinks with the gimmick of table-top beer pumps, staying open into the small hours. Also serves international beers plus tapas and *raciones*. Tues–Sun 1–4pm & 8pm–midnight.

El Paso C/Amanecer 8, Barrio San Francisco. Popular music bar in a *barrio* not known for its wild side. Stays open into the small hours. Tues–Sun 3pm–3am.

El Templo C/Jerez 6. Central and popular *bar-discoteca* with a jazz and rock playlist; shows music videos and occasionally stages live bands.

Pub Baco C/Molino, at the north corner of Plaza del Socorro. Lively music bar popular with a younger crowd. Daily 4pm–late.

Around Ronda

Ronda makes an excellent base for exploring the superb countryside in the immediate vicinity, or for visiting more of the White Towns, including the unusual **Setenil de las**

Bodegas, 15km away, with its curious cave-like streets. If you're attracted by ancient ruins and awesome caves don't miss Ronda's Roman predecessor **Ronda La Vieja** or the **Cueva de la Pileta**, whose remarkable Stone Age cave paintings are unique on the peninsula. To the west are the temptingly scenic villages of **Benaoján** and **Montejaque**, ringed by rugged limestone heights that hold numerous underground caverns such as the Cueva del Gato, a magnet for cavers.

Ronda La Vieja

Some 12km northwest of Ronda are the ruins of **RONDA LA VIEJA**, the first-century Roman town of Acinipo, set in the midst of beautiful hill country. In spite of the site's name there was no relationship between this and modern Ronda, although stone from the ruins of Acinipo was carted away to build up the town of medieval Ronda.

The ruins

Wed–Sun 10am–2pm (although these are susceptible to change; you can check latest times with either tourist office in Ronda or by calling ✆ 670 945 451; English spoken) • Free • There are no bus services to Ronda La Vieja

The **ruins** are reached by leaving Ronda on the Arcos–Seville road (A374). After 6km turn right at a signed turn-off ("Acinipo, Ronda la Vieja") along the MA7402, following this, and its continuation the MA8406, for 16km to reach the site. Upon arrival you will give your details (for statistical purposes) to the guardian and in return will receive a free site plan (in Spanish).

  Based on Neolithic foundations, Acinipo served as a Phoenician outpost but reached its zenith in the first century AD as a Roman town. The piles of stones interspersed with small fragments of glittering marble strewn across the hillside once constituted the forum, baths, temples and other edifices of this prosperous agricultural centre (its coins depicted grapes, a major economic asset), which also had access to iron ore, marble, good building stone and fine potters' clay in close proximity.

  Today only an impressive **Roman theatre** – of which just the stage backdrop and some seating survives – alludes to the importance of Acinipo; inscriptions found here tell of crowds flocking to see the chariot races. Immediately west of the theatre, the ground falls away in a startlingly steep escarpment and from here there are fine **views** towards the hill village of Olvera to the north (see p.232). For reasons not entirely clear, Acinipo declined in the third century and, in the fourth, ceded its power in the area to nearby Arunda (modern Ronda). On your way out take a look at the foundations of some recently discovered prehistoric stone huts beside the farmhouse. From here a track leads off towards Setenil de las Bodegas (see below).

Setenil de las Bodegas

Six kilometres northeast of Ronda La Vieja as the crow flies, and slightly longer along the MA8406, **SETENIL DE LAS BODEGAS** is the strangest of all the White Towns, its cave-like streets formed from the overhanging ledge of a gorge carved through the tufa rock by the Río Trejo. Many of the houses – sometimes two or three storeys high – have natural roofs in the rock that, in places, block out the sky completely. This was once a major wine-producing centre, since the caves made good wine cellars (*bodegas*); hence the latter part of the town's name. The phylloxera plague of the nineteenth century destroyed the vines, however, and brought economic ruin in its wake, from which Setenil has only in recent times recovered.

  From Setenil it's possible to walk the 6km to the ruins of Ronda La Vieja via the hamlets of Campiña and Venta de Leche.

La Encarnación and the castillo

The village's most impressive monument is the Gothic–Mudéjar church of **La Encarnación**, built over the site of the mosque that stood here in Moorish times. If you can gain access (ask the neighbours or contact the tourist office) you'll see a fine, twelve-panelled

1

sixteenth-century Flemish painting that survived Civil War devastation. The ruins of the nearby Moorish **castillo** are worth a look too.

ARRIVAL AND INFORMATION — SETENIL

By bus There is an infrequent bus service from Ronda to Setenil (around 1 daily).

By train Setenil train station is 8km east of the village.

Tourist information Setenil's Turismo (Tues–Sun 10am–2pm & 6–8pm; ⊕956 134 261, ⊛setenil.com) is housed in the former Ayuntamiento at C/Villa 2, below the church. It has a superb Mudéjar *artesonado* ceiling with an inscription dating from September 21, 1484 – the day Isabel and Fernando captured the town. They achieved this triumph only after seven previous attempts (septem nihil – seven times nothing) had failed, giving origin to the first half of Setenil's name today.

ACCOMMODATION AND EATING

El Almendral Ctra Setenil s/n ⊕956 134 029, ⊛tugasa.com. On the road just outside town, with comfortable, recently refurbished rooms, an Olympic-size pool and a good restaurant downstairs. **€60**

Bar-Restaurante Dominguez Plaza de Andalucía s/n. This long-established bar-restaurant at the heart of the village is a solid country hostelry serving up *carnes de caza* (game) in its restaurant, and tapas and *raciones* in the bar. There's a pleasant terrace on the square.

Bar-Restaurante Las Flores Avda. del Carmen 24 (near the river at the opposite end of the town from the church). This welcoming bar with some fine views from its dining room serves tapas, *raciones* and *platos combinados* and there's an economical *menú* for under €10.

El Mirador C/Callejón 10. Reached through an arch uphill from the tourist office, this modern restaurant offers well-prepared meat and fish dishes as well as *jamón* and *salchichón*. There's a weekday *menú* for €8.50 and a special weekend *menú* for €15.

Cueva de la Pileta

Daily 10am–1pm & 4–6pm • Hourly guided tours; final tours leave at 1pm & 6pm (or 5pm Nov–March) • €8

Probably the most interesting trip out from Ronda is to the prehistoric **Cueva de la Pileta**, set in a deep valley and surrounded by a spectacular wall of white rock. These fabulous caverns, with their remarkable Paleolithic paintings, were discovered by a local farmer in 1905 when hunting for guano fertilizer for his fields, and are still supervised by the same family, the Bullóns, one of whom will be your guide.

After the usual jokes, as various "cauliflowers", "castles" and a "Venus de Milo" are pointed out among the stalactites and stalagmites en route, the paintings in the depths of the caves, when you reach them, are genuinely awe-inspiring, particularly those in the central chamber. Etched in charcoal and red and yellow ochres, they depict an abundance of wildlife including fish, the *cabra hispánica* and a pregnant mare, all painted on walls which bear the scorch marks of ancient fires. Other abstract signs and symbols have been interpreted as having some magical or ritual purpose. The occupation of the caves, and the earliest red paintings, dates from about 25,000 BC, thus predating the more famous caves at Altamira in northern Spain, through to the end of the Bronze Age. The section of the caves (and paintings) open to view is only a small part of a more massive subterranean labyrinth, and archeologists will be kept busy for many years to come documenting this Paleolithic art gallery.

ARRIVAL AND TOURS — CUEVA DE LA PILETA

By car Take the A374 Arcos/Seville road northwest from Ronda, turning left after 14km along the MA8403 to Montejaque; the caves are a further 12km from the turn-off, beyond Benaoján.

By bus The bus from Ronda drops you in Benaoján. There's a bar at the train station where you can stock up on drink before the 90min (6km) walk to the caves. Follow the farm track from the right bank of the river until you reach the farmhouse (approximately 30min). From here a track goes straight uphill to the main road just before the signposted turning for the caves.

By train Take an Algeciras-bound local train (4 daily; 20min) to the Estación Benaoján-Montejaque. From the station follow the route described in the bus section above.

By taxi A taxi from Ronda costs around €50 return – get the Turismo to arrange the fare – though renting a car for a day could work out cheaper.

Tours Upon arrival wait at the cave entrance; a strict maximum of 25 people are allowed on each tour and groups larger than four should book ahead (⊕952 167 343; also useful for confirming opening times). Tours are in Spanish (though the guide may speak some English), and last one hour on average. No photography is allowed in the cave and if you leave your vehicle at the car park, make sure to remove any valuables not locked in a secure boot. And finally, remember to bring a sweater as it can get chilly in the caverns.

The Serranía de Ronda

Starkly beautiful and offering some of the best walking terrain in Andalucía, the **Serranía de Ronda** is a region of great natural diversity where wooded ravines, awesome crags and vast forests of cork oaks provide abundant habitats for a rich variety of flora and fauna. The remote hamlets are reachable by road, albeit often with difficulty, but the ideal way to travel this region is with a backpack and compass, from which perspective the landscape – with whitewashed villages set among cherry orchards and vines – becomes an enchanting adventure. Both the Ronda tourist offices (see p.135) should have details on the villages and the limited accommodation available.

ARRIVAL AND INFORMATION

THE SERRANÍA DE RONDA

By bus The heart of the Serranía can be reached by a daily bus from Ronda run by Autobuses Lara (Mon–Fri 2.30pm, returning early morning), passing Parauta, Cartajima, Juzcar, Igualeja, Pujerra, Alpandeire and Farajan.

Tourist information ⓦ serraniaronda.org provides a comprehensive guide to the *pueblos* of the region including places to eat, drink, sleep and camp. The Centro de Iniciativas

Turísticas de la Serranía de Ronda, C/Espíritu Santo, near the Barrio de San Francisco in Ronda (Mon–Fri 10am–1pm; ☏ 952 870 739, ⓦ serraniaronda.org), has a list of *casas rurales* to rent throughout the Serranía.

Maps The best maps of the Serranía are the 1:200,000 IGN Mapa Provincial de Málaga, complemented by the 1:50,000 IGN sheet, number 1065.

ACCOMMODATION

Hotel Bandolero Avda. Havaral 41, Juzcar ☏ 952 183 660 ⓦ hotelbandolero.com. A pleasant country hotel offering good a/c rooms with terrace and *chimenea* (wood-burning fire). The hotel has its own decent restaurant and bar on the ground floor. Free wi-fi. B&B **€58**

Hotel Casa Grande C/Barranco 76, Alpandeire ☏ 952 180 400, ⓦ hotelcasagrande.es. Charming hotel in a refurbished eighteenth-century mansion. The

individually styled rooms come with a/c, heating and satellite TV. B&B **€58**

La Molienda C/Moraleda 59, Benalauría ☏ 952 152 548. In another charming village on the Serranía's western flank, this is an excellent small country restaurant and *casa rural* with four en-suite heated rooms with great views. The very good restaurant below has a terrace with more fine views. **€40–50**

Benaoján

North of the Cueva de la Pileta, **BENAOJÁN** takes its name from the Berber tribal chieftan Ojan (the village's name means "sons of Ojan"). The village was a Moorish stronghold well into Christian times, but its history goes much further back than that and evidence has been found of early human occupation hereabouts dating back some 250,000 years. Neanderthal man also tramped through this sierra landscape, while *homo sapiens* left behind the cave paintings in nearby Cueva de Pileta (see p.140).

There are in fact two villages here: the old village around the church and a smaller hamlet gathered around the train station a good kilometre below The old village is a pleasant enough place, gathered around its sixteenth-century church of Nuesta Señora del Rosario in Plaza San Marcos, itself built on the site of an earlier mosque.

ACCOMMODATION

BENAOJÁN

Los Pintores C/Presbitero José Moreno 20 ☏ 952 167 516, ⓦ hotelrurallospintores.com. Attractive new hotel run by two working artists (hence the name) offering pleasant rooms decorated with the owners' artworks. Also has own restaurant and bar. B&B **€80**

Molino del Santo Bda. Estación, near the train

station, 1km below the village on the Ronda road ☏ 952 167 151, ⓦ molinodelsanto.com. The village's upmarket option is a British-run haven in a converted water-mill with elegantly furnished rooms – many with terraces – surrounded by lush gardens and a pool. B&B **€110**

1

A WALK FROM BENAOJÁN TO JIMERA DE LIBAR

There's a fine, none-too-taxing **walk** from Benaoján to the attractive village of Jimera de Libar, 9km down the railway line linking the two communities. When you've reached Jimera you could take in a well-earned lunch at the *Restaurante Quercus* and return to Benaoján on the afternoon trains – currently leaving Jimera station at 5.09pm (daily) and 8.15pm (weekdays only). Confirm current times with either of the Ronda tourist offices or the *Hotel Inz-Almaraz* (see below). It's useful to take a **map** with you (50:000 IGN sheets 1050 & 1064); alternatively, the walk is described with its own map in Guy Hunter-Watts' *Walking in Andalucía* (see p.593).

The walk begins from the *Molino del Santo* hotel (see p.141). Turn left from the hotel and head downhill until you come to a stop sign at a level crossing. Turn left along the railway line, cross over a river, and at a second level crossing turn right and cross over the railway track. The road drops before crossing the Río Guadiaro and leads up to a sign marking the official start of the walk. The route from here is fairly straightforward except for a fork just beyond a ruined farm (after 3km), where you should veer left, away from the river. At a second fork at a telegraph pole just before Jimera bear right (*not* towards Camino de Huertas Nuevas) to follow the path down to the train station of Jimera de Libar. The walk ends here but see below if you wish to eat at *Restaurante Quercus*. You could also stay overnight at the village's *hotel rural* or its campsite.

ACCOMMODATION AND EATING

Camping Jimera de Libar ☎ 952 180 102, ⟨w⟩ rural -jimera.com. Located near the train station, this leafy campsite also rents out fully equipped en-suite log cabins and has a pool. Two people plus car **€16**, cabins **€56**

Hotel Rural Inz-Almaraz C/Mártires de Igueriben 18 ☎ 952 180 120, ⟨w⟩ inz-almaraz.com. A very pleasant small hotel offering comfortable rooms with TV. It also has its own decent restaurant. The proprietor will pick up guests from and return them to the train station if you ring. B&B **€49**

Restaurante Quercus Bda. Estación s/n ☎ 952 180 041. The food on the mid-priced menu is good – the vegetables come from their own *huerta* – and creatively assembled. Try the *habitas con morcilla* (broad beans with blood sausage). There are vegetarian options and they have a selection of Ronda wines. To reach the restaurant, cross the railway tracks and turn right when you reach the station at the end of the walk – the restaurant is housed in the former station building, actually on the tracks.

EATING

Bar El Encuentro (aka Bar Conejo) Avda. Constitución s/n, opposite the roundabout at the foot of the main street. One of a number of bars in the village proper, offering simple but tasty tapas and *raciónes*. Daily 9am–midnight.

Molino del Santo Bda. Estación. Mid-priced restaurant at the *Molino del Santo* hotel (see p.141), serving up very good food on a terrace beside the tumbling falls that once turned the *molino* (watermill) itself. The cuisine is a mix of *andaluz* and international, with meat, fish and vegetable dishes, plus *menús* (lunch €22, dinner €39). Main dishes €14–24. Daily 1–4pm & 8–10.30pm.

Bar Stop Opposite the train station. A good value bar-restaurant with a shady outdoor terrace. Opens for breakfast and later serves up *venta*-style food along with tapas, *raciones* and a *menú* for €8. Daily except Sat 1–4pm & 8–11pm.

★ **Restaurante El Muelle** Train Station ☎ 952 167 508. One place definitely worth seeking out is this friendly *asador*, actually on the platform at the train station in a converted *muelle* (warehouse). Its speciality is *carnes al horno de leña* (charcoal grilled meats) including game, but fish is also served and comes up fresh on the train from Algeciras. Thurs–Sun 1–4pm & 7.30–11pm.

Montejaque

Some 3km northeast of Benaoján lies the attractive pueblo blanco of **MONTEJAQUE**, cradled between two rocky crags. At its heart it possesses a typically Spanish square – the Plaza de la Constitución – surrounded by bars and a hotel and overlooked by an elegant Ayuntamiento and the sparkling white church of Santiago. Built in the sixteenth-century, with a few later modifications, this is yet another church constructed on the site of a mosque. The narrow, winding streets are a further legacy of the settlement's Moorish roots – the village's name derives from the Arabic *monte-xaquez* (lost mountain), probably referring to the nearby thousand-metre peak of El Hacho.

INFORMATION

Turismo Avda. de Andalucía 45, the entry road into the village (Mon–Sat 10am–2pm & 5–8pm; ☎ 952 167 550).

There's also a small attached shop where you can buy village produce including cheeses and cured meats.

ACCOMMODATION

Casas de Montejaque C/Manuel Ortega 16 ☎ 952 168 120, ⓦ casasdemontejaque.net. A similar operation to the *Casitas de la Sierra* (see below), with a range of refurbished village houses for rent. See the website for offers. **€75.50**

Casitas de la Sierra Avda. Andalucía 1 ☎ 952 167 392, ⓦ casitasdelasierra.com. Fully equipped village houses

with a minimum stay of two nights, assuming there's a property available. **€76.50**

Hotel Montejaque Plaza Constitución 2 ☎ 952 167 252, ⓦ hotelmontejaque.com. Occupying the former ducal palace of the Conde de Benavente on the main square, this charming hotel has comfortable and well-equipped rooms with free wi-fi, plus a restaurant and small pool. B&B **€75**

EATING

Montejaque has no less than fifteen tapas bars. These have recently produced a Ruta de Tapas leaflet with map – available free from the tourist office, *Bar Rincón* (see below) and *Hotel Montejaque* (see above) on the main square.

Bar-Restaurante La Reja Avda. Andalucía 69, on the entry road into the village. A good little bar-restaurant which does tapas and *raciones* as well as full meals. House specials are *cordero a la brasa* (lamb) and *rabo de toro* (stewed bull's tail) and there's a weekday *menú* for €7.50.

Bar Rincón Plaza de la Constitucíon 1. In the corner of the main square (hence the name), this is a friendly bar for tapas and *raciones*. House specials include *ensaladilla de*

patatas (potato salad) and chorizo *al vino* (chorizo in wine). Closed Tues.

Bar Montexaquez Oliva José Vázquez 2, off the main square. Part shop, part bar, this "gourmet" delicatessen is run by builder Juan in his spare time. It also serves up some unusual tapas – and you get a drink and a *tapa* for €1. Try the *setas a la plancha* (grilled mushrooms) or the tasty mature goat's cheese. The shop sells top-quality olive oils, marinaded olives and local cheeses. Open Thurs–Sun.

Cueva del Gato

Ctra Ronda–Benaoján • Open access • Free

Returning to Ronda along the direct road from Benaoján (MA7401), after 2km you'll pass the *Venta Cueva del Gato* (see below) on the left, while a short distance beyond the *venta* a signed road on the left leads down to the *Hotel Cueva del Gato* (see below), where you should park any vehicle.

From just beyond here a path leads to a footbridge across the Río Guadiaro and a tunnel beneath the rail line to arrive at the gaping mouth of the **Cueva del Gato**, a cave fronted by an oleander-fringed lagoon (a popular bathing spot). Continue ahead to a viewing platform overlooking a spectacular waterfall gushing out of the cave. Given the close proximity of the Cueva de la Pileta (see p.140) it seems likely that this cave, too, may well have been occupied by early humans, but no paintings have so far been discovered. The cave is open to all but to penetrate much further than 50m you'll need ropes, lights and some expertise. This is most easily done by contacting climber Jean Hofer at El Chorro (see p.81), who leads fully equipped explorations of the cave and its dramatic subterranean lakes (approximately €90 per person, equipment included).

ACCOMMODATION AND EATING

CUEVA DEL GATO

Hotel Cueva del Gato Ctra. Ronda-Benaoján Km3 ☎ 952 167 296, ⓦ hotelcuevadelgato.com. Comfortable a/c balcony rooms with TV in a stone building facing the cave; also has its own bar and restaurant. B&B **€99**

Venta Cueva del Gato Ctra. Ronda-Benaoján s/n. A couple of kilometres outside the village of Benaoján

towards Ronda, this locally celebrated roadside *venta* is famed for its superb *conejo casero* (grilled rabbit). They also do excellent paella and rice dishes as well as hearty mountain specials like asparagus and vegetable soups. Daily 1–4pm & 8–11pm.

Cádiz province

FERIA IN JEREZ DE LA FRONTERA

Cádiz province

Cádiz province is the most southerly in Andalucía, with a two-hundred-kilometre coastline fronting both the Atlantic and the Mediterranean. Inevitably, the sea has played a large part in the area's history, and most of the province's dozen or so major settlements are within easy distance of a beach. The province's mountainous interior, dotted with numerous picturesque villages, contrasts sharply with the coast and holds two of Andalucía's largest natural parks.

Founded by the Phoenicians over three millennia ago, the provincial capital, **Cádiz**, makes up for in sheer elegance, atmosphere and sea-girthed location what it lacks in the way of irresistible sights. South of Cadiz stretch the broad white beaches of the **Costa de la Luz**, large swathes of which have so far survived the developers' attentions and are often deserted. Resorts such as **Conil**, **Chipiona** and **Sanlúcar de Barrameda** possess a low-key charm, while at the southern tip of the coast, **Tarifa** has developed into a major windsurfing and kitesurfing centre. A short distance to the west lies **Algeciras**, Andalucía's main port for sailings to Morocco, while across the Bay of Algeciras the British colony of **Gibraltar** sits beneath its daunting mountain of rock, regarded uneasily by Spaniards and as a strange, hybrid curiosity to almost everyone else.

Inland, the province offers a fascinating variety of towns and landscapes. Immediately north of Cádiz lies the famous **sherry triangle** between **Jerez**, a fine town in its own right, **Puerto de Santa María** and **Sanlúcar de Barrameda**, with the oldest vineyards in Europe spread across thousands of acres of dazzling white chalk soil. Further west stretches a landscape of rolling hills covered with clumps of walnut trees, pines and Spanish firs, while *toros bravos* – ominous black fighting bulls – graze in the shade of cork oaks and ranches around **Medina Sidonia**.

Further inland still, the northeastern corner of the province is dotted with hill-top White Towns such as **Zahara**, **Olvera** and **Arcos de la Frontera**, while the green oasis of **Grazalema**, the wettest point in Spain, is surrounded by a fine natural park, a paradise for walkers and naturalists. There's further excellent hiking south of here in the vast, rugged **Parque Natural de Los Alcornocales**, home to one of the largest cork oak forests in the world.

KITESURFING IN TARIFA

Highlights

❶ **Gibraltar** This colonial hangover with its vast rock, sterling currency and Barbary apes makes a bizarre contrast with the rest of Andalucía. **See p.151**

❷ **Costa de la Luz** The "Coast of Light" stretching from Tarifa to the Portuguese border has some of the finest – and emptiest – beaches in Spain. **See p.162**

❸ **Tarifa** One of the world's top windsurfing destinations and also home to a wonderfully atmospheric old Moorish town. **See p.162**

❹ **Cádiz** A beguiling air of genteel decay pervades this old sea town, one of the great cities of the Spanish south. **See p.181**

❺ **Jerez** Visit a sherry bodega and sample the legendary aperitivo at one of the town's numerous tapas bars. **See p.214**

❻ **Pueblos Blancos** The White Towns of Cádiz province are picturesque settlements of whitewashed houses set amid spectacular scenery. **See p.226 & p.231**

❼ **Parques naturales** Get away from it all in the natural parks of Sierra de Grazalema and Los Alcornocales, site of Europe's largest cork oak forest. **See p.226 & p.238**

HIGHLIGHTS ARE MARKED ON THE MAP ON P.148

Campo de Gibraltar

Beyond Estepona (p.120) the scenery along the coast road heading south towards the **Campo de Gibraltar** (the administrative area to the north and west of Gibraltar) takes on a wilder and greener aspect as the Sierra Bermeja yields to the Sierra Almenara. The provincial border of Cádiz is crossed and beyond the estuary of the Río Guadiaro, the road turns inland, offering, as it climbs, distant views of the Rock of Gibraltar, its monumental silhouette often girdled with a halo of cloud. The views of the urban sprawl, towers and storage tanks of the Bay of Algeciras's oil refineries signal that this is also a major industrial zone.

San Roque

Now a rather undistinguished small industrial town, **SAN ROQUE**, 18km from the provincial border, was founded in 1704 by the people of Gibraltar fleeing the British,

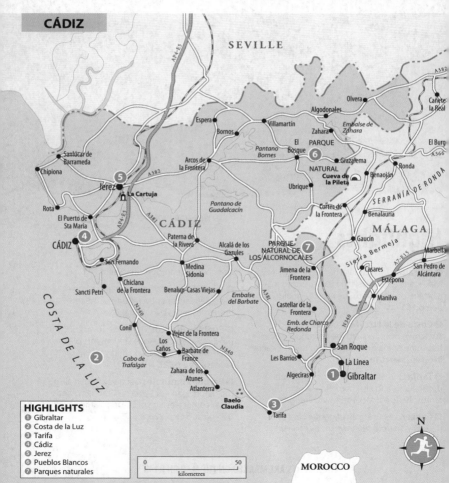

CÁDIZ

SEVILLE

Olvera
Cañete la Real
Algodonales
Espera
Villamartín
Zahara
Bornos
Embalse de Zahara
El Bosque
El Burg
Santúcar de Barrameda
Arcos de la Frontera
Pantano Bornes
PARQUE
Grazalema
Ronda
Chipiona
NATURAL
Cueva de la Pileta
SERRANÍA DE RONDA
Jerez
La Cartuja
Pantano de Guadalcacín
Ubrique
Benaoján
Rota
Cortes de la Frontera
Benalauria
El Puerto de Sta María
CÁDIZ
Paterna de la Riverá
Gaucín
MÁLAGA
Alcalá de los Gazules
CÁDIZ
PARQUE NATURAL DE LOS ALCORNOCALES
Marbella
San Fernando
Benalup-Casas Viejas
Jimena de la Frontera
Casares
San Pedro de Alcántara
Sancti Petri
Chiclana de la Frontera
Medina Sidonia
Estepona
Embalse del Barbate
Castellar de la Frontera
Manilva
Conil
Emb. de Charco Redonda
COSTA DE LA LUZ
Vejer de la Frontera
Los Caños
San Roque
La Linea
Cabo de Trafalgar
Barbate de France
Les Barrios
Zahara de los Atunes
Algeciras
Gibraltar
Atlanterra
Baelo Claudia
Tarifa

N

MOROCCO

HIGHLIGHTS
1. Gibraltar
2. Costa de la Luz
3. Tarifa
4. Cádiz
5. Jerez
6. Pueblos Blancos
7. Parques naturales

0 ——— 50
kilometres

REAL ALE COMES TO ANDALUCÍA

Many British expats who have moved to Spain regret the fact that they've had to give up British real ale as part of the price of changing countries. But a microbrewery based in Los Barrios has now come to the rescue, producing a very good version of English-style real ale using traditional methods. The company, **Fábrica de Cerveza Kettal** (a rather lame pun on the Spanish greeting *Que tal?*), is producing six beers under the direction of head brewer Jonah Jones, a long-time brewmaster from Leigh in Lancashire.

The beers range from La Espiga, a wheat beer, to the treacly El Yunque porter. But the star of the show has to be El Almiar, an IPA with a real mouthful of hoppy flavour. The main difference from beer brewed in Britain – and which would not earn it the approval of CAMRA (the UK's real-ale pressure group) – is that it is kegged and served chilled and under pressure. "Casked beer in wooden barrels just will not survive at this latitude and temperature," says brewer Jones. But he insists that in every other respect this is a real ale made with chemical-free natural ingredients to match the best in Britain.

The brewery has an adjoining and atmospheric brewpub, restaurant and tapas bar (daily noon–midnight) where you can try out the beers for yourself. A taster tray with a mini-glass of all six beers costs a very reasonable €3.80. The brewery is located at C/Brujula 5 in the Poligono Industrial de Palmones III on the outskirts of Los Barrios and isn't the easiest place to find without a taxi or satnav. If you want to visit, you'll find a map on their website (🌐 fabricadecervezakettal.com) or give them a ring on ☎ 956 675 430 and they will provide you with directions.

who had captured the Rock and looted their homes and churches. They expected to return within months, since the troops had taken the garrison in the name of Archduke Carlos of Austria, whose rights Britain had been promoting in the War of the Spanish Succession, but it was the British flag that was raised on the conquered territory – and so it has remained (the Ayuntamiento's council chamber, on the central Plaza de la Iglesia, has a **banner** given to the earlier, Spanish, Gibraltar by Fernando and Isabel). On the same square, the eighteenth-century church of **Santa María Coronada** – built over the ancient hermitage of San Roque – has a fine image of the Virgin, also rescued from the Rock in the flight from the British invaders.

If you're looking for a place to stay, a far better place to overnight is **LOS BARRIOS**, 10km to the west, a tidy and tranquil place away from the somewhat depressing nature of this industrial area.

ACCOMMODATION AND EATING   SAN ROQUE

Los Barrios is a more attractive proposition for accommodation than San Roque, with a couple of pleasant places to stay. Both hotels below have restaurants and there are numerous places to eat along Calle Pablo Picasso, the town's main thoroughfare.

Camping La Casita San Roque, on the N340 (km 126.2) highway just east of the town ☎ 956 780 031, 🌐 campinglacasita.com. Occupying a site with plenty of shade; facilities include a pool and bar-restaurant. Two people plus car **€19.50**

Hotel Montera Plaza Avda. Carlos Cano s/n, on the west side of Los Barrios near the A381 autovía and opposite the plaza de toros ☎ 856 220 220, 🌐 hotel montera.com. Don't be put off by first impressions: behind a fairly humdrum exterior this excellent-value four-star

hotel has smart, well-equipped rooms, many with terrace balcony and views. Add in a good restaurant, gardens, pool, free wi-fi, free car park and friendly staff and you have an exceptional bargain. B&B **€70**

Hotel Real C/Pablo Picasso 7 ☎ 956 620 024. Central, pleasant hotel on this elegant palm-lined avenue (the town's main street) offering a/c balcony rooms with TV. Also has its own decent bar-restaurant and can advise on parking nearby. **€48**

La Línea

Obscured by San Roque's huge oil refinery, the **Spanish-British frontier** is 8km south of San Roque at **LA LÍNEA** ("the line"). When Franco closed the frontier in 1969, it was

2

ANDALUCÍA'S MOROCCAN ENCLAVES

Across the straits from Gibraltar on the north coast of Morocco lie the enclaves of **Ceuta** and **Melilla**, both Spanish territories and officially part of the autonomous region of Andalucía. When they celebrated in 1997 the quincentenary of their founding by the Catholic monarchs Fernando and Isabel, neither King Juan Carlos nor then prime minister José María Aznar saw fit to join in the deliberately low-key festivities – the Spanish establishment acceded to the wishes of Morocco, with which for economic reasons it desires good relations, for minimal observation of the event. This is because Morocco views the territories as China viewed Hong Kong – and as Spain views Gibraltar. Ceuta and Melilla are the remnants of a string of Spanish fortresses built along the coast of North Africa after Andalucía had been reconquered from the Moors. Intended to protect the peninsula from further incursions, they survived into modern times as an anachronism – the United Nations does not even list them as colonies because they were settled long before Morocco existed in its present shape. Their combined populations of 140,000 citizens have the same rights as those on Spain's mainland and vociferously oppose any plans to cede the territories to Morocco.

This opposition has complicated matters for Madrid, who see the enclaves as burning up vast amounts of money in grants and subsidies as well as providing an easy entry point for illegal immigrants into Spain and the EU. In line with what is happening in the former Spanish Sahara, Ceuta and Melilla could eventually gain some form of autonomy within Morocco – but so far the inhabitants are unconvinced and the tug of war between Spain and its North African neighbour seems likely to continue for some time yet.

La Línea that suffered most, as workers lost their jobs on the Rock overnight and the town's population dropped by 35 percent. After sixteen years of Spanish-imposed isolation, the gates were reopened in February 1985, and the five-minute crossing between here and Gibraltar is now routine – except for the odd flare-up when petulant disputes impose long delays on those waiting to cross. La Línea remains in a largely depressed state, a fact that has pushed many of its people into assisting the Rock's smugglers by warehousing contraband tobacco prior to its distribution throughout Spain. There are no sights as such; it's just a fishing village that has exploded in size due to the employment opportunities in Gibraltar and the industrialized zone around the Bay of Algeciras.

ARRIVAL AND DEPARTURE
LA LINEA

By train The closest mainline train station is San Roque–La Línea, 11km west of town, from where you can pick up a train to Ronda and beyond.

By bus The bus station (☎ 956 172 396) is on Plaza de Europa, 250m from the frontier with Gibraltar.

INFORMATION

Turismo Avda. 20 Abril, south of the main Plaza de la Constitución, a large modern square at the heart of La Línea (Mon–Wed 9am–7.30pm, Thurs & Fri 9am–3.30pm, Sat & Sun 9.30am–3pm; ☎ 956 784 138). A very helpful office, their Campo de Gibraltar leaflet has street maps of both La Línea and Algeciras, and they also hand out a free Ruta del Tapeo (tapas route) leaflet.

ACCOMMODATION

Although La Línea's greater number of hotels make it a better overnight bet than Gibraltar, many of its *hostales* are depressingly grim (we've listed a couple of honourable exceptions). Budget accommodation is concentrated around the focal Plaza de la Constitución, while both hotels listed below offer much better value than anything of the same standard in Gibraltar.

Asur Hotel Avda. Príncipe de Asturias s/n, on the seafront ☎ 956 691 211 ⊕ asurhoteles.com. A 5min walk from the Gibraltar border, this is an attractive four-star hotel with spacious and light terrace balcony rooms with sea view, all well equipped with safe, minibar and free wi-fi. Also has a very nice pool and large underground (pay) car park. See website for special offers. B&B **€75**

La Campana C/Carboneras 3, off Plaza de la Constitución ☎ 956 173 059, ⊕ hostalcampana.es. A friendly and recently refurbished *hostal* offering attractive en-suite rooms with a/c, heating and TV and free wi-fi. **€48**

Hostal-Restaurante Carlos C/Carboneras 6 ☎ 956 762 135, ⓦ hostalcarlos.es. Almost opposite La Campana, this is a fractionally cheaper option, with light a/c en-suite balcony rooms, with similar facilities. **€45**

Hotel AC La Línea C/Caireles 2 ☎ 956 175 566, ⓦ espanol.marriot.com. Good four-star option close to the Bay of Algeciras seafront, and a ten-minute walk from the Gibraltar border. It offers well appointed rooms with free minibar and wi-fi and facilities include pool, gym and garage. See website for special offers. **€75**

EATING AND DRINKING

The hostales *Campana* and *Carlos* (see above) have good and economical restaurants – both offering a *menú* for around €9 – with the *Campana*'s perhaps shading it for value. The nearby C/Real, the main pedestrianized shopping street, offers plenty of reasonably priced bars and cafés – good for breakfast pastries – as well as restaurants (while you're here, it's worth having a look at the elegant Casino Mercantil at no.25 dating from 1925). For picnic supplies, head for the market, north of C/Real.

★ **Café Modelo** C/Real 30. Wonderful mid-twentieth-century café boasting a glorious interior full of antique fittings and fixtures and one of La Línea's most fashionable terraces. The kitchen serves up all kinds of tasty snacks from *bocadillos de bacón* to *platos combinados*, or you can take afternoon tea (over twenty different varieties) with pastries.

D'Antonio C/Dr Villar 19, off the north side of C/Real. Decent tapas and *raciones* are served up here as well as *platos combinados*, and there's a small outdoor street terrace.

La Marina Paseo Marítimo s/n ☎ 956 171 531. Northeast of the centre on the beach with great sea views from a delightful terrace (booking advised for a table here), this fairly expensive Michelin-starred fish restaurant is probably the best in town. Now into its eighth decade – one-time customers have included John Lennon, Orson Welles and Gina Lollobrigida – it is renowned for its *langostinos* (from Sanlúcar) and a mouthwatering *arroz con bogavante* (rice with lobster); there's also a *menú de degustación* for around €45. Main dishes €12–20. Worth taking a taxi to get there.

Gibraltar

GIBRALTAR's interest is essentially its novelty: the genuine appeal of the strange, looming physical presence of its rock, and the increasingly dubious one of its preservation as one of Britain's last remaining colonies. This enormous hunk of limestone, 5km long, 2km wide and 450m high – a land area smaller than the city of Algeciras across the water – has fascinated and attracted the people of the Mediterranean basin since Neanderthal times, confirmed by the finds of skulls and artefacts in a number of the Rock's many caves.

The Rock (as it is colloquially known) is a curious place to visit, not least to witness the bizarre process of its opening to mass tourism from the Costa del Sol. Ironically, this threatens both to destroy Gibraltar's highly individual society and at the same time to make it much more British, after the fashion of the expat communities and huge resorts up the coast. The frontier opening has benefited most people: Gibraltarians can buy cheaper goods in Spain, a place ironically where twenty percent of them now have second homes, while expats living on the Costas can shop in familiar British stores like Morrisons and Marks & Spencer. Despite a healthy economy based on tourism, offshore banking and its role as a major bunkering port, the colony has reached yet another crossroads in its tortuous history, and the likely future – whether its population agrees to this or not – is almost certain to involve closer ties with Spain.

Brief history

Although inhabited throughout prehistory, it was the **Phoenicians** who named the Rock "Calpe" (or kalph meaning "hollow", presumably a reference to the Rock's caves) and had a fortified naval base here, barring the way to jealously guarded Atlantic trading destinations such as Tartessus. In **Greek** mythology this was the northernmost of the two pillars erected by Heracles. Following the demise of the Roman Empire, the Rock became the bridgehead for a **Berber** assault on the Visigothic domains of southern Spain. In 711, Tariq ibn Ziryab, governor of Tangier, crossed the straits at the head of an army, defeated the Visigoths and named the Rock "Jabal Tariq" or the Mountain of Tariq, the name – albeit garbled – it still has today.

Gibraltar remained in Moorish hands until taken in 1309 by Guzmán el Bueno, but it was not long before it was recovered. The end finally came when another Guzmán, the duke of Medina Sidonia, claimed it for Spain in 1462. Apart from the raids of Barbarossa, which caused Carlos V to fortify the Rock, Spanish possession was undisturbed until the **War of the Spanish Succession**, when Britain sided with Spain against the French. The outcome of this was the seizure of the Rock in 1704 by the **British** forces whose admiral, Sir George Rooke, gave the inhabitants the choice of swearing allegiance to the Habsburg claimant to the throne – Archduke Charles of Austria – or getting out. Those that left to found San Roque (see p.148) thought their absence would be temporary, but in 1713 the British contrived to have Gibraltar ceded to them "in perpetuity" in the Treaty of Utrecht, no doubt having calculated the military advantages of such a strategic bastion.

GIBRALTAR'S SOVEREIGNTY

Sovereignty over the Rock will doubtless eventually return to Spain, but at present neither side is in much of a hurry. For Britain it's a question of precedent – Gibraltar is in too similar a situation to the Falklands/Malvinas, a conflict that pushed the Spanish into postponing an initial frontier-opening date in 1982. For Spain, too, there are unsettling parallels with the *presidios* (Spanish enclaves) on the Moroccan coast at Ceuta and Melilla (see box, p.150). Nonetheless, the British presence is in practice waning, and the British Foreign Office clearly wants to steer Gibraltar towards a new, harmonious relationship with Spain. To this end they are running down the significance of the military base, and now only a token force remains – most of these working in a top-secret hi-tech bunker buried deep inside the Rock from where the Royal Navy monitors the sea traffic through the straits (accounting for a quarter of the world movement of all shipping). In financial terms this has cut the British government's contribution to Gibraltar's GDP from 65 percent in the early 1980s to less than seven percent today, and the figure is still falling.

The majority of the 28,000 Gibraltarians see all these issues as irrelevant in light of their firmly stated **opposition** to a return to **Spanish control** over the Rock. In 1967, just before Franco closed the border in the hope of forcing a quick agreement, the colony voted on the issue – rejecting it by 12,138 votes to 44 (a poll not recognized, incidentally, by the UN). Most people would probably sympathize with that vote – against a Spain that was then still a dictatorship – but almost half a century has gone by, Spanish democracy is now secure, and the arguments are becoming increasingly tenuous.

GIBRALTAR SAYS "NO"

Gibraltar's current ruling administration is led by **Peter Caruana** at the head of the **Social Democrat party** which ousted the previous long-serving Labour administration from power in 1996 and has held the reins ever since. After talking about opening up a more constructive dialogue with Spain while in opposition, once in power Caruana soon began to voice the traditional Gibraltarian paranoia. Despite attempts by the British and Spanish governments at the start of the new millennium to break the impasse – one idea floated was to give the colony the status of an autonomous region inside Spain – the Gibraltarians remained bitterly opposed to any change of status. The autonomous region proposal was attacked by Caruana who made a speech at the UN castigating Spain's intransigence and claiming the right of Gibraltar to exercise "self-determination." Britain's Blair government then proposed a power-sharing solution with sovereignty to be shared between the two states. Caruana denounced this as an act of treachery and announced that Gibraltar would hold its own **referendum** on the issue. This took place in 2002 and, during a month-long campaign, the old slogan "Give Spain No Hope!" was used as a battle cry. The predictable result was a

In modern times

Despite military and diplomatic attempts by Spain to recover the Rock since, the British have maintained their grip, and Gibraltar played an important strategic role in both World Wars. General **Franco** mounted persistent campaigns to get it back and closed the access link with Spain in 1969, a period of enforced isolation that is indelibly etched into the Gibraltarian collective consciousness.

The Rock, it seems, is destined to be a recurring cause of friction between Britain and Spain; in 1988 three **IRA suspects** were gunned down by British agents near the petrol station at the entrance to the town and close to the frontier. The British government – which went to enormous lengths to obscure the facts of the case – produced a version of events much at odds with that of the Spanish police and once more the issue of a "foreign power on Spanish soil" sparked a national debate.

One more curious twist in the colony's history occurred in the spring of 2004 when Gibraltar voted for the first time ever in **European Parliament elections** after being denied the vote by successive British governments wary of the political and diplomatic complexities involved. However, when the Gibraltarians won a victory in the European Court of Human Rights, the British government was forced into a U-turn and

2

99-percent majority against any sharing of sovereignty with Spain, an outcome that sent shockwaves through the corridors of power in London and Madrid.

AN UNCERTAIN FUTURE

The **new Spanish administration** elected in 2004 and led by José Luis Rodríguez Zapatero has repeated the claims over Gibraltar voiced by all its predecessors and the political stalemate seems set to continue for as long as Britain uses the wishes of the Gibraltarians as a pretext for blocking any change in the colony's status – a policy that infuriates the Spanish government whose former foreign minister, Abel Matutes, stated that the wishes of the residents "did not apply in the case of Hong Kong".

Caruana has regularly been urged by Britain (under pressure from Spain) to crack down on the smuggling of contraband tobacco over the Spanish border and to curb the activities of the Rock's 75,000 "offshore" financial institutions which have mushroomed over recent decades. Many of these companies, Spain claims, are guilty of **drugs money laundering** besides providing a refuge for Russian mafia money, accusations given some credibilty by the EU's decision to start legal proceedings against a number of them in 1999. In 2005 Gibraltar finance companies were also implicated in the uncovering by Spanish police of a huge money-laundering operation based in Marbella (see p.114). With the ending of Gibraltar's tax haven status in 2010 both governments hope that many of these issues will resolve themselves.

What most outsiders don't realize about the political situation is that the Gibraltarians feel very vulnerable: caught between the interests of two big states they are well aware that both governments' concerns have little to do with their own personal wishes. Until very recently people were sent over from Britain to fill all the top civil service and Ministry of Defence jobs, a practice which, to a lesser degree, still continues – the present governor is Vice-Admiral Sir Adrian Johns, a former Royal Navy senior commander.

Locals – particularly on the Spanish side of the border – also vigorously protest about the Royal Navy nuclear-powered and armed submarines that dock regularly at the naval base. Secrecy equally surrounds the issue of whether nuclear warheads and/or chemical and biological weapons are stored in the arsenal, probably deep inside the Rock itself, which is honeycombed with 51km of tunnels.

Yet Gibraltarians stubbornly cling to British status, and all their institutions are modelled on British lines. Contrary to popular belief, however, they are of neither mainly Spanish nor British blood, but an ethnic mix descended from Genoese, Portuguese, Spanish, Menorcan, Jewish, Maltese and British forebears. **English** is the official language, but more commonly spoken is what sounds to an outsider like perfect Andalucian Spanish. It is, in fact, llanito, an Andalucian dialect with odd borrowed English and foreign words reflecting its diverse origins – only a Spaniard from the south can tell a Gibraltarian from an Andalucian.

somewhat bizarrely Gibraltar's twenty thousand voters were appended to the southwest England constituency of Devon and Cornwall, almost one thousand miles away from the Rock – and to where the colony's ballot papers were airlifted once they had been counted. This success has fuelled demands for Gibraltar to have its own Westminster MP, another issue the British government would prefer not to think about. For more on the history of Gibraltar, see Contexts, p.571.

2 | The Rock

Cable car daily 9.30am–6pm, last trip down 5.45pm • £9 return, £7.50 one way

Near the end of Main Street you can hop on the expensive **cable car** which will carry you up to the summit – the **Top of the Rock** as it's logically known. A way to avoid paying the return fare is to walk back down (see p.156). Entry to the Top of the Rock area is 50p for pedestrians but the attractions cost extra.

The cable car ascends via the **Apes' Den** halfway up, a fairly reliable viewing point to see the tailless monkeys (Barbary apes) who live here and hear the guides explain their legend. The story goes that the British will keep the rock only so long as the apes remain too; Winston Churchill was superstitious enough to augment their numbers during World War II when they started to decline. The Top of the Rock gives fantastic views over to the Atlas Mountains in Morocco and the town far below, as well as an

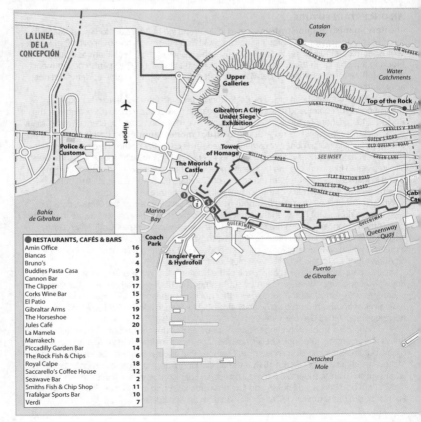

⬤ RESTAURANTS, CAFÉS & BARS	
Amin Office	16
Biancas	3
Bruno's	4
Buddies Pasta Casa	9
Cannon Bar	13
The Clipper	17
Corks Wine Bar	15
El Patio	5
Gibraltar Arms	19
The Horseshoe	12
Jules Café	20
La Mamela	1
Marrakech	8
Piccadilly Garden Bar	14
The Rock Fish & Chips	6
Royal Calpe	18
Saccarello's Coffee House	12
Seawave Bar	2
Smiths Fish & Chip Shop	11
Trafalgar Sports Bar	10
Verdi	7

elaborate water catchment system cut into the side of the rock. This is also an
for observing bird migrations between Africa and the Spanish peninsula.

From the Top of the Rock it's an easy walk south along St Michael's Road pa
another of the apes' dens. Keep a tight grip on your belongings: the unruly pri
prone to stealing tourists' bags and sometimes their cameras – often tossing the items
onto rocks a couple of hundred metres below.

Upper Rock Nature Reserve

Daily 9.30am–7.15pm • 50p • Inclusive ticket to all attractions £10

Much of the area of the upper Rock has now been grandly designated the **Upper Rock
Nature Reserve**, which the resident colony of Barbary apes and a few rare plant species
hardly justifies. To enter this area you will need to pay the pedestrian fee, while you'll
also need to pay again to view attractions inside the reserve such as St Michael's Cave,
the Tower of Homage and the Great Siege Tunnels, plus the **Gibraltar: A City Under
Siege** exhibition.

Saint Michael's Cave

Daily 9.30am–7pm • Covered by inclusive Rock ticket

From the Top of the Rock cable-car station a leafy path leads some 500m east to **Saint
Michael's Cave**, an immense natural cavern that led ancient people to believe the rock

2

was hollow and gave rise to its old name of Mons Calpe (Hollow Mountain). Used during World War II as a bomb-proof military hospital, the cave nowadays hosts occasional concerts. You can arrange at the tourist office for a guided visit to **Lower Saint Michael's Cave**, a series of chambers going deeper down and ending in an underground lake.

Recent discoveries in another cave nearby on the southeast tip of the Rock (not open to the public) suggest that Gibraltar was one of the last habitats of Neanderthal man who may have lived here some 24,000 years ago – much later than previously thought. Earlier finds of flint tools and evidence of camp-fires and cooked meals are regarded as one of the most important **prehistoric** finds in modern times. The cave appears to have been inhabited by both Neanderthals and *Homo sapiens*, and it's hoped that further excavations will provide vital evidence as to the extinction or amalgamation of our species with the earlier race.

The descent from the Top of the Rock

Close to St Michael's Cave at the end of O'Hara's Road, the **Mediterranean Steps** offer one possible route if you want to walk down from the Top of the Rock rather than taking the cable car. They're not very well signposted and you have to climb over **O'Hara's Battery**, a big gun emplacement with a very steep descent most of the way down the east side, turning the southern corner of the Rock. You'll pass through the Jews' Gate and into Engineer Road.

From here, return to town by heading north through the Alameda Gardens and the evocative **Trafalgar Cemetery** (daily 9am–7pm; free), with graves of the Battle of Trafalgar dead and a good line in epitaphs.

Tower of Homage

Daily 9.30am–7pm • Covered by inclusive Rock ticket

On the opposite (northern) side of the rock to St Michael's Cave, the fourteenth-century **Tower of Homage** is the most visible survivor from Gibraltar's original Moorish castle, now filled with wax dummies of British soldiers hacking at the stone and doing battle with the Spanish.

Gibraltar: City Under Siege

Daily 9.30am–7pm • Covered by inclusive Rock ticket

Near the Tower of Homage, in an eighteenth-century former ammunition store on Willis's Road, the **Gibraltar: City Under Siege** exhibition uses tableaux to document the history of the Great Siege and the hardships suffered by both the military and the local population.

The Upper Galleries

Daily 9.30am–7pm • Covered by inclusive Rock ticket

A couple of hundred metres east from here you'll find the **Upper Galleries** (aka the Great Siege Tunnels), blasted out of the rock during the Great Siege of 1779–1782 when the Spanish forces and their French allies attempted to reclaim Gibraltar while the British were distracted by the American War of Independence. The opening of the galleries and the boring of holes in the rock's north face allowed gun emplacements to point down at the Spanish lines.

Gibraltar Museum

Bomb House Lane • Mon–Fri 10am–6pm, Sat 10am–2pm • £2

Perhaps the most interesting item in the town's **museum** are two beautiful, well-preserved fourteenth-century **Moorish Baths**. Resembling the ancient Roman model, the baths had a cold room and hot rooms heated by a hypocaust. Note the star-shaped skylights, and the pillars used in the construction: one Roman, two Visigothic and

2

four Moorish. Otherwise, the museum's collection is an odd assortment including an incongruous Egyptian mummy washed up in the bay, a natural history display of stuffed birds in glass cases, and a rather dreary military section documenting how the British came to rule the roost here.

The museum's star exhibit should be a female skull, dating from around 100,000 years ago and unearthed in 1848 on the Rock's north face. Ironically, because the find was then stored away, it was the later discovery of a skull in Germany's Neander Valley that gave its name to the era we know as Neanderthal, which could just as easily have been termed "Gibraltarian". The museum now retains only a copy, the original having been removed to the research collection of the Natural History Museum in London.

King's Chapel
Daily 9am–7pm • Free

Not far away from the museum, and next door to the Governor's Residence, is the sixteenth-century **King's Chapel**, harking back to pre-colonial days – the seventeenth-century remains of the wife of the last Spanish governor are buried here. It's a fine old church – now rather marred by the military flags, regalia and wall plaques of Empire – and was formerly the chapel attached to the Convent of Franciscan friars (now the Governor's Residence). This should, of course have been titled "Friary" but a mistranslation by early British settlers fixed the erroneous name and this was confirmed as its title in the 1940s by order of King George VI.

Nelson's Anchorage
Mon–Sat 9.30am–6.15pm • £1 or covered by inclusive Rock ticket

At **Nelson's Anchorage** on Rosia Road, to the south of the harbour, a monstruous **100-ton Victorian gun** marks the site where Nelson's body was brought ashore – preserved in a rum barrel – from HMS *Victory* after the Battle of Trafalgar in 1805.

Europa point
Reached by bus #3, which runs along Line Wall Road and Europa Road – its continuation – with a stop at the Rock Hotel

If you have the time to spare you can take a bus south to the tip of the peninsula at **Europa point**. On clear days you get fine views across the strait to Morocco and the sight of the odd leaping dolphin, but there's little else here but a lighthouse, souvenir shop, bus terminal and, interestingly, an impressive mosque donated in the 1990s by King Fahd of Saudi Arabia for the benefit of Muslim immigrants working in Gibraltar.

Catalan Bay
Bus #4 from Line Wall Rd (every 15min)

The best **beach** is at the tiny fishing village of **Catalan Bay**, a characterless stretch of seafront reminiscent of a humdrum British holiday resort whose inhabitants like to think of themselves as distinct from the townies on the other side of the Rock. There's a bus service to Catalan Bay and the other eastern beaches.

DOLPHIN TOURS

A number of companies run rather pricey daily **dolphin-spotting boat trips** and trips around the bay. Most leave from either Marina Bay or the nearby Queensway Quay – ring first to book places or ask the Tourist Office to do it for you. Operators include: Dolphin Safari, Marina Bay (☎ 2007 1914; £25, under 12s £12.50); Dolphin World, Marina Bay (☎ 5448 1000; £20, under 12s £10); Dolphin Adventure, Marina Bay ☎ 2005 0650; £25, under 12s £10).

ARRIVAL AND DEPARTURE

PHONING GIBRALTAR

From Spain dial 00+350 + number
From Europe and UK dial 00 + 350 + number
From North America dial 011 + 350 + number

BY CAR

If you have a car, don't attempt to bring it to Gibraltar – the queues at the border to get in (and out) are often atrocious, and parking on the Rock is limited, due to lack of space. Use the underground car parks in La Línea – there's one beneath the central Plaza de la Constitución – instead (it's worth paying for the extra security) and walk across.

BY BUS

From the frontier at La Línea, where passport checking is a formality, it's a short bus ride (#9, every 15min) or a ten-minute walk across part of the airport's runway to Main Street (La Calle Real), which runs for most of the town's length a couple of blocks back from the port. Services run to La Línea from Algeciras (on the hour and half-hour; 30min).

BY TAXI

Be on your guard at the frontier for touting taxi drivers who offer "tours of the Rock" – they're generally overpriced and very rushed. If you wish to take a taxi tour that includes the Upper Rock Nature Reserve and attractions the current price per person is £22 for up to four and can be booked with the Gibraltar Taxi Association on ☎ 2007 0052.

TO MOROCCO

By boat A catamaran service, the Tanger Jet, sails to Tangier on Fridays at 6.30pm, taking one hour. The return trip from Tangier is on Sundays at 4pm (Moroccan time). Tickets cost £39 one way and £70 return for a foot passenger. Tickets, updated timetables and vehicle rates are available from the agent Turner & Co, 65/67 Irish Town (☎ 2007 8305, ✉ turner@gibtelecom.net).

By plane There are currently no flights between Gibraltar and Morocco.

Travel agents Bland Travel, 6-8 Market Lane, near Irish Town (☎ 2007 7221, ⌨ mbhtravelservices.com; closed Sat & Sun), is the leading travel agent in Gibraltar and runs thrice-weekly day-trips to Tangier in Morocco on Mon, Wed and Fri which includes a guided tour and lunch. The sailing is from Tarifa, to where you are bussed, and the package costs £75.

INFORMATION

Tourist office Casemates Square (Mon–Fri 9am–5.30pm, Sat & Sun 10am–1pm; ☎ 2007 4982, ⌨ visitgibraltar.gi); there's a sub-branch in the customs and immigration building at the border (Mon–Fri 9am–4.30pm, Sat 10am–3pm; ☎ 2005 0762).

Internet The public library in the John Mackintosh Hall (Mon–Fri 9.30am–7.30pm), at the south end of Main Street, which also serves as a cultural centre hosting frequent exhibitions. Slightly east of here, Callshop Gibraltar, 293a Main Street (daily 9am–9pm) is another possibility.

Bookshop The Gibraltar Bookshop at 300 Main St (☎ 2007 1864) is a good source for stocking up on holiday reading and has a wide selection of books on the Rock's history.

Opening hours Much of Gibraltar, including restaurants

and cafés (but with the exception of the cheap booze shops), closes down on Saturday, but the tourist sights remain open, and this can often be a quiet time to visit. Virtually everything closes on Sunday.

Currency The official currency is the Gibraltar pound (same value as the British pound, but different notes and coins – although you'll often find British coins mixed in with your change); ask for your change in euros if you are on a brief day-trip and note that Gibraltar pounds can be hard to change in Spain or anywhere else. Euros are accepted without problems all over Gibraltar, although you generally fork out about five percent more if you pay using these.

Banks ATMs can be found along Main Street along with bureaux de change (which stay open longer).

ACCOMMODATION

Shortage of space on the Rock means that accommodation is at a premium, especially in summer. In addition, most of it isn't overly inviting and (compared to Spain) is expensive too. It's really not worth your while searching out a good place to stay unless you have to: your best bet is to visit on day-trips from Algeciras or La Línea. Other than at the *Cannon Hotel*, you're going to have to pay standard British hotel prices. No camping is allowed on the peninsula, and if you're caught sleeping rough or in abandoned bunkers, you're likely to be arrested and fined.

Cannon Hotel 9 Cannon Lane ☎ 2005 1711, ⌨ cannon hotel.gi. Small, pleasant hotel just off Main St with functional Spanish-*hostal* style rooms with TV but no a/c. En-suite rooms are £10 more expensive than those sharing

bath (the price we quote). B&B **£42**

Emile Youth Hostel Montagu Bastion, Line Wall Rd ☎ 2005 1106, ⌨ emilehostel.net. This privately run youth hostel has the cheapest beds in town, including some

SHOPPING AND SMUGGLING IN GIBRALTAR

Spain's tobacco and alcoholic drinks are among the cheapest in Europe, but Gibraltar – which avoids **excise duty** as it's not part of the European Economic Zone – can do it even cheaper, thus explaining the crowds of plastic-bag-toting individuals passing through the Spanish customs border post at all hours of the day and night. Remember though that this means you are only allowed to take normal duty-free limits back into Spain (200 cigarettes and one litre of spirits per adult), and which also explains why you may be approached by locals asking you to carry a pack of cigarettes over the border into Spain. Think twice about doing so, however, as what may seem to be a simple carton of fags could contain drugs (this is a major supply route from north Africa) and – if searched – you, and not they, will suffer the consequences.

Most of Gibraltar's duty-free booze and tobacco shops along with outlets of major UK stores such as Marks and Spencers, BHS, Body Shop, Next and Mothercare are located on Main Street, while Morrison's supermarket lies northwest of Main Street near the harbour.

claustrophobic dorms and basic but clean shared-bathroom doubles. However, it's not the most attractive location. Dorms **£17**, doubles **£40**

Hotel Bristol Cathedral Square ☎ 2007 6800, ⓦ bristolhotel.gi. Long-established, if rather staid, place with refurbished rooms and a pool. We quote the price for the cheapest interior-facing double but you'll pay a supplement for a sea view. **£81**

Queen's Hotel Boyd St ☎ 2007 4000, ⓦ queenshotel .gi. Decent traditional hotel offering comfortable rooms, many with terrace balconies. We quote the cheapest non-

sea view double (supplement for sea view) **£70**

Rock Hotel 3 Europa Rd ☎ 2007 3000, ⓦ rockhotel gibraltar.com. Gibraltar's flagship hotel, immediately below the Apes' Den, trades on its imperial connections, with photos of the imperial great and good who have stayed here during the days when Gibraltar was an important staging post on the route to and from the imperial east. Rooms are decorated in "colonial style" and come with ceiling fans and a trouser press, and there's also a garden pool, restaurant and hairdresser. **£160**

EATING AND DRINKING

Eating – with a few honourable exceptions – is a bit of a sad affair in Gibraltar: relatively expensive by Spanish standards, with pub grub or fish and chips as the norm and bottled wine prices to make your eyes water. Main Street is crowded with dismal touristy places and fast-food outlets but there are some more inviting places with waterfront terraces in Marina Bay and its continuation Ocean Village, or on the east side of the Rock at Catalan Bay.

RESTAURANTS

The Amin Office 30 Parliament Lane. A good lunch stop specialising in Moroccan and Spanish dishes together with curries. The menu includes couscous, tagines, salads and tandoori chicken. Their street terrace is one of the quieter places around here. Daily 8am–5pm.

Bianca's Marina Bay. Popular all-day local restaurant which kicks off with a giant "English Breakfast" (served from 9am) before moving on to pizzas, snacks and sandwiches – served in the bar – or more elaborate steak and fish dishes (as well as salads and veggie options) in the restaurant. Has reasonable wine prices and a pleasant terrace overlooking the waterfront. Main dishes (in restaurant) £10–18. Daily 9am–late.

Bruno's The Boardwalk, Ocean Village. Chic waterside bar-restaurant with glitzy decor not always matched by the food and service. The menu is Mediterranean and there are salads and seafood pasta dishes. Main dishes £9–16. Daily 10am–late.

Buddies Pasta Casa 15 Cannon Lane, off the east side of Main Street by the cathedral. Decent pasta in all its

varieties is served up here – as well as the ubiquitous fish and chips. Daily noon–10pm.

The Clipper 78 Irish Town. British-style pub grub – a house special is steak and ale pie – served up in a varnished lounge along with a variety of UK beers. Daily 11am–11pm.

Corks Wine Bar 79 Irish Town. A relatively tranquil venue offering a variety of salads and pasta dishes as well as pub-style favourites such as steak and Guinness pie. Daily noon–10pm.

El Patio 11 Casemates Square. This mid-priced Basque-run restaurant is one of the few genuinely Spanish places in town, serving up a decent range of fish and meat dishes in a traditional dining room. Daily 1–4pm & 7.30–10.30pm.

Jules Café 30 John Mackintosh Square. With an attractive terrace on this picturesque square, this another long-established place for fish and meat dishes, with a *menú* offering two courses for £12.75 or three courses for £16.95 (excluding drinks). There are also economical options like jacket potatoes, toasted sandwiches, omelettes and salads. Daily 10am–10pm.

2

La Mamela Catalan Bay. One of the Rock's best fish restaurants (although meat dishes are also served) with good service and an attractive terrace. Try the prawns in spinach, paella or John Dory *a la roteña*. Main dishes £9–15. Daily 12.30–4pm & 7–11pm.

Marrakech 9 Governor's Parade. Moroccan restaurant with a pleasant outdoor terrace which does lamb, chicken and vegetarian couscous along with tagines and other Maghrebi dishes with a set *menú* for under £10. Main dishes £7–12. Daily noon–11pm.

The Rock Fish & Chips Casemates Square. Friendly Moroccan-run chip shop, and they make an excellent job of the British national dish (eat in or takeaway). Does the "heart-attack-on-a-plate" full British breakfast, too – all day. Outdoor terrace. Daily 9am–10pm.

Saccarello's Coffee House 57 Irish Town. A local institution founded in 1888 by a Genoese immigrant and still in the hands of the same family, this has a rather select ambience and makes a great place for afternoon tea (or coffee – they roast their own) and home-made confectionery. They also serve lunches including things like pies, pasta, quiche and salads. Free wi-fi. Daily 9am–6pm.

Seawave Bar Catalan Bay. Economical seafront terrace restaurant with a mainly fish and *mariscos* menu, although fish and chips and burgers and British-style breakfasts also get a look in. Daily 9am–11pm.

Smiths Fish & Chip Shop 295 Main St. Another Rock institution – and if you've suddenly developed a hankering for battered cod, haddock or plaice with chips and mushy peas, wrapped in yesterday's *Gibraltar Chronicle*, then you've hit the jackpot here. Small – stifling in summer – seating area inside. Mon–Sat 11am–6pm.

Trafalgar Sports Bar La Rosia Rd, near the Queen's Hotel. Unless you're a sports nut this is probably not the place to eat when there's a big match on TV (numerous huge screens). Not a bad diner at other times though, with a three-course *menú del día* for £9 including a drink. Also does pub grub, Sunday roast and – of course – fish and chips. Small outdoor terrace. Daily 9am–1am.

Verdi 44 Cornwall's Lane. Lively little kosher vegetarian diner serving pizza and pasta dishes as well as wraps, sandwiches and breakfasts. Daily 9am–10pm.

PUBS AND BARS

Gibraltar's pubs mimic traditional English styles (and prices), but are often rowdy, full of soldiers and visiting sailors.

Cannon Bar Cannon Lane, behind the cathedral. One of Gibraltar's few (relatively) quiet pubs, with friendly staff, decent food and a small terrace. Daily 11am–late.

Gibraltar Arms 186 Main St. British-style boozer in the heart of the action with the usual all-day pub food (including all-day British breakfast). Tends to stay open longer than its neighbours. Daily 11am–late.

The Horseshoe 193 Main St. Serves a range of British and international beers along with hearty pub grub; also has an outdoor pavement terrace. Daily 11am–late.

Piccadilly Garden Bar 3 Rosia Rd, just beyond the Referendum Gates (aka South Port). A garden bar serving breakfasts (British and Spanish) as well as meat and fish dishes; later in the evening it becomes a drinks bar. Daily 11am–late.

Royal Calpe 176 Main St. Pub with outdoor terrace and pub grub – the house special is chicken and mushroom pie, while they also do quiches and salads, backed up by a wide selection of beers. Both kitchen and pub are known to close early when trade is slack. Daily 11am–late.

Algeciras

ALGECIRAS occupies the far side of the bay from Gibraltar, spewing out smoke and pollution in its direction. The last town of the Spanish Mediterranean, it was once an elegant resort; today it's unabashedly a port and industrial centre, its suburbs sprawling out on all sides. When Franco closed the border with Gibraltar at La Línea it was Algeciras that he decided to develop to absorb the Spanish workers formerly employed in the British naval dockyards, thus breaking the area's dependence on the Rock.

Most travellers are scathing about the city's ugliness, and unless you're waiting for a bus or train, or heading for Morocco, there's admittedly little reason to stop. However, Algeciras has a real port atmosphere, and even if you're just passing through it's hard to resist the urge to get on a boat south. This is the main port for Moroccan migrant workers, who drive home every year during their holidays from the factories, farms and mines of Northern Europe. In summer, the port bustles with groups of Moroccans in transit, dressed in flowing djelabas and yellow slippers, and lugging unbelievable amounts of possessions. Half a million cross Spain each year, and at the major Islamic festival periods huge queues build up at the port as the ferries struggle to cope.

Plaza Alta

Once you start to explore, you'll also discover that the old town has some very attractive corners that seem barely to have changed in fifty years, especially around the **Plaza Alta**. This leafy square, arguably the town's only sight of any note, lies a five-minute walk from the bus station/port area and if you're killing time provides a much more pleasant place to sit out than around the port. On the square, the eighteenth-century church of Nuestra Señora de la Palma and the Baroque chapel of Nuestra Señora de Europa – with a fine facade – are worth a look.

Hotel Reina Cristina

Paseo de la Conferencia s/n

Nearer the port, where further impressive but now crumbling edifices echo faded glories, the romantic **Hotel Reina Cristina** is a wonderful throwback to the days of the Grand Tour and steam trains, built in the nineteenth century in British colonial style and set in a park on a rise south of the harbour. Call in for a drink in their terrace bar and take a look at the plaques behind the reception desk bearing the signatures of famous guests, such as Sir Arthur Conan Doyle, W.B. Yeats, Cole Porter and Federico García Lorca.

ARRIVAL AND DEPARTURE
ALGECIRAS

By bus The bus station (☎956 653 456) is at C/San Bernardo 1.2km behind the port.

Destinations: Cádiz (16 daily; 2hr 15min); Jerez de la Frontera (Mon–Fri 7 daily; Sat & Sun 1 daily; 1 hr 30min); La Línea (for Gibraltar; every 30min); Madrid (4 daily; 8hr); Málaga (8 daily; 3hr); Seville (Mon–Fri 7 daily; Sat & Sun 1 daily); Tarifa (every 30min).

By train The train station (☎902 240 202) is just beyond the bus station at Avda. Gesto por la Paz s/n. From here the line heads to Ronda and the Bobadilla Junction, where there are connections with Seville, Málaga, Córdoba and Granada. The stunningly scenic route to Ronda is one of the best journeys in Andalucía; there are four departures a day.

Destinations: Córdoba (1 daily; 3hr 15min); Granada (3 daily; 4hr 20min); Madrid (2 daily; 5hr 20min); Málaga (4 daily, change at Bobadilla; 4hr); Seville (6 daily; 3hr 25min).

TO MOROCCO

Ferry tickets to Morocco are sold at the dozens of travel agents along the waterfront; all agents charge the same prices, though some places may give you a better rate of exchange than others if you want to pay in foreign currency.

Wait until Tangier – or Tetouan if you're going via Ceuta – before buying any Moroccan currency; rates in the embarcation building kiosks are very poor. Check the date and time on your ferry ticket, and beware the ticket sellers who congregate near the dock entrance wearing official Ceuta/Tangier badges: they add a whopping "commission" charge. Convenient tours to Tangier are also offered by Viajes Transafric (see below).

To Ceuta At least twenty departures daily in summer to the Spanish *presidio* of Ceuta (fast ferry 35min), little more than a Spanish Gibraltar with a brisk business in duty-free goods, but a relatively painless way to enter Morocco. Fares are around €25–36 (fast ferry) depending on the company, or €21 (normal ferry).

To Tangier Hourly departures in summer (fast ferry 45min, normal ferry 2hr 30min; around €33 one way for both normal and fast ferries). Note that all ferries to Tangier now dock at the new Tanger-Med port some 40km east of the town itself. The road connections are good but it adds some 30–45min to the journey in both directions. At the time of writing the bus connecting the city with the port was free of charge, but this could change.

INFORMATION

Turismo The helpful Turismo (Mon–Fri 9am–7.30pm, Sat–Sun 9.30am–3pm; ☎956 784 131, ⓦ ayto-algeciras .es) at C/Juan de la Cierva s/n, a pedestrianized avenue near the port, can provide a town map and copious information on the Campo de Gibraltar.

Travel agents The reliable Viajes Transafric (☎956 654 311, ⓦ viajestransafric.com) travel agents, at Avda. Marina

4 near the port, can provide up-to-date information on timetable changes. They also run a daily all-inclusive day-trip (€59) to Tangier by fast-ferry, which includes a guided tour, lunch, and time for shopping.

Internet Locutorio Central, C/Teniente Maroto 2 (daily 10am–10pm), southeast of the market.

2

ACCOMMODATION

Hostal Lisboa C/Juan Morrison 46 ☎ 956 654 452, ⓦ pensionlisboa.com. A couple of minutes' walk from the Turismo this simple but welcoming new *hostal* offers spotless en-suite rooms with TV (most also have balconies), plus free wi-fi and internet. **€36**

Hostal Nuestra Señora de la Palma Plaza de la Palma 12 ☎ 956 632 481, ⓔ hostal_la_palma @hotmail.com. Very spruce place on the market square with spotless en-suite rooms with a/c and TV. **€32–35**

Hotel Don Manuel C/Segismundo Moret 4 ☎ 956 634 606, ⓦ hdonmanuel.es. Reliable two-star hotel opposite the Turismo offering functional, air-conditioned rooms with TV. Free wi-fi. Can advise on parking. **€48**

Hotel Reina Cristina Paseo de la Conferencia s/n ☎ 956 60 26 22, ⓦ reinacristina.es. This grand, historic

four-star hotel (see p.161) has affordable and attractive well-equipped rooms with minibar, safe and satellite TV. Facilities include indoor and outdoor pools and own car park. B&B **€75**

Marina Victoria Avda. de la Marina 7 ☎ 956 650 111, ⓦ hotelmarinavictoria.com. A very pleasant hotel close to the waterfront with air-conditioned balcony rooms overlooking the port and bay with great views towards Gibraltar. **€50**

Youth Hostel Ctra. Nacional 340, 8km west of town on the Tarifa road ☎ 955 035 886, ⓦ inturjoven.com. Algeciras's luxurious youth hostel has a pool, tennis courts and en-suite doubles. Buses heading for Tarifa will drop you outside on request (ask for the "Albergue Juvenil"). Under 26 **€16**, over 26 **€27**

EATING AND DRINKING

The huge number of people passing through the town also guarantees virtually limitless possibilities for food and drink, especially around the port/harbour area, but it's worth venturing a short distance away from here for a bit more quality. Plenty of tapas bars are to be found in the streets surrounding the Plaza Alta, where there are more bars, cafés and popular *heladerías*. The daily markets are useful places to buy food, as well as vibrant and fascinating to visit; the main one, on Plaza Palma down by the port, is a riot of colour on Saturday mornings.

Bar La Casita C/Tarifa 16, slightly west of the market. A typical little *barrio* tapas bar in business for over forty years that gives service with a smile and great-value tapas and *raciones*. Try the paella or *pollo al limón* (chicken with lemon). Puts out tables on this pedestrianized street.

Casa María C/Emilio Castelar 53. Almost opposite *Restaurante Montes* (see below), this is an excellent little restaurant serving meat and fish tapas and *raciones* with a *menú* for €9. House specials are *rapé a la cazuela* (monkfish

casserole) and, in summer, a refreshing gazpacho.

★ **Restaurante Montes** C/Juan Morrison 27. A little north of the bus station, this is an excellent-value traditional restaurant where *pierna de cabrito al horno* (roast kid) is a signature dish. They also offer outstanding fish and *mariscos* too, and there's a great-value *menú* for €9.50. Lower down the hill on the same street, they also have an equally outstanding tapas bar, *Bar Montes*, at the junction with C/Emilio Castelar.

The Costa de la Luz

The villages along the **Costa de la Luz** – the "Coast of Light" between Algeciras and Cádiz – are in a totally different class from the resorts along the Costa del Sol. West from Algeciras the road climbs almost immediately into the rolling green hills of the **Sierra del Cabrito**, a region lashed for much of the year by the ferocious *levante* (east) and *poniente* (west) winds which vie continuously, it seems, for the upper hand. Now cluttered by an inevitable wind farm, from these heights there are fantastic views down to Gibraltar and across the straits to the just-discernible white houses and tapering mosques of Morocco. Beyond, the Rif Mountains hover in the background and on a clear day, as you approach **Tarifa**, you can distinguish Tangier on the edge of its crescent-shaped bay.

Tarifa

TARIFA, spilling out beyond its Moorish walls, was until the mid-1980s a quiet village, known in Spain, if at all, as the southernmost point on the European landmass and for its abnormally high suicide rate – attributed to the unremitting winds that blow across the town and its environs. Occupying the site of previous Carthaginian and Roman

ANDALUCÍA'S BIRD MIGRATIONS

Whilst Andalucía's birdlife is fascinating throughout the year, the region also plays host to one of the remarkable spectacles of the natural world, the great **spring and autumn migrations**, attracting an audience of birdwatchers from far and wide. Many birds spend the winter in warmer African climes, a journey that involves a sea crossing – a major challenge for many large birds such as eagles, vultures and storks who rely on the warm air that rises from the earth to keep them aloft. With no thermals over the sea it's essential that they seek out the shortest possible crossing point: the Strait of Gibraltar.

The main "flight path" across the Strait hits land between Gibraltar and Tarifa. Gibraltar (there's an ornithological information centre on the Upper Rock) and the Punta del Carnero (south of Algeciras) are particularly worth a visit when the wind is in the west, and anywhere along the main Algeciras–Tarifa road is good when there's an easterly breeze. The birds tend to cross in waves so there will inevitably be times when little is visible, and few birds will attempt the crossing in gales or heavy rain. The variety you are likely to see varies from month to month but storks return from Africa in the first months of the New Year. Many black kites, short-toed eagles and other raptors cross the Strait in February and March, but April is the "rush hour" month when huge numbers of honey buzzards are often to be seen aloft and you may even be lucky enough to spot the rare and beautiful black stork.

2

cities, Tarifa takes its name from Tarif Ibn Malik, leader of the first band of Moors to cross the straits in 710, a sortie that tested the waters for the following year's all-out assault on the peninsula.

San Mateo and around

C/Sancho IV El Bravo s/n · Daily 8.30am–1pm & 5.30–9pm · Free

There's great appeal in wandering the crumbling ramparts of Tarifa's old walls, gazing out to sea or down into the network of lanes that surround the fifteenth-century church of **San Mateo**. Don't be fooled by the crumbling Baroque exterior here, fine though it is; this was added in the eighteenth century and hides, inside, a beautiful late-Gothic church with elegant rib-vaulting in the nave and some interesting modern stained-glass windows. A very helpful leaflet in English will guide you around the church's many features, including a fine crucified Christ by the great eighteenth-century sculptor Pedro de Mena, situated along the right aisle. Nearby, a small seventh-century tombstone confirms that there was a Christian presence here before the Moorish invasion of 711. Further along, the *sagrario* (shrine) is a stunning Baroque extravaganza in pink and violet, with an enchanting cupola. The church's stirring finale is at the top of the left aisle, where a copy of the original (and now lost) retablo contains the early seventeenth-century image of San Mateo by Juan Martínez Montañés, Spain's greatest exponent of wood sculpture.

Castillo de Guzmán el Bueno

Entrance from C/Guzmán El Bueno · Tues–Sun 11am–2pm & 4–6pm · €2

The restored **Castillo de Guzmán el Bueno** has great views from its towers and battlements, both over the town and across the water towards Morocco. In origin a tenth-century Moorish *alcázar* constructed by the great Abd ar-Rahman III, ruler of Córdoba, on the ruins of a Roman fort, the building underwent many later alterations. It was also the site of many a struggle as a strategic foothold into Spain. Known today as El Castillo de Guzmán, the appendage refers to Guzmán El Bueno (the Good), Tarifa's infamous commander during the Moorish siege of 1292, who earned this tag for his role in a superlative piece of tragic drama. Guzmán's nine-year-old son had been taken hostage by a Spanish traitor – surrender of the garrison was demanded as the price of the boy's life. Choosing "honour without a son, to a son with dishonour", Guzmán threw down his own dagger for the execution. The story, a famous piece of heroic resistance in Spain, had echoes in the Civil War siege of the Alcázar at Toledo

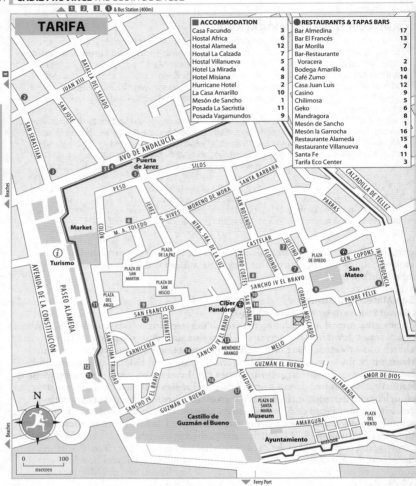

TARIFA

■ **ACCOMMODATION**
Casa Facundo	3
Hostal Africa	6
Hostal Alameda	12
Hostal La Calzada	7
Hostal Villanueva	5
Hotel La Mirada	4
Hotel Misiana	8
Hurricane Hotel	2
La Casa Amarilla	10
Mesón de Sancho	1
Posada La Sacristía	11
Posada Vagamundos	9

● **RESTAURANTS & TAPAS BARS**
Bar Almedina	17
Bar El Francés	13
Bar Morilla	7
Bar-Restaurante Voracera	2
Bodega Amarillo	10
Café Zumo	14
Casa Juan Luis	12
Casino	9
Chilimosa	5
Geko	6
Mandragora	8
Mesón de Sancho	1
Mesón la Garrocha	16
Restaurante Alameda	15
Restaurante Villanueva	4
Santa Fe	11
Tarifa Eco Center	3

in 1936, when the Nationalist commander refused similar threats – an echo much exploited for propaganda purposes.

Plaza de Santa María

Also worth a look is the charming Plaza de Santa María, behind the castle, where you'll find the Ayuntamiento and a small **museum** (currently closed; check with the Turismo) containing an interesting display of artefacts from the Neolithic, Roman and Moorish periods through to modern times. A **mirador** to the east of the square offers more views of the African coast.

Puerta de Jerez

At the northern end of the walled town lies the **Puerta de Jerez**, the only survivor of the four thirteenth-century gates which once led into Tarifa. Sandwiched between two crenellated towers the gate has survived the intervening centuries impressively. A plaque affixed to the wall above its arch records the capture of the town by Sancho El Bravo in

1292. Displayed in a glassed-in alcove inside the arch is a large painting of *El Cristo de los Vientos* (Christ of the Winds) by Tarifa's most famous son, the renowned modern artist Guillermo Pérez Villalta.

A little way beyond the gate to the right as you enter the walled town stands the daily covered **market** (Mon–Sat mornings) with Moorish-style arches – a colourful beehive of activity when in full swing, and with numerous bars in the vicinity doing a roaring trade.

The beaches

The town beaches, separated by a causeway leading to the Isla de las Palomas (not open to the public), include the small, popular and sheltered **Playa Chica** on the Mediterranean side and the **Playa de los Lances** (aka Playa Grande) facing the Atlantic.

Heading **northwest from Tarifa**, towards the Punta Paloma, you'll find some of the loveliest beaches along the whole Costa de la Luz: wide stretches of yellow or silvery-white sand, washed by some magical rollers.

One of these, **Tarifa Beach** arcs around a little bay 9km from town, where there are restaurants and campsites at the base of a tree-tufted bluff. The nearby *Hotel Dos Mares* (see p.166) windsurf centre offers courses and rents out equipment. The same winds that have created such perfect conditions for windsurfing can, however, be a problem for more casual enjoyment, sandblasting those attempting to relax on towels or mats and whipping the water into whitecaps.

ARRIVAL AND DEPARTURE
TARIFA

By bus The bus station (☎ 956 684 038) is at C/Batalla del Salado 13 in the north of town close to the main Algeciras–Cádiz road. From here it's a five- to ten-minute walk along C/Batalla del Salado to the walled old town. Buses run to Cádiz, Jerez and Algeciras.

TO MOROCCO

Day-trips Tangier can be visited as a day-trip by boat from Tarifa using the catamaran fast ferry (around €55 round-trip), which takes 35min to cross from Spain to Morocco. There are eight sailings in each direction in summer between 8am and 11pm, with reduced sailings in winter. The last sailing

back from Tangier runs at 11pm (local time – which is 2hr behind Spanish time in summer, 1hr in winter). You can check current timetables at the Turismo or with the helpful Viajes Baelo Tour, where English is spoken. If you're planning a day-trip, book a few days in advance as groups sometimes make block bookings.

Package tours One- or two-day package tours to Tangier are also available, starting at €60 for the one-day excursion, which includes a sightseeing tour, lunch and all transport. The two-day version (€96) adds in lunch and dinner and a night in a three-star hotel. Details from Viajes Baelo Tour; *Rough Guide* readers can claim a ten-percent discount on

---

THE STRAITS OF DEATH

In Tarifa's cemetery above the town, lines of nameless headstones mark where the dead lie three deep, mostly the remains of unknown Africans washed up on the beach. In recent years the trickle of "wetbacks" eager for a share of European prosperity has turned into a flood, as gangs operating in Tangier offer to get **illegal immigrants** into Spain by evading the Spanish helicopters and coastal patrols. The usual method of transport is *pateras*, flimsy, easily capsized, flat-bottomed fishing boats designed to carry six people. Often packed with as many as thirty – who pay the equivalent of up to €1000 each – these fragile craft set out to cross one of the most treacherous stretches of water in the world. Crooked skippers often tip unfortunates into the water too far out from shore and many non-swimmers drown. More often though, the boats themselves don't make it and the toll of bodies washed up along Spanish beaches has risen to alarming levels in recent years. Of those that do get safely across the straits, many are picked up by the authorities and held in a detention centre on the sealed-off island, Isla de las Palomas, near the harbour, pending extradition. The few that wriggle through the police net face life as non-citizens without papers, drifting between illegal and low-paid jobs or street-selling. The high death toll seems to have no effect on the numbers willing to take their chances on the open seas and the temptation to migrate seems to be getting ever stronger. In the meantime, Tarifa's gravediggers are kept busy as increasing numbers of these desperate boat people perish en route to their promised El Dorado.

tours on production of this guide.

Ticket agents Viajes Baelo Tour, Avda. Constitución 5, near the Turismo (☎ 956 681 242, ✉ viajes-baelo@hotmail .com); the FRS office in the Estación Marítimo building in the harbour (Ferrys Rápido del Sur; ☎ 956 681 830, ⊕ frs .es), plus travel agents along C/Batalla del Salado.

INFORMATION

Turismo The Turismo, at Paseo de la Alameda s/n (April– Sept Mon–Fri 10am–2pm & 4–6pm, Sat & Sun 10am–2pm; Oct–March Mon–Fri 9.30am–1.30pm & 4–6pm, Sat & Sun 9.30am–1.30pm; ☎ 956 680 993, ⊕ aytotarifa.com), can provide a useful town map – also available from many hotels and *hostales* – and a free tapas booklet to help you discover the best places for a snack and a fino.

Internet Ciber Pandor@ (daily 10am–2pm & 5–9pm), C/Sancho IV El Bravo 13a, fronting the *Misiana* hotel.

Vehicle and bike rental Baelotour, Avda. de la Constitución 5 ☎ 956 681 242. Tarifa Eco Center (see "Eating" above) also rents out mountain bikes.

ACTIVITIES

Horseriding The area around Tarifa is good riding country and horses can be hired from the *Hotel Dos Mares* on the N340, 9km northwest of town (☎ 956 236 632, ⊕ aventura equestre.com and ⊕ hoteldosmares.com). They offer single and multiple-day excursions for around €30/hr.

Whale and dolphin-spotting Dolphin- and whale- watching boat trips are run by two non-profit-making organizations: Whale Watch, Avda. de la Constitución 6 (information ☎ 956 682 247, reservations ☎ 639 476 544, ⊕ whalewatchtarifa.net), and FIRMM (Foundation for Information and Research on Marine Mammals; ☎ 956 627 008, ⊕ firmm.org), C/Pedro Cortés 3, slightly west of

---

WATERSPORTS ON THE GULF OF CÁDIZ

The stretch of Atlantic coast around Tarifa provides some of the best conditions in the world for **windsurfing** and **kitesurfing** – according to windsurfing aficionados, Tarifa now ranks alongside Diamond Head in Hawaii and Fuerteventura in the Canaries as one of the top three windsurfing beaches in the world. Equipment rental shops line the main street, and in peak season crowds of windsurfers pack out every available bar and *hostal*. Even in winter, there are windsurfers to be seen, drawn by regular competitions held year-round. Kitesurf novices are advised to get some instruction (especially regarding potential hazards) before striking out on their own. Details of some of the main beaches are given below, while more information as well as details of courses and companies hiring out equipment is available at ⊕ tarifainfo.com/en/surfing.html.

    Board surfing is currently less popular due to the often difficult conditions, but on the right day you can still have some great rides. Courses in all watersports are available in Tarifa and equipment can be rented at numerous shops along C/Batalla del Salado (the Turismo can also supply information).

    The Turismo has an extensive list of companies offering watersports and diving **courses**. One company offering **diving** courses in English is Aventura Marina, Avda. Andalucía 1 (☎ 956 054 626, ⊕ aventuramarina.org). Surfing and kitesurfing courses (in English) are offered by DragonKiteSchool (☎ 660 882 710, ⊕ dragonkiteschool.com) and Hot Stick Kite School (☎ 956 680 419, ⊕ hotsticktarifa.com).

BEACHES

Barbate Sheltered town beach protected by harbour wall. Good option when winds are strong and everywhere else is blown out.

Yerba Buena West-facing beach just beyond Barbate with 200m right-breaking wave off point. Generally needs 2m of swell. North/northeast winds are best. Experienced surfers only.

Caños de Meca South-facing bay approached via pine forest on road from Vejer de la Frontera. Right-breaking wave from point and left-breaking reef breaks. Works on northwest winds. Low tide. Experienced surfers only.

El Palmar West-facing beach with waves from both right and left. Best at mid-to-low tide when waves can reach heights of up to 3m (but is best on 1.5–2m swells).

Conil Good town beach but only works on pushing and dropping tide.

Cabo de Roche (northwest of Conil) Protection from strong east winds. Very fast hollow waves that have tendency to snap boards with no mercy.

La Barrosa (near Sancti Petri) Extensive beach breaks working on same conditions as El Palmar.

the church of San Mateo. You need to book in advance (2 days' notice is preferable; €30 per person; children under 14 €20). Trips last about three hours and if you don't see any dolphins or whales you get a free trip on the next sailing. Whale Watch also runs longer trips to see Orca killer whales. A more commercial operation, Turmares, Alcalde Nuñez 3, at an office on the beach road near the foot of the Paseo de la Alameda (📞 956 680 741, 🌐 turmares.com), also runs whale-spotting trips (€30, kids €20).

ACCOMMODATION

Tarifa has plenty of places to stay although due to its popularity prices tend to be higher than other places along this coast. It's wise to book ahead throughout the year, and especially in August, or whenever there are windsurfing tournaments. As elsewhere, room prices fall sharply (by up to fifty percent) outside July and August. Tarifa's campsites are served by a frequent bus service in July and August from Avda. Andalucía, just to the north of the Turismo.

HOTELS AND HOSTALES

Casa Facundo C/Batalla del Salado 47 📞 956 684 298, 🌐 hostalfacundo.com. Reliable and friendly family *hostal* on the main road into town just outside the walls, offering dorm beds, rooms sharing bath and en-suite rooms with TV. They are also building a grand new hotel across the road, opening in 2012. Dorm beds €25, rooms €71

Hostal Africa C/María Antonia Toledo 12 📞 956 680 220, ✉ hostal_africa@hotmail.com. Charming small *hostal* with clean and simple rooms with and without bath and spectacular sea views from a communal terrace. Rooms 5 and 6, with individual balconies, are the ones to go for. €50

Hostal Alameda Paseo de la Alameda 4 📞 956 681 181, 🌐 hostalalameda.com. Pleasant *hostal-restaurante* on the Alameda with en-suite rooms with TV and sea views (from some), plus free wi-fi. €80

Hostal La Calzada C/Justino Pertiñez 7 📞 956 680 366. Popular and friendly *hostal* in the centre of the old town, close by the church of San Mateo, offering a/c en-suite rooms with TV. Free wi-fi zone. €90

Hostal Villanueva Avda. Andalucía 11 📞 956 684 149. Welcoming and good-value *hostal-restaurante* built into the north wall of the old quarter offering en-suite rooms with TV. €65

Hotel La Mirada C/San Sebastián 41 📞 956 684 427, 🌐 hotel-lamirada.com. Comfortable hotel outside the walls, but only 3min from the beach. Rooms come with balcony and sea view, satellite TV, a/c and safe. B&B €100

Hotel Misiana C/Sancho IV El Bravo 18 📞 956 627 083, 🌐 misiana.com. Stylish hotel above a chic bar offering rooms with arty decor and a mishmash of colour schemes, fabrics and furnishings, some Moroccan. B&B €135

Hurricane Hotel Ctra. Cádiz s/n 📞 956 684 919, 🌐 hotelhurricane.com. Set in dense gardens 7km west of Tarifa at the ocean's edge, this luxurious California-style hotel has tastefully decorated a/c rooms, fully equipped gym, two pools, stables, windsurfing school and its own restaurant. B&B €168

La Casa Amarilla C/Sancho IV El Bravo 9 📞 956 681 993, 🌐 lacasaamarilla.net. Elegant, central and reasonably priced studios and apartments (sleeping two) in a restored nineteenth-century town house. All come with kitchenette, sitting room, a/c and cable TV. Studios €112, apartments €130

Mesón de Sancho Ctra. N340 Cádiz–Málaga, 8km east of town 📞 956 684 900, 🌐 mesondesancho.com. If you can bear being slightly out of the action then this country three-star hotel is a real bargain compared to in-town rates for the same standard of hotel. Leafy surroundings, elegant rooms, garden pool, and very good restaurant – plus a couple of delightful en-suite wood cabins – make this a bit special. Rooms €80, cabins €92

Posada La Sacristía C/San Donato 8, off C/Sancho IV El Bravo 📞 956 681 759, 🌐 lasacristia.net. Stylish boutique hotel in a converted seventeenth-century town house, with elegantly furnished rooms ranged around a central patio. Also has a decent restaurant with sushi and tempura often featuring on the menu. Can organize activities for guests from horseriding to windsurfing and rock climbing. €117 B&B

Posada Vagamundos C/San Francisco 8 📞 956 681 513, 🌐 posadavagamundos.com. Attractive hotel filled with artistic features and furnishings in a restored eighteenth-century town house. All rooms are outward-facing with a/c and TV, and there's also a wi-fi zone. B&B €100

CAMPING

Camping Río Jara On the N340 road 4km northwest of town 📞 956 680 570, 🌐 campingsdetarifa.com. The nearest campsite to the town with plenty of shade and access for disabled campers. Two people plus car €32

Camping Torre de la Peña On the N340 7km northwest of town 📞 956 684 903, 🌐 campingtp.com. Another decent campsite close to the sea with plenty of shade, pool and a decent restaurant. Two people plus car €20

Camping Tarifa On the N340 6km northwest of town 📞 956 684 778, 🌐 camping-tarifa.es. Pleasant site in a pinewood with plenty of shade and its own pool, 100m from the beach. Two people plus car €24

Camping Paloma Los Algarbes 10km northwest of town 📞 956 684 203, 🌐 campingpaloma.com. Not quite as close to the beach as some others, but the magnificent Playa de Valdevaqueros is only 500m distant. There's plenty of shade plus a restaurant, pool and supermarket on site. Two people plus car €21

EATING, DRINKING AND NIGHTLIFE

Tarifa has a wide range of places to eat, divided between the old town inside the walls and the new town beyond. This is another place to try Cádiz's tasty *urta* (sea bream), available all over town. There's little in the way of entertainment beyond a few stylish bars such as those attached to the *Misiana* and *Posada La Sacristía* hotels, and *Bamboo*, at Paseo de la Alameda 2, plus a couple of *discotecas*. It's worth finding out what's happening at the Tarifa Eco Center (w tarifaecocenter .com; see p.169) as they stage frequent concerts (usually Sun) and show films. Tarifa's main summer nightlife scene happens when the town council erects *carpas* (disco tents) on the Playa de los Lances beach at the eastern end of town.

TAPAS BARS AND BARS

Bar Almedina C/Almedina s/n. Popular food and tapas bar in a twelfth-century gatehouse with a battered piano to one side as you enter, and some equally battered-looking regulars propping up the bar. There's a great ambience when it fills up in the evening with the *copas* and cocktails crowd. They also stage live events and flamenco often takes place on Thurs. Daily 9pm–late.

★ **Bar El Francés Paseo** C/Sancho IV El Bravo 21. A highly popular French-owned tapas and *raciones* bar adding a subtly Gallic touch to such staples as *calamares*, *rabo de toro* and *tortilla de camarones*. Has a small street terrace. Daily 10am–5pm & 7pm–2am.

Café Zumo C/Sancho El Bravo IV 26b. Good breakfast bar with a selection of fruit and vegetable juices and a variety of breads and healthy snacks. Daily 9am–2am.

Casino C/Coronel Moscardó s/n, next to the church of San Mateo. Opened in 1875, Tarifa's impressive multi-roomed, tiled and marble-floored Casino is open to all and is splendidly evocative of a bygone age. Its bar serves morning café fare and tasty tapas at lunchtimes, and there's a library with all the papers and space to stretch out. Daily 9am–10pm.

Mesón La Garrocha C/Guzmán El Bueno 22. Very good tapas bar with tables inside to sample their more eleborate fare including their own *jamón ibérico*. Try the *chuleta de vaca retinto* (high-quality beef) or *rabo de toro*. Daily 10am–11pm.

Geko Plaza de Oviedo 1. Fronting the church of San Mateo, this pleasant little terrace bar serves a variety of economical salads, *tablas de queso* (cheese boards) and pasta dishes, as well as *bocadillos* and plenty of vegetarian options. Daily 10am–1am.

RESTAURANTS

Bar Morilla C/Sancho IV El Bravo 2. Central bar where *tarifeños* gather to breakfast or munch early-evening tapas while contemplating the ancient stones of nearby San Mateo. Later, cloths are thrown over the tables as the restaurant hits its stride serving very good fish – *urta a la plancha* (sea bream) is a house special – and meat dishes. Daily 10am–1am.

Bar-Restaurante Voracera C/San Sebastián 28, outside the walls. Great neighbourhood bar-restaurant with tasty tapas and good seafood; *besugo a la espalda* (red bream) is a house special and there's a *menú* (Mon–Fri) for €7.50. Daily 9am–midnight.

Bodega Amarillo C/Sancho IV El Bravo 9. Lots of cool tiles and marble at this bodega serving up *raciones* of *cerdo ibérico jamón*, plus *calamares a la plancha* (fried squid) and in season *atún del almadraba* (the freshest tuna there is). They also own the *Café Central* opposite, another venerable bar-café founded in 1894. Main dishes €8–14. Daily 11am–11pm.

Casa Juan Luis C/San Francisco 15 ☎ 956 681 265. Despite its proximity to the sea this evening-only place is a shrine to meat, in particular pork in all its Iberian variations. The restaurant, housed in a *casa antigua*, also has a beautiful patio and outdoor terrace. *Menú* for about €28. Daily 7pm–midnight.

Chilimosa C/Peso 6, just by the Puerto de Jerez. Lilliputian vegetarian diner with only a few tables, but they also do takeaways. Daily specials feature samosas, *empanadas* (pasties), falafel, quiche, salads and curries. Also makes its own tasty *dulces* and serves organic wine, beer and soft drinks. Daily 12.30–3.30pm & 7–11pm.

★ **Mandragora** C/Independencia 3 ☎ 956 681 291. Located behind the church of San Mateo this is one of Tarifa's best restaurants, and offers dishes from both sides of the straits: in addition to Moroccan couscous and *berenjenas bereber* ("Berber-style" aubergine), it does excellent *raciones*, including *boquerones rellenos* (stuffed anchovies) and fish and vegetarian options. The dining room – decorated with ferns and plants – does justice to the cuisine. Main dishes €10–20. Mon–Sat 7pm–midnight.

Mesón de Sancho ☎ 956 68 49 00. Attached to the hotel (see p.167) of the same name, this is one of the best restaurants in this zone for both fish (*urta a la roteña* – is a house special) and meat dishes. Mid-priced, with a *menú* for around €18. Daily noon–5pm & 8pm–midnight.

Restaurante Alameda Paseo Alameda 4. Popular terrace restaurant outside the western wall, which does reasonable *platos combinados*, fish dishes and a tasty paella. Main dishes €8–15. Daily noon–midnight.

Restaurante Villanueva Avda. Andalucía 11. Excellent little restaurant of the *hostal* of the same name; their *urta* is prepared in five different ways and there's a good-value *menú* for €7.50. Daily 10am–5pm & 8–11pm.

Santa Fe Paseo Alameda s/n, with entry also at C/Santísima Trinidad 19. Excellent mid-priced French-run bistro with a terrace on the Alameda. They serve up a range of fish and meat dishes accompanied by great (French) wines. Their crepes (served in afternoons with tea or coffee as well as to diners at other times) are mouthwateringly authentic. Daily *menú* for €9. Daily 12.30–5pm & 7pm–midnight.

★ **Tarifa Eco Center** C/San Sebastián 4 ☎ 956 627 220. This interesting "alternative" complex has an organic vegetarian restaurant (pasta, pizzas, salads, quiches, *taboulé*, organic hamburgers etc) out front, an eco-shop at the rear and a chill-out zone serving herbal and other teas to the side. Off a courtyard terrace other rooms offer yoga, pilates and other courses. Daily 10am–midnight.

Baelo Claudia

Enseneda de Bolonia s/n • June–Sept Tues–Sat 9am–8pm, Sun 9am–2pm; March–May & Oct–Feb Tues–Sat 9am–7pm, Sun 9am–2pm • €1.50, free with EU passport

Around the coast from Punta Paloma to the west of Tarifa and almost on the magnificent beach at Bolonia Cove are the extensive ruins of the Roman town of **BAELO CLAUDIA**. The site is entered via a new concrete bunker with a car park and visitor centre where you'll find a small museum with finds from the site, historical reconstructions and a photo history of the excavations. Established in the second century BC, the Roman town – rather like modern Zahara and Barbate nearby – became prosperous with the exploitation of tuna and mackerel to make the fish sauce **garum**, of which the Romans were passionately fond. The town reached the peak of its prosperity during the first century AD when it was raised to the status of a municipium or self-governing township by Emperor Claudius, and the buildings you see today date from this period.

The Puerta de Carteia and fish factory

Following the numbered information boards detailed on the leaflet you receive with your ticket, a tour of the site starts by crossing a footbridge over the stream of La Chorrera where you can see the remains of the Punta Paloma **aqueduct**, the longest of the three that formerly supplied the town, bringing water from springs at Punta Paloma, 8km southeast. The route then tracks the remains of the town wall as far as the substantial bastions of what must have been an impressive entry gate – the **Puerta de Carteia** – in the town's eastern wall. You enter the town via this gate as most ancient visitors to Baelo would have done.

The route then follows the decumanus maximus (main street) to the first intersection where it detours left to take in what are probably the most interesting series of buildings, actually on the beach. Here has been revealed a **fish factory** which produced the famous garum, and you can still clearly make out the great stone vats used to make this concoction – always located as near to the sea and as far away from the town as possible because of the stench. The process involved removing the heads, entrails, eggs, soft roes and blood of the fish, layering these in the vats with salt and brine, and leaving them for weeks to "mature". The resulting mixture was then slopped into amphorae and shipped all over the empire, particularly to Rome, where the poet Martial droolingly described it as "made of the first blood of a mackerel breathing still, an expensive gift". The mackerel sauce was the Roman equivalent of beluga and they paid the earth for small quantities of it; the tuna-based variety, however, was less of a luxury and much cheaper.

The forum and around

The route then takes in a well-preserved rectangular **forum**, best viewed from the platform at the northern end supporting a row of **three temples** to Jupiter, Juno and Minerva, the great gods of imperial Rome. Just west of here is a smaller temple dedicated to the Egyptian goddess Isis, and directly ahead, occupying the whole south side of the forum, are the remains of the **basilica**, or law court. At the eastern end of this building stood a colossal white marble statue of the second-century emperor Trajan, the head of which is now preserved in the museum at Cádiz (see p.184). A replica of the statue now occupies the site. On the forum's eastern flank stood a line of tabernae (shops), which seem to have been superseded by the later **macellum** (market), built to the west of the basilica.

2

The route continues west along the main street and then turns north at the town's western gate, the Puerta de Gades (Cádiz), taking in a baths complex en route to the newly restored **theatre**, built into the hillside to take advantage of the slope. The route then crosses the forum's northern end to lead you back to the visitor centre.

ARRIVAL AND DEPARTURE   BAELO CLAUDIA

By bus There are currently three buses per day (10.45am, 3.15pm & 8pm) running from Tarifa bus station to Baelo and returning at 11.30am, 3.45pm and 4.30pm, allowing you to combine a visit to the site with a session on the wonderful beach fronting it.
By car Baelo is a 23km trip from Tarifa via the N340

Tarifa–Cádiz road, with a turn-off down a small side road (signed "Bolonia"), on the left at the *San José del Vallé* hotel-restaurant (which serves a good menú).
By foot You can also walk to Bolonia along the coast from either Punta Paloma west of Tarifa or, coming from the opposite direction, Zahara de los Atunes (3–4hr).

ACCOMMODATION

Hostal Bellavista Near the turn-off into the village of Bolonia ☎ 956 688 553, ⓦ hostalbellavista.es. Decent en-suite rooms with TV above a restaurant – it's worth paying a few euros more to get one with a terrace. Also rents out some studios and apartments nearby. **€50**
★ **Hostal La Hormiga Voladora** C/El Lentiscal 15, at the eastern end of the village ☎ 956 688 562. Delightful garden retreat with individually styled en-suite rooms that are simple but charming. A couple of more expensive

rooms (#7 & #16) have sea views and there are plenty of nooks for lazing around. Breakfast (extra) is served on patio shaded by a prodigious mulberry tree. **€65**
La Posada de Lola C/El Lentiscal 26 ☎ 956 688 536, ⓦ hostallola.com. Attractive *posada* in a beautiful garden run by a friendly, eponymous proprietor. Some rooms have a/c and en suite; others have shared bathroom. Free wi-fi zone. **€50**

EATING AND DRINKING

There are a couple of beach *chiringuitos* actually on the beach serving grilled fish – try the *Bahía de Bolonia* – otherwise most of the places to eat are in the small village of Bolonia itself.

Hostal Bellavista Near the turn-off into the village of Bolonia. This *hostal* restaurant isn't bad and serves standard *venta* food with an economical *menú* for €10.

Las Rejas Close to the Hostal La Hormiga Voladora. Perhaps Bolonia's best restaurant, with fresh *mariscos* and fish – including tuna in season – and a decent lunchtime paella.

Zahara de los Atunes

Eight kilometres north from Bolonia as the crow flies (but a hefty 28km dog-leg by road along the N340), **ZAHARA DE LOS ATUNES** is an ancient fishing village long involved (as its name tells you) in the catching of tuna – now an industry in decline. Linked by an infrequent **bus** service with Barbate (see p.172), Zahara is now beginning to show signs of development, but outside of high summer it remains a slow-moving resort with good tapas bars, hospitable locals and a fabulous eight-kilometre-long **beach**.

ARRIVAL AND DEPARTURE   ZAHARA DE LOS ATUNES

By bus Daily buses link Zahara with Cádiz, Algeciras, Jerez and Málaga.

ACCOMMODATION

Camping Bahía de la Plata 1.5km out of town on the road towards Atlanterra ☎ 956 439 040, ⓦ camping bahiadelaplata.com. Efficient, refurbished campsite with reasonable shade plus a pool, supermarket and restaurant. It also also rents out bungalows and studios, both with cooking facilities. Two people plus car **€26.50**, bungalows and studios **€120**
Gran Sol Avda. de la Playa 20 ☎ 956 43 93 09, ⓦ gransol hotel.com. Excellent three-star seafront hotel (sea-view

rooms cost extra) with comfortable a/c traditional rooms and an extension overlooking a garden pool. Their restaurant is also good and has a daily *menú* for €18. B&B **€120**
Hostal Monte Mar C/Peñón 12 ☎ 956 439 047. A decent budget place bang on the seashore offering simple en-suite rooms with balcony. The service can occasionally be a bit hit and miss but the owners are friendly and usually get there in the end. More of a bargain in spring and autumn than high summer. It's to the right as you cross the bridge

ANDALUCÍA AND THE BLUEFIN TUNA

The catch of the **bluefin tuna** is a ritual that has gone on along the Costa de la Luz since ancient times and today still employs many of the age-old methods. The bluefin is the largest of the tuna family, weighing in at around 200 kilos, and the season lasts from April to June as the fish migrate towards the warmer waters of Mediterranean (*el derecho*) to reproduce, and from early July to mid-August when they return to the high seas (*el revés*). Fishing communities dotted along this stretch of Andalucian coast have been taking advantage of this annual abundance of tuna since the Phoenician period and probably long back into prehistory. The methods used to catch the tuna are still referred to by the Moorish name *almadraba* ("place for hitting"), which involved dragging the giant fish ashore in great nets and clubbing them to death.

Today the fish are caught at sea by herding and corralling them in a huge net stretched between a circle of boats where they are gaffed – their blood turning the sea crimson – before the weakened fish are then hauled aboard. The biggest market is Japan, and Japanese factory ships can often be spotted waiting offshore in season ready to buy up as much of the catch as they can. Once the tuna are on board, the fish are rapidly gutted, washed, filleted and frozen ready to cross another ocean to be eaten raw as sushi. In recent years tuna numbers have been declining and the season shortening – probably the result of overfishing – much to the concern of the people of Barbate, Conil de la Frontera and Zahara de los Atunes, for whom the catch represents an important source of income for fishermen and a provider of employment in the canning factories nearby.

into the village, but new one-way road signing means that with your own transport you may need to ask. €72

Hotel Almadraba & Almadrabeta C/María Luisa 13 ☏ 956 439 274, ⓦ hotelesalmadraba.es. Pleasant and welcoming traditional two-star with perfectly adequate rooms with a/c, TV and terrace balcony. Also has a very good restaurant below. €75

Hotel Antonio C/Atlanterra Km1 ☏ 956 439 141, ⓦ antoniohoteles.com. Decent-value rooms in this two-star

seafront hotel along with more luxurious accommodation in an adjoining four-star extension. Most rooms have terraces and sea views (extra charge) and there's a solarium and a large pool. B&B hotel €120, extension €165

Hotel Doña Lola Plaza Thomson 1, just over the bridge at the entry to the village ☏ 956 439 009, ⓦ dona lolazahara.com. Attractive four-star with light, well-equipped rooms, pool, gardens, *cafetería* and car park. B&B €155

EATING AND DRINKING

Almadraba Hotel Almadraba & Almadrabeta, C/María Luisa 13. This popular hotel restaurant is an excellent place for seafood. Everything is as fresh as can be and the speciality here – not surprisingly – is tuna (*almadraba* refers to netting the tuna catch, see box above).

★ **Antonio** Hotel Antonio, C/Atlanterra Km1 ☏ 956 439 542. Excellent mid-priced fish restaurant almost on the beach with fine sea views. This establishment oozes quality and the fish and *mariscos* are outstanding. Signature dishes include *atún al horno* (baked tuna) and *dorada a la sal* (sea bream baked in sea salt). Has a weekday lunch *menú* for €20.

★ **Casa Juanito** C/Sagasta 7, in the centre of the village. One of the oldest (founded 1948) and the best tapas bars and restaurants on this stretch of coast, serving up deliciously fresh seafood. Try the delectable *tataki de*

atún rojo (red tuna Japanese-style).

El Costero C/Alcalde Ruíz Cana 7. Outstanding new tapas and *raciones* bar, an offshoot of *Casa Juanito* (above) and only a stone's throw away. The interior is light and modern with a long, marble-topped bar and slick service. Among a wide tapas selection (check out the daily specials on a blackboard) featuring fish and *mariscos* their *tapa de mejillones* (mussels) makes a perfect partner for a *copa* of manzanilla.

La Botica C/Real 13 & C/José Antonio 14. A superb bar-restaurant for fish and meat dishes. The bar (in C/Real) does fried fish tapas and *raciones* as well as great *jamón* and *salchichón*. Their restaurant (C/José Antonio, around the corner) offers a variety of fish and meat dishes with the emphasis on tuna. Try the *pescado a la roteña* (fish in onion sauce).

Atlanterra

South from Zahara a road winds down for 4km to the settlement of **ATLANTERRA**, another hamlet seized upon by developers and, a few kilometres beyond this, to a wonderful **beach**, the Playa Camarinal. Atlanterra itself is rapidly being transformed into a warren of holiday apartments ringed around the bland *Hotel Melia*, part of the

2

luxury hotel chain. Just a hundred metres out of this settlement, however, lies the delightful boutique hotel *El Cortijo de Zahara* (see below). Beyond here the road continues for a further 4km passing a few secluded villas (owned by many of Spain's rich and famous) circled by lofty palms before coming to a dead end at the **Playa Camarinal** and, a bit further on, the Faro del Punta Camarinal lighthouse. It's a stunning beach, but there are no facilities whatsoever. With a day to spare you could walk the 5km from here to the Roman ruins at Baelo Claudia (see p.169), but take a map and plenty of water in high summer.

ACCOMMODATION

ATLANTERRA

★ **El Cortijo de Zahara** Avda. de Atlanterra ☎ 902 932 613, ⊛ elcortijodezahara.com. Stunning beach hotel, partly housed in a converted nineteenth-century military barracks (although it has been extended) and surrounded by gardens filled with palms, cactus and hibiscus and a pool. The individually and elegantly styled rooms and suites are equipped to four-star standard and most have a sea view (rooms 7, 106 and 119 are the ones to go for). There's also a bar, cafetería and restaurant. **€155**

Barbate

BARBATE next along the coast and linked by a frequent daily **bus** service with Vejer de la Frontera, is an unkempt and rather featureless little town dominated by its harbour and canning industry which processes the tuna caught along this stretch of coast. As the major fishing port in these parts Barbate has some excellent **tapas bars** and **fish restaurants** along its seafront, but that's about the limit of its appeal. There's a pleasant **walk** (about two and a half hours starting from the west side of the fishing harbour) from here to Los Caños de Meca (see p.173), through a pine forest and passing the Torre de Tajo (a watchtower once used for spotting invading pirates) with great views, but take care at the cliff edges.

Parque Natural de Acantilado

From Barbate, a rolling scenic road winds its way through the verdant pinewoods of the **Parque Natural de Acantilado** (aka Parque Natural La Breña), home to the wonderful El Palomar de la Breña (see below), a superb *hotel rural* with a remarkable eighteenth-century dovecote of immense proportions authenticated by the Guinness Book of Records as the largest in the world. No longer in use, the dovecote's eight thousand nesting places once produced birds for the Spanish Indies fleet who used them to communicate with Spain while out in the Atlantic. At its height the dovecote would have been producing over eighty thousand offspring per year and the huge surplus of birds was a valuable source of meat both for the local population and the navy, who carried doves in cages on board ship to be killed when necessary. A by-product of the thousands of birds nesting here was a fifteen-ton annual supply of guano, considered in those days to be the best organic fertilizer. Doves no longer nest here and their former homes have since been occupied by three pairs of kestrels as well as little owls and barn owls, all serious discouragements should the original occupants try to reclaim their dovecote.

ACCOMMODATION

PARQUE NATURAL DE ACANTILADO

El Palomar de la Breña ☎ 956 435 003, ⊛ palomar delabrena.com. This eighteenth-century *cortijo* has been transformed into a charming 15-room *hotel rural* in the middle of the park. The en-suite rooms are simple but perfectly adequate and come with TV, fridge and a terrace to sit out, plus a pool – or the beaches of Trafalgar are only 5km distant. There's also free wi-fi and the proprietors can advise on many activities in the park including hiking, horseriding, mountain-biking and birdwatching. The hotel is reached via a turn-off from the A2233, 5km out of Barbate, but ring or see their website for precise details. B&B **€98**

Los Caños de Meca

A further 5km beyond the turn-off for El Palomar de la Breña the road descends into **LOS CAÑOS DE MECA** (served by sporadic buses from Barbate to Conil). A small village surrounded by pine groves and a favourite summer escape for *sevillanos*, Los Caños has a long, beautiful beach lined with rocky coves and freshwater springs, marred only by some unfortunate hotel developments on its southern flank. At the western end of seafront, a side road off Avenida Trafalgar (the road running behind the beach) leads to a landmark lighthouse and the historically famous Cabo (or cape) de Trafalgar (see p.178). There used to be a hippy colony here and, although this crowd has now gone, some of the laid-back atmosphere lingers, especially among the groups of naturists who swim out to the more secluded coves along the coast.

ACCOMMODATION
LOS CAÑOS DE MECA

★ **Casas Karen** Camino del Monte 6, down a signed track 500m east of the turning for the lighthouse ☎956 437 067, ⓦcasaskaren.com. Very friendly place run by the eponymous Dutch proprietor with various styles of rooms and apartments (including traditional *chozo* huts) in a wonderful garden setting. High season applies Aug only; see website for special offers. **€85**

Hostal Mar de Frente Avda. Trafalgar 3, 100m beyond the Hotel Fortuna (below) ☎956 437 025, ⓦhotelmardefrente.com. In a brilliant white mansion overlooking the sea and with its own access to the beach. All rooms are en suite with TV and most have a terrace and sea view. Free wi-fi zone. B&B **€77**

Hotel Fortuna Avda. Trafalgar 34, at the eastern end of the seafront ☎956 437 075, ⓦhostalfortuna.com. This friendly family-run hotel has cosy en-suite rooms with balcony (most also have sea view), safe and TV. They also have some attractive seafront chalets nearby sleeping up to four. Free wi-fi and parking. High season applies Aug only. Rooms **€90**, apartments **€180**

Hotel Madreselva Avda. Trafalgar 102 ☎956 437 255,

ⓦmadreselva.grupocalifa.com. A welcoming hotel offering comfortable rooms with terraces surrounding a central plant-filled patio. There's a good-sized pool in the grounds and the beach is just a stone's throw away. The proprietors can advise on horseriding and mountain bike hire and also run surfing and kitesurfing courses with discounts for guests. *Rough Guide* readers with this guide receive a ten percent discount which should be claimed at check-in. B&B **€104**

CAMPSITE

Camping Camaleón Ctra. de Trafalgar s/n ☎956 437 154. This central campsite is a decent option with plenty of shade and its own bar-restaurant. Two people plus car **€27.50**

Camping Caños de Meca Ctra. Vejer a Los Caños, km10, just west of the village ☎956 437 120, ⓦcampingcm .com. The better of Los Caños's two campsites, this is a family oriented site 600m from the beach with plenty of shade provided by pines and eucalyptus. There is also disabled access and the facilities have been recently refurbished. Open Mar–Oct. Two people plus car **€24.50**

EATING, DRINKING AND NIGHTLIFE

El Caña Avda. Trafalgar 53 Good – and reasonably priced – fish restaurant with a shaded terrace giving stunning views over the beach. Specials include *surtido frito* (fried fish) and *urta a la roteña* (sea bream). Main dishes €7–12.

La Aceitera Carril La Aceitera 165 ☎956 437 016. Reached by following the Avda. de Trafalgar 500m west beyond the turn off for the lighthouse, this atmospheric bar-restaurant has an artistic slant (the boss is a woman sculptor). The bar serves tapas (one free with every drink) and they operate a summer barbecue in their garden. The restaurant specialises in Mediterranean cuisine and there are salads and couscous. Live music (flamenco or jazz) is frequently staged at weekends in summer and they also mount art exhibitions.

El Solecito Avda. Trafalgar 51, opposite La Jaima. Popular breakfast and juice bar that stays open late for *copas* and cocktails. Has a small terrace out front.

La Jaima Avda. de Trafalgar s/n. Popular *discoteca* with dancefloor inside an exotically decorated Bedouin tent that attracts quite a crowd in summer. All kinds of drinks are served and the house special is a stiff mojito. Don't bother with their food as it's overpriced and the portions are small.

Las Dunas Ctra. del Cabo de Trafalgar. On the road leading to the lighthouse, this cavernous stone-built bar with a thatched roof serves breakfasts and juices as well as tapas and *raciones*. In summer they also operate a barbecue for grilling *carnes ibéricos* (black pig pork). As dusk falls it metamorphoses into a *copas* and music bar.

Venta Curro C/Zahora s/n ☎956 437 064. Near the *Caños de Meca* campsite, this is perhaps the best-value place to eat in the resort. They do both fish and meat – try the *solomillo ibérico* (pork loin) – dishes well and all the seafood is caught locally. There's also an economical *menú* offering regional specialities.

El Palmar

The coast road northwest from Los Caños (taking a left after 5km and continuing for a further 3km) brings you to **EL PALMAR**, a sleepy and isolated seafront settlement with a waterfront dotted with holiday apartments, bars and restaurants. The narrow, 2km-long blue-flag beach here is popular with surfers, but it never gets overcrowded and this all adds up to about as peaceful a place as you could wish.

ACCOMMODATION AND EATING   EL PALMAR

Hostal Francisco Alferez Paseo de la Playa s/n, southern end ☎ 956 232 134, ⓦ hostalfranciscoalferez .com. Simple but adequate en-suite rooms above a decent fish restaurant with a pleasant sea-view terrace. **€60**

Hostal La Ilusión Playa de El Palmar ☎ 956 232 398, ⓦ la-ilusion.com. Friendly *hostal* at the southern end of the beach, surrounded by an extensive garden. The comfortable rooms come with TV, and most also have sea views. There's also a good restaurant – with €12.50 *menú* – below. B&B **€75**

Hostal-Restaurant Casa Francisco Playa de El Palmar s/n, southern end ☎ 956 232 786, ⓦ casafrancisco eldesiempre.com. Twenty-five metres from the beach, this *hostal* has pleasant en-suite rooms with TV and

sea-view terrace. The outstanding seafood restaurant below is probably El Palmar's best place to eat and has recently made it into Michelin. Recommended dishes include *caribineros con arroz* (scarlet prawns with rice), *tataki de atún rojo* (red tuna Japanese-style) and an outstanding *alcachofas con vieiras* (artichokes with scallops). B&B **€80**

CAMPSITE

Camping El Palmar Playa de El Palmar, southern end ☎ 956 232 161, ⓦ campingelpalmar.es. Set 1km back from the beach this is a very good campsite with a great pool, plenty of shade, restaurant, bar and supermarket, and lots of activities on offer, including trekking, scuba diving and horseriding. Two people plus car **€24.50**

DRINKING

Cortijo El Cartero Ctra. de la Playa s/n, at the northern end of the seafront near an ancient atalaya (watch-tower). This huge *chozo* (traditional thatched hut) is currently the latest rave place at the northern end of

the seafront with terraces and a barnlike interior. They serve food, but most people are here for *copas* and there's often live music (anything from rock to flamenco). Gets packed to the gunwales at weekends.

Vejer de la Frontera

While you're on this stretch of the Costa de la Luz, be sure to take time to head inland and visit **VEJER DE LA FRONTERA**, a classically white, Moorish-looking hill town set in a cleft between great protective hills that rear high above the road from Tarifa to Cádiz. Until relatively recent times the women of Vejer wore long, dark cloaks that veiled their faces like nuns' habits; though still trotted out in many guidebooks, this custom is now virtually extinct outside fiestas.

Maintaining a brooding detachment from the world below for most of its history, Vejer has a remoteness and a Moorish feel as potent as anywhere in Spain. Almost certainly a prehistoric hilltop Iberian citadel, Vejer was utilized as a fortress during the **Phoenician** and **Carthaginian** epochs of the first millennium BC to protect coastal factories and fishing grounds from the warlike Iberians of the interior. Dubbed Besipo by the later **Romans**, it was as the **Moorish** town of Bekkeh that Vejer rose to prominence as an important agricultural centre on the western frontier of the kingdom of Granada. Taken by Fernando III in 1250, it was immediately handed over to Alonso Pérez de Guzmán, founder of the ducal house of Medina Sidonia and later hero of Tarifa.

Vejer is best savoured by randomly exploring the brilliant-white, labyrinthine alleyways, wandering past iron-grilled windows, balconies and patios, and slipping into one of numerous bars.

The castillo

C/Ramón y Cajal s/n • Daily 10am–2pm & 5.30–8.30pm • Free

The **castillo**, in the heart of the old quarter, is Moorish in origin but underwent substantial rebuilding in the fifteenth century when it was used by the dukes of Medina

Sidonia as a summer retreat. The main things to see are a splendid horseshoe arch and some Moorish plasterwork, as well as great views from the terrace. A small **museum** displays ancient and more recent finds discovered in and around the town.

Divino Salvador and around

To the northwest of the castle, the church of **Divino Salvador** (daily 11am–1pm & 5–7pm; free) is a sixteenth-century rebuild of an earlier mosque whose minaret now serves as the tower. The interior is a curious mix of mainly Gothic and Mudéjar styles.

From here, Calle Castrillón descends to the **Plaza de España**, the lovely main square, overlooked by a white-walled Ayuntamiento, and centred on a delightful fountain decorated with nineteenth-century Triana tiles from Seville. North of here, the **Paseo de la Corredera** offers spectacular views over the countryside to the nearby hill towns of Medina Sidonia and Alcalá de los Gazules. The **Torre de la Corredera** halfway along here was a watchtower used for communicating with those towns.

NMAC modern art museum

5km southeast of the town along the N-340 in the grounds of the Dehesa Montenmedio (no bus service) • March–Oct Tue–Sun 10am–2pm & 5–8.30pm; Nov–Feb Mon–Fri & Sun 10am–2.30pm, Sat 10am–2pm & 4–6pm • €5, first Sun of month free • ⑩ fundacionnmac.org

One visit worth making outside Vejer is to the impressive open-air **NMAC modern art museum**. Featuring major works by renowned international artists comprising

2

installations (Fernandez Sánchez Castillo's Fountain, featuring a riot-control truck sunk in the middle of a pond, is a showstopper), sculpture and photography, the route around the artworks passes through stunning parkland and forest replete with birdlife and (in season) nesting storks. For refreshment, the affordable *Café de Kurupay* has an attractive shaded terrace and serves various fish and meat *raciones*, salads and full meals.

ARRIVAL AND DEPARTURE   VEJER DE LA FRONTERA

By bus Buses drop off passengers at the Parque de Los Remedios just to the side of the Turismo from where you'll need to ascend Avda. Los Remedios to reach La Plazuela, the effective centre of town. Services from here connect

with Cádiz, Seville, Jerez and Málaga.
By car It's best to park in the car park at the entrance to the town near the foot of Avda. Los Remedios, as the old town's streets are narrow and convoluted.

INFORMATION

Turismo Next to the car park as you enter Vejer, at Avda. Los Remedios 2 (April–Sept Mon–Sat 10am–2pm & 6–8pm, Sun 11am–1pm; Oct–March Mon–Fri 10am–2pm & 4–6pm, Sat 10am–2pm; ☎ 956 45 17 36, Ⓦ turismovejer.es). Staff here hand out an excellent free town map (also available from the *Hotel Convento*

when the Turismo is closed).
Bookshop Bookend, C/Juan Relinque 45, is a good source of used books in English and does exchange deals.
Internet Vi@.PC, Avda. San Miguel 18 (Mon–Fri 10am–2pm & 5–8pm), slightly out of the centre.

ACCOMMODATION

★ **Casablanca** C/Canalejas 8 ☎ 956 447 569, Ⓦ andaluciacasablanca.com. Chic apartment-style rooms in a house dating back to the thirteenth century. The bright and airy rooms come with a fully equipped kitchen and guests have free use of a roof terrace/solarium (with great views) plus a remarkable cave-like spa carved out beneath the house. The high season price (quoted here) falls by 25 percent outside July and Aug. **€90**
Casa Luisa C/San Filmo 16, close to La Plazuela ☎ 956 450 246. Friendly, economical and clean *pensión* with rooms sharing bath; also has some apartments for rent sleeping up to four. Rooms **€30**, apartments **€50**
Casa Rural Leonor C/Rosario 25, near the castillo ☎ 956 451 085, Ⓦ casaleonor.com. This converted Moorish dwelling has comfortable en-suite rooms with TV, friendly proprietors, and fabulous views towards Morocco from a roof terrace. Also has its own decent restaurant below and rents out some fully equipped apartments nearby sleeping up to four. Rooms **€50**, apartments **€80**
★ **El Cobijo de Vejer** C/La Viña 7 ☎ 956 455 023, Ⓦ elcobijo.com. Excellent-value and welcoming *hostal* inside an enchanting traditional house with a delightful vine-shaded, flower-filled patio and individually styled rooms on various levels. The slightly higher-priced apartment-style rooms Tarifa, Zahara and Xauen (the last has two fabulous terraces) with own kitchens are the ones to go for. All rooms are a/c and come with fridges, satellite TV and free wi-fi. B&B **€85**
Hostal El Mirador C/Cañada de San Lázaro 39, near the bus stop at the entrance to the town ☎ 956 451 713, ✉ hostal_mirador@hotmail.com. Clean and tidy en-suite balcony rooms (with views) plus a/c and TV. **€50**
Hostal La Janda Cerro Clarisas s/n, signposted up a side road on the way in ☎ 956 450 142. Excellent *hostal*

with light and airy en-suite rooms with a/c and TV. Three-night minimum stay in Aug. **€50**
Hostal La Posada Avda. Los Remedios 2, near the top of the hill as you enter the town ☎ 956 450 258, Ⓦ hostal-laposada.com. Good en-suite a/c rooms above a restaurant and most with fine views. Has some singles too, and rents out apartments sleeping up to four. Rooms **€50**, apartments (sleeping up to four) **€25pp**
Hotel Convento de San Francisco La Plazuela s/n ☎ 956 451 001, Ⓦ tugasa.com. Housed in a converted seventeenth-century convent on the smaller of the town's two main squares, this very pleasant and surprisingly reasonably priced hotel has transformed the austere former cells – with exposed stone walls – into attractive a/c rooms with TV. Also has its own restaurant and *cafetería* housed in the convent's former refectory with surviving wall paintings (see p.177). **€67**
★ **La Casa del Califa** Plaza de España 16 ☎ 956 447 730, Ⓦ lacasadelcalifa.com. Stunning hotel created inside a refurbished, part-Moorish house, featuring individually styled rooms decorated with Moroccan lamps and fittings. Guests have use of two patios, a terrace with views, library and there's also free wi-fi and internet. *Rough Guide* readers with this book are entitled to a ten-percent discount, which should be claimed at check-in. B&B **€104**
No.1 La Tripería Plaza de España 16 ☎ 956 447 730, Ⓦ triperia.grupocalifa.com. The *casa rural* of the adjacent *La Casa del Califa* (see above), set in a restored, partly Moorish house with elegantly furnished rooms (most with private terrace) offering fine views and ringed around an inviting pool. Guests have use of a shared kitchen and there's easy parking behind. *Rough Guide* readers with this book are entitled to a ten-percent discount, which should be claimed at check-in. **€120**

CAMPSITE

Camping Los Molinos Ctra. N340 km34.5, Santa Lucía ☎ 956 450 988, ✆ campinglosmolinosvejer.com. Good campsite with plenty of shade, pool and restaurant. It's below the town in the Santa Lucía *barrio* on the main N340 road, close to the *Venta Pinto* restaurant. Two people plus car **€20**

EATING, DRINKING AND ENTERTAINMENT

Vejer has plenty of places for eating and drinking. Nightlife is fairly tame, limited to a few bars around town that keep late hours. Bodegas Gallardo (daily 10am–6pm), on the main Barbate road below the town, welcomes visitors to sample and buy the wines and finos of the region.

Bar Peneque Plaza de España 27. Traditional local bar built into a cave with tables at the back for munching *raciones* should you not feel like joining in the domino games favoured by regulars. Daily 9am–midnight.

Café-Bar La Bodeguita C/Marqués de Tamarón 9, uphill from La Plazuela. Entertaining late-night *copas* bar with a street terrace and an often lively crowd; also does tapas – house specials are *pimiento de piquillo* (peppers stuffed with cod) and *albondigas* (meatballs). Daily 11am–midnight (July & Aug closed for siesta 3.30–7pm).

Casa Varo C/Nuestra Señora de la Oliva 9. New and stylish *raciones* and *media raciones* bar with a pleasant outdoor terrace facing the church. They offer a wide range of meat and fish dishes and ultra-fresh *mariscos*. Try the *cañaillas* (sort of whelk) or any of their tuna offerings. Daily 10am–11pm.

★ **Castillería** Barrio de Santa Lucía s/n ☎ 956 451 497. Wonderful outdoor mid-priced garden restaurant in this rural *barrio* below the town. Specializes in *carnes a la brasa* (charcoal-grilled meats) and excellent salads. Try the *solomillo de vaca retinta* (red cattle beefsteak) or the *magret de pato* (duck). Chef/owner Julian Valdés insists on personally cooking every piece of meat that leaves his kitchen, which can add to waiting times when the place is busy (especially at weekends, when booking is advisable). But it's worth it. Open May–Sept only; daily noon–4pm & 8pm–midnight.

El Jardín del Califa Plaza de España 16. The mid-priced restaurant attached to the hotel of the same name has a Moroccan chef and serves up a variety of Moroccan and Middle-Eastern inspired dishes on a tree-shaded courtyard terrace. Specialities include tagines and spicy Moroccan fish dishes, and there's also a stylish bar with stunning views from its roof terrace. Daily 11am–11pm.

El Palenque C/San Francisco 1, in the market. Bistro-style diner with an outdoor terrace noted for its fried fish and *revueltos*. Daily 12.30–4pm & 7–11pm.

El Refectorio La Plazuela s/n. Comprising the *Hotel Convento de San Francisco*'s restaurant (housed in the ancient convent's former chapel) and cafetería (aka Bar Plaza) in its refectory with an entrance on the square. The latter is a good place for a leisurely breakfast or an early evening *tapa*, whilst the restaurant offers a selection of well-prepared regional dishes with a *menú turístico* for €16. Main dishes €8–18. Bar daily 9am–11pm, restaurant daily noon–4pm & 8–11pm.

La Posada C/Los Remedios 2. The tapas bar and restaurant of the *hostal* of the same name is a good place for economical *platos combinados* and simple meals. Daily 8am–midnight.

Mesón Pepe Julián C/Juan Relinque 7, just off La Plazuela. Popular local bar with *azulejo*-lined walls serving up decent tapas – specials include *chorizo ibérico*, *calamares* (squid) and *carne mechada* (larded meat). Daily 11am–4pm & 7–11pm.

Peña Flamenca Águilar de Vejer C/Rosario 29. Welcoming flamenco *peña* (club) near the castle, where you can sample manzanilla from the barrel and take in occasional weekend flamenco concerts; the Turismo keeps details of upcoming performances.

Venta Pinto La Barca de Vejer s/n ☎ 956 450 069. Down below the town at the road junction with the N340 this is an outstanding mid-priced restaurant with a great range of seafood, fish and game dishes. House specials include *solomillo ibérico* (pork loin) and *rape con azafrán y langostinos* (monkfish with saffron and prawns) and there's a *menú* for around €22. Main dishes €9–20. Daily 7.30am–midnight.

Conil

Back on the coast, a dozen or so kilometres to the northwest of Vejer de la Frontera, is the increasingly popular resort of **CONIL**. Though this former fishing village appears entirely modern when viewed from the beach, it has a distinguished history dating back to ancient times. Founded by the Phoenicians (who were responsible for inventing the *almadraba* method of catching tuna along this coast) it was later a supply base for the Roman navy. Sacked successively by the Vandals, Visigoths and Byzantines, little was heard of the settlement again until, after the *Reconquista*, it once more became a centre of tuna fishing. If you take a stroll around the town you'll see plenty of older buildings that have survived from earlier days. Today, tourism is an important part of the economy too, with the resort's mainly domestic visitors creating a fun, family-oriented, atmosphere.

The beaches

Conil's **beaches** are its *raison d'être:* the central Playa de Los Bateles and Playa de La Fontanilla to the north, which appear as a wide bay of brilliant yellow stretching for miles to either side of town, lapped by an amazingly gentle Atlantic. The area immediately in front of town is the family beach: up to the northwest you can walk to some more sheltered coves; across the river to the southeast is a topless and nudist area. The beach here is virtually unbroken until it reaches the Cabo de Trafalgar, off which Lord Nelson achieved victory but lost his life on October 21, 1805. If the winds are blowing, this is one of the most sheltered beaches in the area. You can get there by road, save for the last 400m across the sands to the rock.

ARRIVAL AND DEPARTURE   CONIL

By bus Most buses drop passengers off at the Transportes Comes station (☎956 442 916) at C/Carretera s/n, just north of the Turismo.

By car The older part of the town is now mostly pedestrianised and parking spaces elsewhere are usually taken (especially in high season). Your best bet arriving by car is to head for the seafront Paseo de Atlántico where there's a kilometre of (free) parking spaces stretching west from the junction with Avda. de la Playa.

INFORMATION

Turismo C/Carretera 1, on the northern edge of the old town, at the junction of C/Carretera and C/Menéndez Pidal (May–Oct daily 9am–2pm & 6–9pm; Nov–April daily 8.30am–2.30pm; ☎956 440 501, ⓦconil.org; a summer office is located in the focal Torre de Guzmán, an ancient tower in the old town (June–Sept; Wed–Sat 11am–2pm & 6.30–9.30pm). The very helpful staff here can provide a useful town map as well as lots of information on the town and nearby coast. Their useful booklet *Conil en su Bolsillo* details all the town's tapas bars, restaurants and much more.

Internet Internet Café El Muro, C/Castillo 5, a stone's throw from the Torre de Guzmán, has plenty of terminals (daily 10.30am–2pm & 5–11pm).

Festival During the second week in June Conil celebrates the Semana del Atún de Almadraba (tuna-catch week) when the first half of the tuna season reaches its peak (see box, p.171) and the town's restaurants participate in a *ruta gastronómica* offering different dishes prepared with the fish at discount prices (details from the Turismo).

ACCOMMODATION

Conil has numerous hotels and *hostales* – most within easy walking distance of the focal Plaza de España, the old quarter's main square. August is the only time when you'll struggle to find a bed, and is also when rates peak. Should you find everything full, you may need to seek out one of a multitude of *casas particulares*, details of which are available from the Turismo.

★ **Casa Alborada** C/G. Gabino Aranda 5, slightly west of Plaza España ☎956 443 911, ⓦalboradaconil.com. Delightful small new boutique hotel with flamboyantly decorated and individually styled bedrooms and bathrooms – the bathroom of room 10 gets the star prize. Also has a stunning roof terrace/solarium with loungers and sofas offering spectacular views of the coast. Outside July and Aug rates halve, making this a real bargain. **€80**

★ **Hipotels Flamenco** Playa Fuente de Gallos ☎956 440 711, ⓦhipotels.com. Set in a tranquil location fronting the Fuente del Gallo beach, this elegant and completely refurbished 100-room four-star is one of the resort's established luxury addresses. Well-appointed rooms have balcony terraces and sea views and there's a bar-restaurant, two garden pools, tennis courts and steps down to a fine beach. When full, the same group has a new four-star hotel nearby, *Hipotels Gran Conil*, with similar facilities. Check website for offers. B&B **€200**

Hostal La Posada C/Quevedo s/n, just northeast of Plaza de España ☎956 444 171, ⓦlaposadadeconil .com. Dapper and welcoming *hostal* with clean and tidy en-suite a/c rooms with TV – many with sea views – above a good restaurant. There's also a charming garden pool and free wi-fi zone. High season is Aug only, outside which rates halve. B&B **€80**

Hostal La Villa Plaza de España 6 ☎956 441 053. Economical en-suite rooms with TV above a bar-restaurant on the old quarter's main square. Open May–Oct only. **€45**

Hostal Sonrisa del Mar C/Huerto 3, close to the seafront Paseo del Atlántico ☎956 442 718. Fronting the town beach (Playa de Los Bateles) this *hostal* has a/c rooms with TV, balcony and sea views. High season applies July–Sept. €80

Hostal Torre de Guzmán C/Hospital 5, southwest of Plaza de España ☎ 956 443 061, ⓦ hostaltorrede guzman.com. Attractive and comfortable en-suite a/c rooms with TV in a beautifully refurbished eighteenth-century mansion close to the Torre de Guzmán. The friendly proprietors also rent out studios with kitchenette and fridge and there's a decent restaurant with patio terrace below. Free wi-fi. Outside high season (Jul–Aug) rates fall by forty percent; see website for special offers. B&B rooms €82, studios €92

Hotel Almadraba C/Señores Curas 4, slightly south of Plaza de España ☎ 956 456 037, ⓦ hotelalmadrabaconil .com. Taking its name from the annual tuna cull, this is a pleasant three-star hotel in yet another modernized eighteenth-century town house. Elegantly furnished, beamed, and well-equipped rooms are ranged around a charming patio and come with minibar, safe and wi-fi. The hotel also has its own bar-*cafetería* and car park. €118

Hotel Diufain Cañada del Rosal s/n, Fuente del Gallo, 3km north of the centre behind the Playa la Fontanilla ☎ 956 442 551, ⓦ hoteldiufain.com. Attractive three-star hotel in its own grounds with large garden pool and a/c sea-view terrace balcony rooms with satellite TV. Free wi-fi and parking. €75

Hotel Oasis C/Carril de la Fuente 3 ☎ 956 442 159, ⓦ alojamientosoasisconil.com. Pleasant traditional small hotel above a restaurant fronting the town beach (Playa de Los Bateles) offering a/c sea-view rooms with minibar and balcony terraces. High season rate applies Aug only, outside which rates halve. €105

CAMPSITE

Camping Fuente de Gallo Urbanización Fuente de Gallo s/n ☎ 956 440 137, ⓦ campingfuentedelgallo .com. The nearest campsite to the town lies a stiff 3km walk (or easy taxi ride) north of the centre and is sited 400m inland from the superb Playa la Fontanilla, with good facilities, bar-restaurant and pool. Two people plus car €20

EATING

Casa Manolo Avda. de la Playa s/n. On the seafront, this is a town favourite where you should be able to try *ortiguillas* – deep-fried sea anemones – a delicious regional speciality. The terrace fills up on summer evenings for *raciones* of *sardinas*, *salmonetes*, *almejas* and lots more.

★ **Francisco Playa de la Fontanilla** Playa de la Fontanilla s/n ☎ 956 440 802. One of Conil's three outstanding seafood restaurants with a terrace on the beach, this is a great place to spend a summer afternoon if you can get a table – not an easy task in high summer. Everything is fresh from the sea whether it be *bogavante* (lobster), *urta* (bream) or one of the house specials such as *lubina al horno* (oven-baked sea bass) or *atún de almadraba* (fresh-landed tuna).

La Bahía Avda. de la Playa s/n. Next door to *Casa Manolo* and sharing the same terrace, this is another very popular seafood bar-restaurant, offering a large selection of *mariscos*. Also has an economical *menú* for under €10.

La Fontanilla Playa de la Fontanilla, next door to

Francisco ☎ 956 440 779. The second of the town's top-rated fish restaurants, and whether you're eating in the beamed dining room or on the terrace you won't be disappointed. House specials here include *arroz con bogavante* (lobster in rice), *gambas con espinacas* (prawns with spinach) and, their pride and joy, *urta a la fontanilla* (bream).

★ **Restaurante Mirador El Roqueo** Urbanización Las Palmeras s/n, at the northern end of the Fuente del Gallo beach ☎ 956 443 337. A kilometre beyond the *Hotel Diufain* (see above), this is another excellent fish restaurant worth making an effort to get to and is perhaps the best of the three (by a whisker). It fronts the beach of El Roqueo and comprises two restaurants in one: the more formal dining room ("El Roqueo") sits on the street behind the seafront "Mirador", which has a great terrace overlooking the shore below. House specials include *carpaccio de pulpo* (octopus), *ijada de atún a la sal* (tuna baked in salt) and an outstanding *salmonete a la plancha* (red mullet). It also offers meat dishes and a variety of salads. Closed Mon.

DRINKING AND NIGHTLIFE

Nightlife centres on the **music** and **drinking bars** in the streets surrounding the Torre de Guzmán and Plaza Santa Catalina to the southwest of Plaza de España. Places worth seeking out near the latter are the *Café de la Habana*, Plaza Santa Catalina 2, a buzzing late-night bar, and the nearby *La Tertulia*, C/Gabino Aranda 12 with a delightful interior patio. *El Sitio* on Plaza Goya is another good place while northeast of the Torre de Guzmán C/José Borrego is a street filled with bars.

Sancti Petri and around

Heading north from Conil along a road (not marked on many maps) which hugs the coast brings you, after 18km, to the isolated fishing village of **SANCTI PETRI**, surrounded by marshes and sand bars and now a popular **watersports** centre. The formerly wild

---

WATERSPORTS AT SANCTI PETRI

There's a small but nice enough beach to the south of the Puerto Deportivo where a number of watersports centres hire out equipment. These include:

Cruceros Sancti Petri ☎617 378 894, ⓦalbarco.com. With a kiosk on the Puerto Deportivo waterfront, this company offers tourist boat excursions to see dolphins and whales as well as trips to the Castillo de Sancti Petri (€11, under-12s €5.50).

Escuela de Vela Zaida ☎956 494 932. Nearer to the Club Náutico, offering sailing and windsurfing courses.

Novo Jet ☎956 49 20 26, ⓦnovojet.net. This long-established centre hires out windsurf boards, kayaks and catamarans and offers scuba diving courses and guided canoe expeditions to the Castillo de Sancti Petri and around the marshes (*marismas*) and watercourses of the Parque Natural de la Bahía de Cádiz to the north.

Sancti Petri Kayak ☎676 363 718 ⓦsanctipetrikayak.net. Kayak courses and hire. Guided tours (€12–15) include trips around the marshes and to the Castillo de Sancti Petri.

---

stretch of coast that precedes it has been developed into a dismal chain of overspill *urbanizaciones* for the sealocked city of Cádiz.

When you reach it (follow signs for the Puerto Deportivo), the village of Sancti Petri itself at the end of a causeway is a place under threat from the encroaching madness to the south and its future remains uncertain. The harbour now contains many more weekend yachts and launches than fishing vessels and, since the tuna-canning factory closed down, there are few jobs. The focal point of the tiny cluster of dwellings is the Club Náutico de Sancti Petri where the few fishermen that are left meet up. On Sunday mornings they sell their catch outside the club, offering some of the freshest oysters and *cañaillas* (murex sea snails) you've ever had for ridiculously low prices. They're best washed down with a beer from the Náutico's bar (they'll also lend you a plate) at a table overlooking the harbour. The bar has recently added an inviting terrace restaurant.

Castillo de Sancti Petri

A kilometre offshore lies an islet occupied by the **Castillo de Sancti Petri**, whose silhouette rises above the horizon. Until recently this was a ruined thirteenth-century castle on an offshore island, but as part of the bicentenary celebration of the Cádiz Córtes (see p.181) it has been partially restored at great cost and can now be visited by boat or kayak (see box above). The castle's gaunt tower – once used as a lighthouse – dominates the horizon as you approach and despite the renovations, which many critics say has destroyed the romance of the ruins, there's not a great deal to see when you get there. A new exhibition centre inside the castle relates its history. Apart from the fortress, however, the site has a much more ancient and distinguished past. The Phoenicians built an important first millennium BC temple to their god Melkaart here which the Romans later turned into a major shrine to Hercules. Hannibal was a visitor to the former, hoping to enlist Melkaart's aid in his projected conquest of Italy, and Julius Caesar to the latter, who while here is said to have had a prophetic dream that he would conquer the world. Important archeological finds have been discovered from both temples which are now on display in the museum at Cádiz.

San Fernando and around

To reach Cádiz, some 30km north of here you'll need to head inland to the rather unexciting town of Chiclana de la Frontera to pick up the A48 *autovía*. Beyond Chiclana you emerge into a weird landscape of marshes, dotted with drying salt pyramids, in the midst of which lies the town of **San Fernando** – once an elegant place (and still so, at its centre) but quickly being swallowed up by industrial and commercial suburbs. These extend until you reach the long causeway that leads to Cádiz, an unromantic approach to what is one of the most extraordinarily sited and atmospheric towns of the south.

Cádiz

Cádiz, from a distance, was a city of sharp incandescence, a scribble of white on a sheet of blue glass, lying curved on the bay like a scimitar and sparkling with African light.   Laurie Lee, *As I Walked Out One Midsummer Morning*

Sited on a tongue of land enclosing a bay and a perfect natural harbour, with some fine beaches besides, **CÁDIZ** has – you would think – all the elements that make for an appealing place to visit. But despite an atmospheric old town and some fine museums, oddly enough the place seems unable to shake off a brooding lethargy when it comes to entertaining visitors, and the world of tourism has largely passed it by. Once you've got through the tedious modern suburbs on its eastern flank, inner Cádiz, built on a peninsula-island entered via the **Puertas de Tierra** (Land Gates) – a substantial remnant of the eighteenth-century walls – looks much as it must have done in the great days of the empire, with grand open squares, sailors' alleyways and high, turreted houses. Literally crumbling from the effect of the sea air on its soft limestone, it has a tremendous atmosphere – slightly seedy, definitely in decline, but still full of mystique. Above all, Cádiz is a city that knows how to enjoy itself. It has always been noted for its vibrant fiestas: the ancient Roman poet Martial was among the many who commented on the sensuous and swirling dances of the townswomen ("they click their Tartessian castanets with a deft hand"), implying a pre-Moorish origin for flamenco. Although settled after the *Reconquista* with immigrants from the northern city of Santander, Cádiz maintains its Roman reputation for joviality with an **annual carnival** in February, acknowledged to be the best – and wildest – in Spain.

Unlike most ports of its size, Cádiz seems immediately relaxed, easy-going, and not at all threatening, even at night. Perhaps this is due to its reassuring compactness, the presence of the sea making it impossible to get lost for more than a few blocks. Although there are plenty of sights to aim for, including an excellent **museum**, a Baroque **cathedral** and some memorable church art, Cádiz is most interesting for its general ambience and for its **vernacular architecture** – elegant *mirador*-fronted facades painted in pastel shades, blind alleys and cafés, and ancient *barrio* backstreets imprisoned behind formidable fortifications.

Brief history
Founded about 1100 BC by the Phoenicians as Gadir, a transit depot for minerals carried from the mining areas of the Río Tinto to the north, Cádiz has been one of Spain's principal ports ever since, and lays claim to being the oldest city in Europe.

Historically Cádiz served as an important base for the navies of Carthage, Rome and – following a long decline under the Moors – imperial Spain. Always prone to attack because of its strategic importance, the city's nose was bloodied on numerous occasions, especially by the English. Drake's "singeing of the king of Spain's beard" occurred here in 1587, followed not long after by Essex's ransacking of the port in 1596, and Nelson's bombardment in 1797.

The city's greatest period, however, and the era from which much of **inner Cádiz** dates, was the eighteenth century. Then, with the silting up of the river to Seville, the port enjoyed a virtual monopoly on the Spanish–American trade in gold and silver: on its proceeds were built the **cathedral**, public halls and offices, broad streets and elegant squares, as well as a clutch of smaller churches. This wealth spawned Spain's first modern middle class which, from early on, was free-thinking and liberal, demanding such novelties as a free press and open debate. One historian has claimed that political dialogue in Spain originated along the Calle Ancha, Cádiz's elegant central thoroughfare, where politicians met informally.

In the early nineteenth century the city made arguably its greatest contribution to the development of modern Spain, when a group of radicals set up the short-lived Spanish parliament or **Cortes** in 1812 during the Peninsular Wars. The Cortes drew up a Constitution (popularly known as "La Pepa") that upheld the sovereignty of the people against the throne and set down a blueprint for a liberal Spain that would take a further century and a half to emerge. Major celebrations throughout 2012 will commemorate the bicentenary of these events and an impressive new bridge, Spain's longest, linking the city with Puerto Real across the bay – and named "Puente de la Pepa" – will provide the city's lasting tribute to its illustrious forebears.

CÁDIZ

FLAMENCO VENUES	
Peña Mellizo	2
La Cava Taberna	3
Flamenca	14
Peña La Perla	12

ACCOMMODATION	
Casa Caracol	11
Hospedería Las Cortes	3
Hostal Bahía	10
Hostal Canalejas	4
Hostal Centro Sol	5
Hostal España	8
Hostal Fantoni	7
Hotel Argantonio	2
Hotel Parador Atlántico	1
Hotel Patagonia Sur	6
Hotel Playa Victoria	13
Hotel Regio	12
Las Cuatro Naciones	9

CLUBS & MUSIC BARS	
Barabass	13
Le Monde	6
Café de Levante	9
El Pay Pay	11
El Poniente	5
Flamenco	14
Habana Café	10
Radio City	15
Imagina	1
Persígueme	4
San Francisco Uno	7
Woodstock	8

Loyal to its traditions, the city relentlessly opposed General Franco during the **Civil War**, even though this was one of the first towns to fall to his forces, and was the port through which the Nationalist armies launched their invasion. Later, when Franco often referred in power to the forces of "Anti Spain" he had in mind the sentiments expressed in the Cádiz Constitution of 1812, ramming home his disapproval by renaming the city's major plazas after himself and other members of the Falangist pantheon. Left-wing Cádiz merely bided its time and now, in the new democracy, these

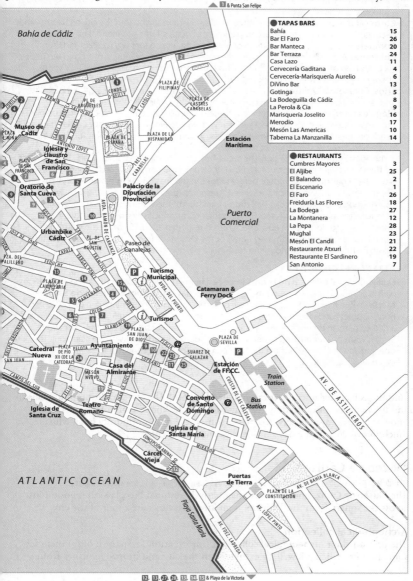

● **TAPAS BARS**

Bahía	15
Bar El Faro	26
Bar Manteca	20
Bar Terraza	24
Casa Lazo	11
Cervecería Gaditana	4
Cervecería-Marisquería Aurelio	6
DiVino Bar	13
Gotinga	5
La Bodeguilla de Cádiz	8
La Perola & Cia	9
Marisquería Joselito	16
Merodio	17
Mesón Las Americas	10
Taberna La Manzanilla	14

● **RESTAURANTS**

Cumbres Mayores	3
El Aljibe	25
El Balandro	2
El Escenario	1
El Faro	26
Freiduría Las Flores	18
La Bodega	27
La Montanera	12
La Pepa	28
Mughal	23
Mesón El Candil	21
Restaurante Atxuri	22
Restaurante El Sardinero	19
San Antonio	7

2

CARNAVAL IN CÁDIZ

Claiming to be saltier than the carnivals of Havana and Río de Janeiro rolled into one, each February Cádiz launches into its riotous **Carnaval**, the most important and wittiest in Spain. Largely a disorganized series of fiestas in origin, it was given its present shape in the late nineteenth century by Antonio Rodríguez Martínez, now known by his nickname El Tío de la Tiza ("Chalky", after the chalk or *tiza* he used in his job) who was improbably employed as a Customs official in the port. He organized the *murgas* or bands – a major feature of Carnaval – into four categories:

Coros Groups of about thirty (formerly all male, now mixed) who tour the city on flamboyantly decorated floats singing to the accompaniment of guitars, lutes and mandolins.

Comparsas Groups of around fifteen people who parade on foot with guitars and drums.

Chirigotas Arguably the most popular with *gaditanos*, these are groups of around ten people accompanied on a reed whistle or *pito*, who tour the bars singing hilarious satirical songs about people and events in the public eye.

Trios, Cuartetos, Quintetos These smaller groups not only sing, but also act out parodies and satirical sketches based upon current events as they tour the town in costume.

Illegales Given the city's innate anarchy these bands do not compete officially (see below), but take to the streets for the sheer hell of it with whatever instruments they can lay their hands on. They include whole families, groups of friends and even collections of drunks, staggering about as they attempt to make music.

The above groups provide only the focus, however, for the real Carnaval which takes place on the streets with everyone dressed up in costume and apparently drunk for ten whole days. The "legal" groups compete before judges in the Teatro Falla in between sessions on the streets and are symbolically awarded a *pelotazo* (good shot) for a bitingly witty composition and a *cajonazo* (a box drum) for a bomb. The various groups work at their repertoire for months before, road-testing their compositions during the two weekends prior to Carnaval (but not in costume, which is regarded as bad form) at the warm-up shindigs of the Erizada (hedgehog party) or the Ostionada (oyster party), great street fiestas which feature sea-urchin and oyster tasting.

ATTENDING CARNAVAL

During Carnaval there are **no rooms** to be had in town at all unless you've made reservations well in advance. One way round this is to see it on **day-trips from El Puerto de Santa María** (a 40min ferry ride across the bay) or Seville, catching an evening train (a couple of hours' journey) and returning with the first train the next day, around 5.30am. These trains are a riotous party in themselves and, packed as they are with costumed carnival-goers from Seville, you'd be well advised to get dressed up yourself if you don't want to stand out. The opening and final weekends are the high points of the whole show; for more information see Ⓦ carnavaldecadiz.com.

landmarks have regained their original designations. The city's tradition of liberalism and tolerance is epitomized by the way *gaditanos* (as the inhabitants of the city are known) have always breezily accepted a substantial **gay** community here, who are much in evidence at the city's brilliant Carnaval festivities.

Museo de Cádiz

Plaza de Mina 5 • Tues 2.30–8.30pm, Wed–Sat 9am–8.30pm, Sun 9.30am–2.30pm • €1.50, free with EU passport

The **Museo de Cadíz**, housed in an imaginatively restored Neoclassical mansion just across the square from the Turismo, is an ideal place to start a tour of the city.

Archeological collection

The ground-floor **archeological collection** (information in Spanish only) includes some fine Phoenician jewellery excavated in the city and bronze figurines from the shrine of the god Melkaart on the island of Sancti Petri (see p.180). Etruscan artefacts found at the same site hint at sophisticated early trading links. Another Phoenician temple to Astarte/Venus on the site of the modern Bastion of Santa Catalina yielded incense burners (*quemaperfumes* – the only ones found in Spain) with Egyptian decoration and a terracotta head with striking negroid features. Two remarkable fifth-century BC **Phoenician carved sarcophagi** in white marble (one male, the other female) are also unique to the western Mediterranean. It's interesting to observe the fusion of influences here: Egyptian for the sarcophagus, Greek for the depiction of the sculpted images. In the same section there's a display of ancient glassware – some of it of a very high standard – from the Phoenician, Greek and Roman periods.

2

The Roman section
In the Roman section a **reconstructed boat wreck** displays various amphorae exported from Cádiz to other parts of the empire; they contained garum (fish sauce), salazones (cured meat and fish), wine and olive oil, and the ship also carried minerals such as copper and lead – all demonstrating the great part played by Spain in making Rome rich. Two enormous anchors nearby, found off Cádiz, attest to the size of vessels that were used. Notable among the Roman statuary is a giant marble sculpture of the second-century emperor Trajan, which prior to excavation stood in the forum of Roman Baelo Claudia at Bolonia (see p.169) near Tarifa.

Museo de Bellas Artes
The second-floor **Museo de Bellas Artes** (fine art museum) is one of the best in Andalucía. The kernel of the collection is a group of 21 canvases by **Zurbarán** in Room 2, including a quite exceptional series of saints brought here from La Cartuja, the Carthusian monastery at Jerez, and one of only three such sets in the country preserved intact, or nearly so (the others are at Seville and Guadalupe). With their sharply defined shadows and intense, introspective air, Zurbarán's saints are powerful and very Spanish, even the English figures such as Hugh of Lincoln, or the Carthusian John Houghton, martyred by Henry VIII, whom he refused to accept as head of the English Church. Perhaps this is not surprising for the artist spent much of his life travelling round the Carthusian monasteries of Spain and many of his saints are in fact portraits of the monks he met.

Highlights of the many other works on display include, in Room 3, Murillo's *Ecce Homo* and *San Pedro y San Paulo*, as well as his final work, the *Mystic Marriage of Santa Catalina* – during the painting of which he fell from a scaffold to his death – and a *Sagrada Familia* by Rubens. The same room also contains *The Vision of San Félix Cantalicio*, a canvas displaying tenebrist influences by seventeenth-century sculptor, painter, architect and all-round genius, *sevillano* Alonso Cano.

A new section here houses a collection of **modern art** featuring, among others, works by Miró, Rafael Alberti and noted Tarifa artist Guillermo Perez Villalta.

The third floor
The museum's third floor has an interesting **ethnological collection** divided into two rooms; the first has examples of traditional *artesanía* including ceramics, basketwork, leatherwork and textiles. The second room contains some wonderful **antique marionettes**, part of a section covering the long tradition of Tía Norica, or satirical marionette theatre, in Cádiz. This art form has often been used to pillory the city's rulers and dignitaries, through the "mouths" of its characters taken from the streets – travelling salesmen, waiters, sailors, fishermen, *toreros*, drunks – often in times when overt political activity was dangerous. The city still holds an annual marionette theatre festival. Fascinating though the puppets are behind glass, they need to be brought to

2

life in a show – for the moment there's a video presentation of a Tía Norica show from the 1980s which you may need to ask to be played.

Iglesia y claustro de San Francisco

Plaza de San Francisco • Open service times Mon–Sat 7–9pm, Sun 9am–1pm • Free

Southeast of the museum, the **Iglesia y claustro de San Francisco** lies on a tiny square of the same name – the square is the site of the church's former orchard. Dating from the eighteenth century the former convent church has a wonderful cloister with a colonnade supported by Tuscan pillars. In the church itself, the high altar's retablo is a magnificent work by Gonzalo Pomar with a central *hornacina* (shrine) holding an image of the Virgen de los Remedios. The flying angels on each side of the retablo are attributed to *sevillaño* sculptor Pedro Roldán, while in the church's *sacristia* are two sculptures, one of San Diego and the other of San Francisco de Assisi attributed to the *andaluz* master, Martínez Montañés.

Oratorio de Santa Cueva

C/Rosario • Tues–Fri 10am–1pm & 4.30–7.30pm, Sat & Sun 10am–1pm • €3

A short walk south from the Museo de Cádiz, the eighteenth-century **Oratorio de Santa Cueva** houses three fine Goya frescoes. The church is divided into two dramatically contrasting parts; in the elliptical **upper oratory** beneath an elegant dome are the three frescoes representing the *Miracle of the Loaves and Fishes*, the *Bridal Feast* (either side of the main altar) and the *Last Supper* (above the entrance), an unexpected depiction of Christ and the disciples dining sprawled on the floor, Roman style. The other works here are depictions of biblical scenes by minor artists.

In sharp contrast to the chapel above is the **subterranean chapel**, containing a sculpture of the Crucifixion whose manifest pathos adds a sombre note. An eighteenth-century work of the Genoa school, the image is said to have inspired visiting composer Joseph Haydn to write his *Seven Last Words* (of Christ) oratorio. Each Good Friday a sermon on the theme of Christ's last words is preached in the chapel, following which Haydn's work is performed. The chapel used to be maintained in a state of unilluminated gloom which is probably how Haydn saw it. Somewhat breaking with tradition, spotlights have been added and a formerly blacked-out lunette has been cleaned, flooding the chapel with light – which inevitably lessens the sculpture's dramatic impact. A small museum has been added between the two chapels giving background information – including a display of Haydn's original score – on the building's history.

Catedral Nueva

Plaza de la Catedral s/n • Cathedral: Mon–Sat 10am–6.30pm & 4.30–7pm, Sat 10am–7pm, Sun 1–7pm • €5 including museum, free entry Sun 11am–1pm • Torre de Poniente: guided visits daily: June–Sept 10am–8pm; Oct–May 10am–6pm • €4

The huge **Catedral Nueva**, so titled because it replaced the former cathedral, Santa Cruz, is one of the largest churches in Spain. Begun in 1722, it took 110 years to finish, and even then the towers – shortened when the money ran out – were completed only in 1853 in an unsympathetic white limestone whose patchwork effect jars with the original sandstone. The time lapse also led to a curious architectural potpourri, strikingly visible on the main facade, where the exuberance of the earlier Baroque below was topped off in a contrastingly sober Neoclassical style. What is more, on closer inspection you'll see that the distinctive "gilded" dome, which appears so impressive from afar, is in fact made from glazed yellow tiles. Sadly, in the latter half of the twentieth century the building fell into an advanced state of decay – caused by sea air calcifying the stone – as chunks of the ceiling started falling on the congregation below. A costly programme of restoration over the last few years has slowly restored the building to its former grandeur.

The interior
Even if you don't normally go for High Baroque, it's hard to resist the attraction of the austere interior. From inside, the soaring 52m-high dome is illuminated by a powdery violet light, the whole perfectly proportioned building decorated entirely in stone with no gold or white in sight. **Artworks** include a sculpture of San Bruno by Martínez Montañés in the chapel of San Sebastián and some other polychrome sculptures including an *Ecce Homo* attributed to Luisa Roldán ("La Roldana"), the daughter of Pedro Roldán. Also worth a look are the wonderful **choir stalls** dating from 1702 which were originally in the Cartuja of Seville and moved here upon the latter's Disentailment in 1835. In the crypt is buried Manuel de Falla, the great *gaditano* composer of such Andalucía-inspired works as *Nights in the Gardens of Spain* and *El amor brujo*.

The cathedral's **museum** holds some dubiously attributed paintings as well as a rather tedious collection of ecclesiastical silver enlivened only by a monstrance – an eighteenth-century bejewelled custodial nicknamed the *Millón* (million), a reference to the number of precious gems and pearls set into the work.

For a magnificent view over the city you can also climb the **Torre de Poniente**, one of the cathedral's twin towers; entrance to the tower is to the right of the main entrance.

Barrio del Populo
The best view of the cathedral is from the waterfront behind, where the golden dome is perfectly set off by the pastel-tinted facades of the adjacent houses along Calle Campo del Sur. To the east of the Plaza de la Catedral fronting the cathedral lies the **Barrio del Pópulo**, a poor, run-down area of narrow alleyways and decaying tenements, a surviving remnant of the thirteenth-century medieval city.

Many of its streets are graced by the odd crumbling *palacio*, formerly residences of merchants made wealthy by empire trade, and now split up into residential blocks. One of these, the **Casa del Almirante** on Calle Posadilla, is a splendid Baroque pile with an ebullient facade featuring barley-sugar and Tuscan columns in rose-tinted Italian marble. At the time of writing there are plans to turn this into a luxury hotel. An ancient, seventeenth-century inn, though recently restored as a community centre, the **Mesón del Pópulo** at Calle Mesón Nuevo 11 – at the crook in the street – has the typical layout of these travellers' hostelries with stables below and living quarters above. Calles Sopranis and Santa María – where the Palacio Lasquetty (no. 11) and the church of Santa María are also worth a look – are other good places to sample the typical atmosphere of this quarter.

Iglesia de Santa Cruz
Plaza Fray Félix s/n • Mon 5.30–7.45pm, Tues–Sat 10am–1pm & 5.30–7.45pm, Sun 10am–noon & 6.15–7.30pm • Free

Just east of the Catedral Nueva stands the "Old" Cathedral, the **Iglesia de Santa Cruz**. Originally a thirteenth-century church built on top of a mosque, it was almost destroyed by the Earl of Essex during the English assault on Cádiz in 1596, and is effectively a seventeenth-century rebuild with only occasional vestiges such as the entrance arch surviving from the earlier Gothic structure. The sober grey stone interior contrasts with the magnificent seventeenth-century gilded retablo, a beautiful work with sculptures by Martínez Montañés, as is the Capilla de los Genoveses, its own stunning retablo of red, white and black Italian marble now wonderfully restored.

Teatro Romano

Avda. Campo del Sur s/n • Daily 10am–2.30pm • Free

Just behind the church of Santa Cruz is the **Teatro Romano** (Roman theatre), dating from the first century BC. Discovered in 1980, it is partly cut into by a corner of the Iglesia de Santa Cruz and was built over by a later Moorish *alcazaba*. It was one of the earliest and largest theatres constructed by the Romans in Spain with a cavea (semicircular auditorium) more than 120 metres in diameter and capable of seating an audience of twenty thousand. It merited a mention in the letters of the orator Cicero who relates that one actor was knighted following a memorable performance here, while another was sent for execution after an abysmal flop. The theatre fell into disuse in the late third century and the building was used as a stone quarry by the builders of the Moorish and medieval periods. A number of the remaining banks of seats have been restored.

Casa del Obispo

Plaza Frey Félix 5 • Daily June–Sept 10am–8pm, Oct–May 10am–6pm • €4

Across the square from the Iglesia de Santa Cruz the **Casa del Obispo**, former residence of the bishops of Cádiz, contains beneath its recently excavated floor and basement evidence of a Phoenician burial site and Roman cisterns and wall paintings from a later Roman temple that superseded this. The fragmentary paintings have been reconstructed and portray images of Melpomene, the muse of tragedy and Clio, muse of history in addition to the god Apollo and his lover Coronis.

Plaza de las Flores and Mercado Central

Heading west from the cathedral, it's a couple of blocks to the **Plaza de las Flores** (aka Plaza Topete), one of the city's most emblematic squares. Fronted by the striking early twentieth-century Correos, the square is a riot of colour most days due to the many flower sellers that have their stalls here. There are a couple of elegant mansions, too: **no. 1** with a portal decorated with pilasters in the Cádiz Baroque style dates from 1746 and, around the corner in Calle Libertad, numbers **15** and **16** are a couple more eighteenth-century mansions with *torres-miradores* (lookout towers).

Fronting these two, the whole of Plaza de la Libertad is taken up by the early nineteenth-century **Mercado Central**, an elegant neoclassical construction with a colonnade of Doric pillars enclosing the central area. Following a five-year refurbishment, the building has been restored to its former glory with vendors' stalls modernised to comply with current hygiene requirements. On weekday mornings the market is once again a vibrant beehive of activity.

Hospital de Mujeres

C/Hospital de Mujeres • Mon–Thurs 10am–1.30pm & 5.30–8pm, Fri & Sat 10am–3.30pm • €1.50 (ask the porter for admission)

Northwest of the Mercado Central the Hospital Misericordia, known now as the **Hospital de Mujeres** on the street of the same name. One of the finest Baroque buildings in the city, it was built as a hospital for women arriving in the port – many seeking a passage on boats to the Americas – who got sick and frequently died in the doorways and colonnades of public buildings.

The hospital's main **chapel**, dedicated to San Francisco, is an exuberant Baroque extravaganza and displays a brilliant El Greco, *St Francis in Ecstasy*. It's one of the Cretan artist's finest portrayals of the saint, albeit a rather sombre study using copious shades of grey. Don't miss also the hospital's two elegant patios linked by an unusual double-sided staircase.

CLOCKWISE FROM TOP LEFT CATEDRAL NUEVA (P.186); PICKING GRAPES ON THE COSTA DE LA LUZ; CASTILLO DE SAN SEBASTIÁN (P.191) >

Oratorio de San Felipe Neri

C/San José • Mon–Sat 10am–1.30pm • €2.50

The eighteenth-century oratory of **San Felipe Neri**, to the northwest of Plaza de las Flores, is one of the most important historical buildings in Spain, evidenced by the number of commemorative plaques from countries as far apart as Chile and the Philippines attached to the exterior. It was here, on March 29, 1812, that a group of patriotic radicals defied the Napoleonic blockade and set up the Cortes, or parliament, which drew up a liberal constitution (popularly known as "La Pepa") enshrining the principles of universal male suffrage, freedom of the press and land reform.

The church itself, an elegant oval structure, has a double tier of balconies which would once have echoed with the roar of fierce debate, and above which eight *ventanillas* in the dome allow the brilliant light to illuminate the sky-blue decor and the central nave punctuated by seven chapels. The high altar's retablo is crowned with a fine *Inmaculada* by Murillo.

Museo de las Cortes de Cádiz

C/Santa Inés • Tues–Fri 9am–1pm & 5–7pm, Sat & Sun 9am–1pm • Free

Next door to the oratory, the **Museo de las Cortes de Cádiz** was set up in 1912 to commemorate the first centenary of the 1812 Constitution. The highlights of the museum are a large Romantic-style mural depicting the events of 1812 together with a number of the original documents of the Cortes, and an enormous eighteenth-century scale model of the city – almost filling a room – made of mahogany and ivory at the behest of King Carlos III.

Plaza de España

Four hundred metres northwest of the museum, the Plaza de España is dominated by a rather pompous **monument to the Constitution**, also set up in 1912 and now crowned with the rather impertinent addition of a crane's nest. Gaditanos like to claim that it's the only monument in the world honouring and topped by a book – a representation of the 1812 Constitution.

Torre Tavira and Calle Ancha

C/Marqués del Real Tesoro 10 • Daily 10am–8pm (Oct–May closes 6pm) • €5

Just southeast of the Museo de las Cortes de Cádiz, the **Torre Tavira** is an eighteenth-century mansion with the tallest tower in the old city, which you can climb to get a great view over the white roofs below and the sea beyond. Many houses had these towers added so that shipowners and merchants could see ships arriving in the port. The tower also holds a camera obscura, which gives equally dramatic views, and the rooms below contain historical displays covering Cádiz and its past.

A couple of blocks north, the **Calle Ancha** – an historic thoroughfare (see p.181) that is today an attractive pedestrianized shopping street – makes a pleasant place for a stroll.

Barrio de la Viña

Squeezed between Calle Campo del Sur and the Playa de la Caleta on the west side of the centre lies the **Barrio de la Viña**, the old fishermen's quarter, typically *gaditano* and traditionally renowned for the spirited and sarcastic humour of its inhabitants. Its main street is the **Calle Virgen de la Palma**, close to the eastern end of which lies the tiny Plaza Tío de la Tiza, a charming square (filled with terraces for seafood tapas and *raciones* in summer) named after the man who, in the late nineteenth century, gave the famous Carnaval the form it has today (see p.184).

Playa de la Caleta

The western flank of the Barrio de la Viña faces the **Playa de la Caleta**, an over-popular – and often none too clean – beach in a small bay sandwiched between the most impressive of Cádiz's eighteenth-century sea fortifications, the **Castillo de Santa Catalina** and the **Castillo de San Sebastián**, the latter constructed on an islet and reached by a causeway. This is believed to be the site of the ancient Phoenician harbour where, tradition has it, there once stood an impressive temple to the Phoenician god Melkaart.

A walk along the seafront here can be wonderfully bracing day or night (when cooling breezes blow in off the Atlantic and many of the monuments are floodlit), with the possibility of a stroll through the Parque Genovés, planted with palms and cypresses as far as the bastion of Candelaria, or onwards to the Alameda Apodaca, another waterfront garden, beyond.

Beaches south of the centre

On the opposite, southern side of the city centre, the **Playa Santa María del Mar** is town's main beach, lying some five hundred metres east of the cathedral. However the city's main beach and the one with all the action – including restaurants and *chiringuitos* – is the **Playa de la Victoria**, 2km of excellent sand, cleaner and usually less crowded than the two town beaches. Getting here is an easy thirty-minute walk from the old town – just find the seafront on the south side of the peninsula and head east – or there's a bus (#7) which starts out from the Parque Genovés and follows the coast as far as the *Hotel Playa Victoria*.

The **Playa Cortadura** begins where the Playa de la Victoria ends and it's an altogether less commercialized affair – in fact there are no bars or *chiringuitos* at all. To reach the Playa Cortadura by public transport you can take bus #7 (see above) and walk east from the Hotel Playa Victoria bus terminus or take the train from the main station; leaving every twenty minutes or so, there are stops at Segunda Aguada (for Playa de la Victoria) and Cortaduras, from where the Playa de la Cortadura is a short walk.

ARRIVAL AND DEPARTURE

CÁDIZ

By train The train station (☎902 432 343) is on Plaza Sevilla at the periphery of the old town, close to the Plaza San Juan de Dios, busiest of the city's many squares.

Destinations: Córdoba (3 daily; 3hr); El Puerto de Santa María (13 daily; 30min); Granada (5 daily, change at Seville; 4hr); Jerez de la Frontera (14 daily; 35min); Seville (15 daily; 2hr).

By bus The bus station is currently located on Plaza Sevilla, alongside the train station, although a new bus station is planned and will probably be sited on the east (or opposite) side of the train station on Avda. de Astilleros. The tourist offices will be able to advise on this.

Destinations: Alcalá de los Gazules (Mon–Fri 5 daily, Sat & Sun 2–3 daily; 1hr 40min); Algeciras (8 daily; 2hr 30min); Arcos de la Frontera (4 daily; 1hr 30min); Córdoba (3 daily; 4hr); El Puerto de Santa María (23 daily; 35min); Granada (4 daily; 5hr 15min); Jerez de la Frontera (Mon–Fri 13 daily, Sat & Sun 1 daily; 45min); Los Caños de Meca (2 daily; 1hr 15min); Málaga (4 daily; 4hr); Ronda (Mon–Fri 4 daily, Sat & Sun 1 daily; 3hr); Seville (9 daily; 1hr).

By car Coming in by car you're best off taking accommodation with a garage (all the hotels will assist with parking) or heading for a car park rather than

looking for street parking. Two of the most central car parks inside the city walls are by the train station and along Paseo de Canalejas near the waterfront. A useful tip if you're coming in for a day-trip is to park in the huge underground car park of the El Corte Inglés department store (just off the bottom right of our city map at the end of Avda. de Astilleros) and take the bus from outside which goes to the centre. Note that the car park closes with the store at 10pm.

By boat Local ferries sail across the bay to El Puerto de Santa María and the beach resort of Rota (see p.203), leaving from the dock on the south side of the Puerto Comercial. There are seven departures daily to Rota (50min; €8.40 return) plus more frequent departures to El Puerto de Santa María either aboard *El Vapor* (5 daily; 40min; €5 return; ⓦvapordeelpuerto.com) or a faster catamaran (every 30min between 7.45am–9.25pm; 30min; €4.30 return; ⓦcmtbc.es). A useful site for checking all the latest ferry schedules is ⓦdirectferries.co.uk. The only long-distance ferry services from Cádiz are to the Canary Islands. Trasmediterranea, Estación Marítima (☎956 227 421, ⓦtrasmediterranea.es) currently operates a weekly sailing (Tues 5pm) to Las Palmas (39hr) and Tenerife (48hr).

INFORMATION

Turismo Avda. Ramón de Carranza s/n (Mon–Fri 9am–7.30pm, Sat–Sun 10am–2.30pm; ☎ 956 203 191), just north of Plaza San Juan de Dios. This office hands out current transport and ferry timetables as well as general information, a detailed street map and a useful *Ruta de Tapas* leaflet. Also has details of the various performances – from Beethoven to folk music, dance and flamenco – which are held throughout the summer at the city's theatres and concert venues.

Turismo Municipal Paseo de Canalejas (April–Sept Mon–Fri 9am–7pm, Sat & Sun 9am–5pm; Oct–Mar Mon–Fri 8.30am–6.30pm, Sat & Sun 9am–5pm; ☎ 956 241 001). Just 70m from the above, this is another useful office for maps and information. They also produce their own *Ruta de Tapas* leaflet and self-guided themed walking-tour leaflets.

Listings *El Diario de Cádiz* (☑ diariodecadiz.es) is the city's daily paper – good for local information, upcoming flamenco concerts and entertainment details.

Online information Information on the city is available at ☑ infocadiz.com, ☑ cadiz.es, ☑ cadizturismo.com and ☑ andalucia.org. For information on Cádiz province see ☑ cadiznet.com.

GETTING AROUND

City buses These offer a handy way of getting around and a route map is available from the Turismo. A ten-trip Bonobus travelcard (€6.35 from *estancos* – tobacconists, bus kiosks and many newspaper stands) gives you a healthy discount compared to buying single-journey tickets.

Open-top bus tour One way to get to grips with the city is to do an open-top bus tour – especially good if you're pressed for time. City Sightseeing Cádiz (daily 10am–9pm; €10.99 for a one-day ticket; ☑ city-sightseeing.com) runs a hop-on, hop-off clockwise service around the peninsula with stops at or near Plaza San Juan de Dios, the Cathedral, the Parque Genovés, the Playa de la Victoria and places in between.

Cycle hire Cycles can be hired from UrbanbikeCádiz, C/Marqués Valde Iñigo 4 near Plaza San Agustín (☎ 856 170 164) for around €2/hr or €15/day.

ACCOMMODATION

In tune with the city itself, much of Cádiz's budget accommodation has seen better days, and although things are slowly improving there's still a shortage of good quality accommodation in all categories. Except during the Carnaval, and July and August, finding a place to stay shouldn't be a problem. Again it's worth noting that outside high season (the price we quote) rates fall considerably.

BUDGET

★ **Casa Caracol** C/Suárez de Salazar 4 ☎ 956 261 166, ☑ hostel-casacaracol.com. Friendly backpackers' place in a large house with dorm beds, some double rooms sharing bath and pricier en-suite rooms in a new *hostal* nearby. Rates includes breakfast, free wi-fi and internet access, and use of a kitchen. Dorms **€18**, rooms **€40**

Hostal España C/Marqués de Cádiz 9 ☎ 956 285 500, ☑ pensionespana.com. In an elegant restored nineteenth-century *casa palacio* and offering a mix of rooms, either with shared bath or en suite with TV and fan. Can arrange parking. **€45–60**

Hostal Fantoni C/Flamenco 5 ☎ 956 282 704, ☑ hostal fantoni.es. Pleasant en-suite rooms with a/c, TV and free wi-fi in a charming renovated eighteenth-century house filled with *azulejos* and cool marble. **€70–75**

Las Cuatro Naciones C/Plocia 3 ☎ 956 255 539. Centrally located, clean, unpretentious place with low-priced rooms sharing bath, plus free wi-fi zone. **€40**

MODERATE TO EXPENSIVE

★ **Hospedería Las Cortes** C/San Francisco 9 ☎ 956 220 489, ☑ hotellascortes.com. Splendid hotel in a stylishly restored *casa señorial*. The attractive rooms have a/c, minibar and free wi-fi, while facilities include a sauna, gym, *cafetería* and restaurant. Can advise on parking. High-season price Aug only, and good value at any time of the year. B&B **€150**

Hostal Bahía C/Plocia 5 ☎ 956 259 061, ☑ hostalbahia @hostalbahia.info. Reasonable-value and conveniently located hostal offering en-suite rooms with a/c and TV. Ask for one of the more attractive exterior balcony rooms. Can arrange parking. **€78**

Hostal Canalejas C/Cristóbal Colón 5 ☎ 956 264 113, ☑ hostalcanalejas.com. Pleasant two-star *hostal* in completely restored townhouse. The en-suite rooms come with a/c and TV, and there's a wi-fi zone plus pay car park nearby. Avoid the windowless interior rooms though. **€80**

Hostal Centro Sol C/Manzanares 7 ☎ 956 283 103, ☑ hostalcentrosolcadiz.com. Slightly pricey for what you get, but the en-suite rooms – arranged above a pleasant patio – are smart, and come with a/c and TV. Has its own café-bar. Free wi-fi. **€75**

Hotel Argantonio C/Argantonio 3 ☎ 956 211 640, ☑ hotelargantonio.com. Newish and very pleasant hotel housed in an elegant nineteenth-century town house and decorated throughout with Moroccan furnishings and fittings (many of them for sale). All rooms come with plasma TV, minibar and free wi-fi. The top floor outward-facing rooms are the ones to go for. B&B €108

Hotel Parador Atlántico Parque Genovés 9 ☎956 226 905, ⍵parador.es. Spanking new state-of-the-art rectilinear construction fronting the sea. Opening its doors in early 2012 it's planned to hold 124 rooms and suites, all with terrace balcony and sea view. Features include full-size pool, solarium, bars, restaurant and gardens. €180

Hotel Patagonia Sur C/Cobos 11 ☎956 174 647, ⍵hotelpatagoniasur.com. Stylish new hotel in a renovated town house. The well-equipped a/c rooms come with minibar, safe, plasma TV and free wi-fi. Either of the attic suites is worth the few euros extra – #52 has its own expansive sun-terrace with loungers and cathedral view. B&B €115

Hotel Playa Victoria Glorieta Ingeniero La Cierva 4 ☎956 205 100, ⍵palafoxhoteles.com. If you're looking for a beachfront location, this giant four-star hotel fronting the Playa de la Victoria has well-appointed rooms with terraces and sea views (especially from rooms 609–11), while facilities include a pool, solarium, restaurant, bars, own garage and beach hammocks. €160

Hotel Regio Avda. Ana de Viya 11 ☎956 279 331, ⍵hotelregiocadiz.com. Catering mainly to the corporate sector, this modern three-star is nevertheless convenient and comfortable, with parking nearby and a bus stop (for transport into the centre – a five-minute ride) almost outside. €130

EATING AND DRINKING

Cádiz's best **cafés**, **tapas bars** and **restaurants** tend to be clustered around its many grand squares, especially Plaza San Juan de Dios, dominated by the delightful wedding-cake facade of the late eighteenth-century Ayuntamiento (whose bells sound the hour with notes from de Falla's *El amor brujo*) and the pleasant Plaza de Mina. Across the old town there are more places to hunt down in and around the adjoining Plaza de las Flores and Plaza de la Libertad, the latter containing the **market**, while the atmospheric C/Sagasta, almost bisecting the peninsula north to south, is another place to find more typically earthy watering holes. The old seamen's quarter, the Barrio de la Viña, is where *gaditanos* make for on warmer nights to scoff *caballa a la gaditana* (mackerel) and shellfish at economical *marisquerías* in the narrow streets around Plaza Tío de la Tiza and along C/Virgen de la Palma. The city's summer playground, the Paseo Marítimo – the long boulevard fronting the Playa de la Victoria – is lively and fun all season, with tapas bars, restaurants and beach *chiringuitos* (*Marimba* and *Marea* are recommended) all doing a roaring trade. A great **snack** at any time of the day are *empanadas gallegas* (fish or meat pies), obtained from the only Galician bakery in town, Casa Hidalgo, at Plaza Catedral 8, fronting the cathedral.

RESTAURANTS

El Aljibe C/Plocia 25 ☎956 266 656. Good restaurant serving up a range of traditional *andaluz* and Mediterranean dishes on a menu that changes four times a year. Also serves very good tapas in its bar. *Menú de degustación* €32 including wine; main dishes €10–15. Daily 1–5pm & 8pm–midnight.

★ **El Balandro** C/Apodaca 22 ☎956 220 992. Highly popular venue with a view of the Bay of Cádiz offering a range of excellent seafood tapas (try the *papas aliñados con bacalao* – marinated potatoes with cod) served at the bar or *raciones* and fresh fish and meat dishes on the promenade terrace – a wonderful place to watch the sun set. Their interior restaurant is also good and serves a range of dishes with a creative slant. They offer a range of fresh pasta dishes too, plus some delicious desserts. Extensive and fair-priced wine list. Main dishes €11–20. Tues–Sat 1–4pm & 8pm–midnight, Sun 1–4pm.

★ **El Faro** C/San Félix 15 ☎956 211 068. In the heart of the Barrio de la Viña, this is one of the best fish restaurants in Andalucía. House specialities include *pulpo* (octopus), *merluza* (hake), *urta* (sea bream), and a delicious *arroz marinero* (Andalucian paella). There's a *menú de degustación* for €45 (excluding wine) and a *menú* for around €20 (Mon–Fri) which you may need to ask for. Their tapas bar (see p.194) is also well worth a visit. Daily 12.30–3.30pm & 5.30–11.30pm.

★ **Freiduría Las Flores** Plaza de las Flores. One of the best *freidurías* in town. You can get an economical takeaway and eat it at the terrace tables of the nearby bar *La Marina* (facing the post office), who don't seem to mind, as long as you buy a drink; alternatively, you can eat at *Las Flores* itself in their new café-restaurant. Another good place is the nearby *Freiduría Europa*, C/Hospital de Mujeres 21 (at the junction with C/Sagasta). Daily 9am–4pm & 8pm–midnight.

La Bodega Paseo Marítimo 23, on the Playa de la Victoria seafront and close to Cádiz's football stadium ☎956 275 904. Excellent mid-priced restaurant and tapas bar with a wide range of meat and fish dishes. Just the place if you're looking for a place to eat while at the beach. Daily 1–5pm & 8pm–1am.

La Montanera C/Sacramento 39. Good economical place for carnivores in this fish-crazy city. The lamb dishes, especially, are excellent, and they are famous for their quality *jamón ibérico* and *hamburguesa montanera* (hefty hamburger). The *ensalada montanera* (cheese and pepper salad) is also recommended, and don't forget to check out the dish of the day. Daily 1–5pm & 8pm–midnight.

Mughal C/Plocia 13, off the east side of Plaza San Juan de Dios. Atmospheric and authentic small Bangladeshi restaurant offering well prepared tikka, korma and Punjabi dishes accompanied by naan bread. Try their mixed appetiser

2

plate which feeds two for under €9. Also has vegetarian options. Tues–Sun 1.30–4pm & 8pm–midnight.

La Pepa Paseo Marítimo 14, beyond the Hotel Playa Victoria. Excellent family-run terrace restaurant at the eastern end of the Paseo Marítimo serving excellent fish and rice dishes. Try their *paella gaditana* (with meat and *mariscos*). Thurs–Sun 1–4pm & 8pm–midnight.

Mesón El Candil C/Abreu 7. Very pleasant restaurant whose popularity has led to its occupying premises on both sides of this small plazuela with a charming terrace between. The chef has been fronting the *fogón* (stove) here for four decades so he should know by now how to prepare the house special *pescado plancha a la Pepe*. Meat is also on offer and there's a *menú* for €8. Daily 1–4pm & 8–11.30pm.

★ **Restaurante Atxuri** C/Plocia 7 ☎ 956 253 613. This outstanding and popular (booking advisable) mid-priced Basque fish restaurant is one of the city's top tables. The kitchen turns out a fusion of *andaluz* and Basque dishes served in a very pleasant dining room beyond a small (and very good) tapas bar at the entrance. Try the *almejas a la marinera* (clams) or *bacalao al pil-pil* (salted cod casserole). Mon–Wed & Sun 10am–4.30pm, Thurs–Sat 10am–4.30pm & 8pm–midnight.

Restaurante El Sardinero Plaza San Juan de Dios 4. Traditional *gaditano* fish restaurant offering good-quality fish dishes served on a pleasant terrace, plus some meat dishes. Main dishes €7–18. Daily 10am–midnight.

San Antonio Plaza San Antonio 9 ☎ 956 212 239. Good, mid-priced and typically *gaditano* restaurant with a small terrace on this attractive square and an extensive menu featuring a variety of local meat and fish dishes. Main dishes €12–25. Daily 1–5pm & 8pm–midnight.

TAPAS BARS

Bahía Avda. Ramón Carranza 29. Wonderful old harbourfront bar that does excellent fino and delicious *guisos* – tapas in sauce; there's no frying here. Try the *costillas de cerdo* (pork ribs) or *papas aliñas* (potatoes in garlic sauce). Mon–Sat 9am–midnight, closed Sat eve & Sun.

★ **Bar El Faro** C/San Félix 15. Tapas bar of the renowned restaurant (see p.193), and probably the best in town. A stand-up place where the finos are first rate, the service is slick and the seafood tapas are mouthwateringly delicious. House specials include *tortillitas de camarones* (shrimp fritters) and *tostaditas de pan con bacalao* (cod). Daily 1–4pm & 8pm–midnight.

Bar Manteca Corralón de los Carros 66, near C/San Félix. Great old place in the Barrio de la Viña run by a retired *torero* and decorated with bullfighting memorabilia. Excellent fino and *oloroso*. House specials include *chicharrones* (pork crackling), *lomo* (cured pork loin) and *salchichón* (cured sausage) all served up on a square of greaseproof paper. Impromptu flamenco often takes place here too.

El Pescador, opposite, is also good. Tues–Sun noon–4.30pm & 8.30pm–1am.

Bar Terraza Plaza de la Catedral. Facing the cathedral and founded in 1952, despite a touristy location this is a good tapas bar and fish restaurant with a very pleasant terrace on the most scenic square in town (which is why the prices here are slightly higher than elsewhere). Daily noon–4pm & 7pm–1am.

Cumbres Mayores C/Zorilla 4. Excellent and atmospheric restaurant and tapas bar located in a century-old former brewery where *carne* (particularly Huelva *jamón*) is king. The tapas bar has daily specials and in winter serves up a delicious *berza* – a chickpea and *morcilla* (blood sausage) based broth. Daily 12.30–4.30pm & 8–11.30pm.

Casa Lazo C/Barrié 17, northeast of the Torre Tavira. Charming little shop/bar with tasty tapas selection. Try their *jamón*, *boquerones en vinagre* (anchovies) or *croquetas caseras* (croquettes). Their delicatessen sells fine *jamón*, cheeses and regional wines. Mon–Sat 11am–4pm & 7–11.30pm.

Cervecería Gaditana C/Zorilla 3. Fine bar – the tasty *montaditos* (tapas on bread) are wonderful; try the salmon and Roquefort and their *bombita* (baby bomb), a ball of potato with onion and tuna fish. Daily noon–4pm & 8pm–1am.

★ **Cervecería-Marisquería Aurelio** C/Zorilla 1, near Plaza Mina. Vibrant and outstanding seafood tapas bar with excellent manzanilla to wash them down with. Founded by the late and legendary Aurelio, who sold shellfish outside the entrance for many years; specials include *merluza rebozada* (hake) and *ortiguillas* (fried sea anemones). They'll also serve you a great fish supper at tables in a side room. Daily 12.30–5pm & 8.30pm–1am.

DiVino Bar Plaza Candelaria, at the corner with C/Zapata. Stylish new tapas and *raciones* bar with a pleasant terrace on this leafy square serving both hot and cold dishes. The house speciality is *ibéricos* (Iberian black pig cured meats and salamis); try a *gran surtido de ibéricos* (selection) to share for €15. They also have a decent wine selection and serve desserts so you could easily make a meal of it. Free wi-fi throughout the bar. Tapas €3–5, *raciones* €8–20. Daily noon–5pm & 8pm–1am.

Gotinga Plaza del Mentidero 15. German-run bar with an inviting terrace on one of Cadiz's most delightful (and little-known) squares, dotted with jacaranda trees. Offers a wide tapas and *raciones* range, including plenty of vegetarian options, and also makes its own cakes and pastries which go well with a range of teas. Later in the evening regulars gather to drink international beers or cocktails. Mon–Sat 12.30pm–1am, Sun 12.30–8pm.

La Bodeguilla de Cádiz C/San Pedro 20. Fine little tapas and *raciones* bar also serving up *platos combinados*. Try a *chapata ibérico* (ciabatta with *salchichón*). Daily noon–4pm & 8pm–2am.

La Perola & Cia C/Canovas del Castillo 34, southwest of the Santa Cueva chapel. Modern tapas and *raciones* bar popular with a younger clientele and serving over seventy different tapas. Try the *chocos con garbanzos* (baby squid with chickpeas) or the *tortilla de papas a la marinera* (Spanish seafood omelette). Daily 9am–5pm & 8pm–1am.

Marisquería Joselito C/San Francisco 38. Venerable old (but recently modernized) haunt and one of a chain of tapas bars, but none the worse for that. House specials include *salpicón de mariscos* (seafood cocktail) and *gambas al ajillo* (garlic prawns). There's a sister branch just around the corner (with a pleasant terrace), facing the port on Avda. Ramón Carranza. Daily 11am–4pm & 8pm–1am.

Merodio Plaza Libertad 4, fronting the market. One of the city's best-loved old bars, which gets riotous during Carnaval and really buzzes on Sunday lunchtimes.

Specializes in *erizos de mar* (sea urchins) in season, as well as shellfish. Daily noon–5pm & 7pm–midnight.

Mesón Las Americas C/Ramón y Cajal 1. Very good South American tapas and *raciones* bar housed in a vaulted former warehouse – try their *bombitas de patata* (croquettes). Their other speciality is Argentinian meat dishes and steaks, and they also serve a selection of salads. Mon–Sat 12.30–4.30pm & 8.30pm–2am.

Taberna La Manzanilla C/Feduchy 18, north of Plaza Candelaria. Wonderful atmospheric eighteenth-century bodega serving the odd *tapa* in addition to excellent manzanilla decanted from huge butts. If you ask, the proprietor will show you his cellar with some classic vintages. The nearby *El Cañon* (junction of C/Feduchy & C/Rosario) is another good tapas place. Mon–Fri 10am–3pm & 6.30–10.30pm, Sat & Sun 10am–3pm.

NIGHTLIFE

Outside carnival and fiesta times, nightlife in Cádiz centres on the areas around the Plaza de Miña and Plaza de España, while a new nightlife copas (drinks) zone has opened up in the Barrio del Pópulo centred on *calles* Mesón Nuevo and Silencio, and Plazuela San Martín. However, many places close during July and August and in summer much of the nightlife scene migrates to the Paseo Marítimo, behind the beaches to the east of the centre (C/Muñoz Arenillas, behind the *Hotel Playa Victoria* is the focus), where you'll find most of the bars and clubs. In winter revellers flock to the Punta de San Felipe (there's a less frenetic scene here in summer, too), known locally as La Punta, the peninsula beyond the harbour to the northeast of Plaza de España.

CLUBS AND BARS

Barabass C/Muñoz Arenillas, off Glorieta Ingeniero La Cierva and behind the Paseo Marítimo. In a street packed with clubs and bars which get full to bursting in high summer, this is a fairly big place with 60s decor and a great atmosphere when the dancing gets going. Mon–Thurs 8pm–5am, Fri–Sun 8pm–7am.

Café de Levante C/Rosario 23, near Plaza de San Agustín. Relaxed bar with a cultural ambience, often staging literary events, live music and even flamenco. Daily 8pm–1am.

El Pay Pay C/Silencio 1, Barrio del Pópulo. Large café-bar with a long history as a former sailors' hangout. Now renamed and revamped, it stages live music, theatre and poetry readings and there are noticeboards with information on cultural events around the city. This is now a major *copas* zone and the adjoining C/Mesón Nuevo is filled with late-night bars and clubs such as *La Favorita*, *El Malagueño* and *Mesón de la Posadilla*.

El Poniente C/Diego Beato 14, near Plaza de España. Busy and upbeat gay (but not exclusively so) bar with house music and frequent drag shows. Wed–Sun 11pm–5am.

Flamenco Paseo Marítimo 14, 300m east of the Hotel Playa Victoria on the seafront. A good place for those wanting to escape the more frenetic nightlife in nearby C/Muñoz Arenillas, and a favourite for watching the sun go down. Daily 1pm–1am.

Habana Café C/Rosario 21, near Plaza San Francisco. Stylish bar for late-night drinking. The house speciality is cocktails and they claim to make the best mojitos and daiquirís in town. Tues–Sun 12.30pm–2am.

Imagina Punta de San Felipe. Good, popular salsa club – which only lifts off at 3am – with a view of the Bay of Cádiz on this frenetic street. A highly popular venue appealing to a lively young crowd and featuring showboating salsa dancers who command the floor. South of here a string of bars and clubs all add to the action. 10pm–6am.

Le Monde C/Manuel Rancés 2, just west of Plaza de España. A relaxed and friendly late-night *copas* and music bar open until after 4am which tends to fill up on weekends. There are quite a few other lively places in this street. Daily 8pm–2am.

Persígueme C/Tinte, near Plaza de Mina. Trendy music bar very popular in summer. It gets lively at weekends and sometimes stages live bands. Thurs–Sat 8pm–3am.

Radio City C/Virgen de las Angustias 6, in the Paseo Marítimo zone, slightly east of the Hotel Playa Victoria. Entertaining den of a club that manages to do a bit of everything: live concerts (including flamenco), theatre, big football games on a large screen and free nightly salsa classes. Thurs–Sun 6pm–7am.

San Francisco Uno Plaza San Francisco 1. This pleasant bar with a terrace on this delightful square is good for breakfast coffee and perfect for late-night liqueurs or even a wine from their extensive list.

2

Woodstock C/Canovas del Castillo, old town, at the corner with C/Sagasta and Paseo Marítimo 11. Two lively branches of this bar at each end of the town serving up eighty-plus of the world's top beers to the accompaniment of rock, blues, jazz and the occasional blast of Celtic pipes. During winter the old town branch is more popular; in summer head for the one on Paseo Marítimo, which has panoramic windows overlooking the beach.

FLAMENCO

Flamenco is an irregular feature at private *peñas* or clubs, and isn't always that easy to find. We've listed a few places below, but check with the Turismo for more, as well as for details of "barrio flamenco" staged by bars and restaurants across the city; these are amateur shindigs but often hugely enjoyable. The Turismo will also give details of special concerts and festivals at venues such as the Teatro Falla and the Diputación (regional government building) in Plaza de España.

Baluarte de Candelaria On the northern tip of the peninsula. This sea bastion is the venue for some wonderfully authentic open-air flamenco concerts by the Peña Flamenco Enrique Melliza staged every Thurs evening from mid-July to late Aug (entry €20). It gets going

about 10.30pm and there's food and drink. Reservations are advised on ☎ 956 221 985 (Spanish only), or get either tourist office do it for you.

La Cava Taberna Flamenca C/Antonio Lopez 16, near the Plaza de la Mina ☎ 956 211 866, ⓦ flamencolacava .com. Tourist-oriented place where the performers are reasonably serious. Shows Feb–June & Oct-Nov Tues, Thurs and Sat at 9.30pm; Jul–Sept Tue–Sat at 9.30pm. €22 entry includes a drink.

Peña La Perla C/Carlos Ollera s/n ☎ 956 259 101. Down a tiny street behind the Cárcel Vieja (Old Prison), to the east of the cathedral, this wonderfully atmospheric old *peña* (where many "greats" have performed) is open to visitors and is somewhere that flamenco can happen spontaneously on any night of the week, with a regular performance on Fri at 10pm (not July and Aug). Enquire in their bar, give them a ring, or alternatively, check with the Turismo.

Peña Mellizo Paseo de San Felipe s/n, close to the Punto de San Felipe. Very friendly bar (open daily) and flamenco theatre. Outside July and Aug there are performances of flamenco here on Fri & Sat at 9pm (free). Again, details are available on ☎ 956 221 985 or from either tourist office.

DIRECTORY

Banks There are ATMs throughout the city centre, with several banks around Plaza San Juan de Dios and Avda. Ramón de Carranza (facing the port).

Bookshop Quorum, C/Ancha 27, is the city's best bookshop and stocks a decent selection of books in English.

Football C.F. Cádiz, nicknamed Submarino Amarillo ("Yellow Submarine" – they play in canary shirts), is the town's team, currently languishing in Division 2. Their ground is the Estadio Ramón Carranza, Plaza Madrid, behind the Playa de la Victoria (☎ 956 070 165, ⓦ cadizcf .com). Tickets can be purchased at the ground.

Hospital For urgent medical treatment go to the *urgencias* (emergency) department of the Residencia Sanitaria Hospital, Avda. Ana de Viya 21, near the *Hotel Playa Victoria* (☎ 956 002 100).

Internet Ciber Columela, C/Columela 2 off Plaza de las Flores (daily 9am–10.30pm); Novap Computers, Cuesta de

las Calesas 45, near the train station (daily 10am–11pm).

Police In emergencies dial ☎ 091 for the Policía Nacional (serious crimes) and ☎ 092 for the Policía Local (theft and petty crime). Both police forces have their headquarters in the Playa de la Victoria zone: the national police are located on Avda. de Andalucía and the local police are on the Avda José León de Carranza, next to the football stadium.

Post office Plaza de las Flores, near the market (Mon–Fri 8.30am–8.30pm; Sat 9am–2pm).

Shopping Cádiz's branch of the El Corte Inglés department store is at Avda. de las Cortes de Cádiz s/n (☎ 956 205 122) 1.5km east of the train station; buses #5 or #8 from a stop at the eastern end of Avda. del Puerto (close to the train station) will take you there. For the latest designer fashions head for C/Columela running between C/San Francisco and Plaza Flores, where many international designer labels have their outlets.

The Sherry Triangle

The northwest corner of Cádiz province is sherry country, a dramatic landscape of low, rolling hills and extensive vineyards. The famous triangle of sherry towns – **Jerez de la Frontera**, **El Puerto de Santa María** and **Sanlúcar de Barrameda** – are the main production centres, but smaller places like **Chipiona** and even tiny **Rota** manage to muscle in on the action.

Besides their bodegas, many of which can be visited, all the sherry towns make interesting places for a stopover in themselves. Jerez and El Puerto de Santa María both have sufficient churches, museums and architectural sights to take up at leas[t] of days, while coastal Sanlúcar has a castle and also offers the chance to take into the wilderness of the **Doñana National Park**, Spain's largest. Sanlúcar is to some of the finest seafood bars and restaurants in Andalucía, while the r sands – the setting for some exciting horse-races in summer – are another attractio[n] are the further string of magnificent **beaches** which stretch along the 40km stretch of coastline between here and El Puerto de Santa María. In fact, when Cádiz's city beaches are full it's only a 30-minute trip by catamaran across the bay to El Puerto, where you'll find superb beaches with space to breathe all summer long.

El Puerto de Santa María

Just 10km across the bay from Cádiz, **EL PUERTO DE SANTA MARÍA** is the obvious choice for a day-trip from the provincial capital. It's a traditional family resort for both *gaditanos* and *sevillanos* – many of whom have built villas and chalets along

ACCOMMODATION	
Camping Playa Las Dunas	11
Casa de los Leones	4
Casa No. 6	6
Hostal Loreto	3
Hotel Duques de Medinaceli	1
Hotel Los Cantaros	5
Hotel Santa María	10
Monasterio San Miguel	2
Palacio Bartolomé	7
Pensión Guadalete	9
Pensión Santa María	8

NIGHTLIFE	
Bar & Company	1
La Cristalera	3
La Pontona	2
Milwaukee	4

EL PUERTO DE SANTA MARÍA

● RESTAURANTS & CAFÉS					
Aponiente	6	Las Capuchinas	2		
Bodega Jerezana	13	Pasta Gansa	5		
Casa Flores	7	Romerijo	9		
El Faro de El Puerto	1				

● TAPAS BARS				
Bar Tapia	3	Nuevo Portuense	8
Bar Vicente	4	Sol y Sombra	10
La Dorada	12		
La Galera	11		

2

fine **Playa Puntilla** which you'll pass as the boat comes in to dock at the Muelle del Vapor in the estuary of the Río Guadalete. The town itself, some distance from the beach, has an easy-going air and, despite some ugly modern development on its periphery, is surprisingly picturesque, with many narrow, white-walled streets and plant-filled balconies, plus an impressive medieval castle, imposing *casas palacios*, some fine churches and Spain's third most prestigious bullring. On the cultural front, El Puerto will always be associated with one of the major Spanish poets of the twentieth century, **Rafael Alberti**, who was born here in 1902 and died here in 1999; his birthplace at Calle Santo Domingo 25 is now a museum (see p.199).

Today one of the three centres of **wine** production (along with Jerez and Sanlúcar) that make up the sherry triangle, El Puerto de Santa María came to prominence in the eighteenth century as a botanical garden where plants brought from the New World were cultivated for seed. This and other trading enterprises helped increase local prosperity, as demonstrated by the numerous mansions around the town, which was once known as the *ciudad de los cien palacios* (city of a hundred palaces).

El Fuente de las Galeras

Arriving by ferry, close to the landing quay, the Muelle del Vapor, you'll immediately spot the fine six-spouted eighteenth-century fountain, **El Fuente de las Galeras**, constructed, as the Latin inscription on it tells you, to provide galleys leaving for the Americas with water. Voyages from here in the years following the discovery of the Americas in 1492 charted much of the New World's coastline and in 1500 El Puerto resident and sea captain Juan de la Cosa produced his famous **mapamundi**, the first map to include the continent of America and show Cuba surrounded by water (Columbus never believed that it was an island).

Castillo de San Marcos and Antigua Lonja

Plaza de Alfonso El Sabio • Tours Tues 7pm, 8pm & 9pm; Wed–Sat 10.30am, 11.30am, 12.30pm, 1.30pm & 7pm, 8pm & 9pm • €5, €2 kids, free on Tues morning if booked in advance on ☎ 956 851 751

West of El Fuente is the **Castillo de San Marcos**, a thirteenth-century fort built by Alfonso X on the site of a Moorish watchtower and mosque. The towers of the castle bear the stirring (restored) proclamations of devotion to the Virgin, a symbol of the victory over the vanquished Moors. So besotted was the king with her that he sang the Virgin's praises in a surviving poetic work, *Las Cantigas*, and renamed El Puerto after her. Inside the fort – today owned by the Luis Caballero bodega – Alfonso also constructed a triple-naved Mudéjar church, in which the mosque's ancient *mihrab* can still be identified. The current proprietors have long used one of the castle's halls as a sherry bodega, stacked with butts. You can take a full tour of the castle, leaving via the bodega, where you'll be invited to taste (and buy) their finos.

Slightly southwest of here the elegant eighteenth-century **Antigua Lonja** (aka El Resbaladero) on Calle Micaela Aramburu served for two centuries as the town's fishmarket – note the piscatorial reliefs decorating its exterior.

Iglesia Mayor Prioral

Plaza Mayor • Mon–Fri 8.30am–12.45pm & 6–8.30pm, Sat 8.30am–noon & 6–8.30pm, Sun 8.30am–1.45pm & 6.30–8.30pm • Free

Following the pedestrianized Calle Luna west into town from the ferry quay will bring you to El Puerto's **Plaza Mayor** (officially the Plaza de España) fronted by the **Iglesia Mayor Prioral**. A thirteenth-century Gothic edifice, it has suffered much rebuilding and the shell is now largely Baroque, but don't miss its superb Plateresque south entrance. Inside, a richly gilded retablo in the Capilla de la Virgen de los Milagros holds La Patrona, a thirteenth-century image of the Virgin formerly housed in the castle of San Marcos and to which the town is devoted. Note also some fine choir stalls richly carved in walnut and cedar.

Museo Municipal

C/Pagador 1 • Tues–Fri 10am–2pm, Sat & Sun 10.45am–2pm • Free

Across Playa Mayor from the church lies the **Museo Municipal**, housed in another mansion, the **Casa de la Marquesa de Candia**. The museum contains archeological finds from the surrounding area plus a selection of indifferent artworks only relieved by a couple of paintings by Alberti (see below).

Fundación Rafael Alberti

C/Santo Domingo 25 • Tues–Sun 10.30am–2pm • €5 • ⓦ rafaelalberti.es

Around the corner from the Museo Municipal lies the **Fundación Rafael Alberti**, an excellent museum dedicated to El Puerto's great poet and artist, Rafael Alberti, who was born here. A communist and supporter of the Republic, Alberti fled abroad following the victory of Franco in 1939 and spent time in Argentina, Paris and Rome before returning to Spain in 1977 after the dictator's death. Aged 76, shortly after his return he was elected deputy for Cádiz in the new Spanish parliament. He died here in 1999, in the same house where he had been born 97 years earlier. Many of his vibrant engravings decorate the walls and a fascinating photographic biography illustrates his life, contacts and friendships with many of Spain's twentieth-century literary and artistic giants including Lorca and Picasso.

Plaza de Toros

Plaza Elías Ahuja s/n • Tues–Sun 11am–1.30pm & 5.30–7pm • Free

A few blocks south of the Plaza Mayor the **Plaza de Toros** is one of the largest in Spain (third only to Madrid and Seville) and among the most celebrated by aficionados. Opened in 1880 with a capacity of fifteen thousand, the bullring has hosted all the great names. A mosaic inside the entrance records the words of the legendary *sevillano* bullfighter Joselito, who fought here: "He who has not seen bulls in El Puerto does not know what bullfighting is."

The palacios

Scattered all over town are the **palacios** left behind by the great eighteenth-century families of El Puerto and decorated with their shields. The Turismo's town map marks them all, but three of the most outstanding are **Casa de Vizarrón** (aka Casa de las Cadenas) near the El Resbaldero market, with an elegant escutcheoned doorway; the **Casa de los Leones**, now the *Casa de los Leones* hotel (see p.200), with a fine facade and patio; and **Palacio de Aranibar**, with another elegant portal fronting the Castillo de San Marcos, and which now houses the Turismo.

The beaches

The closest beaches, **Playa La Puntilla** and **Playa Valdelagrana**, are some distance from town (15min walk or local buses from the ferry dock at Plaza Las Galeras: #1 and #2 for La Puntilla or #3 for Valdelagrana) and are pleasant places to while away an afternoon with lots of lively *marisquerías* and beach bars. For fewer crowds you're better off on the **Playa Santa Catalina** to the west of Playa La Puntilla; bus #3 (direction Fuenterrabía) from Calle Micaela Aramburu near the ferry dock will take you there.

| ARRIVAL AND DEPARTURE | EL PUERTO DE SANTA MARÍA |

By train The train station is on Plaza de la Estación s/n (☎ 902 240 202), on the northern periphery of the old town. Exit the station and turn left along C/Albareda to reach the centre. There are frequent trains to Cádiz and Jerez.

By bus Arriving by bus you'll be dropped by the Plaza de Toros – the "bus station" is little more than a couple of bus stands. There are frequent services from here to Cádiz, Sanlúcar and Jerez.

By car El Puerto has the usual problem of too many cars and too few parking spaces. A good tip is to head for the riverfront facing the *Hotel Santa María* where a large car park (shown on our map) charges €1 for 24hr. Make sure you are in the right car park, however, as a neighbouring car park charges €1 per hour.

By boat The "Vapor" ferry (40min; €5 return) leaves from the Fuente de las Galeras for Cádiz roughly every two hours between 11am and 5pm. The last sailing back from Cádiz is at 6.30pm. South of here opposite the *Hotel Santa* *María* is the Catamaran ferry dock with seventeen faster sailings (30min; €4.40 return) on weekdays (twelve on weekends) between 7.10am and 9.25pm with the last sailing back from Cádiz at 10pm.

INFORMATION

Turismo The Turismo, at Palacio de Aranibar, Plaza del Castillo facing the Castillo de San Marcos (daily: May–Sept 10am–2pm & 6–8pm; Oct–April 10am–2pm & 5.30–7.30pm; ☎956 483 715, ⓦturismoelpuerto.com), is handily sited for picking up a detailed street map as well as a Ruta del Tapeo leaflet to help find the best tapas bars. Many of the main sights (including the Castillo San Marcos) are covered in a two-hour guided tour leaving from the Turismo (July–Sept Tues & Sat 10.30am; April–June & Oct Sat 11am; free).

Internet Locutoro Santa María, C/Santa María 2 near Plaza de España (daily 10am–3pm & 6–10pm).

Festival The town stages a cultural festival each summer (July & Aug) with concerts (mainly classical) taking place on Thursday evenings in the Castillo San Marcos; details from the Turismo.

ACCOMMODATION

Many visitors come to El Puerto for the day, but should you be tempted to stay – and it makes a great break from Cádiz – there are plenty of rooms within easy walking distance of the ferry. Bear in mind that things get tight during August, when it's worth ringing ahead. If you have problems, ask at the Turismo for assistance; they also keep a list of apartments for longer stays.

Casa de los Leones La Placilla 2 ☎956 875 277, ⓦcasadelosleones.com. Enchanting eighteenth-century *casa palacio* – with a fabulous exterior – converted into an elegant apart-hotel with a/c apartments featuring bedroom and sitting room plus kitchen equipped with washing machine, fridge and microwave. Higher apartments have more light. **€132**

Casa No. 6 C/San Bartolomé 14 ☎956 877 084, ⓦcasano6.com. Rooms in a delightful *casa palacio* lovingly restored by an Anglo-Spanish couple; the en-suite rooms above a gorgeous patio are well furnished and come with fans and there are also two fully equipped rooftop apartments with terraces. Free wi-fi zone. B&B **€80**

Hostal Loreto C/Ganado 17 ☎956 542 410 ⓦpension loreto.com. Pleasant *hostal* with a delightful patio. Rooms come with or without bath; en suites have ceiling fans, fridge and TV. **€42**

Hotel Duques de Medinaceli Plaza de los Jazmines 2 ☎956 860 777, ⓦhotelesjale.com. A palatial hotel housed in the former mansion of the Irish sherry family Terry, this eighteenth-century edifice has been restored to its former glory with a stunning patio, opulent furnishings and rooms decorated with original artworks. There are all the trimmings of a five-star hotel but sometimes the standard of service falls slightly below this. Elegant public areas include a small pool, sauna and restaurant, plus a magnificent botanical garden in the hotel's grounds (open to the public daily noon–10pm). Free parking but pay wi-fi. See website for special offers. B&B **€310**

Hotel Los Cantaros C/Curva 6 ☎956 540 240, ⓦhotel loscantaros.com. Central hotel – housed in a former women's prison – offering a/c rooms with TV and minibar. Light sleepers may be disturbed by nearby music bars. Free wi-fi. **€139**

Hotel Santa María Avda. Bajamar s/n ☎956 873 211, ⓦhotelsantamaria.es. Good-value three-star riverfront hotel in a converted eighteenth-century *palacio* with a/c rooms, restaurant, garage (or there's easy parking by the river) and rooftop pool. **€123**

Monasterio San Miguel C/Larga 27 ☎956 540 440, ⓦhotelesjale.com. One of the best accommodation options in town, this sixteenth-century monastery has been converted into a luxurious four-star hotel complete with patios, pool and rooftop solarium. Try for a balcony room on the interior patio overlooking the pool, as street-facing rooms get some noise. See website for offers. Own garage and pay wi-fi. **€160**

Palacio San Bartolomé C/San Bartolomé 21 ☎956 850 946, ⓦpalaciosanbartolome.com. A beautifully converted eighteenth-century *casa palacio* with 11 attractive, well-equipped rooms and five suites. The basement also has a gym, spa, sauna and pool for use of guests. Free wi-fi. **€120**

Pensión Guadalete C/Veneroni 1 ☎956 870 90, ⓔhostalguadalete@gmail.com. Housed in the crumbling but nonetheless impressive early nineteenth-century Aduana (customs building), this *hostal* offers rooms with and without en suite, all with TV and fans. **€36**

★ **Pensión Santa María** C/Pedro Múñoz Seco 38 ☎956 853 631. Very welcoming family *pensión* offering spotless rooms with or without bath (with a negligible difference in price), run by an ebullient *dueña andaluza* (female proprietor). She'll even do a bit of washing for you. If you want to practise your Spanish, here's the place to stay. **€30**

CAMPSITE

Camping Playa Las Dunas Paseo Marítimo, Playa la Puntilla ☎956 872 210. Just behind the Playa Puntilla this site has modern facilities and plenty of shade. Take bus #2 from Plaza de Galeras by the ferry dock. Two people plus car **€19.50**

EATING AND DRINKING

The best areas in town for places to eat are the Ribera del Marisco, a street upstream from the ferry dock lined with a variety of seafood restaurants and bars serving tapas and *raciones*, and the nearby Plaza de la Herrería. You should also try the beaches of La Puntilla and Valdelagrana for their cluster of friendly bars.

CAFÉS AND RESTAURANTS

Aponiente Puerto Escondido 6 ☎956 851 870. El Puerto's newest top-end seafood restaurant has arrived with a bang, winning a Michelin star in its first year. Under chef Ángel León who is a prophet of the El Bulli school – flavours matter more than stuffing your stomach – the menu is creatively slanted to testing out new fusions: "oyster in plankton foam" and suchlike. A *menú de degustación* for €60 (excluding wine) has been described by one critic as "a shameless scam with pigmy portions on big plates and lots of seaweed" and by another as "the pinnacle of the creative chef's art." Take your pick. Tues–Sat 1–4pm & 8–11pm, Sun 1–4pm.

Bodega Jerezana Avda. de la Paz, Valdelagrana seafront. Briny tapas bar and traditional restaurant offering a wide range of well-prepared tapas in its bar and more elaborate seafood dishes in the restaurant. Main dishes €9–20. Daily noon–5pm & 8pm–midnight.

Casa Flores Ribera del Río 9 ☎956 543 512. Long-established fish and *mariscos* restaurant. *Lomo de urta al brandy de Jerez* (bream with brandy sauce) is a signature dish, and there are also various *marisco raciones* in its tapas bar, including good *almejas* (clams). Main courses €15–25. Daily 1–5pm & 8pm–midnight.

El Faro de El Puerto 0.5km along the Rota road ☎956 870 952. Outstanding seafood and meat dishes produced under the direction of top chef Fernando Córdoba in this stylish establishment (the twin of the restaurant of the same name in Cádiz). Widely regarded as having the best wine-cellar in the province, and also has a very pleasant garden terrace and a *menú de degustación* for around €60. Main dishes €12–25. Mon–Sat 1–4pm & 9–11pm, Sun 1–4pm.

Las Capuchinas Monasterio San Miguel, C/Larga 27. The *Monasterio* hotel's swish *cafetería* serves up good-value *platos combinados* and has a *menú* for around €12. Daily 1–4pm & 8.30–11pm.

Pasta Gansa C/Puerto Escondido 1, near the Ribera del Marisco. Stylish Italian restaurant with reasonably priced pizzas and risottos served on an attractive patio. Daily 1–4.30pm & 8.30pm–1am.

⭐ **Romerijo** Ribera del Marisco. This enormous, economical and justifiably popular seafood bar dominates the strip. You can get a takeaway of *mariscos* in a *cartucho* (paper funnel) from their shop and eat it at outdoor tables where buckets are provided for debris and waiters serve beer; the *cóctel de mariscos* (seafood cocktail) or any of the six types of *langostinos* are delicious. The same firm's *freiduría* restaurant over the road is equally excellent, and a generous *frito variado* (assorted fried fish) easily serves two. Daily noon–midnight.

TAPAS BARS

⭐ **Bar Tapia** C/Mayorga 7. Excellent and friendly small tapas and *raciones* bar with a charming summer patio. Specials include *arroz casero* (house paella) and *mariscos*. Daily noon–4pm & 8.30pm–12.30am.

Bar Vicente C/Abastos 7. This wonderful old bar first opened its doors well over a century ago and is now part of El Puerto folklore. Show an interest and the latest Vincente (in a long line) will tell you its story and show you an atmospheric photo of the bar in its early days (the wall tiles are the originals). Also serves decent tapas and *raciones* and a house special is *tortillita de camarones* (shrimp fritters). Daily 7am–3pm & 8–11pm.

La Dorada Avda. Bajamar 26, 150m south of the ferry dock. Inexpensive, meal-sized *raciones* with a terrace overlooking the river – the *pescado frito* is superb, and house specials include *choco a la plancha* (cuttlefish). Tues–Sun 1–4pm & 8–11.30pm.

La Galera Plaza de las Galeras, close to the Muelle del Vapor. Good bar for beer and seafood tapas and *raciones* while waiting for a boat, with a pleasant terrace overlooking the river. Daily 9am–11pm.

Nuevo Portuense C/Luna 31. Good, busy central bar with a wide range of seafood tapas and *raciones* (*sardinas empanadas* are a special) and there's a *menú* for around €9. Mon–Sat noon–4.30pm & 8pm–midnight.

Sol y Sombra Plaza de Ahuja, facing the bullring. Taking its name from the nearby bullring's seating arrangements, this is an often lively venue – especially on fight days – offering good and cheap tapas with house specials including *fideos con almejas* (vermicelli with clams) and paella. Its restaurant is also recommended and does a lunchtime *menú* for €10. Mon, Tues & Thurs–Sun 8am–midnight.

NIGHTLIFE

Nightlife in El Puerto means just that – in summer many places don't even open until around 11pm. The action centres on the bars around the eighteenth-century former fishmarket (El Resbaldero) and the focal Plaza Herrería, nearby C/Jesús de los Milagros and the river area.

Bar & Company Plaza de la Herrería s/n. A roomy place that features lots of dancing to top-40 hits plus frequent live gigs, especially at weekends.

La Cristalera Plaza de las Galeras s/n. On the river near the ferry dock this glass-walled bar – just to the north of the Galeras fountain – is a laid-back late-night music venue.

La Pontona Parque Calderon s/n. Moored just upstream of *La Cristalera*, *La Pontona* is a pontoon music bar with a dance floor and popular roof terrace. Things tend to start late here and go on till dawn.

Milwaukee Avda. de Bajamar 10. Cavernous riverfront bar with frequent live performances by local and national rock, jazz and punk bands.

Rota

Much of the 15km between El Puerto and the town of **ROTA** is occupied by one of the three major **US military bases** in Spain. Installed in the 1950s as part of a deal in which Franco exchanged strips of Spanish sovereign territory for economic aid and international "respectability", the base is surrounded by a seemingly endless barbed-wire fence bristling with military gadgetry. Behind the wire it's possible to glimpse farms and whole villages linked by their own bus service along a road system where

---

THE SHERRY BODEGAS OF EL PUERTO DE SANTA MARÍA

The long, whitewashed warehouses flanking the streets and the banks of the Río Guadalete belong to the big sherry bodegas: Luís Caballero, Terry, Osborne and Duff Gordon, the last three founded in the eighteenth and nineteenth centuries by Irish and English families. Osborne (pronounced "Osbornay" in Spanish) and Duff Gordon are now co-owned after a takeover by Osborne, although separate production is maintained and the Duff Gordon brand is sold only outside Spain. Osborne is also the largest producer of Spanish brandy, and its black-bull logo – long used as a billboard perched on hills throughout Spain – has become a familiar part of the country's landscape.

In sherry circles, El Puerto is noted for a lighter, more aromatic fino with more *flor* aroma imparted due to its humid geographical location, close to the sea (see the box on p.207 for details of sherry styles).

VISITING THE BODEGAS

It's easy enough to visit the bodegas; all welcome visitors for tours and tastings, although you'll need to call in advance to Osborne and Caballero to book a place. Other bodegas also do visits and the Turismo can supply a full list with opening hours.

Osborne and Duff Gordon C/Los Moros 7 (tours Mon–Fri: 10.30am in English, noon in Spanish; Sat 11am in English, noon in Spanish; ☎956 869 100, ✆osborne.es; €7.50). The biggest of El Puerto's sherry producers. The beautiful old bodega dates from 1837, while its vinification plant is one of the most modern.

Fernando de Terry C/Toneleros 1 (tours in Spanish/English Mon–Fri at 10.30am & 12.30pm, Sat at noon [booking required for this tour]; ☎956 151 500, ✆bodegasterry.com; €8). Situated in a beautiful converted seventeenth-century convent with its own museum. The bodega was founded in 1883 by an Irish family which had settled in Spain in the sixteenth century; the family sold up

in 1981 and the bodega is now owned by a multinational conglomerate.

Gutiérrez Colosía Avda. de Bajamar 40, near the *Hotel Santa María* (tours in English Mon–Fri 1pm, Sat 12.30pm & 1.30pm; ☎956 852 852, ✆gutierrez-colosia.com; €4). Highly rated small producer with a wonderfully atmospheric old bodega founded in the early nineteenth century.

Caballero C/San Francisco 32 (tours in English Tues–Sat 11am; ☎956 851 751, ✆caballero.es; €10). Another old wine family, the Caballeros have been making wine here since the late eighteenth century and their bodega is yet another "wine cathedral" with thousands of sleeping vats.

signs are in English. Huge Ford trucks trundle to and from Rota's harbour from where the base services and supplies the US Sixth Fleet – including nuclear submarines. In the autumn of 2011 the Spanish and US governments announced that the base was to be expanded as part of NATO's anti-ballistic missile defence system with a significant increase in personnel.

The US military population tends to keep to itself, however, and Rota exudes an affable character very much its own, with an attractive *casco antiguo* and some excellent tapas bars. In season, the resort fairly bounces with life, its magnificent **beach**, the Playa de la Costilla, being the main attraction for the crowds who flock here in August. The town's sights can be seen in under an hour.

Castillo de Luna
C/Cuña 2 • Sat & Sun 1–5pm • Free

Highlights in the old quarter include a thirteenth-century castle now housing the Ayuntamiento and Turismo – the frequently remodelled and much-restored **Castillo de Luna**, with a stunning fifteenth-century patio. Built on the ruins of a Moorish fort, it passed into the hands of two of Spain's great dynastic families, the Guzmán and the Ponce de León (their arms appear throughout the building), who used it until the middle of the eighteenth century. It then fell into a ruinous state and changed hands numerous times. The Ayuntamiento subsequently took it over in 1987 and spent a fortune restoring the building to the rather too-perfect-looking edifice you see today.

Nuestra Señora de la Expectación
Plaza Padre Eugenio s/n • Daily 9am–1pm and 6.30–9pm • Free

Also worth a look is the sixteenth-century Gothic church, **Nuestra Señora de la Expectación** (known locally as Nuestra Señora de la O). Behind a box-like exterior lies a fine single-naved church with elegant vaulting, magnificent choir stalls depicting the twelve apostles by Diego Roldán and – in the chapel of Jesús Nazareno – a delightful eighteenth-century image of the Last Supper crafted in azulejos from Triana in *Sevilla* (the barely surviving image of Judas has received some rough treatment over the years).

Capilla de San Juan Bautista
Plaza Andalucía • Open service times only, try early evening 7–8pm

Worth a visit is the **Capilla de San Juan Bautista** (aka Capilla de la Caridad), near the Turismo, with a spectacular Baroque *altar mayor* (high altar) by Diego Roldán, one of the finest in the province.

ARRIVAL AND DEPARTURE ROTA

By bus The bus station (☏ 956 810 499) is at C/Zoilo Ruíz Mateos s/n, just off Plaza del Triunfo, a ten-minute walk or an easy bus ride south to the centre along C/Calvario. Frequent services connect the town with Cádiz, Seville, El Puerto de Santa María, Chipiona and Sanlúcar de Barrameda.

By car Parking in the centre is almost impossible and car parks tend to fill up quickly. Make your way to the seafront (the *Hotel Duque de Najera* is a good place to aim for,

see p.204) where there are street parking spaces along Avda. San Juan de Puerto Rico and its continuation Paseo Marítimo Cruz del Rompidillo.

By boat There's a useful and enjoyable catamaran service across the Bay of Cádiz linking Rota to Cádiz (eight services daily between 7am and 9pm from a quay in the Puerto Deportivo; last boat from Cádiz at 8.30pm; 25min; €8.60 return). Services are sometimes reduced at weekends.

INFORMATION

Turismo The very helpful Turismo (July–Sept Mon–Fri 9.30am–1.30pm & 5.30–8.30pm, Sat & Sun 10am–2pm & 6–9pm; Oct–June Mon–Fri 9.30am–1.30pm & 5–7.30pm, Sat & Sun 10am–2pm; ☏ 956 846 345, ⍟ turismorota .com) is located in the Castillo de Luna, C/Cuna 2 in the old

quarter on the town's southern flank. They can provide a useful town map.

Festival Rota's big festival is the mid-August Fiesta de la Urta, when all the restaurants in town compete to win the prize for the best *urta*-based dish (see p.204).

2

ACCOMMODATION

Duque de Najera C/Gravina 2 ☎ 956 846 020, ⊛ hotel duquedenajera.com. The town's flagship hotel, with seaview rooms overlooking the harbour in an elegant four-star. Facilities include a pool, two restaurants, bar, gym and sauna. See website for offers. **€193**

Hostal Macavi C/Écija 11, off the main Avda. Sevilla ☎ 956 813 336. Excellent and friendly *hostal* with en-suite a/c rooms with TV, a mere 50m from the beach, and a decent restaurant. Parking can be tricky in high summer – call ahead for advice. **€60**

Hostal Sixto Plaza Barroso 6 ☎ 956 846 310, ⊛ hostal sixto.com. Enchanting small *hostal* in a restored town house in the heart of the old quarter with attractive a/c rooms with TV set around a pretty patio in the house or above their nearby (and good) restaurant a few metres away. Free wi-fi. B&B **€85**

★ **Hostal El Torito** C/Constitución 1, near the Plaza de España in the old town ☎ 956 813 369, ⊛ eltoritoderota.com. This stunningly minimalist *hostal* has to rank as one of Andalucía's most original, with individually styled a/c rooms (and bathrooms) decorated with cutting-edge furnishings and artworks with large-lettered Zen quotes running across the walls. Room #5 with its own terrace is a gem. Facilities include a shared guests' kitchen and free w-fi. **€60**

CAMPSITE

Camping Playa Aguadulce 7km from Rota along the A491 to Chipiona ☎ 956 847 078, ⊛ playaaguadulce .com. Fronting a magnificent beach this is the nearest campsite to Rota with decent services and plenty of shade. Two people plus car **€21**

EATING AND DRINKING

The modern town fans out from the central Plaza Jesús Nazareno fronting the beach, and it's here that you'll find most of the bars, restaurants and nightlife. Look out for the town's very own speciality, the outstandingly tasty *urta a la roteña* (sea bream in a caramelized onion and tomato sauce). Note also that the *urta* season lasts June–Sept, outside which many restaurants revert to *mero a la roteña* (grouper). Rota's tapas bars tend to be better value than the restaurants, many of which are overpriced and bland. For tapas head down atmospheric C/La Mina, a little northwest of the Castillo de Luna, where a number of bars line the pedestrianized street.

Bar–Restaurante La Costilla C/Higuereta 68, facing Plaza Jesús Nazareno. With a busy bar and a more relaxed dining room this is a great place to sample the town's signature *urta a la roteña* or their tasty *arranque roteño* (a variation on gazpacho). Plenty of other *mariscos* on offer too – try the *deditos fritos* (sea bass) or the *chocos fritos* (fried squid).

Bar Torito C/Italia 2. A stone's throw from the chic *hostal* of the same name (see above); less cutting-edge than the *hostal* but a cosy place with tapas, *raciones* and some cool sounds. Try their *tortilla Española*.

Casa Raul C/Mina 20. Another excellent tapas haunt for fish and *mariscos*. The house special is *caballa a la plancha* (mackerel) but the *urta* is good too, and there's also paella and some meat dishes.

Emilio C/Mina 30. Excellent small family-run tapas bar with fresh fish and *mariscos*. Try their *tortillita de camarones* (shrimp fritters).

La Mina C/Mina 27. Fine little tapas bar with a good selection of meat and fish tapas – house specials include *angulas* (baby eels) and *tortillas de camarones* (shrimp fritters).

Mesón Alicantino Avda. Sevilla 39, near the Hostal Macavi (see above). Pleasant bar-restaurant with a street terrace. Serves good local fish and seafood and does a variation on the town's signature dish with *corvina a la roteña* (meagre). Also offers paella and some meat dishes *a la plancha*. Closed Wed.

Restaurante Sixto Hostal Sixto, Plaza Barroso 6. Yet another place to sample *urta* at its best, with an inviting terrace on a pedestrianized street. Two of the signature dishes are *carrillera de cerdo ibérico* (Iberian pigs' cheeks) and *lubina rellena de langostinos* (sea bass filled with deep-water prawns).

Chipiona

From Rota the road north winds inland behind a coast lined with further golden sand beaches to **CHIPIONA**, 18km away, on a point at the edge of the estuary of the Guadalquivir. The town is now famed for its lighthouse – the tallest in Spain (see p.205). There has been a lighthouse here since the first century BC, when the Roman consul, Quinto Servilius Caepion, ordered the construction of a beacon to help shipping navigate the hazardous offshore rocks and currents. The lighthouse became known as Caepionis Turris, which lent its name to the settlement as well.

An image of the Roman lighthouse and its Latin name now comprise the town's coat of arms.

Presenting itself as a modest, straightforward seaside resort crammed with family *pensiones* and small hotels, Chipiona is a great place to spend a few days, and has some magnificent beaches. It's perhaps best avoided in August, however, when the town's charms are all but submerged beneath an onslaught of mainly Spanish visitors.

Nuestra Señora de Regla

Avda. Nuestra Señora de la Regla s/n • Daily 8am–noon & 5–7.30pm • Free

Older tourists come here for the spa waters, channelled into a fountain at the fourteenth-century church of **Nuestra Señora de Regla**, which incorporates a delightful *claustro gótico* (Gothic cloister) adorned with seventeenth-century Triana *azulejos* – although it's kept shut (try to find a priest or churchwarden to open it for you).

The main altar displays the **Virgen de la Regla**, the town's iconic patroness. This curious black Virgin is said to have been the image to which Saint Augustine prayed when the Vandals were about to attack his city, Hippo in North Africa in the fifth century. He died and, so the story goes, his Virgin was carried off to Spain and safety by his disciple Saint Cyprian. She was venerated for three centuries in Chipiona prior to the Moorish invasions when Augustinian monks hid her in an underground cistern where she remained for five hundred years. After the *Reconquista* she was retrieved and – following numerous miracles – the shrine was built which finally grew into the church we see today.

The old quarter

The town has a charming **old quarter** on its northern flank, cut through by sinuous, white-walled alleyways. The major thoroughfare here is the pedestrianized Calle Isaac Peral (and its continuation Calle Miguel Cervantes), lined with shops, bars and some elegant buildings and hotels.

El Faro de Chipiona

Plaza de las Americas • Visits May, June & Sept Tues & Thurs 11am, 11.45am & 12.30pm; July & Aug Tues–Fri 11am, 11.45am & 12.30pm; April & Oct Thurs only 11am, 11.45am & 12.30pm • €5

Constructed in 1863–67 over the remains of its Roman predecessor, the giant 72m-high **Faro de Chipiona** is the tallest lighthouse in Spain, the third highest in Europe and the fifth loftiest in the world. It's 344 steps to the top, so should give you a good appetite for a few tapas later.

Beaches

For most visitors to Chipiona it is the twelve kilometres of beaches that are the lure. Stretching south of the town beyond the lighthouse is the long **Playa de la Regla** and its continuation **Playa Camarón**, both best avoided in August, although for much of the year it's possible to leave the crowds behind. In the opposite direction lie **Playa de las Canteras**, **Playa Cruz del Mar** and – beyond the Puerto Deportivo – the tranquil **Playa Micaela**. Northeast of here, towards Sanlúcar, are sand bars and rocks with fine views towards the Marismas de Doñana and the Guadalquivir estuary.

ARRIVAL AND DEPARTURE	CHIPIONA

By bus The bus station (☎ 956 377 010 or ☎ 956 341 063) is at the junction of Avda. de Almería and Avda. de Andalucía at the eastern end of town. To reach the centre (a ten-minute walk or take a taxi), follow Avda. de Andalucía and its continuation Avda. del Ejército until you reach the junction with C/Isaac Peral, the old quarter's main pedestrianized artery. Services include buses to Seville, Jerez, Cádiz and Sanlúcar.

By car Outside August coming into Chipiona by car shouldn't present any great problems and street parking is plentiful and easy to find.

INFORMATION

Turismo The well-organized Turismo is at C/Castillo 5, in the restored castle on the seafront (June–Sept daily 9am–2pm & 6–9pm; Oct–May Mon–Fri 10am–2pm & 5–7pm, Sun 10am–2pm; ☎956 929 065, ⓦturismo chipiona.es). Staff can help with maps, information, accommodation plus a list of tapas bars. A museum in the same castle building (Tues–Sun 10am–2pm; €2) mounts an interesting exhibition entitled Cádiz y El Nuevo Mundo (Cádiz and the New World) documenting with displays and multimedia Cádiz's role in the history of the Americas from the days of Columbus to the decline of the Spanish empire.

ACCOMMODATION

Hostal Andalucía C/Larga 14, close to the seaward end of C/Isaac Peral ☎956 370 705, ⓦhostal-andalucia .com. Welcoming, central place with recently refurbished and spotless a/c en-suite rooms. There's also a pleasant patio, rooftop solarium and free wi-fi zone. **€60**

Hostal Belén Avda. del Ejército 5, close to the central C/Miguel Cervantes ☎956 372 680. Simple, clean and economical rooms, some en-suite and others sharing bath (but with no difference in price). **€40**

★ **Hostal Gran Capitán** C/Fray Baldomero González 3, close to the seaward end of C/Isaac Peral ☎956 370 929, ⓦhostalgrancapitan.com. Very attractive and friendly *hostal* housed in a venerable *casa antigua* now owned and run by one of the descendants of Spain's eponymous fifteenth-century military commander Gran Capitán Gonzalo de Córdoba. The attractive a/c en-suite rooms come with TV and free wi-fi and the proprietor also rents out bicycles. **€65**

Hostal San Miguel Avda. de la Regla 79 ☎956 372 976.

Comfortable en-suite rooms in a charming Art Nouveau mansion close to the church of Nuestra Señora de la Regla. The friendly proprietors also rent some apartments nearby sleeping up to 4. Rooms **€65**, apartments **€70**

Hotel Al Sur de Chipiona Avda. de Sevilla 101, facing the church of Nuestra Señora de la Regla ☎956 370 300, ⓦhotelalsur.com. Fifty metres from the Playa de la Regla, this comprises an older, elegant hotel (and listed building) with a new wing – complete with pool and gardens – tacked on. Easily the best value of the more exclusive places, with well-appointed rooms, all with terrace balcony and many with sea view. **€115**

Hotel La Española C/Isaac Peral 4 ☎956 373 771, ⓦhotellaespanola.com. Superbly renovated and good-value old hotel – the front door is a mere 20m from the waves and many rooms have sea views. Free wi-fi zone and parking in the underground garage, but you may prefer staff to park your vehicle as the entry is tortuously crooked. **€70**

EATING AND DRINKING

Chipiona has a gratifying range of restaurants, all excelling in seafood. For tapas and bars – some with music – take a stroll along the pedestrianized C/Isaac Peral. The bars also serve up Chipiona's excellent moscatel wine made in numerous small bodegas around the town.

Bar Paquito C/Isaac Peral 36, at the junction with Plaza Pío XII. Long-established tapas and *raciones* bar with a small outdoor terrace. Try their *ventresca de atún rojo* (red tuna) or *pulpo a la gallega* (octopus).

Bar La Parra C/Isaac Peral 14. Excellent bar-restaurant serving a wide range of tapas and *raciones*. It's noted for its *almejas* (clams) and *coquinas* (wedge-shell clams) but also does meat dishes such as *cola de toro* (stewed bull's tail) and a tasty *carrillada ibérica* (black pig's cheek). Has some tables on an outdoor terrace, and authentic *chocolate con churros* on Sunday mornings – not to be missed. Oct–March open weekends only.

★ **Bar Peña Bética** C/Larga 46 at the junction with C/Isaac Peral. Highly popular and wonderfully atmospheric *gaditano* bar. It matters little that it's the Chipiona branch of the Real Betis supporters' club (one of Seville's two big football teams), the fried fish is excellent and the welcome ebullient. Try the *chipirones en salsa verde* (small squid). Closed Mon.

Bar-Restaurante Repostaero C/Dr Tolosa Latour 7, running behind the seafront near the Turismo. Boisterous seafood *chiringuito* with a great atmosphere late at night when impromptu flamenco sometimes gets going. *Sardinas asadas* (grilled sardines) and *pescados fritos* (fried fish) are house specials.

★ **Las Canteras** Playa de Las Canteras s/n ☎956 373 633. A superb seafront fish and *mariscos* restaurant with a shady terrace and fine sea views at the end of the tiny Playa de Las Canteras close to the lighthouse. Everything is fresh from the sea and the *urta* and *dorada* are recommended, as are the *boquerones fritos* (anchovies) – and they do pretty good *patatas fritas* (chips) too. Main dishes €5–20. Closed Tues Oct–May.

★ **Los Corrales** Playa de las Canteras s/n ☎956 375 129. Next to *Las Canteras* at the northern end of this small beach and just as good as its rival, with its own great seafront terrace. House specials include *arroz de mariscos* (shellfish paella), *salmonetes fritos* (red mullet) and wonderful *langostinos de Sanlúcar* (deep water prawns). Main dishes €10–25.

La Pañoleta C/Isaac Peral 5. Belonging to (and in the same building as) the *Hotel La Española*, this restaurant offers a varied menu of fish and meat dishes, plus a mid-priced *menú* for under €15.

Sanlúcar de Barrameda

Like El Puerto de Santa María, **SANLÚCAR DE BARRAMEDA**, 8km beyond Chipiona, is a major sherry town. A substantial place with an attractive old quarter set at the mouth of the Guadalquivir, it is the main depot for **manzanilla** wine – a pale dry fino variety with a salty tang – highly regarded by connoisseurs and much in evidence in the bars round here. Sanlúcar is also one of the best places in Andalucía for **seafood**, for which manzanilla is the perfect accompaniment.

The town is split into three distinct quarters, the older and formerly walled **Barrio Alto** on the hill, the **Barrio Bajo** below and the town's former port – the **Bajo de Guía** – 1km away on the river. Many of the monuments are in the Barrio Alto, where a good

2

SANLÚCAR'S MANZANILLA BODEGAS

The delicate taste of Sanlúcar's distinctive manzanilla is created by the seaside environment in which the wine is matured, and by the fact that it's not fortified with alcohol (as happens in Jerez and El Puerto). The humid microclimate necessary for the growth of the dense *flor* (yeast) inside the wine butts is added to by the moist *poniente* (westerly) wind that blows across the Coto de Doñana, imparting the characteristic saltiness to this driest of all sherries.

Sanlúcar is less aggressive than Jerez in its public relations (despite manzanilla recently overtaking fino sales on the peninsula for the first time), and only a few of Sanlúcar's bodegas are open for visits and tastings. We have quoted the bodega's guided tours in English; visit their websites for visits in other languages. Note that unlike many bodegas in Jerez or El Puerto, in Sanlúcar it's not necessary to book a place for a bodega visit

VISITING THE BODEGAS

Antonio Barbadillo C/Sevilla 25, near the castle (tours Tues–Sat 11am; ☎ 956 385 500, ⓦ barbadillo.com; €3). The town's major producer, founded in 1821, is responsible for seventy percent of all manzanilla, and also makes *manzanilla pasada*, an exceptional fifteen-year-old wine (as against the normal four for standard fino), as well as one of Andalucía's best white table wines (Castillo de San Diego) from the same Palomino grape. The bodega's Museo de Manzanilla (Tues–Sat 10am–3pm; free) is located slightly east of the castle and has a shop attached where you can buy their produce.

Bodegas La Cigarrera Plaza Madre de Dios s/n, near the *Hotel Los Helechos* (Mon–Sat 10am–2pm; ☎ 956 381 285, ⓦ bodegaslacigarrera.com; €2.85). Another family-controlled bodega, La Cigarrera (the name means "cigarette seller", whose image appears on their bottles) dates from the eighteenth century. Their leading brand is the La Cigarrera manzanilla, although they also produce *oloroso* and amontillado wines.

Bodegas Herederos de Argüeso C/Mar 8 (tours Mon–Sat 10.30am & noon; ☎ 956 385 116, ⓦ argueso.es; €6). Founded in 1822, this is another old established firm, makers of San León manzanilla, another highly popular brand.

Bodegas Hidalgo C/Banda Playa 24 (tours Mon–Fri 11am & noon, Sat & Sun 11am; ☎ 956 360 516, ⓦ lagitana.es; €5). Founded at the end of the eighteenth century, this is another long-established bodega which produces the La Gitana brand, one of Spain's most popular manzanillas. To visit first go to the Hidalgo shop on Calzada de la Duquesa Isabel (formerly the Calzada del Ejército) who will issue you with a ticket. The bodega is a short walk away around the corner.

Bodega de Velasco C/Truco s/n, near the market (Mon–Fri 8am–3pm). Friendly and intimate family-run place (a junior offshoot of Bodegas La Cigarrera) where they'll serve you their La Cigarrera brand manzanilla to try (and buy) straight from the butt.

Pedro Romero C/Trasbolsa 84, east of the Plaza del Cabildo (tours Mon–Sat at noon, also Tues–Fri at 5pm; ☎ 956 360 736, ⓦ pedroromero.es; €6). A family-run bodega founded in the late nineteenth century.

SHOPPING FOR SHERRY

La Abuela Lola C/Caballeros 21 near the *Posada de Palacio*. Stocks all the major brands and does tastings.

Bodegas Hidalgo Opposite the Turismo on the Calzada de la Duquesa Isabel (formerly Calzada del Ejército).

2

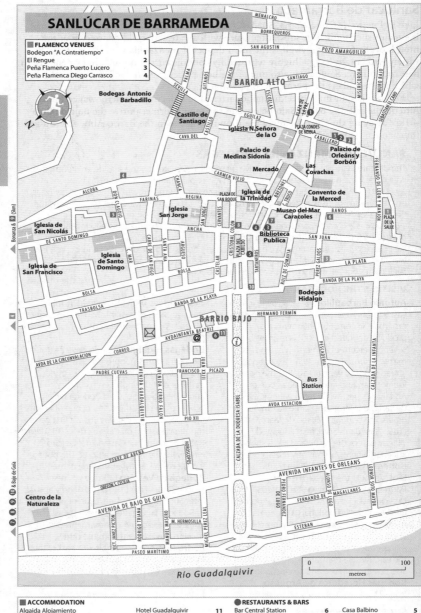

SANLÚCAR DE BARRAMEDA

▌FLAMENCO VENUES
Bodegon "A Contratiempo" — 1
El Rengue — 2
Peña Flamenca Puerto Lucero — 3
Peña Flamenca Diego Carrasco — 4

Bonanza & 9 (5km)

Río Guadalquivir

0   100
metres

▌ACCOMMODATION				●RESTAURANTS & BARS			
Algaida Alojamiento Rural	9	Hotel Guadalquivir	11	Bar Central Station	6	Casa Balbino	5
Hospedería Duques de Medina Sidonia	3	Hotel Los Helechos	6	Bar El Cura	4	Casa Juan	7
		Hotel Tartaneros	10	Bar Joselito Huerta	10	El Espejo	2
Hostal Alcoba	4	Pensión Blanca Paloma	7	Bar Juanito	3	Mirador de Doñana	9
Hostal Gadir	2	Pensión Bohemia	5	Bar Parada "El Gallego"	1		
Hotel Barrameda	8	Posada de Palacio	1	Bar-Restaurante El Bigote	8		

number of bodegas and their warehouses are also to be found, emitting a pleasant hint of sherry into the air.

Brief history

Although there was a small settlement here in Roman times and the Moors built a fort to guard the vital Guadalquivir estuary from sea raiders, it was only after the recapture of the town in 1264 by Alfonso X that Sanlúcar grew to become one of sixteenth-century Spain's leading ports. **Columbus** sailed from here on his third voyage to the Americas and it was also from here in 1519 that Magellan set out to circumnavigate the globe. Decline in the eighteenth century, however, was exacerbated by the War of Independence and the town revived only in the mid-nineteenth century when the duke of Montpensier built a summer palace here. Since then Sanlúcar has grown into the popular resort it is today.

Plaza del Cabildo and around

The **Plaza del Cabildo**, a charming, palm-fringed square ringed with bars and sporting a splendid fountain, is a good place to start your explorations. Directly southwest of the square, Plaza de San Roque adjoins the **morning market** which is one of the town's great shows when it's in full swing – Saturday mornings are best when burly señoras give no quarter while attempting to get their hands on the best fish.

Just off this square, the interior of the fifteenth-century **Iglesia de la Trinidad** (Mon–Sat 10am–1pm; free) has a fine Mudéjar ceiling. West of here and parallel to Calle Bretones lies the curious **Museo del Mar Caracoles** (daily 10am–7pm; €2), exhibiting the bizarre lifetime collection of objects retrieved from the sea by eccentric proprietor Garrido García, who resembles a latter-day Long John Silver and conducts tours around his house/museum with a tame feral pigeon perched on one shoulder.

Iglesia de San Jorge

C/San Jorge • Mon–Sat 10am–1pm • Free

The sixteenth-century **Iglesia de San Jorge** was constructed by English sherry merchants with special permission from the duke of Medina Sidonia, who was keen to encourage their lucrative trade. Henry VIII of England allowed the merchants to levy the substantial English community for funds to build the church, but soon after its completion in 1517 it became embroiled in Henry's struggles with Rome. A document dated 1591 records that Sanlúcar's English community – the majority still loyal to Rome – decided to hand over the church to some Irish monks who themselves had been chased out of England by Henry's daughter, Elizabeth I. After serving as a church and a hospital for the poor the church was rebuilt in the eighteenth century in the Baroque style, funded by the duke of Medina Sidonia and the town council. Inside, a magnificent retablo by Juan González de Herrera is topped off by a mounted San Jorge (St George) slaying the dragon.

Iglesia de Santo Domingo

C/Ancha • Open 30min before services which are held Mon–Fri 9.30am & 8pm, Sat 8pm, Sun 10.30am, noon and 7.30pm • Free

Sanlúcar's only church built entirely of stone, the sixteenth-century **Iglesia de Santo Domingo** was formerly the church of a Dominican monastery to which it was attached. Inside, there are a couple of fine retablos and the interesting tombs of a seventeenth-century duke and duchess of Niebla on either side of the main altar.

Iglesia San Francisco

C/Ancha • Open for services or call ☎ 956 360 126 • Free

Northeast of Iglesia de Santo Domingo lies the sixteenth-century church of **San Francisco**, founded by Henry VIII of England – while he was married to Catherine of Aragón – as a hospital for British sailors. Rebuilt in the eighteenth century in the Baroque style, the unusually bare white interior has a fine ungilded wooden retablo.

2

VISITING THE COTO DE DOÑANA NATIONAL PARK

Access to the vast, marshy expanse of the Coto de Doñana National Park (see p.330), on the shore opposite Sanlúcar, is strictly controlled to protect Europe's largest wildlife sanctuary and a vital wetland for a variety of migrating birds. However, a four-hour **boat cruise** aboard the *Real Fernando* allows visitors to access the park, giving a wonderful introduction to this remarkable area. The boat – which has a *cafetería* on board – leaves from the Bajo de Guía (March, April, May & Oct daily 10am & 4pm; June–Sept Mon–Sat 10am & 5pm; Nov–Feb daily 10am; booking essential on ☎956 363 813, ⓦvisitasdonana.com; €16.35). The trips allow two short guided walks led by wildlife experts inside the park where you'll visit a hamlet of *chozas* (traditional Doñana huts) and should see *jabalí* (wild boar), wild horses, flamingos and a profusion of birdlife including buzzards, herons, kites, cranes and eagles, as well as stunning wild flowers, depending on your luck and season. In summer it's best to book as early as you can, since the trips are limited to 94 passengers; binoculars (essential) can be hired on board.

Collect your tickets (at least 30min in advance of the sailing) from the Fábrica de Hielo, Bajo de Guía s/n (daily 9am–8pm), virtually opposite the *Real Fernando*'s jetty. This extravagant exhibition centre in Sanlúcar's old ice factory was created by the National Park authority and contains stunningly unimaginative displays of the park's flora and fauna. Viajes Doñana, C/San Juan 20 (☎956 362 540), also do all-terrain **vehicle-based trips** into the park (Tues & Fri; booking essential; €40) starting from the Bajo de Guía at 8.30am and 4.30pm (Oct–April 8.30am & 2.30pm) and covering about 70km in four hours.

Las Covachas

C/Bretones

The Barrio Alto is reached by following Calle Bretones uphill from the Plaza San Roque. To the left, beyond the market you pass the remarkable fifteenth-century **Las Covachas** (market stalls) with an elegantly carved, if worn, Gothic frontage. Built at the behest of the second duke of Medina Sidonia, next to the *alcaicería* or silk market, this was Sanlúcar's first shopping centre, comprising ten (now glassed-in) ogival arches separated by pillars decorated with serpents. Soon established as the town's commercial district, with the construction of the adjoining market in the eighteenth century so it has remained.

Convento de la Merced

C/Bretones • Enquire at the Turismo about visits • Free

Continuing uphill the way bends left, passing the seventeenth-century **Convento de la Merced**. The religious order abandoned the ruinous convent in 1960, after which it fell into a dilapidated state. The then owner, the Duchess of Medina Sidonia (see box opposite), finally ceded ownership to the Ayuntamiento of Sanlúcar, who restored the building as a concert hall, the function it serves today. Designed by Juan de Oviedo and Alonso de Vandelvira, son of the more famous Andrés (see p.366), the interior has fabulous stone vaulting, while a rather plain white-walled facade on Calle Bretones has a soberly worked entrance portal with tympanum flanked by six stone porthole windows.

Palacio de Orleáns y Borbón and gardens

C/Bretones • Mon–Fri 8am–1.30pm; free guided tours are run by the Turismo (Tues, Thurs, Sat & Sun at 10.45am leaving from the Turismo), although there are no visits when the Ayuntamiento is being used for an official function

Beyond the Covento de la Merced stands the neo-Mudéjar **Palacio de Orleáns y Borbón**, a flamboyantly decorated nineteenth-century summer palace of the dukes of Montpensier, now occupied by the Ayuntamiento. You are allowed to step inside the building's entrance to take a look at an impressive patio but the building's other rooms – decorated in a pot-pourri of neo-Mudéjar, rococo and ancient Egyptian styles – are off-limits outside guided visits. The palace's true glory, however, are the magnificent **gardens** behind (access via the Ayuntamiento), filled with palms, follies and fountains as well as offering magnificent views over the town and river.

Nuestra Señora de la O

Plaza de las Condes de Niebla • Fri–Sat 11am–1pm (also open for daily Mass Mon–Sat at 8pm, Sun 9am, noon & 8pm) • Free

Taking a left at the top of Calle Bretones into Calle Caballero will bring you to – on the right – **Plaza de la Paz**, another delightful small square, and, almost opposite, the church of **Nuestra Señora de la O**, Sanlúcar's oldest, founded in the thirteenth century but much altered since and recently restored. The exterior has an exquisite Gothic-Mudéjar portal depicting lions bearing coats of arms and, inside, there's an impressive *artesonado* ceiling.

Palacio de los Duques de Medina Sidonia

Plaza de las Condes de Niebla • Tours Sun 11am & noon (advance booking required on ☎ 956 360 161) • Gardens open Mon–Fri 8.30am–1pm & 3–5pm, Sat–Sun 9am–1pm • ⓦ fcmedinasidonia.com • €4

Nuestra Señora de la O is connected to the *palacio* of the **duques de Medina Sidonia**, whose sixteenth- to eighteenth-century interior houses the family's important historical archive and has wonderful views over the Coto de Doñana. Until her death in 2008 the duchess of Medina Sidonia (see box below) lived here. The guided tour of the house and its beautiful gardens takes an hour and proceeds through impressive rooms stuffed with works by Spanish masters such as Roelas, Morales and Goya. The *cafetería* in the *Hospedería Duques de Medina Sidonia* (see p.213) opposite the palace entrance, with a charming patio, is open daily from 8.30am–9pm.

Castillo de Santiago

C/Sevilla • Tues–Sat tours on the hour 11am–1pm, plus July–Aug at 8pm & 9pm • €7

Heading northeast from the palace brings you to the recently restored fifteenth-century **Castillo de Santiago** where guided visits enable you to see the castle's barbicans, Plaza de

---

THE RED DUCHESS

In 2008, Sanlúcar mourned the passing of **Luisa Isabel Álvarez de Toledo**, more formally known as the Duchess of Medina Sidonia or by her nickname "La Duquesa Roja" (the Red Duchess). The great ducal family of Medina Sidonia – Spain's oldest dynasty, founded in 1455 – has had a hand in most of the country's great historic events from the *Reconquista* to the launching of the Spanish Armada – which was commanded by the seventh Duke of Medina Sidonia.

A free-thinker from her earliest days, she was expelled from numerous convent schools due to her tomboyish and nonconformist behaviour. Upon the death of her father in 1955 Isabel inherited the title of the ducal house and moved into the palace in Sanlúcar. She joined the then illegal Socialist Workers Party (PSOE) and displayed contempt for Franco and his regime at every opportunity. One of her anti-Franco activities – supporting farmers in Almería who had been affected by the nuclear incident at Palomares in 1966 (see p.552) – landed her in jail for eight months in 1969. The Franco government – embarrassed when the story hit the world headlines – offered her a pardon providing she repented. Typically she refused and served out the full sentence. She then wrote a devastating indictment of prison conditions, shaming the government into a programme of reforms. A fervent believer in land reform, she gave away vast tracts of her estates to form rural cooperatives, until only the Palace of Medina Sidonia remained in her hands. A historian, she spent most of her time organizing the massive and important historical archive of the ducal family and set up the foundation that now continues the work.

She died as she had lived, controversial to the end. On her deathbed – thanks to Spain's new law permitting same-sex marriages – she married her secretary and long-time companion Liliana Dahlmann who, as its president, now runs the Fundación Casa Medina Sidonia. Her memory is much cherished here, and in 2009 the town honoured the duchess by renaming one of its major thoroughfares after her. The former Calzada del Ejército (Boulevard of the Army), an avenue leading down to the river, now bears the name Calzada de la Duquesa Isabel. As a pacifist, she would no doubt have approved.

2

Armas and towers with stunning views. It is still unclear at the time of writing what the new exhibition areas inside the castle will contain (details from the Turismo).

A flight of steps beside the castle leads back down to the Barrio Bajo.

Río Guadalquivir

Bus #3 or #4 from the Calzada de la Duquesa Isabel or a €4 taxi ride from Plaza del Cabildo • Ferry to Coto de Doñana runs daily 8am to 9pm (€6 return)

A good kilometre walk from the centre, Sanlúcar's shell-encrusted **river beach** – unfortunately marred by a lengthy and rather ugly concrete esplanade – is nevertheless a nice place to while away some time, and is usually quite deserted. The beach is also the setting for some exciting **horse-races**.

From April to September, a *barcaza* (ferry barge) carries passengers to the Coto de Doñana's beaches on the opposite bank of the Guadalquivir. It leaves from a quay at the Bajo de Guía, near the *Real Fernando* jetty (see box, p.210) and is operated by the same company. The Doñana's beaches suffer from pollution but do provide a change of scene and some bird-spotting possibilities. There are absolutely no facilities, so be sure to take along liquid refreshment, food and perhaps a parasol. And remember that no incursions into the national park are allowed; wardens are on patrol and tend to be severe with those who flout the regulations.

Bonanza

Four kilometres upstream from Sanlúcar, the small port of **Bonanza** is where the town's sizeable fishing fleet is based, their catch sold at entertaining auctions (Mon–Sat at 5pm) on the harbourside. This is also the very spot from where Columbus and Magellan set sail on their epic voyages. Bonanza can be reached by taxi from the Plaza del Cabildo for around €5 or by bus #1 from the top of the Calzada de la Duquesa Isabel.

ARRIVAL AND DEPARTURE — SANLÚCAR DE BARRAMEDA

By bus The bus station is at Avda. Guzmán El Bueno, between the river and the centre, to the east of the main avenue Calzada de la Duquesa Isabel. There are services to Chipiona, Cádiz, Seville and Jerez run by Amarillos (☎ 956 385 060) and Linesur (☎ 956 341 063).

By car It's best to avoid the congested central zone and find a parking place along the Calzada de la Duquesa Isabel. When this is full, there's a subterranean pay car park at this avenue's southern end (nearest the centre).

INFORMATION

Turismo At Calzada de la Duquesa Isabel s/n (July–Aug Mon–Fri 10am–2pm & 6–8pm, Sat & Sun 10am–2pm; March–June & Sept–Nov Mon–Fri 10am–2pm & 5–7pm, Sat–Sun 10am–2pm; Dec–Feb Mon–Fri 10am–2pm & 4–6pm, Sat–Sun 10am–2pm; ☎ 956 366 110, ⓦ turismo sanlucar.com or ⓦ sanlucardebarrameda.es). Staff can provide a detailed street map and a tapas guide.

Internet Ciber Guadalquivir, C/Infanta Beatriz s/n (daily 10am–11pm), near the *Hotel Guadalquivir*. The Biblioteca Pública (public library: Mon–Sat 9.30am–1.30pm) at Plaza San Roque s/n, is another possibility, with two terminals (free); the library is also a free wi-fi zone – the password key (*llave*) you need to enter the system is posted on the

notice board as you enter.

Festivals The fiesta of the Virgen de la Caridad takes place on August 15, honouring the town's patron, the Virgin of Charity; the central C/Ancha is the site of a colourful spectacle, laid end to end with a carpet of colourful "flowers" – actually tinted sawdust. The town's other big knees-up is the Feria de la Manzanilla at the end of May, an excuse to celebrate the town's famous wine, with much drinking and dancing. In early and late August, the beach is the setting for some exciting horse-races, a tradition dating from 1845, accompanied by lots of betting and riotous partying by revellers filling the bars and restaurants along the Bajo de Guía riverfront.

ACCOMMODATION

There's a shortage of budget accommodation in Sanlúcar, and in August you'll be pushed to find anything at all. This is when a number of *casas particulares* open to mop up the overflow. Enquire at the Turismo for information about these, and for longer stays they have a list of apartments for rent (minimum three nights), plus *casas rurales* in and around the town.

Algaida Alojamiento Rural Calle 1, no. 4 Colonia Monte Algaida, 5km out of town beyond the village of Bonanza ☎ 956 387 372. This friendly rural option offers rooms sharing bath in a large house in a village close to the Guadalquivir estuary. You'll need your own transport and to call ahead for directions. B&B **€50**

★ **Hospedería Duques de Medina Sidonia** Plaza Condes de Niebla 1 ☎ 956 360 161, ⓦ ruralduques medinasidonia.com. The best address in town, in the palace of the dukes of Medina Sidonia, one of Spain's most blue-blooded dynasties. The *hospedería* has nine excellent-value beamed rooms and suites with original features and tasteful furnishings surrounding a charming patio – suites also come with private terrace. B&B rooms **€75**, suites **€100**

★ **Hostal Gadir** C/Caballeros 19 ☎ 956 360 078, ⓔ info@hostalgadir.com. Wonderful friendly new family-run *hostal* with sparkling a/c rooms (including singles); all come with TV and free wi-fi, while some have a terrace and others a Jacuzzi. Rooms 3, 4, 5, & 10 (with Jacuzzi) have a superb view of the gardens of the Palacio de Orleáns y Borbón opposite. A bargain in high season, and an absolute steal at other times of the year. **€50**

★ **Hostal Alcoba** C/Alcoba 26, slightly east of the Plaza del Cabildo ☎ 956 383 109, ⓦ hostalalcoba.com. New and superbly designed ultra-modern *hostal* offering bright and elegant rooms with plasma TV and free wi-fi and stylish public areas, with a plunge pool and decked patio at the rear. The friendly proprietors rent out bikes, as well as flamenco dress for festivals. All rooms adapted for disabled use. **€70**

Hotel Barrameda C/Ancha 10 ☎ 956 385 878, ⓦ hotel barrameda.com. A newish, central and welcome addition to the town's accommodation options offering light and airy a/c rooms with plasma TV, some with balcony. Also has a pleasant patio, solarium roof terrace and wi-fi throughout. **€80**

Hotel Guadalquivir Calzada de la Duquesa Isabel 20 ☎ 956 360 742, ⓦ hotelguadalquivir.com. Modern hotel towering over the thoroughfare leading to the river. The functional rooms come with a/c, while some also have balcony, and there are good views from higher ones. High season applies July–Aug only; see website for offers. **€125**

Hotel Los Helechos Plaza Madre de Dios 9 ☎ 956 361 349, ⓦ hotelloshelechos.com. Smart, very reasonably priced three-star central hotel in converted former bodega with attractive rooms around two charming patios and lots of traditional features. Free wi-fi zone. **€84**

Hotel Tartaneros C/Tartaneros 8 ☎ 956 362 044, ⓦ hoteltartaneros.com. Despite an impressive late nineteenth-century façade – designed by noted architect Aníbal González – this is a rather dull, old-fashioned hotel with a/c rooms and a dubious collection of dolls and effigies dotted around the staid interior. **€120**

Pensión Blanca Paloma Plaza de San Roque ☎ 956 363 644, ⓔ hostal_blanca_paloma@yahoo.es. Good-value and friendly *pensión* with simple rooms sharing bath in a central position. **€30**

Pensión Bohemia C/Don Claudio 5 ☎ 956 369 599. Comfortable en-suite a/c rooms with TV – albeit slightly dark due to windows facing an internal corridor – in a quiet street. **€47**

★ **Posada de Palacio** C/Caballeros 11 ☎ 956 364 840, ⓦ posadadepalacio.com. Elegantly converted eighteenth-century *casa palacio* with a delightful patio and tastefully furnished rooms with character. Rooftop terraces, bar and an intimate atmosphere make this rather special. **€109**

EATING, DRINKING AND ENTERTAINMENT

Sanlúcar is renowned for the quality of its seafood, and the place to head for is the Bajo de Guía, the old fishing district upstream from where the Alameda meets the river. Numerous bars and restaurants lining the waterfront have terrace views towards the Coto de Doñana and serve excellent seafood, washed down with manzanilla. In the Barrio Bajo, the Plaza del Cabildo has a number of good tapas and breakfast bars, while higher up, Plaza de la Paz is a tranquil little square with various tapas bars.

RESTAURANTS

★ **Bar-Restaurante El Bigote** Bajo de Guía 10 ☎ 956 362 696. Celebrated establishment and one of the "big two" on the waterfront – and which has recently edged ahead of its neighbour. There's excellent tapas in their lively bar or more formal dining in the restaurant, with outstanding fish and *arroz de marisco* (seafood paella). Don't miss the succulent local *langostinos* (prawns) too. An upstairs dining room offers panoramic views across the river. Main dishes €10–20; reservation advised. Mon–Sat 1–4pm & 8.30–11.30pm.

Casa Juan Bajo de Guía 26. Another Bajo de Guía favourite with a great river-view terrace and house specials including *arroz a la marinera*, *rape al cerco* (monkfish) plus excellent *langostinos* (deep-water prawns) and *coquinas* (clams). Daily noon–4.30pm & 7–11.30pm.

Mirador de Doñana Bajo de Guía s/n ☎ 956 364 205. The second of the Bajo de Guía's "big two" occasionally rests on its laurels, but is nevertheless an outstanding restaurant with a summer terrace overlooking the river. Try their *mi barca Doñana* (white fish in a tomato sauce served in an edible "boat") or *sopa de Galeras*, a special *marisco* soup of which they're deservedly proud. When not busy, the waiters in the tapas bar will be happy to give you a master class in the thirty-plus brands of manzanilla on offer. Main dishes €9–20. Tues–Sun 1–4pm & 8–11.30pm.

BARS

Bar Central Station C/Infanta Beatriz 1, by the side of the Hotel Guadalquivir. Highly original bar created by its train-mad owner and featuring a steam engine and a full-size reconstruction of a wagon from the old Orient Express with sofa-style seats, lots of polished wood and a gleaming copper tea urn. Daily 9am–11pm.

Bar El Cura C/Amargura 2, off Plaza del Cabildo. Relatively cheap and cheerful *platos combinados* at this pleasant bar-restaurant. They also do decent tapas and there's a *menú* for €8. Daily 10am–11pm.

Bar Joselito Huerta Bajo de Guía s/n, at the upstream end of the strip. Friendly seafood restaurant, slightly less expensive than its neighbours and with a popular river terrace. The *pescaíto frito* (fried fish), *almejas* (clams), *cazón con tomate* (shark) and *acedías* (baby sole) are all excellent, and they also serve good tapas at the bar. Daily 1–4pm & 8–11pm.

Bar Juanito Plaza San Roque 18. Popular local tapas venue, noted for its seafood (try the *almejas*) and *chacinas* (cured pork meats), and with a terrace on this lively square. Daily 9am–11pm.

Bar Parada "El Gallego" Plaza de la Paz 6. Galician bar that serves excellent *raciones* at economical prices. *Bacalao con tomate* (cod), *pulpo a la gallega* (octopus) and their *jamones* are all good. Daily 1.15–5.30pm & 7.30pm–1am.

★ **Casa Balbino** Plaza del Cabildo 11. Behind an unassuming facade lies one of the best tapas bars in Andalucía. Long established, its walls are hung with faded photos and the obligatory bulls' heads, and the smoothly efficient bar staff will guide you through a daunting tapas menu. The manzanillas are outstanding and their *tortillita de camarones* (shrimp fritter) is justly famous. There is a (self-service) terrace on the square. Daily noon–5pm & 8pm–1am.

El Espejo C/Caballeros 11. Entertaining new *raciones* gastro-bar with a bright, white and modern interior. Seating is bar-stools and high tables and the dishes are creatively edged. Try the *carpaccio de presa ibérica* (pork), *pastel de ortiguillas* (sea anemone) or one of their interesting salads. *Raciones* €7–22. Daily 1–5pm & 7.30pm–1am.

FLAMENCO

Bodegón "A Contratiempo" C/San Miguel 5 ☎673 071 099. Flamenco performances in an atmospheric small theatre (Fri–Sat 11pm; €5–15 depending on artist performing; admission includes one drink).

El Rengue Avda. V Centenario s/n (at the end of C/San Juan). Late-night *rociero* (loyal to the traditions of the El Rocío *romería* – see p.335) bar with a great atmosphere. Often stages impromptu flamenco, especially at weekends.

Peña Flamenca Diego Carrasco Callejón de la Guía 38, to the northeast of the Calzada de la Duquesa Isabel ☎678 055 491. Free performances of flamenco every Saturday evening (except Aug).

Peña Flamenca Puerto Lucero C/La Plata 50 ☎956 368 595. Wonderful old flamenco *peña* with walls lined with photos under a high beamed room. The bar is open daily but performances are irregular; ask at the Turismo.

ACTIVITIES

Horseriding A number of companies run guided tours in the Río Guadalquivir area. The reliable Club Equestre La Arboleda (☎630 867 672, ⓦclubecuestrelaarboleda .com) is one, charging around €20 per hour; the Turismo can provide details of others.

Jerez de la Frontera

Encircled by vines planted in the chalky, *albariza* soil, **JEREZ DE LA FRONTERA**, 22km inland from Sanlúcar and 35km from Cádiz, is the home and heartland of sherry (itself an English corruption of the town's Moorish name, Xerez) and also, less known but equally important, of Spanish brandy. Once you've penetrated some architecturally bleak suburbs, the town centre possesses a charming *casco antiguo* and a number of elegant, palm-fringed squares, as well as a handful of notable Renaissance and Baroque churches and palaces.

Jerez's biggest attractions are indisputably the great **sherry bodegas** located in the heart of the town. The sherry dynasties that own these companies (or used to own them, as many have been taken over by international conglomerates) are renowned as some of the biggest snobs in Spain, and take a haughty pride in aping the traits and customs of the English upper-middle class – their strutting around on polo horses, wearing tweeds and speaking Spanish with an affected accent has earned them the nickname of *señoritos* or "toffs".

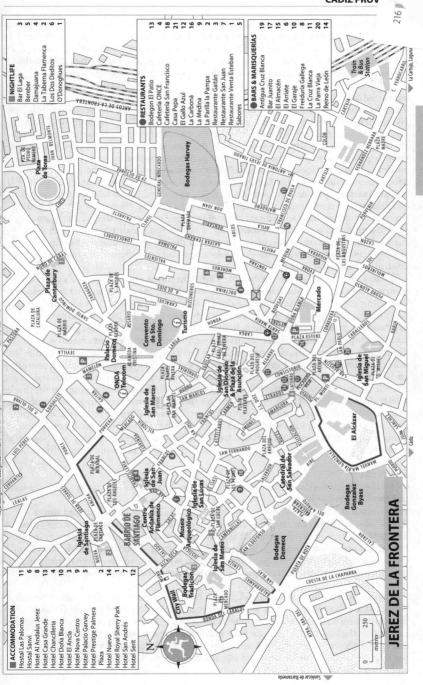

JEREZ DE LA FRONTERA

ACCOMMODATION
Hostal Las Palomas	11
Hostal Sanvi	6
Hotel Al Andalus Jerez	8
Hotel Casa Grande	13
Hotel Chancilleria	4
Hotel Doña Blanca	10
Hotel El Ancla	3
Hotel Nova Centro	9
Hotel Palacio Garvey	5
Hotel Prestige Palmera Plaza	
Hotel Nuevo	14
Hotel Royal Sherry Park	1
Hotel San Andrés	7
Hotel Serit	12

NIGHTLIFE
Bar El Laga	3
Bereber	5
Damajuana	4
La Taberna Flamenca	2
Los Dos Deditos	6
O'Donoghues	1

RESTAURANTS
Bodegon El Patio	13
Cafeteria ONCE	4
Cafeteria San Francisco	18
Casa Pepa	21
El Gallo Azul	12
La Carboná	16
La Medina	9
La Parilla la Pampa	2
Restaurante Gaitán	3
Restaurante San Juan	7
Restaurante Venta Esteban	1
Sabores	5

BARS & MARISQUERIAS
Antigua Cruz Blanca	19
Bar Juanito	17
El Almacén	15
El Arriate	6
El Garaje	10
Freiduría Gallega	8
La Cruz Blanca	11
La Parra Vieja	20
Reino de León	14

Sherry bodegas apart, the town has many other worthwhile sights, not least the **Barrio de Santiago**, a fascinating and authentic white-walled *gitano* (gypsy) quarter to the north of the cathedral. Conveniently, all the major sights and most of the bodegas are within just a few minutes' walk of the central, elegant and palm-fringed **Plaza del Arenal**, dominated by a bronze statue of the 1920s dictator Primo de Rivera.

Brief history

The area around Jerez has been inhabited since Neolithic times. In the first millennium BC the settlement here may have been founded by – or had trading links with – the lost city of Tartessus (see p.564), while the Phoenicians were active in the area around the same time. It was later, however, under the Romans that the city – now known as Asta Regia – grew to prominence. The vine is inextricably linked with Jerez's fortunes and the conquering legions discovered a town already producing **wine** (the Greek geographer Strabo states that the Phoenicians first planted the grape here). Under Roman tutelage, production methods were improved and it was soon being exported to Rome where the "Vinum Ceretensis" acquired a healthy reputation. The Moorish occupation did nothing to dampen the region's wine industry – despite the Koran's prohibition – and it seems the production of raisins and the drinking of alcohol for medical purposes served as pretexts to maintain the city's wine output. Briefly, in the eleventh century the city became an independent *taifa* state before passing under the control of Arcos and later Seville.

In 1264 the city fell to the conquering Christian forces under Alfonso X, a great sherry aficionado who purchased vineyards here. Later, the city prospered through its trading connections with the newly discovered Americas (wine was allocated one third of the cargo space on all merchant vessels bound for the New World) as well as European markets, particularly Britain and the Low Countries. This prosperity continued throughout the seventeenth and eighteenth centuries and created a flourishing aristocracy and bourgeoisie. They were responsible for the arrival of the railway, a water supply and gas-powered street lighting by the mid-nineteenth century and electricity and the telephone before 1900. It was only in the latter half of the twentieth century that the **sherry industry** began to show signs of flagging and in the 1980s alone exports fell by fifty percent. This trend has caused serious jobless problems in a city with few other sources of employment. The recent world economic downturn has further exacerbated matters, but it's a fairly safe bet that a wine loved by Chaucer, Shakespeare, Pepys, Columbus, Magellan, Pérez Gáldos and Hemingway will bounce back once again, as it has done so many times before in its three-millennia history.

The Alcázar

C/M. María González • July–Sept Mon–Fri 9.30am–7.30pm, Sat & Sun 9.30am–2.30pm; Feb–June & Oct Mon–Fri 9.30am–5.30pm, Sat & Sun 9.30am–2.30pm; Nov–Jan daily 9.30am–2.30pm • €3, €5.40 including camera obscura

Constructed in the twelfth century by the Almohads, though much altered since, Jerez's substantial **Alcázar** has been extensively excavated and restored in recent years. The **gardens** have received particular attention: the plants and arrangements have been modelled as closely as possible – using historical research – on the original. The interior contains a well-preserved mosque complete with *mihrab* from the original structure, now sensitively restored to its original state after having been used as a church for many centuries.

There's also a **bathhouse** modelled, by the Almohads, on those of the earlier Romans with cold and hot plunges, which contains wonderfully preserved *bóvedas* (vaults). The complex is surrounded by impressive walls and eighteen towers on the site's outer perimeter. The eighteenth-century **Palacio de Villavicencio** constructed on the west side of the Alcázar's Patio de las Armas (parade ground) houses a **camera obscura** offering views of the major landmarks of the town, as well as the sherry vineyards and the sea beyond.

The Cathedral
Tues–Sat 11am–1pm & 6–8pm; open for viewing prior to Mass Sun (12.30pm) & Mon (8pm) • Free

Immediately north of the Alcázar, the eighteenth-century **Catedral de San Salvador** was rather harshly dismissed by Richard Ford as "vile Churrigueresque" because of its mixture of Gothic and Renaissance styles, but an elegant facade – largely the work of Vincente Acero – is not without merit. Inside, over-obvious pointing gives the building an unfinished, breeze-block aspect, while, in the sacristy, there's a fine, little-known painting by Zurbarán, *The Sleeping Girl*. The most exciting time to be here is September, when the wine harvest celebrations begin with the crushing of grapes on the broad cathedral steps below the free-standing bell tower – actually part of an earlier, fifteenth-century Mudéjar castle.

Plaza de la Asunción
Iglesia de San Dionisio: Tues–Sat 11am–1pm (also open for Mass Tues–Sat 7.30pm, Sun 11.30am & 1.30pm) • Free

A few minutes' walk to the northeast of Plaza del Arenal lies the town's most charming square, the **Plaza de la Asunción** (known as Plaza San Dionisio to *jerezanos*), where a sixteenth-century former **Ayuntamiento** features – on its elegant Plateresque facade –

SHERRY – JEREZ'S LIQUID GOLD

It's believed that the Phoenicians brought the vine to this area early in the first millennium BC. The Romans shipped wine from here to all parts of their empire, and the Roman settlement of Asido Caesaris may well be the town from which Jerez derives its name, later corrupted to **Xerez** (pronounced "Sherrish") by the Moors.

British merchants were attracted here in the fourteenth century and, following the expulsions of Moors and Jews in the wake of the *Reconquista*, they established firms that first traded, and later produced, Falstaff's "sack" (probably derived from the Spanish *sacar* – to draw out – referring to the *solera* system, see below). Some of the bodegas, or cellars, were founded by British Catholic refugees, barred from careers at home by the sixteenth-century Supremacy Act. The names of the great sherry firms today testify to the continuing love affair of the British with this wine: Britain, along with the Netherlands, still consumes up to seventy percent of all exports.

It's a particular combination of climate, soil and grape variety that gives **sherry wine** its distinctive style. The chalky, white *albariza* soil of the region is the natural habitat for the Palomino sherry grape, and though the resulting wine is fairly ordinary stuff, it's what happens inside the bodegas that transforms it into sherry. Here the wine is transferred to oak butts with loose stoppers to let in air. Then the **flor** – a puffy layer of scum (actually yeast) – magically appears on the surface of the wine not only preventing oxidization, but feeding on it too, in the process adding a special flavour and bouquet. It is the subtle nature of the *flor*, the ingredient that cannot be duplicated by competitors, that imparts a different flavour to the sherries of Jerez, El Puerto de Santa María and especially Sanlúcar, where it absorbs the salty breezes off the sea, producing the most delicate fino of all, manzanilla. The bodegas of Jerez, unlike in other wine-producing areas, are situated above ground in order to maintain the humid conditions necessary for the growth of this *flor* – helped by sprinkling the sand-covered floors with water.

The final stage in the creation of sherry – but not manzanilla – is the fortification of the wine with alcohol (up to fifteen percent in the case of fino sherry) before it enters the **solera** system. Because sherry is not a vintage, or yearly, wine it is always blended with older wines through the *soleras* and *criaderas*, as many as six rows of butts placed on top of each other from which the wine is gradually transferred from the topmost to the bottommost over a period of time. This process, mixing the new, younger, wine with the greater quantity of mature, older, wine, "educates" it to assume its character. The wine drawn off at the end for bottling has an even consistency year after year, conveniently with none of the problems of "good" and "bad" years. The classic sherry is the bone-dry fino, but variations on the theme include amontillado (where the *flor* is allowed to "die" in the butt, imparting a nutty flavour), oloroso (produced as fino but minus the *flor*) and cream – pronounced "cray-am" in Andalucía – a purely British concoction where sweet grapes are blended with oloroso.

ornamental statues of Hercules and Julius Caesar. It's flanked by the fifteenth-century Gothic-Mudéjar **Iglesía de San Dionisio** with a graceful bell tower and a triple-naved interior with three Baroque retablos and a fine *artesonado* ceiling.

Barrio de Santiago

Jerez's ancient *gitano* quarter, the **Barrio de Santiago**, stretches uphill from the cathedral in a maze of narrow lanes and alleys to the church of Santiago on its northern boundary. Part of the attraction of visiting the *barrio* is its many fascinating churches. The sixteenth-century Gothic **Iglesía de San Mateo** (Mon 5–9pm, Sat 7.30–9pm, also open for Mass Mon–Sat 8.30pm; free), with a fine retablo and superb vaulting over the chapels, is one of a quartet of churches dotted around the *barrio* dedicated to the four Evangelists: the other three, dedicated to saints Marcos, Lucas and Juan, all to the east of San Mateo, are also worth seeking out. All three have similar visiting and Mass times as San Mateo.

Museo Arqueológico

Plaza del Mercado • June–Aug Tues–Sun 10am–2.30pm; Sept–May Tues–Fri 10am–2pm & 4–7pm, Sat & Sun 10am–2.30pm • €3

Located inside a renovated eighteenth-century mansion close to San Mateo is the delightful **Museo Arqueológico**. A plant-filled patio leads to the early rooms dealing with prehistory; upstairs, Room 3 has some curious **Chalcolithic** (early second millennium BC) cylinder-shaped idols with starburst eyes from Cerro de las Vacas, 20km to the north of the town. Room 4 has a wonderfully preserved **Greek** military helmet dating from the seventh century BC which was found on the banks of the nearby Río Guadalete. This was a time when the early Greeks were colonizing sites all around the Mediterranean, and they evidently expected to meet resistance from the Iberian tribes. Also in Room 4 are finds from the ancient town of **Asta Regia**, as Pliny, Strabo and Ptolemy referred to Jerez in Roman times. A wide range of amphorae, funerary stones and sculptures evidence Asta's importance.

More Roman amphorae – some stamped with the maker's name – appear in Room 5, once used for the shipping of garum (see p.169), olive oil and other products around the Mediterranean. Room 6 has items from the **Visigothic** period and in Room 7 there's an interesting chronological display of **coins** found around Jerez; a good image of the Roman emperor Tiberius (no. 44) is followed by dirhams of rulers Al-Hakam and Abd Ar-Rahman (no. 84) from the period of the Cordoban emirate. Upstairs again, you'll find a *cafetería* with roof terrace, and Rooms 8 and 9, both holding the Moorish and medieval collections, with some fine Moorish ceramics, especially a tenth-century Caliphal bottle vase with Kufic script, found near Jerez.

Before leaving, take a look at the striking works placed around the ground-floor patio. Among them, there's a powerful third- to first-century BC Iberian sculpture of a lion mauling a ram, found nearby, and an intriguing seventh-century Visigothic sarcophagus from La Peñuela carved with curious vegetable, animal and human symbols.

Iglesia de Santiago

Plaza de Santiago s/n • Open daily for services 7.30–8.30pm • Free

To the north of the archeological museum, Calle Muro is flanked by a substantial chunk of the original Moorish **city wall**. You can follow these north to another Gothic church, the fifteenth-century **Iglesia de Santiago**, with wonderfully florid Plateresque portals. Inside there's some beautiful Gothic vaulting and a celebrated sixteenth-century sculpture of the *Prendimiento* – or arrest of Christ – attributed to La Roldana, the sculptor daughter of Pedro Roldán. This image forms the centrepiece of Jerez's Semana Santa processions when it's carried through the streets on a float.

On the small square opposite the church stands a bronze bust dedicated to Fernando Terremoto, one of many legendary **flamenco artists** the *barrio* has produced. You'll come across others dotted around this quarter (including one of Tío José de Paula behind the church), all testifying to the *barrio*'s great pride in its contribution to Andalucía's musical heritage.

Centro Andaluz de Flamenco

Plaza de San Juan • Mon–Fri 10am–2pm, also Wed 4.30–7pm • ⓦ centroandaluzdeflamenco.es • Free

Housed in the elegant eighteenth-century Palacio de Pemartín, the **Centro Andaluz de Flamenco** is home to a library of *flamencología* (plus sound and vision archive) dedicated to preserving the works and performances of past greats, while a dance room on the top floor is used to teach students from all over the world. The staff are welcoming and anyone is free to use the video archive to see performances by flamenco masters past and present – just give them a name and they'll do the rest. There's also a good audiovisual presentation in Spanish, *El Arte Flamenco* (hourly, on the half-hour, in Spanish and English), which – if you know little about flamenco – will give you a grasp of the basics and an understanding of why it is so important to *andaluzes*.

Convento de Santo Domingo

C/Larga • Open for services daily 9.30am, noon & 8pm • Free

The northern end of the pedestrianized **Calle Larga** is dominated by the august frontage of the **Convento de Santo Domingo**. Although badly damaged by fire in the Civil War, it has been diligently restored and, in common with many of the town's other religious buildings, has a curious mixture of styles: in this case Mudéjar, Romanesque and Gothic. The church's seventeenth-century *retablo mayor* is an orgy of gilded wood, with the Virgen de la Consolación – the city's patroness, carved in Italian marble – as its centrepiece.

South from here, at the junction with Calle Santa María, stands the old **Café Cena Cirullo** (now the *El Gallo Azul* café), a fine modernist building which used to be the great meeting place of Jerez's salon society.

Palacio Domecq

Alameda Cristina s/n • Tours April–Oct Tues & Thurs 10am & 11am, Sat noon • €10

Just to the north of the Convento de Santo Domingo stands the eighteenth-century **Palacio Domecq**, a grand pile still owned by the Domecq sherry family. The palace was built in 1778 by the Marqués de Montana, and typifies the opulent mansions being constructed at the time by Jerez's wealthy farmers and winemakers. However, the Marqués and his family lived here for only seven years prior to his death in 1785. The house then lay empty until it was purchased in 1855 by Juan Pedro Domecq and became the sherry dynasty's home. Beyond an entrance flanked by barley-sugar pillars and topped by an ornate balcony, visits take in an exquisite marble-floored and porticoed Baroque patio as well as rooms richly decorated with period furniture, artworks, carpets, tapestries, clocks and countless other *objets d'art* assembled by the Domecq family.

Iglesia de San Miguel

Plaza San Miguel 1 • Mon–Fri 10am–1pm (also open for services Mon–Sat 8pm, Sun noon & 8pm) • Free

One other church worth a visit is the fifteenth-century Gothic **Iglesia de San Miguel**. An ornate classical facade added in the eighteenth century climbs dizzily to a pretty bell tower adorned with blue and white *azulejos*. The Gothic interior exhibits some fine vaulting, and the main altar has a magnificent retablo by Juan Martínez Montañés, one of Andalucía's greatest sculptors.

Museo del Tiempo

C/Cervantes 3 • Tours Tues–Fri 9.30am–1.15pm • €6

At the northern end of town, a ten-to-fifteen-minute walk from the centre along *calles* Guadalete and Pozo de Olivar, the recently revamped and enlarged **Museo del Tiempo** (aka Museo de Relojes), claims to have the largest collection of fully functioning antique clocks and watches in Europe, all chiming on the hour.

2

Real Escuela Andaluz del Arte Ecuestre

Avda. Duque de Abrantes s/n • ☎ 956 318 008, ⓦ realescuela.org • **Performances**: Tues & Thurs noon, plus (Aug only) Fri noon • €19–25 • **Stable visits, plus rehearsals**: Mon, Wed & Fri 10am–2pm (except Aug) • €10

A ten-to-fifteen-minute walk north of the Alameda Cristina (same directions as for the Museo del Tiempo above, turning from Calle Pozo de Olivar into Avenida Duque de Abrantes), the nineteenth-century Palacio de las Cadenas, the former seat of the Duques de Abrantes, is home to the famous **Real Escuela Andaluz del Arte Ecuestre** (Royal Andalucian School of Equestrian Art). Here you can see teams of horses performing to music: a mesmerising spectacle that has been described as "an authentic equestrian ballet." It doesn't come cheap, however, and watching the almost as interesting training and rehearsals (without music), which includes a visit to the stables and museum, is more affordable.

THE BODEGAS OF JEREZ

The tours of the sherry and brandy bodegas in Jerez provide a fascinating insight into the mysteries of sherry production, although sampling – nowadays restricted to a couple of tots at the end of a tour – is hardly as much fun as when Richard Ford was here in the nineteenth century and saw visitors emerging "stupefied by drink". There are a great many bodegas to choose from and, with the exception of August when all but a few firms close down, most welcome visitors throughout the year. Some companies insist that you book at least a day in advance (see listings below). The following bodegas offer tours throughout the whole or part of August; should you wish to visit some of the smaller establishments, get hold of a complete list from the Turismo. Details of many of these, together with visiting times, maps and contact details appear on ⓦ sherry.org or on the Turismo's site at ⓦ turismojerez.com. Visiting hours frequently change and it's worth confirming these in advance with the bodega or getting an updated list from the Turismo.

Each bodega has its celebrity barrels signed by famous visitors – Martin Luther King, Orson Welles, Queen Victoria, Cole Porter and Franco (protected by a glass screen) are some of the big names in the González collection while in 1965 Williams and Humbert managed to get the Beatles to sign a barrel each. All the bodegas also have a transparent butt that allows you to see the action of the magical *flor* on the sherry.

BRANDY

Many of Jerez's bodegas are today as renowned for their brandies as their finos – some are as good as any in the world. As with sherry, the *solera* system (see box, p.217) is used here too, with the spirit being transferred from one vat to another, creating Jerez brandy's unique character. The barrels themselves are also old sherry vats and impart an oaky subtlety, a further distinctive feature. As with wine and sherry, brandy has its own *consejo regulador* (regulatory body) and the brandies are ranked into three grades of quality: *solera*, *solera reserva* and *solera gran reserva*, the last of which must spend at least three years in the barrel. The inexpensive mass-market *solera* brands – which tend to give Spanish brandies a "cheap and cheerful, but not much else" reputation – do not have the same cachet as Jerez's more sophisticated labels, where great care is taken over grape quality and production methods. These are worth seeking out and we mention a few below.

VISITING THE BODEGAS

González Byass (aka Bodegas Tío Pepe) C/Manuel González s/n, behind the Alcázar (Aug & Sept tours daily in English on the hour 11am–2pm & 5–7pm; Oct–July Mon–Sat 11am–7pm, Sun 11am–2pm; ☎ 902 440 077, ⓦ bodegastiopepe.com; €10 with wine tasting). The city's most central bodega and one of the two giants of Jerez, founded in 1835 by Manuel María González – the bodega's buildings now form almost a small town in their own right. The González cellars are perhaps the oldest in Jerez and, though no longer used, preserve an old circular chamber, La Concha, designed by Eiffel (of Eiffel Tower fame). Among their brands are the most

---

La Cartuja de Santa María de la Defensión

4km out of town on the road to Medina Sidonia • Daily 9.30am–6pm; mass Tues–Sat 8.15pm, Sun & Mon 5.30pm; vespers Tues–Sat 6pm, Sun 5pm • Free

The remarkable Carthusian monastery of **La Cartuja de Santa María de la Defensión** lies 4km from town in the midst of lush countryside and surrounded in summer by a sea of sunflowers. The monastery was founded in 1477 and, following great destruction by billeted French troops in 1810, was abolished in 1835 during the Liberal backlash against the church and male religious orders.

After serving as a military barracks for almost a century, La Cartuja was restored to the Carthusians in 1949, since when the handful of monks here have dedicated themselves to restoring and maintaining this beautiful building. The Baroque **facade** you see today – added in the 1660s – is one of the most spectacular in the

2

famous fino of all, Tío Pepe ("Uncle Joe" named after the founder's uncle), and an exceptional Lepanto brandy.

Domecq C/San Ildefonso 3 (Mon–Fri tours on the hour 10am–1pm; Sat noon; April–Oct also tours Mon–Fri on the hour 5–7pm; reservations required for Sat tour only; ☎ 956 151 500, ⊕ bodegasfundador pedrodomecq.com; €9). Jerez's other major firm, founded in the eighteenth century by an Irish immigrant who married into a French immigrant family called Domecq. Pedro Domecq took over the business in 1816 and dramatically expanded the firm with the help of a brilliant British agent, John Ruskin, the father of the Victorian art critic. With an extensive bodega, Domecq are the makers of the top-selling La Ina fino and the excellent Carlos I brandy.

Sandeman C/Pizarro 10 (Mon, Wed & Fri tours at 11.30am, 12.30pm, 1.30pm, & 2.30pm; Tues & Thurs 10.30am, noon, 1pm & 2pm; ☎ 956 312 995, ⊕ sandeman.eu; €7). Founded by Scottish grandee George Sandeman in the late eighteenth century, the bodega is famous for its trademark depicting the don in the black cape. The seventh generation of Sandemans are still involved in running the company which makes the less well-known but excellent amontillado brand Royal Esmerelda and the Capa Negra brandy.

Williams & Humbert Ctra. Nacional IV km641.75, Seville road (reservation required; tours Mon–Fri 10am, noon & 2pm; ☎ 956 353 406, ⊕ bodegas-williams -humbert.com; €7.10). Alexander Williams married Amy Humbert and, with backing from his father-in-law, founded W&H in

1877. It went on to become one of the great sherry houses, just behind the big two. Its best-known fino is Dry Sack (formerly Pando) and it also produces Gran Duque de Alba brandy.

Harveys C/Pintor Muñoz Cebrian s/n (reservation required; tours Mon–Fri noon; ☎ 956 151 500, ⊕ bodegaharveys.com; €8). The originally Bristol-based company was founded in 1796 but, despite a high reputation for its wines, had no presence in Jerez until it bought out another bodega (noted for its fine gardens) in 1970. Harveys is known in Britain and the US (but not in Spain) for its Bristol Cream sherry, but its amontillado and *palo cortado* finos are much appreciated on the peninsula.

Tradición Plaza Cordobeses 3 (reservation required; tours April–Sept Mon–Fri 9.30am, 11.30am, 1.30pm & 5pm (also April–June & Sept Sat 10am English, midday Spanish); ☎ 956 168 628, ⊕ www.bodegastradicion .es; €16.50). An interesting newcomer, this bodega was created in 1998 by three members of old Jerez families who bought a derelict bodega in the old quarter of the city and completely renovated it. They then filled it with very old wines purchased from bodegas that had ceased trading, and so founded their own top-notch *soleras*. Their wines have been critically acclaimed: the Tradición Oloroso is one of their best finos while their Gold brandy is also top quality. The visit includes a tasting of four wines (including old rare sherries) and two brandies as well as a tour of their *pinacoteca* (art gallery) displaying works by Goya, Velázquez, Zurbarán, Sorolla and Solana among many others.

whole of Spain. Unfortunately, access is restricted to the building's exterior (with a magnificent main doorway), gardens and (occasionally) cloister; currently the impressive church and its artworks may be seen only by those attending mass or vespers.

Laguna de Medina

11km southeast of Jerez: take the A381 out of Jerez for about 11km towards Medina Sidonia; the entrance to the lake area is signposted immediately opposite a cement factory, and there's a small car park

If you have transport, you could make another excursion from Jerez to the **LAGUNA DE MEDINA**, a small freshwater lake which – from late August on – attracts a great number of migrating birds returning from northern Europe to Africa. Two paths skirt the lake from where, among a variety of waders, it's possible to spot white-headed duck, spoonbills and the greater flamingo in season. Fringed with reeds and tamarisk trees, the shallow lagoon is also home to numerous frogs, snakes and lizards. Because of its close proximity to the Coto Doñana across the Guadalquivir, many birds – particularly flamingos – use this as an alternative food source, especially if the Doñana's marshes are drier than normal towards the end of the summer.

ARRIVAL AND DEPARTURE   JEREZ

By plane Jerez airport (☎ 956 150 000) lies 7km northeast of the centre on the NIV *autovía* with connections to Madrid, Barcelona and other Spanish airports, as well as international flights to Britain and Germany. Buses (Mon–Fri roughly hourly 6.30am–9.45pm, Sat & Sun every 3hr; €1.10) link the airport with the town. If you arrive outside these times you'll need to take a taxi (about €16–20) to the centre.

By bus The bus station (☎ 956 149 990) is at Plaza Estación s/n, 1km east of Plaza del Arenal. To reach the centre, take the #10 urban bus (painted lurid lilac) from outside the station. Frequent bus services link Jerez with Cádiz, Arcos,

Vejer, Tarifa, Algeciras and destinations further afield.

By train The train station (☎ 902 240 202) is at Plaza de Estación s/n, 1km east of Plaza del Arenal. To reach the centre, take #10 urban bus from outside the station. Trains link Jerez with Cádiz, Seville and Córdoba.

By car Street parking is at a premium and you'd be advised to use the car park at your hotel or *hostal* if it has one (and for which you'll pay extra), or one of the pay car parks signed in the centre. An alternative is to park further out and walk to the centre. A huge car park lies under the focal Plaza del Arenal and there's another handy one northwest of the Turismo beneath Plaza Mamelón.

INFORMATION

Turismo At C/Larga 39, next door to the Convento de Santo Domingo (June–Sept Mon–Fri 10am–3pm & 5–7pm, Sat & Sun 10am–2.30pm; Oct–May Mon–Fri 9am–3pm & 4.30–6.30pm, Sat & Sun 9.30am–2.30pm; ☎ 956 341 711, ⊛ turismojerez.com). It's well stocked with information about the town and staff can supply a detailed map.

Internet Centrally located internet cafés include Onda Telecom, C/Porvera 18 (Mon–Sat 10am–2pm & 5–10pm), and Ciber Jerez, C/Santa María 3 (Mon–Sat 10am–10.30pm, Sun 5–10.30pm). The city also has free internet zones – ask at the Turismo for a map and the necessary password key (*llave*).

FESTIVALS IN JEREZ

The city's big festival is the **Feria del Caballo** (horse fair) in the first half of May, perhaps the most refined or (depending on your viewpoint) snooty of Andalucian *ferias*. Held at the Recinto Ferial (fairground) to the northeast of the centre, this is a huge knees-up with exhibitions of horsemanship and dressage along with singing and dancing in the couple of hundred *casetas* (marquees) open to all. The **Festival de Jerez** is a two-week flamenco-fest held at the end of February or the start of March featuring many big-name flamenco artists at various venues around the town. Details from the Turismo or their website. The annual **Fiesta de la Vendimia** held during the last third of September (details from the Turismo) celebrates the end of the grape harvest with concerts of flamenco, bullfights, equestrian events and a procession of the Virgin, Nuestra Señora de la Merced.

ACCOMMODATION

There's usually no problem finding rooms in Jerez except during the period March to May when Semana Santa, the Festival de Jerez, the World Motorcycle Championship (held at the town's Formula 1 racing circuit) and the Feria del Caballo come one after the other and fill the town to bursting point; make sure to ring ahead if you are planning to visit at this time. The high-season prices we quote below are for this period, outside of which rates (especially for hotels) tend to fall by up to fifty percent. Most of the budget accommodation is conveniently located within a few minutes' walk of the bus and train terminals. More possibilities are to be found in the streets surrounding the church of San Miguel.

BUDGET

Albergue Juvenil Avda. Blas Infante 30 ☎955 035 886, ⓦinturjoven.com. Jerez's modern youth hostel has a fine pool but lies out in the suburbs; all rooms are en suite doubles with a/c (no dorms). Bus #9 from outside the bus station or from Plaza de las Angustias will take you there. Under 26 **€21**, over 26 **€27**

Hostal Las Palomas C/Higueras 17 ☎956 343 773, ⓦhostal-las-palomas.com. In a quiet street, this *hostal* offers clean, simple rooms sharing bath plus some en suite (negligible price difference); fans are available and there's a free wi-fi zone. **€32**

Hostal Sanvi C/Morenos 10 ☎956 345 624. Sparklingly clean *hostal* with lots of *azulejos* and friendly proprietors offering economical, a/c en-suite rooms with TV and free wi-fi. Garage parking available for €6. **€33**

Hotel Nova Centro C/Arcos 13 ☎956 332 138, ⓦhotel novacentro.com. Pleasant and very central small hotel offering rooms with a/c, satellite TV, safe and free wi-fi. Request a higher room to avoid street noise. Paid parking available. **€45**

Hotel Nuevo C/Caballeros 23 ☎956 331 600, ⓦnuevo hotel.com. Attractive and excellent-value hotel set in a lovely nineteenth-century *casa palacio*; rooms come with a/c and TV. See website for offers. **€45**

★ **Hotel San Andrés** C/Morenos 12 & 14 ☎956 340 983, ⓦhotel-sanandres.com. Great-value hotel and *hostal* side by side. The charming and friendly *hostal* has en-suite rooms (with a/c and TV) and others sharing bath, plus a pleasant, plant-filled patio. The hotel's rooms are slightly more comfortable. Free wi-fi and internet terminal. Can advise on parking places nearby. *Hostal* **€40**, hotel **€45**

MODERATE TO EXPENSIVE

Hotel Al Andalus Jerez C/Arcos 29 ☎956 323 400, ⓦalandalusjerez.es. Comfortable hotel with two pretty patios. Recently refurbished rooms – the better ones are off the inner patio – are equipped with a/c and TV and free wi-fi. Can advise on parking. **€54**

Hotel Casa Grande Plaza de las Angustias 3 ☎956 345 070, ⓦcasagrande.com.es. Beautifully presented three-star in a restored nineteenth-century *casa señorial*. Rooms are bright and comfortable, while breakfast (extra) can be taken on a delightful roof terrace. Free wi-fi. **€95**

★ **Hotel Chancillería** C/Chancillería 21 ☎956 301 038, ⓦhotelchancilleria.com. Welcoming, recently constructed (in an eco-friendly manner) 14-room hotel in the Barrio Santiago with attractive a/c rooms with plasma TV sharing a balcony overlooking a garden backed by Jerez's ancient walls. There's a wonderful roof terrace, rooms come with CD and DVD players (films may be borrowed from hotel library) and there's free internet and wi-fi. Disabled access in most rooms. Can advise on parking nearby. B&B **€90**

Hotel Doña Blanca C/Bodegas 11 ☎956 348 761, ⓦhoteldonablanca.com. In a quiet street, this is one of the most central and intimate of the upper-range places with well-equipped a/c balcony rooms with minibar and satellite TV, plus garage. **€60**

Hotel El Ancla Plaza Mamelón 15 ☎956 321 297, ⓦhotelancla.es. Dapper hotel with friendly proprietors on an attractive square. Rooms overlooking the street (quieter at night) are compensated with views of square and fountains. All rooms have a/c, TV and free wi-fi. Reduced-rate parking in public car park under the square. **€54**

Hotel Palacio Garvey C/Tornería 24 ☎956 326 700, ⓦsferahoteles.com. Beautiful 16-room four-star in the former mansion of the Garvey family, one of the great sherry dynasties in nineteenth-century Jerez. The elegant and spacious rooms have modern designer furnishings, large beds and come with free minibar, wi-fi, CD player and satellite plasma TV. **€120**

Hotel Prestige Palmera Plaza C/Pizarro 1 ☎956 031 500, ⓦprestigehotels.com. New five-star oasis housed in a refitted former bodega. The sumptuously furnished rooms come with large beds, marble bathroom or wet room and all have a balcony views over the delightful palm-filled gardens, where there's also a pool. Rooms have safe and minibar, while facilities include a gym, sauna and car park. Occasionally the service falls below five-star, but this is a very attractive hotel. See website for offers. B&B **€160**

Hotel Royal Sherry Park Avda. Alvaro Domecq 11 ☎956 317 614, ⓦhipotels.com. Along with the above, this is the nearest of the peripheral luxury hotels to the centre; notwithstanding its four-star rating, this is a rather bland and modern affair with sober rooms furnished for the corporate market, although it has an attractive pool and gardens, plus car park. **€134**

Hotel Serit C/Higueras 7 ☎956 340 700, ⓦhotelserit .com. Central and friendly traditional hotel with bright and airy a/c rooms equipped with satellite TV and free wi-fi. Own car park for €8. **€60**

EATING AND DRINKING

Jerez's booming sherry trade ensures that the town's restaurants are kept busy, and a few of these are very good indeed. Befitting the capital of sherry production Jerez also has a range of great bars where fino – the perfect partner for tapas – can be sampled on its own turf.

RESTAURANTS AND CAFÉS

Bodegón El Patio C/San Francisco de Paula 2 ☎956 340 736. Housed in a former bodega, this mid-priced *ambiente jerezano* restaurant offers carefully prepared meat and fish dishes. *Cochinillo asado* (suckling pig) is a house special and there's a *menú* for around €18. Main dishes €10–25. Mon–Sat 11.30am–4pm & 8pm–midnight.

Cafetería ONCE C/Gaitán 10. The spotless, a/c *cafetería* of Spain's powerful charity for the blind serves up one of the cheapest three-course *menús* in town for €7 (including wine) – an excellent deal. Mon–Fri 12.30–4pm & 8–11pm (lunchtime only during July & Aug), Sat & Sun 12.30–4pm.

Cafetería San Francisco Plaza Estebe 2, near the market. This popular tiled bar-restaurant does tapas (often for a euro), *raciones* and *platos combinados* throughout the day, plus a *menú* for around €7. Daily 9am–midnight.

Casa Pepa Plaza Madre de Dios 14, near the train and bus stations. Long established *barrio* restaurant overseen by the eponymous *dueña* Pepa with *cocinera* Isabel running the kitchen. Good, inexpensive meat and fish dishes – try the *dorada* (bream) or *solomillo* (pork loin) – or there's a *menú del día* for around €8. Daily 9.30am–5pm & 8pm–midnight.

El Gallo Azul C/Larga 2. Iconic building by noted architect Aníbal González constructed by the Domecq family at the time of the 1929 World Fair in Seville (and still owned by them). Once the city's most fashionable meeting place, today it's a bar-restaurant serving decent tapas (or coffee and ices) downstairs, with the town's best terrace for people-watching. Upstairs, a recently added restaurant serves *raciones* and salads as well as a range of fish and meat dishes: *atún al amontillado viejo* (tuna in sherry) is a house special. Main dishes (restaurant) €9.50–18. Mon–Sat 8am–10.30pm.

La Carboná C/San Francisco de Paula 2 ☎956 347 475. Cavernous but wonderfully atmospheric top-notch restaurant inside an old bodega, specializing in charcoal-grilled fish and meat dishes (the house speciality is Cantabrian beef T-bone steaks) and – in season – fresh tuna. Main dishes €10–20, plus a *menú* for around €32. Daily except Tues 12.30–4pm & 8–11.30pm.

★ **La Medina** Zoco de Artesanía Jerez, Plaza de Peones s/n, north of the cathedral. Inside this crafts centre (on the first floor), this is a terrific little bar-restaurant with a wonderful vibe. Husband and wife team Pablo and the ebullient Araceli watch over the stoves and bar and produce some pretty good tapas and *raciones* – from *couscous de pollo* to moussaka – at giveaway prices. There are also plenty of veggie options, plus an outstanding *menú* for just €6 (or €5 on Thursdays, *día del trabajador* –

workers' day). You can eat in the cosy bar or out on the craft centre's terrace-patio. Mon–Wed & Sun noon–9pm, Thurs–Sat noon–2am.

La Parilla la Pampa C/Guadalete 24. Very good Argentine restaurant with an excellent-value five-course meal (for two) of Argentine specialities including steaks – the meat is flown in from South America – a bottle of wine and *cafés argentinos*. Expect to pay around €40 for two. Daily except Weds 12.30–4.30pm & 8pm–midnight.

Restaurante Gaitán C/Gaitán 3 ☎956 168 021. Attractive, long-established upmarket restaurant very popular with *jerezanos* and specializing in Basque and *andaluz* dishes, although it's resting on its laurels a bit these days. There's a range of fish and meat dishes including house specials *cordero al brandy* (lamb) and – in season – tuna. Main dishes €12–16. Mon–Sat 1–4.30pm & 8–11.30pm, Sun 1–4.30pm.

Restaurante San Juan Plaza Malgarejo s/n ☎956 326 471. Excellent Italian restaurant in a beautiful old bodega fronting the church of San Juan in the Barrio de Santiago. Offers a wide range of meat and fish courses as well as salads and authentic pizzas. Main dishes €10–20. Tues–Sat 1–4pm & 8.30pm–midnight, Sun 1–4pm.

★ **Restaurante Venta Esteban** Colonia de Caulina, off the Arcos de la Frontera road ☎956 316 067. Arguably Jerez's best-value restaurant, this is a little way out of town near the airport and has four attractive dining rooms and a wonderful terrace. Both the welcome and the cooking are top notch and everything is done with panache, with traditional *andaluz* and *gaditano* cuisine at its best. Try the outstanding *urta a la roteña* (bream in onion sauce), any of the meat dishes or a whole *bogavante* (lobster) if you feel like pushing the boat out. Main dishes €10–15. There's also a *menú* for €20 including drinks. Mon–Sat noon–midnight.

Sabores Hotel Chancillería, C/Chancillería 21 ☎956 301 038. Very good restaurant with a charming patio terrace offering *andaluz* traditional cuisine with a creative twist, including house specials *carillada de ternera con cremosa de calabaza* (cow's cheek with pumpkin sauce). As they work with *raciones* and *medias* (a half *ración*), you can order as much (or little) as you wish. They also serve tapas in their bar. Main dishes €13–19. Daily 1.30–4pm & 8–11pm, closed lunchtimes in Aug.

BARS AND MARISQUERÍAS

Antigua Cruz Blanca Plaza del Arenal s/n. In the southern corner of the city's main square, this pleasant new *cervecería* sports a minimalist interior featuring stripped wood tables, chairs and stools. The tapas are mainly *mariscos* with what's on offer chalked up on a big board inside. Try the *langostinos* (prawns), *cañaillas* (whelks), *mejillones* (mussels), *pimientos asados* (roasted peppers) or *salmorejo* (Córdoba-style gazpacho).

Bar Juanito C/Pescadería Vieja 4. In a small passage off the west side of Plaza del Arenal, this is one of the best and most celebrated tapas bars in town, with a menu as endless as the number of excellent *finos* on offer. Specials include *berza a jerezano* (chickpea stew) and their celebrated *alcachofas* (artichokes). Mon–Sat noon–5pm & 8.30pm–midnight.

El Almacén C/La Torre 2. Atmospheric tapas bar installed in an old grocery shop (*almacén*). Tapas and *raciones* include *pinchos de pollos* (fried chicken) and *kebap* (kebab) as well as *tablas de quesos* (cheese boards), plus various vegetarian options. Mon–Thurs 8.30pm–midnight, Fri–Sun 1–4.30pm & 8.30pm–1am.

El Arriate C/Francos 43, in the Barrio de Santiago. Flamenco and jazz bar whose amiable proprietor is an aficionado of both traditions. Also does a decent selection of tapas. Daily 9am–midnight.

★ **El Garaje** Plaza Peones 4, slightly north of the cathedral. Light and airy new bar (inside a former garage) with stylish decor and a youthful ambience. It kicks off with breakfasts and then moves onto tapas and *raciones* for lunch. Following the siesta they're open for dinner – try the *presa ibérica* (pork shoulder) or *gazpacho de fresa* (made with strawberries) washed down with a bottle of house Rioja for

€8. Later the *copas* and cocktails crowd arrives, and cool sounds fill the bar. Mon–Sat 8am–4pm & 7pm–midnight.

Freiduría Gallega C/Arcos 5, near the market. Founded in 1934, this is a justly popular bar serving up Galician-style fried fish and *mariscos* prepared *a la gallega* by proprietors originally hailing from the northwestern Spanish province of Galicia; eat in or take away. Daily 9am–4pm & 7pm–midnight.

La Cruz Blanca C/Consistorio 16. Very good restaurant offering traditional and creatively slanted tapas and *raciones* to an unusually high standard – including the signature *solomillo con foie y salsa de Pedro Ximénez* (pork loin). There's an attractive and popular terrace, although they don't take reservations so you may have to wait to get a table. Daily 11am–4pm & 8–11pm.

La Parra Vieja C/San Miguel 9. One of Jerez's oldest tapas bars (over a century in business), in an alleyway downhill from the Iglesia de San Miguel. Specials include *croquetas de jamón* and *mollejas de cordero* (sweetbreads). There's a small restaurant too, with a *menú* for €9. The nearby *La Marea* at no. 3 in the same street is also worth a call for its excellent fried-fish tapas. Tues–Sun 11am–4pm & 8pm–midnight.

Reino de León C/Latorre 8, slightly northeast of Plaza del Arenal. Very good tapas bar that once carried off the prize (competed for by all the city's bars) for the best tapa a couple of years back; the winner, *milhojas de foie* (millefeuille with paté), still features on their menu. Mon 8.30am–4.30pm, Tues–Sun 8.30am–4.30pm & 8.30pm–12.30am.

NIGHTLIFE

Much of Jerez's nightlife centres around the bars and discos near the bullring and the zone around the Avda. de Mexico to the northeast of here. One place which is very popular with younger *jerezanos* is Plaza de Canterbury, C/Nuño de Cañas s/n, a renovated plaza pulsing with numerous bars and *discotecas* where live music is frequently staged. The local paper *El Diario de Jerez* is a good place to find out about upcoming concerts and festivals.

Bar El Laga Plaza del Mercado, next to the Archeological Museum ☎ 956 338 334. Authentic (if somewhat touristy) flamenco bar with recitals and dancing Mon to Sat starting at 10.30pm; tapas and *raciones* are

FLAMENCO IN JEREZ

Given Jerez's great flamenco traditions, it's worth trying to hear some of the real stuff at one of the many *peñas* (clubs) concentrated in the old *gitano* quarter of Santiago, north of the cathedral (though be careful in this area after dark). The following are some of the best; turning up at around 10pm at weekends (although they're open at other times, too) should provide an opportunity to hear some authentic performances. Otherwise consult the Turismo, who also publish a sheet listing all of Jerez's *peñas*; the Centro Andaluz de Flamenco (see below), who also have details of the special flamenco festivals held in town over the summer; or the local paper *El Diario de Jerez*, which has a special flamenco listings page on Fridays.

Centro Andaluz de Flamenco Plaza San Juan 1, Santiago ☎ 956 349 265.
Peña Antonio Chacón C/Salas 12, Santiago ☎ 956 347 472.
Peña La Buena Gente Plaza San Lucas 9, Santiago ☎ 956 338 404.

Peña Los Cernícalos C/Sancho Vizcaíno 25, south of the church of San Miguel ☎ 956 333 871.
Peña Tío José de Paula C/La Merced 11, Santiago ☎ 956 320 196.

served. Tables can be reserved if you want to get a good view. €18 including a drink.

★ **Bereber** C/Cabezas 10, near the archeological museum. Spectacular transformation of a sixteenth-century *palacio* (with original wall paintings) into a multi-patio garden bar and flamenco club. The heart of the complex holds two (soundproofed) *discotecas*, one playing sixties to eighties sounds, the other more contemporary stuff. Daily 3pm–late.

Damajuana C/Francos 18. Delightful café-bar in a fabulous seventeenth-century mansion with two charming patios. The music varies from flamenco and blues to rock and soul and there are frequent live concerts of flamenco and jazz in the patios, while a *crepería* serves sweet and savoury crêpes plus a variety of other snacks. Also has a gallery featuring shows by contemporary artists. Daily 8.30pm–2am.

La Taberna Flamenca Angostillo de Santiago 3 ☎ 956 323 693. Tucked down the west side of the Iglesia de Santiago. Slightly touristy flamenco bar-restaurant offering shows by professional artistes. May–Oct flamenco performances daily at 10.30pm; plus (Tues, Wed & Sat) 2.30pm. Ring for winter schedule. Show with dinner (including wine) €38, show with one drink €15.

Los Dos Deditos Plaza Vargas 1 off the end of C/Pescadería Vieja s/n, off Plaza del Arenal. Relaxed *copas* (drinks and music) bar – except when there are live performances of rock, jazz or blues. Popular with over 30s.

O'Donoghues C/Nuño de Cañas 16, next door to the Plaza de Canterbury. Music bar that packs them in after midnight, especially at weekends – but stays serious enough to stock a good supply of Hibernian whiskies plus decent Guinness in pint glasses.

The Sierra de Grazalema

The green lung at the heart of Cádiz's province, the **Sierra de Grazalema** was one of the first *parques naturales* (natural parks) to be established in Andalucía. Covering around 550 square kilometres it has been a UNESCO biosphere reserve since 1984 and contains a wealth of some 1,300 plant species including a large number of orchids. The park is also home to many of the celebrated "pueblos blancos" or white towns (more often villages). Among these the sparkling whitewashed town of **Grazalema** itself, **El Bosque** and the enchanting village of **Zahara de la Sierra** stand out.

Grazalema

Some 18km west of Ronda as the crow flies lies **GRAZALEMA**, the central point of the Sierra de Grazalema, and its natural park. A pretty white village beneath the craggy peak of San Cristóbal, with lots of sloping narrow streets and window-boxes full of

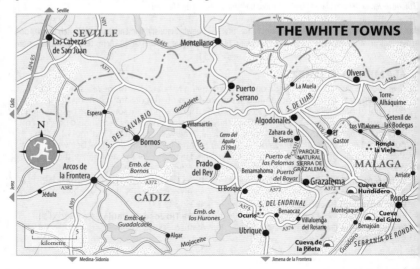

EXPLORING THE PARQUE NATURAL SIERRA DE GRAZALEMA

Bounded by the towns of Grazalema, Ubrique, El Bosque and Zahara, plus Algodonales and Olvera to the north, the **Parque Natural Sierra de Grazalema** is an important mountain wilderness, unique to Andalucía. The limestone mass of the Sierra was formed in the Jurassic and Triassic periods and the close proximity of the range to the sea – which traps many of the clouds drifting in from the Atlantic – has produced a microclimate where numerous botanical species dating from before the Ice Age have survived. The most famous of these is the rare **pinsapo**, or Spanish fir, native only to this area of Europe, which grows at an altitude of between 1000m and 1700m. The high rainfall here, plus the wet, cool summers, are essential to its survival. The Sierra also supports a wealth of **birdlife**: eagles (Bonelli's, booted, and golden), vultures (griffon and Egyptian), as well as various owls and woodpeckers are all common. The streams and riverbanks are the domain of water voles and otters, the latter not popular with a number of fish farms in the area. On the Sierra's higher reaches the magnificent Spanish ibex has been reintroduced to a craggy habitat, and its numbers are increasing.

The best way to appreciate the park is by **walking**, but to protect wildlife and nesting birds access is restricted to different sections at certain times, and in July and August many routes are closed due to the high fire risk.

INFORMATION

The natural park's main **information office** (Centro de Visitantes; Mon–Sat 10am–2pm & 4–6pm, Sun 10am–2pm, Aug daily 10am–2pm; ☎ 956 709 733) is at El Bosque, C/Federico García Lorca s/n, next to the Plaza de Toros, and there is a smaller branch in Zahara de la Sierra. The main office issues access *permisos* (permits; free) and takes bookings for the Itinerario del Pinsapar, guided walks through the major stands of the *pinsapo* Spanish fir. If you contact them they will fax the permit free of charge to the tourist offices in Grazalema (p.228) and/or the natural park office in Zahara de la Sierra (p.231) to save you a journey. The office also stocks park maps with walking routes.

Horizon, at C/Corrales Terceros 29 in Grazalema (☎ 956 132 363, ☻ horizonaventura.com), organizes a broad range of **outdoor activities** in the park, including hiking (with English-speaking guides), mountain-bike tours, Land Rover trips and much more. They also conduct a variety of wildlife and birdwatching excursions and can even arrange accommodation for you.

blooms in summer, it makes an ideal base for delving into the park. This is also the spot with the country's highest rainfall – and there's often quite a bit of snow in winter too – which explains the lush vegetation covering the surrounding area, home to a spectacular variety of flora and fauna. Quite apart from the attractions of the park, the village has its own charms too, and often fills up in summer with hikers and climbers and in winter with more sedentary Spanish tourists.

If the weather's warm enough, you could try out the communal **swimming pool**, which is spectacularly sited on the Arcos/Benamahoma road at the village's eastern edge.

Brief history

The earliest traces of the village are connected with the remains of a Roman settlement named Lacidulia which traveller Richard Ford described as "plastered like a martlet-nest on the rocky hill." In the Moorish period the area was populated by Berbers who gave the town the name of Raisa lami Suli, which eventually passed down to Ben-salama "son of Zulema" who was often referred to in Spanish as Gran Zulema. Following the *Reconquista* the town was assigned to the estates of the Duke of Arcos – whose crest still forms the town's coat of arms today – and the name was changed to Zagrazalema, soon shortened to its current form.

In the seventeenth century the woollen industry became an important activity and the town grew rapidly as the fame of Grazalema shawls, blankets and cloaks spread. Attacks by Napoleonic troops in the War of Independence caused extensive damage but the town soon recovered and grew in size to almost ten thousand inhabitants by 1850 (compared with today's couple of thousand). The prosperity was so impressive that its name was often appended with the tag "Cádiz Chico" (Little Cádiz), favourably comparing its affluence with the provincial capital. However, the industrial revolution that reached Spain in the later nineteenth century decimated the town's cottage industry as large factories in Catalunya began to produce blankets and textiles much more cheaply. The industry went into decline and today only a couple of producers make the once-renowned Grazalema shawls. It is only with the creation of the Parque Natural – and with it the development of rural tourism – that some measure of prosperity has returned.

Plaza de España

The simple main square, the **Plaza de España**, is the hub of activity here, as it has been for a couple of centuries. At the southern end stands the eighteenth-century church of **Nuestra Señora de la Aurora** with a sober, unadorned façade topped off by a trio of belfries. Facing it at the elongated square's northern end lies the elegant and porticoed **Ayuntamiento**, with a four-spouted eighteenth-century fountain nearby. On the western side lies the early twentieth-century **Casino**, a tranquil place (open to visitors) where (mainly) male members of the community gather to play dominoes, cards, read the papers and down the odd *carajillo* (or two). The centre of the square, fronting the Ayuntamiento, is adorned with an emblematic **pinsapo** fir tree (see box, p.227).

Neilson Gallery of Contemporary Art

C/Mateos Gago 50 • Tues–Sat 11am–2pm & 6–8.30pm • ⓦ neilsongallery.com • Free

The Neilson Gallery opened its doors in 2003 and mounts works by a range of artists both Spanish and non-Spanish, in a variety of mediums. The gallery hosts shows both by established artists and younger talent and invites artists to spend periods in Grazalema developing their work. Artists that have used this scheme include Erika Saito (Japan), David López Panea (Spain), Carol Misch (UK), Quico Rivas and Gonzalo Torné (both Spain).

ARRIVAL AND INFORMATION   **GRAZALEMA**

By bus Grazalama is connected by daily buses with Ronda, Málaga and, in the opposite direction, Ubrique. There is no bus station; buses pull up and leave from outside the Ayuntamiento on the main square, Plaza de España.

Turismo Grazalema's tourist office (daily 10am–2pm & 3.30–7pm; ☎ 956 132 052), at Plaza Asomaderos 3, just east of the main square, sells walking maps and car provide information about the park and activities such as horseriding. Lots of useful background information on the Sierra's towns and villages and their histories as well as the natural park's flora and fauna is available on ⓦ sierradecadiz.com.

LOCAL CRAFTS IN GRAZALEMA

Grazalema has long been a centre of **wool production** and famous for its woven cloaks and blankets. One of the two factories carrying on the tradition, Artesanía Textil de Grazalema (Ctra. de Ronda s/n, Mon–Fri 9am–2pm & 5–8pm; ☎ 956 132 008) can be visited and their products, including blankets, scarves and ponchos, are on sale in the factory shop. As you approach the village from Ronda the factory is up a signed turning on the right just after the petrol station.

Leatherwork has also been a strong tradition here since medieval times and although the Sierra's main centre of production is in Ubrique (see p.236), there are quality craftsworkers here too. La Tienda Chica, at C/Agua 25 close to the main square, turns out creative work by Fernando García including bags, belts, wallets and accessories made from the finest Ubrique leather.

The goat and sheep **cheeses** produced in the Sierra are also highly prized and Finca La Huzuelas, a cheese factory making the famous Payoyo brand of cheese, can be visited (daily 10am–2pm & 4–8pm, ☎ 956 234 018). The factory is below the village on the right as you enter from Ronda and its cheeses can be purchased from their shop.

LUNES DE TORO CUERDO

One of Grazalema's major events is the **Lunes de Toro Cuerdo** festival, held on a Monday during the third week in July, when a full-size *toro bravo* (fighting bull) is released in the streets of the village. It's the oldest such event in Spain, dating back to the eighteenth century, and the town fills up with thousands who line the streets to taunt the animal but attempt to get out of the way when he charges. Not always successfully, however, and one spectator was seriously gored in 2011.

ACCOMMODATION

Casa de las Piedras C/Las Piedras 32 ☎ 956 132 014, ⊛ casadelaspiedras.org. Sited above the main square, this *hostal* is the village's only budget option, offering rooms with and without bathroom. They also rent out two-person apartments for slightly more. Something of a walkers' refuge due to its use by organized groups; the proprietors can provide information on trekking in the area and arrange transport to the start of walks. Free wi-fi. Rooms **€40**, apartments **€55**

Hotel Fuerte Baldío de los Alamillos ☎ 956 133 000, ⊛ fuertehoteles.com. Four kilometres out of the village at the start of the Ronda road, this huge modern four-star caters to the mainly Spanish winter trade, offering well-equipped rooms with fine views plus pool, tennis courts, restaurant and large car park. Activities such as horse-riding are on offer and there's free wi-fi. Three-night minimum stay in July–Aug. **€110**

Hotel Peñon Grande Plaza Pequeña 7 ☎ 956 132 434, ⊛ hotelgrazalema.com. Pleasant and central two-star hotel close to the main square with clean, light and airy a/c rooms. **€55**

Hotel Puerta de la Villa Plaza Pequeña 8 ☎ 956 132 376, ⊛ hotelpuertadelavilla.com. Just off the main square, this is a reasonably good-value four-star hotel in a refurbished mansion next to the sparkling white church of Nuestra Señora de la Encarnación (the early morning bells may disturb you if you're a light sleeper). The spacious rooms are well equipped while facilities include a restaurant, jacuzzi, sauna, gym and even a tiny plunge pool. Free wi-fi. **€90–100**

★ **La Mejorana** C/Santa Clara 6 ☎ 956 132 327, ⊛ lamejorana.net. Perhaps the most attractive place to stay, housed in an elegant *casa señorial* reached by following C/Mateos Gago 300m uphill from Plaza de España. With welcoming proprietors and charming en-suite rooms (some with great views – try for "Mejorana") plus a pool, this is a winner. Free wi-fi. Street parking possible nearby. B&B **€58**

CAMPSITE

Camping Tajo Rodillo 400m above the village at the end of C/Las Piedras ☎ 956 132 418, ⊛ campingtajo rodillo.com. Grazalema's campsite is pleasantly shady and rents out fully equipped cabins in addition to the usual facilities. There's a pool and restaurant and its office has literature on the park and can provide information about walks and horse-treks in the Sierra. They also rent out mountain bikes. Two people plus car **€16.50**, cabins **€75**

EATING AND DRINKING

The bars and restaurants on the focal Plaza de España have terraces and are reasonably priced for tapas and *raciones*, while the nearby C/Agua off the square's east side has another cluster of bars and restaurants.

Bar Posadilla C/Agua 19. A good-value and popular bar for tapas and *raciones* with a terrace on this small square. Try the *chorizo frito* or *rabo de toro* (stewed bull's tail). Closed Thurs.

Bar Zulema C/Agua 44. This is another decent tapas and *raciones* bar with good-value tapas, *raciones* and *platos combinados*. Also offers an economical lunchtime *menú* and has an outdoor terrace.

Cádiz El Chico Plaza de España 8. Located on the main square, this is one of the town's better restaurants and specializes in dishes of the sierra – *cordero al horno de leña* (lamb baked in a wood-fired oven) is a signature dish. There's a *menú* for €14.

Casa de las Piedras C/Las Piedras 32. The restaurant at this *hostal* (see above) is also worth a try and serves game and rabbit dishes in addition to *trucha de El Bosque* (trout) and a good-value *menú* for €12.

Restaurante El Pinsapar C/Mateos Gago 22. Uphill from the main square, this is another good place for traditional sierra cuisine. Has a menú for €10. Closed Wed.

Torreón C/Agua 44. Reliable, traditional restaurant for dishes of the sierra including game and venison. The *sopa de grazalema* is the region's hearty mountain soup, and there are also fish dishes and salads. The wine list is fair priced and you can eat in the cosy dining room upstairs or, in better weather, on a street terrace below. Main dishes €8–15.

El Bosque and around

Located on the park's western flank, the village of **EL BOSQUE**, surrounded by slopes of planted pine, is easily reached from Grazalema via a delightfully wooded drive along the A372, which bisects the park. It provides an alternative to Grazalema as a base for visiting the park.

When travel writer Richard Ford passed through here in the 1830s he described it as a "robbers' lair" and counted "fifteen monumental crosses in the space of fifty yards" – victims of the ruthless bandits who preyed on travellers. He advised his readers to make sure they carried a watch to buy off these brigands, preferably one with a gaudy gilt chain, "the lack of which the bandit considered an unjustifiable attempt to defraud him of his right". Today it's a far more peaceful place, although the tranquillity is interrupted in August when nearby summer camps increase the two thousand-odd population threefold.

A walk along the Río Majaceite

The nearby settlement of **Benamahoma**, another picturesque sierra village some 4km east of El Bosque, provides the starting point for a particularly scenic walk along the Río Majaceite back to El Bosque (the walk is more easily tackled starting from Benamahoma rather than El Bosque). Starting from the *El Bujío* bar (a taxi will drop you there if you don't fancy the walk from El Bosque), make for some green gates at the end of the car park. Step through a small stand of eucalyptus to the right of the gates and keep ahead along the left bank of the river. As you follow the river back to El Bosque, there are plenty of opportunities for bird-spotting and picnicking.

ARRIVAL AND DEPARTURE — EL BOSQUE AND AROUND

By bus El Bosque's bus station (call Ubrique on ☎956 468 011 for information) is on the Ctra. Benamahoma–Grazalema s/n, the main road running through the village, with connections to Ubrique, Jerez and all parts of the province and beyond.

ACCOMMODATION

EL BOSQUE

Albergue El Bosque ☎956 716 212, ⓦinturjoven.com. Tucked away in the woods above the village, this recently constructed youth hostel occupies a wonderful wooded setting, with double and triple en-suite rooms, restaurant and pool. To get there, follow the road that bends up behind the *Hotel Las Truchas*. Under 26 **€21**, over 26 **€27** including breakfast.

Hotel Enrique Calvillo Avda. Diputación 5 ☎956 716 105. Decent *hotel rural* with modern rooms in the centre of the village. Also has a pool and restaurant. Free wi-fi. B&B **€50**

Hotel Las Truchas Avda. Diputacíon 1 ☎956 305 611 ⓦtugasa.com. Named after the village's local speciality, trout (El Bosque has Europe's most southerly trout river – the Río Majaceite), this is a pleasant enough place with attractive rooms and a restaurant below. Own car park. **€60**

BENAMAHOMA

Camping Los Linares C/Nacimiento s/n ☎956 716 275, ⓦcampingloslinares.com. Sited above the village with plenty of shade, a superb pool and its own restaurant. Also rents out some attractive fully equipped wood cabin apartments. Two people plus car **€21**, cabins **€65**

EATING AND DRINKING

EL BOSQUE

Hotel Enrique Calvillo Avda. Diputación 5. The restaurant at this hotel is not a bad place to eat for sierra specialities such as *jabalí* (wild boar) and pork dishes, and also has a pleasant terrace and a *menú* for €9.

Hotel Las Truchas Avda. Diputación 1. The hotel's restaurant specialises in sierra and *andaluz* cuisine; given its name it's no surprise that fresh trout from the nearby river features strongly on the menu, often with a slice of *jamón serrano* tucked inside. Main dishes €12–18.

Mesón Majaceite Reached by following the road to the Albergue El Bosque that climbs behind the Hotel Las Truchas. Opposite the *piscifactoría acuario* (fish farm) this *venta* does the freshest trout you can get as part of a €10 *menú*.

Venta Julian Avda. Diputación 11. Near the bus station, this is a reliable place for *platos combinados*, tapas and *raciones*. Also has an economical *menú* for €9 plus a pleasant terrace that's popular on warmer evenings.

Zahara de la Sierra

It's worth going back to Grazalema from El Bosque to take the spectacular CA9104 road, which climbs to the Puerto de las Palomas (Pass of the Doves, at 1350m the second-highest pass in Andalucía). A little before the pass you'll see on the left an entrance to the forest of the *pinsapo* Spanish fir – this is the start of the Itinerario del Pinsapar walking route (see box, p.227). Once over the pass the road embarks on a dramatic descent to **ZAHARA DE LA SIERRA** (or *de los Membrillos* – "of the Quinces"), surrounded by olive groves. This is perhaps the most perfect of Andalucía's fortified hill pueblos, a landmark for miles around, its red-tiled houses huddled round a church beneath a ruined castle on a stark outcrop of rock. It was once an important Moorish town, and its capture by the Christians in 1483 opened the way for the conquest of Ronda – and ultimately Granada.

The heart of the village, which was declared a national monument in 1983, is an orange tree-fringed main street connecting the churches of San Juan and the eighteenth-century Baroque church of Santa María de la Mesa with a vermilion painted exterior and tower. Inside, the latter has a fine retablo with a sixteenth-century image of the Virgin. The surviving tower of the twelfth-century Moorish castle (open daily; free) – constructed over a previous Roman one – looms over the village and incorporates the remains of an early church.

Embalse de Zahara y El Gastor reservoir

The terrain near to the village has changed dramatically over recent years due to the creation of the **Embalse de Zahara y El Gastor reservoir**, the waters of which now lap the foot of its hill on the northern and eastern flanks. The Río Guadalete, once crossed by a Roman bridge, was dammed in the late 1980s and the valley took six years to flood, creating the immense lake-like dam that dominates the landscape today. It was controversial when built but now provides vital water for irrigation and livestock and is today a great attraction for fishermen and kayakers, and even boasts its own artificial beach.

ARRIVAL AND INFORMATION   ZAHARA DE LA SIERRA

By bus Zahara is connected by services (weekdays only) to and from Ronda. There is no bus station and buses park up and leave from a stop near the entrance to the village close to the Guardia Civil barracks.

Parque Natural Information Centre At the eastern end of the main street C/San Juan and fronting the church of Santa María (daily 10am–1.30pm; ☎ 956 123 114), the centre can provide information on the village and the park, and acts as a booking office for a number of local *casas rurales* and farmhouses.

ACCOMMODATION

Al Lago C/Félix Rodríguez de la Fuente 11, on the edge of the village going towards Grazalema ☎ 956 123 032, ⓦ al-lago.es. This restaurant (see p.232) has now become a boutique hotel with the addition of four elegant rooms with a/c, walk-in wet rooms and plasma TV. There's also a solarium, and staff can arrange horseriding excursions and kayaking on the reservoir. **€90**

Casas Rurales El Vínculo Ctra. Zahara-Grazalema Km1 ☎ 956 123 002, ⓦ molinoelvinculo.com. Very pleasant rural apartments next to a (still working) eighteenth-century olive oil mill. The apartments are well equipped and come with kitchen; some also have terraces with views over the reservoir. The welcoming proprietor will show you around his mill and will sell (or give) you some olive oil to sample. **€96**

Hostal Marqués de Zahara C/San Juan 3 ☎ 956 123 061, ⓦ marquesdezahara.com. A pleasant small *hostal* on the village's main street offering en-suite a/c balcony rooms above a shady patio with TV and free wi-fi. If closed enquire at the nearby *Los Naranjos* restaurant fronting the church of San Juan. B&B **€50**

Hotel Arco de la Villa Camino Nazari s/n ☎ 956 123 230, ⓦ tugasa.com. On the road leading up to the castle, this stylish three-star has decent a/c rooms with spectacular views over the nearby reservoir, along with its own restaurant and bar, and free wi-fi. **€60**

Hotel Rural Los Tadeos Paseo de la Fuente s/n ☎ 956 123 086. Towards the swimming pool on the eastern edge of the village, this former *hostal* – still run by the same family – has had a complete makeover to become a *hotel rural*. The terrace balcony a/c rooms have wet rooms (a couple have Jacuzzis) and there are great views, a restaurant, free wi-fi and infinity pool. **€60**

2

EATING AND DRINKING

For tapas and *raciones* there is a cluster of bars around the church of Santa María. Both the *Hotel Arco de la Villa* and the *Hostal Marqués de Zahara* have decent restaurants of their own.

Al Lago C/Félix Rodríguez de la Fuente 11, on the edge of the village going towards Grazalema. Interesting mid-priced restaurant with the village's most attractive terrace, overlooking the reservoir, and creative Mediterranean-influenced dishes (with numerous vegetarian options) including salads and paella, as well as a curry night. There's also a five-course tasting *menú* for €27 (excluding wine) and a weekday lunch *menú* for €12. Main dishes €10–15.
Mesón Los Estribos C/El Fuerte 3 ☎ 956 123 145.

Up the street to the side of the church of Santa María, this is another good restaurant specializing in dishes from the sierra. Try their *jabalí al horno* (oven-baked wild boar). There's a weekday *menú* for under €10.
Los Naranjos C/San Juan 15. The restaurant of the *Hostal Marqués de Zahara* (see p.231), this reliable place serves up the usual standards as well as tapas and *raciones*. There's also an economical *menú* and a pleasant terrace on the square facing the church of San Juan.

Algodonales

Enclosed by the folds of the Sierra de Líjar, **ALGODONALES**, 6km north of Zahara, is an unassuming farming settlement with a long, central plaza dominated by the lofty tower of the eighteenth-century Neoclassical church of Santa Ana. Although lying a couple of kilometres beyond the park boundary, the village is endeavouring to make itself an activity centre for the park.

Valeriano Bernal's guitar workshop

C/Ubrique 8 • Mon–Fri 10am–1.30pm & 5–8pm, Sat 10am–2pm • ☎ 956 137 280, ⓦ valerianobernal.com

One place worth a visit in Algodonales is the workshop of renowned guitar maker **Valeriano Bernal**, whose beautiful instruments are sought after by many of the leading classical and flamenco guitarists in Spain. His modest workshop is a two-minute walk from *Hostal Sierra de Líjar*, whose proprietor can provide directions. Should you want to take a guitar home, prices range from €500 for a student's model to €5000-plus for a virtuoso instrument.

ARRIVAL AND DEPARTURE ALGODONALES

By bus The village's proximity to the main A382 *autovía* means that it has frequent daily bus connections with Seville, Jerez, Cádiz and Ronda as well as a bus to Zahara (Mon–Fri only) currently running at 1.45pm with the return to Algodonales at 7.50am or 2pm. Otherwise a taxi to Zahara will cost you about €20 one way.

ACCOMMODATION

Albergue de Algodonales C/Zahara de la Sierra 13, at the entrance to the village ☎ 956 137 882, ⓦ al-qutun.com. Very friendly and pleasant private youth hostel with dorm beds and en-suite doubles; they also rent out *casas rurales* nearby, sleeping two. There's also a garden pool and staff can advise on all kinds of activities in the park including guided hikes, hang-gliding, canoeing, caving and canyoning. Dorms €13, rooms €36, *casas rurales* €70

Hostal Sierra de Líjar C/Ronda 5 ☎ 956 137 065, ⓔ hostalsierradelijar@hotmail.com. Just below the main square, this welcoming, family-run *hostal* has en-suite a/c rooms with TV, a free garage, and a very good restaurant serving tapas and *raciones*, with a *menú* for €9. B&B €45

Olvera

OLVERA, 18km beyond Algodonales in an area thick with olives (from which the town's name may derive), couldn't look more dramatic: a great splash of whitewashed houses tumbling down a hill below the twin towers of its giant church and fine Moorish castle. You can ascend the hill along the town's long main street, the aptly named Calle Calvario and its continuation Calle Llana, to reach the church, La Encarnación. However, up close it's a somewhat uninspiring nineteenth-century edifice built on the site of a fifteenth-century Gothic-Mudéjar church, thought too small for the town's growing population, which was cleared to make way for it.

Moorish castle

Tues–Sun 10.30am–2pm & 4–7pm (Oct–March closes 6pm) • €2

More interesting than the church is the somewhat over-restored twelfth-century **Moorish castle**, which formed part of Nasrid Granada's line of defence against the Christian lands – communication between these forts was apparently carried out by means of reflecting light with mirrors. Entry is via a gate to the side of no.3 on the Plaza de la Iglesia, facing the church. Inside, you can appreciate how the castle has been built into the triangular shape of the huge rock on which it sits, and a vertiginous spiral staircase in the tower leads to the summit from where there are great views over the town and to the surrounding hill villages.

Museo de la Frontera

Tues–Sun 10.30am–2pm & 4–7pm • €2

The castle's **Museo de la Frontera**, entered via the tourist office (see below), uses tableaux and information boards to explain the fortress's history and its evolving role between the eighth and fifteenth centuries as a military outpost on the frontier with Christian Castile. Separate sections have details on daily life as lived in the castle as well as in the town during the same period.

Via Verde

w fundacionviaverdedelasierra.com

An imaginative development in Olvera is the transformation of the disused rail line – running 34km east to Puerto Serrano through rolling, wooded hill country – into a track for cyclists and walkers, known as the **Via Verde**, with stations along the route transformed into hotels and ventas. You can hire a mountain bike (or a tandem) for around €12 per day from Olvera's dapper station-hotel, the *Hostal Estación Verde* (see below). They will give you a route map and ring ahead to book rooms at your next stop. If you don't want to do the return journey you can deposit the bike in Puerto Serrano. Alternatively you can rent a bike for a half-day (€9) to do part of the route.

ARRIVAL AND INFORMATION

OLVERA

By bus Olvera's bus station (☎605 027 477) is on C/Bellavista, slightly northeast of the focal Plaza de la Concordia in the lower town. Daily services connect with Ronda, Málaga, Cádiz and Jerez.

Turismo The Turismo (Tues–Sun 10.30am–2pm & 4–6pm, closes 7pm April–Sept; ☎956 120 816, w olvera .es), at Plaza de la Iglesia s/n facing the La Encarnación church, can provide a town map and information on nearby birdwatching sanctuaries for viewing such species as vultures, eagles, owls and falcons.

ACCOMMODATION

Hostal Estación Verde ☎661 463 207, e estacion verde@hotmail.com. This pleasant *hostal* has a/c ensuite rooms with TV in the old train station along with new and fully-equipped apartments inside converted railway wagons in the sidings next door. It also has its own bar-restaurant. Rooms €50, apartments €90

Hotel Sierra y Cal Avda. Nuestra Señora de los Remedios 2 ☎956 130 303, w tugasa.com. Slightly out of the centre, this comfortable hotel offers pleasant a/c rooms and has its own bar-restaurant. €60

Pensión Medina C/Sepulveda 6 ☎956 130 173. In the town proper at the foot of C/Calvario, and off Plaza de la Concordia, this friendly small *hostal* has clean and simple rooms, all en suite. €30

EATING

Bar Mi Pueblo Plaza de Andalucía 1, about halfway up the hill. Flanked by the square's impressive fountain, this place serves up meat and fish tapas and *raciones* along with *revueltos* (scrambled egg dishes) and salads.

Bar Pepe Rayas Plaza del Ayuntamiento 9, just below the Encarnación church. Traditional bar in the upper village, now taken over by British proprietors, serving up tapas and *raciones* and with outdoor seating on a terrace on the square.

Sierra y Cal Avda. Nuestra Señora de los Remedios 2. The bar-restaurant of the *Sierra y Cal* hotel has a decent kitchen and serves tapas in its bar or more elaborate fare in the restaurant. Weekday *menú* for €10.

From Grazalema towards Cádiz

East from Grazalema a spectacular route heads towards Cádiz via the appealing villages of **Villaluenga** and **Benaocaz**, the remarkable site of Roman **Ocuris** and the larger settlements of **Alcalá de los Gazules** and **Medina Sidonia**. A detour north from here enables a trip to the stunning hilltop town of **Arcos de la Frontera**, with the towers of its castle and churches silhouetted against the sky.

The route also takes you through the southern sector of the natural park of the Sierra de Grazalema and the northern zone of the huge **Parque Natural de Los Alcornocales**, with one of the world's largest cork oak (*alcornoque*) forests. There's more excellent walking country here and a wealth of opportunities for spotting birds and other wildlife. *Walking in Andalucía* by James Hunter–Watts (see p.593) details half-a-dozen walks in the park.

The route is a wonderful drive but can also be done by bus – all the main towns are connected by frequent services.

Villaluenga del Rosario

Some 13km southwest of Grazalema, the tiny village of **VILLALUENGA DEL ROSARIO** is the highest in Cádiz Province. Tucked beneath a great crag, it's a simple place, with narrow streets, flower-filled balconies and pantiled roofs, frequently enveloped by mountain mists.

In the twilight years of the Nasrid Emirate of Granada and after Ronda had fallen to the Christians in 1485, an unprotected Villaluenga was conquered and repopulated with settlers from Arcos de la Frontera and Villamartín. Some impressive brick-built ancient Moorish wells can be seen in the fields along the roadside to the left as you approach. Recent research suggests that these wells were part of a much more sophisticated water supply system and were linked to create a form of subterranean aqueduct.

The twentieth-century Civil War was also bitterly fought here when one of the village's two churches was torched: its gutted ruin, located at the top of the village, now serves as the cemetery. Villaluenga's curious **Plaza de Toros**, partly hacked out of the rock, is also worth a look and sees action once a year during the annual *feria* (see below).

The village is also famous for its goats' cheeses, which can be purchased at the multi-award-winning Payoyo cheesemaker's factory on the south side of the main road running through the village.

ARRIVAL AND INFORMATION VILLALUENGA

By bus The village is served by two daily buses to and from Ronda and Málaga. From here buses also head west to Ubrique. Buses stop on the main road, close to the Payoyo cheesemaker's factory.

Festival Villaluenga's major festival takes place in the first week of September and honours the village's *patrona*, the Virgen del Rosario. The bullring comes into action with top *toreros* performing and there are many performances of flamenco and other events.

ACCOMMODATION

Hotel La Posada C/Torre 1 ☎ 956 126 119, ⓦ tugasa .com. The village's only place to stay, the charming *Hotel La Posada* lies in the upper village near the ruined church, housed in a beautifully renovated stone-built *casa señorial*. Not all the rooms have views, so it's worth requesting one that does (try for room 4). The hotel also has a bar-restaurant and rents out some pleasant apartments nearby. Rooms **€60**, apartments **€69**

EATING AND DRINKING

Bar Alameda Plaza Alameda 2. On the main square, the village's liveliest (and friendliest) bar fills up for major football matches and *corridas* but at other times is an inviting place for a drink and a *tapa* or *ración*. Try the *carillada en salsa* (pork cheeks). There's also an open-air terrace at the back with a fine view across the valley.

La Velada Avda. Los Arbolitos s/n. On the village's western edge, this family-run place is perhaps the best place to eat. There's a bar for tapas and the restaurant specializes in *carnes de monte* such as charcoal-grilled *jabalí* (wild boar) and *venado* (venison). You might also want to sample the goat-milk cheese which they make themselves. There is a small outdoor terrace.

Benaocaz

From Villaluenga the A2302 road descends through a spectacular pass, La Manga de Villaluenga, an area that has yielded many prehistoric artefacts and dolmens and is traversed by the remains of a medieval road. This road was laid on top of an ancient Roman road that connected Ocuris (see p.236) to Lacidulia (Grazalema) and Arunda (Ronda). Once through the pass, the road turns north to the farming settlement of **BENAOCAZ**, another ancient village founded by the Moors in the eighth century. A series of wall plaques dotted around the Barrio Nazarí – with substantial Moorish ruins and cobbled streets – in the upper village provides information (in Spanish) on buildings and locations from this period. The village's main Baroque church of San Pedro has more vestiges of Moorish days and is built over the former mosque, part of whose minaret was used to make its tower.

Museo Histórico

C/Jabonería 7, near the Ayuntamiento • Sat & Sun 11.30am–1.30pm (if closed during these hours enquire at the Ayuntamiento) • Free

The village's very well presented **Museo Histórico** includes background on life in the Sierra ranging from the times of the prehistoric cave-dwellers through to the colourful *bandoleros* who preyed on travellers in these parts until well into the twentieth century. There are also sections devoted to the nearby cave of La Pileta (see p.140) and displays focusing on the village's Roman and Moorish periods, with interesting ceramic displays from both.

The Roman road

If you want to stretch your legs, there's a fine 6km downhill walk from here to Ubrique along a superbly preserved **Roman road** complete with culverts to protect it from flooding. The start of the route (marked by an information board) is across the road from the bus stop on the main road below the village. If you time your arrival to coincide with the afternoon bus from Ubrique to Benaocaz (currently running at 3.30pm), this will save you the walk back up the hill.

ARRIVAL AND INFORMATION · BENAOCAZ

By bus Buses stop on the main road, with twice-daily services to and from Ronda and Málaga, plus Ubrique.

Tourist information Staff in the elegant eighteenth-century Ayuntamiento (Mon–Fri 9am–2pm, ☎956 125 500) on the main square, Plaza de las Libertades 1, can provide a village map as well as tourist information on the village and the surrounding area.

Festival The village's annual *feria* takes place in the middle of August to coincide with the feast of the Ascension (of the Virgin). There are numerous concerts, and other events over the three days.

ACCOMMODATION

Benaocaz makes a pleasant place to stop over, with a few attractive places to stay. The Ayuntamiento (see above) can also provide a list of apartments to rent around the village.

El Parral Laderas del Parral 1 ☎956 125 565, ⓦ elparralbenaocaz.com. At the village's western edge beyond the *Hostal San Antón*, this *hostal-rural* has simple en-suite rooms sharing an outdoor terrace and small pool, with a bar-restaurant below. **€50**

Hostal San Antón Plaza de San Antón 5 ☏ 956 125 577, ✉ refugio-benaocaz@hotmail.com. Pleasant, fully equipped two- and four-person apartments, some with fine views, plus two village houses nearby which can also be rented. Apartments **€40**, houses **€20pp**

Los Chozos Sendero Ojo del Moro s/n ☏ 954 637 205, ⓦ loschozos.com. Just outside the village on the Ubrique road, *Los Chozos* rents out *chozos* (modern versions of traditional circular thatched-roofed dwellings) sleeping two or more in a scenic location. Free wi-fi. Substantial reductions for stays of two nights or more. Open April–Sept only. **€100**

EATING AND DRINKING

Bar Las Vegas Plaza de las Libertades 5, opposite the Ayuntamiento. The village's main bar has a decent kitchen offering a weekday lunchtime *menú* for €7 and a more sophisticated à la carte menu at weekends when the speciality is a tasty *jabalí al horno* (oven-baked wild boar). The bar also serves a vital role as the vendor of daily newspapers for this corner of the Sierra. Closed evenings.

El Parral Laderas del Parral 1 The restaurant at this *hostal* (see p.235) produces tapas and *raciones* in addition to typical sierra dishes – *carnes asados* (charcoal-grilled meats) are a speciality. Also does salads and some vegetarian options, and there's a pleasant terrace. Open Fri–Sun only.

Mesón El Refugio Plaza San Anton 5, in the same building as Hostal San Antón. A decent sierra restaurant where the house speciality is *carnes a la brasa* (charcoal-grilled meats), while salads, tapas and *raciones* are also available, along with a weekday *menú* €7.50. Closed Tues.

Ocuris

Daily 11am–7pm • €1 (tickets available from the Venta Ocuris bar-restaurant at the site)

Four kilometres west of Benaocaz, close to the junction with the A373, a small road on the right (signed "Consorcio Bahía de Cádiz") leads to the spectacularly situated Roman site of **OCURIS**. The road is easy to miss and if you reach the petrol station at the junction beyond it you will need to turn around. Leave any transport at the *Venta Ocuris* fronting the site entrance, who will issue you with a ticket.

Beyond the entry gate a paved path climbs into the woods for a good kilometre to the site of the former Roman town, located on the crest of the hill above. Just before you arrive at the ruins, to the left stands a well-preserved (although partly restored) first-century AD **columbarium** tomb with wall niches for burial urns. This is followed by some impressive Cyclopean dry-stone **walls** that date from the site's origin as an Iberian *oppidum*, or tribal settlement, in the pre-Roman era – the Romans would have had to overcome defences like these during the subjugation of the peninsula in the first and second centuries BC.

Once through the walls, you enter the heart of the Roman settlement where the substantial remains of **dwellings**, **baths** and huge **cisterns**, with their mortar linings still intact, surround the ancient **forum**. Archeologists are still busy excavating here and it will be some time before the remains are entirely revealed and understood. On all sides of the site the hill falls sharply away and there are wonderful **views** over the Sierra and the town of Ubrique, far below. There's plenty of shade and lush grass up here and, if you've brought provisions, it's hard to imagine a better place for a picnic.

Ubrique

From Benaocaz the road corkscrews down from the mountainous sierra until the snow-white vista of **UBRIQUE** comes into view below, spreading along the valley of the Río Ubrique with the daunting knife-edged crag of the Cruz de Tajo rearing up behind. Despite this stunning first appearance, on closer contact it's a rather large and dull industrial centre, but the town's bustling prosperity ensures a good variety of place to eat and drink on and around Avenida Dr Solis Pascual, the tree-lined main artery.

A place that has always bred tenacious guerrilla fighters and which fought against the French in the War of Independence (actually defeating a contingent of the Imperial Guard near Gaucín), Ubrique is a natural mountain fortress which was one of the last Republican strongholds in the Civil War. Today, it's a relatively wealthy if unexciting town, surviving largely on its medieval guild craft of **leather manufacturing**, the products of which are sold in numerous shops lining the main street, where most of the bars and restaurants are also gathered. Although the town has been badly hit by the economic downturn in recent years – partly as a result of cheap leather imports from Asia – the most highly skilled of Ubrique's leather workers keep busy working for many of the big designer names like Loewe, Luis Vuitton and Gucci.

ARRIVAL AND INFORMATION   UBRIQUE

By bus The bus station is at northern end of town Avda. Manuel de Falla s/n (☎ 956 461 070) with frequent services to Cádiz, Jerez, Grazalema, El Bosque, Ronda, Málaga and other destinations.

Turismo The Turismo (Mon–Fri 10am–2pm & 4–7pm, Sat & Sun 11am–2pm & 4–7pm; ☎ 956 464 900), on Moreno de Mora 19, the continuation of Avda. Dr Solis Pascual, can provide a town map and has information on the town and local area including Ocuris.

ACCOMMODATION

Hotel Ocurris Avda. Dr Solis Pascual 49, close to the main junction and roundabout as you enter the town from the north ☎ 956 463 939, ⊛ hotelocurris .com. Two-star hotel on the main street offering pleasant enough en-suite rooms with TV plus its own bar and restaurant. **€56**

Hotel Sierra de Ubrique Avda. Sierra de Ubrique 1 ☎ 956 466 805, ⊛ hotelsierradeubrique.com. On the road leading out of town towards Alcalá, this is an attractive three-star hotel with well-equipped rooms, plus a restaurant and bar, pool, solarium, free wi-fi and car park. **€75**

EATING AND DRINKING

La Tasca de Juande Avda. de España 85. Excellent little tapas and *raciones* bar with a terrace near the southern end of this pedestrianized street. All the tapas are good, with house specials including *revuelto campero de morcilla* (eggs with blood sausage) and *higaditos de pollo* (sautéed chicken livers).

★ **Restaurante El Laurel** C/San Juan Bautista s/n, just behind the main street ☎ 956 460 284. One of the best restaurants in the Sierra with an untypically creative

approach, matched by the restaurant's modern decor. All the dishes are prepared with style – try the *solomillo de cerdo con salsa de oporto* (pork loin with port sauce), *confit de pato* (duck confit) or the *milhojas de espinacas* (millefeuille with spinach). The desserts are pretty mouthwatering, too. Also does pizzas and there's a weekday *menú* for €12. Main dishes €8–15. *El Laurel Tapas*, their tapas and *raciones* bar across the street, is also highly recommended.

Southwest from Ubrique

The A373 road from Ubrique towards Alcalá, 44km to the southwest, runs through the **Parque Natural de Los Alcornocales**, with magnificently rugged but sparsely populated mountain scenery. Close to the Sierra de Aljibe to the south, the road skirts the provincial border with Málaga before ascending to the Puerto de Galis pass, at the junction with the CA8201. Beyond here the road joins the valley of the Río Barbate for the final descent into the White Town of Alcalá de los Gazules (see below), the geographical centre of the province of Cádiz.

EATING   PARQUE NATURAL DE LOS ALCORNOCALES

★ **Venta del Puerto de Galis** Junction of A373 and CA8201. Isolated but excellent lunch stop, popular with

local hunters, and often featuring game on its menu.

Alcalá de los Gazules

A cascade of white dwellings gathered beneath its ruined *alcázar*, **ALCALÁ DE LOS GAZULES** is a sleepy little place today. Apart from the winding, narrow streets, little remains of the later Moorish settlement founded by a Berber family the Gazules, who gave their name to the town in the twelfth century when this was a *taifa* state of the kingdom of Granada.

In the Plaza Alta in the upper town stands the fifteenth-century Gothic church of **San Jorge**, built over the mosque that was razed to make way for it. It has an imposing tower (probably the mosque's minaret) and, inside, a beautifully carved choir and an effigy attributed to Martínez Montañes, but not much else.

Alongside the church is the sixteenth-century **Casa del Cabildo**, which until the last century served as Alcalá's Ayuntamiento. In the lower town the **Plaza de Toros** has been turned into a *discoteca*, somewhat blasphemously given the surrounding bull-breeding country.

Brief history

When the Romans were conquering this area early in the second century BC, they tried to divide and rule the Iberian tribes by granting the status of *colonia* to selected settlements – a crucial first step on the way to full Roman citizenship and all the privileges such status could bestow. One such settlement so rewarded was the Iberian Turris Lascutana, as Alcalá then was, and this was an attempt by Rome to win its allegiance away from the Turditanian tribal capital at Asta Regia near Jerez. A unique bronze plaque (in the national archeological museum in Madrid) records the decree of the Roman governor, Lucius Aemelius Paullus, in 189 BC, which granted Turris possession of the fields and town that they had formerly held as a fief of Asta.

ARRIVAL AND DEPARTURE   **ALCALÁ DE LOS GAZULES**

By bus Services from Jerez, Cádiz and Medina Sidonia arrive and depart from the central Avda. Alcornocales.

THE CORK OAK STRIPPERS

Whether a supermarket bottle of wine is stopped with a **cork** or with a screw-top cap may be a matter of indifference to most wine buyers, but it's a hot topic in and around the forest of **Los Alcornocales**. Each summer *tiradores* (cork strippers) head deep into the forest with their mules to strip the cork bark from the *alcornoques* (cork oak trees) that are ready. They use long pointed lances called *burjas* and special axes to split and strip the outer bark leaving a bright orange inner layer – the *casca* – which gives a stand of freshly stripped trees a rather surreal stark-naked appearance.

It's tough work for these gangs of men who toil far from any road or track, which is where the mules come in. The mule drivers load up their beasts with the *panos* – square chunks of bark about half the size of a door – and take them to the patio where it is weighed – the *tiradores* are paid by weight collected. Then they are carried to a point where a truck can access the forest edge. These vehicles' trailers, loaded with thousands of neatly stacked *panos*, are a common sight on the roads of Cádiz all summer long. The *tiradores* camp out in the forest during the cutting season and drinking and singing around their campfires is a long tradition.

However, the wine industry is in a state of revolution as cork is abandoned for more economical means of bottle closure. A wine cork costs about 30 US cents as against 6 US cents for a plastic cork or a cap, and there lies the rub. The Australians now bottle only fifty percent of their wine with cork, many wine-producing countries are following them, and this has got the *tiradores* worried for their future. Perhaps just in time, the naturalists have now taken up their cause. Recent reports by bodies such as the WWF (World Wide Fund for Nature) and RSPB (Royal Society for the Protection of Birds) argue that cork oak forests like Los Alcornocales are unique **ecosystems** vital to a whole food chain of insects, flora and fauna which in turn support species such as Bonelli's eagle, the Iberian lynx, the spectacular azure-winged magpie, otters, mouflon, wild boar, roe deer, the Egyptian mongoose and many more. The cork oak forests are protected, but if the trees lose their economic value there will be sustained pressure to make other use of the land. Which is why, next time you buy a bottle of wine, you may just decide to take the one with the cork.

TOROS BRAVOS

This part of Cádiz province is **bull country**, and the roads around the towns of Álcala de los Gazules and Medina Sidonia are lined with the ranches of the breeders of fighting bulls destined for bullrings all over Spain. Behind warning signs posted on roadside fences it's often possible to catch a view of the mean, black *toros bravos*, or fighting bulls used in the *corridas*. These magnificent beasts weighing 500 to 600 kilos, the descendants of the *bos taurus ibericus* of ancient times, graze on pastures shaded by olives and holm oaks, and are tended by mounted *vaqueros* who guard them while noting their potential for valour. This is eventually tested in the *tienta* or trial ring, an important first step in deciding whether the bull will die in the *corrida* or the abattoir. The *vaqueros* are always on the lookout for the exceptional bull displaying outstanding bravery and physical construction and these are separated from the herd to be used exclusively at stud, to improve the breed. The bulls that leave these ranches to fight in the ring usually die there, although very occasionally bulls displaying exceptional bravery and spirit will receive the *indulto*, or pardon, to be returned to their ranch of origin for stud.

If you'd like to see a bull-breeding ranch, **A Campo Abierto** (☎ 956 304 312) offers visits to the renowned Domecq ranch to the west of Medina Sidonia (Wed, Fri & Sat at 11.30am; €18, under 12s €9). The visit includes displays of herding the *toros bravos* as well as riding by the *vaqueros*. Get details from the Turismo in Medina or from their website ⓦ acampoabierto.com.

ACCOMMODATION AND EATING

Hostal Pizarro Paseo de la Playa s/n ☎ 956 420 103. The proprietors of *Restaurante Pizarro* (see below) also run this comfortable *hostal* with plain, but satisfactory en-suite rooms with TV. €35
Hotel San Jorge C/Antonio Alzaga 51 ☎ 956 413 255. Uphill from the *hostal*, this is a two-star hotel with light,

well-equipped rooms with a/c and TV, plus bar-restaurant and free car park. €60
Restaurante Pizarro Paseo de la Playa 9. Decent mid-priced restaurant on the main street serving up typical dishes of the sierra. *Carne de caza* (game and venison) is a speciality here, and they also serve a weekday lunchtime *menú* for €8.

Tajo de las Figuras

Wed–Sun 9am–3pm • Check current visiting arrangements with the Ayuntamiento in Benalup-Casas Viejas, C/Cantera s/n ☎ 956 417 733 or the Turismo in Medina Sidonia (see p.240) • Free

From Alcalá the A381 *autovía* heads west to Medina Sidonia. An alternative route heads 17km southwest to **BENALUP-CASAS VIEJAS** allowing you to visit the **Tajo de las Figuras** caves, home to important Neolithic **cave paintings.** Discovered in 1913, the vivid paintings depict a variety of birds, as well as deer and human figures, perhaps hunters.

The caves and *abrigos* (rock shelters) with the paintings lie 7km south of Benalup-Casas Viejas along the A5203, signed on the left; the *abrigos*, some half-a-kilometre distant, can be seen from the road. Park by a metal gate and go through this heading towards the rock cliffs where you will eventually make out a steel ladder to the main cave above. If closed, wait around and the site's guardian (who shelters among the rocks) will eventually emerge to unlock them. He can also guide you to another cave nearby with more paintings of animals and human figures (one with a child) and, below this, to some remarkable anthropomorphic **sarcophagus tombs** – some for children – carved into the rocks. You may want to give the guardian a small consideration for his trouble.

Medina Sidonia

Some 19km northwest of Alcalá along the A381 autovía, a turn-off left leads to the ancient town of **MEDINA SIDONIA**, sited on a low hill and huddled below the tower of its ancient church. Legend has it that the town's Phoenician founders (from Sidon) gave it the latter part of its name while the Moors added Medina. Following its reconquest by Alfonso X in 1264, Medina became one of Spain's most prestigious ducal seats, supplying the admiral who led the Armada against England. The title of Duque de Medina Sidonia was bestowed upon the family of Guzmán El Bueno for his valiant role in battles against the Moors, a line which continues, and was led by the firebrand socialist duchess of Medina Sidonia up to her death in 2008 (see p.211). Today Medina is an atmospheric little town where tidy narrow cobbled streets lined with *reja*-fronted houses circle the lower slopes of a peak dominated by the striking church of Santa María.

Plaza de España

A good place to begin a look around is the elegant **Plaza de España**, dominated at its southern end by the wonderful porticoed facade of the seventeenth-century Ayuntamiento. The facade reflects the history of its construction: the columned ground floor is seventeenth-century Baroque while the second floor – added later – is Neoclassical with pediments above the windows. The third floor, finished in the nineteenth century, has square windows placed to each side of a central clock.

At the plaza's northern end lies the **Mercado de Abastos**, or market, dating from 1871. Part of the building will house the new tourist office following refurbishment.

Santa María la Coronada

Daily: April–Sept Mon–Fri noon–2pm & 4.30–7pm, Sat & Sun 11.30am–2pm & 4.30–7pm; Oct–March 10.30am–2pm & 4–7pm • €2.50

To the rear of the Ayuntamiento, at the top of a steeply climbing road (Calle Arrieros), is the **Plaza Iglesia Mayor**, dominated by the tower and portal of **Santa María la Coronada** church, built over an earlier mosque. Inside is an enormous and exquisite **retablo** depicting scenes from the life of Christ – a stunning sixteenth-century work of craftsmanship in polychromed wood by the *sevillano* school. There's also an imposing sculpted image of *Cristo del Perdón* attributed to Luisa Roldán ("La Roldana") and a fine wood sculpture of *San Francisco de Asís* by Juan Martínez Montañes. On the church's eastern aisle are two sixteenth-century benches used by the Inquisition.

The Roman sewers

C/Ortega 10 • April–Sept Tues–Sun 10.30am–2pm & 5.30–8pm; Oct–March Tues–Sun 10.30am–2pm & 4–6.30pm • €3.50

Medina's importance in Roman times, when it was known as Asido Caesarina, is evidenced by some remarkable **Roman sewers** ("Cloacas Romanas") buried beneath the town's northern flank. Dating from the first century AD, the extensive stone-built sewers stand over two metres in height and are a tribute to Roman engineering skills. The same building also holds a small **museum** displaying sculptures, mosaics, coins and amphorae unearthed in various excavations around the town.

The same ticket covers entry beneath another building nearby to see a remarkably well preserved stretch of paved **Roman road** – complete with guttering, sewers and pavement – lying below the town's main street, Calle San Juan. Don't miss the child's game etched into one of the paving stones, which adds a wonderfully human touch.

The Moorish gates

Medina Sidonia also boasts three **Moorish gates** – all shown on the Turismo map – of which the tenth-century Arco de la Pastora, close to the Jerez road, is the best preserved. The others, the twelfth-century Arco de Belén and the Puerta del Sol, are also worth a look.

ARRIVAL AND INFORMATION   **MEDINA SIDONIA**

By bus Buses to and from Cádiz and other locations throughout the province use the bus station on Avda. del Mar (☎956 807 059), a few minutes' walk north of the focal Plaza de España.

Turismo The Turismo (daily: April–Sept 10.30am–2pm & 5.30–8pm; Oct–March 10.30am–2pm & 4.30–6.30pm;

☎956 412 404, ⓦmedinasidonia.com) is at C/Ortega 10, in the same building as the Roman Sewers. Staff can provide a useful town map, plus information about visits to local bull-breeding ranches. Note that the Turismo will be moving to the Mercado de Abastos (on Plaza de España) once the new building is ready.

ACCOMMODATION

★ **Casa Rural Los Balcones** C/La Loba 26 ☎ 956 423 033, ⓦ losbalcones.net. Inside an elegant nineteenth-century mansion offering delightful a/c rooms with kitchenette and fridge. €̄55̄

Hotel Medina Sidonia Plaza Llanete de Herederos 1 ☎ 956 412 317, ⓦ tugasa.com. The best conventional option in town, offering attractive rooms in a tastefully restored *casa señorial* with an exquisite patio. Also has its own restaurant and bar. €̄67̄

★ **La Casa de Abú** C/Espíritu Santo 6, west of Plaza de España ☎ 956 412 463, ⓦ lacasadeabu.es. Delightful

new *casa rural* in a beautifully restored nineteenth-century flour mill with five apartments ranged around a leafy patio. The a/c apartments come with state-of-the-art kitchens and bathrooms plus satellite TV and free wi-fi. Most have terraces to sit out and there's a solarium. The quoted rate halves outside high season. €̄90̄

La Tagarnina C/Moritos 10 ☎ 956 423 067, ⓦ la tagarnina.com. This old mill and bakery has been converted into an intimate *casa rural* hotel with delightful patio. Rooms are light and airy and individually styled and come with a/c and TV. B&B €̄65̄

EATING AND DRINKING

Bar-Restaurante Ortega Plaza de España 10. On the main square – and with fewer pretensions than the neighbouring *Restaurante Cádiz* – this is a popular tapas and *raciones* place with a terrace on the square. Also does fish and meat *platos combinados* and there's a *menú* for €8.

Hotel Medina Sidonia Plaza Llanete de Herederos 1. This hotel restaurant is good for regional dishes and also does a variety of salads and a daily *menú* for €13. Main dishes €10–14.

Restaurante Cádiz Plaza de España 13. The best restaurant in town, offering a wide choice of local dishes – including *venado* (venison), *jabalí* (wild boar) and *solomillo de cerdo* (pork loin) – plus an interesting selection of wines (local and national) and some tasty desserts. They also offer a *menú* for €12 (weekdays) and €15 (weekends) and their

tapas bar – with terrace – is also good.

Sobrina de las Trejas Plaza España 7. Medina was noted in Moorish times for its sweets and pastries, a tradition continued here – the *alfajores* (sugary tubes containing honey, almonds and dried fruit) are delicious.

★ **Venta la Duquesa** Ctra. Medina-Vejer Km3 ☎ 956 410 836. Excellent restaurant masquerading as a humble *venta* in the countryside just outside Medina. But there's nothing humble about the kitchen – under the direction of head chef Carmen Prieto – which pushes out a variety of traditional *gaditano* specialities from the sierra and the sea. Any of the meat dishes are recommended (particularly the lamb) and *rabo de toro* (stewed bull's tail) is a signature dish. They also offer a variety of salads and there's a tapas bar and pleasant terrace. Main dishes €10–20.

Arcos de la Frontera

Some 35km northeast of Medina Sidonia, the ancient hill town of **ARCOS DE LA FRONTERA** straddles the notional border between the Sierra de Cádiz to the east, and the parched, wine-growing flatlands of Jerez de la Frontera to the west. From whichever direction you approach it, your first view of Arcos – the westernmost of the White Towns – will be fabulous. In full sun the town shimmers magnificently on its great double crag of limestone high above the Río Guadalete. This dramatic location, enhanced by low, white houses and fine sandstone churches, gives the town a similar feel and appearance to Ronda – except Arcos is rather poorer and, quite unjustifiably, far less visited. By far the best thing to do here is take a stroll around the tangle of narrow streets, lined with a mix of Moorish and Renaissance buildings. Most of Arcos's monuments are located in the higher old town – where you'll be spending much of your time. The new town has spilled out to the west and east of here at the foot of the crag.

Brief history

Dating from Iberian times and known as Arco Briga to the Romans, Arcos came to prominence as the Moorish town of Arkos within the Cordoban caliphate. When Córdoba's rule collapsed in the eleventh century, Arcos existed as a petty *taifa* state until its annexation by al-Mu'tamid of Seville in 1103. The seizure of Arcos by Christian forces under Alfonso El Sabio (the Wise) in 1264 was a real feat against what must have been a wretchedly impregnable fortress. In the following three centuries most of Arcos's churches were built and, in a less warlike age, the town expanded beyond its walls for the first time when the "new town" of La Corredera was created. In the nineteenth

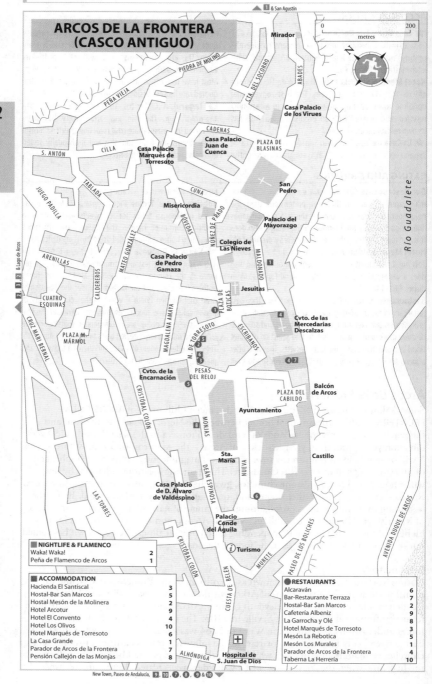

ARCOS DE LA FRONTERA (CASCO ANTIGUO)

0   metres   200

Mirador

Casa Palacio
de los Virues

PIEDRA DE MOLINO

CTA. DEL SOCORRO

ABADES

PEÑA VIEJA

CADENAS

CILLA

S. ANTÓN

Casa Palacio
Marqués de
Torresoto

Casa Palacio
Juan de
Cuenca

PLAZA DE
BLASINAS

TABLADA

CUNA

San
Pedro

JUEGO PADILLA

Misericordia

BÓLEDAS

NÚÑEZ DE PRADO

Palacio del
Mayorazgo

ARENILLAS

MATEO GONZÁLEZ

Colegio de
Las Nieves

& Lago de Arcos

CALDEREROS

Casa Palacio
de Pedro
Gamaza

MALDONADO

Jesuitas

CUATRO
ESQUINAS

MAGDALENA AMAYA

PLAZA DE BOTILLAS

CRUZ MARI BERNAL

PLAZA M.
MÁRMOL

M. DE TORRESOTO

ESCRIBANOS

Cvto. de las
Mercedarias
Descalzas

Cvto. de la
Encarnación

PESAS
DEL RELOJ

PLAZA DEL
CABILDO

Balcón
de Arcos

Ayuntamiento

CRISTÓBAL COLÓN

MONJAS

Sta.
María

NUEVA

Castillo

LAS TORRES

DEAN ESPINOSA

Casa Palacio
de D. Álvaro
de Valdespino

Palacio
Conde
del Águila

AVENIDA DUQUE DE ARCOS

PASEO DE LOS BOLICHES

Río Guadalete

ⓘ Turismo

MURETE

CRISTÓBAL COLÓN

CUESTA DE BELEN

ALHÓNDIGA

Hospital de
S. Juan de Dios

& San Agustín

■ **NIGHTLIFE & FLAMENCO**

| Waka! Waka! | 2 |
| Peña de Flamenco de Arcos | 1 |

■ **ACCOMMODATION**

Hacienda El Santiscal	3
Hostal-Bar San Marcos	5
Hostal Mesón de la Molinera	2
Hotel Arcotur	9
Hotel El Convento	4
Hotel Los Olivos	10
Hotel Marqués de Torresoto	6
La Casa Grande	1
Parador de Arcos de la Frontera	7
Pensión Callejón de las Monjas	8

● **RESTAURANTS**

Alcaraván	6
Bar-Restaurante Terraza	7
Hostal-Bar San Marcos	2
Cafetería Albeniz	9
La Garrocha y Olé	8
Hotel Marqués de Torresoto	3
Mesón La Rebotica	5
Mesón Los Murales	1
Parador de Arcos de la Frontera	4
Taberna La Herrería	10

New Town, Paseo de Andalucía, 9, 10, 7, 8, 9 & 10

century an outbreak of yellow fever decimated the population while the Napoleonic invasions caused extensive damage to much of the town, including the castle and many churches. The town only really recovered in the latter part of the last century with the arrival of mass tourism, from which Arcos gains most of its income today.

Santa María de la Asunción

Mon–Fri 10am–1pm & 4–7pm, Sat 10am–2pm, Sun 8.30am for Mass • €2, tower €3

At the heart of the *casco antiguo* or monumental quarter is the **Plaza del Cabildo**, easily reached by following the signs for the *parador*. Flanking another two sides are (behind the Ayuntamiento) the castle walls and towers (the castle is privately owned and off-limits) and the large fifteenth-century Gothic-Mudéjar church of **Santa María de la Asunción**, built over an earlier mosque; one side is left open, offering spectacular plunging views to the river valley and the *vega*. Santa María's Plateresque south facade with later additions is a stunning work, although an unfinished bell tower unbalances the whole – the original was destroyed by the Lisbon earthquake of 1755 and the plan was to raise this new one to 58m, second in height only to Seville's Giralda. Three years later, however, the money ran out and the tower was left at a relatively feeble 37m. The tower can be visited and offers views over the town and surrounding countryside. The church's gloomy interior has fine Gothic vaulting as well as a stunning retablo, exquisitely carved choir stalls by Pedro Roldán, and a treasury with all the usual collection of church silver and some dubiously attributed artworks.

San Pedro

C/Núñez de Prado • Mon–Fri 9.30am–2pm & 4–7pm, Sat 9.30am–2pm • €1

At the northeastern end of the old town, the Gothic church of **San Pedro**, perched precariously on the cliff edge, was rebuilt in the sixteenth century over an original Moorish fort. The later imposing Baroque exterior and tower are in strong contrast to the interior, where a fine sixteenth-century retablo (the oldest in the province) documents the life of San Pedro and San Jerónimo. To each side of this are paintings of *San Ignacio* and *La Dolorosa* by Pachecho, the tutor of Velázquez. There's also the rather grisly undecomposed body of San Victor (thankfully behind glass) and an image of the Virgin attributed to Luisa Roldán ("La Roldana"), the sculptor daughter of Pedro Roldán. You can climb the tower, but you'll need a good head for heights, as there are few guardrails on the top to prevent a fall.

San Agustín and Casa Cuna

Further east lies the convent of **San Agustín** (daily except Tues 10.30am–1pm & 3.30–6.30pm; free), on the narrow neck of the spur, whose church contains a fine seventeenth-century carved wood retablo and the town's most venerated image of Jesús Nazareno (Christ bearing the Cross). Nearby on Calle Cuna stands the **Casa Cuna**, formerly the synagogue of the old Jewish ghetto.

The river beaches and Lago de Arcos

East of town, the A372 road to Ronda leads down to a couple of sandy **beaches** on the riverbank, while to the north of here the **Lago de Arcos** (actually a reservoir) is a good spot for swimming. The lake is served by eleven daily buses (weekdays with reduced service weekends) in each direction (Sun service only July & Aug) leaving from the Plaza de España, below the old town.

ARRIVAL AND DEPARTURE   ARCOS DE LA FRONTERA

By bus The bus station (☎ 956 704 977) is in the new town on C/Corregidores below and to the south of the Paseo de Andalucía. It is served by the Comes and Amarillo companies, with regular buses to Cádiz and Jerez. The station currently has no ticket office; tickets must be purchased on the bus. A useful minibus service (Mon–Sat until 9.15pm; €0.90) runs back and forth between Plaza de España and the Paseo de Andalucía in the new town and

2

FERIA DE SAN MIGUEL

Each September 29 (and the two days before and after), Arcos celebrates the **Feria de San Miguel**, honouring the town's patron saint, with parades, concerts of music and flamenco and wine tasting. Since the eighteenth century each Easter Sunday Arcos has celebrated Christ's resurrection with the Aleluya Toro (Hallelujah Bull), when a fighting bull is released. During this *encierro*, the town's narrow streets echo to the screams of hundreds of children who lift themselves clear of the rampaging *toro*'s horns by grabbing an overhanging balcony. It's a truly nail-biting sight, yet remarkably few seem to get injured.

Plaza del Cabildo in the *casco antiguo* – saving you a climb.

By car Parking in the narrow streets of the old town is tricky (although all the hotels have their own arrangements) and you'd be much better off trying to find space on the Paseo de Andalucía or using a pay car park (there's one beneath the Paseo itself).

INFORMATION

Turismo The Turismo (April–Sept Mon–Sat 9.30am–2pm & 3–7.30pm, Sun 10am–2pm; Oct–March Mon–Sat 9.30am–6.30pm, Sun 10am–2pm; ☎956 702 264, ⓦarcosdelafrontera.es), at Cuesta de Belén 5, can provide a detailed map, which you'll need to find your way around the new town. The same building houses a new Centro de Interpretación (same hours as Turismo; free) covering the town's history.

Tours The Turismo does weekday guided tours of the monuments and patios of the old town, departing from their office Mon–Fri at 11am (€4).

Internet Locutorio El Barrio, Plaza de las Aguas s/n in the new town (Mon–Sat 10am–2pm & 5–9pm). The Turismo also has a single computer for public use.

ACCOMMODATION

A number of *hostales* providing budget accommodation have recently opened up in the old town, formerly the exclusive preserve of a clutch of upmarket hotels. Lower down, the new town has many more options, including a renovated old *fonda* on the main street, C/Corredera. Staying a little out of town at the Lago de Arcos, where there's a *hostal* and a couple of inviting hotels, is another possibility – though you'll need insect repellent in summer. There's a bus service to the lake from the bus station (see p.243). It's worth noting that outside high season prices can fall by up to fifty percent.

Hacienda El Santiscal 3km out of town on the lakeside ☎956 708 313, ⓦsantiscal.com. Small country hotel in a beautiful converted hacienda, partly dating from the sixteenth century, with attractively furnished a/c rooms, restaurant and a pool in the grounds. Horseriding available. See website for special offers. **€85**

Hostal-Bar San Marcos C/Marqués de Torresoto 6 ☎956 700 721. Excellent small *hostal* in the old town offering pleasant a/c en-suite rooms with free wi-fi. Also has its own bar-restaurant below. **€35**

Hotel Arcotur C/Alta 1, in the new town ☎956 704 525, ⓦarcoturhotel.com. Welcoming small hotel offering good value a/c en-suite rooms with TV and balcony (some also have great views); there's also a roof-terrace café for breakfast. **€37**

★ **Hotel El Convento** C/Maldonado 2 ☎956 702 333, ⓦhotelelconvento.es. Stunning hotel in a seventeenth-century former convent whose comfortable a/c rooms – 8 & 9 are recommended – have spectacular views over the *vega*. Breakfast is served in a charming courtyard and there's free wi-fi. **€71**

Hotel Los Olivos C/San Miguel 2, in the new town ☎956 700 811, ⓦhotel-losolivos.es. Charming and friendly little hotel near the Paseo de Andalucía gardens, in a superbly restored *casa antigua*. Some of the light a/c rooms have fine views and there's a plant-filled interior patio and further views from a rooftop terrace. Also has free wi-fi and a car park. **€85**

Hotel Marqués de Torresoto C/Marqués de Torresoto 4 ☎956 700 717, ⓦhotelmarquesdetorresoto.com. Attractive, good value a/c rooms with minibar and satellite TV in a converted seventeenth-century mansion, the former seat of the *marqueses* de Torresoto. The delightful colonnaded patio – complete with Baroque chapel – now serves as the hotel restaurant (open to the public). Has rooftop terrace plus rooms for non-smokers. Free wi-fi. **€54**

★ **La Casa Grande** C/Maldonado 10 ☎956 703 930, ⓦlacasagrande.net. Perched along the same cliff top as the *parador*, this elegant hotel has beautiful individually styled rooms (and more expensive suites) – some with terrace – inside a restored *casa señorial* with a columned inner patio and a sensational view from the bar terrace across the river valley. **€85**

Mesón de la Molinera Lago de Arcos ☎956 708 002, ⓦmesondelamolinera.com. Tranquil hotel-*hostál* on the waterfront with stunning views across the lake towards Arcos on its hill top. Comfortable balcony rooms with minibar and safe are offered in the hotel while chalet-style bungalows comprise the *hostal*. There's also a sun terrace, great pool and easy parking. Also has its own bar and restaurant. B&B hotel **€80**, hostal **€60**

★ **Parador de Arcos de la Frontera** Plaza del Cabildo ☎ 956 700 500, ⓦ parador.es. One of the region's smaller and more intimate *paradores*, occupying the former Casa del Corregidor (house of the king's magistrate) with parts dating from the sixteenth century. The striking building is perched on a rock pedestal with reassuringly reinforced foundations to prevent it from sliding over the cliff and elegant balconied rooms from which to enjoy the view. There's also a delightful patio (open to the public for drinks and afternoon tea) and the *cafetería*'s "crow's nest" terrace has the best views in town. Parking on the square outside. **€163**

Pensión Callejón de las Monjas C/Dean Espinosa 4 ☎ 956 702 302, ⓦ hotelelpatio.com. Decent if cramped *pensión* with en-suite rooms in the heart of the old town; some slightly pricier rooms come with a/c, TV and terrace. Also rents out some fully-equipped apartments nearby. Free wi-fi. Rooms **€30–35**, apartments **€66**

EATING AND DRINKING

Alcaraván C/Nueva 1, close to the castle walls. Atmospheric cave restaurant serving tapas, *raciones*, *carnes asados* (roasted meats) and a variety of salads. Tues–Sun 11am–4pm & 7.30–midnight.

Bar-Restaurante Terraza C/Múñoz Vásquez s/n. Below the old town, in the gardens of the Paseo de Andalucía, this is a pleasant place to sit out and serves a wide variety of inexpensive *platos combinados* and a *menú* for €9. Daily 9am–11pm.

Cafetería Albeniz C/Muñoz Vázquez 10, close to Bar-Restaurante Terraza. Pleasant café-bar serving a variety of salads, fish and meat dishes as well as paella; has a small terrace. Daily noon–midnight.

Hotel Marqués de Torresoto C/Marqués de Torresoto 4. Situated in this hotel's elegant seventeenth-century patio and worth a try for tapas and *raciones* – as is their next-door *cafetería*. There's also a *menú* for €7. Mon & Weds–Sun 12.30–4pm & 7.30–10.30pm.

Hostal-Bar San Marcos C/Marqués de Torresoto 6. Cosy downstairs bar-restaurant serving tapas – try the *salchichón ibérico* (salami) or *platos combinados* such as *solomillo de cerdo* (pork loin). There's also a *menú* for €7. Daily 9am–11pm.

La Garrocha y Olé Cerro de la Reina 8, off Plaza de España. Modern bar-restaurant serving decent and reasonably priced pizzas and *platos combinados* on a terrace in a revamped plaza. Daily 9am–11pm.

Mesón Los Murales Plaza de Boticas 1. One of the best low-priced options in the old town, close to the church of San Pedro, and serving tapas and *montaditos* (tapas on bread) plus salads. Has an economical *menú* for €9 and a small street terrace. Main dishes €7–12. Daily except Thurs noon–4pm & 8–11pm.

Mesón La Rebotica C/Marques de Torresoto 1. New bar-restaurant with a roomy interior and a good selection of tapas and *raciones*. Try the *solomillo ibérico* (pork loin) or (at weekends) paella.

Parador de Arcos de la Frontera Plaza del Cabildo. The *parador*'s restaurant has a recommended *menú* for €32 which includes local specialities. On the à la carte menu *salmorejo de aguacate* (avocado gazpacho) and *conejo de Serranía de Cádiz* (rabbit with honey) are signature dishes. Also offers vegetarian and diabetic menus. Daily 1–4pm & 8–11pm.

Taberna La Herrería Plaza de las Aguas s/n, in the new town. Atmospheric and popular tapas and *raciones* bar serving a wide range of tapas in a flamenco venue, with frequent performances at weekends (not Aug). Daily 10am–midnight.

NIGHTLIFE

Arcos locals tend to gravitate to the bars and restaurants for nightlife; however, in summer there are quite a few free outdoor events, such as flamenco (and even rock) concerts and it's worth checking with the Turismo, or perusing the local weekly paper, *Arcos Información*, to see what's coming up.

Peña de Flamenco de Arcos Plaza de la Caridad 4 ☎ 956 701 251. The welcoming Peña de Flamenco de Arcos, east of the old quarter, stages regular – and authentic – flamenco, with *actuaciones* (shows) most weekends (not July & Aug), normally Saturdays after 10.30pm, but ring first (Spanish only) to check.

Waka! Waka! Open-air *discoteca* which livens up the lakeside in summer, and gets going after 11pm.

Seville and Huelva

SAN LUÍS, SEVILLE

Seville and Huelva

The irresistible city of Seville, Andalucía's capital, has many of the region's most beautiful monuments: the Giralda tower, a magnificent Gothic cathedral and a fabulous Mudéjar Alcázar are just the highlights. Add to these the stunning Museo de Bellas Artes, the nearby Roman site of Itálica and a number of remarkable Renaissance mansions – not to mention the atmospheric *barrios*, each with its own strong character and traditions – and you're looking at a stay of at least two days. Beyond Seville, the central and western regions of Andalucía are little visited – a great pity, as the city's province and its neighbour Huelva can spring a variety of surprises, both scenic and cultural, on visitors who wander off the beaten track to find them.

3

East of Seville, a clutch of smaller towns on the way to Córdoba includes Moorish **Carmona**, which possesses a remarkable Roman cemetery, and Baroque **Écija**, with its striking churches and mansions. Also in Seville's Campiña – the name given to this broad and fertile agricultural plain watered by the Guadalquivir – are the towns of **Osuna** and **Estepa**, both with their own Renaissance architectural gems. To the north, the wooded hills of the **Sierra Morena** offer welcome respite from the intense summer heat, with charming small towns making excellent base-camps for hiking.

The **province of Huelva**, which stretches from Seville to the Portuguese border, hardly deserves its tag as the least-visited province of Andalucía. The area boasts the huge **Parque Nacional de Doñana** spreading back from the Guadalquivir estuary in vast expanses of *marismas* – sand dunes, salt flats and marshes. The largest roadless area in western Europe, the park is vital to scores of migratory birds and to endangered mammals including the Iberian lynx, and is also home to Andalucía's rumbustious Whitsuntide pilgrimage and fair, the Romería del Rocío. **Huelva**, the provincial capital, although scarred by its industrial surrounds, tries its best to be welcoming and does have a number of things to see; it also makes a convenient base for trips to local sites associated with the voyages of Columbus, which set out from here. It was at the nearby monastery of **La Rábida** that the explorer's 1492 expedition was planned and from the tiny port of **Palos de la Frontera** that he eventually set sail to discover a new route to the

GRUTA DE LAS MARAVILLAS, SIERRA DE ARACENA

Highlights

❶ La Giralda and Catedral, Seville The city's landmark building and the world's largest Gothic church, whose soaring minaret – now the bell tower – is one of the most beautiful of all Moorish monuments. **See p.258**

❷ Alcázar, Seville A Moorish fortress-palace adorned with breathtakingly beautiful stuccowork, tiles and coffered ceilings within, and relaxing gardens without. **See p.263**

❸ Tapas bars, Seville The city that invented tapas has some of Spain's very best bars to sample them – two not to miss are *Bar Giralda* and *El Rinconcillo*. **See p.293**

❹ Semana Santa, Seville The solemn pomp and pagan ecstasy of the Holy Week processions are the most impressive and moving in Spain. **See pp.300–301**

❺ Coto de Doñana National Park Europe's largest and most important wildlife sanctuary. **See p.330**

❻ Costa de la Luz Huelva's stretch of the Atlantic coast has a string of enjoyable resorts and some of the finest beaches in Andalucía. **See p.335**

❼ Sierra de Aracena A landscape of wooded hills, babbling streams and attractive villages which produce the best cured ham in Spain. **See p.347**

HIGHLIGHTS ARE MARKED ON THE MAP ON PP.250–251

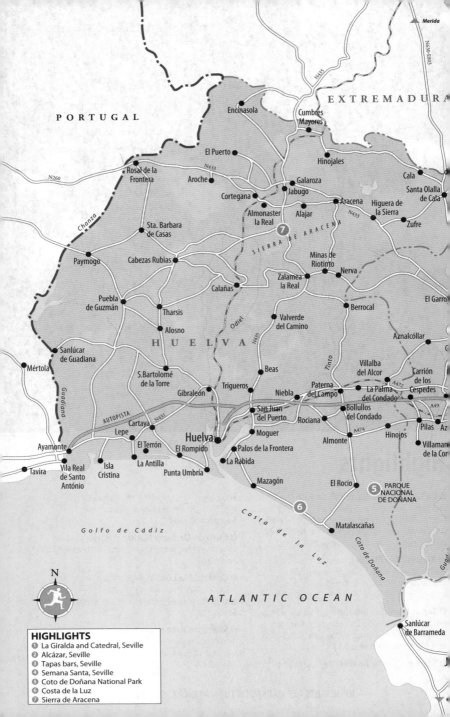

PORTUGAL

EXTREMADURA

Merida

N435

N630-E803

Encinasola

Cumbres
Mayores

El Puerto

Hinojales

Cala

Rosal de la
Frontera

N433

Aroche

Galaroza

Santa Olalla
de Cala

N260

Cortegana

Jabugo

Chanza

Sta. Barbara
de Casas

Almonaster
la Real

Alajar

Aracena

Higuera de
la Sierra

Zufre

N433

Paymogo

Cabezas Rubias

Calañas

SIERRA DE ARACENA

7

Minas de
Riotinto

Nerva

Puebla
de Guzmán

Tharsis

Zalamea
la Real

El Garro

Alosno

H U E L V A

Odiel

Valverde
del Camino

Berrocal

Aznalcóllar

Sanlúcar
de Guadiana

N435

Beas

Villalba
del Alcor

Mértola

S.Bartolomé
de la Torre

Trigueros

Tinto

Carrión
de los
Céspedes

Gibraleón

Niebla

Paterna
del Campo

La Palma
del Condado

A472

Guadiana

AUTOPISTA

N431

Cartaya

San Juan
del Puerto

Rociana

Bollullos
del Condado

A49

Ayamonte

Lepe

Huelva

Moguer

Almonte

Hinojos

Pilas

Az

El Terrón

Palos de la Frontera

A474

Villaman
de la Cor

Tavira

Vila Real
de Santo
António

Isla
Cristina

La Antilla

El Rompido

La Rábida

Punta Umbría

Mazagón

El Rocío

5 PARQUE
NACIONAL
DE DOÑANA

Golfo de Cádiz

C o s t a   d e   l a   L u z

6

Matalascañas

Coto de Doñana

Guad

N

ATLANTIC OCEAN

Sanlúcar
de Barrameda

HIGHLIGHTS
1 La Giralda and Catedral, Seville
2 Alcázar, Seville
3 Tapas bars, Seville
4 Semana Santa, Seville
5 Coto de Doñana National Park
6 Costa de la Luz
7 Sierra de Aracena

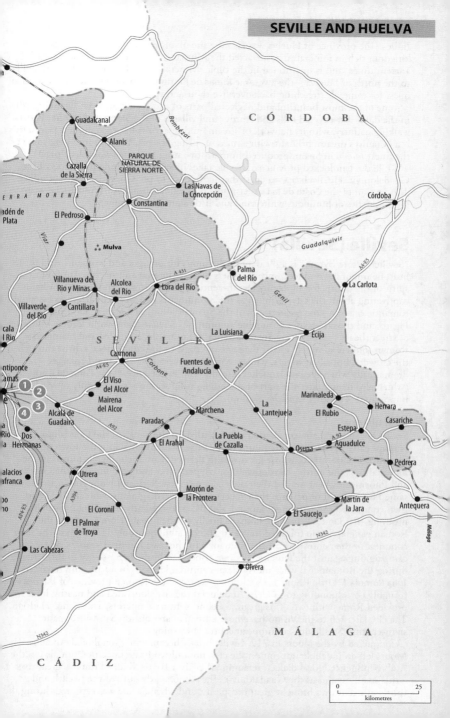

CÓRDOBA

Guadalcanal

Alanis

Cazalla
de la Sierra

PARQUE
NATURAL DE
SIERRA NORTE

Las Navas de
la Concepción

Córdoba

SIERRA MORENA

adén de
Plata

El Pedroso

Constantina

Viar

Mulva

Bembézar

Guadalquivir

A-4/E-5

Villanueva del
Rio y Minas

Alcolea
del Rio

Lora del Río

A 431

Palma
del Río

La Carlota

Villaverde
del Rio

Cantillara

Genil

cala
l Río

La Luisiana

Écija

SEVILLE

Carmona

Carbone

Fuentes de
Andalucía

A-364

ntiponce
amas

El Viso
del Alcor

Mairena
del Alcor

Marinaleda

Herrara

La
Lantejuela

El Rubio

Alcalá de
Guadaira

Paradas

Marchena

A 92

Estepa

Casariche

Dos
Hermanas

A-92

La Puebla
de Cazalla

Aguadulce

Osuna

Pedrera

El Arahal

Río
a Hermanas

Utrera

Palacios
afranca

Morón de
la Frontera

Martín de
la Jara

Antequera

Málaga

El Coronil

El Palmar
de Troya

El Saucejo

N-342

Las Cabezas

A-4/E-5

Olvera

MÁLAGA

CÁDIZ

N-342

0 — 25
kilometres

Indies. The province of Huelva was also the site of ancient Tartessus, a legendary kingdom rich in minerals that attracted the Minoans, Phoenicians and Greeks in ancient times, and is mentioned in the Bible. Minerals are still extracted from the hills to the north of Huelva – the awesome **Minas de Ríotinto** display evidence of the human quest for minerals stretching back over five thousand years.

Some of the most beautiful and neglected parts of this region are even further north, in the dark, ilex-covered hills and sturdy rural villages of the **Sierra de Aracena**. Perfect walking country, with its network of streams and reservoirs between modest peaks, this is a botanist's dream, brilliant with a mass of spring flowers. You also find here some of the finest *jamón* in Spain, produced from acorn-eating *cerdos ibéricos* (black pigs).

While the landlocked province of Seville takes its relaxation along the banks of the Guadalquivir, Huelva has a sea coast that harks back to pre-Costa del Sol tranquillity. This section of the **Costa de la Luz** has some of the finest beaches in Andalucía, with long stretches of luminous white sand and little sign of development.

Seville (Sevilla)

"Seville," wrote Byron, "is a pleasant city, famous for oranges and women." And for its heat, he might have added, since summers here are intense and start in April, but the spirit of the quote, for all its nineteenth-century chauvinism, is about right. What is captivating about the city, as much as the monuments and works of art, is its essential romantic quality – the greatest city of the Spanish south, of Carmen, Don Juan and Figaro, and the archetype of Andalucian promise. *Sevillanos* are world leaders in the art of street theatre, too. During **Semana Santa**, for example, sandalled and helmeted Roman soldiers sombrely escort the *paso*, or effigy, of the condemned Christ through the crowded but silent streets, while a couple of weeks later the mood changes dramatically when the city launches into the wild exuberance of the **Feria de Abril** (which also inaugurates the start of the bullfighting season – second only to Madrid's in importance – another *sevillano* passion).

Brief history

Seville began when ancient Iberian tribes settled on the banks of the Guadalquivir perhaps early in the first millennium BC. The settlement grew into the town now known as **El Carambolo**, whose great wealth derived from the minerals mined in the mountains to the north. The demand for copper, silver and gold lured in the Greeks and Phoenicians, who traded their own ceramics, jewellery and ivory goods. It was the same Phoenicians, or perhaps their successors the Carthaginians, who attacked and then conquered the settlement around 500 BC, subsequently renaming it **Hispalis**, meaning "flat land". When the **Romans** finally wrested Spain from Carthage the Roman general Scipio founded **Itálica** in 206 on a hill overlooking the river. The final conquest of the peninsula cost the Romans a further two hundred years of dogged campaigning against the ferocious Iberian tribes and in the latter stages of this struggle, during the Roman civil war, Julius Caesar captured Hispalis in 45 BC and renamed it **Julia Romula** ("Little Rome"). As a leading centre of the Roman province of Baetica (roughly corresponding to modern Andalucía) the city flourished and nearby Itálica provided Rome with two of its greatest second-century emperors, Trajan and Hadrian. The city later fell to the **Visigoths**, whose Christian archbishop San Isidro made sixth-century Seville into a European centre of learning.

Conquered by the **Moors** in 712, Seville briefly became the capital of al-Andalus. The Moors left an indelible imprint on the city, not only in its architecture, but also in the Arabic-influenced local dialect, renaming the River Baetis Wadi El Kabir ("great river"), a title it still retains as the Guadalquivir. The Almohad dynasty of the twelfth and thirteenth centuries brought great prosperity, and when Seville was captured during the

Reconquista by Fernando III in 1248 the city became a favoured residence of the Spanish monarchy, in particular Pedro the Cruel, who was responsible for the construction of the outstanding Alcázar. Religious intolerance racked the city in the wake of the Reconquest, however, and in 1391 the Jewish quarter in the Barrio Santa Cruz was sacked – a harbinger of the banishment of all Jews from Spain, to be proclaimed by Fernando and Isabel a century later.

The fifteenth century also saw, as well as the construction of the Cathedral, the **discovery of the New World** – an event that would catapult the city to the forefront of Spanish affairs. Seville's navigable river, with access to the Atlantic, made it a natural choice for the main port of commerce with the Americas. In the 1500s, as fabulous wealth poured in from the empire, Seville was transformed into one of the great cities of Europe and, with a population of over 150,000, one of the largest.

The **silting up of the Guadalquivir** in the 1680s deprived Seville of its port and with it the monopoly of trade with the Americas. The merchant fleet was transferred to Cádiz and the city went into a decline exacerbated by the great earthquake of 1755 which, although centred on Lisbon, caused much destruction. The city was further ravaged by the **Napoleonic occupation** of 1810–12 and was largely bypassed by the industrial revolution which permeated slowly from the north. It was only in the later nineteenth century that Seville was rediscovered by travellers such as Richard Ford, who declared it to be "the marvel of Andalucía".

While wealthy European travellers flocked to the city in the wake of Ford and other writers, life in the early twentieth century for the majority of *sevillanos* was harsh. The huge Spanish Americas Fair of 1929 (see p.270) was intended to launch the city into an economic revival but – coming at the time of a world recession – instead bankrupted it. In 1936 Seville was the first major city to fall to Franco's Nationalist forces at the start of the Civil War and the infamous General Queipo de Llano then subjected the city to a murderous repression in order to root out "villainous Marxists" in the working-class *barrios*. The long years of poverty that followed were only alleviated with the return of democracy and the election of a *sevillano* prime minister, Felipe González, in1982. During his years in power he pumped significant funds into his native city culminating with the AVE high-speed train connection to Madrid and a massive investment in infrastructure connected with the staging of Expo 92, a world fair to mark the quincentenary of Columbus's voyage to the Americas. In what was almost a re-run of the 1929 event, this once again left the city with colossal debts. Seville today projects a prosperous air despite many serious social, and not always visible, problems.

SEVILLE ORIENTATION

The **old city**, where you'll be spending most of your time, takes up the east bank of the Guadalquivir. At its heart, side by side, stand the three great monuments: the **Giralda** tower, the **Cathedral** and the **Alcázar**, with the cramped alleyways of the **Barrio Santa Cruz**, the medieval Jewish quarter and now the heart of tourist life, extending east of them. North and west of the *barrio* is the main shopping and commercial district, **El Centro**, its most obvious landmarks the **Plaza Nueva** and **Plaza Duque de la Victoria**, and the smart pedestrianized **Calle Sierpes** which runs between them. To the north lies the gritty **Macarena** quarter, from whose church the *paso* of the bejewelled Virgin of Macarena – the most revered in Seville – sails forth on the Maundy Thursday of Semana Santa to enormous popular acclaim. Just beyond the walls here in the converted sixteenth-century **Hospital de las Cinco Llagas** ("Five Wounds of Christ") is the permanent seat of the Andalucian parliament.

Across the river is the earthier, traditionally working-class district of **Triana**, flanked to the south by **Los Remedios**, the former business zone and now an upmarket residential quarter. Adjoining this to the south lie the grounds where Seville's Feria de Abril is held, and also on this bank, to the north of Triana, lie the remains of the **Expo 92 exhibition ground**, at Isla de la Cartuja.

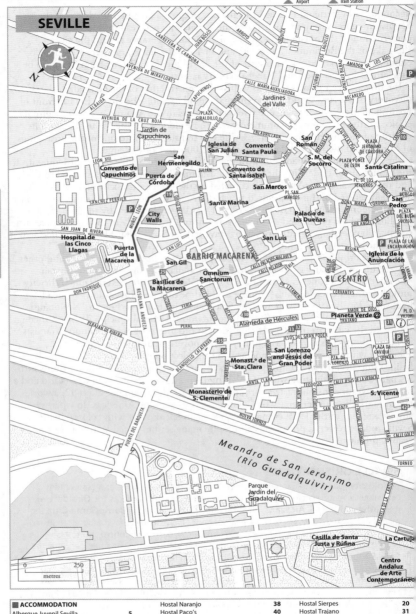

ACCOMMODATION		Hostal Naranjo	38	Hostal Sierpes	20
Albergue Juvenil Sevilla	5	Hostal Paco's	40	Hostal Trajano	31
Camping Villsom	6	Hostal Pérez Montilla	3	Hostería del Laurel	12
Casa La Luna	18	Hostal Puerta Carmona	1	Hotel Adriano	34
Hostal Alameda	33	Hostal Redes	42	Hotel Alcántara	9
Hostal Atenas	15	Hostal Romero	43	Hotel Alfonso XIII	17
Hostal Doña Feli	35	Hostal Santa María	22	Hotel Alminar	23
Hostal La Muralla	19	Hostal Santa María de la Blanca	7	Hotel Amadeus	13

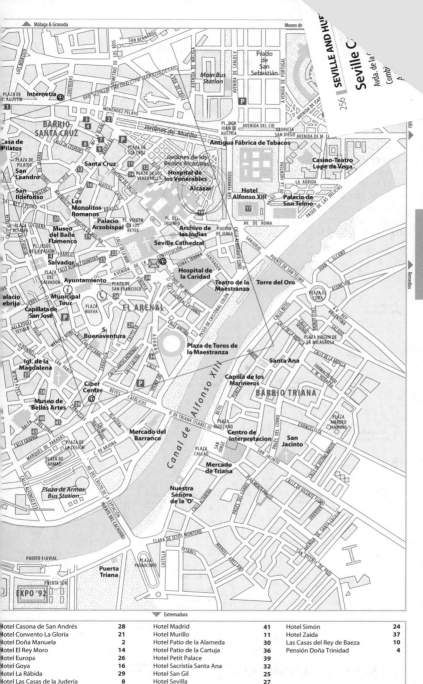

Málaga & Granada

Museo de

SEVILLE AND HUE

Seville C

256

3

Remedios

Extremadura

Hotel Casona de San Andrés	28	Hotel Madrid	41	Hotel Simón	24
Hotel Convento La Gloria	21	Hotel Murillo	11	Hotel Zaida	37
Hotel Doña Manuela	2	Hotel Patio de la Alameda	30	Las Casas del Rey de Baeza	10
Hotel El Rey Moro	14	Hotel Patio de la Cartuja	36	Pensión Doña Trinidad	4
Hotel Europa	26	Hotel Petit Palace	39		
Hotel Goya	16	Hotel Sacristía Santa Ana	32		
Hotel La Rábida	29	Hotel San Gil	25		
Hotel Las Casas de la Judería	8	Hotel Sevilla	27		

athedral

onstitución s/n • July & Aug Mon–Sat 9.30am–4pm, Sun 2.30–6pm; Sept–June Mon–Sat 11am–5pm, Sun 2.30–6pm •
ed ticket for cathedral and Giralda €8, under-16s free • Ⓦ catedraldesevilla.es

After the reconquest of Seville by Fernando III (1248), the Almohad mosque was consecrated to the Virgin Mary (the church's full name is La Catedral de Santa María de la Sede) and kept in use as the Christian cathedral. As such it survived until 1402, when the cathedral chapter dreamed up plans for a new and unrivalled monument to Christian glory: "a building on so magnificent a scale that posterity will believe we were mad". To this end the Almohad mosque (see box, p.261) was almost entirely demolished, and the largest Gothic church in the world, Seville's **Cathedral**, was completed, extraordinarily, in just over a century (1402–1506). As Norman Lewis said, "it expresses conquest and domination in architectural terms of sheer mass". Built upon the huge, rectangular base-plan of the old mosque whose minaret, the **Giralda**, now serves as the bell tower, it was given the extra dimension of height by the Christian architects, probably under the direction of the French master architect of Rouen Cathedral. It was previously reckoned to be the third-largest church in the world – after St Paul's in London and St Peter's in Rome – but

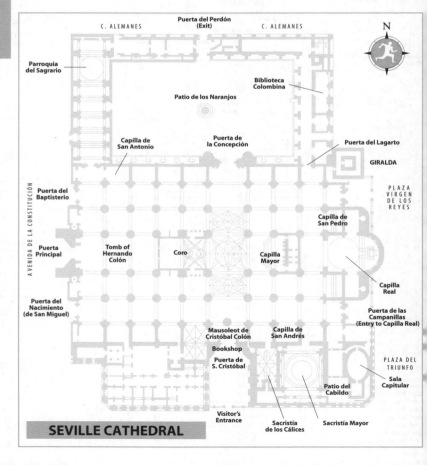

SEVILLE CATHEDRAL

new calculations based on cubic measurements have now placed it in the number one position, a claim upheld by the *Guinness Book of Records*, a copy of whose certificate is proudly displayed in the church.

Entry to the cathedral is through the **Puerta de San Cristóbal**, on the building's south side where, beyond a reception area displaying minor artworks by Murillo and Zurbarán among others, you enter the church to the west of the portal itself. If you're interested in studying the abundant artworks dotted around the various chapels en route, visit the bookshop at the entrance to obtain a copy of the official *Guide to the Cathedral of Seville*, which deals with them in detail.

Mausoleo de Cristóbal Colón

The enormous late nineteenth-century **Mausoleum of Christopher Columbus** (Cristóbal Colón in Spanish), by *sevillano* sculptor Arturo Mélida, may or may not house the navigator's remains. It was originally intended to be erected in the Cuban cathedral of Havana, then a Spanish colony, where it would have become a sepulchre for Columbus's remains, but the Spanish–American War – and Cuba's subsequent independence – intervened. As a result the plans were changed and the work was placed here. The mariner's coffin is held aloft by four huge allegorical figures, representing the kingdoms of León, Castile, Aragón and Navarra; the lance of Castile should be piercing a pomegranate (now inexplicably missing), the symbol of Granada (and the word for the fruit in Spanish), the last Moorish kingdom to be reconquered.

In the **nave**, first impressions are of the sheer size and grandeur of the place, but as you grow accustomed to the gloom, two other qualities stand out: the rhythmic balance and interplay between the parts, and an impressive overall simplicity and restraint in decoration. Successive ages have left monuments of their own, but these have been limited to the two rows of side chapels. In the main body of the cathedral only the great box-like structure of the **coro** (choir) stands out, filling the central portion of the nave.

Capilla Mayor

The **Capilla Mayor** (main chapel) is dominated by a vast and fabulous Gothic retablo composed of 45 carved scenes from the life of Christ. Begun in 1482 and the lifetime's work of a single craftsman, Fleming Pieter Dancart, this is the supreme masterpiece of the cathedral – the largest and richest altarpiece in the world and one of the finest examples of Gothic woodcarving. Above the central tabernacle, the Virgen de la Sede (Virgin of the Chair) is a stunning thirteenth-century Gothic figure of silver-plated cedar. Just to the right, a panel depicts an image of the Giralda as it appeared prior to any Renaissance additions.

Sacristía de los Cálices

In the church's southeast corner is the **Sacristía de los Cálices**, where many of the cathedral's main art treasures are displayed. Among some outstanding works are a masterly *Santas Justa y Rufina* by Goya, depicting Seville's patron saints who were put to death in 287 during the Roman emperor Diocletian's persecution of the Christians, and a powerful *Cristo Crucificado* by the same artist.

Sacristía Mayor

Behind the **Capilla de San Andrés**, which has an exceptional polychromed image of the crucified Christ by Juan Martínez Montañés, lies the grandiose sixteenth-century **Sacristía Mayor** designed in 1528 by Diego de Riaño. It's a prime example of the rich Plateresque style, and Riaño was one of the foremost exponents of this predominantly decorative architecture of the late Spanish Renaissance. Forming a veritable church-within-a-church it induced Philip II to remark to the members of the chapter: "Your sacristy is finer than my Chapel Royal". The sacristy houses more paintings, including a poignant *Santa Teresa* by Zurbarán, and the **treasury**, a dull collection of silver reliquaries and monstrances. Also here are the keys presented to Fernando III by the Jewish and Moorish communities on the surrender of the city in 1248; sculpted into the Moor's key in stylized Arabic script are the words "May Allah render eternal the dominion of Islam in this city". Nearby is a polychromed image of Fernando by Pedro Roldán, one of Andalucía's great eighteenth-century sculptors.

Sala Capitular
Passing through a small antechamber beyond the diminutive Patio del Cabildo brings you into the remarkable oval-shaped **Sala Capitular** (Chapter House), whose elaborate domed ceiling is mirrored in the outstanding geometric marble decoration of the floor. The stone benches provide seats for the members of the chapter. It contains a number of paintings by Murillo, a native of Seville, the finest of which, a flowing *Concepción Inmaculada*, occupies a place of honour high above the bishop's throne.

Capilla de San Antonio
On the southwest side of the cathedral is the **Puerta del Nacimiento**, the door through which pass all the *pasos* and penitents who take part in the Semana Santa processions; from here, turning right (north) along the west wall, passing the **Puerta Principal**, takes you to the northwest corner. Here the **Capilla de San Antonio** contains the *Vision of St Anthony*, a magnificent work by Murillo, depicting the saint in ecstatic pose before an infant Christ emerging from a luminous golden cloud. Try and spot where the restorers joined San Antonio back into place after he had been crudely hacked out of the picture by thieves in the nineteenth century. He was eventually discovered in New York and returned to the cathedral. The *Baptism of Jesus* above this is another fine work by the same artist.

Capilla Real
Entry from Plaza Virgen de los Reyes • Sat 8am–2pm & 4–7pm, Sun for services between 8.30am & 6pm • Free

The nave's north side leads to the **Puerta de la Concepción**, where an altar on the left side has a fine portrayal of the Virgen de Belén painted in 1635 by *granadino* artist Alonso Cano. Before exiting here, head for the northeast corner to view the domed Renaissance **Capilla Real**, built on the site of the original royal burial chapel and containing the body of Fernando III (El Santo) in a suitably rich, Baroque silver sepulchre before the altar. The large tombs on either side of the chapel are those of Fernando's wife, Beatrice of Swabia, and his son, Alfonso the Wise. The entrance to the chapel from the cathedral is normally closed, meaning that to view the interior you'll need to use the street entrance in the Plaza Virgen de los Reyes. As the chapel is used for services and private prayer no photography or conversation is allowed.

Capilla de San Pedro
To the north of the Capilla Real, the **Capilla de San Pedro** has a fine seventeenth-century retablo by Diego López Bueno with nine Zurbarán scenes depicting the life of St Peter (except for the image of God, which is a later replacement). Also here is the **Puerta del Lagarto** (Door of the Alligator), so named in commemoration of a stuffed reptile given to Alfonso X by the sultan of Egypt in 1260. A wooden replica now hangs in place of the perished original.

The Giralda
Unquestionably the most beautiful building in Seville, the **Giralda**, named after the sixteenth-century *giraldillo* or weather vane on its summit, dominates the skyline and, with its perfect synthesis of form and decoration, is one of the most important examples of Islamic architecture in the world.

WHERE LIES CHRISTOPHER COLUMBUS?

The dispute about Christopher Columbus's birthplace – claimed by both Italy and Spain – is matched by the labyrinthine controversy surrounding the **whereabouts of his remains**. After his death in **Valladolid** in 1506, Columbus was originally buried there, but three years later his remains were removed to **Seville** and interred at the monastery of Santa María de las Cuevas, across the river on La Cartuja island, to be joined shortly afterwards by those of his son Diego. But Diego's widow was determined to have both bodies interred in **Hispaniola** (modern Haiti and the Dominican Republic), the site of Columbus's first landfall in 1492, the capital of Spanish America and where Diego had served as governor. Following an intervention by the emperor Carlos V supporting her wishes, in 1544 the remains of both bodies were packed into lead coffins and shipped to the island, where they were placed in the cathedral. The remains of Columbus's grandson, Luís, were interred in the same cathedral in 1783.

Later, during repairs to the cathedral in Hispaniola, it seems that the coffins were mislaid, then opened, and the names mixed up. It did not take the authorities long to resolve the dilemma of which was which, by having all three sets of remains placed in one coffin. Shortly after 1795, when Spain was forced to cede Santo Domingo to the French, the remains were moved to Cuba and the cathedral in **Havana**, still Spanish territory. When Cuba was lost in 1898 the remains were transported back across the Atlantic and placed in the tomb in Seville. The lingering uncertainty lies in the accidental discovery in 1879 of another lead coffin in the cathedral in **Santo Domingo** bearing a silver plate inscribed with Columbus's name. This box of remains then disappeared, and despite the government of the Dominican Republic's claim to have recovered them (now enshrined in a national monument), numerous coffins of bones claiming to be the same have made frequent appearances at auction houses ever since.

Were the correct remains dispatched from Santo Domingo to Havana in 1795? Was the discovery of 1879 a fraud? Are the remains in the tomb today really those of Christopher, Diego and Luís? The only certainty in the story is that one member of the Columbus family, at least, was buried in Seville's cathedral and has stayed here – Christopher's bookish son **Hernando**, who wrote a biography of his father and donated his large library to what became the cathedral's Biblioteca Colombina. His tombstone lies in the centre of the pavement towards the main west door, the Puerta Principal, flanked by smaller slabs portraying sailing vessels.

In 2002, science was called on to try to resolve the mystery and a plan was drawn up to subject all the known remains of Columbus family members to **DNA testing** in the hope that a common genetic code could be established. Initial reports on samples taken from the Seville tomb by scientists at Granada university were inconclusive due to the poor condition of the remains, although the tests did indicate that there were matches with other members of the family. A request was then made to test the remains in Santo Domingo which – if this proved negative – would go some way to confirming the authenticity of those in Seville. After initially agreeing to this request the government of the Dominican Republic had second thoughts. An announcement by scientists that the Santo Domingo remains are not those of Columbus would be hugely embarrassing for a country where the navigator is a national hero. Thus in early 2005 the republic's government stated that it didn't have sufficient confidence in the reliability of DNA testing to allow the research to go ahead. When the Spanish ambassador announced that Spain would not make an issue of the matter the outcome of this tortuously tangled tale was, for the time being, put on hold, leaving the location of Columbus's remains a mystery for at least a few more years yet.

Some experts are convinced that Columbus's remains may lie in both the Dominican Republic and Seville, as the remains found in the cathedral tomb do not make up a complete skeleton. When the Dominican Republic eventually allows access to their remains it could well be proven that the navigator's bones lie on both sides of the Atlantic: a messy but probably apt ending to the story. Experts are now using the DNA samples to try to unravel the other prickly problem – where he was born.

3

Formerly the minaret of the mosque that once stood here, the Giralda was the culmination of **Almohad architecture** and served as a model for those at the imperial capitals of Rabat and Marrakesh. Said to be built on a foundation of destroyed Roman statuary, it was designed by the architect of the original mosque, Ahmed ibn Baso, and was used by the Moors both for calling the faithful to prayer and as an observatory. They so worshipped the building that they planned to destroy it before the Christian conquest of Seville, but were prevented from doing so by the threat of Alfonso (later King Alfonso X) that "if they removed a single stone, they would all be put to the sword". Instead the

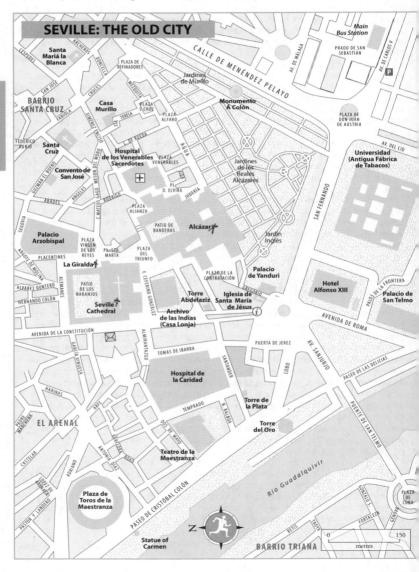

MOORISH SEVILLE

Seville was one of the earliest **Moorish conquests** (in 712) and, as part of the caliphate of Córdoba, became the second city of al-Andalus. When the caliphate broke up in the early eleventh century it was by far the most powerful of the independent states (or *taifas*) to emerge, extending its power over the Algarve and eventually over Jaén, Murcia and Córdoba itself. This period, under a series of three Arabic rulers from the **Abbadid** dynasty (1023–91), was something of a golden age. The city's court was unrivalled in wealth, luxury and sophistication, developing a strong chivalric element and a flair for poetry – one of the most skilled exponents was the last ruler, al Mu'tamid, the "poet-king". But with sophistication came decadence, and in 1091 Abbadid rule was usurped by a new force, the **Almoravids**, a tribe of fanatical Berber Muslims from North Africa, to whom the Andalucians had appealed for help against the threat from the northern Christian kingdoms.

Despite initial military successes, the Almoravids failed to consolidate their gains in al-Andalus and attempted to rule through military governors from Marrakesh. In the middle of the twelfth century they were in turn supplanted by a new Berber incursion, the **Almohads**, who by about 1170 had recaptured virtually all the former territories. Seville accepted Almohad rule in 1147 and became the capital of this last real empire of the Moors in Spain. Almohad power was sustained until their disastrous defeat in 1212 by the combined Christian armies of the north, at Las Navas de Tolosa in Jaén. Within this brief and precarious period Seville underwent a renaissance of public building, characterized by a new vigour and fluidity of style. The Almohads rebuilt the Alcázar, enlarged the principal mosque and erected a new and brilliant minaret, a tower over 100m tall, topped with four copper spheres that could be seen from miles around: the Giralda.

3

Giralda went on to become the bell tower of the Christian cathedral. The Patio de los Naranjos (see below), the old entrance to the mosque, also survives intact.

The structure took twelve years to build (1184–96) and derives its firm, simple beauty from the shadows formed by blocks of brick trelliswork or *ajaracas*, different on each side, and relieved by a succession of arched niches and windows. The original harmony has been somewhat blemished by the Renaissance-era addition of balconies and, to a still greater extent, by the four diminishing storeys of the belfry – added, along with the Italian-sculpted bronze figure of Faith which surmounts them, in 1560–68, following the demolition by an earthquake of the original copper spheres. The fact that a weather vane blown by the four winds should epitomize the ideal of constant faith, or that this female figure should possess a masculine name ("Giraldillo"), has never seemed to trouble whimsical *sevillanos*.

From inside the cathedral you can **climb to the bell chamber** for a remarkable view of the city – and, equally remarkable, a glimpse of the Gothic details of the cathedral's buttresses and statuary. Keep an eye out, too, for the colony of kestrels which has long nested in the tower – the descendants no doubt of the "twittering, careering hawks" seen by Ford when he climbed up here in the 1830s. Most impressive is the tower's inner construction, a series of 35 gently inclined ramps wide enough for two mounted guards to pass.

The Patio de los Naranjos

The **Patio de los Naranjos** takes its name from the orange trees that now shade the former mosque's entrance courtyard where ritual ablutions were performed prior to worship. In the centre of the patio a Moorish fountain incorporates a sixth-century carved marble font, a surviving remnant of the earlier Visigothic cathedral which was itself levelled to make way for the mosque. Cross to the patio's northern side and the **Puerta del Perdón**, the mosque's original entrance. Although sadly marred by Renaissance embellishments, there remains some exquisite Almohad plasterwork and the original great doors made from larchwood faced with bronze. Minute Kufic script inside the lozenges proclaims that "the empire is Allah's". The pierced bronze door-knockers are copies of the beautiful hand-crafted twelfth-century originals now preserved inside the church (not currently on view).

The Archivo de las Indias

Avda. de la Constitución 3 • Mon–Sat 9.30am–4.45pm, Sun 10am–1.45pm • Free

If you've been inspired by the Columbus saga after seeing his monument in the cathedral, visit the **Casa Lonja**, opposite the cathedral. Built in the severe and uncompromising style of El Escorial near Madrid, and designed by the same architect, Juan de Herrera, it was the former merchants' commodity exchange (*lonja*), adapted in the eighteenth century to house the remarkable **Archivo de las Indias**, a monumental storehouse of the archives of the Spanish empire. Following a three-year restoration programme the archive (holding 38,000 documents and files covering four centuries of Spanish rule) has been moved around the corner to the Cilla Cabildo on Calle Tormes, revealing Herrera's masterpiece in all its splendour. The exterior is defined by four identical facades, with corner pyramids supporting weather vanes. Inside, the sumptuous marble floors, bookcases in Cuban wood, arcaded central patio and grand staircase in pink and black marble are a visual feast. The upper floor houses temporary exhibitions of interesting documents from the archive; these frequently include items such as Columbus's log and a letter from Cervantes (pre-*Don Quixote*) petitioning the king for a position in the Americas – fortunately for world literature, he was turned down.

The Ayuntamiento

Avda. de la Constitución • Tours Tues, Wed & Thurs 5.30pm & 6pm; closed Aug • Free • ☎ 955 470 243 (Spanish)

North of the cathedral, the sixteenth-century **Ayuntamiento** is also well worth a visit, with a richly ornamented Plateresque facade by Diego de Riaño, one of the finest in Spain. Substantially enlarged early in the nineteenth century, the building's western exterior facing Plaza Nueva dates entirely from this time and forgoes the exuberant decoration of the original. The interior – decorated with numerous artworks including canvases by Zurbarán and Murillo – features Riaño's star-vaulted *vestíbulo* (entrance hall), the elaborately ornate Sala de Consistorio (council chamber) and a Sala de Consistorio above it, with a ravishing gilded coffered ceiling dating from the time of Philip II.

During the Semana Santa processions **Plaza de San Francisco** in front of the Ayuntamiento is part of the official route leading to the cathedral, and huge temporary grandstands fill the square providing prime vantage points for the city's dignitaries and their families and friends. The pointed *capirote* hoods worn by the penitent brotherhoods are eerily identical to those worn by the inquisitors of the Spanish Inquisition who, between the fifteenth and eighteenth centuries, sentenced an untold number of "heretics" to death by burning in public autos-de-fe, or trials, held in this same square.

WHO WILL BUY MY BEAUTIFUL ORANGES?

Sevillanos love to tell each other stories of seeing tourists picking oranges from trees in the streets of Seville only to spit out their first mouthful of the bitter, tart tasting fruit. However, because of its high pectin content, compared with the sweet orange, the **Seville orange** (*Citrus aurantium*) is prized by marmalade manufacturers as it gives a better set and higher yield. The Seville orange is also used for compotes and orange-flavoured liqueurs. Each year workers from the Seville town hall harvest 150,000 tonnes of fruit from the city's forty thousand trees the best of which is then shipped off to British marmalade factories. In recent years though, the amount exported has fallen due to contamination of the fruit by the city's traffic fumes and changing tastes in Britain. Increasingly, the unsold, inferior and contaminated oranges are turned into fertilizer.

The Alcázar

Entrance on Plaza del Triunfo • April–Sept daily 9.30am–7pm; Oct–March Mon–Sat 9.30am–5pm, Sun 9.30am–1.30pm • €7.50 •
Ⓦ patronato-alcazarsevilla.es

Rulers of Seville occupied the site of the **Alcázar** from the time of the Romans. The fortified palace was probably founded in the eighth century on the ruins of a Roman barracks, with the surrounding walls being added in the ninth. In the eleventh century it was expanded to become the great court of the **Abbadid** dynasty, who turned the wealth gained from the production of olive oil, sugar cane and dyes into a palace worthy of their hubris. This regime reached a peak of sophistication and decadence under the ruthless al Mu'tamid, a ruler who further enlarged the Alcázar in order to house a harem of eight hundred women, and decorated the terraces with flowers planted in the skulls of his decapitated enemies. Later, in the twelfth and thirteenth centuries under the **Almohads**, the complex was turned into a citadel, forming the heart of the town's fortifications. Its extent was enormous, stretching to the Torre del Oro on the bank of the Guadalquivir. Parts of the Almohad walls survive, but the present structure dates almost entirely from the Christian period following the fall of the city in 1248.

Seville was a favoured residence of the Spanish kings for some four centuries after the *Reconquista* – most particularly of **Pedro the Cruel** (Pedro I, 1350–69) who, with his

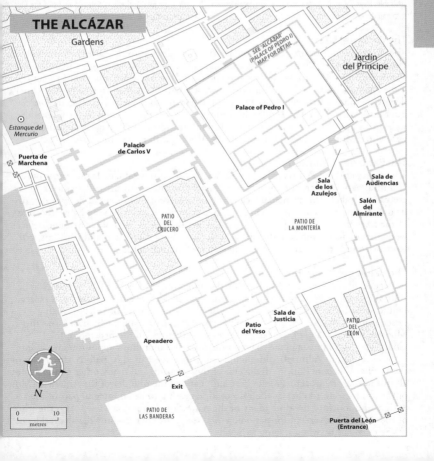

mistress María de Padilla, lived in and ruled from the Alcázar. Pedro embarked upon a complete rebuilding of the palace, utilizing fragments of earlier Moorish buildings in Seville, Córdoba and Valencia. Pedro's works form the nucleus of the Alcázar as it is today and, despite numerous restorations necessitated by fires and earth tremors, offer some of the best surviving examples of Mudéjar architecture – the style developed by Moors working under Christian rule.

Later monarchs have also left many traces and additions. In the **fifteenth century** Isabel built a new wing in which to organize expeditions to the Americas and control the new territories; in the sixteenth century Carlos V married a Portuguese princess in the palace, adding huge apartments for the occasion; and under Felipe IV (c.1624) extensive renovations were carried out to the existing rooms. On a more mundane level, kitchens were installed to provide for General Franco, who stayed in the royal apartments whenever he visited Seville.

INFORMATION   **THE ALCÁZAR**

Visiting the Alcázar The pressure of visitors to the Alcázar has resulted in the introduction of a flow-control system whereby 750 people are allowed in every 20–30min. It's still advisable, however, to visit early morning or late afternoon to savour the experience in relative calm.

Guidebooks An official guidebook to the complex is on sale at the gift shop in the Apeadero (see p.267) near the exit (there's a short cut to it from the Patio de la Montería – ask a guardian); this has detailed maps of the palaces and information on the gardens beyond.

The Patio del León

The Alcázar is entered from the Plaza del Triunfo, adjacent to the cathedral, through the **Puerta del León**, which bears a heraldic image of a lion in fourteenth-century glazed tiles above the lintel. The gateway, flanked by original Almohad walls, opens onto a courtyard – the **Patio del León** – where Pedro (who was known as "the Just" as well as "the Cruel", depending on one's fortunes) used to give judgement; to the left is the Sala de Justicia built by Alfonso XI in the 1340s with exquisite *yesería* (plasterwork) in the Grenadine style and a beautiful *artesonado* ceiling. Beyond, the restored **Patio del Yeso** is the only visible surviving remnant of the Almohads' Alcázar, with more fine plasterwork.

The Patio de la Montería

The main facade of Pedro's palace stands at the end of the **Patio de la Montería**, or "hunting patio", where the royal hunt gathered; on either side are galleried buildings erected by Isabel. This principal facade is pure fourteenth-century Mudéjar and, with its delicate, marble-columned windows, stalactite frieze and overhanging roof, is one of the finest features of the whole Alcázar. The castles, lions and other heraldic devices were intended to emphasize the king's power over both Christians and Muslims, but Kufic lettering still proclaims that "There is no God but Allah".

The Salón del Almirante

It's a good idea to look round the **Salón del Almirante** (or Casa de la Contratación de Indias), the sixteenth-century building on the right, before entering the main palace. Founded by Isabel in 1503 as an office where personnel could be hired to man expeditions to the New World, this gives you a standard against which to assess the Moorish forms. Many of the early voyages were planned in the first room, the Cuarto del Almirante, a name that commemorates Columbus's appointment as Gran Almirante (Senior Admiral), although he probably never used it. Balboa, discoverer of the Pacific, Vincente Pinzón, discoverer of the Amazon, and many other conquistadors all spread their maps across tables here and planned the plunder of the Americas. Most of the rooms seem too heavy, their decoration ceasing to be an integral part of the design, and much of the time many of them are closed to public view – as is the whole of the upper floor (except for periodic visits, see p.265), which provides the residence of the royal family when staying in Seville.

The only notable exception, architecturally speaking, is the **Sala de Audiencias** (or Capilla de los Navegantes), with its magnificent *artesonado* ceiling inlaid with golden rosettes. Within is a fine early sixteenth-century retablo by Alejo Fernández depicting the Virgin of the Navigators spreading her protective mantle over the conquistadors and their ships – which are so well portrayed that they have been of great assistance to naval historians. Columbus (dressed in gold) is flanked by the Pinzón brothers who sailed with him on his first voyage to the New World, while Carlos V (in a red cloak) shelters beneath the Virgin. In the rear to the left are the kneeling figures of the Indians to whom the dubious blessings of Christianity had been brought by the Spanish conquest. The painting synthesizes the sense of a divine mission – given to Spain by God – prevalent at the time. Beside the altarpiece stands a model of the Santa María, Columbus's first flagship. Slightly further along the patio to the right lies the entrance to the **Sala de los Azulejos** containing a display of relatively modern tilework and, beyond, a couple of delightfully serene patios.

The Palacio Real Alto

Tours daily every 30min 10am–1.30pm; 30min; 30min • €4.20 (maximum of 15 persons per visit)

The royal apartments, known as the **Palacio Real Alto**, are open for visits when not in use and shouldn't be missed. Tours take in the **royal chapel**, with an exquisite early sixteenth-century retablo consisting of painted *azulejos* (tiles) by Nicola Pisano, the so-called bedroom of Pedro I, with fine early Mudéjar plasterwork and *artesonado* ceiling, and the equally splendid Sala de Audiencias – with more stunning plaster and tile decoration – which is still used by the royal family when receiving visitors in Seville.

The Palace of Pedro I

As you enter the main **Palace of Pedro I**, the "domestic" nature of Moorish and Mudéjar architecture is immediately striking. This involves no loss of grandeur but simply a shift in scale: the apartments are remarkably small, shaped to human needs, and take their

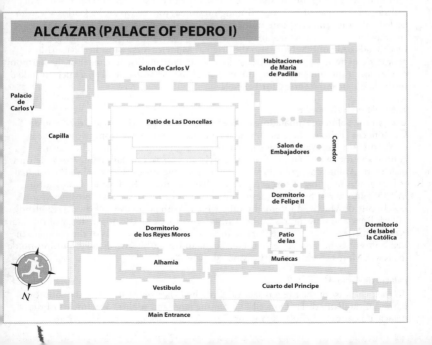

ALCÁZAR (PALACE OF PEDRO I)

- Salon de Carlos V
- Habitaciones de Maria de Padilla
- Palacio de Carlos V
- Capilla
- Patio de Las Doncellas
- Salon de Embajadores
- Comedor
- Dormitorio de Felipe II
- Dormitorio de Isabel la Católica
- Dormitorio de los Reyes Moros
- Patio de las Muñecas
- Alhamia
- Vestibulo
- Cuarto del Principe
- Main Entrance

N

beauty from the exuberance of the decoration and the imaginative use of space and light. There is, too, a deliberate disorientation in the layout of the rooms, which makes the palace seem infinitely larger and more open than it really is.

Patio de las Doncellas

From the entrance court a narrow passage leads beyond the **Vestíbulo**, where visitors removed their outer clothing, straight into the central courtyard, the **Patio de las Doncellas** (Patio of the Maidens), its name recalling the Christians' tribute of one hundred virgins presented annually to the Moorish kings. The heart of the patio has been restored to its original fourteenth-century state after being buried under a tiled pavement for four centuries. Archeologists have replanted the six orange trees that once grew in sunken gardens to either side of a central pool, filled with goldfish – as it was in the time of Pedro I – a medieval method of eliminating mosquitoes in summer. The court's plaster frieze and dado composed of polychrome *azulejos* and doors are all of the highest Granada craftsmanship, and are the finest in the palace. Interestingly, it's also the one location where Renaissance restorations are successfully fused – the double columns and upper storey were added by Carlos V, whose *Plus Ultra* ("Yet still further") motto recurs in the decorations here and elsewhere.

The Salón de Embajadores

Beyond the **Salón de Carlos V**, distinguished by a truly magnificent *artesonado* ceiling, are three rooms from the original fourteenth-century design built for María de Padilla (who was popularly thought to use magic in order to maintain her hold over Pedro – and perhaps over other gallants at court, too, who used to drink her bath water). These open onto the **Salón de Embajadores** (Salon of the Ambassadors), the most brilliant room of the Alcázar, with a stupendous wooden dome of red, green and gold cells, and horseshoe arcades inspired by the great palace of Medina Azahara outside Córdoba. An inscription in Arabic states that it was constructed by craftsmen from Toledo and completed in 1366. Although restored, for the worse, by Carlos V – who added balconies and an incongruous frieze of royal portraits to commemorate his marriage to Isabel of Portugal here – the salon stands comparison with the great rooms of Granada's Alhambra. Note also the original Mudéjar tiles, with their Moorish geometric patterns expressing artistically the fundamental Islamic tenet of the harmony of creation. Adjoining are a long dining hall (*comedor*) and a small apartment installed in the late sixteenth century for Felipe II.

The Patio de las Muñecas

Beyond the **Salón de Embajadores** is the last great room of the palace, the **Patio de las Muñecas** (Patio of the Dolls), which takes its curious name from two tiny faces decorating the inner and outer surfaces of one of the smaller arches. The elegant columns in the tenth-century Caliphate style are believed to have come from the ruins of Medina Azahara near Córdoba. Thought to be the site of the harem in the original palace, it was here that Pedro is reputed to have murdered his brother Don Fadrique in 1358; another of his royal guests, Abu Said of Granada, was murdered here for his jewels, one of which – an immense ruby which Pedro later gave to Edward, England's "Black Prince" – now figures in the British Crown Jewels. The upper storey of the court is a much later, nineteenth-century restoration. On the other sides of the patio are the bedrooms of Isabel and of her son Don Juan, and the arbitrarily named Dormitorio de los Reyes Moros (Bedroom of the Moorish Kings).

Palacio de Carlos V

To the northeast of the main palace (and reached via a stairway out of the southeast corner of the Patio de las Doncellas) loom the large and soulless apartments of the **Palacio de Carlos V**. With its many tapestries (eighteenth-century copies of the sixteenth-century originals now in Madrid) and pink-orange or yellow paintwork, the apartments' classical style asserts a different and inferior mood to the main palace.

The Alcázar gardens

The beautiful and relaxing Alcázar **gardens** are the rambling but enticing product of several eras. Here are the vaulted **baths** in which María de Padilla was supposed to have bathed (actually an auxiliary water supply for the palace), and the **Estanque del Mercurio**, a pool with a bronze figure of the messenger of the gods at its centre, specially built for Felipe V (1733), who whiled away two solitary years at the Alcázar fishing here and preparing himself for death through religious flagellation. In the gardens proper – and close to an unusual maze of myrtle bushes – lies the pavilion (*pabellón*) of Carlos V, the only survivor of several he built in the gardens. This one, designed by Juan Hernández, was completed in 1543 and has the king's motto, *Plus Ultra*, displayed on the tiles of the steps leading to the pavilion's entrance.

The gardens are a spacious and tranquil haven – filled with birdsong and the cries of resident peacocks – to escape the crowds; particularly the **Jardín Inglés** on the southwest side, which would make an ideal place for a picnic. A *cafetería* can be reached via the Puerta de Marchena, to the left of the Estanque del Mercurio, which has a pleasant terrace overlooking the gardens.

The way out is via the **Apeadero**, a large coach hall built for Philip V in the eighteenth century, which housed not only the coaches used by the royals, but also legions of servants who slept on the floor. Beyond lies the impressive **Patio de las Banderas** (Patio of the Flags) edged with orange trees and until fairly recently the parade ground of the military barracks surrounding it, now luxury apartments. The flags of the various regiments were assembled here and reviewed by the king prior to battle. Exit from this square to the street, where you emerge on the edge of the Barrio Santa Cruz.

The Barrio Santa Cruz

Spreading away to the east side of the cathedral the **Barrio Santa Cruz** is very much in character with Seville's romantic image, its streets narrow and tortuous to keep out the sun, the houses brilliantly whitewashed and festooned with flowering plants. Many of the windows are barricaded with *rejas* (iron grilles) behind which girls once kept chaste evening rendezvous with their paramours who were forced to *comer hierro* ("eat iron") as passion mounted. Almost all of the houses have patios, often surprisingly large, which in summer become the principal family living room. Most of the time they can be admired from the street beyond the wrought-iron screen inside the doorway, something the residents don't appear to mind.

Hospital de los Venerables Sacerdotes

Plaza Venerables • Tours daily 10am–2pm & 4–8pm • €4.75

One of the most beautiful patios is within the **Baroque Hospital de los Venerables Sacerdotes**, on the northeast side of the Alcázar, originally a home for infirm clerics. Built around the patio, the hospice and church now house an outstanding gallery including sculptures by Martínez Montañés, Pedro and Luisa Roldán, a painting of the Last Supper by Lucás Valdés, plus some wonderfully restored frescoes by the same artist and his son Valdés Leal. The museum is also home to the new **Centro Velázquez** which, besides works by the master – including an image of Santa Rufina and a spectacular *Inmaculada Concepción* – displays canvases by Pacheco, Murillo and Zurbarán.

South of the Cathedral

South of the cathedral stand a number of buildings of note: the **Hotel Alfonso XIII**, the **Palacio de San Telmo** and the **Fábrica de Tabacos**, the city's old tobacco factory and the

A WALK AROUND THE BARRIO SANTA CRUZ

The Barrio Santa Cruz is a great place for a stroll with no set route to follow. The following walk highlights just a few of the *barrio*'s many features.

Starting out from **Plaza Virgen de los Reyes**, behind the cathedral, the **Palacio Arzobispal** (free access to the patio if open) conceals, behind a Baroque facade, a remarkable staircase made entirely of jasper. Along C/Mateos Gago, **Bar Giralda** at no. 2 incorporates part of a Moorish hammam (steam baths), while over the road and up a bit, at no. 20, is one of Seville's institutions, the hole-in-the-wall **bodega of Juan García Aviles** (see p.294) with its prized gleaming bar counter of Spanish mahogany, well over a century old and one of the few remaining in the city. Juan García passed away in 1996, and the bar has been officially retitled *Bar Alvaro Peregil* – both names are visible on the building – but otherwise it remains as its original owner left it.

When you've downed a *manzanilla*, continue east and turn right into C/Mesón del Moro where the slightly incongruous **San Marco** pizzeria at no. 4 is another establishment operating inside a splendid Moorish bathhouse. Further up C/Mateos Gago, a left turn will bring you into C/Guzmán El Bueno where, at no. 10, the charming sisters at the **Convento de San José** will allow you to view (outside siesta period; free, but a small contribution is appreciated) some remarkable Mudéjar plaster decoration (its ornate appearance is on a par with the Alcázar) in what was the salon, and is now the chapel, of this former fourteenth-century palace. This street has some particularly lovely **patios** – take a look at no. 4, with its plants, *azulejos*, wall-mounted bulls' heads and Roman statuary.

Retracing your steps and following C/Mesón del Moro will bring you – via C/Ximénez de Enciso (a left and then a right) – to C/Santa Teresa where, at no. 8, you'll find the **Casa Murillo** (currently closed for refurbishment). Located in the artist's seventeenth-century home, this house-museum is furnished with contemporaneous artworks, craftsmanship and furniture, but, somewhat disappointingly, none of Murillo's original paintings.

PLAZA SANTA CRUZ AND SANTA MARÍA LA BLANCA

Continuing along C/Santa Teresa – note the old grindstones sunk into the wall on the left – will bring you to the delightful **Plaza Santa Cruz** where, until the French burned it down in 1810, stood the church which gave the square (and the *barrio*) its name and in which Murillo was

setting for Bizet's *Carmen*. Further south, but still just ten minutes from the Giralda, lies the **Plaza de España** and adjoining **Parque de María Luisa** (María Luisa park) – laid out in 1929 for a gargantuan "Fair of the Americas", these are among the most impressive public spaces in Spain. Within the park the **Museo Arqueológico** houses Andalucía's most important archeological collection.

Hotel Alfonso XIII

C/San Fernando 2 · Daily · Free

The **Hotel Alfonso XIII**, Seville's grandest, is worth a look inside – no one minds as long as you aren't dressed too outrageously. Named after the ill-starred monarch Alfonso XIII who was forced to abdicate soon afterwards, it was built to house important guests attending the 1929 exhibition, and an elegant neo-Baroque facade conceals one of the city's most beautiful patios, best enjoyed over a beer or afternoon tea.

Palacio de San Telmo

Avda. de Roma s/n · Tours Mon–Fri (must be booked in advance) · Free · ☎ 955 001010, ✉ visitasantelmo@juntadeandalucia.es

Slightly west of the *Hotel Alfonso XIII*, the **Palacio de San Telmo**, built as a marine training academy for the Indies fleet and completed in 1734, is another expression of Seville's full-tilt Baroque period. During the mid-nineteenth century, it was purchased by the dukes of Montpensier, a member of whose family – the dowager duchess María Luisa – in 1893 presented part of the palace's vast grounds to the city, which became the park now named after her. The palace's main facade overlooks Avenida de Roma and has a marvellous Churrigueresque entrance arch topped – in a central niche – by San Telmo (of St Elmo's fire fame), patron saint of navigators. The building fell into a buried. The French consulate appears to see no irony in occupying a building directly overlooking the scene of Napoleonic devastation. The attractive seventeenth-century **cross**, circled by rose bushes, marks the centre of the original church and was placed here when the plaza was created in 1918.

Heading east along *calles* Mezquita and Doncellas brings you to the ancient Gothic-Baroque church of **Santa María La Blanca**, on the street of the same name, which has, built into its south wall in C/de los Archeros, the entrance to the original synagogue, the only surviving architectural remnant of the Jewish quarter. The church's main portal is flanked by Visigothic columns probably from a church pre-dating both the synagogue and the Moorish period, while the interior has lots of *azulejos* from Triana as well as an extravagant filigree stucco ceiling and two artistic gems: a moving *piedad* (pietà) by the sixteenth-century artist Luís de Vargas, and a fine *Last Supper* by Murillo, the latter a rare tenebrist work.

In the next street along from the church on the right heading north, the tiny C/Dos Hermanas has, at no. 7, the **Casas de la Judería** hotel – a restored *casa señorial* formerly the residence of the dukes of Bejar – whose beautiful patio is worth a look, perhaps over a drink from the bar.

JARDINES DE MURILLO AND THE PLAZA DE LOS VENERABLES

An alternative route heads south from Plaza de Santa Cruz to the **Jardines de Murillo**, another peaceful oasis and a place to get your breath back in the midst of shady arbours decorated with Triana tiles.

Alternatively, head west from the plaza along Callejón del Agua back towards the town centre. The **Corral del Agua** restaurant (at Callejón del Agua 6) has yet another fine patio quickly followed by the charming, plant-bedecked **C/Pimienta** (Pepper St), thought to take its name from a Jewish spice merchant who once lived here.

Turn right along here, at the end turning right again to reach the **Plaza de los Venerables** where, if you don't want see the artworks inside the Hospital de los Venerables (see p.267) you could visit the plaza's celebrated tapas bars: the **Hostería del Laurel** and the **Casa Román**. Otherwise, heading north and then west along C/Jamerdana and the Pasaje Vila returns you to the C/Mateos Gago, just before which (on the tiny C/Rodrigo Caro) there's the **Bodega Santa Cruz**, another – and cheaper – Seville tapas institution.

3

ruinous state in the latter part of the twentieth century and a five-year refurbishment was completed in 2010. The building now houses the office of the President of the Junta de Andalucía (the region's autonomous government) and other regional government departments. Inside, highlights include two beautiful pillared patios, marble staircases as well as a church with an exquisite painted cupola.

Santa María de Jesús

Near the Palacio de San Telmo, on the northeast side of the Puerta de Jerez road junction – a name referring to its former importance as one of the twenty gates in the city's ancient walls – on the corner of Calle San Gregorio, lies the small former mosque and now chapel of **Santa María de Jesús** (open during service times). Converted into a Christian church in 1248, it was frequently visited by Columbus on his trips to the city.

Antigua Fábrica de Tabacos

C/San Fernando 4 • Access to public areas Mon–Fri 10am–8pm & Sat 10am–2pm • Free

The **Antigua Fábrica de Tabacos**, or Old Tobacco Factory, just behind the *Hotel Alfonso XIII* along Avenida San Fernando, was where Carmen – in the nineteenth-century story by Mérimée made into an opera by Bizet – worked as a cigar maker. A beautiful and sensual *gitana* (gypsy), she falls in love with Don José, a corporal, who deserts his regiment to join her band of smugglers. When Carmen tires of him and transfers her affections to the toreador Escamillo, an insanely jealous Don José stabs her to death outside the bullring where a statue of "Carmen" now stands. Legions of foreign travellers later made pilgrimages to Seville in search of their own Carmen. The disillusion of the 1930s Irish traveller Walter Starkie was typical: he said that he had never seen "an uglier collection of women in my life", and was then hounded out of the workshops with a chorus of obscene abuse.

Now part of the university and only open during term time, this massive structure – 250m long by 180m wide – was built in the 1750s and still retains its position as the largest building in Spain after El Escorial in Madrid. Above the main entrance – facing Calle San Fernando – perches a marble angel, a trumpet to its lips, which malicious popular legend has it would only sound when a virgin entered the factory for the first time. The entrance arch below aptly incorporates medallion busts of Columbus (discoverer of the tobacco lands) and Cortés (reputedly Europe's first smoker) – in effect the factory's founding fathers.

The building was divided into residential quarters below with the work areas on the upper – and lighter – level. The entrance leads through a vestibule into the Clock Patio (with fountain), off which is a cafeteria. At its peak in the nineteenth century the factory was also the country's largest single employer, with a workforce of some ten thousand women *cigarreras* (cigarette makers) – "a class in themselves" according to Richard Ford and forced to undergo "an ingeniously minute search on leaving their work, for they sometimes carry off the filthy weed in a manner her most Catholic majesty never dreamt of". Production of cigars, cigarettes and snuff – originally ground by two hundred donkey-driven rolling mills – continued here until 1965 when its operations were moved to a new factory across the river close to the Puente de Los Remedios.

The Plaza de España

The **Plaza de España** lies beyond the Avenida del Cid – the latter, incidentally, the site of the Inquisition's *quemadero*, or burning platform, where for three hundred years convicted heretics were put to death; the last witch was burned here in 1781. The vast semicircular complex was designed as the centrepiece of the Spanish Americas Fair, which was somewhat scuppered by the Wall Street Crash abroad and political upheavals at home. Designed by Anibal González with theatrical towers, sprinkling fountains, majestic stairways and masses of brick and tile work, its flamboyance would seem strange in most Spanish cities but here it looks entirely natural, carrying on the great tradition of civic display. At the fair, the Plaza de España was used for the Spanish exhibit of industry and crafts, and around the crescent are *azulejo* scenes and maps of each of the provinces: an interesting record of the country at the tail-end of a monied era. After falling into disrepair in the latter part of the twentieth century, an expensive renovation has made it once again one of the city's major architectural sights. Locals and tourists alike again come out to the plaza to sit on the many benches or potter about in the little boats rented out on its tiny strip of canal.

Parque de María Luisa
Avda. de la Palmera s/n • daily 8am–10pm • Free

The **Parque de María Luisa**, which adjoins the Plaza de España, is a favourite haven for *sevillanos* who need to hide from the sun or escape the crowds. With its tree-shaded avenues, ornamental pools and decorative bridges and follies, it is just the place to linger for an hour or two in the heat of the city's summer afternoons. The park is designed, like the plaza, in a mix of 1920s Art Deco and mock-Mudéjar. Scattered about, and round its edge, are more buildings from the fair, some of them amazingly opulent, built in the last months before the Wall Street Crash undercut the scheme's impetus.

The Museo Arqueológico
Plaza de América s/n • Tues–Sat 9am–8.30pm, Sun 9am–2.30pm • €1.50 (free with EU passport)

Towards the southern end of the park, the grandest mansions from the Spanish Americas Fair have been adapted into museums, of which the **Museo Arqueológico** is the most important of its kind in Andalucía. The collection's wide remit, divided among 27 rooms on two floors, spans the period from prehistory to the end of the Moorish age.

Starting in the basement with the prehistoric sections, Room 4 displays a collection of funerary stelae from the Iberian period, while Room 6 has a unique eighth-century BC bronze statuette of **Astarte-Tanit**, the Phoenician fertility goddess once worshipped throughout the Mediterranean. This room also contains the stunning **Carambolo Treasures** discovered in the Seville suburb of Camas in 1958. This remarkable hoard of gold jewellery further fuelled the debate surrounding the whereabouts and existence of the ancient land of Tartessus, known to the Greeks and mentioned in the Bible as Tarshish. The legendary mineral wealth of Tartessus probably indicates a location in the area between Seville and the mineral-rich hills of Huelva, but despite investigations by archeologists for most of the last hundred or so years it has never been found.

Rooms 11 to 24 on the ground floor contain the substance of the **Roman collection** with an interesting display of kitchen equipment in Room 13, including what appears to be a modern-looking fork, contradicting the theory that the implement was a medieval invention. The same room also has a fine third-century mosaic from Écija depicting the god Bacchus being transported on a chariot drawn by tigers. In Room 17 there's a sensitive, second-century sculpture of Venus from Itálica, which was imported from Greece.

There's yet more statuary in rooms 19 and 20, as well as portrait busts of the emperors Augustus and Nero and local boys Trajan and Hadrian, the latter particularly striking. In a small room off Room 19 you'll find a number of remarkable **bronze plaques** inscribed with the "Lex Irnitana", a rare set of laws illustrating how the Romans – the inventors of jurisprudence – went about ruling their empire. The laws make a fascinating read but are sadly translated only into Spanish. Rubric 72 of the code deals with the freeing of public slaves whilst number 82 relates to the upkeep of roads, tracks, irrigation channels, drains and sewers, all vital to the Roman way of life. The laws are sanctioned by the despotic emperor Domitian, whose name appears at the end of the document dated April 10, 91 AD. A portrait bust of Domitian is displayed in Room 20.

Finally, rooms 26 and 27 display **post-Roman finds** including early Christian tombstones and Mudéjar ceramic works, among which a fifteenth-century green-glazed baptismal font stands out.

Museo de Costumbres Populares

Plaza de América 3 • Tues–Sat 9am–8.30pm, Sun 9am–2.30pm • €1.50 (free with EU passport)

Opposite the archeological museum is the fabulous-looking **Museo de Costumbres Populares** (Popular Arts Museum) with, inside, an equally fine patio, which despite displays of costumes, implements, furniture, photos and posters describing life in eighteenth- and nineteenth-century Andalucía, feels a bit lifeless. The basement ceramics displays are the highlight, illustrating the regional developments of this craft inherited from the Moors. In spring there are also special exhibitions devoted to Semana Santa and the April *feria*.

Along the river to the Maestranza

The Río Guadalquivir is Seville's historic artery, and a number of important monuments and museums are to be found along or close to its banks, including the Moorish **Torre del Oro**, the **Maestranza** bullring, second in prestige only to Madrid's Las Ventas.

Torre del Oro and the naval museum

Naval museum Tues–Fri 9.30am–1.30pm, Sat & Sun 10.30am–1.30pm; closed Aug • €2; free on Tues

On the Río Guadalquivir to the west of the Alcázar, the main riverside landmark is the twelve-sided **Torre del Oro** (Tower of Gold), built by the Almohads in 1220 as part of the Alcázar fortifications. It was connected to another small fort across the river by a chain which had to be broken by the Castilian fleet before their conquest of the city in 1248. The tower later saw use as a repository for the gold brought back to Seville from

---

BOAT TRIPS ON THE RÍO GUADALQUIVIR

Cruceros Turísticos (☎ 954 561 692, ⓦ cruceros torredeloro.com) have a quayside office below the Torre del Oro and run an hour-long cruise (daily every 30min 11am–9pm; €16) which takes in all the major riverside sights, including a view of the Expo 92 site. On Saturdays (May–Oct) they also run a scenic downriver cruise to Sanlúcar de Barrameda, leaving the Torre del Oro at 8.30am (€35 round-trip). The cruise docks at 1pm at Sanlúcar's Bajo de Guía with its outstanding fish restaurants. A bus departing at 5.30pm returns you to Seville, arriving around 7pm.

Pedalos To see the river under your own steam, pedalos (€10/hr) can be hired from Acuaterraza (daily noon until sunset; ☎ 679 194 045), on the east bank of the river near the Puente de Isabel II. They also hire out rowing boats, canoes and motor boats.

---

the Americas; hence its name. It now houses a small **naval museum**, which exhibits charts and engravings of the port in its prime.

The Hospital de la Caridad

C/Temprado 3 • Mon–Sat 9am–1pm & 3.30–7pm, Sun 9am–12.30pm • €5 • ⓦ santa-caridad.es

One block east of the Torre del Oro is the **Hospital de la Caridad**, founded in 1674 by Don Miguel de Mañara, who may well have been the inspiration for Byron's Don Juan. According to the testimony of one of Don Miguel's friends, "there was no folly which he did not commit, no youthful indulgence into which he did not plunge … (until) what occurred to him in the street of the coffin". What occurred was that Don Miguel, returning from a wild orgy, had a vision in which he was confronted by a funeral procession carrying his own corpse. He repented his past life, joined the Brotherhood of Charity (whose task was to bury the bodies of vagrants and criminals), and later set up this hospital for the relief of the dying and destitute, for which it is still used. Touchingly, whenever a patient dies here, the chapel is closed on the day of the funeral.

Between 1670 and 1674 Don Miguel commissioned a series of eleven paintings by Murillo for the chapel, seven of which remain after Marshal Soult looted four of them during the Napoleonic occupation. Murillo always created pictures "made to measure" for the available light, and it's a real treat to see the pictures in the place they were originally intended to hang. Among the surviving works are a colossal *Loaves and Fishes* depicting Christ feeding the Five Thousand, and "a *San Juan de Dios* equal to Rembrandt" as Richard Ford, a fervent Murillo fan, described it. Mañara himself posed as the model for the saint. Alongside them hang two *Triumph of Death*s by Valdés Leal. One, portraying the fleeting nature of life, features a skeletal image of Death pointing to the message *in ictu oculi* ("in the blink of an eye"), while the other depicts a decomposing bishop being eaten by worms (beneath the scales of justice labelled *Ni más, Ni menos* – "No More, No Less"). Murillo found this so repulsive that he declared "you have to hold your nose to look at it". The mood of both works may owe a lot to the vivid memory of the 1649 plague that killed almost half the population of the city. The main altar's retablo features a superlative *Burial of Christ* carved by Pedro Roldán, and the steps to the left of this descend to a crypt where Mañara is buried.

As you're leaving the Caridad, step inside the private car park and look across to the **Torre de la Plata** (Tower of Silver), a castellated Moorish watchtower, at Calle Santander 13. It probably got its name to correspond with the nearby Torre del Oro, although there is no evidence to suggest that it was once coated with silver tiles or was ever a silver store, as local legends have it.

Plaza de Toros de la Maestranza and around

Paseo de Cristóbal Colón 12 • Tours daily: May–Oct 9.30am–8pm; Nov–April 9.30am–7pm; fight days 9.30am–3pm • €6.50

The **Plaza de Toros de la Maestranza** (Maestranza bullring) is the most famous and, for aficionados, the most beautiful bullring in the world. It was completed in the latter half of the eighteenth century to provide a home for the Real Maestranza de Caballería

(Royal Equestrian Society). Subsequently altered, it is still one of the finest in Spain and has featured in numerous novels, poems and films – most enduringly in Bizet's *Carmen*. Once inside the arena, you will see a metal frame in the roof holding a furled canvas. On fight days this is unfurled – not to give spectators more shade but to temper the wind, which often whips up over the river causing the capes of the matadore to behave in unpredictable and possibly dangerous ways. The Maestranza's museum has the usual posters, prints, photographs and memorabilia. A monument to "Carmen" (see p.269) stands opposite the entrance to the bullring, across the road near the river.

Three blocks downriver – with a dome that's hard to miss – is the **Teatro de la Maestranza** concert hall and opera house. Built as part of the Expo 92 improvements, it incorporates the remains of the Artillería ammunition works that previously occupied the site. The rather dominating and uninspired design caused much controversy when it was unveiled because of its detrimental effect on the magnificent view of the city from across the river.

The Museo de Bellas Artes

Plaza del Museo 9 · Tues–Sat 9am–8.30pm, Sun 9am–2.30pm · €1.50 (free with EU passport)

A ten-minute walk north of the Maestranza bullring, and fronted by a formidable bronze statue of Murillo, lies the **Museo de Bellas Artes**. Housed in recently modernized galleries in a startlingly beautiful former convent, the Convento de la Merced, it ranks second in Spain only to the Prado in Madrid. Founded in the thirteenth century by Fernando III after Seville had been taken from the Moors, the convent was subsequently remodelled and reached its present form in the eighteenth century, although it lost most of its own commissioned paintings during the nineteenth-century Disentailment when it was secularized, and it opened as a museum in 1838. You should be aware that the museum has a policy of rotating its collection and not all the works mentioned here may be exhibited. A Sunday morning **art market** (9am–3pm) takes place in the plaza fronting the museum where local artists and craftworkers sell their work.

The downstairs galleries

Among the highlights of an outstanding collection is a wonderful late fifteenth-century painted terracotta sculpture in Room 1, *Lamentation over the Dead Christ*, by the *andaluz* **Pedro Millán**, founding father of the Seville school of sculpture. A marriage of Gothic and expressive naturalism, this style was the starting point for the outstanding seventeenth-century period of religious iconography in Seville – a later example, in Room 2, is a magnificent *San Jerónimo* by the Italian **Pietro Torrigiano**, who spent the latter years of his life in Seville. Ever his own man, Torrigiano once broke the nose of his contemporary Michelangelo in a quarrel and eventually died at the hands of the Inquisition in Seville, condemned for impiety after he had smashed his own sculpture of a Virgin when the duke of Arcos refused to pay the price asked. His *Virgen de Belén* here is another powerful work. This room also has **El Greco**'s portrait of his son, Jorge Manuel Theotokopoulos.

Room 3 has a retablo of the Redemption, c.1562, with fine woodcarving by **Juan Giralte**. Originally made for the Convento de Santa Catalina in Aracena, tableaux 6 (the crowning with thorns) and 10 (Mark writing his gospel) are especially fine. Here also is displayed the grisly terracotta sculpture of the severed head of John the Baptist by **Núñez Delgado**, not something you want to see too soon after lunch. Dated 1591, this work is a prototype of the Baroque images later carried on the *pasos* during Semana Santa.

A monumental *Last Supper* by **Alonso Vásquez** painted for the monastery of La Cartuja covers an end wall of Room 4, where you'll also find works by **Pacheco**, one of the protagonists of the Mannerist school and the father-in-law and tutor of Velázquez. His series of canvases for the Convento de la Merced is represented here by images of San Pedro and San Ramón Nonato. There's also a **Velázquez** work here, a portrait of Don

3

> ## MURILLO IN ALL HIS GLORY
>
> Born in Seville in 1618 and orphaned ten years later, **Bartolomé Esteban Murillo** grew up in the home of his brother-in-law. After enrolling as a student under Juan de Castillo he came to the attention of another *sevillano*, Velázquez, who was by then established in Madrid. Murillo studied with Velázquez for three not very happy years in the capital, where he found the social scene oppressive, but was apparently much impressed by the works of the Flemish and Italian schools he saw in the royal collections there.
>
> Once back in his native city Murillo started work in earnest, often using poor *sevillanos* from districts such as La Macarena as his models. In 1682, still at the height of his artistic powers he was painting an altarpiece for the Capuchin church in Cádiz when he fell from the scaffold, suffering serious injury. He was brought back to Seville where he died in the Convent of San José near to his home in the Barrio Santa Cruz.
>
> Downgraded by critics in the nineteenth century for his sentimentalism – a view largely based on the genre paintings of rosy-faced urchins that had found their way across Europe – Murillo's reputation has since been restored. A greater familiarity with the powerful works that remained in Seville, such as those in the Caridad, substantiates Richard Ford's proclamation: "At Sevilla Murillo is to be seen in all his glory … a giant on his native soil."

Cristóbal Suarez de Ribera produced in his teens, betraying sure signs of the master's touch as well as an unparalleled ability to illuminate his figures from within.

Beyond a serene patio and cloister, Room 5 is located in the monastery's former church. The restored paintings on the vault and dome by the eighteenth-century *sevillano* **Domingo Martínez** are spectacular. Here also is the nucleus of the collection: **Zurbarán**'s *Apotheosis of St Thomas Aquinas* as well as a clutch of **Murillos** in the apse crowned by the great Immaculate Conception – known as "la colosal" to distinguish it from the other work here with the same name. In an alcove nearby you'll see the same artist's *Virgin and Child*. Popularly known as *La Servilleta* because it was said to have been painted on a dinner napkin, the work is one of Murillo's greatest. In the same room are more Murillos and also works by the early seventeenth-century *sevillano* **Roelas**, including a magnificent *Martirio de San Andrés*.

The upstairs galleries

Room 6 displays works from the Baroque period, among which a moving *Santa Teresa* by **Ribera** – Spain's master of *tenebrismo* (darkness penetrated by light) – and a stark *Crucifixión* by Zurbarán stand out. The same artist's *Niño de la Espina* and a luminous *Virgen del Rosario* are also outstanding. Room 7 is devoted to Murillo and his school and has a superb *San Agustín y la Trinidad* by the master.

In Room 8, eighteenth-century *sevillano* **Valdés Leal** symbolizes the city's enduring fascination with agony and mortality: his depiction of Fray Juan de Ledesma wrestling with the devil disguised as a serpent has the brooding intensity of much of his work. Room 9 contains works from the **European Baroque**, among which there's an outstanding *La Adoración de los Pastores* (Adoration of the Shepherds) by the Flemish painter Pieter Van Lint and an *Adoración de los Reyes* (Adoration of the Kings) by his compatriot Cornelis de Vos, both connected with the school of Rubens.

There's more sculpture in Room 10, this time by the sixteenth-century genius **Martínez Montañés**, whose early *Saint Dominic in Penitence* and *San Bruno* from his mature period display mastery of technique. Also here are imposing canvases by Zurbarán: San Hugo visiting the Carthusian monks at supper (*San Hugo in the Refectory*), *The Visit of San Bruno to Pope Urban II* and the *Virgen de los Cartujos* were all painted for the monastery of La Cartuja across the river. There's also another almost sculptural crucifixion to compare with his earlier one in Room 6.

The collection ends with works from the Romantic and Modern eras where an austere late work by **Goya**, in Room 11, of the octogenarian *Don José Duaso* compensates for some not terribly inspiring works accompanying it. There's also a portrait of the incompetent and indolent ruler Alfonso XIII painted in 1929 by Gonzalo Bilbao, which tells you all you need to know about this monarchical disaster. The same artist has more works in Room 12 – his *Las Cigarreras* is a vivid portrayal of the wretched life of women in the tobacco factory during the early years of the last century. Room 13 has an evocative image of *Sevilla en Fiestas* dated 1915 by Gustavo Bacarisas and the monumental canvas by José Villegas Cordero, *La Muerte del Maestro*, depicting the death of a *torero*. Finally, in Room 14 there's *Juan Centeño y su cuadrilla* by Huelvan artist Daniel Vásquez Díaz, who worked in Paris and was a friend of Picasso. This stirring image of the *torero* and his team provides an appropriately *andaluz* conclusion to a memorable museum.

El Centro

El Centro, the central zone, lies north of the cathedral at the geographical heart of the city. It contains the main shopping areas, including **Calle Sierpes**, the city's most fashionable street, as well as the museum of flamenco dance. Here, too, you'll find many of Seville's finest churches, displaying a fascinating variety of architectural styles. Several are converted mosques with belfries built over their minarets, others range through Mudéjar and Gothic (sometimes in combination), Renaissance and Baroque. Most are kept locked except early in the morning, or in the evenings from about 7 until 10pm – a promising time for a church crawl, especially as they're regularly interspersed with tapas bars.

The Casa de Pilatos

Plaza de Pilatos 1 • Daily: March–Sept 9am–7pm; Oct–Feb 9am–5.30pm • €6 ground floor only; both floors €8 (including audioguide); Wed 3–7pm free with EU passport

Of Seville's numerous mansions, by far the finest is the **Casa de Pilatos** in the Plaza de Pilatos, close to northern edge of the Barrio Santa Cruz. Built by the Marqués de Tarifa of the Ribera family on his return from a pilgrimage to Jerusalem in 1519, the house was popularly – and erroneously – thought to have been an imitation of the house of Pontius Pilate, supposedly seen by the duke on his travels. In fact it's a harmonious mixture of Mudéjar, Gothic and Renaissance styles, featuring brilliant *azulejos*, a tremendous sixteenth-century stairway and the best domestic patios in the city. After the Civil War the dukes of Medinaceli returned to live here and inaugurated a programme of restoration that has gradually brought the house back to its original splendour.

The lower floors

Entering by the **Apeadero**, where the old carriages were boarded, and which for most of the year is a riot of magenta bougainvillea, brings you to a gateway leading into the wonderful **Patio Principal**. Here, Muslim elements such as the irregular arches, plasterwork and glazed tiles combine with Gothic tracery on the upper balustrades and an Italian Renaissance fountain and columns below. The imposing statues in each corner of the patio are classical originals, of which the Athene (bearing a spear) is attributed to the fifth-century BC school of the Greek master, Phidias; the others are Roman. Antique Italian busts of Roman emperors and men of letters such as Trajan, Hadrian and Cicero occupy niches in the arcades.

The **Salón Pretorio** is notable for its coffered ceiling, incorporating the Ribera family's coat of arms. The Roman sculptures – collected in Italy by the sixteenth-century duke of Alcalá – in the nearby Zaquizamí corridor are extremely fine, especially the slumbering Venus and a marble relief fragment, depicting weapons, above. Passing the Jardín Chico (Small Garden), the Chapel of the Flagellation (its central column is supposed to represent the one at which Christ was scourged) and Pilate's "study", you reach the **Jardín Grande**, a verdant oasis with palms, pavilions and a bower, not to mention a wonderful abundance of orange trees. A tradition associated with this garden relates that the first duke of Alcalá obtained from Pope Pius V the ashes of the emperor Trajan (born in nearby Itálica), which were then displayed in a vase in the library. Later, a servant is supposed to have dumped them in the garden thinking the urn to be full of dust. The legend grew that an orange tree sprouted up wherever the ashes had fallen.

The upper floors

The **upper floors** (still partly inhabited by the Medinaceli family) are reached from the Patio Principal via the fine, tiled staircase with a gilded, sixteenth-century semicircular dome, but can be seen only by guided tour (frequent, on an informal basis). The rooms are decorated with various frescoes, canvases by Goya (a tiny bullfighting scene), Ribera and Jordáns, and objets d'art collected by the family. Outstanding here is the **Salón de Pacheco** with the *Apotheosis of Hercules* painted on the ceiling in 1603 by the *sevillano* artist after whom the room is named.

San Ildefonso

C/Rodríguez de Marín 4 • Open service times Mon–Sat 7pm, Sun 10am–noon • Free

San Ildefonso is a fourteenth-century church later rebuilt in the classical style. Inside, behind the altar on the north aisle, there's a fresco of the Virgin dating from the original building. The church also has some seventeenth-century wood sculptures by Roldán and a bas-relief, *The Trinity*, by Martínez Montañés dated 1609.

Museo del Baile Flamenco

C/Manuel Rojas Marcos 3 • Daily 9am–7pm • €10 • ☎ 954 340 311, ⓦ museoflamenco.com

A few minutes' walk to the west of the Casa de Pilatos lies the **Museo del Baile Flamenco**, an innovative and entertaining museum dedicated to the history and evolution of this emblematic *andaluz* art form. Set up in collaboration with celebrated flamenco dancer Cristina Hoyos, the museum is interactive (and multilingual), employing the latest sound and image technology to illustrate the origins of flamenco and the range of dance styles (*palos*). The final section of the museum displays photos of, as well as costumes used by, some flamenco greats. There is also a shop selling books and CDs, a dance school (sampler classes possible) and frequent live performances in the museum's theatre.

Not far away, and heading in a more or less westerly direction, Calle Boteros will bring you to **Plaza Alfalfa**, the site of the forum of Roman Hispalis and a good place for tapas bars.

Los Monolitos Romanos

A couple of blocks south of Plaza Alfalfa are three enormous columns, known as **Los Monolitos Romanos,** which once belonged to what must have been a gigantic Roman temple dating from the second century. There were originally five surviving pillars here but in the nineteenth century two were transferred to the Alameda de Hércules where they now act as plinths for statues of Julius Caesar (who granted the city its first urban statute) and Hercules (mythical creator of Hispalis), the city's "founding fathers".

Plaza del Buen Suceso

Heading north from Plaza Alfalfa, along calles Sales y Ferré and Padre Llop will lead you to the **Plaza del Buen Suceso** on which lies the **convent** of the same name. Inside, there's a marvellous sculpture of St Anne with the Virgin by Martínez Montañés.

San Pedro and around

North from Plaza del Buen Suceso, Calle Velilla leads to the Gothic church of **San Pedro**, with a Mudéjar tower modelled on the Giralda, and where a marble tablet records Velázquez's baptism. Just behind the church on Calle Dueñas, the splendid **Palacio de las Dueñas** was the birthplace (marked by a plaque) of another *andaluz* genius, the poet Antonio Machado.

Palacio Lebrija

C/Cuna 8 • July & Aug Mon–Fri 9am–3pm, Sat 10am–2pm; Sept–June Mon–Fri 10.30am–7.30pm, Sat 10am–2pm & 4–6pm, Sun 10am–2pm • €5 one floor, €8 both floors • ⊕ palaciodelebrija.com

A stroll west from San Pedro along Calle Imagen passes the Renaissance Iglesia de la Anunciación on Calle Laraña leading to Calle Cuna on the left where, at no. 8, stands the sixteenth-century **Palacio Lebrija** housing a vast collection of Iberian and Roman antiquities gathered by the Condesa (countess) de Lebrija who acquired the house in 1900. She transformed the interior to incorporate some fine Roman mosaics – particularly that of the deity Pan – from the Roman site at Itálica. As well as the antiquities carted away from Itálica – before there were laws to prevent this – there are marbles plundered from the Moorish site at Medina Azahara as well as various exhibits purchased on her travels and a number of artworks.

Alameda de Hércules

A route directly north from the Palacio Lebrija brings you to the tree-lined **Alameda de Hércules**, once a swamp and converted in the sixteenth century into a promenade. The southern end has two pillars taken from a Roman temple on Calle Mármoles – hence the promenade's name. King Alfonso X believed that only Hercules (the city's mythical founder) could have raised these pillars and it was later alleged (without evidence) that the Roman temple had been dedicated to the Greek god and thus, via this convoluted thought process, the Alameda acquired its name. Once fashionable, in the latter part of the last century the area went to seed and became the city's red-light district. However, in recent years a costly makeover has transformed it, attracting numerous new bars and hotels and the Alameda is re-emerging as a vibrant centre of *sevillano* life.

Jesús del Gran Poder

Plaza de San Lorenzo • Mon–Thurs 8am–1.30pm & 6–9pm, Fri 7.30am–10pm • Free

West of the Alameda lies the church of **San Lorenzo** and, next to it, the modern church of **Jesús del Gran Poder**. In the latter's retablo is displayed the much venerated figure of Jesús del Gran Poder (Christ bearing his cross) by Juan de Mesa, carved in 1620. This image is borne in procession in the small hours of Good Friday morning.

Plaza de San Francisco

In the shadow of the Giralda, the **Plaza de San Francisco**, slightly north of the cathedral, takes its name from the great monastery that once covered much of this and the Plaza Nueva to the west. The plaza is overlooked on its western flank by the fabulous plateresque facade of the sixteenth-century Ayuntamiento (see p.262), one of Seville's iconic buildings.

Calle Sierpes

Leading out of Plaza de San Francisco you'll find the true heart of Seville, **Calle Sierpes**, where, according to Cervantes – who spent some time in prison here serving a sentence for his tax debts – "all the social classes of the city come together". This narrow pedestrianized street, today lined with souvenir stores, private clubs and smart *pastelerías* (cake shops), is a wonderful place to stroll. It's particularly dramatic – though quite uncharacteristic – during Semana Santa, when the brotherhood of El Silencio passes through in total silence in the early hours of Good Friday, watched by an equally hushed crowd lining the route.

Look out for Seville's most famous *pastelería*, **La Campana**, at no. 1 (the northern end). At no. 65 a wall plaque indicates the site of the **Cárcel Real**, or royal prison, where Cervantes was incarcerated and where – according to legend – he scribbled the first notes that were eventually to be transformed into *Don Quijote*. A short way down on the left, on Calle Jovellanos, lies the small **Capillata de San José**, one of the best examples of full-blown Baroque in the city with a beautiful gilded retablo.

Otherwise, just behind Calle Sierpes in the parallel Calle Tetuán, a detour will lead you to a wonderful old tiled **billboard** advertising a 1924 Studebaker Special Six convertible. The Triana tiles are hand painted and the work of noted ceramicist Enrique Orce Mármol (who did much of the tile work on the Plaza de España), and it prompts the question of just how long the company (now out of business for fifty years) expected the model to remain in production. It's sited opposite the C&A department store.

El Salvador

Plaza del Salvador • July–Aug Mon–Sat 10am–5pm, Sun 3–7pm; Sept–June Mon–Sat 11am–5.30pm, Sun 3–7pm (also service times 6.30–9pm) • €3, or free with cathedral ticket

To the east of Calle Sierpes, the collegiate church of **El Salvador** was built on the site of a ninth-century – and the city's first – Friday mosque. Most of what you see today dates from the seventeenth century, with remnants of the mosque preserved in its tower, formerly the minaret, and its patio, originally the ablutions courtyard. Inside, there's a magnificent Churrigueresque retablo as well as a number of sculptures, among them the renowned *Jesús del Pasión* by the great master of wood sculpture, Juan Martínez Montañés, who also embellished the church's exterior and whose bronze monument stands in the plaza outside.

Plaza de la Encarnación

A couple of blocks north of Plaza del Salvador lies another of the city's major squares, **Plaza de la Encarnación**, created in 1819 after Napoleon's invading forces demolished the convent of the same name that stood on the spot. Long criticised for its bleakness – its main function throughout the twentieth century was to serve as a market and then bus terminal – at the start of the new millennium the city government decided to spectacularly raise its profile with a breathtaking piece of modern architecture.

Las Setas

Taking seven years to build, the **Metropol Parasol** is a 30m-high, 150m-long structure comprising a series of undulating, wood-waffle flat-topped mushroom structures on giant concrete pillars. Claimed by its German architect, Jürgen Mayer, to be the world's largest timber construction, it incorporates a market, shopping mall, restaurant and a basement museum displaying the ruins of Roman Hispalis – complete with mosaics – discovered in the preliminary excavations. The structure's high point (in all senses) is a spectacular undulating pedestrian walkway winding across the roof to a sky deck with stunning views over the city.

Many critics argue that the Metropol Parasol has no place in a square surrounded by Baroque edifices, while supporters claim it has launched the city into the new millennium with a flourish. Typically, the structure's official name did not last more than a couple of days after the unveiling – *sevillano* wags took one look and tagged it **Las Setas** (the mushrooms), the name everyone uses today.

The Barrio Triana

The **Barrio Triana**, an endearingly scruffy, lively and not at all touristy neighbourhood, across the river from the old town, is generally believed to have taken its name from the Roman emperor Trajan who was born at nearby Itálica. This was once the heart of the city's *gitano* (gypsy) community and, more specifically, home of the great flamenco dynasties of Seville. The gypsies lived in extended families in tiny, immaculate communal houses called *corrales* around courtyards ablaze with flowers; today only a handful remain intact. Triana has also long been a centre of glazed-tile production, and you'll see plenty of examples of this fine ceramic work as you stroll around the streets.

Triana is still the starting point for the **annual pilgrimage to El Rocío** (at the end of May), when myriad painted wagons leave town, drawn by elephantine oxen. And one of the great moments of **Semana Santa** occurs here in the early hours of Good Friday when the candlelit *paso* of the Virgin Esperanza de Triana is carried back over the Puente de Triana (Isabel II) to be given a rapturous welcome home by the whole *barrio* assembled on the other side.

Plaza de la Virgen de la Milagrosa

In the centre of **Plaza de la Virgen de la Milagrosa** is a modern statue to **Rodrigo de Triana**, a sailor on Columbus's initial voyage who was the first to set eyes on the New World. In spite of his name, however, more recent research suggests that he hailed not from Triana, but Lepe, in the neighbouring province of Huelva. Determined not to be put off by this academic meddling with their history, the *barrio* erected the sculpture anyway with the laconic "Tierra" ("Land") inscribed on its base, the word an unidentified Rodrigo is presumably yelling as he clings to the mast.

Calle Gonzalo Segovia

Calle Gonzalo Segovia was the site of the **former gunpowder factory** that supplied the vessels of the Indies fleet. An enormous explosion here in 1579 not only destroyed half of Triana but also blew the stained-glass windows out of the cathedral across the river. In Roman times, clay was collected from this riverbank to make the amphorae used to transport cereals, wine, oil and pickled fish to the imperial capital – much of the broken pottery piled up in ancient Rome's towering rubbish dump at Monte Testaccio has now been identified as coming from Triana. The same clay also made the bricks for the Giralda and many more of the city's houses and monuments.

Church of Santa Ana

Mon–Sat 11am–1pm & 6.30–8.30pm, Sun 9.30am–1pm & 6.30–8pm • Free

Triana's main church, the **Church of Santa Ana**, is the oldest parish church in Seville. Built for Alfonso X in the thirteenth century, it includes many later additions: note, for example, the Mudéjar tower with blocked lobed windows topped by a Renaissance belfry. Should you be able to gain entry look out for the fine sixteenth-century retablo of the Virgen de la Rosa and the church's baptismal font – Pila de los Gitanos – from which, according to tradition, the gifts of flamenco singing and dancing are bestowed on the newborn infants of the *barrio*.

Capilla de los Marineros

C/Pureza 5 • Mon–Sat 9.30am–1pm & 6–9pm, Sun 10am–1.30pm

The eighteenth-century chapel of **Capilla de los Marineros** is now seat of the Cofradía de Jesús de las Tres Caídas y Nuestra Señora de la Esperanza (Brotherhood of Jesus of the Three Falls and Our Lady of Hope), one of the major brotherhoods who march in the Semana Santa processions. The chapel's Baroque retablo incorporates the figure of the Virgin known as the Esperanza de Triana to which the *barrio* is devoted.

From the Capilla de los Marineros to the Puente de Triana

A walk from the Capilla de los Marineros – perhaps taking a detour to the **Bar Anselma** (fronting Calle Pages), a great old tiled place with occasional impromptu flamenco (see p.299) – will bring you to sixteenth-century **church of Nuestra Señora de la "O"** at Calle Castilla 30, with its splendid tiled tower. The interior, as well as holding some fine ceramics, contains a seventeenth-century sculpture of Jesús Nazareno by Pedro Roldán. Heading south, with the river to your left, a small alley bears the name Callejón de la Inquisición. This was the site of the northern flank of the former **Castillo de Triana** (Triana Castle), the original residence of the Inquisition until it was forced out by a flood in 1626 or, as Ford colourfully puts it, until "the Guadalquivir, which blushed at the fires and curdled with the bloodshed, almost swept it away as if indignant at the crimes committed on its bank". Almost opposite, *Cervecería Casa Cuesta* is a welcoming bar with tiled interior serving good tapas. Continuing around the corner you'll come to the spectacular tiled facade of **Cerámica Santa Ana** at Plaza Callao 12. The city's oldest working ceramics factory, over a century old, this is a good place to buy hand-painted Triana pots and tiles. South of here is **Plaza Altozano**, where there are monuments to the *barrio*'s great flamenco traditions and another to Triana's famous *torero*, Juan Belmonte. The latter sculpture by Venancio Blanco nestles against the **Puente de Triana** – designed by Gustave Eiffel of "tower" fame.

Mercado de Triana

Centro de Interpretación Entrance alongside the market • Mon–Fri 9am–2pm, Sat & Sun 10am–2pm • Free

Sitting next to the bridge between Triana and the centre, the **Mercado de Triana** (market) has been cunningly constructed over excavations of the old Castillo de Triana, with parts viewable through a glass floor. A new **Centro de Interpretación**, alongside the Mercado Triana, incorporates parts of the remains of the Castillo de Triana in a walk-through museum where multimedia tableaux describe the horrors once perpetrated here in the name of religion.

La Cartuja

C/Américo Vespucio 2 • Tues–Sat 11am–9pm, Sun 11am–3pm • €3 (free Sat & Tues–Fri 7–9pm with EU passport); includes entry to Centro Andaluz de Arte Contemporáneo • Buses #C1 or #C2 from the Prado de San Sebastián bus station or the Puente de los Remedios

Across the river from El Centro and accessible either by bus or by the Pasarela de la Cartuja, a pedestrian bridge constructed for Expo 92, is the fourteenth-century **La Cartuja**, a former Carthusian monastery. Founded in 1399 on the site where there had been an apparition of the Virgin in some pottery workshops (*cuevas*) installed here during the Almohad era, the monastery of Santa María de las Cuevas was expanded by the Carthusians in the fifteenth and sixteenth centuries with donations from Seville's leading families.

This was where Columbus lodged on his visits to Seville, where he planned his second voyage to the New World, and where he was buried for a few years. The core of the monastery suffered eighteenth-century Baroque additions and was made the headquarters of the notorious Marshal Soult's garrison during the Napoleonic occupation of 1810–12, when the monks were driven out and fled to Portugal. A final indignity was visited on the place when, after Disentailment in 1836, it was purchased by a Liverpudlian, Charles Pickman, and turned into a ceramics factory, which it remained until 1982. The whole complex – including the towering brick kilns and

---

EXPO 92

The staging of Expo 92 secured a year of publicity and prosperity for Seville during which the sybaritic *sevillanos* started to believe their own hype, billing it as the "event of the century". After the fuss died down and the visitors departed, the city was left with a staggering debt of sixty billion pesetas (€360 million), financial scandals, endless recriminations, and a dilapidated site which no one knew what to do with. Plans to turn it into a science park came to nothing and the western side of the complex has now been split between the University of Seville and a technological/industrial park.

Expo's artificial lake on the east side of the site has been revamped as the focus of the **Isla Mágica** amusement and theme park (April–Nov daily 11am–7.30pm, open until 11pm July & Aug; €29; evening-only tickets €27; reductions for kids; Ⓦ islamagica.es), with rides and attractions (included in ticket price) based on the theme of the sixteenth-century Spanish empire.

The remains of the Expo site lying beyond this and to the south of La Cartuja are mostly a hotchpotch of desolate and overgrown structures, including the **Navigation Pavilion** celebrating Columbus's voyages, the soaring but rusting **Torre Mirador** plus gimmicks such as the **Omnimax** giant cine screen. All have been closed to the public for some years.

chimney that can be glimpsed from outside the site, and which are now regarded as industrial history – was restored for **Expo 92** at enormous cost.

The Capilla de Afuera and the monastery church

The visit begins at the **Capilla de Afuera** where the chapel's gilded Baroque retablo has lost its central effigy of the Virgen de las Cuevas, a carved work in cedar and once the monastery's most venerated image. In the chapels of **Santa Catalina** and **San Bruno** (the founder of the Carthusian order) there are fine Triana tiles; Felipe II used the latter as his oratory when he visited Seville in 1570.

Apart from a few surviving architectural fragments, the monastery's **church** is now bare, but maintains a serene dignity after its use as a workshop in the ceramics factory. Off it, the chapel of Santa Ana contains **the tomb of Christopher Columbus** where the navigator's bones rested for 27 years prior to beginning their travels (see p.259). Also here in wall niches are the remains of some fine polychrome tile panels depicting San Juan Evangelista and San Mateo.

The cloister, chapter house and refectory

Also off the church are the elegant Mudéjar **cloister**, the centre of Carthusian community life and home to more tile work, and the **Capítulo de Monjes** (chapter house), with the sixteenth-century tombs of the Ribeira family and finely sculpted retablos made in Italy. Finally, the **refectory**, with more partially tiled walls and a tiled pulpit, retains a beautiful *artesonado* ceiling which was used by the French for target practice. The visit ends with a chance to view Pickman's enormous bottle-shaped kilns close up en route to the *huerta* (market garden) of the former monastery, which has been transformed once again into a tranquil oasis as the recently planted trees mature.

Casilla de Santa Justa y Rufina

Along the garden's northwest wall you can see the pumps which once drew water from the river to irrigate the garden, while from a mirador in the reconstructed **Casilla de Santa Justa y Rufina** there is a great view over the whole complex to the west, the river and city to the east and, to the north, the rather forlorn and weed-festooned site of Expo 92.

Centro Andaluz de Arte Contemporáneo

C/Américo Vespucio 2 • €3 (free Sat & Tues–Fri 7–9pm with EU passport); includes entry to La Cartuja • 𝕨 caac.es

A separate building within the La Cartuja complex now houses the **Centro Andaluz de Arte Contemporáneo**, one gallery of which displays changing selections from a large and interesting collection of contemporary work by *andaluz* artists including canvases by Antonio Rodríguez de Luna, Joaquín Peinado, Guillermo Pérez Villalta, José Guerrero and Daniel Vásquez Díaz. Two other galleries stage temporary exhibitions by international artists and photographers.

The Barrio Macarena

"The Macarena, now as it always was, is the abode of ragged poverty, which never could or can for a certainty reckon on one or any meal a day." Things have changed considerably for the better since Ford was in the **barrio Macarena** in the middle of the nineteenth century, and since Murillo used the *barrio*'s beggars and urchins as models for his paintings. Northwest of the Centro and enclosed by the best surviving stretch of the city's ancient walls, Macarena's very unfashionability, along with its solid working-class traditions, have helped prevent its wholesale dismemberment at the hands of speculators and builders. The result today is an area full of character, with many attractive cobbled streets, and quite a few jewels to show off in the way of churches and convents. The Macarena's pride was further enhanced when it was decided that the *barrio* would become the home of the newly autonomous Andalucian parliament in the converted Renaissance hospital of the Cinco Llagas.

Plaza de los Terceros

A good place to start a tour around La Macarena is the **Plaza de los Terceros**, some 250m to the north of the Casa de Pilatos (see p.275). Here you'll find the fourteenth-century Mudéjar church of **Santa Catalina** with a tower modelled on the Giralda and topped off with Renaissance embellishments. The interior (access is difficult but try 6.30–7.30pm) has some interesting Mudéjar features including an elegant panelled ceiling as well as – in the Cristo de la Exaltación chapel (the most easterly on the south side) – a fine sculpture of Christ by Roldán. Within spitting distance of the church (on the corner of C/Gerona) lies another of Seville's great institutions, the bar *El Rinconcillo* (see p.298), founded in 1670 and believed to be the oldest in the city.

Convento de Santa Paula

Plaza Santa Paula • Tues–Sun: April–Sept 10am–1pm; Oct–May 10am–1pm & 4.30–6.30pm • €3

Following Calle Sol out of the Plaza Terceros will bring you to **Plaza San Román,** where another fourteenth-century Gothic-Mudéjar church, **San Román,** has a fine coffered ceiling. North of the church is the fifteenth-century **Convento de Santa Paula**, renowned for its beautiful belfry and church. It's entered through an imposing fifteenth-century Gothic doorway built with Mudéjar brickwork and decorated with Renaissance *azulejos* by Pedro Millán, with ceramic decoration by Niculoso Pisano. Inside there's a sumptuously gilded San Juan Evangelista retablo by Alonso Cano with a magnificent central figure of St John by Martínez Montañés dated 1637.

The **convent museum**, crammed with treasures, is entered through a small patio to the left of the church entrance. Guided tours (in Spanish) are led by one of the convent's 48 nuns, who has been given a special dispensation to break the order's vow of silence. The first room has a painting of San Jerónimo by Ribera, and, almost as beautiful, a view out onto a seventeenth-century patio cloister. In Room 2 there's a fascinating maquette made by Torrigiano before starting on his full-size masterpiece of *San Jerónimo Penitente*, which is now in the Museo de Bellas Artes (see p.273). Room 3 holds two outstanding, though damaged, painted sculptures by Pedro de Mena, a *Virgin* and an *Ecce Homo*. Immediately before the exit there is also a *Crucifixión* by Zurbarán. The hard-working sisters are famous for their *dulces* and *mermaladas* (including a tomato jam), which you can buy from their small shop.

The city walls

The **Puerta de Córdoba** (Córdoba Gate), with its horseshoe arch, is the best surviving section of the **city wall**. The Almoravids constructed the wall in the early twelfth century, possibly on Roman foundations, and it was further strengthened by the later Almohads as wars against the Christians intensified. This stretch of the fortification – which once spanned twelve gates and 166 towers – owes its survival to the poverty of the *barrio* during the nineteenth century when, elsewhere in the city, the wall was pulled down to allow expansion.

Basílica de la Macarena

Puerta de la Macarena • Daily 9am–2pm & 5–9pm • Church free; treasury museum €5

Just beyond the **Puerta de la Macarena** (a city gate reconstructed in the eighteenth century and the only one to retain its pre-Christian name), stands the **Basílica de la Macarena** which, despite an apparently Baroque facade, dates from the 1940s. The basilica's importance, however, derives from the revered image of the Virgen de la Esperanza Macarena it was constructed to house. Inside the church, to the left, is the solid silver *paso* used to carry the image around the city during the Semana Santa processions. To the right is a second *paso* (the brotherhoods normally carry them in pairs), Jesús de la Sentencia, depicting Pilate washing his hands with a fine, but now modestly cloaked, Christ by the seventeenth-century sculptor, Felipe Morales. The retablo of the main altar is dominated by a seventeenth-century image of La Macarena, as the Virgin is popularly called by this city of fanatical devotees. Depicted in the trauma of the Passion when her son has been condemned, the work is attributed to La Roldana – largely based on the *sevillano* sentiment that only a woman could have portrayed the suffering of a mother with such intensity. La Macarena's elaborate costume is often decorated with five diamond and emerald brooches bestowed on her by Joselito el Gallo, a famous *gitano torero* of the early part of the last century, and on which he spent a considerable fortune. She didn't return the favours though – he died in the ring in 1920. Despite this mishap, the Virgin is still regarded as the patron of the profession and all matadors offer prayers to her before stepping out to do business in the Maestranza. The basilica's **treasury museum** features a rather gaudy display of the Virgin's other jewels and regalia.

Hospital de las Cinco Llagas

C/San Juan de Ribera • Free afternoon guided tours Sept–June twice weekly; must be booked in advance • ☎ 954 592 100

The sixteenth-century **Hospital de las Cinco Llagas** (aptly, of the Five Wounds Of Christ), was one of the first true hospitals of its time and the largest in Europe. Sited outside the walls because hospitals then were places of pestilence and contagion, the restored building is now the seat of Andalucía's autonomous government (and many *sevillano* wags drily comment that nothing's changed). The enormous edifice, once capable of holding a thousand beds, is noted for a fine Mannerist facade with a Baroque central doorway of white marble. The interior – including the hospital's impressive former church, now the debating chamber – is open for public view when parliament is not sitting.

Santa Marina

C/San Luis

The Gothic-Mudéjar church of **Santa Marina** is set back from the road in a *plazuela*. Founded in the thirteenth century, the oldest feature here must be the doorway, dating

---

THE FORGOTTEN BROTHERHOOD

The Macarena church of Santa Marina is home to the **Cofradía del Resucitado** (Brotherhood of the Resurrection), the newest of all the brotherhoods who march in the Semana Santa processions. Founded in 1969, it has never been taken to its heart by a citizenry whose apparent lack of interest in this celebration of the Redeemer's return is in marked contrast with the grisly enthusiasm they evidence for each act in the Passion leading up to his death. However, this apathy is the visitor's opportunity, for when El Resucitado leaves Santa Marina at four-thirty in the early dawn of Easter Sunday you'll get a perfect view of the intricate manoeuvres performed by the *costaleros* (porters) to negotiate the two *pasos* – the Risen Christ and the aptly titled Vírgen de la Aurora (Virgin of the Dawn) – through the church's doors, which are normally obscured by vast crowds elsewhere. And as there are no seats lining the atmospheric C/Sierpes, which is almost impossible to get near during the other processions, you will be able to accompany the *pasos*, the band and the masked, candle-bearing *nazarenos* (penitents) in their all-white tunics along here as the dawn breaks – calling in at nearby bars for a café and maybe a *churro* or two.

The procession then passes through a sombre Plaza de San Francisco where the normally packed grandstands are eerily empty. Security is also lax at the cathedral, and with a bit of nimble footwork you should be able to follow the *pasos* through the church and past the enormous monstrance inside to emerge in a sunlit Plaza Vírgen de los Reyes beneath the Giralda tower, where a few *sevillanos* have usually gathered to pay their respects. If you wanted to follow El Resucitado back to Santa Marina it's a great (if slow) meander until they arrive home at about two in the afternoon.

from around 1300, which has Gothic archivolts, or arch mouldings, with Mudéjar star decoration on the outer band. Another church badly damaged in the Civil War, Santa Marina was in ruins for decades, and only spruced up for Expo 92 when the interior was entirely restored. It is now home to the Cofradía del Resucitado, the Brotherhood of the Resurrection (see box, p.283).

San Luís
C/San Luis • Sept–June Tues–Thurs 9am–2pm, Fri & Sat 9am–2pm & 5–8pm • Free

The church of **San Luís** is a glorious eighteenth-century structure, preserved in 1995 from demolition after the city government had said they couldn't afford to save it. Public outcry forced a change of heart and the riot of a Churrigueresque facade, topped by glazed-tile domes, has now been restored along with the interior, which features a fine fresco by Lucas Valdés on the central dome. The church is also floodlit at night to spectacular effect.

San Marcos
Plaza San Marcos

The fourteenth-century **San Marcos** sits in the plaza of the same name. Another fine Macarena church built on the site of an earlier mosque, it has a Mudéjar tower – note the Giralda-style *sebka* brickwork – and a superb Gothic-Mudéjar entrance. Although gutted by fire during the Civil War and since restored, its interior uniquely preserves the original Mudéjar horseshoe arches dividing nave and aisles. At the head of the north aisle there's a seventeenth-century sculpture in painted wood of San Marcos, by Juan de Mesa. Cervantes used to climb San Marcos's tower to view the plant-filled and peaceful patio of the convent of Santa Isabel just behind the church. You can see why.

ARRIVAL   **SEVILLE**

BY PLANE
Seville's **airport** (☎ 954 449 000) lies 12km northeast of town along the A4 (NIV) *autovía* towards Córdoba. From here the airport bus (daily 5am–1.10am; roughly every 30min; reduced service Sat & Sun; 30min; €2.40) runs to the Avda. del Cid (also the departure point), close to the Prado de San Sebastián bus station, with a stop at the train station en route. Taxis officially cost €25 (plus €1/bag and modest surcharge after 9pm and on Sun).

BY TRAIN
The city's train station, **Santa Justa** (☎ 954 540 202), is some way northeast of the centre, on Avda. Kansas City. Bus #32 will get you from the station to the central Plaza Ponce de León (close to the church of Santa Catalina), while bus lines #28 or #C1 take you to the main Prado de San Sebastián bus station.

Destinations Algeciras (5 daily; change at Bobadilla); Almería (4 daily; 5hr 40min); Cádiz (14 daily; 1hr 50min); Córdoba (AVE 19 daily; 45min; 5 daily; 1hr 20min); Granada (4 daily; 3hr 10min); Jaén (3 daily; 3hr 12min); Huelva (3 daily; 1hr 38min); Málaga (10 daily; 2hr 30min); Osuna (9 daily; 1hr).

BY BUS
The **Prado de San Sebastián bus station** (☎ 954 417 111), on the eastern edge of the Barrio Santa Cruz, is the city's main bus station. However, services from and to northern Seville (including Itálica), Extremadura (provinces of Cáceres and Badajoz), Huelva province, Madrid and international destinations arrive and depart from the station at **Plaza de Armas** (☎ 954 908 040) by the Puente del Cachorro, on the river; from here, bus #C3 will get you to the Prado de San Sebastián bus station.

Destinations Algeciras (4 daily; 3hr 30min); Almería (3 daily; 5hr 15min); Aracena (1 daily; 1hr 45min); Arcos de la Frontera (3 daily; 2hr); Ayamonte (access to Portugal's Algarve; 3 daily; 2hr); Cádiz (10 daily; 1hr 45min); Carmona (16 Mon, Fri; 7 Sat, Sun; 30min); Constantina (9 daily; 1 hr 40min); Córdoba (8 daily; 1hr 45min); Écija (9 Mon-Fri; 5 Sat,Sun; 1hr 15min); El Rocío (4 daily; 1hr); Matalascañas (3 Mon–Thurs, Sat,Sun; 1 Fri; 1hr 30min); Huelva (20 daily; 1hr 15min); Jaén (1 daily; 4hr); Jerez de la Frontera (7 daily; 1hr 15min); Málaga (6 daily; 2hr 30min); Madrid (4 daily; 6hr); Málaga (6 daily; 4hr); Torremolinos (3 daily; 2hr); Osuna (9 daily; 1hr); Ronda (6 Mon-Sat; 1 Sun; 2hr); Santiponce (Itálica up to 30 daily; 45min).

BY CAR
Driving in Seville is an ordeal, especially in the narrow streets of *barrios* such as Santa Cruz, and parking spaces are almost impossible to find. Your best bet for parking is to find a pay car park, or to choose accommodation with a garage (see p.286).

FROM TOP PARQUE MARÍA LUISA, SEVILLE (P.268); FLAMENCO, SEVILLE (P.298); PLAZA DE ESPAÑA, SEVILLE (P.270) >

3

INFORMATION

Turismo Seville's Turismo, just south of the cathedral at Avda. de la Constitución 21 (Mon–Fri 9am–7.30pm, Sat 10am–3.30pm; ☎ 954 7875 78), can provide good city maps and an excellent free monthly listings guide, *El Giraldillo* (ⓦ elgiraldillo.es), but is often overwhelmed in high season. There's a quieter municipal tourist office (Mon–Fri 9am–7.30pm, Sat & Sun 10am–2pm; ☎ 954 471 232, ⓦ visitasevilla.es) in the Edificio Laredo building at the northern end of Plaza de San Francisco.

Map The *Guía Verde Callejero* street guide, available from *Kioskos* and bookshops, is an invaluable aid to finding your way around the city's more convoluted corners.

Newspapers Seville's best all-round daily paper is *El Diario de Sevilla*, although the older *El Correo* also sells well; both are good for entertainment listings and local news.

Online See ⓦ visitasevilla.es and ⓦ exploreseville.com.

GETTING AROUND

By bus All bus journeys have a flat fare of €1.30. If you're planning on getting around a lot by bus, invest in a *tarjeta multiviaje* (card pass) which works out at €0.64 per journey. The card can be bought for €1.50 from Tussam (Seville's bus company) kiosks in the Prado de San Sebastián bus station or the Plaza Ponce de León, or from any of the over 700 participating *kioskos* (news stands) throughout the city. You then load the card with any amount from €6.40 to €50 and recharge as needed. A Tussam route map is available from the same kiosks or tourist offices, or on their website (ⓦ tussam.es). Useful buses are #C1, #C3 (clockwise), #C2 and #C4 (anticlockwise) lines, which roughly circle the city centre.

Bus tours Sevilla Tour offers hop-on/hop-off open-top bus tours, stopping at or near the main sites (every 30min from the Torre del Oro; ☎ 902 101 081; €16).

By tram Seville's tram system (tickets €1.35) presently runs only from Plaza Nueva to the Prado de San Sebastián bus station (just over 1km) but will be expanding in the years to come.

By metro A new metro system will eventually crisscross the city, the first sections of which – linking the southern suburbs to the Puerto de Jerez and Triana – opened in 2009.

By taxi The main central taxi ranks are in Plaza Nueva, Plaza de la Victoria, the Alameda de Hércules, and the Plaza de Armas and Prado de San Sebastián bus stations. The basic charge for a short journey is around €4–5. Reliable taxi services include Radio Taxi ☎ 954 580 000 and TeleTaxi ☎ 954 622 222.

ACCOMMODATION

Rooms in Seville are relatively expensive, and in **high season** (early summer, Semana Santa and Feria de Abril) you can find yourself paying ridiculous amounts for what is little more than a cell (while for Semana Santa and the April *feria* you should also book as far ahead as possible). At other times, however, prices can drop dramatically, and it's worth checking websites for special offers. We have quoted the *temporada media* (mid-season) rate below, which applies to the rest of the year outside high season, barring January and February, when prices are at their lowest. By far the most attractive (and priciest) area to stay is the **Barrio Santa Cruz**, while other central but more reasonably priced options lie around the churches of Santa Catalina and San Pedro, and clustered around the Alameda de Hércules. Many hotels have **garages** or can assist with parking (usually €15–20/day).

BARRIO SANTA CRUZ AND CATHEDRAL AREA

Casa La Luna C/Mariana de Pineda 9 ☎ 954 218 389, ⓦ lacasadelaluna.es; map pp.254–255. Cosy *hostal* with smart if simple rooms – all en suite with a/c, TV and safe – in a quiet pedestrian street. **€56**

Hostal Atenas C/Caballerizas 1 ☎ 954 218 047, ⓔ atenas@hostal-atenas.com; map pp.254–255. A pretty, plant-festooned passage leads to a charming *pensión* decorated with *azulejos*; the proprietors are welcoming and all rooms are en suite and have a/c. Free wi-fi. **€59**

Hostal Pérez Montilla Plaza Curtidores 13 ☎ 954 421 854, ⓔ info@pensionperezmontilla.com; map pp.254–255. Spotless *hostal* on a tranquil square. More expensive rooms come with bath and a/c. Quoted prices can drop when business is slack. **€35**

Hostal Puerta Carmona Plaza de San Agustín 5 ☎ 954 988 310, ⓦ hostalpuertacarmona.es; map pp.254–255. Very pleasant *hostal* owned by the proprietors of *Hotel Maestre* in Córdoba (see p.384). Good-value modern en-suite rooms with a/c, TV and free wi-fi. They can advise on where to park nearby. **€55**

Hostal Santa María C/Hernando Colón 19 ☎ 954 228 505, ⓔ juanibort@hotmail.com; map pp.254–255. Small, simple, cheap and friendly place on a busy street in the Giralda's shadow. All rooms are en suite, with a/c and TV. **€40**

Hostal Santa María de la Blanca C/Santa María La Blanca ☎ 954 421 174; map pp.254–255. Friendly small *hostal* above a shop, through which you gain entry; there are some en-suite a/c rooms plus cheaper ones sharing bath. Check the room you are offered as some lack light. **€35**

Hostal Sierpes Corral del Rey 22 ☎954 224 948, ⓦwww.sierpes.com; map pp.254–255. Welcoming *hostal* with light and airy en-suite a/c rooms (#104 & #306 are particularly spacious) arranged around a central patio. Has own restaurant and garage. **€76**

Hostería del Laurel Plaza de los Venerables 5 ☎954 220 295, ⓦhosteriadellaurel.com; map pp.254–255. Comfortable a/c en-suite rooms with TV above a very good restaurant and tapas bar – a superb location, although it can get a bit overrun with visitors in high season. B&B **€114**

Hotel Adriano C/Adriano 12, ☎954 293 800, ⓦadrianohotel.com; map pp.254–255. Close to the bullring, this stylish two-star hotel has elegantly furnished a/c rooms with satellite TV (half are no-smoking). There's also a roof terrace, compact gym/spa, plus free wi-fi and a garage. **€140**

Hotel Alcántara C/Ximénez de Enciso 28 ☎954 500 595, ⓦhotelalcantara.net; map pp.254–255. Smart, compact and good-value two-star hotel close to Plaza Santa Cruz, with light, tastefully furnished a/c rooms (including some singles) with safe. There's also free wi-fi and a pleasant breakfast patio. **€79**

Hotel Alfonso XIII C/San Fernando 2 ☎954 917 000, ⓦluxurycollection.com/alfonsoxiii; map pp.254–255. A monument in its own right (see p.268), this has a fair claim to being Seville's number-one hotel; the public rooms and patio are stunning but unless you're into pompous decor (which a substantial refurbishment may be about to change), a visit to the bar or restaurant might be better than overnighting here. **€426**

Hotel Alminar C/Álvarez Quintero 52 ☎954 293 913, ⓦhotelalminar.com; map pp.254–255. Recently created small hotel inside a former textile workshop, 50m from the Giralda. Elegantly furnished exterior balcony rooms are equipped with a/c, TV, CD player and minibar, while up top there are two pricier superior rooms, each with ample roof terrace and stunning views. Free wi-fi. The hotel can advise on public car parks nearby. **€95**

★ **Hotel Amadeus** C/Farnesio 6, near the Iglesia de Santa Cruz ☎954 501 443, ⓦhotelamadeussevilla .com; map pp.254–255. Welcoming hotel – housed in an eighteenth-century *casa señorial* – owned by an *aficionada* of the great composer. There's a grand piano for use by guests (other instruments can be borrowed), and the soundproofed and stylish rooms come with a/c, satellite TV and free wi-fi. The house is topped off with a stunning roof terrace for taking breakfast, where there's also a telescope for night-time astronomical contemplations. Public car park nearby. **€103**

Hotel Convento La Gloria C/Argote de Molina 26 ☎954 293 670, ⓦhotelconventolagloria.es; map pp.254–255. Charming three-star hotel inside a former convent with many features – such as painted ceilings, *azulejos* and patios – surviving from its former incarnation. The rooms are comfortable and well equipped and with safe and a/c; six have views of the Giralda and cathedral. Public garage nearby. **€149**

Hotel Doña Manuela Paseo de Catalina de Ribera 2 ☎954 546 400, ⓦhoteldonamanuela.com; map pp.254–255. Good-value two-star hotel in a great location, with rooms on the west side overlooking the Jardines de Murillo. Rooms come with a/c, satellite TV, safe and free wi-fi, and there's a roof terrace with sun loungers (while the three top-floor suites have with their own terraces). Car park. **€89**

Hotel El Rey Moro C/Lope de Rueda 14 ☎954 563 468, ⓦelreymoro.com; map pp.254–255. Attractive boutique hotel with beautifully furnished rooms (with wi-fi and plasma TV) and bathrooms overlooking two patios. Ask for a room (any of nos.10–25) on the quieter "interior" patio – the other gets noise from the hotel's restaurant. Free wi-fi and garage nearby. Free cycle hire for guests. See website for offers. **€180**

Hotel Goya C/Mateos Gago 31 ☎95 421 11 70, ⓦhotel goyasevilla.com; map pp.254–255. Small traditional hotel in the heart of Santa Cruz with a good range of attractive a/c en-suite rooms equipped with satellite TV and free wi-fi. **€85**

Hotel La Rábida C/Castelar 24 ☎954 501 280, ⓦvincci hoteles.com; map pp.254–255. Recently refurbished traditional four-star hotel inside a *casa palacio* with a nice patios, lots of marble and good facilities. Rooms in the older part have more character, but all come well equipped and there's free wi-fi. Special offers (see website) can reduce rates considerably. **€188**

★ **Hotel Las Casas de la Judería** C/Callejón de Dos Hermanas 7 ☎954 415 150, ⓦcasasypalacios.com; map pp.254–255. Housed in a stunningly beautiful old aristocratic mansion and now incorporating numerous other adjacent buildings, this is a serene four-star hotel with pastel-tinted rooms sporting sumptuous and delightfully varied furnishings. Exquisite patios, gardens and a restaurant complete the picture. Good value for this category. Parking available. **€180**

Hotel Murillo C/Lope de Rueda 7 ☎954 216 095, ⓦhotelmurillo.com; map pp.254–255. Excellent-value traditional hotel with amusingly kitsch features such as suits of armour in the lobby, and paint-palette room key rings. Housed in a restored mansion, the attractive modern rooms come with all facilities including wi-fi, and there's a stunning rooftop bar with Giralda view. Also rents some equally attractive and fully equipped studios and apartments nearby (sleeping 1–5) for not much more than the room price (details on website). Public parking close by. Outstanding value in July and Aug. Rooms **€50**, apartments **€70**

Hotel Simón C/García de Vinuesa 19 ☎954 226 660, ⓦhotelsimonsevilla.com; map pp.254–255.

Eighteenth-century mansion with elegant patio and excellent position near the cathedral. Rooms are adequate, with a/c and individual styling, although they vary in size – those on the first floor are the most spacious, while the top floor has the pokiest. Free wi-fi zone and public parking nearby. **€65**

Las Casas del Rey de Baeza Plaza Jesús de la Redención 2 ☎ 954 561 496, ⓦ hospes.es; map pp.254–255. Ultra-cool four-star boutique hotel with rooms arranged around an eighteenth-century *corral sevillano*. The plant-bedecked interior patio is charming and the stylishly furnished rooms come with traditional exterior *esparto* blinds, a neat finishing touch – and there's a rooftop pool to cool off in. Can arrange parking. **€275**

Pensión Doña Trinidad C/Archeros 7 ☎ 954 541 906, ⓦ donatrinidad.com; map pp.254–255. Sparkling *hostal* with simple but pleasant a/c en-suite rooms (some single) around a central patio. Free wi-fi and public parking nearby. **€55**

YH Giralda C/Abades 30 ☎ 954 228 324, ⓦ yh-hoteles .com. Despite the name this is not a youth hostel but a welcoming and very pleasant small hotel in a restored eighteenth-century *casa de abades* (abbot's residence) only 100m from the cathedral. Most of the rooms are high-ceilinged and beamed and come with tasteful furnishings and free wi-fi. Public parking nearby. **€90**

PLAZA NUEVA, REYES CATÓLICOS AND MUSEO DE BELLAS ARTES

Hostal Naranjo C/San Roque 11 ☎ 954 225 840, ⓦ www.bandbsevilla.com; map pp.254–255. Welcoming and competitively priced *hostal* close to the Museo Bellas Artes offering decent a/c en-suite rooms with TV and safe, plus free wi-fi. B&B **€65**

Hostal Paco's C/Pedro del Toro 7, off C/Gravina ☎ 954 217 183, ⓦ sol.com/hostales-sp; map pp.254–255. Friendly, basic place with clean and economical en-suite rooms. The same proprietor has a number of similar *hostales* nearby (some sharing bath are even cheaper). **€42**

Hostal Redes C/Redes 28 ☎ 954 901 946, ⓦ hostal -redes-sevilla.com; map pp.254–255. Clean and tidy *hostal* offering en-suite rooms with TV and a/c (only charged for if used), plus free wi-fi. B&B **€30**

Hostal Romero C/Gravina 21 ☎ 954 211 353, ⓦ pension romerosevilla.es; map pp.254–255. Basic but efficient, clean and friendly *hostal* with plant-bedecked patio and rooms (all a/c) either sharing bath and with en suite – the latter also come with TV. Free wi-fi and public parking nearby. **€30**

Hotel Europa C/Jimios 5 ☎ 954 214 305, ⓦ hotel europasevilla.com; map pp.254–255. Elegant, traditional and welcoming hotel in an eighteenth-century mansion offering comfortable if soberly furnished rooms with safe and satellite TV. Own garage. **€119**

Hotel Madrid C/San Pedro Mártir 22 ☎ 954 214 306, ⓦ hotelmadridsevilla.es; map pp.254–255. Pleasant, recently refurbished family-run hotel in a vibrant part of the city offering functional a/c balcony rooms with TV and free wi-fi. Can advise on parking. **€55**

Hotel Petit Palace C/Canalejas 2 ☎ 954 210 773, ⓦ hthoteles.com; map pp.254–255. The former *Hotel Plaza-Sevilla* has a new name but the stunning Neoclassical facade – the work of Aníbal González, architect of the Plaza de España – remains the same. The rather compact but well-equipped rooms come with PC and exercise bike. Free wi-fi. See website for offers. **€150**

Hotel Zaida C/San Roque 26 ☎ 954 211 138, ⓦ hotel zaida.com; map pp.254–255. Charming and intimate hotel in an eighteenth-century neo-Mudéjar mansion with a fine exterior and an interior replete with plasterwork and *azulejos*. The comfortable rooms come with bath, TV and a/c, although some single rooms lack light. **€65**

SANTA CATALINA, SAN PEDRO, ALAMEDA DE HÉRCULES

Hostal Alameda Alameda de Hércules 31 ☎ 954 900 191, ⓦ hostalalameda.es; map pp.254–255. Modern, pleasant and very friendly *hostal* offering a mixture of rooms (en suite or shared bath) with a/c, TV, free wi-fi and a balcony view of the Alameda. Can assist with parking. **€35**

★ **Hostal Doña Feli** C/Jesús del Gran Poder 130 ☎ 954 901 048, ⓦ hostaldonafeli.com; map pp.254–255. At the northern end of the atmospheric Alameda de Hércules this is a very pleasant (and economically priced) small *hostal* with neat and tidy en-suite rooms equipped with a/c and TV. Own garage with low rates. **€50**

Hostal Trajano C/Trajano 3 ☎ 954 382 421, ⓦ hostaltrajano.com; map pp.254–255. This friendly *hostal* has basic but decent value a/c en-suite rooms with TV. Also has a free wi-fi zone, and there's a public car park nearby. **€50**

Hotel Casona de San Andrés C/Daóiz 7 ☎ 954 915 253, ⓦ casonadesanandres.com; map pp.254–255. Former nineteenth-century *casa palacio*, recently transformed into a pleasant hotel, with attractive balcony rooms facing either a pedestrianized square or two interior patios. Free wi-fi. **€50**

Hotel Patio de la Alameda Alameda de Hércules 56 ☎ 954 904 999, ⓦ patiodelaalameda.com; map pp.254–255. Partly sixteenth-century *casa palacio* revamped into an elegant hotel with light and airy balcony rooms plus three patios and own garage. Free wi-fi. **€90**

Hotel Patio de la Cartuja C/Lumbreras 8 ☎ 954 900 200, ⓦ patiosdesevilla.com; map pp.254–255. Unique, stylish and good-value apart-hotel created from an old *corral sevillano* with balconies around a tiled patio. All rooms have kitchen and *salón* and there's a garage. **€60**

★ **Hotel Sacristía Santa Ana** Alameda de Hércules 22 ☎954 915 722, ⓦhotelsacristia.com; map pp.254–255. Beautiful boutique hotel with delightful rooms inside an eighteenth-century religious building with many original features including a delightful patio, *artesonado* ceilings and antique furnishings. The nicer external rooms have Alameda views and there's also free wi-fi. Public parking nearby. **€106**

Hotel Sevilla C/Daóiz 5 ☎954 384 161, ⓦwww.hotel -sevilla.org; map pp.254–255. Revamped and refurbished old hotel with a nice patio and stylishly furnished rooms with a/c and TV. Those at the front offer balcony views onto a pleasant *plazuela*. **€80**

LA MACARENA

Hostal La Muralla C/Fray Diego de Cádiz 39 ☎954 371 049, ⓦhostalmurallamacarena.com; map pp.254–255. Pleasant and good-value *hostal* facing the medieval walls. All rooms are en suite and come with bath, a/c and TV. Own car park with low rates. **€30**

Hotel San Gil C/Parras 28 ☎954 906 811, ⓦhotel sangil.com; map pp.254–255. Luxurious hotel in a beautifully restored early 1900s *casa palacio*. Rooms are bright, spacious and stylishly furnished and come with minibar and free wi-fi. Public facilities include a garden with palms and cypresses, rooftop pool, restaurant, garage, and an interior decorated with mosaics and *azulejos*. **€80**

OUT OF TOWN

Albergue Juvenil Sevilla C/Isaac Peral 2 ☎955 035 886, ⓦinturjoven.com; map pp.254–255. Seville's leafy if sometimes crowded youth hostel has basic en-suite double and triple rooms. It's also some way out: take bus #34 from Puerta de Jerez by the Turismo or from Plaza Nueva. Note that they tend not to answer the phone. Under 26 **€21**, over 26 **€27**

Camping Villsom N-IV, km554.8, 10km out of town on the main Cádiz road ☎&☎954 720 828; map pp.254–255. This recently overhauled campsite with a pool is the nearest to the city. Half-hourly buses from C/La Rábida (near the Fábrica de Tabacos) take 20min. Make sure to take the bus M-132 signed "Dos Hermanas por Barriadas", which will drop you outside the campsite. Two people plus car **€20**

EATING AND DRINKING

Seville is tremendously atmospheric in the evening, packed with lively and enjoyable bars and clubs. That the city has never been particularly noted for its restaurants may have a lot to do with its strong **tapas** tradition (see p.293). Great though this is, even the most enthusiastic *tapeadores* eventually tire of "plate-pecking" to seek out a place to sit down for a more conventional meal.

RESTAURANTS

BARRIO SANTA CRUZ AND CATHEDRAL AREA

To eat well without breaking the bank, you generally have to steer clear of the restaurants around the major sights and in the Barrio Santa Cruz. However, there are some reasonable options: the streets around the *barrio's* northern edge (framed by *calles* Menéndez Pelayo and Santa María la Blanca) are a good hunting ground.

Bar Modesto C/Cano y Cueto 5; map pp.290–291. More a touristy terrace restaurant these days than purely a bar, it is still renowned for its tapas which (unless trade is slow) you'll need to eat at the bar. The kitchen is pretty good at straightforward meals, too, and there's a *menú* for around €20. Main dishes €11–20. Daily 8am–2am.

Café Rayuela C/Miguel de Mañara 9; map pp.290–291. Pleasant lunchtime venue serving economically priced *raciones* (and *media raciones*), *montaditos* (*tapa* on bread) and salads at outdoor tables in a pedestrianized street. Weekday *menú* for €9.50. Daily 9am–11pm.

Corral del Agua Callejón del Agua 6 ☎954 220 714; map pp.290–291. Very good if pricey restaurant serving *cocina andaluza* in a lovely, plant-filled patio. Try their *ajo blanco* (chilled almond soup) or the house special *lubina al Tío Pepe* (sea bass with a sherry sauce). There's an unpublicized weekday lunchtime *menú* for around €22 (including wine) which you may need to ask for. Main dishes €17–25. Mon–Sat noon–4pm & 8pm–midnight.

Doña Francisquita C/Álvarez Quintero 58, near the cathedral; map pp.290–291. A good lunch stop for authentic and tasty pizzas cooked in a wood-burning oven, although the rest of the Italian-style menu isn't up to the same standard. Mon–Sat noon–1.30am.

Duplex C/Don Remondo 1; map pp.290–291. Pleasant and economical new-style *sevillano* diner serving a series of two course *menús* for €8–12.50 as well as a range of *platos combinados*. Also salads and tapas (€3–4). Daily noon–midnight.

El Cabildo Plaza del Cabildo s/n ☎954 227 970; map pp.290–291. Elegant mid-priced traditional restaurant specializing in Mediterranean cuisine. *Arrozes* (rice dishes) and paella are house specialities, and there's a daily €18 *menú* which you may need to ask for. Main dishes €15–25. Daily 1–5pm & 8pm–midnight.

Kaede C/Sta. María la Blanca 32; map pp.290–291. Authentic and entertaining Japanese restaurant. Sushi, sashimi or tempura are included on a good-value *menú* for €15. Daily 1–4pm & 8pm–midnight.

La Albahaca Plaza Santa Cruz 9 ☎954 220 714; map pp.290–291. Charming and excellent traditional restaurant housed in a converted mansion with three

SEVILLE RESTAURANTS, TAPAS BARS AND NIGHTLIFE

RESTAURANTS

As-Sawïrah	74
Bar Dueñas	28
Bar Modesto	5
Bar-Restaurante Casa Manolo	83
Café Rayuela	27
Casablanca	31
Contenedor	26
Corral del Agua	15
Doña Francisquita	32
Duplex	24
El Búcaro	75
El Cabildo	45
El Manijero	80
Horacio	59
Kaede	4
La Albahaca	8
La Judería	3
La Primera del Puente	57
Lar Gallego	1
Mama Terra	33
Mesón del Pulpo	39
Mesón Serranito	56/69
Nueva Victoria	84
Pando	71
Restaurante Enrique Becerra	51
Restaurante Japonés Samurai	63
Restaurante Las Piletas	79
Restaurante Los Gallegos	61
Río Grande	47
Taberna El Alabardero	64
Zarabanda	67

TAPAS BARS

Bar Alicantina	38	Bar Europa	34	Bodega de Juan		Casa Román	11
Bar Anselma	85	Bar Feli	70	García Aviles		Cervecería	
Bar Antonio		Bar Giralda	25	Bodega Paco Góngara	54	Internacional	49
Romero	58	Bar Hermanos		Bodega Santa Cruz		El Bacalao	17
Bar Bistec	66	Gómez	6	Bodega Siglo XVIII	72	El Faro de Triana	82
Bar Dos de Mayo	73	Bar Quita Pesares	14	Café Universal		El Rincón Gallego	46
Bar Enrique		Bar Santa Ana	68	Casa Los Caracoles	30	El Rinconcillo	22
Becerra	52	Bar Sol y Sombra	87	Casa Morales	40	Entrecárceles	42
Bar Eslava	76	Bodega Belmonte	18	Casa Robles	35	Freiduría La Isla	44

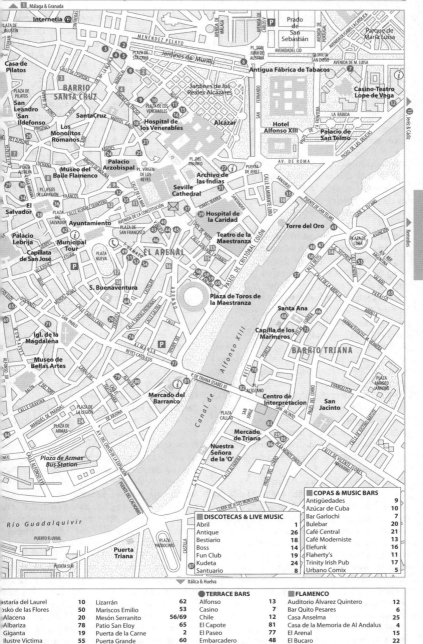

3

■ DISCOTECAS & LIVE MUSIC

Abril	1
Antique	26
Bestiario	18
Boss	14
Fun Club	19
Kudeta	24
Santuario	8

■ COPAS & MUSIC BARS

Antigüedades	9
Azúcar de Cuba	10
Bar Garlochi	7
Bulebar	20
Café Central	21
Café Moderniste	13
Elefunk	16
Flaherty's	11
Trinity Irish Pub	17
Urbano Comix	5

● TERRACE BARS

Alfonso	13
Casino	7
Chile	12
El Capote	81
El Paseo	77
Embarcadero	48
Puerto de Cuba	41

■ FLAMENCO

Auditorio Álvarez Quintero	12
Bar Quito Pesares	6
Casa Anselma	25
Casa de la Memoria de Al Andalus	4
El Arenal	15
El Bucaro	22
La Carbonería	3
Los Gallos	2
Teatro Central	23

...staría del Laurel	10	Lizarrán	62	
...osko de las Flores	50	Mariscos Emilio	53	
...Alacena	20	Mesón Serranito	56/69	
...Albariza	78	Patio San Eloy	65	
...Giganta	19	Puerta de la Carne	2	
...Ilustre Victima	55	Puerta Grande	60	
...Moneda	37	Sopa de Ganso	29	
...s Golondrinas	86	Taberna Coloniales	23	
...s Teresas	9	Taberna Coloniales II	43	

intimate period rooms featuring chandeliers and original paintings. Signature dishes include *jabalí al horno* (oven-baked wild boar) and a delicious orange mousse dessert. There's a *menú* for around €20. Main dishes €15–25. Mon–Sat noon–4pm & 8pm–midnight.

La Judería C/Cano y Cueto 13 ☎954 426 456; map pp.290–291. Popular and pleasant mid-priced restaurant with a daily *menú* for €20. The restaurant is noted for its *revueltos* (scrambled egg dishes) and house specials include *cordero lechal* (suckling lamb) and *urta a la roteña* (sea bream). Main dishes €10–18. Daily 1–3.30pm & 8.30–11.30pm.

Mesón del Pulpo C/Tomás Ibarra 10; map pp.290–291. Excellent little Galician restaurant popular with locals. Specializes (as its name implies) in *pulpo a la gallega* (octopus), and there's a decent *menú* for €10. Daily 9am–4pm & 8pm–midnight.

THE RÍO GUADALQUIVIR AND TRIANA

Across the river, **Triana** offers some excellent restaurants. Near the Puente San Telmo, a number of restaurants along C/Salado cater for workers from the Los Remedios business quarter, and along C/Betis close to the water's edge are a number of restaurants with terraces looking out over the city. Around C/García Vinuesa to the west of the cathedral there's an abundance of reasonable *bocadillo* bars and delis for picnic food.

As-Sawïrah C/Galera 5; map pp.290–291. Superb Moroccan restaurant with a great ambience offering a variety of North African dishes including a delicate couscous and their house special *tajin de cordero con membrillos* (lamb with quinces). Weekday lunch *menú* €12. Mon–Sat 2–4pm & 9.30pm–midnight.

Bar-Restaurante Casa Manolo C/San Jorge 16; map pp.290–291. Buzzing Triana bar-restaurant with tapas and *raciones* (or breakfast) in the bar or economical *platos combinados* in a dining room just off it. Daily 9am–6pm & 8pm–1am.

Casablanca C/Adolfo Rodríguez Jurado 12, facing the Turismo; map pp.290–291. Smart, mid-priced restaurant and tapas bar that is noted for its excellent fish dishes – including *mero con frambuesa* (grouper with raspberries) – but also does meat. Their tapas include a tasty *tortilla* and they also make their own desserts. They insist that their tapas bar was once visited by an incognito King Juan Carlos to sample their *papas aliñas* (marinated potatoes). Mon–Fri 7am–5pm & 8.30pm–12.30am. Closed Aug.

El Manijero C/Trastamara 15; map pp.290–291. Excellent and economical neighbourhood bar-restaurant with a tapas and *raciones* bar at the front and a dining room off this. Try the *secreto* pork, *solomillo ibérico* (pork loin) or *gambas rebozadas* (prawns in batter). Daily 12.30–4pm & 8–11pm.

Horacio C/Antonia Díaz 9 ☎954 225 385; map pp.290–291. Moderately priced fish and meat dishes at this very

pleasant small restaurant near the bullring. *Escalopinas en oloroso* (veal in a sherry sauce) is a house special and they also offer seasonally changing creative *menús* (from €32 including wine) and paella (€26 for two). Main dishes €12–17. Daily 12.30–4pm & 7.30pm–midnight.

La Primera del Puente C/Betis 66; map pp.290–291. One of the city's best options for economical yet generous *raciones* of fried fish, meat and *mariscos*; their wines are also reasonably priced. Sweet talk a waiter to get a frontline table for the spectacular river view from their terrace. Daily except Wed 11.30am–4.30pm & 8pm–1am.

Mamma Terra Corner of Paseo Colón and Avda. Cristina; map pp.290–291. Organic *cafetería* with large selection of vegetarian food ranging from grilled vegetable pitas to tofu burgers. There's also a *menú* for €10. Daily 12.30–9pm.

Mesón Serranito C/Antonia Díaz 11; map pp.290–291. Twin restaurant of the one near El Corte Inglés (see p.293) and with similar dishes and economical *platos combinados* and – due to the location – a line of bulls' heads gazing down from the walls. *Menú* for €9. Daily 1.30–4pm & 8–11pm.

★ **Nueva Victoria** C/Torneo 85; map pp.290–291. Superb new place comprising a bright and airy bar with terrace and more serious starched table-linen and flowers-on-the-table restaurant further in. Both serve up excellent food at moderate prices. Tapas in the bar are in fact *media raciones* (around €5–7): try the *queso gratinado con pimientos* (goat's cheese with peppers) or, in the restaurant, the succulent *venado* (venison), *solomillo* (pork loin) and *carrillada* (pork cheek). Main dishes (restaurant) €6–18; *menús* €14–20. Daily noon–midnight.

Restaurante Enrique Becerra C/Gamazo 2 ☎954 213 049; map pp.290–291. Mid-priced restaurant in a rambling seventeenth-century house (complete with Roman pillars lifted from Itálica) with a solid reputation for well-prepared *andaluz* dishes such as *cola de toro* (bull's tail) and *pez espada al amontillado* (swordfish). Main dishes €10–25. Mon–Sat 1–5pm & 8.30pm–midnight.

Restaurante Japonés Samurai C/Salado 6; map pp.290–291. Interesting little Japanese restaurant with versions of Oriental dishes slanted towards Spanish palates; it's more about price than culinary perfection, with an economical *menú* for €6.50. Mon–Sat noon–4.30pm & 7.30pm–12.30am.

Río Grande C/Betis 70 ☎954 273 956; map pp.290–291. One of the best places for a lunchtime feast of traditional meat and fish dishes. Whether you're seated behind the panoramic windows or on the terrace, the view across the river to the Torre del Oro and Giralda, illuminated at night, is stunning. Their next-door tapas bar – with the same terrace view – is worth a visit too. There's a *menú de degustación* for around €40. Main dishes €12–20. Daily 1–4pm & 8pm–midnight.

★ **Taberna El Alabardero** C/Zaragoza 20 ☎954 502 721; map pp.290–291. Elegant nineteenth-century *casa palacio sevillana* with attractive decor – chandeliers and artworks – and an upmarket clientele. The pricey but outstanding restaurant upstairs is one of the region's best for *andaluz* dishes served with a creative edge. Everything is done with panache and there's a *menú de degustación* for €60 (€70 with wine); however, the daily, excellent-value *menú* for €12.90 (or €17.50/€19.90 Sat & Sun lunch/evening) in the patio bar below comes from the same kitchen and is one of Seville's best-kept secrets. Main dishes €15–25. Daily 1.30–4.30pm & 8.30pm–midnight; closed Aug.

EL CENTRO, LA MACARENA, ALAMEDA AND SANTA JUSTA

Many parts of **El Centro** still possess a seedy charm, especially in its southern reaches and the remoter bits of La Macarena. This is where *sevillanos* tend to do their eating and drinking, away from the tourist sights, and you'll have no trouble finding low-priced *comidas* in and around streets such as C/San Eloy which runs into Plaza Duque de la Victoria, as well as all the main arteries of La Macarena. The Alameda de Hércules is a formerly dubious area now heading upmarket with new places opening all the time.

Bar Dueñas C/Dueñas 1, on the corner of three streets; map pp.290–291. Ancient and atmospheric *barrio* bar and just the place for a good lunch with delicious home cooking and a *menú* for €8. Their longstanding tapas specials are *riñones al jerez* (kidneys in sherry) and *menudo de ternera* (tripe stew). Daily 9am–midnight.

Contenedor C/San Luís 50; map pp.290–291. Relaxed and friendly diner with daily specials such as *arroz con setas y pato* (duck and mushroom rice) as well as curries and fish and meat dishes. There's a piano for any customers inclined to tinkle the ivories and they stage art exhibitions. Daily 9–11pm. Fri–Sun also 1.30–4pm.

El Búcaro Alfonso XII 30; map pp.290–291. Vibrant bar-diner serving up decent *raciones* – try the *queso de cabra al horno* (baked goat's cheese) or *patatas fritas con salsa brava* (in a spicy sauce). There's also a *menú* for €7 and free flamenco starting at 9.30pm on Sat evenings. Daily 11am–midnight.

★ **Lar Gallego** C/Gonzalo Bilbao 20, close to the Santa Justa train station ☎954 419 303; map pp.290–291. Excellent mid-priced Galician bar-restaurant serving *platos típicos gallegos* – fish and *mariscos* (shellfish) including oysters, scallops and *langostinos* in the restaurant – and equally good tapas at the bar. Daily 9am–2am.

Mesón Serranito C/Alfonso XII 9, behind El Corte Inglés; map pp.290–291. Cosy and economical little restaurant beyond the tapas bar out front, serving up good fish and meat dishes. *Rosada a la vasca* (rockfish) and

rabo de toro (stewed bull's tail) are house specials. Daily 8am–midnight.

Pando C/San Eloy 47; map pp.290–291. Lively, stylish and economical *raciones* restaurant which also does salads. The cooking is well done and a *frito variado* (fried fish) for €12.90 will serve two. An ideal lunch stop. Mon–Sat 8am–5pm & 8pm–2am, Sun 8am–5pm.

Restaurante Las Piletas C/Marqués de Paradas 28 ☎954 220 404; map pp.290–291. Diminutive, atmospheric (bulls' heads and framed photos) and typically *sevillano* mid-priced restaurant with tapas bar (listing 50 possibilities) and small outdoor terrace attached. Specialities include fish and *mariscos* as well as *cola de toro* (stewed bull's tail) which is heaved over from the nearby Maestranza ring. Main dishes €10–15. Daily 1–3pm & 8pm–midnight.

Restaurante Los Gallegos C/Capataz R Franco; map pp.290–291. Friendly and inexpensive Galician restaurant in a tiny alley off C/Martín Villa, serving *gallego* specialities – try the excellent *pulpo gallego* (spicy boiled octopus) – or there's a wide range of *platos combinados*. The dessert list is headed by a home-made *tarta de Santiago*. *Menú* for €10 (lunch) or €14 (eve). Daily 11am–11pm.

Zarabanda C/Padre Tarín 6, off C/Jesús del Gran Poder; map pp.290–291. Friendly and intimate family restaurant with an Italian slant. They offer pizzas and very good traditional *sevillano* dishes such as *carillada ibérica* (stewed pork), as well as a variety of salads and *revueltos* (scrambled egg with sautéed vegetables) and a few adventurous desserts such as *mousse de dulce de leche al Carlos III* (whipped cream mousse with brandy). A good lunch stop. Main dishes €8–15. Mon noon–5pm, Tues–Sun noon–5pm & 8pm–12.30am.

TAPAS BARS

A popular saying here is *En Sevilla no se come sino que se tapea* ("In Seville you don't eat, you *tapear*"). As the city that claims to have invented tapas, Seville knocks spots off the competition. There is simply nowhere else in Andalucía – or even Spain – with such a variety of places to indulge this culinary art. **El tapeo** means eating "on the go" and *sevillanos* do it on their feet, moving from bar to bar where they stand with a manzanilla or beer – leaving the seats to tourists – whilst wolfing back fistfuls of whatever tapas take their fancy. Locals tend to drink the cold, dry **fino** with their tapas, especially *gambas* (prawns), but often change to beer in high summer. Another popular tapas partner is a **tinto de verano** – the local version of sangría – consisting of wine mixed with lemonade and ice. Finally, don't think that because the servings are small they are always cheap. Some seafood tapas can be pricey, as can the cured *jamón*, and the plates have a tendency to mount up. Making your way to some of the bars listed below will lead you into areas

3

where tapas outlets tend to congregate, enabling you to make discoveries of your own – an essential part of becoming a *tapeador*.

BARRIO SANTA CRUZ AND THE CATHEDRAL AREA

The ancient heart of Seville is filled with tapas possibilities and has a few of the very best places in town.

★ **Bar Enrique Becerra** C/Gamazo 2; map pp.290–291. The outstanding and atmospheric bar of the popular restaurant. House specials include *bocadito de mejillones* (mussels) and *ajo blanco* (almond gazpacho) as well as their famed *croquetas de rabo de toro* (croquettes stuffed with bull's tail). Their tapas – slightly pricier than elsewhere, but worth it – are served only in the bar. Mon–Sat 1–5pm & 8pm–midnight.

Bar Europa Junction of C/Alcaicería de la Loza and C/Siete Revueltas; map pp.290–291. Fine old watering hole with lots of cool tiled walls plus excellent manzanilla and a variety of tapas – try their *croquetas de espinaca* (spinach croquettes) or *butifarra* (catalan sausage) – served on marble-topped tables. There's an outdoor terrace, but the waiter service here can be hit and miss. Daily 9am–midnight.

★ **Bar Giralda** C/Mateos Gago 1; map pp.290–291. One of the city's leading bars, occupying a Moorish bathhouse with arched doorways and lots of *azulejos*, and serving a wide selection of tapas. House specials include *magret de pato* (duck), *pate de cabracho* (fish mousse), *cazuela Tío Pepe* (meat stewed with fino) and the *sevillano* favourite *espinacas con garbanzos* (spinach with chick-peas). Mon–Sat 9.30am–12.30am.

Bar Hermanos Gómez Jardines de Murillo; map pp.290–291. A branch of a chain of similar places offering excellent value for money, with economical tapas and *raciones* served on a big garden terrace. House specials include *bacalao con tomate* (cod) and *habas con jamón* (broad beans), and there's also a low-priced *menú* for €6. Tues–Sun 8am–midnight.

Bodega Belmonte C/Mateos Gago 24; map pp.290–291. A classic place with vibrant ambience and superb *raciones* (and *medias raciones*) – try their *papas arrugas* (baked potatoes) or tasty *pan de ajo con carne mechada* (garlic bread with larded meat) or *alcachofas salteados* (sautéed artichokes). Daily 11am–11pm.

Bodega de Juan García Aviles C/Mateos Gago 20; map pp.290–291. Also known as *Bar Álvaro Peregil*, this ancient and renowned bathroom-sized spit-and-sawdust place serves top-notch manzanilla and range of tapas – try the *tomate aliñado* (marinated tomatoes) as well as *jamón*, olives and manchego cheese. An interesting house speciality is *vino de naranja* (orange flavoured wine). Daily 1–5pm & 8pm–12.30am.

Bodega Santa Cruz (aka Las Columnas) C/Rodrigo Caro 1; map pp.290–291. Close to the Hospital de Venerables, this is another popular favourite, with long-in-the-tooth waiters who survived a recent refurb; standing at the bar you'll get your bill chalked up on the counter in front of you. Serves up generous tapas portions and house specials include a very good *ensaladilla* (potato salad with crab) and *pollo frito* (chicken nibbles). Daily 10am–1am.

Casa Morales C/García de Vinuesa 11; map pp.290–291. Pleasant old bar, founded in 1850, which once served barrelled Valdepeñas wine from great butts (now empty) behind the counter. Today a few simple tapas such as cheese are served on *tablas* (wooden boards); other possibilities include *pringa* (meat stew) and *menudo con garbanzos* (fried giblets with chick-peas). Mon–Sat noon–4pm & 8pm–midnight.

SWEET-TOOTH SEVILLE

Many of Seville's *conventos de clausura*, or enclosed orders of nuns, earn money to support themselves by turning out **dulces** (confectionery), and supply many of the city's leading restaurants with their desserts. Other good places to head for cakes and pastries are the *pastelerías* along C/Sierpes.

Convento de San Leandro Plaza Ildefonso 1. Renowned for its *yemas*, a sugar, syrup and egg-yolk concoction.

Convento de Santa Inés C/Doña María Coronel 5, near the church of San Pedro. The speciality here are *bollitos* (sweet buns) and *tortas almendradas* (almond cakes).

Heladería Rayas C/Almirante Apodaca 1 (near the church of San Pedro). To cool down in Seville's intense summer heat, head for the city's favourite ice-cream maker. They have the best selection, and there's a terrace, too.

★ **Horno de San Buenaventura** C/García de Vinuesa 10, on the cathedral's doorstep. Two-floor cake shop where *sevillanos* love to indulge themselves with creamy pastries and *andaluz* classics such as *tocino de cielo*.

La Campana C/Sierpes 1. The most celebrated *pastelería* in town.

Santa Paula In the heart of Macarena. Famous for its nineteen varieties of jams and marmalades, this convent also gets into the *dulces* business with Andalucía's signature dessert, the egg-yolk confection *tocino de cielo* (translated, very inadequately, as "heavenly lard").

Casa Robles C/Álvarez Quintero 58; map pp.290–291. Fronting the cathedral, with an inevitably tourist-dominated clientele, this remains a first-rate tapas venue with an equally fine mid-priced restaurant. House specials include *ortiguillas* (sea anemones), *bacalao con garbanzos* (cod with chick-peas) and a very tasty *alcachofas con salmón* (artichokes with salmon). Daily 1pm–1am.

Casa Román Plaza de los Venerables 1; map pp.290–291. Ancient and renowned tapas institution with prices a tad higher than the norm specializing in *jamón*, eaten at the bar or around the elf-sized tables outside. Other signature plates include *carillada* (stewed pork) and *chorizo de Jabugo*. Mon–Sat 9.30am–4pm & 7.30pm–midnight, Sun 9.30am–4pm.

Cervecería Internacional C/Gamazo 3; map pp.290–291. High-ceilinged beer bar with 15 world beers on draught and many more by the bottle. Also offers tapas such as *garbanzos con bacalao* (cod with chick-peas), *costillas de cerdo* (pork ribs) and *pan con jabalí* (wild boar on bread) to go with them. Mon–Sat noon–4pm & 8pm–midnight.

El Rincón Gallego C/Harinas 21; map pp.290–291. Tiny outpost of Galicia serving daily changing tapas from this northwestern province. House specials include *pulpo a la feira* (octopus with paprika) and *empanada* (Galician pie). Daily 10.30am–4.30pm & 7–11pm.

Entrecárceles C/Manuel Cortina s/n; map pp.290–291. Tiny, 150-year-old Dickensian-style bar on the site of the prison that once housed Cervantes. Specials include *anchoas con queso* (anchovies with cheese) and *melva con pimientos* (tuna with peppers), while it also serves a magnificent, rare and pricey (around €20) Fino Imperial sherry by the glass. Mon–Thurs 8pm–1am, Fri & Sat noon–5pm & 8.30pm–2am, Sun noon–5pm.

Freiduría La Isla C/García de Vinuesa 13; map pp.290–291. Great little *freiduría* serving up a wide variety of mouthwatering fried fish. The nearby *freiduría* El Arenal on C/Arfe is another excellent place, where you can take your *cartucho* (paper cone) of fish into the *El Arenal* bar almost next door (providing you buy a drink). Mon–Sat 11.30am–12.30am.

Hostería del Laurel Plaza de los Venerables 5; map pp.290–291. Historic and popular bar whose superb decor with Triana tiles is complemented by hanging *jamones* and excellent tapas. House specials include *riñones al jerez* (kidneys in fino), *zarzuelita de mariscos* (shellfish cocktail) and *patatas alioli* (potatoes in garlic mayonnaise). Daily 11.30am–4.30pm & 8pm–midnight.

La Alacena C/Águilas 6; map pp.290–291. New-style tapas bar with shop attached selling high-class *andaluz* products like *jamón* and cheese. Good tapas range includes *bacalao en aceite* (cod), and they also do desserts. Daily 12.30–4pm & 8pm–midnight.

La Moneda C/Almirantazgo 4; map pp.290–291. Lively, upscale place with prices to match serving up superb – if not over-generous – tapas and excellent manzanilla. Specials include *langostinos con bacon* (prawns wrapped in bacon) and *calamares rellenos* (stuffed squid). Also has its own attractive little mid-priced restaurant. Daily 1–4.30pm & 8.30pm–midnight.

★ **Las Teresas** C/Santa Teresa; map pp.290–291. Atmospheric, traditional L-shaped bar with cured hams hanging above tiled walls lined with photos of *toreros* and bottles of vintage sherry. Also a nice place to relax over breakfast. Specials include *queso viejo* (mature cheese), *pulpo al gallego* (octopus) and a tasty *arroz dominical* ("Sunday rice"), served only on the sabbath. Daily 9am–midnight.

Puerta de la Carne C/Santa María La Blanca 36; map pp.290–291. Not strictly a tapas bar but a *freiduría* where you can buy a *cartucho* of delicious fried fish and – with a beer from the bar – eat it out of the paper on a very pleasant terrace. Tasty things to order include *puntillitas* (small squid) and *gambas fritas* (fried prawns). Mon–Thurs 6.30pm–midnight, Fri & Sat noon–4pm & 6.30pm–midnight.

★ **Taberna Coloniales II** C/Fernandez y González 36 (at the junction with C/Jimios); map pp.290–291. Twin establishment to the original bar in Plaza Cristo de Burgos (see p.298), and up to the same high standard. Tapas are served at the bar but cornering a table will allow you to feast on a wide range of tapas including *solomillo al whisky* (pork loin) and *pollo en salsa de almendras* (chicken in almond sauce); and they also let you round it off with café and desserts. Good deals on bottled wine. Daily 12.30pm–midnight.

THE RÍO GUADALQUIVIR AND TRIANA

The streets near the river surrounding the Maestranza bullring have always been a prime spot for tapas bars, no doubt to serve the gargantuan appetites of fight fans. Triana is another excellent tapas hunting ground, both on the riverfront along C/Betis, and further into the *barrio*.

Bar Anselma C/Pagés del Corro 49; map pp.290–291. This fine old tiled place with neo-Moorish façade was designed by noted architect Aníbal González and is owned by a formidable *dueña* (the eponymous female proprietor) who bosses the bar and makes sure everyone has bought a drink. The place has many (Romería de) Rocío connections (every night at midnight the lights are dimmed and the Rocío hymn is sung) and if you're lucky you may just catch some of the best impromptu flamenco in town. House specials include *caldereta* (lamb stewed in fino), and *pisto* (stewed vegetables). Mon–Sat 11pm–until dawn.

Bar Antonio Romero C/Antonia Díaz 19; map pp.290–291. A real *tapeador's* bar that is much visited by the Maestranza crowd before and after *corridas*. Specials are *muslo de pato* (duck) and *salmón ahumado con alcaparras*

3

(smoked salmon with capers). The *anchoas en salazón* (anchovies in olive oil) is a delicious (if extravagant at €7) mini-feast. They have another bar slightly east of here at C/Gamazo 16. Daily noon–midnight.

Bar Bistec C/Pelay Correa 34; map pp.290–291. Ancient and hearty Triana hostelry opposite the church of Santa Ana, with outdoor tables in summer. Specials include *cabrillas* (spicy snails), *codorniz en salsa* (quail) and *pan de mi pueblo* (cod gazpacho). Daily except Wed 11.30am–4.30pm & 8pm–1am.

Bar Feli (aka Bar F. Rollan) C/Zaragoza 15; map pp.290–291. Atmospheric little bar with a great kitchen which turns out a range of tasty tapas. Try their gazpacho, paella, *solomillo al whisky* (pork loin), *atún al ajillo* (tuna with garlic) or a mouthwatering *higaditos de pollo* (chicken liver). There's also a *menú* for €7.90 and great beer. Daily noon–4.30pm & 7.30pm–midnight.

Bar Santa Ana C/Pureza 82; map pp.290–291. Lively *barrio* bar fronting the church of Santa Ana, with outdoor tables and a wide range of tapas and *raciones*. House special is *tortillitas de camarón* or *bacalao* (shrimps or cod in batter). Mon–Sat 7.30am–midnight, Sun noon–4pm.

Bar Sol y Sombra C/Castilla 151; map pp.290–291. At the northern end of Triana, this is another favourite with bullfight fans, and an atmospheric bar in its own right. House specials include *cola de toro* (oxtail), *almejas* (clams), and *cazuela Tío Pepe* (stew with fino). Tues–Sun 1–4pm & 8pm–midnight.

Bodega Paco Gongora C/Padre Marchena 1; map pp.290–291. Wonderful and atmospheric tapas bar in another ancient house serving a wide range of fish and meat tapas and *raciones*. Try the *mojama de atún* (blue fin tuna) or the *tortillitas de camarones* (shrimp fritters). Daily noon–4pm & 8pm–midnight.

Bodega Siglo XVIII C/Pelay Correa 32; map pp.290–291. Solid Triana establishment with pretty tiles, plenty of *corrida* posters and good tapas. House specials include *tortilla española* and *espinacas con garbanzos* (spinach with chick-peas). Tues–Sun 12.30–4pm & 8pm–1am.

El Faro de Triana Puente de Triana; map pp.290–291. Sitting atop the western end of the bridge (aka Puente de Isabel II), the dining room and roof terrace here give amazing river views. Tapas at the bar and *raciones* at the tables consist of their noted *pescaito frito* (fried fish) as well as meat and *mariscos*. Tues–Sun 11am–4.30pm & 7.30pm–12.30am.

Kiosko de las Flores C/Betis s/n, on the river; map pp.290–291. A Seville institution, this upscale *freiduría* has a prime riverside location with fine views. In season you can eat *raciones* at outdoor tables on an attractive terrace. Specials include *coquinas* (clams) and a celebrated *sardinas asadas* (grilled sardines). Tues–Sun 11am–4pm & 5pm–midnight, Sun 11am–4pm.

La Albariza C/Betis 6; map pp.290–291. Triana bar fitted out like a Jerez bodega with butts used as tables. House specials include *tortilla de camarones* (shrimps in batter) and *caña de lomo* (cured pork) as well as excellent *salchichón* (salami) and *jamón*. Mon–Sat 1–4pm & 9pm–12.30am.

★ **Las Golondrinas** Antillano Campos 26; map pp.290–291. Outstanding bar on two floors filled with Triana *azulejos* and serving quality tapas. Specials include *punta de solomillo* (sirloin steak), *alcachofas aliñados* (artichokes), *chuletitas de cordero* (lamb chops) and *rabanillos* (radishes). They've recently opened a new branch around the corner at C/Pagés del Corro 76. Daily 1–4.30pm & 8pm–12.30am.

Mariscos Emilio (aka Cervecería La Mar) C/Génova 1; map pp.290–291. Excellent and long-established bar specializing in self-service seafood tapas. House specials include *almejas* (clams), *ostras* (oysters) and *cañaíllas* (murex shellfish). Equally good Triana offshoots of the same bar are to be found at C/López de Gomara 18 (with a terrace) and C/San Jacinto 39 (corner with C/San Romero). Daily noon–midnight.

Puerta Grande C/Antonia Díaz 33, facing the Maestranza bullring; map pp.290–291. This popular bar-restaurant takes its name from the gate in the neighbouring bullring through which successful matadors get carried shoulder high. Serves up tasty *raciones* in the bar – try the *acelgas con pasas* (Swiss chard with raisins) or the inevitable house special *cola de toro* (stewed bull's tail). There's also a stylish restaurant decked out with bullfighting regalia and a decent-value *menú* for around €20. Mon–Sat 1–5pm & 9pm–1am.

EL CENTRO, ALAMEDA DE HÉRCULES AND LA MACARENA

El Centro is the bustling heart of Seville in a culinary as well as geographical sense. The areas surrounding four of the *barrio*'s focal landmarks – the Museo de las Bellas Artes, the vibrant C/Sierpes, Plaza Alfalfa and the Iglesia de Santa Catalina – provide rewarding hunting grounds for the *tapeador*, while the rejuvenated Alameda de Hércules is also now a vibrant new area for tapas bars and nightlife.

Bar Alicantina Plaza del Salvador 2; map pp.290–291. Famous bar with outdoor tables on a pleasant pedestrianized square. There's excellent tapas – served only in the bar – and *raciones* with house specials including a celebrated *ensalada rusa* (Russian salad), *pavías de bacalao* (cod croquettes) and *filetitos de corvina* (sea bass). Mon–Sat 11am–1am, Sun 11am–5pm.

Bar Dos de Mayo Plaza de la Gavidia s/n; map pp.290–291. Popular and vibrant bar with a terrace on the square and good tapas including *solomillo al whisky* (pork loin in grog), *pastel de berenjena* (aubergine terrine) and a tasty paella. Daily 12.30–4pm & 7pm–midnight.

FERIA DE ABRIL (P.301) >

3

Bar Eslava C/Eslava 3, facing the Iglesia de San Lorenzo; map pp.290–291. Excellent, very popular tapas venue with low prices and a great atmosphere. House specials include *costillas a la miel* (ribs with honey), *solomillo al eneldo* (pork loin with dill) and *boquerones rellenos* (stuffed anchovies). Also has an equally good small restaurant next door. Tues–Sat 1–4.30pm & 8.30–11.30pm, Sun 1–4.30pm.

Café Universal C/Blanca de los Rios 3; map pp.290–291. Quality tapas in pleasant surroundings with a small terrace; house special is *patatones* (potatoes with various dips), and the *tortilla de verduras* (vegetable omelette) is a good veggie option. Also does *platos combinados*. Daily 1pm–1am.

★ **Casa Los Caracoles** (aka Casa Antonio) C/Pérez Galdós, just off Plaza Alfalfa; map pp.290–291. Classic tapas bar in the vibrant Alfalfa *barrio*. There's a spacious bar for winter dining but in summer everyone sits out on their expansive terrace. House specials include (you've guessed it) *caracoles* as well as *brocheta de rape* (monkfish kebab), *solomillo al whisky* (pork loin in grog) and *bacalao a la Bilbaina* (cod in chilli sauce). Daily 12.30–4.30pm & 8pm–midnight.

El Bacalao Plaza Ponce de León 15; map pp.290–291. This venue is devoted to *bacalao* (cod) in all its manifestations, but they do have other dishes too. Specials to try are their *tortillas*, *croquetas* and *taquitos* (all cod) or the *bacalao al arroz* (paella). Tues–Sun noon–4pm & 7.30pm–1am, Sun noon–4pm.

★ **El Rinconcillo** C/Gerona 32; map pp.290–291. Seville's oldest bar (founded in 1670), just off Plaza Los Terceros, and full of atmosphere. A meeting place for the city's literati; excellent tapas are often washed down with a *coronel* ("colonel"), an ample glass of Valdepeñas red wine. Renowned for its *jamón* and cheese tapas, other specials include *espinacas con garbanzos* (spinach with chick-peas) and *bacalao con tomate* (cod). Also has an intimate little restaurant upstairs. Daily 1pm–1am.

La Giganta C/Alhóndiga 6 (facing church of Santa Catalina); map pp.290–291. Taking its name ("The Big Lady") from the city's nickname for the figure of Faith atop the Giralda tower, with numerous images of her throughout its interior. House special is *tablas* (boards of cheese or meat) and it has a wide tapas range including *costillas* (ribs) and *lomo a la cerveza* (beef stewed in beer). Tues–Sat 11.30am–midnight, Sun noon–4.30pm.

La Ilustre Víctima C/Dr Letamendi 35; map pp.290–291. Great tapas and drinking bar with original decor, street terrace, laid-back music and an eclectic tapas and *raciones* menu including dishes from Mexico as well as Asia, the Middle East and Spain. House specials include *couscous de legumbres* (vegetable), *shoarmas* (kebabs), falafel and tacos. Mon–Fri 9am–2am, Sat & Sun noon–2am.

Lizarrán C/Javier Lasso de la Vega 14; map pp.290–291. Cheap, cheerful and busy bar serving Basque-style *pintxos* (snacks on sticks). There's a wide variety to choose from (around €1 each) and when you want to pay, the barman/woman counts up the number of sticks on your plate (no cheating). Daily 10am–midnight.

Mesón Serranito Alfonso XII 9, behind El Corte Inglés; map pp.290–291. The bar adjoined to the restaurant of the same name (see p.293) is also worth a mention for great-value tapas. The house special, *serranito* (*bocadillo* with pork loin and *jamón*) uses the diminutive ironically – it's a meal in itself. Daily 8am–midnight.

Patio San Eloy C/San Eloy 9; map pp.290–291. Youthful, bustling and economical bar on a busy pedestrianized street with a giant tiled "bleachers staircase" at the back where everyone sits to eat their *bocadillos*; other options include *salmón ahumado* (smoked salmon) and *montaditos* (titbits on bread). Daily 11.30am–5pm & 6.30pm–midnight.

Sopa de Ganso ("Duck Soup") C/Pérez Galdós 8; map pp.290–291. Young, lively bar in one of the city's main nightlife zones. On offer are *tagarninas* (a pasty) and *pudín de verduras* (vegetable bake). Daily 1pm–3am.

★ **Taberna Coloniales** Plaza Cristo de Burgos 19; map pp.290–291. Typical ancient *sevillano* tavern decorated with photos of the town's bygone days serving up outstanding, generous and fair-priced tapas. House specials include *champiñones rebozados* (fried mushrooms), *croquetas de espinacas* (spinach croquettes) and *pluma ibérica* (pork shoulder). Has a very pleasant terrace that you'll need to queue for in summer (add your name to the blackboard inside). When busy, table service can verge on the brusque. Daily 12.30pm–midnight.

NIGHTLIFE

Seville has plenty to offer in the way of nightlife, from expensive, touristy **flamenco** shows to atmospheric, tucked-out-of-the-way drinking holes. On summer evenings bar terraces by the river (see p.301) often put on live musical entertainment. Major **concerts** take place in one of the football stadiums or in the Auditorio de La Cartuja across the river. Throughout the summer the Alcázar, the Prado de San Sebastián gardens and other squares host occasional free concerts.

Information and booking The Turismo, the local press and the *El Giraldillo* listings magazine have information on nightlife; La Teatral, C/Velázquez 12, near Plaza Duque de la Victoria (☎ 954 228 229), are the official ticket agents for many concerts.

FLAMENCO

Flamenco – now strutting more proudly than ever after being recognized as an intangible world heritage art form by UNESCO in 2010 – music and dance are on offer at dozens of places around the city, some of them extremely

FLAMENCO FESTIVALS AND FREE SHOWS

Various **festivals**, such as the Bienal de Flamenco, A Palo Seco (Cante Jondo) and Un Verano de Flamenco, as well as concerts staged by the various *barrios*, take place throughout the summer, offering a good chance of hearing something special – and you're guaranteed to hear authentic flamenco at the Triana *barrio*'s annual festival **Velá de Santa Ana** in the final week in July. There are flamenco performances (free) every night starting around 10 or 11pm in the **Plaza del Altozano** and along the waterfront **C/Betis**. Performances by top artistes are also staged at the **Museo del Baile Flamenco** (see p.276). All festivals and shows are widely advertised, and the Turismo and local press should have details.

tacky and overpriced. Finding flamenco *puro* isn't easy, possibly because – like good blues or improvised jazz with which flamenco shares an affinity– its spontaneous nature is almost impossible to timetable. Visitor demand for this romantic Spanish art form has resulted in a form of "theatre flamenco", where you can pay to see two shows a night – a far cry from the time when the *gitanos* sang in their *juergas* (shindigs) for as long and as often as the mood took them.

Auditorio Álvarez Quintero C/Álavarez Quintero 48 ☎ 954 293 949; map pp.290–291. New flamenco venue in a traditional *sevillano* house with *cante, guitarra y baile* (song, guitar and dance) by reliable performers. Shows daily 9pm; €16.

Bar Quita Pesares Plaza Jerónimo de Córdoba, near the church of Santa Catalina; map pp.290–291. A tapas bar by day run by the flamenco singer Peregil, after dark it metamorphoses into a frequently chaotic flamenco venue where there's often spontaneous music, especially at weekends. Things get lively around midnight and, more importantly, when the owner is on song. If he isn't, he'll sell you a CD of an occasion when he was. Mon–Sat 11am–late.

El Búcaro C/Alfonso XII 30 ☎ 954 225 116; map pp.290–291. Vibrant flamenco takes here behind a normal bar (see p.293) out front. In a space behind, younger flamenco talent gets a chance to show what it can do. Shows on Fri & Sat at 9pm (officially, although they often don't get going until around 10pm).

Casa Anselma C/Pages del Corro 49; map pp.290–291. Lively, rumbustious bar staging free flamenco most nights starting around 10.30pm; it may not be *flamenco puro* but what it lacks in finesse it more than makes up for in atmosphere.

Casa de la Memoria de Al Andalus C/Ximénez de Enciso 28, Barrio Santa Cruz ☎ 954 560 670; map pp.290–291. Cultural centre with fine patio mounting excellent and reasonably priced concerts of flamenco throughout the year. Shows usually start daily at 9pm as the programme changes monthly you'll need to ring or pick up a leaflet to confirm this. Tickets (which need to be booked in advance) €15.

El Arenal C/Rodo 7 ☎ 954 216 492; map pp.290–291. Most palatable of the pricey tourist flamenco spots, and run by a former dancer who sees to it that the spectacle

doesn't veer too far into burlesque. Tickets for shows at 9pm and 11pm cost a steep €37 (including one drink), €59 with tapas and drinks or €72 for show and dinner. If they're not too busy, after the first show you can stay to see the second for free.

La Carbonería C/Levies 18; map pp.290–291. Excellent bar that often has spontaneous flamenco – Thursday is the best night, but not before 10pm. Once a coal merchant's building (hence the name), this is a large, welcoming place, run by flamenco expert Paco Lira, with its own patio at the back. They also do tapas and *raciones*. Tricky to find, but well worth the effort. Daily noon–late.

Los Gallos Plaza de Santa Cruz ☎ 954 216 981; map pp.290–291. Reputable flamenco show using a professional group of singers and dancers who sometimes get close to the real thing, although a nagging feeling persists that the performers are just going through the motions. Performances at 8pm & 10.30pm; €30 including one drink.

Teatro Central C/José de Gálvez 6, Isla de la Cartuja ☎ 955 037 200; map pp.290–291. It's worth checking on this venue in the local press or with the Turismo, as they often stage festivals featuring up-and-coming flamenco talents as well as established performers.

DISCOTECAS AND LIVE MUSIC

Earlier on in the evening, Seville's *discotecas* attract a young crowd of 17- to 20-year-olds; the serious action starts after midnight and often lasts till well beyond dawn. For live music the bars around Plaza Alfalfa and Alameda de Hércules tend to have the best of what's on offer. In summer as the town heats up, much of the action switches to the terrace bars along the river to the north of the Puente de Triana as far as the Puente de la Barqueta.

Abril C/Luis Montoto 118. Cavernous and loud, this is the ultimate in trendy *sevillano* nightlife, hosting well-known international DJs. Specializes in house – if you're in the mood to dance, this is the place. Wed & Thurs 11.30pm–dawn.

Antique Avda. Matemáticos Rey Pastor y Castro s/n; map pp.290–291. Popular with Seville's smarter crowd, this place comes with a transparent dancefloor, a summer terrace ("Rosso") and music that goes from Latin pop to heavier stuff. Thurs–Sat from midnight.

3

Bestiario C/Zaragoza 33, at the Plaza Nueva end; map pp.290–291. Disco-bar throbbing with manic techno and house sounds, usually attracting an over-30s crowd. Sunday is the big day/night of the week here. Daily 3pm–3am.

Boss C/Betis 67; map pp.290–291. Cavernous *discoteca* which takes off after midnight; popular with the study-abroad student crowd (attracted by bars serving €1 shots) and has a penchant for house, pop and techno. Thurs–Sat 11pm–late.

Fun Club Alameda de Hércules 86; map pp.290–291. Popular weekends-only music and dance bar with live bands. Entry charge (€6) after midnight. Thurs–Sat from 9pm (if there's live music; otherwise 11pm) until dawn.

Kudeta Plaza Legión 8, inside the Plaza de Armas shopping mall; map pp.290–291. Three storey Asian-fusion resto-lounge-*discoteca* where you can follow a meal by smoking a hookah on terrace loungers or take a drink in the *discoteca*.

Santuario C/Cuesta del Rosario; map pp.290–291. Attractive and upmarket smaller club playing techno, funk, soul and hip-hop to a predominantly over-30s clientele. Sometimes hosts live bands.

COPAS AND MUSIC BARS

Copas bars (drinking bars) are scattered all over the centre. Clusters of good ones are to be found in the Alameda de Hércules and Plaza Alfalfa zones in El Centro, with more gathered to the north of the Maestranza bullring – where there's also a gay scene – and along C/Betis in Triana.

Antigüedades C/Argote de Molina 10; map pp.290–291. Arty music bar with paintings and sculptures hanging from the ceiling, many the work of the owner. Good place to kick-start the evening. Daily 5pm–3am.

Azúcar de Cuba Paseo de las Delicias 3; map pp.290–291. A corner of Cuba in Seville where the proprietors (from Havana) play salsa sounds accompanied by authentic nibbles. Live music on Thurs & Sun. Tues–Sun 6pm–late.

Bar Garlochí C/Boteros 4, one block northeast of Plaza Alfafa; map pp.290–291. The city's most eccentric bar, a wonderfully kitsch "religious shrine" complete with incense, candles and flying angels. Their sacrilegious

---

SEMANA SANTA AND THE FERIA DE ABRIL

Seville boasts two of the largest festival celebrations in Spain. The first, **Semana Santa** (Holy Week), always spectacular in Andalucía, is here at its peak with extraordinary processions of masked penitents and lavish floats. The second, the **Feria de Abril**, is unique to the city – a one-time market festival, now a week-long party of drink, food and flamenco. The *feria* follows hard on the heels of Semana Santa so if you have the energy, experience both.

SEMANA SANTA

Semana Santa may be a religious festival, but for most of the week solemnity isn't the keynote – there's lots of carousing and frivolity, and bars are full day and night. In essence, it involves the marching in procession of **brotherhoods** of the church (*cofradías*) and **penitents**, followed by *pasos*, elaborate **floats** on which sit seventeenth-century images of the Virgin or of Christ. For weeks beforehand, the city's fifty-plus *cofradías* painstakingly adorn the hundred or so *pasos* (each brotherhood normally carries two; Christ and a Virgin), spending as much as €350,000 on flowers, costumes, candles, bands and precious stones. The **bearers** (*costaleros*, from the padded *costal* or bag protecting their shoulders) walk in time to traditional dirges and drumbeats from the bands, which are often punctuated by impromptu street-corner **saetas** – short, fervent, flamenco-style hymns about the Passion and the Virgin's sorrows.

Each procession leaves its district of the city on a different day and time during Holy Week and finally ends up joining the official route at La Campana (off Plaza Duque de la Victoria) to proceed along C/Sierpes, through the cathedral and around the Giralda and the Bishop's Palace. **Good Friday** morning is the climax, when the *pasos* leave the churches at midnight and move through the town for much of the night. The highlights then are the procession of El Silencio – the oldest *cofradía* of all, established in 1340 – in total silence, and the arrival at the cathedral of La Esperanza Macarena, an image of the patron Virgin of bullfighters, and by extension of Seville itself.

On **Maundy Thursday** women dress in black and it's considered respectful for tourists not to dress in shorts or T-shirts. Triana is a good place to be on this day when, in the early afternoon, Las Cigarreras (the *cofradía* attached to the chapel of the new tobacco factory) starts out for the cathedral with much *gitano* enthusiasm.

To see the climax of all the processions – save that of the Cofradía del Resucitado (Resurrection) on Easter Sunday – there's always a crush of spectators outside the cathedral and along C/Sierpes. However, without a **seat** (the best of which are rented by the hour and

Sangre de Cristo crimson cocktail is a must. Daily 9pm–late.

Bulebar Alameda de Hércules 83; map pp.290–291. Late-opening bar with a plant-filled terrace facing the Alameda. Often stages theatre, music (from classical to jazz) or other events and serves tapas and *pasteles* (cakes). Daily 7pm–late.

Café Central Alameda de Hércules s/n; map pp.290–291. As it's always the last bar to close on the Alameda this bar attracts an eclectic, international crowd. The atmosphere is laid-back and conversational – just the place to chill out. Daily 11am–4am.

Café Moderniste C/Dos de Mayo 28, near the Maestranza theatre; map pp.290–291. Pleasant, relaxing bar that fills up on opera and concert nights, often with the musicians and performers themselves. Noted for its mojitos. Also does breakfasts. Daily 8am–2am.

Elefunk C/Adriano 10, near the bullring; map pp.290–291. Modish *copas* bar with goldfish hanging in water-filled globes above the bar, funky Latino and techno sounds, frequent live bands, and late hours. Daily 3pm–late.

Flahertys C/Alemanes 7, next to the Cathedral; map pp.290–291. Popular Irish bar which, due to its location, inevitably attracts many tourists. Lots of Anglo-American sports with big screens, rowdy supporters and pub grub. Daily 10.30am–late.

Trinity Irish Pub C/Madrid s/n, just off Plaza Nueva; map pp.290–291. For those with a fondness for Guinness, this is Seville's nearest approximation to a Dublin hostelry, with plenty of nooks to converse and ruminate. Daily 10.30am–1.30am.

Urbano Comix C/Matahacas 5, near the Convento de Santa Paula in Macarena; map pp.290–291. Popular student bar – with hippie overtones – featuring zany urban decor and grunge metal, rock, punk and R&B sounds plus live bands, often staying open till dawn. Daily 9.30am–late.

SUMMER TERRACE BARS

On sultry summer nights it's worth doing what *sevillanos* do and making a beeline for these riverside oases which are the only place to stay really cool in July and August (and booked up weeks in advance; contact the Turismo for details) or an invitation to share someone's balcony, viewing spots near the cathedral are almost impossible to find. A good **place to stand** is beneath the Giralda, where the processions exit into Plaza de la Virgen de los Reyes, but even here it gets chaotic. The best way of all to see the processions is to pick them up on the way from and to their *barrios*, which is where you'll see the true *teatro de la calle* – the theatre of the streets.

During Semana Santa the pattern of events changes daily, and while newsstands stock the official programme – **Programa de la Semana Santa** – they quickly sell out. A daily detailed timetable is issued with local papers (*El Correo* and *Diario de Sevilla* both do coloured route maps) and is essential if you want to know which processions are where. The ultra-Catholic *ABC* paper has the best background information, and the Turismo's *El Giraldillo* listings magazine prints a brief programme, whilst the banks and bigger hotels tend to produce their own guides. The national *El País* and *El Mundo* newspapers also carry excellent daily supplements with all the routes and *cofradías* tunics listed in colour. A dedicated website, ⓦ lapasion.net also has lots of background information and links.

THE FERIA DE ABRIL

The nonstop, week-long Feria de Abril takes place in the second half of the month when a vast area on the west bank of the river, the **Real de la Feria**, is taken over by rows of *casetas*, canvas pavilions and tents of varying sizes. Some of these belong to eminent *sevillano* families, some to groups of friends, others to clubs, trade associations or political parties. Each one resounds with flamenco singing and dancing from around 9pm until perhaps 6am or 7am the following morning. Many of the men and virtually all the women wear traditional costume, the latter in an astonishing array of brilliantly coloured, flounced gypsy dresses.

The sheer size of this spectacle makes it extraordinary, and the dancing, with its intense and knowing sexuality, is a revelation. But most infectious of all is the universal spontaneity of enjoyment; after wandering around staring, you wind up a part of it, drinking and dancing in one of the "open" *casetas* which have commercial bars. Earlier in the day, from 1pm until 5pm, *sevillana* society parades around the fairground on carriages or on horseback in an incredible extravaganza of display and voyeurism with subtle but distinct gradations of dress and style. Each day, too, there are **bullfights** (at around 5.30pm; very expensive tickets in advance from the ring), generally reckoned to be the best of the season.

often in June and September too). Note that these bars open June–Sept only and some only for a season, opening up the next year under different names and owners but usually in the same location.

Alfonso Avda. de la Palmera, Parque de María Luisa; map pp.290–291. Popular terrace bar in the park for cooling off over a long drink. The neighbouring *Bilindo* and *Libano* opposite are similar relaxing places. Thurs–Sat 11pm–late.

Casino Avda. María Luisa s/n, in the gardens of the Lope de Vega theatre; map pp.290–291. The Lope de Vega gardens and theatre provide a scenic backdrop to this tropical-themed terrace. The crowd is always dressed to impress, but far from stuffy. July–Sept daily 11.30pm–dawn.

Chile Paseo de las Delicias, near the Parque de María Luisa; map pp.290–291. Housed in the old Chile pavilion of the 1929 Fair of the Americas, this a colourful bar with a pleasant terrace – recently enlarged to accommodate smokers who can no longer puff inside – sometimes

featuring live music. Daily 11pm–late.

El Capote Next to the Puente de Triana (aka Isabel II); map pp.290–291. Highly popular riverside bar with outdoor terrace which has DJs spinning cool sounds and often stages live bands in summer.

El Paseo C/Paseo de Colón 2, opposite the Puente de Triana; map pp.290–291. Small gay bar playing 1970–90s music. Daily 11pm–late.

Embarcadero C/Betis 69; map pp.290–291. Down a narrow passage to the side of the *Río Grande* restaurant, this is a great little *copas* and music bar (top 40 and golden oldies) with a riverside terrace and a stunning view towards the Torre del Oro and cathedral across the river. Daily 5pm–late.

Puerto de Cuba C/Betis s/n; map pp.290–291. Tucked beneath the San Telmo bridge this dual-level club is frequented by the city's smart set. The upper level is mellow with a nautical theme while the ground floor overlooking the river reverberates with pop dance hits and eternal favourites. Wed–Sat 11pm–dawn.

SHOPPING

Seville is a great place to shop, offering everything from regional crafts and ceramics to chic designer fashions and accessories. Shops – except for the larger department stores such as El Corte Inglés – generally close during the afternoon siesta (roughly 1.30–5.30pm) and stay open until 8 or 9pm.

MARKETS

Entertaining **Sunday markets** (*mercadillos*; roughly 10am–2pm depending on weather) take place on the Plaza del Cabildo opposite the cathedral (stamps, coins, ancient artefacts) and the Plaza del Museo fronting the Museo de las Bellas Artes (art, tiles and woodcarvings). Calle Feria's long-standing **El Jueves** (Thursday) market near the Alameda de Hércules, with secondhand articles and antiques, is another good one. An excellent *artesanía* market, **El Postigo**, C/Arfe s/n, just west of the cathedral, displays a range of fans, glassware, ceramics, silverware and jewellery with innovative designs made by local craftspeople.

POTS AND TILES

Beatriz Rengifo Ruiz C/Antillano Campos 10. Interesting potter whose pottery shop has a wonderfully ebullient nineteenth-century exterior. Mixes traditional styles with more modern designs.

Cerámica Rocio-Triana C/Antillano Campos 8. Displaying work by Rafael Muñiz, a creative potter producing pieces with a modern slant. He can also create customized painted tile images (any size) to take home or have sent.

Cerámica Santa Ana C/San Jorge 31, near the Puente de Triana. Good for typically Andalucian souvenirs, with a wide selection of Triana pots and tiles.

FLAMENCO

As well as El Corte Inglés (see below), flamenco dresses to sport during the *fería* or take home are also available from Doña Ana, C/San Eloy 14 near the Museo de Bellas Artes; Flamenk, C/Francos 15, slightly north of the cathedral; Molina, C/Sierpes 11; and the celebrated Asunción Peña, close by at C/Francos 12.

Casa Damas C/Asunción 43, near the San Telmo bridge, Triana ☎ 954 272 421. Wide range of flamenco CDs and books.

El Corte Inglés Plaza Duque de la Victoria. Stocks a wide range of flamenco dresses leading up to the *feria*; prices start at around €180 but you can sometimes pick up a bargain for half this.

DESIGNER FASHIONS

Cutting-edge women's designer fashions are sold by Purificación García, C/Rioja 13 (off C/Sierpes); Loewe, Plaza Nueva 12; and Vittorio & Lucchino, C/Padre Luís María Llop 4, near the Iglesia de Santa Catalina. Cuqui Castellanos, C/Rosario 8, and Antonio Ortíz, C/Sierpes 3, both craft whimsical women's shoes.

BOOKS AND NEWSPAPERS

Beta C/Sierpes 25 and C/San Pablo 12 (near the Museo de las Bellas Artes). This chain stocks English-language guides and maps: central branches include the cavernous branch at C/Sierpes 25.

Casa del Libro C/Velázquez 8, just east of C/Sierpes. A wide range of books in English (and other languages).
El Corte Inglés Plaza Duque de la Victoria. Stocks English titles and the international press.
Press kiosk Plaza de la Campana outside La Campana

pastelería. Comprehensive range of international newspapers.
Vértice C/San Fernando 33, near the Alcázar. Good for a variety of books, including English-language and other European titles.

DIRECTORY

Banks and currency exchange Numerous banks around the centre, specifically on the Avda. de la Constitución and around Plaza Duque de la Victoria, have ATMs. Bureaux de change can be found on Avda. Constitución near the cathedral but banks offer better rates.
Bullfights The main *corridas* are staged during the April *feria*. Tickets from the Plaza de Toros (☎ 902 223 506) or (with commission) the nearby Impresa Pagés ticket office at C/Adriano 37 or the booking agency La Teatral (see p.298).
Consulates UK, contact the Málaga consulate (see p.79); Ireland, Avda. de Jerez 46 ☎ 954 690 689; USA, Plaza Nueva 8 ☎ 954 218 751.
Hospital English-speaking doctors are available at Hospital Universitario Virgen Macarena, C/Dr Marañón s/n ☎ 955 008 000, behind the Andalucía parliament building to the north of the centre. For emergencies, dial ☎ 061.
Internet There are numerous internet cafés around the centre and several hotels now have pay-as-you-go computers or wi-fi. Two central internet cafés are Cibercenter, C/Julio César 8 (Mon–Fri 9am–10pm) and Planeta Verde, C/Trajano 8 (daily 10am–10pm).
Laundry Tintorería Vera, C/Arjona 3, close to the Plaza de Armas bus station (Mon–Fri 9.30am–1.30pm & 5–8pm, Sat 10am–1.30pm); Lavandería Roma, C/Castelar 4, east of the bullring (Mon–Fri 9.30am–1pm & 5–8.30pm, Sat 10am–2pm).
Left luggage There are coin-operated lockers (ask for

the *consigna*) at the Santa Justa train station. The Prado de San Sebastián bus station has a left-luggage office (daily 9am–9pm), and there's another *consigna* at the Plaza de Armas bus station (9.30am–1.30pm & 3–6pm) – note that it's not inside the bus station but around the right side of the building by the taxis.
Lost property Oficina de Objetos Perdidos, C/Manuel V. Sagastizabál 3, next to the Prado de San Sebastián bus station (Mon–Fri 9.30am–1.30pm; ☎ 954 420 703).
Maps and hiking equipment For made-to-measure maps (1:50,000, 1:100,000 and 1:200,000) for a defined area, contact Francisco Marquez, C/Las Cruzadas 7, immediately behind the Plaza de España (☎ 954 423 063). The excellent LTC, Avda. Menéndez Pelayo 42 in Santa Cruz (☎ 954 425 964), and Risko, C/Sinai 37 close to Santa Justa train station (☎ 954 570 849), also stocks maps, and has a wide range of outdoor equipment.
Police For emergencies dial ☎ 092 (local police; less serious matters) or ☎ 091 (national; violent crime and so on). Central local police stations are at C/Arenal 1 (☎ 954 275 509) and C/Crédito 11 (☎ 954 289 555), off the north end of the Alameda de Hércules. Petty crime in the city is a notorious problem, but violent crime is rare; avoid leaving anything at all in a car parked on the street overnight; the guarded underground car parks are a possible alternative.
Post office Avda. de la Constitución 32, by the cathedral; poste restante (*lista de correos*) is also held here. (Mon–Fri 8.30am–8.30pm, Sat 9.30am–2pm).

North of Seville: Itálica and around

The Roman ruins and remarkable mosaics of **Itálica** and the exceptional Gothic monastery of **San Isidoro del Campo** lie some 9km to the north of Seville, just outside the village of **Santiponce**. Both can be easily visited by bus as a day-trip from Seville and there are excellent places to eat near the archeological site.

Itálica

Avda. de Extremadura 2 • April–Sept Tues–Sat 8.30am–9pm, Sun 9am–3pm; Oct–March Tues–Sat 9am–6.30pm, Sun 10am–4pm • €1.50 (free with EU passport)

As you survey the dusty, featureless landscape of the site of **Itálica** today, it's hard to believe that this was once the third largest city of the Roman world, surpassed only by Alexandria and Rome itself (a free site map from the ticket office helps you identify the main features). Itálica was the birthplace of two emperors (Trajan and Hadrian) and one of the earliest Roman settlements in Spain. Founded in 206 BC by Scipio Africanus after his decisive victory over the Carthaginians at nearby Alcalá del Río, it became a settlement for many of his veterans, who called the place "Italica" to remind them of home. With a thriving port – now beneath Santiponce – the city rose to considerable military importance in the second and third centuries AD, when it was richly endowed during the reign of Hadrian (117–138). Grand buildings dripped with fine marble brought from Italy, Greece, Turkey and Egypt, and the population swelled to half a million. Itálica declined as an urban centre only under the Visigoths, who preferred Hispalis (Seville). Eventually the city was deserted by the Moors after the river changed its course, disrupting the surrounding terrain.

In the Middle Ages the ruins were used as a source of stone for Seville, and, from the eighteenth century onwards, lack of any regulation allowed enthusiastic amateurs to indulge their treasure-hunting whims and carry away or sell whatever they found. The Duke of Wellington spent some time "excavating" here during the Peninsular Wars and later the Countess of Lebrija conducted her own "digs" to fill her palace in Seville with mosaics and artefacts (see p.277). Somehow, however, the shell of its enormous **amphitheatre** – the third largest in the Roman world and originally standing outside the city walls – has survived. It is crumbling perilously, but you can clearly detect the rows of seats for an audience of 25,000, the access corridors and the dens for wild beasts.

Beyond, within a rambling and unkempt grid of streets and villas, about twenty **mosaics** have been uncovered in what was originally the northern, richer sector of the city. Look for the outstanding Neptune mosaic in the house of the same name, as well as the colourful bird mosaic in the Casa de los Pájaros depicting 33 different species. Towards the baths, in the Casa del Planetario, there's a fascinating representation of the Roman planetary divinities who, in the Roman calendar, gave their names to the days of the week. Finally, on the site's western edge, the **Hadrianic baths** – named the Termes Mayores to distinguish them from a smaller baths discovered in the village of Santiponce – are divided into those for men to the centre and right, and those for women to the left.

On the site's southern edge, to the rear of the still-functioning walled cemetery of Santiponce – which was here long before excavations began – is the recently unearthed **Traianeum**, a great religious complex constructed by Hadrian and dedicated to the worship of his adoptive father Trajan.

Outside the site, in the village of **Santiponce** itself – beneath which lies another sizeable chunk of unexcavated Itálica – there's also a well-preserved Roman theatre and the Termes Menores baths (both Tues–Thurs 8am–3pm, Fri–Sat 8am–3pm & 4–7pm, Sun 10am–3pm; free), both a five-minute walk away from the site entrance and signposted from the main road.

Monasterio Isidoro del Campo

C/San Isidoro s/n • April–Sept Wed & Thurs 10am–2pm, Fri & Sat 10am–2pm & 5.30–8.30pm, Sun 10am–3pm; Oct–March Wed & Thurs 10am–2pm, Fri & Sat 10am–2pm & 4–7pm, Sun 10am–3pm • Free

A little over 1km south of Santiponce on the road back to Seville lies the splendid former Cistercian **Monasterio Isidoro del Campo**. Founded by the thirteenth-century monarch Guzmán El Bueno of Tarifa fame (see p.163), the monastery is a masterpiece of Gothic architecture which, prior to its confiscation during the nineteenth century Disentailment, was occupied by a number of religious orders. Among these were the *ermitaños jerónimos* (Hieronymites) who, in the fifteenth century, decorated the central cloister and the Patio de los Evangelistas with a remarkable series of **murals** depicting images of the saints – including scenes from the life of San Jerónimo – as well as astonishingly beautiful floral and Mudéjar-influenced geometric designs. In the sixteenth century the monastery was renowned for its library and in 1569 a member of the order, Casiodoro de Reina, made the first translation of the Bible into Castilian Spanish (a copy is on display). But when de Reina and others began to display an over-zealous interest in the Protestant ideas of Martin Luther the community fell foul of the Inquisition and was dissolved, with some monks being executed and others escaping abroad.

The monastery was then assigned to the non-hermitic main order of San Jerónimo which employed the seventeenth-century sculptor Juan Martínez Montañés to create the magnificent **retablo mayor** in the larger of the complex's twin churches. Depicting scenes from the Nativity, the Adoration of the Kings and San Jerónimo himself, this is one of the greatest works by this *andaluz* master of wood sculpture. In wall niches alongside the retablo – and positioned above their tombs – are images of Guzmán El Bueno and his spouse, also by Montañés.

Other highlights of this remarkable building include the **Sala Capitular** (chapter house) with more wall paintings and the **Refectorio** (refectory), with a fine mural of the *Sagrada Cena* (Last Supper) occupying an end wall and displaying more geometric designs worked into the table linen.

ARRIVAL AND INFORMATION

ITÁLICA AND AROUND

By bus Itálica and Monasterio Isidoro del Campo are easily reached by bus from the Plaza de Armas bus station in Seville (Bus #M-172; Mon–Sat every 30min, Sun hourly; 20min; €1.30). The bus passes the monastery on its way to the terminus outside the archeological site entrance. Ask the bus to drop you at the monastery stop ("Parada Monasterio") on the outward journey. When you've seen the monastery you can then cover the 1.5km (a 15min walk, or take a later bus) through the village of Santiponce to the Itálica site entrance, from where buses return to the city. If you plan to see both monuments on the same day it's worth noting the differing opening hours.

Turismo Santiponce has a Turismo at C/La Feria s/n (Tues–Fri 9am–3pm, Sat & Sun 10am–2pm; ☎ 955 998 028).

ACCOMMODATION AND EATING

Hotel Anfiteatro Romano Avda. Extremadura 18, facing the Itálica site entrance ☎ 955 996 700. Comfortable a/c rooms in a hotel attached to the *Ventorrillo Canario* restaurant (see below). **€56**

★ **La Caseta de Antonio** C/Rocío Vega 10, Santiponce ☎ 955 996 306. Fifty metres down a side street behind the *Ventorrillo Canario*, this is undisputably the place to go for fish or an outstanding paella. Main dishes €8–20.

Daily noon–4pm & 7.30–11pm.
Ventorrillo Canario Avda. de Extremadura 13, Santiponce. For a meal before or after your visit to Itálica, try this popular restaurant almost opposite the site entrance; it does good *platos combinados* and is famous for its charcoal-grilled steaks served with *papas arrugadas* – small baked potatoes in *mojo* spicy sauce. Tends to fill at weekends. Main dishes €6–16. Daily 12.30–4pm & 8–11.30pm.

East from Seville

The direct route east by train or car along the valley of the Guadalquivir heading towards Córdoba is a flat and largely unexciting journey. The more interesting route follows the A4-E5 route just to the south of this (the one used by most buses), via **Carmona** and **Écija**, both ancient towns with plenty to see. To the south of Écija lies the ducal town of **Osuna** and its neighbour **Estepa**, both with compelling architectural delights. With good bus connections to Seville (and trains running from Osuna), these towns are all easily reached on a day-trip – Carmona in particular is an easy 30km journey.

Leaving Seville, the A4-E5 crosses **La Campiña**, a rich and undulating lowland framed between the Guadalquivir to the north and the hills of Penibetic Cordillera to the south. It's a sparsely populated area, its towns thinly spread and far apart – a legacy of post-*Reconquista* days when large landed estates were doled out to the nobility by the crown. The feudal nature of this system of *latifundia* (great estates where the nobles owned not only the towns but also the inhabitants and the serfs on the land) wrought much bitterness in Andalucía, vividly described in Ronald Fraser's book, *Pueblo*.

Carmona

Sited on a low hill overlooking a fertile plain planted with fields of barley, wheat and sunflowers, **CARMONA** is a small, picturesque town that has burst beyond its ancient walls. Founded by the Carthaginians in the third century BC probably on the site of a Turditani Iberian settlement, they named it Kar-Hammon (City of Baal-Hammon) after their great deity – the origin, via the Roman "Carmo", of its present name. A major Roman town (from which era it preserves a fascinating subterranean necropolis), it was also an important *taifa* state in Moorish times. Following the *Reconquista*, Pedro the Cruel built a palace within its walls, which he used as a "provincial" royal residence – it's now the modern *parador*.

The majority of Carmona's monuments and churches lie inside the ancient walls. The only site involving a bit of effort to get to is the remarkable Necrópolis Romana (Roman cemetery) on the west side of town, a ten-minute walk from the old quarter.

San Pedro

C/San Pedro s/n • Thurs–Mon 11am–2pm • €1.20

The fifteenth-century church of **San Pedro**, near the main bus stop, is a good place to start exploring Carmona. With its soaring tower built in imitation of the Giralda and added a century later, San Pedro evokes a feeling of Seville – entirely appropriate since the two towns share a similar history, and under the Moors Carmona was often governed by a brother of the Sevillian ruler. Inside, the church has a superb Baroque *sagrario* (side chapel) by Figueroa.

Just behind the church at the top of Avda. de Portugal lies a famous fifteen-spouted **fountain** which has figured in many flamenco songs and poems about the town.

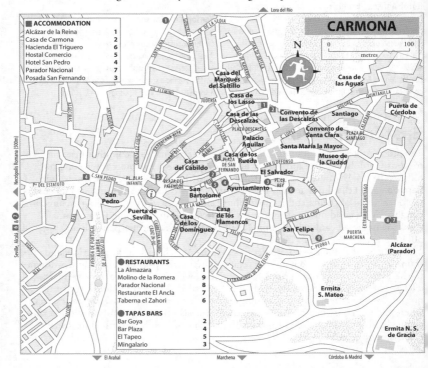

Puerta de Sevilla

Plaza Blas Infante • Tours (organized by the Turismo) Mon–Sat 10am–6pm, Sun 10am–3pm • €2, Mon free

The old town – circled by 4km of ancient walls containing substantial Carthaginian, Roman and Moorish elements – is entered by the **Puerta de Sevilla**, an impressive double gateway. Although most of what you see now is of Roman origin there has been a gate of some form here since Iberian times: remains dating back to the late second millennium BC have been found in recent excavations. Through this gate passed the great Vía Augusta on its way from Hispalis (Seville) to Corduba (Córdoba). During the Moorish period a fortified *alcázar* was added, creating the great bastion that still dominates the town's western flank today.

Plaza de San Fernando

Inside the walls, narrow streets wind upwards past Mudéjar churches and Renaissance mansions. Follow Calle Prim uphill to the **Plaza de San Fernando** (or Plaza Mayor), modest in size but overlooked by splendid Moorish-style buildings, including the Casa del Cabildo (the old Ayuntamiento).

A striking Renaissance facade fronts the town's present **Ayuntamiento** (Mon–Fri 8am–3pm; free) in the square's southeast corner, worth a visit to view a striking geometric-patterned Roman mosaic with a head of Medusa in its patio.

Behind the plaza (reached by taking Calle Sacramento and turning right along Calle Dominguez de Aposanto) there's a bustling **fruit and vegetable** market in an elegant porticoed square.

Santa María La Mayor

Plaza El Salvador s/n • Mon–Fri 9am–2pm & 5.30–7.30pm, Sat 9–11.30am, closed second half Aug & first half Sept • €3

Moving east from the Ayuntamiento, you'll reach **Santa María la Mayor**, a fine fifteenth-century Gothic church built over the former Almohad Friday (main) mosque, whose elegant patio it retains, complete with orange trees and horseshoe arches. Like many of Carmona's churches it's capped by a Mudéjar tower, possibly utilizing part of the old minaret. One of the patio's pillars is inscribed with a Visigothic liturgical calendar, said to be the oldest in Spain. The church's high altar has a splendid Renaissance retablo and, in the third chapel to the right, a fifteenth-century triptych by Alejandro Fernández. Off the patio is a museum containing artworks by Zurbarán, Roldan and Bocanegro.

Museo de la Ciudad

C/San Ildefonso 1 • Mon 10am–2pm, Tues–Fri 10am–2pm & 6.30–8.30pm, Sat & Sun 9.30am–2pm • €3, free on Tues

Housed in the elegant eighteenth-century Casa del Marqués de las Torres is the **Museo de la Ciudad**, documenting the history of the town with mildly interesting displays of artefacts from the prehistoric, Iberian, Carthaginian, Roman, Moorish and Christian epochs. The most entertaining feature is a series of interactive screens in a section dedicated to the role of flamenco in Andalucian culture – enabling you to call up a flamenco style of your choice and fill the museum with the sound. There's little in the way of bars in this area so the museum's *cafetería* provides a useful refreshment stop.

The Alcázar

Looming above the town's southeastern ridge are the massive ruins of Pedro's **Alcázar**, an Almohad fortress transformed into a lavish residence by the fourteenth-century king – employing the same Mudéjar craftsmen who worked on the Alcázar at Seville – but which was destroyed by an earthquake in 1504. It received further architectural attentions from Fernando (after Isabel's death) but later fell into ruin, until it was more recently renovated to become a remarkably tasteful *parador*, entered through an imposing Moorish gate.

Puerta de Córdoba

To the northeast of the Alcázar, beyond and below Pedro's palace, the town comes to an abrupt and romantic halt at the Roman **Puerta de Córdoba**, a second-century gateway with later Moorish and Renaissance additions, from where the old Córdoba road (now a dirt track) drops down to a vast and fertile plain. Following this ancient route for a few kilometres will lead you to a five-arched **Roman bridge**, just visible on the plain below. Near to the gate, the **church of Santiago**, at the end of Calle Calatrava, is another impressive fourteenth-century Mudéjar building with an elegant brick tower decorated with *azulejos*.

Convento de Santa Clara and around

C/Torno de Santa Clara • Fri–Mon 11am–1.30pm & 5–7pm • €2

Following Calle Dolores Quintanilla and its continuation, Calle López, from the Puerta de Córdoba back to the centre, you'll pass by more *palacios* and churches, among them the fifteenth-century **Convento de Santa Clara**, with a *mirador* tower on the left and paintings by Valdés Leal in its church, while beyond lie the eighteenth-century **Convento de las Descalzas** and the Baroque **Palacio de los Águilar** (on the right), with a fine facade.

The Necrópolis Romana

Guided tours only (English spoken): Tues–Fri 9am–6pm, Sat & Sun 9am–3.30pm • €2, free with EU passport

Lying on a low hill outside the walls, as was the Roman custom, Carmona's remarkable **Necrópolis Romana** (Roman cemetery) is one of the most important in Spain. To get there, walk out of town from San Pedro along Paseo del Estatuto and its continuation Calle Enmedio, parallel to the main Seville road, for about 450m. Here, amid the cypress trees, more than nine hundred family tombs dating from the second century BC to the fourth century AD were excavated between 1881 and 1915. Enclosed in subterranean *columbaria* – chambers hewn from the rock – the tombs are often frescoed in the Pompeian style with images of garlands, birds and fruit, and contain a series of niches in which many of the funeral urns remain intact.

Some of the larger tombs, such as the **Tumba del Elefante** (complete with a stone elephant, perhaps symbolic of long life) are enormously elaborate, in preparation for the ceremonies that went with burial and after, when the tomb became a focus for family rituals centred on the dead. Alongside its burial chamber, a bath, pantry and kitchen with chimney as well as stone benches and tables for funeral banquets are wonderfully preserved. Most spectacular is the **Tumba de Servilia**, a huge colonnaded temple with vaulted side chambers and separate *columbaria* for the servants of the family. The tours lead you in gratifying detail round this extraordinary site, pointing out the various types of tombs, together with the cremation pits where the corpse would have been burned while members of the family (and hired mourners if they were rich) threw clothes and food into the flames for use in the afterlife. The paths between the tombs were also used in Roman times, and it doesn't take a lot of imagination to visualize a slow procession of grieving relatives and mourners preceded by flute players or trumpeters making their way to the family vault.

The site also has a small **museum** with finds from the tombs including gravestones, mosaics and vases. Opposite is a partly excavated second-century amphitheatre.

ARRIVAL AND INFORMATION   **CARMONA**

By bus The bus from Seville will drop you on the Paseo del Estatuto in sight of the Moorish Puerta de Sevilla, a grand and ancient fortified gateway to the old town. The Paseo del Estatuto is also the halt for buses from Córdoba and Éjica.

By car The subterranean car park beneath the Paseo del Estatuto is central and convenient. Parking places also become free along the main C/San Pedro during siesta and after 7pm.

Turismo Carmona's efficient Turismo is located inside the Puerta de Sevilla (Mon–Sat 10am–6pm, Sun 10am–3pm; ☏ 954 190 955, ⊚ turismo.carmona.org).

ACCOMMODATION

Carmona has a shortage of places to stay, especially in the budget category, and particularly in spring and high summer it's worth ringing ahead. The cheaper places lie outside the walls, whilst a clutch of more upmarket options all occupy scenic locations in the old town and have their own restaurants and garages. Prices below are for the *temporada media* (shoulder season), which covers the months of May, September and October. All other periods are low season when (particularly hotel) prices will be significantly cheaper.

Alcázar de la Reina C/Hermana Concepción Orellana 2 ☎ 954 196 200, ⓦ alcazardelareina.com. Rather bland addition to Carmona's luxury hotel list. Fully equipped rooms have internet access and free wi-fi and there's also a pool. **€150**

Casa de Carmona Plaza de Lasso 1 ☎ 954 191 000, ⓦ casadecarmona.com. Stylish transformation of a seventeenth-century *casa palacio* into a serene hotel with individually styled rooms decorated with genuine antiques and artworks. **€110**

★ **Hacienda El Triguero** 4km southwest of town along the A398, direction El Viso ☎ 955 953 626, ⓦ eltriguero.com. With your own transport this elegant *cortijo* is an inviting rural possibility, with cosy en-suite rooms, a restaurant (evening meal €18), a fine garden pool and some great walks nearby. Ring ahead before turning up. B&B **€65**

Hostal Comercio C/Torre del Oro 56 ☎ 954 140 018. Built into the Puerta de Sevilla gateway, this charming small *hostal* offers compact a/c en-suite rooms (without TV) around a pretty patio. **€50**

Hotel San Pedro C/San Pedro 3 ☎ 954 190 087. Pleasant central budget option, with clean and functional a/c en-suite rooms with TV above a bar-*cafetería*. B&B **€59**

★ **Parador Nacional** Alcázar Rey Don Pedro ☎ 954 141 010, ⓦ parador.es. Its superb location, patios and swimming pool ensure that this is still the most appealing of the luxury places in town. Pay a few euros extra for a room with a balcony. It's worth calling in for a drink at the bar, to enjoy the fabulous views from the terrace. **€180**

Posada San Fernando Plaza San Fernando 8 ☎ 954 141 408, ⓦ posadasanfernando.com. New and attractive small hotel on this focal square with individually styled rooms with a/c, minibar and plasma TV. Free wi-fi. **€65**

EATING AND DRINKING

There are plenty of places to eat both in the old and new town and you don't need to spend a fortune to dine well. However, a step up in price will allow you to sample some of the best food in the province. In addition to the places below, all the upmarket hotels have their own restaurants, often with a reasonably priced *menú*. Carmona has its fair share of tapas bars too – the Turismo produces a free tapas guide and map, *Des Tapa Carmona*.

RESTAURANTS

La Almazara C/Santa Ana 33 ☎ 954 190 076. Slightly out of the centre, this excellent, stylish restaurant and tapas bar in a refurbished old oil mill (*almazara*) offers a *menú* for around €30, and is definitely worth the walk. *Cabrito* (roasted kid), *cochinilla* (suckling pig) and game dishes are among its specialities. Main dishes €12–18. Daily 1–4.30pm & 8–11.30pm.

★ **Molino de la Romera** C/Pedro s/n ☎ 954 142 000. Housed in a former Moorish oil mill with a great terrace view across the Campiña, this pleasant restaurant serves up regional dishes, with a good-value *menú* (around €12) and *dulces* prepared by the nuns of the nearby Convento de Santa Clara. Main dishes €7–15. Daily 1–4pm & 8–11pm.

Parador Nacional Alcázar Rey Don Pedro ☎ 954 141 010. The restaurant of the *parador* is a model of baronial splendour. The *menú del día* for €33 includes many local dishes, and they also offer vegetarian and diabetic *menús*. Main dishes €10–20. Daily 1.30–4pm & 8–11pm.

Restaurante El Ancla C/Bonifacio IV, about 500m along the Alcalá road ☎ 954 143 804. Out of the centre but well worth the effort, this is a great fish restaurant;

there's also an outstanding tapas bar with a tempting *menú* for under €10. Thurs–Tues noon–4pm & 8–11pm.

Taberna El Zahorí Costanilla del Pozo Nuevo s/n. Atmospheric *taberna* housed in refurbished former stables of a nearby *casa señorial*. Has a good tapas range – try the *alcochofas a la plancha* (artichokes) – in its bar while more elaborate meat, fish and game dishes are served in the restaurant. Tues–Sun 1.30–4pm & 8–11.30pm.

TAPAS BARS

Bar Goya C/Prim 42. A good tapas bar off the west side of Plaza de San Fernando, with a nice terrace. House specials include *alboronías* (ratatouille) and *rabo de toro*. Daily 8am–1am.

Bar Plaza Plaza de San Fernando s/n. Focal tapas bar on the main square and well worth a try. Specials include *carillada* (stewed pork cheeks) and *berenjenas con miel* (aubergine). Daily 9am–11pm.

El Tapeo C/Prim 9. Tapas bar-restaurant offering a decent tapas selection – try the *espinacas con garbanzos* or *berenjenas fritas* (aubergine) – while the restaurant serves up various meat and fish dishes plus a good-value *menú* (€10). Daily 8am–4pm & 7–11pm.

3

Mingalario Plaza Cristo del Rey 1. Popular and atmospheric tapas bar noted for its *charcutería ibérica* (cured pork meats) and *gambas al ajillo* (prawns with garlic). **Daily 10am–midnight.**

Écija

One of the most distinctive and individual towns of Andalucía, **ÉCIJA** lies almost midway between Seville and Córdoba, in a basin of low sandy hills. The town is known, with no hint of exaggeration, as *la sartenilla de Andalucía* (the frying-pan of Andalucía) and once registered an alarming 52°C on the thermometer. In mid-August the only way to avoid this heat is to slink from one tiny shaded plaza to another, putting off sightseeing until late in the day. It's worth the effort, since Écija has eleven superb, decaying church towers, each glistening with brilliantly coloured tiles. The town also has a unique domestic architecture – a flamboyant style of twisted or florid forms, displayed in a number of fine mansions close to the centre.

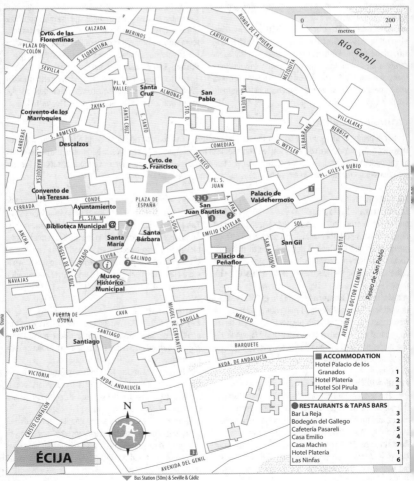

ACCOMMODATION

Hotel Palacio de los Granados	1
Hotel Platería	2
Hotel Sol Pirula	3

RESTAURANTS & TAPAS BARS

Bar La Reja	3
Bodegón del Gallego	
Cafetería Pasareli	5
Casa Emilio	4
Casa Machin	7
Hotel Platería	1
Las Ninfas	6

ÉCIJA

Bus Station (50m) & Seville & Cádiz

Brief history

The Romans knew Écija as Astigi (the modern inhabitants are known as *astigitanos*), probably the name of an earlier Iberian settlement. It was an important and prosperous olive-growing town, trading the prized Baetican oil all over the empire during the first and second centuries. In the early Christian era Écija became a bishopric, but in Moorish times (now named Estadja) sank into relative obscurity as part of the caliphate of Córdoba. Conquered by Fernando III in 1240, it was only in the seventeenth and eighteenth centuries that it staged a recovery, when the prosperity brought by the new *latifundia* – harking back to the great slave-worked Roman estates – encouraged the nobility to build impressive mansions in the town. Following the devastation wrought by the Lisbon earthquake of 1755, Écija's ruined churches were restored at great cost; hence the magnificent collection of late Baroque towers that are the glory of the place today.

Plaza de España

Écija's most important churches and palaces are all within a few minutes' stroll of the once delightful arcaded and palm-shaded **Plaza de España** (known locally as the Plaza Mayor), although a controversial revamp to create an underground car park has turned the plaza into a rather desolate, modernistic space jarring with the Baroque splendours surrounding it. A Roman bath discovered in the course of these works – only one of many archeological discoveries – can now be viewed under a canopy in the plaza's southeast corner.

At the plaza's western end stands the **Ayuntamiento** which contains – in the imposing council chamber – a fine second-century Roman mosaic depicting the mythological Dirce being dragged by a bull as a punishment meted out by the two sons of Antiope, Zethus and Amphion – whose mother she had mistreated. Ask in the reception for permission to view.

Just behind the Ayuntamiento, overlooking the southwest side of Plaza España, stands the lyrically beautiful tower of **Santa María** (Mon–Sat 10am–1pm & 5.30–8pm, Sun 10am–1pm; free) – one of the eighteenth-century rebuilds. Inside, a cloister displays archeological finds from the surrounding area.

Museo Histórico Municipal

C/Canovas de Castillo • June–Sept Tues–Fri 10am–2pm, Sat 10am–2pm & 8–10pm; Oct–May Tues–Fri 10am–1.30pm & 4.30–6.30pm, Sat 10am–2pm & 5.30–8pm, Sun 10am–3pm • Free

Behind Santa María, on Calle Canovas de Castillo, lies the magnificent eighteenth-century Palacio de Benamejí, with a fine portal in contrasting tints of marble. The palace now houses the Turismo and the **Museo Histórico Municipal**, providing an opportunity to view this imposing mansion and its patio.

Inside the museum, exhibits cover the town's history, from Neolithic hunters and gatherers through the Romans – there's a particularly good section on Astigi's role in the olive-oil trade – to the Moorish and medieval epochs. In 2002 excavations in the Plaza Mayor unearthed the remarkable **Amazona de Écija**, a stunning, first-century AD Roman statue, over 2m high and depicting an Amazon resting against a pillar. Of the highest craftsmanship and still bearing traces of ochre paint, the image has become the museum's dramatic focal exhibit and the town's civic icon. At the time of writing the museum is being extended to display a wonderful collection of Roman mosaics unearthed in recent local excavations.

Santa Cruz

Plaza Nuestra Señora • Mon–Sat 9am–1pm & 5–9pm, Sun 10am–1pm & 6–8pm • Free

North of Plaza España lies the church of **Santa Cruz**, whose brick tower was once a minaret, with tenth-century Arabic inscriptions recording the setting up of public fountains. Inside, there are more superb retablos and an early Christian sarcophagus, all beneath a lofty cupola. The charming *plazuela* fronting the church has two fine old iron crosses on a plinth, backed in summer by a wonderful avalanche of crimson bougainvillea down the wall behind.

San Juan Bautista

Plaza San Juan • Tues–Sat 10am–1pm & 5–8pm, Sun 10am–2pm

Heading along a narrow street out of the Plaza España's northeast corner you'll soon spot the ornate belfry of **San Juan Bautista**, perhaps the best of all Écija's Baroque towers. In its churchyard are the substantial ruins of the earlier church destroyed in the eighteenth-century earthquake.

Palacio de Peñaflor

Continuing east leads you to the sixteenth-century **Palacio de Valdehermoso**, with a Plateresque facade incorporating Roman pillars and, almost opposite and running along Calle Castellar, the enormous eighteenth-century **Palacio de Peñaflor** (currently closed; enquire at the Turismo), where a magnificent painted curved frontage is complemented by a full-blown Baroque portal topped with twisted barley-sugar columns. Formerly the residence of the marquises of Peñaflor until the line became heirless in 1958, the edifice was sold to the town council for the nominal sum of 50,000ptas (€300). The cost of restoration and maintainance, however, may result in the palace being sold again, it is rumoured, to be converted into a luxury hotel. The interior has a fine staircase with intricate stuccowork and cupola off a twin-tiered arched central patio.

San Gil and around

Plaza de San Gil • Tues–Thurs 11am–1pm, Fri 9am–1pm & 5–9.30pm, Sat & Sun 10am–1pm • Free

The Gothic-Mudéjar church of **San Gil** is famed for its pencil-slim tower, and has a restored interior with an elegant retablo in its *sagrario*. Just beyond San Gil more **archeological excavations** are in progress and have so far revealed the foundations of enormous Roman buildings, plus some extremely fine mosaics which will soon be displayed in the town museum. The progress of the excavations can be viewed through the surrounding fence.

ARRIVAL AND INFORMATION   ÉCIJA

By bus Frequent daily buses to and from Seville and Córdoba stop at the station on Avda. Andalucía.

Turismo In the Museo Histórico Municipal (daily 10am–2pm, closed Sat & Sun July & Aug; ☎ 955 902 933, ⓦ turismoecija.com).

Internet The Biblioteca Municipal (public library; Mon–Fri 9.30am–1.30pm & 4–8.30pm, Sat 9.30am–1.30pm) off the western end of the Plaza Mayor has free internet and wi-fi.

ACCOMMODATION

Hotel Palacio de los Granados C/Emilio Castelar 42 ☎ 955 905 344, ⓦ palaciogranados.com. Beautifully restored eighteenth-century mansion with delightful patios, small pool and rooms decorated with original contemporary artworks. B&B **€129**

Hotel Platería C/Garcilópez 1 ☎ 955 902 754, ⓦ hotel plateria.net. Off the east side of the Plaza Mayor, this comfortable hotel has modern a/c rooms and its own restaurant. Can advise on parking. **€67**

Hotel Sol Pirula C/Miguel de Cervantes 50 ☎ 954 830 300, ⓦ hotelpirula.com. South of the centre, with decent a/c rooms above its own restaurant (*menú* €9). Free wi-fi. **€71**

EATING AND DRINKING

Bar La Reja C/Garcilópez 1. Next door to the *Hotel Platería*, this popular bar serves a wide choice of tapas and *raciones*. Specialities include fish and *mariscos* as well as excellent *jamón ibérico*. Daily noon–midnight.

Bodegón del Gallego C/A. Aparicio 3. A little pricey, but serves fish, shellfish and meat dishes to a high standard

and is noted for its *arroz marinero* (seafood paella). Mon–Sat 2–5pm & 8pm–midnight.

Cafetería Pasareli Pasaje Virgen del Rocío, off C/Emilio Castelar. Serves a range of fish and meat dishes – including *atún fresco de almadraba* (fresh tuna) in season and offers a budget *menú* for €10. Also has a small terrace.

Tues–Sat 8.30am–midnight, Sun 8.30am–4pm.

Casa Emilio Plaza Mayor. Decent stop on the main square for tapas and *raciones*; try their local cheeses and *charcutería* (cured pork) or *jamón*. Daily 10am–11pm.

Casa Machín C/Galindo 4. Mid-priced restaurant, housed in an elegant *casa señorial* and popular with locals. House specials include *carrillada ibérico* (pork cheeks) and *dorada a la sal* (bream baked in salt). Main dishes €8–15. Daily noon–midnight.

Hotel Platería C/Garcilópez 1. This reliable hotel restaurant serves a bargain weekday *menú* for €7. Main dishes include *solomillo ibérico* (pork loin). Daily noon–4pm & 7.30–10.30pm.

Las Ninfas C/Elvira 1. This mid-priced restaurant is situated inside the Palacio de Benamejí, with a terrace in the palace's spectacular courtyard. Signature dishes include *arroz con perdiz* (partridge) and *rabo de toro*. Main dishes €9–15. Tues–Sun 1–5pm & 8pm–midnight.

Osuna

Some 34km south of Écija along the A351, **OSUNA** is one of those small Andalucian towns which are great to explore in the early evening: slow and quietly enjoyable, with elegant streets of tiled, whitewashed houses and some of the finest Renaissance mansions in Spain.

Another settlement of obscure Iberian origin, Osuna first came to prominence as the Roman town of Urso, and ten bronze tablets from this period recording the town's statutes are preserved in Madrid's Archeological Museum. In Moorish times the town was of little note and it was during the post-*Reconquista* period, when it became the seat of the dukes of Osuna with enormous territories, that it was embellished with most of the outstanding buildings that make it so attractive today. Osuna's major sights are its collection of stunning **Renaissance mansions** and, on the hill to the east of the centre, the old **university**, the **Collegiata** church and the convent of **La Encarnación**.

Plaza Mayor

Osuna's main square is the elegant Plaza Mayor in the heart of the town and here it's worth taking a look at the eighteenth-century **Ayuntamiento** and, on the west side, the sixteenth-century **Convento de la Concepción** (open service times), with a fine eighteenth-century retablo.

One other place not to miss here is the wonderful **Casino** on the east side; with 1920s Mudéjar-style decor and a grandly bizarre ceiling it's open to all visitors and makes an excellent place for a drink (or breakfast) while lounging in armchairs overlooking the square.

Museo de Osuna

C/Sevilla 37 • Tues–Sat 10am–2pm & 5–7pm, Sun 10am–2pm • €2

Directly opposite the Palacio de Govantes y Herdera lies the new **Museo de Osuna**, housed in yet another stunning eighteenth-century *casa palacio*, the Palacio de Arjona y

---

OSUNA'S PALACIOS

The best of the mansions erected in Osuna by its aristocrats and wealthy landowners are on the streets off Calle Carrera, running north from the Plaza Mayor, particularly Calle San Pedro. Many have an information board outside. On C/San Pedro the **Cilla del Cabildo** (at no. 16) has a superb geometric relief round a carving of the Giralda. Further along, the eighteenth-century **Palacio Marqués de Gomera** is another Baroque extravaganza with undulating ornamentation, balcony and solomonic columns beneath the family crest; it has now been converted into an upmarket restaurant and hotel (see p.316). Calle de la Huerta, south of the Plaza Mayor, has further interesting buildings, including the **Palacio de los Cepadas** (now the palace of justice) with an elegant patio and staircase, and nearby slightly north, on Calle Sevilla, the **Palacio de Puente Hermoso**. On the same street are more fine *palacios*, with the outstanding – but tragically crumbling – **Palacio de Govantes y Herdara** in urgent need of salvation. More *casa palacios* are to be found on calles Gordillo and Compañia (a street off the latter) to the west of the Plaza Mayor.

OSUNA

●RESTAURANTS & TAPAS BARS	
Bar San Agustín	7
Casa Curro	6
Doña Guadalupe	3
Hostal Caballo Blanco	1
La Casa del Marqués	4
Mesón del Duque	5
Taberna Raspao	2

■ACCOMMODATION	
Hospedería del Monasterio	4
Hostal Caballo Blanco	2
Hostal Granadino	5
Hotel Esmeralda	6
Hotel Palacio Marqués de la Gomera	3
La Casona de Calderón	1

Cubas. The museum has more information on the history of the *palacios* as well as artworks and exhibits illustrating the life and times of the town and its countryside over the last three hundred years.

Old University

C/Cuesta del Calvarios • Patio open term-time Mon–Fri 10am–7pm, closed July & Aug

On a hilltop overlooking the town, the **Old University**, now part of the Universidad de Sevilla, has an elegant arcaded Renaissance patio. Founded in 1548 by one of the predecessors of the dukes of Osuna, it was later suppressed by the reactionary Fernando VII in 1820 and only recently recovered its academic status.

Colegiata

Plaza de la Encarnación • Guided tours only (English spoken): Tues–Sun: May–Sept 10am–1.30pm & 4–7pm; Oct–April 10am–1.30pm & 4–6.30pm • €3

Looming over the town from a hilltop near the Old University is the lavish sixteenth-century **Colegiata** – a fine Renaissance building with a Plateresque west doorway damaged, so the story goes, by French soldiers in the War of Independence who used it for target practice. Inside, a guide will point out a sumptuous gilded retablo and the remarkable seventeenth-century *Expiración de Cristo* (Crucifixion) by Ribera – one of the artist's greatest works. Also in the church some exquisite sculptures include a superb Crucifixion by Juan de Mesa, from the same period. More Riberas are to be seen in the *sacristía*, which now holds the church's impressive **art collection**. His *San Jerónimo*, *San Pedro* and a moving *Martirio de San Bartolomé* are all of the highest quality.

The highlight of the visit's latter stages is the descent to the subterranean depths to view the gloomy **pantheon and chapel of the dukes of Osuna**, where these descendants of the kings of León and former "Lords of Andalucía" are buried in niches in the walls. Some of the Renaissance ornamentation and sculpture is extremely fine, especially the polychrome wooden *Santo Entierro* (Burial of Christ), as well as panels from the Flemish school and a fine relief of San Jerónimo. The tour ends with the guide pointing out an antique portable sixteenth-century **organ** – one of few to survive from the period.

La Encarnación

Plaza de la Encarnación • Tues–Sun: May–Sept 10am–1.30pm & 4–7pm; Oct–April 10am–1.30pm & 4–6.30pm • €2.50

Opposite the entrance to the Colegiata is the Baroque convent of **La Encarnación**, founded in the seventeenth century by a duchess of Osuna. The highlight of the nun-led guided tour is a fine plinth of eighteenth-century Sevillian *azulejos* (from Triana) round its cloister and gallery, depicting curiously secular scenes. Complete your visit by filling up on the tasty convent *dulces* sold here.

Torre de la Merced

From La Encarnación it's a pleasant walk north and then west along Calle Abades and the Cuesta de Marruecos to the **Torre de la Merced**, the tower of the former convent church of the same name, with its stupendously carved late Baroque tower and portal by Alonso Ruiz Florindo.

Roman Urso

Las Canteras is the site of **Roman Urso**, Osuna's ancient predecessor. The site is still in the process of investigation, but you will soon make out the foundations of once significant buildings and here also you'll find a necropolis with tombs quarried from the sandstone, as well as the vague remains of a theatre, fort and a gigantic quarry – with steps leading down into it – where the Romans obtained the stone to build the city.

Museo Arqueológico

Plaza de la Duquesa s/n • Tues–Sat 10am–1.30pm & 4–7pm, Sun 10am–1.30pm • €2.50

Sited on the more direct descent to the town from the Colegiata, the **Museo Arqueológico** is housed in the Torre del Agua, a twelfth-century Almohad tower. The small museum displays finds discovered hereabouts, none unfortunately spectacular so far although this situation is bound to change as excavations of the Roman town (see above) progress. Disappointingly, many of the best items are copies, with the originals having been sent to Madrid.

Osuna's other churches

Mon–Sat from 7pm is the best time to find the churches open

Other churches around the town worth seeking out include the sixteenth-century **Santo Domingo**, towards the northern end of Calle Carrera, a fine Renaissance church with a couple of superb Mudéjar chapels; nearby, **Nuestra Señora de la Victoria** has an impressive Baroque retablo by José Mora.

To the west of the Plaza Mayor, the **Convento del Carmen**, on the street of the same name, has another stunning sixteenth-century retablo in carved wood, while to the south of the Plaza Mayor the recently refurbished sixteenth-century **San Agustín** has a beautiful single-naved interior and more fine retablos.

ARRIVAL AND INFORMATION

By train The train station is on Avda. de la Estación s/n (☎ 902 432 343), on the western edge of town. Osuna lies on the Seville–Granada line and is served by six daily trains from the provincial capital.

By bus The bus station lies southeast of the centre on Avda. de la Constitución s/n (☎ 954 810 146), with frequent services to Seville and (less frequently) to Málaga and Granada.

Turismo 300m northwest of the Plaza Mayor at C/Carrera 83 (Tues–Sat 9.30am–1.30pm & 4–6pm, Sun 9.30am–1.30pm; ☎ 954 815 732, ⊕ turismosuna.es). Staff can provide a detailed town map.

ACCOMMODATION

Accommodation in Osuna is not plentiful, but outside of national holiday periods and the local *feria* (third or fourth week in May) there's usually no great problem finding a place to stay. All the same, it's worth ringing ahead.

Hospedería del Monasterio Plaza de la Encarnación 3 ☎ 954 821 380 ⊕ hospederiadelmonasterio.com. Stunning new hotel housed in an ancient building alongside the Colegiata. Individually styled rooms come with tiled floors, iron bedsteads and elegant furnishings and there's a wonderful terrace pool outside. Free wi-fi. **€90**

Hostal Caballo Blanco C/Granada 1 ☎ 954 810 184. Welcoming and comfortable *hostal* with en-suite a/c rooms with TV in a remodelled old coaching inn. It has an equally good restaurant and large car park at the back. **€55**

Hostal Granadino Plaza Salitre 1 ☎ 954 810 184. Slightly out of the centre to the southwest of the Plaza Mayor, this is a friendly place offering clean and tidy a/c en-suite rooms above a restaurant. **€41**

Hotel Esmeralda C/Tesorero 7 ☎ 955 821 073, ⊕ hotelesmeralda.es. Charming and recently refurbished hotel with attractive a/c rooms with safe and minibar. The rooftop terrace has a small pool and fine views towards the hilltop Colegiata. Free parking for guests. **€55**

★ **Hotel Palacio Marqués de la Gomera** C/San Pedro 20 ☎ 954 812 223, ⊕ hotelpalaciodelmarques .es. Dreamy four-star option, set inside one of the most beautiful *casas palacios* in the country. A monument in its own right, this eighteenth-century mansion has a breathtakingly beautiful patio with a Baroque chapel just off it and all rooms are tastefully and individually furnished. The irresistibly romantic Room 10 is in the palace's tower. B&B **€78**

La Casona de Calderón Plaza de Cervantes 16 ☎ 954 815 037, ⊕ casonacalderon.es. Charming, recently arrived hotel in a restored eighteenth-century *casa palacio* with regally furnished and well-equipped rooms, wet-room-style bathrooms, elegant patio, small pool and its own restaurant. **€75**

EATING AND DRINKING

There are places to eat and drink all over town; many of the accommodation options also have restaurants of their own.

Bar San Agustín C/San Agustín 15. Good little neighbourhood bar-restaurant to the south of the Plaza Mayor open for breakfast and, later in the day, economical *platos combinados*. Daily except Thurs 9am–11pm.

★ **Casa Curro** Plaza Salitre 5. The town's best (and liveliest) tapas and *raciones* bar cooks up a tasty range of seafood and meat dishes. Try the *pescaíto frito* (fried fish) or *patatas bravas*. There's a superb restaurant in the back, too, serving up dishes with more than a touch of creative flair – try the *carrillada ibérica con crema de queso y Pedro Ximénez* (pork cheeks with cheese and sherry sauce). Tues–Sun 1–4pm & 8–11pm.

Doña Guadalupe Plaza Guadalupe 6 ☎ 954 810 558. The town's top mid-priced restaurant specializes in *cocina andaluza* and has a terrace on this pleasant square. *Lomo ibérico en salsa de almendras* (pork loin) is a signature dish and there's a *menú* for around €18. Main dishes €12–19. Daily except Tues 1–4pm & 8–11pm.

Hostal Caballo Blanco C/Granada 1. The *hostal's* restaurant is very good for *comida casera* serving up dishes such as *redondillo guisado* (beef stew) and *gachas de osuna* (local gruel) as well as the usual standards. Daily 1–4pm & 7.30–10.30pm.

La Casa del Marqués C/San Pedro 20. The very good restaurant of the *Hotel Marqués de Gomera* is on the high side of mid-priced, and rather formal; try their slightly cheaper courtyard brasserie, the *Asador del Marqués* (June–Sept) where *Cola de toro en vino tinto* (bull's tail in wine) and croquetas de gambas (prawn croquettes) are house specials. Main dishes €9–26. Daily 1–4pm & 8–11pm.

★ **Mesón del Duque** Plaza de la Duquesa 2. Excellent little mid-priced restaurant, with the best terrace in town. Wide range of meat and fish dishes including *lomo a la almendra* (pork loin with almonds) and a weekday *menú* for around €10. Daily 10am–midnight.

Taberna Raspao Plaza de la Merced 7. A very good neighbourhood restaurant for fish – try their *bacalao de la casa* (cod) – and meat tapas and *raciones*, with a pleasant terrace on the square. Tues–Sun 1pm–midnight.

Estepa

Another delightful Baroque town, **ESTEPA**, 24km east of Osuna, resembles a miniature version of its larger neighbour. Originally a Carthaginian settlement, it took the side of the North African state during the Punic Wars with Rome, and when the victorious Romans finally took the city in 208 BC they found that the citizens had burned their possessions and killed themselves rather than surrender. Repopulated, it eventually became the Roman Ostipo and, later, the Moorish Istabba. The town climbs up the slopes of San Cristóbal to its peak, where stands the impressive church of **Santa María** and the ancient **Moorish fort**. In the lower *barrios* – the main focus of life in Estepa today – there are quite a few churches and monuments worth a look.

Iglesia de la Santa María de la Asunción

Cerro de San Cristóbal s/n • Mon–Thurs 8.30am–2.30pm & 4–6pm, Fri 8am–3pm • €1

Crowning the hill above the town and reached by following Calle Saladillo, the fifteenth-century **Iglesia de la Santa María de la Asunción** is built on the remains of a tenth-century *mezquita*, and is one of Estepa's oldest churches. Currently undergoing a gradual restoration, the Gothic interior, entered via the tourist office – as well as a museum – has various treasures, many rescued from other churches and monasteries. Look out for a fine sculpture of *San Juan Evangelista* by Juan de Mesa.

Iglesia de Santa Clara

Cerro de San Cristóbal s/n • Daily 7–9pm • €1

Just east of the church of Santa María, the **Iglesia de Santa Clara** is another impressive convent church, dating from the late sixteenth century. Inside, the gilded seventeenth-century Plateresque retablo by Pedro Ruíz Paniagua is regarded as one the finest in the provinice.

Torre de la Victoria

C/Ancha

The spectacular Baroque **Torre de la Victoria** is all that remains of the eighteenth-century convent of the same name. A Civil War casualty, the convent was demolished in 1939 but the 50m-high tower, designated a national monument in 1955, survived to become the town's iconic symbol.

Iglesia del Carmen

Plaza del Carmen s/n • Mon–Sat 7–9pm, Sun noon–1pm • Free

From the Torre de la Victoria, heading north and downhill for a couple of blocks along *calles* Toralba and Libertad leads to the Plaza del Carmen and the stunning eighteenth-century **Iglesia del Carmen** with an exuberant Baroque facade in black and white stone and a stunningly ornate interior, recently restored.

Palacio de los Marqueses de Cerverales and around

C/Castillejos 16 • Mon–Fri 9am–1pm • €4 including Iglesia de la Asunción

From the Plaza del Carmen, following Calle Mesones (and its continuation, Calle Castillejos) west through the town, you pass another fine church, the **Iglesia de la Asunción**, known locally as Estepa's Sistine Chapel due to a splendid painted ceiling depicting scenes from the life of the Virgin. The church was originally the chapel of one of Estepa's best mansions, the **Palacio de los Marqueses de Cerverales** next door, a superb eighteenth-century palace with barley-sugar columns supporting its balcony and delightful patio within.

One block south from here, **Calle Nueva** has some of the town's oldest mansions; among them nos. 12 and 14 are good examples and, at no 2, take a look at a pair of ancient Visigothic columns built into the doorway of a much later house, and probably scavenged from some ancient site.

ARRIVAL AND INFORMATION

By bus Estepa's new bus station is on the Avda. Andalucía close to the *Hostal Balcón de Andalucía* (see below) and is served by buses from Córdoba, Sevilla and Málaga.

Turismo Estepa's Turismo, Cerro de San Cristóbal s/n (Mon–Thurs 8.30am–2.30pm & 4–6pm, Fri 8am–3pm; ☎ 955 912 717), is in an annexe of the church of Santa María (see p.317).

ACCOMMODATION AND EATING

Hostal Balcón de Andalucía Avda. de Andalucía 23 ☎ 955 912 680, ⓦ balcondeandalucia.com. A decent *hostal* offering functional, clean a/c rooms with TV. The lively bar below serves decent meals and *platos combinados*, specializing in charcoal-grilled meat and fish.

Free parking on the wide road outside. **€50**
Hostal Rico Avda. de Andalucía 135. A rustic tapas and *raciones* bar which also does *platos combinados* and has an economical *menú*.

West from Seville

With your own transport, the fastest – but dullest – way from **Seville west to Huelva** is via the A49 *autovía*. More tranquil and interesting is the A472, which cuts through the area to the west of the city called **El Aljarafe** by the Moors (the "high lands", although they're actually rather flat), planted with olives, vines and orange trees.

La Palma del Condado and around

West of Seville along the A472, in the province of Huelva, is the wine-producing town of **LA PALMA DEL CONDADO**. It's highly probable that this terrain, an area first planted with vines by the Greeks, produced the local wine taken on the voyage to the New World by Columbus when he sailed from nearby Palos. The wine produced here today is the Condado de Huelva, which hardly ranks with Spain's top-drawer vintages, although the dry whites are an excellent partner for seafood. With its impressive eighteenth-century Baroque church of San Juan Bautista towering over a palm-fringed central plaza, this slow-moving, white-walled country town makes a good stopping point for a drink of the local brew at one of the central bars.

Some 6km south of La Palma, **BOLLULLOS DEL CONDADO** is a busy little town filled with bodegas and *ventas* (called *bodegones* here) – big, high-ceilinged places capable of seating over a hundred diner-imbibers at long trestle tables. A number of them line the main street – *Abuelo Curro*, *Tío Paco* and *El Postigo* are all worth a try for their local wines and great tapas. The A483 continues south from Bollullos to El Rocío (p.333) and the Coto de Doñana.

EL BULLI IN ANDALUCÍA

Some 12km west of Seville, the slow-moving village of **SANLÚCAR LA MAYOR** is now home to the *andaluz* outpost of celebrated Catalán chef Ferran Adrià's culinary empire. To reach the complex, follow the signs on entering the village.

Hacienda Benazuza ☎ 955 703 344, ⓦ elbullihotel .com; from €350. A venture into the world of *hostelería* by Spain's internationally renowned chef. Created inside a restored and partly Moorish hacienda (from which it takes its name), this hotel and restaurant complex is the last word in luxury and pampered living. Bougainvillea-draped courtyards with tinkling fountains, evocative belfries, aromatic herb and jasmine-scented gardens

with palms and orange trees surround the extravagant and individually styled bedrooms and salons.
La Alquería Three on-site restaurants in the *Hacienda Benazuza* include the Michelin double-starred *La Alquería* (*menú de degustación* €130) under former *El Bulli* chef Rafael Zafra, serving up a changing selection of Adrià's greatest "*cocina experimental*" hits from twenty years of his famous *El Bulli* restaurant in Catalunya.

ACCOMMODATION AND EATING   **LA PALMA DEL CONDADO**

Hostal Garle C/Circunvalación s/n ☎ 959 400 750. This roadside *venta* on the junction of the A472 has basic but clean en-suite rooms above its restaurant (*menú* €6). **€36**

★ **La Agencia** C/Real 19. This stylish restaurant (a few minutes away from the A472 in the town proper) is the best place to eat. They serve tapas and *raciones* in the bar as well as excellent and reasonably priced dishes in the main room – dishes of the sierra such as *solomillo ibérico* are a good choice. Main dishes €8–15. Daily noon–4pm & 8–11pm.

Niebla and around

Twelve kilometres west from La Palma along the A472, the salmon-pink ancient walls and towers of **NIEBLA** make a spectacular sight. The approach is wonderful, almost a medieval fairytale come true – this is a real walled town and looks the part. The Roman bridge you cross to reach it – probably built in the second century during the reign of Trajan – is remarkably well preserved and carried traffic for two thousand years until it was blown up during the Civil War (though it's now been meticulously restored). Once inside the 2km-long encircling walls, Niebla's tidy streets of whitewashed houses and small squares are a delight to explore.

Brief history

Little is known about a Phoenician settlement here or the possible Iberian village of the Turditanian tribe which may have preceded it. However, coins found dating from the Roman period gave the town's name as Ilipla, which is probably derived from the Iberian name. Described by the Roman writer Pliny as a fortified city of strategic importance, it was a crucial link in the massive Roman mining operations carried out upriver at the Río Tinto mines. The metals – mostly silver – were moved down the river by barge and then transferred to galleys here for the voyage to Rome and other parts of the empire. A bishopric under the Visigoths, after the Moorish conquest it became successively part of the Almoravid and then Almohad domains until, as an independent *taifa* state, it experienced its greatest period of prosperity during the twelfth century, trading in saffron and raisins. After falling to the Christian forces under Alfonso X in 1262, Niebla was passed around as a fief of various rulers, until in 1369 it came into the hands of the Guzmán dynasty, following which it entered a long period of decline.

Santa María de Granada

Plaza Santa Maria • Open service times: Mon–Sat 7.30–8.30pm, Sun noon–1pm • Free

The Puerta del Socorro leads from the Seville–Huelva road to the Plaza Santa María in the heart of the town, dominated by the church of **Santa María de Granada**. The key is available from the custodian of the Casa de Cultura (itself the former fifteenth-century Hospital de Nuestra Señora de los Ángeles) almost facing the church.

Entered through a splendid Mozarabic eleven-lobed portal, the original tenth-century church is believed to have been constructed over a Visigothic cathedral, and was used by Christians during the Almoravid period. It was converted into a mosque by the Almohads in the thirteenth century: the *mihrab* in the side wall and the elegant tower – the former minaret – both date from this period. The pillars in the second-floor windows of the tower, incidentally, are believed to have come from the original Visigothic church. Outside the entrance, a patio is dotted with remnants of the building's chequered history – various Visigothic, Christian and Moorish stones and pillars.

Among the artefacts dotted around the austere and much restored Mudéjar-Gothic interior are a couple of Roman altars and the remarkable, stone-carved Silla Episcopal, the throne of the Visigothic bishops.

San Martín

Plaza San Martín • Fri 9.30am–noon • Free

Only the apse, bell tower and a chapel survive of the ruined church of **San Martín**, near the town's main gate and sliced through by a plazuela. It was built in the fifteenth century on the site of a former synagogue donated in more tolerant times by Alfonso X as a concession to the Jews of Niebla, and before the Inquisition began its grisly work. The chapel contains a fifteenth-century sculpture of Christ being scourged.

Castillo de Guzmán

C/Niebla 1 • Daily 10am–6pm • €4

The town's four **gates** are worth seeking out, each with its Moorish horseshoe arch and features, as is the **Castillo de Guzmán,** to the east of the main entrance arch into the walled town, with views from its towers. In origin the Moorish *alcázar*, but much added to by Enrique de Guzmán in the fifteenth century, it later fell into decay and was ruined after Marshal Soult used it as a barracks for French troops during the War of Independence. Inside you can see the fort's barracks, stable and church and various tableaux depict life as it would have been lived in medieval times. Today it stages concerts and theatrical productions as part of Niebla's annual summer festival of theatre and dance.

ARRIVAL AND INFORMATION   NIEBLA

By train Niebla's train station, on the Seville–Huelva line, is served by two trains daily in each direction. The station lies at the end of C/Walabonso, heading downhill between the Casa de Cultura and the church of Santa María.

Turismo You can pick up a map and visitor information at the town's Turismo (daily 10am–2pm & 4–6pm; ☎ 959 362 270, ⊛ www.niebladigital.com), inside the Castillo.

EATING

Brasería Las Almenas C/Padre Marchena 2. Among a number of restaurants, bars and *ventas* lining the main road outside the walls the best value is perhaps to be had at

this *brasería* specializing in charcoal-grilled meat. It also offers a daily *menú* for €10. Open daily.

Huelva and around

Large, sprawling and industrialized, the city of **HUELVA** struggles to present an attractive face to visitors. Still, once you've got past the messy suburbs with their fish canneries, cement factories and petrochemical refineries, the tidy city centre – perched on a peninsula between the confluence of the Odiel and Tinto river estuaries – comes as a pleasant surprise. Huelva's populace escapes the city in summer to enjoy the Atlantic beaches and sea breezes at the resorts of Punta Umbría and El Rompido across the Río Odiel estuary to the south and southwest.

Brief history

Huelva was born as **Onuba**, a trading settlement founded by the Phoenicians early in the first millennium BC (modern inhabitants still call themselves *onubenses*). These early merchant traders were attracted by the minerals in the mountainous areas to the north, and by the time the Carthaginians came to dominate the area in the third-century BC, Onuba was an established port, conveying these minerals throughout the Mediterranean world. When Spain fell into **Roman** hands the mining operations at Río Tinto were dramatically expanded to satisfy the empire's insatiable demand for metals such as silver and copper and the city prospered even more. Following Rome's demise the **Visigoths** and **Moors** displayed little interest in mineral extraction; the latter concentrated on dominating the seaborne trade with North Africa.

Huelva's maritime prowess gained for the city its crowning glory when **Columbus** set out from across the Río Tinto to find a new sea passage to India in ships manned

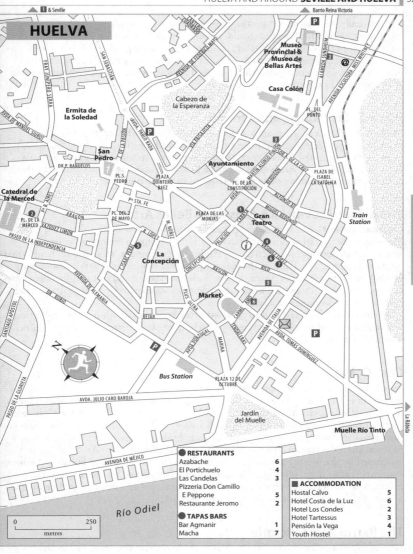

HUELVA

RESTAURANTS
Azabache	6
El Portichuelo	4
Las Candelas	3
Pizzeria Don Camillo E Peppone	5
Restaurante Jeromo	2

TAPAS BARS
Bar Agmanir	1
Macha	7

ACCOMMODATION
Hostal Calvo	5
Hotel Costa de la Luz	6
Hotel Los Condes	2
Hotel Tartessus	3
Pensión la Vega	4
Youth Hostel	1

by hardy Huelvan sailors. The city enjoyed a boom when the Extremadurans to the north of Huelva – the men who conquered the Americas – used the port as a base for their trade with the new territories overseas, but eventually Seville, and later Cádiz, came to dominate the silver and gold routes from the Americas and Huelva was squeezed out. Largely flattened by the Lisbon earthquake of 1755, it is only in the last century that the place has begun to regenerate itself: first as the base for mineral exports from Río Tinto in the early 1900s, when the **British Río Tinto Mining Company** largely ruled the roost here, and later when Franco established a petrochemical industry in the 1950s.

Incidentally, the British workers employed in the mines were also responsible for the importation of **football** into Spain, helping set up Huelva's league club, Recreativo – the oldest in the country – in 1889. It's a pedigree hardly matched by the club's record, however, which has been to languish for more than a hundred years in the lower leagues. In recent seasons they managed to hold down a place among the elite of the Spanish first division – before slipping back into the second.

Plaza de las Monjas and around

Many of Huelva's key sights are a short walk from **Plaza de las Monjas**, the city's palm-lined and pedestrianized main square. Just south of the plaza along Calle Vásquez López is the impressive Neoclassical **Gran Teatro**, while south of the square at Calle Rico 26 you'll find the Art Nouveau **Clínica Sanz de Frutos** (now the Conservatorio de Música), one of a number of elegant buildings in the centre.

The Museo Provincial & Museo de Bellas Artes

Avda. Alameda Sundheim 17 • Tues 2.30–8.30pm, Wed–Sat 9am–8.30pm, Sun 9am–2.30pm • Free

The best place to start a tour of the city is at Huelva's **Museo Provincial**, where the interesting archeological collection has exhibits of equipment, tools and oil lamps used by slave miners at Río Tinto in the Roman period as well as information about early mining in the north of the province. The museum's star exhibit (located in a huge glass case next to the entrance) is a magnificent Roman water-wheel – used to drain water from the mine-workings at Río Tinto.

On the second floor, the **Museo de Bellas Artes** houses a fairly humdrum collection of works alleviated by a few canvases by Huelvan artist and friend of Picasso, Daniel Vásquez Díaz.

Casa Colón

Plaza del Punto • Mon–Fri 9am–3pm • Free entry to public areas

Just south of the Museo Provincial lies the elegant pink-and-white **Casa Colón**, Huelva's first luxury hotel, which played a large part in the story of "*Huelva británica*", housing many of the Río Tinto Mining Company's visitors and providing a venue for important functions. The hotel was built in the final years of the nineteenth century in a variety of styles around a central courtyard with palms and a fountain, and was subsequently purchased by the mining company (who used it to house guests and families of mining employees) after it ran into financial difficulties. Now owned by the city council, it functions as a conference centre and holds the municipal archive. You are free to take a look at the public areas and view the central court.

The Barrio Reina Victoria

One of Huelva's more bizarre features is a whole quarter designed by English architects. The **Barrio Reina Victoria** (or Queen Victoria housing estate), east of the Museo Provincial alongside the Avenida de Guatemala, was constructed by the Río Tinto Mining Company in the early years of the twentieth century to house its British workers. It's a truly weird experience to stroll along the tree-lined avenues flanked by bungalows with rose gardens and semis with dormer windows and mock-Tudor gables – more resembling Acacia Avenue, Essex, than an Andalucian town. Even the street names have a colonial symmetry about them: Calle A, Calle B and so on. Given the drab uniformity it's little wonder that the present native occupants have attempted to relieve these humdrum northern exteriors with a few primary colours.

The Muelle Río Tinto

Another legacy of the British era is the **Muelle Río Tinto** (Río Tinto pier), on the east side of the harbour, a huge nineteenth-century ironwork structure formerly used to ship out the minerals which arrived by train from the mines to the north. Designed by the British engineer George Barclay Bruce and finished in 1874, the redundant pier's decaying ironwork curves gracefully out into the estuary, and today serves as a boardwalk for loungers and courting couples.

Catedral de la Merced

Plaza de la Merced • Open for services: Mon–Wed 9am; Sun 11am, 1pm & 7pm

The **Catedral de la Merced**, to the north of Plaza de las Monjas, was one of the few buildings to survive the eighteenth-century earthquake, resulting in its upgrading to cathedral status which – apart from a brilliant-white Baroque interior and an interesting salmon-pink colonial facade with elegant belfries – it hardly merits. It's worth looking inside at the image of the Virgen de la Cinta (the city's patron) attributed to Martínez Montañés.

Virgen de la Cinta

Avda. de la Cinta s/n • Daily 9am–1pm & 4–7pm • Free • #6 bus from the bus station; ask for the "Parada escuela Montessori" on Avda. de Manuel Suirot, which will leave you close to the sanctuary

More interesting than the cathedral, the restored fifteenth-century **Virgen de la Cinta** lies 3km further north along Avenida Cristóbal Colón (with a signed turn-off along Avenida de la Cinta). This simple white-walled sanctuary set on a low hill overlooking the sea is where Columbus is said to have prayed before setting out on his voyage. Inside, beneath the Mudéjar roof, you can see a medieval fresco of the Virgin, a fine altar grille, and a series of 1920s faïence tiles by the painter Daniel Zuloaga depicting scenes from the explorer's life.

ARRIVAL AND INFORMATION
HUELVA

By train Frequent trains to Seville (and at least one through-train a day to Madrid) leave from the splendid neo-Moorish train station (☎ 902 432 343), a short distance southeast of the centre on Avda. Italia.
Destinations Almonaster (2 daily; 2hr 44min); Jabugo (2 daily; 2hr); Seville (3 daily; 1hr 30min).

By bus Huelva's bus station is at Avda. Dr Rubio s/n (☎ 902 114 492), west of Plaza de las Monjas. The Autobuses Damas (✇ damas-sa.es) timetable lists all services throughout the province – handy if you're going to be using the town as a base.
Destinations Aracena (1 daily; 2hr); Ayamonte/Portuguese

border (9 daily; 1hr); Granada (1 daily; 4hr); Isla Cristina (14 daily; 1hr); La Antilla (7 daily; 45min); Matalascañas (5 daily; 3 on Sat & Sun; 50min); Moguer (14 daily; 40min); Palos de la Frontera (15 daily; 30min); Punta Umbría (17 daily; 30min); Seville (23 daily; 1hr 15min).

By car Finding street parking can often verge on the impossible. The easiest solution is to use a pay car park: the one immediately north of the bus station is convenient.

Turismo Plaza Coto Mora 2, opposite the Gran Teatro (Mon–Wed 9am–7.30pm, Thurs & Fri 9am–3.30pm, Sat & Sun 9.30am–3pm; ☎ 959 650 200).

ACCOMMODATION

Finding a place to stay is usually not a problem this far off the tourist trail, although budget options are severely limited. The town's nearest campsite is in Punta Umbría, a 15min bus ride away (see p.325).

Hostal Calvo C/Rascón 35 ☎ 959 249 016. Uninspiring but central, clean and welcoming place offering rooms (including a few singles) with shared bath. **€22**
Hotel Costa de la Luz C/José María Amo 8 ☎ 959 253 214, ✇ hotelcostaluzhuelva.com. Good two-star option near the market offering rooms with a/c and TV; those on

higher floors also have balconies. **€48**
Hotel Los Condes Avda. Alameda Sundheim 14 ☎ 959 282 400, ✇ hotelfamiliaconde.com. Comfortable hotel near the museum, with serviceable a/c rooms and its own bar-restaurant, plus parking and free wi-fi. B&B **€72**

3

Hotel Tartessus Avda. Martín Alonso Pinzón 13 ☎ 959 282 711, ⓦ eurostarshotels.com. Business-oriented four-star with soberly furnished a/c rooms with minibar and safe. There's also a gym, and parking is available in a nearby public garage. Free wi-fi. **€129**

Pensión La Vega Avda. Alemán 96 ☎ 959 244 544. Pleasant and friendly *hostal* near the cathedral offering clean and tidy en-suite rooms with TV, some with balcony. Free wi-fi. **€46**

Youth Hostel Avda. Marchena Colombo 14, in the northern suburbs (bus #6 from the bus station) ☎ 959 650 010. Modern and well-run hostel with double and triple en-suite rooms and cafeteria. Under 26 **€21**, over 26 **€27**

EATING AND DRINKING

Azabache C/Vásquez López 22. Excellent tapas bar and mid-priced restaurant with a modern, tiled interior. Offers fish, meat and *jamón*-based dishes (*cerdo ibérico al vino* is a house special) with a *menú* for €38. Main dishes €8–20. Mon–Fri 1.30–4pm & 8.30–11.30pm, Sat 1.30–4pm.

Bar Agmanir C/Carasa 9. Great and atmospheric local bar with outdoor tables and a wide tapas range including the house special *mojama de atún* (cured tuna). Daily 9am–11pm.

El Portichuelo C/Vázquez López 15. Pricey but good restaurant offering a variety of fish and meat dishes. *Raciones* (but not meals) are served on a pleasant terrace. Main dishes €12–15. Mon–Sat noon–4pm & 7.30pm–midnight.

★ **Las Candelas** 7km from town at the Aljaraque crossroads on the road to Punta Umbría ☎ 959 318 301. An old *venta*, and one of Huelva's best seafood venues, this place is worth making the effort to get to,

with outstanding food complemented by impeccable service. Without your own transport you'll need to take the Punta Umbría bus or take a taxi. Main dishes €12–19. Mon–Sat 12.30–5pm & 8.30pm–12.30am.

Macha C/Vázquez López 22. Recently opened modern "style" tapas bar with swish furnishings and decor and offering a range of fish and *mariscos*. Daily noon–4pm & 7.30pm–midnight.

Pizzeria Don Camillo e Peppone C/Isaac Peral s/n. Italian-owned pizzería serving up authentic and delicious pizzas, plus pasta and salads. Daily 1–4.30pm & 8.15pm–midnight.

Restaurante Jeromo Plaza de la Merced 6. Attractive and economical little bar-restaurant near the cathedral with a lunchtime *menú* (€8.50) in its bar or more elaborate fare in a pleasant dining room. *Rabo de toro* is a house special. Main dishes €7–15. Daily 9.30am–5.30pm & 7.30pm–midnight.

Punta Umbría

PUNTA UMBRÍA, 20km southwest of the city and sitting astride a finger of land between the Atlantic and the Tinto-Odiel river estuary, is Huelva's nearest – and biggest – seaside resort. The mineworking processes used in the nineteenth century by the Río Tinto Mining Company (see p.341) in the north of the province involved emitting noxious fumes into the atmosphere and many workers became ill. In the early 1880s the company built a rest and recovery centre at Punta Umbría for its employees. Shortly after this, and attracted by the point's unspoilt beauty, senior management began to build holiday homes here and the tourist resort was born. Quite a few of their dwellings, built in the British colonial style, survived until the 1970s; they have gone now, however, and the only vestige from this era is the *barrio*'s name, Los Ingleses.

Casa Museo de los Ingleses

Avda. Ciudad de Huelva s/n, close to the Turismo • April–Sept Tues–Fri 10.30am–1.30pm & 7–9pm; Oct–March 11.30am–1.30pm • Free

The resort has paid a belated tribute to its British founders by reconstructing one of the curious British stilted dwellings that the company's architects designed for its senior staff. This now houses the **Casa Museo de los Ingleses**, decorated with typical period furnishings and reconstructed living and cooking areas. There's also a photo history and a fascinating video about the life of the British community in Punta Umbría.

The beaches

Punta Umbría's later growth into a seaside town has produced a tidy if uninspiring resort which does, however, have magnificent **blue-flag beaches** flanking the north and south sides of its *punta* (point). It makes a reasonable place to stop over if you don't want to stay in the city; be warned, though, that for the latter part of July and most of August every room will be taken.

ARRIVAL AND INFORMATION — PUNTA UMBRÍA

By bus There are hourly buses from Huelva bus station.

Turismo At the junction of Avda. de Andalucía and Avda. Ciudad de Huelva near the Ayuntamiento (June–Sept Mon–Sat 9am–2pm & 7–9pm, Sun 10am–1pm; Oct–May Mon–Sat 11.30am–1.30pm; ☎ 959 495 160, ⓦ puntaumbria.es); they stock copious amounts of information and a useful town map.

Boat trips Turismar (☎ 959 315 526) runs boat trips around the estuary and nature reserve of Marismas del Odiel from the Muelle Viajeros quay near the fishing harbour.

Internet Znet (daily 5.30–10.30pm) C/Delfín 2, near the fishing harbour on the north side of the point.

ACCOMMODATION

Most places to stay are within walking distance of the Turismo behind the beaches on each side of the point.

Camping Playa La Bota 6km west of Punta Umbría, near the hamlet of La Bota ☎ 959 314 537. Close to the beach with plenty of shade; they also rent *cabañas* (cabins) sleeping up to four. Two people plus car €29, cabins €102

Hostal Manuela C/Carmen 8 ☎ 959 310 760 ⓦ hostal manuela.com. Near the harbour on the *punta's* river flank, this recently renovated *hostal* offers sparkling a/c en-suite rooms with TV. Free wi-fi. €55

Hostal Playa Avda. del Océano 95 ☎ 959 310 112 ⓦ hostalplaya.net. Very pleasant *hostal* on the west side of the point, with light and airy en-suite rooms 50m from the sand. Many rooms come with sea view. Free wi-fi. €45

Hotel Barceló Avda. del Océano s/n ☎ 959 495 400, ⓦ barcelopuntaumbria.com. Situated between two nature reserves, this beachfront four-star is one of the resort's top addresses, with luxurious rooms (most with sea view) and a huge garden pool plus bars, restaurant and a spa and wellness centre. €150

Hotel Emilio C/Ancha 21 ☎ 959 311 800, ⓦ hotelemilio .com. Close to the Atlantic side of the point, this is a decent small hotel offering a/c rooms with safe and fridge (some also with balcony or terrace and sea views). Also has its own bar-restaurant and parking. €90

Youth Hostel Avda. del Océano 13 ☎ 959 524 129. High-season pressure on rooms could mean that the very pleasant youth hostel, with a seafront location and some double en-suite rooms, is the only option. Under 26 €21, over 26 €27

EATING AND DRINKING

For food and drink, *chiringuitos* – open-air bars on the seafront serving snacks – are popular, and the resort is full of the usual *freidurías* and *marisquerías*.

Antonio C/Combes Ponzones 10. Popular *freiduría* serving up the usual favourites including *cazón* (smooth hound shark) and *urta* (sea bream) Similar to *Juanito Coronel* (see below), while *Antonio* around the corner is also popular. Daily 10am–6pm & 9pm–12.30am.

Camarón Avda. Océano s/n. Next to the *Hotel Barceló*, this is a popular beachfront *chiringuito* serving a wide range of fresh fish and *mariscos*. Specially noted for its *bogovantes* (lobster) and *langostas* (crayfish). Daily 9am–midnight.

Juanito Coronel Avda. del Río s/n. On the river side of the point, opposite the fishing harbour, this is a good place for inexpensive fried fish. Daily noon–5pm & 8–11pm.

Miramar C/Miramar 3. Welcoming place near the youth hostel and with a seafront terrace. They serve *platos combinados* and *fritados variados*, with house specials including *pargo con crema de marisco* (bream with a shellfish sauce) and paella. Daily 1–4pm & 8.30pm–midnight.

Restaurante El Tiburón Avda. del Océano s/n. A reliable restaurant on the west side of the point which claims to serve every kind of fish (except shark), plus meat and game dishes. Daily noon–6pm & 9pm–12.30am.

The Columbus Trail

Huelva's greatest source of pride lies with the momentous expeditions of **Christopher Columbus** to the New World, the first of which sailed from Palos de la Frontera (or simply Palos), across the Tinto estuary from the city. When he was unable to get backing for his voyages, Columbus cooled his heels for many years in and around Huelva and the La Rábida monastery until he finally managed to obtain a commission from the king and queen in the spring of 1492. The main sites connected with

Columbus – **La Rábida**, **Palos** and **Moguer** – are all within a 30km round-trip from Huelva. Buses running between Huelva and Moguer call at all three locations.

La Rábida and around

The monastery of **LA RÁBIDA**, 8km from Huelva, can be reached by bus (roughly hourly from Huelva) or, with your own transport, by taking the Mazagón road southeast across the Río Tinto road bridge. At the Punta del Sebo – the tip of land where the Tinto and Odiel rivers meet – stands a **monument to Columbus** dating from the 1920s. Although most Huelvans think the 37m-high monster statue of a cowled figure clutching a huge Tau cross is that of the navigator himself, it actually represents a monk from the nearby Franciscan monastery at La Rábida (the Tau or "T"-form cross is a symbol of the Franciscan order) in recognition of the role the monks played in the Columbus story. A Cubist-inspired work, sculpted by Gertrude Vanderbilt Whitney in 1929, it was donated to the province by the USA.

The monastery

Plaza la Rábida • Tours hourly: Tues–Sat 10am–1pm & 4–7pm, Sun 10.45am–1pm & 4–7pm • ⓦ monasteriodelarabida.com • €3

Situated amid a forest of umbrella pines (which serve to mask the petrochemical refineries across the polluted river estuary), the small whitewashed Franciscan **monastery** is a surprisingly pleasant oasis once you reach it. The monastery lies at the end of Avenida de la América, linking it with Palos and lined with ceramic pavement tiles marking all the countries of the New World. Dating from the fourteenth century, the buildings suffered structural damage during the Lisbon earthquake of 1755 and have been extensively restored.

The tour begins with a room containing stylized modern **frescoes** of the explorer's life by distinguished Huelvan artist Daniel Vásquez Díaz. At the building's heart is a tranquil fifteenth-century Mudéjar **cloister**, opening off the monks' **refectory** where Columbus would have dined during his many stays here. You will also see the **cell** where the abbot, Juan Pérez, and Columbus discussed the explorer's ideas. Beyond the cloister, a fourteenth-century **church** contains an alabaster statue of the Virgin and Child to which the mariner and his men prayed before setting sail.

Upstairs, above the refectory, lies the **Sala Capitular** (Chapter House), an impressive beamed room with heavy period furniture where Fray Pérez, Columbus and the Pinzón brothers discussed the final plans before the first voyage set sail. In other rooms on the same floor you can see models of the three caravels, as well as navigation charts, cases containing various artefacts brought back from the expedition and "team pictures" of the crew.

Don't miss the curious **Sala de Banderas**, or Flag Room, where, beneath flags of the various South American nations of the New World, is a casket of earth donated by each. If some of these caskets look a bit roughed-up it's probably due to visiting South Americans who, after reverentially handling the soil of their fatherland, often treat the caskets of their neighbours with some disrespect.

Muelle de la Carabelas

June–Sept Tues–Fri 10am–2pm & 5–9pm, Sat & Sun 11am–8pm; Oct–May Tues–Fri 10am–7pm • €3.55

The reconstructed **Muelle de la Carabelas** (Harbour of the Caravels), on the nearby Río Tinto estuary, has impressive full-size replicas of the three caravels that made the epic voyage to the New World. Realistic displays on board reconstruct the grim realities of life at sea, while the surrounding quays are lined with recreations of fifteenth-century quayside bars and market stalls. In the adjoining museum are displays illustrating Columbus's life (including facsimiles of some of his geographical books annotated in a surprisingly delicate hand), video presentations on a giant screen and a *cafetería*.

By bus There are frequent buses from Huelva to the monastery. In summer a tourist road train links La Rábida with Palos de la Frontera.

Information The monastery's gardens contain an information office as well as a pleasant bar-restaurant with terrace tables.

Palos de la Frontera

Four kilometres north of La Rábida along the Río Tinto estuary lies **PALOS DE LA FRONTERA**, a rather featureless village but an important site in the Columbus story. It was from the silted-up bay below the church of San Jorge – then a major harbour and sea port – that Columbus's three caravels, the *Niña*, the *Pinta* and the *Santa María*, set out to reach Asia by crossing the western ocean.

San Jorge

C/Fray Juan Pérez 19 • Mon–Fri 10am–noon & 6–7.30pm • Free

O Palos, no one can equal your glory.
Not Memphis, nor Thebes nor eternal Rome.
Not Athens nor London.
No city can dispute your historical fame!

This modern poem fixed to the exterior wall of the fifteenth-century parish church of **San Jorge** leaves you in no doubt of how Palos views its role in world history. It was here that Columbus and his crewmen attended Mass before taking on water for their voyage from the nearby **La Fontanilla**, a medieval well tarted up in 1992 as the centrepiece of a dismal park to mark the quincentenary. Near the fountain a statue has been recently erected honouring the Pinzón brothers (see below). The harbour lay to the west of the fountain in an area now marshland, and it was due to the river's silting up that the decline of Palos set in. The church has a simple, bare-brick interior containing some mural fragments as well as a distinctive wrought-iron pulpit – from which the edict was read ordering an initially reluctant Palos to provide ships, crew and provisions for the voyage – and some thirteenth- and sixteenth-century alabaster sculptures of Santa Ana and the Crucifixion.

On that August morning in 1492 Columbus is supposed to have left the church through its southern Mudéjar portal flanked by his captains Martín Alonzo Pinzón and his younger brother Vincente, both from Palos. It is these native sons that Palos today celebrates, even more than its Columbus connection, claiming that their contribution to the epic voyage has been eclipsed. Indeed, at the time the Pinzón family insisted that Martín – a mariner of great local repute – had planned such a voyage long before Columbus.

Casa Museo Martín Alonso Pinzón

C/Colón 24 • Mon–Fri 10am–2pm & 5–9pm • Free

South of San Jorge on the main street, the **house of Martín Alonso Pinzón** survives, and is well worth a visit. It has been converted into a museum with lots of background information on the Pinzón brothers and their role in the voyages to the New World as well as reconstructions of daily life, fashions and food preferences in the sixteenth century.

By bus There are frequent buses to and from Huelva.
Tourist information The Ayuntamiento (Mon–Fri 9am–3pm; ☎959 350 100), facing Plaza Mayor on

C/Rábida 3, the main street, can provide information and a town map, as well as assistance in viewing the church and museum outside formal opening hours.

3

THE VOYAGES OF COLUMBUS

Probably born in Genoa around 1451 to the son of a weaving merchant, Christopher Columbus (in Spanish, Cristóbal Colón) went to sea in his early teens. After years of sailing around the Mediterranean, in 1476 he was shipwrecked off the coast of Portugal and it was in **Lisbon** – then the world leader in navigation – that Columbus learned the skills of map-making. In 1479 he married into a high-ranking Portuguese family and spent the following years on trading voyages to the British Isles and elsewhere, including in 1482 a journey down the coast of **West Africa** to Ghana, a major source of spices, ivory and slaves.

During this time the idea germinated in his mind of attempting to **sail west to reach the Indies and the Far East**, thus shortening the route that Portugal was then exploring around the coast of Africa. He built up an enormous library of ancient and contemporary geographical writings now preserved in Seville, all heavily annotated in his own hand. By some optimistic interpretations of these works and a misreading of an Arab geographer, Alfraganus, Columbus seriously undercalculated the earth's circumference, believing that Marco Polo's fabulous island of Cipangu (Japan) lay a mere 2400 miles west of the Canaries instead of an actual 10,600.

Trying to find backers, when the Portuguese monarch, still more interested in the African route, demurred, Columbus turned to Spain. In 1486 at **Córdoba** he presented his plan to reach the gold-rich Orient to Fernando and Isabel, still involved in the protracted and costly war against the Moors. Desirous of the gold to boost their fortunes but wary, after consultations with advisers, of Columbus's calculations, they both refused support. Now desperate, Columbus turned to France and then to Henry VII of England, with no success.

During his earlier journey from Portugal to Córdoba, Columbus had stayed at **La Rábida** Franciscan monastery. It was to here that he returned frustrated and depressed in the autumn of 1491. The explorer's luck turned when **Juan Pérez**, the abbot of La Rábida and a former confessor to Isabel, was moved to write to the queen on Columbus's behalf. It was a timely moment. In January of 1492 Granada had fallen, the treasury was empty, and the promise of gold and glory for a resurgent Spain now attracted the monarchs.

Columbus set out from Palos on **August 3, 1492**, with three small vessels, the *Santa María*, the *Niña* and the *Pinta*, carrying a total of 120 men recruited from Palos and Moguer by the Pinzón brothers. Columbus's discovery of the **Atlantic wind patterns** ranks alongside his other feats; he sailed via the Canaries to take advantage of the trade winds, but the incredible voyage almost ended in mutiny by crews who believed that they would never find a wind to bring them home. This was avoided when, on October 12, Columbus made landfall on **Watling Island** (aka San Salvador) in the Bahamas. Watched by naked and silent natives he took the island in the name of Spain and gave thanks to God. After leaving a colony of men on Hispaniola (modern Haiti) he returned to Palos on March 15, 1493, to enormous acclaim.

Successful as a mariner, Columbus was disastrous as a **colonizer**, epitomized by his forcing of the native population of Hispaniola into the gold mines in a brutal process that reduced their numbers from a quarter of a million in 1492 to sixty thousand fifteen years later. In 1500, Columbus was removed from office as governor and sent back to Spain in chains and disgrace. He was eventually released and made his final voyage in 1502 – a last desperate attempt to find a strait leading to India – but ended up stranded in Jamaica for a whole year after losing his ships to sea worms. Columbus died at Valladolid in 1506, still believing that he had reached the East Indies.

ACCOMMODATION AND EATING

Hotel La Pinta C/Rábida 75 ☎ 959 350 511, ⊛ hotella pinta.com. Attractive small hotel with comfortable a/c balcony rooms with TV and safe, plus its own restaurant and car park. **€65**

Restaurant El Paraíso Avda. America 15, near *Hotel*

La Pinta. The village's best restaurant, offering a wide selection of both fish and meat dishes. The *carnes a la brasa* (charcoal-grilled meats) are particularly good, and there's an excellent-value weekday *menú* for €9. Daily noon–5pm & 8–11pm.

Moguer

The compact and beautiful whitewashed town of **MOGUER**, 8km north of Palos, also takes pride in its Columbus connections: many of the crew members were recruited here. Quite apart from this, it's a place with plenty to see, and achieved worldwide fame in 1956 as the birthplace of the Nobel prize-winning poet **Juan Ramón Jiménez**.

Plaza del Cabildo

Starting from the **Plaza del Cabildo** in the centre – where there's a bronze statue of Jiménez – it's easy to find your way around. First take a look at the elegant eighteenth-century **Ayuntamiento** (Mon–Fri 8.30am–2pm) on the same square, a quintessentially Andalucian edifice in cream and brown paint.

Convento de Santa Clara

Plaza de las Monjas s/n • Tours hourly Tues–Sat 10.30am–12.30pm & 4.30–6.30pm, Sun 10.30am–12.30pm • €3

Close to Plaza del Cabildo in Plaza de las Monjas lies the Gothic-Mudéjar **Convento de Santa Clara**. Founded in the fourteenth century, this housed nuns from the order of St Clare until 1898, but is now a museum. Inside, a Mudéjar cloister leads into the nuns' former quarters, which include a kitchen, refectory and a large sixteenth-century dormitory. The **church** possesses a fine retablo and some notable alabaster tombs of the Portocarrero family, the convent's founders, as well as – at the entry to the choir – a seventeenth-century diptych of the Sienese school portraying the Immaculate Conception.

Look out for an inscription in the right aisle, which tells of **Columbus's visit** to offer thanksgiving for his safe return. He is reputed to have spent the whole night in prayer here upon returning from his first voyage in March 1493, in fulfilment of a vow he made in the middle of a terrifying storm. Other parts of the tour take in sculptures by La Roldana, Martínez Montañés and many other beautiful if anonymous works from the fourteenth, fifteenth and sixteenth centuries.

San Francisco

Plaza de San Francisco s/n • Mon–Fri 11am–2pm • Free

Behind the convent of Santa Clara lies the fifteenth-century monastery of **San Francisco**, with its stunning ochre-tinted Mudéjar brick church from where legions of missionaries were sent out to the New World. The monastery's elegant Mannerist patio/cloister can be viewed by going through the archival museum next door.

Nuestra Señora de la Granada

C/Trasera Iglesia 1 • Mon–Fri 10am–2pm • Free (donations welcome)

To the east of the centre the eighteenth-century church of **Nuestra Señora de la Granada** was raised over a church of the same name which was flattened in the Lisbon earthquake of 1755. It boasts a scaled-down, whiter version of Seville's Giralda tower "which from close up looks like Seville's from far away", wrote Jiménez. An impressive triple-naved interior is complemented by some fine vaulting.

JUAN RAMÓN JIMÉNEZ IN MOGUER

The work that most Andalucians remember Jiménez for today is **Platero y yo** ("Platero and I"), the story of a little donkey who is a "friend of the poet and children" based on his own donkey, Platero, in whose company he often toured Moguer's streets. Glazed plaques on walls around town mark streets or buildings that occur in the story, and there are a couple of worthwhile sites dedicated to the author.

Jiménez museum C/Jiménez 5. The house where Jiménez was born has been restored as an interesting museum displaying mementoes from the poet's life. Tours hourly Tues–Sat 10.15am–1pm & 5.15–7pm, Sun 10.15am–1pm; €3

Jiménez gravesite Avda. Hermanos Niño, the road leading towards the Seville–Huelva highway. Moguer's cemetery has the grave of the poet and his wife, Zenobia. His body was returned to the town he loved for burial in 1958 after twenty years spent in exile in Puerto Rico, to where he had emigrated after Franco came to power.

3

ARRIVAL AND INFORMATION

By bus Buses from and to Huelva drop off and leave from C/Coronación to the north of Plaza Cabildo.

Turismo Moguer's Turismo (April–Sept Mon–Sat 10am–2pm & 5–7pm; Oct–March Mon–Sat 10am–2pm & 4.30–7pm, Sun 10am–3pm; ☏ 959 371 898,

ⓦ aytomoguer.es) lies just off the main square, inside the former castle at C/Castillo s/n.

Festival Festival de Flamenco, held annually in the middle of September.

ACCOMMODATION

Hostal Platero C/Aceña 4, slightly east of Plaza del Cabildo ☏ 959 372 159. Central *hostal* offering serviceable en-suite rooms with TV. Can advise on parking nearby. €30

Hotel Plaza Escribano Plaza Escribano 5, south of the

Plaza del Cabildo ☏ 959 373 063 ⓦ hotelplazaescribano .com. Elegant, gleaming-white small hotel with newly decorated a/c rooms equipped with minibar, plasma TV and safe. Free wi-fi. €50

EATING AND DRINKING

Mesón El Lobito C/La Rábida 31. Unique bar with eccentric decor including vast numbers of unidentified objects hanging from the ceiling, chickens in cages in a patio and walls completely covered in graffiti (which you're welcome to add to). There's usually a good atmosphere if you turn up after 10pm. Daily 10am–midnight.

Mesón Restaurante Parala Plaza de las Monjas 22. Opposite the entrance to Santa Clara, this is the best restaurant in town, and serves up excellent regional fish and meat dishes, plus tapas and an inexpensive *menú* (around €10). Main dishes €8–15. Daily 1–4pm & 8–11pm.

Coto de Doñana National Park

Sited at the estuary of the Guadalquivir, the vast roadless area of the **COTO DE DOÑANA** is Spain's largest wildlife reserve, a world-class wetland site for migrating birds and one of Europe's greatest wilderness areas. The seasonal pattern of its delta waters, which flood in winter and then drop in the spring, leaving rich deposits of silt, raised sandbanks and islands, give the Coto de Doñana its special interest. Conditions are perfect in winter for ducks and geese, but spring is most exciting: the exposed mud draws hundreds of flocks of breeding birds. In the marshes and amid the cork oak forests behind you've a good chance of seeing squacco heron, black-winged stilt, whiskered tern, pratincole and sand grouse, as well as flamingos, egrets and vultures. There are, too, occasional sightings of the Spanish imperial eagle, now reduced to a score of breeding pairs. In late summer and early autumn, the swamps – or *marismas* – dry out and support far less birdlife. The park is also home to an estimated 25 pairs of the pardel or Spanish lynx, now in severe peril of extinction, although a captive breeding programme has had some success in reversing the trend.

Inevitably, it seems, the park is under threat from development, and several lynx have been killed by traffic on the road to the beach resort at Matalascañas. Even at current levels the drain on the water supply is severe, and made worse by pollution of the Guadalquivir by farming pesticides, Seville's industry and Huelva's mines. The seemingly inevitable disaster finally occurred in April 1998, when an upriver mining dam used for storing toxic waste burst, unleashing millions of litres of pollutants into the Guadiamar river which flows through the park. The noxious tide was stopped just 2km from the park's boundary, but catastrophic damage was done to the surrounding farmland, with nesting birds decimated and fish poisoned. The mining dams have not been removed (the mines are a major local employer) but merely repaired. Proposals for a huge new tourist centre – to be known as the **Costa Doñana** – on the fringes of the park have been shelved, but the pressure for development remains. Bitter demonstrations organized by locals who saw the prospect of much-needed jobs in the Costa Doñana development have abated into an uneasy truce, further exacerbated by the economic downturn of recent years. Some experts have proposed that "green tourism", allowing a greater but controlled

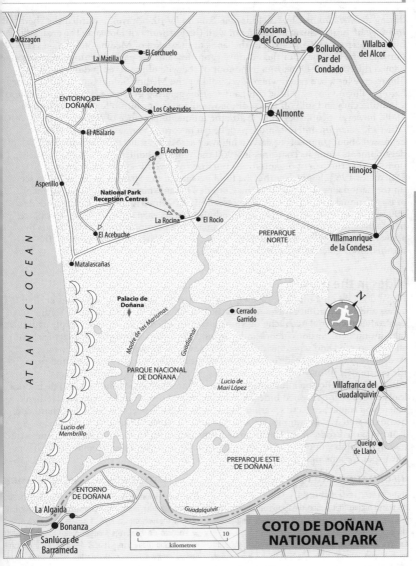

COTO DE DOÑANA
NATIONAL PARK

public access to the park, and thereby providing an income for the local community, is the only way to bring both sides together.

Brief history

This area was known to the Romans as **Ligur**, and in the 1990s archeologists were surprised to discover a Roman quayside 3km into the swamps, showing just how much the area has expanded in the ensuing two millennia. It was Alfonso X, however, who claimed the territory of Las Rocinas as a hunting reserve for the Spanish crown in 1262 during the *Reconquista*. In 1294 his heir, Sancho IV (the Brave), rewarded the "hero" of the siege of Tarifa, Guzmán El Bueno, with the territories of Doñana. The area, still a hunting reserve, remained part of the lands of the dukes of Medina Sidonia – as the Guzmán line became – for the next five centuries, and the park's hunting lodge was named the palace of Dona Aña in honour of the wife of the seventh duke in 1595. The reserve hit a bad patch when it was sold by the Medina Sidonias in 1897 to sherry baron William Garvey, whose company is still operating in Jerez. Garvey turned it into a hunting club and sold off much of the woodland for profit; following his death in 1909, however, people began to realize the unique importance of the area.

In 1957 scientific interest in the park began in earnest and, as a result of concern expressed about proposals to carve a highway across the zone and build tourist developments along its coastline, in 1969 the World Wildlife Fund (Spain) was set up following the parent organization's purchase of seventy square kilometres of Doñana in 1963. Soon after this the fund persuaded the Spanish government to set up the national park. Since then the Coto de Doñana, now under the management of the National Institute for the Conservation of Nature (ICONA), has expanded to 190,000 acres (750 sq km). The park's administrators then enlisted divine assistance in safeguarding its future when they diplomatically petitioned the brotherhoods to allow the Virgin of Rocío (see p.335) to become the National Park's patron. The brotherhoods graciously acceded to this request.

Hides in the park

If you don't go on a tour (see below), you're currently restricted to the **hides** at three access and information centres open to the public. The five hides adjacent to the **Centro Recepción del Acebuche** overlook a lagoon where marbled teal, purple gallinule (aka swamphen), various grebes and – around the trees – azure-winged magpies have all been spotted and where, with luck, you may even glimpse the extremely rare Audouin's gull. You'll need to bring your own binoculars or they can be hired from the centre (€1.50/hr).

Beyond the **La Rocina** information centre, a 3km route called the "Charco de la Boca" leads to five well-concealed hides in marshland, pine woods and along the riverbank, where you might see Cetti's warbler, the spectacular hoopoe, red-crested pochard and herons as well as – in summer – flamingos and a plethora of singing nightingales. A 1.5km marked route from **El Palacio de Acebrón** threads from the centre, circling a lake mainly through woodland, and offering possibilities to sight the rare hawfinch. It's a great spot for a picnic.

INFORMATION AND TOURS

COTO DE DOÑANA NATIONAL PARK

INFORMATION OFFICES

It's worth noting that during the Pentecost *romería* (the seventh week after Easter) all three visitor centres are closed.

Centro Recepción del Acebuche The starting point for bus tours into the park (see p.333), this information office (daily: April–Sept 8am–9pm; Oct–March 8am–7pm; ☎959 430 432, English spoken, ⓦ parquenacional donana.com), 4km north of Matalascañas towards El Rocío and Almonte, then 1.5km up a signed road on the left, can supply a useful free map and has a bookshop, a natural history exhibition, a rather tedious audiovisual presentation and a *cafetería* with an economical *menú*.

La Rocina Nine kilometres north of the Centro Recepción del Acebuche, close to the El Rocío bridge (daily 9am–3pm

& 4–7pm). Information centre (free maps), car park and a small open-air museum with historical reconstructions of life in the *marismas*.

El Palacio de Acebrón Along a minor road 5km west of La Rocina (daily 9am–3pm & 4–7pm). An impressive former hunting lodge with another information centre housing an ethnographic exhibition dealing with the area's history and development.

OFFICIAL TOURS

Visiting the Coto de Doñana still involves – understandably – a certain amount of frustration. At present the heart of the reserve is still open only to brief, organized **bus tours**, though you can also take a **boat cruise** into the park from Sanlúcar de Barrameda (see p.210).

BUS TOURS

Cooperativa Marismas del Rocío tours Cooperativa Marismas del Rocío uses all-terrain 24-seater buses to tour the park (May–Sept daily 8.30am & 5pm; Oct–April Tues–Sun 8.30am & 3pm; €27). Book at the Centro de Recepción del Acebuche. Either call in at the centre or phone ahead. Outside July, August and holiday periods you should be able to get on to the next day's trip, otherwise you'll need to book at least a week in advance. Tours consist of an 80km, four-hour trip sampling the park's various ecosystems: dunes, beach, *marismas* and woodland, with the guide pointing out only spectacular species such as flamingo, imperial eagle, deer and wild

boar. Binoculars are essential, and although the centre has some available for rent (€2.50/tour), you'd be well advised to bring your own.

Tailor-made tours If you're a serious ornithologist or naturalist, the tour isn't for you and you should consider a group booking, which costs a little more than the daily excursion and lets you create your own itinerary (details from the centre).

Other tour operators Other operators running trips into the park are: Discovering Doñana (☎ 959 442 466, ⓦ discoveringdonana.com), Doñana Bird Tours (☎ 955 755 399, ⓦ donanabirdtours.com) and Doñana Nature (☎ 959 442 160, ⓦ donana-nature.com).

El Rocío

3

Set on the northwestern tip of the marshes, **EL ROCÍO** is one of the most atmospheric places in Andalucía: a tiny cluster of white cottages, sandy streets and an imposing church where the most famous pilgrimage-fair of the south occurs annually at Pentecost. As the cowboy-hatted farmers nonchalantly ride horses along the wide sandy streets and tie up at Wild West-style hitching rails in front of their timber cabins, you half expect Clint Eastwood to emerge from a nearby saloon chewing on a cheroot. And this frontier-like feeling isn't altogether accidental, as it was from this area that many of the colonizers of the New World set out, exporting their vernacular architectural preferences with them. In the evening the street lights do little to undermine the time-warp quality of an area unchanged for centuries. A new **Museo Histórico** (daily 10am–2pm; €2), on the opposite side of the main A483 road from the village, has interesting displays relating to the history of El Rocío and the annual *romería*.

Beyond the village's core, ghostly streets of dwellings belonging to the **brotherhoods** – all with hitching rails and verandas – stand empty most of the year waiting to be put to service each May or June in the *romería*, when the ninety or so brotherhoods use them to house their members.

Nuestra Señora del Rocío

C/Ermita s/n • Daily 8.30am–7.30pm • Free

Centre of the town's Pentecost celebrations, the church of **Nuestra Señora del Rocío** was, despite its Baroque appearance, built in the 1960s on the site of a church which collapsed in the eighteenth-century Lisbon earthquake. It holds the venerated image of the **Virgen del Rocío**, a thirteenth-century work in carved wood.

ARRIVAL AND INFORMATION

EL ROCÍO

By bus There are at least three buses a day to and from Seville en route to Matalascañas, enabling a stop to be made at the La Rocina or El Acebuche National Park visitor

centres – make sure to let the driver know you want to be dropped off. Getting to or from Huelva is more complicated, requiring a change at Almonte.

INFORMATION

Turismo El Rocío's Turismo (daily 10am–2pm; ☎ 959 442 166) is housed in the Museo Histórico, Camino de Moguer s/n, on the opposite side of the main A483 road from the village. Staff can supply a village map and lots of information about the national park including a 5km scenic walk along the Raya Real to the Palacio del Rey, northeast of the village, where deer, wild boar and the Spanish lynx have all been spotted.

ATMs The village now has a number of cash machines and a bank (sited alongside the *Hotel Rocío Doñana*).

Tours On the opposite side of the main A483 road to the village, Doñana Reservas (☎ 959 442 474, ⓦ donana reservas.com) offers jeep tours into Doñana National Park. They also offer horseriding and landau excursions in and around the park lasting from one day to a week.

ACCOMMODATION AND EATING

El Rocío makes a nice place to stay – except during the *romería* at Pentecost when rooms (costing a whopping €200–500/night) are booked up months, even years, in advance. All the hotels and *hostales* have restaurants – note that El Rocío's eating places tend to close earlier than is normal in Andalucía and start shutting down around 10.30–11pm. Tapas and *raciones* are served at many other restaurants and bars on and around the village's main street – but to eat out on their terraces after sundown in summer you'll need plenty of mosquito protection.

Camping La Aldea ☎ 959 442 677, ⓦ campinglaaldea.com. El Rocío's campsite lies on the village's northern edge along the Almonte road (A483), offering good facilities and a reasonable amount of shade. Two people plus car **€26**

Hospedería Puente del Rey Avda. Canaliega 1 ☎ 959 442 575, ⓦ rociodonana.com. Enormous and rather incongruous upmarket three-star alongside the A483. The comfortable and spacious rooms come with fridge, TV and safe. **€70**

Hostal Cristina C/Real 58, behind the church ☎ 959 442 413. Welcoming and economical option offering en-suite rooms with TV in a corral (patio) behind. Also has a good restaurant with a good-value *menú* and a bar. **€50**

Hostal Isidro Avda. Los Ansares 59 ☎ 959 442 242. Pleasant *hostal* on the village's eastern side, offering good-quality en-suite a/c rooms with TV above a restaurant with an economical *menú*. **€48**

Hotel La Malvasia C/Sanlúcar 38 ☎ 959 443 870, ⓦ lamalvasiahotel.com. A couple of hundred metres beyond *Hotel Toruño* and on the edge of the *marismas* this hotel is housed in a former *casa señorial* with stylish, well-equipped rooms around a patio and a sensational view over the *marismas* from its suite (Room 13), as well as a rooftop *mirador*. **€65**

★ **Hotel Toruño** Plaza Acebuchal 22 ☎ 959 442 323, ⓦ toruno.es. The best of the more expensive places, with comfortable rooms overlooking the *marismas*. The best view is from Room 225 but some of the ground floor rooms (#109, #111 & #115) also allow you to spot flamingos, herons, avocets and lots more whilst lying in bed. Free wi-fi. The bar-restaurant, opposite the hotel itself, is the village's best place to eat. A range of tapas and *raciones* are served in the cosy bar, while the elegant dining room – with a stunning panoramic view over the *marismas* – offers fish and *mariscos* as well as *cerdo ibérico* (pork from black pigs) and organic beef raised in the national park. Also has a *menú* for €15. Main dishes €8–15. Restaurant daily 9am–11pm. **€80**

BIRDWATCHING AROUND EL ROCÍO

In the spring, El Rocío is probably the best birdwatching base in the area. The *marismas* and pine woods adjacent to the town itself are teeming with birds, and following tracks east and southeast along the edge of the reserve you'll see many species from white stork, herons and egrets to masked great grey shrike and honking wild geese.

At the water's edge 150m east of the *Hotel Toruño* (see above) the **Centro Ornitológico Francisco Bernis** (Tues–Sun 9am–2pm & 4–7pm, ⓦ seo.org) has copious information on the birds to be seen plus a rooftop hide overlooking the *marismas*. The **Boca del Lobo** ("wolf-breath") sewage treatment plant a further 400m east of the centre is an unlikely-sounding bird-spotting location, but vultures and storks are frequent patrons there.

El Rocío bridge, on the village's southern edge (carrying the A483), has been described by one naturalist as "the best free birdwatching site in Europe". From this spot, red kite – a common sight here – soaring flocks of whiskered terns, disturbed by the ominous approach of a majestic booted eagle, and migrating greenshank, ruff and sandpiper are all to be seen in season. In high summer, though, the marshes dry out and are grazed by horses while the birdlife is restricted to coot and avocets breeding by the river. The view across the marshes towards the village and church of El Rocío from here is also superb.

With your own transport another great birdwatching location is the **Cerrado Garrido** (aka Centro José Antonio Valverde; June–Sept 10am–8pm; Oct–May 10am–6pm; ☎ 671 564 145) on the park's northern fringes. To get there from El Rocío follow the signs from the centre of the village, a 30km trip via Villamanrique de la Condesa. Approaching the centre the route traverses the Preparque along unmade tracks and is quite feasible in summer; after heavy rains access may not be possible and you should check with the El Acebuche visitors' centre (see p.332). Cerrado's visitors' centre has a *cafetería*-bar, as well as telescopes and hides. You'll have plenty of other birdwatching and wildlife-spotting opportunities en route – keep an eye out for purple gallinules (aka swamphen) in the ditches between the paddy fields. The sunrises and sunsets over the *marismas* at Cerrado Garrido are quite spectacular, too.

THE ROMERÍA DEL ROCÍO

The Romería del Rocío, a Whitsun pilgrimage to the sanctuary of the Virgen del Rocío, is one of the most extraordinary spectacles in Europe, with whole village communities and some ninety local **"brotherhoods"** from Huelva, Seville, Málaga and even one from Gibraltar converging on the village on horseback and in lavishly decorated ox-carts. The event is part pilgrimage and part jamboree as the intense emotions awakened by the two- to four-day journey (not to mention the drinking) often spill over uncontrollably.

The brotherhoods coming from Sanlúcar de Barrameda have a special dispensation to follow their ancient route across the heart of the Parque de Doñana which takes them three nights and four days, with all the attendant fire risks en route. The army is employed to get them and their carts over the Guadalquivir safely, and the park's rangers set up campsites for them and provide firewood for their great feasts in the woods. Sadly, the rubbish left behind by these large crowds is the cause of many wildlife fatalities as species such as boar choke on the plastic containers they attempt to devour. Throughout the *Romería*, which climaxes on the Saturday evening, everyone parties in fiesta costume, while by the time the carts arrive at El Rocío they've been joined by hundreds of busloads of pilgrims.

What they have all come for – apart from the spectacle itself – is the commemoration of the miracle of **Nuestra Señora del Rocío** (Our Lady of the Dew). The miracle concerns the venerated statue believed to have been found on this spot by a shepherd in the thirteenth century – conveniently after the eviction of the Moors – which, so it is said, resisted all attempts to move it elsewhere. A shrine was built, miraculous healings and events were reported, and El Rocío was suddenly on the map. In the early hours of **Pentecost Sunday** when many of the revellers either are gripped by religious frenzy or lie prostrate in an alcoholic stupor, the image of the Virgin, credited with all kinds of magic and fertility powers, is paraded before the faithful as she visits each one of the brotherhoods' houses (which lie empty for the rest of the year).

In recent years the sheer size of the Romería has begun to worry the authorities as it has exploded from a few thousand pilgrims in the 1970s to an incredible half a million in the early years of the new century. Despite the whole affair having become a spectacular TV event with arc lamps, amplified music and fireworks, popular enthusiasm is undiminished. The brotherhoods wrestle with each other to carry the Blanca Paloma ("the White Dove", as the Virgin is fondly known) one more time in procession before she's returned to her shrine for another year, and the weary homeward trek begins.

Accompanying one of the brotherhoods on their pilgrimage to El Rocío is a memorable and exhilarating experience. Anyone is entitled to be a pilgrim: just turn up when the processions leave the major villages in the provinces of Seville and Huelva in the days leading up to Pentecost, taking with you a sleeping bag and some food and water. The walking is easy with plenty of stops for dancing and liquid refreshment, and the nightly encampments, when folk songs are sung around campfires, are magical.

Beaches south of El Rocío

With your own transport, you can explore many fine, empty dune-backed **beaches** to the northwest of the humdrum resort of Matalascañas, 16km south of El Rocío. These fabulous strands retain their tranquillity thanks to the lack of settlements along the 30km of coastline flanking the A494 west of here. There are a number of access points to beaches such as the signed **Playa Cuesta de Maneli**; here boardwalks cross the pine- and juniper-covered dunes to a magnificent swathe of golden sand, stretching far into the distance in both directions – you will rarely see another soul. A few kilometres further, near the resort of Mazagón, lies the Costa de la Luz's most attractive hotel, the **Parador Cristóbal Colón** (☎959 536 300, ⓦparador.es) set on its own fabulous strand (see p.36).

Along the coast to Portugal

The stretch of coast between the **Guadiana** – which marks the border with Portugal – and **Tinto** rivers is lined with some of the finest **beaches** in Andalucía and a scattering of low-key resorts that rarely see a foreign tourist. There's no train service, but plenty of buses run along this main route to the Portuguese frontier, easily crossed by a spectacular road bridge over the Guadiana estuary.

From Huelva the **coast road to Portugal** loops around the Marisma de San Miguel, passing through the dull towns of **Cartaya** and **Lepe**. Geoffrey Chaucer (whose father was a vintner), in the *Pardoner's Tale*, wrote that the potent white wine of Lepe "creepeth subtilly … that whan a man hath dronken draughtes three, and weneth he be at hoom in Chepe, He is in Spaigne, right at the toune of Lepe" – an out-of-body experience no doubt familiar to many modern inebriates. Lepe's main claim to fame today, however, is as the butt of hundreds of "did you hear about the man from Lepe …?" jokes, in which the town's supposedly gormless inhabitants are pilloried by the rest of the nation.

Playa de la Antilla

The road hits the coast 5km south of Lepe at **LA ANTILLA**, a low-key beach resort with a wide, sandy blue-flag beach backed by a palm-lined promenade. There are some very good seafood restaurants close to the seafront making it an invitingly peaceful place to stay outside high season.

ACCOMMODATION   PLAYA DE LA ANTILLA

You won't find a room in Playa de la Antilla in August without pre-booking. Places to stay cluster around the junction of Avda. Castilla and C/La Parada, which is also where the bus drops you.

Camping Luz Ctra. La Antilla-Isla Cristina s/n ☏ 959 341 142. Five kilometres west of the resort towards Isla Cristina, this is a decent campsite with plenty of shade, good facilities and a large pool. Two people plus car €24

Hostal El Álamo Avda. Castilla 82 ☏ 959 481 018, ⓦ elalamoplaya.com. Around the corner from C/La Parada, this welcoming *hostal* has distinctively decorated en-suite rooms with lots of primary colours and stencil designs. Some slightly more expensive rooms come with

a/c, fridge and sea-view terrace. €60

Hostal Azul La Parada 9 ☏ 959 480 700, ⓦ hostalazul .com. The nearest to the seafront of a line of places along La Parada, this dapper *hostal* has en-suite balcony rooms with sea views plus an attractive roof terrace with loungers. Free wi-fi. €75

Hostal La Parada Plaza La Parada s/n ☏ 959 480 726. Friendly *hostal* with newly refurbished a/c en-suite rooms with TV above a bar restaurant. €65

EATING AND DRINKING

There's a good spread of bars and cafés near the seafront plus a scattering of *marisquerías* and restaurants to choose from. Many of these line the main street, Avda. Castilla, a couple of blocks in from the sea.

Bar-Restaurante Feria Avda. Castilla 16. This is an excellent place for fresh fish; unusually for this area it is also noted for its *jamón* and *carnes a la brasa* (charcoal-grilled meats). Main dishes €8–18. Daily 12.30–4pm & 8–11pm.

Bar-Restaurante Lino Avda. Castilla 2. Another great place for fresh fish and *mariscos* including *almejas a la marinera* (clams in wine). Check the daily specials. Daily noon–4pm & 8–10.30pm.

Café-Restaurante Coral C/Estrella del Mar 3. A good

stop for breakfast snacks, with sea views and pleasant terrace; from lunchtime onwards it also does *platos combinados*. Daily 8.30am–11pm.

Casa Rodri C/Adelfa s/n, just off Avda. Castilla. Excellent fish and shellfish – the *dorada* (bream) and *lubina* (sea bass) are recommended – and there's also an astonishingly good-value *menú* for €6.50. Daily noon–4pm & 8–11pm.

Cervecería Estoril Avda. Castilla. Locals pack this popular *cervecería* to munch *mariscos* and various other seafood tapas and *raciones*. Daily 10am–midnight.

La Islantilla

On the western edge of La Antilla the coast road passes some pretty awful beach development as well as, a couple of kilometres further, the newly created coastal nightmare of **La Islantilla**, where a clutch of tasteless upmarket hotels and *urbanizaciones* are flanked to the right of the road by a sprawling 25-hole golf course

– a misguided joint venture by Lepe and Isla Cristina to attract well-heeled visitors. Beyond the campsites Luz (see p.336) and *Taray*, the vista clears to provide a pleasant few kilometres of pine woods and, behind the dunes, more good beaches.

INFORMATION
LA ISLANTILLA

Turismo La Islantilla has a conveniently located Turismo (daily: March–Oct 10am–2pm & 5–7pm; Nov–April 10am–2pm; ☎ 959 646 013), on the left of the through road, with stacks of information on the whole Costa de la Luz.

Isla Cristina

ISLA CRISTINA, 8km beyond La Islantilla, was, as its name implies, once an island, but infilling has transformed it into a pleasant resort surrounded by *marismas* and tidal estuaries. For most of the year the town's prevailing atmosphere is one of nonchalant tranquillity, punctuated only in August by the annual invasion of *sevillanos*, who fill its holiday apartment blocks and beaches to bursting point. The commercial centre is concentrated around the **port** which is the second most important in the province and from where shellfish and wet fish are transported overnight on ice to the markets, bars and restaurants of Seville, Córdoba and Madrid.

Life in town revolves around the central **Plaza de las Flores**, from where it's an easy ten-minute walk down Carretera de la Playa, shaded by giant eucalyptus trees, to the town's fine sandy **beach**, which somewhat makes up for a drab seafront. Alternatively there's a half-hourly bus (except during the siesta) from the bus station close to the same square.

ARRIVAL AND INFORMATION
ISLA CRISTINA

By bus The bus station (☎ 959 331 652) is on Avda. de Huelva, a couple of blocks east of Plaza de las Flores. There are frequent daily buses from Huelva and Seville, while buses (May–Sept) also go from here to the beach.

Turismo Slightly northwest of Plaza de las Flores at C/San Francisco 12 (March–Oct Mon–Fri 10am–2pm & 5.30–7.30pm, Sat & Sun 10am–2pm; Nov–April daily 10am–2pm; ☎ 959 332 694). Staff can provide a town map.

Festival The big event in Isla Cristina is the town's Carnaval, held annually in February.

ACCOMMODATION

Due to the severe shortage of accommodation, if you want to stay – in August especially – you'll need to book ahead. We quote August rates; prices tend to fall dramatically outside this period.

Camping Giralda 2km from town on La Antilla road ☎ 959 343 318, ⊚ campinggiralda.com. The nearest campsite to the resort with adequate shade, good services and a pool, plus canoeing and sailing. **€6.90** per person, **€6.90** per tent, **€5.75** per vehicle

Hotel Brisamar C/Baja 187 ☎ 959 331 130. The most central place to stay in town (to the southeast of the central zone), this pleasant, recently refitted hotel offers sparkling, light and airy rooms equipped with fridge and kitchenette. **€80**

Hotel Paraíso Playa Carretera de la Playa s/n ☎ 959 331 873, ⊚ hotelparaisoplaya.com. Comfortable hotel, slightly inland from the beach, with attractive balcony rooms plus pool, car park and free wi-fi. **€120**

Hotel Sol y Mar Paseo Marítimo s/n ☎ 959 332 050, ⊚ hotelsolymar.org. Right on the beach, this inviting hotel has pleasant rooms with terrace balcony and sea views, plus its own car park and a very good bar-restaurant. **€110**

EATING

★ **Casa Rufino** Carretera de la Playa ☎ 959 330 810. Less than 100m from the beach and with an outdoor terrace, this is one of the town's best – and priciest – fish restaurants. Specials include *atún de almadraba* (tuna) and a superb *arroz negro de marisco* (rice with squid); plus a good-value *menú* (around €20) and a "*tonteo*", featuring eight different kinds of fish. Main dishes €10–25. Mon–Thurs noon–4pm, Fri–Sun noon–4pm & 8–11pm.

★ **Hermanos Moreno** Avda. Padre Miravent 39. A stone's throw from the fishing harbour, you won't get fish any fresher than at this popular and reasonably priced bar-restaurant. Everything served in the tapas bar below is straight from the sea, while their upstairs restaurant is also outstanding – *atún* (tuna) and *urta* (sea bream) are specialities. Weekday *menú* €8; main dishes €8–15. Daily 10am–11pm.

Ayamonte and around

Although the sprawling, slightly down-at-heel border town of **AYAMONTE** lies just 8km from Isla Cristina, the road has to dogleg 16km around the *marismas* to get there. With Portugal only a few hundred metres away on the opposite bank of the Río Guadiana – and easily visitable – there's a pronounced Portuguese feel to the town, and in the *horario comercial* the streets hum with the conversations of cross-border visitors who come over to do their shopping.

The old town

The warren of narrow streets behind the main square, **Paseo de la Ribera** (and its continuation Plaza de la Coronación) overlooking the harbour, leads up to the old town. Here, the fourteenth-century **Iglesia de San Francisco** (open service times; try 7–9pm), has a beautiful Mudéjar *artesonado* ceiling; following the same street, Calle San Francisco, further north will bring you to the fifteenth-century **Iglesia de San Salvador** (Mon–Sat 5–8pm; free) with a striking tower which you can climb for fine views across the river to Portugal.

The beaches

Ayamonte's beaches, the blue-flagged **Playa Isla Canela**, 7km south of town, and its eastward continuation, the **Playa Punta del Moral**, are excellent places for a bit of basking in the sun, although what was once an attractively wild stretch of coast has undergone a mammoth building programme turning the Punta del Moral into a complex of high-rise holiday apartments and hotels with the gargantuan and tasteless *Hotel Ríu* as its centrepiece. Playa Isla Canela can be reached by half-hourly bus (April–Sept) from the bus station.

Punta del Moral

The picturesque old fishing village of **PUNTA DEL MORAL** sits on an inlet slightly north of Ayamonte, warily eyeing the concrete monsters dominating the skyline to the south. It's worth seeking out this tiny place for a line of excellent tapas bars along its only recently asphalted main street: *Bar Nuevo Simón*, *Chiringuito III* and the excellent-value *El Contrabando* are all good for fresh fish, *raciones* and a wide range of tapas.

ARRIVAL AND INFORMATION | AYAMONTE

By bus Frequent daily buses from Huelva and Seville arrive at the bus station (☎ 959 256 900) on Avda. de Andalucía, slightly north of the Paseo de la Ribera.

Turismo C/Huelva 17, slightly northwest of the Paseo de la Ribera (May–Sept Mon–Fri 10am–9pm, Oct–April 10am–8pm; ☎ 959 320 737, ⊛ ayto-ayamonte.es). Staff can provide a town map and information.

Internet Todoapc internet café (daily 10am–9pm), Avda. Villa Real de Santo Antonio 5, on the waterfront facing the fishing harbour.

ACCOMMODATION

Places to stay are limited and rooms can be hard to find, especially in summer; if things become really tight one option may be to cross the Guadiana to the Portuguese side and the town of Vila Real de Santo Antonio on the opposite bank.

Hostal Las Robles Avda. Andalucía 119 ☎959 470 959. This welcoming *hostal* is one of the best-value options in town, with pleasant a/c en-suite rooms with TV. It's opposite the petrol station as you enter Ayamonte from Isla Cristina. **€46**

Hotel Ayamonte Center Avda. Ramón y Cajal 2 ☎959 470 250, ⊛ ayamontecenter.com. East of the harbour along the beach road, this recently refurbished hotel offers very pleasant a/c rooms with terrace balcony.

Try for a third-floor room at the rear (eg 310) overlooking the leafy zoological garden. Rates fall by up to fifty percent outside July & Aug. **€116**

Hotel Luz del Guadiana Avda. Andalucía 121, next door to Hostal Las Robles ☎959 322 002. Recently opened and comfortable hotel offering good-value and attractive en-suite rooms with a/c and TV. **€65**

Parador Costa de la Luz ☎959 320 700, ⊛ parador .es. Overlooking the Río Guadiana and its spectacular bridge, this is the town's luxury address with elegant, well-equipped rooms, many with river views, plus pretty gardens and a pool. A bar and restaurant (with river views and a *menú* for €32) complete the picture. Own car park and free wi-fi. **€138**

EATING AND DRINKING

Cafetería Restaurante Barberi Paseo de la Ribera 13. Worth a try for *platos combinados* and more elaborate dishes in the restaurant, while its café next door has an inexpensive *menú del día* for around €9. Daily 9am–11pm.

Casa Luciano C/Palma 2 ☏ 959 470 171. For a feast, the town's best place – especially for fish – is this attractive mid-priced restaurant on the east side of the harbour. House specials include *salmorejo de gambas* (shrimp gazpacho) and *atún al horno* (baked tuna). Main dishes €10–20. Mon–Sat 1–4.30pm & 8pm–midnight.

La Casona C/Lusitania 2. This bar-restaurant consists of a cosy tapas bar out front with an equally cosy restaurant behind, plus exterior and interior terraces. The bar offers more than twenty different tapas and the restaurant – serving both fish and meat dishes has *menús* starting at €10. Main dishes €7–15. Daily 11am–4pm & 8pm–midnight.

Mesón Juan Macías Paseo de la Ribera 2. On the west side of the main square, this place serves up fish and meat dishes with the emphasis on the province's famous *jamones* and *chorizos*. When busy the service tends to deteriorate. Daily 11am–4pm & 7.30–11pm.

★ **Ultramarínos Orta** C/Lusitania 8, near La Casona. Founded in 1863, this is a wonderful bar-shop selling wines, cheeses and *jamones* out front, while an atmospheric bar uses barrels for tables and serves tapas in the back. Mon–Fri 10.30am–3pm & 6–11pm, Sat 10.30am–3pm.

Inland to Río Tinto

Of the potential routes to the mountainous north of the province, the Sierra de Aracena and Sierra de Morena, the westernmost, from near Ayamonte, is the least interesting. Here the road ploughs on endlessly through a dreary landscape dominated by stands of voracious and alien eucalyptus which have sucked the lifeblood from the soil.

Far more attractive is the **N435** heading northeast from Huelva to Aracena which offers – with your own transport – an interesting detour to the mines of **Río Tinto** (see p.341). The bus uses the same route to reach Aracena or you could take a train, which will drop you at Almonaster La Real at the Sierra de Aracena's western end.

Huelva to Minas de Ríotinto

Once clear of Huelva the N435 climbs steadily towards **Trigueros**, a pleasant agricultural village and the market town of **Valverde del Camino**, noted more for its leather footwear factories than its charms. A further 10km on, a turn on the right towards the hamlet of El Pozuelo allows you to see three **dolmens** from the third

millennium BC. Following this minor road for about 2km brings you to a signed road just before a cemetery on the outskirts of the village. Follow this on foot or by car as it loops around the village for a further 2km to reach a rest area and information board. Leave any transport here and follow the track on the right which ascends the hill through trees for about 100m to the first dolmen, from where the other two can be seen on hills nearby. The first is the most impressive and has three burial chambers, two with their

capstones still in place. The second has four burial chambers, and the last is in ruins. A further six dolmens displayed on the information board are not so easy to spot.

Return to the N435, which soon begins to wind into the wooded hill country of the **Sierra Morena** until – just beyond Zalamea La Real – a right turn along the A461 leads you into the area of the **Río Tinto mines**.

Minas de Ríotinto and around

Set in an area dramatically scarred by open-cast mineworkings, where the exposed faces of mineral-rich rock are streaked with glinting rivulets of ochre, rust and cadmium, the village of **MINAS DE RÍOTINTO**, 6km east of the N435, was created by the Río Tinto mining company in the early twentieth century after they had dynamited its predecessor – complete with Baroque church – which had stood in the way of mining operations.

Barrio de Bella Vista

As you approach it from the west, watch out on the left for the **Barrio de Bella Vista**, or what the locals refer to as the "English colony". This estate of Victorian villas, complete with mock-Gothic Presbyterian church and village green, was constructed to house the largely British management and engineering staff when the mines passed into Anglo-German hands in the nineteenth century. The attitude of this elite to the surrounding village – where the mineworkers lived – is indicated by the estate's high perimeter wall and once-guarded entry gates intended rigorously to exclude "the natives", as they were disdainfully described. In a company policy with racist overtones these "colonialists" were forbidden from living in Bella Vista if they dared to marry a Spanish woman, thus deterring any dangerous interbreeding.

The estate now houses local people and no one minds if you wander in for a look around. The former "**Social Club**", membership of which was exclusively male (women were allowed only as guests), is now a bar named *Club Inglés* with a terrace overlooking the former village green/cricket pitch with a recently added pool (open to patrons of the bar).

The mining museum (see p.341) recently acquired a house in Bella Vista which has been wonderfully restored in late nineteenth-century style. Known as **Casa No. 21**

AÑO DE LOS TIROS

In 1888 the village of Ríotinto was the setting for possibly the first **ecological protest** in modern times. The Río Tinto Mining Company was using a copper processing method (banned many years before in Britain) that polluted the village and surrounding agricultural zone with a *"manta"* (blanket) of toxic fumes. Unable to convince the company or the Spanish governmental authorities (who were very much in awe of the company) to end a practice which was grievously affecting the health of the miners' families and children, the whole community staged a protest demonstration on February 4, 1888 culminating in a march to the Ayuntamiento where miners' representatives had requested a meeting with the mayor, company officials and the provincial governor. The latter had brought with him a regiment of Spanish troops to ensure that order was maintained.

While the meeting was taking place within, the troops outside received an order (it is unclear who gave it) to open fire on the peaceful demonstrators. In what is now infamously known as the **Año de los Tiros** (Year of the Shootings) up to two hundred men, women and children lost their lives. In an attempt to obscure the scale of the tragedy many corpses were disposed of in disused mine shafts which is why the precise death toll was never known.

For more, read *Corazón de la Tierra* (Heart of the Earth), a novel centred on these events, written by Juan Cobos Wilkins, a native of Río Tinto and the descendant of an English Río Tinto employee. His work in Spanish, *La Huelva Británica* (published in 2007) is a fascinating history of the British in Huelva and particularly in the village of Bella Vista.

(same ticket and hours as the mining museum) it uses period furnishings, clothing, domestic appliances, and fascinating photos of the village and its social life to recreate a bygone age.

The Museo Minero

Plaza del Museo s/n • Daily 10.30am–3pm & 4–7pm • €4

At the village's western edge on a hill above the Río Tinto company's former offices lies the Río Tinto Foundation's remarkable **Museo Minero**. Housed in the company's former hospital, the museum presents an interesting panorama of mining in the area from prehistoric to modern times. The Roman period is the best represented, with exhibits illustrating their mining methods, daily life and burial practices in addition to a variety of coins and statuary. A recently opened section here has a walk-through reconstruction of a Roman mineworking gallery discovered in the nearby mining area. The actual site cannot be visited as it lies within the zone of the modern mineworkings and is thus dangerous, but the museum has done an excellent job in recreating it. The section includes a functioning reconstruction of a *noria*, or water-wheel, which were worked by slaves and used to drain the mines of flood water. Modern mining is also covered, as well as the geology, flora and fauna of the area. Don't miss the luxurious **wagon of the maharaja**, built in 1892 by the Birmingham Railway Carriage and Wagon Company to be used by Queen Victoria on her proposed visit to India. When this didn't happen it was sold to the Río Tinto company and used for the visit of King Alfonso XIII to the mines.

THE MINES OF RÍO TINTO

The **Río Tinto** (Red River) takes its name from the oxidized iron minerals that flow down from the fissured crags of this strange, forbidding landscape, turning the river blood-red. Evidence of mineral exploitation here goes back at least five millennia – popular tradition asserts that these were the legendary mines of King Solomon, as seen in place names such as Cerro (or hill) de Saloman and Zalamea La Real. More secure historical evidence shows it was the **Phoenicians** (giving the name Ur-yero – "river of fire" – to the Río Tinto) who encouraged exploitation here early in the first millennium BC, during the age of the fabled kingdom of Tartessus from where they acquired the copper to smelt with the tin of Cornwall to make bronze. It was not copper but silver, however, which attracted the **Romans** in the second century BC. Production was dramatically stepped up during the late republic and early empire using remarkable – if brutal – systems to combat flooding, the perennial hazard in deep mining. This they overcame by means of slave-operated *norias*, or water-wheels; in some workings as many as eight pairs of these wheels were used in relays to raise water from depths of 100m and more. For the shackled slave miners working with primitive tools by the light of small clay lamps in warrens of cramped, dark galleries (now vividly reconstructed in the Río Tinto mining museum), life must have been wretched. The scale of the Roman operations can be judged from the fifty million tons of visible slag left behind.

After the Romans had gone, the **Visigoths** worked out the Roman shafts but the mines were then run down during the **Moorish** period – although Niebla built part of its prosperity on its rights of ownership by granting permits. The **Reconquista** brought further decline in its wake as cheap mineral wealth flooded into Spain from the New World. Loss of empire and hard times induced efforts to restart the industry which, in 1873, resulted in the Spanish government selling the mines to a consortium of British and German bankers. Out of this the **Río Tinto Mining Company** was born, bringing numerous northern Europeans to work here. In 1954 control of the company returned into Spanish hands but falling world mineral prices led to it being sold on to a succession of multinational companies before, in 1995, it was purchased by its 523 employees for the symbolic price of one peseta. The worker-owned company also ran into difficulties and went bankrupt. After lying dormant for over a decade, the soaring price of copper on world markets led to another multinational, Emed Mining, purchasing the mines in 2010 with a view to returning them to full production in 2012.

> **THE RÍO TINTO AND OUTER SPACE**
>
> The almost Martian landscape of much of the Río Tinto area has attracted scientists from Madrid University's Centro de Astrobiologia and the Astrobiological Institute of NASA, who have begun joint research into the remarkable **microbial life** that has developed here in some of the most inhospitable conditions on the planet. The enormous diversity of eukaryotic life forms (organisms with genetic cells) able to prosper in the poisonous and highly acidic waters of the Río Tinto mining zone initially astonished experts, who went on to discover a variety of previously unknown life forms here. Now formally known as the **MARTE Project** (Mars Astrobiology Research and Technology Experiment; ⓦ marte.arc.nasa.gov) it comprises of researchers who hope that the thousands of species of micro-organisms that have evolved here over millennia in the toxic depths of the Red River will provide clues as to how life may have developed and evolved in other parts of the universe, including Mars.

The museum can also provide information on visits to old underground mine workings at **Peña de Hierro**, the source of the Río Tinto river and the site where NASA and Spanish academics are carrying out their research for the Mars project (see box above). A *cafetería* serves snacks and drinks and its adjoining shop sells a wide variety of souvenirs.

The Río Tinto Foundation also runs **train trips** through the mining area (daily: March–May Mon–Fri 1pm, Sat & Sun 4.30pm; June to mid-July 1.30pm; mid-July to Sept 1.30pm & 5.30pm; 2hr; call ☎959 590 025 or consult ⓦparqueminerode riotinto.com for winter timetable; €10), aboard century-old restored rolling stock – on the first Sunday of each month they use a 120-year-old steam locomotive. Buy tickets from the museum.

ARRIVAL AND DEPARTURE   **MINAS DE RÍOTINTO**

By bus Minas de Ríotinto is connected by bus with Aracena and Seville (Mon–Fri) and Huelva (at least 3 daily).

By car To reach the village proper from Barrio de Bella Vista head east along the A461 and turn right following the "*centro urbano*" signs. The road leads to a roundabout with palms on its central island, with the former Río Tinto Mining Company's offices (now the Ayuntamiento) to the left. The village's centre lies to the left (east) from here while the mining museum is reached by taking a right uphill from the roundabout. On foot, from the west side of the same roundabout you can follow a path which ascends through the pine and eucalyptus woods to emerge at the museum.

ACCOMMODATION

★ **Cortijo Zalamea** 8km west of Minas de Ríotinto, off the main N435 close to the village of Zalamea La Real ☎959 561 027, ⓦcortijozalamea.es. With your own transport the *Cortijo Zalamea* provides a delightful oasis in leafy surroundings with accommodation in self-contained, fully equipped cottages; there's also a pool, plus horseriding, mountain-biking and walking. **€80**

Hostal-Restaurante Atalaya Avda. de Esquila 13 ☎959 592 854, ⓦhostalrestauranteatalaya.com. At the top of the hill near the mining museum, this inviting, recently opened *hostal* offers comfortable en-suite rooms with TV and also has a decent restaurant (*menú* €9). **€40**

EATING AND DRINKING

Minas de Ríotinto has plentiful bars and a number of eating options in addition to the restaurant of the *Hostal Atalaya* (see above).

Bar La Esquila Avda. Esquila 3. Slightly down the hill on far side of the museum to one side of the entrance to the hospital, this bar serves up a variety of tapas and *platos combinados* as well as a *menú* for €8.50. Daily 9am–11pm.

Restaurante Epoca Paseo de los Caracoles 6. Heading 150m west downhill from the *Galán* and *Esquila* restaurants, this is another very good place offering sierra cuisine such as *churrasco minero* (grilled pork) and *pollo a* *la Inglesa* (roast chicken "English style"); also does a range of salads and has a daily *menú* for €9. Daily except Fri 1–4pm & 8.30pm–midnight.

Restaurante Galán Avda. de la Esquila 10. Just around the corner from the museum this reliable bar-restaurant specializes in *carnes de la sierra* (black pig pork), with an inviting terrace and a lunchtime *menú* for €12. Daily 9am–11pm.

Northeast to La Dehesa

Two kilometres northeast of Minas de Ríotinto, along the A461 as it heads north towards Aracena, you pass two spectacular open-cast mines: the **Corta Atalaya**; and, with 5000 years of exploitation, the **Cerro Colorado**, set in an awesome landscape of rock cliffs glittering with iron pyrites, copper, silver and gold. From a viewing platform by the roadside you can see into the giant elliptical basin of the Corta Atalaya, which at 1200m long and 330m deep is one of the biggest open-cast mines in the world – far below, enormous trucks are dwarfed by the immense walls of rock.

Another 2km further on, at **LA DEHESA**, the Río Tinto Company headquarters are backed by a **Roman graveyard** discovered in the 1990s featuring a number of interesting tombstones. Alarmingly close to the present mining operations which rumble on in the background, the graveyard (signed "Necropolis Romana") can currently only be viewed behind a fence, set slightly back from the road.

Nerva

NERVA, 4km east of Minas de Ríotinto, is a pleasant little place, its pedestrianized main street fringed with orange trees and overlooked by a splendid redbrick Ayuntamiento with a wonderful minaret-inspired octagonal tower. Leaving the mining area by the A461, beyond **Campofrío** the landscape softens as the road progresses through verdant forests of cork and holm oaks, chestnut and walnut trees towards Aracena.

Centro de Arte Contemporáneo

Opposite the Ayuntamiento • May–Sept Tues–Sun 11am–2pm & 6–9pm; Oct–April Tues–Sat 11am–2pm & 5–8pm, Sun–Mon 10am–2.30pm • Free

The extravagant **Centro de Arte Contemporáneo** honours Daniel Vázquez Díaz (a Paris contemporary and friend of Picasso), who was born in Nerva. In addition to a handful of canvases by Díaz, the museum also displays an indifferent collection of works by other *nerveuses*, plus temporary exhibitions to fill the rather cavernous interior.

ARRIVAL AND DEPARTURE   NERVA

Two **buses** currently run from Nerva to Aracena (Mon–Sat noon & 3.45pm).

ACCOMMODATION AND EATING

Cervecería Robles Avda. de Andalucía 9. On the main street almost opposite the Ayuntamiento, this is a popular bar for *copas* and tapas – try their locally cured chorizo or *jamón*. Daily 10am–midnight.

El Círculo Comercial (aka Círculo Mercantil) Avda. de Andalucía s/n. Facing the fountain on the main street in the elegant town casino, with a grand and spacious interior with plenty of comfortable chairs to sit and eat tapas and *raciones*. Everything is good and any of the fried fish or grilled pork dishes is worth a try. Daily 9am–11pm.

Hostal El Goro C/Reina Victoria s/n ☎ & ☎ 959 580 437. Pleasant and friendly family-run *hostal*, close to the centre, with clean and well-equipped en-suite rooms with TV. **€30**

Hotel Vázquez Díaz C/Cañadilla 51 ☎ 959 58 09 27, ⓦ hotelvazquezdiaz.es. Reached by turning first left into the town coming from Minas de Ríotinto, this is a welcoming rural hotel with tidy rooms above a bar-restaurant serving a *menú* for €14. **€48**

The Sierra Morena

The longest of Spain's mountain ranges, the **Sierra Morena** extends almost the whole way across Andalucía from Rosal on the Portuguese frontier to the dramatic pass of Despeñaperros, north of Linares. Its hill towns once marked the northern boundary of the old Moorish caliphate of Córdoba and in many ways the region still signals a break today, with a shift from the climate and mentality of the south to the bleak plains and villages of Extremadura and New Castile. The range is not widely known – with its highest point a mere 1110m, it is not a dramatic sierra – and even Andalucians can have trouble placing it. All of which, of course, is to your advantage if you like to be alone. Tracks are still more common in these hills than roads, and rural tourism, which the government of Andalucía is keen to encourage, has so far led to little more than a handful of signs pointing out areas of special interest. The wealth of good walking country invites organizing your routes around **hikes** if you want to spend any amount of time here. **Cycling**, too, is an option, though you'll need a sturdy bike with plenty of gears, especially on the winding and muscle-taxing hill roads.

This is also an area rich in **wildlife** – including frogs, turtles, lizards, dragonflies, bees, hares and foxes – while bird fanciers should keep an eye out for imperial and booted eagles, as well as goshawks, peregrine falcons and the rare black vulture. In villages such as Cortegana, Zufre and Santa Olalla del Cala the black stork nests on the church towers. The Sierra de Aracena sector of the sierra has been designated as a ZEPA (Zona de Especial Protección a las Aves) in recognition of its importance as a bird sanctuary. The sierra is also home to one of two surviving populations of Spanish lynx on the peninsula, although, with only thirty or so pairs eking out an existence as their forest habitat is gnawed away, you're unlikely to spot one. Locals maintain that while the last bears disappeared only a short time ago, there are still a few wolves in remoter parts.

The **climate** is mild – sunny in spring, hot but fresh in summer – but it can get very cold in the evenings and mornings. A good time to visit is between March and June, when the flowers, perhaps the most varied in the country, are at their best. You may get caught in the odd thunderstorm but it's usually bright and hot enough to swim in the reservoirs or splash in the springs and streams, most of which are good to drink from.

GETTING AROUND   THE SIERRA MORENA

By bus East–west transport in the Sierra is limited, but with a little planning most places mentioned in our account can be reached on public transport. For the area east of Aracena, specifically the terrain beyond the main N630-E803 in Seville Province, bus services are radial and north–south, with Seville as the hub.

ACCOMMODATION

RAAR Rural tourism accommodation has really taken off in recent years and there are also a great number of villas and farmhouses to rent in lovely settings. Try RAAR (Red Andaluza de Alojamientos Rurales; ☎ 902 442 233, English spoken, ⊛ raar.es).

Aracena

Clustered beneath its hilltop medieval castle, the attractive town of **ARACENA** is the highest conurbation in the Sierra Morena as well as the gateway to its own **Sierra de Aracena** to the south and west. Sheltered by this offshoot of the larger Morena range, Aracena is blessed by remarkably sharp, clear air – all the more noticeable, and gratifying, if you've arrived from the heat of Seville.

Although traces of Paleolithic occupation of this area have been found, it was only in the Middle Ages that more concrete historical events happened here, namely the passing of this territory into the kingdom of Castile by a treaty of 1267 following a long struggle with Portugal. Once inside the domains of Castile, Alfonso X ceded the zone around Aracena to the **Knights Templars** to maintain and protect the Sierra. They constructed the castle, one of many erected in this frontier zone, and ruled the roost here until 1312. Today, the town's main role is as a centre of agriculture and cattle breeding, assisted by the tourist magnet of the **Gruta de las Maravillas** (Cave of Wonders).

Iglesia del Castillo

Plaza del Castillo • Daily 10.30am–5pm, April–Sept until 7pm • Free

The town's southern flank rambles up the side of a hill topped by the **Iglesia del Castillo** – or, more correctly, Nuestra Señora de los Dolores – an impressive thirteenth-century Gothic-Mudéjar church built by the Knights Templar around the remains of a Moorish castle. Its tower was formerly the *alminar* (minaret) of the castle's twelfth-century

RESTAURANTS & TAPAS BARS

Café-Bar Manzano	1
Casas	3
La Serrana	4
Restaurante José Vicente	2

ACCOMMODATION

Camping Aracena Sierra	8
Casa Manolo	6
Finca Valbono	3
Hospedería Reina de Los Angeles	9
Hostal Molino del Bombo	2
Hotel Aracena Park	1
Hotel de los Castaños	7
Hotel Sierra de Aracena	5
La Casa Noble	4

Almohad mosque, destroyed by the Templars. Decorated with some exquisite *sebka* brickwork above two polylobed arches, it is reminiscent of Seville's Giralda. Inside the church there's an unusual and finely made glazed clay tomb of the sixteenth-century prior, Pedro Vásquez de Miguel.

The climb to the **castle** offers good views over the town from the imposing sixteenth-century brick gate, complete with belfry, which gives access to the castle.

Plaza Alta

The track up to the Iglesia del Castillo begins from the Plaza Alta, where there's the unfinished church of **Nuestra Señora de la Asunción** (open service times; Mon–Sat 7.30–9pm, Sun noon–1pm; free) with remnants of Renaissance craftsmanship, flanked by a sixteenth-century *cabildo viejo* or old **Ayuntamiento**, the oldest in the province, which now houses the Natural Park information centre. The building's imposing main portal is by Hernán Ruíz II and dates to 1563.

Gruta de las Maravillas

C/Manuel Suirot • Daily 10am–1.30pm & 3–6.30pm (tours every hour, or every 30min at weekends; 50min) • €8.50 • ☎ 663 937 876

Aracena's principal attraction is the **Gruta de las Maravillas**, the largest and arguably the most impressive cave in Spain, discovered, so they say, by a local boy in search of a lost pig. Due to the cave being damaged by the overwhelming number of visitors, there's now a maximum of 35 visitors per tour. The best time to visit is before noon; if you're planning an afternoon visit (the time favoured by coach tours) call them to see whether you will be able to gain entry. It can be chilly inside, so bring a sweater.

A guide takes you round the cave and the "marvels" are explained in Spanish only (leaflet in English). Although the garish coloured lighting is more Santa's Grotto than geological wonder, the cave is still astonishingly beautiful, and entertaining too – the last chamber of the tour is known simply as the **Sala de los Culos** (Room of the Buttocks), its walls and ceiling an outrageous, naturally sculpted exhibition, tinged in a pinkish orange light. You might care to ponder why this section of the caves did not appear in the film *Journey to the Centre of the Earth*, much of which was shot here.

In the Plaza de San Pedro outside the Gruta there's a **contemporary sculpture garden** featuring 34 donated works by many noted artists including *Reconocimiento del Vacío* by the famous Basque sculptor Eduardo Chillida, a graceful cube-like structure, and Carmen Perujo's *Paloma*, near the cave entrance.

Museo del Jamón

Gran Via s/n • Tours (some in English) every 40min daily 11am–2pm & 3.30–6.30pm • €3

A recent new attraction in the town is the **Museo del Jamón**, dedicated to explaining the story of the Sierra de Aracena's celebrated *jamón ibérico* hams: how they're produced and the importance of the *dehesa* (evergreen parklands with sparse plantations of holm and cork oaks), where the pigs are pastured. The traditional and modern methods of slaughter and subsequent curing of the *jamones* is informatively explained.

A separate (free) section of the museum deals with the sierra's **setas** (wild mushrooms) – almost seven hundred species have been identified in the sierra. It's possible to go on *setas* field trips run by Doñana Aracena Aventura (Sept–Dec; ☎959 127 045, ⦿donana -aracena-aventura.com; $10); their pick-up point is the Gruta de las Maravillas.

ARRIVAL AND INFORMATION   ARACENA

By bus Aracena's bus station, Avda. de Sevilla s/n (☎959 127 003), lies on the southeast side of town close to the Parque Municipal and operates services to and from Seville as well as throughout the Sierra de Aracena.

Turismo Beneath the Gruta de las Maravillas ticket office (daily 10am–2pm & 4–6pm; ☎959 127 953, ⦿sierrade aracena.net); staff can provide information and a town map. Information on the surrounding Parque Natural Sierra de Aracena y Picos de Aroche is obtainable from the

information centre in the old Ayuntamiento, Plaza Alta 5 (Tues–Sun: July–Aug 10am–2pm & 6–8pm; Sept–June 10am–2pm & 4–6pm). They can also supply information on the town, including a useful town map.

Internet Servicio Informática, C/Constitución s/n near Plaza del Marqués de Aracena (Mon–Fri 10.30am–2pm & 5.30–8.30pm, Sat 10.30am–2pm) and the publicly funded Centro Guadalinfo, Plaza de Doña Elvira (Mon–Fri 5–7pm; free).

ACCOMMODATION

Camping Aracena Sierra Ctra. Sevilla-Lisboa km 83 ☎959 501 004. Excellent site, with plenty of shade and good facilities. To reach it, head 3km along the Seville road, then turn left for 500m towards Corteconcepción. **€3.50** per person, **€3.50** per tent, **€3.50** per vehicle

Casa Manolo C/Barberos 6 ☎959 128 014. Simple, clean and friendly budget place with rooms sharing bath. Outside summer make sure to get an exterior room as the inside ones (which get no sun) can be freezing. **€22**

Finca Valbono Ctra Carboneras, km 1 ☎959 127 711, ⦿fincavalbono.com. Rural hotel set in thirty acres of scenic woodland, 1km north of town on the road to Carboneras. The rustic-style self-contained *casas rurales* come equipped with *chimeneas* (wood-burning stoves) or

there are conventional rooms with mini bar, satellite TV, heating and a/c. Facilities include a bar, restaurant and pool, while hiking and horseriding excursions are on offer. Rooms **€97**, *casas rurales* **€108**

Hospedería Reina de los Angeles Avda. Reina de los Angeles s/n ☎959 128 367, ⦿hospederia reinadelosangeles.com. Located close to the Gruta de las Maravillas, this rather institutional hotel betrays its origins as a former student hostel. Redecorated and refitted, its ninety en-suite and rather spartan rooms (some single) are nevertheless clean, bright and good value. **€50**

Hostal Molino del Bombo C/Ancha 4, close to the bullring in the upper town ☎959 128 478, ⦿molino delbombo.com. Charming newish *hostal rural* in a refurbished town house offering bright, comfortable en-suite rooms with optional breakfast. **€47**

Hotel Aracena Park Ctra Sevilla–Lisboa km 88 ☎959 127 959, ⓦaracenapark.es. Luxury four-star option at the north end of the town on the main N-433 road coming from Seville. The spacious rooms (many with views) are well-equipped with minibar and satellite TV, while public areas include three bars, two restaurants, pool and spa. Free wi-fi. Ring or check website for frequent special offers. **€120**

Hotel de los Castaños Avda. de Huelva 5 ☎959 126 300, ⓦloscastanoshotel.com. Decent, if rather formally furnished, rooms (aimed at business travellers) with

heating, a/c and TV. Facilities include a restaurant and garage. Free wi-fi. **€60**

Hotel Sierra de Aracena Gran Via 21 ☎959 126 175, ⓦsierradearacena.es. Refurbished traditional hotel with pleasant, decent-sized rooms (including ten singles), all with heating and a/c, some with views. Public areas include a bar-cafetería. **€60**

La Casa Noble C/Campito 35 ☎959 127 778, ⓦlacasanoble.net. The "pamper yourself" option: six sumptuously furnished luxury suites in an elegant early twentieth-century mansion with many original features including a fine patio plus roof terrace with outdoor hot tub. The spacious rooms come with sofas, and the tiled bathrooms are palatial. B&B **€105**

EATING

Aracena has plenty of places to eat, some of which are excellent – and many hotels also have their own restaurants. As Aracena is at the heart of a prestigious *jamón*-producing area, anything with *cerdo ibérico* (black-pig pork) is highly recommended, as are the delicious wild asparagus (spring to autumn), mushrooms (Sept onwards) and local snails (June–Aug).

Café-Bar Manzano Plaza del Marqués de Aracena. One of the town's most popular bars, serving a range of well-prepared tapas and *raciones* and with a terrace on the square. Their new restaurant (just around the corner) serves up economical sierra cuisine and has a *menú* for €15. Daily except Tues 8am–midnight.

Casas Pozo La Nieve 39. One of the town's three top restaurants, this is sited near the Gruta de las Maravillas and only open lunchtimes. All the pork-based dishes are excellent, as is the *jamón* and *salchichón* (salami), plus there's a *menú* for around €20. Main dishes €8–16. Daily 12.30–4.30pm.

La Serrana Pozo de la Nieve s/n ☎959 127 613. The third of Aracena's best restaurants, located opposite *Casas*, and showcasing sierra cooking is at its best. All the pork dishes are recommended, and there's a *menú* for around €20. Main dishes €8–20. Daily 1–5pm.

★ **Restaurante José Vicente** Avda. Andalucía 51 ☎959 128 455. For a memorable splurge this is the place to come. Arguably the town's best restaurant, patrons gather to savour the five grades of Jabugo *jamón ibérico* (black-pig ham) under the approving gaze of owner/chef

Vicente Sousa, who is an expert on the sierra's mushrooms. The €20 *menú*, which often includes a mouthwatering *solomillo ibérico* (black-pig loin), is recommended. His shop next door sells natural products from the sierra. Daily except Tues 1.30–5pm & 8.30pm–12.30am.

CAFÉS AND TAKE-OUT FOOD

Casino C/Mesones 2. For breakfast or evening drinks, sit with the locals at the outdoor tables of the casino (the town's men's club) above the main square, from where you get a wonderful view towards the castle. The elegant early twentieth-century building is the work of noted architect Aníbal González (who also designed the Plaza de España in Seville). Tues–Sun 8.30am–10pm.

Confitería Casa Rufino C/Constitución 3. For superb *dulces*, this 125- year-old *confitería* and *pastelería*, just off the main square, is a must; their *tocino de cielo*, *vitorías* (liqueur-soaked, iced cakes) and *sultanas* (filled coconut cakes) are truly memorable. In the afternoon do what everyone else does, and take your cakes to *Café-Bar Manzano*'s terrace for an afternoon tea or coffee. Daily 9am–2pm & 5.30–9pm, Sun 9am–2pm.

The Sierra de Aracena

With a few days to spare, the rugged villages perched on the **Sierra de Aracena** to the west of Aracena make a fine walking tour. Along the route you'll find a number of good places to stay and plenty of tracks to follow through a rich landscape of orange and lemon orchards and forests of cork oaks, chestnut and gum trees. In spring the profusion of flowers is extraordinary: rosemary, French lavender, peonies and Spanish irises are most common, and you may also be lucky enough to see the rare brown bluebell and members of the orchid family. The hills are one of the last native habitats (outside the Coto de Doñana) of the rarely sighted Spanish lynx, while the skies are home to black vultures and peregrine falcons on patrol and even the occasional

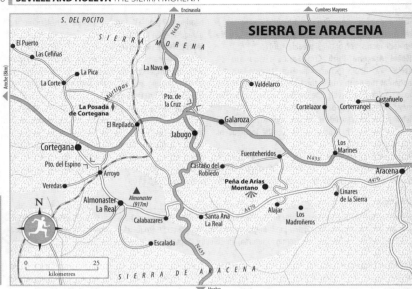

imperial eagle, a stirring image as they glide regally above their domain. You might also be lucky enough to see one of the rare black storks that are known to nest in the church towers of Cortegana and Zufre.

ARRIVAL AND INFORMATION

SIERRA DE ARACENA

By bus Buses run between Aracena and the villages of Alájar, Almonaster, Cortegana and Aroche (2 daily Mon–Sat 1pm & 5.30pm, the latter terminating at Cortegana) and between Aracena and Galaroza, Jabugo, Cortegana and Aroche (5 daily Mon–Sat 7.10am, 10.30am, 1.15pm terminating at Cortegana, and two at 5.30pm – one via Linares, Alájar and Cortegana; the other travelling via the main N432; also Sun at 10.30am). Similar services return in the reverse direction. All leave from Aracena's bus station on Avda. de Sevilla s/n near the Parque Municipal.

Walking guides The useful *Sierra de Aracena* by David & Ros Brawn (see p.592) has clear descriptions of 27 walks in the sierra ranging from 4 to 14km. An accompanying map for the book is sold separately and all walks also have GPS waypoints identifying key locations en route. *Walking in Andalucía* by Guy Hunter-Watts (see p.593) also covers half a dozen walks in the Sierra de Aracena. Alternatively, the Aracena and Huelva Turismos give out the free *Senderos de la Sierra de Aracena y Picos de Aroche* map listing 23 waymarked routes, and there's the more detailed *Mapa Guía de la Sierra de Aracena y Picos de Aroche* on sale at the Aracena Turismo. It's also worth enquiring at all the Ayuntamientos along your route, as many of them are now producing their own walking guides, literature and lots of useful local information.

Linares de la Sierra

Leaving Aracena by the minor A470, after about 7km a turn-off left leads to the tiny village of **LINARES DE LA SIERRA**, a fairly simple and impoverished place huddled around its eighteenth-century Baroque church, a typical example of the sierra style, and curious bullring plaza. The latter's sandy surface has recently been paved over but the *barreras*, behind which the *toreros* dodge the fearsome fighting bulls, survive and seem a somewhat eccentric aberration considering that the ring is put to use only a couple of times a year in the village's fiestas. There's no accommodation, but *Bar Riandero* in the bullring/plaza serves tapas and sometimes meals when they're in the mood.

EATING

LINARES DE LA SIERRA

⭐ **Mesón Arrieros** C/Arrieros 2, below the church and off a street to the right ☎ 959 463 717. This outstanding mid-priced restaurant has arguably the sierra's most creative chef, Luis Miguel López. Its main room has a homely, rustic whitewalled interior and any of the *cerdo ibérico* dishes are highly recommended – the house *solomillo ibérico* is a classic; *setas* (wild mushrooms) also feature in season. Make sure to leave some room for the delicious desserts. Also offers a *menú de degustación* for around €35. Main dishes €12–20. Tues–Sun 1–5pm.

Alájar

Some 4km beyond Linares de la Sierra, along the A470, lined with chestnut orchards and great clumps of oregano, a turning on the left descends to **ALÁJAR**, a delightful, cobble-streeted hamlet at the foot of the Peña de Arias Montano. There's another eighteenth-century Baroque church here – dedicated to San Marcos – with the typical spire, besides plenty of places to eat or have a beer, all clustered around the main square. Each September 7 and 8, the village holds a pilgrimage to the hermitage of the Virgen de los Ángeles on the Peña de Arias Montano hill, 1km above the village. This involves the young men of the village in the *polleo*, a rite of passage in which they race horses along the narrow streets and then up the steep slope to the shrine. The horses are spurred mercilessly and arrive foaming and bleeding at the top of the climb.

ACCOMMODATION

ALÁJAR

Hotel La Posada C/Emilio González 2, off the west side of Plaza Constitución ☎ 959 125 712, ⊛ laposada dealajar.com. In the heart of the village this is a pleasant small hotel with comfortable rooms with bath and heating (but no TV), with an ample breakfast included in the price. The proprietors can provide information and maps for walking and mountain-biking, and horse-trekking is also on offer. B&B **€60**

Molino Río Alájar 1km from the village in the direction of Santa Ana La Real ☎ 959 501 282, ⊛ molinorioalajar.com. Attractive *cortijo* hotel comprising six superbly equipped cottages sleeping between two and six persons. There's also a pool and donkey-riding, and the Dutch proprietor has produced a pamphlet of half-a-dozen walks all starting and ending here. Minimum stay two nights. **€112**

A WALK FROM ALÁJAR TO LINARES DE LA SIERRA

A fine walk (6km) from Alájar to Linares de la Sierra takes in the delightful isolated hamlet of Los Madroñeros, whose grassy streets can only otherwise be reached by tractors and off-road vehicles. To find the **start of the walk** take the street left along the north side of Alájar's church to a plazuela (small square) and follow the street downhill to an open area. The path follows the old road, climbing beyond a board (detailing the walk) on the far side. Should you lose the way, ask for the *camino antiguo a Los Madroñeros*.

Once on the track it soon leads away from the village running between drystone walls behind which are cork oaks sheltering *pata negra* black pigs, soon to be turned into the region's prized *jamón*. The settlement of **Los Madroñeros** is a tranquil haven: a huddle of traditional white-walled dwellings topped by distinctive chimney-pots with green grass all around. You'll be lucky to see any inhabitants as they seem to keep a low profile, unlike their numerous cats who will eye you curiously as they sun themselves on rooftops or any convenient flat stone.

The *camino* (with frequent yellow and white PR – Pequeño Recorrido – waymarks to guide you) leads on eastwards away from the village, gently climbing and falling with only one place which may confuse. Just after crossing a stream, about half way between Los Madroñeros and Linares, you'll come to a deserted **semi-ruined farmhouse**; the path here isn't immediately clear but you need to go through the gateway of the farmhouse to pick up the track on the other side. Soon after this, you reach Linares. To return to Alájar you can retrace your route or follow the road back (the A470). In David and Ros Brawn's book (see p.592) they describe an alternative route back to Alájar with one steep climb. Alternatively you could time your arrival to meet up with Alájar-bound buses (see p.349) passing through about 1.20pm or 5.50pm. Going in the other direction the Aracena bus currently passes through at 4.10pm.

3

EATING AND DRINKING

Bar-Restaurante El Corcho Plaza España 3. Atmospheric place serving up hearty sierra dishes at reasonable prices – all the fittings in the dining rooms (even the "glasses" and menu) are made from cork. Daily except Thurs 10am–11pm.

Casa El Padrino C/Miguel Moya 2. Sited to the rear of the church this is another very good restaurant with a rustic dining room and pleasant patio terrace. Specials include *presa el padrino* (pork steak) and *lomo con castañas* (pork with chestnut sauce). Main dishes €8–15. Daily 1–4pm & 9–11pm.

La Peña Peña de Arias Montano ☎959 501 340.

Opposite the *ermita* (see below) at the top of the cliff above the village this first-rate place serves tapas in its bar and a variety of dishes made with sierra products in its restaurant – *cochinillo ibérico al horno* (oven-baked suckling pig) is a signature dish. There's a *menú de degustación* for around €20. Main dishes €10–22. Tues–Sun noon–8pm.

Mesón El Molino C/Alta 9. Quality restaurant housed in a converted old mill and specialising in *carnes a la brasa* (charcoal-grilled meats). To get there follow the street uphill from the main square for 50m, turning left into a narrow alley; the restaurant lies at the end of here. Main dishes €8–18. Daily noon–4pm & 8–11pm.

Peña de Arias Montano

On quieter days the **Peña de Arias Montano**, the rock cliff that towers above the village, is a beautiful leafy spot set among woods of cork oaks, with cold springs surrounding the sixteenth-century **ermita** (hermitage) of the Virgen de los Ángeles. The Sierra Morena is liberally dotted with these buildings, almost always in isolated spots and dedicated to the Virgin. The site here has been hallowed since prehistoric times, and Iberian shamans are reputed to have gained their "second sight" from the hallucinogenic *amanita muscaria* mushroom which grows in the woods here – don't experiment yourself though as some species can kill in thirty minutes. The hermitage itself – filled with ex-votos from pilgrims and distinguished more by the beauty of its setting than for any architectural qualities – was formerly the retreat of humanist Benito Arias Montano, confessor and librarian to Philip II, who was born nearby in 1527 and gave his name to the site. The belfry to the side of the church dates from the same period and offers glorious views over Alájar beneath, and the Sierra beyond. A **cavern** below the car park is said to be where magical and religious ceremonies were carried out in ancient times and where Philip II is supposed to have meditated during a visit here – giving it the name Sillita del Rey (The King's Chair), a reference to the huge boulder at the cave's mouth.

The true peace of the place is best appreciated by leaving the visitors' area – and its stalls selling honey, garish pots and religious tack – and heading along the track into the woods of cork oaks where there are plenty of likely picnic spots, and more fine views over the Sierra. Continuing along the track for a couple of kilometres will bring you to a ferociously steep climb leading to the "true" *peña* (peak) where Arias Montano is said to have done much of his meditating, with a **mirador** at the summit offering fine views.

Santa Ana La Real

Six kilometres west of Alájar the modest but pretty white-walled village of **SANTA ANA LA REAL** – with another crumbling eighteenth-century church at its heart – is worth a detour. Traditionally the village was known for it *arrieros* (mule drivers), who carried the products of the sierra to Seville. In the age of the truck these are long gone together with countless others who emigrated to find work. The village population today consists of four hundred souls, mostly elderly, and is still shrinking.

ACCOMMODATION   SANTA ANA LA REAL

Hostal El Cruce Junction of the A470 and the N435 ☎959 122 333. Convenient and good-value *hostal* a couple of kilometres beyond Santa Ana, set amid fine scenery. The modern, flower-bedecked building has

en-suite rooms (heated in cooler seasons) plus a lively tapas bar and popular restaurant with a pleasant terrace and an economical *menú*. **€33**

Almonaster La Real

Continuing west of Santa Ana La Real for another 6km brings you to the main village in this corner of the Sierra, the picturesque agricultural centre of **ALMONASTER LA REAL**, huddled in a river valley below the peak of the same name, which at 912m is the sierra's highest summit.

La Mezquita

Daily 9am–7pm • Free

Almonaster has an impressive Moorish past, and an important tenth-century **mezquita**, or **mosque**, still stands on a hill south of town. The mosque may have Roman and Visigothic antecedents, and after it became Christianized in the thirteenth century was little altered, thus preserving its square minaret, the *mihrab* (said to be the oldest in Spain) and beautiful interior of five naves with brick horseshoe arches supported by what are probably recycled Roman columns. It should be open, but if not, ask at the Ayuntamiento, Plaza de la Constitución, for the key. Tacked on to the mosque/church is the village bullring where each August a *corrida* is staged during Almonaster's annual fiesta (see box below). The mosque's tower is a favourite with the kids of the village at this time, as it provides a free (if dangerously precarious due to a lack of barriers) view of the ring.

ARRIVAL AND INFORMATION

ALMONASTER LA REAL

By train The station lies 3km north of the village (actually nearer to Cortegana), with infrequent services to Huelva.

By bus For bus services in the Sierra see p.344.

Tourist information The village has no tourist office, but basic information is available from the Ayuntamiento, Plaza de la Constitución s/n (☎ 959 143 003, ⓦ www .almonasterlareal.es).

COUNTRY CORRIDAS

Like many country rings, the bullring at Almonaster does not see much action. In fact, the prohibitive cost of mounting a **corrida** with six bulls, three matadors and their retinues often restricts a small village to one *corrida* each year, usually in the middle of its annual fiesta. To see a bullfight at places like Almonaster, however, is to get a fascinating insight into many of the secrets of the *corrida* as, with the ring barely big enough to contain the crowd, bulls and matadors, many of the preparations have to take place outside.

First of all, while the arena is doused from a water tanker, the *picadores* select their 8ft-long lances from a couple of dozen leaning against the wall of the ring. When they've chosen, a blacksmith attaches one of three lethal-looking steel points, again selected by the *picador*. Meanwhile, below the walls of the mosque, the grooms prepare the horses – whose vocal chords have been severed so as not to alarm the crowd with their terrified shrieks – by fastening on the *peto* (heavy padding) protection against the bull's ferocious horns. Next the horses' ears are stuffed with oil-soaked rags and securely tied to block out the sound of the crowd and the bull. Finally, they are blindfolded over the right eye, the side from which the bull will attack.

Fifteen minutes before the *corrida* is due to start the village band marches up the hill playing a lively tune before disappearing into the arena. Once inside, they strike up a *paso doble* for the pre-fight parade before the grotesque figure of the helmeted and armoured *picador* is pushed through the small doorway into the ring and a great cheer goes up from the crowd inside. They are soon yelling "*fuera!*" (away), however, because they don't want the bull too weakened by the lance to be able to put up a decent fight. A few minutes later the trumpets sound and the door opens to allow the *picador* to exit the arena. With fresh blood dripping from his lance, the image of this warrior is almost medieval. Big-name *toreros* appear in these village *corridas* because the pay is good, but equally the risks are high. The primitive nature of rings such as the one at Almonaster means a long journey to reach a hospital with adequate facilities should the matador be seriously gored, a factor that has, in the past, proved fatal.

WALKS AROUND ALMONASTER

There are some superb **walks** around Almonaster, following the old cobbled mule paths and village tracks (*senderos*). The paths are well preserved, on the whole – though at times you are forced on to the tarmac road – and are waymarked with paint-splashes on trees and rocks. You need sharp eyes to spot the beginning of the paths, below the road – if possible, get hold of the *Senderos de la Sierra de Aracena y Picos de Aroche* walks pamphlet, which the *ayuntamientos* in Almonaster, Cortegana or Jabugo should stock. This is easy to follow with minimal Spanish and has route descriptions and an excellent fold-out survey map. Cortegana also produces its own leaflet, *Senderos de Pequeño Recorrido en el Entorno de Cortegana*, with a good map and covering much of the same ground, which is usually available from the Ayuntamiento (if they haven't run out). You'd be advised also to take a decent 1:100,000 or 1:50,000 map (CNIG sheets 895 & 916 for the latter), just in case you lose the way.

One of the most enjoyable walks, starting from Almonaster, is the **PRA-5** which leads off to the left of the Cortegana road, around 1km out of Almonaster. This takes you through woodland peppered with streams to the hamlets of Arroyo and Veredas (2hr), where there are bars with food, and on to Cortegana (3hr). Alternatively, if it's just a brief country ramble you're after, follow the sign to Acebuches along the **PRA-5-2** path, under an hour from Almonaster, and again endowed with a small bar.

Another fine walk from Almonaster is to head straight up the hillside northeast of the village along the **PRA-5-1**. This is actually a paved Roman track, presumably built for some kind of quarrying. It takes a couple of hours' strenuous walking to get up to the summit, and, if you're making a day of it, you could continue on to Cortegana or Jabugo.

ACCOMMODATION

Hotel Casa García Avda. San Martín 2 ☎ 959 143 109. Comfortable sierra hotel at the entrance to the village. Rooms at the front have great views, and there's a decent bar-restaurant with terrace downstairs. **€53**

Las Palmeras C/Carretera s/n ☎ 959 143 240, ⓦ laspalmerasrural.com. Modern, heated and fully equipped apartments are available at this welcoming establishment located opposite the restaurant of the same name (see below). Apartments come with *chimenea* (wood-burning fireplace), TV and DVD. **€50**

EATING AND DRINKING

El Rincón de Curro C/Carretera s/n, on the Cortegana road a short distance beyond Casa García. Small family restaurant serving up *platos de la sierra – solomillo de cerdo ibérico* (pork loin) is a house special. Main dishes €8–16. Daily 1–5pm & 8–11pm.

★ **Las Palmeras** C/Carretera s/n. Perhaps the most entertaining place for food is the plant-bedecked Las Palmeras on the road into the village before Casa García. Voluble proprietor Alejandro produces everything on the economical (and ecological) menu himself, from the tasty *caña de lomo* (cured ham from his own black pigs) to the salads (which shouldn't be missed) from his *huerta* (vegetable garden). Daily noon–5pm & 8–11pm.

Cortegana

Roughly 2km out of Almonaster the road forks left to **CORTEGANA**, a bustling and populous *pueblo* of almost five thousand people spreading along the valley of the Río Carabaña below a heavily restored castle.

The Castillo

Plaza del Castillo s/n • Officially May–Sept Tues–Sun 11am–2pm & 6–8pm; Oct–April 11am–2pm & 4–6pm; otherwise enquire at the Ayuntamiento, C/Maura 1, just off the Plaza de la Constitución • €1.50

Built in the thirteenth century during the frontier disputes with the Portuguese, the heavily restored **Castillo** provided a necessary observation post and today gives fine views from its battlements. It is flanked by the fourteenth- to fifteenth-century *ermita* of **Santa María del Castillo** whose chapel has been recently refurbished with the addition of some rather tedious modern frescoes. To reach the castle take the Almonaster road – signed from the N433 on the village's eastern edge. After 100m you come to a junction where a driveable road (or a ten-minute walk) on the left climbs to the castle.

Iglesia del Divino Salvador

Plaza de la Iglesia • Open service times only (try 7–9pm) • Free

The town's major church, the **Iglesia del Divino Salvador** was started in the late sixteenth century but has later elements including the bell tower, constructed after the original collapsed in the earthquake of 1755. The interior has a finely worked Baroque pulpit, and the eighteenth-century retablo in the *capilla* (chapel) of Nuestra Señora del Rosario is the only one of the church's original nine to survive the Civil War conflagration when local churches became a part of the ideological battleground.

Cortegana's big annual knees-up is the **Jornadas Medievales** *feria*, held in the first or second week in August with archery contests, falconry, various tournaments and re-enactments of the storming of the castle walls – accompanied by much music, drinking and dancing. Its other main *feria*, **Fiestas Patronales**, occurs in early September with *corridas*, processions and concerts.

ACCOMMODATION
CORTEGANA

Antigua Estación Estación de Tren Almonaster–Cortegana ☎ 650 414 869, ⊛ casasantiguaestacion.com. Although trains still stop here (two daily in both directions) the former station has now been converted into a charming *casa rural* with railway-inspired decor throughout its three fully equipped apartments. **€65**

Hostal Sancho IV Avda. Pedro Maestro 24 ☎ 959 131 880, ⊛ hostalsanchoIV.com. Close to the N433 at the north end of town, this new *hostal* is a hotel in all but name and the only upmarket option in town. Somewhat overpriced, it offers light and functional a/c en-suite rooms with TV. Free wi-fi. B&B **€75**

La Posada de Cortegana Ctra. El Repilado–La Corte s/n ☎ 959 503 301, ⊛ posadadecortegana.es. Charming hotel buried deep in the countryside to the north of Cortegana consisting of log cabins set in woodland with a restaurant and reception housed in the main building nearby. It can be easily reached with transport by following a badly potholed minor road (signed to the hotel) just east of the village of El Repilado for about 4km. **€90**

★ **Los Gallos** ☎ 959 501 167 or ☎ 687 365 754, ⊛ alojamientolosgallos.com. A tempting option for a longer stay, this leafy and tranquil oasis rents out cottages and apartments in and around a restored farmhouse set in spectacular countryside, with gardens and a pool. It lies on the Almonaster road, a couple of kilometres to the southeast of the village, close to the delightfully rustic Almonaster-Cortegana train station. **€50**

Pensión Cervantes C/Cervantes 27 ☎ 959 131 592, ⊛ pensioncervantes2000.com. This welcoming *hostal* lies just off the focal Plaza Constitución, offering small but clean and comfy heated en-suite rooms with a/c and TV; try for a room overlooking a peaceful garden at the rear. B&B **€33**

★ **Villa Cinta** Avda. de las Minas 61 ☎ 959 131 522, ⊛ casaruralvillacinta.com. Friendly and very pleasant guesthouse at the start of the road out towards Almonaster, 200m east of the bullring (with a Casa Rural sign). The attractive rooms (or slightly more expensive suites) come with en suite and stunning views, while more views – towards the castle – are to be had from a roof terrace. B&B **€50**

EATING AND DRINKING

Casino Plaza de la Constitución s/n. The town's elegant casino – a stately turn-of-the-twentieth century building with tiled interior – makes a pleasant breakfast or morning-coffee stop and stocks all the daily newspapers. Daily 8.30am–10pm.

El Aceitón Avda. de Portugal 5. Reasonably priced restaurant close to the Guardia Civil barracks on the main N433, a five-minute walk from the centre along C/Talero.

House specials include *solomillo de cerdo con castañas* (pork loin with chestnut sauce). Daily noon–4pm & 8–11pm.

Los Peroles C/Eritos 32. Atmospheric *venta* housed in an old bodega and offering a good tapas and *raciones* selection plus *platos combinados* and an economical *menú* (under €10). To reach it find your way to *El Aceitón* (see above), then continue up the same street and turn left into C/Eritos. Daily 12.30–4.30pm & 8–11pm.

Aroche and around

Heading west for 14km from Cortegana along the N433 brings you to **AROCHE**, in sight of the border with Portugal. Perched on a hill dominated by its castle with a fertile plain below, it's a neat little place, with white-walled, cobbled streets where – because it gets so few visitors – you can be sure of a hearty reception. Aroche was originally the Roman town of Arruci Vetus, but many more ancient vestiges of habitation have been discovered here, including giant prehistoric single standing stones, or menhirs, erected in the Megalithic period. Arriving with your own transport take the first – and fully asphalted – entry on the left into the town coming from Aracena; using the other entry road to the east leads up into a warren of steep cobbled backstreets which are difficult to negotiate.

A pleasant walk out of the village starts on the opposite (north) side of the main N433 to the twelfth- to fourteenth-century Gothic-Mudéjar **Ermita de San Mamés** and the impressive remains of Roman **Turóbriga**. The (driveable) track leading to both is signed between the two entry roads to the town.

The Castillo
See p.353 for access details

Once you have made it up the hill to the village, the obvious place to aim for is the **Castillo**. Constructed by the Almoravids in the twelfth century, the fort was remodelled after the *Reconquista* – but the most bizarre alteration of all was to make the interior into a full-scale bullring. A curiosity here are the sallyports – narrow openings in the arena's stone wall – used by the *toreros* to dodge the bull, instead of the normal *barrera* (fence).

La Cilla convent and archeological museum
C/Fray J Bross s/n • Fri–Sun: June–Sept 11am–3pm; Oct–April 11am–2pm & 3–5pm; see p.356 for access details • Free

In the same building as the Centro de Visitantes (see p.356), the splendid seventeenth-century former convent of **La Cilla** – incorporating an olive-oil pressing room from the original edifice – also houses the town's **archeological museum**. The interesting collection has numerous finds from the Roman and Moorish periods as well as ceramics and other artefacts from Turóbriga, a first-millenium BC Iberian and later important Roman settlement discovered 3km north of the town (see p.356).

Nuestra Señora de la Asunción
See p.356 for access details

Just below the castle, the parish church of **Nuestra Señora de la Asunción** was started in 1483, with a mixture of Mudéjar, Gothic and Renaissance styles being added by the time it was completed 150 years later. Behind a dour, buttressed exterior, the triple-naved church has a trio of retablos: the image of Christ lowered from the cross at the top of the right hand (or south) nave is by La Roldana; the representation of Christ *nazareno*, bearing his cross, in the retablo at the end of the left aisle is a seventeenth-century work by Alonso Cano. Along the north wall nearby, another retablo has – below and to the left of Nuestra Señora de Los Remedios, the town's patron – a small and sensitively worked image of the Virgin perched on an inverted half-moon and coiled serpent, another seventeenth-century work by La Roldana. The church's other treasures (only viewable when the *cura* or priest is available due to their value) include the fifteenth-century crucifix of Cardenal Mendoza of Seville, the supporter of Isabel, as well as a seventeenth-century Russian icon from St Petersburg.

Museo del Santo Rosario
C/Ordoñez Valdes s/n • Fri–Sun: June–Sept 11am–3pm; Oct–April 11am–2pm & 3–5pm; see p.356 for access details • Free

There are some pretty strange museums in Andalucía, but Aroche's **Museo del Santo Rosario** (Museum of the Holy Rosary) has to be one of the most eccentric. Located a little downhill to the east of the Ayuntamiento and near the *correo* (post office), the exhibits consist of well over a thousand rosaries donated by such leading religious luminaries as Pope John XXIII and Mother Teresa, in addition to others from *toreros* and soccer players and one each from John F. Kennedy and King Juan Carlos. Those sent in by Richard Nixon and General Franco betray suspiciously little sign of wear.

Ermita de San Mamés

Tues–Thurs 8am–3pm, Fri–Sun 10am–5pm (May–Sept closes 3pm) • €1

Following the (driveable) track signed between the two entry roads to the town for 2km leads to the **Ermita de San Mamés**. A triple-naved church built on the site – and using the walls – of an important building, perhaps the basilica or law court, adjoining the Roman forum, the church has some remarkable fourteenth-century fresco fragments including a spectacular painting (recently discovered beneath centuries of whitewash) of the Last Supper.

Turóbriga

Behind the Ermita de San Mamés are the extensive and recently revealed remains of the first-century BC to third-century AD Roman town of **Turóbriga**. Substantial buildings surrounding the forum alongside the *ermita* have been unearthed, including the foundations of temples plus administrative and judicial buildings. The archeological excavations are now uncovering the substantial town that surrounded the forum and various streets with dwellings as well as a bathhouse and exercise gymnasium have come to light. A leaflet (available free from the site guardian) provides more information on the finds.

INFORMATION   AROCHE

Visiting the monuments For access to all the town's sights (except the Ermita de San Mamés and Roman Turóbriga), including the Castillo, you'll need to call at the Centro de Visitantes (Fri–Sun: June–Sept 11am–3pm; Oct–April 11am–2pm & 3–5pm) at C/Fray J Bross s/n, close to the main square, Plaza Juan Carlos 1. When the office is closed the Ayuntamiento (also on the main square) can usually help out with information and provide a map.

ACCOMMODATION

There is currently no hotel or *hostal* accommodation in Aroche, although a new hotel was under construction at the time of writing – the visitor centre should have details of this.

Apartamentos Picos de Aroche Ctra. Las Peñas s/n ☎667 756 445, ⓦpicosdearoche.com/bayon.htm. On the west side of the village this is a possible option for overnighting here. The apartments are well-equipped with two bedrooms and can sleep two or five. The same proprietor also rents out a fully equipped house for up to eight people. €75

A WALK FROM EL REPILADO TO LOS ROMEROS

Returning to Aracena from Aroche by the N433 takes you through the village of **El Repilado** from where a picturesque five-kilometre walk heads south along the Río Caliente to the charming village of **Los Romeros**. Leave Repilado by the N433 road towards Cortegana and after crossing the bridge over the river, turn left along the HV-111 going to Los Romeros. Where the road traverses to the east bank of the river, follow the track along the west bank which leads through woods of chestnut and black poplar, and where in spring you'll see a profusion of wild flowers. When the road recrosses the river, use the bridge to gain access to the tiny and picturesque village of Los Romeros, a place devoted to *jamón* production (it takes its name from a major ham family).

ACCOMMODATION

Finca La Silladilla Just outside Los Romeros ⓦsilladilla.com, ☎959 501 350. *Cortijo* with lodgings in several refurbished farmhouses, with a bar, restaurant and pool. €160 for up to four

Hermanos Marquez supermarket Los Romeros ☎959 124 450. Houses for rent in and around Los Romeros (minimum two nights, sleeping two to four people). €60

EATING AND DRINKING

Bodegón Los Romeros Plaza del Valle Florido (by the church), Los Romeros. Good tapas and *raciones* and has a terrace.

La Albardería 100m up a signed road beyond the church in Los Romeros. A smart but still economical place with a good selection of sierra *platos típicos*.

EATING AND DRINKING

Cafetería Las Peñas Plaza Juan Carlos I s/n. This popular *cafetería* is a good breakfast stop and later serves tapas and *raciones*. House specialities include seafood tapas and cured meats of the region, and there's an inviting terrace on the square. Daily 9am–11pm.

Centro Cultural Las Peñas C/Real 8. Near the church of La Asunción, a wonderfully atmospheric bar and social centre. Tapas and *raciones* are served at lunchtime and early evening and the fried fish – try the *bacalao frito* (cod) or *chocos* (cuttlefish) – is excellent. Daily 9am–midnight.

Mesón Los Arcos C/Bellido 9. Below the church, this is another popular tapas haunt and also serves *platos combinados*. The *ibérico* pork products are favourites here. Daily 11am–11pm.

Mesón San Mamés C/Del Postigo 2, downhill from the main square along C/Dolores Rosada, and left after 50m. Decent restaurant offering a range of seafood and meat dishes including good pork and *embutidos* (cured sausages) from the sierra. Daily noon–4pm & 8–11pm.

Jabugo

The mere mention of the name of **JABUGO** is enough to make any Spaniard's mouth water, and once you've tasted what all the fuss is about it's easy to understand why. As roadside billboards depicting smiling pigs proclaim, *jamón* is king in Jabugo. To get stuck into ham sampling, when you approach the village from the N433, ignore the sign directing you to the *centro urbano* and continue straight on. You'll pass half a dozen bars and restaurants all eager to sell you a *bocadillo* stuffed with *jamón de Jabugo* – or even a whole ham shank should you feel like splashing out. *Bodega Restaurante Jabugo* and *Mesón Cinco Jotas* are probably the best. There are tapas, too, but keep an eye on the prices as the *pata negra* (from acorn-fed black pigs) doesn't come cheap.

Ham apart, the village of Jabugo is a sleepy place gathered around a charming square, the aptly named **Plaza de Jamón**, with a central fountain overlooked by the Casino – a relaxing place for a beer – and the restored, Baroque **Iglesia de San Miguel**. The nearby **Casa Irene**, at the opposite side of the square, is another good source for the pork products of the region.

THE KING OF HAMS

Surrounding Jabugo is a scattering of attractive but economically depressed villages mainly dependent on the *jamón* industry and its curing factory, which is the major local employer. Things were little different when Richard Ford passed through here a century and a half ago, describing these mountain villages as "coalitions of pigsties", adding that it was the duty of every good pig to "get fat as soon as he can and then to die for the good of his country".

Sought out by classical writers such as Strabo for its distinctive flavour, and produced since long before by the peoples of the Iberian peninsula, **jamón serrano** (mountain ham from white pigs) is a *bocadillo* standard throughout Spain – the English words "ham" and "gammon" are both derived from the Spanish. Some of the best ham of all, *jamón ibérico* or *pata negra* (both acorn-fed ham), comes from the Sierra Morena, where herds of sleek black pigs grazing beneath the trees are a constant feature. In October the acorns drop or are beaten down by their keepers and the pigs, waiting patiently below, gorge themselves, become fat and are promptly whisked off to the factory to be slaughtered and then cured in the dry mountain air. The meat of these black pigs is exceptionally fatty when eaten as pork but the same fat that marbles the meat adds to the tenderness during the curing process. This entails first of all covering the hams in coarse rock or sea salt to "sweat", after which they are removed to cool cellars to mature for up to two years. *Jamón serrano* from mass-produced white pigs is matured for only a few weeks, hence the incomparable difference in taste. At Jabugo the best of the best is then further graded from one to five *jotas* (the letter "J" for Jabugo) depending on its quality – a whole leg of *cinco jotas jamón* will set you back anything from €250 to €350.

The king of hams also demands an etiquette all of its own: in bars and restaurants everywhere it has its own apparatus (*la jamonera*) to hold it steady, and carving is performed religiously with a long, thin-bladed knife. The slices must not be wafer-thin nor bacon rashers, and once on the plate *jamón ibérico* becomes the classic partner for a glass of fino.

The **villages around Jabugo** – Aguafría, Castaño del Robledo and Fuenteheridos – all make rewarding destinations for walks amid splendid wooded hills, though all are equally ill-served by public transport and you may well find yourself in for a walk both ways.

There is currently no accommodation in the village itself.

Castaño del Robledo

Four kilometres southeast of Jabugo, but a few kilometres more by road, lies the isolated village of **CASTAÑO DEL ROBLEDO**, which has not one but two outsized **churches** for its meagre population. Both named Santiago, they attest to a time in the seventeenth and eighteenth centuries when the population here was growing so rapidly that the church of Santiago la Mayor, then under construction, had to be enlarged. However, the population declined as quickly as it had grown and the crumbling, cavernous and now little-used church was left unfinished, while the congregation remained in the older and smaller of the two churches built in the sixteenth century. The larger Neoclassical hulk – containing a rare and recently restored eighteenth-century organ – today looks down grimly on the surrounding pantiled roofs. Other remnants from more illustrious days are a number of decaying mansions along the village's narrow, cobbled streets.

ACCOMMODATION   CASTAÑO DEL ROBLEDO

Posada del Castaño C/José Sánchez Calvo 33 ☏ 959 465 502, ⓦ posadadelcastano.com. A very pleasant place to stay just a short walk from the focal Plaza del Álamo. Run by an expat Scottish couple who are enthusiastic hikers and can advise on walking in this zone, the en-suite rooms are comfortable and overlook a garden where you can take breakfast. B&B **€50**

EATING AND DRINKING

Bar La Bodeguita Plaza del Álamo. On the compact main square, this is a pleasant old place with photos on the walls from bygone days serving decent tapas and *raciones*. Daily 9am–11pm.

Bar-Restaurant El Roble C/Arias Montaño 8. Welcoming place close to the main square with a wood fire in winter and an outdoor terrace in summer. The pork dishes – try the *presa ibérica* (pork steak) – are outstanding and the desserts aren't bad either, including a tasty *flan de turrón* (crème caramel with nougat). Also serves tapas and *raciones* in the bar. Main dishes €7–15. Daily 10am–11pm.

Maricastaña Plaza del Álamo ☏ 654 248 583. A surprisingly swish place for a village of this size, this mid-priced restaurant turns out a small number of creative dishes. Recommended are the *entrecot de buey con verduras* (ox steak) and *capricho serrano* (pork loin with goat's cheese sauce). There's also a small patio terrace. Main dishes €12–20. Fri–Sun 1–4.30pm & 8–11pm.

Galaroza and around

The N433 east from Jabugo rolls along through country filled with dense oak woods surrounded by dry stone walls, where you may catch a fleeting glimpse of a herd of *cerdos ibéricos*, the celebrated black pigs of the Sierra. The enlongated village of **GALAROZA**, encircled by chestnut and fruit orchards, seems awash with water which for much of the year splashes and bubbles in its fountains and along the culverts lining the narrow streets. This may explain its annual **Fiesta de los Jarritos** during which everyone – including visitors – gets soaked as the town goes water mad. September 6 is the date to avoid if you want to stay dry – and if you do turn up take note that the crazy crowds are no respectors of visitors or their cameras when the *cubos de agua* (buckets) start flying.

A **water sculpture** in the focal Plaza los Álamos celebrates the Fiesta de los Jarritos, although the fiesta's focal point is the nearby **Fuente del Carmen** – colloquially known as Fuente de los Doce Caños (twelve spouts) – a nineteenth-century fountain with evocative washing stones once used by the village women before the age of washing machines.

At the eastern end of Plaza los Álamos stands the seventeenth-century church of **Nuestro Señora del Carmen** (open service times Mon–Sat 7.30pm, Sun 12.30pm; free) – not especially interesting inside excepting a unique seventeenth-century image of a pregnant Virgin by La Roldana.

ACCOMMODATION GALAROZA

Aparthotel Sierra de Galaroza C/De la Cultura 21, at the eastern end of the village behind the church ☏ 959 123 414, ✆ galaroza.net. New apart-hotel with fully equipped two- and four-person modern apartments consisting of one or two bedrooms plus *salón*. Also has an excellent garden pool plus its own restaurant. Free wi-fi. €80

Hostal Toribio C/Primo de Rivera 2 ☏ 959 123 073, ✆ hostaltoribio.com. At the village's western end, this

comfortable *hostal* has pleasant en-suite a/c rooms with heating and TV and its own restaurant below. Free wi-fi. €57

Hotel Galaroza Sierra Just west of the village on the Jabugo road ☏ 959 123 237, ✆ hotelgalaroza.com. Attractive, upmarket country hotel with pool and restaurant in its own grounds. Rooms are light and well-equipped and come with TV, and the hotel also rents out fully equipped bungalows sleeping up to four. Free wi-fi and parking. Rooms €65, bungalows €85

EATING AND DRINKING

Bar Alonso Avda. Ismael González 8. Earthy bar on the square on the right as you come in from Aracena (eastern entry) serving a variety of tapas and *raciones* including *jamón* and *salchichón* (salami). Daily 9am–11pm.

Bar La Fuente Plaza Alcalde Luis Navarro s/n. Fronting the square at the entry to the village at its western end, this is a humble place with an eccentric proprietor and good economical tapas – try the *jamón con tomate*. Daily 10am–10pm.

Bar-Restaurante La Salina Tío Máximo 3. Near to the

Plaza los Álamos (you may need to ask for directions) this decent bar-restaurant with an attractive courtyard terrace serves up tasty and economical tapas, *raciones* and *platos combinados*. Daily 1–4pm & 8–11pm.

El Encinar Hotel Galaroza Sierra (see above). Perhaps the village's best restaurant, serving up typical dishes of the sierra – any of the game and *cerdo ibérico* dishes are worth trying – which also has a *menú* for €13. Main dishes €8–15. It also does breakfasts. Restaurant daily 1–4pm & 8–11pm.

Fuenteheridos

Some 5km east of Galaroza, a right turn brings you almost immediately to **FUENTEHERIDOS**, one of the most picturesque of the Sierra *pueblos* – a huddle of whitewashed dwellings with contrasting red pantiled roofs. The typical tiled Sierra spire of its fine eighteenth-century Neoclassical **Iglesia del Espíritu Santo** hovers above the rooftops.

The village's interesting **Jardín Botánico** (botanical garden; daily 10am–dusk; free) is planted with specimens from all over the globe. It lies to the west of the village and north of the main road, close to the Molino de Fuenteheridos (see below).

ACCOMMODATION FUENTEHERIDOS

Bar-Restaurante Biarritz C/Virgen de la Fuente s/n ☏ 959 125 088, ✆ biarritzrural.com. This bar-restaurant also lets a number of charming and well-equipped cottages and apartments in and around the village sleeping up to four. €70

Camping El Madroñal 500m out of the village towards Castaño Robledo ☏ 959 501 201, ✆ camping elmadronal.com. Good campsite, with mature trees providing plenty of shade and decent facilities including a large pool. Two people plus car €13

Finca La Media Legua Ctra. N433 km91 (3km towards Aracena near the village of Los Marines) ☏ 669 490 648, ✆ fincalamedialegua.es. Inviting rural retreat in the midst of dense chestnut woods offering stylishly decorated two- to six-person apartments with kitchenette, plus a pool. Mountain bikes can be hired and the complex

has its own bar and restaurant. See website or ring for frequent special offers. €100

Hostal Carballo C/La Fuente 16 ☏ 959 125 108, ✆ hostalcarballo.com. Welcoming *hostal* with a variety of light and spacious en-suite balcony rooms, plus a pleasant roof terrace with views and easy parking nearby. €33

Molino de Fuenteheridos Ctra. N433 km97 (down a side road off the north side of the main road signed "Villa Onuba") ☏ 670 051 519, ✆ molinosde fuenteheridos.es. This luxury option comprises a series of adobe-style chalets in wonderfully verdant woodland surrounding the main building, a former *cortijo* with many original features. Most chalets have terraces and all come with Jacuzzi and are tastefully furnished with pastel-tinted walls, hangings and artworks. The public areas include a lounge with enormous fireplace and a garden pool. €108

3

EATING AND DRINKING

★ **Bar-Restaurante Biarritz** C/Virgen de la Fuente s/n. Very good restaurant, just off the main square, with tasty tapas and a weekday *menú* for €6.50 (which you may need to ask for). Main dishes €7–15. Daily noon–4pm & 8–11pm.

Casa Andrés Plaza Mayor s/n. Perhaps the best of the bars on the main square and a good place for lunchtime tapas or *raciones*, or breakfast on its shady terrace. Daily 10am–11pm.

La Caldera C/Charneca s/n. Pleasant little *asador* (charcoal-grill restaurant) uphill from the main square, with an elegant dining room and patio terrace for warmer days. Food comprises a variety of well-prepared sierra dishes – anything with *cerdo ibérico* is recommended. Main dishes €8–15. Daily Fri–Sun 1–4pm & 8–11pm.

Zufre and east towards Cazalla

East of Aracena there's more good – if slightly less wooded – hiking country along the northern frontier of Seville Province, which traverses the **Parque Natural de Sierra Norte**, a wildlife and nature zone stretching across the north of Seville province to the border with Córdoba. The park's comprehensive website (⑩sierranortedesevilla.es) has information on most of the towns and villages in the sierra, including accommodation and lots of useful links. See p.363 for details of the natural park information centre.

Zufre

ZUFRE, about 25km southeast of Aracena, must be one of the most spectacular villages in Spain, hanging like a miniature Ronda on a high palisade at the edge of a ridge. Below the crumbling Moorish walls, the cliff falls away hundreds of feet, terraced into deep green gardens of orange trees and vegetables.

In town, and sharing a charming and leafy plazuela, the arcaded **Ayuntamiento** and parish church of **Purísima Concepción** – built of brick and pink stone – are both interesting sixteenth-century examples of the Mudéjar style, the latter built on the foundations of a mosque. In the basement of the Ayuntamiento is a gloomy line of stone seats, said to have been used by the Inquisition. For access, enquire at the Ayuntamiento during working hours for the key.

Zufre's real centre, however, is the **Paseo**, a little park with rose gardens, balcony and a bar at one end and a casino at the other, with spectacular views over the sierra from its open southern flank. The villagers gather round here for much of the day – there's little work either in Zufre or the surrounding countryside, and even the local bullring, cleverly squeezed on to a rock ledge above the Paseo, only sees use twice a year: at the beginning of the season in March, and at the town's September *feria*.

ARRIVAL AND INFORMATION   ZUFRE

By bus Buses from Aracena (1 daily; Mon–Sat 5.30pm) connect with the bus from Seville.

By foot You can walk from Aracena to Zufre (a day-long, 25km hike); the free map (available from the Turismo in Aracena), *Senderos de la Sierra de Aracena y Picos de Aroche*, details the route and shorter alternatives. The 1:25000 IGN maps, *hojas* (sheets) 917 and 918, are also useful.

Information Staff at the Ayuntamiento (Mon–Fri 8am–3pm; ☏ 959 198 009), Plaza de la Iglesia, can provide information.

ACCOMMODATION

La Posá C/Cibarranco 5 ☏ 959 198 110 or ☏ 658 972 705 (mobile). Friendly and central *hostal* close to *Bar Los Benitos* (see below) offering tidy en-suite rooms with fine views. As the proprietors don't live on site, you may need to use their mobile number. **€45**

EATING AND DRINKING

Bar Los Benitos Plaza La Quebrada s/n. On the village's main square and good for breakfast, as well as for tapas, *raciones* or *platos combinados* later in the day. Daily 9am–midnight.

Casa Pepa C/Portales 1, just off Plaza La Quebrada. Pleasant little country restaurant (run by the family who own *Bar Los Benitos*) serving up tasty sierra standards such as *solomillo* (pork loin) and *rabo de toro*. Main dishes €7–15. Fri–Sun 1–4pm & 8–11pm.

Cazalla and the Central Sierra

The next place of any size beyond Zufre, **CAZALLA DE LA SIERRA** lies some 50km further east, the latter stages of the journey following a mountainous and lonely route, stunning to drive, but a real test on foot.

When you finally reach it, Cazalla de la Sierra feels like a veritable metropolis: a charming country town with a number of sights and an ideal base for exploring the surrounding Sierra Norte Natural Park. An ancient Iberian settlement, Cazalla became the Roman Callentum and later the Moorish Kazalla ("fortified city") from which the modern name derives. Its importance in post-*Reconquista* days was as a staging post along the route to Extremadura and the north. The place was noted in Roman times for its vines and wines, a tradition which survives today in the production of *aguardiente* and *anis* (aniseed liqueur), sold in bodegas around the town. The Turismo can advise on where to find them if you're interested.

Nuestra Señora de la Consolación

Plaza de la Iglesia • Tues–Sat 11am–1pm (also service times; Mon–Sat 7.30pm, Sun 7pm) • Free

Cazalla's main attraction is the huge, fortress-like church of **Nuestra Señora de la Consolación** at the southern end of town, an outstanding example of *andaluz* mix-and-match architecture begun in the fourteenth century in Gothic-Mudéjar style, with some later Renaissance touches, and finally completed in the eighteenth century. The interior has a fine sixteenth-century retablo and an image of San Bruno by Juan Hernández.

Fronting the church's northern door, Calle Virgen del Monte – lined with some elegant *casas señoriales* – leads to the **market area**, a colourful and bustling place on weekdays.

Cartuja

Daily 9am–2pm & 4–8pm • €5 • W cartujadecazalla.com

A little out of town, Cazalla's fifteenth-century **Cartuja**, or Carthusian monastery, was until recently a near ruin; it's now being gradually and privately restored as an upmarket hotel and arts centre. What remains, particularly a beautiful portal and the cupola of a church with Mudéjar frescoes, is set in picturesque surroundings. The proprietors have now added an art gallery and there are frequent artistic and musical events held here. To reach it, take the A455 for 3km towards Constantina, turning off along a signposted side road.

ARRIVAL AND INFORMATION

By train Cazalla is also served by trains on the Seville–Mérida line, but as the station lies 7km east of town and buses are infrequent, you'll need to take a taxi (☎ 954 884 094) if you don't fancy the walk.

By bus Cazalla is one of the few places in the Sierra with regular buses, which run daily between here and Seville.

Turismo On the Plaza Mayor, next to the church of Nuestra Señora de la Consolación (Tues–Sun 10am–2pm, plus Thurs–Sat 4–6pm; ☎ 954 883 562, W cazalladela sierra.es). Staff can provide a town map and have copious information on the town and Parque Natural de Sierra Norte.

ACCOMMODATION

El Palacio San Benito C/San Benito s/n ☎ 954 883 336, W palaciodesanbenito.com. Housed in a magnificent fifteenth-century former hospice of the knights of the Order of Calatrava, which gave shelter to pilgrims travelling the Via de la Plata to Santiago de Compostela. All rooms are sumptuously decorated with period furniture and artworks, and there's a glittering Mudéjar chapel plus bar, library and pool. B&B €160

★ **Hospedería La Cartuja** ☎ 954 884 516, W cartuja decazalla.com. Out of town and surrounded by rolling hill country, the enchanting La Cartuja monastery (see above) has its own atmospheric inn with pool and eight elegantly styled rooms in what was formerly the monastery's gatehouse; also has its own restaurant and *cafetería*. B&B €80

Hostal Castro Martínez C/Virgen Monte 36 ☎ 954 884 039. Near the main street, this is the best budget choice, offering a/c en-suite rooms, some of which come with terraces and views. €30

La Plazuela C/Caridad 2 ☎ 954 421 496, ⓦ casarural
-laplazuela.es. Charming new *casa rural* in a refurbished
town house in the heart of the town with well-equipped,
individually styled rooms with tiled floors, wooden beams
and elegant bathrooms. **€60**

★ **Las Navezuelas** 3km out of town along the A432
road to El Pedroso (signed on the left) ☎ 954 884 764,
ⓦ lasnavezuelas.com. An inviting option, offering
delightful rooms and studios in a white-walled sixteenth-
century *cortijo* and mill set among woods and olive groves;
it also has a pool and its own reasonably priced restaurant,
and the owners can arrange horseriding excursions and
advise on trekking routes. Rooms **€63**, studios **€93**

Posada del Moro C/Paseo del Moro s/n ☎ 954 884 858,
ⓦ laposadadelmoro.com. A five-minute walk southeast
from the Turismo, this attractive hotel offers comfortable
tile-floored rooms – as well as superior rooms and suites
– overlooking a patio garden and pool. **€65**

EATING AND DRINKING

Bar Gonzalo C/Caridad 3. Friendly, popular and central
bar serving various tapas, *raciones* and *platos combinados*,
plus a daily *menú* for around €7. Daily 9am–11pm.

Bar Torero C/Virgen del Monte 56. This central bar, near
the former Convento de San Francisco (now a bodega),
serves good breakfast standards as well as tapas and
raciones later in the day. Daily 9am–midnight.

Cafetería-Restaurante Manolo Paseo del Moro s/n.
Close to the *Posada del Moro* (above) this is a decent
restaurant specializing in sierra cuisine, particularly
carnes a la brasa (charcoal-grilled meat), and also does
barbecues on its terrace in summer. Main dishes €7–15.
Daily except Tues 1–4pm & 8–11pm.

Casino La Plazuela C/La Plazuela 1. The town's casino is
an great place for a beer and tapas including *boquerones
en vinagre* (anchovies) and very good *jamón*. Daily
9am–10pm.

La Agustina Plaza del Consejo s/n, off the top end of
the Paseo del Moro. Stylish little restaurant serving tapas
(try the *queso de cabra con miel*) in the bar below and
full meals – *carillada ibérica* (pork cheeks) is a house
special – in a restaurant above. Main dishes €11–18.
Wed–Sun 1–4.30pm & 9–11.30pm.

Los Mellis C/La Plazuela s/n. This long established
bar-restaurant is a town favourite. Tapas and *raciones*
are served in the bar, while the restaurant specializes
in game – *caldareta de jabalí* (stewed wild boar) and
venado (venison) frequently appear on the menu. Daily
10am–11pm.

Restaurante Posada del Moro Posada del Moro,
C/Paseo del Moro s/n. This hotel restaurant is a serious
venture and has won many critical plaudits. Julia and
Lucia, the English chefs, use the riches of the sierra to
embellish their traditional dishes with a creative edge.
Setas a la plancha (sierra mushrooms) and *cola de toro*
(stewed bull's tail) are two signature dishes, and there's
a *menú* (€18) and more elaborate *menú de degustación*
(€45). Main dishes €12–20. Tues–Sun 1–4pm & 8–11pm.

Constantina and around

Eighteen kilometres southeast of Cazalla lies **CONSTANTINA**, an important and
beautiful mountain town and the main administrative centre for Seville's section of
the Sierra Morena. For hikers this is as good a place as any to cut back to Seville if
you're not counting on continuing across the provincial border into Córdoba. Founded
in the fourth century by the Romans during the reign of the emperor Constantine,
and named after his son, this was an important centre of wine-production which sent
a vintage named *cocolubis* to the imperial capital. The town is a delightful place to
wander around, particularly the old quarter, which is dotted with a number of notable
eighteenth-century mansions. With transport you can make a trip to **La Pantalla** lake
for swimming and fishing. It is reached by heading east for 3km along the A452 road
to El Pedroso.

Castillo de la Armada

Topping the hill flanking the western edge of town and high above the streets below,
the **Castillo de la Armada** is an impressive medieval fortress surrounded by shady
gardens descending in terraces to the old quarter.

La Encarnación

Plaza Llano del Sol 8 · Daily 7–8pm · Free

At the foot of the hill below the castle you'll find the sixteenth-century parish church
of **La Encarnación**, once again with a Mudéjar tower – Moorish influence having died
hard in these parts – and a splendid, if crumbling, Plateresque portal by Hernán Ruíz,

the architect of the cathedral inside the Mezquita at Córdoba and the belfry added to the Giralda in Seville. The church's *altar mayor*, a magnificent gilded work by Juan de Oviedo, is also worth a look.

ARRIVAL AND INFORMATION

By train The nearest train station is at Cazalla de la Sierra, 12km away (see p.361) with daily trains to Seville. There is no bus service to the station but the Turismo can help with booking a taxi.

By bus There are daily buses from and to Seville.

Turismo There's a Turismo cabin (daily 10am–1pm; ☎ 955 881 297, ⓦ constantina.org) on Avda. Andalucía, near the entry to the town from El Pedroso; staff here can provide a useful town map. When closed, you can also pick up the map from the Ayuntamiento, C/Eduardo Dato 7, near La Encarnación church.

CONSTANTINA

El Robledo Centro de Visitantes Two kilometres out of the town on the El Pedroso road, this is the visitor centre (Tues–Thurs 10am–2pm, Fri 10am–2pm & 6–8pm, Sat 10am–2pm & 4–6pm, Sun 10am–2pm; ☎ 955 581 597) for the Sierra Norte natural park and has lots of maps, guidebooks and information on activities such as horseriding and hiking in the park. There's also a botanical garden (same hours; free) displaying a wide variety of the park's flora.

Festival Constantina's *feria* (last week in Aug) is a rumbustious affair, with horseriding contests plus drinking, dancing and singing galore.

ACCOMMODATION

Albergue Juvenil C/Cuesta Blanca s/n ☎ 955 889 500. The cheapest place to stay in Constantina, slightly out of the centre, uphill behind a petrol station at the southern end of the town. The modern hostel has double rooms and shared showers, plus some fully equipped apartments. Under 26 **€21**, over 26 **€27**

Hotel San Blas C/Miraflores 4 ☎ 955 880 077,

ⓦ fp-hoteles.com. Pleasant three-star hotel with attractive rooms, pool and own car park in an elevated location at the northern end of town. **€48**

La Casa Mari Pepa C/José de la Bastida 25 ☎ 955 880 282. The town's only *hostal*, occupying a *casa señorial* which has been lovingly transformed into a delightful series of distinctively decorated en-suite rooms. B&B **€60**

EATING AND DRINKING

There are numerous good tapas bars along and around C/Mesones, the pedestrianized main street, plus, a few minutes' walk away, some outstanding places to eat.

Bar Bullhy C/Mesones 30. Another of the town's topnotch tapas bars, serving up further sierra specialities including *solomillo al whisky* (pork loin in whisky). Daily 11am–midnight.

La Bodeguita Alférez C/Cabrera 1. Well worth seeking out, this tapas bar with *taurino* traditions specializes in *setas* (mushrooms), *carillada* (pork cheeks) and *venado* (venison). Daily 10am–11pm.

★**Cambio de Tercio** C/Virgen del Robledo 53 ☎ 955 881 080. Arguably the town's best restaurant, taking its name from the stages of a *corrida* and continuing the theme with an amusing entrance imitating a bullring. This is also the place where King Juan Carlos gets his victuals during sessions gunning down the local wildlife (in one of his favourite hunting zones) – they deliver elaborate picnics to him in the

field, as a photo on one wall shows. There's a lively bar for tapas and *platos combinados* – with its own economical *menú* for €8 – in the front and a pleasant room at the back for more formal dining. All is reasonably priced and the *solomillo de cerdo* (pork loin) is excellent. Main dishes €7–18. Daily 1–4pm & 8pm–midnight.

Casino de Labradores C/Mesones 36. Lively tapas haunt serving up a decent selection of tapas and *raciones*. Daily 11am–11pm.

El Mesón de la Abuela Paseo de la Alameda 39. Atmospheric and friendly bar-restaurant for tapas and *raciones*. *Carnes a la brasa* (charcoal-grilled meats) are the speciality here, and they also offer a range of salads. Daily noon–4pm & 8–11pm.

Marisquería El León Paseo de la Alameda. A good little place specializing in fried fish and shellfish tapas. Daily.

Córdoba
and Jaén

CÓRDOBA

Córdoba and Jaén

Andalucía's most northerly province, Córdoba is bisected by the fertile valley of the Río Guadalquivir which meanders across it from east to west. On the river's northern bank, the provincial capital is a handsome city whose outstanding attraction is its twelve-hundred-year-old Moorish Mezquita, one of the world's great buildings. In the tangled lanes of the Judería, the old Jewish quarter, that partially surrounds it, the sense of Córdoba's history as the centre of a vast empire is overwhelming. After the brilliance of the Mezquita the rest of the city, particularly modern Córdoba, can seem like an anticlimax, but persist and you'll discover a host of striking post-*Reconquista* churches, elegant convents and mansions. Despite a reputation for sobriety among its neighbours, Córdoba has some of the most distinctive old bars in Andalucía, where taking a drink and a *tapa* is a particularly unique experience.

A few kilometres from the city there's more Moorish splendour at the ruins of **Medina Azahara**, a once-fabulous palace of the caliphs now being painstakingly restored, while south of the river lies Córdoba's **Campiña**, a rolling landscape of grainfields, olive groves and vineyards, where Montilla, the province's rival to the wines of Jerez, is made. Little visited, the more elevated southern reaches of this area are particularly delightful, with towns and villages such as **Baena**, **Cabra** and **Zuheros** ringed by excellent hiking country. The equally unsung town of **Priego de Córdoba**, further south still, has a clutch of spectacular Baroque churches that are worth a trip in themselves. To the north of the capital, the hardy mining towns in the foothills of the **Sierra Morena** attract even fewer visitors, but there's a rich variety of birdlife here, and the higher slopes are home to deer and wild boar zealously stalked by hunters in winter.

The **province of Jaén** has been regarded since Moorish times as Andalucía's gateway – through the **Despeñaperros Pass** – to Castile and the cities of Toledo and Madrid to the north. Although often used as this gateway's doormat and something of a forgotten entity, the region's poorest province has some surprisingly worthy sights. The **city of Jaén** has a fine **Renaissance cathedral** as well as impressive **Moorish baths** but is more often used as a stop on the way to the magnificent twin Renaissance towns of **Baeza** and **Úbeda**. Sharing a similar history, the nobilities of these two conurbations competed in using their sixteenth-century wealth to employ some of the best architects and builders around. These craftsmen, such as the great architect **Andrés de Vandelvira** – whose imprint is everywhere – have left behind a monumental treasure in golden

MEZQUITA, CÓRDOBA

Highlights

❶ Córdoba The city of Córdoba is a feast of museums and palaces, with an old Jewish quarter and some excellent tapas bars and restaurants. **See p.370**

❷ Mezquita, Córdoba This twelve-hundred-year-old mosque is one of the world's Moorish architectural masterpieces. **See p.371**

❸ Medina Azahara The ruins of this sumptuous tenth-century Moorish palace evoke the dazzling grandeur of the Córdoba caliphate. **See p.390**

❹ Zuheros A delightful white village perched on a ridge in the midst of stunningly picturesque walking country. **See p.404**

❺ Priego de Córdoba The Baroque showpiece of Córdoba province, this charming town is crammed with fine churches and monuments. **See p.405**

❻ Baños Arabes, Jaén One of the largest and best-preserved Moorish bath complexes in Spain. **See p.422**

❼ Baeza and Úbeda The twin Renaissance jewels of Jaén province are filled with a wealth of magnificent monuments in honey-tinted stone. **See p.426 & p.431**

HIGHLIGHTS ARE MARKED ON THE MAP ON PP.368–369

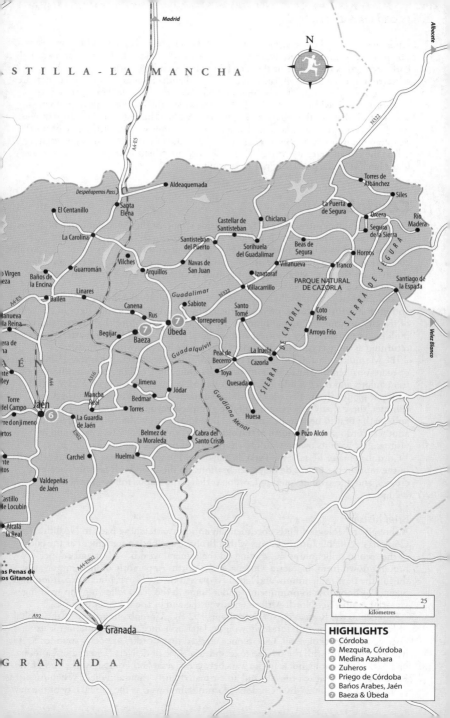

CASTILLA-LA MANCHA

Madrid

Albacete

N

Aldeaquemada

Despeñaperros Pass

El Centanillo

Santa Elena

La Carolina

Torres de Albánchez

Siles

La Puerta de Segura

Orcera

Río Madera

Castellar de Santisteban

Chiclana

Segura de la Sierra

o Virgen eza

Baños de la Encina

Guarromán

Vilches

Santisteban del Puerto

Sorihuela del Guadalimar

Beas de Segura

Villanueva

Hornos

Guarromán

Linares

Arquillos

Navas de San Juan

Iznatoraf

Tranco

PARQUE NATURAL DE CAZORLA

anueva la na

Bailén

Canena

Rus

Sabiote

Villacarrillo

Santiago de la Espada

era de na

Begíjar

Baeza

Torreperogil

Úbeda

Santo Tomé

Coto Ríos

Velez Blanco

JAÉN

Ey

Torre del Campo

Jaén

Mancha Real

Jimena

Jódar

Bedmar

Torres

Peal de Becerro

La Iruela

Arroyo Frío

Cazorla

Toya

Quesada

La Guardia de Jaén

Belmez de la Moraleda

Cabra del Santo Cristo

Huesa

Carchel

Huelma

Pozo Alcón

Valdepeñas de Jaén

astillo e Locubín

Alcalá la Real

as Penas de os Gitanos

Granada

GRANADA

0   25
kilometres

HIGHLIGHTS
1. Córdoba
2. Mezquita, Córdoba
3. Medina Azahara
4. Zuheros
5. Priego de Córdoba
6. Baños Arabes, Jaén
7. Baeza & Úbeda

sandstone, one of the marvels not only of Andalucía, but of Spain and Europe as well. The province's mountainous eastern flank now forms the heart of the **Cazorla Natural Park** and cradles the source of the Guadalquivir. Extending northeast from the town of **Cazorla**, the park's vast expanse of dense woodlands, lakes and spectacular crags are crowned by eagles' and vultures' nests and patrolled by the agile ibex. Its northerly reaches are guarded by many ruined Moorish castles, the most astonishing of which sits on the hill above the village of **Segura de la Sierra**. The rest is mainly **olive groves**, which cover a vast area of Jaén, and whose exclusive cultivation is the cause of much seasonal unemployment. But there is a beauty in the orderly files of trees, stretching across the red and creamy white hills to the horizon, which seem "to open and close like a fan," as Lorca poetically put it, as you pass.

Córdoba

CÓRDOBA stands upstream from Seville beside a loop of the Guadalquivir, which was once navigable as far as here. It is today a minor provincial capital, prosperous in a modest sort of way, but a mere shadow of its past greatness. The city's name – a possible corruption of the Syrian *coteba* or "oil press" – is believed to be of Phoenician origin dating from the time when merchant venturers sailed up the river to carry away the region's much-prized olive oil.

Córdoba is now principally famous for a single building, the **Mezquita** – the grandest and most beautiful mosque ever constructed by the Moors. It stands right in the centre of the city, surrounded by the **Judería**, the old Jewish and Moorish quarters, and is a building of extraordinary mystical and aesthetic power. Head for it on arrival and keep returning as long as you stay; its beauty and power increase with each visit.

The Mezquita apart, Córdoba is a city of considerable charm. It has few grand squares or mansions, tending instead to introverted architecture, calling your attention to the tremendous and often wildly extravagant **patios**, yet another Moorish legacy. Filled with pot plants, decorative tiles, tinkling fountains and a profusion of flowers in summer, these shady oases can usually be glimpsed beyond a forged iron *verja* (gate), and are the best to be seen in Andalucía. Besides the city's Moorish treasures, there is another Córdoba, to the **north of the old quarter**, an area rarely touched upon by visitors, but with its own rewarding churches and palaces, not to mention bars.

Córdoba's major fiesta is the **Feria de Mayo**, held in the final week in May. Earlier in the month, the **Cruces de Mayo** celebrations fill the town with lavishly decorated crosses, and a festival devoted to Córdoba's delightful patios follows immediately behind.

Brief history

Although archeological finds document an antiquity stretching back to Neolithic times, Córdoba's verifiable history begins with a Bronze Age **Iberian** settlement at the end of the second millennium BC trading on the mineral wealth – silver and copper – brought down from the Sierra Morena to the north. Apparently of little importance during the next millennium, and largely bypassed by the Carthaginian expansion into Spain, Córdoba rose to prominence under **Rome** in the years following the crushing victories against her North African enemy at the end of the third century BC.

Founded as the Roman city of **Corduba** in 152 BC, Córdoba flourished as the capital of Hispania Ulterior and, foreshadowing its later brilliance, became famous for its poetry as well as its olive oil. Cicero once cracked that Cordoban poetry sounded as if it had got mixed up with the oil due to its guttural style of delivery. Later, after Córdoba had backed the wrong horse in the wars between Caesar and Pompey at the end of the Republic, Caesar sacked the city and an estimated thirty thousand died. When Augustus reorganized Spain in 27 BC, Córdoba's fortunes improved as the capital city of the new province of Baetica, roughly corresponding to modern Andalucía. A brilliant period followed during which the city produced the poets **Lucan** and **Seneca** whilst prosperity – based on oil, wool and minerals – increased. Córdoba's importance continued for another three centuries evidenced by recent excavations opposite the city's new train and bus station complex where the remains of a huge fourth-century **palace** constructed by the emperor Maximian have been unearthed.

As Roman power waned in the fifth century the area was overrun first by **Vandals** and then by **Visigoths** before falling to the **Moors** early in the eighth century. In 756 Córdoba became the capital of Moorish Spain and the succeeding three centuries – when the city formed the heart of the Western Islamic Empire – were Córdoba's golden age, as it grew to rival Cairo and Baghdad as a centre of Muslim art and learning. Though later its political power declined, Córdoba remained a centre of culture and scholarship and was the birthplace of the twelfth-century thinkers **Averroës**, the great Muslim commentator on Aristotle, and **Maimónides**, the Jewish philosopher. After conquest by **Fernando III** in 1236, Córdoba's glory vanished as the city sank into a long and steady decline. Such aspects of civilized life as the elaborate Moorish systems of water supply and sewage disposal fell into ruin and the mosques were turned into churches. Little of the wealth of imperial Spain found its way here, although the city's leatherworkers, silversmiths and *parfumeurs* (all continuing Moorish traditions) achieved some renown in the sixteenth century. Plagues in the next century decimated the population and when Ford arrived in the 1830s he found "a poor and servile city". Córdoba suffered terrible repression in the wars against the **French** as it was to do again in the twentieth century when, during the Civil War, it was captured by the **Nationalists** who carried out brutal atrocities. Local voters took belated revenge for this in the first post-Franco elections of 1979 when it elected a **communist** council – the only major city in Spain to do so.

Today, Córdoba boasts a progressive air and is a city of learning once again. The university was re-established in 1971 – its latest faculty is devoted to the study of Muslim history and culture.

The Mezquita

April–Sept Mon–Sat 10am–7pm, Sun 8.30–10am & 2–7pm; Oct–March Mon–Sat 10am–6pm, Sun 2–6pm. Also year round Mon–Sat 8.30–10am for services in the cathedral; you are allowed to visit the mosque at this time but silence must be observed and lighting is dimmed • €8; free Mon–Sat 8.30–10am during cathedral services

As in Moorish times, the **Mezquita** is approached through the **Patio de los Naranjos**, a classic Islamic ablutions court with fountains for ritual purification before prayer, which still preserves its orange trees. None of the original ablutions fountains survives, the present ones being purely decorative later additions. Originally, when in use for the Friday prayers, all nineteen naves of the mosque were open to this court, allowing the rows of interior columns to appear as an extension of the trees. Today, with all but one of the entrance gates locked, the image is still there, though subdued by the loss of those brilliant shafts of sunlight filtering through. The mood of the building has been distorted a little, from the open and vigorous simplicity of the mosque, to the mysterious half-light of a cathedral.

The Mihrab

The mosque's overall uniformity was broken only by the culminating point of al-Hakam II's tenth-century extension – the domed cluster of pillars surrounding the mosque's great jewel, the sacred **Mihrab**. Even here, although he lengthened the prayer hall by a third, al-Hakam carefully aligned the new *mihrab* at the end of the same central aisle which had led to the previous two. The *mihrab* had two functions in Islamic worship: it indicated the direction of Mecca and it amplified the words of the *imam*, or prayer leader.

CÓRDOBA

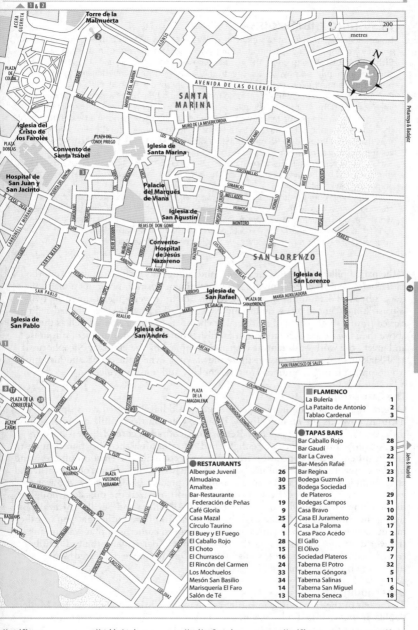

FLAMENCO

La Bulería	1
La Pataito de Antonio	2
Tablao Cardenal	3

TAPAS BARS

Bar Caballo Rojo	28
Bar Gaudí	3
Bar La Cavea	22
Bar-Mesón Rafaé	21
Bar Regina	23
Bodega Guzmán	12
Bodega Sociedad de Plateros	29
Bodegas Campos	31
Casa Bravo	10
Casa El Juramento	20
Casa La Paloma	17
Casa Paco Acedo	2
El Gallo	8
El Olivo	27
Sociedad Plateros	7
Taberna El Potro	32
Taberna Góngora	5
Taberna Salinas	11
Taberna San Miguel	6
Taberna Seneca	18

RESTAURANTS

Albergue Juvenil	26
Almudaina	30
Amaltea	35
Bar-Restaurante Federación de Peñas	19
Café Gloria	9
Casa Mazal	25
Círculo Taurino	4
El Buey y El Fuego	1
El Caballo Rojo	28
El Choto	15
El Churrasco	16
El Rincón del Carmen	24
Los Mochuelos	33
Mesón San Basilio	34
Marisquería El Faro	14
Salón de Té	13

Hostal Plaza Corredera	8	Hotel Amistad Córdoba	12	Hotel Las Casas de la Judería	22
Hostal Santa Ana	29	Hotel González	19	Hotel Los Omeyas	18
Hostal Séneca	11	Hotel Hespería Córdoba	31	Hotel Marisa	16
Hotel Albucasis	7			Hotel Mezquita	21

Hotel Plateros	10
Parador Nacional Arruzafa	1
Pensión Los Arcos	23

4

DESIGNING THE MEZQUITA

Inside the Mezquita, a forest of supporting pillars stretches away into the distance. This was an early and sophisticated architectural improvisation to gain height. The original architect, **Sidi ben Ayub**, working under the instruction of Abd ar-Rahman I, had at his disposal columns in marble, porphyry and jasper from the old Visigothic cathedral and from numerous Roman buildings, as well as many more shipped in from all parts of the former Roman Empire. This ready-made building material could bear great weight, but the architect was faced with the problem of the pillars' varying sizes: many were much too tall but the vast majority would not be tall enough, even when arched, to reach the intended height of the ceiling. The long pillars he sank in the floor, whilst his solution for the short pillars (which may have been inspired by Roman aqueduct designs) was to place a second row of square columns on the apex, serving as a base for the semicircular arches that support the roof. For extra strength and stability (and perhaps also deliberately to echo the shape of a date palm, much revered by the early Spanish Arabs), he introduced another, horseshoe-shaped arch above the lower pillars.

A second and purely aesthetic innovation was to alternate brick and stone in the arches, creating the red-and-white striped pattern that gives a unity and distinctive character to the whole design. This architectural *tour de force* was unprecedented in the Arab world and set the tone for all future enlargements – excepting the Christian cathedral – of the building. Most impressively, it was completed within a year of its commencement in 785.

The paired pillars that flank the *mihrab* and support its arch were taken from the earlier *mihrab* of Abd ar-Rahman I, their prominent position no doubt a mark of respect by al-Hakam to his great predecessor. The inner vestibule of the niche (which is frustratingly fenced off) is quite simple in comparison, with a shell-shaped ceiling carved from a single block of marble. The chambers to either side, as well as the dome above the *mihrab*, are decorated with exquisite **mosaics** of gold, rust-red, turquoise and green, the work of Byzantine craftsmen supplied by the emperor Nicephorus II at al-Hakam's request. These constitute the *maksura*, where the caliph and his retinue would pray, a fitting monument to this scholarly and sensitive ruler.

The Cathedral

Originally the whole design of the mosque would have directed worshippers naturally towards the *mihrab*. Today, though, you almost stumble upon it, as in the centre of the mosque squats a Renaissance **cathedral coro**. This was built in 1523, nearly three centuries of enlightened restraint after the Christian conquest, and in spite of fierce opposition from the town council. The erection of a *coro* and *capilla mayor*, however, had long been the "Christianizing" dream of the cathedral chapter and at last they had found a monarch, predictably Carlos V, who was willing to sanction the work. Carlos, to his credit, realized the mistake (though it did not stop him from destroying parts of the Alhambra and Seville's Alcázar); on seeing the work completed he told the chapter, "You have built what you or others might have built anywhere, but you have destroyed something that was unique in the world." Some details are worth noting, though, particularly the beautifully carved Churrigueresque **choir stalls** by Pedro Duque Cornejo, created with mahogany brought from the New World.

Other additions

To the left of the *coro* stands an earlier and happier Christian addition, the Mudéjar **Capilla de Villaviciosa**, built by Moorish craftsmen in 1371. Beside it are the dome and pillars of the **earlier mihrab**, constructed under Abd ar-Rahman II. The mosque's original and finely decorated timber-coffered ceiling was replaced in the eighteenth century by the present Baroque cupolas. Further post-Reconquest additions include the **Capilla Real**, installed by Alfonso X in the thirteenth century, with *azulejo* panels and lobed niches in Mudéjar style, and the early eighteenth-century **Capilla del Cardinal** (Chapterhouse – now housing the cathedral's treasury), the *tesoro* (treasury) and *sacristía*, none of which detracts from the building's imposing majesty.

The evocative belfry, the **Torre del Alminar** (currently closed to visitors) at the corner of the Patio de los Naranjos, is built on the site of the original minaret and contemporary with the cathedral addition. The belfry was designed by Hernán Ruíz, who used the earlier tower as a core to support two additional sections more than

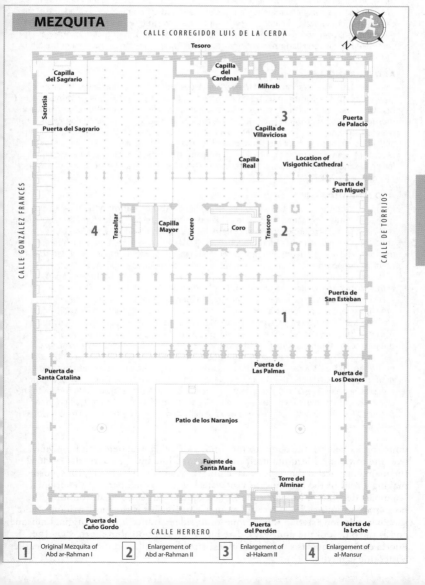

MEZQUITA

CALLE CORREGIDOR LUIS DE LA CERDA

N

Tesoro

Capilla del Sagrario

Capilla del Cardenal

Mihrab

Sacristía

Puerta del Sagrario

Puerta de Palacio

3

Capilla de Villaviciosa

Capilla Real

Location of Visigothic Cathedral

Puerta de San Miguel

CALLE GONZÁLEZ FRANCES

CALLE DE TORRIJOS

4

Trasaltar

Capilla Mayor

Crucero

Coro

Trascoro

2

Puerta de San Esteban

1

Puerta de Santa Catalina

Puerta de Las Palmas

Puerta de Los Deanes

Patio de los Naranjos

Fuente de Santa Maria

Torre del Alminar

Puerta del Caño Gordo

CALLE HERRERO

Puerta del Perdón

Puerta de la Leche

| **1** Original Mezquita of Abd ar-Rahman I | **2** Enlargement of Abd ar-Rahman II | **3** Enlargement of al-Hakam II | **4** Enlargement of al-Mansur |

MOORISH CÓRDOBA AND THE BUILDING OF THE MEZQUITA

Córdoba's domination of **Moorish Spain** began thirty years after the conquest – in 756, when the city was placed under the control of **Abd ar-Rahman I**, the sole survivor of the Umayyad dynasty which had been bloodily expelled from the eastern caliphate of Damascus. He commenced the building of the **Great Mosque** (La Mezquita), purchasing the site of the former Visigothic Cathedral of Saint Vincent from the Christians. This building which, divided by a partition wall, had previously served both communities had itself been constructed on top of an earlier Roman temple dedicated to the god Janus. Demolishing the church as they built, Abd ar-Rahman's architects, for reasons of speed and economy, incorporated one of the cathedral's original walls – that facing west – into the new structure and this is the reason why the *mihrab*'s prayer wall is not precisely aligned towards Mecca. This original mosque was completed by his son **Hisham** in 786 and comprises about one-fifth of the present building, the first dozen aisles adjacent to the Patio de los Naranjos.

ABD AR-RAHMAN II

The Cordoban emirate soon began to rival Damascus both in power and in the brilliance of its civilization. **Abd ar-Rahman II** (822–52) initiated sophisticated irrigation programmes, minted his own coinage and received embassies from Byzantium. He in turn substantially enlarged the mosque. A focal point within the culture of al-Andalus, this was by now being consciously directed and enriched as an alternative to Mecca; it possessed an original script of the Koran and a bone from the arm of Muhammad, and, for the Spanish Muslim who could not go to Mecca, it became the most sacred place of **pilgrimage**. In the broader Islamic world it ranked fourth in sanctity after the Kaaba of Mecca, the city of Medina in Saudi Arabia, and the Al Aksa mosque of Jerusalem.

ABD AR-RAHMAN III

In the tenth century Córdoba reached its zenith under **Abd ar-Rahman III** (912–61), one of the great rulers of Islamic history. He assumed power at the age of 23 after his grandfather had killed his father during a period of internal strife. During his reign, according to a contemporary historian, he "subdued rebels, built palaces, gave impetus to agriculture, immortalized ancient deeds and monuments, and inflicted great damage on infidels to a point where no opponent or contender remained in al-Andalus. People obeyed en masse and wished to live with him in peace." In 929, with Muslim Spain and a substantial part of North Africa firmly under his control, Abd ar-Rahman III adopted the title of "caliph", or successor of the Prophet. It was a supremely confident gesture and was reflected in the growing splendour of Córdoba itself which, with a population approaching 500,000, had become the largest, most prosperous city of Europe, and outshone both Byzantium and Baghdad (the new capital of the eastern caliphate) in science, culture and scholarship. At the turn of the tenth century it could boast some 27 schools, 50 hospitals (with the first separate clinics for the leprous and insane), 600 public baths, 60,300 noble mansions, 213,077 houses and 80,455 shops. One of Córdoba's most magnificent buildings during this and later periods would have been the Umayyad palace of the caliphs, of which little except a bath complex remains (see p.380). Extending to the west of the Mezquita from Calle Torrijos to the city walls and southwards to the river, the palace was connected to the Mezquita by a secret passage. Built in the ninth century to allow the caliph privileged access to the mosque at all

doubling its height. The climb to the top is a dizzying experience and the **views** over the town and Mezquita itself tremendous. Close by, the **Puerta del Perdón**, the main entrance to the patio, was rebuilt in Moorish style in 1377. It's worth making a tour of the Mezquita's **outer walls** before leaving; parts of the original "caliphal" decoration (in particular some exquisite latticework) surrounding the portals are stunning. The west wall along Calle Torrijos is the most striking where the **Puerta de San Esteban** was an important side entrance into the original mosque and is the oldest of the doorways, dated by an inscription above it to 855. The **Puerta de San Miguel** is sited in the oldest stretch of wall, and dates from the earlier Visigothic cathedral.

times, traces of this tunnel (not on view) have been found in the building's southwest corner. The construction of a glorious new palace at **Medina Azahara** in the 930s as well as further development of the Great Mosque paralleled these new heights of confidence and splendour. Abd ar-Rahman III provided the Mezquita with a new minaret 80m high, topped by three pomegranate-shaped spheres, two of silver and one of gold and each weighing a ton. The minaret was badly damaged in a storm in 1589 and was later used as the core of the sixteenth century Torre del Alminar which replaced it.

AL-HAKAM II

The caliph's successor **al-Hakam II** (961–76) was a man from another mould than that of his warrior father, best epitomized by his advice to his own son:

Do not make wars unnecessarily. Keep the peace, for your own wellbeing and that of your people. Never unsheathe your sword except against those who commit injustice. What pleasure is there in invading and destroying nations, in taking pillage and destruction to the ends of the earth? Do not let yourself be dazzled by vanity; let your justice always be like a tranquil lake.

In tune with these sentiments, al-Hakam was a poet, historian and the builder of one of the great libraries of the Middle Ages. This cultured ruler was also responsible for the mosque's most brilliant expansion, virtually doubling its extent. After demolishing the south wall to add fourteen extra rows of columns, he employed Byzantine craftsmen to construct a new *mihrab* or prayer niche. This has survived due to having been bricked up following the Christian Reconquest. Only rediscovered in the nineteenth century, it remains complete and is perhaps the most beautiful example of all Moorish religious architecture.

AL-MANSUR

Under the vizier-usurper **al-Mansur** (977–1002), who used his position as regent to push al-Hakam's child successor, Hisham II, into the background, repeated attacks were carried out on the Christians in the north, including the daring expedition to Santiago de Compostela in 997, when the pilgrimage cathedral's bells were seized. This military might was built on the incorporation of thousands of Berbers from North Africa into al-Mansur's army – a policy that was to have devastating implications for the future when the same Berbers turned on their paymasters and sacked and plundered the city, destroying al-Hakam's treasured library in the process. Within less than thirty years the brilliant caliphate of Córdoba had collapsed in a bloody turmoil as short-lived puppet caliphs attempted to stave off the inevitable.

When he was not away on his military campaigns, al-Mansur gave his attention to further embellishing the Great Mosque. As al-Hakam had extended the building as far to the south as was possible, he completed the final enlargement by adding seven rows of columns to the whole east side. This spoiled the symmetry of the mosque, depriving the *mihrab* of its central position, but Arab historians observed that it meant there were now "as many bays as there are days of the year". They also delighted in describing the rich interior, with its 1293 marble columns, 280 chandeliers and 1445 lamps. Hanging inverted among the lamps were the bells of the cathedral of Santiago de Compostela. Al-Mansur had made his Christian captives carry them on their shoulders from Galicia – a process which was to be observed in reverse after Córdoba was captured by Fernando el Santo (the Saint) in 1236.

Museo Diocesano

C/Torrijos 12 • July & Aug Mon–Sat 9.30am–3pm, Sept–June 9.30am–1.30pm & 4–6pm • €1.50, free with Mezquita ticket • ☏ 957 496 474

Opposite the Mezquita's west wall on the site of the former Moorish *alcázar* lies the **Museo Diocesano**. This elegant seventeenth-century building with a fine patio and fountain is now a **museum of religious art**, mainly sculpture. In the early rooms are some outstanding examples of medieval wood sculpture – a great Spanish tradition. The anonymous thirteenth-century *Virgen de las Huertas* in Room 1 is finely worked, as is a striking fifteenth-century *Calvario Villaviciosa* or Crucifixion. In Room 3, an anonymous early sixteenth-century pietà has the agonized expressions of the onlookers beautifully portrayed. The remainder of the museum comprises more wood sculpture from later periods – including an image of *Santo Tomás* by José de Mora – plus tapestries, furniture, and, in Room VI, a vibrant eighteenth-century image of San Miguel Arcángel attributed to La Roldana, the daughter sculptor of Pedro Roldán. On the ground floor, there's a beautiful Baroque **chapel** dedicated to the Virgin (which may be closed).

The Alcázar

Plaza Campo Santo de los Martires s/n • July & Aug Tues–Sun 10am–2pm; Sept–June Tues–Fri 8.30am–7.30pm, Sat 9.30am–4.30pm, Sun 9.30am–2.30pm • €4 includes access to Baños Califales; free on Wed • ☎ 957 420 151

Dating from the time of the *Reconquista*, the **Alcázar de Los Reyes Cristianos**, a palace fortress, was completed in the fourteenth century and now houses a small municipal museum. The original Moorish *alcázar* stood beside the Mezquita, on the site presently occupied by the Palacio Episcopal. After the Christian conquest it was rebuilt a little to the west and used by monarchs – including Fernando and Isabel who were visited here by Columbus in 1486 – when staying in the city. That the buildings retain little of their original opulence today is due to their use as the residence of the **Inquisition** for three centuries prior to 1821, and later as a prison until as recently as 1951.

The palace underwent extensive Mudéjar rebuilding during the fifteenth century, when the attractive **Moorish-style gardens** were added. One of the glories of Córdoba today with lots of arbours and shady corners, the gardens are dotted with hefty chunks of Roman columns and other masonry testifying to the city's importance in the Roman era. From the tower's belvedere there are great **views** over the town and river, while the **interior** of the Alcázar features fifteenth-century royal baths and some fine **Roman mosaics** discovered in the city. The second-century depiction of *Polyphemus and Galatea* is outstanding and the monochrome mosaic beside it is one of the largest complete mosaics in existence. A fine third-century carved sarcophagus is also worth a look; a half-ajar portal on the sarcophagus's side indicates that access is open to the person within.

Baños Califales

Plaza Campo Santo de los Mártires s/n • July & Aug Tues–Sun 10am–2pm; Sept–June Tues–Fri 8.30am–7.30pm, Sat 9.30am–4.30pm, Sun 9.30am–2.30pm • €2 (free with Alcázar ticket); free on Wed

In the gardens across the plaza to the north of the Alcázar are the impressive remains of a tenth-century Moorish *hammam*, or bathhouse, the **Baños Califales**, constructed in the reign of al-Hakam II. As their name implies, the baths were possibly attached to the Umayyad palace that once covered most of this area. Inside you can see various bathing rooms, which would have had gradated temperatures, lit by star-shaped windows set in barrel-vaulted ceilings; the western rooms date from the post-califal Taifa, Almoravid and Almohad periods. The baths would originally have been surrounded by plant-filled gardens and arbours where bathers could relax and chat; in the afternoon they normally passed into feminine hands, when a towel would be hung outside to warn absent-minded males of the change of use. Travellers to Moorish Córdoba record between three and six hundred bathhouses similar to these throughout the city, which would probably not be excessive for a population of half a million inhabitants. See p.380 for details on visiting a modern reconstruction of the Moorish bathing experience.

Jardín Botánico

Avda. de Linneo s/n • April–June Tues–Sun 10am–8pm; July & Aug Tues, Fri & Sat 9am–2pm, Wed & Thurs 9am–2pm & 8pm–midnight, Sun 10am–3pm; Sept–March Tues–Sat 10am–6pm, Sun 10am–3pm • €2 • ⓦ jardinbotanicodecordoba.com

Some 300m downriver of the Alcázar, Córdoba's extensive **Jardín Botánico** features hothouses with exotic species of succulents, ferns and prickly plants, as well as a rose garden. At the garden's northern end a paleobotanical museum – housed inside a medieval water-mill – displays 150,000 specimens of fossil plant life. The nearby arboretum exhibits trees and shrubs from all over the world including samples of Andalucía's own arboreal rarity, the **pinsapo** Spanish fir, transplanted from its only European habitat in the Sierra de Grazalema. Other features include a garden for the visually impaired with a collection of plants recognizable by their aroma and texture and a **cafetería**.

The Puente Romano and around

The pedestrianized **Puente Romano** is an impressive 250m-long Roman bridge across the Río Guadalquivir probably built during the first or second centuries AD. Inscriptions record repairs to it carried out in Moorish times by the *wali* or governor Al-Samh in the eighth century, and by Al-Hakam II in the tenth, but the structure still retains much Roman stonework. A controversial refurbishment of the bridge in 2007, which replaced its former cobblestones with a redstone pavement, added modern lighting and remodelled the support walls, outraged many architectural experts and archeologists.

Torre de la Calahorra

Puento Romano s/n • Daily: May–Sept 10am–2pm & 4.30–8.30pm; Oct–April 10am–6pm • €4.50

Guarding the southeastern end of the Puente Romano is the **Torre de la Calahorra**, a medieval tower that now houses a **museum** full of hi-tech gimmicks including weird tableaux, an illuminated Alhambra, a model of the Mezquita prior to its Christian alterations and, improbably, a multimedia presentation on the history of man. From the tower you get a wonderful panoramic **view** towards the Mezquita and city beyond.

Albolafia water-wheel

Just west of the Puente Romano at its northern end, the reconstructed **Albolafia** is the sole survivor of a number of ancient **Moorish water-wheels** that once crossed the river here and which, besides grinding flour, pumped water to the Alcázar's gardens. So noisy were this wheel's rumblings that Queen Isabel – resident at the Alcázar during a royal visit – had it dismantled when it disturbed her sleep.

La Judería

Between the Mezquita and the beginning of the Avenida del Gran Capitán lies the **Judería**, Córdoba's old Jewish quarter. A fascinating network of lanes, it's just as atmospheric as Seville's Barrio Santa Cruz, although here too tasteless souvenir shops are beginning to gain ground.

Sinagoga

C/Maimónides 18 • Daily 9.30am–2pm & 3.30–5.30pm • €0.30, free with EU passport

Near the heart of the Judería is the **Sinagoga** (synagogue), one of only three in Spain – the other two are in Toledo – that survived the Jewish expulsion of 1492. This one, built in 1315, is minute, particularly in comparison to the great Santa María in Toledo, but it has some fine stuccowork elaborating on a Solomon's-seal motif together with Hebrew texts in the Mudéjar style, and it also retains its women's gallery.

Capilla de San Bartolomé

Plaza del Cardenal Salazar s/n • June–Sept Mon 5.30–8.30pm, Tues–Sat 10.30am–1.30pm & 5.30–8.30pm, Sun 10.30am–1.30pm; Oct–May Mon 5.30–6.30pm, Tues–Sat 10.30am–1.30pm & 3.30–6.30pm, Sun 10.30am–1.30pm • Free

Fifty metres east of the synagogue, the **Capilla de San Bartolomé** is a superb Gothic– Mudéjar chapel built in the fifteenth century. Recently restored, the chapel's exquisite vaulting, original brick floor, glazed tiles and *yesería* (plasterwork) are well worth a look.

Museo Taurino

Plaza de Maimónides s/n • Tues–Sat 10am–2pm & 5.30–7.30pm, Sun 9.30am–2.30pm • €3, free on Fri

The small **Museo Taurino** (Bullfighting Museum) warrants a look, if only for the kitschy nature of its exhibits: among a number of mounted bulls' heads (some dating from the nineteenth century), two of them were given this "honour" for having killed matadors. Beside a copy of the tomb of Manolete, most famous of the city's fighters, is exhibited the hide of his taurine nemesis, Islero; you can also see the bloodstained vest from his ill-fated bullfight in 1947. Other displays include eighteenth-century bullfight posters and a series of photos from 1914 depicting a bullfighter being gored and killed.

Callejón de las Flores

The **Callejón de las Flores**, which lies close to the Mezquita's northeast corner, is the most famous street in town, a white-walled alley from whose balconies and hanging pots cascades a riot of geraniums in summer. When viewed from its northern end, the *callejón* neatly frames the Mezquita's belfry – the picture that decorates every postcard rack in town.

Plaza del Potro

A short walk east from the Mezquita along Calle Corregidor Luís de la Cerda and its continuation, Calle Lucano, is the **Plaza del Potro**, one of Córdoba's more historic landmarks. This fine old square is named after the colt (*potro*) that adorns its sixteenth-century fountain. Originally a livestock market dealing in horses and mules, the area once had a villainous reputation, as did the remarkable inn opposite, the **Posada del Potro**, which Cervantes mentions in *Don Quijote*, and where he almost certainly stayed. Sensitively restored, the building, with an atmospheric cattle yard, is now a centre for the study of the art of flamenco and stages exhibitions and occasional concerts.

Museo de Bellas Artes

On the eastern side of Plaza del Potro • Tues 2.30–8.30pm, Wed–Sat 9am–8.30pm, Sun 9am–2.30pm • €1.50, free with EU passport • ☎ 957 355 550

The former Hospital de la Caridad, founded in the sixteenth century, now contains the **Museo de Bellas Artes**. Among a fairly unremarkable collection is an *Immaculate Conception* by Murillo as well as works by Valdés Leal and other minor *andaluz* painters. The ground floor has a small archeological collection, as well as a collection of modern sculpture and paintings. Look out for a recently acquired Dalí-esque work *Mujeres Vela* (women sailing) by noted Montoro painter Antonio Rodríguez de Luna (see p.414).

Museo Julio Romero de Torres

Plaza del Potro 1 • May–Sept Tues–Sat 10am–2pm & 5.30–7.30pm, Sun 9.30am–2.30pm; Oct–April Tues–Sat 8.30am–2.30pm, Sun 9.30am–2.30pm • €4, free on Fri • ☎ 957 760 269, ⊛ museojulioromero.cordoba.es

Across the courtyard from the Museo de Bellas Artes is a small museum devoted to the Cordoban artist **Julio Romero de Torres** (1874–1930), painter of some sublimely dreadful canvases, most of which depict reclining female nudes with furtive male guitar players. Though he's attacked by feminists and dubbed "the king of kitsch" by critics, the *cordobeses*, won't have a word said against him. Depending on your tastes, you might find a trip to *Bodegas Campos*, just east of here at Calle Lineros 32 (see p.387), rather more rewarding.

Hammam Baños Arabes

C/Corregidor Luis de la Cerda 51 • Daily, but reserve in advance (by phone is fine); 2hr sessions 10am–midnight • Prices start at €27 for a simple soak • ☎ 957 484 746, ⊛ hammamspain.com

Slightly southwest of the Plaza del Potro, back towards the Mezquita, the **Hammam Baños Arabes** is a full-scale Moorish bath complex that recreates the architecture and atmosphere of a medieval *hammam*. You'll need a bathing suit.

Plaza de la Corredera

To the north of Plaza del Potro, in an area which was once the *plateros* or silversmiths' quarter, you'll find **Plaza de la Corredera**, a wonderfully refurbished colonnaded square, much resembling Madrid's or Salamanca's Plaza Mayor. Unique in Andalucía, the square was completely enclosed in the seventeenth century, creating a suitable space for all kinds of spectacles. These have included burnings by the Inquisition as well as bullfights, from which event the tiny **Callejón Toril** (Bull Pen) on the eastern side takes its name. Today bars and restaurants fill the square, their terraces popular places to sit out on summer evenings.

Museo Arqueológico

Plaza de Jerónimo Páez 7 · Tues 2.30–8.30pm, Wed–Sat 9am–8.30pm, Sun 9am–2.30pm · €1.50, free with EU passport · ⓦ museosdeandalucia.es/cultura/museos/MAECO/?lng=en

To the northeast of the Mezquita lies the excellent **Museo Arqueológico**. The collection here is essential to gaining an understanding of Córdoba's importance as a Roman city in particular, as so little from this period survives above ground today. Housed in a new building, the basement incorporates elements of a **Roman theatre** which can be seen from the entry foyer. On the first floor, the **prehistoric section** has a selection of Iberian sculptures unearthed throughout the province, while among sculptures in the **Roman section** a first-century head of Drusus (son of the Emperor Tiberius) is outstanding. The **Moorish period** is represented by a number of exhibits including some fine Caliphal ceramics and *azulejos* (tiles).

The lower floor is themed around the daily life of Córdoba's Roman and Moorish civilizations. Look out for the famous second-century **sculpture of Mithras** slaying the bull from a mithraeum excavated at Cabra in the south of the province. This conventional image, which was placed in the *retablo* position in the small mithraic cult temples, shows Mithras plunging his dagger into the bull whose blood, initiates believed, gave birth to all living things, hence the dog and the snake trying to get their share. The ever-present problem of evil is portrayed by the symbolic scorpion attacking the bull's vitals. Nearby is a fine fourth-century relief of Daniel in the lions' den and a reconstruction of the tenth century *alminar* or minaret of the Mezquita which was replaced by the current belltower in the sixteenth century.

The new museum is only half-finished and many former exhibits, including an outstanding collection of Roman sculptures, mosaics and sarcophagi, will not be displayed again until the second phase of construction – incorporating the **Casa Páez**, a stunning sixteenth-century mansion next door – is completed, probably sometime in the next decade.

North of the monumental quarter

Many visitors to Córdoba make a stopover at the Mezquita and then leave without ever discovering the other Córdoba, to the north of the monumental quarter and the Judería, where the city's everyday life is carried on. Here, interspersed among the modern streets – many still built on the ancient grid – are **Gothic churches**, **convents** and **Renaissance palaces** that are little visited but well worth an hour or two. Note that churches are usually locked outside service times: early mornings or evenings (about 7–9pm) are the most promising times to catch them open, perhaps visiting a few of the area's excellent tapas bars en route.

Plaza Tendillas and around

Plaza Tendillas is the vibrant centre of modern Córdoba, as it was in Roman times. Dominated by the bronze equestrian statue of El Gran Capitán, a Cordoban general whose Italian campaigns in the late fifteenth century helped to project post-*Reconquista* Spain onto the world stage, it also features fountains – spurting water 2m into the air from the pedestrianized pavement – that are a big hit with tourists, children and dogs.

Off the east side of the plaza, along Calle Claudio Marcelo, lies the **Templo Romano**, the tortuously reconstructed remains (mostly pillars) of a first-century Roman temple thought to have been of a similar form to the Maison Carrée at Nîmes.

Iglesia de San Pablo and around

C/San Pablo • Access most likely in early mornings or evenings (about 7–9pm)

A fine Romanesque-Gothic church, dating from the period following the *Reconquista*, the **Iglesia de San Pablo** has undergone numerous later modifications including a Baroque facade. Its interior retains a fine Mudéjar dome and coffered ceiling as well as a seventeenth-century sculpture of the Virgin, *Nuestra Señora de las Angustias* (*Our Lady of the Sorrows*), a masterpiece by Juan de Mesa, himself a native of Córdoba.

Northwest from here, at Calle Alfonso XIII 14, is the striking **Círculo de la Amistad**, a *Casino* founded in 1842 and set inside a former convent. Ask the porter to let you see the marvellous Renaissance **patio**, originally the convent's cloister. Continuing east again, beyond San Pablo lies **San Andrés**, another post-*Reconquista* church and, further on, at the end of Calle Santa María de la Gracia, is the Gothic **San Lorenzo**, whose converted Moorish minaret tower, outstanding rose window and triple-arched portico combine to make it the best-looking church in the city. Inside, the apse has some fine fifteenth-century frescoes depicting scenes from the Passion.

Turning north along Calle Roelas, passing the nineteenth-century Neoclassical Iglesia de San Rafael, you'll come to another *Reconquista* church, **San Agustín**, in the plaza of the same name. Originally a Gothic church, it was substantially altered in the sixteenth century; inside it has frescoes and another sculpture of the Virgin by Juan de Mesa.

Palacio del Marqués de Viana

Plaza de Don Gome 2 • Guided tours (45min) June–Sept Tues–Sun 9am–3pm; Oct–May Tues–Fri 10am–7pm, Sat & Sun 10am–3pm • €6, patios only €3

The **Palacio del Marqués de Viana**, one of Córdoba's finest palaces, was the seat of the marquises of Viana until the family sold up to a bank in 1981, after which it was opened – apparently just as the family left it – to the public. Started in the fourteenth century, the building has had numerous later additions, including most of the **twelve outstanding patios**, filled with flowers, the main attraction for many visitors today.

The compulsory tour shunts you around a bewildering number of drawing rooms, gaudy bedrooms (one with a Franco portrait), kitchens and galleries, linked by creaking staircases, while the Spanish commentary (foreign-language room descriptions are available) points out a wealth of furniture, paintings, weapons and top-drawer junk the family amassed over the centuries.

Iglesia de Santa Marina

Plaza de Santa Marina s/n • Access most likely in early mornings or evenings (about 7–9pm)

North of the Palacio de Viana, the fortress-like **Iglesia de Santa Marina** dates from the thirteenth century (with Baroque modifications) and is one of the city's oldest churches, built shortly after the city was taken from the Moors. It shares the charming plaza of the same name with a monument to the celebrated Cordoban *torero* **Manolete**, who was born in the Santa Marina *barrio* and died in the ring in 1947.

Convento de Santa Isabel

C/Santa Isabel 13 • Shop usually open Mon–Sat 9.15am–12.45pm & 5–7.30pm, Sun 9.30am–1pm

At the western end of Plaza de Santa Marina, strictly speaking the Plaza del Conde Priego, the fifteenth-century Franciscan **Convento de Santa Isabel** has a delightful patio with an imposing cypress. The *capilla mayor* inside the convent's church has sculptures by Pedro Roldán. In the convent's shop the nuns also sell their home-made *dulces* – one nun is given a special dispensation from the order's rule of silence to serve you.

Cristo de los Faroles

Plaza de los Capuchinos

The simple white-walled Plaza de los Capuchinos is the site of **Cristo de los Faroles** (Christ of the Lanterns), an eighteenth-century sculpture of the Crucifixion which is the centre of much religious fervour. At night, when the lanterns flanking the cross are illuminated, the place has an unearthly, mystical ambience.

Torre de la Malmuerta

Plaza de Colón s/n

Close to the northeast corner of the garden square of Plaza de Colón, the **Torre de la Malmuerta** (Tower of Bad Death) is an early fifteenth-century battlemented tower that was once part of the city walls. It takes its name from a crime of passion when a guard posted here is supposed to have killed his adulterous spouse. At the foot of the tower is one of the city's best loved *tabernas*, the *Casa Paco Acedo* (see p.388), housed in part of a former barracks.

Convento de la Merced

Plaza de Colón s/n • Entry to patio daily 9am–2pm & 5–9pm • Free

The west side of the Plaza de Colón is dominated by the lavishly ornate facade – adorned with barley-sugar pillars and twin belfries – of the eighteenth-century former **Convento de la Merced**, now the seat of the provincial government, and the biggest and best example of full-blown Baroque in town. Inside is an exquisite Renaissance patio with paired columns, elegant staircases and a central fountain.

Iglesia de San Miguel

Plaza de San Miguel s/n

The imposing **Iglesia de San Miguel** is yet another *Reconquista* church founded in the thirteenth century by Fernando III, with a magnificent rose window above the early Gothic entrance. Built on the foundations of a former mosque (one of the original horseshoe-arched entrances to this survives) the triple-naved interior has some elegant vaulting and a Baroque *retablo* in pink marble. Tucked behind the church lies one of Córdoba's most atmospheric taverns, the **Taberna San Miguel** (see p.388).

ARRIVAL AND DEPARTURE   CÓRDOBA

By train Córdoba's impressive train station (☎902 240 202) is on Plaza de las Tres Culturas, off Avda. de America to the northwest of the old town. To reach the centre, pick up Avda. de los Mozárabes, then veer east onto the broad Avda. del Gran Capitán which will lead you to the old town and the Mezquita, 15min to the south. Bus #3 from outside the bus station will take you to the focal Plaza Tendillas and C/de San Fernando on the old quarter's eastern flank.
Destinations Algeciras (2 daily; 3hr 12min); Granada (2 daily; 2hr 20min); Jaén (4 daily; 1hr 40min); Málaga (AVE 11 daily; 50min); Ronda (2 daily; 1hr 48min); Seville (3 daily; 1hr 20min; AVE 13 daily; 45min).
By bus The bus station (☎957 404 040) is in the same complex as the train station. Each bus company has its own *ventanilla* (sales window).

Destinations Algeciras (1 daily; 6hr 45min); Almería (1 daily; 5hr 30min); Cádiz (2 daily; 4hr); Écija (6 daily; 55min); Granada (8 daily; 2hr 30min); Jaén (8 Mon–Fri, 5 on Sat, 4 on Sun; 1hr 45min); Málaga (4 daily; 3hr); Seville (7 daily; 4hr).
By car Arriving by car can be a pain, especially during rush hour in the narrow streets around the Mezquita. Parking is also a major headache, so the best solution is to park your vehicle for the duration of your stay in a hotel garage or (stripped of any valuables) on a street out of the centre and get around the city on foot, which is both easy and enjoyable. On-street parking spaces are often to be found on Avda. de la República Argentina on the western edge of the old quarter and across the river in the streets either side of the *Hotel Hesperia* (see p.385).

INFORMATION

Turismo Palacio de Congresos y Exposiciones, C/Torrijos 10 (Mon–Fri 9am–7.30pm, Sat & Sun 9.30am–3pm; ☎957 355 179). The city's main tourist office faces the Mezquita's west wall, and has a detailed town plan.

Tourist kiosks Turismo Consorcio, Córdoba's municipal tourist office (☎957 201 774, ⓦturismodecordoba.org) has joined forces with a private company to provide information from three *kioskos*; one in the Plaza Campo de los Mártires almost facing the Alcázar (daily 9am–2pm & 5–7.30pm); another in the Plaza de las Tendillas (daily 10am–1.30pm & 5.30–8pm); and the third on the main concourse of the train station (daily 9.30am–2pm & 5–7.30pm). All keep copies of the monthly *Welcome y Olé*, a free bilingual listings magazine detailing the main events, and hand out useful guide maps.

Monument opening hours Córdoba changes its monument opening hours more than any other town in Andalucía; check in advance with with any tourist office.

Hiking maps 1:50,000, 1:100,000 and 1:200,000 maps are available from CNIG branch office (National Geographic Service; ☎957 989 268), Plaza de la Constitución 1, west of the Judería.

Newspapers Córdoba's daily paper, *El Diario Córdoba* (ⓦdiariocordoba.com), is good for local and provincial news, events and entertainment.

Internet Most hotels and many *hostales* now have wi-fi (in the room or a zone). Central internet cafés include Ch@t (Mon–Sat 10am–2pm & 5–9.30pm), C/Claudio Marcelo 15, near Plaza Tendillas, and *Hostal El Pilar del Potro* (daily 10am–1pm & 5–10pm), C/Lucano 12.

Online information ⓦayuncordoba.es, ⓦinfocordoba .com and ⓦturiscordoba.es.

City guided walks Turismo Consorcio offers guided walks around the old city (Paseos por Córdoba; English spoken; 9.30pm; 2hr; €16); they start from the Plaza de las Tendillas office and end up at a typical *cordobés* tavern.

ACCOMMODATION

Places to stay can be found all over Córdoba, but the majority are concentrated in the narrow maze of streets around the Mezquita. If you can resist the urge to lodge on the Mezquita's doorstep, a five minute walk in any direction leads to some real bargains. Finding a room at any time of the year – except during **Semana Santa** and the **May festivals** (the city's high season, and the rates we quote here) – isn't usually a problem. Upmarket places often drop their prices considerably in July and August, so its always worth checking their websites for offers. Where listings below have a garage, unless otherwise stated you will be charged a daily rate for parking (around €15–20).

AC Córdoba Palacio Jardines de la Victoria s/n ☎957 298 066, ⓦac-hotels.com. A controversial "rusting skin" metal facade has been applied to Cordoba's oldest luxury hotel (now part of the AC chain) and an internal refurb has added plenty of five-star frills. There's a pool, restaurant, wi-fi and you're a minutes' walk from the Judería. Garage. **€150**

Casa de los Azulejos C/Fernando Colón 5 ☎957 470 000, ⓦcasadelosazulejos.com. Charming small hotel with distinctive, individually styled rooms, featuring iron bedsteads and artworks, arranged around a leafy patio that's used for art shows. More expensive rooms come with their own terraces. Free wi-fi and can arrange garage parking. **€120**

Casa de los Naranjos C/Isabel Losa 8 ☎957 470 587, ⓦcasadelosnaranjos.com. In the north of the town near the Plaza de Colón, this is a small two-star hotel in a nineteenth-century town house with lots of charm and rooms overlooking a leafy patio. Free wi-fi and can help with parking. B&B **€85**

Fonda Agustina C/Zapatería Vieja 5 ☎957 470 872. Charming, spotless little *fonda* in a tranquil location, with basic rooms sharing bath. **€40**

Hospedería de Churrasco C/Romero 38 ☎957 294 808, ⓦelchurrasco.com. Elegant, welcoming nine-room hotel in the Judería belonging to the restaurant of the same name. Entry is through a double patio and chintzy rooms are classically furnished; some have sit-out terraces.

Facilities include minibar, computer with internet in all rooms (free) and rooftop terrace/solarium. Own garage. B&B **€173**

★ **Hostal & Hotel Maestre** C/Romero Barros 4 & 16 ☎957 475 395 (hostal), ☎957 472 410 (hotel), ⓦhotel maestre.com. Friendly *hostal* with fine patio and attractive en-suite rooms (room 22 has its own terrace); rooms both here and at the nearby hotel (which are slightly larger) have a/c and TV. They also let a number of nearby apartments. *Rough Guide* readers with this guide get free underground parking (except April–May). *Hostal* **€45**, hotel **€55**, apartments **€66**

★ **Hostal Alcázar** C/San Basilio 2 ☎957 202 561, ⓦhostalalcazar.com. Comfortable and welcoming family-run *hostal* with a nice patio and range of a/c rooms (most en suite) with TV. Also some good-value fully equipped apartments opposite (sleeping up to four; minimum stay two nights). Wi-fi zone and own garage nearby (€6). B&B **€45**, apartments **€80**

Hostal Almanzor C/Corregidor Luís de la Cerda (aka Cardenal González) 10 ☎957 485 400, ⓦhostal -almanzor.es. Attractive central *hostal* where sound-proofed en-suite rooms come with TV and a/c. Free use of their car park. **€60**

Hostal El Portillo C/Cabezas 2 ☎957 472 091, ⓦhostalelportillo.com. Beautiful old *hostal* in an early nineteeth-century mansion with elegant tiled patio and friendly management. Recently refurbished rooms – many with balconies – come with showers and include a few singles. Wi-fi zone. **€45**

Hostal El Triunfo C/Corregidor Luís de la Cerda (aka Cardenal González) 79 ☎957 498 484, ⓦhostaltriunfo.com. Traditional hotel-style *hostal* on the Mezquita's east face. Some of the pleasant rooms at the front have a Mezquita view; attic rooms share a rooftop terrace with stunning views over the river and Mezquita. Rooms come with safe and free wi-fi and there's a decent bar and restaurant below. Garage. **€120**

Hostal La Fuente C/San Fernando 51 ☎957 481 478, ⓦhostallafuente.com. Welcoming *hostal* in a refurbished town house with a delightful patio and pristine en-suite rooms with strongbox, TV and a/c. Also rents out some nearby apartments for two. Wi-fi zone and parking nearby. Rooms **€55**, apartments **€85**

Hostal La Milagrosa C/Rey Heredia 12 ☎957 473 317, ⓦlamilagrosahostal.es. Attractive and welcoming *hostal* with a beautiful patio and lots of plants, plus clean and attractive marble-floored en-suite a/c rooms. Own garage. **€50**

Hostal Lineros 38 C/Lineros 38 ☎957 482 517, ⓦhostallineros38.com. This Moorish extravaganza of a *hostal* has been lovingly created by its friendly proprietors inside an ancient Mudéjar mansion. The comfortable rooms continue the theme and furnishings and fittings are all Moorish-inspired with arabesques and horseshoe arches everywhere. Some single rooms. Own parking (€10). **€58**

Hostal Luís de Góngora C/Horno de la Trinidad 7 ☎957 295 399, ⓦhospederialuisdegongora.com. Attractive a/c en-suite rooms in a friendly *hostal* in a pleasant location on the northern edge of the Judería. A couple of rooms are dark and gloomy so check what you're offered. **€70**

Hostal Osio C/Osio 6 ☎957 485 165, ⓦhostalosio.com. Charming *hostal* in a refurbished mansion with two fine patios (one a listed monument) and attractive a/c en-suite rooms. The friendly proprietors speak English. Free wi-fi and can arrange parking. **€50**

Hostal Plaza Correredra C/Rodríguez Marín 15 ☎957 470 581, ⓦhostallacorredera.com. This refurbished *pensión* on the wonderful old Plaza Correredra has spacious beamed rooms sharing bath and some with great views over the plaza. There are some singles, plus a roof terrace above and a bar below for breakfast. Wi-fi zone and own car park. **€47**

Hostal Santa Ana C/Corregidor Luís de la Cerda (aka Cardenal González) 25 ☎957 485 837, ⓦhostalsantaana.com. Good upmarket *hostal* with a nice roof terrace and a/c en-suite rooms with TV. Free wi-fi and own garage. **€60**

★ **Hostal Séneca** C/Conde y Luque 7 ☎957 473 234, ⓦsensesandcolours.com Delightful *hostal* in ancient house with a stunning patio complete with original Moorish pavement. Rooms with and without bath, and some singles. In summer you'll need to book ahead. **€80** with breakfast.

Hotel Albucasis C/Buen Pastor 11 ☎957 478 625, ⓦhotelalbucasis.com. Charming small hotel with ivy-clad courtyard, spotless en-suite marble-floored bedrooms with a/c and TV plus breakfast bar. Garage. **€85**

Hotel Amistad Córdoba Plaza de Maimónides 3 ☎957 420 335, ⓦnh-hoteles.com. Four-star hotel (now part of the *NH* chain) incorporating two eighteenth-century mansions with Mudéjar patio and staircase. Internet access and car park available. **€139**

Hotel González C/Manríquez 3 ☎957 479 819, ⓦhotel-gonzalez.com. Converted sixteenth-century *casa palacio* in the heart of La Judería with comfortable, spacious rooms overlooking a brilliant white-walled, geranium-filled patio. **€99**

Hotel Hesperia Córdoba Avda. Fray Albino 1 ☎957 421 042, ⓦhoteles-hesperia.es. Luxurious four-star with great views across the river towards the Mezquita and city from rooms at the front. Facilities include restaurant, *cafetería*, pool and rooftop bar (with the same view) and there's easy access to the town across the pedestrianized Puente Romano. Frequent special offers. Own garage or easy street parking nearby. Free wi-fi. **€250**

Hotel Las Casas de la Judería C/Tomás Conde 10 ☎957 202 095, ⓦcasasypalacios.com. Córdoba's latest five-star hotel is under the same proprietors as the similarly named hotel in Seville. This also is an exquisitely charming restoration of an ancient *casa palacio* with elegant rooms arranged around patios with tinkling fountains and fragrant flowers. Rooms are decorated with period furnishings and artworks and come with satellite TV and all the five-star frills. Spa, restaurant and garage. **€315**

Hotel Los Omeyas C/Encarnación 17 ☎957 492 267, ⓦhotel-losomeyas.com. Attractive and airy hotel built around a nice marble floored patio; well-equipped rooms come with a/c, TV, wall safe and free wi-fi. Garage. **€95**

Hotel Marisa C/Cardenal Herrero 6 ☎957 473 142, ⓦhotelmarisacordoba.es. You won't get closer to the Mezquita than this. Rather plain hotel where functional rooms come with a/c (but not TV). Garage. **€85**

Hotel Mezquita Plaza Santa Catalina 1 ☎957 475 585, ⓦhotelmezquita.com. Atmospheric, central hotel in a converted sixteenth-century mansion facing the Mezquita's eastern wall. Attractive rooms equipped with satellite TV. Wi-fi zone. **€105**

★ **Hotel Plateros** Plaza Seneca 4 ☎957 496 785, ⓦhotelplateros.com. Small, friendly hotel belonging to the *Plateros* chain of tapas bars and housed in an elegant refurbished old mansion on a charming plazuela. Pleasant a/c rooms have internet access and there's a wi-fi zone. The *Plateros* tapas bar below incorporates the ancient house's bodega (where the proprietor still makes his own wine) whose walls were once part of the ancient Roman theatre. The hotel encourages cyclists and can store bikes. **€80**

Parador Nacional Arruzafa Avda. de la Arruzafa s/n, 5km north of town in El Brillante suburb ☎957 275 900, ⓦparador.es. Attractive, modern *parador* with elegant, spacious rooms. Features include pool, tennis courts, shooting range and views over the city. Worth a trip for a drink in its gardens or a good-value meal (lunch *menú* €23.50, dinner €32) in its terrace restaurant. **€156**

Pensión Los Arcos C/Romero Barros 14 ☎957 485 643, ⓦpensionlosarcos.com. Simple rooms (some en suite) with fans in a quiet street behind the Plaza del Potro; it's a charming place, with a great plant-filled patio. Free wi-fi and can arrange parking. **€39**

YOUTH HOSTEL

★ **Albergue Juvenil** Plaza Judá Leví s/n ☎957 355 040, centralized bookings ☎902 510 000, ⓦinturjoven .com. There are 81 double, triple and four-person rooms with en-suite bath/shower at this modern, relaxed and superbly located hostel. You'll need to book ahead at busy periods. Wi-fi throughout. Under 26 **€21**, over 26 **€27**

CAMPSITE

Campamento Municipal El Brillante Avda. Brillante s/n, 2km north on the road to Villaviciosa ☎957 403 836. Good site with pool, reached by bus #10 or #11 from the station. Open all year. **€7** per person, **€5** tent, **€5** vehicle

EATING AND DRINKING

If you have come from Seville or the coast, the **nightlife** in Córdoba will seem rather tame by comparison. Places start closing at around 11pm, and by midnight the empty streets around the Mezquita, lit by lanterns, have a melancholy air. When they are open, however, many of the city's bars and restaurants are among the best in Andalucía.

RESTAURANTS

Córdoba's restaurants are on the whole reasonably priced – and quite a few of the upmarket establishments are really excellent. Be sure to try Córdoba's two specialities, *rabo de toro* (slow-stewed bull's tail) and *salmorejo* (a chunky gazpacho with pieces of ham and egg), available all over town.

Albergue Juvenil Plaza Judá Leví s/n ☎957 035 886, ⓦinturjoven.com. The youth hostel's cafetería (open to all) has some of the cheapest food in town with three-course lunch and dinner *menús* for a bargain €8. Daily 2–3pm & 8.30–9.30pm.

Almudaina Plaza Campo Santo de los Mártires 1 ☎957 474 342, ⓦrestaurantealmudaina.com. Top-notch restaurant with four stylish rooms in an atmospheric sixteenth-century mansion facing the walls of the Alcázar. Among many fine dishes *rabo de toro a la cordabesa* is a house special. It's expensive (main dishes €15–24), but there's a *menú* for about €25. Mon–Sat 12.30–4pm & 8.30pm–midnight, Sun 12.30–4pm.

★ **Amaltea** C/Ronda de Isasa 10 ☎957 491 968. Excellent organic restaurant with lots of veggie options where specialities include couscous and *carpaccio de cecina* (described as cured ham made with beef). There are plenty of organic wines and a few special beers, and occasional art exhibitions. Main dishes €8–12. Tues–Sun 12.30–4pm & 8.30pm–midnight.

Bar-Restaurante Federación de Peñas C/Conde y Luque 8. Moorish-style patio dining room offering a variety of economical *menús* featuring meat and fish dishes. Thurs–Tues 12.30–4pm & 7.30–11pm.

Café Gloria C/Claudio Marcelo 15. Attractive café-diner done out in Art Deco style with big windows onto the street; offers economical *platos combinados* and a variety of menús starting at around €8. Daily 7.30am–midnight.

Casa Mazal C/Tomás Conde 3 ☎957 941 888, ⓦcasa mazal.com. New *sefardí* restaurant and cultural centre with a cuisine based on the Sephardic dishes of Spanish Jews. The wide-ranging seasonal menu features at least a dozen vegetarian dishes. Recommended include *atún a lo Hebrea* (tuna Hebrew-style) and *pollo a la miel* (chicken with honey). Musical events are staged at weekends. Main dishes €9–16. Daily noon–4pm & 8–11.30pm.

★ **Círculo Taurino** C/Manuel María de Arjona 1 ☎957 715 256. In the modern town, this is an excellent, mid-priced, family establishment offering a wide range of local dishes and a place where *cordobéses* come to eat. There's an elegant dining room at the rear and a tapas and *raciones* bar out front. As you'd expect with its bullfighting connections, the *rabo de toro* is outstanding. Main dishes €9–20 with very reasonable wine prices. Mon–Sat noon–6pm & 8pm–12.30am.

El Buey y El Fuego C/Benito Pérez Galdós 1 ☎957 491 012. Excellent new restaurant serving traditional dishes using top-quality ingredients. The speciality of the house is *carne a la brasa* (grilled meat) and the signature *buey asado en horno de leña* (grilled ox) is recommended. They also offer a *menú ejecutivo* (Mon–Fri €23), and *menú de degustacion* (€40). Main dishes €15–30. Mon–Sat 1–5pm & 7.30pm–midnight.

El Caballo Rojo C/Cardenal Herrero 28 ☎957 475 375, ⓦelcaballorojo.com. Beneath the Mezquita's belfry, this is one of Córdoba's choicest restaurants, despite its café-style interior. The Moorish-influenced menu offers such specialities as *cordero a la miel* (lamb in honey) and tasty desserts like *canutillo de almendra* (almond pastry). Expensive (main dishes €13–23) but offers a *menú de degustación* for around €40. Daily 1–4.30pm & 8–11.30pm.

El Choto C/Almanzor 10 ☎957 760 115. Attractive small restaurant offering well-prepared fish and meat dishes including its signature dish *choto asado* (roast kid). Comfortable – if slightly formal – dining room plus a small terrace at the entrance (which you will need to book for). There's a four-course *menú de degustación* (Tues–Fri) for €35 including wine and a *menú de la casa* for around €22. Main dishes €15–25. Tues–Sat 1–5pm & 7.30pm–midnight, Sun 1–5pm.

★ **El Churrasco** C/Romero 16 (not C/Romero Barros) ☎957 290 819, ⍟elchurrasco.com. One of the best of Córdoba's top restaurants, with sumptuously decorated dining rooms and patio in a traditional *cordobés* townhouse. It has a long-standing reputation for its *churrasco ibérico* (a kind of grilled black-pig pork steak, served with pepper sauces). Prices match its reputation (main dishes €15–25), although there's an interesting set *menú* at €32. Daily 1–4pm & 8pm–midnight. Closed Aug.

El Rincón del Carmen C/Romero 4. Small, pleasant café-restaurant, with a charming patio terrace below and restaurant upstairs, serving reasonably priced *raciones* and *media raciones* of fish and meat, along with salads and a €15 *menú*. Daily 10am–midnight.

Los Mochuelos C/Agustín Moreno 51. Traditional tapas and *raciones* restaurant with large variety of dishes including *mochuelitos* (spicy meat); plenty of atmosphere, stacked butts, bullfight posters and a pleasant patio. Daily 8.30am–4.30pm & 7pm–midnight.

Mesón San Basilio C/San Basilio 19. Excellent little neighbourhood restaurant with a nice patio, friendly service and *menús* at €12 (weekday lunch) and €18 (evenings and weekends). House specials include *presa ibérica* (pork steak) and *berenjenas fritas* (fried aubergine). Mon–Sat 1–4pm & 8–11.30pm, Sun 1–4pm.

Marisquería El Faro C/Ricardo de Montís 1. Small upmarket restaurant with good seafood *raciones* and *menús* for €8.50 and €12.50 (Mon–Fri) and a decent paella (€20 for two). Daily 1–4pm & 9pm–midnight.

Salón de Té C/Buen Pastor 13 ☎957 487 984, ⍟lacasaandalusi.com. To the northwest of the Mezquita's belfry is this very attractive Moroccan tea salon with a charming patio offering over fifty varieties, including a special *hierba buena* (mint tea), as well as snacks. Daily 11am–11pm.

TABERNAS AND TAPAS BARS

The *cordobeses* are proud of their **tabernas** – and with good reason, for few places anywhere can match them for sheer character and variety, not to mention tapas. Remember, too, when ordering fino that the equivalent brew here is **Montilla** and the best way to get up a barman's nose is to ask for any of the wines of Jerez, the product of the upstart province downriver. If you're new to Montilla-Moriles, to give it its full title, or have been unimpressed with the insipid concoctions sold abroad under the Montilla name, prepare for a pleasant surprise. Montilla, which vaguely resembles a mellow, dry

sherry, is a giant on its native soil, and is considered a healthier tipple by the *cordobeses*; whereas Jerez sherry is fortified with alcohol, here the process is totally natural, leading (they insist) to fewer hangovers (see p.396).

AROUND THE MEZQUITA AND JUDERÍA

Bar Caballo Rojo C/Cardenal Herrero 28 ☎957 475 375, ⍟elcaballorojo.com. The smoothly efficient – and slightly pricey – bar of the famous restaurant has excellent tapas and *raciones* including *boquerones en vinagre* (anchovies in vinegar). Daily 1–4.30pm & 8–11.30pm.

Bar La Cavea Plaza Jerónimo Páez, near the archeological museum. Pleasant little bar with nice terrace where you can knock back a *jarrón* of beer with meat and fish tapas and *raciones*. Also *platos combinados*. Tues–Sun 9am–4.30pm & 8pm–midnight.

Bar-Mesón Rafaé C/Deanes 2. North of the Mezquita in the Judería, this appealing old bar offers a broad tapas range, well-kept Montilla and a reasonably priced *menú*. Daily noon–4pm & 7–11pm.

★ **Bodega Guzmán** C/Judíos 7. Cavernous old bar frequented by bullfight aficionados, with a small *taurino* "museum" in its inner sanctum and outstanding Montilla served from a butt behind the bar. A very tasty *salmorejo* plus *albondigas* (pork meatballs) are house specials here. Fri–Wed 11.30am–4pm & 8.30–11.30pm.

Casa Bravo Puerta de Almodóvar s/n. This atmospheric tiled bar has outdoor *botas* (barrels) for tables where you can eat tapas and *raciones*. Try their *berenjenas fritas a la miel* (fried aubergine with honey). Mon–Sat 11.30am–4pm & 8pm–midnight, Sun 11.30am–4pm.

El Olivo Avda. Dr Fleming 25, close to the Plaza Maimónides. Inviting little bar-restaurant with a very agreeable evening terrace which is just the place for enjoying a few tapas or *raciones* (*jamón* is a speciality).

AROUND THE PLAZA DEL POTRO

★ **Bodega Sociedad de Plateros** C/San Francisco 6. Headquarters of the *Plateros* chain, and in a converted former convent. What started in 1868 as a mutual benefit society for Córdoba's silversmiths eventually branched out into the bodega business, presently owning three excellent bars around the city. This bar – over a century old and serving a wide range of tapas – is light and airy with a glass-covered patio with hanging plants and *azulejos*. Try their *rabo de toro* or tasty *croquetas de bacalao* (cod croquettes), perfect partners for any of their own brands of Montilla. Mon–Sat 8am–4pm & 8pm–midnight.

Bodegas Campos C/Lineros 32 ☎957 497 500, ⍟bodegascampos.org. A wonderful, rambling old bodega where you can see the cellars – stacked with giant oak *botas* (barrels) – in which the company matures its wine. As is the tradition in the sherry and Montilla worlds, many of the vats are signed by famous visitors – big names here include the members of the Spanish royal family and ex-British premier Tony Blair. The bar at the entrance sells their own excellent Montilla, where there are also excellent (if pricey) tapas. There's an expensive, highly rated – and rather stuffy – restaurant behind. Daily 1–4pm & 8.30–11.30pm.

Taberna El Potro C/Lineros 2, near the Plaza del Potro. Despite being in the tourist zone and somewhat over-adorned with reproductions of Julio Romero de Torres's (an ex-customer) "art works" it has a solid reputation for its tapas; try the *salmorejo* or *flamenquines* (stuffed rolls of ham). Also offers a variety of economical *menús* and has a pleasant outdoor terrace. Tues–Sun 8.30am–1am.

AROUND AND NORTH OF PLAZA TENDILLAS

Bar Gaudí Avda. Gran Capitán 22 ☎ 957 471 736 ⓦ cafegaudi.net. Named after the great architect and aptly decorated in wonderful Art Nouveau style, this place serves excellent tapas (try their *bonito en escabeche* – marinated tuna) and a range of European beers. Daily 8am–midnight.

Casa Paco Acedo Beneath the Torre de Malmuerta C/Adarve 28. Fine old bar serving up a superb range of tapas, including *salmorejo* and all kinds of fried fish. The house speciality is a memorable *rabo de toro*, the perfect complement to the house Montilla, and best eaten at the tables outside. Daily noon–4pm & 8.30pm–midnight.

Taberna Góngora C/Torres Cabrera 4. Welcoming modern bar carrying on the tapas tradition and much favoured by *tapeadores*. Specials include *berenjenas fritas* (fried aubergine), *carne de monte* (cured meats) and *boquerones al limón* (anchovies with lemon). Daily 12.30–4pm & 7–11.30pm.

★ **Taberna San Miguel** Plaza San Miguel 1 ☎ 957 470 166, ⓦ casaelpisto.com. Known to all as *El Pisto* (the barrel) and virtually unchanged for over a century, this is one of the city's legendary bars and not to be missed. Wonderful Montilla and tapas; *rabo de toro* and *callos en salsa picante* (tripe in a spicy sauce) are big favourites, as is the house *pisto* (type of ratatouille). Mon–Sat noon–4pm & 8.30pm–12.30am. Closed Aug.

Taberna Seneca Plaza Seneca 4 ☎ 957 496 785, ⓦ hotelplateros.com. In the same building as the *Hotel Plateros* (see p.385) this is another bar in the *Plateros* chain with the same great tapas and Montilla. House specials include *puntas de solomillo* (pork loin) and *patatas bravas* (potatoes in spicy sauce). Mon–Sat 1–3.30pm & 8.30–11.30pm, Sun 1–3.30pm.

AROUND PLAZA CORREDERA AND BEYOND

Bar Regina Plaza de Regina. Century-old bar with plenty of bullfight memorabilia, a nice patio and good tapas, including their noted *salmorejo* and *patatas bravas*. Mon–Sat 9am–4pm & 8pm–midnight.

Casa El Juramento C/Juramento 6. Atmospheric old bar with a charming patio and a good tapas selection. House specials include *croquetas de espinacas* (spinach croquettes) and *pimientos rellenos* (stuffed peppers) the favourite *tapa* of artist Julio Romero de Torres who was a regular. Wed–Fri, Sun & Mon 1.15–4pm & 9.15–11.30pm, Sat 1.15–4pm.

Casa La Paloma Plaza Corredera 5. A good, economical bar on this atmospheric enclosed square, serving vegetarian dishes, *raciones* and *media raciones*, soups and fish. House specials include *japuta en adobo* (marinated fish) and *carillada ibérica* (pork cheeks). Tues–Sun 9am–4pm & 8pm–midnight.

★ **El Gallo** C/María Cristina 6. Fine old *cordobés* drinking hole which has changed little since it opened in 1936. Good

---

FLAMENCO IN CÓRDOBA

As in many of Córdoba's provincial capitals, plenty of **flamenco** is on offer – but much of it is dire and tourist oriented. The places below can be depended upon for some reasonably authentic stuff. Free flamenco performances are also mounted by the local council in summer and various other concerts are staged at the Gran Teatro, Avda. Gran Capitán 3, and in the Alcázar gardens (details from the Turismos).

La Bulería C/Pedro López 3, near Plaza de la Corredera ☎ 957 483 839, ⓦ flamencolabuleria.com. Nightly flamenco performances with *cantante* El Calli and his family forming the core of the show. They are serious and it gets near enough to the real thing, although corners are sometimes cut when trade is slack. Food also served. Performances daily 10.30pm; €12, includes a free drink.

La Pataito de Antonio C/Barroso 3 ☎ 957 491 544. This bar-restaurant stages reasonably authentic flamenco. The early show (without music) is flamenco song only, while the later shows comprise flamenco song and dance. Fri & Sat; first performance 4–6pm, free with the price of a drink; second performance 10pm; €12.

Tablao Cardenal C/Torrijos 10, next door to the Turismo ☎ 957 483 320, ⓦ tablaocardenal.com. Córdoba's best non-membership flamenco *tablao*, where you can catch performances by established artists in a pleasant open-air patio. It's worth ringing in advance to reserve a frontline table. Mon–Sat 10.30pm; €20, includes first drink.

tapas selection includes *calamares*, *bacalao* (cod), *croquetas* and *gambas rebozadas* (fried prawns). The outstanding *amargoso* Montilla comes from their own bodega and is also sold by the bottle. There's a street terrace. Daily 1–5pm & 7pm–1am.

Sociedad Plateros C/María Auxiliadora 25 ☎ 957 470 304, ⓦ sociedadplateros.com. Aficionados of the *Plateros* chain will enjoy this cavernous old mini-Mezquita serving up excellent *raciones* and *medias*. Some way from the centre, it's definitely worth the walk. House specials include *venado en salsa* (venison), and *bacalao al pil-pil* (cod in garlic). Daily noon–midnight.

★ **Taberna Salinas** C/Tundidores 3 ☎ 957 480 135, ⓦ www.tabernasalinas.com. Century-old *taberna* with dining rooms around a charming patio and an outstanding range of tapas and *raciones*; try their delicious *bacalao con naranja* (cod with orange and olive oil), *setas en salsa* (mushrooms), *rabo de toro* or *cochifrito* (fried lamb). Mon–Sat 12.30–4pm & 8–11.30pm. Closed Aug.

SHOPPING

Córdoba is known for **silver** jewellery and embossed **leather** goods, both on offer at many workshops in the streets around the Mezquita.

Almacen Rafael C/Dr Barraquer 5, to the northeast of the Alcázar ☎ 957 203 183. A well-stocked bodega selling most of Córdoba's Montilla wines. Mon–Sat 9am–1.30pm & 5–9pm.

Beta C/Córdoba de Veracruz 2, 100m west of the El Corte Inglés department store ☎ 957 497 515, ⓦ www .libreriasbeta.com. One of the town's biggest and best bookstores. Mon–Fri 10am–2pm & 5.30–9pm, Sat 10am–2pm.

El Corte Inglés Avda. del Gran Capitán, at the junction with Avda. Ronda de los Tejares ☎ 957 481 506, ⓦ elcorteingles.es. Córdoba's branch of the nationally famous department store. Mon–Sat 10am–10pm.

Espaliu C/Corregidor Luis de la Cerda 3 ☎ 957 491 790. Stylish silver jewellery on sale near the Mezquita; they fabricate their own designs. Mon–Sat 10am–2pm & 5–9pm.

Librería Luque C/Jesús y María 6 (slightly south of Plaza Tendillas) ☎ 957 498 046, ⓦ librerialuque.es. A good selection of books and walking maps. Mon–Fri 9.45am–1.45pm & 5.15–8.30pm, Sat 10am–1.30pm.

Meryan Callejón de las Flores 2 ☎ 957 475 902, ⓦ meryancor.com. A wide selection of leather goods. Mon–Sat 9am–8pm.

Sombrería Rusi C/Conde de Cardenas 1, near the Roman temple ☎ 957 479 446. A remarkable hat shop, founded in 1903 and still making hats by hand on site. They stock a wide range of headwear including the flat-topped *cordobés* style worn by men at fiesta times. Mon–Fri 10am–2pm & 5.30–9pm, Sat 10am–2pm.

Zoco (market) C/de los Judíos close to the synagogue. A particularly good place to find Córdoba's filigree silver jewellery. Mon–Sat 10am–10pm.

DIRECTORY

Banks Numerous banks with ATMs are located along Ronda de los Tejares and Avda. del Gran Capitán. In the Judería there are ATMs in C/Magistral González Francés near the Mezquita and along C/Judería, off its northwest corner.
Hospital Hospital Reina Sofía, Avda. Menéndez Pidal s/n (☎ 957 010 000), southwest of the centre. Cruz Roja, Avda. del Dr Fleming s/n (☎ 957 420 666); for emergencies dial ☎ 061.
Laundry Seco y Agua, C/Dr Marañon 3, slightly northwest of the Alcázar (Mon–Fri 9.30am–1.30pm & 5.30–8.30pm, Sat 9.30am–1.30pm), is an efficient *tintorería* who will wash, dry and fold 5kg of clothes the same day for around €17.
Police A local police station is located in Plaza Judá Levi, near the Mezquita (☎ 957 290 760). For emergencies dial ☎ 092 (local police), ☎ 091 (national).
Post office The main office is at C/Cruz Conde 15, just north of Plaza Tendillas (Mon–Fri 8.30am–8.30pm; Sat 9am–2pm).

West of Córdoba

Just a few kilometres from the city is the historic site of **Medina Azahara**, a must for those on the Moorish trail, and with a fascinating eighteenth-century hermitage nearby. As you continue west along the southern fringes of the Sierra Morena, following the course of the Rio Guadalquivir, you will come to **Almodóvar del Río**, which has a remarkable castle, and can stop off at a string of charming rural towns. This area also features Córdoba province's largest natural park, the **Parque Natural de la Sierra de Hornachuelos**, a wonderful spot for birdwatching.

Medina Azahara

Some 7km to the west of Córdoba lie the vast and rambling ruins of **Medina Azahara**, a palace and administrative complex built on a dream scale by **Caliph Abd ar-Rahman III**. Naming it after a favourite wife, az-Zahra (the Radiant), he spent one-third of the annual state budget on its construction each year from 936 until his death in 961. Since the first archeological excavations were carried out in 1911, work has been going on more or less continuously to piece together the fragments of this once fabulous creation, which is the reason it is currently only possible to visit a fraction of the excavated site. In 2011 archeologists released a report that stated that they had so far excavated a mere ten percent of the site and only five percent is currently open to the public. Note also that the same archeological and restoration work is ongoing and the route described below may have to be altered to allow for this.

Dar al–Wuzara and Plaza de Armas

The **site** is entered by the **Puerta Norte**, the typically Moorish "twisted gate" which forced would-be invaders to double back on themselves, thus making them easy targets. Behind you at this point lies the Dar al-Mulk or royal palace (currently not open to visitors) which is thought to have been the residence of Abd ar-Rahman III. The signed route leads to **Dar al-Wuzara** (House of the Viziers, aka Edificio Basilical), believed to have been the bureaucratic heart of the complex with administrative rooms, archives and a grand salon (with reconstructed horseshoe arches), originally fronted by a patio, now a garden. To the east of here, the route leads to the elegant arched **portico** and the **Plaza de Armas** – formerly a grand parade ground – beyond, still awaiting excavation. The portico is thought to have supported a balcony terrace from where the caliph reviewed his troops. Turning south, you can see the **Aljama mosque** below, one of the first buildings to be constructed on the site, oriented towards the southeast and Mecca. Its ground plan allows you to make out the main entrance, flanked by the base of a minaret (*alminar*), with patio, prayer hall – the floor of which was covered with esparto mats found in the excavations – and *mihrab*. The route now veers west passing the princely baths to the right, with washing fountains and marble surfaces, beyond which lay the royal apartments.

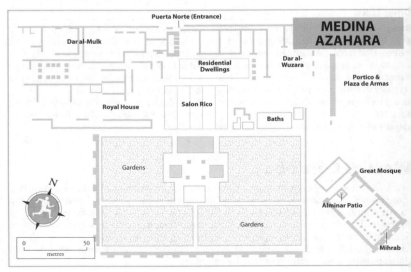

MEDINA AZAHARA

Puerta Norte (Entrance)

Dar al-Mulk

Residential Dwellings

Dar al-Wuzara

Portico & Plaza de Armas

Royal House

Salon Rico

Baths

Gardens

Great Mosque

Gardens

Alminar Patio

Mihrab

N

0   50
metres

THE RISE AND FALL OF MEDINA AZAHARA

Ten thousand workers and 1500 mules and camels were employed in the construction of **Medina Azahara** in the early tenth century, and the site, almost 2000m long by 900m wide, stretched over three descending terraces above the Guadalquivir valley. Roman masonry was taken from sites throughout Andalucía and reused, while vast quantities of marble were shipped in from North Africa. In addition to the palace buildings, the complex contained a zoo, an aviary, four huge fish ponds, three hundred baths, four hundred houses, weapons factories, two barracks for the royal guard as well as numerous baths, markets, workshops and mosques. Visitors, so the chronicles record, were stunned by its wealth and brilliance: one conference room contained a pile of pure crystals, creating a rainbow when lit by the sun; another was built round a huge shallow bowl of mercury which, when the sun's rays fell on it, would be rocked by a slave, sending sunbeams reflected from its surface flashing and whizzing around the room, apparently alarming guests but greatly amusing the caliph.

Medina Azahara was a perfect symbol of the western caliphate's dominance and greatness, but it was to last for less than a century. Al-Hakam II, who succeeded Abd ar-Rahman, lived in the palace, continued to endow it, and enjoyed a stable reign. However, distanced from the city, he delegated more and more authority, particularly to his vizier Ibn Abi Amir, later known as al-Mansur (the Victor). In 976 al-Hakam was succeeded by his eleven-year-old son Hisham II but after a series of sharp moves al-Mansur assumed the full powers of government, keeping Hisham virtually imprisoned at Medina Azahara, to the extent of blocking up connecting passageways between the palace buildings.

Al-Mansur was equally skilful and manipulative in his wider dealings as a dictator, and Córdoba rose to new heights of prosperity, retaking large tracts of central Spain and raiding as far afield as Galicia and Catalunya. But with his death in 1002 came swift decline as his role and function were assumed in turn by his two sons. The first died in 1008; the second, Sanchol, showed open disrespect for the caliphate by forcing Hisham to appoint him as his successor. At this a popular revolt broke out and the caliphate disintegrated into civil war and a series of feudal kingdoms. Medina Azahara was looted by a mob at the outset and in 1010 was plundered and burned by retreating Berber mercenaries – splashes of molten metal from this conflagration are still to be seen in the Salon Rico. The ruins slowly disappeared under the earth until archeologists arrived at the site in the early twentieth century. But it was never secure and as late as the 1930s a visiting Gerald Brenan saw stones being carted off to service other buildings. In the 1960s academic study, excavation and reconstruction of the complex began in earnest, and this is set to continue for many decades to come.

Royal House

For centuries, the site was looted for building materials; parts, for instance, were used in the Seville Alcázar and much of the surrounding town served as a quarry for the fifteenth-century construction of the monastery of San Jerónimo (now privately owned) at the end of the track which climbs above the ruins. In 1944, however, excavations unearthed the buried materials from a crucial part of the palace, the **Royal House**, where guests were received and meetings of ministers held. This has been meticulously reconstructed and, though still fragmentary, its main hall, the **Salón Rico de Abd al-Rahman III** – currently undergoing an extensive restoration – decorated with exquisite marble carvings, must rank among the greatest of all Moorish rooms. Modelled on the Roman basilica, it has a different kind of artistic representation from that found in the palaces at Granada or Seville – closer to natural and animal forms in its intricate Syrian Hom (Tree of Life) motifs. Unlike the later Spanish Arab dynasties, the Berber Almoravids and the Almohads of Seville, the caliphal Andalucians were little worried by Islamic strictures on the portrayal of nature, animals or even men – the beautiful stag in the site museum is a good example (see p.392) – and it may well have been this aspect of the palace's artistic decor that led to such zealous destruction during the civil war. The reconstructed palace gives a scale and focus to the site, while elsewhere work continues in restoring and rebuilding more ruined structures. Beyond these there are little more than foundations, gardens and the odd horseshoe arch to fuel your imaginings, amid an awesome area of ruins, hidden beneath bougainvillea and rustling with cicadas.

The gardens

Over a decade ago biologists from Córdoba University carried out a study of soil samples from the site to gain an understanding of exactly which plants and flowers the Moors had cultivated in the extensive **gardens**. When the study was completed, planting began in an attempt to reconstruct the gardens of Medina Azahara as accurately as possible. The planted trees, shrubs, plants and herbs are now maturing into a delightful and aromatic garden the caliphs would recognize.

The museum

Among the exhibits at the new **museum** inside the Centro de Interpretación are outstanding examples of ceramics, glassware and carved stone and marble unearthed in the excavations. One superb work transferred from Córdoba's archeological museum is an exquisite tenth-century **bronze stag** – a gift of the Byzantine emperor Constantine VII to Abd ar-Rahman III – and found at the Moorish palace where it was used as the spout of a fountain.

ARRIVAL AND DEPARTURE · MEDINA AZAHARA

All visitors must arrive at the **Centro de Interpretación**, a state-of-the-art complex incorporating a museum, shop and *cafetería* as well as research facilities for scholars and archeologists. Here you are required to park any vehicle and pick up your entry tickets. Once you have your ticket you are free to walk the 2km to the site, but it is all uphill; best to take a bus (every 10–20min; €2.10 return) from the car park outside the Centro.

By bus A dedicated bus service links Córdoba with the site (April–Sept Tues–Sat 10.15am & 5pm, Sun 9.30am & 10.15am; Oct–March Tues–Sun 9.30am & 10.15am; €7 return, which includes the bus to the site itself). The bus departs from a signed stop on the Glorieta (roundabout) Cruz Roja at the southern end of Paseo de la Victoria (confirm this at the tourist office); note that tickets must be bought in advance from any municipal tourist office *kiosko*. You could also take bus #01 from Avda. de la República Argentina (at the northern end, near a petrol station); this will drop you off at the intersection, from where it's a 1km walk to the Centro de Interpretación. Ask the driver for "El Cruce de Medina Azahara".
By car To drive to Medina Azahara Centro de Interpretación from Córdoba, follow Avda. de Medina Azahara west out of town onto the road to Villarubia and Posadas. About 4km down this road, make a right turn (signed for the site), after which it's another 1km to the Centro de Interpretación. You have to park your car at the Centro de Interpretación and take the dedicated bus (or walk) to the site; you may, however, drive along the road that passes the site to reach the nearby restaurants (see below).
By taxi A taxi will cost you about €25 one-way for up to five people, or there's a special round-trip deal ("Taxi-Tour Córdoba") for €45, which includes a one-hour wait at the site while you visit. A convenient taxi rank is located outside the Turismo on the west side of the Mezquita.
Guided tours Córdoba Vision runs guided trips to the site (Tues–Sun 11am; €20; ☎ 957 299 777, English spoken); buses leave from the same stop at the Glorieta Cruz Roja (see above) as the dedicated bus service.

INFORMATION

Opening hours May–Sept Tues–Sat 10am–8.30pm, Sun 10am–2pm; Oct–April Tues–Sat 10am–6.30pm, Sun 10am–2pm. Confirm winter hours with the site (☎957 352 860) or at Córdoba's tourist offices.
Entry fee €1.50, free with EU passport, but a ticket still needs to be collected (see above).

EATING AND DRINKING

Bar-Restaurante El Cruce Ctra. de Trassiera km7. Accessible if you have your own transport, this is an atmospheric and economical place to eat near Medina Azahara; it's a 3km climb from a signed junction near the entrance to the site. Sit on the leafy terrace and try the *jabalí* (wild boar). Daily 11am–11pm.

Los Almendros Ctra. de Trassiera km8. A kilometre along the road beyond the *El Cruce* restaurant, this is a good *venta* serving typical *cordobés* cuisine including *rabo de toro* and *salmorejo* as well as venison and fish. There's also a €10 *menú* (Mon–Fri). Daily noon–11pm.

Las Ermitas

Tues–Sun: April–Sept 10am–1.30pm & 4.30–7.30pm; Oct–March 10am–1.30pm & 4.30–6.30pm • €1.50

A scenic signed road climbs for 4km beyond the *Bar-Restaurant El Cruce* (see p.392) to **Las Ermitas**, a beautiful jasmine-scented hermitage filled with cypresses, olives and cacti. Here you can see twelve cells dating from the eighteenth century – spaced out around a central shrine – where hermit monks once flagellated themselves in splendid isolation. These hills were inhabited by hermits from the earliest days of Christianity through the Visigothic and Muslim periods and solitaries occupied the hermitage until as recently as 1957. There are dramatic **views** over the valley of the Guadalquivir from the *mirador* of the giant cross, La Cruz del Humilladero.

Almodóvar del Río

Buses run from Córdoba to **ALMODÓVAR DEL RÍO**, where an impressive multi-turreted **castle** (April–Sept Mon–Fri 11am–2.30pm & 4–8pm, Sat & Sun 11am–8pm; Oct–March closes 7pm; €5) sits on a hill high above the town dominating the landscape. Dating originally from the eighth century, and significantly expanded by Abd al-Rahman II in the ninth, the fortress underwent many later additions and restorations, most of them following its fall to the Christian army of Fernando III in 1240. Today the castle is owned by the Marqués de Motilla. It's a pleasant walk up to the castle from the town, and though there's little to see in the over-restored interior – now filled with rather tedious "historical" tableaux –there are fine **views** from the battlements over the valley of the Guadalquivir. Watch your step, as there are few handrails.

Parque Natural de la Sierra de Hornachuelos

Some 20km west of Almodóvar del Río along the A431, a turn on the right (the A2212) leads after 8km to **HORNACHUELOS**, the gateway village to the extensive **Parque Natural de la Sierra de Hornachuelos**, a heavily wooded area on the lower slopes of the Sierra Morena. The park, rich in birdlife, is home to Andalucía's second largest colony of black vultures, along with a wide range of wildlife including the threatened Iberian lynx, deer, wild boar and, in the river valleys, otters.

INFORMATION   **PARQUE NATURAL DE LA SIERRA DE HORNACHUELOS**

Turismo C/Ctra. de San Calixto s/n (Mon–Fri 8am–3pm, Sat & Sun 10am–2pm; ☎957 640 786). This helpful office, signed on the right as you enter Hornachuelos, can provide information on the park as well as a map.

Centro de Visitantes Huerta del Rey This is the park's main information centre, 2km beyond Hornachuelos heading into the park and signed on the left (Mon–Fri 10am–2pm & 4–7pm, Sat 10am–7pm; ☎957 641 140). It has informative displays on the park's flora and fauna and can provide maps and information on numerous waymarked walking routes.

ACCOMMODATION

Bar-Casa Alejandro Avda. Guadalquivir 4, on the village's southern edge ☎957 640 098. Friendly *hostal* with simple but clean en-suite rooms above an inexpensive bar-restaurant with a daily *menú*. The *venado* (venison) and *jabalí* (wild boar) are recommended. **€35**

El Alamo Ctra. Comarcal 141 ☎957 640 476, ⒲ elalamo hostal.com. A short distance up the road from *Bar-Casa Alejandro*, this is a more upmarket motel-style option where a/c en-suite rooms come with a parking space. The main building also has its own bar-restaurant. **€50**

The Campiña

To the south of Córdoba, and stretching to the mountains of the province's southern border, lies the **Campiña Cordobesa**. A fertile, undulating region of wheatfields, olive groves and productive vineyards, it has been renowned since Roman times when the eminent Roman writers Pliny and Martial praised its artichokes, fruit, wool and the excellence of its olive oil. The town of **Baena** keeps up the tradition with an oil so good that it carries an official *denominación de origen* label. Each of the villages of the Campiña has its own interesting castle, church, palace or Roman villa and sometimes a bodega – and there are towns such as **Priego de Córdoba**, a Baroque architectural feast and well off the tourist trail, that are undiscovered jewels. Even the smallest villages usually have a *hostal* or hotel, which opens up the possibility of **walks** exploring some of the Campiña's delightful countryside including – in its lower reaches – the **Parque Natural de las Sierras Subbéticas**, replete with wooded hills and river valleys. Many of the tourist offices in this zone stock a free bilingual booklet, *La Subbética Senderismo Guide*, which details fourteen walks in the park.

The Ruta del Vino

Leaving Córdoba by the A4–E5 (or more directly via the new A45) and, after 14km forking left along the N331, brings you to **Fernán Núñez**, a pleasant hill village a further 14km down the road. Among a number of interesting places along this route are **Montilla**, the centre of Córdoba's wine production, **Rute**, where *anís*, a far stronger brew, is concocted, and the beautiful lakeside village of **Iznájar**, in the midst of some good trekking country.

Montemayor

Just beyond the village of Fernán Núñez is **MONTEMAYOR**, a charming and typical *campiña* village with a fourteenth-century **castle**. Off its neat little central plaza is the sixteenth-century church of **Nuestra Señora de la Asunción** with a beautifully painted stucco *sagrario* and a sixteenth-century carved baptismal font, still used to initiate the newborn of the parish. You'll need to find the priest, Padre Pablo Moyano, to open the church and he may well be in the *Casino*, a fine old institution across the square. If you ask, he will also let you see his personal **archeological collection** (daily 9–10.30am & 6.30–8pm; free), kept in a vault beneath the church and for which he is famous for miles around. This enormous accumulation of artefacts includes coins, agricultural implements, grindstones, jewellery and sculpture – most of it from Ulia, as Montemayor was in Roman times – and has been collected on his walks over the years in the surrounding fields.

ACCOMMODATION AND EATING   **MONTEMAYOR**

Hotel Castillo de Montemayor Ctra Córdoba–Málaga km35 ☎957 384 253, ⓦhotelcastillodemontemayor.com. Close to the village on the N331, this is the best of a clutch of accommodation options around this road junction. The rooms are comfortable (get one at the back overlooking their garden pool to avoid highway noise) and below there's an efficient and a decent-value restaurant with an outdoor terrace. **€60**

Montilla

Beyond Montemayor the A45 highway presses on into the Sierra de Montilla and endless rows of vines begin to creep across the landscape as you enter Córdoba's **wine-producing region**. The tough Pedro-Ximénez vines planted here have to withstand searing summer temperatures, and send their roots deep down into the whitish-grey *albariza* soil searching for moisture. Eleven kilometres beyond Montemayor, **MONTILLA**, the capital of Córdoba's wine country, comes into view. Hardly the region's prettiest town, it does however boast one of its leading **bodegas**, a picturesque place founded in the eighteenth century.

ACCOMMODATION AND EATING   **MONTILLA**

Don Quijote C/Bailén 4 ☎957 651 271. This very popular and spacious bar-restaurant in the heart of town specializes in *carnes a la brasa* (charcoal-grilled meat). Also serves salads and fish dishes and a *menú* for under €10.
Hostal Bellido C/Enfermería 57 ☎957 651 915, ⓦhostalbellido.com. Comfortable en-suite rooms at this welcoming and good value *hostal* housed in an elegantly refurbished mansion a stone's throw from *Don Quijote* restaurant. **€53**
Restaurante Camachas Avda. de Europa 3, on the main road at the entrance to the town ☎957 650 658.

MONTILLA–MORILES: NO HANGOVER GUARANTEED

The Romans and later the Moors (in spite of the Prophet's prohibition) developed the Campiña as a wine region. The great wine of Córdoba, **Montilla** (often called Montilla-Moriles, the latter village being its partner in production to the south) has suffered over the years from comparison with the wines of Jerez, with which it shares similar characteristics. The reasons for this are largely historical as, prior to the 1940s, much of Córdoba's vintage was sold to the great fino houses of Jerez and eventually marketed as sherry. In 1944 this was made illegal, since when Montilla was granted its own *denominación*, but the notion that the wines of this region are merely a less expensive alternative to sherry has been a tag that the industry here has found hard to shake off.

The most visual difference in the production of Montilla is the great *tinajas* – huge, earthenware urns in which the wine undergoes its fermentation. These Ali-Baba jars, the direct descendants of the Roman dolium, have pointed ends which are buried in the earth inside the bodegas and are believed to impart a unique character to the wine. As in Jerez, the wine in these great vats also develops a flor (a thick layer of yeast) which covers the narrow neck of the urns. Later, the solera system (see p.217), during which the wine is aged and blended in oak butts for two years, is used to finish the process. The response you get around these parts should you bring up the subject of comparisons with the finos of Jerez is the assertion that Montilla is a natural product, whilst the wines of Jerez need to have their alcohol added. The Pedro-Ximénez grape used for Montilla is baked in the furnace heat of the Campiña sun and produces wines of sixteen percent proof which, the bodegas here like to claim – unlike that synthetic *jerezano* – never give you a hangover.

Alvear SA Avda. María Auxiliadora 1 ☎957 664 014, ⌨ alvear.es. Founded in 1729 by Diego Alvear and still in the hands of the same family, this major producer of Montilla wines offers visits and tastings daily at 12.30pm. €3.80 weekdays, €5 Sat & Sun. Shop open Mon–Fri 10am–2pm & 4.30–6.30pm, Sat 11am–2pm.

A very good, long-established restaurant renowned for its traditional *cordobés* cuisine – *paletilla de cordero lechal* (roast suckling lamb) and *rabo de toro* are signature dishes. There's a good-value weekday *menú* for €11. Main dishes €12–20.

Aguilar

AGUILAR, 7km south of Montilla, perched on top of a hill, is worth a visit to see its wonderful eighteenth-century octagonal plaza of **San José**, probably inspired by the better-maintained one at Archidona in Málaga. The rest of the town is equally charming, its sloping streets lined with white-walled houses, their windows protected by *rejas*, or iron grilles. From the **Torre del Reloj**, a Baroque clock tower and local landmark, there are excellent views over the Campiña. At the top of the Cuesta de Jesús, the sixteenth-century **Santa María del Soterraño** (open service times 7–9pm), with an *artesonado* Mudéjar ceiling, Plateresque doorway and an impressive *sagrario* with a sculpture of Christ in a *camarín* by Donaire Trexo, is Aguilar's best church.

INFORMATION AGUILAR

Turismo Cuesta de Jesús 2 (daily 10am–2pm; ☎957 661 567). This office can provide you with a wide range of information both on the town as well as the Sierra Subbética.

ACCOMMODATION AND EATING

Hostal-Restaurante Queen C/Pescadería 6 ☎957 660 222. Just off the Plaza de San José, this is a good overnight stop and has decent a/c en-suite rooms with TV above a restaurant. €45

★ **La Casona** Avda. Puente de Genil 6 ☎957 660 439. Aguilar's best place to eat lies on the edge of town along the Puente Genil road. The main room is rustic *andaluz* with traditional green chairs and painted beams, and there's also a bar serving tapas. The restaurant offers well-prepared *venta*-style food – *solomillo* (pork loin), *salmorejo* and *salchichón ibérico* are specials – with large helpings, reasonable prices and a weekday *menú* for around €8. Main dishes €7–15.

Laguna de Zóñar

Some 4km southwest of Aguilar along the A309 and easily walkable, the **Laguna de Zóñar** is the largest of a group of little-known inland salt lakes. Visited in winter by large numbers of **migrating waterfowl**, this time of the year is best for spotting white-headed duck, a species that once almost disappeared but is now on the increase. Other species that can be seen here include red-crested pochard, mallard, great-crested grebe, tufted duck and marsh harrier. In summer there's less to see, although sometimes flamingos fly in from the Fuente de Piedra in nearby Málaga, for a change of scene. You can gain access to routes around the lake and the hides when the centre is closed. Other lakes in this group include the Laguna del Rincón, north of Moriles, and the Laguna de Tiscar, north of Puente Genil, both of which, unlike this one, tend to dry up in summer.

INFORMATION	LAGUNA DE ZÓNAR

Laguna de Zoñar Centro de Información Displays relating to the lagoon's flora and fauna, particularly birdlife. Outside on the edge of the lagoon are observation hides (July–Sept Fri–Sun 9am–2pm & 6–8pm; Oct–June Tues–Fri 9am–2pm, Sat & Sun 9am–2pm and 4–6pm; ☎ 957 335 252).

Cabra

Some 22km from Aguilar along the A45, turning east after 12km east along the A342, lies **CABRA**, another pleasant Campiña town. Possessing an old quarter with steep, winding streets lined with *rejas* – many holding pots sprouting colourful geraniums in summer – and a number of Baroque mansions, it's a lovely place to wander for an hour or so, or even stop over.

At the end of the town, near the castle, the Baroque **Iglesia de la Asunción** (open service times; try 7–9pm), built over a mosque, is surrounded by palms and cypresses. It has a fine portal with twisted marble Solomonic pillars, and inside, an altar of red and black jasper together with fine choir stalls. The church of **San Juan Bautista** (open service times; try 7–9pm) in the old quarter – Visigothic in origin but much altered since – is reckoned to be one of Spain's oldest, with Moorish and Baroque features added. The Casa de Cultura, Calle Martín Belda 27, holds a modest **archeological museum** (July & Aug Mon–Fri 9am–2pm; Sept–June Mon–Fri 10am–2pm & 6–9pm, Sat & Sun 10am–2pm; free) with local finds from the prehistoric, Visigothic, Roman and Moorish periods. Just to the north of the central Parque Alcántara Romero, the town's ancient **Plaza de Toros**, built in 1857, is also worth a look (its gate is usually left open and you're free to look around).

INFORMATION	CABRA

Turismo C/Mayor s/n, close to the Asunción church (Mon–Fri 10am–1.30pm & 5–7.30pm, Sat & Sun 10am–2pm; ☎ 957 523 493, ⓦturismodecabra.es). Plenty of information on the town and Campiña.
Internet access Ciberia, C/Santa Rosalla 5 (daily 11am–2pm & 6–8pm).

THE VÍA VERDE

The decline of the railway in the area south of Córdoba has had a beneficial knock-on effect for walkers and cyclists. The old line of the Tren de Aceite (olive oil train) which was closed in the 1980s has now been transformed into the **Vía Verde** (ⓦviasverdes.com), a rambling and biking route linking the towns and villages of Puente Genil, Lucena, Cabra, Doña Mencía, Zuheros and Luque with a further extension planned to the east. Some of the stations along the route have been transformed into bars, restaurants and information centres. There are two outdoor activity centres and at its eastern end the route passes La Laguna del Conde (aka Laguna Salobral), the largest lagoon in the Subbética with a wealth of birdlife and its own information centre.

Vía Verde Centro de Interpretación Near the Fuente del Rio, in Cabra's former railway station, signed on the left along the Avda. de Gongóra 500m before the Fuente itself (Mon–Fri 10am–4pm, Sat & Sun call for details; ☎ 957 523 156). Information for all the Vía Verde with details on walking and cycling (mountain bikes can be hired) along the route. Also a *cafetería* and museum – complete with an original steam engine from the *Tren de Aceite* (oil train) – documenting the history of the line.

4

THE ERMITA DE LA VIRGEN

On the road leading east out of Cabra towards Priego de Córdoba, there's a wooded picnic and swimming area, **La Fuente del Río**, centred around a natural spring which is the source of the Río Cabra. Seven kilometres beyond this, a road on the left climbs 6km to the **Ermita de la Virgen de la Sierra**, a hermitage sited at an altitude of over 1200m from where there are stupendous **views** west towards the valley of the Guadalquivir, and east to the mountains of the Sierra Nevada. This is also the starting point for a hike to Zuheros (see p.404).

★ **Venta Los Pelaos** C/del Priego km5, at the start of the road to the Ermita de la Virgen. This outstanding restaurant is a great place for a meal, with economically priced dishes and a terrace, though you'll struggle to get a table on Sunday lunchtimes.

ACCOMMODATION

Hospedería Horno Grande C/Muñiz Terrones 17 ☎ 957 524 477, ⓦ hospederiahornogrande.com. An upmarket option to the west of the Turismo, this offers attractive a/c en-suite rooms in a superbly refurbished elegant town house with a rooftop pool. Superior rooms, costing slightly more, come with their own terrace. **€60**

Hotel Fuente Las Piedras Avda. Fuente de Piedras s/n ☎ 957 529 740, ⓦ mshoteles.com. On the outskirts of town along the A318 heading towards Baena, this is a pleasant three-star hotel with light and spacious rooms plus an on-site restaurant and inviting garden pool. B&B **€70**

Pensión Guerrero C/Pepita Jiménez 7, close to the Parque Alcántara Romero ☎ 957 520 507, ⓔ pension guerrero_s.l.l@hotmail.com. A very friendly budget *hostal* with a/c en-suite rooms with TV. Also some singles. *Rough Guide* readers carrying this guide can claim a ten percent discount. **€45**

EATING

Mesón El Vizconde C/Martín Belda 26, near the tourist office ☎ 957 521 702. One of Cabra's top restaurants, with excellent service and superb food. On a menu with many *cordobés* specialities *alcachofas al hierbabuena* (artichokes with mint) and *carillada ibérico* (black-pig cheeks) are signature dishes. There's also a weekday *menú* for around €10. Main dishes €9–25. Closed Tues & July.

Mesón San Martín Plaza de España 6 ☎ 957 525 131. Very pleasant Michelin-recommended restaurant facing the Ayuntamiento on an attractive square and with a small pavement terrace. A range of local specialities include *lomo de rosada a la cordobesa* (dogfish) and *codillo de cerdo ibérico* (pork knuckle). Main dishes €8–15. Closed Thurs.

Rincón Gallego Avda. de Andalucía 1. Facing the bullring, this atmospheric little Galician restaurant offers a very good weekday *menú* for €9, tapas at the bar and excellent barrelled *sidra* (cider). Specials in the restaurant include *pulpo gallego* (spicy octopus) and *brochetas de marisco* (shellfish kebabs). Closed Mon.

Lucena

Surrounded by hills covered with vines and olives, **LUCENA**, 11km down the N331 from Monturque, is a large industrial town that makes its money from furniture production and the manufacture of the great *tinajas*, or earthenware urns, used in the making of Montilla. Once you've penetrated the rather drab outskirts, Lucena's revamped town centre is not without charm and there are a handful of sights well worth a look. A centre of learning in Moorish times, Lucena fell into Christian hands in 1240 when it was besieged by the armies of Fernando III El Santo, following which event most of its churches and other monuments were erected.

Castillo del Moral

Plaza de Espana s/n; museum entered through the Turismo • Tues–Fri 9am–2pm & 5–8pm, Sat & Sun 11am–2pm & 6–8pm • Free

The focal **Plaza del Coso** (aka Plaza de España) is overlooked by the **Castillo del Moral** whose tower, the Torre del Moral, is the surviving remnant of an earlier castle where Boabdil, the last sultan of Granada, was briefly imprisoned by Isabel la Católica in 1483. The castle now houses the tourist office and an interesting **archeological museum** which focuses on Lucena's role in Roman times as a centre of *alfarería* (pottery).

San Mateo

Plaza Nueva s/n • Mon–Sat 7.30am–1.30pm & 6.30–9pm, Sun 9.30am–noon • Free

The church of **San Mateo** on the Plaza Nueva, a short walk northwest of the castle, houses one of the Baroque glories of the province. The church was started in the fifteenth century over a former mosque and has a superb Mannerist *retablo* and a beautiful eighteenth-century Baroque *sagrario*, with painted stucco cherubs and a feast of decorative detail topped off by a remarkable cupola, all the work of local artist Antonio de Castro.

Santuario de Nuestra Señora de Araceli

Daily 8am–9.30pm • Free

At the town's southern end, a road (CP 157) climbs to the **Santuario de Nuestra Señora de Araceli**, Lucena's much-venerated 900m-high hill-top shrine to the Virgin. The 6km trip is only really worth doing if you've got your own transport, though note that at weekends and in fine weather the car park and small café at the summit are often full to bursting point. The eighteenth-century Baroque shrine has plenty of over-the-top polychrome decor and an image of the Virgin in a *camarín*. Perhaps the best reason for a trip here is the stunning **views** which, weather permitting, allow you to look out over five of Andalucía's eight provinces.

INFORMATION

LUCENA

Turismo Castillo del Moral, Plaza de España s/n (Tues–Fri 9am–2pm & 5–8pm, Sat & Sun 11am–2pm & 5–8pm; ☎957 513 282, ⓦturlucena.com). A helpful office with lots of information on the town and surrounding area.

ACCOMMODATION

Hotel Santo Domingo C/Juan Jiménez Cuenca 16 ☎957 511 100, ⓦmshoteles.com. A few minutes' walk northwest of the Turismo, the eighteenth-century former Convento de Nuestra Señora de la Victoria has been converted into a four-star hotel and must rank as one of the most beautiful in Andalucía. The rooms – many once nuns' cells – are comfortable and well equipped and there's also a bar and good restaurant with a daily *menú* for €15. The convent's former cloister has been transformed into a stunning patio lounge (where non-guests can enjoy a drink). **€90**

Hostal Sara C/Cabrillana 49 ☎957 516 151, ⓦpension saradelucena.com. The best of the budget options, 500m northwest of the Turismo. Clean and tidy en-suite rooms come with TV and a/c. Free wi-fi zone. **€36**

Hotel Veracruz C/Veracruz 1 ☎957 500 300, ⓔhotel veracruz@infonegocio.com. A couple of blocks north of the Turismo, this decent-value and welcoming small hotel offers functional a/c rooms with TV. **€50**

EATING

El Valle C/Federico García Lorca 14 ☎957 501 512. Reached by following C/El Peso east from Plaza Nueva near the Turismo, this is another excellent restaurant for *cocina andaluza* – any of the pork or game dishes are recommended. Its tapas bar has a weekday *menú* for around €11, and there's a attractive street terrace. Main dishes €8–18.

Golem Condesa Carmen Pizarro 8, 100m south of the Turismo ☎957 514 626. An appealing bar-restaurant partly housed inside a former eleventh-century synagogue. Food is *andaluz* with a modern slant (main dishes €7–15). They also mount art shows and cultural events, and the bar hosts jazz and flamenco concerts (except in July and Aug).

Horquillo C/Montenegro 14. Good tapas bar, with plenty of atmosphere.

Olympo C/El Peso 35. Another recommended tapas bar, serving *media raciones* and which also has a restaurant attached.

Rute

The scenic A45 Málaga road continues south from Lucena to **Benamejí**, 20km away, a pleasant agricultural village with a couple of *fondas*, close to the provincial border. However, the more interesting route lies along the road (CP167) which turns off left off the A45 8km out of Lucena, heading towards the small town of **RUTE**. Twelve kilometres from the turning, the whitewashed town, sited picturesquely on a hill overlooked by the hazy Sierra de Rute behind, comes into view. Beyond a ruined Moorish castle and a Baroque church, it has few monuments. Rute's fame throughout Andalucía is based on a far more potent allure: the manufacture of a lethal **anís** (aniseed apéritif) with springwater

4

4

SAVE THE DONKEY

Founded by local draper Pasqual Rovira in 1989, ADEBO (Association for the Defence of the Donkey) is Spain's oldest **donkey refuge**, and well worth a visit. The country's donkey population has shrunk dramatically from over one million fifty years ago to a current 100,000 – most of which are crossbreeds. Only a few hundred remain of the five breeds of pure Spanish *burro* that have existed on the peninsula since pre-Roman times. One of these, the *raza córdobes*, was so renowned in the eighteenth century for its strength that George Washington asked the Spanish king, Carlos III, to send him some for his farm.

Used for centuries as beasts of burden, the donkeys often receive brutal treatment at the hands of uncaring owners. Working with scarce resources, and using the meagre profits from the family drapery business, Pasqual and his wife Quica have devoted their lives to ending this cruelty and saving the Spanish breeds – including the *cordobés* – from extinction. They were greatly helped in this when Queen Sofía rang Pasqual some years ago after reading about his work and offered her support, and suddenly, previously sceptical politicians in Córdoba and Madrid became enthusiastic about the venture.

The work of the sanctuary continues with the aid of voluntary contributions, and both the queen and her husband King Juan Carlos have sponsored donkeys, as have the late writer Camilo José Cela, Bill Clinton (remarking that the donkey is the mascot of the Democratic Party) and Fidel Castro. Tenor Placido Domingo also donated royalties from his recorded version of the popular Christmas carol *Arre, Borriquito* ("Gee up, donkey") to the centre.

ADEBO To get to the donkey sanctuary, continue uphill from the Museo de Anís in the Paseo del Fresno, Rute, following the road for the campsite. Call them on ☎ 957 532 032, ☎ mobile 610 841 720 for directions, or ask at the tourist office (see below), who can supply a map. Usually daily 9am–noon.

---

from the Sierra. It comes in varying strengths and can be tasted at the twenty or so small bodegas scattered around the town; *Bodega Machaquita*, Paseo del Fresno 7, is regarded as one of the best.

Museo del Anís

Paseo del Fresno 2 • Mon–Sat 9am–2pm & 4–7pm • €1 • ☎ 957 532 991, ⓦ museodelanis.com

A guided tour at the **Museo del Anís** on the Paseo del Fresno in the upper town will tell you all you need to know about the making of *anís* and its history, with a chance to taste and buy at the end.

INFORMATION   RUTE

Municipal tourist office Parque Nuestra Señora del Carmen (Mon–Fri 8am–3pm; ☎ 957 532 929). Near the main road through the town and close to the landmark Anís monument, this office can provide a useful town map.

ACCOMMODATION AND EATING

Rute has just two hotels, near each other at the southern end of the town. Both have their own decent restaurants serving economical *menús*.

Hotel El Mirador Ctra. Rute-Encinas Reales s/n ☎ 957 539 404, ⓦ miradorderute.com. A pleasant hotel with well-equipped rooms offering views towards the sierra. It also has its own pool and bar-restaurant. €61
Hotel María Luisa Ctra. Lucena–Loja 22 ☎ 957 538 096, ⓦ hotelmarialuisa.es. Comfortable three-star hotel with light and airy rooms overlooking a garden and excellent pool. There's a bar-restaurant on site. B&B €65
Restaurante Primavera de Rute C/Blas Infante s/n, near the Anís monument on the main road. The best of the in-town places to eat, this is good option for solid sierra cooking – *cerdo ibérico* (black-pig pork) is a house speciality – and has a daily *menú* for around €8.

Iznájar

Reached by following the scenic A331 road for 13km from Rute, **IZNÁJAR** is a picturesque, whitewashed farming village, with a spectacular location overlooking a reservoir. Despite the beauty, this is a place of long-standing poverty; it was here in 1861 that peasants, or *braceros*, revolted against the injustices of the landowning class – an uprising that was viciously suppressed.

Of Moorish origin (from the Arabic *hizn*, fort, and *achar*, refuge), Iznájar's ruined **Alcazaba** was constructed in the eighth century, and the church of **Santiago** was added to its interior in the sixteenth.

INFORMATION IZNÁJAR

Municipal tourist office At the top of the village close to the arch leading to the church (Mon–Fri 9.30am–1.30pm & 4.30–7.30pm, Sat & Sun 10am–2pm; ☎ mobile 649 218 783, ⌨ iznajar.net).

ACCOMMODATION AND EATING

Camping Valdearenas beach, just beyond the Hotel Caserío de Iznájar (see below). You can camp for the odd night or two on this beach fronting the *embalse*. There are no facilities, and you must clear your own rubbish.

Cortijo La Haza C/Adelantado 19 ☎ 957 334 051, ⌨ cortizolahaza.com. Pretty farmhouse in olive groves 7km out of the village, with rustically furnished, beamed rooms ranged around a pool. It also has its own very good restaurant with vegetarian options and a *menú* for €25; ring for directions (English spoken). **€92**

Finca La Bobadilla Ctra. Iznájar–Salinas ☎ 958 321 861, ⌨ la-bobadilla.com. Twenty kilometres south of Iznájar, close to the junction with the A92 *autovía*, a signed entrance on the left indicates a long drive leading to one of the most exclusive hotels in Spain. Surrounded by vast tracts of woodland and built on the model of a "typical" Andalucian village, it has appealed to guests as diverse as Tom Cruise, King Juan Carlos and many Japanese tourists, for whom this is a favourite place to get married. Facilities include heliport, spa, fitness centre and upmarket restaurant (supplied by the hotel's farm). Call in for a drink at the bar if you're curious. **€355**

Hotel Caserío de Iznájar Ctra. de Valdearenas s/n ☎ 957 508 011 ⌨ zercahoteles.com. Sited on a headland overlooking the lake/reservoir, and surrounded by gardens with a fine pool, this charming hotel has light, spacious rooms with a/c, plus a restaurant and bar. *Rough Guide* readers with this guide can claim a ten percent discount. B&B **€71**

Restaurante Rosi Ctra. Lucena–Loja. Good *venta* below the village close to the *embalse*, serving decent and economical food. Try the *solomillo* (pork loin) or *calamares a la romana*.

The Ruta del Aceite

The **Ruta del Aceite** (Olive Oil Route), follows the N432 southeast out of Córdoba towards Priego de Córdoba. It takes in the olive-oil producing region centred on **Baena** before visiting some of the province's most picturesque villages, including **Luque** and **Zuheros**.

Espejo

At **ESPEJO**, 31km south of Córdoba, an impressive Moorish castle looms above the white-walled village, vineyards and olive groves spread out below. The fourteenth-century Gothic-Mudéjar **castillo** is the property of the dukes of Osuna, the great ruling family based to the southwest (see p.313), which once owned an enormous tract of Andalucía. The nearby and recently restored Gothic-Renaissance church of **San Bartolomé**, dating from the fifteenth and sixteenth centuries, is also worth seeking out for its superb *retablo mayor* by Pedro Romana and a fine *artesonado* ceiling.

Castro del Río

Sited on a low hill on the north bank of the Río Guadajoz, **CASTRO DEL RÍO**, 9km on from Espejo, has a **Roman bridge** spanning the river and a ruined Moorish **castle** built on the foundations of a Roman fort. The village also claims a footnote in Roman history as this is believed to be the place where Pompey's troops rested up prior to their showdown battle with Caesar in 45 BC at nearby Montilla (Munda) which ended the civil war and, briefly, gave Caesar control of the whole Roman world. The **Iglesia de la Asunción**, founded in the thirteenth century with later additions, has a fine if somewhat eroded Plateresque portal, and the **Ayuntamiento** preserves the prison in which Cervantes was locked up for a week in 1568 when, then working as a tax collector, he was falsely accused of fiddling the books. A modern sculpture of Don Quijote, honouring the great writer's literary creation, now adorns the exterior.

Baena

The Sierra Subbética Cordobesa, a rugged, rambling spur of the Cordillera Bética range in the province's southeastern corner, is now officially designated the **Parque Natural de las Sierras Subbéticas** (ⓦsubbetica.es). Beyond Castro del Río the N432 climbs gently through hills covered with olive groves until it reaches Andalucía's most celebrated oil production centre, **BAENA**, famous for centuries for the high quality of its olive oil. Baena was an important and populous place in the Moorish period, but the town shrank as a result of emigration in the twentieth century. In recent years it has made a comeback based upon its oil and agricultural wealth and today exudes a busy and prosperous air, with huge metal tanks for storing the oil lining the roads on the outskirts of town. Most of Baena's sights lie in the upper town, reached by following Calle Juan Rabadán from the focal Plaza de España to the Plaza de la Constitución. The eighteenth-century arcaded **almacén** (warehouse) here houses a cultural centre and *Mesón Casa del Monte*, a good tapas bar and restaurant (see p.403).

Museo Archeológico

Casa de la Tercia, C/Henares s/n • Tues–Thurs 11am–2pm, Fri & Sat 11am–2pm & 4–7pm, Sun 11am–2pm • Free

The Casa de la Tercia is an elegant eighteenth-century *casa señorial* which now houses the town's interesting **archeological museum**. Spread over three floors, the museum has interesting exhibits from prehistory and Roman Baena (with a section dealing with ancient olive oil production), as well as the Moorish and medieval periods.

BAENA'S OIL FOR CONNOISSEURS

Spain produces, and probably consumes, more **olive oil** than any other country in the world. However, this wasn't always so, and when the Greeks introduced the olive to the peninsula in the first millennium BC, it was regarded with suspicion by the native Iberians who went on using their traditional lard. Only with the arrival of the Roman legions did they begin to acquire a taste for it, and under Roman supervision Hispanic oil became the finest and most expensive in the empire. Later, sophisticated Moorish invaders taught the Iberians better cultivation techniques, as well as culinary and medicinal possibilities. The Moorish, and now Spanish, names for oil and the olive, *aceite* and *aceituna*, are a legacy of this time.

Today, Spaniards are great connoisseurs of quality oil and **Baena** has its own official **denominación de origen**, backed by an official regulatory body, the *Consejo Regulador*, guaranteeing the standards attained by strict methods of production. Baena's finest oil stands comparison with the best in Europe, and *almazaras* (oil mills), such as that operated for several generations by the Núñez de Prado family in the town, take a great amount of care at every stage in the production process. The olives cultivated on the estate are all harvested by hand prior to being ground to a paste on ancient granite stone mills. The "free run" oil – with no further pressure applied – that results from this process is regarded as the *grand cru* of the oil trade and it takes eleven kilos of olives to yield just one litre of such oil. With a markedly low acid content and an unfatty, concentrated flavour, this oil is far too good (and expensive) for cooking and is sparingly used to flavour gazpacho – in Córdoba province, *salmorejo* – or tasted on a morsel of bread as a *tapa*.

Núñez de Prado mill Avda. de Cervantes 15 close to Plaza de España ☎957 670 141. With parts dating from the eighteenth century, this mill can be visited all year, although most of the action takes place between November and February when the harvested olives are pressed. Their shop sells a range of oils, including the celebrated *flor de aceite*, at bargain prices. June–Sept Mon–Sat 8am–2pm; Oct–May Mon–Fri 9am–1pm & 4–6pm; €6

Santa María

Plaza del Angel s/n • Fri & Sat noon–2pm & 5–7pm, Sun noon–2pm • Free

At the top of Calle Henares, veering to the left brings you to the early sixteenth-century Gothic church of **Santa María** with a fine portal and a Moorish tower, probably the minaret of a former mosque. Ruined and roofless for many years after being put to the torch during the Civil War, this beautiful church has undergone a substantial restoration, and features a magnificent new wooden vaulted roof. The fine iron *reja* (altar screen) survives, while an image of what was lost, including a precious retablo, is preserved in a faded photograph in the sacristy (the Turismo also displays a copy in its lobby).

Madre de Dios

Plaza Palacio s/n • Fri & Sat noon–2pm & 5–7pm, Sun noon–2pm • Free

Behind the church of Santa María is the sixteenth-century Mudéjar convent of **Madre de Dios** with a fine late Gothic porch, and equally fine retablo, *coro* and *artesonados* in its church.

Museo del Olivar

C/Cañada 7 • Tues–Thurs 11am–2pm, Fri & Sat 11am–2pm & 4–6pm, Sun 11am–2pm • Free • ☏ 957 691 641

A little way northwest of the Plaza de España, the **Museo del Olivar** pays tribute to the history and development of olive oil production in the area, including a section on the modern uses of oil and its by-products – Baena has a power station fuelled by olive waste. You can also sample and buy the famed oils.

INFORMATION
BAENA

Turismo C/Virrey del Pino 5, slightly east of the Plaza de España (Tues–Sat 10am–2pm & 6–8pm; ☏ 957 671 757).
Festival Besides oil, Baena is also famous for its Semana Santa rituals, which include a drum-rolling contest when the streets are filled with the deafening sound of up to two thousand drums being struck simultaneously. From Wednesday to Friday during Holy Week is the time to avoid, unless you have ear plugs.

ACCOMMODATION

Albergue Ruta del Califato C/Coro 7 ☏ 656 252 717, ⊛ baenarural.com. Perhaps the most attractive budget option is the Ayuntamiento's youth hostel, close to the church of Santa María in the upper town. Most rooms are doubles (sharing bathrooms) and there are also dorms. Plus spectacular views, and a bar-restaurant with a €7.50 *menú*. B&B under 26 €14 per person, over 26 €18.50 per person
Casa Grande Avda. Cervantes 35 ☏ 957 671 905, ⊛ lacasagrande.es. Near the Turismo, this is an elegant and very comfortable three-star hotel with spacious rooms inside a converted nineteenth-century mansion. Street parking outside. €61
Hostal Rincón C/Llano del Rincón 13, off Plaza de España ☏ 957 670 223. This central and friendly *hostal* has en-suite a/c rooms with TV above a very good bar-restaurant with a *menú* for €10. Can advise on parking nearby. €40

EATING AND DRINKING

Mesón Casa del Monte Plaza de la Constitución. This restaurant, facing the Ayuntamiento, is a cut above the rest, serving well-prepared regional dishes – *solomillo* ibérico (pork loin) is a house special – with an economical *menú*.
★ **Mesón de los Arcos** On the eastern side of the Parque Ramón Santaella. A superb place to eat. Along with tapas and *raciones* – *salmorejo* and *ventresca de atún* (tuna) are big favourites – it also offers an excellent-value weekday lunch *menú* for €7.50 and has a pleasant terrace.
Primero de la Mañana C/Llano del Rincón 14, off Plaza de España. A good place for breakfast, and for tapas later in the day. *Pescaito frito* (fried fish) is a house special.

Luque

Seven kilometres beyond Baena, a right turn leads to the attractive village of **LUQUE**, spread out below a daunting rocky outcrop topped by the almost obligatory castle. Dating from the thirteenth century, the ruins of the Moorish **castillo** are worth a look, and beside them is the golden limestone facade of the Gothic-Renaissance **church of La Asunción** with a retablo whose central image of San Juan is attributed to Martínez Montañés. There is no accommodation, but a couple of good places for food.

EATING AND DRINKING LUQUE

Bar-Restaurante La Plancha Plaza España 12, across from the church. A lively local meeting place, serving up tapas and *raciones* as well as *platos combinados*.

Casa Frasco C/Padrón 6. A worthwhile haunt specializing in *carnes de monte* – *venado* (venison) is a house special – and *mariscos* (game and shellfish).

Zuheros and around

Nestling in a gorge backed by steep rock cliffs some 5km west of Luque, **ZUHEROS** is another stunningly beautiful Subbética village. A cluster of white houses tumbles down the hill below a romantic Moorish **castle** built on and into the rock. Later Christian additions were made after it fell to Fernando III (El Santo) in 1240 and became a frontier bastion against the kingdom of Granada. The nearby early seventeenth-century **Iglesia de los Remedios** (open service times 6.30–8.30pm) has a fine retablo as well as a tower built on the remains of a minaret from an earlier mosque, while on the neighbouring small square a **mirador** gives a great view over the surrounding countryside. At the eastern end of the village, on Calle Santo, the well-presented **Museum of Customs and Popular Arts** displays implements, furniture and decor from bygone days (April–Sept Fri–Sun 10.30am–2.30pm & 5–8.30pm; Oct–March Fri–Sun 10.30am–2.30pm & 4–7pm; €3).

Museo Arqueológico and Castillo

Guided tours April–Sept Mon–Fri 10am–2pm & 4–7pm, Sat, Sun & hols on the hour 10am–6pm; Oct–March Mon–Fri 4–6pm, Sat & Sun 10am–6pm on the hour; outside these times ask at the Hotel Zuhayra or call • €1.90 including guided castle visit • ☎ 957 694 545

On the edge of a small square, facing *Bar-Mesón de los Palancos* (see below), the village's **archeological museum** displays fascinating finds from the Cueva de los Murciélagos (see below) as well as exhibits from the Roman and Moorish periods. The visit concludes with a visit to the **castle**, which offers great **views** from its tower.

Cueva de los Murciélagos

Guided tours April–Sept Sat, Sun & hols 11am, 12.30pm, 2pm, 5pm & 6.30pm; for winter hours and to see the cave outside these times ask at the *Hotel Zuhayra* or call • €5 • ☎ 957 694 545

In the hills above the village, reached by a paved, 4km road, the spectacular **Cueva de los Murciélagos**, first explored in 1938, is well worth a visit. Its name means "cave of the bats" and the hour-long tour (bring a sweater) takes in impressive stalagmites, stalactites and awesome rock formations while the guide relates the fascinating story (revealed by recent excavations) of the remarkable **Neolithic cave paintings** and human remains found here.

INFORMATION ZUHEROS

Municipal Tourist office Just below the village on the Baena road (April–Sept Tues–Thurs10am–2pm, Fri & Sat 10am–2pm & 4.30–7.30pm, Sun 10am–2pm; Oct–March

closes 6pm; ☎ 957 694 692); they have information about renting *casas rurales* in the area.

ACCOMMODATION

★ **Hotel Zuhayra** C/Mirador 10 ☎ 957 694 693, ⓦ zercahoteles.com. Downhill from the castle, this charming place to stay makes a perfect base to explore the surrounding natural park. They stock copies of local resident and walking guide Clive Jarman's book *Walking in the Subbética Natural Park*, which details a number of excellent hikes, and can can also arrange canoeing, mountain biking

and birdwatching excursions. Guests get free use of the village swimming pool. There's also a good and economical restaurant on site, with a daily *menú*. Ten percent discount for *Rough Guide* readers with this guide. B&B **€71**

Señorío de Zuheros C/Hornos 3 ☎ 957 667 574, ⓦ subbeticaviva.com. Fully equipped studios and apartments available to rent. **€50** per night

EATING

Bar-Mesón Los Palancos C/Llana 45, facing the castle. Lively restaurant and tapas bar with an inviting terrace on the square. Both fish and meat dishes are served; *carnes asados* (grilled meats) and *conejo al ajillo* (rabbit in garlic)

are favourites.

Mesón Atalaya C/Santo 58, at the eastern end of the village, next to the turn-off to the Cueva de los Murciélagos. A good bar for tapas and *raciones* with a restaurant at the back. A variety of regional dishes include *rabo de toro* (stewed bull's tail) and *salmorejo* (thick gazpacho) and they offer a nice line in local goat-milk cheeses (which the village is noted for).

Doña Mencía

Not quite as pretty as some of its neighbours, **DOÑA MENCÍA**, 5km west of Zuheros, is a sizeable oil and wine centre lying at the foot of a slope covered with silver-leaved olives, interrupted by the occasional vineyard. On the town's western flank there are the walls and bastions of a fifteenth-century **castle** next to which there's an elegant carved stone **portal**, all that remains of an eighteenth-century Dominican monastery destroyed in the Civil War and now incorporated into a new municipal open-air theatre.

Museo Histórico-Arqueológico

C/Juan Ramón Jiménez 5 • Mon–Fri 11am–1pm • ☎ 957 695 075

Off the main square at the end of Calle Juan Valera is a small **archeological museum**, with exhibits from the prehistoric, Roman and Moorish periods found in the surrounding area. The museum occupies the site of the house of the nineteenth-century novelist Juan Valera who was born here, and whose best-known work, *Pepita Jiménez*, was set in nearby Cabra.

ACCOMMODATION AND EATING	DOÑA MENCÍA
⭐ **Casa Morejón** C/Obispo Cubero 3, just off the Plaza Andalucía ☎ 957 676 169. Excellent, welcoming small *hostal* offering perhaps the best-value en-suite rooms in Andalucía. The rooms are functional but spotless and arranged around a charming tiled interior patio; there is also an excellent restaurant with a bargain *menú* for €8. **€20**	**Mesón la Cantina** On the southern edge of town at the junction with the A318, near the turn-off to Zuheros. A lively *venta* housed in the town's disused railway station; the former platform is now a terrace, looking out on to the Vía Verde cycling and hiking route. There's a good-value *menú*.

Priego de Córdoba and around

The tranquil town of **PRIEGO DE CÓRDOBA**, 20km southeast of Luque, is capital of the Subbética and one of Andalucía's little-known Baroque wonders, with a feast of superb churches and a remarkable fountain. It's situated beneath the province's highest mountain, the 1600m **La Tiñosa**; the northern approach presents a dramatic view of the whitewashed buildings of its old quarter, laid out along the edge of a picturesque escarpment known as the Adarve.

Plaza de la Constitución, an elegant square fronted by the **Ayuntamiento**, forms the town's core; all the monuments are within easy walking distance from here. It should be possible to see most of the main **churches** (all free) on the same day; though note that some of them close on Sunday and Monday. Priego is also in the centre of a major **olive oil** zone, which produces some of Spain's finest oils. Many of the *almazaras* (oil mills) are open for visits and tastings; details are available from the Turismo (see p.409).

The towns and villages around Priego generally lack anything compelling in the way of sights, but two outstanding exceptions are the village of **Almedinilla**, where a remarkable Roman villa has recently been discovered, and, a little further afield, the picturesque town of **Montefrío** and its nearby prehistoric site.

Brief history

Despite evidence of long prehistoric habitation in nearby caves and a later Roman settlement, it was under the Moors that Medina Bahiga, as Priego was then known, flourished as part of the kingdom of Granada. Following a tug of war between the Moors and Christians during the fourteenth century, in which the town changed hands three times, it finally fell to the Christians in 1341. Recovery from the aftermath of this turbulent era came only in the eighteenth century when, in 1711, Priego became a dependency of the dukes of Medinaceli. An economic resurgence based on the

PRIEGO DE CÓRDOBA

● RESTAURANTS	
Balcón del Adarve	3
El Aljibe	1
El Virrey	2

● TAPAS BARS	
Bar Río	4
Mesón el Telar	5

■ ACCOMMODATION	
Hostal Rafi	6
Hotel Huerta de las Palomas	4
Hotel Zahori	2
La Posada Real	3
Río Piscina	1
Villa Turística	5

production of silk and textiles poured great wealth into the town and it was during this time that most of the **Baroque churches**, Priego's outstanding attraction today, were constructed or remodelled. In the nineteenth century, though, the industry found it hard to compete with cheap cotton textiles produced in Catalunya and Britain, and a slow decline set in. The Europe-wide slump in textiles in the 1950s and 1960s caused by imports from Asia accelerated the problems and, as factories closed, many people emigrated to seek work elsewhere. Today the remnants of the textile industry, along with farming, are the town's main employers.

Castillo

Plaza de la Abad Palomino • Tues–Sat 11.30am–1.30pm & 4.30–6.30pm, Sun 11.30am–1.30pm • €2 (ticket also valid for Carnicerías Reales)

From the Plaza de la Constitución, head northeast towards the **Barrio de la Villa**, the old quarter, which contains most of Priego's principal monuments. A good place to begin is with the austere Moorish **castle** whose impressive keep, the Torre del Homenaje, dominates the small Plaza del Abad Palomino. There are spectacular views from the other towers.

Carnicerías Reales

C/San Pedro de Alcantara s/n • Sun & Mon 11.30am–1.30pm, Tues–Sat 11.30am–1.30pm & 5–7pm • €2 (ticket also valid for castillo)

Near the castillo, to the rear of the church of San Pedro, the **Carnicerías Reales** is a sixteenth-century abattoir and meat market with a fine cobbled patio.

Iglesia de la Asunción

Plaza del Abad Palomino • Mon 7.15–8pm, Wed 11.30am–1.30pm, Tues & Thurs–Sun 11.30am–1.30pm & 7.15–8pm • Free

The first and most important of the Baroque churches is the **Iglesia de la Asunción**, its modest whitewashed exterior dating from the sixteenth century. The original Gothic building was remodelled in the Baroque style in the eighteenth century by Jerónimo Sánchez de Rueda, an architect who did a similar job on many of Priego's other churches.

It is inside, however, that the surprises begin: an ornate white stucco Baroque interior leads towards a stunningly beautiful carved Mannerist **retablo** with images attributed to Juan Bautista Vázquez. The greatest surprise of all, though, lies through a portal on the left aisle where you enter the breathtaking **sagrario**, one of the masterpieces of Spanish Baroque. Here, a dazzling symphony of wedding-cake white stuccowork and statuary, punctuated by scrolls and cornices, climbs upwards beyond a balcony into a fabulous cupola illuminated by eight windows. The frothy depth of the stucco plaster was achieved by the use of esparto grass to lend it additional strength – a material which has played a remarkable part in the craft history of Andalucía, even found in hats, baskets and sandals discovered in the Neolithic caves of Granada. This recently restored octagonal chapel is the work of Francisco Javier Pedrajas, a native of Priego and one of a number of leading sculptors, carvers and gilders working in the town at this time. The *altar mayor* and the *sagrario* have been declared national monuments.

Barrio de la Villa

Before taking in more Baroque mastery, the nearby and delightful **Barrio de la Villa** provides a welcome opportunity for a stroll. The ancient Moorish part of the town, a maze of sinuous whitewashed alleys with balconies and walls loaded with pot plants, leads to a number of typical plazuelas. You should eventually stumble on one of the most charming, the **Plazuela de San Antonio**, replete with palms and wrought-iron *rejas*. Behind the Iglesia de la Asunción, Calle Bajondillo leads to the **Paseo de Adarve**, a superb, and originally Moorish, promenade with a spectacular **view** over the valley of the Río Salado and undulating groves of olives stretching to the distant hills.

Iglesia San Pedro

Plaza de San Pedro s/n • Mon–Sat 10.30am–1pm • Free

Just to the west of the castillo, the **Iglesia de San Pedro** is another Baroque treat with more stucco and a wonderful **altar mayor** in painted wood and stucco with a delightful domed *camarín* (shrine) behind, which holds a stirring image of the *Inmaculada*. The side chapel of the **Virgen de la Soledad**, with another *camarín*, has an image of the Virgin at the centre of its retablo by Pablo de Rojas.

Iglesia de San Juan

C/San Juan de Dios s/n • Mon–Sat 10.30am–1pm • Free

A short distance west of San Pedro, the church of **San Juan** is an early example of Priego Baroque, completed in 1717. Beyond a stone portal designed by Santaella (see p.408), the triple-naved interior has a finely crafted cupola, and – in the Capilla de la Virgen de la Soledad – a *camarín* and retablo by Pedrajas.

Iglesia de la Aurora

C/Álvarez s/n • Tues–Sun 10am–12.45pm, plus Sat midnight–1am • Free

To the south of the Barrio de la Villa stands the church of **La Aurora**, yet another Baroque gem remodelled from a former *ermita*, whose exuberant facade, with Corinthian and Solomonic pillars topped by a Virgin and flanked by exquisite stone and marble decoration, is only a prelude to the interior. This, now restored to its full glory, is a single-naved Baroque explosion in painted wood and stucco descending from the grey and white cornices, with polychromed figures on its ceiling, dome and walls, to an animated and sumptuously theatrical **retablo**. This retablo is a glittering amalgam of *vegetal* and geometrical forms, and the crowning achievement of Juan de Dios Santaella, another native Priego talent, born here in 1716. The church is also home to the **Cofradía de la Aurora**, a brotherhood whose sixteenth-century articles of foundation stipulate that they must proceed through the streets in musical procession every Saturday at midnight. Thus, whatever the weather, this band of men, hatted and cloaked, gather behind their banner and a huge lantern to proceed through the streets singing hymns to *La Aurora* (Our Lady of the Dawn) accompanied by guitars, accordions and tambourines.

Iglesia de San Francisco

C/San Francisco s/n • Mon–Sat 10am–1pm & 6–8pm, Sun 9.30am–12.45pm • Free

Just south of the church of La Aurora on an elegant old square, the **Iglesia de San Francisco** is another late-Gothic church that Santaella had a hand in remodelling and which has recently been restored to its former splendour. Once you've admired the facade and portal (both by Santaella), employing contrasting tones of marble, look inside: the *retablo mayor* is a splendid gilded work by Santaella again. The **chapel of Jesús Nazareno** has a sumptuous gilded and polychromed wood and stucco retablo by Pedrajas, the creator of the *sagrario* in the Asunción, and is topped off by another extravagant cupola by Santaella. The altarpiece's central image of *Jesús Nazareno* (Christ bearing the Cross) is a fine work, attributed to Pedro de Mena.

The Fuente del Rey and around

At the southwestern end of the town, and easily reached by following Calle Río – a street dotted with many fine Baroque portals – to its end, lies the **Fuente del Rey**, a spectacular sixteenth-century 180-jet fountain (with many later additions) which pours water into a number of basins. The highest of these has a sculpture of a lion struggling with a serpent, while the second contains a larger late eighteenth-century depiction of Neptune and Amphitrite, the king and queen of the sea. Amphitrite is clutching the dolphin that returned her to Neptune after her attempted escape, incidentally emphasizing the power of the king, the work's intended ideological message, given that over the border in France, monarchs were losing their heads. There are in fact two fountains here, the second being the **Fuente de la Salud**, to the rear of the plaza, a sixteenth-century Italianate work built on the spot, according to legend, where the conquering Alfonso XI pitched his camp in 1341. One of the most tranquil squares in Andalucía, this leafy area is a wonderful place to relax and get away from it all, which is why there are so many seats.

From just beyond the square you can **walk** to the Ermita del Calvario from where there are fine **views** over the town. Take the steps to the left of the Fuente de la Salud.

Museo Niceto Alcalá Zamora

C/Río 46 • Tues–Sat 10am–1.30pm & 4.30–7pm, Sun 10am–1.30pm • Free • ☎ 957 543 030, ⓦ epriego.com/niceto/

Another historic building on Calle Río at no. 46 is the birthplace of, and now **museum** dedicated to, **Niceto Alcalá Zamora**, first president of the ill-fated Spanish republic from 1931 to 1936. On a visit to Scandinavia when the Civil War broke out, he never returned to Spain but spent the rest of his life in France and then Argentina where he died in 1949, unwilling to recognize the Franco regime. Much of the original furniture of this middle-class nineteenth-century family mansion survives intact, and you are free to look around.

Iglesia del Carmen

C/Río s/n • Mon–Tues & Thurs–Sun 6.15–7pm plus Sun 11.15am–noon • Free

The **Iglesia del Carmen** is another church remodelled in the eighteenth century by Santaella. A brilliant white interior and cupola has a fine gilded retablo with a *camarín* also by Santaella.

Iglesia de las Angustias

C/Río s/n • Sat 11am–1pm • Free

Just off the Plaza de la Constitución at the start of Calle Río, the **Iglesia de las Angustias** is a charming small church and another work by Santaella. The interior has a fine cupola with typically exuberant polychromed stucco decoration.

Iglesia de las Mercedes

Carrera de la Monjas s/n • Mon,Tues & Thurs 5.45–6.30pm, Wed 6.15–7pm, Fri 10.30am–1pm & 5.45–6.30pm, Sat 10.30am–1pm, Sun 9.45–10.30am • Free

East of the Plaza de la Constitución, the **Iglesia de las Mercedes** was an ancient hermitage prior to its remodelling in the latter part of the eighteenth century when its interior was decorated in Rococo style by Pedrajas, highlighted by the four winged archangels at the scalloped corners. Another stunningly ornate snow-white cupola (which is almost Pedrajas's trademark), is balanced by an elegant retablo below. The exterior is an incomplete later addition.

Museo Histórico

Carrera de las Monjas 9 • Tues–Sat 10am–1.30pm & 6–8.30pm, Sun 10am–1.30pm • Free • ☎ 957 540 947

Almost opposite the Iglesia de las Mercedes, Priego's **Museo Histórico** is housed in an elegant *señorial* mansion with a fine patio. The interesting collection displays finds from the surrounding area dating from the Paleolithic down to the Roman and Moorish periods.

ARRIVAL AND INFORMATION   PRIEGO DE CÓRDOBA

By bus Buses drop you in the central Plaza de la Constitución, although the actual bus station is a 5min walk to the west of the centre on C/Nuestra Señora de los Remedios. There are easy connections with Córdoba, Granada and Málaga.

Turismo Plaza de la Constitución 3 (Mon–Sat 10am–2pm & 4.30–7pm, Sun 10am–2pm; ☎ 957 700 625,

🔲 turismodepriego.com). This is an efficient office with copious information on the town and the Subbética and details (repeated on their website) on *casas rurales* in the surrounding area.

Internet Ceballos Recreativos, Paseo de Colombia 4 (daily noon–2.30pm & 5–11pm).

ACCOMMODATION

Priego offers some very pleasant, reasonably priced places to stay, and, outside the first week in September, when the town celebrates its annual **Feria Real**, there's usually no great demand.

Hostal Rafi C/Isabel la Católica 4 ☎ 957 540 749, 🔲 hostalrafi.es. In a tiny street near the main square, this welcoming *hostal*, housed in a refurbished mansion, is an excellent deal. Comfortable a/c en-suite rooms come with satellite TV; own car park and restaurant, with a *menú* for €9. **€46**

Hotel Huerta de las Palomas Ctra. Priego-Zagrilla km3 ☎ 957 720 305, 🔲 zercahoteles.com. Four kilometres northwest of town along the CO8211 (direction Zagrilla), this is a stylish four-star hotel with well-equipped and spacious rooms in rolling Subbética countryside; facilities include gym, pool and restaurant. It also offers activities including mountain biking, tennis and hiking. Ten percent discount for *Rough Guide* readers with this guide. B&B **€106**

Hotel Zahori C/Real 2 ☎ 957 547 292, 🔲 hotelzahori .es. In the picturesque Barrio de la Villa, this charming small hotel offers excellent a/c en-suite rooms in a refurbished town house, and a good mid-priced restaurant. **€54**

La Posada Real C/Real 14 ☎ 957 541 910, 🔲 laposadareal.com. Another possibility in the Barrio de la Villa, this is an attractive, flower-bedecked little place with cosy, a/c en-suite balcony rooms with TV. Also rents some apartments nearby. Rooms B&B **€55**, apartments **€80**

Río Piscina ☎ 957 700 186, 🔲 hotelriopiscina.com. Spacious a/c terrace rooms overlooking a garden pool. Other features include restaurant, tennis court, gardens and a car park. **€56**

Villa Turística Aldea de Zagrilla s/n, 3km beyond the Huerta de las Palomas hotel along the CO8233 leading to Zagrilla ☎ 957 703 503, 🔲 villadepriego.com. Built on traditional lines with lots of Moorish-inspired decor, this country hotel has 52 apartment/chalets sited in gardens where water features set the mood. Offers a range of outdoor activities including horseriding and mountain biking. **€82**

EATING AND DRINKING

The bars around the main square are good for breakfast and tapas. In addition to those listed below, the restaurant attached to *Hostal Rafi* (see p.409) is especially good, and *Hotel Zahori* (see p.409) is also worth a try.

Balcón del Adarve Paseo de Colombia 36 ☎ 957 547 075. Priego's most celebrated restaurant is close to the promenade it's named after and part of which it uses as a pleasant terrace; specialities include *rabo de toro* (stewed bull's tail), *carillada ibérica* (pork cheeks) and a wide range of other dishes of the region. There's a *menú de degustación* for around €20. Main dishes €11–18. Tues–Sun 1–4pm & 8pm–midnight.

Bar Río C/Río 3. A highly popular tapas and *raciones* bar noted for its *calamares fritos* and *flamenquines* (deep-fried pork and *jamón* roll). Daily 9am–11pm.

El Aljibe C/Abad Palomino 7, opposite the Iglesia de la Asunción ☎ 957 701 856, ⓦ restaurante-elaljibe.com. Built over a Moorish bathhouse (which you can glimpse through a glass floor in the lower dining room). The menu features some Moorish-inspired dishes – *asado de cordero con membrillo* (lamb with quince) is one – plus a lunch *menú* for €11; there's also an attractive outdoor terrace. Main dishes €7–15. Daily 1–4.30pm & 8pm–midnight.

El Virrey C/Solana 16, off Plaza San Pedro. A good neighbourhood restaurant preparing a wide range of local dishes such as *lomo ibérico* (pork loin) and *salmorejo*. There's also a weekday *menú* for €10 which you may need to ask for. Main dishes €6–15. Daily noon–4pm & 7.30–11pm.

Mesón El Telar C/Buen Suceso 2, close to the Iglesia de San Francisco. Excellent tapas and *raciones* bar where the specialities of the house include *berenjenas a la miel* (fried aubergine in honey) and *rabo de toro*. Mon–Sat noon–4pm & 8–11pm.

Carcabuey

Seven kilometres west of Priego and reachable by bus, **CARCABUEY** is a charming place laid out on a hill topped by a ruined castle. The Gothic-Renaissance church of **La Asunción** lower down has a handsome Renaissance portal flanked with marble pillars, and inside an elegant **retablo** with the central figure of Christ attributed to Pedro de Mena and Alonso Cano. It is usually locked, so you'll need to ask at the nearby houses for the key.

ACCOMMODATION AND EATING · CARCABUEY

La Zamora Ctra. Cabra-Priego, A339 km14 ☎ 957 704 208, ⓦ hostal-lazamora.com. This motel-style *hostal* on the nearby main highway, 3km towards Cabra, is the only place to stay. The en-suite rooms are simple but clean and the welcome is warm; the restaurant below serves tapas, *raciones* and full meals and has a *menú* for under €10. Free parking. **€40**

Almedinilla

ALMEDINILLA, 9km east of Priego on the Jaén border, is a characteristic Subbética village squatting along the valley of the Río Caicena. Hardly worth a second glance until recently, it has catapulted itself onto the tourist map with the discovery of a remarkable **Roman villa** with unique features as well as a fine **museum**.

Villa Romana de El Ruedo

At the northern edge of Amedinilla close to the main A340 highway • March–Sept Wed–Fri & Sun 10.30am–1.30pm, Sat 10.30am–1.30pm & 6–7.30pm; Oct–May Wed–Fri & Sun 10.30am–1.30pm, Sat 10.30am–1.30pm & 4.15–6pm; guided tours daily 1.30pm • ☎ 957 703 317, ⓦ almedinillaturismo.org • €2.20

Discovered in 1989, the **Villa Romana de Ruedo** is now recognized as one of the most important Roman villas in Andalucía. Once inside the entrance you will pass to the left the remains of an ancient **pottery kiln**. This would have provided the numerous ceramic containers necessary for the substantial oil and grain farming centred on the villa. Beyond this and beneath a canopy lies the villa proper, constructed and inhabited between the first and fifth centuries AD. Laid out around a central patio or **atrium**, with remains of walls well over a metre high, the bedrooms and living rooms – many bearing vestiges of frescoes and laid with mosaic floors – are adjoined by a bath and kitchen as well as bodegas for storing wine, the ruins of an oil mill and warehouses for holding grain. But it is on the north side of the patio in the dining room, or **triclinium**, where the most sensational finds were discovered. In the centre of this room is a well-preserved **podium** upon which diners would have reclined whilst eating. Behind this and set into the wall are the remains of a spectacular artificial **cascade** fed by a diverted nearby stream, unique in Spain and added when the villa was substantially remodelled in the third century AD, providing an aural backdrop to the diners' meals. Also unearthed here were a number of outstanding sculptures; the major work, a bronze figure of Hypnos, in Greek mythology the god of sleep, is now displayed in the Museo Histórico (see below).

To the north and east of the villa lie the remains of a **necropolis** that would have served the Roman settlement here, as well as the remnants of numerous other Roman dwellings. It is planned to excavate these too, eventually transforming the whole area into an archeological park. At the moment a **museum-information centre** (same hours), with reconstructions and exhibits discovered during the excavations, stands opposite the entrance to the villa.

Museo Histórico

April–Sept Wed–Fri & Sun 10am–1.30pm, Sat 10am–1.30pm & 6–8pm; call for winter hours • €2.20 • ☎ 957 703 317, ⓦ almedinilla.es /museo-historico-cultural

Almedinilla's **Museo Histórico**, on the east side of the village, is housed in a former oil and flour mill, El Molino de Fuente Ribera, whose grindstones were powered by the adjacent Río Caicena. The exhibits are distributed on three floors with the ground floor displaying the mill's grindstones, once used for making olive oil. Taking its theme from this machinery, the rest of the room charts the development of olive oil production from Iberian and Roman times to the present day – not losing an opportunity to remind visitors that the oil produced here today is as highly prized as it was in Roman times, carrying its own *denominación de origen*. The second floor is devoted to the **Iberian period**, particularly finds from Cerro de la Cruz, a hill settlement discovered on the crag behind the village by archeologists early in the last century. The remains displayed – pottery, burial goods, weapons and tools – detail a well-planned urban development existing between the fourth century BC and the first century AD. The museum can provide information about guided visits to the Cerro de la Cruz site.

The third floor houses the **Roman collection** with the finds from the Roman villa of El Ruedo. Pride of place goes to the sculptures, particularly the fine and superbly restored bronze of the Greek god of sleep **Hypnos**, discovered in the villa's dining room, and a work of exceptional quality. For the Greeks (and the Romans who knew him as Somnus) Hypnos was the personification of sleep and his mission was to lead the soul to a peaceful death, as in a dream. Made from individual casts of bronze later welded together, in his left hand he would have held an opium poppy to induce sleep, and in his right a horn from which he cast the night as he flew across the sky with the aid of wings protruding from his temples. Almost as fine is a bronze **hermaphrodite** depicting the dancing figure staring into a mirror held in its right hand (now lost) which would have reflected the feminine parts thus exciting the masculine side of its androgynous nature. This ancient fascination with dualism – as in life and death, darkness and light, male and female – is undoubtedly the work's underlying message. Other sculptures in stone include a genius of the house, perhaps depicting spring, a partially damaged image of Perseus and Andromeda, and a head of Dionysos. A **maquette** of the Roman villa gives you an idea how it would have looked when in use.

INFORMATION ALMEDINILLA

Ayuntamiento Should you have any problems gaining access to the Roman villa or museum, call at the Ayuntamiento, Plaza de España s/n (☎ 957 703 085, ⓦ almedinillaturismo.org), who should be able to help.

ACCOMMODATION AND EATING

Bar-Restaurante La Bodega Plaza de España, in front of the Ayuntamiento. The village's main bar-restaurant serves tapas in its bar and a range of *cordobés* cuisine – including *salmorejo* and *rabo de toro* – in its restaurant. There's also midday *menú* for €8.

Mesón Rural La Era Plaza La Era 1 ☎ 957 703 201. Excellent and well-equipped en-suite a/c rooms in the heart of the village at this cunningly recreated copy of an ancient town house which, despite appearances, is completely new. It also has its own bar-restaurant. B&B **€65**

Alcalá La Real

ALCALÁ LA REAL, 27km east of Priego, is a pleasant country town at the foot of a hill dominated by one of the most impressive Moorish forts in eastern Andalucía. Later reconstructed as the **Castillo de la Mota** (daily: July–Sept 10.30am–1.30pm & 5–8pm; Oct–June 10.30am–6.30pm; €5), it preserves among its earlier gates the Moorish **Puerta de la Imagen**. After the fort had been taken during the *Reconquista*, Alfonso XI built – and this became the custom – the Renaissance church of **Santa María la Mayor** inside the walls. Designed by the leading architect of the sixteenth century, Diego de Siloé, and now magnificently restored, its interior floor conserves scores of Visigothic burial niches from an earlier building on the site. Displays in the church's small museum evidence activity on this hill going back to prehistoric times. The fort's imposing **Torre de la Homenaje** also has an interesting small **museum** with great views from the top of the tower.

Turismo The castle's ticket office doubles as the Turismo (daily: July–Sept 10.30am–1.30pm & 5–8pm; Oct–June 10.30am–6.30pm; ☎ mobile 639 647 796).

ACCOMMODATION AND EATING

Hotel Torrepalma C/Conde de Torrepalma 2 ☎ 953 581 800, ⊛hoteltorrepalma.com. This three-star hotel lies just off the town's main street, Avda. de Andalucía, and has comfortable and well-equipped a/c rooms with free wi-fi. Also has its own bar-restaurant. **€60**

Montefrío

MONTEFRÍO, 24km southeast of Priego (or 32km by road), and just over the Granada border, is one of the more spectacularly sited towns in this part of the region. Cradled between two rocky outcrops, each topped by a church which can be visited, the town has the even bigger Neoclassical **Iglesia de la Encarnación** (daily 10am–2pm & 8–9pm; free) at its heart, with an enormous dome and bizarre acoustics. The most interesting of the hill-top churches is the sixteenth-century **Iglesia de la Villa** (daily noon–2pm; €2.50, a superb building designed by Diego de Siloé, and now converted into a themed museum based on the reconquest of this part of Andalucía from the Moors. The interior has some exquisite **vaulting** and is surrounded by the ruins of the Moorish *alcazaba*; there are fine **views** over the town and beyond from its tower. The church is reached by a bracing climb along the road which ascends beyond the Turismo (see below).

Turismo Plaza de España 1, just uphill on the left from the Encarnación church (Mon–Fri & Sun 10am–2pm, Sat 10am–2pm & 4–6pm; ☎ 958 336 004, ⊛montefrio.org). This office can supply information on Las Peñas de los Gitanos (see p.413).

ACCOMMODATION

Casas rurales A number of *casas rurales* are available for rent in and around the town – including one on the outcrop just below La Villa church. Ask at the Turismo or call ☎ 958 310 124 (English spoken).

Hotel La Enrea Ctra. Tocón s/n ☎ 958 336 662, ⊛laenreahotel.com. Reached by following the Granada road out of the centre (an easy five- to ten-minute walk) this is the town's best hotel, housed in a converted nineteenth-century water-mill in a picturesque river gorge. Marble-floored a/c rooms are light and airy and have free wi-fi. Also has its own bar-restaurant. B&B €65

EATING

Bar-Restaurante Pregonero Plaza de España 3, next door to the Turismo. This place serves tapas (in the bar) and *platos combinados* in the restaurant, which has a pleasant outdoor terrace. They also offer a weekday lunchtime *menú* for less than €10.

Bar Uno Más Plaza Virgen de los Remedios 3. A good place to try the acclaimed local chorizo and *morcilla* (blood pudding), facing the Encarnación church.

Las Peñas de los Gitanos

Some 8km east of Montefrío along the GR3410 towards Illora, and signposted

Six kilometres long and demarcated by limestone outcrops, the remarkable Neolithic site of **Las Peñas de los Gitanos** was occupied by Stone-Age people in the third millennium BC. The overhanging rocks and caves were used as shelters by bulls, goats, sheep and other ancient beasts and this food source attracted early humans who would have hunted these animals in groups. These ancient hunters left behind paintings inside the caves (currently not on view), various **stone tombs** – some with carvings of animals and horns – and the remains of later stone and clay dwellings when they became Chalcolithic (copper-age) village dwellers. Make sure to see Dolmen 23 (fronted by an information board) which is the best preserved of the group, with a finely worked entrance still intact. A detailed leaflet (in Spanish) is available from the Turismo in Montefrío, but many of the dolmens and other remains are hard to find, so a **guided visit** is recommended.

ARRIVAL AND INFORMATION   LAS PEÑAS DE LOS GITANOS

To visit the site, which is on private land, you will need to contact **Las Peñas de Los Gitanos S.L.** (☎ 628 305 337; English spoken). Having arranged a visit and arrived at the site, park at the signed entry road (with locked gate barring vehicles) on the left where Sra. Paqui Sanchez will normally meet you.

Guided visits Guided tours (2 daily, morning and late afternoon; 2hr; €10) must be booked at least 24 hours in advance through Paqui Sanchez. The meeting point is normally at the site entrance.

Auto-guided visits You can visit the site independently (€7) with the aid of a map, but will still need to contact Sra. Sanchez to book and be allowed access.

Northeast of Córdoba

The A4–E5 highway which heads northeast out of Córdoba along the valley of the Guadalquivir is the main road to Madrid and one of the great historical highways of Andalucía. Not only was this the bullion route between Madrid and its imperial seaports of Seville and Cádiz, but over a millennium and a half earlier, as the Vía Augusta, it formed the vital overland link joining Roman Spain with Gaul, Italy and Rome itself. Transport is easy, with buses linking Córdoba to most places, and trains to Montoro, Andujar and Bailen. The route has a number of delightful stopovers including the handsome small town of **Montoro**, an outstanding Moorish castle at **Baños de Encina** and the historic **Despeñaperros Pass**.

Montoro

MONTORO lies 43km from Córdoba, beyond the villages of El Carpio and Pedro Abad, and just off the A4–E5. Dramatically sited on an escarpment above a horseshoe bend in the Guadalquivir, the town is a centre of olive-oil production obtained from extensive groves planted in the foothills of the Sierra Morena to the north. A labyrinth of narrow, white-walled streets surrounds the main square, the Plaza de España, dominated by the lofty tower of its Gothic-Mudéjar church, **San Bartolomé**. The interior, behind the red sandstone facade, has a fine *artesonado* ceiling inlaid with mother-of-pearl, recently recovered from under layers of whitewash. On the same square is the sixteenth-century **Ayuntamiento**, an old ducal mansion with a fine Plateresque frontage. The narrow main street (Calle Corredera) connects Plaza de España with **Plaza del Charco** (aka Plaza Caridad), which contains the town's main **bars** and two *casinos*, the larger Casino de los Ricos (Rich) and the Casino de los Pobres (Poor), reflecting the bitter class divisions that once existed here and to some extent persist.

Santa María de la Mota archeological museum

Plaza Santa María s/n · Sat, Sun & hols 11am–1pm, outside these times contact the Turismo on ☎ 957 160 089 · Free

A narrow street uphill out of the north side of the square leads into an atmospheric old quarter whose main feature is the thirteenth-century church of **Santa María de la Mota**, with some interesting Romanesque capitals, now converted into a small **archeological museum**.

Casa de las Conchas

C/Grajas 17 (signed from Plaza de España)

One curiosity that shouldn't be missed is the **Casa de las Conchas**. Here the owners have covered both the exterior and interior with thousands of seashells; the proprietor or his wife will proudly show you around and relate the story behind their 30-year-old obsession.

Museo Antonio Rodríguez de Luna

Plaza del Charco 18 · Sun & hols 11am–1pm, or contact the Turismo on ☎ 957 160 089 · Free

Slightly uphill from the Plaza del Charco and housed in the eighteenth-century Capilla de San Jacinto, lies the **Museo Antonio Rodríguez de Luna** housing some powerful abstract works by the Montoro-born artist who spent part of his life in Paris and Mexico and died in 1985.

Puente de Las Donadas

The elegant sixteenth-century bridge of **Las Donadas** over the Guadalquivir was paid for by local women who, tradition holds, sold their jewellery to place the town on a more direct, and lucrative, route to the north. Across the bridge, the Cardeña road leading up into the hills offers superb **views** back over the town.

ARRIVAL AND INFORMATION   MONTORO

By train Montoro is served by trains on the Córdoba–Linares–Madrid line.

Turismo C/Corredera 23 (Mon–Fri 9.30am–3pm, Sat 10am–1pm, Sun 10am–2pm; ☎ 957 160 089).

ACCOMMODATION AND EATING

Bar Yepez Plaza del Charco 4 ☎ 957 160 123. Popular and bustling local bar with a wide tapas range. House specials include *berenjenas con salmón* (aubergine with salmon) and *alcachofas con rabo de toro* (artichokes with bull's tail stew).

Mirador de Montoro Cerro de la Muela s/n ☎ 957 165 105, ⓦ zercahoteles.com. This three-star hotel at the southern end of town offers light and pleasantly furnished a/c rooms, many with terraces offering great views over the river valley. Facilities include a pool, restaurant and free wi-fi. *Rough Guide* readers with this guide can claim a ten percent discount. **€80**

Andújar

Lying some 32km beyond Montoro, **ANDÚJAR** is a sizeable if simple country town which claims to be the world's biggest centre of sunflower-oil bottling. There's also a thriving commercial ceramics industry, as well as a couple of churches worth a visit for their artworks. The road into the town crosses a fifteen-arched Roman **bridge** spanning the Guadalquivir, which has been considerably restored from Moorish times onwards. There are also a number of elegant **Renaissance palaces** within walking distance of the centre; the Turismo can provide a map detailing their locations.

Plaza de España

The central **Plaza de España**, a baking furnace in the heat of high summer, is overlooked by the impressive Gothic church of **San Miguel** (April–Sept Mon–Sat 7.30–9pm, Sun 11.30am–1.30pm; Oct–March Mon–Sat 6.30–8pm, Sun 11am–1.30pm) with a fine stone tower and Plateresque features. It is flanked by an equally striking late-Baroque **Ayuntamiento** – recently restored to its full glory – with elegant portals.

Iglesia de Santa María

Plaza de Santa María • April–Sept Tues–Sun 11.30am–1.30pm & 7–9pm; Oct–March closes 8pm • Free

The most interesting church in town is the **Iglesia de Santa María** on the plaza of the same name, reached by following Calle La Feria from Plaza de España. Built on the site of a former mosque, the free-standing bell tower probably replaced the mosque's minaret and now houses a small tourist office (see below). Inside, a chapel on the left has a fine *Christ in the Garden of Olives* by **El Greco**, a startling surprise in a nondescript country church. The superb **reja** which stands before the El Greco is the work of Master Bartolomé of Jaén, who also created the more famous one in the Capilla Real at Granada.

Archeological museum

C/Don Gome • June–Sept Tues–Sat 10am–2pm; Oct–May 11am–1pm & 4–6pm • Free

The town's **archeological museum** is housed in the striking seventeenth-century Palacio Don Gome, Calle Don Gome, to the southeast of Plaza de España, decorated with moustached figures of feathered Indians inspired by the burgeoning Spanish American empire. The collection consists of mainly Roman ceramics.

ARRIVAL AND INFORMATION   ANDÚJAR

By train Trains on the Córdoba–Linares–Madrid line stop at Andújar.

Turismo Torre del Reloj, Plaza de Santa María s/n (July &

Aug Mon–Sat 8.30am–2.30pm; Oct–March Mon–Fri 9am–2pm & 5.30–7pm, Sat 9am–1.30pm; ☏ 953 504 959).

ACCOMMODATION

The most attractive accommodation options in the area are in the Parque Natural (see p.416).

Hotel Logasasanti C/Dr Fleming s/n ☏ 953 500 500, ⓦ logasasanti.com. The best place to stay in town, this has functional a/c rooms, free wi-fi and a bar-restaurant with a €9 *menú*. **€51**

EATING AND DRINKING

Bar-Restaurante Los Naranjos C/Guadalupe 4. A very good tapas bar – try their *perdiz en escabeche* (marinaded partridge) – and restaurant combined. House specials in the restaurant include *ensalada de conejo en salsa* (rabbit salad) and there's also a €10 *menú*. Tues–Sun 1–4pm & 8pm–midnight.

Mesón El Churrasco Corredera de Capuchinos 12, east of Plaza de España ☏ 953 502 120, ⓦ restauranteel churrascoandujar.com. Excellent and popular town centre

restaurant for meat and fish dishes. *Carnes de monte* (wild boar and venison) are popular here and the bar also serves excellent tapas and *raciones*. Daily 12.30–4pm & 8.30pm–midnight.

Mesón Ortega Plaza de España. A lively tapas bar on this focal square with a pleasant outdoor terrace. House favourites include *carrillada ibérica* (pork cheeks) and *ensalada de pimientos* (red pepper salad). Tues–Sun 8.30am–4.30pm & 7–10.30pm.

4

Parque Natural Sierra de Andújar

A wonderful thirty-kilometre drive into the **Parque Natural Sierra de Andújar** to the north of Andújar along the A6177 leads to the thirteenth-century hermitage of **Nuestra Virgen de la Cabeza**, one of the most revered of Andalucía's shrines. To break the journey, on the way up there are three decent **ventas** (see below).

Once you arrive at the shrine, there's not much left of the ancient building, which was destroyed in the Civil War when two hundred Guardia Civil officers seized it, declaring their support for Franco's rebellion. Bombarded for eight months by Republican forces, the sanctuary was eventually set alight and the guards captured on May 1, 1937. The distasteful rebuild flanked by equally bleak Guardia Civil monuments was carried out during the Franco period, but the famous *romería* – in which brotherhoods and pilgrims converge on the shrine from all over Andalucía and Spain on the last Sunday in April – carries on undaunted. In a crypt to the side of the church is a display of hundreds of crutches, Zimmer frames and all kinds of surgical supports and braces left behind by "healed" pilgrims – a bizarre testament to the Virgin's curative powers.

INFORMATION   PARQUE NATURAL SIERRA DE ANDÚJAR

Centro de Visitantes As you drive up into the park, at the 13km point (April–Sept Thurs & Sun 10am–2pm, Fri & Sat 10am–2pm & 6–8pm; Oct–March Thurs–Sun 10am–2pm & 4–6pm; ☎ 953 549 030). The centre has displays on the natural park's flora and fauna including the threatened *lince ibérico* (pardel lynx); they can also provide a map of the park and have leaflets detailing hiking routes.

ACCOMMODATION AND EATING

El Toledillo Crta. del Santuario ☎ 953 505 800. Decent *venta* on the route into the natural park, serving up the usual standards such as *solomillo* (pork loin) and *churrasco* (pork steak). They also offer an economical weekday *menú del día*.

El Tropezón Crta. del Santuario km3 ☎ 953 506 921, ⓦ restauranteeltropezon.es. On the drive into the park, this roadside restaurant specializes in *carnes a la brasa* (grilled meats) and *pescados al horno* (oven-baked fish). There's also a weekday *menú del día* for around €10. Daily 9am–1pm.

La Mirada Virgen de la Cabeza ☎ 953 549 111. A hotel-bar-restaurant close to the shrine, with functional a/c rooms and an adjoining small mini-market. €71

Los Pinos Crta. del Santuario km14.2 ☎ 953 549 023, ⓦ lospinos.es. Tourist complex with cosy en-suite rooms, *apartamentos rurales* and cottages in a pleasant woodland setting with a pool. There's a good restaurant, too, with an economical *menú*. Doubles €49, apartments and cottages €97

Sierra Luna 6km down a road heading west (direction Alcaparrosa) from near the Centro de Visitantes ☎ mobile 653 805 129, ⓦ sierra-luna.com. A rural option with accommodation in fully equipped wood cabins sleeping up to four. €73

Villa Matilde 3km down a track heading east from Los Pinos (signed "La Jandula") ☎ 953 549 127, ⓦ villa matilde.org. A pleasant rural retreat offering (mostly) en-suite rooms in a converted villa with a pool and a restaurant that also caters for vegetarians. €44

Baños de la Encina

Just beyond Andújar, the A4-E5 turns away from the Guadalquivir valley to head northeast to **Bailén**, a dull farming town where Napoleon's troops suffered a crushing defeat in 1808. From here it pushes on for another 45km to Andalucía's border with La Mancha at the Despeñaperros Pass (see p.419) and Madrid. Other **possible routes** from this junction lead south to the city of Jaén, or east to Baeza and Úbeda via Linares.

Some 6km after Bailén a left turn leads to the sizeable village of **BAÑOS DE LA ENCINA**, which has one of the most impressive Moorish castles in Andalucía. Crowning a low hill above the village, the tenth-century **Alcázar** is a magnificent sight with its fourteen square towers and enormous keep spaced out along a crenellated curtain wall.

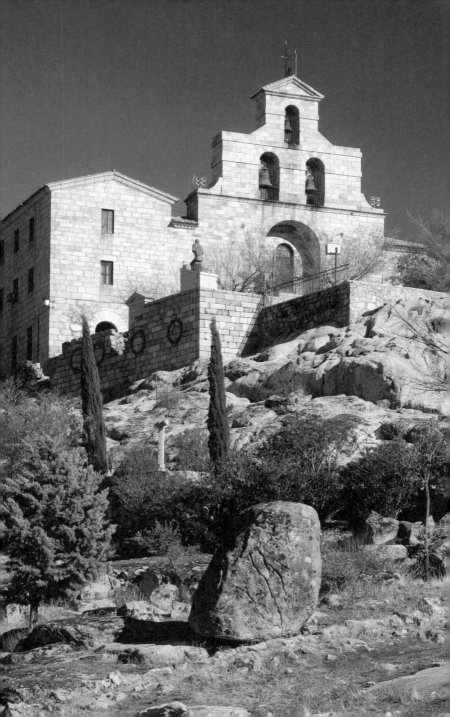

Alcázar

C/Santa María s/n • Guided tours: April & May Tues–Fri 11am & noon, Sat & Sun 10.30am–1.30pm & 5.30–7.30pm; June–Sept Tues–Fri 11am & noon, Sat & Sun 10.30am–1.30pm & 6–8pm; Oct–March Tues–Fri 11am & noon, Sat & Sun 10.30am–1.30pm & 4.30–6.30pm • €2 (buy your ticket from the tourist office first)

Baños de la Encina's **Alcázar** was built by al-Hakam II of Córdoba in 967, in an attempt to control the rugged and mountainous territory to the north, the domain of various unruly Iberian clans, as well as the entry to Andalucía through the Despeñaperros pass and along the nearby valley of the Guadalquivir. During the *Reconquista* the castle changed hands twice in the twelfth century and it was only in 1225 that it finally fell to Fernando III (El Santo) to be incorporated into the dominion of Castile. Entered through a double-horseshoe arch, where a plaque in Arabic script dates the edifice to year 357 of the *hegira* (967 AD), the fort has an oval ground plan and from the battlements there are **fine views** over the village and towards the Sierra de Cazorla to the east and the less impressive reservoir behind.

San Mateo

Plaza de la Constitución s/n • Open service times: April–Sept 7pm; Oct–June 8pm • Free

The splendid fifteenth-century red stone Gothic-Renaissance church of **San Mateo** dominates the main square. The most striking exterior feature is an elegant octagonal tower, while the interior has some wonderful vaulting and an exquisite *sagrario* (sanctuary) constructed in ebony and adorned with silver, marble and tortoiseshell.

Ermita de Cristo del Llano

Plaza Ermita s/n • Daily 10.30am–1pm & 4.30–6pm • Donation requested

It is worth heading out to the **Ermita de Cristo del Llano**, an eighteenth-century hermitage in the upper village that's a ten-minute walk from the tourist office. During the hours listed above the nuns will let you in to view the remarkable church and its startlingly beautiful **Baroque camarín** with stellar decoration and stucco polychromed angels and saints climbing to the roof.

INFORMATION

BAÑOS DE LA ENCINA

Municipal tourist office Callejón del Castillo 1, just off the main square (April–June & Sept Tues–Sun 10am–1.30pm & 5–7pm; July & Aug Tues–Sun 10am–1.30pm; Oct–March Tues–Sun 10am–1.30pm & 4.30–6.30pm; ☎ 953 613 229, ⓦ bdelaencina.com).

Tours The municipal tourist office offers a 90min guided tour of the castle and monuments (June–Sept Sat & Sun 11am & 6pm; April & May Sat & Sun 11am & 5pm; Oct–March Sat & Sun 11am & 4.30pm; €8).

ACCOMMODATION AND EATING

Bar-Restaurante Mirasierra C/Bailén s/n. A tapas bar and restaurant near the tourist office that does good full meals.

Hotel-Restaurante Baños Cerro de la Llaná s/n ☎ 953 614 068, ⓦ hotelbanos.com. Pleasant hotel on a hill behind the castle, with good-value balcony rooms many with stunning castle views (room 101 has the best). The restaurant offers tempting regional meat and game dishes, with a lunchtime weekday *menú* for €9. **€56**

La Carolina

LA CAROLINA, 20km northeast of Baños de la Encina, is the most important of the new towns set up by Carlos III in the eighteenth century to protect the bullion route from Cádiz to Madrid. As with the other settlements it was named after a member of the royal family – in this case the king himself – settled with foreign immigrants and laid out on a regular grid-pattern street plan that still survives today. The town's central square, the Plaza del Ayuntamiento, has the imposing, honey-coloured sandstone **Palacio de Pablo de Olavide**, built for Carlos III's radical minister, the force behind the Nuevas Poblaciones idea. De Olavide did not long enjoy the fruits of his labours, however, for the clergy, who were denied access to these new towns, wreaked their vengeance by denouncing him to the Inquisition. Arrested in 1776, he was divested of his property and confined to a convent in La Mancha subject to whatever penances the monks thought appropriate. He subsequently escaped to France. Flanking the *palacio*, the parish church of **La Concepción** contains a fine Baroque image of the *Virgen de las Angustias* in alabaster. The square is linked by a thoroughfare to an impressive tree-lined avenue entered via a gateway bearing images of Carlos III, at the far end of which lies the municipal **swimming pool**.

ACCOMMODATION AND EATING   LA CAROLINA

El Retorno C/Sanjurjo 5. A good neighbourhood restaurant next to *Los Jardineros hostal* serving up meat and fish tapas with a small street terrace. Daily noon–5pm & 8–11pm.

La Perdiz On the main A4-E5 highway, km268, at the edge of town ☎953 660 300, ⓦ nh-hoteles.es. Lovely, luxurious hotel with well-equipped rooms and stunning garden pool. Not be confused with the uninviting *Orellana Perdiz* nearby. **€100**

Los Jardineros C/Sanjurjo 1 ☎953 660 812. A friendly *hostal* a few blocks north of the Plaza de España and opposite the market, with clean and tidy en-suite rooms with TV. **€30**

The Despeñaperros Pass

Two kilometres beyond La Carolina, slightly before the village of Navas de Tolosa, a huge roadside **monument** marks the site of the important battle that took place in 1212 between the Christian armies under Alfonso VIII and the Almohad forces. The Moors suffered a crippling defeat, opening the way for the *Reconquista* of Andalucía. The monument depicts the Christian monarchs as well as the shepherd, an apparition of St Isidore in disguise, who, according to Christian belief, guided them through the well-defended Sierra Morena, thus enabling a surprise attack on the Moorish army who fled after defeat through the Despeñaperros Pass. This event, in fact, gave the pass its name – meaning the "overthrow of the dogs" (or Moors).

The **Despeñaperros Pass**, 14km further on, is the dramatic gateway between Andalucía and La Mancha and the only natural breach in the 500km length of the Sierra Morena. This narrow defile, flanked by daunting crags and slopes covered with dense pine woods, was for centuries the main point of entry into Andalucía from the north and many travellers have left vivid accounts of arriving in the lush promised land of the south after traversing the dry and arid plains of La Mancha (from the Moorish *manxa*, or parched earth). George Borrow, however, also related the sense of foreboding

4

DON QUIJOTE AND THE DESPEÑAPERROS PASS

Cervantes would have been familiar with the route through the Despeñaperros Pass, connecting La Mancha with Seville and Córdoba, where he lived both as a child and in later life. The brooding and threatening nature of the pass – probably greater before it was blasted to make room for road widening and the railway line – appealed to him, for he used it in two of the most memorable scenes in the adventures of **Don Quijote** and Sancho Panza. The centre of the pass is where Don Quijote ran mad and played "the desperate, the raving, the furious lover", in order that Sancho could convey news of this penance to his fantasized Lady Dulcinea del Toboso, in reality a slatternly country lass named Alonza Lorenzo. About 1km further on, the *Venta de Cardenas* was the inn that the deluded knight errant imagined to be a castle. When the morning after a night's hospitality the innkeeper demanded payment, Quijote refused with the explanation that knights never paid for their accommodation and made his exit. Sancho, however, was not so lucky and was given a violent tossing in a blanket to teach him a lesson. The old *venta* apparently survived until the nineteenth century, when it was seen by Borrow. However, it was subsequently demolished and a characterless hotel now stands on the site. It's still a stopover on this major transportation route and the lines of lorries parked outside belong to the truck drivers who use this inn today, the successors of the muleteers, drovers and carriers of Cervantes's time.

due to the pass's evil reputation "on account of the robberies which are continually being perpetrated in its recesses". Ford, when going the other way, described the land beyond the pass as where "commences the *paño pardo*, the brown cloth, and the *alpargata*, or the hempen sandal of the poverty-stricken Manchegos". The whole area surrounding the Despeñaperros Pass is now a **Parque Natural**.

INFORMATION   DESPEÑAPERROS PASS

Centro de Visitantes Just off the A4-E5 at Santa Elena (Tues–Sun 9am–2pm & 4–7pm; ☎953 664 307). The visitor centre for the natural park has exhibitions of flora and fauna and lots of information on activities and accommodation.

Jaén

Surrounded by olive groves and huddled beneath the fortress of Santa Catalina on the heights above, **JAÉN**, the provincial capital and by far the largest town in the province, is an uneventful sort of place. Its name derived from the Arabic *Geen*, meaning a stop on the caravan route, the modern town is more northerly than Andalucian in its appearance and character, doubtless stemming from its resettlement with emigrants from the north following the *Reconquista,* and the subsequent long centuries spent as the front line bulwark of Christian Spain against Moorish Granada. At the centre of an area impoverished by lack of economic development and chronic unemployment, while you would hardly want to go out of your way to get here, the city makes an easy stop over en route to destinations such as Baeza, Úbeda and Cazorla to the northeast. And, given a chance, it has a surprising number of worthwhile sights, including an outstanding **cathedral**, the largest **Moorish baths** in Spain, some elegant old churches and mansions and an important museum. To the northeast of Jaén along the Baeza road lies the **La Laguna** complex, with a comprehensive museum dedicated to explaining the history and development of olive oil production.

Most of Jaén's sights lie within a few minutes' walk of the rather characterless main thoroughfare, the **Paseo de la Estación**. This cuts through the heart of the city from north to south linking the train station with the Plaza de la Constitución, the major hub of activity. The *paseo* is interrupted only by the Plaza de las Batalles, a square dominated by a grotesque sculpture commemorating the battles of Nava de Tolosa (against the Moors) and Bailén (against the French).

Brief history

Although the area around the city is liberally dotted with Iberian settlements, it was probably as the Roman settlement of *Auringis* that Jaén was born. A centre noted for its **silver mines** and settled by the Moors shortly after the conquest of 711, judging by the number of mosques it must have been a thriving place. The Moors also made use of the **hot springs** that had been known to the Romans and utilized them in the construction of several baths. Fernando III's Christian forces captured the city – then part of the newly founded Nasrid kingdom of Granada – in 1246 and made its ruler Ibn al-Ahmar (aka Muhammad ibn Yusuf ibn Nasr) into a vassal, obliged to pay annual tribute. It was from Jaén, too, and a half centuries later, that the final assault on Boabdil's Granada was launched. The city then entered into a slow decline which gathered pace in the seventeenth and eighteenth centuries and led many of its citizens to emigrate to the imperial colonies, evidenced by towns with the same name in countries as far apart as Peru and the Philippines. Although Jaén's strategic importance played a part in the War of Independence, the economic disruption caused brought further decline in its wake, from which the city never really recovered. The province and city continually register the lowest income levels in the region, with well over fifty percent of the population describing themselves as living in poverty.

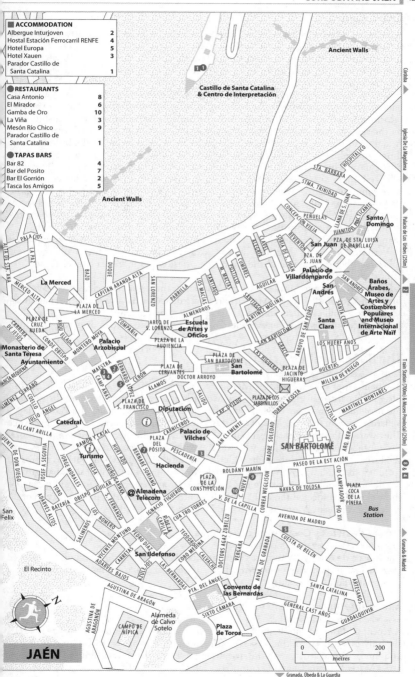

ACCOMMODATION	
Albergue Inturjoven	2
Hostal Estación Ferrocarril RENFE	4
Hotel Europa	5
Hotel Xauen	3
Parador Castillo de Santa Catalina	1

RESTAURANTS	
Casa Antonio	8
El Mirador	6
Gamba de Oro	10
La Viña	3
Mesón Río Chico	9
Parador Castillo de Santa Catalina	1

TAPAS BARS	
Bar 82	4
Bar del Posito	7
Bar El Gorrión	2
Tasca los Amigos	5

Ancient Walls

Castillo de Santa Catalina & Centro de Interpretación

Ancient Walls

JAÉN

0   200
metres

Granada, Úbeda & La Guardia

The Catedral

Plaza Santa Maria • **Cathedral** Mon–Sat 10am–2pm & 4–7pm, Sun 10am–noon & 4–7pm; ritual display of the lienzo del Santo Rostro Fri 11.30am–1pm • Free **Museum** Daily 10.30am–1pm & 5–8pm • €5

Jaén's massive and magnificent **cathedral** dwarfs the city. Begun in 1492 after the demolition of the great mosque that had previously occupied the site, the cathedral was not completed until 1802. A number of architects turned their hand to the project during this period, including the great Andrés de Vandelvira, whose work had the most influence over the building as it looks today. The spectacular **west facade**, flanked by twin 60m-high towers framing Corinthian pillars and statuary by the seventeenth-century master, Pedro Roldán, is one of the masterpieces of Andalucian Renaissance architecture. Inside, the overall mood of the building is more sombre, with bundles of great Corinthian columns surging towards the roof of the nave. Fine sixteenth-century **choir stalls** have richly carved images from the Old Testament as well as a number of grisly martyrdoms. The dim side chapels also have some interesting artworks, among them an eighteenth-century *Virgen de las Angustias* (Our Lady of the Sorrows) by José de Mora in the fifth side chapel to the right. The church fills up on Friday mornings when the **lienzo del Santo Rostro** is ritually removed from its coffer behind the high altar. This Byzantine cloth icon bearing a likeness of Christ is believed locally to be the napkin with which St Veronica wiped his face en route to Calvary. Long queues form to kiss the icon (preserved behind glass) and the attending priest wipes it with a handkerchief after each devotee.

The sacristy **museum** displays works by artists of the region as well as the *tenebrario*, a fifteen-armed candlestick by Master Bartolomé de Jaén who also made the magnificent *reja* in the Capilla Real at Granada. Two fine seventeenth-century sculptures by Martinéz Montañés, *San Lorenzo* and *Cristo Nazareno*, are also on display.

The Baños Árabes

Palacio de Villardompardo • Tues–Sat 9am–9.30pm, Sun 9.15am–2.45pm • Free

The **Baños Árabes**, a remarkable Moorish *hammam*, is the largest to survive in Spain. Originally part of an eleventh-century Moorish palace, the baths fell into disuse after the *Reconquista* and were used as a tannery. In the sixteenth century the Palacio de Villardompardo, now the **Museo de Artes y Costumbres Populares**, was built over them. They were rediscovered early last century and in the 1980s were painstakingly restored. Recent modifications now lead you into the baths over a glass floor allowing views of the Roman and Moorish remains which surround the complex. The various rooms (cold, tepid and hot) have wonderful brickwork ceilings with typical star-shaped windows, and pillars supporting elegant horseshoe arches. An underground passage (now closed) connected the baths with the centre of the Moorish palace, on top of which was built the Monastery of Santo Domingo (see p.423).

Museo de Artes y Costumbres Populares

Tues–Sat 9am–9.30pm, Sun 9.15am–2.45pm • Free

The **Museo de Artes y Costumbres Populares** contains a fascinating and well-presented folk history of the province on three floors using artefacts, clothing, toys, ceramics, photos and audiovisual aids.

Museo Internacional de Arte Naïf

Tues–Sat 9am–9.30pm, Sun 9.15am–2.45pm • Free

A recent addition to the Baños Árabes complex is the **Museo Internacional de Arte Naïf**, the only museum of its kind in Spain. The museum displays works by (mainly) Spanish and international artists with the star attraction being the thirty paintings by Navarran artist María Victoria Otano Lecumberri.

South of the Baños Árabes

Just to the southeast of the Baños Árabes on Calle San Andrés stands the **church of San Andrés** (Mon–Sat 11.30am–12.30pm, Sun 11.30am during services; ☎953 237 422) which, in the sixteenth-century Santa Capilla, contains a fabulous *reja* (altar screen) depicting the *Holy Family* and the *Tree of Jesse* by Maestro Bartolomé of Jaén, creator of the *reja* in the Capilla Real in Granada.

A block south of the Baños Árabes on Plaza de San Juan lies the ancient post-*Reconquista* church of **San Juan** (Mon–Thurs 9am–2pm & 5–8pm; free), with an elegant Romanesque tower and, inside, a fine sixteenth-century sculpture of the Crucifixion by Sebastián de Solís. A couple of streets north, Calle Santísima Trinidad leads to a **path** which climbs, ruggedly in parts, to the castle of Santa Catalina (see p.424), a much shorter route than the 3km-plus road. The path starts from the *Bar Sobrino Bigotes*.

North of the Baños Árabes

Standing to the north of the Baños Árabes on Calle Santo Domingo, the **Monastery of Santo Domingo** (patio can be viewed Mon–Fri 9am–2pm; free), erected over a Moorish palace, was originally a fourteenth-century Dominican monastery and later became Jaén's university. Later still it was a seat of the Inquisition, before being transformed in more recent times into the office of the provincial historical archive (Archivo Histórico). From its earlier incarnations a fine sixteenth-century **portal** by Vandelvira and a beautiful **patio** with elegant twinned Tuscan columns survive.

A little further north still on Plaza de la Magdalena, the **Iglesia de La Magdalena** (Fri & Sun 11am–1pm, Sat 11am–1pm & 5–7pm; free), the oldest in Jaén, was built over a mosque, the minaret of which is now its bell tower, and a patio at the rear preserves a pool used in Moorish times for ritual ablutions. In the cloister you can still see a few Roman tombstones used in the construction of the original Moorish building; this quarter was also the centre of the ancient Roman town. Inside, the church has a superb **retablo** by Jacobo Florentino depicting scenes from the Passion.

San Bartolomé

Plaza San Bartolomé; entry through the sacristy • Tues, Wed & Fri 9.30am–11am & 6–8pm, Sun 10.30am–12.30pm & 7–8pm • Free

Between the cathedral zone and the Baños Árabes area, the sixteenth-century **San Bartolomé** is worth a look. A handsome church with a stone facade and triple belfry, the interior has a fine Mudéjar *artesonado* ceiling, an equally fine retablo by Sebastián de Solís plus a fifteenth-century Gothic ceramic font and an outstanding *Expiration of Christ* by José de Medina.

Museo Provincial

Paseo de la Estación 27 • Tues 2.30–8.30pm, Wed–Sat 9am–8.30pm, Sun 9am–2.30pm • Free

Five minutes' walk northeast of the centre, the excellent **Museo Provincial** has a remarkable collection of Iberian stone **sculptures**, among the most important in Spain.

Iberian collection

Housed in a separate building to the side of the museum, the museum's **Iberian sculptures** were found near the town of Porcuna, close to the province's western border, and date from the fifth century BC. One is of a magnificent bull, while another is a strange fragment – titled *grifomaquia* – depicting a struggle between a man and a griffon. All the works betray the artistic influence of the classical Greek world on the fertile Iberian imagination. The strange fact revealed by the archeological excavations when these works came to light is that they had been deliberately broken a short time after their execution and then laid in a long trench. No satisfactory explanation for this has yet been put forward. More sculptures are being put on show each year as they are uncovered by archeologists. Work has started converting a former prison near the museum into what will become Spain's national museum for Iberian art. No opening date has been set; check with the museum or Turismo.

Main building

Items on display in the main building include Phoenician jewellery and ointment phials, Greek vases, as well as Roman mosaics and sculpture, including an outstanding fourth-century **sarcophagus** found near Martós depicting seven miracles of Christ including the transformation of water into wine. A recent addition here is a complete full-scale walk-in reconstruction of the remarkable fourth-century BC Iberian necropolis **tomb** at Toya near Cazorla. Room 11 deals with Jaén's significant **Moorish period** and has lamps and stoneware as well as a whole jugful of money that someone buried and never came back to collect. This room also has some fine **ceramics** that verify the Moorish origin of the green glazed plates and vases, still the hallmark of the pottery of Jaén province. A Visigothic section has examples of jewellery, vases and metalwork from this hazy period in Spanish history.

Upstairs, the **Museo de Bellas Artes** starts out with some interesting medieval wood sculpture before quickly degenerating into a hotchpotch of fairly awful stuff from the nineteenth and twentieth centuries, although there are a few laughs, not to mention a large number of steamy nudes. The tedium is somewhat relieved by a work by Huelvan artist Daniel Vasquéz Díaz, an engraving by Picasso and some interesting drawings and paintings by Manuel Angeles Ortiz, a native of Jaén who was a great friend of both Picasso and García Lorca.

Castillo de Santa Catalina

Ctra. del Castillo s/n • Daily: April–Sept 10am–2pm & 3.30–7.30pm; Oct–March 10am–2pm & 3.30–6pm • €3.50 • Taxis (about €6 one way) leave from Plaza Coca de la Piñera by the bus station. You can also walk to the castle on a 3km, near-vertical hike, or take a much shorter (but still pretty taxing) path up from C/Santísima Trinidad, to the east of Santo Domingo

The **Castillo de Santa Catalina**, dominating the crag that rises behind the city, was in origin a Moorish fortress constructed in the thirteenth century by Ibn al-Ahmar. After the Reconquest, the castle was much altered and today part of it has been stylishly converted into a modern *parador*, and little of the Moorish edifice now survives. What does remain has been reconstructed as a **Centro de Interpretación** housing in the fort's five towers a series of hi-tech interactive audiovisual gadgets explaining the building's history. A number of secret passageways connected the Moorish fortress with the town below and a few of these have been discovered.

A path from the *parador* car park leads to the older and ruined part of the edifice at the castle's southern tip where a *mirador* beneath a huge, whitewashed cross gives a **spectacular view** of the city laid out below your feet and dominated by the massive cathedral. Beyond, Jaén's wealth and misery, the endless lines of olive groves, disappear over the hills into the haze. Nonresidents are welcome to use the *parador's* bar and restaurant.

ARRIVAL AND DEPARTURE   JAÉN

By train The train station (☎ 953 270 202) is at the end of Paseo de la Estación, a good 10min walk (or an easier ride on bus #19) from the centre. There are train connections to Córdoba and Madrid.
Destinations Andújar (4 daily; 40min); Córdoba (4 daily; 1hr 40min); Seville (3 daily; 3hr).
By bus Jaén's bus station (☎ 953 250 106, ⓦ epassa.es for details of all Jaén's provincial services) is on Plaza Coca de la Pinera, just off the Paseo de la Estación. There are

frequent daily services to and from Úbeda and Baeza and less often, Cazorla.
Destinations Almería (4 daily; 4hr); Almuñecar (1 daily; 3hr 45min); Baeza/Úbeda (15 daily; 1hr 25min); Cazorla (2 daily; 2hr 30min); Córdoba (8 Mon–Fri, 5 on Sat & Sun; 2hr); Granada (14 daily; 1hr 15min); La Guardia (8 daily; 20min); Málaga (4 daily; 3hr 30min); Seville (1 daily; 4hr).
By car Arriving by car, either use the signed pay car park around the centre or ask your lodging to advise.

INFORMATION

Turismo C/Ramon y Cajal s/n (Mon–Fri 9am–7.30pm, Sat & Sun 9.30am–3pm; ☎ 953 190 455, ⓦ aytojaen.es).
Provincial tourist office Diputación Provincial building,

Plaza de San Francisco (Mon–Fri 8am–3pm; ☎ 953 248 000).
Internet access Almadena Telecom, C/Hurtado 18 (daily 11am–3pm & 5–11pm).

ACCOMMODATION

Accommodation in Jaén is limited and – with the exception of the youth hostel – relatively expensive. However, there's usually no difficulty in finding a place to stay at any time of the year, and there are no seasonal rate changes. Mosquitoes can be a real problem during high summer, when places with air-conditioning come into their own.

★ **Albergue Inturjoven** C/Borja s/n ☎ 953 313 540, ⓦ inturjoven.com. This youth hostel, with the imposing facade of a former eighteenth-century hospital, has excellent rooms – modern, minimalist, en-suite a/c doubles and "apartments" (which have a salon but don't actually come with a kitchen). There's also a pool, and, somewhat incongruously, a full-blown spa where the variety of luxurious detox and anti-*edad* (ageing) cures will cost you far more than the rooms. Under 26 €21, over 26 €27

Hostal Estación Ferrocarril RENFE Estación de Tren ☎ 953 274 614, ⓦ hostalestacionferrocarril.com. The train station's own *hostal* at the front of the station is a rather swish affair with comfortable a/c rooms with TV, wi-fi throughout and a car park. €61

Hotel Europa Plaza de Belén 1 ☎ 953 222 700, ⓦ hoteleuropajaen.es. Perhaps the best of the more upmarket places in the centre, where attractive a/c rooms come with strongbox, satellite TV and free wi-fi. Garage. B&B €85
Hotel Xauen Plaza Deán Mazas 3 ☎ 953 240 789, ⓦ hotelxauenjaen.com. A reasonable option with decent a/c rooms with TV. Own garage. €92
★ **Parador Castillo de Santa Catalina** Castillo, 3km above the town ☎ 953 230 000, ⓦ parador.es. For a truly memorable experience you could stay at Spain's most spectacularly sited hotel. The very comfortable and elegantly furnished rooms have fine balcony views with a sheer drop to the valley below; facilities include a pool, restaurant, bar, free wi-fi and ample parking. €161

EATING AND DRINKING

Jaén tends to shut down after dark and in the absence of much nightlife you'll probably compensate by eating and drinking. In the centre, the best place to find food is on the east side of Plaza de la Constitución. Here, the tiny **C/Nueva** has a whole row of tapas bars and places to eat. Near the cathedral, **C/Arcos del Consuelo** is another good tapas hunting ground.

RESTAURANTS

Casa Antonio C/Fermín Palma 3, north of the bus station ☎ 953 270 262. The top culinary choice, this upmarket place offers innovative *jiennense* and Basque-inspired dishes; house specials include *cochinillo* (suckling pig) and *jarrete de cordero* (stewed lamb). *Menú de degustación* €50. Main dishes €16–25. Tues–Sun 1.30–3.30pm & 8.30–11.30pm. Closed Aug.

El Mirador Ctra. de Jabalcuz km7.9 ☎ 953 243 658. A popular haunt with *jiennenses* – especially on Sun – this great family-run restaurant offers excellent local dishes with *carnes a la brasa* (charcoal-grilled meats) a speciality. There's also an economical *menú* and fine views from its terraces. Tues–Sun noon–5pm & 8–11pm.

Gamba de Oro C/Nueva 3 ☎ 953 241 746, ⓦ restaurantelagambadeoro.es. Excellent and popular seafood (but not exclusively so) bar–restaurant serving fresh crustaceans and fish in a lively room. Try the *tortillitas de camarones* (shrimp fritters). Thurs–Tues 11am–5pm & 8pm–midnight.

La Viña C/Maestra 8. Stylish *cervecería*, restaurant and *raciones* bar close to the cathedral with a pleasant terrace on a pedestrianized street. House specials include *paté*

de perdiz (partridge), *berenjenas a la miel* (aubergine with honey) and *solomillo al jerez* (pork loin in fino). Daily noon–5pm & 8pm–midnight.

Mesón Río Chico C/Nueva 12. Compact, atmospheric bar-restaurant with the dining room upstairs. Reasonably priced fish and meat dishes include *bacalao estilo mesón* (cod house style) and *pierna de choto braseado* (grilled kid). Main dishes €8–15. Tues–Sat noon–4pm & 8pm–midnight, Sun noon–4pm.

Parador Castillo de Santa Catalina Castillo, 3km above the town ☎ 953 230 000, ⓦ parador.es. To feast in baronial splendour you'll need to climb – or take a taxi – to this spectacularly located restaurant inside the *parador* (see above). In a recreated medieval banqueting room, dine on superb cooking with many local specialities – try the *morcilla* (blood sausage), *andrajos de bacalao* (cod and shellfish soup) and *pipirrana* (*jamón* and vegetable salad) – and a good-value *menú*, costing around €33.

TAPAS BARS

Bar 82 C/Arcos del Consuelo. Excellent small bar noted for its *embutidos* (sausages) and *calamares* (fried squid).

4

Bar del Pósito Plaza del Pósito 10, above the west side of the Plaza de la Constitución. A popular tapas, *raciones* and *copas* venue with a lively terrace on this charming square.

Bar El Gorrión C/Arcos del Consuelo. One of the city's most vibrant and atmospheric bars, noted for its *jamón*

ibérico and *salchichón* (salami); they also offer a range of cooked tapas.

Tasca Los Amigos C/Bernardo López 10. A block north of the cathedral, this cosy tapas bar serves a range of fried fish tapas. Its *jamón* and *morcilla* (blood pudding) are also favourites.

Baeza and around

Campo de Baeza, soñaré contigo cuando no te vea.
Fields of Baeza, I will dream of you when I can no longer see you.

Antonio Machado (1875–1939)

Fifty kilometres from Jaén along the winding A316, **BAEZA** is a tiny, compact and provincial country town with a perpetual Sunday air about it. Sited on the escarpment of the Loma de Úbeda, both Baeza and the neighbouring town of Úbeda have an extraordinary density of exuberant **Renaissance palaces**, richly endowed churches and magnificent public squares which are among the finest in Spain. Most of Baeza's main

BAEZA

■ ACCOMMODATION
Hostal Aznaitin	7
Hotel Baeza	5
Hotel Baeza Monumental	2
Hotel Fuentenueva	3
Hotel Juanito	1
Hotel Puerta de la Luna	6
La Casona del Arco	4

● TAPAS BARS
Arcediano	4
Bar Cafetería Mercantil	6
Bar Mibel	2
Bar Pedrito	3
La Bodega	10

● RESTAURANTS
Casa Juanito	1
El Pasaje	8
El Sarmiento	7
El Señorío de Baeza	5
La Almazara	9

attractions lie within a few minutes' walk of the pleasant central joined squares of **Plaza de España** and the larger **Paseo de la Constitución**. There are no charges to enter any of the monuments but you may offer the guardian a small *propina* (tip).

Brief history

Important in Roman times as Beatia, Baeza was later a Visigothic bishopric and then a prosperous commercial and agricultural centre under the Moors. After a prolonged and bitter struggle the town fell to the Christian forces in 1227, and *hidalgos* or nobles were granted estates in the surrounding countryside with orders to defend this frontier zone. The power of these noble houses was so untrammelled that they were soon warring among themselves for control of the town (a favoured place of battle being Baeza's Alcázar – until Isabel had it demolished). It was later, in the sixteenth century, however, that Baeza embarked on its most prosperous period. The nobility, made rich by farming and textile production, endowed the town with numerous striking Renaissance buildings as the population expanded.

Paseo de la Constitución

On the eastern side of the bar-lined **Paseo de la Constitución** is **La Alhóndiga**, an elegant porticoed sixteenth-century corn exchange and, almost opposite across the gardens, the arcaded eighteenth-century **Casa Consistorial**, or old town hall, which once fronted the old market square. At the southern end of the *paseo*, you'll find the **Plaza de los Leones** (also called the Plaza del Populo), a delightful cobbled square enclosed by Renaissance buildings. A central fountain incorporates Roman lions and a statue – which locals believe is Imilce, the Iberian wife of the Carthaginian general, Hannibal. The fountain is overlooked by some remarkable buildings including the **Antigua Carnicería** (old slaughterhouse), bearing the arms of Carlos V, and beside the arch at the far end, the Audiencia housing the Turismo (see p.429). Also here, on a rounded balcony flanking the double arch of the Arco de Villalar and the Puerta de Jaén, the first Mass of the *Reconquista* is reputed to have been celebrated. The Puerta de Jaén was a memento (or rebuke) left by Carlos V to the town that had opposed him, and commemorated the Germanic ruler's procession through here in 1526 en route to marry Isabel of Portugal.

Palacio de Jabalquinto

Plaza de Santa Cruz • Patio Mon–Fri 9am–2pm • Free

The stepped street behind the Plaza de los Leones ascends (via Calle Romanones and Calle Juan de Ávila) to a cluster of monuments that includes the finest of Baeza's palaces, the **Palacio de Jabalquinto** – now a seminary – with an elaborate "Isabelline" front showing marked Moorish influence in its stalactite decoration. Built in the fifteenth century by the Benavides family, the tranquil interior patio has a double tier of arcades around a central fountain and a superb Baroque **staircase** with fine carving.

Antigua Universidad

C/Beato Juan de Ávila s/n • Patio daily 10am–2pm & 4–7pm • Free

Next to the Palacio de Jabalquinto, the **Antigua Universidad** (old university) was founded in 1538 and, after functioning for nearly three centuries as a centre of study and debate, its charter was revoked in 1824 during the tyrannical reign of Fernando VII. From 1875 it was used as a school until, in 1979, the building once again became a centre of higher learning – as a summer school for the University of Granada. The interior has an elegant patio and, next to a sixteenth-century lecture hall, the preserved **classroom** used by the great *sevillano* poet and writer Antonio Machado when he served as a teacher here from 1912 to 1919. This experience must have provided much of the material for his most famous prose work, *Juan de Mairena*, the observations on life and culture of a fictional schoolmaster.

Santa Cruz

Plaza de Santa Cruz s/n • May–Sept Mon–Sat 11am–1pm & 5–7pm, Sun 11am–1pm; Oct–April Mon–Sat 11am–1pm & 4–6pm, Sun 11am–1pm • Free

The remarkable church of **Santa Cruz** is Baeza's oldest, built shortly after the *Reconquista* in the thirteenth century, although later much restored. Converted from an earlier mosque, the church betrays a combination of late Romanesque and early Gothic architectural styles. The austere, white-walled interior has slender stone columns as well as some fourteenth- and fifteenth-century frescoes, and (in the east aisle) the preserved arch of the *mihrab*.

Tienda Museo del Padre Sifón

C/Arco de las Escuelas 2 • Mon–Sat 8.30am–2pm & 5–10pm • Free

On Calle Arcos de las Escuelas you will find one of Baeza's quirkier attractions – a shop ostensibly selling local ceramics. Passing beyond the shelves of pots and a bottling plant for mineral water (thus the sculptor's nickname, "Father Siphon"), you'll enter a studio with a series of remarkable **marble replicas** of Baeza's famous buildings, including the Ayuntamiento, cathedral and the Palacio de Jabalquinto, all created in eye-straining detail by the shop's self-taught proprietor and local character, Diego Lozano.

The Catedral

Plaza de Santa María s/n • Tues–Sat 10am–2pm & 4–6.30pm, Sun 10am–2pm • Church free, museum €2

The **Plaza de Santa María** is another of Baeza's glorious squares, with a few welcome, shade-providing trees, fronted by a nucleus of fine Renaissance buildings. The rather squat sixteenth-century **Catedral de Santa María** dominates the square and inside has a fine nave by Andrés de Vandelvira which is, in many ways, a scaled-down version of his cathedral at Jaén. Like several of Baeza's and Úbeda's churches, the cathedral also has painted *rejas* by Maestro Bartolomé, a local craftsman who was responsible for some of the finest examples of this uniquely Spanish contribution to Renaissance art. His work enclosing the choir, with its depictions of a Virgin and Child accompanied by angels and cherubs, is stunning. In the Gothic **cloister**, part of the old mosque – which the church replaced – has been uncovered, but the cathedral's real novelty is a huge silver *custodia* cunningly hidden behind a painting of St Peter which whirls aside on the insertion of a coin. To the east of the cathedral, and beyond Plaza de Arcediano, a narrow street leads to a *mirador* with a fine **view** over the olive groves in the valley of the Guadalquivir towards the distant Cazorla mountain range beyond.

Adjoining the cathedral on the north side is the old Renaissance **Casas Consistoriales Altas** (town hall) with Plateresque features, formerly the palace of the Cabrera family who have another mansion in the town. In the centre of the **Plaza de Santa María** is a sixteenth-century fountain erected by the same family, with pilasters and crude caryatids supporting the arms of Felipe II. Beyond this are the graffiti-covered walls of the sixteenth-century seminary of **San Felipe Neri** where students record their names and dates in bull's blood – a traditional way of celebrating graduation. The building now houses the International University of Andalucía.

Ayuntamiento

C/Benavides • Main hall viewing Mon–Fri 9am–2pm

West of the Paseo de la Constitución, the magnificent **Ayuntamiento** was originally the Palace of Justice and prison. Completed in 1559, its richly ornamented facade is

BAEZA'S RENAISSANCE PALACES

Heading north from the Plaza de España, pedestrianized C/San Pablo has a number of interesting Renaissance palaces, many with impressive facades, dating from the sixteenth century. In addition to the Gothic **Palacio Garcíez** (or Salcedo), now an upmarket hotel with a fine patio, and the **Casa Acuña**, the following are well worth a look.

Casa Cabrera C/San Pablo. A *palacio* that's specially notable for its elegant Plateresque facade, which incorporates a double window and frieze over the entrance.

Palacio Cerón C/San Pablo. This palace played an important role in the cultural life of the town as Baeza's *Casino*; ask to be shown the wonderfully evocative *salon* upstairs with elegant mirrors and velvet curtains. Former member Antonio Machado gave poetry readings here, and you can see the piano once played by a visiting Federico García Lorca.

Palacio de los Elorza C/Intendente P Olavide. The remains of what must have been a fine sixteenth-century mansion, featuring a wonderfully exuberant Renaissance portal.

exuberantly Plateresque with elegant balconies, coats of arms and, above, a phalanx of gargoyles decorating the cornice. Inside, the main hall upstairs has a fine coffered ceiling. At the end of the street and facing the same edifice is the charming (now privately owned) little **house of Antonio Machado**, marked with a plaque, where the poet lived for most of his time in Baeza.

Hospital of the Purísima Concepción

Calle San Francisco passes the exterior of the **Hospital of the Purísima Concepción** with an elegant Renaissance facade. Adjoining it is the ruined convent of **San Francisco**, designed by Vandelvira and badly damaged during the War of Independence. Sections of both buildings have now been converted into a hotel, banqueting hall and restaurant.

ARRIVAL AND DEPARTURE   BAEZA

By train The nearest train station is Estación Linares-Baeza (☎ 902 432 343) 14km away and served by frequent trains from Seville, Córdoba and Granada. Buses connect with weekday trains, or it's a €20 taxi ride into town. Fronting the station is a good *hostal* and restaurant, *Las Palmeras* (☎ 953 698 979; €40).

By bus The bus station (☎ 953 740 468), officially at Paseo de Elorza Garat 1, is actually at the end of C/San Pablo and along the Paseo Arca del Agua. All services (around 14 daily) between Jaén and Úbeda, 9km further east, call in at Baeza.

Destinations Cazorla (4 daily; 1hr 30min); Granada (11 daily; 2hr 20min); Jaén (20 daily; 1hr); Úbeda (18 daily; 15min).

INFORMATION

Turismo Plaza del Populo s/n (Mon–Fri 9am–7.30pm, Sat & Sun 9.30am–3pm; ☎ 953 779 982). Housed in the splendid sixteenth-century former *Audiencia* (appeal court), this office can supply maps and information as well as a *Ruta del Tapeo* booklet and details of guided city tours.

Internet Micro Ware (Mon–Sat 10.30am–1pm & 5.30–9.30pm), C/Portales Tundidores 13, facing the Paseo de la Constitución.

Festivals Baeza's lively annual *feria* takes place during the second and third weeks in August and is a wonderfully rural affair with processions of *gigantones* (carnival giants), fireworks and an enormous funfair on the edge of town.

Flamenco There are occasional flamenco peformances at the Peña Flamenca, C/Romanones 6; ask the Turismo for details.

ACCOMMODATION

Baeza has a decent range of places to stay, some of which are architectural gems. There's usually no problem finding rooms except during the *feria* in mid-August and even then you should have no trouble if you ring ahead. **Prices** are often far lower if you don't stay on a Friday or Saturday.

★ **Hostal Aznaitin** C/Cabreros 2 ☎ 953 740 788, ⓦ hostalaznaitin.com. Splendid new *hostal* in the old quarter with well-equipped, pristine and stylish en-suite a/c rooms. Facilities include a pool, library, *cafetería*, garage

(€8) and free wi-fi. B&B Sun–Thurs €43, weekend €53

Hotel Baeza C/Concepción 3 ☎953 748 130, �🌐trh hoteles.com. Three-star hotel with attractive a/c rooms, partly housed in a converted Renaissance monastery with a glassed-in patio. Call or check the website for good deals. B&B €170

Hotel Baeza Monumental C/Cuesta de Prieto 6 ☎953 747 282, �🌐hotelbaezamonumental.com. Very nice small hotel with attractive rooms with plasma satellite TV, minibar, strongbox and free wi-fi. B&B Sun–Thurs €50, weekend €70

★ **Hotel Fuentenueva** C/del Carmen ☎953 743 100, �🌐fuentenueva.com. Delightful and friendly small hotel in a stylishly refurbished nineteenth-century town house with *cafetería* and garden plunge pool. Ultra-modern rooms come with minibar, safe, satellite TV, free wi-fi and power shower or jacuzzi. *Rough Guide* readers with this guide can claim a ten percent discount. Sun–Thurs €70, weekend €88

Hotel Juanito Paseo Arca del Agua s/n ☎953 740 040, �🌐juanitobaeza.com. Very reasonably priced hotel for pleasant rooms with a/c and TV above the top-notch restaurant of the same name. Ask for a west-facing room at the back or a high room on the front (both with views) to avoid odours from the *gasolinera* next door. €47

★ **Hotel Puerta de la Luna** C/Pintada Alta s/n ☎953 747 019, ⤬hotelpuertadelaluna.com. Beautiful four-star hotel in a refurbished seventeenth-century *casa palacio*. The comfortably furnished tiled-floor rooms are airy and well equipped and have free wi-fi. Facilities include two delightful patios, restaurant, gym, library, spa, small pool and a car park. Sun–Thurs €70, weekend €89

La Casona del Arco C/Sacramento 3 ☎953 747 208, ⤬lacasonadelarco.com. Comfortable, classically furnished rooms with exposed beams in a wonderfully restored eighteenth-century *casa palacio*. Also squeezes in a small pool. B&B Sun–Thurs €65, weekend €80

EATING AND DRINKING

CAFÉ

Pastelería Martínez C/San Pablo, next to the Palacio Cabrera ☎953 748 219. Enjoy teatime treats at this café, which serves delicious pastries made on the premises. Mon–Sat 9am–2pm & 5–9pm, Sun 10am–2pm.

TAPAS BARS

Arcediano C/Barbacana s/n ☎953 748 184. An excellent tapas bar off the east side of Plaza de España. They specialize in local cheeses and *salchichón* (salami) and offer a wide selection of wines. Wed–Sun 1–4pm & 8–11pm.

Bar Cafetería Mercantil Overlooking Plaza de España ☎953 740 971. This atmospheric tapas bar is the town's most popular haunt, well over a century old and once patronized by Antonio Machado. It's noted for its *conejo* (rabbit) and *cordero* (lamb) tapas. Tues–Sun 9am–11pm.

Bar Mibel C/San Pablo 44 ☎953 744 453. A popular tapas bar, north of Plaza de España, with a nice outdoor terrace on a pedestrianized street. House specials include *cordoniz en escabeche* (partridge) and *gambas rebozadas* (battered prawns). Tues–Sun 1–4pm & 8pm–midnight.

Bar Pedrito C/San Pablo 42 ☎953 742 234. Next door to *Bar Mibel* (see above), with an adjoining terrace, this equally popular bar is renowned for its *bombas* (meatballs) and *champiñones a la plancha* (sautéed mushrooms). Wed–Mon noon–4pm & 8pm–midnight.

La Bodega C/San Francisco 49 ☎953 740 375. Good bar serving up a range of tapas including *solomillo* (pork loin) and *lomo de orza* (conserved pork). There's also a decent restaurant. Wed–Mon noon–4pm & 8pm–midnight.

RESTAURANTS

Casa Juanito Paseo Arca del Agua s/n ☎953 740 040. Opened in 1952 and attached to the hotel of the same name, Baeza's most celebrated restaurant has walls covered with photos of the great and the good who have dined here over the decades. It's famed for its traditional approach with dishes such as *ensalada de perdiz*, *bacalao con tomate* (cod) and *cabrito al horno* (roast kid); these often feature on a *menú de degustación* for around €40. Main dishes €16–27. Tues–Sat 1–4pm & 8–11pm, Mon 1–4pm.

El Pasaje C/Benavides 3. A reliable place with a terrace offering a variety of fish and meat dishes – *ensalada de perdiz* (partridge) and *pierna de choto* (roast kid) are specials – with a *menú* for around €11. Tues–Sun 1–4pm & 7–11.30pm.

El Sarmiento C/Plaza del Ardeciano 10 ☎953 740 323, ⤬restauranteelsarmiento.com. Excellent restaurant with a terrace on this attractive square behind the cathedral. Specializes in charcoal-grilled meat dishes and has a Tues–Fri *menú* for €17. Main dishes €10–20. Tues–Sat 1.30–4.30pm & 8–11.30pm, Sun 1.30–4.30pm.

El Señorío de Baeza C/Concepción 3 ☎953 748 130, ⤬trhhoteles.com. The restaurant of the *Hotel Baeza* is popular with locals; its good-value *menú* includes local dishes such as *pipirrana* (*jamón* and vegetable salad) for around €15 (€11.50 Mon–Fri). Daily 1.30–3.30pm & 8.30–11.30pm.

La Almazara C/Cardenal Benavides 15 ☎953 741 650, ⤬restaurantelaalmazarabaeza.com. Opposite the sixteenth-century Ayuntamiento, this is a good new restaurant with a weekday *menú* for €11 plus a wonderful outside terrace where you can feast your eyes on the beautiful building across the way. Signature dishes include *alcachofas rellenos de bacalao* (artichokes with cod) and *berenjenas con salmorejo* (aubergine). Main dishes €8–20. Thurs–Tues 1–4pm & 7–11.30pm.

La Laguna

9km southwest of Baeza; 2km down a signed right turn off the A316 just beyond the village of Puente del Obispo • **Museo de la Cultura del Olivo** Daily: April–June 10.30am–1.30pm & 4.30–7pm; July & Aug 10.30am–1.30pm & 5.30–8pm; Sept–March 10.30am–1.30pm & 4–6.30pm • €3.60 • ☎ 953 765 142, ⓦ museodelaculturadelolivo.com

La Laguna, a former hacienda or olive-oil estate and mill bought in 1992 by the Junta de Andalucía, now houses the impressive **Museo de la Cultura del Olivo**, outlining the history of the olive and production methods used since Roman times. The patio garden has examples of olive species from all over the world. La Laguna also possesses its own farm and lake (*laguna*) and houses the province's hotel and catering school.

ACCOMMODATION AND EATING LA LAGUNA

Hotel La Laguna La Laguna ☎ 953 771 005, ⓦ ehlaguna.com/hotel. The complex's adjoining hotel, with good-value modern and attractively furnished a/c rooms with TV. Mini-suites come with a jacuzzi. B&B **€57**

Restaurante La Campana La Laguna ☎ 953 771 005. The hotel school's excellent mid-priced restaurant, where trainee chefs serve up their creations, is partly housed in the hacienda's former chapel, with a stunning painted domed ceiling. Their *menú de degustación* (around €31) is recommended, and often includes specialities such as *vieras en mascarpone* (scallops) and *helado de aceite* (olive oil ice cream). Main dishes €13–18. Oct–June Mon–Sat 1.30–4pm & 8–11pm.

Úbeda

Some 9km east of Baeza and built on the same escarpment overlooking the valley of the Guadalquivir, **ÚBEDA** looks less promising when you reach it. Don't be put off, though, for hidden away in the old quarter is one of the finest Renaissance architectural jewels in the whole of Spain, and perhaps even in Europe.

Brief history

Little is known of **Úbeda's** previous incarnation as the Roman town of Betula, and it was only in the **Moorish** period that Obdah, as it became, grew into a prosperous and important centre endowed with walls and a castle. Following the Christian victory over the Moors at Navas de Tolosa in 1212, the Moors from Baeza moved into the city, feeling it provided a more secure refuge against the Christian forces. Despite this, Úbeda was taken a week later and, although an interlude of further freedom for the Muslim occupants was purchased from the Christian armies with massive donations, the town fell conclusively to Fernando III (El Santo) in 1234. As happened in Baeza, numerous noble families were then established by the king and built their mansions in the town. These haughty "**lions of Úbeda**", as they styled themselves, were soon warring amongst each other, the Arandas fighting the Traperas, and the Molinas against the Cuevas. The fighting got so bad at one point that in 1503 Fernando and Isabel ordered the destruction of the town's walls and towers, to enable the unruly aristocrats to be kept in check. Twelve of these noble families are represented by the twelve lions on the town's coat of arms.

In common with Baeza, it was in the sixteenth century, as a producer of textiles traded across Europe, that Úbeda's fortunes reached their zenith and members of the same noble families came to hold prominent positions in the imperial Spanish court. This was the age of the houses of **Cobos** and **Molinos**, two families who, linked by marriage, dominated the town's affairs. They were also responsible for employing **Andrés de Vandelvira** as their principal architect, whose buildings are the glory of Úbeda today. This prosperity, however, was short-lived and the town declined in the seventeenth century as sharply as it had flourished in the sixteenth, which explains its architectural unity and lack of any significant Baroque edifices. Today, Úbeda is a moderately prosperous provincial town.

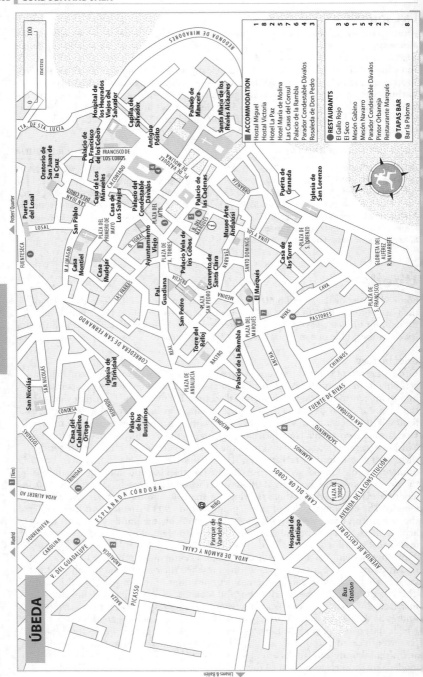

ÚBEDA

ACCOMMODATION
Hostal Miguel	1
Hostal Victoria	8
Hotel La Paz	2
Hotel María de Molina	5
Las Casas del Consul	7
Palacio de la Rambla	6
Parador Condestable Dávalos	4
Rosaleda de Don Pedro	3

RESTAURANTS
El Gallo Rojo	3
El Seco	6
Mesón Gabino	1
Mesón Navarro	5
Parador Condestable Dávalos	4
Pintor Orbaneja	2
Restaurante Marqués	7

TAPAS BAR
Bar la Paloma	8

Plaza de Vázquez de Molina and around

Follow the signs for the "Zona Monumental" and you'll eventually reach the **Plaza Vázquez de Molina**, a magnificent Renaissance square at the heart of the old town. Most of the buildings around this square are the late sixteenth-century work of **Andrés de Vandelvira**, the architect of Baeza's cathedral and of numerous churches in both towns.

Palacio de las Cadenas

Plaza Vázquez de Molina

At the western end of the plaza, the **Palacio de las Cadenas** (or "chains", which once decorated the facade) was built by Vandelvira for the secretary of Felipe II, Juan Vázquez de Molina, whose family arms crown the doorway of a beautiful classical facade. The interior, these days occupied by the Ayuntamiento, features a superb double-tier arcaded patio. To see it you'll need to go to the back of the building and the Ayuntamiento entrance where the security guard will allow you a peep.

Santa María de los Reales Alcázares

Plaza Vázquez de Molina

Opposite the Palacio de las Cadenas, and between the lions marking the edge of the mansion's domain, lies the church of **Santa María de los Reales Alcázares**, built on the site of a former mosque, and now set to reopen after years of renovation works. Behind the facade, topped by a double belfry, an elegant Gothic cloister encloses what was once the ablutions patio of the mosque. The church contains a fine *reja* by Maestro Bartolomé of Jaén depicting the Tree of Jesse.

Palacio del Condestable Dávalos

Plaza Vázquez de Molina

The **Palacio del Condestable Dávalos**, which Vandelvira had a hand in designing, is the former dwelling of the chaplain of the church of El Salvador. This elegant building now houses what must be the most impressive *parador* in Andalucía (see p.436). A stunning arcaded interior patio now serves as the hotel's bar, and is best contemplated over a cool drink.

Capilla del Salvador

Plaza Vázquez de Molina • Mon–Sat 10am–2pm & 4.30–7pm, Sun 11.15am–2pm & 4.30–7.30pm • €3

At the eastern end of the Plaza Vázquez de Molina, Vandelvira erected the **Capilla del Salvador**, Úbeda's finest church and one of the masterpieces of Spanish Renaissance architecture. Vandelvira was in fact working to a design created in 1536 by Diego de Siloé (architect of Málaga's and Granada's cathedrals) but typically added his own flourishes. The church was originally the chapel of the mansion – which later burned down – of Francisco de Cobos y Molina, secretary of state to Carlos V and one of the most powerful men of his time. This remarkable building is almost unique in Spain for being built within a very short period (1540–1556) with hardly any later alterations. It also preserves many of its interior furnishings. The exterior **facade** has a carving of the Transfiguration of Christ flanked by statues of San Pedro and San Andrés with a wealth of Plateresque detail. Above the north door around the corner, Vandelvira has placed an image in the tympanum which is almost his trademark – Santiago the Moor slayer, used in Baeza and on the hospital of Santiago in the north of the town.

Entry to the church is via the doorway on the south side. The single naved interior with a beautiful cupola has a brilliantly animated retablo on the high altar representing the Transfiguration with a sensitively rendered image of Christ by Alonso de Berruguete who studied under Michelangelo; this is the only part of the altarpiece that completely survived the Civil War. The **reja** fronting the altar is yet another fine work by Maestro Bartolomé de Jaén. In the **sacristy** (all Vandelvira's work) there's a photograph of a statue by Michelangelo given to Francisco de Cobos by the state of Venice, which alas was another Civil War casualty.

Behind El Salvador, and beyond the sixteenth-century **Hospital de los Honorados Viejos del Salvador** (another Vandelvira work), Úbeda comes to a sudden halt at a **mirador** with fine views over a sea of olive groves backed by the Sierra de Cazorla.

Palacio Vela de los Cobos

C/Juan Montilla s/n • Viewing of interior by reservation at the Turismo

Just behind Plaza Vázquez de Molina, the Plaza del Ayuntamiento has the **Palacio Vela de los Cobos**, another impressive building by Vandelvira dating from the middle of the sixteenth century, with an interesting corner balcony and an elegant facade topped off by a delightful arcaded gallery.

Oratorio de San Juan de la Cruz and around

C/Carmen 13

To the north of Plaza Vázquez de Molina (easily reached along Calle Francisco de los Cobos), the **Oratorio de San Juan de la Cruz** is where San Juan (St John of the Cross), an accomplished poet and mystic, died of gangrene in 1591. The original monastery was damaged in the Civil War and little of it survives, although a small **museum** (Tues–Sun 11am–1pm & 5–7pm; €2) preserves memorabilia from the saint's lifetime as well as his writing desk and the cell in which he died.

At the end of Calle San Juan de la Cruz facing the monastery, the **Plaza del Primero de Mayo** (formerly the Plaza del Mercado) is a charming acacia-lined square with a bandstand at its centre marking the site of the fires of the *autos-de-fé* that were once carried out here on the orders of the Inquisition. The Town Council presided over these grisly events from the superb arcaded sixteenth-century **Ayuntamiento Viejo** on the square's western side.

San Pablo

Plaza Primero de Mayo s/n • Mon 11am–noon, Tues & Wed 11am–noon & 5–7.30pm, Thurs & Fri 11am–1pm & 5–7.30pm, Sat 11am–1pm, Sun 12.15–1.30pm • Free

Dominating the northern flank of the **Oratorio de San Juan de la Cruz** is the idiosyncratic **Iglesia de San Pablo**, incorporating various Romanesque, Gothic and Renaissance additions and crowned by a Plateresque tower. It boasts a thirteenth-century balcony (a popular feature in Úbeda), and a superb portal. The interior has a fine *capilla* by Vandelvira (chapel of Camarero Vago) as well some intricate carving in the Capilla de la Mercedes and superb *rejas* (altar screens).

Around Plaza del Primero de Mayo

Calle Horno Contado, which leaves **Plaza del Primero de Mayo** at the southeast corner, has two palaces you might want to see: a short way down on the right, the **Casa de los Manueles** has a fine facade and, a little further down on the left, the fifteenth-century **Casa de los Salvajes** (savages) is named after the two figures clothed in animal skins supporting the arms of its founder, Francisco de Vago. In reality they are probably natives of the imperial colonies, from whose exploitation much of this conspicuous wealth was derived.

Calle Melchor Almagro, leaving the square on the north side of San Pablo, has another mansion, the wonderful Plateresque **Casa Montiel**, and, further along, a sixteenth-century Carmelite convent.

Museo Arqueológico

C/Cervantes 6 • Tues 2.30–8.30pm, Wed–Sat 9am–8.30pm, Sun 9am–2.30pm • Free • ☎ 953 795 077

Off the north side of Plaza del Primero de Mayo stands a fine fourteenth-century building whose elegant Mudéjar **patio** has pointed horseshoe arches. It also houses a

ÚBEDA'S POTTERS' QUARTER

Leaving the Plaza del Primero de Mayo by the C/Losal in its northeast corner leads to the **Puerta del Losal**, a magnificent thirteenth-century Mudéjar gate with a double-horseshoe arch which was formerly one of the main entrances to the old walled town. Through the arch you enter C/de la Merced, soon arriving at Plaza Olleros (Potters' Square). Leading off this, C/Valencia is the old **potters' street** where the workshops of Úbeda's main ceramic craftsmen are located. In addition to the workshop of Paco Tito you can see those of other potters – including Juan and Antonio Almarza, and Góngora – all famous throughout Spain. Paco Tito's equally well-known brother, Juan, also has a workshop on the west side of the Plaza del Ayuntamiento, near the Turismo.

Alfarería y Museo Tito C/Valencia 22 ⓦ pacotito .com. One of the friendliest pottery workshops in town, where renowned ceramic artist Paco Tito will usually give you a demonstration on the potter's wheel. Nearby in the yard is the kiln, where the system used to fire the pots – many glazed and tinted with Úbeda's traditional deep green – is inherited from the Moors; once the wood is burning, olive stones are introduced into the fire which creates smoke and soaks up oxygen, producing a more even heat with superior results in both colour and glaze. There are only six of these traditional kilns left in the whole of Spain and three are in this street. The museum/ gallery upstairs is devoted to Paco's more ambitious works including statuary, huge amphorae and a completely ceramic (and fully functioning) bathroom. He is famous also for his sculptures and has sculpted many eminent Spaniards including King Juan Carlos. Mon–Sat 8am–2pm & 4–8.30pm.

small **archeological museum** displaying ceramics, sculpture and many other artefacts from the Roman, Moorish and medieval periods.

Plaza San Pedro and around

On the Plaza San Pedro, the thirteenth-century **Convento de Santa Clara** contains a patio with a fine Gothic-Mudéjar multi-lobed portal. The convent also sells its home-made *dulces* – tasty cakes, biscuits and pastries. Just south from here along Calle Narvaez at no. 11 the private **Museo de Arte Andalusi** (daily 11am–2pm & 5–7pm; €2) is housed in a sixteenth-century mansion filled with period artefacts from other houses around the town. Heading west from Plaza San Pedro you come to another mansion, the **Palacio de la Rambla**, at the end of Calle Medina. The facade is another graceful work by Vandelvira; inside, there's an upmarket hotel (see p.436). Across the square, the church of **San Pedro**, with a noteworthy portal, leads into Calle Pascua where, on the junction with Calle Real, stands the impressive tower of the **Palacio del Conde de Guadiana**, one of the most striking of all Úbeda's palaces. The tower is, in fact, a seventeenth-century work and the richly ornamented balconies are a delight.

Hospital de Santiago

C/Obispo Cobos • Mon–Fri 8am–2.30pm & 5–10pm, Sat & Sun 10am–2.30pm & 4–9.30pm • Free

Five minutes west of the Plaza de Andalucía, along the pedestrianized Calle Obispo Cobos, is Vandelvira's huge **Hospital de Santiago**, commissioned by Bishop Cobos y Molina and begun in 1562. Perhaps the scale put Vandelvira off, for the exterior decoration is untypically restrained. You enter via a flight of steps flanked by a set of "lions of Úbeda" (see p.431), beyond which Vandelvira has inserted his trademark – Santiago the Moor slayer – above the arch. The equally restrained interior has a patio with columns of Genoa marble and a staircase with stunning vaulting, in addition to a striking chapel.

ARRIVAL AND DEPARTURE ÚBEDA

By train Estación Linares-Baeza (☎ 902 432 343) is the nearest train station, about 15km from Úbeda and served by frequent trains from Seville, Córdoba and Granada (connecting buses for trains Mon–Sat; a taxi costs around €20).

By bus The main bus station (☎ 953 795 188) is on C/San José, west of the centre beyond the Hospital de Santiago; there are currently 14 buses a day from Jaén (all stopping en route at Baeza).

Destinations Baeza (up to 20 daily; 15min); Cazorla (5 daily; 1hr); Córdoba (4 daily; 2hr 45min); Granada (6 daily; 2hr 30min); Jáen (up to 20 daily; 1hr 15min); Seville (4 daily; 4hr 20min).

By car On-street parking places are difficult to find. Most hotels have car parks or can advise. A central car park lies beneath the focal Plaza de Andalucía.

INFORMATION

Turismo In the elegant eighteenth-century Palacio del Marqués del Contadero, C/Baja del Marqués 4 (Mon–Fri 8.30am–7.30pm, Sat & Sun 9.30am–3pm; ☎ 953 779 204).

Internet Cibernetworld, C/Niño 22 (daily 11am–2pm & 4.30–10pm), close to the Parque de Vandelvira to the west of the old quarter.

Festivals During April and May Úbeda's annual International Festival of Music and Dance attracts big names from the fields of flamenco, rock, opera, jazz, blues and ballet. Día de San Miguel, on September 29, is when carnival giants, fireworks and a flamenco festival honour the town's patron saint.

Tours The Turismo has details of daily guided tours of the town.

ACCOMMODATION

The only budget places to stay are within walking distance of the bus station, in the modern part of town. The *casco antiguo* has a great choice of more upmarket places, some in stunning ancient palaces and mansions. Úbeda's **high season** is in April and May and thus hotel (but not *hostal*) rooms tend to be significantly cheaper in July and August. Many hotels apply a surcharge on Fridays and Saturdays.

Hostal Miguel Avda. Libertad 69 ☎ 953 752 049. One of Úbeda's cheapest *hostales* lies a 10min walk away from the centre in the north of town, offering decent en-suite rooms with a good and inexpensive restaurant below. **€40**

Hostal Victoria C/Alaminos 5 ☎ 953 791 718. Comfortable, welcoming *hostal* near the bus station offering pleasant, a/c en-suite rooms with TV. Own car park, too. **€40**

Hotel La Paz C/Andalucía 1 ☎ 953 750 848, ⓦ hotel-lapaz.com. This decent two-star hotel has functional but spacious a/c balcony rooms with TV and free wi-fi. Request a room on the fourth or fifth floors to reduce traffic noise. Facilities include *cafetería* and own garage (€9). **€80**

Hotel María de Molina Plaza del Ayuntamiento s/n ☎ 953 795 356, ⓦ hotelmariademolina.es. In the heart of the old quarter, this hotel is housed in a magnificent sixteenth-century *casa palacio* with a superb patio. Attractively furnished rooms come with a/c, strongbox and satellite TV, and some have balconies. The restaurant has a good-value *menú* at €15. Sun–Thurs **€79**, weekend **€89**

Las Casas del Consul Plaza del Marqués 5 ☎ 953 795 430, ⓦ lascasasdelconsul.com. Attractive hotel in a beautifully refurbished seventeenth-century *casa palacio*. Elegant, well-equipped rooms, many with beams or exposed stone walls, come with free wi-fi. There's also a wonderful patio and a garden pool. Sun–Thurs **€95**, weekend **€115**

Palacio de la Rambla Plaza del Marqués 1 ☎ 953 750 196, ⓦ palaciodelarambla.com. In the old quarter, this upmarket *casa palacio* is owned by the Marquesa de la Rambla. The lavish interior – with eight palatial rooms set around a stunning Renaissance patio designed by Vandelvira – contains valuable furnishings and artworks, so you have to use an entryphone to get in. Price includes breakfast – brought to your room if you wish. Closed mid-July to mid-Aug. B&B **€130**

★ **Parador Condestable Dávalos** Plaza de Vázquez de Molina 1 ☎ 953 750 345, ⓦ parador.es. On arguably the most beautiful plaza in Andalusia, Úbeda's *parador* is housed in a fabulous sixteenth-century Renaissance mansion, with gorgeous patio and sumptuously furnished rooms and suites overlooking the square. Free wi-fi. Call in for a drink if you're not staying. **€180**

Rosaleda de Don Pedro C/Obispo Toral 2 ☎ 953 795 147, ⓦ rosaledadedonpedro.com. Efficient and good-value three-star hotel offering well-equipped rooms with satellite TV and free wi-fi; facilities include bar-restaurant (with a *menú del día* for €15) and library, and there's a small pool in their terrace garden at the rear. Own garage. Sun–Thurs **€54**, weekend **€69**

EATING, DRINKING AND NIGHTLIFE

Most reasonably priced restaurants are in the modern part of town, along the **Avda. Ramón y Cajal**, but many of the town's more memorable places to eat are located in the **old quarter**.

FROM TOP LEFT BATH HOUSE, CÓRDOBA (P.378); IGLESIA DE LA AURORA, PRIEGO DE CÓRDOBA (P.407); CAZORLA (P.438) >

Bar La Paloma Junction of calles Rastro and Cava ⓣ953 750 027. A small corner bar and good tapas haunt. Specialities include *jamón ibérico* and *boquerones en vinagre*. Tues–Sun 12.30–4pm & 8–11pm.

El Gallo Rojo C/Torrenueva 3. Set back from the road on a small plazuela, this is one of the town's better and more reasonably priced restaurants, offering local specialities such as *rabo de toro* and venison, as well as a *menú* for €12. There's a pleasant outdoor terrace. Daily 1–4pm & 7.30–11pm.

El Seco C/Corazón de Jesús 8 ⓣ953 791 452, ⓦrestauranteelseco.com. This mid-priced restaurant is a cut above the norm; it is noted for its tasty *potaje carmelitano* (chick-pea, leek and cod soup) but also does excellent meat and game dishes such as *pierna de cordero* (lamb). Weekday *menú* €15; main dishes €12–20. Mon–Thurs & Sun 1–4pm, Fri & Sat 1–4pm & 8.30–11pm.

Mesón Gabino C/Fuente Seca ⓣ953 757 553, ⓦmesongabino.com. A good place for meat and fish *raciones*, in a converted ancient cellar on the northern edge of the old quarter near the Puerta del Losal. Its mid-priced restaurant also does decent fish and game dishes; a house special is a tasty *solomillo* (pork loin). There's a daily four-course *menú* for €20, and main dishes from €10–20. Tues–Sun noon–5pm & 8pm–midnight, Mon noon–5pm.

Mesón Navarro Plaza del Ayuntamiento. In the old quarter, behind the Palacio de las Cadenas, this popular place is one of only a handful of restaurants in the area; it also has a lively tapas and *raciones* bar with an outdoor terrace. Main dishes €10–15. Daily 9am–midnight.

Parador Condestable Dávalos Plaza de Vázquez de Molina 1 ⓣ953 750 345, ⓦparador.es. If you want to dine in style in the old quarter, try the *parador's* expensive restaurant. Superbly prepared regional dishes are available on a tasting *menú* (€36); house specialities include *andrajos de Úbeda* (stew of cod, prawns and pasta) and *pierna de cabrito con tomillo* (kid baked with thyme). Main dishes €10–25. Tues–Sun 1–4pm and 8–11pm, Mon 1–4pm.

Pintor Orbaneja C/Virgen de Guadalupe 5. Just north of *El Gallo Rojo* (see above), this is a lively *barrio* bar-restaurant serving well-prepared meat and fish dishes and with a *menú* for €13. The bar also offers pretty good tapas. Thurs–Tues 12.30–11pm.

Restaurante Marqués Plaza Marqués de la Rambla 2. Attractive restaurant serving a good-value *menú* for €15 often featuring *merluza con almejas y espárragos* (hake with clams and asparagus). In summer, the inviting terrace on the square allows you to contemplate the Palacio de la Rambla's elegant exterior. Main dishes €12–20. Daily 1–4pm & 8–11pm.

Cazorla and around

From Úbeda, the next destination for most travellers is the spectacular **Cazorla Natural Park** (officially titled the Parque Natural de Cazorla, Segura y Las Villas), a wilderness area filled with deep ravines and wooded valleys and which, in its mountains, gives birth to the mighty Río Guadalquivir. The main route into the park from Úbeda, and the one also taken by the bus, is via the attractive small town of **CAZORLA**, the park's main gateway, located on its southern edge.

Some 50km southeast of Úbeda, at an elevation of 900m, Cazorla huddles towards the top of a valley that runs from the rugged limestone cliffs of the Peña de los Halcones. This rocky bluff, with its wheeling buzzards and occasional eagle, marks the southwestern edge of the park, containing the sierras of Cazorla and Segura and the headwaters of the Río Guadalquivir.

Brief history

Little about the town today would lead you to believe that Cazorla has been around for over two thousand years. However, not only were there significant Iberian and Roman settlements here, this was also the see of one of the first bishoprics of early Christian Spain. Under the Moors it was a strategic stronghold and one of dozens of fortresses and watchtowers guarding the Sierra. Taken after a bitter struggle in 1235, during the *Reconquista*, the town then acted as an outpost for Christian troops. Nowadays, the two castles that dominate the village testify to its turbulent past; both were originally Moorish but later altered and restored by their Christian conquerors.

Plaza de la Corredera and around

A few minutes' walk south from the Plaza de la Constitución along the main Calle Dr Muñoz leads to the **Plaza de la Corredera** (or *del Huevo*, "of the Egg", because of its

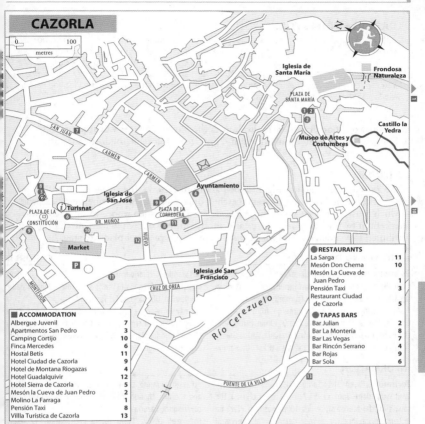

CAZORLA

0   100
metres

ACCOMMODATION
Albergue Juvenil	7
Apartmentos San Pedro	3
Camping Cortijo	10
Finca Mercedes	6
Hostal Betis	11
Hotel Ciudad de Cazorla	9
Hotel de Montana Riogazas	4
Hotel Guadalquivir	12
Hotel Sierra de Cazorla	5
Mesón la Cueva de Juan Pedro	2
Molino La Farraga	1
Pensión Taxi	8
Villla Turística de Cazorla	13

RESTAURANTS
La Sarga	11
Mesón Don Chema	10
Mesón La Cueva de Juan Pedro	1
Pensión Taxi	3
Restaurant Ciudad de Cazorla	5

TAPAS BARS
Bar Julian	2
Bar La Montería	8
Bar Las Vegas	7
Bar Rincón Serrano	4
Bar Rojas	9
Bar Sola	6

4

shape). This is the traditional meeting place for the *señoritos*, the class of landowners and their descendants who, through influence and privilege, still lay claim to the most important jobs and mould local destiny. The Ayuntamiento is here too – a fine Moorish-style palace off the far end of the plaza. The arrival of the *Hotel Ciudad de Cazorla* on the square's east side caused a controversy in the town because of its jarring architectural style.

Plaza de Santa María and around

Beyond Plaza de la Corredera, Calle Gómez Calderón is one of a labyrinth of narrow, twisting streets descending to Cazorla's liveliest square, the **Plaza de Santa María**. This takes its name from the sixteenth-century cathedral church of **Santa María**, designed by Andrés de Vandelvira, which was damaged by floods in the seventeenth century and later torched by Napoleonic troops. Its impressive ruins, now preserved, and the fine open square with a Renaissance fountain form a natural amphitheatre for concerts and local events as well as being a popular meeting place. Just behind the church lies the **Frondosa Naturaleza** (Tues–Sat 10am–2pm & 5–8pm; free), a Centro de Visitantes for the Parque Natural with information and displays on the park's flora and fauna. The square itself is dominated by **Castillo la Yedra**, the austere, reconstructed tower of the

> ### CAZORLA TAPAS TRAIL
>
> A few of Cazorla's excellent tapas bars (see p.442) provide the route for an entertaining **bar crawl** between the town's three squares. On Plaza de la Constitución you'll find the superb *Bar Sola* and the nearby *Bar Rojas*, which is just as good. Head then south to Plaza de la Corredera, where you'll find the popular *Bar La Montería*, *Bar Las Vegas* and *Bar Rincón Serrano*. You can round off your trail by heading downhill from here to the picturesque Plaza de Santa María and the lively terrace of *Bar Julián*.

lower of two Moorish castles. It also houses the **Museo de Artes y Costumbres** (Tues 3–8pm, Wed–Sat 9am–8pm, Sun 9am–2pm; free), a notable folklore museum.

La Iruela

Some 2km up the road heading into the park from Cazorla, the village of **LA IRUELA** has another ruined Moorish **fortress**, perched on a daunting but picturesque rock peak – which must have been a wretched struggle for the Christian troops to subdue. It was later rebuilt by the Templars. There's also another ruined church here, Santo Domingo, attributed to Vandelvira. The village has a number of upmarket **places to stay**.

ARRIVAL AND DEPARTURE

CAZORLA

By bus The terminus is on C/Hilario Marco, 300m downhill from the busy Plaza de la Constitución, the town's main square. Up to five buses a day (currently Mon–Fri 10am, 1.30pm, 2.30pm, 6pm & 7.30pm) go from Úbeda to Cazorla. The same buses leave Baeza 30min earlier, and there are also buses from Jaén and Granada. Alsina Graells (@alsa.es), the main bus operator, has a ticket office at the bus stand in C/Hilario Marco.

Destinations Granada (3 daily; 3hr 45min); Jaén (4 daily; 2hr 15min); Úbeda (5 daily; 55min).

By car Arriving by car, once you reach the Plaza de la Constitución you should head downhill to the car park; trying to find a place to park anywhere else can be futile, especially in high summer.

INFORMATION

Turismo C/Paseo del Santo Cristo 19 (April–Sept Wed–Sun 10am–2pm; @953 710 102, @cazorla.es). The town's official tourist office lies 100m north of Plaza de la Constitución, and can provide details on all aspects of the park and activities.

La Despensa del Parque Plaza de la Constitución 5 (daily 10am–2pm & 5–8pm; @953 720 115). This privately run tourist office also acts as an agent for Turisnat (@turisnat.es) one of the major providers of activities in the park. The staff are friendly but the office exists to promote Land Rover excursions, photo safaris and the like, though they do sell the Alpina map series covering the Cazorla park.

Internet Dynos, Plaza de la Constitución 12 (daily 10am–2pm & 5–9pm).

Festivals On May 15, Cazorla honours its patron, San Isicio, with a vibrant *romería* preceded the night before by La Hoguera (bonfires). In mid-September there's the fiesta de Cristo del Consuelo, with fairgrounds, fireworks and religious processions.

ACCOMMODATION

Outside August, finding a place to stay is usually no problem, as most visitors are either en route to, or leaving, the Cazorla Natural Park. It's worth noting that outside high summer it can get quite chilly in the evenings and while all the hotel rooms have heating, not all the *hostales* do – check in advance if you think this may be a problem.

CAZORLA

Albergue Juvenil Plaza Mauricio Martínez 6 @955 035 886, @inturjoven.com. Cazorla's tidy youth hostel, housed in a former convent, has some double rooms and a pool, and is reached by following C/Juan Domingo (reached via steps) from Plaza de la Constitución. B&B under 26 **€21**, over 26 **€27**

Camping Cortijo Camino San Isicio s/n @953 721 280, @campingcortijo.com. Cazorla's campsite is located beyond the Castillo de la Yedra, 1km from the centre; to get there, follow the Camino San Isicio from the Plaza de Santa María. The campsite has good facilities, plenty of shade and a pool. **€4.30** per person, **€3.50** per tent, **€3** per vehicle

Hostal Betis Plaza de la Corredera 19 @953 720 540. Central location, friendly proprietor and good-value accommodation in simple but spotless rooms sharing bath; rooms at the rear (nos. 101–104) have great views. **€26**

Hotel Ciudad de Cazorla Plaza de la Corredera 8 ☎ 953 721 700, ⓦ rlhoteles.com. Cazorla's newest hotel caused a ruckus when it was unveiled (see p.439), but inside modern a/c rooms come with minibar and safe, some have terraces. There's a circular pool at the back. Free wi-fi throughout and own garage. B&B Sun–Thurs **€60**, weekend **€76**

Hotel de Montaña Riogazas 7km south of Cazorla along the road to El Chorro and the Nacimiento del Río Guadalquivir ☎ 953 124 035, ⓦ riogazas.com. An appealing country option in the Sierra de Cazorla with rooms inside a handsome *casa forestal* with pool and restaurant. They offer a wide range of park-based activities from guided hikes to wildlife photography courses and 4x4 excursions. **€60**

Hotel Guadalquivir C/Nueva 6 ☎ 953 720 268, ⓦ hguadalquivir.com. Charming, recently refurbished and very friendly small hotel in a central location offering comfortable a/c en-suite rooms with fridge, TV, heating and free wi-fi. **€49**

Mesón La Cueva de Juan Pedro Plaza Santa María ☎ 953 721 225, ⓦ turismoencazorla.com/juanpedro .html. Rustic, friendly restaurant that also offers simple but clean en-suite rooms and excellent-value studio apartments nearby with kitchen, TV and terrace. Surcharge in Aug. Rooms **€30**, two-person apartment **€40**

⭐ **Molino La Farraga** Camino de la Hoz s/n, 5min from Plaza Santa María ☎ 953 721 249, ⓦ molinola farraga.com. An enchanting *casa rural* with tastefully furnished, cosy en-suite rooms (many with terraces) in a densely wooded garden location above the valley of the Río Cerezuelo with great pool and friendly proprietors. B&B **€70**

Pensión Taxi Travesía de San Antón 7 ☎ 953 720 525, ⓦ turismoencazorla.com/taxi. Up steps off the east side of Plaza de la Constitución, this is a friendly budget option

with a good-value *comedor* (dining room). Clean and tidy en-suite rooms have a/c, heating and TV. **€40**

Villa Turística de Cazorla Ladera de San Isicio s/n, reached by crossing the bridge over the river below Plaza de la Constitución ☎ 953 724 090, ⓦ villacazorla .com. One of the most attractive of the upmarket in-town places and set in leafy surroundings, it comprises a series of attractive, self-contained, a/c chalets with terraces plus communal pool and restaurant. Own car park (free). Surcharge in Aug. Sun–Thurs **€56**, weekend **€75**

LA IRUELA

Apartamentos San Pedro Ctra. de la Sierra s/n, La Iruela ☎ 953 720 015, ⓦ hotelsierradecazorla.com. Pleasant apartments sleeping from two to six. All come with kitchen, TV, washing machine and heating, and there's a small pool too. Residents can use the facilities at the nearby *Hotel Sierra de Cazorla*. Surcharge in Aug. **€66**

⭐ **Finca Mercedes** Ctra. de la Sierra 1, La Iruela ☎ 953 721 087, ⓦ lafincamercedes.es. At the end of the village where the road heads into the park, this is a rustic, very friendly and excellent-value country inn. The en-suite rooms are cosy and those at the rear are the quietest with the best views. There's also a very good and economical restaurant plus pleasant garden with a superb pool. Free wi-fi and parking. **€42**

Hotel Sierra de Cazorla 2km outside Cazorla, La Iruela ☎ 953 720 015, ⓦ hotelsierradecazorla.com. Modern complex comprising three- and four-star hotels plus a spa. The three-star option is particularly good value with terrace balcony rooms, many (rooms A10–A17 particularly) having a spectacular view of the castle behind; there's also a restaurant, bar and great pool. They produce their own walks guide for guests. Sun–Thurs **€48/€68**, weekend **€60/€77**

EATING AND DRINKING

RESTAURANTS

⭐ **La Sarga** Plaza del Mercado s/n ☎ 953 721 507. On the market square, this is the town's top restaurant. A pleasant traditional dining room hung with artworks makes a nice setting to eat regional standards prepared with flair; *lomo de jabalí en salsa de castañas* (wild boar with chestnut sauce) and *conejo al ajo arriero* (rabbit with garlic) are signature dishes, and there's also a *menú* for €18, a bargain *menú de degustación* for €27, and an evening tapas *menú* for €9.50 which gets you five creative tapas – just the accompaniment for a glass or two of fino. Don't miss the excellent and innovative desserts. Wed–Sun 1.30–4pm & 8–11pm, Mon 1.30–4pm.

Mesón Don Chema C/Doctor Muñoz s/n. Despite its address, this *mesón* is in a narrow alley down some steps off the west side of C/Muñoz. It's rustically decorated with plenty of mounted deer horns and specializes in *carnes de*

monte (venison and wild boar), although salads and *platos combinados* are also on offer. They also serve tapas and *raciones* and a good-value *menú* for €12. Daily 1–4pm & 8–11pm.

Mesón La Cueva de Juan Pedro Plaza Santa María 10. An entertaining bar-restaurant which has been in the Muñoz family for more than a century. Authentic regional food is on offer; the house speciality is *carnes a la brasa* (meats cooked on a wood-fired range), and the *conejo* (rabbit) and a *jabalí* (wild boar) are recommended. There's also a *menú* for €12 often featuring venison, trout and lamb. Daily noon–4.30pm & 8pm–midnight.

Pensión Taxi Travesía de San Antón 7 ☎ 953 720 525, ⓦ turismoencazorla.com/taxi. The *hostal's* pretty good restaurant serves up authentic sierra cuisine – and tasty winter soups – on an excellent-value *menú* for €10. Daily 1–4pm & 7.30–11.30pm.

Restaurante Ciudad de Cazorla Plaza de la Corredera 8 ☎ 953 721 700, ⊕ rlhoteles.com. The hotel of the same name's restaurant is a popular spot, serving dishes of the region including *solomillo ibérico con salsa de boletus* (black-pig loin in mushroom sauce). There's also a *menú* (including wine) for €14. Daily 1.30–4pm & 8–11pm.

TAPAS BARS

Bar Julián Plaza de Santa María ☎ 953 710 532. Delicious *choto con ajos* (baby kid with garlic), *caracoles* (snails) and *alcachofas fritas* (fried artichokes) are just a few of the many dishes popular with locals who fill the terrace of this lively tapas bar all summer.

★ **Bar La Montería** Plaza de la Corredera 20. Justly popular tapas bar serving a very tasty range – for a selection of them all, try the famous *plato olímpico* for €5.

Bar Las Vegas Plaza de la Corredera 17. With a very nice terrace on the busy square, the *Las Vegas*'s kitchen offers a creative tapas menu including *noruegos* (a variation on Scandinavian smørbrød) and *matrimonios* (anchovies on toast).

Bar Rincón Serrano Plaza de la Corredera 12. Near the Ayuntamiento, this old favourite has a pleasant terrace by the ancient fountain (used as a seat when the bar fills up), and provides a free *tapa* with every drink. Try the ever-popular *pavías de bacalao* (cod fingers) or *montaditos* (tapas on bread).

Bar Rojas Plaza de la Constitución 2 ☎ 953 721 936. One of two excellent tapas bars on this square, this bustling option is noted for its *navajas* (razorshell clams) and *pescado frito* (fried fish).

Bar Sola Plaza de la Constitución ☎ 953 720 058. The best in town, according to many locals. Favourites include *lomo con tomate* (pork in tomato) and *conejo* (rabbit).

Cazorla Natural Park

The **Cazorla Natural Park** – or **Parque Natural de Cazorla**, Segura y Las Villas to give its official name – is not as lofty as the Sierra Nevada (the highest peaks are 2000m), but outdoes it for beauty, slashed as it is by river gorges and largely covered in forest. The towering rock cliffs are the preserve of the acrobatic ibex, whilst the valleys and gorges swarm with birdlife and are home to unique pre-Ice Age plants. Covering an area of more than two thousand square kilometres, it is the largest protected area in Spain and the second largest in Europe. As the largest of Andalucía's natural parks, Cazorla also functions as an important **nature reserve**, with close to one and half thousand catalogued species. Judging from the number of *cabra hispánica* (Spanish mountain goat), *ciervo* (deer), *jabalí* (wild boar), *nutrias* (otters), birds and butterflies that even the casual visitor is likely to spot, the reserve appears to be fulfilling its role handsomely. Ironically, though, much of the best wildlife viewing will be at the periphery, or even outside the park, since the wildlife is most successfully stalked on foot and walking opportunities within the park itself are, surprisingly, somewhat limited although things are slowly improving.

HIKING IN CAZORLA NATURAL PARK

Few hiking routes in the park are waymarked. Of these one leads from the Empalme de Valle to the Puente de las Herrerías via the Fuente del Oso (2km one way); another of about 1.7km curls round the Cerrada (Narrows) del Utrero near Vadillo-Castril village; the best-marked segment, through the lower Borosa gorge (see box, p.444), is also a mere 1.7km long.

Good **hiking guides** for the park include Guy Hunter-Watts' *Walking in Andalucía*, which details five walks of between five and nineteen kilometres (see p.593); also it's advisable to take a reliable map (see below) when doing any serious walking here. Before heading into the park, it's worth stopping at the private **tourist office**, La Despensa del Parque, in Cazorla (see p.440). Both they and the Torre del Vinagre Centro de Interpretación (see p.447) should have copies of the 1:40,000 **map and guide packs** titled *Mapa y Guía Excursionista* (Editorial Alpina). This series splits the park in two parts: *Sierra de Cazorla* (covering the southern zone) and *Sierra de Segura* (the central and northern sectors). These are now the most accurate maps available on the park and detail *senderos* (footpaths), mountain bike routes, refuges, campsites and hotels. The accompanying booklet (in Spanish or English versions) has useful background information on the park's flora and fauna as well as villages, and includes half a dozen described walks.

Chiclana de Segura

El Campillo

Camporredondo

Sorihuela del Guadalimar

Fuente de la Torre

Gutar

Villanueva del Arzobispo

Iznatoraf

Villacarrillo

Santo Tomé

Almansas

Burunchel

La Iruela

Castillo

Cinco Esquinas

El Chorro

Quesada

Huesa

Tiscar

Peñolite *(1247m)*

(1086m)

Beas de Segura

Cuevas de Ambrosio

Cañada Morales

(1331m)

Tranco

La Platera

(1010m)

Cañada de la Madera

(1432m)

Bujaraiza

Blanquillo *(1830m)*

Coto Ríos

(1577m)

Torre del Vinagre

Arroyo Frío *(1736m)*

Nava de Pablo

Nava de San Pedro

Gilillo *(1847m)*

(708m)

(1411m)

Cabañas *(2028m)*

Peña de Quesada *(1336m)*

(1835m)

Cazorla

Orcera

Los Arroyos

Segura de la Sierra

Las Herrerías

Yelmo *(1809m)*

Río Madera

Cortijos Nuevos

El Parralejo *(1794m)*

Hornos

Casicas del Río Segura

Embalse del Tranco

Venta de la Muela

Pontones *(1609m)*

Santiago de la Espada

Matea

(1964m)

(2064m)

R. Guadalquivir

Río Borosa

(1993m)

(2381m)

Doña Ana

Moncayo *(1531m)*

(2106m)

Tornajuelos *(2133m)*

Embalse de San Clemente

Buitre *(2013m)*

Moro *(1833m)*

Cubo *(1369m)*

Castril

Huéscar

SIERRA DE CAZORLA

SIERRA DE LA CABRILLA

SIERRA DE SECA

SIERRA DE SEGURA

SA. DE LA SAGRA

SA. DE MONTILLA

SA. DE MARMOLANCE

Río Guadalquivir

Río de la Vega

Río Guadalentín

Río Madera

Río Segura

N322 · A312 · A314 · A317 · IH7048 · A319 · LV7701 · A915 · A326 · NE33 · GR700 · GR110

0   10
kilometres

■ **ACCOMMODATION**
Parador El Adelantado ... 1

SIERRAS DE CAZORLA AND SEGURA

N

Baza & Granada

4

The best **times to visit** are late spring and early autumn. The winters can be uncomfortably wet and cold, and roads are often closed due to snow. In high summer, although walking is pleasant before noon, the climate tends to be hot and dry.

Arroyo Frío

The road into the park from Cazorla passes **Burunchel** and climbs over the Puerto de las Palomas with spectacular views before descending into the valley of the Guadalquivir. A little further on there's a turning for the scenically sited **parador** (25km from the turning) which, with your own transport, makes a nice stop-off for a drink or a meal (see p.447).

Back on the road into the heart of the park, beyond the turning, you will soon pass the hamlet of **ARROYO FRÍO**, which has a couple of accommodation options offering outdoor activities. **Horseriding** is available from a ranch, *Picadero Campillo* (☎609 704 137, ⓦturismoencazorla.com/empresas/picaderocampillo/), next door to the *Los Enebros* complex; they can provide tuition and rent out horses for guided half- and full-day treks.

Torre del Vinagre

The Río Borosa walk (see box below) begins at **TORRE DEL VINAGRE**, 9km from Arroyo and 34km from Cazorla; there is also a **visitors' centre** here (see p.447), and, alongside it, a **botanical garden** (Tues–Sun: April–Sept 10am–2pm & 5–8pm; Oct–March 10am–2pm & 3–5pm) with living specimens of the park's flora. Following the road downhill from opposite the Torre del Vinagre building leads to yet another information centre, **Río Borosa** (see p.447).

Coto Ríos

Some 5km beyond Torre del Vinagre, **COTO RÍOS** is a pleasant village with a river beach on the Guadalquivir; there's a campsite here, and lots of accommodation nearby (see p.447). It's possible to reach the village from Cazorla by bus (see p.446) – taking the early departure allows you to do the classic **walk along the Río Borosa** as a day-trek (see box below; confirm all the above times in Cazorla to avoid being stranded).

Parque Cinegético

Eight kilometres northeast of Coto Ríos, keeping to the river's west bank, at the southern end of the Embalse del Tranco reservoir, is the **Parque Cinegético**, a wildlife

---

THE RÍO BOROSA WALK

The **Río Borosa walk**, one of the most popular walks inside the park, follows the Río Borosa upstream. From the visitors' centre at **Torre del Vinagre**, cross the road and take the path to the side of the Jardín Botánico. When you reach an electricity pylon turn left onto a downhill track. After passing a campsite and sportsfield on the left cross a footbridge over the river and turn right, aiming for a white building peeping above the trees. Soon you'll pass a small campsite (with an open-air bar in summer) and about 1km from the footbridge you'll come to a car park at a *piscifactoría* (trout hatchery).

From here follow the path as it crosses back and forth over the Borosa, swift and cold even in summer. After some 6km a signposted footpath diverges to the right; this also marks the beginning of the **Cerrada de Elías gorge**. Two or three wooden bridges now take the path back and forth across the river, which is increasingly confined by sheer rock walls. At the narrowest points the path is routed along planked catwalks secured to the limestone cliff. The walk from Torre del Vinagre to the end of the narrows takes about two hours.

Here the footpath rejoins the track; after another half-hour's walk you'll see a turbine and a long metal pipe bringing water from two **lakes** – one natural, one with a small dam – up the mountain. The road crosses one last bridge over the Borosa and stops at the turbine house. When you get to the gate, beyond which there's a steeply rising gully, count on another full hour up to the lakes. Cross a footbridge and start the steep climb up a narrow track over the rocks below the cliff (at one point the path passes close to the base of the palisade – beware falling stones). At the top of the path is a cavernous amphitheatre, with a waterfall in winter. The path ends about halfway up the cliff, where an artificial tunnel has been bored through the rock; walk through it to get to the lake.

Allow three and a half hours' walking time from Torre del Vinagre for the whole route, slightly less going down. It's a full day's excursion but you should have plenty of time to catch the afternoon bus back, which currently passes the visitors' centre at around 4.15pm, but it would be a good idea to confirm this before starting out. This walk is clearly detailed on the *Editorial Alpina* **map** (see p.442).

park which eventually hopes to include specimens of all the park's fauna including ibex and mouflon, although at present you'll be lucky to see some rather bewildered deer and the odd wild boar from the viewing balcony. To reach the viewing areas, park at the entrance and walk a good kilometre through the woods to get to the first viewing hide. Early morning and evening are the best times to see the animals not struck down by midday torpor. It's worth noting that there are no further campsites or places to stay beyond here until you get to Tranco.

Tranco

Beyond the Parque Cinegético, the road continues along the west bank of the river, passing more picnic spots and *ventas* along the way, en route to **TRANCO**, 21km north, where the Guadalquivir is dammed to create the Embalse de Tranco reservoir. The island in the centre of the lake contains the ruined castle of **Bujaraiza**, all that remains of the village of the same name that disappeared beneath the waters when the dam was created. Apart from a few holiday villas, a lakeside bar, and a **campsite** (see p.448), 4km north of the village, Tranco has little to detain you, but there are a couple of good places **to stay** beyond here (see p.448).

Hornos

From Tranco, the road heads north and circles around the northern end of the reservoir before turning into the valley of the Río Hornos. Here you can glimpse the village of **HORNOS**, perched on a daunting rock pinnacle beneath the tower of its Moorish castle. When you reach it, the village has an isolated air with plenty of Moorish atmosphere. Its narrow, white-walled streets are perfect for meandering, and the castle is worth a look, although once you've got up close there isn't much to it apart from the tower. The Plaza Mayor is overlooked by a solid sixteenth-century church, the **Iglesia de la Asunción**, with an early, if worn, Plateresque portal. Close by and reached through a small arch off the square lies a *mirador* with wonderful **views** over the reservoir, flanked by the heights of the Sierra de Segura. The waters, which lapped the foot of the outcrop below, have receded dramatically in recent years – a symptom of Andalucía's chronic and continuing drought. A stretch of the village's ancient walls is still intact, complete with a horseshoe-arched Moorish gateway.

You can **stay** in Hornos (see p.448), and a pleasant **walk** can be made along the reservoir's eastern banks to the hamlet of **LA PLATERA** (where there is another pleasant place to stay p.448) and the hill of Montero, with views along the reservoir, 4km

4

THE RETURN OF THE BONE-BREAKER

The magnificent **Lammergeier** or **bearded vulture** was once a frequently spotted resident of the Sierras of Segura and Cazorla as it soared and glided around the crags in search of prey. Then in the Sixties and Seventies the species declined dramatically, largely due to the drying up of the supply of carrion that these scavengers rely on to survive. The last sighting of the bird here occurred in the early Eighties. However, in the spring of 2008 four young birds were liberated in the park as part of a programme to reintroduce the species to Cazorla. Two of the juveniles were bred in a rearing centre in the park while the others came from the mountains of the Pyrenees and Austria. All the birds have been fitted with radio transmitters enabling the park's naturalists to monitor their adaptation to their new environment. There are now eleven birds here but as the Lammergeier takes eight years to reach breeding condition the growth of the colony will inevitably be slow. The vultures are known as *quebrantahuesos* (bone-breakers) in Spanish, after their practice of hoisting the leg bones of victims high into the air and dropping them onto a rock below – nearly always the same one – splitting them open to allow the birds to extract the marrow.

beyond. The rock faces above the pine-covered slopes are home to a variety of plants, including yellow-flowered flax and throatwart. Common **bird** species in this area include azure-winged magpies, kestrels and sparrowhawks, but you will be extremely lucky to see the **Lammergeier** or bearded vulture in this, its only habitat in Spain outside the Pyrenees (see box, p.445).

Segura de la Sierra

Scenic though Hornos is, it is overshadowed in every sense by the Cazorla park's most spectacularly sited village, **SEGURA DE LA SIERRA**, 20km to the northeast. With a romantic castle crowning an almost conical 1100m-high hill top, beneath which the tiered village streets seem in danger of collapsing into the olive groves far below, it's a landmark for miles around. Segura's top-notch **olive oil** (including an organic variety) is famed throughout Spain, for which it has a coveted *denominación de origen* label (one of only twenty in the whole country); though the oil is not always easy to find in the village itself, the *almacen* near the church should have a few bottles, or ask at Segura's tourist office (see p.447) who now have their own small shop selling products of the Sierra.

Once you've managed to climb the road that snakes up to it and passed through the medieval gate, you will find Segura to be a warren of narrow streets left behind by its former Moorish occupants. But its **history** goes back much further, perhaps as far as the Phoenicians who, local historians claim, called it Tavara. Greeks, Carthaginians, Romans and Visigoths came in their wake, until the last of these were prised out of this mountain eyrie by the invading Moors who constructed the castle they called Saqura. When it fell to the Christian forces under Alfonso VIII during the thirteenth century, the fort became a strategic outpost on the frontiers of the kingdom of Granada, whose borders were framed by the Guadalquivir and Segura river valleys.

El Castillo

C/Regidor Juan de Isla 1 • April–Sept Tues–Sun 10.30am–2pm & 4.30–8pm; Oct–March Wed–Sun 11am–2pm & 4–7pm • €3

Segura's **castle** – now somewhat over-restored after being torched by French troops during the War of Independence – is open to visitors. Started in the eleventh century, it was much altered after the *Reconquista*. A Moorish bath survives from its earliest days, as well as the impressive *Torre de Homenaje* (keep) with spectacular **views** from its summit, and there is a vaulted chapel from the Christian period. You'll also see a crucial *aljibe* (well) without which the castle would have been vulnerable in times of siege.

On your way up, take in the views over the country for miles around, including a primitive rectangular **bullring** below.

Baños Árabes and around

C/Caballeros Santiaguistas s/n • April–Sept Tues–Sun 10.30am–2pm & 4.30–8pm; Oct–March Wed–Sun 11am–2pm & 4–7pm • Free

Segura's **Baños Árabes** is a splendid eleventh-century Moorish bathhouse off the central Plaza Mayor and behind the church. Inside, three well-preserved chambers are illuminated by overhead light vents and contain elegant horseshoe arches. To reach the baths, follow a descending street to the right-hand side of the parish church of Nuestra Señora Collado which brings you to a superb Moorish double arch in a preserved tower of the ancient walls. The baths are facing this.

Incidentally, a waymarked footpath, the GR147, leaves the double arch for Río Madera, a downhill none-too-challenging 15km hike.

ARRIVAL AND DEPARTURE	CAZORLA NATURAL PARK

By bus The only public transport is from Cazorla, via Torre del Vinagre, to the village of Coto Ríos, 39km into the park (2 daily; April–Sept Mon–Fri; Oct–March Mon & Fri). One bus currently runs at 7.15am, the other at 2.30pm, with return buses from Coto leaving at 9am and 4.15pm (but always confirm these times, and the winter timetable, with the bus company, Carcesa: ☎ 953 721 142).

GETTING AROUND

The number of campsites in the park makes it feasible to do a walking tour, but distances between points are enormous, so to explore well you'll need to be prepared for long hikes. To see the most, of course, you will need to drive.

INFORMATION

Torre del Vinagre Centro de Interpretación Torre del Vinagre (Tues–Sun: April–June 10am–2pm & 4–7pm; July & Aug 10am–2pm & 5–8pm; Oct–March 10am–2pm & 4–6pm; ☎953 713 040). This visitors' centre, packed with motoring tourists in high summer, features a series of interactive sections dealing with the park's flora and fauna, and has a shop and café.

Río Borosa Following the road downhill from opposite the Torre del Vinagre Centro de Interpretación brings you to another *centro* (July & Aug daily 10am–2pm & 5–9pm; Sept–June Wed–Sun 10am–2pm & 5–9pm), with information and displays relating to the park's fluvial wildlife.

Segura Turismo Paseo General Navarro s/n (daily 10.30am–2pm & 6.30–8.30pm; ☎953 480 280, ⓦseguradelasierra.com). The village's municipal tourist office lies down a street forking left before the main road climbs the hill to the village proper.

ACCOMMODATION AND EATING

There are a number of **campsites** – both *camping libre* (free camping) and official sites – dotted around the park; the Turismo at Cazorla (see p.440) will provide a complete list and map. In addition, there are various places to stay – hotels, apartments, villas and wood cabins – throughout the park, many of them very attractive indeed if you want to get away from it all. Note, however, that while for most of the year you should be able to find accommodation with ease, they tend to fill up in August, when ringing ahead is strongly advised. The **high-season prices** quoted here apply only to August. **Food** is available at many places along the main roads inside the park and most hotels have their own restaurant and bar.

SIERRA DE CAZORLA

Parador El Adelantado Ctra. JF-7094, in the park ☎953 727 075, ⓦparador.es. Some 25km from Cazorla and reached via a signed turn-off 12km south of Arroyo Frío, this somewhat featureless modern building is made attractive by its wonderful setting inside the park and a garden swimming pool. Rooms are comfortable (make sure to get one with a view – rooms 4–11, 18–22 and all suites have the best) and well equipped. Also a café-bar and very good restaurant with a good-value set *menú* featuring sierra cuisine for €28. €144

ARROYO FRÍO

Hotel Cazorla Valle ☎953 727 100, ⓦcazorlavalle .com. Rooms and apartments to rent, with a restaurant and pool. Numerous outdoor activities on offer. B&B €58

Hotel Montaña In the centre of the village ☎953 727 011, ⓦhmontana.com. A straightforward affair with restaurant, bar and pool. B&B €84

Los Enebros ☎953 727 110, ⓦlfhoteles.com. A campsite, hotel and restaurant that also rents out heated freestanding wood cabins; there's a wide range of activities on offer here too, such as mountain biking, canoeing and guided walks. B&B €100

Monte Piedra Aparthotel 4km out of Arroyo ☎953 713 145, ⓦturismoencazorla.com/monte piedra.html. Good-value rooms, great views, a pool and restaurant. Apartments (sleeping up to six) are available for day-lets outside August, when you're looking at one-week minimum. Rooms €50, apartments €60

TORRE DEL VINAGRE

Hotel Noguera de la Sierpe A couple of kilometres south of Torre del Vinagre ☎953 713 021, ⓦlfhoteles .com. One of a string of relatively upmarket hotels close to the road, partly housed in a converted *cortijo* with views over a lake and the Guadalquivir valley. It's frequented in winter by the hunting fraternity; the *patrón* is a hunting fanatic and images of his exploits plus trophies (including a stuffed lion) litter the foyer and public rooms. They also rent out some self-catering *casas rurales* overlooking the lake (sleeping up to four), and there's a pool and horse stables. Hotel €65, self-catering €130

COTO RÍOS

Camping Chopera de Coto-Ríos Coto Ríos ☎953 713 074. One of the three good campsites in these parts, well shaded, and with a restaurant and pool. €5.50 per person, €4.40 per tent, €3.40 per vehicle

El Hoyazo Some 7km further along the Tranco road from Coto Ríos ☎953 124 110, ⓦturismoen cazorla.com/hoyazo.html. Well-equipped apartments and bungalows sleeping up to four, with a fine pool. €59

Fuente de Pascala 2km north of Coto Ríos ☎953 713 028. This campsite is marginally cheaper than the other two in the area, but also has plenty of shade, good facilities, a restaurant and a pool. €3.75 per person, €3.75 per tent, €2.75 per vehicle

★ **Hotel La Hortizuela** A couple of kilometres south of Coto Ríos ☎953 713 150, ⓦturismoencazorla.com /alojamiento/hortizuela. Good-value accommodation in

> ## MOVING ON FROM CAZORLA NATURAL PARK
>
> With your own transport, you can avoid backtracking to Cazorla and take an alternative and attractive **route out of the park** heading south from Hornos along the A317 through the Sierra de Segura to Pontones and **Santiago de Espada**, on the border with **Granada**. There are plenty more campsites signed along this route, and Santiago has hotels and *hostales*. The same road continues to **Puebla de Don Fadrique**, where there is another recommended hotel-restaurant. From here you have a choice between the routes to Granada and Almería.
>
> The Granada route via the cattle town of **Huéscar**, following the A330, takes in the interesting towns of Baza and Guadix and provides an opportunity en route to see the remarkable prehistoric discoveries at Orce (see p.556); otherwise the A317 heads across the deserted but picturesque wheatfields of Granada province's eastern panhandle towards **Vélez Blanco** (see p.555) with an impressive castle and prehistoric caves, and eventually hits the coast near the Almerian resort of Mojácar (see p.549).
>
> ### ACCOMMODATION
>
> **Hotel San Francisco** Santiago de Espada ☎ 953 438 072, ⓦ www.hotelsan-francisco.com. A pleasant two-star hotel on the border with Granada, offering functional but perfectly satisfactory rooms. Also has its own bar and a decent restaurant. **€50**
>
> **Puerta de Andalucía** Puebla de Don Fadrique ☎ 958 721 340, ⓦ www.puertadeandalucia.com. On the main road through the village, this is a reliable country hotel offering comfortable rooms above a lively bar-restaurant. **€40**

a delightfully serene hideaway with garden pool and restaurant serving specialities of the sierra including trout and game. B&B **€54**

Hotel Mirasierra Just south of Coto Ríos ☎ 953 713 044, ⓦ turismoencazorla.com/mirasierra .html. Welcoming, comfortable place with air-conditioned rooms. They serve excellent *ciervo* (deer) and trout in its restaurant. **€54**

Hotel Paraíso de Bujaraiza Just south of the Parque Cinegético ☎ 953 124 114, ⓦ paraisode bujaraiza.com. Small, friendly and good-value lakeside hotel with comfortable rooms, pool, restaurant and plenty of greenery. B&B **€70**

Llanos de Arance campsite On the opposite bank of the river, 1km north of Coto Ríos ☎ 953 713 139. Shady spot, with a pool, restaurant and excellent facilities. **€5.50** per person, **€4.40** per tent, **€3.40** per vehicle

TRANCO

★ **Hotel Los Parrales** 3km beyond Tranco ☎ 953 126 170, ❶ mobile 699 834 049. Attractive, friendly hotel in a woodland setting with excellent en-suite rooms and a pool. **€50**

Hotel Losam 7km beyond Tranco ☎ 953 495 088, ⓦ hotellosam.com. A functional, modern roadside place with clean and tidy en-suite rooms and a decent restaurant serving a weekday *menú* for €9. **€35**

Montillana campsite 4km north of Tranco ☎ 953 126 194. A well-run campsite with plenty of shade, and good facilities including a pool, bar-restaurant and supermarket. **€3.85** per person, **€3.75** per tent, **€3** per vehicle

LA PLATERA

★ **El Mesoncillo** La Platera ☎ 646 810 252, ⓦ mesoncillo.com. Delightfully rustic cottages in leafy countryside sleeping up to four. Each cottage comes with its own *chimenea* (wood-burning stove), fully equipped kitchen, TV and garden with barbecue. Two nights minimum. **€80**

HORNOS

Hostal El Cruce C/Puerta Nueva s/n ☎ 953 495 035. Pleasant *hostal-restaurante* whose prominent garden terrace is hard to miss as you enter the village. Offers good-value a/c en-suite rooms with TV. **€30**

Hostal El Mirador C/Puerta Nueva 7 ☎ 953 495 019, ⓦ pensionelmirador.es. Decent rooms above a bar-restaurant near the heart of the village. Rooms come with or without bath, and there are fine views over the *embalse* from some. Shared bath **€28**, en-suite **€35**

Raisa Apartamentos C/Enmedio 5 ☎ 953 495 023, ⓦ apartamentosraisa.es. On the right (and just before *Hostal El Cruce*) as you enter from Cazorla, this place offers pleasant en-suite a/c rooms and apartments with a restaurant below. Rooms **€60**, apartments **€70**

Restaurante El Cruce C/Puerta Nueva s/n ☎ 953 495 035. The leafy terrace of the *hostal's* restaurant is arguably the best place to eat in Hornos. Hearty sierra cuisine includes *solomillo de cerdo* (pork loin), and there's a weekday *menú* for €10.

Restaurante Raisa C/Enmedio 5, about 30m from the church in the heart of the village. A reliable place to eat offering fish and meat *platos combinados*.

SEGURA DE LA SIERRA

Camping El Robledo 4km east of Cortijos Nuevos, on the road from Hornos ☎953 126 469, ⓦcamping elrobledo.com. This is the nearest campsite to Segura with decent facilities including a rustic bar-restaurant; there's plenty of shade but the ground tends to be hard. Organizes plenty of activities such as hiking, horseriding and mountainbiking. **€3.50** per person, **€4.50** per tent, **€3.50** per vehicle

El Mirador Messia de Leiva C/Postigo 1 ☎953 480 806, ⓦmessiadeleiva.com. Rustically decorated and fully equipped apartments and studios. There's also an economical restaurant offering local specialities. **€66**

La Mesa Segureña C/Postigo 2, above the church ☎953 482 101, ⓦlamesadesegura.com. Modern and well-equipped studios and apartments in the heart of the village near the restaurant of the same name. The restaurant is very good, with a welcoming terrace and a daily €10 *menú*. **€60**

★ **Los Huertos de Segura** C/Castillo 11, in the upper village ☎953 480 402, ⓦloshuertosdesegura.com. This is the village's most attractive place to stay, offering comfortable studios and apartments with kitchenettes and terrace or balcony and fine views. The friendly English-speaking proprietor has produced a set of walking leaflets for guests and can provide maps and advice. **€63**

4

Granada and Almería

THE ALHAMBRA, GRANADA

5

Granada and Almería

There is no more convincing proof of Andalucía's diversity than its eastern provinces: Granada, dominated by the Spanish peninsula's highest mountains, the snowcapped Mulhacén and Veleta peaks of the Sierra Nevada; and Almería, a waterless and, in part, semi-desert landscape. For most visitors, the city of Granada is one of the great destinations of Spain, home to Andalucía's most precious monument, the exquisite Moorish Alhambra palace and gardens. The city preserves, too, the old Moorish quarter of Albaicín and gypsy *barrio* of Sacromonte – places filled with the lingering atmosphere of this last outpost of Muslim Spain – as well as a host of Christian monuments. Granada is also an atmospheric place to be during Semana Santa, and a place of literary pilgrimage through its associations with Spain's greatest modern poet, Federico García Lorca.

South of Granada rear the peaks of the **Sierra Nevada** and its lower slopes, **Las Alpujarras**, a series of wooded valleys sprinkled with attractive whitewashed villages. This is wonderful country for walks and wildlife, with ancient cobbled paths connecting many of the villages, among them **Yegen**, one-time base of author Gerald Brenan, and **Trevélez**, Spain's highest village, famed for its snow-cured *jamón serrano*. The province's boast that you can ski in the Sierra Nevada's snowcapped peaks in the morning and swim on the coast in the afternoon is true: the resorts of **Almuñécar**, **Salobreña** and **Castell de Ferro**, along the **Costa Tropical**, all have fine beaches and less development than the Costa del Sol.

There's less of interest west and east of Granada. To the west, **Alhama de Granada** is a delightful spa on a scenic back road to Málaga. To the east, amid a landscape of dusty hills covered with clumps of esparto grass, lies **Guadix**, famous for its cave dwellings hacked out of the soft tufa rock, and the red stone Renaissance castle of **La Calahorra**. Beyond here, Granada's panhandle extends past the ancient country town of **Baza** to a lonely landscape of rolling *sierras* where small farms and isolated villages watch over fields of wheat, fruit orchards and pasture.

The **province of Almería** is a strange corner of Spain. Inland it has an almost lunar landscape of desert, sandstone cones and dried-up riverbeds; on the coast, with a few

PORTICO DEL PARTAL, THE ALHAMBRA

Highlights

❶ The Alhambra, Granada One of the world's great monuments and the pinnacle of Moorish architectural splendour in Spain. **See p.460**

❷ The Albaicín, Granada Granada's ancient, atmospheric Moorish quarter. **See p.470**

❸ Capilla Real, Granada Stunning Gothic chapel built to house the remains of Isabel and Fernando, conquerors of Moorish Granada. **See p.474**

❹ Las Alpujarras A wildly picturesque mountain region dotted with traditional villages and many other vestiges of a Moorish past. **See p.497**

❺ Los Millares This third millennium BC settlement is one of the most important prehistoric sites in Europe. **See p.517**

❻ Alcazaba, Almería One of Andalucía's finest Moorish forts dominates the provincial capital. **See p.527**

❼ Cabo de Gata Natural Park Desert plants and volcanic hills are the features of this natural park edged with coastal resorts where the beaches are often deserted. **See p.542**

❽ Mojácar Attractive "sugar cube" village on a rocky hill with a lively beach resort below. **See p.549**

❾ Mini Hollywood The Almería deserts have provided the backdrop for many Westerns and some of the movie sets can still be visited. **See p.557**

HIGHLIGHTS ARE MARKED ON THE MAP ON PP.454–455

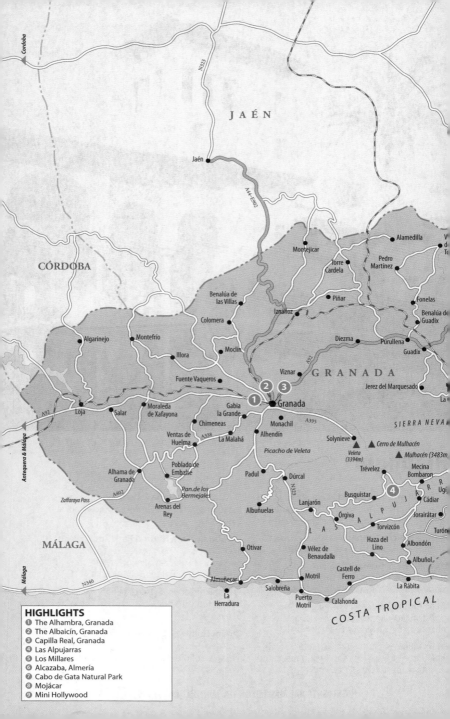

HIGHLIGHTS
1. The Alhambra, Granada
2. The Albaicín, Granada
3. Capilla Real, Granada
4. Las Alpujarras
5. Los Millares
6. Alcazaba, Almería
7. Cabo de Gata Natural Park
8. Mojácar
9. Mini Hollywood

GRANADA AND ALMERÍA

N

MURCIA

MEDITERRANEAN SEA

PARQUE NATURAL SIERRA DE MARÍA

Puebla de Don Fadrique

Castril
Huéscar
Gálera
Castilléjar
Venta Micena
Orce
Cortes de Baza
Fuente Nueva
María
Cueva de los Letreros
Vélez Blanco

Cúllar Baza
Las Vertientes
Vélez Rubio

A92N
A92N

Baza
Caniles

SIERRA DE LAS ESTANCIAS

Oria

Tíjola
Purchena
Albox
Serón
Cantoria

Macael
Albánchez
Huércal-Overa
San Juan de los Terreros

Cóbdar
Cuevas del Almanzora

ALMERÍA

Lubria
Vera
Palomares

Uleila del Campo
Garrucha
Mojácar
8

DE LOS FILABRES

Fiñana
Sorbas
PARAJE NATURAL KARST EN YESOS

Gérgal
A92
Lucainena de las Torres
SIERRA CABRERA

A348
Canjáyar
Tabernas
N340
Carboneras

Fondón
Mini Hollywood
9
Los Millares
5

Alhama de Almería
Gádor
Pechina
SIERRA DE ALHAMILLA
Níjar

Huercal de Almería
Viator
Agua Amarga

CAMPO DE DALÍAS
Almería
6

Fernán Perez
PARQUE NATURAL DE CABO DE GATA
Las Negras
Rodalquilar

SIERRA DE GÁDOR
A7-E15
Aguadulce

Dalías
El Ejido
Roquetas de Mar
El Cabo de Gata
Los Escullos
San José
7

Almerimar
Cabo de Gata

COSTA DE ALMERÍA

0   25
kilometres

5

exceptions, it's relatively unspoilt, with development thwarted by sparse water supplies. The beach resorts are worth considering during what would be "off-season" elsewhere; Almería is Spain's hottest province, and summers start well before Easter and last into November. In midsummer it's incredibly hot – frequently touching 35°C in the shade – while year round there's an intense, almost luminous, sunlight.

The provincial capital and port, **Almería**, enjoyed a brief period of prosperity under the Moors but has been something of a backwater ever since, overlooked by the largest castle the Moors built in Andalucía, the **Alcazaba**, below whose walls is a cave quarter, still populated by gypsies. East of the capital lie the province's best **beaches and resorts**, the least developed of the Spanish Mediterranean. One of the nicest, the small resort of **San José**, lies inside the **Cabo de Gata Natural Park**, a wildlife and wetland area that is home to some interesting desert plants as well as a breeding ground for enormous flocks of **flamingos** in summer. As you head north, you'll find **Los Escullos**, **Las Negras** and **Agua Amarga**, all attractively low-key places fronting a crystal-clear blue sea and sandy strands that see few visitors. North again, things liven up at **Mojácar**, Almería's most fashionable resort, an ancient hilltop village with an enjoyable seafront quarter. To the west of Almería city a dismal sea of plastic tents – *invernaderos* – covers the **plain of Dalías** from the hills to the coast: a bonanza of drip-irrigation agriculture where exotic vegetables are force-grown to supply northern European markets all year round.

Inland, northeast of the provincial capital, begins the most remarkable **desert landscape** in Europe: badlands of twisted gulches, dry riverbeds and eroded hills that have long attracted film producers. Much of *Lawrence of Arabia* was shot here, along with scores of spaghetti westerns, whose sets have been preserved at **Mini Hollywood**, near Tabernas: a fun visit, especially if you have kids to entertain. This weird scenery also shelters some interesting villages such as **Níjar**, a long-established ceramics centre, and the cliff-top **Sorbas**.

The province of Almería also maintains relics of a rich **prehistoric** past, when the rains were regular and the landscape verdant. In the northeast, near the village of **Vélez Rubio**, is the **Cueva de los Letreros**, whose prehistoric cave paintings are among the most important in Spain, while north of the provincial capital, in the Almerian reaches of Las Alpujarras, is the exceptional archeological site of **Los Millares**.

Granada and around

Los dos ríos de Granada
Bajan de la nieve al trigo…

Granada's twin rivers
Tumble down from the snow to the wheat…   Federico García Lorca

The city of **GRANADA** has one of the most dramatic locations in Spain, poised below a magnificent backdrop of the snowcapped peaks of the Sierra Nevada. It's the perfect setting for a near-perfect edifice, the extraordinary **Alhambra** – the most exciting, sensual and romantic of all European monuments. It was the palace-fortress of the Nasrid kings, rulers of the last Spanish Muslim realm, and in its construction Moorish art reached a spectacular yet serene climax. The building, however, seems to go further than this, revealing something of the whole brilliance and spirit of Moorish life and culture. It should on no account be missed – and neither should the city itself.

If you're spending just a couple of days in Granada it's hard to resist spending both of them in the Alhambra. There are, however, a handful of minor Moorish sites in and around the run-down medieval streets of the **Albaicín**, the largest and most characteristic such quarter to survive in Spain. After the delights of Moorish Granada it takes a distinct readjustment and effort of will to appreciate the city's later Christian monuments – although the **Capilla Real**, at least, demands a visit, and Baroque enthusiasts are in for a treat at the **Cartuja**.

Brief history

Before the arrival of the Moors, Granada's mark on history was slight. An early Iberian settlement here, Elibyrge, was adapted by the **Romans** as Illiberis, but although its fertility was prized, it was greatly overshadowed by the empire's provincial capital at Córdoba. Later, after the region had come under **Visigothic** control in the sixth century, the old Roman town, centred on the modern-day Albaicín, grew a **Jewish suburb**, Garnatha, on the south slope of the Alhambra hill. Popular tradition has it that friction between this Jewish settlement and the Christian town led to the Jews assisting the **Moors** to take the city shortly after the invasion of 711.

The Moors adapted the name to Karnattah, and for three centuries it was an important city under the control of the Cordoban caliphate and, when this fell in 1031, under the Almoravid and Almohad Berber dynasties of Seville. When, however, Almohad power crumbled in the thirteenth century as the Christian *Reconquista* gathered momentum, an astute Arab prince of the **Nasrid** tribe, which had been driven south from Zaragoza, saw his opportunity to create an independent state. The kingdom, established in the 1240s by **Ibn al-Ahmar** (aka Muhammad ibn Yusuf ibn Nasr), was to outlast the vanished al-Andalus by a further two and a half centuries.

Nasrid Granada

Nasrid Granada was always a precarious state. Ibn al-Ahmar proved a just and capable ruler but all over Spain the Christian kingdoms were in the ascendant. The Moors of Granada survived only through paying tribute and allegiance to Fernando III of Castile – whom they were forced to assist in the conquest of Muslim Seville – and by the time of Ibn al-Ahmar's death in 1273 Granada was the only surviving Spanish Muslim kingdom. It had, however, consolidated its territory, which stretched from just north of the city down to a coastal strip between Tarifa and Almería, and, stimulated by Muslim refugees, developed a flourishing commerce, industry and culture. Over the next two centuries, Granada maintained its autonomy by a series of shrewd manoeuvres, its rulers turning for protection, as it suited them, to the Christian kingdoms of Aragón and Castile and the Merinid sultans of Morocco. The city-state enjoyed its most confident and prosperous period under **Yusuf I** (1334–54) and **Muhammad V** (1354–91), the rulers responsible for much of the existing Alhambra palace.

But by the mid-fifteenth century a pattern of coups and internal strife became established and a rapid succession of rulers did little to stem Christian inroads. In 1479 the kingdoms of Aragón and Castile were united by the marriage of Fernando and Isabel and within ten years had conquered Ronda, Málaga and Almería. The city of Granada now stood completely alone, tragically preoccupied in a **civil war** between supporters of the sultan's two favourite wives. The Reyes Católicos made escalating and finally untenable demands upon it, and in 1490 war broke out. **Boabdil**, the last Moorish king, appealed in vain for help from his fellow Muslims in Morocco, Egypt and Ottoman Turkey, and in the following year Fernando and Isabel marched on Granada with an army said to total 150,000 troops. For seven months, through the winter of 1491, they laid siege to the city. On January 2, 1492, Boabdil formally surrendered its keys. The Christian reconquest of Spain was complete.

Christian Granada

There followed a century of repression for Granada, during which Jews and then Muslims were treated harshly and finally expelled by the **Christian state and Church**, both of which grew rich on the confiscated property. The loss of Muslim and Jewish artisans and traders led to gradual economic decline, which was reversed only

■ ACCOMMODATION
Albergue Juvenil	40
Casa del Aljibe	8
Casa del Aljarife	14
Casa del Capitel Nazari	17
Casa Morisca	4
Cuevas el Abanico	1
El Ladrón de Agua	15
El Numero 8	11
Hostal Arteaga	27
Hostal Austria	25
Hostal Britz	24
Hostal Costa Azul	30
Hostal La Ninfa	19
Hostal Landázuri	22
Hostal Márquez	35
Hostal Meridiano	37
Hostal Moni Albayzín	7
Hostal Navarro Ramos	21
Hostal Salvador	34
Hostal San Joaquin	32
Hostal Santa Ana	20
Hostal Suecia	13
Hostal Zurita	36
Hotel Albero	9
Hotel Alhambra Palace	10
Hotel América	6
Hotel Guadalupe	3
Hotel Hespería	31
Hotel Inglaterra	28
Hotel Los Angeles	29
Hotel Los Tilos	33
Hotel Macía Plaza	26
Hotel Molinos	23
Hotel Palacio Santa Inés	12
Hotel Reina Cristina	38
Hotel Santa Isabel la Real	16
Palacio de Mariana Pineda	18
Parador de San Francisco	5
Pensiones La Milagrosa y Matilde	39
Posada Doña Lupe	2

■ BARS & CLUBS
Afrodisia	13
Camborio	1
Chupitería	17
Fondo Reservado	6
Granada 10	12
La Estrella	9
La Sal	14
Makeba	16
Peatón Pub	18
Planta Baja	19
Potemkin	10
Quilombo	5
Six Colours	15
Son	11

■ FLAMENCO VENUES
El Niño de las Almendras	8
Jardines de Zoraya	4
Los Faroles	2
Peña Platería	3
Sala Vimaambi	7

● RESTAURANTS
Bar-Restaurante Sevilla	43	Café-Bar Oliver	48	El Ladrillo II	10	La Mimbre	2
Botánico	52	Carmen de Aben Humeya	9	El Trillo del Reca	12	La Ninfa	16
Café-Bar 380	27	Casa Cepillo	47	Juanillo	1	Lago de Como	13
		Casa López Correa	23	La Esquinita	14	Las Cuevas	24

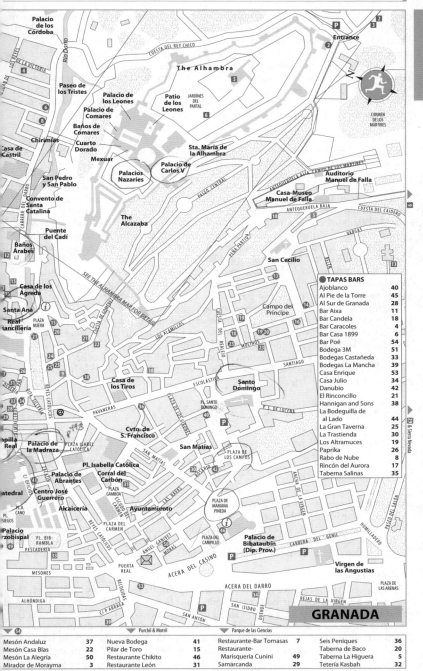

TAPAS BARS

Ajoblanco	40
Al Pie de la Torre	45
Al Sur de Granada	28
Bar Aixa	11
Bar Candela	18
Bar Caracoles	4
Bar Casa 1899	6
Bar Poë	54
Bodega 3M	51
Bodegas Castañeda	33
Bodegas La Mancha	39
Casa Enrique	53
Casa Julio	34
Danubio	42
El Rinconcillo	21
Hannigan and Sons	38
La Bodeguilla de al Lado	44
La Gran Taverna	25
La Trastienda	30
Los Altramuces	19
Paprika	26
Rabo de Nube	8
Rincón del Aurora	17
Taberna Salinas	35

GRANADA

Mesón Andaluz	37	Nueva Bodega	41	Restaurante-Bar Tomasas	7
Mesón Casa Blas	22	Pilar de Toro	15	Restaurante-Marisquería Cunini	49
Mesón La Alegría	50	Restaurante Chikito	46	Samarcanda	29
Mirador de Morayma	3	Restaurante León	31		

Seis Peniques	36
Taberna de Baco	20
Taberna La Higuera	5
Tetería Kasbah	32

5

temporarily in the seventeenth century, the period when the city's Baroque monuments – La Cartuja monastery and San Juan de Dios hospital – were built. The city suffered heavily under **Napoleonic occupation**, when even the Alhambra was used as a barracks, causing much damage, and, although the nineteenth-century Romantic movement saw to it that the Alhambra suffered few more such violations, the sober *granadino* middle class have been accused repeatedly since of caring little for the rest of their city's artistic legacy. Over the last century and a half, they have covered over the Río Darro – which now flows beneath the town centre – and demolished an untold number of historic buildings to build avenues through the centre of the city.

Modern Granada

Lorca described the *granadinos* as "the worst bourgeoisie in Spain", and they are regarded by many other Andalucians as conservative, arrogant and cool, like a colony somehow transplanted from northern Spain. A strong small-shopkeeper economy – which discouraged industrial development – and a society where military and clerics were dominant inhibited innovation and liberal ideas through the early part of the twentieth century. This introverted outlook perhaps contributed also to the events of the **Civil War**, one of the greatest stains on the city's name. In 1936, following Franco's coup, a fascist bloodbath was unleashed during which an estimated seven thousand of the city's liberals and Republicans were assassinated, among them poet and playwright **Federico García Lorca**. The poet deserved better from his native city, of which he had written, "The hours are longer and sweeter here than in any other Spanish town … Granada has any amount of good ideas but is incapable of acting on them. Only in such a town, with its inertia and tranquillity, can there exist those exquisite contemplators of water, temperatures and sunsets."

In recent years the Andalucian parliament has had to block a preposterous plan by the city council to cover much of the Alhambra hill with a luxury housing estate – the bulldozers had actually begun digging. The council's latest plan to build a lift and tunnels connecting the Paseo de los Tristes with the Alhambra's Moorish palace was turned down by the monument's governing board in 2011 as being likely to cause serious archeological damage.

The Alhambra

The Sabika hill sits like a garland on Granada's brow,
In which the stars would be entwined
And the Alhambra (Allah preserve it)
Is the ruby set above that garland.   Ibn Zamrak, vizier to Muhammad V (1362–91)

One of the most sensual architectural creations in the world and the greatest treasure of Moorish Spain, the **Alhambra** sits on a hill overlooking the city it has captivated for seven centuries. There are three distinct groups of buildings on the Alhambra hill (known as Sabika to the Moors): the **Casa Real** (Royal Palace or Palacios Nazaríes), the palace gardens of the **Generalife**, and the **Alcazaba**.

Brief history

The Alcazaba, the fortress of the eleventh-century Ziridian rulers, was all that existed when the Nasrids made Granada their capital, but from its reddish walls the hilltop had already taken its name: Al Qal'a al-Hamra in Arabic means literally "the red fort". The first Nasrid king, **Ibn al-Ahmar**, rebuilt the Alcazaba and added to it the huge circuit of walls and towers that forms your first view of the castle. Within the walls he began a palace, which was supplied with running water by diverting the Río Darro nearly 8km to the foot of the hill; water is an integral part of the Alhambra and this engineering

5

A WALK TO THE ALHAMBRA

The standard approach to the Alhambra is along the **Cuesta de Gomérez**, a narrow, semi-pedestrianized road that climbs uphill from Plaza Nueva. The only traffic allowed to use this road are taxis and residents' vehicles. Should you decide to walk up (a pleasant 20min stroll from Plaza Nueva), after a few hundred metres you reach the **Puerta de las Granadas**, a massive Renaissance gateway topped by three pomegranates which became the city's symbol (*granada* is the fruit's Spanish name). Beyond the gate the path on the right climbs up towards a group of fortified towers, the **Torres Bermejas**, parts of which may date from as early as the eighth century, along with some other interesting sights. The left-hand path heads through woods of closely planted elms and past a huge terrace-fountain (courtesy of Carlos V), eventually reaching the main gateway of the Alhambra in Moorish times, the **Puerta de la Justicia**. A magnificent tower that forced three changes of direction, making intruders hopelessly vulnerable, it was built by Yusuf I in 1348 and preserves above its inner arch the Koranic symbol of a key (for Allah, the opener of the gates of Paradise) and, over the outer arch, an outstretched hand whose five fingers represent the five Islamic precepts: prayer, fasting, alms-giving, pilgrimage to Mecca and the oneness of God. A Moorish legend stated that the gate would never be breached by the Christians until the hand reached down to grasp the key. To reach the ticket office, continue uphill for 400m. Leaving the Alhambra, a lovely alternative route down to the city is the **Cuesta de los Chinos**, and its continuation the Cuesta del Rey Chico, which descends beneath two arches to the right of the *La Mimbre* restaurant near the Alhambra's ticket office. It winds gradually down, passing beneath the Alhambra's northern walls, to the Río Darro and a terrace of riverside cafés.

feat was Ibn al-Ahmar's greatest contribution. The Casa Real was essentially the product of his fourteenth-century successors, particularly **Muhammad V**, who built and decorated many of its rooms in celebration of his accession to the throne (in 1354) and conquest of Algeciras (in 1369). Also within the citadel stood a complete "government city" of mansions, smaller houses, baths, schools, mosques, barracks and gardens.

After their conquest of Granada, **Fernando and Isabel** lived for a while in the Alhambra. They restored some rooms and converted the mosque but left the palace structure unaltered. As at Córdoba and Seville, it was their grandson **Emperor Carlos V** who wreaked the most insensitive destruction. He demolished a whole wing of rooms in order to build yet another grandiose Renaissance palace. This and the Alhambra itself were simply ignored by his successors and by the eighteenth century the Royal Palace was in use as a prison. In 1812 it was taken and occupied by **Napoleon's forces**, who looted and damaged whole sections of the building, and on their retreat from the city tried to blow up the entire complex. Their attempt was thwarted only by the action of a crippled soldier (José García) who remained behind and removed the fuses; a plaque honouring his valour has been placed in the Plaza de los Aljibes.

Two decades later the Alhambra's "rediscovery" began, given impetus by the American writer **Washington Irving**, who set up his study in the empty palace rooms and began to write his marvellously romantic *Tales of the Alhambra* (on sale all over Granada – and good reading amid the gardens and courts). Shortly after its publication the Spaniards made the Alhambra a **national monument** and set aside funds for its restoration. This continues to the present day and is now a highly sophisticated project, scientifically removing the accretions of later ages in order to expose and restore meticulously the Moorish creations.

The Alcazaba

Having made your way from the ticket office (see p.468), go through the **Puerta del Vino** – named from its use in the sixteenth century as a wine cellar – and across the Plaza de los Aljibes you are confronted by the walls of the **Alcazaba**, the earliest, though most ruined, part of the fortress. Quite apart from filling in time before your ticket

5

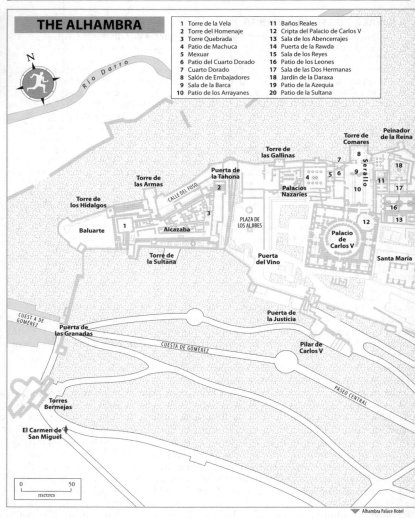

THE ALHAMBRA

1 Torre de la Vela	11 Baños Reales
2 Torre del Homenaje	12 Cripta del Palacio de Carlos V
3 Torre Quebrada	13 Sala de los Abencerrajes
4 Patio de Machuca	14 Puerta de la Rawda
5 Mexuar	15 Sala de los Reyes
6 Patio del Cuarto Dorado	16 Patio de los Leones
7 Cuarto Dorado	17 Sala de las Dos Hermanas
8 Salón de Embajadores	18 Jardín de la Daraxa
9 Sala de la Barca	19 Patio de la Azequia
10 Patio de los Arrayanes	20 Patio de la Sultana

Alhambra Palace Hotel

admits you to the Palacios Nazaríes, this is an interesting part of the complex and one where you can get a grip on the whole site.

Once inside, thread your way through remnants of the barracks to the Alcazaba's summit, the **Torre de la Vela**, named after a huge bell on its turret which until recent years was rung to mark the irrigation hours for workers on the *vega*, Granada's vast and fertile plain. The views from here are spectacular: west over the plunging ravine of the Darro with the city and the *vega* beyond, and north towards the Albaicín and Sacromonte hills, with the Alhambra itself behind and the snowcapped peaks of the Sierra Nevada forming a backdrop. It was on this same parapet at 3pm on January 2, 1492, that the Cross was first displayed above the city, alongside the royal standards of Aragón and Castile and the banner of St James. Boabdil, leaving Granada for exile in the Alpujarras, turned and wept at the sight, earning from his mother Aisha the famous rebuke: "Do not weep like a

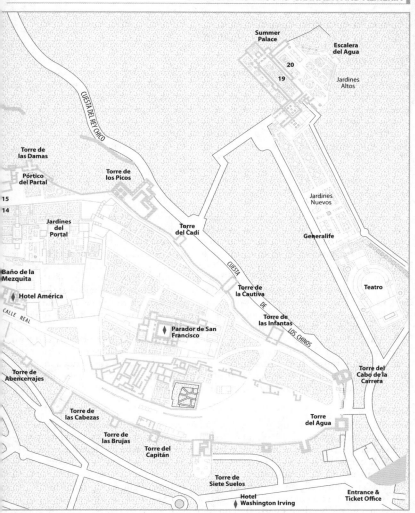

woman for what you could not defend like a man." The visit route continues via the **Jardín de los Ardaves**, a delightful seventeenth-century garden laid out along the fort's southern parapets with creepers, fountains and sweet-scented bushes.

To gain access to the palace you need to recross the **Plaza de los Aljibes** (where there's a very welcome drinks kiosk). In Nasrid times this area was a ravine dividing the hill between the Royal Palace on one side, and the Alcazaba on the other. Following the *Reconquista* the ravine was filled in to hold two rainwater cisterns (*aljibes*) and the surface above laid out with fortifications. During the construction of Carlos V's palace in the sixteenth century, the area was cleared of these structures to create a parade ground, the rather desolate form it retains today. The underground **cisterns** can now be seen only as part of a guided visit (see p.468). Follow the arrows indicating the Palacios Nazaríes (Nasrid Palaces) to reach the royal palace. Fronting the entrance to the palace

5

a **Sala de Presentación** has a small exhibition – with some informative maquettes – detailing the development of the Alhambra.

The Palacios Nazaríes

It is amazing that the **Palacios Nazaríes** has survived, for it stands in utter contrast to the strength of the Alcazaba and the encircling walls and towers. It was built lightly and often crudely from wood, brick and adobe, and was designed not to last but to be renewed and redecorated by succeeding rulers. Its buildings show a superb use of light and space but they are principally a vehicle for ornamental stucco decoration. This, as Titus Burckhardt explains in *Moorish Culture in Spain*, was both an intricate science and a philosophy of abstract art in direct contrast to pictorial representation:

With its rhythmic repetition, [it] does not seek to capture the eye to lead it into an imagined world, but, on the contrary, liberates it from all pre-occupations of the mind. It does not transmit any specific ideas, but a state of being, which is at once repose and inner rhythm.

Burckhardt adds that the way in which patterns are woven from a single band, or radiate from many identical centres, served as a pure simile for Islamic belief in the oneness of God, manifested at the centre of every form and being.

Arabic inscriptions feature prominently in the ornamentation. Some are poetic eulogies of the buildings and builders, others of various sultans – notably Muhammad V. Most, however, are taken from the Koran, and among them the phrase "Wa-la ghaliba illa-Llah" (There is no Conqueror but God) is tirelessly repeated. It's said that this became the battle cry of the Nasrids upon Ibn al-Ahmar's return from aiding the Castilian war against Muslim Seville; it was his reply to the customary, though bitterly ironic, greetings of *Mansur* (Victor).

The palace is structured in three parts, each arrayed round an interior court and with a specific function. The sultans used the **Mexuar**, the first series of rooms, for business and judicial purposes. In the **Serallo**, beyond, they would receive embassies and distinguished guests. The last section, the **Harem**, formed their private living quarters and would have been entered by no one but their family and servants.

The Mexuar

The council chamber, the main reception hall of the **Mexuar**, is the first room you enter. It was completed in 1365 and hailed (perhaps obsequiously) by the court poet and vizier Ibn Zamrak as a "haven of counsel, mercy and favour". Here the sultan heard the pleas and petitions of the people and held meetings with his ministers. At the room's far end is a small **oratory**, one of a number of prayer niches scattered round the palace and immediately identifiable by their angular alignment to face Mecca.

This "public" section of the palace, beyond which few would have penetrated, is completed by the Mudéjar **Cuarto Dorado** (Golden Room), redecorated under Carlos V, whose Plus Ultra motif appears throughout the palace, and the **Patio del Cuarto Dorado**. This latter has perhaps the grandest facade of the whole palace, for it admits you to the formal splendour of the Serallo.

The Serallo

The **Serallo** was built largely to the design of Yusuf I (1333–54), a romantic and enlightened sultan who was stabbed to death by a madman while worshipping in the Alhambra mosque. Its rooms open out from delicate marble-columned arcades at each end of the long **Patio de los Arrayanes** (Myrtles) with its serene fountain and pool flanked by clipped myrtle bushes. At the court's northern end is the **Sala de la Barca**, with a fine copy of its original cedar ceiling (destroyed by fire in the nineteenth century), and beyond this the fortified **Torre de Comares**, two floors of which are occupied by the royal throne room.

This room, known as the **Salón de Embajadores** (Hall of the Ambassadors), is the palace's largest and most majestic chamber. It was where the delicate diplomacy with the Christian emissaries would have been transacted – the means by which the Nasrid dynasty preserved itself – and as the sultan could only be approached indirectly it stands at an angle to the entrance from the Mexuar. It is perfectly square, with a stunning wooden dome, a superb example of *lacería*, the rigidly geometric "carpentry of knots" domed roof, and with a complex symbolism representing the seven heavens of the Muslim cosmos. The walls are completely covered in tile and stucco decoration and inscriptions, one of which states simply "I am the Heart of the Palace". It was here, symbolically, that Boabdil signed the terms of his city's surrender to the Reyes Católicos, whose motifs (the arms of Aragón and Castile) were later worked into the dome. Here, too, so it is said, Fernando met with Columbus to discuss his planned voyage to find a new sea route to India – the trip that led to the discovery of the Americas.

Carlos V tore down the rooms at the southern end of the Patio de los Arrayanes. From the arcade there is access (frequently closed) to the gloomy **chapel crypt** (*cripta*) of his palace; it has a curious "whispering gallery" effect, whereby words whispered on one side of the crypt can be heard quite clearly on the opposite side.

The Harem

The visit route continues to the **Patio de los Leones** (Court of the Lions), which has become the archetypal image of Granada, and constitutes the heart of the harem section of the palace. It was this area that moved Washington Irving to write in his *Tales of the Alhambra*:

It is impossible to contemplate this scene, so perfectly Oriental, without feeling the early associations of Arabian romance, and almost expecting to see the white arm of some mysterious princess beckoning from the gallery, or some dark eye sparkling through the lattice. The abode of beauty is here as if it had been inhabited but yesterday.

The stylized and archaic-looking lions beneath its fountain probably date, like the court itself, from the reign of Muhammad V, Yusuf's successor; a poem inscribed on the bowl tells how much fiercer the beasts would look if they weren't so restrained by respect for the sultan. The court was designed as an interior garden and planted with shrubs and aromatic herbs; it opens onto three of the finest rooms in the palace, each of which looks directly onto the fountain.

The most sophisticated rooms in this part of the complex, apparently designed to give a sense of the rotary movement of the stars, are the two facing each other across the court. The largest of these, the **Sala de los Abencerrajes**, has the most fabulous ceiling in the whole Alhambra complex: sixteen-sided, supported by niches of astonishing stalactite vaulting and lit by windows in the dome. Based on Pythagoras's theorem, the whole stupendous design – with a final and deft artistic flourish – is reflected in a fountain on the floor. Its light and airy quality stands at odds with its name and history, for it was here that Abu al-Hassan, Boabdil's father, murdered sixteen princes of the Abencerraj family, whose chief had fallen in love with his favourite, Zoraya. The stains in the fountain are popularly supposed to be indelible traces of blood from the severed heads thrown into it – but are more likely to be from rust.

At the far end of the court is the **Sala de los Reyes** (Hall of the Kings), whose dormitory alcoves preserve a series of unique paintings on leather. These, in defiance of Koranic law, represent human scenes. They were probably painted by a Christian artist in the last decades of Moorish rule and were once thought to portray images of the Nasrid rulers – hence the room's name.

The second of the two facing chambers on the court's north side, the **Sala de las Dos Hermanas** (Hall of the Two Sisters), is more mundanely named – from two huge slabs of white marble in its floor – but just as spectacularly decorated, with a dome of over five thousand honeycomb cells. It was the principal room of the sultan's favourite,

5

opening onto an inner apartment and balcony (with surviving fragments of Moorish tinted glass in the dome), the **Mirador de la Daraxa** (Eyes of the Sultana); the romantic garden patio below was added after the Reconquest.

Beyond, you are directed along a circuitous route through **apartments** redecorated by Carlos V (as at Seville, the northern-reared emperor installed fireplaces) and later used by Washington Irving. Eventually you emerge at the **Peinador de la Reina** (Queen's Pavilion), which served as an oratory for the sultanas and as a dressing room for the wife of Carlos V; perfumes were burned beneath its floor and wafted up through a marble slab in one corner.

From here, passing the **Patio de la Lindaraja** added in the sixteenth century (though the basin of its marble fountain was taken from outside the Mexuar), you come to the **Baños Reales** (Royal Baths), wonderfully decorated in rich tile mosaics and lit by pierced stars and rosettes once covered by coloured glass. The central chamber was used for reclining and retains the balconies where singers and musicians – reputedly blind to keep the royal women from being seen – would entertain the bathers. At present, entry is not permitted to the baths, though you can make out most of the features through the doorways.

The visit route exits via the exquisite **Portico del Partal** with a tower and elegant portico overlooking a serene pool. What appears no more than a garden pavilion today is in fact the surviving remnant of the early fourteenth-century Palace of the Partal, a four-winged structure originally surrounding the pool, the Alhambra's largest expanse of water. The **Jardines del Partal** lie beyond this and the nearby gate brings you out close to the entrance to the Palacio de Carlos V.

The Palacio de Carlos V

Entering the **Palacio de Carlos V** strikes a totally different mood to what has gone before. The architecture of the palace with its rigid symmetries and dour exterior could not be more different from that of the Nasrid palaces. The building is dominated by its interior circular courtyard, where bullfights were once held. The palace itself was begun in 1526 but never finished – the coffered ceilings of the colonnade were added only in the 1960s before which the Ionic columns had projected into open sky – as shortly after commissioning it, Carlos V left Granada never to return, his plan to turn the city into the seat of the Spanish monarchy forgotten. Despite seeming totally out of place, however, the edifice is a distinguished piece of Renaissance design in its own right – the only surviving work of Pedro Machuca, a former pupil of Michelangelo. Lorca once referred to the stylistic clash between the two palaces as symbolic of "the fatal duel that throbs in the heart of each of Granada's citizens".

Museo de la Alhambra

Tues–Sat 9am–2.30pm (June–Sept closes 2pm) • €1.50, free with EU passport

The lower floor of the Palacio de Carlos V houses the **Museo de la Alhambra,** a wonderful collection of artefacts that visitors are often too jaded to take in after the marvels of the Moorish palace outside. As well as fragments of sculptured plaster arabesques, wood carving and tilework saved from the Alhambra and a splendid ceramic collection, look out for some outstanding fourteenth- and fifteenth-century Nasrid paintings and equally stunning carved wood panels and screens. The rare and beautiful fifteenth-century **Alhambra Vase** (Jarrón de las Gacelas) is the museum's centrepiece. Almost 1.5m high, and made for the Nasrid palace from local red clay enamelled in blue and gold with leaping *gacelas* (gazelles), it is the ceramic equal of the artistic splendours in the palace.

Museo de Bellas Artes

March–Oct Tues 2.30–8pm, Wed–Sat 9am–8pm, Sun 9am–2.30pm; Nov–Feb closes 6pm • €1.50, free with EU passport

On the upper floors of the Palacio de Carlos V is the **Museo de Bellas Artes**, a cavernous gallery whose paintings and sculpture might command more attention elsewhere. In

5

Room 1 there's a fine sixteenth-century woodcarving of the *Virgin and Child* by Diego de Siloé. Room 2 is dedicated to the works of Alonso Cano, the seventeenth-century *granadino* painter and sculptor. His powerful portrayals of *San Diego de Alcalá* and *San Antonio* stand out, as does a head of *San Juan de Dios*, the latter made with some assistance from Granada's other great sculptor, Pedro de Mena. Room 3 has more examples of the Andalucian sculptural tradition, including an *Ecce Homo* and a *Dolorosa* by José de Mora. Room 4 displays some minor Flemish works from the Golden Age, while the later rooms, devoted to paintings from the nineteenth and twentieth centuries, are fairly forgettable. Exceptions here are a typical work by Mariano Fortuny of Granada's *Ayuntamiento Viejo* and a handful of vibrantly coloured abstract works by Granada-born José Guerrero (see p.475). The final couple of rooms are devoted to temporary exhibitions.

The Baño de la Mezquita
Behind Carlos V's palace are the remnants of the town (with a population of forty thousand during the Nasrid period) that once existed within the Alhambra's walls. The main street, Calle Real, today lined with tedious tourist shops, guides you east towards the Generalife; on the way it's worth looking into the well-preserved **Baño de la Mezquita**, where ablutions were performed prior to entering the Alhambra's main mosque. The mosque itself was demolished to make way for the undistinguished sixteenth-century church of Santa María de la Alhambra.

Convento de San Francisco
At the southern end of Calle Real the fifteenth-century **Convento de San Francisco** is also worth a visit. Built by Fernando and Isabel on the site of another Moorish palace, this is now a *parador* whose marvellous plant-filled patio, dominated by a soaring cypress projecting above the roof, preserves part of the chapel where the Catholic monarchs were buried – commemorated by a marble slab – before being removed to the cathedral. It's tricky to find, and you'll need to ask for directions at the hotel's reception. At the rear of the *parador*, there's a restaurant and a very pleasant terrace bar, both open to nonresidents.

The Generalife
Paradise is described in the Koran as a shaded, leafy garden refreshed by running water where the "fortunate ones" may take their rest under tall canopies. It is an image that perfectly describes the **Generalife**, the gardens and summer palace of the Nasrid rulers. Its name means literally "garden of the architect" and the grounds consist of a luxuriantly imaginative series of patios, enclosed gardens and walkways.

By chance, an account of the gardens during Moorish times, written rather fancifully by fourteenth-century Moorish historian, poet and palace vizier Ibn Zamrak, survives. The descriptions that he gives aren't all entirely believable but they are a wonderful basis for musing as you lounge around by the patios and fountains. There were, he wrote, celebrations with horses darting about in the dusk at speeds that made the spectators rub their eyes (a form of festival still indulged in at Moroccan *fantasías*); rockets shot into the air to be attacked by the stars for their audacity; tightrope walkers flying through the air like birds; men bowled along in a great wooden hoop, shaped like an astronomical sphere.

Today, even devoid of such amusements, the gardens remain deeply evocative, above all, perhaps, the **Patio de la Sultana** (aka Patio de los Cipreses), a dark and secretive walled garden of sculpted junipers where the sultana Zoraya was suspected of meeting her lover Hamet, chief of the unfortunate Abencerrajes. The trunk of the seven-hundred-year-old **cypress tree** (marked by a plaque) is where legend says their trysts took place and where the grisly fate of the Abencerraj clan was sealed. Nearby is the inspired flight of fantasy of the **Escalera del Agua** (aka Camino de las Cascadas), a staircase with water flowing down its stone balustrades. At its base is a wonderful little **Summer Palace**, with various decorated belvederes.

5

ARRIVAL AND DEPARTURE   THE ALHAMBRA

By bus A dedicated minibus service, the Alhambrabus (#30; daily 7am–10pm, every 10min; €1.20), links the Plaza Isabel La Católica in the centre with the Alhambra palace.

By car To approach the Alhambra by car, use the signed route heading from Puerta Real along the Paseo del Salón and the Paseo de la Bomba to the Alhambra's car park on the eastern edge of the complex.

On foot The standard approach to the Alhambra is along the Cuesta de Gomérez (see box, p.461).

INFORMATION

Opening hours The Alhambra is open daily (April–Oct 8.30am–8pm; Nov–March 8.30am–6pm; last admission 1hr before closing time; €13; ⓦ alhambra-patronato.es).

Admission To protect the complex, only 6600 daily admissions are allowed. All tickets will state whether they are for morning (8.30am–2pm) or afternoon (2–8pm; Nov–March 2–6pm) sessions. You must enter between the stated times; once inside you may stay as long as you wish, but note that you will not be allowed to enter the complex (even with pre-booked tickets) less than 1hr before closing time. To alleviate overcrowding, tickets are stamped with a 30min time slot during which you must enter the Palacios Nazaríes. You will not be allowed to enter before or after this time, but again, once inside the palace you can stay as long as you like. Note also that the Museo de la Alhambra (see p.466) and the Museo de las Bellas Artes (see p.466), both in the palace of Carlos V, have different hours and admission fees to those of the Alhambra. Note, however, that only the palaces, museums and Generalife require a ticket to gain entry – the rest you are allowed to wander around freely.

BUYING TICKETS

Buying tickets in advance The method strongly recommended by the Alhambra to guarantee entry on a specific day is to book in advance on one of two websites: ⓦ alhambra-tickets.es and ⓦ servicaixa.com. Internet reservations carry a booking fee of €1 per ticket. You can also book by phone (from Spain) ☎ 902 888 001 or (from abroad) ☎ 934 923 750 (24hr; English spoken). Either way, you will be allocated a time slot for visiting the Palacios Nazaríes (see p.464). Collect your tickets from the reservation counter in Alhambra's ticket office, at least 1hr before this time. You'll need your reservation number (issued with all internet and phone transactions), the same credit card with which you made the booking, and your passport for identification.

Buying tickets on the day If you are buying your tickets in person you have two options. They can be bought at the entrance (the ticket office opens at 8am), but queues can be long and there is no guarantee of getting in. It may be possible to avoid the queues by paying with a credit card. Signed off the car park near the entrance with a board in English and Spanish stating "Credit Cards/Tarjetas de Crédito" is a small building with *ServiCaixa* ticket machines operated by the La Caixa bank. Insert your card into the machine and request a day and time (morning or afternoon); if tickets are available for that slot the machine will issue tickets and debit your card. (Note, however, that for technical reasons not all credit cards will work on these machines, and that the tickets put on sale in this manner are only what remain after the advance sales have taken priority.)

Night visits The Palacios Nazaríes is also open for floodlit night visits (March–Oct Tues–Sat 10–11.30pm; Nov–Feb Fri & Sat 8–9.30pm; €13). Ticket offices open 15min before to 15min after each opening time and the availability of tickets (which can be pre-booked) is subject to the same terms as for daytime visits.

Guided visits Themed guided tours (in Spanish; Sept–June; €5) allow visitors to view parts of the complex (many in the process of restoration) not normally open to the public. A schedule, *Programa de Visitas Guiadas*, is available from the Alhambra ticket office; tours need to be booked at an office in the Corral de Carbón, slightly south of the cathedral.

PLANNING A ROUTE

The ticket office entrance to the Alhambra brings you into the complex at the eastern end, near to the Generalife gardens. However, your time slot for entering the Palacios Nazaríes (usually up to 1hr ahead) means that it makes sense to start your visit with the Alcazaba, the oldest part of the complex, at the Alhambra's opposite (western) end. To get here from the entrance, walk up the short avenue lined with cypresses to a three-way fork, taking the signed path to the Alhambra. Cross the bridge over the "moat" (actually the Cuesta de los Chinos) following signs to the Alcazaba and Palacios Nazaríes. You will eventually pass the gates of the *Parador de San Francisco* (right) and the *Hotel América* to enter the Calle Real. Continue alongside the palace of Carlos V to reach the Puerta del Vino.

ESSENTIALS

Bookshops On the lower floor of the Palacio de Carlos V is one of the three official Alhambra bookshops (*Librería de la Alhambra*) with a wide variety of texts and postcards relating to the monument; the others are next to the ticket office at the entrance and along the Calle Real.

Eating and drinking If you're looking for a place to eat lunch or have a refreshing drink between palaces and museums, the shady terrace of *Restaurante La Mimbre* is one of the best-value places on the hill (see p.486).

The Alhambra Hill: other sights

After taking in the delights of the Alhambra and Generalife, most visitors are too tired to even think of more sightseeing – which is a pity, for there are a number of other sights on the hill worthy of a visit. These are not connected with the Alhambra but are very much part of Granada's more recent past and, in the case of the **Carmen de los Martires**, make a wonderful place to while away an hour before returning to the city.

Casa-Museo Manuel de Falla

C/Antequerela s/n • Sept–June Tues–Sun 10am–2pm; July & Aug Thurs–Mon 10am–2pm; guided visits, last visit 1.30pm • €2

From the Puerta de las Granadas, taking the right-hand path uphill leads, in its higher reaches, to the **Casa-Museo Manuel de Falla**, the former home of the great Cádiz composer. The tiny house has been recreated to appear just as he left it in 1939 – with piano, domestic clutter, medicine bottles by his bed (he was a life-long hypochondriac), and stacks of books – before quitting fascist Spain for an exile spent in Argentina where he died in 1946. The walls and surfaces are dotted with mementos and gifts from friends – including a series of sketches by Picasso – and the pretty garden with its bench and vista is where the composer relaxed ("I have the most beautiful panoramic view in the world," he wrote to friends). A summer café (April–Sept) here serving *pasteles* (cakes) and drinks opens from 8.30pm to 1am. Occasional concerts of de Falla's works are performed in the nearby **Auditorio Manuel de Falla**, Paseo de los Mártires s/n, on Saturday evenings and Sunday mornings throughout the year (details from the Turismo).

Carmen de los Mártires

Paseo de los Mártires s/n • March–Oct Mon–Fri 10am–2pm & 6–8pm, Sat & Sun 10am–8pm; Nov–Feb Mon–Fri 10am–2pm & 4–6pm, Sat & Sun 10am–6pm • Free

The enchanting **Carmen de los Mártires** is a turn-of-the-twentieth-century house set in a delightfully tranquil garden filled with palms, cypresses and tinkling fountains. Throughout the garden you'll come across grottoes, statues, and follies as well as peacocks and black swans paddling around an artificial lake. After a visit to the Alhambra this makes a wonderfully tranquil oasis to get your breath back.

Hotel Alhambra Palace

Peña Partida 2–4 • ☎ 958 221 468, ⓦ h-alhambrapalace.es

Just opposite the de Falla Museum, the terrace of the exclusive neo-Moorish **Hotel Alhambra Palace** (open to the public providing you're decently dressed), with fine **views** over the city, is a great place for a drink. Ask at reception to see the hotel's charming **theatre**, also in pseudo-Moorish style and where on June 7, 1922, an evening of poetry and song launched the career of a youthful Federico García Lorca (the guitarist Segovia appeared on the same bill). It is, of course, also possible to stay at the hotel (see p.482).

Hotel Washington Irving

Paseo del Generalife 2

Just north of the *Hotel Alhambra Palace*, the nineteenth-century **Hotel Washington Irving** is another of Granada's hotels with many historical associations. Opened in 1820, it played host to many of the nineteenth century's Romantic travellers including Irving himself. Today the hotel – which closed its doors in 2001 – is run down and in serious need of attention but it is to be hoped that such an important part of Granada's modern history will at some point be rehabilitated. In 1928, *New York Times* journalist Mildred Adams met Federico García Lorca here for the first time and fell under his spell. The poet sat down at the hotel's battered, out-of-tune piano in the lobby and sang her a ballad about the arrest and death of a local flamenco singer. "In gesture, tone of voice, expression of face and body, Lorca himself was the ballad," she wrote later. The lobby can be glimpsed through the glass entry doors.

5

The Albaicín

Bus #32 from Plaza Nueva goes to Plaza del Salvador in the heart of the *barrio*, and Plaza San Nicolás, near the famous mirador. Roughly one bus per hour (#35) deviates from this route to take in the adjoining *barrio* of Sacromonte

Declared a World Heritage Site by UNESCO in 1994, the **Albaicín** stretches across a fist-shaped area bordered by the Río Darro, Sacromonte hill, the old town walls and the winding Calle de Elvira (which runs parallel to the Gran Vía). From the centre, the best approach is from the Plaza Nueva and along the Carrera del Darro, beside the river. Coming from the Alhambra, you can make your way down the Cuesta de los Chinos – a beautiful path and a short cut.

Plaza Nueva and around

Before starting a tour of the Albaicín from the **Plaza Nueva**, take a look at the square itself. It was constructed just after the *Reconquista* as a new focus for the city, and soon served as the site of an act of stunning Christian barbarity: a bonfire of eighty thousand books from the former Muslim university. The square's elegant sixteenth-century fountain, the **Pilar del Toro**, is the last known work by the eminent Renaissance architect Diego de Siloé.

Flanking the plaza's north side is the austerely impressive **Real Chancillería** (Royal Chancery), built at the same time as the square, and now the law courts. Beyond its monumental entrance lies an elegant two-storeyed **patio** designed by Diego de Siloé with marble Doric columns and a staircase with stalactite ceiling.

Cuesta de Gomérez

The **Cuesta de Gomérez** leads up from south of Plaza Nueva to the Alhambra. It's here that many of Granada's renowned **guitar** manufacturers are gathered. Behind the windows of these places you may catch sight of a major concert or flamenco musician trying out a new instrument; they are not averse to giving the shop's customers a free concerto or two.

Santa Ana

Plaza Nueva • Open service times; 6–7.30pm • Free

Perched over the Río Darro at the Plaza Nueva's eastern end is the sixteenth-century church of **Santa Ana** whose elegant bell tower is the converted minaret of the mosque it replaced. The church's interior has flamboyantly decorated Baroque side chapels and a fine *artesonado* ceiling.

Hammam

C/Santa Ana 16 • Bath €22; reservations plus swimsuit required • ☎ 958 229 978

To get an idea of what a functioning **Moorish bathhouse** would have been like, head for this recreated **hammam** just behind the church of Santa Ana. Here you can wallow in the graded temperatures (cold, tepid and hot) of the traditional bath surrounded by

---

PERSONAL SAFETY IN THE ALBAICÍN

There has been an increasing number of **thefts** from tourists in the Albaicín in recent years. The preferred method is bag snatching, and is rarely accompanied by violence. However, don't let the threat put you off visiting one of the city's most atmospheric quarters; applying a few common-sense measures should ensure that you come to no harm. Firstly, do not take any valuables (including airline tickets and passports) or large amounts of cash with you when visiting the Albaicín and keep what you have on your person, not in a bag. If your bag is snatched don't resist – the thief will be concerned only with making a speedy getaway. Finally, try not to look like an obvious tourist (map/guidebook in hand is a dead giveaway) or flaunt expensive-looking photographic equipment, and keep to streets where there are other people around, especially at night.

marble pavements, mosaic wall decor and plaster arabesques. There's also a nice *tetería* (tearoom) upstairs.

Carrera del Darro

Following the river's northern bank from the Plaza Nueva along the **Carrera del Darro**, glance back to where the river disappears from sight under the city and "moans as it loses itself in the absurd tunnel" as the young Lorca put it.

Baños Árabes

Carrera del Darro 31 • Tues–Sat 9am–2.30pm • Free

A little way up the Carrera at no. 31 are the remains of the **Baños Árabes**, a marvellous and little-visited Moorish public bath complex. Built in the eleventh century, the sensitively restored building consists of a series of brick-vaulted rooms with typical star-shaped skylights (originally glazed) and columns incorporating Roman and Visigothic capitals. When Richard Ford was here in the 1830s he found it being used as a wash house by the local women because "one of the first laws after the conquest of the Catholic sovereigns was to prohibit bathing by fine and punishment".

Convento de Santa Catalina

Carrera del Darro 39 • Sept–July daily

The nuns at the convent of **Santa Catalina de Zafra**, housed in a sixteenth-century Mudéjar palace, are renowned for their convent *dulces* and will gladly supply you (through a *turno*) with their speciality, *glorias* (almond cakes); they're open daily except in August.

Casa de Castril: the Museo Arqueológico

Carrera del Darro 43 • Tues 2.30–8.30pm, Wed–Sat 9.30am–8.30pm, Sun 9.30am–2.30pm • €1.50, free with EU passport

A hundred metres beyond the Baños Árabes lies **Casa de Castril**, a Renaissance mansion with a fine Plateresque facade and doorway, which houses the city's **Museo Arqueológico** with its interesting exhibits of finds from throughout the province.

Rooms 1 and 2 cover the Paleolithic and Neolithic periods, among which are some remarkable artefacts from the **Cueva de los Murciélagos** near Albuñol. In this fourth-millennium BC Neolithic cave, alongside a dozen cadavers arranged in a semicircle around that of a woman, were found some modern-looking esparto grass sandals and baskets, as well as a **golden diadem**. Room 3 has some interesting reconstructions of social life and culture in the Bronze Age and one exhibit shows how copper weapons and tools were manufactured using primitive moulds. Room 4 contains the Iberian and pre-Roman collection with some fine examples of early lapidary work, including a hefty carved stone bull, stone vases and outstanding alabaster vessels. The finds from the necropolis at **Punté Noye** near Almuñécar (the Phoenician Sexi) suggest a large colony here trading as far afield as Egypt and Greece from where the vases (some bearing pharaonic titles) were imported. The Roman section in Room 5 has a striking third-century bronze statue of a man in a toga as well as some interesting **early Christian lamps** from the fourth century.

Pride of place in the **Moorish section** (Room 7) is a fourteenth-century **bronze astrolabe**, demonstrating the superior scientific competence of the Arabic world at this time. The instrument was adopted by the Arabs from ancient Greece and used for charting the position of the stars in astrology, precisely orienting the *mihrab* of the mosques towards Mecca, determining geographical coordinates as well as trigonometry and converting Muslim dates into Christian ones. Its transmission from the Arab to the Christian world made possible the voyages of discovery to both east and west. More Moorish symmetry is evident in the designs on the vases, wooden chests and amphorae also displayed here.

5

SACROMONTE: GRANADA'S GITANO QUARTER

Granada has an ancient and still considerable **gitano** (gypsy) population, from whose clans many of Spain's best flamenco guitarists, dancers and singers have emerged. Traditionally the gypsies inhabited cave homes on **Sacromonte hill**, and many still do, giving lively displays of dancing and music in their *zambras* (shindigs). These were once spontaneous but are now blatantly contrived for tourists, and are often shameless rip-offs: you're hauled into a cave, leered at if you're female, and systematically extorted of all the money you've brought along (for dance, the music, the castanets, the watered-down sherry …). Which is not to say that you shouldn't visit – just take only as much money as you want to part with. Turn up mid-evening; the lines of caves begin off the Camino de Sacromonte, just above the Casa del Chapiz. When the university is in session, the cave dwellings are turned into **discotecas** and are packed with students at weekends.

MUSEO CUEVAS DEL SACROMONTE

Barranco de los Negros s/n • March–Oct Tues–Sun 10am–2pm & 5–8.30pm; Nov–Feb Tues–Sun 10am–2pm & 4–7pm • €5

An intriguing museum depicting the life and times of the *barrio*. In this area – and Sacromonte generally – it would also be wise to heed our warnings on personal security (see p.470).

Paseo de los Tristes and around

Continuing along the Río Darro from the Casa de Castril you'll eventually come to **Paseo de los Tristes** (aka Paseo del Padre Manjón), a delightful esplanade beside the river overlooked by the battlements of the Alhambra high on the hill above, a great spot for a drink and especially so at night when the Alhambra is floodlit. There are several terrace bars fronting the river.

Two streets off here also contain **Moorish houses**: Calle del Horno de Oro (no. 14) and, two streets further along, Cuesta de la Victoria (no. 9). The street after this, the **Cuesta del Chapiz**, climbs left into the heart of the Albaicín, passing first, on the right, the **Casa del Chapiz**, in origin a Moorish mansion – with a charming patio – and today reclaimed as a school of Arabic studies. The **Camino del Sacromonte**, just beyond it, heads east towards the *barrio* of **Sacromonte**'s celebrated caves where, after sundown, the *gitanos* (gypsies) will attempt to entice you in for some raucous but often dubious flamenco (see p.489).

Iglesia del Salvador

Plaza Salvador s/n • Daily 10.30am–1pm & 4.30–7.30pm • €1

The **Iglesia del Salvador** is built on the site of a mosque of which the **courtyard** – with whitewashed arches and Moorish cisterns – is beautifully preserved. Diego de Siloé, the architect of the sixteenth-century church, which was badly damaged in the Civil War, converted the mosque's original **minaret** into its tower.

Plaza Larga

From San Salvador, Calle Panaderos leads into **Plaza Larga**, the busy heart of the Albaicín, with a concentration of restaurants and bars. The nearby Calle Agua has more **Moorish dwellings**: take a look at nos. 1, 37, 28 and 19. A busy little **market** is held in Plaza Larga on Saturday mornings selling the usual fruit and vegetables as well as potted plants and bootleg CDs and DVDs.

Mirador de San Nicolás

The **Mirador de San Nicolás** is justly famous for its panoramic **view** of the Sierra Nevada, the Alhambra and Granada spread out below. To get here from Plaza Larga, go through the Arco de las Pesas, an old arch in the west corner, and turn sharply left up Callejón de San Cecilio. When you reach it, the fifteenth-century church of San Nicolás is of little note but the nearby **aljibe** (fountain) is a Moorish original, one of many in the Albaicín to survive from the time when every mosque – there were more than thirty of them – had its own.

Convento de Santa Isabel la Real

C/Santa Isabel la Real • Tues, Thurs & Fri guided visits 10am & 11.30am • Free

Below the Mirador de San Nicolás, Calle Nuevo de San Nicolás descends into Calle Santa Isabel la Real, passing, on the right, the early sixteenth-century **Convento de Santa Isabel la Real** with a superb patio. The **convent church** has a superb Plateresque doorway and, inside, a fine Mudéjar ceiling, and holds sculptures by Pedro de Mena and José Mora.

La Daralhorra

C/Santa Isabel la Real • Tues & Thurs 10am–2pm • Free

The Santa Isabella convent was partly constructed within a fifteenth-century Nasrid palace – part of which was the adjoining **La Daralhorra**, of which only the patios and some arches survive. This was the residence of Aisha, the mother of the last king of Granada, Boabdil.

Plaza de San Miguel Bajo and around

Calle Santa Isabel drops into one of the Albaicín's most delightful squares, **Plaza de San Miguel Bajo**, lined with acacia and chestnut trees. The church of **San Miguel** on its eastern side is a sixteenth-century work by Diego de Siloé, built over yet another mosque, and preserves its original thirteenth-century *aljibe* (fountain) where the ritual ablutions would have been performed before entering. The square also has a clutch of good bars, whose terraces are extremely popular at night. The opposite end of the plaza leads to the **Mirador del Carril de la Lona** with its views over the western side of the city. You could also detour north from here – climbing uphill beyond the walls – to the church of **San Cristóbal**, which has another fine **view** of the Alhambra from its own *mirador*.

A pleasant walk back to the centre from Plaza de San Miguel is to head roughly south along calles San Miguel and San José, eventually meeting up with calles Calderería Nueva and Calderería Vieja which have been transformed into a vibrant and delightful "Little Morocco" with food shops, restaurants and excellent teahouses (see p.484).

Palacio de la Madraza

C/Oficios s/n • Mon–Sat 10.30am–1pm & 3.30–6.30pm, Sun 11am–1pm; hours may change during special exhibitions • Free

Outside the Albaicín is a further group of Moorish buildings. The most interesting of them, and oddly one of the least known, is the so-called **Palacio de la Madraza**, a vividly painted building opposite the Capilla Real. Built in the early fourteenth century at the behest of Yusuf I – though much altered since – this is a former Islamic college (*medressa* in Arabic) and retains part of its old prayer hall, including a magnificently decorated **mihrab**.

Corral del Carbón

Off C/de los Reyes Católicos

Slightly south of the Palacio de la Madraza lies the **Corral del Carbón**, a fourteenth-century caravanserai (an inn where merchants would lodge and, on the upper floors, store their goods) that is unique in Spain. A wonderful horseshoe arch leads into a courtyard with a marble water trough. Remarkably, the building survived intact through a stint as a sixteenth-century theatre – with the spectators watching from the upper galleries – and later as a charcoal burners' factory, the origin of its present name. The building is a little tricky to find: it lies down an alleyway off the Calle de los Reyes Católicos, opposite the **Alcaicería**, the old Arab silk bazaar, burned down in the nineteenth century and poorly restored as an arcade of souvenir shops.

5

Casa de los Tiros

C/Pavaneras 19 • Tues 2.30–8.30pm, Wed–Sat 9am–8.30pm, Sun 9am–2.30pm • Free

East of the Corral del Carbón, an impressive Mudéjar mansion, the **Casa de los Tiros**, stands just behind Plaza de Isabel Católica. This was built just after the *Reconquista* ended and has a curious facade adorned with various Greek deities and heroes as well as a number of *tiros* (muskets) projecting from the upper windows. Above the door is a representation of the sword of Boabdil that the family who lived here claimed they held in custody. The interior – which is worth a look – now houses the mildly interesting **Museo Casa de los Tiros** exhibiting documents, furniture, engravings and photos from the city's past.

Capilla Real

Daily: April–Sept 10.30am–1.30pm & 4–7.30pm; Oct–March 10.30am–1.30pm & 3.30–6.30pm • €3.50

The **Capilla Real** (Royal Chapel) is Granada's most impressive Christian building, flamboyant late Gothic in style and built ad hoc in the first decades of Christian rule as a mausoleum for Los Reyes Católicos, the city's "liberators". Before entering, note the stone frieze above the entrance that romantically alternates the initials of the two monarchs. Isabel, in accordance with her will, was originally buried on the Alhambra hill (in the church of the San Francisco convent, now part of the *parador*) but her wealth and power couldn't safeguard her wishes; both her remains and those of her spouse Fernando, who died eleven years later in 1516, were placed here in 1522. Isabel's final indignity occurred in the 1980s, when the candle that she asked should perpetually illuminate her tomb was replaced by an electric bulb – after many protests the candle was restored. But, as with Columbus's tomb in Seville, there is considerable doubt as to whether any of the remains in these lead coffins – so reverentially regarded by visiting Spaniards – are those of the monarchs at all. The chapel and tombs were desecrated by Napoleon's troops in 1812 and the coffins opened and defiled.

The tombs

The monarchs' **tombs** in a plain underground crypt below are as simple as could be imagined: Fernando and Isabel, flanked by their daughter Juana ("the Mad") and her husband Felipe ("the Handsome"), rest in lead coffins placed in a plain crypt (a not easily spotted "F" marking that of the king on the left of the central pair). The smaller coffin to the right is that of the infant Príncipe de Asturias who died before reaching the age of two. Above them, however, is an elaborate Renaissance monument, with sculpted effigies of all four monarchs – the response of their grandson Carlos V to what he found "too small a room for so great a glory". The figures of Fernando and Isabel are easily identified by the rather puny-looking lion and lioness at their feet. Popular legend has it that Isabel's head sinks deeper into the pillow due to the weight of her intelligence compared with that of her husband; this is not without some truth; Fernando was never much more than a consort. Carved in Carrera marble by the Florentine Domenico Fancelli in 1517, the tomb's **side panels** depict the Apostles and scenes from the life of Christ and are especially fine. The Latin inscription at the monarchs' feet is brutally triumphalist in tone: "Overthrowers of the Mahometan sect and repressors of heretical stubbornness." The tomb of Juana and Felipe, a far inferior work, is by Ordóñez.

The reja

Near the tombs, and dating from the same period, is an equally magnificent **reja**, or gilded grille. The work of Maestro Bartolomé of Jaén, it is considered one of the finest in Spain. Its outstanding upper tier features scenes from the life of Christ and the Crucifixion.

5

The retablo
The altar's striking **retablo** is by Felipe Vigarny, dated 1522, depicting in one scene San Juan being boiled in oil; beneath the kneeling figures of Fernando and Isabel – sculptures possibly by Diego de Siloé – are images depicting events close to both their hearts, Boabdil surrendering the keys of Granada for him, the enforced baptism of the defeated Moors for her.

The Sacristy
In the capilla's **Sacristy** are displayed the **sword of Fernando**, the **crown of Isabel**, and the banners used at the conquest of Granada. Also here is Isabel's outstanding personal collection of **medieval Flemish paintings** – including a magnificent **El Descendimiento** (Descent from the Cross) triptych by Dirk Bouts. Here too, are important works by Memling, Bouts and van der Weyden – as well as various Italian and Spanish paintings, including panels by Botticelli, Perugino and Pedro Berruguete.

Centro José Guerrero
C/Oficios 8 • Tues–Sat 10.30am–2pm & 4.30–9pm, Sun 10.30am–2pm • Free • Ⓦ centroguerrero.org

South of the Capilla Real, along Calle Oficios, stands the **Centro José Guerrero**, a museum dedicated to the city's most famous modern artist and brilliant colourist José Guerrero (1914–91). Influenced early on by Cubism and later by Miró, in 1950 Guerrero moved to New York where he became a leading exponent of American Expressionism, before returning to Spain in 1965. The museum displays arresting works from all his major periods of artistic development.

Granada Catedral
Gran Vía s/n • April–Sept Mon–Sat 10.45am–1.30pm & 4–8pm, Sun 4–8pm; Oct–March Mon–Sat 10.45am–1.30pm & 4–7pm, Sun 4–7pm • €3.50

For all its stark Renaissance bulk, Granada's **Catedral**, adjoining the Capilla Real and entered from a door on Gran Vía, is a disappointment. It was raised on the site of the Great Mosque, with work commencing in 1521 – just as the royal chapel was finished – but it was then left uncompleted until well into the eighteenth century. However, the main west facade by Diego de Siloé and Alonso Cano is worth a look. It still carries a provocative inscription honouring Primo de Rivera, founder of the fascist Falange Party, added in the Franco period, and, significantly for Granada today, never removed.

Inside, the church is delightfully light and airy due to its painted stonework and twenty giant pillars which push the central dome to a height of above 30m. The Capilla Mayor has figures by Pedro de Mena of Fernando and Isabel at prayer, with, above them, oversized busts of Adam and Eve by *granadino* Alonso Cano, who also left quite a bit of work in the other chapels and is buried in the crypt – a marble and bronze plaque next to the main door honours him.

In the eighteenth-century **sagrario** there are more works by Cano as well as a fine *Crucifixión* by Martínez Montañés. In the side chapels are a triumphant sculpture of *Santiago* (St James) in the saddle, by Pedro de Mena (Capilla de Santiago) and an **El Greco** *St Francis* (Capilla de Jesús Nazareno).

Hospital de San Juan de Dios
North of the cathedral, and ten minutes' walk along Calle San Jerónimo, the Renaissance **Hospital de San Juan de Dios** is well worth a visit. It was founded in 1552 by Juan de Robles (Juan de Dios) as a hospital for the sick and a refuge for foundlings, and its elaborate facade has a statue by José de Mora depicting the saint on his knees holding a cross, which popular legend says is how he died. The hospital itself still

5

functions and you'll have to pass the entrance hall to reach two marvellous **patios**. The outer and larger one is a beautiful double-tiered Renaissance work with a palm at each of its four corners and a fountain in the centre; the inner patio – with orange trees in the corners here – has delightful but deteriorating frescoes depicting the saint's miracles. Next door, the impressive church, a Baroque addition, has a Churrigueresque retablo – a glittering, gold extravaganza by Guerrero.

Monasterio de San Jerónimo

C/Rector López Argüeta 9 • Daily: April–Sept 10am–1.30pm & 4–7.30pm; Nov–March 10am–2pm & 3–6.30pm • €3.50

One block south of San Juan de Dios lies a little-known jewel: the sixteenth-century **Convento de San Jerónimo** founded by the Catholic monarchs, though built after their death. This has an exquisite pair of Renaissance **patios** (or cloisters in this context), the largest an elegant work by Diego de Siloé with two tiers of 36 arches. The **church**, also by Siloé, has been wonderfully restored after use as cavalry barracks and has fabulous eighteenth-century frescoes, another monumental carved and painted retablo, and, on either side of the altar, monuments to "El Gran Capitán" Gonzalo de Córdoba and his wife Doña María. The remains of this general, responsible for many of the Catholic monarchs' victories, may lie in the vault beneath, but the Napoleonic French were here too and, as Ford noted not much later, had "insulted the dead lion's ashes before whom, when alive, their ancestors had always fled". The church is little visited, and in late afternoon you may hear the nuns singing their offices in the railed-off choir loft above. A small shop at the entrance sells the convent's marmalade and *dulces*.

LORCA'S GRANADA

One of the ghosts that walks Granada's streets and plazas is that of Andalucía's greatest poet and dramatist **Federico García Lorca**. Born in 1898 at Fuente Vaqueros, a village in the *vega*, the fertile plain to the west of the city, he moved to Granada eleven years later. But it was his childhood spent growing up on the family farm, where he soaked up both the countryside and the folklore of its people, that was to have an enduring influence on his work.

Lorca published his first book of essays and poems while still at university in Granada, in 1918. It was in 1928, however, that he came to national prominence with *El Romancero Gitano*, an anthology of gypsy ballads. This success led to a trip to New York in 1929 where he spent a year at Columbia University ostensibly learning English, but actually gathering material for the collection of poems, *Poeta in Nueva York*, published after his death.

He returned to Spain in 1931 at the advent of the Spanish Republic and was given a government grant to run a travelling theatre group, La Barraca (the cabin). From this period the poet's major works for the stage – *Bodas de Sangre* (Blood Wedding) and *Yerma* – emerged.

In July 1936, on the eve of the Civil War, Lorca went back to Granada for the summer. This visit coincided with Franco's coup and control of the city was wrested by the Falangists, who initiated a reign of terror. Lorca, as a Republican sympathizer and declared homosexual, was hunted down by fascist thugs at the house of a friend – now the *Hotel Reina Cristina* (see p.481). Two days later he was murdered in an olive grove near the village of Viznar. His body was never found.

Anyone with an interest in tracing the **key locations** in Lorca's life should check out the places listed below; it's also possible to visit his death site in **Viznar** (see p.490). More avid followers should get hold of the excellent *Lorca's Granada* by Ian Gibson, his biographer.

HUERTA DE SAN VICENTE

Granada, west of the centre • April–Oct Tues–Sun 10am–12.30pm & 5–7.30pm; Nov–March Tues–Sun 10am–12.30pm & 4–6.30pm; guided tours every 45min • €3, Wed free • ⓦ huertadesanvicente.com • Take the southbound bus #4 from Gran Vía or Plaza del Carmen (direction Palacio de Deportes), or a taxi

West of the centre is the Huerta de San Vicente, an orchard where the poet's family used to spend the summer months. It spreads back from C/de la Virgen Blanca, behind *Los Jardines Neptuno Flamenco* nightclub. The house – now restored and opened as a museum – is set in the

Hospital Real

A few blocks to the northeast of the Hospital de San Juan de Dios • Mon–Fri 9am–2pm • Free

The **Hospital Real** is a magnificent Renaissance building designed by Enrique Egas. Formerly known as the Hospital de los Locos, it was founded by the Catholic monarchs and finished by Carlos V. As its former name implies, it was one of the first lunatic asylums in Europe, though it now houses the main library of the University of Granada. Inside, a beautiful arcaded patio and some fine *artesonado* ceilings are worth a look.

La Cartuja

Paseo de Cartuja s/n • Daily 10am–1pm & 4–8pm; Nov–March closes 6pm • €3.50 • Bus #8, going north along Gran Vía, passes by, or it's a 10- to 15min walk beyond the Hospital Real

Granada's **Cartuja**, on the northern outskirts of town, is the grandest and most outrageously decorated of all the country's lavish Carthusian monasteries. The monastery was founded in 1516 on land provided by "El Gran Capitán", Gonzalo de Córdoba (see p.476), though the building is noted today for its heights of Churrigueresque-inspired Baroque extravagance – added, some say, to rival the Alhambra. The **church** is of staggering wealth, surmounted by an altar of twisted and coloured marble described by one Spanish writer as "a motionless architectural earthquake". There are Bocanegra paintings and a seventeenth-century sculpture of the *Assumption* by José de Mora.

The **sagrario** drips with more marble, jasper and porphyry and has a breathtakingly beautiful gilded and frescoed **cupola** by Antonio Palomino, while the **sacristía** pulls out yet more stops with another stunning painted cupola and fascinating sculptural features

---

centre of what is now the largest rose garden in Europe, the Parque Federico García Lorca, the city's belated tribute. When the Lorcas had it, the five-acre holding was planted with vegetables and fruit trees. Then a tranquil rural plot on the city's edge, it has since been enveloped by ugly urban sprawl and it's hard to square the scene today with the poet's description of a "paradise of trees and water and so much jasmine and nightshade in the garden that we all wake up with lyrical headaches". The light and airy rooms contain some of their original furniture including, in Lorca's bedroom, his work desk, bed, a poster of the Barraca theatre company and the balcony (from outside, the furthest left of the three) looking towards the Sierra Nevada, which inspired one of his best-known poems, *Despedida* (Farewell). In a *hornacina* or wall niche outside is the tiny image of San Vicente placed there by Lorca's father – and where it has remained ever since – when he bought the house in 1925 and changed its name to that of the saint.

LORCA MUSEUM

C/Poeta García Lorca, Fuente Vaqueros, 17km west of Granada • July & Aug Tues–Sun 10am–2pm; April–June & Sept Tues–Sat 10am–1pm & 5–6pm, Sun 10am–1pm; Oct–March Tues–Sat 10am–1pm & 4–5pm, Sun 10am–1pm; guided visits on the hour • €1.80 • ☎ 958 516 453, ⓦ museogarcialorca.org • Take one of the services operated by Ureña (hourly from 9am; last bus returns to Granada at 8pm; 20min), which leave from Granada's Avda. de Andaluces in front of the train station

Lorca's birthplace, in the tranquil farming village of Fuente Vaqueros, is now a house museum, lying just off the village's main square. Now a charming shrine to the poet's memory, the museum is stuffed with Lorca memorabilia, manuscripts and personal effects. The tour also includes a DVD with footage of Lorca and his engaging smile. After you've seen the house, you could also pay a visit to the parish church (open service times, 7–9pm) at the end of the street opposite, where Lorca's mother took him regularly as a child. The old stone font where Lorca – or "Federico" as he is known to all the world here – was baptized is still there.

CASA-MUSEO DE FEDERICO GARCÍA LORCA

C/Iglesia 20, signed from the main road into Valderrubio, 4km northwest of Fuente Vaqueros • Tues–Sat 9am–2pm • €1

The Lorca family had a house 4km to the northwest of Fuente Vaqueros in the pleasant village of Valderrubio, which is now open as a museum. Each year the family moved here at harvest time (Lorca's father was a wealthy landowner) and the infant Lorca spent many summers playing in surrounding fields. The house remained in the family until 1986.

5

influenced by the art of the Aztec and Maya civilizations encountered in the New World. Here also are fine sculptures of *San Bruno* by José de Mora in a side niche, and an *Inmaculada* by Alonso Cano.

Parque de las Ciencias

Avda. de las Ciencias s/n • Tues–Sat 10am–7pm, Sun 10am–3pm • €6; planetarium extra €2.50 • Bus #1, going south along Gran Vía, will drop you outside

The last thing you might think of visiting in Granada is a **science park**, but this mammoth enterprise is a genuinely fun visit and especially good if you've got kids to entertain. Filled with interactive gizmos and gadgets, it features a number of themed pavilions – one is dedicated to a journey through the human body, another deals with the history of science in Andalucía, with plenty on the Moorish contribution, and the "natural spaces" pavilion has a stunning walk-in tropical butterfly garden featuring many exotic species. They also host big-name special exhibitions: dinosaurs, the *Titanic* and M. C. Escher's "infinite universes" have featured in recent years. The showstopper is a planetarium that gives you a breathtaking ride through the universe, passing seven thousand stars along the way.

ARRIVAL AND DEPARTURE — GRANADA

BY PLANE

Granada **airport** (T 958 245 200), 17km west of the city on the A92 *autovía*, handles domestic flights to Madrid and Barcelona as well as international and budget flights. Buses (14 daily; 5am–8pm; 40min; €3) take you into town. You can also get out to the airport from a stop on the east side of Gran Vía opposite the cathedral; check with the operator, Gonzalez S.L. (T 958 490 164, W autocaresjosegonzalez.com), or the tourist offices for the latest timetable. A taxi from the airport will cost about €20–25 into town.

BY TRAIN

The **train station** (T 902 240 202) lies 1km or so northwest of the centre on Avda. de Andaluces, off Avda. de la Constitución; to get into town take bus #11 which runs a circular route: inbound on the Gran Vía de Colón and back out via the Puerta Real and Camino de Ronda. Buses #3, #4, #6, and #9 also run between the station and Gran Vía.

Destinations Algeciras (3 daily; 4hr 20min); Almería (4 daily; 2hr 20min); Córdoba (2 daily; 2hr 20min); Guadix (4 daily; 1hr 10min); Málaga (8 daily; change at Antequera; 2hr 40min); Ronda (3 daily; 2hr 30min); Seville (4 daily; 3hr 30min).

BY BUS

Bus stations The city's main bus station, Ctra. de Jaén s/n (T 913 270 540), is some way out of the centre in the northern suburbs, and handles all services, including those to the Sierra Nevada but not to Viznar. City buses #3 and #33 buses leave from outside and will drop you in the centre on Gran Vía Colón near the cathedral (15min).

Services and timetables For information on bus services and timetables check with the companies, which are all – except for the service to Viznar – based at the bus station. Alsa (T 958 185 480, W alsa.es) serves Almería, Alpujarras (high and low), Córdoba, Jaén, Málaga, Motril, Úbeda, Seville and the coast. Empresa Autedia (T 902 422 242, W maestra-autedia.com) heads for Baza and Guadix, and Autocares Bonal (T 958 465 022) goes to Veleta and the north side of Sierra Nevada.

Destinations Almería (8 daily; 4hr); Almuñécar (10 daily; 1hr 40min); Baeza/Ubeda (10 daily; 2hr 15min); Baza (10 daily; 1hr 30min); Cádiz (4 daily; 5hr); Cazorla (2 daily; 4hr); Córdoba (8 daily; 2hr 30min); Guadix (15 daily; 1hr); Jaén (14 daily; 1hr 15min); La Herredura (7 daily; 1hr 50min); Madrid (17 daily; 4hr 30min); Mojácar (4 daily; 4hr); Montefrío (2 daily; 1hr 15min); Motril (9 daily; 1hr 45min); Nerja (4 daily; 2hr 15min); Salobreña (6 daily; 1hr); Seville (10 daily; 3hr 40min). For the Sierra Nevada/Alpujarras, the following buses all pass Lanjarón and Órgiva; current departure times are 8.30am & 6pm to Ugíjar (also passing Albondón, Cádiar and Yegen); noon & 5.30pm to Bérchules (also passing Pampaneira, Bubión, Capileira, Busquístar and Trevélez); Berja (2 daily, via Motril or Órgiva).

BY CAR

Central Granada is often choked with more traffic than its streets are able to bear, and finding on-street parking can be close to impossible. If you do arrive **by car**, you're best off leaving it in a car park or garage for the duration of your stay. Note that the city's main artery, Gran Vía, is part of a **city-centre traffic exclusion zone**. You may enter it only if your hotel is actually *on* this street. Carefully read all signs in the central zone. If you make a mistake your number plate will be photographed and you (or your hire company) will be fined €80.

CLOCKWISE FROM TOP LEFT GENERALIFE, GRANADA (P.467); LA CARTUJA, GRANADA (P.477); JAMÓN IN GRANADA >

5

GETTING AROUND

Practically everything of interest in Granada, including the hills of **Alhambra** (to the east) and the **Albaicín** and **Sacromonte** (to the northeast), is within easy walking distance of the centre. The only times you'll need a local bus or taxi are if you're arriving or leaving on public transport, since both the bus and train stations are some way out. **Gran Vía (de Colón)** is the city's main street, cutting its way through the centre along a roughly north–south axis between the Jardines del Triunfo and **Plaza Isabel la Católica**. It forms a T-junction at its southern end with **C/Reyes Católicos**, which runs east to the **Plaza Nueva** and west to the **Puerta Real**, Granada's two focal squares.

INFORMATION

Turismo Municipal The city's best tourist office, at Plaza Mariana Pineda 10 (Mon–Fri 9am–8pm, Sat 10am–7pm, Sun 10am–3pm; ☎958 247 128), east of Puerta Real; they also stock information on the province of Granada.

Turismo C/Santa Ana 2 (Mon–Fri 9am–7.30pm, Sat 9.30am–3pm & 4–7pm, Sun 9.30am–3pm; ☎ 958 575 202). The official Turismo is rather lethargic compared to the Turismo Municipal, and frequently runs out of maps and printed materials; it's located up steps to the right of the church of Santa Ana, off Plaza Nueva. They also have a branch in the Alhambra's ticket office (open same hours as the monument).

Information office Inside the Ayuntamiento on Plaza del Carmen (Mon–Fri 10am–2pm & 4.30–8pm). Another source of city maps and transport information.

Maps A detailed city map (€1.20) can be obtained from a machine in the central Plaza Isabel La Católica, near the cathedral.

BonoTurístico The Bono Turístico (City Pass), valid for five days, gives you access to eight of the city's monuments including the Alhambra, Capilla Real, Catedral, La Cartuja and Parque de Ciencias for €30. You may enter each monument once only, and when buying it can choose a time for visiting the Alhambra's Palacios Nazaríes (subject to availability). It also includes nine bus journeys and a ride on the Granada sightseeing bus. The card doesn't save you a great deal unless you intend to visit all the monuments, but it does guarantee you entry to the Alhambra, which is a benefit – even when the Alhambra is sold out this scheme has a guaranteed 250 places per day. The Bono can be bought from the Audioguías: This is Granada kiosk in Plaza Nueva (commission-free) or the Caja Granada bank at Plaza Isabel La Católica 6 (during business hours; plus €2.50 commission).

Bus tour City Sightseeing Granada (☎ 902 535 028) offer hop-on hop-off open-top bus tours, making a roughly circular tour around the city with stops at the Cathedral (starting point), Alhambra, Museo García Lorca and Plaza Nueva among others. Tickets (€18) are valid for 48hr from the time of purchase.

Walking tours An officially approved guided walking tour taking in the city's major sights (not the Alhambra) is operated by Cicerone Granada (☎mobile 607 691 676, ☎ciceronegranada.com; March–Oct daily 10.30am; Nov–Feb Wed–Fri & Sun 11am; English & Spanish; 2hr; €15; booking recommended in high season). The walks take place in all weather, and leave from the green-and-white kiosk in the northeast corner of the Plaza de Bib-Rambla.

Useful websites ☎ granadatur.com, ☎turgranada.es, ☎ granadainfo.com, ☎andalucia.org and ☎albaicin -granada.com.

Newspapers and listings The monthly *Pocketguía de Granada* (available from newspaper kiosks or free from the municipal tourist office; €1) has cultural and entertainment listings, though it tends to be less up to date than the city's rather staid daily paper, *Ideal*, which has a more reliable entertainment guide, particularly in its weekend editions. Foreign press is sold by the *kioskos* in Plaza Nueva and Puerta Real.

Festivals Granada has a number of good festivals, including the Theatre Festival at the end of May, and the International Music and Dance Festival at the end of June (☎ granadafestival .org), during which you may just be lucky enough to see a performance under the stars in the Alhambra. There's also an annual jazz festival in October or November. Information is available from any tourist office and tickets are sold at a *kiosko* on Acero del Casino, near the post office on Puerta Real.

ACCOMMODATION

Finding **a place to stay** in Granada usually isn't a problem, except during Semana Santa (Easter week) and very occasionally during August. Note that spring and early autumn are the high seasons here. In addition to the central zone, the atmospheric **Albaicín** quarter also makes a wonderful place to stay and while most of its addresses are upmarket, a few recent arrivals also cater for budget travellers. **Self-catering accommodation** (minimum stay two nights) is also an option: we've listed a couple below but for a wider choice visit ☎ granadahotel.com. With your own transport, staying in one of the **rural villages** to the south of the city is also an option.

HOTELS AND HOSTALES

Unless we state otherwise, where hotels or *hostales* have a garage expect to pay around €10–20 per vehicle per day.

AROUND PLAZA NUEVA AND TOWARDS THE ALHAMBRA

Hostal Austria Cuesta de Gomérez 4 ☎ 958 227 075,

ⓦpensionaustria.com. Efficient, friendly, Austrian-run *hostal* in a quiet street. The compact en-suite a/c rooms come with TV and free wi-fi, and it has its own garage. **€45**

Hostal Britz Cuesta de Gomérez 1 ☎ 958 223 652, ⓦlisboaweb.com. Small, welcoming, very comfortable and well-placed *hostal* near the Plaza Nueva. Some rooms are en suite and there are a couple of singles. En suite **€48**, sharing bath **€36**

Hostal Landázuri Cuesta de Gomérez 24 ☎ 958 221 406, ⓦhostallandazuri.com. Good-value rooms, some en suite, plus its own restaurant, bar and a roof terrace with a view of the Alhambra. Some single rooms. Free wi-fi. Garage. En suite **€45**, sharing bath **€34**

Hostal Navarro Ramos Cuesta de Gomérez 21 ☎ 958 250 555, ⓦpensionnavarroramos.com. Very appealilng small *hostal* en route to the Alhambra; neat and tidy rooms with and without bath and some singles. No TV or a/c but has fans in summer. En suite **€36**, sharing bath **€30**

Hostal Santa Ana C/Hospital de Sta. Ana 8 ☎ 958 225 820. Elegant *hostal* inside a restored 200-year-old mansion. Attractive en-suite rooms come with a/c and TV. Wi-fi zone. Free parking. B&B **€50**

Hotel Macía Plaza Plaza Nueva 4 ☎ 958 227 536, ⓦmaciahoteles.com. Centrally located modern hotel, offering stylishly furnished well-equipped a/c rooms, many overlooking the square. Free wi-fi. Garage. *Rough Guide* readers with this guide can claim a ten percent discount. **€120**

CATHEDRAL AREA

Hostal Arteaga C/Arteaga 3 ☎ 958 208 841, ⓦhostal arteaga.com. Central and economical *hostal* offering simple but brightly decorated en-suite a/c rooms with TV in a quiet street. Free wi-fi. **€48**

★ **Hostal Costa Azul** C/Rosario 5 ☎ 958 222 298, ⓦhostalcostaazul.com. Friendly, refurbished small *hostal* with good en-suite rooms with heating and a/c. Also has its own restaurant and free wi-fi, and rents out luxurious apartments nearby. *Rough Guide* readers with this guide can claim a fifteen-percent discount on apartments. Rooms **€55**, apartments **€65**

Hostal Salvador C/Duende 6 ☎ 958 261 955, ⓦcasa salvador.net. Small and comfortable *hostal* in a quiet pedestrianized street. All rooms are en suite with a/c and TV, and rooms 303 & 304 come with terrace. There's a decent restaurant too. **€40**

Hotel Hesperia Plaza Gamboa s/n ☎ 958 018 400, ⓦhesperia-granada.com. Stylish four-star luxury hotel in a beautiful old mansion with delightful patio. The comfortable if rather staid rooms are less inviting, but frequent special offers can reduce rates by up to sixty percent; ring or check website for details. Free wi-fi. Own car park. **€142**

Hotel Inglaterra C/Cetti Meriem 6 ☎ 958 221 559, ⓦnh-hoteles.com. Three-star hotel offering comfortable,

sober, a/c rooms with satellite TV, internet and minibar in a stylishly modernized building. Car park available. Sun–Thurs **€70**, weekend **€130**

Hotel Los Tilos Plaza de Bib-Rambla 4 ☎ 958 266 712, ⓦhotellostilos.com. Pleasant, two-star hotel on this atmospheric square. The functional rooms have TV, but make sure to request one on the exterior as the interior rooms are gloomy. Higher rooms 401 & 402 or 301 & 302, with Alhambra views, are the ones to go for. Car park nearby. B&B **€80**

PLAZA DE LA TRINIDAD AND AROUND THE UNIVERSITY

Hostal Márquez C/Fábrica Vieja 8 ☎ 958 275 013, ⓔhostal-marquez@ozu.es. An appealing refurbished *hostal* with some en-suite rooms, plus a few singles, all with a/c. The lobby is dominated by a snarling boar's head bagged by the *patrón*. Parking spaces. En suite **€42**, sharing bath **€34**

Hostal Meridiano C/Angulo 9 ☎ 958 250 544, ⓦhostal pensionmeridiano.com. Friendly and efficient *hostal* offering bright a/c rooms with and without bath. There's free internet access and wi-fi available to guests, and they can assist with parking. En suite **€40**, sharing bath **€34**

Hostal San Joaquin C/Mano de Hierro 14 ☎ 958 282 879, ⓦpensionsanjoaquin.com. A great, rambling old place with simple but clean en-suite rooms (some with fridge, a/c and TV) and charming patios. **€40**

Hostal Zurita Plaza de la Trinidad 7 ☎ 958 275 020, ⓦpensionzurita.com. Welcoming *hostal* where immaculate balcony rooms come with and without bath. All have TV, a/c and free wi-fi. Garage. En suite **€42**, sharing bath **€38**

Hotel Reina Cristina C/Tablas 4 ☎ 958 253 211, ⓦhotelreinacristina.com. Modern and welcoming hotel inside an older building – with fine patio – where Lorca spent his last days before being seized by the fascists. Twin-bedded rooms tend to be larger. They also have a good restaurant and garage. Rates are forty percent lower in July & Aug. **€120**

Pensiones La Milagrosa y Matilde C/Puentezuelas 46 ☎ 958 263 429, ⓦmilagrosaymatilde.com. Two clean and serviceable if rather spartan *pensiones* under the same ownership. Some rooms en suite. En suite **€38**, sharing bath **€33**

ALBAICÍN, SACROMONTE AND NORTH OF THE CENTRE

★ **Casa del Aljarife** Placeta de la Cruz Verde 2 ☎ 958 222 425, ⓦcasadelaljarife.com. Delightful, small upmarket *hostal* in a restored sixteenth-century house, near the heart of the Albaicín; three beautiful en-suite rooms (two with Alhambra views) and patio, plus free wi-fi and use of internet. **€95**

★ **Casa del Aljibe** C/Aljibe de Trillo 26 ☎ 958 227 843, ⓦcasadelaljibe.com. Charming two- to four-person

5

rooms and apartments in a refurbished, traditional *casa andaluza* with tastefully furnished and well-equipped balcony rooms, charming patio, garden and Alhambra views. Rooms **€65**, apartments **€80**

★ **Casa del Capitel Nazari** Cuesta de Aceituneros 6 ☎ 958 215 260, ✆ hotelcasacapitel.com. Beautiful sixteenth-century *palacio* transformed into an enchanting small hotel with elegantly furnished beamed or *artesonado* (coffered ceilinged) rooms overlooking a triple-tiered patio; room 22 has an Alhambra view. Welcoming staff, *cafetería* and free wi-fi make this rather special. Special offers in Jan, Feb, July & Aug can cut prices significantly. Parking nearby. **€110**

★ **Casa Morisca** Cuesta de la Victoria 9 ☎ 958 221 100, ✆ hotelcasamorisca.com. Stunningly romantic small hotel inside an immaculately renovated (for which it won an award) fifteenth-century Moorish mansion with an exquisite patio below the walls of the Alhambra in the Albaicín. Rooms are sumptuously equipped and there are recreated Moorish furnishings throughout (the splendid Mudéjar wooden ceilings are original). Room 15, with Alhambra views, is the one to go for. Exterior rooms cost more. Street parking outside or own garage. Free wi-fi. **€125**

Cuevas el Abanico Verea de Enmedio 89 ☎ 958 226 199, ✆ el-abanico.com. Fully equipped and stylishly renovated en-suite cave-dwellings with kitchen, available for a minimum stay of two nights. Free wi-fi. **€70**

El Ladrón de Agua Carrera del Darro 13 ☎ 958 215 040, ✆ ladrondeagua.com. Beautiful hotel inside a restored sixteenth-century Mudéjar *palacio* with lots of exposed brick, cool marble, understated decor and a charming patio. Some of the exquisitely furnished beamed rooms come with Alhambra views. **€118**

El Número 8 C/Virgen Carmen s/n ☎ 958 220 682, ✆ elnumero8.com. Charming and good-value self-catering apartments and studios in a small street in the Albaicín. All are tastefully furnished and come with radio/CD player and there's a rooftop terrace with Alhambra views and a cinema for guests. The owner lives off-site, so you'll need to make contact before turning up. **€65**

★ **Hostal Moni Albayzín** Plaza San Bartolomé 5 ☎ 958 285 284, ✆ hostalmoni.com. The Albaicín's first budget *hostal* – and it's a cracker. The proprietors provide a hearty welcome and the en-suite rooms – with TV and a/c – are spotless. The roof terrace has views of the Alhambra and Sierra Nevada and guests have use of fridge and washing machine. Parking and garage. **€50**

★ **Hotel Palacio Santa Inés** Cuesta de Santa Inés 9 ☎ 958 222 362, ✆ palaciodesantaines.com. Sumptuous eleven-room hotel in a beautiful, restored sixteenth-century Mudéjar mansion on the south side of the Albaicín with Alhambra views – especially from rooms 32–36. The nearby, similarly priced and equally delightful *Carmen de Santa*

Inés, Placeta de Porras 7, off C/San Juan de los Reyes, is owned by the same proprietors and occupies an equally attractive restored Moorish *carmen*. **€100**

Hotel Santa Isabel la Real C/Santa Isabel la Real 19 ☎ 958 294 658, ✆ hotelsantaisabellareal.com. Enchanting and welcoming small hotel housed in a wonderfully restored sixteenth-century Albaicín mansion close the church of San Nicolás. Elegantly furnished beamed rooms (some with Alhambra views) are equipped with minibar. Free wi-fi and a car park. B&B **€105**

★ **Palacio de Mariana Pineda** Carrera del Darro 9 ☎ 958 216 158, ✆ palaciomarianapineda.com. Fabulous five-room boutique hotel in a stunning seventeenth-century mansion, birthplace of the eponymous *granadina* heroine about whom Lorca wrote a play. Above a delightful patio, the beamed rooms are opulently furnished and decorated, and some have four-poster beds and Alhambra views. Garage and free wi-fi. **€150**

INSIDE AND AROUND THE ALHAMBRA

Hostal La Ninfa Campo del Príncipe s/n ☎ 958 227 985, ✆ hostallaninfa.net. On one of the nicest squares in town, this place – with an exterior studded with multicoloured stucco flowers – is easy to find. The interior offers pleasing white-walled, en-suite rooms with individual furnishings, a/c and TV. Rooms with *cama de matrimonio* (double bed) are cheaper than those with two beds. **€55**

Hostal Suecia Huerta de los Ángeles 8 ☎ 958 225 044, ✆ pensionsuecia.es. Charming, good-value small *hostal* – with some en-suite rooms – in a quiet, leafy area below the Alhambra with a charming garden terrace to eat breakfast. Rooms have heating but no TV. Relatively easy parking and free wi-fi. En suite **€50**, sharing bath **€43**

Hotel Albero Avda. Santa María de La Alhambra 6 ☎ 958 226 725, ✆ hotelalbero.com. This excellent-value, attractive and friendly small hotel lies on the access road to the Alhambra to the south of the centre. Sparkling a/c balcony rooms come with TV and there's easy street parking. Ring if you have problems finding them and they will advise (English spoken). **€40**

Hotel Alhambra Palace Peña Partida 2–4 ☎ 958 221 468, ✆ h-alhambrapalace.es. On the Alhambra hill and a 5min walk from the palace entrance, this opulent four-star *belle époque* hotel in neo-Moorish style offers every service you would expect for the price, except a pool. Many of the classically furnished rooms have spectacular balcony views over the city and the same views can be enjoyed from the bar's terrace (open to the public). Car park. The high season price halves in July & Aug. **€235**

Hotel América Real de la Alhambra 53 ☎ 958 227 471, ✆ hotelamericagranada.com. Charming small hotel in the Alhambra grounds, bang opposite the *parador* so you can get an early march on the queues. You pay for the location rather than creature comforts (a/c rooms but no TV) and prices have risen steeply (and somewhat unjustifiably) here. Free wi-fi. €120

Hotel Guadalupe Paseo de la Sabica ☎958 223 423, ⓦhotelguadalupe.es. Smart, recently refurbished three-star hotel a stone's throw from the Alhambra's entrance. The a/c rooms are styled with either traditional or ultra-modern furnishings and some come with partial Alhambra views. There's also free wi-fi and outside April and May rates drop by up to fifty percent. Guests get reduced-rate parking in Alhambra car park, and the Alhambrabus from Plaza Isabel La Católica stops nearby. €100

Hotel Los Angeles Cuesta Escoriaza 17 ☎958 221 423, ⓦhotellosangeles.net. Attractive four-star hotel on a leafy, quiet avenue in walking distance of the Alhambra. Elegant, individually styled rooms come with minibar, satellite TV and terrace balcony and there's a pool. Own car park. €85

Hotel Molinos C/Molinos 12 ☎958 227 367, ⓦeel.es /molinos. In the heart of the vibrant Realejo *barrio* and little over 4m wide, this place is listed in the *Guinness Book of Records* as the narrowest hotel in the world. Pleasant a/c en-suite rooms (some with balcony), and friendly proprietors. Own garage. €68

★ **Parador de San Francisco** Real de la Alhambra ☎958 221 440, ⓦparador.es. Without doubt the best hotel in Granada – a converted fifteenth-century monastery (itself created from a Nasrid palace) in the Alhambra grounds. Alas, this top-of-the-range *parador* is also the most expensive in the city; rooms are elegantly furnished and well equipped and all superior rooms and suites have Alhambra or Generalife views. Booking is advised at least four months ahead in summer or over Easter. Free wi-fi and own car park. Non-guests can call in for a drink in the terrace bar or use the restaurant (see p.486). Standard room €320

Posada Doña Lupe Avda. Generalife-Alhambra s/n ☎958 221 473, ⓔposadadonalupealhambra@yahoo .es. Rambling and potentially inviting place on the Alhambra hill blighted by a student hostel atmosphere (toilet paper and towels are doled out at check-in); there are numerous permutations of prices, some exceptionally cheap. Many rooms are en suite and there's a *cafetería* and small swimming pool. Easily reached by the Alhambrabus from Plaza Nueva. €30

OUT OF TOWN: LA ZUBIA

Balcón de Cumbres Verdes Cerro del Caballo, La Zubia, 8km south of Granada ☎958 891 058, ⓦhotelcumbresverdes.es. Fifteen minutes from the city centre, this is an attractive rural hotel in rolling countryside beyond the village of La Zubia. Rooms come with kitchenette and there's a pool. €67

Hotel El Balcón de las Nieves C/Alayos 174, in the village of Cumbres Verdes beyond La Zubia ☎958 892 062, ⓦelbalcondelasnieves.es. This is another charming place in the foothills of the Sierra Nevada but within easy striking distance of the city. Comfortably furnished rooms have satellite TV and there's a pool plus a decent restaurant (*La Gitarra*) over the road. €76

YOUTH HOSTEL

Albergue Juvenil Avda. Ramón y Cajal 2, off the Camino de Ronda ☎958 035 886, ⓦinturjoven.com. Recently renovated and with lots of facilities, Granada's hostel is handy for the train station: from there, turn left onto Avda. de la Constitución and left again onto the Camino de Ronda – it's the large white building by a sports stadium (Estadio de la Juventud); from the bus station take bus #3 to the cathedral and then bus #11, which will drop you outside. All rooms are en-suite doubles, the staff are friendly but the food is institutional. An excellent alternative is the hostel at Viznar, in the hills above the city (see p.491). Under 26 €21, over 26 €27

CAMPSITES

Camping Reina Isabel 4km along the Zubia road to the southwest of the city ☎958 590 041, ⓦreina isabelcamping.com. With a pool, less noise and more shade than *Camping Sierra Nevada*, this makes a pleasant rural alternative and – with your own transport – the city is within easy reach. €6 per person, €4.50 per tent, €4.50 per vehicle.

Camping Sierra Nevada Avda. de Madrid 107, northwest of the centre and 200m south of the bus station ☎958 150 062, ⓦcampingsierranevada.com. Easiest reached from the centre on bus #3, this is the most convenient city site, and – with a pool – probably the best too. €6 per person, €6 per tent, €6 per vehicle.

EATING AND DRINKING

Granada is quite a sedate place, at least compared to Seville or Málaga, and if it weren't for the university, you sense the city would go unnaturally early to bed. However, on a brief stay, there's more than enough to entertain you, with some decent restaurants and plenty of animated bars, especially in the zone between **Plaza Nueva** and **Grand Vía**, the plazas of the **Albaicín** quarter, whose streets make for enjoyable (if confusing) evening wanderings, around the **Campo del Príncipe**, a spacious square with outdoor eating and drinking, at the foot of the west slopes of the Alhambra hill, and along the **Carrera del Darro**.

RESTAURANTS

Granada is not noted for the quality of its **restaurants**, and service and standards even at the best places often

leave a lot to be desired. That said, good-value food is to be found all over town, and there are a number of places worth paying a bit more for, too. Beware, of course, the

5

TEAHOUSES IN GRANADA

The **teterías** (teahouses) in the "Little Morocco" district on and around the *calles* Calderería Nueva and Calderería Vieja are a colourful part of Granada's social scene and well worth a visit.

Al-Faguara C/Calderería Nueva 7. A classic for teas (try their "té Pakistani"), juices and crepes.

As-Sirat C/Calderería Nueva 5. The friendly, Moroccan-run "bridge between earth and paradise", is one of the oldest of Granada's teahouses and offers eighty-plus teas in its Moorish-inspired interior.

Dar Ziryab C/Calderería Nueva 11. Frequent live concerts of Middle-Eastern and North African music; its cultural centre offers classes in guitar and Maghrebi music.

Pervane C/Calderería Nueva 24. At the top of the hill, this multi-storeyed place is popular with a younger crowd.

Repostería Morisca C/Calderería 12. A bakery selling Moroccan cakes, pastries and pies – try their *pastela*, a delicious spicy chicken- and egg-filled filo pastry.

Tetería Tuareg C/Corpus Cristi 5, just off the foot of C/Calderería Vieja. A popular, atmospheric teahouse with a cave-like interior that recesses into candlelit gloom. Come here to sip teas with crepes in the summer, or with *pasteles* in the winter.

---

inevitable tourist traps, particularly around the Plaza Nueva and on the Alhambra hill. It's worth remembering that you can also get substantial meals at many of the bars listed on pp.486–488.

PLAZA NUEVA AND CATHEDRAL AREA

Bar-Restaurante Sevilla C/Oficios 12 ☎958 221 223. One of the few surviving pre (Civil) war restaurants, this place is steeped in literary history and Lorca spent many happy hours here. The kitchen – headed by noted chef Dany Álvarez – is traditional *granadino*, there's a *menú* for €36 and, in the evenings (May–Sept), tables outside give a view of the Capilla Real. Main dishes €10–20. Sept–June Tues–Sun 12.30–4.30pm & 8pm–midnight; July & Aug Tues–Sat 12.30–4.30pm & 8pm–midnight, Sun 12.30–4.30pm.

Café-Bar 380 C/Imprenta 3, off Plaza Nueva. Stylish small diner serving breakfast snacks, and later in the day tapas, *raciones* and crepes to finish. Free *tapa* with every drink and plenty of veggie options. Daily 9am–1am.

Las Cuevas C/Calderería Nueva. Crepes, couscous, *dulces árabes*, tagines and pizzas cooked in a wood-burning oven make this a popular place with locals. Has a *menú* for €9. There's a small terrace facing San Gregorio church. Daily 11am–11pm.

Mesón Andaluz C/Cetti Meriem 10 ☎958 227 357. Reliable restaurant with a renowned *fritura mixta* (fried fish platter), good *platos combinados* and a *menú* for €12.50. Daily noon–5pm & 7.30pm–midnight.

Nueva Bodega C/Cetti Meriem 9. Good-value local *bodega* that serves up basic tapas, *bocadillos* and *platos combinados* with a *menú* for €12. Daily 1.30–4pm & 8pm–midnight.

Pilar de Toro C/Hospital de Santa Ana 12 ☎958 223 847. Stylish, medium-priced bar-restaurant inside a former seventeenth-century *casa señorial* with exterior *terraza*, elegant patio bar (serving tapas) and, upstairs, a mid-priced restaurant with its own leafy and secluded patio. There's a *menú* for €11. Main dishes €12–18. Mon–Sat noon–4pm & 8pm–midnight.

Restaurante León C/Pan 3. Long-established economical *cordobés* restaurant serving many *carne de monte* (game) dishes and *migas* (fried breadcrumbs) and an economical *menú* for €11. Thurs–Mon 1–4pm & 8–11.30pm, Tues 1–4pm.

Samarcanda C/Calderería Vieja 3. Excellent Lebanese restaurant (with quite a few vegetarian options), this is the best of the few places in "Little Morocco" where it's worth having a full meal. You could try their *menú de la casa* for two for €30. Thurs–Tues 1–4.30pm & 7.30–11.30pm.

Tetería Kasbah C/Calderería Nueva 4. Styled as a "tea-house" serving delicious *pasteles árabes* (cakes) and crepes, this little Moroccan place also offers more elaborate dishes including couscous and tagines and has a vegetarian *menú* for €8.50. Daily noon–1am.

ALBAICÍN

Carmen de Aben Humeya C/Cuesta de las Tomasas 12. Superb Alhambra views from the terrace of this *bar-cafetería* serving tea and *pasteles* in the afternoon, and salads, meat and fish dishes in the evenings. Main dishes €8–15. Thurs–Tues 1–5pm & 8pm–midnight.

El Ladrillo II Plazoleta de Fatima. This place specializes in *barcos* (boats) of fried fish, served at economical prices on tables beneath the stars – all of which make the climb here worthwhile. Thurs–Tues noon–5pm & 8pm–midnight.

★ **El Trillo del Reca** Callejón del Aljibe del Trillo 3 ☎958 225 182. Enchanting little mid-priced restaurant in an Albaicín *carmen* (villa and garden) offering Basque-influenced cuisine: *bacalao al pil-pil* (salted cod with garlic) is a signature dish. It has outdoor tables on a delightful garden patio shaded by pear and quince trees. Main dishes €12–20. Wed–Mon 1.30–3.30pm & 7.30–11.30pm.

Juanillo Camino del Monte 81. Well-known low-price restaurant in Sacromonte serving typical no-nonsense bu well-prepared *raciones*, paella and other rice dishes with great views of the Alhambra. Take the bus from Plaza Nueva if you can't face the hike. Tues–Sat 1–5pm & 8pm–midnight, Sun 1–5pm.

Mesón Casa Blas Plaza San Miguel Bajo 3. Probably the best of this attractive square's bar-restaurants with an excellent kitchen. Their terrace is very popular with *granadinos*, especially at weekends. For cooler days a pleasant interior is furnished rustic *andaluz* style. House specials include *rabo de toro* (stewed bull's tail), *pastel de berenjena* (aubergine terrine) and *salmorejo*. There's a *menú* for €16. Tues–Sat noon–5pm & 8pm–midnight, Sun noon–5pm.

Mirador de Morayma C/Pianista García Carrillo 2 ☎ 958 228 290. Situated in a gorgeous Albaicín *carmen* with a fine view of the Alhambra, this place offers traditional food and many *granadino* specialities: *conchinillo al horno* (baked suckling pig) is a signature dish, and the desserts are made by the sisters at the Convento de Santa Catalina. Insist on a terrace table (fine weather) or ground floor or first floor table (but refuse the cellar). Main dishes €10–20; *menú* for around €35. Mon–Sat 1–3.30pm & 8–11.30pm.

⭐ **Restaurante-Bar Tomasas** Carril de San Agustín 4, just below the Mirador de San Nicolás ☎ 958 224 108. Mid-priced summer restaurant serving *cocina andaluz* in a huge and beautiful *carmen* with a stunning terrace view of the Alhambra. *Ajo blanco* (almond gazpacho) is a speciality. You can also nurse a drink here if you don't want to eat. Main dishes €12–22. June–Oct Tues–Sat 8.30pm–midnight; Dec & Feb–May Wed–Sun 2–4pm & 8.30–11.30pm.

Taberna La Higuera Horno de Hoyo 6. Economical and highly popular place with a delightful terrace under a huge fig tree (*higuera*). The cuisine has a Basque flavour and *salmón marinado* is a house special. There's also a *menú* for around €7.50. Daily 11am–11pm.

PLAZAS BIB-RAMBLA AND TRINIDAD

Botánico C/Málaga 3. A fusion restaurant with a healthy eating slant, with a menu influenced by Asian, Mexican and North African cuisines. Its Scandinavian-style dining room is open from breakfast till late, so it also serves a variety of healthy snacks, juices and infusions and there's a *menú* for €12. They have a small street terrace. Daily 8.30am–midnight.

Café-Bar Oliver Plaza Pescadería 12, slightly northwest of the Plaza de la Trinidad. Good *raciones* bar and upmarket restaurant with cosy interior rooms and a popular (with the *granadino* smart set) outdoor terrace. Traditional cuisine. Main dishes €12–21. Mon–Sat noon–4.30pm & 8pm–midnight.

Casa Cepillo Plaza Pescadería 8 – a marketplace linking Plazas Bib-Rambla and Trinidad. Cheap and cheerful *comedor* with an excellent-value *menú* for €10; the soups are especially good here. Mon–Sat 1–4pm & 8–11pm.

⭐ **Restaurante-Marisquería Cunini** Plaza Pescadería 14 ☎ 958 250 777. A gleaming, marble-topped bar serves standing customers with high-quality fish tapas and *raciones* plus there's a pricier and equally excellent seafood restaurant to the side (for which reservation is advised). Specialities include *caldereta de marisco* (fish casserole) and *pescado cocinado en barro* (fish cooked in earthenware pot). There's a *menú* for €19.50. Main dishes €11–20. Tues–Sat noon–4pm & 8pm–midnight, Sun noon–4pm.

PLAZA MARIANA PINEDA AND THE SOUTH CENTRAL AREA

Mesón La Alegría C/Moras 4, east of Puerta Real. This economical *mesón* is a favourite of *granadinos* working nearby and specializes in *carnes a la brasa* (charcoal-grilled meats). Daily 1–5pm & 8.30pm–midnight.

Restaurante Chikito Plaza del Campillo 9 ☎ 958 223 364. Fronted by four towering plane trees, and formerly the *Café Alameda* where Lorca, de Falla and the *Rinconcillo* group met. Literary lights from abroad such as Kipling and H.G. Wells all visited the bar's corner table (*rincón*). Today's restaurant – with outdoor terrace – is one of Granada's better ones for à la carte, but the medium-priced *menú* is unexciting. *Bacalao con bresa de pimientos* (cod in pepper sauce) is a house special, and their *sopa sevillana* (fish and rice soup) is mouthwatering. Decent tapas (free with each drink) in the bar. Main dishes €10–20. Thurs–Tues 1–4pm & 7.30–11pm.

Seis Peniques Plaza de Padre Suárez. Excellent and economical little *barrio* bar-restaurant with a small terrace facing the Casa de los Tiros; they serve great tapas in the bar, or you can take a table to eat *platos combinados – habas con jamón* (broad beans with *jamón*) is a house special – and there's a good *menú* for €8.50. Daily 9am–midnight.

ALHAMBRA AND CAMPO DEL PRÍNCIPE

⭐ **Casa López Correa** C/de los Molinos 5, in the Realejo barrio. Wonderfully cosy and atmospheric English-run neighbourhood café-restaurant. An eclectic menu includes excellent salads and pastas and lots more – try their chilli con carne or tandoori chicken. There's a *menú* for €10 and Friday night jam sessions (after 10pm) feature locals who bring along instruments to play jazz, rock, blues, flamenco or whatever. Cocktails are on offer nightly after 10pm. Mon–Fri noon–4pm & 8pm–1am, Sat 8pm–1am.

El Carmen de San Miguel Plaza Torres Bermejas 3 ☎ 958 226 723. One of Granada's top places to eat, with a fabulous terrace looking out over the city. An innovative approach (occasionally overdone) to *andaluz* cuisine is illustrated by a signature dish, *cochinillo confitado a la vainilla con pure de manzana y ciruelas* (confit of suckling pig with vanilla plus apple and plum purée). Main dishes €20–22, *menú de mercado* for around €30. Mon–Sat 1.30–4pm & 8.30–11.30pm.

5

La Esquinita Campo del Príncipe s/n. One of this plaza's best places for reasonably priced *cocina andaluz*, it's renowned for its fried fish. You can eat tapas and *raciones* at the bar or on a nice terrace. Main dishes €10–20. Mon–Sat 1–4pm & 8pm–midnight.

Lago di Como Campo del Príncipe 8. Slightly pricier than *La Ninfa* (see below), this two-storey Italian restaurant is also good and is more likely to have a table. Specialities include *pappardelle con crema de queso manchego* (pasta with cheese sauce) and thirty-five types of pizza. Main dishes €7–18. Daily 1.30–4.30pm & 8.30pm–12.30am.

La Mimbre Paseo del Generalife s/n, near the Alhambra's entrance. With a delightful terrace shaded by willows (*mimbres*) this is one of the best restaurants on the Alhambra hill and just the place for a lunch between monuments. The food is well prepared but they are sometimes overwhelmed in high season. There's a *menú* for around €17.50, which you may need to ask for. Main dishes €10–25. When full the nearby restaurant of the *Hotel Guadalupe* (see p.483) with a *menú* for €12 (but no terrace) is a decent alternative. Daily: May–Sept 1–4pm & 8.30pm–midnight; Oct–April 1–4pm.

La Ninfa Campo del Príncipe. Popular Italian restaurant for pizza, pasta and salads that puts out tables on the plaza and has a roof terrace as well. Its popularity means that it's often full to bursting at weekends. Be wary of the off-menu daily specials (pushed by the waiters), which can be pricey. Main dishes €7–15. Daily 1–4.30pm & 7.30pm–midnight.

Parador de San Francisco Alhambra ☎958 221 440. The *parador*'s restaurant is one of the best in an upmarket chain often noted for its blandness. It boasts fine views and offers a varied and not-too-bank-breaking *menú* for around €34. À la carte includes *granadino* specialities such as *sopa de espárragos de la vega* (asparagus soup) and *lubina asada a la sal con pomelo* (sea bass baked in a salt crust). Main dishes €14–24. Daily 1–4pm & 8–11.30pm.

Taberna de Baco Campo del Príncipe 22. Economical Peruvian-run diner famous for its *pastela* (Peruvian corn, beef and tomato pie). They also do great tapas: try the *surtido* (selection) that includes stuffed mushrooms, honey ribs and fillets with mango sauce. Their lamb's lettuce, goat cheese and raisin salad with balsamic vinaigrette is also a winner. Daily noon–4pm & 7.30–11.30pm.

OUT OF THE CENTRE

★ **Ruta del Veleta** Ctra. de Sierra Nevada 136 (Cenes de la Vega) ☎958 486 134. Three kilometres out of town along the Sierra Nevada road, this is currently Granada's top restaurant. The cooking – traditional *granadino* with a creative slant – is outstanding, as is the wine list. Signature dishes include *calderetas de arroz con bogavante* (lobster) or *cordero segureño* (lamb with rosemary). If you're going to be up in the Solynieve ski resort (see p.495) they have an offshoot there, too. Main dishes €12–30; *menú de degustación* €60. Mon–Sat 1–4pm & 8pm–midnight, Sun 1–4pm.

TAPAS BARS AND DRINKING BARS

Granada's proximity to the Sierra Nevada brings a coolness to the city that means you're just as likely to find locals ordering a glass of rioja as the beloved fino preferred in the rest of Andalucía. One local **wine** worth trying is *vino de la costa* (coast wine – ironically made in the mountains of the Alpujarras); amber in colour, fairly potent, but relatively easy on hangovers, it's the ideal partner for a *tapa*. The **bars** recommended below are mainly for drinking, though most serve tapas and *raciones* and you could happily fill up and forget about going to a restaurant. The city has quite a reputation for its **tapas**, which are more elaborate than is usual in Andalucía and in most bars one comes free with each drink – a laudable trait in a city generally regarded as penny-pinching by most *andaluzes*.

PLAZA NUEVA AND CATHEDRAL AREA

Al Pie de la Torre C/Pie de la Torre s/n. Close to the foot of the cathedral's tower this is an atmospheric little bar for tasty tapas – try the *tortitas de camarones* (shrimp fritters) – out front with an intimate and very good small restaurant for fish and meat dishes behind. Main dishes €12–20. Tues–Sat noon–4pm & 8–11pm, Sun noon–4pm.

★ **Bodegas Castañeda** C/Almireceros 1, at the corner of C/Elvira, across Gran Vía from the cathedral. A *granadino* institution and one of the city's oldest bars, though much refurbished and prettified; it's still an attractive first stop of an evening. Good tapas include generous paté and cheese boards (*tablas*), *montaditos* (small open sandwiches), baked potatoes and gazpacho.

Bodegas La Mancha C/Joaquín Costa 10. Monumental spit-and-sawdust establishment (slightly more refined since refurbishment) hung with hams, and with great wine vats stationed behind the bar like rockets on a launch pad. Tasty tapas on offer include *jamón de Trevélez* and *tortilla española*; they also sell excellent hot and cold *bocadillos* to eat in or take away.

Casa Enrique Acera de Darro 8, near the Puerta Real. This hole-in-the-wall has been open for almost 150 years and is a popular daytime or early-evening haunt with an extensive – but no freebies here – tapas selection. Specializes in *jamón ibérico* and chorizo from Salamanca. Wide-ranging wine list. Tues–Sun noon–4pm & 7.30pm–midnight.

Casa Julio C/Hermosa, off Plaza Nueva. A pocket-sized boozers' bar lined with fine old *azulejos* that nonetheless turns out some excellent fried seafood tapas. Treat yourself to the fried *berenjenas* (aubergine) or a refreshing gazpacho (served in a glass) which – the bar's clientele will assure you – is the best in town.

El Rinconcillo C/Hospital de Santa Ana 7, on south side of Plaza Nueva. Friendly and compact bar with lively summer *terraza* serving good tapas and *raciones*. Try the *morcilla ibérica* (blood sausage). Mon–Sat noon–4pm & 8pm–midnight.

★ **Hannigan and Sons** C/Cetti Merriem s/n. Independent Irish house whose owner *is* named Hannigan. The usual range of beers and stouts are on offer and the place has an airy feel to it with a snug, decorative stained glass and the only wooden floor in town. House specials include baked potatoes and a "gourmet" Angus-steak burger. On Sat & Sun they do a slap-up Irish breakfast brunch (starting at 1pm) popular with late risers in to watch live football games on TV. Mon–Fri 4.30pm–4am, Sat & Sun 1pm–4am.

La Bodeguilla de al Lado C/Tendillas de Sta. Paula 4, just north of the cathedral. Pricey but authentic tapas (from ancient family recipes) in a cosy bar where the charming female proprietor is an authority on Spanish wines, many of which are on sale by the glass. Closed July & Aug. Tues–Sat noon–midnight.

La Gran Taverna Plaza Nueva 12. This elegant tiled-floor tapas bar hung with photos is popular with bus drivers and the Guardia Civil (from the nearby courthouse) attracted by a particularly good midday selection. House specials include *montaditos* (tapas on bread) and *palometa* (Ray's bream).

La Trastienda C/Cuchilleros 11, on a small plaza just off C/Reyes Católicos. Plush little drinking den hidden behind a shop selling wine, cheese and ham. Once you've negotiated your way around the counter it's surprisingly cosy in the back. Best tapas to go for are the *jamón ibérico* and *salchichón*. Mon–Sat 8pm–1am.

Taberna Salinas C/Elvira 13, slightly west of Plaza Nueva. Elegant brick-and-wood taverna serving *tablas* (boards) of cheese and *ahumados* (smoked fish and meat); *pastel de merluza* (fish pie) is a house special and it has international beers on draught. There's also a small dining room. Daily noon–midnight.

ALBAICÍN

★ **Al Sur de Granada** C/Elvira 150, near the Moorish Puerta de Elvira arch. Great modern little bar-shop serving delicious cheeses, ham and *salchichón* tapas. Each drink comes with a generous free *tapa* and they stock a wide selection of Granada wines (now acquiring a reputation) to try and buy. Often stages exhibitions of work by local artists on its walls. Daily 10am–midnight.

Bar Aixa Plaza Larga. Welcoming bar with terrace tables serving well-prepared tapas and *raciones*. Try their *migas* (breadcrumbs) stir-fried with crispy pork fat and green peppers or fresh anchovies. Daily noon–4pm & 8pm–midnight.

Bar Caracoles Plaza Aliatar, slightly northeast of the Iglesia del Salvador. Popular and atmospheric tapas place on this attractive square. It's famous for its *caracoles* (snails) as well as *almejas* (clams), *gambas* (prawns), and fish stir-frys. Daily 12.30–4.30pm & 8pm–midnight.

Danubio C/Rosario 10. Stylish modern bar in the Realejo *barrio* with cheese and meat tapas and some veggie options. Offers a bottle of good rioja and ten tapas for €17.50. Daily 1–4pm & 8pm–2am.

Paprika Cuesta de Abarqueros 5. Stylish and somewhat pricey vegetarian bar-restaurant very popular with a younger international crowd. They serve world cuisine-inspired tapas and *raciones* as well as risottos, rice dishes, hummus and *curry Thai* accompanied by laid-back sounds including jazz. There's a summer street terrace. Main dishes €8–18. Daily 1–4pm & 8pm–midnight.

Rincón del Aurora Plaza San Miguel Bajo 7. Another good bar with outdoor tables on this square offering a mix of north African and Spanish cuisines. Try the *fritura* (fried fish), *croquetas* (croquettes) or *berenjenas con miel* (aubergine with honey). Daily noon–4pm & 8pm–midnight.

CAMPO DEL PRÍNCIPE AND CARRERA DEL DARRO

Ajoblanco C/Palacios 17, close to the church of Santo Domingo. Charming, cosy bar with creative tapas such as *queso con semillas de granada* (cheese decorated with pomegranate seeds) or *cabrales* (blue cheese with cinnamon and walnuts). Daily 9pm–1am.

Bar Candela C/Panaderos 9. A mixture of students and neighbourhood artists fill this atmospheric Basque bar every night. They serve *jamón*, cheese and chorizo tapas. Daily 1–4pm and 8.30pm–midnight.

Bar Casa 1899 Paseo de los Tristes 3. Another decent tapas place on this atmospheric square with an old *bodega* inside and terrace seats – with Alhambra view – for summer evenings. House specials include *rabo de toro* (stewed bull's tail) and *berenjenas gratinadas* (aubergine au gratin). Daily 12.30–4pm & 7.30pm–midnight.

Los Altramuces Campo del Príncipe s/n. Lively bar with a varied selection of *raciones* – a *media ración* should be enough for two. Good choices include *croquetas* (croquettes), *boquerones fritos* (fried anchovies), *berenjenas fritas* (aubergine) or the house special *caracoles* (snails). There's a good outdoor terrace. Daily noon–midnight.

Rabo de Nube Paseo de los Tristes 5. One of many terrace bars on this plaza – at the far end of the Carrera del Darro – and a wonderful place to sit out at night with a drink whilst gazing up at the Alhambra's illuminated battlements. They serve *tablas* (paté and cheese boards) and house specials include *pimientos rellenos* (stuffed peppers) and *lomo con ajos* (pork in garlic). Daily 12.30–4.30pm & 8pm–midnight.

UNIVERSITY ZONE

★ **Bar Poë** C/Verónica de la Magdalena 40. Highly original bar frequented by colourful characters and run

5

by an Angolan-Brit couple, Ana and Matt, who serve an exotic free *tapa* with every drink. "Not any old *tapa*", as their publicity says, but all kinds of delights ranging from Portuguese *piri-piri* and Thai chicken to *feijoada* (Brazilian bean stew) and Italian vegetable bake – and, unlike most bars in Granada, you get to choose your *tapa*. Wide range of drinks, *chupitos* (shots) and cocktails including an electrifying *absintio* (absinthe). Daily 8pm–2am.

Bodega 3M C/Santa Bárbara 12, near the Hospital de San Juan de Dios. Classic old-style, spacious *bodega* serving great tapas – try the *salazones* (smoked fish) – and whose Portuguese proprietor is known to cook up plates of *bacalao* at weekends. They often host exhibitions by local artists. Mon–Sat noon–4pm & 8pm–midnight; open on Sun when a group has ordered a bacalao lunch (in which case most of the clientele get a free plate too).

NIGHTLIFE

Granada's *discotecas* – mostly dismal teenage hangouts – are mainly concentrated along **C/Pedro Antonio de Alarcón** to the west of the centre, which turns into one big clubbing zone at weekends. For serious drinking into the early hours head out to the bars along the same street, as well as *calles* Gran Capitán and San Juan de Dios, both in the university area.

DISCOBARES AND DISCOTECAS

Conventional **discotecas** aren't too popular with the restrained *granadinos*, though the university guarantees a bit of action during term time and particularly at weekends; C/Pedro Antonio de Alarcón, to the west of the centre, is where the action is and the stretch between Plaza Albert Einstein and Obispo Hurtado is the main focus. There are, as everywhere in Spain, a fair scattering of **discobares** – drinking bars with loud sound systems, trendy decor and a fashion-conscious clientele. Granada also has a lively **gay** scene, with some good bars.

Afrodisia C/Almona de Boquerón s/n. One of Granada's best *discobares* for funk, hip hop, reggae, and soul with a clientele spread over a broad age range. Stages frequent live gigs. Tues–Sun 10.30pm–late.

Camborio Camino del Sacromonte s/n, Sacromonte. Fashionable *discobar* housed in a series of caves; it's especially lively at weekends from about 4am. Other similar late-night venues run along the same street and are lots of fun in the early hours. Be alert for bag snatchers in this area. Tues–Sat 10pm–late.

Chupitería C/Pedro Antonio Alarcón 69. Popular music and shots bar that has a hundred selections listed on a board. If you can't choose, they'll mix your own poison. A dubious bonus is that each shot you buy gets you a token that can be exchanged for prizes. Daily 9pm–3am.

Fondo Reservado C/Santa Ines 4, northeast of Plaza Nueva. Funky gay and straight bar with a hilarious drag show and party nights every weekend. Thurs–Sat 10pm–4am.

Granada 10 C/Carcél Baja 10, off Gran Vía near the cathedral. Small and popular central *discoteca* inside a beautifully restored retro cinema. Sounds are mainly Top-40 and golden oldies. Daily 11.30pm–late.

La Estrella C/Cuchilleros near Plaza Nueva. Compact, congested *discobar* with a good mix of people and great sounds. Daily 9pm–3am.

La Sal C/Santa Paula 11, off the west side of Gran Vía.

The city's oldest gay and lesbian bar. Originally a lipstick lesbian dance bar, but now attracting gay males too. Daily 11pm–3am.

Peatón Pub C/Socrates 25, off C/Pedro Antonio de Alarcón. Rock bar popular with a student crowd. Other lively places nearby include *Babel*, *Van Gogh* and *Genesis*. Daily 9pm–3am.

Planta Baja Horno de Abad, off Carril del Picón and slightly northwest of Plaza de la Trinidad ⓦplantabaja.net. Long-established *discobar* – garage is big here – now in a new home with plenty of live gigs. Daily 9pm–4am.

Makeba Placeta de Sillería, east of the cathedral. Lively and popular African and Russian-run Reggae/African bar. They have a special reggae night on Wed, with free tapas. Daily 10pm–late.

★ **Potemkin** Plaza Hospicio Viejo s/n. Great pint-sized *copas* bar with cool sounds (mainly early twentieth-century jazz) which also stages art exhibitions. Japanese chef Hide's tapas are excellent, and he also does sushi nights (Tues–Thurs) when even more mouthwatering tapas from his homeland are on offer. There's also a noon lunch special (with a veggie option) for €8. Mon–Sat 1–4pm & 9pm–1am.

Quilombo C/Carril de San Cecilio 21, uphill from the Campo del Príncipe. Vibrant bar with a pool table and big dancefloor that gets humming around 3am; techno and house are the main sounds. Sometimes stages live music. Wed–Sat 11pm–7am.

Six Colours C/Tendillas de Santa Paula 11 ⓦsixcolours .com. This is currently the hottest gay place in town. The exotically decorated café-pub opens in late afternoon and goes on until the small hours. The main action begins after midnight. Tues–Sun 4.30pm–very late.

Son C/Joaquín Costas 3, slightly west of Plaza Nueva. Ultra-cool two-level bar with older salsa scene upstairs – where Cuban rum cocktails are a house speciality – and a cavernous, smoky (not tobacco smoke) dance bar below with a younger heavy-metal scene. Daily 9pm–3am.

5

ENTERTAINMENT

Like many cities in Andalucía, Granada lays claim to the roots of **flamenco**, though you'd hardly believe it from the travesties dished up these days in the gypsy quarter of Sacromonte (see p.472). The bus-'em-in "flamenco shows" on offer in the city aren't much better, either, being geared firmly to the tourist trade. However, up in the Albaicín there is one genuine *peña* (club), with consistently good artists and an audience of aficionados, and we also review here a number of other places that are reasonably authentic. Generally more rewarding are the **festivals** held throughout the year (see p.480). It's worth watching out for street posters, as well as checking listings in the local daily paper *Ideal* or the monthly listings mags *Guía del Ócio* (⊕ guiadelocio.com) and *Pocketguía de Granada* (⊕ pocketguia.es) on sale at *kioskos*.

FLAMENCO

El Niño de las Almendras C/Muladar de Doña Sancha, at the junction with C/La Tiña and southeast of Plaza San Miguel Bajo, Albaicín. This tiny, unsigned bar – done up inside to resemble a cave – is owned by the flamenco singer of the same name. It's only open one night a week, but there's unforgettable flamenco when it happens. Fri from midnight.

Jardines de Zoraya C/de los Panaderos 32 ☎ 682 158 819. Pretty good Albaicín café-restaurant that offers nightly flamenco shows (€15) often featuring big names. For the evening shows they offer a flamenco *cena* (dinner; €35) which includes a three-course meal. Their terrace garden is also very attractive. Mon–Fri 8pm & 10.30pm; Sat & Sun 3pm, 8pm & 10.30pm.

Los Faroles Sacromonte. Almost at the very end of the line of "caves" – ask anyone for directions – this is a good place for a lunchtime or evening drink, with a view of the Alhambra from its terrace. The genial owner, Quiqui, is a flamenco *cantante* besides being a fount of information on flamenco. You may well be lucky enough to catch an authentic, spontaneous show here after dark. Wed–Sun noon–midnight.

Peña Platería Plazoleta de Toqueros 7, Albaicín ☎ 958 210 650, ⊕ laplateria.org.es. Private club devoted to the celebration of Andalucía's great folk art. There are frequent flamenco performances (Thurs or Sat are your best chances; €8), and visitors are generally welcomed so long as they show a genuine interest and aren't in too large a group. You'll need to speak some Spanish and use a bit of charm. Also food from 8pm onwards. Thurs & Sat shows start at 10.30pm. Closed Aug.

Sala Vimaambi Cuesta de San Gregorio 30, Albaicín ☎ 958 227 334, ⊕ vimaambi.com. A cultural and craft centre with frequent presentations of flamenco and *raices* (roots) music from North Africa and South America. Concerts usually take place on Fri and Sat (€15 including a drink) but ring or check their website for the current programme. Fri & Sat 9pm & 10.30pm.

SHOPPING

Granada has a substantial **Maghrebi** community; for a wide range of Moroccan/traditional Spanish fruits and groceries try C/Calderería Nueva and neighbouring C/Calderería Vieja.

Casa Ferrer Cuesta de Gomérez 26 ☎ 958 221 832. Granada's oldest guitar-maker, who has made instruments for many famous names including Paco Lucía. Mon–Fri 10.15am–1.45pm & 5–8.30pm, Sat 10.15am–1.45pm.

Castellano C/Almireceros 6, between C/Elvira and Gran Vía. One of the city's best places to buy *jamón serrano*, including the province's famed Trevélez hams. They also stock regional wines and brandies. Mon–Sat 9am–2pm & 5–8.30pm.

Deportes de Aire Libre C/Paz 20, just southeast of Plaza de la Trinidad ☎ 958 523 361. This is a good outdoor pursuits shop selling climbing, camping and trekking gear. Mon–Fri 10am–1.30pm & 5–8.30pm, Sat 10am–1.30pm.

El Corte Inglés Carrera del Genil 22 ☎ 958 223 240. Granada's branch of Spain's major department store is on the Acera del Darro, to the south of Puerta Real. The basement supermarket is great, with a wide range of Spanish and international food and wines. Mon–Sat 10am–10pm.

El Piano C/Gran Capitán 7, near the Hospital San Juan de Dios ☎ 646 018 110. Interesting little shop selling international foods as well as doubling up as a vegetarian-vegan deli and takeaway – ideal for picnics. Mon–Fri 9am–10pm, Sat 1–9pm, Sun 1–11pm.

La Casa de Los Tés C/Calderería Vieja s/n. Shop selling herbs and spices, incenses and exotic teas and much more. Mon–Sat 9am–2pm and 5–10pm.

La Oliva C/Rosario 9, close to Plaza Mariana Pineda ☎ 958 225 754. Wonderful shop specializing in the *gastronomía* of the province as well as the rest of Andalucía (olive oil, wines, cheeses, honey). You can sample before you buy. Mon–Fri 9am–2pm & 5–8.30pm, Sat 9am–2pm.

Librería Atlantida Gran Vía 9 ☎ 958 224 403. A good bookshop with a wide selection, including lots on different aspects of Granada. Mon–Fri 9am–2pm & 5–9pm, Sat 9am–2pm.

Market Plaza San Agustín. The city's main market is an ultramodern affair just north of the cathedral. Mon–Fri early until 1.30pm.

Metro C/Gracia 31, off C/Alhóndiga, southwest of Plaza de la Trinidad ☎ 958 261 565. The city's best international

5

bookshop, with a good range of titles on Granada and Lorca, plus some useful walking maps. Daily 10am–2pm & 5–8.30pm, Sat 10am–2pm.

DIRECTORY

Banks There are numerous banks and ATMs along C/Reyes Católicos and Gran Vía.

Hiking maps Maps of the Sierra Nevada and Las Alpujarras can be obtained from the Turismo, though for a more specialist selection try Cartográfica del Sur, C/Valle Inclán 2, southwest of the train station in the university zone (T 958 204 901, W cartograficadelsur.com), which sells a wide range, including military maps. The CNIG (National Geographic Institute), C/Divina Pastora 7, by the Jardines del Triunfo (T 958 909 320), also sells 1:50,000 and 1:25,000 maps. The Metro bookshop (see p.489) is also a good source.

Hospital Cruz Roja (Red Cross), C/Escoriaza 8 (T 958 222 222), or Hospital Clínico San Cecilio, Avda. del Doctor Olóriz, near the Plaza de Toros (T 958 023 000). For advice on emergency treatment phone T 061.

Internet There are internet cafés throughout the city centre and many bars and cafés offer free wi-fi. A couple of central internet cafes are *Free Memory*, C/San Jerónimo 14 (daily 10am–2.30pm & 4.30–10pm) and *Locutorio Azahara*, C/Colcha s/n (daily 9am–midnight), southwest of Plaza Nueva.

Laundry Lavandería Duquesa, C/Duquesa 24, near the church of San Jerónimo (Mon–Fri 9.30am–2pm & 4.30–9pm, Sat 9.30am–2pm; T 958 280 685), is very efficient and will wash, dry and fold 4kg the same day for €15.

Left luggage There are lockers at both train and bus stations as well as a *consigna* (left luggage office) at the latter.

Police For emergencies dial T 091 (national) or T 092 (local). The Policía Local station is at Plaza de Campos 3 (T 958 808 502). There is also a property lost-and-found section in the Ayuntamiento building on Plaza del Carmen (T 958 248 103).

Post office Puerta Real (Mon–Fri 9am–8pm, Sat 9am–2pm).

Viznar

The village of **VIZNAR**, 10km northeast of Granada, will always be linked with the **assassination of Federico García Lorca** (see box, pp.476–477) in August 1936. After his arrest in Granada, he was held for two days at a farmhouse called La Colonia before being taken to a bleak gully (*barranco*) nearby and shot. A poem of Lorca's seemed eerily prescient about his own end:

I realized I had been murdered.
They searched cafés and cemeteries and churches,
they opened barrels and cupboards,
they plundered three skeletons to remove their gold teeth.
They did not find me.
They never found me?
No. They never found me.

From the centre of the village the road towards La Fuente Grande passes the site of **La Colonia** (later demolished), near a white-walled cottage. From here, the road curves around the valley to the **Parque Federico García Lorca**, a sombre monumental garden marking the *barranco* and honouring all the Civil War dead. Climb the steps to the garden and veer left up more steps: the site of Lorca's murder was here, beneath a solitary olive tree. After the killing – he was shot with three others – a young gravedigger threw the bodies into a narrow trench. The supposed site is marked by a granite memorial. In 2009 an **archeological excavation** here attempted to discover Lorca's remains but came to a halt when it was discovered that the supposed burial site had only a thin layer of soil – not enough to dig a grave – beneath which lay solid rock. Lorca experts were stunned by this revelation and it is now possible that the poet's remains will never be found.

ARRIVAL AND ACCOMMODATION — VIZNAR

By bus Viznar is served by Fernandez de la Torre buses (T 958 405 413) from Granada's Arco de Elvira terminal on the Plaza del Triunfo at the northern end of Gran Vía (Granada to Viznar Mon–Fri hourly 8.30am–9.30pm;

reduced service Sat & Sun; Viznar to Granada Mon–Fri hourly 8.50am–9.50pm; reduced service Sat & Sun; 25min).

Youth hostel Camino Fuente Grande ☎ 958 893 524. This excellent hostel has a swimming pool open to all. Under 26 €21, over 26 €27

West towards Málaga

Travelling from Granada to Málaga by bus will take you along the fast but dull A92 *autovía*, which crosses the *vega* to the west of the city. With your own transport and time to spare, you could take a more interesting and scenic route, stopping off at the delightful but little-visited town of **Alhama de Granada** and traversing the dramatic **Zaffaraya Pass**, descending into Málaga by way of the ruggedly beautiful **Axarquía** region.

To do this, leave Granada by the route for Motril and the coast, along the A44 *autovía*. Four kilometres southwest of the city take the exit signed Armilla, and from here, follow the A338 heading west towards the village of **La Malahá** (which has a fine roadside *venta*), and, 10km beyond, **Ventas de Huelma** where *Luciano* is another excellent *venta* stop. From here the road twists and climbs into the Sierra de la Pera and, after descending to the lakeside village of **Poblado del Embalse** – where there's a good **campsite**, *Los Bermejales* (see p.494) – continues through a rich landscape of bubbling streams and rocky gulches overlooked by hills planted with olives, to Alhama de Granada, 14km further.

Alhama de Granada

Scenically sited along a ledge overlooking a broad gorge or *tajo* created by the Río Alhama, the spa town of **ALHAMA DE GRANADA** is one of the unsung gems of Granada province and makes a wonderful overnight stop or a base for exploring the surrounding hill country. It has a couple of striking churches in a well-preserved old quarter, and its baths, dating back to Roman and Moorish times (Al Hamma in Arabic means "hot springs"), still draw in numerous visitors to take the waters. They were greatly treasured during Moorish times, and the Spanish expression of regret "¡Ay de mi Alhama!" was the cry of sorrow attributed to Abu al-Hacen (the Mulhacen after whom the Sierra Nevada peak is named) when he lost the town in a crucial battle here against the Christian forces in 1482. It was this loss that severed the vital link between Granada and Málaga (and hence North Africa), foreshadowing the end of eight centuries of Moorish rule. Settlement started here much earlier, however, and the ancient Iberian town on the site was referred to by the Romans as Artigi.

Most of Alhama's sights are within a short walk of **Plaza de la Constitución**, the main square fronted by bars and restaurants. To see the interior of some of them, however, you will need to take a **guided tour** organized by the Turismo (see p.493).

El Castillo

Plaza de la Constitución

At the northern end of Plaza de la Constitución stands the Alhama's **castle**, now privately owned. Although constructed in Moorish times, the castle suffered serious damage in sixteenth- and seventeenth-century confrontations and today only fragments of its original walls remain; these can be seen on Calle Adarve Remedios, on the building's northwest flank. The castle was substantially rebuilt and remodelled in the early twentieth century, when it suffered the unfortunate addition of crenellated battlements.

Iglesia del Carmen and around

Cuesta del Carmen s/n • Open service times (7–8pm) or on a Turismo tour (see p.493)

Close to the castle's eastern flank, the sixteenth- to eighteenth-century **Iglesia del Carmen** is Alhama's prettiest church, overlooking the **Tajo** and fronted by a

5

RICHARD FORD AND THE HANDBOOK FOR SPAIN

Very few books have been written about Spain that do not draw on **Richard Ford** and his 1845 *Murray's Handbook for Spain* – arguably the best, the funniest and the most encyclopedic guidebook ever written on any country. Born in 1796 into a family of means, Ford studied law but never practised, and in 1824 married Harriet Capel, the daughter of the Earl of Essex. When she received medical advice to seek a warmer climate for her health, Ford – inspired by Irving's recent publication of the *Conquest of Granada* – took his family off to Spain where they lived for three years, wintering in Seville and spending the summers living in part of the Alhambra in Granada.

Ford spent most of his time traversing the length and breadth of the country – but particularly Andalucía – on horseback, making notes and sketches. It's hard to believe that all this was not meant for some literary purpose, but it was only back in England – and six years after his return – when publisher John Murray asked him to recommend someone to write a Spanish travel guide, that Ford suggested himself. His marriage now broken, he settled in a Devon village in a house to which he added many Spanish features (including some souvenirs from the Alhambra) to work solidly for nearly five years on what became the *Handbook for Spain*. When Murray and others took exception to the final manuscript's often caustic invective, Ford was advised to tone it down and a revised – but still gloriously outspoken – edition finally appeared in 1845 to great acclaim. Curiously, although he became *the* resident expert on Spain, he never returned to the country that had put him on the literary map.

Ford's blind spots, such as British prejudice against Baroque architecture (the more extravagant styles of which he dismissed as "vile Churrigueresque"), are often irritating, and the High Tory attitudes sometimes verging on jingoism, added to a splenetic francophobia, often threaten to tip over into the worst kind of churlishness. However, the author's enduring fascination with Spain and all things Spanish – he personally introduced amontillado sherry and Extremaduran *jamón serrano* into England – allied to a crisp writing style and a dry wit, invariably save him, and some of his passages, related with a wry irony, are still hilariously funny. His description of the hostelry at Alhama is typical:

The posada at Alhama, albeit called La Grande, is truly iniquitous; diminutive indeed are the accommodations, colossal the inconveniences; but this is a common misnomer, en las cosas de España. Thus Philip IV was called El Grande, under whose fatal rule Spain crumbled into nothing; like a ditch he became greater in proportion as more land was taken away. All who are wise will bring from Málaga a good hamper of eatables, a bota of wine, and some cigars, for however devoid of creature comforts this grand hotel, there is a grand supply of creeping creatures, and the traveller runs risk of bidding adieu to sleep, and passing the night exclaiming, Ay! de mi, Alhama.

twin-basined ancient fountain where farmers water their donkeys on sultry summer evenings. The simple stone and white-walled interior focuses on a main altar featuring a Virgin in a *camarín*. Just off to the right here, with its back to the Tajo, is Artesanía Los Tajos, Calle Peñas 34, selling local **ceramics** as well as some remarkable traditional clay water-whistles called *canarios*. Once used by local shepherds and goatherds, they make an ear-splitting racket, as the proprietor will eagerly demonstrate. About 50m east of the Iglesia del Carmen on Calle Baja Iglesia lies the so-called **Casa de la Inquisición**, which may have nothing to do with the Inquisition at all but is noted for its fine Isabelline Gothic facade. Beyond here Calle Baja Iglesia ascends to Plaza de los Presos and the church of La Incarnación.

Iglesia Mayor de Santa María de la Encarnación
Plaza de los Presos s/n • Open on a Turismo tour (see p.493)

The town's main church, always referred to as **La Encarnación**, dominates the Plaza de los Presos, an agreeable little square with a central fountain. Donated by Fernando and Isabel after the conquest of the town from the Moors, the church was completed in the first half of the sixteenth century by some of the major architects of the time – among them Enrique Egas and Diego de Siloé, the designers of the Capilla Real and cathedral at Granada. Siloé was responsible for the striking and massive Renaissance belfry that towers above the town. The restrained single-naved interior displays some elegant vaulting and the *sacristía* has fifteenth-century vestments with embroidery attributed to Isabel herself.

Around the Iglesia de la Encarnación

Opposite the La Encarnación church, on Plaza de los Presos, is an ancient **posito** (granary) dating from the thirteenth century but incorporating parts of an earlier synagogue. Just downhill from here the sixteenth-century **Hospital de la Reina**, Calle Vendederas s/n (open on a Turismo tour; see below), was the first building of this kind to be built in the kingdom of Granada. Leaving the square to the right of the church along Calle Alta Iglesia takes you past the misleadingly named **Casa Romana** on the right, an eighteenth-century mansion believed to have been constructed on the site of a Roman villa. The same street returns to the Plaza Mayor.

The Balneario and around

Alhama's only other site of note is a well-preserved first-century BC Roman **bridge** at the edge of the town, close to the A338 to Granada, a short distance along the road to the **Balneario** (baths). Beyond here, a (signed) twisting road leads 1km to the baths (daily 2–4pm; €1) that give the town its name. Although little remains of the Roman baths seen by Ford in the nineteenth century, elements of the Moorish *hammam* survive and can be seen by enquiring at the *Balneario de Granada*, a member of whose staff will conduct you into the depths to see some astonishing Moorish arches and the odd stone inscribed in Latin.

ARRIVAL AND DEPARTURE

ALHAMA DE GRANADA

By bus Alhama is served by three buses in both directions (1 on Sat & Sun) from Granada and one daily bus from Torre del Mar (p.93) in Málaga province. Full details are available from the bus company Alsa (⚑ alsa.es). The bus stop is on Plaza del Duque de Mandas in the lower town.

INFORMATION

Turismo Paseo Montes Jovellar s/n (daily: April–Sept 9.30am–2.30pm & 5–7pm; Oct–March 9.30am–2.30pm & 4–6pm; ☎ 958 360 686, ⚑ turismodealhama.com). This helpful office close to the Plaza de la Constitución can provide maps and information on walking in the area. They also run guided tours of the town and its monuments (Tues, Thurs & Sat; €3), which depart from in front of the building at noon.

Swimming pool Alhama's municipal swimming pool, with plenty of shade, lies just outside town along the Málaga road.

Cycling Cycling Country, C/Salmerones Bajo 18 (☎ 958 360 655, ⚑ cyclingcountry.com), offer guided or self-guided bike tours around the spectacular countryside (from one day to two weeks), with top-quality bikes and equipment.

ACCOMMODATION

Things have improved immeasurably on the **accommodation** front since Ford was here (see box opposite) and the dreaded *La Grande* is no more. Except in August (when it's wise to reserve in advance) there's usually no problem finding a room at any of the places listed below.

Balneario de Granada Ctra. del Balneario s/n, 1km off the road into town from Granada ☎ 958 350 011, ⚑ balnearioalhamadegranada.com. The *balneario's* three-star spa hotel is pleasant enough and the comfortable parquet-floored rooms come with a/c and TV. However, despite being situated in dense pinewoods, when it's full with visitors taking the waters it has the ambience of a sanatorium. €95

Cortijo Moyano Ctra. de Játar ☎ 676 474 443, ⚑ cortijo moyano.com. Welcoming and very agreeable rural option 4km out of town along the road to Játar. The main farmhouse houses a restaurant while behind, modern and comfortable en-suite a/c rooms come with TV and underfloor heating. The restaurant uses organic fruit and vegetables from its garden and serves its own olive oil and organic wine; the house speciality is *carnes a la brasa* (charcoal-grilled meats). The proprietor can arrange horseriding and trout fishing trips, as well as advising on walking routes in the area. B&B €60

Hostal San José Plaza de la Constitución 27 ☎ 958 350 156. Bang on the main square, this is a simple but clean *hostal* offering en-suite rooms; it also has a few singles. €35

Hotel El Ventorro 3km out of town on the Málaga road (take the turn-off for Játar) ☎ 958 350 438, ⚑ el ventorro.net. An attractive rural alternative, this fronts a

5

lake and has its own decent restaurant (which, in recognition of the fact that there has been a *venta* on this site since the eighteenth century, offers a few eighteenth-century dishes). You can choose between delightfully decorated and furnished cave rooms or conventional rooms, all of them en suite. There is a full-blown cave spa and a public swimming pool next door. B&B cave rooms **€70**, conventional rooms **€60**

★ **La Seguiriya** C/Las Peñas 12 ☏ 958 360 801, ⓦ laseguiriya.com. This charming *hospedería rural* and restaurant (see below) lies 50m uphill off the main square, in an eighteenth-century house with fine views over the Tajo from its back garden. The friendly proprietor is a retired flamenco *cantante*, and the comfortably furnished en-suite rooms are appropriately named after flamenco styles. They also offer outdoor activities including hiking, canoeing and mountain biking. B&B **€60**

CAMPSITE

Camping Los Bermejales Arenas del Rey, Poblado de Embalse ☏ 958 359 190, ⓦ losbermejales.com. Attractive lakeside campsite 14km outside town, with plenty of shade plus good facilities, pool and restaurant. **€5** per person, **€3** per tent, **€4** per vehicle

EATING AND DRINKING

Bar Ochoa Plaza de la Independencia s/n ☏ 958 350 643. A friendly tapas and *raciones* place, just off the main square, serving up a range of tasty tapas including *gambas a la plancha* (prawns with garlic) and *setas* (mushrooms cooked in herbs and oil). In cooler periods don't be surprised to find a *brasero* (hot coals footwarmer) under your table. When the mood takes them impromptu flamenco sessions take place in the back room. Fri–Sun 10am–2pm & 7pm–midnight.

Bar Ohana Carrera de Francisco de Toledo 2 ☏ 633 271 855. Despite its address this bar is on the main square. Besides snacks and *raciones* it also offers *platos combinados* and *carne en salsa de almendras* (meat in almond sauce) is a special. Daily noon–midnight.

El Tigre Plaza de la Constitución 1 ☏ 958 350 445. Small and entertaining bar-shop on the main square specializing in *jamón* and *salchichón* (salami) *ibérico*, both from the Spanish black pig. They also offer *tostadas* (toast) with various toppings (tomato and anchovy are good) and *fritura de pescado* (fried fish). Mon–Sat 9am–4pm & 8pm–midnight.

★ **La Seguiriya** C/Las Peñas 12 ☏ 958 360 801, ⓦ laseguiriya.com. The attractive restaurant of the *hospedería rural* (see above) is the town's best place to eat. Chef Lola Maiztegui hails from the Basque country and the small menu has a mixture of dishes from northern and southern Spain. House specials include *sopa de espárragos con almendras* (asparagus and almond soup), *lomo con ciruelas pasas* (pork with prunes) and *atún a la roteña* (tuna). The menu also features a range of salads and in summer you can dine on the terrace with a spectacular Tajo view. Main dishes €8–15. Mon–Sat 2–4pm & 8–10pm.

★ **Los Caños de Alcaicería** Ctra. Alhama–Vélez km10 ☏ 958 350 325. Ten kilometres out of Alhama in the direction of the Zaffaraya pass, this excellent, rustically decorated *venta* specializes in *carnes de monte* (meat and game). Recommended dishes include *churrasco de cerdo* (pork steak) and *solomillo* (pork loin) and there's an economical weekday *menú*. Also sells its own honey, *jamón* and *salchichón* (salami) produced on the premises. Daily 9am–11pm.

Mesón Diego Plaza de la Constitución 12 ☏ 958 360 121. Long-established restaurant with a terrace on the square serving up the usual standards; *bacalao arriero* (cod) and *solomillo* (pork loin) are two of the specialities. There's a *menú* for around €8. Mon–Fri 8am–11pm.

From Alhama to the Zaffaraya Pass

South of Alhama, the A402 climbs towards Ventas de Zaffaraya passing, 10km out, a great-value *venta*, *Los Caños de Alcaicería* (see above), with an economical weekday *menú*. The road then toils on, cutting through a rich agricultural area to the isolated hamlet of Ventas de Zaffaraya, 6km after the *venta*. Just beyond here the spectacular **Zaffaraya Pass**, which slips through a cleft in the Sierra de Tejeda and was part of the old coach route, provides a dramatic entrance into the Axarquía region of Málaga Province, with superb **views** to the distant Mediterranean. Roughly 6km beyond the pass lies the deserted medieval village of **Zalía**, after which the road continues to Vélez-Málaga (p.94) and the coast.

Sierra Nevada National Park

Southeast from Granada rise the mountains of the **SIERRA NEVADA**, designated Andalucía's second **national park** in 1999, a startling backdrop to the city, snowcapped

5

THE SIERRA NEVADA'S FLORA AND FAUNA

The Sierra Nevada is particularly rich in **wild flowers**. Some fifty varieties are unique to these mountains, among them five gentians, including *Gentiana bory*, the pansy *Viola nevadensis*, a shrubby mallow *Lavatera oblongifolia*, and a spectacular honeysuckle, the 7- to 10m-high *Lonicera arborea*.

    Wildlife, too, abounds away from the roads. One of the most exciting sights is the *Cabra hispanica*, a wild horned goat which you'll see standing on pinnacles, silhouetted against the sky. They roam the mountains in flocks and jump up the steepest slopes with amazing agility when they catch the scent of a walker on the wind. The higher slopes are also home to a rich assortment of **butterflies**, among them the rare Nevada Blue as well as varieties of Fritillary. **Birdwatching** is also superb, with the colourful hoopoe – a bird with a stark, haunting cry – a common sight.

---

for most of the year and offering skiing from November until late May. The ski slopes are at **Solynieve**, an unimaginative, developed resort just 28km away (40min by bus). Here, the direct car route across the range stops, but from this point walkers can make the relatively easy two- to three-hour trek up to **Veleta** (3394m), the second highest peak of the sierra and the second-highest summit on the Spanish peninsula (see p.496).

    The main A395 access road from Granada to the national park has been a mixed blessing for the delicate ecosystem of the sierra, and the expanding horrors of the Solynieve ski centre, which was chosen to hold the 1995 World Ski Championships (subsequently cancelled due to lack of snow and then held in 1996), has only made things worse.

Monachil

Before the road was constructed in the 1920s few *granadinos* ever came up to the sierra, but one group who had worn out a trail since the times of the Moors were the *neveros*, or icemen, who used mules to bring down blocks of ice from the mountains, which they then sold in the streets. Their route to Veleta can still be followed beyond **MONACHIL**, a village on the Río Monachil southeast of Granada. It's worth stopping off here; there are places to stay (see p.497) and a number of companies offering adventure activities in the park (see p.497).

Solynieve

The route to Solynieve leaves Granada via the Paseo del Salón (where the bus picks up and drops off); two wagons stand as a memory to the tram service which, from the 1920s until 1970, used to ascend as far as Güejar Sierra. Beyond Pinos de Genil the road begins to climb seriously, passing a number of alpine-style roadside **ventas** which do good business in season. After some 17km, with your own transport you could make a stop at the **Balcón de Canales** with fine **views** over the Río Genil and its dam. At the 23km point you will pass the "El Dornajo" Sierra Nevada National Park Visitors' Centre (see p.496), and a further five kilometres on, the ski resort of **SOLYNIEVE** ("Sun and Snow") appears.

    Solynieve is a hideous-looking resort and regarded by serious alpine skiers as something of a joke. But with snow lingering so late in the year (Granada's Turismo should be able to advise on the state of this, or contact Sierra Nevada Club on ☏902 708 090 or visit ⊛sierranevada.es) it has obvious attractions for anyone determined to ski in southern Spain. From the middle of the resort a lift takes you straight up to the main ski lifts, which provide access to most of the higher **slopes**, and when the snow is right you can ski a few kilometres back down to the *zona hotelera* (the lifts run only when there's skiing). There are plenty of places to rent gear. If you intend to ski (or walk) here be sure to double your **skin protection** as this is the most southerly ski centre in Europe, with intense sun at high altitudes.

5

Ascending Veleta

The ascent of **Veleta** is a none-too-challenging hike rather than a climb but should only be attempted between May and September – unless you're properly geared up – but even then you'll need warm and waterproof clothing. From the *Albergue Universitario* (see p.497) the **Capileira-bound road** – now permanently closed to traffic to protect the sierra's delicate environment – actually runs past the peak of Veleta. Recently asphalted – somewhat removing the sense of adventure from the trek – it is perfectly, and tediously, walkable (bikes are allowed but it's a fierce climb). However, most hikers follow the well-worn shortcuts between the hairpins the road is forced to make. With your own transport it's possible to shave a couple of kilometres off the total by ignoring the no-entry signs at the car park near to the *Albergue Universitario* and continuing on to a second car park further up the mountain from which point the road is then barred. Although the peak of the mountain looks deceptively close from here you should allow two to three hours to reach the summit and ninety minutes to get back down. Make sure to bring **food and water** as there's neither en route and a picnic at the summit is one of the best meals to be had in Spain, weather permitting.

With a great deal of energy you could conceivably walk from Veleta to Capileira (see p.506) – but bear in mind that it's a good 30km distant, there are no facilities along the way and temperatures drop pretty low by late afternoon. En route, an hour beyond Veleta, you pass just under **Mulhacén** – the tallest peak on the Iberian peninsula at 3483m. Should you decide to detour from the Capileira route and climb it, be aware that an ascent involves two hours of exposed and windy ridge-crawling from the road, and a sudden, sheer drop on its northwest face. There is a gentler slope down to the Siete Lagunas valley to the east. The easiest way of scaling Mulhacén, though, is from Capileira (see p.506).

ARRIVAL AND INFORMATION   SIERRA NEVADA NATIONAL PARK

MONACHIL

Monachil is connected by frequent **buses** to Granada, running from the terminal at the Paseo del Salón.

SOLYNIEVE

Throughout the year Autocares Bonal runs daily **buses** from Granada to Solynieve and, just above this, to the *Albergue Universitario* (see p.497). From April to Sept services leave Granada bus station at 10am and 5pm, returning from the *Albergue Universitario* at 4pm and 6pm (and passing Solynieve 10min later). For the winter service (Oct–March) ring the bus company (see p.478) or check with any Turismo. Tickets to Solynieve (€8 round trip) should be bought in advance at the bus station, although you can pay on board if the bus is not full.

INFORMATION

"El Dornajo" Sierra Nevada National Park Visitors' Centre Ctra. de Sierra Nevada km23 (Tues–Sun 10am–2pm & 4–6pm; ☎ 958 340 625). Signposted just off the A395, this is the national park's main information centre. Its shop sells guidebooks, maps and hats (sun protection is vital), has a permanent exhibition on the park's flora and fauna, provides hiking information (English spoken), and rents out horses and mountain bikes. The centre also has a *cafetería* with a stunning terrace view beyond the ancient tram parked in a garden behind.

Maps The best general map of the Sierra Nevada and of the lower slopes of the Alpujarras is co-produced by the Instituto Geográfico Nacional and the Federación Española de Montañismo (1:50,000). Not far behind is the Editorial Alpina's

---

RUTA INTEGRAL DE LOS TRES MIL

The classic **Ruta Integral de los Tres Mil**, a complete traverse of all the sierra's peaks over 3000m high, starts in Jeres del Marquesado on the north side of the Sierra Nevada (due south of Guadix) and finishes in Lanjarón, in the Alpujarras. It's an exhausting three- to four-day itinerary described in detail in Andy Walmsley's book *Walking in the Sierra Nevada* (see p.593). For any serious exploration of the Sierra Nevada, essential equipment includes a tent, proper gear and ample food. It's a serious mountain where lives have been lost so come prepared for the eventuality of not being able to reach (or find) the refuge huts, or the weather turning nasty.

Sierra Nevada y La Alpujarra (1:40,000) map, which has the bonus of a booklet (with an English edition) describing fourteen hikes in the Sierra as well as useful background information on the zone. The CNIG's 1:25,000 sheets are more detailed for trekking purposes, and all three can be obtained in Granada or from the El Dornajo visitor centre (see p.496).

Ride Sierra Nevada C/San Miguel s/n, Monachil (☎ 958 501 620, ⓦ ridesierranevada.com). Located in the centre of Monachil, this company organizes all kinds of outdoor pursuits including mountain biking, horseriding, climbing and hiking in the spectacular Los Cahorros gorge; they also act as an information centre for the village. Besides their own rooming house (see below) they can also provide information on renting *casas rurales* and cave dwellings for longer stays.

Emergencies Inside the park, to report any emergencies, including forest fires, stranded hikers or personal injuries, there's a coordinated emergency service contactable on ☎ 112; the park's Guardia Civil unit can be reached on ☎ 062.

ACCOMMODATION

MONACHIL

Casa Aurel Contact Ride Sierra Nevada, C/San Miguel s/n ☎ 958 501 620, ⓦ ridesierranevada.com. Rooms in a refurbished village house, rented out by the adventure activities company Ride Sierra Nevada. €45

El Molino de Rosa María Serrano Avda. del Río 23, Monachil, 11km southeast of the city ☎ 958 301 914, ⓦ molino-rosa-maria-serrano.com. Very good-value rural hotel in this pretty village, a mere 10min from the city centre, with attractive rooms and its own restaurant. B&B €65

SOLYNIEVE

The Granada Turismo and the Sierra Nevada Club (☎ 902 708 090, ⓦ sierranevada.es) can advise on places to stay at the ski resort (many hotels open only during the ski season). We review some of the resort's budget options below, but other places can be very expensive in season, when you should expect to pay at least €80–100 per night for a double room.

Albergue Juvenil C/Peñones 22 ☎ 955 035 886, ⓦ inturjoven.com. The resort's cheapest accommodation is the modern and comfortable youth hostel, on the edge of the ski resort, where you can get good-value doubles and four-bed studios and apartments, all en suite. They also rent out skis and equipment in season (Dec–Feb) when room prices increase slightly. Open all year. Under 26 €21, over 26 €27

Albergue Universitario Peñones de San Francisco, 3km above the ski resort ☎ 958 480 122, ⓦ nevadensis .com. At an altitude of 2500m and often snowed in winter, this isolated mountain hostel is an attractive option if seclusion is what you're seeking. Sited just off the main road where the bus drops you, it offers bunk rooms and doubles sharing bathrooms and there's also a bar-restaurant (daily *menú* €10). It's a stunning location for exploring the national park (the hostel can advise on walking routes) but without transport extremely isolated. The Granada bus (which only runs beyond the ski resort in summer) turns around at the *Albergue* and this marks the start of the Veleta ascent (see p.496). Half-board for two €44 (April–Oct), €90 (Nov–March)

Camping Ruta del Purche Ctra. de Sierra Nevada km16 ☎ 958 340 407, ⓦ rutadelpurche.com. Signed down a turnoff 16km out of Granada (the site is a further 3km from here) this is a well-run campsite with plenty of shade. Facilities include a bar-restaurant, supermarket, pool and free wi-fi zone. It also rents out en-suite wood cabins sleeping up to four. €4.50 per person, €8.50 per tent & vehicle, cabins €130

Las Alpujarras

The N323 road south from Granada to Motril crosses the fertile *vega* after leaving the city and then climbs steeply until, at 850m above sea level, it reaches the **Puerto del Suspiro del Moro** – the Pass of the Sigh of the Moor. Boabdil, last Moorish king of Granada, came this way, having just handed over the keys of his city to the Reyes Católicos in exchange for a fiefdom over the Alpujarras. From the pass you catch your last glimpse of the city and the Alhambra. The road then descends and beyond Padul crosses the valley of Lecrín planted with groves of orange, lemon and almond trees, the latter a riot of pink and white blossom in late winter. To the east, through a narrow defile close to Béznar, lie the great valleys of **Las Alpujarras**, first settled in the twelfth century by Berber refugees from Seville, and later the Moors' last stronghold.

The so-called **High Alpujarras** – the villages of **Pampaneira**, **Bubión** and **Capileira** – have all been scrubbed and whitewashed and are now firmly on the tourist circuit, as popular with Spanish as foreign visitors. Lower down, in the **Órgiva area**, are the main concentration of expatriates – mainly British, Dutch and Germans, seeking new

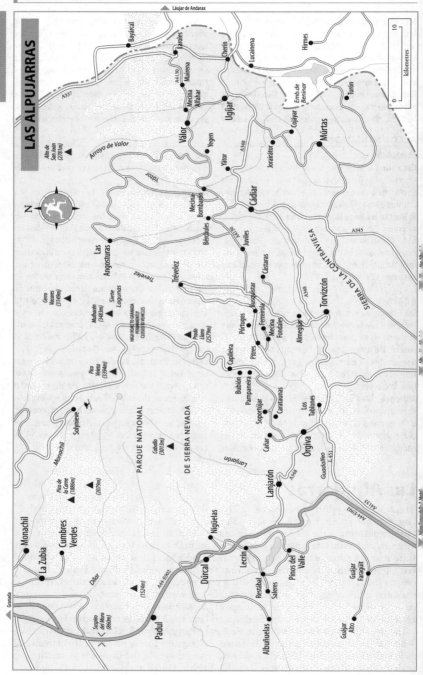

Mediterranean lives. Most seem to have moved here permanently, rather than establishing second homes (though there are houses for rent in abundance), and there's a vaguely alternative aspect to the new community, which sets it apart from the coastal expats. In addition to property owners, the area has also attracted groups of New Age travellers. The locals, to their credit, seem remarkably tolerant of the whole scene.

Brief history

The valleys are bounded to the north by the Sierra Nevada, and to the south by the lesser *sierras* of Lujar, La Contraviesa and Gador. The eternal snows of the high *sierras* keep the valleys and their seventy or so villages well watered all summer long. Rivers have cut deep gorges in the soft mica and shale of the upper mountains, and over the centuries have deposited silt and fertile soil on the lower hills and in the valleys; here the villages have grown, for the soil is rich and easily worked. The intricate terracing that today preserves these deposits was begun perhaps as long as two thousand years ago by **Visigoths** or **Ibero-Celts**, whose remains have been found at Capileira.

The **Moors** carried on the tradition, and modified the terracing and irrigation in their inimitable way. They transformed the Alpujarras into an earthly paradise, and there they retired to bewail the loss of their beloved lands in al-Andalus. After the fall of Granada, many of the city's Muslim population settled in the villages, and there resisted a series of royal edicts demanding their forced conversion to **Christianity**. In 1568 they rose up in a final, short-lived revolt, which led to the expulsion of all Spanish Moors. Even then, however, two Moorish families were required to stay in each village to show the new Christian peasants, who had been marched down from Galicia and Asturias to repopulate the valleys, how to operate the intricate irrigation systems.

Through the following centuries, the villages fell into poverty, with the land owned by a few wealthy families, and worked by peasants. It was one of the most remote parts of Spain in the **1920s**, when the author Gerald Brenan settled in one of the eastern villages, Yegen, and described the life in his book *South from Granada*, and things changed little over the next forty-odd years. During the **Civil War**, the occasional truckload of Nationalist youth trundled in from Granada, rounded up a few bewildered locals, and shot them for "crimes" of which they were wholly ignorant; Republican youths came up in their trucks from Almería and did the same thing. In the aftermath, under Franco, there was real hardship and suffering, and in the **1980s** the region had one of the lowest per capita incomes in Spain, with – as an official report put it – "a level of literacy bordering on that of the Third World, alarming problems of desertification, poor communications and high under-employment".

Ironically, the land itself is still very fertile – oranges, chestnuts, bananas, apples and avocados grow here, while the southern villages produce a well-known dry rosé wine, *costa*. However, it is largely the recent influx of **tourism** and foreign purchase of houses and farms that has turned the area's fortunes around, bringing pockets of wealth and an influx of new life to the region.

ARRIVAL AND DEPARTURE	LAS ALPUJARRAS

By bus There are several buses a day from both Granada and Motril, and one a day from Almería, to Lanjarón and Órgiva. One operated by Alsina Graells (☏ 902 422 242, ⦿ alsa.es) direct to the High Alpujarras, via Trevélez as far as Bérchules, leaves the main Granada bus station (daily noon & 4.30pm): in the other direction it leaves Bérchules at 5.50am and 5.05pm, passing Trevélez 30min later, to arrive in Granada at 9.25am or 8.50pm respectively. There's also a service from Granada to Ugíjar in the Low Alpujarras, via Lanjarón, Órgiva, Torvizcón, Cádiar, Yegen and Valor (currently 8.30am & 5pm); this takes a little over

4hr to the end of the line. The return journey from Ugíjar currently runs at 5.45am and 3pm. There are also frequent daily buses between Granada and Órgiva (three via Lanjarón) and vice versa, and three daily buses link with Pampaneira, Bubión, Capileira and Pitres.

By car From Granada, the most straightforward approach to the Alpujarras is to take the Lanjarón turning – the A348 – off the Motril road (E902). Coming from the south, you can bear right from the road at Vélez de Benaudalla and continue straight along the A346 to Órgiva, the market town of the western Alpujarras.

INFORMATION

Guidebooks There are many walkers' guides to the Alpujarras. Useful publications include Charles Davis's *34 Alpujarras Walks*, Jeremy Rabjohns' *Holiday Walks in the Alpujarras* and *GR142: Senda de la Alpujarra* (in Spanish) by Francisco Jiménez Richarte; there are also half a dozen Alpujarras treks featured in *Andalucía and the Costa del Sol* by John and Christine Oldfield and an equal number in Guy Hunter-Watts' *Walking in Andalucía* (see p.593 for details of all these publications). See p.490 for details on maps of this area.

Lanjarón

LANJARÓN has known tourism and the influence of the outside world for longer than anywhere else in the Alpujarras due to the curative powers of its **spa waters**. These gush from seven natural springs and are sold in bottled form as mineral water throughout Spain. Between March and December, when the spa baths are open, the town fills with the aged and infirm and the streets are lined with racks of herbal remedies, all of which imparts a rather melancholy air. This might seem good reason for passing straight on to the higher villages, though to do so would be to miss out on some beautiful local walks, and a town centre that, now a bypass has removed much of the traffic, grows on you.

Like so many spa towns, Lanjarón is Roman in origin, though today the place is largely modern, with a ribbon of buildings flanking its attractive, tree-lined main thoroughfare, split into three sections running west to east: Avenida de Andalucía, Avenida de La Alpujarra and Calle Real.

Lanjarón castle

Free

Below the main street, and beyond the town's new bypass, marking Lanjarón's medieval status as gateway to the Alpujarras, is a **Moorish castle**, newly refurbished and now permanently open for visits. It was here on March 8, 1500, that the Moorish population made its final heroic stand against the Christian troops under the command of Fernando. Pounded by artillery, hundreds died as the town was taken. A ten-minute stroll reveals its dramatic setting – follow the signs downhill from the main street and out onto the terraces and meadows below the town.

Balneario de Lanjarón

Western end of the village • March–Dec • Basic soak about €15 • ☎ 958 770 137, ⓦ balneariodelanjaron.com

It's fun to take the waters at Lanjarón's **Balneario** – go for a basic soak, or reckon on add-ons for massage, mud baths, pressure showers and all kinds of other alarming-sounding treatments such as *drenajes linfáticos* and *pulverizaciones faríngeas*.

ARRIVAL AND INFORMATION   LANJARÓN

By bus Midway along the main street at C/Real 123 is the Alsina Graells bus terminal (☎ 958 770 003).

Turismo Municipal Avda. de Andalucía s/n (Mon–Sat 10am–2pm & 4.30–8.30pm, Sun 10am–2pm; ☎ 958 770 462). Located opposite the Balneario at the village's western end the town's municipal tourist office can provide information on the town and the Alpujarras.

Internet Cyberplay Lanjarón (daily except Wed 6pm–

WALKS FROM LANJARÓN

The countryside and **mountains around Lanjarón** are spectacularly beautiful. Wander up through the backstreets behind the town and you'll come across a track that takes you steeply up to the vast spaces bordering on the Reserva Nacional de la Sierra Nevada.

For a somewhat easier day's **walk**, go to the bridge over the river just east of town and take the sharply climbing, cobbled track which parallels the river. After a walk of 2hr–2hr 30min, through small farms with magnificent views and scenery, a downturn to a small stone bridge lets you return to Lanjarón on the opposite bank. Allow a minimum of 6hr for a leisurely expedition.

midnight), Avda. de Andalucía 30, near the La Caixa bank.

Festivals Lanjarón puts on a stirring Semana Santa – one of the best in the province, and worth going out of your way to see if you're in the area. Its other great shindig is the water festival on the eve of San Juan (June 24) when the unaware get drenched by cascades falling from balconies and "water bombs" are thrown around with abandon.

ACCOMMODATION

Thanks to the Balneario, there's no shortage of **places to stay** in town, most sited along the main street. In high summer it's essential to book ahead, while in winter many places close in January and February.

Camping Puerta de la Alpujarra Ctra. Lanjarón–Órgiva, 7km out of Lanjarón in the direction of Órgiva, ☎958 784 450, ⓦcampingpuertadelaalpujarra.com. Decent campsite with ample shade and panoramic views where services include pool, bar-restaurant and shop. €4 per person, €3.80 per tent, €3.80 per vehicle

Hotel Alcadima C/Francisco Tarrega 3, down a signed turn-off from the main street ☎958 770 809, ⓦalcadima.com. A good-value hotel with the best pool and prettiest restaurant terrace in town. Many of the comfortable rooms have stunning balcony views towards the castle and guests may use the small gym. They also have a number of two-bedroomed family suites. Free wi-fi and internet access. €85

Hotel El Sol Avda. de La Alpujarra 30, ☎958 770 130, ⓦhotelelsol.es. Good-value choice if you're here in winter or early spring as there is reliable heating in their en-suite rooms. Guests also have use of sauna and jacuzzi. B&B €82

Hotel España Avda. de La Alpujarra 42, near the Balneario ☎958 770 187, ⓦlanjaron.biz. This great-value hotel, with an air of faded grandeur, has hosted such luminaries as García Lorca (Room 107) and Manuel de Falla in its time. It comes with friendly staff, comfortable tile-floored rooms, its own bar-restaurant and a pool. €45

Hotel Miramar Avda. de Andalucía 10 ☎958 770 161. For a step up in price you can enjoy the relative luxury of one of the town's top hotels where a/c rooms come with strongbox and (in some) a balcony. It also has a bar, restaurant, pool, garden and garage. €66

Hotel Nuevo Palas Avda. de La Alpujarra 24 ☎958 770 111, ⓦhotelnuevopalas.com. Pleasant three-star hotel with a/c rooms, rooftop pool, gym and – in the bar – pool tables. B&B €76

Hotel Paris Avda. de La Alpujarra 23 ☎958 770 056, ⓦhotelparislanjaron.com. A charming and very good-value main street hotel. Marble floored rooms come with TV and many have fine views. Facilities include a good-value restaurant, pool, free wi-fi zone and own garage. €44

EATING AND DRINKING

Plenty of **bars and restaurants** line the Avda. de Andalucía and many of the hotels and *hostales* have good-value meals and tapas, too – especially the hotels *España* and *El Sol*. On the Avda. de Andalucía's "main square", midway between the Balneario and the church, lies Lanjarón's celebrated *churrería*, claimed by some to sell the best home-made potato crisps in Andalucía, opposite which are a couple of good ice-cream parlours.

Bar Galvez C/Real 95, at the eastern end of the main street. A popular bar-restaurant serving up economical *platos combinados* and with a *menú* for €11. Daily 9am–11pm.

Café-Bar Health C/Señor la Expiración s/n. Downhill at the extreme eastern end of the main street and beyond the Ayuntamiento, this cosy eco-café serves breakfasts and full meals with many vegetarian options and often has live music in the evenings. Also serves a range of British and continental beers. Daily 10am–10pm.

Hotel Alcadima C/Francisco Tarrega 3, down a signed turn-off from the main street ☎958 770 809, ⓦalcadima .com. Probably the most romantic choice for dining out is the terrace restaurant of the *Hotel Alcadima* – pretty much the perfect place to while away a summer evening with a superb view of the castle. House specials include *jarratillo de cordero* (jugged lamb) and there's a *menú* for €15. Main dishes €8–15. Daily 1.30–3.30pm & 8–11.30pm.

Jamones Gustavo Rubio Avda. de Andalucía 38, about half way down the main street. This justly popular bar is worth a visit for its excellent tapas and is tucked behind a shop selling the wines, cheeses, *jamones* and other products of the region. Mon–Sat 9am–9pm.

★ **Los Mariscos** Avda. de Andalucía 6, near the "main square". Excellent and very friendly *marisquería* serving up a range of seafood. Specialities include *sopa de mariscos* (shellfish soup) and *fritura de pescado* (fried fish). There's a daily *menú* for €12. Sunday lunch is very popular with local families. Main dishes €7–15. Tues–Sun noon–4pm & 8–11pm.

Venta El Buñuelo 1km from the centre along the Órgiva road. Rustic but entertaining roadside *venta* with a terrace and lively bar; they serve good low-priced *alpujarreño* cooking with a weekday *menú* for €8. Thurs–Tues 8am–11pm.

5

Órgiva (Órjiva)

Heading east out of Lanjarón brings you after 7km to a turn-off for Las Barreras, notable for its campsite *Puerta de la Alpujarra* (see p.501). Three kilometres further lies **ÓRGIVA**, the market centre of the western Alpujarras. It's a lively little town, with a number of good bars and hotels, and an animated and entertaining **Thursday market**. The contrast between the timeworn *campesinos* and their pack-mules, and some of the foreign New Age travellers who seek their indulgence and charity, is as bizarre as anything this side of Madrid. Many of the New Agers here inhabit a **tepee village**, *El Beneficio*, above the town where a polyglot community of mainly northern Europeans and their offspring endure freezing winters under canvas. Another local resident is writer and farmer **Chris Stewart** who moved with his wife to an isolated *cortijo* (farmhouse) on the outskirts of Órgiva over twenty years ago. His trilogy of books (see p.588) wittily describing life among the peasants, shepherds, New Age travellers and expats of the western Alpujarras proved highly popular and helped to place this area of Andalucía on the map.

Órgiva's other sights line the main street, Calle González Robles: the sixteenth-century Baroque **church** of Nuestra Señora de la Expectación, whose towers add a touch of fancy to the townscape, and a once crumbling but now over-restored Moorish **palace** that today houses the Ayuntamiento.

ARRIVAL AND INFORMATION
ÓRGIVA (ÓRJIVA)

By bus Daily buses from the Alsa stop, on Avda. González Robles, serve the Low Alpujarras to Ugíjar (currently passing Orgiva at 10.15am & 6.45pm), as well as the High Alpujarran villages (passing at 11.30am, 1.30pm & 6pm).

Local information There's a useful noticeboard for locals and visitors in the wholefood shop Herbolario La Alacena, downhill from the Ayuntamiento.

Internet Ananda's Mundo, C/Cristo de la Expiración 4 (daily 10am–2pm & 6–10pm), behind the church.

Festivals Órgiva comes to life with its annual fiesta on the days each side of September 29, the feast day of San

Miguel, when the population doubles as prodigal sons and daughters all return to join in the fun. A more eccentric festival is the Día del Señor on the second Friday before Easter. This opens with a terrifying salvo of rockets on the Thursday before, when the town's womenfolk attack the church until they are able to make off with the effigies of El Señor (Christ) and the Virgin. On the Friday evening both Christ and his mother are paraded around town before re-entering the church in the early hours accompanied by great displays of emotion – not to mention more deafening rocketry.

ACCOMMODATION

Camping Órgiva Ctra. A-348 km19 ☎ 958 784 307, ⓦ campingorgiva.com. The town's campsite lies 2km south of the centre beyond the *Hotel Taray* and has plenty of shade plus clean facilities and a restaurant and pool. It can also advise on walking routes and renting horses in the nearby Sierra de Lújar. €5 per person, €5 per tent, €4 per vehicle

Hostal-Bar Semáforo Avda. González Robles 14 ☎ 958 784 309, ⓦ elsemaforo.es. Close to the town's main traffic junction (its name means "traffic lights"), this is a decent *hostal* for clean and tidy a/c en-suite rooms with TV above a bar. Free wi-fi. €50

Hotel Mirasol C/González Robles 3 on the entry road from Lanjarón ☎ 958 785 108, ⓦ hotelmirasol.es.

Comfortable a/c en-suite rooms come with TV and wi-fi. €45

Hotel Taray Ctra. A-348 km18 ☎ 958 784 525, ⓦ hoteltaray.com. Just over 1km along the A348 south of the town, this inviting three-star rural hotel is easier to get to with your own transport. The attractive rooms are surrounded by lovely gardens with a superb pool and there's also a bar-restaurant. They have frequent special offers. €110

Pensión Alma Alpujarreña C/González Robles 49 ☎ 958 784 085. Just beyond the traffic lights at the town's main intersection, this is a pretty, economical and friendly *hostal* with en-suite rooms (some single), plus a restaurant beneath a vine trellis. Outside high season (Aug) prices drop by thirty percent. €50

EATING

Many of the hotels and *hostals* have decent restaurants – *Hotel Mirasol* and *Hotel Taray* are both worth trying – and there are a few tapas bars gathered around the square in C/García Moreno fronting the church.

Baraka C/Estación 12, in the upper village near the market. A very nice small Moroccan café and *tetería*

offering felafel, couscous and tagines along with Hispanic dishes including guacamole and gazpacho. They make their

5

own ices in summer and also offer a variety of international teas. There's an outdoor terrace. Daily noon–11pm.

Bar Santiago C/García Moreno, almost opposite the church. Lively bar offering a good tapas range as well as a wide selection of beers and wines; unusually this bar lets you choose your own (free) *tapa* with each drink – a bonus for vegetarians. Daily 10am–11pm.

El Limonero C/Yanez 27, off the main road to the right 50m below La Almazara (see below). An interesting restaurant that does a range of creative dishes such as *cordero en especias de Marruecos* (braised lamb with Moroccan spices) as well as curries, risottos and pizzas. It has a good-looking terracotta-tinted room but no terrace. Main dishes €10–20. Tues–Sat 1–4pm & 8–11pm, Sun 1–4pm.

La Almazara Avda. González Robles 53, almost next door to the Pensión Alma Alpujarreña. A very good restaurant with a cosy wood-tabled interior room and a leafy garden terrace for warmer days. It offers a range of dishes such as *carrillada gratinada* (pork cheek au gratin) and *bacalao confitado* (confit of cod), and also does excellent freshly made pizzas. There's also a daily *menú* for €12.50. Main dishes €7–15. Thurs–Tues 1–4pm & 8–11.30pm.

Pensión Alma Alpujarreña C/González Robles 49 ☎ 958 784 085. The *hostal's* economical restaurant has a decent kitchen and a terrace for alfresco dining in summer. House specialities include paella and *pescado frito* (fried fish) and there's a good-value *menú* for €8.50. Daily 1–4pm & 8–11pm.

The High Alpujarras

From Órgiva, you can reach the High Alpujarran villages by car or bus, or you could walk – the best way to experience the region. There is a network of paths in this area, though to avoid getting lost it's wise to equip yourself with a compass and the Instituto Geográfico Nacional/Federación Española de Montañismo 1:50,000 map, which covers all the territory from Órgiva up to Berja. A reasonable knowledge of Spanish is also invaluable.

At their best, Alpujarran **footpaths** are remnants of the old Camino Real, the mule routes that crossed Spain, and are engineered with cobblestones, and beautifully contoured, alongside mountain streams, through woods of oak, chestnut and poplar, or across flower-spangled meadows. In their bad moments they deteriorate to incredibly dusty firebreaks, forestry roads or tractor tracks, or (worse) dead-end in impenetrable thickets of bramble and nettle. Progress is slow, gradients are sharp and the heat (between mid-June and Sept) is taxing. Over the past few years part of the path network through the High Alpujarras has been upgraded as the final section of the **European long-distance footpath** that begins in Athens and ends in Algeciras. Designated as footpaths E4 or GR7 in Spain, the full route is now waymarked (in theory – you'll still need a good map where the posts are missing or misplaced) with red and white ringed posts.

Soportújar and around

Following the high road from Órgiva, the first settlements you reach, almost directly above the town, are the isolated but pretty **CAÑAR** – at the end of a sinuous 5km drive off the main road – and **SOPORTÚJAR**, a maze of picturesque white-walled alleys bridged by numerous *tinaos* (see box opposite). Like many of the High Alpujarran villages, they congregate on the neatly terraced mountainside, planted with poplars and laced with irrigation channels. Both have **bars** where you can get a meal, and Soportújar can

---

HIGH ALPUJARRAS HIKES: THE HIGHLIGHTS

Rewarding **hikes** in the High Alpujarras include:

Pitres to Mecina Fondales A short (20min) hike to Mecina Fondales, and then a good hour-plus from neighbouring Ferreirola to Busquistar.

Busquístar to Trevélez One hour's hike, and then two-plus hours of road walking.

Pórtugos to Trevélez Two hours, meeting the tarmac a little beyond the end of the Busquistar route.

Trevélez to Bérchules Four hours, with the middle 2hr on a dirt track.

Trevélez to Juviles Three hours, including some sections of firebreak.

ALPUJARRAN ARCHITECTURE

Alpujarran **village houses** are unlike any others in Spain – though they are almost identical to Berber houses across the straits in the Rif mountains of Morocco, where many of the Moorish refugees settled. They are built of grey stone, flat-roofed and low; traditionally they are unpainted, though these days *cal* (whitewash) – a luxury until recent times – is increasingly common. The coarse walls are about 75cm thick, for summer coolness and protection from winter storms. Stout beams of chestnut, or ash in the lower valleys, are laid from wall to wall; on top of these is a mat of canes, ilex or split chestnut; upon this flat stones are piled, and on the stones is spread a layer of **launa**, the crumbly grey mica clay found throughout the area, which is made waterproof when pressed down.

The *launa* must – and this maxim is still observed today – be laid during the waning of the moon (though not, of course, on a Friday) in order for it to settle properly and thus keep rain out. Gerald Brenan wrote in *South from Granada* of a particularly ferocious storm: "As I peered through the darkness of the stormy night, I could make out a dark figure on every roof in the village, dimly lit by an esparto torch, stamping clay into the holes in the roof."

Another feature peculiar to the Alpujarras are the **tinaos**, a kind of portico or bridge that enables access from a dwelling in one row to another in an upper or lower row. In summer, time is passed on the roof terrace or *terrao*, especially once the sun has cooled in early evening. Bubión, Capileira and Pitres all have good examples of the traditional architectural style.

---

provide accommodation. Perched precariously on the steep hillside, both villages share a rather sombre view of Órgiva in the valley below, and on a clear day the mountains of North Africa over the ranges to the south. Each village has a sixteenth-century church, both of which fell into a terrible state of disrepair at the end of the last century, and both of which, thankfully, have now been refurbished and saved.

Carataunas

Just below Soportújar, the tiny hamlet of **CARATAUNAS** is particularly attractive, with a labyrinth of narrow, whitewalled streets overlooked by the elegant tower of its sixteenth-century church of Nuestra Señora de la Paz. The village is famous for its *embutidos* (sausages) as well as a rousing start to its Semana Santa on Palm Sunday, when an effigy of Judas is tossed on a bonfire.

The Lower Poqueira Gorge

Shortly beyond Carataunas the road swings to the north after passing the turn-off to the Buddhist monastery of Osel Ling (see p.506), and you have your first view of the **Gorge of the Poqueira**, a huge gash into the heights of the Sierra Nevada. Trickling deep in the cleft is the Río Poqueira, which has its source near the peak of Mulhacén. The steep walls of the gorge are terraced and wooded from top to bottom, and dotted with little stone farmhouses. Much of the surrounding country looks barren from a distance, but close up you'll find that it's rich with flowers, woods, springs and streams. A trio of spectacular villages – **Pampaneira**, **Bubión** and **Capileira** – teeter on the steep edge of the gorge among their terraces. They are, justifiably, the most touristy villages in the region and a bit over-prettified, with craft shops and the like, but nonetheless well worth it, as is some walking on the local mule paths. A number of fine **walking routes** are detailed with maps in *Landscapes of Andalucía and the Costa del Sol* (see p.593).

Pampaneira

PAMPANEIRA, the first of the Poqueira villages, is a neat, prosperous place, and a bit less developed and spoilt than its neighbours. Around its main square, Plaza de la Libertad, fronting the sixteenth-century Gothic-Mudéjar church of Santa Cruz are a number of bars, restaurants, *hostales* and craft shops, one of which, just down the hill, is a weaving workshop that specializes in traditional Alpujarreño designs.

5

Monastery of Osel Ling

Open to visitors daily 3–6pm • ☎ 958 343 134 • The monastery is reached by a track on the left – signed "camino forestal" – 1km east of the turning to Soportújar

Above Pampaneira, on the very peak of the western flank of the Poqueira gorge in a stunning location, is the small Tibetan Buddhist **Monastery of Osel Ling** (Place of Clear Light) founded in 1982 by a Tibetan monk on land donated by the communities of Pampaneira and Bubión. The simple stone-built monastery, complete with stupas and stunning **views** across the Alpujarras, welcomes visitors; lectures and courses on Buddhism are held regularly and there are simple cabins dotted around the site for those who wish to retreat. Should you have trouble finding it, ask at Nevadensis (see p.509) or Rustic Blue (see p.510).

Bubión

BUBIÓN, backed for much of the year by snowcapped peaks, lacks the focus of a proper main square and is probably the least attractive of the high villages but – perhaps because of this – it certainly seems the most peaceful. The tranquillity may not last long, though, if the property developers have their way, and already there is quite a bit of building taking place on the lower slopes. There are no sights other than a municipal **museum**, the Casa Alpujarreña (Tues–Fri 11am–2pm, Sat & Sun 11am–2pm & 5–7pm; €1.80), just off Plaza de la Iglesia near the church, which displays aspects of the folklore, daily life and architecture of the Alpujarras in a traditional house. Towards the end of August, Bubión celebrates its **Fiestas Patronales** with music, dance, fireworks and copious imbibing.

Capileira

CAPILEIRA is the highest of the villages of the Lower Poqueira Gorge, and the terminus of Europe's highest road across the heart of the Sierra Nevada from Granada. This is now closed to traffic except for a summer bus service (see p.509). A picturesque and tranquil place, except in high summer when it is deluged with visitors and coach tours, Capileira makes a fine base from which to explore the Poqueira Gorge, or you could even strike out for Trevélez about five hours to the northeast. Capileira's **museum** (Tues–Sun 11.30am–2.30pm; €1), just downhill from the *kiosko*, contains displays of regional dress and handicrafts as well as various bits and pieces belonging to, or produced by, Pedro Alarcón, the nineteenth-century Spanish writer, born in Guadix, who made a trip through the Alpujarras and wrote a (not very good) book about it.

On the Sunday prior to August 5, Capileira embarks on its annual **romería** to the summit of Mulhacén and the *ermita* of the Virgen de las Nieves.

SCALING MULHACÉN – THE EASY WAY

In summer (June–Oct depending on weather) the Parque Nacional authority runs a daily minibus service along the closed road from Capileira to the **Mirador de Trevélez** (with spectacular **views** on clearer days) and on to the **Alto del Chorrillo**, some 20km above the village. The 75-minute trip (with on-board guide) is great to do in itself but why not add in the conquest of the peninsula's highest peak as well?

From the Alto del Chorrillo bus stop it's a roughly 4hr hike to make the ascent and descent of Mulhacén – clearly described in Charles Davis's *34 Alpujarras Walks* (see p.593). The *kiosko* can provide a simple map, but you'd be wise to take the *Editorial Alpina* map along, too (see p.496). Outward-bound morning buses currently leave from Capileira at 8.30am, 11am, 3pm and 5.30pm with the return from Alto del Chorillo at 9.45am, 12.15pm, 4.15pm and 6.45pm (confirm the timetable at the *kiosko* or when booking). Seats on the bus (€10 return) should be booked **in advance** – from the *kiosko* from where the buses depart, or by phone on ☎ 958 763 090 or ☎ 671 564 406. As you'll be in the high mountains you should come prepared for sudden changes in weather conditions and equip yourself accordingly.

5

WALKS IN THE HIGHER POQUEIRA GORGE

Capileira is a handy base for easy day walks in and around the higher part of the **Poqueira Gorge**. For a not-too-strenuous ramble, take the northernmost of the three paths below the village, each of which spans bridges across the river. This one sets off from alongside the Pueblo Alpujarreño villa complex and winds through the huts and terraced fields of the river valley above Capileira, ending after about an hour and a half at a dirt track within sight of a power plant at the head of the valley. From here, you can either retrace your steps or cross the stream over a bridge to follow a dirt track back to the village. In May and June, the fields are laboriously tended by hand, as the steep slopes dictate.

A number of reasonably clear paths or tracks also lead to **Pampaneira** (2–3hr; follow the lower path to the bridge below Capileira), continuing to **Carataunas** (a further 1hr, mostly road) and **Órgiva** (another 45min on an easy path) from where – if you time it right – you can get a bus back.

In the other direction, taking the Sierra Nevada road and then the first major track to the right, by a ruined stone house, you can reach **Pitres** (2hr), **Pórtugos** (30min more) and **Busquístar** (45min more). Going in the same direction but taking the second decent-sized track (by a sign encouraging you to "conserve and respect nature"), **Trevélez** is some five hours away. Rather than doing Mulhacén the "easy way" (see box opposite), more skilled, equipped and ambitious climbers may wish to attempt the whole circuit, starting from Capileira. The summit of **Mulhacén**, the peninsula's highest peak at 3483m, is achievable in a day from here, but is perhaps more sensibly done over two days with an overnight stop at the *Refugio Poqueira*.

Refugio Poqueira At the head of the Poqueira valley ☎ 958 343 349. Marked on the *Editorial Alpina* map (see p.496), this *refugio* is open all year – but you need to book in advance.

The Tahá villages

PITRES is far less picturesque and less developed than the trio of high villages to its west and, like its equally unpolished neighbour, **PÓRTUGOS**, offers more chance of a room during high season. All around, too, spreads some of the best Alpujarran walking country.

Down below the main road are a trio of villages – **MECINA FONDALES**, **FERREIROLA** and **BUSQUÍSTAR** – which along with Pitres and Pórtugos and a couple of smaller settlements formed a league of seven villages known as the **Tahá** (from the Arabic "Tá" meaning obedience) under the Moors. These are among the most unspoilt of the Alpujarra *pueblos* where you can find plenty of examples of typical regional architecture (see box, p.505). Ferreirola and Busquístar – the latter a huddle of grey *launa* roofs – are especially attractive, as is the path between the two, clinging to the north side of the valley of the Río Trevélez. You're out of tourist country here and the villages display their genuine characteristics to better effect.

Trevélez

The cut into the mountain made by the Río Trevélez is similar to the Poqueira, but grander and more austere. **TREVÉLEZ** village stands on a flank at the end of the ravine and its altitude – this is Spain's highest conurbation – makes it a cool place even in high summer when many of the inhabitants continue to don sweaters and coats. It's built in traditional Alpujarran style, with a lower and two upper *barrios* overlooking a grassy, poplar-lined valley where the river starts its long descent. The upper *barrios* (*alto* and *medio*) are the best places to stay; the lower (*barrio bajo*) is more touristy, filled with stalls and shops selling the village's famed *jamones dulces*, crystals, earrings and herbal remedies and attracting streams of visitors, especially at weekends. There are fine walks in the valley and you can swim, too, in a makeshift pool by the bridge. The village is well provided with **places to stay** (see p.511) in both the lower and upper squares; if you are susceptible to low temperatures, outside July and August you may want a place with efficient heating.

5

A WALK AROUND THE TAHÁ

A circuit of the Tahá villages – with many fine stopping places for a picnic – is a good introduction to the Alpujarras, offering opportunities to appreciate both typical architecture and landscape within a compact area. The following walk around the **Southern Tahá** is an easy two-hour hike, although you'll probably want to take the diversion down to the picturesque Trevélez Gorge which adds another half-hour or so; allow three hours for the full circuit. There's little shade on parts of the route, so avoid the afternoon sun in summer. Remember that the second (uphill) part of the walk is the most strenuous.

The route starts in **Pitres**. Follow the narrow path, which begins as a concrete driveway curving behind *Restaurante La Carretera* (on the main road to the right as you enter the village) and descends southwards – veering left – to **Mecinilla**, which is soon visible below; you should be aiming for the left of the church tower. Ignoring turnings, after fifteen minutes or so you emerge in the upper part of the village (Mecilla). Cross the main Pitres–Ferreirola road into the lower village (Mecinilla), following the road past the *Hotel Albergue de Mecina* (with a decent tapas bar and restaurant) and the church on the left. Just after the *Bar El Aljibe* (on the left), go through a gap and take an immediate right. After a drinking fountain (marked "1964"), turn left; continue downwards through the narrow streets, eventually leaving the village beneath a *tinao* (see p.505). Initially following the edge of a ravine, the path continues downwards through orchards (crossing the road once but continuing clearly a little to the right) until reaching the maze of narrow, white streets that make up **Mecina Fondales** – this should take another half-hour or so. Take your time here, partly as it's one of the most peaceful and least spoilt villages, but also as the maze of streets makes it easy to get lost and the vociferous dogs zealously guarding their patches can be off-putting; ask for directions if you can.

From here, for the **shorter route**, take the Camino Real towards Ferreirola, a well-maintained mule track leaving the centre of the village heading east. For the **longer route**, head to the wash area known as "La Fuente" in the village's southeast corner – veer downhill to the left from the road to pass beneath an elaborate *tinao* topped by a vine trellis – to reach the five-basined wash place. From here take the track descending towards the river, bearing left where there's any confusion. After a while the gushing waters become audible below, and the path emerges high above the gorge with the Trevélez bridge visible ahead. Immediately before the bridge, turn left up a small path which crosses the Río Bermejo, before climbing steeply over rocks (ignore the right-hand fork) and continuing uphill to **Ferreirola**.

In Ferreirola, head for the church square; close by is another wash place. Take the path rising north alongside it, which, after another steepish climb, leads to **Atalbéitar**. The path actually emerges on the road below the village from where you turn left to continue the walk, but first you should visit Atalbéitar, another unspoilt hamlet, well off the usual tourist trail. Leaving the village, passing a lifeless oak tree and rubbish container on the right, turn left as the road bends to the right and follow this track in the direction of Pitres (now visible above) past a few houses. The path twice briefly joins the "road" (more of a dirt track); each time, take the path to the left where the road bends right. Leaving the track the second time, just before it joins the "main road", the path first skirts the Bermejo Gorge but then drops sharply to cross the river – some welcome greenery here hides the bridge until you're close to it. Across the river, the path climbs to an *acequia* (irrigation channel); turn right here and continue along the wooded path, past the *Albergue*, till emerging on the main road slightly to the east of **Pitres**.

Trevélez is traditionally the jump-off point for the high **Sierra Nevada** peaks (to which there is a bona fide path) and for treks across the range (on a lower, more conspicuous track). The latter begins down by the bridge on the eastern side of the village. After skirting the bleak Horcajo de Trevélez (3182m), and negotiating the Puerto de Trevélez (2800m), up to which it's a very distinct route, it drops down along the north flank of the Sierra Nevada to Jerez del Marquesado.

Juviles

Heading east from Trevélez, either by vehicle or on foot, you come to **JUVILES**, a great centre of silk production in Moorish times, and today an attractive village straddling

ON HORSEBACK TO LAS SIETE LAGUNAS

In late spring and summer (when the mountain snows have retreated) you might want to try a trip on horseback from Trevélez to **Las Siete Lagunas**, a spectacular collection of mountain lakes in a valley on the upper slopes of the mighty Monte Mulhacén. It's a five-hour journey each way and you spend a night on the mountain at an altitude of 3000m; you'll need your own sleeping bag and it's possible to pitch a tent at Siete Lagunas, although this is not essential. The highpoint of the trip is the sun rising above the Sierra de Gador in the east.

The route can also be done **on foot**, and although the ascent is signed ("Siete Lagunas") in its early stages you'd be much better off following the trekking route clearly described in Jeremy Rabjohns' book *Holiday Walks in the Alpujarras* (see p.593). If you don't plan to sleep out at the lakes you should allow at least ten hours walking time to get up and down the same day.

Rutas de Caballo Virgen de Las Nieves C/Puente s/n, in the barrio alto, Trevélez ☎958 858 601, ☎mobile 619 031 821 (Spanish only). Horseriding trips to Las Siete Lagunas, starting from Trevélez, cost around €140 per person (meals included) for two people (marginally cheaper for larger groups). This is to ride both ways; if you decided to walk down the price would be €70. It is also possible to ride up and descend the same day for €70 but this entails a full day in the saddle. The same company also do shorter trips (a couple of hours or a half-day; €15/hr). Note that a little Spanish would help (although this is not a major problem) and that no insurance cover is provided, so check your policy.

the road. At its centre is an unwhitewashed, peanut-brittle-finish church with a clock that's usually running slightly slow (like most things around here). The villagers don't appear to have taken to their renovated plaza with its jarring ornamental fountains, lamp-standards and trees in brick boxes, and in the evening people still promenade in the road, knowing that there will be no traffic. Juviles also takes its share of the **jamón** business and a large attractive building on the main road as you exit towards Ugíjar houses Jamones de Juviles S.A. (🖳jamonesdejuviles.com), a curing factory for this *alpujarreño* delicacy. Ring the doorbell and you will be invited inside to taste their fine hams, which can be bought whole or in smaller cuts.

Bérchules
BÉRCHULES, a high village of grassy streams and chestnut woods, lies just 6km beyond Juviles, but a greater contrast can hardly be imagined. It is a large, abruptly demarcated settlement, three streets wide, on a sharp slope overlooking yet another canyon.

Cádiar
CÁDIAR, just below Bérchules and the central town – or "navel" as Gerald Brenan termed it – of the Alpujarras, is in fact a fairly humdrum market town whose life centres on its main square, fronted by a sixteenth-century stone church, where a colourful produce market takes place on the 3rd and 18th of every month, sometimes including livestock.

ARRIVAL AND DEPARTURE   THE HIGH ALPUJARRAS

By bus There are daily buses to Capileira from Granada. Buses out of Capileira to Órgiva and Granada currently leave at 7am, 4.45pm and 6.15pm.

INFORMATION

PAMPANEIRA
Nevadensis Plaza de la Libertad (Tues–Sat 10am–2pm & 4–6pm, Sun & Mon 10am–3pm; ☎958 763 127, 🖳nevadensis.com; English spoken). A private, efficiently run information centre for the National Park of the Sierra Nevada. As well as providing information, they sell large-scale topographical maps of the area, walking guidebooks and outdoor clothing. They also organize themed guided walks in all seasons and offer activities and excursions including mountain biking, climbing, canyoning, hiking, and cross-country skiing. You can pick up a list of hostels, village houses, and farmhouses for rent throughout the Alpujarras.

5

BIRDWATCHING IN THE HIGH ALPUJARRAS

This corner of the Alpujarras is an excellent place for **birdwatching**, particularly in late spring. Quiet roads, an abundance of footpaths and dirt tracks make access easy. At this time of the year, most of the species associated with the upland areas of southern Spain can be found in the **Poqueira Gorge** and the Trevélez River Valley. Above the village of **Capileira**, a walk from the end of the metalled road in areas clear of pine woods can turn up sightings of southern grey shrike, rock thrush, black-eared wheatear and the striking black-eyed race of northern wheatear as well as Ortolan bunting. Higher up, in autumn, honey buzzards can occasionally be seen heading for the Straits of Gibraltar and winter quarters in Africa. Higher still, the alpine accentor is to be spotted around mountain huts.

The more wooded parts of the **Trevélez Valley** have booted eagle, buzzard, raven and the short-toed treecreeper, whilst lower down, near **Pitres**, Scops owl and red-necked nightjar can be heard at dusk, and in late summer bee eaters congregate for their migration south. Throughout these areas golden eagle, crag martin, black redstart and rock bunting are also to be seen and, with a little more persistence and patience, the members of the warbler family – Dartford, spectacled, selodius and Bonelli's – can be turned up in suitable habitats.

BUBIÓN

Rustic Blue Barrio La Ermita s/n (Mon–Fri 10am–7pm, Sat 11am–2pm; ☎ 958 763 381, ⓦ rusticblue.com; English spoken). This private information office, at the entrance to the village on the right, is a useful source of local knowledge and stocks walking guides to the area as well as organizing week-long guided treks and horseriding tours. It can also provide information on renting apartments and houses in the village and throughout the Alpujarras.

Horseriding For horseriding trips of one to five days,

the friendly Rancho Rafael Belmonte (☎ 958 763 135, ⓦ ridingandalucia.com), at the bottom of the village near Rustic Blue, or Dallas Love (☎ 958 763 038, ⓦ spain-horse-riding.com), are the places to contact.

CAPILEIRA

Information The national park *kiosko* (daily 10am–2pm & 5–8pm) at the centre of the village, near where the bus drops you, sells newspapers, large-scale walking maps, hands out a free village map and acts as an information office.

ACCOMMODATION

PAMPANEIRA

Hostal Pampaneira C/José Antonio 1 near the bus stop at the entrance to the village ☎ 958 763 002, ⓦ hostalpampaneira.com. Friendly place offering functional en-suite rooms above a popular bar-restaurant. **€42**

Hotel Estrella de las Nieves C/Huertos 21, 200m up the road from the bus stop ☎ 958 763 981, ⓦ estrelladelasnieves.com. The village's luxury option, this is a recently built hotel with surprisingly modern and attractive rooms behind a traditional exterior. All are well equipped and many come with a terrace balcony (worth requesting this) and fine views. There's also a garden pool. Free wi-fi. B&B **€70**

BUBIÓN

La Locana C/Real s/n ☎ 958 763 095, ⓔ lurdes.lalocana@gmail.com. Just behind the museum in the lower village, this is a welcoming small *pensión* with en-suite rooms plus a charming fully equipped studio with kitchenette. Rooms **€35**, studio **€50**

Las Terrazas Plaza del Sol 7 ☎ 958 763 034, ⓦ terrazasalpujarra.com. Comfortable en-suite rooms and apartments with TV, close to the main road at the top of the village. Many rooms have great views. Free wi-fi. Rooms **€35**, apartments **€48**

Los Tinaos C/Parras s/n, downhill from the main road ☎ 958 763 217, ⓦ lostinaos.com. Excellent apartments with heating, garden terrace, kitchen, satellite TV and fine views. **€60**

CAPILEIRA

Cortijo Catifalarga Ctra. de Sierra Nevada s/n ☎ 958 343 357, ⓦ catifalarga.com. Some 500m beyond the *Ruta de Las Nieves* hotel (see p.511) and signed up a track on the left, this is a delightful hideaway with charming rooms inside a traditional *alpujarreño cortijo*, along with fabulous views and a pool. Also has its own bar-restaurant. **€65**

Cortijo Prado Toro 3km up the mountain from Cortijo Catifalarga ☎ 958 343 240, ⓦ pradotoro.es. For those seeking even more solitude. At an altitude of 1500m, this delightful stone-built apart-hotel has beamed rooms with tiled floors and stylishly rustic furnishings. There's also a great pool and garden plus spectacular views. **€90**

El Cascapeñas Ctra. de la Sierra 5 ☎ 958 763 011, ⓦ elcascapeñas.com. Good-value en-suite rooms, split between a *hostal* and hotel, near the bus stop. All have TV. **€45**

Finca Los Llanos Uphill from the bus halt ☎ 958 763 071, ⓦ hotelfincalosllanos.com. Rather luxurious possibility with apartment-style rooms with kitchenettes and terraces. There's also a pool and a good restaurant. B&B **€75**

Hostal Atalaya To the right as you enter the village ☎ 958 763 025, ⓦ hostalatalaya.com. A nice little place with en-suite rooms and terrific views from those at the front (costing a few euros more). **€30**

Mesón-Hostal Poqueira Near the bus stop ☎ 958 763 048, ⓦ hotelpoqueira.com. En-suite heated rooms, some with terraces and views, at this welcoming option; there's also a pool and good restaurant with a *menú* for around €10. It also has some attractive apartments sleeping up to four for longer stays, and they are building a new hotel in the centre of the village, to be completed in 2012. *Hostal* **€40**, hotel **€60**, apartments **€50**

Ruta de Las Nieves Ctra. de Sierra Nevada s/n ☎ 958 763 106. Further up the mountain road beyond *Finca Los Llanos*, this is a pleasant stone-built hotel with well-equipped attractive rooms and studios (with kitchenette) many with terrace balconies and fine views. There's also a good heating system which you'll be glad of outside high summer and the hotel has its own bar-restaurant. Rooms **€42**, studios **€48**

Villa Turística de Bubión Barrio Alto s/n, above the main road ☎ 902 006 490, ⓦ villasdeandalucia.com. Recently refurbished, the village's four-star luxury option consists of chalet-style villas in a rustic setting. Classically furnished interiors come with terrace balconies and fine views and there's also a restaurant and pool. **€85**

PITRES

Balcón de Pitres Ctra. Orgiva–Ugíjar km.51 ☎ 958 766 111, ⓦ balcondepitres.com. Pitres's campsite occupies a stunning position on the village's western edge, and has plenty of shade, swimming pool, restaurant and great views. Closed Nov–Feb. **€5** per person, **€5** per tent, **€4.50** per vehicle.

Hotel San Roque C/Cruz 1 on the main road at the east side of the village ☎ 958 857 528. Currently the only en-suite room option in the village, offering rooms with TV and (on the south side) views. B&B **€58**

Refugio Los Albergues C/Cruz s/n ☎ 958 343 176, ⓦ losalbergues.org. Near the *Hotel San Roque* and down a track on the opposite side of the road, this is an old Civil War hostel rustically refurbished to provide dormitory beds; there is also one double room sharing bath. Facilities include a communal kitchen, outdoor toilets, and a library but no TV – and mobiles must be turned off inside the premises. It's signposted from the main road, but if you get lost ask for "Casa Barbara (Hauck)", the name of the friendly German who runs it. Dorm **€10**, double **€30**

THE TAHÁ

Casa Sonia C/San Francisco 5, Busquístar ☎ 958 857 503, ⓦ casasoniaenbusquistar.com. This charming small hotel in the heart of the village near the church offers elegant en-suite a/c rooms, some with great views. Breakfast can also be provided (€5 extra). **€65**

Hotel Albergue de Mecina C/La Fuente 2, Mecina Fondales ☎ 958 766 241, ⓦ hoteldemecina.com. Very good two-star hotel with attractive rooms, many with terrace balcony and views. Has its own bar-restaurant and there's also an excellent garden pool. Information is also available on hiring horses and mountain bikes. Fifteen-percent discount for *Rough Guide* readers with this guide. B&B **€88**

L'Atelier C/Alberca 21, Mecina Fondales ☎ 958 857 501, ⓦ ivu.org/atelier. The French vegetarian restaurant (see p.513) lets a few comfortable en-suite rooms above its restaurant in the heart of the village. It also acts as agent for some delightful apartments and *casas rurales* close to the village, most with views, gardens and pool (two-night minimum). B&B **€50**, apartments **€65**, houses **€80**

★ **Sierra y Mar** C/Albaycin 3, Ferreirola ☎ 958 766 171, ⓦ sierraymar.com. Wonderful Scandinavian-run rural hotel in leafy surroundings with cosy rooms, most with fine views. The owners – enthusiastic walkers – will advise on routes in the area and guests also have use of a kitchen to prepare their own food. To get here, take the road to the right of the fountain out of the main plaza. B&B **€62**

TREVÉLEZ

Alcazaba de Busquístar Some 5km south along the A4132 road which descends along the east side of the ravine to meet the A4130 ☎ 958 858 687, ⓦ hotel alcazaba.com. One of the most attractive places to stay in this area is this tranquil four-star hideaway. The luxurious apart-hotel has traditionally styled Alpujarran dwellings (no. 411 is recommended) with *lauña* roofs and fine views, while facilities include bar, restaurant and pool; horseriding, mountain biking, trekking and fishing are some of the activities on offer. Heating comes from a *chimenea* (wood-burning stove) that you feed yourself. **€104**

Camping Trevélez Ctra. Trevélez–Órgiva km1 ☎ 958 858 735, ⓦ campingtrevelez.net. The village's campsite has decent facilities and good shade. Although officially open all year, you can expect arctic conditions in midwinter. It also rents out some heated cabins. **€4.50** per person, **€4** per tent, **€4** per vehicle, cabins **€30**

Hostal Fernando C/Pista del Barrio Medio s/n ☎ 958 858 565. A welcoming option in the *barrio medio*, offering en-suite rooms with great terrace views (from some); it also lets out a couple of excellent-value apartments with kitchen and terrace. All come with heating and there's easy parking. Rooms **€30**, apartments **€35**

Hostal Mulhacén Ctra. Ugíjar s/n ☎ 958 858 587. In the lower *barrio* and 100m along the Juviles road from Plaza Francisco Abellán, this is another good possibility for rooms with and without bath, and offers great views down the valley. **€45**

5

★ **Hotel La Fragua I & II** C/San Antonio 4 ☎958 858 626, ⊕hotellafragua.com. Beside the Ayuntamiento in the *barrio alto*, this is probably the most attractive of the village places with pine-furnished, en-suite, heated rooms with fine views. Their more recently built second hotel at the end of the same street is also good. As this is a popular place with walking places, it may be worth ringing ahead. Hotel I €48, hotel II €58

Hotel Pepe Alvarez Plaza Francisco Abellán 16 ☎958 858 503. Decent hotel on the lower *barrio*'s main square with heated en-suite rooms with TV, some with views. €38

JUVILES

Pensión Tino C/Altillo Bajo 38 ☎958 769 174. At the western end of the main road running through the village, this small *hostal* offers clean and tidy en-suite rooms above a bar-restaurant. Some rooms have views and there's a pretty, flower-filled roof terrace for taking breakfast. The restaurant is also reliable, and has a *menú* for under €10. €33

BÉRCHULES

Alojamiento Rural La Tahoma C/Baja de la Iglesia s/n ☎958 76 90 51, ☎ mobile 628 281 882. Excellent-value apartments with kitchen, *salon* and TV; one-night stays are possible. €35

El Mirador de Bérchules Plaza de Zapata 1, in the barrio alto ☎958 767 690, ⊕miradordeberchules.com. Welcoming place with fully equipped studios and apartments with terraces and views. It also has its own good restaurant (with economical *menú*), tapas bar and pool. €60

Hotel Bérchules Ctra de Bérchules 20 ☎958 852 530, ⊕hotelberchules.com. On the main road into the village from Juviles, this is an agreeable two-star hotel with comfortable rooms above its own restaurant. There's also a pool. €52

CÁDIAR

Alquería de Morayma Ctra. A-348 km50 ☎958 343 303, ⊕alqueriamorayma.com. Upmarket apart-hotel in a converted Alpujarran *cortijo* in 86 acres of farmland; there are charming and traditionally styled rustic rooms and apartments (almost the same price), many with terraces, plus a pool and good restaurant (open to visitors). It offers guests mountain biking and horseriding and there are plenty of hiking trails. €65

EATING AND DRINKING

PAMPANEIRA

Bar Belezmín Plaza de la Libertad 11. On the leafy main square, this is a good bet for well-prepared regional dishes. They specialize in *carnes asados* (charcoal-grilled meats) and there's a pleasant terrace on the square. Daily 10am–11pm.

★ **Bodega La Moralea** C/Veronica 12, down a narrow street off Plaza de la Libertad. Wonderfully atmospheric and entertaining little bar-shop selling fine *alpujarreño jamones* (from Juviles and Pampaneira) which hang from the ceiling. You'll usually get a sample cut from one of these as a free *tapa* when you order a drink. Also sells the oils, wines and cheeses of the region as well as other local products. Daily 10am–10pm.

Casa Diego Plaza de la Libertad 15. An attractive restaurant with a rustically decorated interior dining room and a terrace. House specials include *chuletón ibérico* (black pig chop) and *croquetas caseras* (croquettes); there's also a *menú* for €9. Daily noon–4pm & 8–11pm.

Casa Julio Avda. de la Alpujarra 9, up some steps near the bus halt. This is perhaps the village's best restaurant with a delightful terrace. The kitchen produces hearty mountain food such as *choto en salsa de almendras* (kid in almond sauce) and *patatas a lo pobre* (potatoes with garlic) and a selection of salads. There's also an €8 *menú*. Daily 1–4.30pm & 8–11pm.

Hostal Pampaneira C/José Antonio 1 near the bus stop at the entrance to the village ☎958 763 002, ⊕hostalpampaneira.com. The *hostal*'s bar-restaurant is a good place for breakfast and, later in the day, full meals. They offer many *alpujarreño* dishes such as *potaje de garbanzos* (chick-pea soup) and *carnes asados* (charcoal-grilled meats) and have a *menú* for €9. Daily 9am–11pm.

BUBIÓN

Estacion 4 C/Estación 4. In the heart of the village, this is perhaps the most ambitious of the eating options. The dining room is bright and appealing, and the kitchen produces a variety of Mediterranean-influenced dishes including pasta and risottos as well as fish and meat courses. Vegetarian possibilities include couscous, hummus and salads. Main dishes €8–15. Tues–Fri 5–11pm, Sat 1–11pm.

La Artesa C/Carretera 2, on the main road above the village. This reliable village restaurant serves regional dishes such as *migas con tropezones* (fried breadcrumbs with meat) and a range of salads. Also a weekday *menú* for €8.50. Tues–Sat 1–4pm & 8–11pm, Sun 1–4pm.

Teide C/Carretera s/n. Opposite *La Artesa* on the main road, and probably the better of the two restaurants; the kitchen turns out hearty soups as well as a variety of *alpujarreño* specialities – *pierna de cordero al horno* (baked lamb) is a speciality – and there's a good value *menú* for €9. Sit in the leafy garden terrace on warmer days. Wed–Mon 1.30–4pm & 8–10.30pm.

CAPILEIRA

Bodega La Alacena Callejón de las Campanas s/n. An atmospheric bar-shop that's a popular place to sample the wonderful *jamón* and cheese of the Alpujarras. It also offers excellent *salchichón* (sausage) and salads while the shop sells its own *miel* (honey) and locally produced confectionery and wines.

Casa Ibero C/Parra 1, near the museum. This restaurant offers a fusion of Moroccan, Alpujarreña and Indian cuisines. Lamb couscous is a house speciality, and there are some interesting starters and desserts. Plenty of vegetarian options too, including curries and vegetarian rice dishes, and a *menú* for €18. Main dishes €11–16. Thurs–Sat, Mon & Tues 1–4pm & 8–11pm, Sun 1–4pm.

La Casa de Paco y Pilar Ctra. de la Sierra 16. Uphill from the *Finca Los Llanos*, serving well-prepared mountain dishes such as *choto al ajillo* (roast kid with garlic) and *migas* (fried breadcrumbs), along with some vegetarian dishes; it's also a good place to sample the local *jamones* and cheeses. There's a nice garden terrace and they offer a daily €10 *menú*. Daily: April–Sept 1.30–3.30pm & 8–11.30pm; Oct–March 1.30–3.30pm.

Mesón Rural Panjuila Ctra. de la Sierra 24, a little way uphill from the bus halt on the right. Serving *alpujarreña* cuisine in a rustic setting, with specialities including *potaje gitano* (mountain soup) and *cazuela de arroz* (baked rice and meat). There's also a €9.50 *menú*. Daily 1–4pm & 8–11pm.

Restaurante El Tilo Plaza Calvario 1. In the lower village, this is a very good stop for *platos combinados* or watching-the-world-go-by drinks and tapas on its tranquil terrace shaded by a lime tree. Tapas specialities include the *jamones* and cheeses of the region. Daily 10am–11pm.

PITRES

Hotel San Roque C/Cruz 1 on the main road at the east side of the village ☎ 958 857 528. The hotel restaurant is the best place to eat in town. Other than this, you have a choice between the bars on the village's main square, Plaza de la Alpujarra, and the campsite.

THE TAHÁ VILLAGES

Bar Paco C/Carretera s/n, Busquístar. Just below the main road as you pass through the village, this is a reliable option for tapas and *raciones* and serves a weekday *menú* for around €8. Daily 9am–11pm.

FaRe C/Soledad s/n, Ferreirola. *Tetería-cafetería* (Arabic tearoom) with a beamed interior and a terrace, offering a wide range of teas, home-baked confectionery, wines and cheeses. It's at the bottom of the village. Thurs–Sun 10am–11pm.

★ **L'Atelier** C/Alberca 21, Mecina Fondales. Mecina's best place for food: a French-run restaurant specializing in vegetarian/vegan cuisine with a Moroccan slant, located in the old village bakery. House specialities include couscous and a *gratinado andaluz* made with red lentils, and the arab-style puddings are delicious. Booking is advised at weekends. Mon, Wed & Thurs 1–4pm, Fri–Sun 1–4pm & 7–11pm.

TREVÉLEZ

Casa Julio Plaza de la Iglesia s/n in the barrio medio. Popular *barrio* bar-restaurant serving *carnes a la brasa* (charcoal-grilled meats) as well as pizzas. They also have tapas in the bar and an outdoor terrace. Tues–Sun 8.30am–5pm & 7pm–midnight.

Jamones Jiménez C/Carretera 5, 50m before the bridge in the barrio bajo. A good place to buy and try *jamón* and many other local products such as *salchichón* (salami) and *morcilla* (blood sausage). Mon–Sat 9am–2pm & 5–9pm.

Mesón del Jamón C/Carcel s/n. Head here to sample Trevélez's celebrated *jamónes* – the restaurant also serves up regional specials such as *choto al ajillo* (kid) and *trucha* (trout). The panoramic terrace has great views. Daily 10am–11pm.

Mesón Haraicel C/Real s/n, just above the main square in the lower barrio. Good-value place, offering economical *platos combinados* and pasta dishes – plus tapas and *raciones* in its bar. Daily: April–Oct 8.30am–midnight; Nov–March 8.30am–7pm.

Mesón Joaquín At the entrance to the village in the barrio bajo. One of the village's *jamón* specialists, its ceiling hung with hams. Regional specialities include *habas con jamón* (beans with ham), *plato alpujarreño* (mixed fry-up with blood pudding, *jamón* and egg), *trucha con jamón* (river trout) and hearty mountain soups. There's also a €9 *menú*. Daily 9am–7pm.

★ **Mesón La Fragua** C/San Antonio s/n. The hotel restaurant is Trevélez's best place to eat, serving well-prepared dishes in a rustic two-storey bar-restaurant. *Venao en salsa* (venison) and *pollo a la gitana* (chicken) feature among a wide range of specialities, and there is a range of salads and vegetarian dishes, too. Daily 1–4pm & 8–11.30pm.

Piedra Ventana Ctra. Bérchules s/n. This compact restaurant, a little way out along the Ugíjar road, is a good place for traditional *alpujarreño* cuisine. The main dining room has great views over the ravine and the house specialities include *trucha con jamón* (trout), *venao* (venison) and chorizo. There's a *menú* for €8. Daily 9am–10pm.

JUVILES

Bar Fernández C/Carretera 23. On the main street close to the square, this atmospheric bar-restaurant does inexpensive meals and will be delighted to serve you with a *tapa* of the local *jamón*. Daily 9am–10pm.

CÁDIAR

Alquería de Morayma Ctra. A-348 km50 ☎ 958 343 303, ⊕ alqueriamorayma.com. The *Morayma*'s own organic farm and vineyard, the bodega of which is open to visitors, also supplies its restaurant and provides its virgin olive oil and bottled wine. The restaurant cooks a range of *alpujarreño* specialities including *estofados* (stews), *arroces* (rice dishes) and *choto al ajillo* (roast kid). Daily 1–4pm & 8–11pm.

5

The eastern and southern Alpujarras

Cádiar and Bérchules mark the end of the western Alpujarras, and a striking change in the landscape; the dramatic, severe, but relatively green terrain of the Guadalfeo and Cádiar valleys gives way to open, rolling and much more arid land. The villages of the **eastern Alpujarras** display many of the characteristics of those to the west but as a rule they are poorer and less visited by tourists. There are attractive places nonetheless, among them **Yegen**, which Gerald Brenan wrote about, the market centre of **Ugíjar**, plus a remarkable museum at **Jorairátar**.

Yegen

YEGEN, some 7km northeast of Cádiar, is where author and historian **Gerald Brenan** lived during his ten or so years of Alpujarran residence (see box below). Brenan connections aside, Yegen is an appealing place, with its two distinct quarters (*alto* and *bajo*), cobbled paths and cold-water springs.

Mecina Bombarón

From Yegen there's an easy 4km **walk** up to the hamlet of **MECINA BOMBARÓN**, along one of the old cobbled mule paths. This starts out from the old bridge across the gorge and is easy to follow from there, with Mecina clearly visible on the hill above. Mecina is also reachable by road.

Válor

Six kilometres beyond Yegen, and sited between deep ravines, **VÁLOR** is a charming and sleepy hamlet, a fact which belies its history as a centre of stubborn resistance in the sixteenth-century revolt by the Moors against the "insults and outrages" of the Christian ascendancy. These events are "celebrated" in the annual **Fiestas Patronales** in mid-September when the whole story – including battles between Moors and Christians – is colourfully re-enacted in the main square.

Ugíjar

UGÍJAR, 6km beyond Válor, is the largest community in these parts, and an unassuming, quiet market town. There are easy and enjoyable walks to the nearest villages – up the valley to Mecina-al-Fahar, for example – and a handful of **places to stay**.

GERALD BRENAN: SOUTH FROM GRANADA

Gerald Brenan's autobiography of his years in the Alpujarras, **South from Granada**, is the best account of rural life in Spain between the wars, and also describes the visits made here by Bloomsburyites Virginia Woolf, Bertrand Russell and the arch-complainer Lytton Strachey who attributed his Iberian ailments to "crude olive oil, greasy tortillas and a surfeit of *bacalao*" and proclaimed when he got home that "Spain is absolute death". Disillusioned with the strictures of middle-class life in England after World War I, Brenan rented a house in Yegen and shipped out a library of two thousand books, from which he was to spend the next eight years educating himself. Since only a handful of the inhabitants of Yegen were literate, the reserved, lanky stranger was regarded as an exotic curiosity by the villagers. With glazed windows in only two dwellings, no doctor, electricity or telephone and no road to the outside world, Yegen's rustic isolation together with its characters, traditions, superstitions and celebrations provided the raw material for his great work.

Towards the end of his stay he became involved in a number of scandals and, after getting a young teenage girl pregnant, moved to the hills of Churriana behind Torremolinos, with his wife, US writer and poet Gamel Woolsey. Here he died in 1987, a writer better known and respected in Spain (he made an important study of St John of the Cross) than in his native England. The contribution he made to informing the world about the Alpujarras, its history and culture, is recorded on a plaque fixed to his former home, now the **Casa de Brenan**, just along from the fountain in Yegen's main square.

Jorairátar

With your own transport you may wish to detour 10km to **JORAIRÁTAR** to take in the remarkable **Museo Histórico de las Alpujarras,** a labour of love devoted to the disappearing traditions and way of life of the people of the Alpujarras.

Museo Histórico de las Alpujarras

Daily 1–8pm • Free, but a contribution to the museum's upkeep will be much appreciated • ☎ 958 853 114 (Spanish only) • To get to Jorairátar from Ugíjar, take the A348 in the direction of Cádiar, turning off (after 5km) along the GR5202

Occupying two floors of an enormous old building, the **Museo Histórico de las Alpujarras** is spread over numerous rooms. Highlights include a reconstructed kitchen kitted out as it would have been a century ago, and a schoolroom complete with period desks. You can also see firewater stills, musical instruments, books and maps, plus a host of other fascinating paraphernalia. When you arrive in the village, a charming place in itself, make for the *barrio alto* (upper village) and ask for the house of the museum's guardian, Señora Angelita Martínez, and her husband Juan Soría who will give you an enthusiastic tour (a little Spanish would be an advantage).

ARRIVAL AND DEPARTURE

THE EASTERN AND SOUTHERN ALPUJARRAS

UGÍJAR

By bus Buses, which stop in Ugíjar's central plaza, run onwards to Almería (3hr) or back to Granada (3hr 30min).
By car Slightly west of Ugíjar, a road heads north to Laroles

to join the A337, which climbs over Puerto de la Ragua pass (see p.526), descending beyond to the spectacular castle of La Calahorra (see p.524) on the northern slopes of the Sierra Nevada.

ACCOMMODATION

YEGEN

Alojamientos Las Eras C/Carretera 39 ☎ 958 851 191, ⓦ alojamientoslaseras.com. A reliable option for modern, fully equipped apartments with TV and terrace. They also have a pool. **€50**

Bar La Fuente C/Real 46, opposite the fountain in the square ☎ 958 851 067, ⓦ pensionlafuente.com. The *barrio alto*'s main bar rents out en-suite rooms and apartments and serves tapas and *raciones* in a room dotted with Brenan memorabilia and photos. The proprietor can provide a leaflet of walks (in Spanish; one route is named after Brenan) around the village. **€40**

El Rincón de Yegen La Carretera s/n, on the main road heading east out of the village ☎ 958 851 270, ⓦ elrincondeyegen.com. Decent two-star hotel with heated rooms with TV and views (some) plus a pool. Also rents out rooms and apartments in the village (prices on request). **€55**

El Tinao La Carretera s/n ☎ 958 851 212, ⓔ eltinao yegen@hotmail.com. Bright and airy en-suite rooms are offered at this bar-*hostal* on the main road through; they also let fully equipped village houses (prices on request) and serve meals. **€30**

MECINA BOMBARÓN

Casas Blancas C/Casas Blancas 24 ☎ 958 851 151, ⓦ casasblancas.org. Mecina's rural hotel is a pleasant place to stay, where studio rooms come with TV, kitchenette and sun balcony. The new *Apartamentos Altas Vistas* next door is owned by a branch of the same family with similar prices and is also good. **€70**

VÁLOR

Balcón de Válor C/Torrecilla s/n, on the main road through ☎ 958 851 821, ⓦ balcondevalor.com. On the village's eastern edge, this option has attractive fully equipped apartments with terraces and sharing a pool. **€75**

Hostal Las Perdices C/Torrecilla s/n, on the main road through ☎ 958 851 821. Comfortable *hostal* offering en-suite rooms with TV. **€52**

UGÍJAR

Hostal-Restaurante Vidaña Ctra. de Almería s/n ☎ 958 767 010. Decent *hostal* with en-suite, heated rooms with TV above a restaurant with a good-value *menú* for €8.50. It's on the Almería road out of town. **€32**

EATING AND DRINKING

YEGEN

Bar Muñoz C/Iglesia s/n. This is one bar worth finding your way to in the village's *barrio bajo* (lower quarter) where on cooler nights locals gather around the fireplace to enjoy *jamón serrano* cured on the premises by the

proprietor; if someone decides to unhook one of the guitars from the wall, sessions of singing can continue late into the night. Daily 9am–11pm.
El Rincón de Yegen La Carretera s/n, on the main road heading east out of the village ☎ 958 851 270,

5

ⓦ elrincondeyegen.com. The hotel's very good restaurant produces a selection of regional dishes. There's also a weekday *menú* for €10. Main dishes €8–18. Wed–Sun 12.30–4pm & 8–10.30pm.

MECINA BOMBARÓN

Casa Joaquín Avda. José Antonio Bravo 66, just below the church. Popular village bar-restaurant serving a range of tapas and *raciones* in the bar and good hearty dishes in its restaurant – *rabo de toro* (stewed bull's tail) and *costillas* (spare ribs) are house specials; there's also a *menú* for under €10. Daily 8.30am–11.30pm.

VÁLOR

Restaurante Aben Humeya C/Bolos s/n. Popular bar-restaurant just off the main street. The dishes – *chotillo al ajillo* (kid with garlic) is a special – are well prepared and there's a *menú* for €10. Daily 1–4pm & 8–11pm.

UGÍJAR

Bar La Peña Ctra. Granada s/n. One of the town's two best tapas bars, on the corner of the main road by the church. You can choose from a good range of tapas here, or opt for the bargain €9 *menú* (their *sopa de picadillo* is delicious). A huge *tapa* comes with every drink. Daily 9am–11pm.

Bar Progreso Plaza Iglesia s/n. Just a few metres away from *Bar La Peña* up a side street, this is another excellent bar with a good tapas range: try the locally cured *jamón* or the *costillas* (spare ribs). Daily 9.30am–11.30pm.

Pepe Aguado Trasera de la Iglesia 8, behind the church. The town's best place to eat, specializing in *carnes a la brasa* (charcoal-grilled meats). Specials include *perdices en escabeche* (partridge) and *rabo de buey* (stewed oxtail). They also serve tapas and *raciones* in their cosy bar. Daily noon–4pm & 7.30pm–midnight.

The Almerian Alpujarras

From Ugíjar the A348 toils eastwards and, once across the Río de Alcolea, enters the province of Almería where the starker – but no less impressive terrain – gradually takes on the harsh and desiccated character of the deserts that lie ahead. There are still the odd oases to be found, however, in **Láujar de Andarax** and the spa of **Alhama de Almería** and, just beyond the latter, a remarkable prehistoric site, **Los Millares**.

Laroles

If you're in no hurry to reach Láujar, a scenic detour along the A337 and AL5402 through the hamlets of **LAROLES** and Bayárcal offers a chance to see some of the National Park's magnificent upland terrain, and the possibility of overnighting at two attractive bases for exploring an area rich in trekking possibilities and on the route of the E4 (marked GR7 on Spanish maps) pan-European footpath.

Bayárcal

Spme 5km beyond Laroles, beyond the hamlet of **BAYÁRCAL**, is the mountain hotel of *Posada de los Arrieros* (see p.519) built on the site of an old muleteers' inn on this important commercial route between the Alpujarras and Almería. There are spectacular **walks** from the hotel, including one to the Puerto de la Ragua, which at 2000m is Andalucía's highest pass. Information on this and other walks in the area is available from the hotel's friendly English-speaking staff, and horseriding, mountain biking and archery are also on offer. The cool temperatures at this altitude (even in Aug) make walking in this area pleasant all summer, although you still need to protect yourself from the sun.

Láujar de Andarax

It was at **LÁUJAR DE ANDARAX**, 16km east of Ugíjar, at the source of the Río Andarax, that Boabdil, the deposed Moorish king of Granada, settled in 1492 and from where he intended to rule the Alpujarras fiefdom granted to him by the Catholic monarchs. But Christian paranoia about a Moorish resurgence led them to tear up the treaty and within a year Boabdil had been shipped off to Africa, an event which set in train a series of uprisings by the Alpujarran Moors, ending in their suppression and eventual deportation, to be replaced by Christian settlers from the north.

The **Río Andarax's source**, at the town's eastern edge – signposted "*nacimiento*" – is a shady spot, with a restaurant, the *Mesón El Nacimiento*, serving hearty *platos*

5

combinados at lunchtime, beside the falls. If you're here on a Sunday you'll find the falls a hive of activity as families pour in to make barbecues under the trees. In Láujar's centre the **Plaza Mayor** has a seventeenth-century four-spouted fountain – one of many dotted around the town – and an elegant late eighteenth-century **Ayuntamiento**, where you can pick up a street map. This will enable you to find four crumbling seventeenth-century **palacios** as well as an impressive Mudéjar-style seventeenth-century church of **La Encarnación**, which contains a sculpture of the Virgin by Alonso Cano.

Láujar is the centre of a burgeoning **wine industry**, and although smoother and slightly less potent than the *costa* wines further west, the brew is just as palatable. The **Cooperativo Valle de Láujar**, on the main road 2km west of town, was founded in 1992 and is beginning to commercialize these wines both within Spain and abroad. At their small shop (Mon–Sat 8.30am–noon & 3.30–7.30pm) you can taste and buy their four good reds as well as whites, a rosé and a *cava*, plus cheeses and other local produce.

East of Láujar de Andarax

The road east of Láujar de Andarax passes a series of unremarkable villages, surrounded by slopes covered with vine trellises, little changed since Moorish times and little visited today. Among them is **FONDÓN**, whose church tower was the minaret of the former mosque, and **PADULES**, 11km beyond Láujar, where the municipal swimming pool might prove a greater lure in the baking heat of high summer. The prettier village of **CANJÁYAR**, 4km further on, also has a swimming pool, and becomes a centre of frenetic activity during the autumn *vendimia*, when the grapes are gathered in. The road then trails the course of the Andarax river valley through an arid and eroded landscape, skirting the Sierra de Gádor before climbing slightly to **ALHAMA DE ALMERÍA**, 16km further on. This is an appealing spa town, dating back to Moorish times, and most of its visitors are here to take the waters – hence the rather incongruous three-star hotel sited on the location of the original baths.

Los Millares: the Chalcolithic settlement

Wed–Sun 10am–2pm, but call to confirm • Free • ☎ 950 011 131 or mobile ☎ 677 903 404 • Although Alhama de Almería is served by bus from Almería it's worth noting that there is no public transport from either place to the Los Millares site, although the 5km distance is just about walkable (with fierce temperatures in summer) at a push, or you could take a taxi (about €8 one-way); for more details on the limited transport to Los Millares, contact the Alhama Turismo (see p.519)

Leaving Alhama, after 5km the Almería road passes a signed turn-off leading to the remarkable pre-Bronze Age settlement of **LOS MILLARES**, one of the most important of its kind in Europe. Situated on a low triangular spur between two dried-up riverbeds, it was exposed in 1891 during the construction of the Almería-to-Linares railway line that passes below the site today. Two Belgian mining engineers, Henri and Louis Siret, who were also enthusiastic amateur archeologists, took on the excavations at the beginning of the twentieth century, funding them from their modest salaries. What they revealed is a Chalcolithic or Copper Age (the period between the Neolithic and the Bronze Age) **fortified settlement**. It dates from c.2700 BC and was occupied until c.1800 BC, when both stone and copper but not bronze were used for weapons and tools. Whilst it is not entirely clear who the occupants were – possibly emigrants from the eastern Mediterranean or perhaps an indigenous group – the settlement they left behind is exceptional. Spread over twelve acres it consists of four sets of defensive walls, with a number of advanced fortlets beyond these, as well as an extraordinary cemetery with over one hundred **tombs** which are without equal in Europe.

Looking over the barren landscape that surrounds the site today, it's hard to believe that five thousand years ago this was a fertile area of pine and ilex forests, inhabited by deer and wild boar. The nearby Río Andarax was then navigable and the inhabitants used it to bring copper down from mines in the Sierra de Gádor to the west. The population – perhaps as many as two thousand – not only hunted for their food but bred sheep, goats and pigs, grew vegetables and cereals, made cheese and were highly

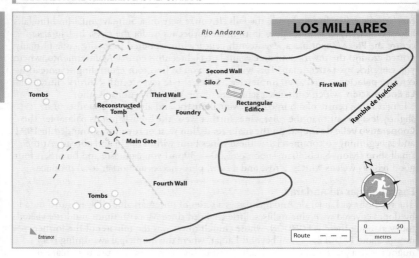

Rio Andarax

LOS MILLARES

Second Wall
Silo
First Wall

Tombs
Third Wall
Reconstructed Tomb
Rectangular Edifice
Foundry

Rambla de Huéchar

Main Gate

N

Fourth Wall

Tombs

Entrance

Route — — —

0   50
metres

skilled in the manufacture of pottery, basketwork and jewellery, as is evidenced by the finds now in museums in Almería (see p.532) and Madrid.

Excavations are continuing at the site and information boards (in English and Spanish) have been set up at various points; a map on the wall of the entrance office shows **walking routes** outside the site which take in dolmens and ten forts related to the Los Millares settlement discovered in the surrounding hills. The most impressive of the forts (with fine **views** over the Los Millares site), Fortin Uno (Fort One), lies up a track on the opposite side of the road from the site entrance and the site guardians will advise how to reach it.

The site

A tour of the **site** begins with the outermost of four exterior **walls** which were constructed successively further west as the settlement expanded across the escarpment in the latter part of the third millennium BC. An impressive structure, 4m high when built, the fourth (and last) wall was lined with outward-facing bastions or towers, and at 310m is the longest wall known in Europe from this period. Its layout bears a striking similarity to a wall of the same epoch at the early Cycladic site of Halandriani on the island of Síros in Greece, suggesting a possible link with the Aegean. The **main gate**, towards the centre, is flanked by watchtowers, beyond which a walled passage gave access to the settlement.

A little way north of here are the remains of a primitive **aqueduct** which cut through the wall to carry water from a spring near to the village of Alhama into the populated area. Fifty metres east of the main gate remains can be seen from the third wall. Close to here also are the remains of a number of circular **huts** – one of which has been partially reconstructed – in which the inhabitants of the site lived. Six to seven metres in diameter with pounded earth floors, they consisted of cavity stone walls filled with mud and pebbles, with a roof probably made from straw. Inside the huts the excavators found remains of hearths as well as grindstones, pottery and a variety of utensils.

Moving east again, beyond the second wall lies a primitive **foundry** where the copper ore was crudely smelted by means of fire and bellows before being hammered into the required form. Moulds arrived only in the later Bronze Age. Further north, on the line of the wall, lies a **silo** used for storing grain. Behind this wall are the foundations of a **rectangular edifice**, 32m in length, whose function is as yet unknown. The settlement at first appeared to lack a hierarchical social structure due to the overall similarity of the huts, but after the discovery of this building – much larger than the rest – some have speculated that it could have served as a form of council chamber or even a royal palace.

The remains of the first wall, enclosing what may have been the citadel, lie further back still and excavations here recovered many of the patterned, bell-shaped vases to be seen in the museum at Almería.

The necropolis

Retracing your steps to the outer (or fourth) wall will bring you to one of the reconstructed tombs, part of the ancient **necropolis**. This "beehive" tomb, originally sited outside the third wall, was encompassed by the later fourth wall. It is one of more than a hundred tombs (the rest lie west of this wall), and the typical structure of a low corridor punctuated by perforated slate slabs leading to a domed burial chamber bears a striking resemblance to tholos tombs of a similar date from the Aegean, particularly southern Crete. It has been suggested that early Cretans (for whom the bull was religiously significant) may have found their way here and that the importance of bulls and bullfighting on the Iberian peninsula may owe something to this link. Present academic thinking, however, tends towards the idea that the civilization here was of local origin.

More tombs, most in a collapsed state, in which clan members were buried together with their possessions such as arms, tools and what appear to be ceramic idols (suggesting the existence of a cult), lie beyond the outer wall. Originally, and again as in the Aegean, the tombs were covered with an earth mound or tumulus. Resist climbing over them; many are in a fragile condition and it's hard to overstate the importance of this site for posterity.

ARRIVAL AND INFORMATION   THE ALMERIAN ALPUJARRAS

LÁUJAR DE ANDARAX

The eastern panhandle of the Sierra Nevada National Park lies 15km to the north of Láujar; you'll find a **National Park information office**, the Centro de Visitantes (Wed–Sun: April–Sept 10am–2pm & 6–8pm; Oct–March 10am–2pm & 4–6pm) on the edge of the town as you come in from Ugíjar.

ALHAMA DE ALMERÍA

Alhama de Almería is served by bus from Almería (but note that transport to Los Millares from here is more difficult than you might imagine; see p.517). Information on transport to Los Millares is available from a central **Turismo**, C/Médicos 13 (Mon–Fri 10am–2pm & 6–8pm, Sat 9am–1pm; ☎ 950 640 469).

ACCOMMODATION

LAROLES

Camping Alpujarras Ladera Sur de Sierra Nevada ☎ 958 760 231. Laroles's campsite is on the village's western edge with good facilities, plenty of shade and a pool. €4 per person, €4 per tent, €4 per vehicle
Refugio de Nevada C/Mairenas s/n ☎ 958 760 320, ⓦ refugiodenevada.com. A very good option for comfortable en-suite heated rooms with TV and stunning views, or slightly more expensive fully equipped studios. Food is available at their own good restaurant or at the nearby village bars, and the attractive village swimming pool is at the rear of the building. Rooms €44, studios €56

BAYÁRCAL

Posada de los Arrieros Ctra. Bayarcal-Puerto de la Ragua s/n ☎ 950 524 001, ⓦ posadadelosarrieros.com. This is a wonderful stone-built hotel, well equipped to withstand the winter snows that engulf it until well into spring. There are comfortable heated en-suite rooms and Swiss-style chalets nearby sleeping up to four people.

There's also a bunkhouse (bring your own sleeping bag), and an on-site restaurant. Rooms B&B €59, chalets €100, bunkhouse €29 per person (including half board).

LÁUJAR DE ANDARAX

Hostal Nuevo Andarax C/Canalejas 27, west of the centre along the main street ☎ 950 513 113. Plain but functional en-suite rooms above a bar-restaurant in town. €50
Hotel Almirez Ctra Láujar–Orgiva km1.6, at the western edge of town ☎ 950 513 514, ⓦ hotelalmirez .es. With your own transport (or a 15min walk from the centre), this offers better value than the *Hostal Nuevo*, with spacious balcony rooms in a leafy setting. They also have a restaurant. €50
Villa de Láujar de Andarax Paraje Cortijo de la Villa s/n ☎ 950 608 050, ⓦ villasdeandalucia.es. A luxury four-star hotel in a park down a side road at the town's eastern end. Attractive rooms and studios are set in a rural landscape, and there's a bar-restaurant and a fine garden pool. Good weekday special offers. €70

5

ALHAMA DE ALMERÍA

Hotel San Nicolás C/Baños s/n ☎951 641 361, ⓦbalneariosannicolas.es. Sited over the baths with a slightly institutional ambience, this is the place where people taking the waters tend to stay. The rooms are three-star standard and there is also a restaurant and bar. **€86**

Pensión Chiquito C/Pablo Picasso 5, near the church ☎950 640 231, ☎ mobile 625 379 850. Unsigned *hostal* with very attractive a/c en-suite rooms with TV. **€35**

EATING

LAROLES

Refugio de Nevada C/Mairenas s/n ☎958 760 320, ⓦrefugiodenevada.com. The *Refugio*, a recommended accommodation option (see p.519) has its own restaurant dishing up good, tasty food.

BAYÁRCAL

Posada de los Arrieros Ctra. Bayarcal-Puerto de la Ragua s/n ☎950 524 001, ⓦposadadelosarrieros.com. The hotel's restaurant – serving hearty *alpujarreño* specialities – is recommended, and has a good-value *menú* for €14.50.

LÁUJAR DE ANDARAX

Hotel Almirez Ctra Laujar–Orgiva km1.6, at the western edge of town ☎950 513 514, ⓦhotelalmirez .es. A 15min walk from the centre, this is a decent hotel restaurant with a *menú* for €14.

ALHAMA DE ALMERÍA

Hotel San Nicolás C/Baños s/n ☎951 641 361, ⓦbalneariosannicolas.es. Other than a couple of *raciones* bars along the main street, C/Medicos, the hotel restaurant is the main place to eat in Alhama.

From Guadix to Almería

An alternative route from Granada to Almería – via the N342 and A92 and covered by Empresa Autodía buses from the main bus station – goes via **Guadix**, a crumbling old Moorish town with a vast and extraordinary cave district. For those with transport, the route also offers the opportunity for a detour to the impressive Renaissance castle of **La Calahorra**.

To the northeast, the A92N *autovía* speeds traffic from Guadix towards Lorca and Murcia, and there is a possible stop at the market town of **Baza** beyond which the road pushes on through a sparsely populated landscape for the 70km between here and the towns of Vélez Rubio (p.554) and Vélez Blanco with a fine castle (p.555).

Guadix

Sited on the banks of the Río Guadix, in the midst of a fertile plain, **GUADIX** is a ramshackle, windblown sort of town, often coated in the red dust that gusts in from the surrounding hills. It's not a particularly attractive place and were it not for its remarkable **cave district** there would be little reason to stop. However, Guadix's old quarter is still largely walled, and the circuit includes an imposing Moorish gateway, the Puerta San Turcuato.

Brief history

An ancient settlement, dating back to Paleolithic times, became the Roman town of Julia Gemella Acci in 45 BC, established by Julius Caesar as a base for exploiting seams of silver in the surrounding hills. Following a period of decline during the Visigothic era, the conquering Moors revived its fortunes, renaming the town Guadh-Haix ("River of Life"), and it rapidly grew in size, soon becoming a rival for Granada. It was renowned for its poetry, and bards such as Ibn Tofayl sang the praises of Guadix's beauty and its valley. It was also during the Moorish period that the town developed an important silk industry, whose mulberry trees can still be seen along the river. More recently, industrial development was based upon the production of esparto grass products and cutlery. Guadix endured terrifying atrocities during the Civil War, which Gerald Brenan vividly described in *South from Granada*.

Gaudix Catedral

Plaza de la Catedral s/n • Mon–Sat: April–Sept 10.30am–2pm & 5–8pm; Oct–March 10.30am–2pm & 4–6pm • €3.50

Inside the ancient walls, the *barrio antiguo* is dominated by the imposing red sandstone towers of its sixteenth-century **Catedral** – circled on Saturdays by a lively **market** – built on the site of a former mosque. The edifice has been much hacked around and embellished over the years and the exterior is eighteenth-century Corinthian, the work of Vincente Acero. The sombre, late-Gothic interior was designed by Diego de Siloé, based on that of the cathedral at Málaga. Its best feature is the superb Churrigueresque choir stalls by Ruíz del Peral. Civil War reminders from both sides of the conflict include the defaced and destroyed heads of the saints on the carved marble pulpit and, near to the entrance, two plaques recording the names of local priests "killed by Marxism".

Plaza Mayor and around

Just across from the cathedral entrance, beneath an arch, stands the elegant **Plaza Mayor** (aka Plaza de la Constitución), an arcaded Renaissance square which was reconstructed after severe damage in the Civil War. A right turn in the stepped street (Calle Santisteban) at the far end of the square leads up to the Renaissance **Palacio de Peñaflor** with a twin towered brick facade featuring an interesting *balconada* (corner balcony). After a prolonged programme of refurbishment is completed, visitors will be able to see the stunning columned interior patio. Nearby, in the Placeta de Santiago, the whitewashed church of **Santiago** (daily 6.15–7pm; free), another work by de Siloé, has an imposing Plateresque entrance and, inside, a beautiful *artesonado* ceiling.

Next to the Peñaflor mansion, a former theological seminary alongside the sixteenth-century church of **San Agustín** gives access to the conclusively ruined ninth-century Moorish **Alcazaba**. At the time of writing a major programme of rebuilding and restoration had begun; contact the Turismo for more details on when it might be open again. From the Alcazaba's battlements there are **views** over the cave district of Santiago and beyond towards the Sierra Nevada.

The cave district

South of the Alcazaba and sited in a weird landscape of pyramidal red hills, the **Barrio de las Cuevas** or cave district still houses some ten thousand people (most of whom, and contrary to popular belief, are not *gitanos* or gypsies), and to take a look round it is the main reason for most visitors stopping off.

The quarter extends over around 2.5 square kilometres in area, and the lower caves, on the outskirts, are really proper cottages sprouting television aerials, with upper storeys, electricity and running water. But as you walk deeper into the suburb, the design quickly becomes simpler – just a whitewashed front, a door, a tiny window and a chimney – and the experience increasingly voyeuristic. Penetrating right to the back you'll come upon a few caves which are no longer used: too squalid, too unhealthy to live in, their whitewash faded to a dull brown. Yet right next door there may be a similar, occupied hovel, with a family sitting outside, and other figures following dirt tracks still deeper into the hills.

Be aware that offers to show you around the interior of a cave will often be followed by a demand for substantial sums of money when you emerge.

Cueva Museo

Plaza Padre Poveda, opposite the church of San Miguel, and signed along C/San Miguel heading south from the centre • Oct–March Mon–Fri 10am–2pm & 4–6pm, Sat 10am–2pm; April–Sept Mon–Fri 10am–2pm & 4–7pm, Sat 10am–2pm • €2.50

The easiest way to get an understanding of cave culture is to visit the **Cueva Museo**, or cave museum. Sited in a series of rehabilitated cave dwellings, it documents the history and reality of cave living with audiovisual aids and reconstructed rooms.

ARRIVAL AND INFORMATION
GUADIX

By bus The bus station (frequent services to and from Granada and Almería), to the southeast of the centre off Avda. Medina Olmos, is a 5min walk from the walls and cathedral.

By train Guadix station (4 services daily to and from Granada and Almería) is on the northeast side of town,

1.5km out along Avda. de Buenos Aires (the Murcia road).

Turismo Plaza de la Constitución 15, close to the cathedral (Mon–Fri 9am–1.30pm & 4–6pm; ☎958 662 804 or ☎958 699 574).

Internet *Habana Café Internet*, Plaza de la Constitución 4, near the cathedral.

ACCOMMODATION

Hostal Chez Jean & Julia C/Ermita Nueva 67 ☎958 669 191, ⊛altipla.com/jj. Spotless and good-value cave *hostal* where you have a choice of a double "cave room" sharing bath or pricier en-suite cave apartments with salon, kitchen and washing machine. It's near the cave museum; to find it, make your way there and give the proprietors a ring for directions (English spoken). B&B €35

Hostal El Retiro Avda. Mariana Pineda 38 ☎958 669 520. A budget option on the Granada road out of town, offering functional, clean and tidy rooms above a bar-restaurant. €40

★ **Hotel Abentofail** C/Abentofail s/n ☎958 669 281, ⊛hotelabentofail.com. Stunning new boutique hotel in a refurbished Mudéjar medieval building 70m south of the Plaza de la Constitución. All the rooms are beautifully presented and most have beams and exposed brickwork;

the slightly pricier options have more space. Two delightful rooftop suites come with their own terrace and Jacuzzi plus DVD & CD player. There's also a very good bar-restaurant. Free wi-fi. B&B €70

Hotel Comercio C/Mira de Amezcua 3 ☎958 660 500, ⊛hotelcomercio.com. Just south of the Plaza de la Constitución, this is an elegant turn-of-the-twentieth-century hotel with a spa complex. Stylish rooms come with a/c, minibar, room safe and TV and there's also an excellent restaurant. Guests get a free sample session in the spa and sauna. €70

Pedro Antonio Alarcón A couple of kilometres north of the centre along Avda. de Buenos Aires ☎958 664 986, ⊛cuevaspedroantonio.com. A cave hotel on the other side of town beyond the train station, with a luxurious complex of nineteen caves with pool, gardens and restaurant. €80

EATING, DRINKING AND NIGHTLIFE

Boabdil C/Manuel de Falla 3, 200m northwest of the cathedral. A decent and economical option with great salads. *Carnes a la brasa* (charcoal-grilled meat) is the house speciality. Daily 1–4pm & 7.30–11.30pm.

Cafetería Cart Luis Plaza de Naranjos s/n. This lively square 100m northeast of the cathedral is a good hunting ground for cheap eats. The popular *Cart Luis* bar-café is usually buzzing with clients who've dropped in for a *ración* of *salchichón ibérico* or tasty *setas a la plancha* (sautéed mushrooms). Mon–Sat 10am–11pm.

★ **Hotel Comercio** C/Mira de Amezcua 3 ☎958 660

500, ⊛hotelcomercio.com. The restaurant of this top hotel is one of the best in town and very reasonably priced. The menu offers a range of local specialities such as *conejo al ajillo* (rabbit with garlic) and any of the *perdiz* (partridge) dishes are recommended. There's also a good-value *menú* for €12. Main dishes €9–18. Daily 1–4pm & 8–11pm.

La Bodeguilla C/Doctor Pulido 4, 300m northeast of the cathedral. A wonderfully atmospheric old bodega-bar with a nice range of tapas and *raciones*. Try the *jamón* or *pimentón con sardinas*. Daily 10am–11pm.

FIESTA DE CASCAMORRAS

Guadix and Baza are linked by old rivalries that are kept alive in the annual **Fiesta de Cascamorras** from September 6–9. At the outset of this festival, a man dressed as a jester and carrying a sceptre travels from Guadix to Baza in an attempt to retrieve an ancient image of the Virgin, over which the two towns have disputed ownership since the sixteenth century. However, to retrieve the sacred image from the church, he must remain unblemished and so, as he nears Baza, a huge reception committee awaits him armed with drums of used engine oil at the ready.

Needless to say, he is coated from head to toe in the stuff within seconds of crossing the city limits – as are a whole crowd of the Virgin's protectors – and the oily mass then squelches its way to the Plaza Mayor where, amidst the tolling of church bells, the mayor (from the safety of a balcony) proclaims that Guadix has blown it yet again, after which the town lets rip on a three-day binge of celebration.

Baza

5

BAZA, 44km northeast of Guadix along the A92N, is another old Moorish town, well worth a detour if you have time and transport. Approached through an ochre landscape dotted with weird conical hillocks covered with esparto grass, the town is slightly smaller than Guadix, with a web of streets encircling its ancient central plaza. As with many towns in these parts, it has a history dating back well into prehistoric times. A prosperous Iberian settlement here named *Basti* produced the remarkable *Dama de Baza* sculpture (see below) and the town remained a considerable centre under the Romans, and later, like Guadix, a focus of silk production under the Moors; it was especially renowned for its silk prayer mats. Taken by Christian forces in 1489 after a long siege, the town has had a less-than-glorious past few centuries, in part due to trouble from earthquakes, which have crumbled away most of the old Moorish Alcazaba. Like Guadix, Baza also has a **cave quarter**, albeit less touristic, on the northern side of town, close to the bullring.

As you head on from Baza, possible destinations include the Cazorla Natural Park, to the north, or the Almería coast via the A92N *autovía* with the option of a detour to Orce, the site of sensational finds concerning early humans in Spain, and the prehistoric cave paintings at Vélez Rubio.

Santa María

Plaza Mayor • Open during services; daily 7–9pm • Free

The impressive Renaissance collegiate church of **Santa María** and its eighteenth-century brick tower – added when the previous one collapsed during an earthquake – leads you to the pedestrianized Plaza Mayor. Built over an earlier mosque, the church's elegant **Plateresque main door** – attributed to Diego de Siloé – is worth a look and inside there's an interesting marble pulpit and elegant vaulting.

Museo Arqueológico

Plaza Mayor s/n (entry to museum is in C/Alhóndiga) • Mon–Fri 9am–2pm, Sat 11am–2pm • Free

The town's small **Museo Arqueológico** preserves finds from the town's ancient past, including a copy of the *Dama de Baza*, a magnificent life-size fourth-century BC Iberian painted sculpture unearthed in 1971 in a necropolis on the outskirts of the town. The original is now in Madrid, where it is exhibited alongside the century-later *Dama de Elche*, another iconic work of Spain's early artistic tradition.

Baños Árabes

C/Caniles 19 • Wed–Sun 11am–1pm & 6–8pm • Free

A few minutes' walk east of Plaza Mayor, following Calle Cabeza then turning left along Calle del Agua, and then right into Calle Caniles leads to the **Baños Árabes**, an impressive tenth-century Moorish bath complex – one of the oldest and most complete surviving in Spain. The building has been sensitively restored – winning it a national architectural prize – and the cold, lukewarm and hot rooms are wonderfully preserved as are the stunning brickwork walls, *bóvedas* (vaults) and star-shaped ceiling windows. Recent excavations have revealed the heating furnace and wood store.

Iglesia de Santiago

Plaza de Santiago • Open during service times only, try 7–8pm • Free

Close to the Baños Arabes, the **Iglesia de Santiago** is a fine sixteenth-century church built over a former mosque and inside has a magnificent Mudéjar *artesonado* coffered and painted ceiling in nave and apse.

ARRIVAL AND DEPARTURE

BAZA

By bus The bus station (with frequent connections to Guadix and Granada) is on Avda. Reyes Católicos to the west of the centre, and an easy 5min walk to the Plaza Mayor.

5

INFORMATION

Turismo municipal Plaza Mayor s/n (April–Sept Mon 10am–2pm, Tues–Fri 10am–2pm & 5.30–7pm, Sat & Sun 11am–2pm; Oct–March Mon–Fri 4.30–6.30pm, Sat & Sun 11am–2pm; ☎ 958 861 325).

Turismo Museo Arqueológico, Plaza Mayor (Mon–Fri 9am–2pm, Sat 11am–2pm).

ACCOMMODATION

Hostal Casa Grande Ctra. de Ronda 28, a 10min walk south of the centre ☎ 958 702 732, ⓦ hostal casagrande.es. A welcoming and excellent-value *hostal* with immaculate non-smoking en-suite rooms with a/c, heating and TV. It also has its own very good restaurant next door with a superb value €7 *menú*. **€38**

Hotel Anabel C/María de Luna 3, four blocks east of the Plaza Mayor ☎ 958 860 998, ⓦ hotelanabelbaza.com. This very comfortable hotel is the town's only central option, with modern rooms and a bar-restaurant. Free wi-fi. **€45**

EATING AND DRINKING

Bar Los Canteros Plaza Arcipreste Juan Hernández, 100m south of the Plaza Mayor. Good bar-restaurant serving up tapas and *raciones* including *entrecot de buey* (ox steak) and *pulpo a la brasa* (grilled octopus). Daily 10am–midnight.

Casino Plaza Mayor s/n. The town's *Casino* has a nice terrace on the south side of the Plaza Mayor – a great place for a leisurely breakfast. They also serve up tapas later in the day. Daily 8.30am–10pm.

La Curva C/Corredera 3 ☎ 958 700 002. A few blocks northeast of the Plaza Mayor, this excellent bar-restaurant is renowned for its seafood, although meat is also on the menu. Try *pierna de cordero* (roast lamb), which is a house special, or

the *salmonete* (red mullet), a noted fish platter. There's also a weekday *menú* for €10. Tues–Sun 1–4pm & 8–11pm.

Mesón los Moriscos C/Cava Alta 3, 100m southwest of the Plaza Mayor. A little restaurant that lives up to its name and dishes up fine tapas and *platos combinados* in a mini-Alhambra-inspired dining room. Daily 12.30–4.30pm & 8–11pm.

Mesón Siglo XX C/Solares 5, northeast of the Plaza Mayor. This is the kind of splendid local restaurant that Andalucía excels in; an all-female kitchen team cooks up a range of local delicacies including great soups, stews and a tasty paella, and the *menú* is a gift at €9. Mon–Sat 1–4pm & 8–10.30pm, Sun 1–4pm.

La Calahorra

If you continue southeast of Guadix along the A92 to Almería, the spectacular domed Renaissance **castle** of La Calahorra heaves into view at the 16km point. A turn-off to the right takes you the 4km to the village of **LA CALAHORRA**, where, on a hill above it, this brooding red stone monster dominates the landscape.

Castillo La Calahorra

Plaza del Castillo • Wed only, 10am–1pm & 4–6pm; outside these times access is possible by visiting C/de los Claveles 2 in the village (☎ 958 677 098; avoid siesta time), home of the guardian, Antonino Tribáldoz, who (for a consideration) will open it for you • €3

Constructed between 1509–12, **Castillo La Calahorra** was owned by one Rodrigo de Mendoza, the bastard son of the powerful Cardinal Mendoza, who did much to establish Isabel on the throne. Rodrigo, created marquis of Zenete by Isabel, acquired a taste for the Renaissance during an Italian sojourn, and ordered the castle to be designed by an Italian architect as a wedding gift for his wife, María de Fonseca. The bleak situation proved unattractive both to them and to their descendants, however, and it was rarely used.

Once inside, you'll be able to view an exquisite Renaissance **patio** – the last thing you'd expect behind such a dour exterior. The doorways, arches and stairway of this two-storey courtyard are beautifully carved from Carrara marble. Some of the palace's rooms have finely crafted *artesonado* ceilings and there's also a curious women's prison. Leave any vehicle at the bottom of the boulder-strewn track leading up to the castle and walk up to avoid severe damage to the underside of your car.

ACCOMMODATION AND EATING	LA CALAHORRA

Hospedería del Zenete Ctra. La Ragua 1 ☎ 958 677 192, ⓦ hospederiadelzenete.com. This four-star hotel is the village's luxury option, with great views of the castle from most rooms (make sure to request this). If you ring at

SAN JOSÉ (P.545) >

5

least 24 hours ahead they will arrange a visit to the castle for you. The bar-restaurant is good for *raciones* and more formal meals. **€90**

Hostal-Restaurante La Bella Ctra. de Aldeire 1 ☎ 958 677 000, ⊛ hostallabella.com. A budget option in the village proper, with comfortable a/c rooms with TV; a couple on the front also have castle views. The restaurant below is pretty good too, and offers a decent weekday *menu* for €9. **€40**

Puerto de la Ragua

From La Calahorra, a lonely but scenic mountain road – the A337 – toils south to the **Puerto de la Ragua**, at 1993m Andalucía's highest all-weather pass. The hairpin climb offers spectacular views back over the plain of the Hoya de Guadix and the rose-tinted La Calahorra castle. When you reach the pass – where it can be chilly even in high summer – you'll find a pleasant **refuge**.

Beyond the pass the road forks, offering alternative descents to the Alpujarras villages of Válor or Ugíjar to the west, and Láujar de Andarax in the east. Forking left towards Láujar would bring you to Bayárcal and the superb mountain hotel *Posada de los Arrieros* (see p.519).

INFORMATION AND ACCOMMODATION
PUERTO DE LA RAGUA

National park information centre In the *Refugio* (Thurs, Fri & Sun 10am–2.30pm, Sat 10am–2.30pm & 5–7pm; T950 524 020). They can provide maps of the area.

Refugio Puerto de la Ragua ☎ 958 760 223 (English spoken), ⊛ puertodelaragua.com. Comfortable bunk accommodation and a restaurant; to be certain of a bed you should ring ahead. The wardens can provide details of fine walks in the vicinity and (in winter) cross-country skiing, with ski-hire available.

Towards Almería

East beyond La Calahorra, the A92 crosses the border into Almería and passes by **FIÑANA**, with another **castle**, this time Moorish and in a more ruinous state, and a well-preserved Moorish **mezquita**. Some 25km further on there's a turn-off for **GÉRGAL**, with another well-preserved fortress and, on the highest summit of the Sierra de los Filabres behind, an observatory housing one of the largest telescopes in Europe, sited here by a German–Spanish venture to take advantage of the almost constantly clear skies (see p.557). The A92 gradually descends into the valley of the Río Andarax – where you could detour to the prehistoric site of Los Millares (see p.517) – which it follows for the final 15km to Almería.

Almería

Cuando Almería era Almería
Granada era su alquería

When Almería was Almería
Granada was but its farm.

Traditional Almerian couplet

ALMERÍA is a pleasant and largely modern city, spread at the foot of a stark grey hill dominated by a magnificent Moorish fort. Founded by the Phoenicians and developed by the Romans, who named it Portus Magnus, it was as a Moorish city – renamed al-Mariyat (The Mirror of the Sea) – that Almería grew to prominence. The sultan Abd ar-Rahman I began the building programme soon after the conquest, in 713, with an arsenal beside the port, and the great **Alcazaba**, still the town's dominant feature, was added in the tenth century by Abd ar-Rahman III when the city formed part of the Cordoban caliphate.

The city's other sights pale by comparison, though it is worth taking time to look over the **cathedral** and, nearby, Andalucía's regional **photographic museum**. More sights surround the focal **Puerta de Purchena** where some remarkable **air-raid shelters** from the Civil War have been opened up for visits while to the east lies the city's striking **archeological museum** which should not be missed.

The city **beach**, southeast of the centre beyond the railway lines, is long but crammed for most of the summer. For a day-trip, the best options are Cabo de Gata or San José, both easily accessible by bus.

Brief history

The splendours created here by the **Moors** – most of which have been lost – inspired the popular rhyme at the beginning of this section, contrasting this early prosperity with the much later glories of Nasrid Granada. After the collapse of Moorish Córdoba, Almería's prosperity was hardly affected and, as a principality or *taifa* state, it became the country's major port, famed for its exports of silk, as well as a pirates' nest feared around the adjacent coasts. This period ended when the city fell to the forces of Fernando in 1490 and the Moors were expelled. Their possessions and lands were doled out to the officers of the conquering army, forming the basis for the *señoritismo* which has plagued Almería and Andalucía throughout modern times. Predictably, there followed a prolonged decline over the next three hundred years, reversed only by the introduction of the railway and the building of a new harbour in the nineteenth century, as well as the opening up to exploitation of the province's vast mineral wealth, particularly iron, lead and gold.

The **Civil War** interrupted this progress. The city's communist dockworkers gave staunch backing to the Republic, at one point in 1937 causing Hitler to order that the city be subjected to aerial bombardment and shelled from offshore by the German fleet (see p.532). It was one of the last cities to fall to Franco's forces in 1939, after which many suicides took place to avoid the fate planned for the most bitter enemies of the new order.

Although still the centre of one of the poorest areas in Europe, Almería today is seeking a more prosperous future based upon intensive vegetable production in the surrounding *vega*, in tandem with gaining a greater share of Spain's tourist economy. Whilst even its most devoted admirers wouldn't describe it as a beautiful place, the provincial capital deserves more visitors than it gets. Enjoying something of a recent renaissance, the city has sunk enormous funds into smartening up the town centre, which has areas with considerable charm. Add to this a handful of fascinating sights and a friendly welcome in some great bars and restaurants, and you may be induced to give it a bit longer than the customary one-night transit.

The Alcazaba

C/Almanzor s/n • Tues–Sun: April–Oct 9am–8.30pm; Nov–March 9am–6.30pm • €1.50, free with EU passport

The **Alcazaba**, begun by Abd ar-Rahman III of Córdoba in 955, was just one part of a massive building programme that included a great mosque and city walls. During the eleventh century when the city enjoyed a period of prosperous independence, between the fall of the Cordoban caliphate and its capture by the Almoravids, the medina (walled city) here contained immense gardens and palaces and housed some twenty thousand people. It was adapted after the *Reconquista* by the Catholic monarchs but severely damaged during a great earthquake in 1522. A programme of restoration in recent years has begun to reverse the centuries of crumbling decay.

It can be reached by following any of the narrow streets which climb the hill west of the cathedral, aiming for the entrance below the walls in the Plaza Joaquín Santisteban, at the end of Calle Almanzor. Through the **Puerta Exterior**, a zigzagged entrance ramp – a traditional Moorish architectural feature to make attack precarious – leads to the

5

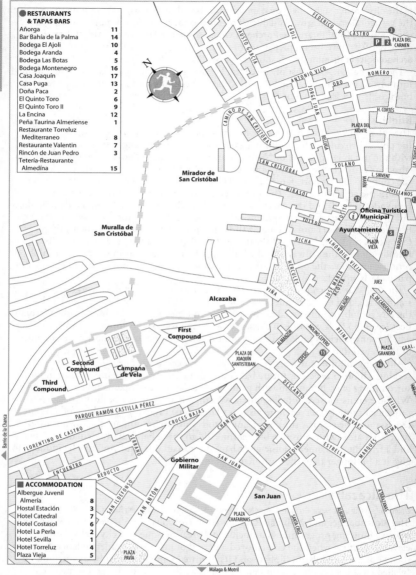

● RESTAURANTS & TAPAS BARS	
Añorga	11
Bar Bahía de la Palma	14
Bodega El Ajoli	10
Bodega Aranda	4
Bodega Las Botas	5
Bodega Montenegro	16
Casa Joaquín	17
Casa Puga	13
Doña Paca	2
El Quinto Toro	6
El Quinto Toro II	9
La Encina	12
Peña Taurina Almeriense	1
Restaurante Torreluz Mediterraneo	8
Restaurante Valentin	7
Rincón de Juan Pedro	3
Tetería-Restaurante Almedína	15

■ ACCOMMODATION	
Albergue Juvenil Almería	8
Hostal Estación	3
Hotel Catedral	7
Hotel Costasol	6
Hotel La Perla	2
Hotel Sevilla	1
Hotel Torreluz	4
Plaza Vieja	5

Puerta de la Justicia, the gateway to the first of the Alcazaba's three great compounds. Halfway up the ramp to the right is the **Tower of Mirrors**, a fifteenth-century addition, where mirrors were employed to communicate with ships approaching the port below.

The first compound

The first compound is the largest of the three. Now filled with delightful gardens and aromatic plants, it was originally designed as a military camp and an area in which the

populace could seek protection when under siege. A **well** in the centre of this area raised water from a depth of 70m to supply the site. At the eastern end of the enclosure, the **Saliente Bastión** was a lookout point over the town below, and the sea beyond.

Below the north side of the compound, the **eleventh-century wall** (Muralla de San Cristóbal) descends the hill; it originally formed part of a great complex of walls, not only surrounding the city but also dividing it internally. Above the wall, which divides

5

the first and second compounds, is the **Campana de Vela**, a bell erected during the eighteenth century to announce ships sighted nearing the port, or to summon soldiers to their battle stations.

The second compound

The second compound accommodated the Moorish kings, when resident in the city, and at other times served as the governor's quarters. In the eleventh century, when Almería was the wealthiest, most commercially active city of Spain, the buildings here were of unparalleled brilliance. Their grandeur was even reputed to rival the later court of Granada, but the ruins that remain today make a valid comparison impossible.

What you can see, however, are the remains of **cisterns**, the old **mosque** – converted into a chapel by the Reyes Católicos – and once palatial dwellings, but sadly no sign of the magnificent stuccowork said to equal that of the Alhambra, the last remnants of which were sold off by the locals in the eighteenth century. The **Ventana de Odalisca**, a *mirador* window in the compound's northern wall, is a poignant reminder of lost glory. A legend attached to this concerns an eleventh-century Moorish slave-girl, Galiana, the king's favourite, who fell in love with a prisoner and arranged to help him to escape. But the guards discovered them in the attempt and the prisoner threw himself from this window into the valley below, whilst Galiana died of a broken heart a few days later. Recent archeological excavations here have uncovered Moorish bath houses and other structures.

The third compound

The third and highest compound demonstrates the starkly contrasting style of the conquering Christians. When they took the city, the Catholic monarchs found the fortress substantially damaged due to an earthquake a couple of years before. They therefore built walls much stronger than the original Moorish structure, to cope with both potential future earthquakes and the recent innovation of artillery. Triangular in form, this upper fort is guarded by three semicircular towers built of ashlar masonry, both features at odds with the earlier Moorish design.

To the right, the **Torre del Homenaje** (Tower of Homage) bears the crumbling escutcheon of the Catholic monarchs and looks out over the **Patio de Armas** (Courtyard of Arms) where the guard would be assembled. From the **Torre de Pólvora** (Gunpowder Tower) and the battlements (take care as there are few handrails) fine views are to be had of the coast and of Almería's *gitano* cave quarter – the Barrio La Chanca – on a low hill to the west.

La Catedral

Plaza de la Catedral s/n • Mon–Fri 10am–2pm & 4–5pm, Sat 10am–2pm • €3

Like the Alcazaba, the **Catedral**, in the heart of the old quarter, also has a fortress look about it. Begun in 1524 on the site of the great mosque – conveniently destroyed by the 1522 earthquake – it was designed in the late-Gothic style by Diego de Siloé, the architect of the cathedral at Granada. Because of the danger of attack in this period from Barbarossa and other Turkish and North African pirate forces, the corner towers once held cannons. The threat was real and not long after its construction the cathedral chapter is recorded purchasing guns, muskets and gunpowder.

Like many of Andalucía's cathedrals, it was never completely finished and it may be that the city's inhabitants had no great affection for this austere giant, preferring instead their more intimate parish churches. The **exterior** is of little interest apart from a curious, pagan-looking relief of a garlanded radiant sun on the eastern wall – that is, facing the rising sun. Echoing the Roman Sol Invictus, or unconquerable sun, its appearance on the church has been put down to a sixteenth-century bishop with masonic leanings, but its true significance will probably never be known. Appropriately, as the province with the highest sun-hours statistic in Spain, Almería now uses the image as its official logo.

The interior

The cathedral is entered through the Puerta Principal, an elegant Renaissance doorway flanked by buttresses. Within, the sober Gothic **interior** is distinguished by some superb sixteenth-century choir stalls carved in walnut by Juan de Orea. Just behind this, the **retrochoir** is a stunning eighteenth-century altar in contrasting red and black jasper. Behind the Capilla Mayor (or high altar) with some elegant and sinuous vaulting, the Capilla de la Piedad has a painting of the *Annunciation* by Alonso Cano and *Immaculate Conception* by Murillo, whilst the Capilla de Santo Cristo – next door to the right – contains the sixteenth-century sculptured tomb of Bishop Villalán, the cathedral's founder, complete with faithful hound at his feet. Further along again, a door (often closed) leads to the sacristy and a rather uninspiring Renaissance cloister – relieved by a small garden with palms and orange trees. The church also contains a number of fine **pasos** of the Passion carried in the Semana Santa processions at Easter; among these, *El Prendimiento* (the Arrest of Christ) is outstanding.

Centro Andaluz de la Fotografía

C/Pintor Diaz Molina s/n • Daily 11am–2pm & 5.30–9.30pm • Free

A couple of blocks south of the cathedral, and housed in a converted nineteenth-century theatre, the **Centro Andaluz de la Fotografía** is Andalucía's first photo museum, often staging interesting exhibitions of work by *andaluz* and international photographers.

San Juan

C/General Luque s/n • Daily 6–6.30pm • Free

Some 300m west of the cathedral stands the seventeenth-century church of **San Juan**, built over the Moorish city's tenth-century main mosque. As with the Alcazaba, this was raised at the behest of Abd ar-Rahman III in 965 with three naves and a capacity for nine thousand worshippers. Inside, the church's southern wall survives from the original mosque and preserves the *mihrab* (prayer niche) of the original building. Now largely bare stone, this was once decorated with the finest *yesería* (plasterwork) tantalising fragments of which survive. Next to this, there's another niche that would have contained the *minbar* or wooden pulpit used for readings from the Koran.

Plaza Vieja

To the north of the cathedral the **Plaza Vieja** (officially Plaza de la Constitución) is a wonderful pedestrian square which – because of its restricted entrance – you would hardly know was there. It contains the **Ayuntamiento**, a flamboyant early twentieth-century building with a brown-and-cream facade, and a monument to citizens put to the firing squad in 1824 for opposing the tyrannical reign of Fernando VII. After decades of neglect the square has been refurbished and has begun to realize its potential with the arrival of a restaurant, hotel and one of the main tourist offices.

Around the Puerta de Purchena

Further sights, including the city **market** (see p.535), are located within a couple of minutes' walk of the **Puerta de Purchena**, the city's major traffic intersection, taking its name from a Moorish gate – long gone – where al-Zagal, the city's last Moorish ruler, surrendered to the Catholic monarchs in 1490.

5

Los Aljibes

C/Tenor Iribarne s/n • Mon–Fri 9am–2pm • Free

On the west side of the Puerta de Purchena junction are some well-preserved eleventh-century Moorish water cisterns – known as **Los Aljibes**. Constructed at the command of Jairán, the then *taifa* (independent) ruler of Almería, the *aljibes* were supplied by underground conduits channeling water obtained from springs in the surrounding hills. Capable of holding more than six hundred thousand litres of water, this was sufficient to supply thirty thousand inhabitants, the size of the city's population at that time. Inside, you can see the cistern's three brick-constructed naves and caliphal arches as well as the odd recycled Roman pillar.

Los Refugios

Plaza Manuel Pérez García s/n • Guided visits Tues–Thurs 10am–2pm, Fri–Sun 10am–2pm & 5–9pm; book in advance by phone to guarantee entry • €2 • ☏ 950 268 696

Off the southwest side of the Puerta de Purchena is the remarkable **Los Refugios**, a series of underground air-raid shelters used by the city's population during the Civil War bombardments by Nazi and Italian aircraft and naval forces. Between February 1937 and the spring of 1938 city engineers (using experience gained in the province's mining industry) constructed no less than 4.5km of tunnels beneath the city with 67 access points to shelter 35,000 citizens. Much of the rest of the then fifty thousand population took cover in the caves of the La Chanca district, now inhabited by the city's *gitano* community. Now open to the public as a museum, the tunnels are superbly constructed with ventilation pipes and shields to prevent fifth columnists throwing in hand-grenades, and there is also an operating theatre. Visible too throughout the tunnels are the poignant graffiti and children's sketches scratched into the walls by those who sheltered here.

Calle de las Tiendas and around

Just west of the Puerta de Purchena **Calle de las Tiendas** – the oldest street in the city – was formerly called Calle Lencerías (Drapers' Street) and in the nineteenth century was Almería's most fashionable shopping thoroughfare. Some of the street lamps survive from this period, although the place has now become rather seedy.

Iglesia de Santiago

Mon–Fri 9.30–11.30am & 6.30–7pm • Free

The **Iglesia de Santiago** dates from the same period as the cathedral, and is built with stone from the same quarry. A fine Plateresque portal incorporates a statue of Santiago slaying the Moors as well as scallop shells associated with the saint's shrine in Galicia, plus the coat of arms of the all-powerful Bishop Villalán, the cathedral's founder.

East of the centre

Some 300m east of the market, the **Avenida de Federico García Lorca**, formerly an unsightly dry river-bed bisecting the city from north to south, has been dramatically transformed into a stately avenue with palms, fountains and newsstands. It's a great place for a stroll, perhaps taking a coffee or a beer on a terrace of one of its numerous cafés.

Museo Arqueológico

Ctra. de Ronda 91 • Tues 2.30–8.30pm, Wed–Sat 9am–8.30pm, Sun 9am–2.30pm • €1.50, free with EU passport

Almería's **Museo Arqueológico**, an impressive hi-tech museum to the east of the city centre, is well worth a visit. The main attraction for most visitors is the first-floor display of finds from the remarkable Chalcolithic site at **Los Millares** (see p.517), which are superbly displayed. There is also an informative maquette depicting how the site would have looked at its zenith in the third millennium BC. The second floor displays

5

more finds from Los Millares plus other prehistoric sites in the province, and has sections dealing with funerary rites and burial customs. The third floor is devoted to Almería province's Roman and Moorish past, with some particularly outstanding ceramics displayed in the latter.

Barrio de la Chanca

To the west of the centre lies the **Barrio de la Chanca**, an area of grinding poverty occupied by *gitanos* and hard-pressed fisherfolk which has hardly changed since Brenan vividly described it in his *South from Granada*; there are some occupied cave dwellings here, too, but it's not a place to visit alone after dusk.

ARRIVAL AND DEPARTURE
ALMERÍA

By plane Almería's airport (☎ 950 213 700), 8km east from the city along the coast, handles scheduled budget services from the UK and other parts of Europe. Local buses make the journey from the centre; take line #20 (every 30min 7am–9pm) labelled "El Alquián" from the junction of the Avda. Federico García Lorca and C/Gregorio Marañón.
By train and bus Almería's bus (☎ 950 262 098) and train (☎ 902 240 202) stations have been combined into a striking Estación Intermodal, Crta. de Ronda s/n, a couple of blocks east of the Avda. de Federico García Lorca. Train tickets are available at the station and the RENFE office at C/Alcalde Muñoz 7, behind the church of San Sebastián near the Puerta de Purchena.
Destinations by train Granada (4 daily; 2hr 20min); Guadix (6 daily; 1hr 20min); Seville (4 daily; 5hr 30min).
Destinations by bus Agua Amarga (6 daily; 1hr 30min); Aguadulce (every 30min); Almerimar (3 daily; 1hr 30min); Cabo de Gato via Retamar (6 daily; 55min); Carboneras (4 daily; 1hr 15min); Córdoba (1 daily; 4hr); Garrucha (5 daily; 1hr 15min); Granada (7 daily; 4hr); Guadix (5 daily; 2hr

15min); Jaén (4 daily; 4hr); Láujar de Andarax (2 daily; 2hr); Las Negras (2 daily; 1hr 15min); Málaga (7 daily; 3hr 30min); María (1 daily; 3hr 15min); Mojácar (5 daily; 1hr 40min); Mini Hollywood (4 daily; 40min); Níjar (2 daily Mon–Fri; 35min); Rodalquilar (1 daily; 1hr); Roquetas de Mar (every 30min; 30min); San José (4 daily; 1hr 15min); Seville (3 daily; 5hr 45min); Sorbas (4 daily; 1hr); Tabernas (7 daily; 40min); Úbeda (1 daily; 3hr); Vélez Blanco (1 daily; 3hr 15min); Vélez Rubio (1 daily; 2hr 50min).
By boat There is a daily boat to Melilla on the Moroccan coast throughout the summer (less often out of season). It's a 6hr journey, but one that cuts out the haul to Málaga or the usual port for Morocco, Algeciras. In summer (June–Sept) a high-speed vessel does the trip in 4hr. For information and tickets contact the Compañía Tras-mediterránea (☎ 950 236 956, ⊕ trasmediterranea .es), Parque Nicolás Salmerón 19, near the port. The daily 6hr route to Nador (south of Melilla) is operated by Ferrimaroc (☎ 950 274 800, ⊕ ferrimaroc.com) who have an office in the port.

INFORMATION

Turismo Parque Nicolas Salmerón s/n, at the junction with C/Martínez Campos (Mon–Fri 9am–7.30pm, Sat & Sun 9.30am–3pm; ☎ 950 175 220).
Oficina Turística Municipal Plaza de la Constitución s/n (Daily: July & Aug 9am–2pm & 4–7pm; Sept–June 9am–5pm; ☎ 950 280 748). This helpful office has lots of information on the town and province and gives out a free tapas-bar guide. They also offer a guided tour of the town (Sat & Sun 11am; €1.50) departing from their office.
Festivals In August the city holds its annual music and arts festival, the Fiesta de los Pueblos Ibéricos y del Mediterráneo, with concerts and dance events, many of

them free, taking place in the squares and various other locations throughout the city (details from either tourist office). Tacked on to the end of this is the Festival de Flamenco with big-name artists performing on a stage set up in the atmospheric Plaza de la Constitución. During the last week of the month, the city's main annual fiesta, the Romería de Augusto, also takes place with lots of street parties and spectacular processions with carnival giants. Details of the exact dates for all these again are available from the tourist office.
Useful websites ⊕ almeria-turismo.org, ⊕ turismode almeria.com, ⊕ almeriacultura.com and ⊕ andalucia.org.

ACCOMMODATION

Albergue Juvenil Almería C/Isla de Fuerteventura s/n ☎ 950 175 136, ⊕ inturjoven.com. Almería's swish and friendly youth hostel has 150 double rooms and some singles, all en suite. It lies on the east side of town next to the Estadio Juventud sports arena; take bus #1 from the

Paseo de Almería in the centre. Under 26 **€21**, over 26 **€27**
Camping La Garrofa Ctra. 340-A km435 ☎ 950 235 770, ⊕ lagarrofa.com. Almería's nearest campsite lies 5km west of town, on the coast at La Garrofa, and is easily reached by the buses to Aguadulce and Roquetas de Mar

5

(where there's another, giant site). There's plenty of shade and facilities include a bar-restaurant and supermarket. €5 per person, €5.50 per tent, €5.50 per vehicle

Hostal Estación C/Calzada de Castro 37 ☎ 950 267 239. Close to the train and bus stations, this *hostal* offers decently furnished en-suite rooms and garage parking (extra). €45

Hotel Catedral Plaza de la Catedral 8 ☎ 950 278 178, ⓦ hotelcatedral.net. Elegant new hotel in a nineteenth-century *casa señorial* 20m from the cathedral's doorstep. Rooms are bright and stylishly furnished and the hotel has its own bar-restaurant. Garage and free wi-fi. €70

Hotel Costasol Paseo de Almería 58 ☎ 950 234 011, ⓦ hotelcostasol.com. Central, comfortable hotel with spacious rooms; some on the front have terrace balcony. High season rates drop by thirty percent outside July and Aug. Own garage and free wi-fi. €70

Hotel La Perla Plaza del Carmen 7 ☎ 950 238 877, ⓦ githoteles.com. The city's oldest hotel has played host to John Lennon and Clint Eastwood as well as various Spaghetti Western stars in its time and has a/c rooms with satellite TV. Some at the rear can be rather cramped, so check what you're offered. Can advise on parking. Rates fall by 25 percent outside July and Aug. €60

Hotel Sevilla C/Granada 25 ☎ 950 230 009, ⓦ hotel sevillaalmeria.com. Welcoming, modern, small hotel for en-suite rooms equipped with a/c and TV. Public car park nearby. €63

Hotel Torreluz Plaza Flores 2 ☎ 950 234 399, ⓦ torreluz.com. One of the town's leading hotels with outstanding-value two-star and three-star options in the same complex. It's aimed at the corporate sector, which is reflected in the rather staid rooms. Garage and free wi-fi. Two-star €40, three star €45

Plaza Vieja Plaza de la Constitución 4 ☎ 950 282 096, ⓦ plazaviejahl.com. Stylish new boutique hotel on this delightful square (traditionally known as Plaza Vieja) where rooms come with cutting-edge designer furnishings and decor and lots of luxuries such as bathrobes and minibar. Public areas include a bar-restaurant and *baño árabe* (Moorish style baths). Garage and free wi-fi. €120

EATING AND DRINKING

Almería has a surprising number of interesting and good-value places to **eat and drink**. Most of the best are around the Puerta de Purchena and in the web of narrow streets lying between the Paseo de Almería and the cathedral. The best place for early-evening **tapas** is around the Puerta de Purchena, where – especially at weekends – the whole town turns out during the evening *paseo* to see and be seen. Places around the cathedral and old town are more lively at lunchtime.

AROUND THE PUERTA DE PURCHENA

Bodega Aranda Rambla del Obispo Orbera 8, near the Puerta de Purchena. This great tapas bar hums with life at lunch when local professionals come to grab a bite. In former days it was the "sordid" *pensión* where a penurious Gerald Brenan put up in 1921 (sleeping 6 to a room) while waiting for a letter with money from England – which never came. Daily noon–4pm & 7–10pm.

Bodega Las Botas C/Fructuoso Pérez 3, just south of the Puerta de Purchena. Very good tapas place with hanging *jamón serrano* shanks and upturned sherry butt tables; the excellent fino and *manzanilla* (served with a free *tapa*) go well with the house special, *merluza en escabeche* (marinated hake). Daily noon–4pm & 7.30pm–midnight.

Doña Paca C/Murcia 69, 400m northeast of the Puerta de Purchena. Wonderful little *barrio* restaurant serving up hearty and economical food – including tapas, *raciones* and *platos combinados*. There's a great-value *menú* for €10. Mon–Sat noon–5pm & 7.30pm–midnight.

★ **El Quinto Toro** C/Reyes Católicos 6. Top-notch atmospheric tapas bar taking its name from the fifth bull in the *corrida* (reputed to always be the best). Friendly service and their legendary and mouthwatering *patatas a lo pobre* (potatoes baked with garlic; lunchtimes only) are reason enough for a visit. The same proprietor also runs *El Quinto Toro II* at the junction of C/Javier Sanz with C/Padre Santaella which is also excellent. Mon–Sat 9.30am–4pm & 7pm–midnight, Sun 9.30am–4pm.

La Encina C/Marín 16 ☎ 950 273 429. This excellent little mid-priced restaurant has rising chef Francisca Pérez fronting the *fogón* (stove). They serve outstanding tapas in the bar at the front and creative and innovative rice, fish and meat dishes in a cosy restaurant at the rear (where you can see a Moorish well found during the restaurant's refurbishment). The *menú de degustación* costs €35. Tues–Sun noon–4pm & 8.30pm–midnight.

Peña Taurina Almeriense C/Las Cruces 14, northeast of the Puerta de Purchena. Great old bar where *corrida* aficionados gather to talk about fights past, present and to come, looked down on by historical photos and paraphernalia. Mon–Sat 10am–11pm.

Restaurante Torreluz Mediterráneo Plaza Flores 1 ☎ 950 281 425. Close to the hotel of the same name, this is a very good mid-priced restaurant with a creative bent. Try their outstanding *pluma de cerdo ibérico* (pork shoulder). They offer a *menú gourmet* for €25. Main dishes €10–20. Daily 1–4pm & 8–11pm.

Restaurante Valentín C/Tenor Iribarne 19 ☎ 950 264 475. Owned by the same people as *Bodega Las Botas* (see above), this is a stylish upscale restaurant and tapas bar noted for its seafood and *mariscos*. Main dishes €16–26. Tues–Sun 1–4pm & 8pm–midnight.

Rincón de Juan Pedro C/Federico de Castro 2 ☎950 235 819. Reasonably priced fish and meat dishes in a small and intimate restaurant. The friendly and eponoymous host oversees the kitchen and paella (€23 for two) and *solomillo* (pork loin) are house specials. There's also a good-value *menú* for €12. Tues–Sat 1–4pm & 8–11pm, Sun 1–4pm.

★ **Teteria-Restaurante Almedína** C/Paz 2. Very friendly little Moroccan-run *tetería* (tearoom) which serves full meals later in the day including tasty couscous and chicken and lamb tagines with many vegetarian possibilities. They often stage live concerts of flamenco and north African music at weekends. Daily 1–11pm.

AROUND THE CATHEDRAL

Añorga C/Padre Alfonso, slightly south of the Iglesia de San Pedro. Basque tapas bar with a range of *pinxtos* (tapas on sticks) and *raciones*. Has a small terrace on this pedestrianized street. Daily 1–4pm & 8pm–midnight.

Bar Bahía de la Palma Plaza Administración Vieja 1, next to Plaza Vieja. Great old bar and a good lunchtime tapas stop; they also serve *platos combinados* and there's a *menú* for €12. Recorded flamenco music is often the accompaniment to the drinking here and some evenings they even put on live sessions. Mon–Sat 8am–3pm & 8pm–midnight.

Bodega El Ajoli C/Padre Alfonso s/n. Opposite *Añorga* (see above), this tapas and *raciones* bar also has outdoor tables. They specialize in pork dishes – ordering their *surtido* gets you a bit of everything. Tues–Sun 1.30–4.30pm & 8.30pm–midnight.

Bodega Montenegro Plaza Granero, just west of the cathedral. Delightful neighbourhood bar, stacked with barrels. Once they've got over the initial novelty of seeing a foreigner walk through the door, they serve up great local wines and seafood tapas. Tues–Sun 8am–3pm & 6.30–10pm, Mon 8am–3pm.

Casa Joaquín C/Real 111, near the port. Fine and popular tapas bar which buzzes with contented drinkers most evenings. All tapas and *raciones* are excellent, especially the seafood. Tues–Sat noon–4pm & 8pm–midnight, Sun noon–4pm.

★ **Casa Puga** Corner of C/Lope de Vega and C/Jovellanos. With hams hanging from the ceiling, marble-topped tables and walls covered with *azulejos*, this is an outstanding tapas bar – founded in 1870 – with a great atmosphere and loyal clientele; try the *atún en escabeche* (marinated tuna) or *boquerones en vinagre* (fresh anchovies in vinegar). If you can beat the rush you may be able to corner a table and make a meal of it. They also have one of the best wine-cellars in Andalucía. Mon–Sat noon–4pm & 8pm–midnight.

SHOPPING

Librería Picasso C/Reyes Católicos 17. Just south of the market, this bookshop stocks walking guides and hiking maps.

Market C/Aguilar de Campo. Across the Paseo de Almería, the main street that leaves the Puerta de Purchena from its southern side, the colourful market is well worth a look. Mon–Sat 7am–2pm.

DIRECTORY

Banks The major banks, most with ATMs, are along the Paseo de Almería and close at 2pm; there is also an ATM at the airport.

Hospital The main infirmary is Hospital Torrecárdenas (☎950 016 000) in the northeastern suburbs.

Internet Ciber del Puerto, C/Alvarez de Castro 24 (daily 10am–10pm), 50m from the Turismo.

Left luggage There are coin-operated lockers at the Estación Intermodal (train-bus) station.

Police Contact the Policia Municipal C/Santos Zárate 11, off the north end of the Avda. Federico García Lorca, to report thefts or lost property (☎950 621 205). In case of emergency dial ☎092 (local police) or ☎091 (national).

Post office Plaza Cassinello 1 (Mon–Fri 9am–8pm, Sat 9am–1.30pm), near Plaza del Ecuador, off Paseo de Almería.

The Costa Tropical

Almería's best beach resorts lie on its eastern coast, the Costa de Almería, between the city and Mojácar. To the west of the city, the nearest beaches such as **Aguadulce**, **Roquetas de Mar** and **Almerimar** are overdeveloped and the landscape is dismal, backed by an ever-expanding plastic sea of *invernaderos*, hothouses for cultivation of fruit and vegetables for the export market (see box, p.536). The plastic sea has now expanded west to cover most of the 30km-long Campo de Dalías plain and well beyond, and there's little to detain you until, past the large and ugly industrial town of Motril, you reach the **Costa Tropical**, the name given to Granada Province's 60km

5

PLASTICULTURA: ALMERÍA'S ELDORADO

West of Almería, and stretching from beneath the hills of the Sierra de Gador to the sea, lies the **Campo de Dalías**, a vast plain of salt flats and sand dunes which has become a shining sea of *plasticultura* – the forced production of millions of tons of tomatoes, peppers, cucumbers, strawberries and exotic flowers. This industry has wrought quite a revolution in impoverished Almería, covering a once-barren wilderness with a shimmering sea of 64,000 acres of polythene canopies (producing twenty thousand tons of plastic waste annually) propped up by eucalyptus supports.

The boom is all due to the invention of drip-feed irrigation and it has led to phenomenal increases in the year-round production of crops, allowing cheap tropical fruit and flowers to fill the supermarket shelves of northern Europe throughout the year. The future of this miracle, however, may be precarious. Scientists have serious worries about the draining of the province's meagre water resources through the tapping of countless artesian wells – many as deep as 100m. A plan hatched by the Partido Popular government in 2002 to solve this problem by diverting water from the Río Ebro in northern Spain met with outraged resistance from the inhabitants and farmers of the Ebro delta and the plan was dropped by the incoming PSOE regime in 2004. The Almerian farmers have now placed their hopes in the construction of a mammoth seawater desalination plant at Carboneras.

of coastline. Here, along a coast of rugged cliffs peppered with inviting coves, lie the appealing resorts of **Salobreña**, **Almuñécar** and the more laid-back **La Herradura**, all well worth a visit.

Salobreña

Beyond Motril, the N340 road passes slopes dotted with almond and custard apple trees until, after some 10km, a spectacular vista opens up to reveal **SALOBREÑA**, a White Town tumbling down a hill topped by the shell of its Moorish castle and surrounded by a sea of sugar-cane fields. Comparatively undeveloped, the town is set back a two-kilometre hike from the sea (although there are hourly buses), and is thus less marketable for mass tourism, making it a far more relaxed destination than Almuñécar, its neighbour to the west. Beginning life as a Phoenician city dedicated to Salambo (the Syrian goddess of love), the town retained some importance in Moorish times – as the much restored **Alcázar** reveals – but then languished in poverty until rescued by more recent prosperity, generated, in part, by its new trickles of tourism.

Below the Alcázar, down at the foot of the hill, the sixteenth-century church of **Nuestra Señora del Rosario** (open service times) stands on the site previously occupied by a Moorish mosque. A stone's throw away, the old Ayuntamiento houses the town **museum** (Daily: June–Oct 10am–2.15pm & 4.15–8.30pm; Nov–May 10am–2.15pm & 4.15–7pm; €3 including Alcázar) which displays artefacts from all periods of Salobreña's history. There's also an animated **market** each Tuesday and Friday morning in the central Plaza del Mercado, but that's about as far as sightseeing goes.

The Alcázar

C/Andrés Segovia s/n • Daily: June–Oct 10am–2.15pm & 4.15–8.30pm; Nov–May 10am–2.15pm & 4.15–7pm • €3 (including town museum)

On the eastern side of town, the **Alcázar** is worth a look, not least for the fine **views** from its crenellated towers. The hill topped by the fortress has long served a defensive role, and the first bastion here was built by the Phoenicians. This was expanded and added to by the later Romans, but it was in the Moorish period that the form it now has was finalised. The Nazarí rulers from Granada used it first as a prison before turning it into a summer palace.

5

ARRIVAL AND INFORMATION

SALOBREÑA

By bus Buses arrive and depart from the Plaza de Goya at the entrance to the town just off the N340.

Turismo Plaza de Goya s/n (June–Sept Wed–Sun 11am–2pm & 4–9pm; Oct–May Mon–Fri 9am–3pm; ☎ 958 610 314, ⊛ ayto-salobrena.org). They offer their own bilingual (Spanish and English) book of coastal and hill walks, *Rutas y Senderos de Salobreña* (€6) and lead guided visits to the old town (July–Sept Fri 6.30pm; €6). A kiosk (same hours) opens in summer on the Paseo Marítimo near El Peñon, the seafront promontory.

Internet Video Mania, C/Muñoz Seca 3 (daily 11am–2pm & 5–11pm), 300m south of the Turismo.

ACCOMMODATION

Hostal Jayma C/Cristo 24 200m east of the Turismo ☎ 958 610 231, ⊛ hostaljayma.com. This is a good new option in the upper town, with sparkling en-suite rooms, roof terrace and free wi-fi. Rates fall by 25 percent outside July & Aug. **€65**

Hostal Mary Tere C/Fábrica Nueva 7 300m southwest of the Turismo ☎ 958 610 126, ⊛ hostalmarytere.com. Attractive *hostal* with a/c en-suite balcony rooms with TV above its own bar-restaurant. Free wi-fi. **€52**

Hostal Miramar C/Arrabal Villa 37, 250m southwest of the Turismo ☎ 958 828 534. A very good-value *hostal* offering a/c en-suite rooms with TV in a street behind the bar of the same name. **€48**

★ **Hostal San Juan** C/Jardines 1 ☎ 958 611 729, ⊛ hostalsanjuan.com. Perhaps the best deal in town is this friendly French-run *hostal*, a couple of minutes' walk southeast from the Turismo. Situated in a beautifully restored townhouse with elegant patio, the attractive en-suite rooms come with a/c and TV. High season rates apply July & Aug only. **€58**

Pensión Castellmar C/Nueva 21 ☎ 958 610 227. Close to Avda. García Lorca, the main avenue winding down from the town to the beach, this is a welcoming *hostal* with spick and span rooms sharing bath. Some rooms have terraces and delightful sea views. **€35**

Pensión Mari Carmen C/Nueva 32 ☎ 958 610 906, ⊛ pensionmaricarmen.com. A friendly option, offering clean and tidy rooms with fans, some of them en suite and others, cheaper, sharing private bath. **€35**

EATING AND DRINKING

El Molino Paseo Marítimo s/n, to the east of El Peñon. A very good *chiringuito* with a sea-view terrace, and a great place for fish and *mariscos*. *Almejas al ajillo* (clams in garlic) and paella (€18 for two) are house specials and there's a *menú* for €10.

El Peñon Paseo Marítimo 1. Sited on the seafront promontory (*peñon*) from which it takes its name, this is an extremely popular seafood restaurant with close-up views of the sea from its terrace. Although good, it tends to exploit its location by charging higher prices. *Arroz con bogavante* (lobster rice) is a signature dish, and costs around €40 for two. Tues–Sun 12.30–5pm & 7.30–11pm.

La Bahía Playa del Peñon s/n. Slightly further back from the sea, but still with excellent views from its terrace, this is a better deal then the nearby *El Peñon* (see above). House specialities include *fritura de pescado* (fried fish), seafood paella and fresh *sardinas* cooked in a boat on the beach. Tues–Sun noon–4pm & 8pm–midnight.

La Bodega Avda. de Motril s/n, effectively the Plaza de Goya. Reliable bar-restaurant offering well-prepared *granadino* cuisine – both fish and meat – in a rustic dining room. *Silla de cordero* (saddle of lamb) is a signature dish, and there's a good wine list plus a reasonably priced lunchtime *menú del día* for €9. Main dishes €9–23. Daily 1–4pm & 8–11pm.

Emilio Paseo Marítimo s/n. One of a number of good seafront *chiringuitos* near *El Peñon* (see above), this specializes in fish and *mariscos* and has a lunchtime *menú* for €9. There is a seafront terrace at the rear. Tues–Sun noon –4.30pm & 7–11pm.

La Portería C/Fábrica Nueva 1, 50m southwest of the Turismo. Perhaps the best of the economy options in town. It's an excellent place for breakfast and, later in the day, tapas, *raciones* and full meals. As well as meat and fish they also offer decent salads and there's a lunchtime *menú* for €9. Mon–Sat 8am–4pm & 8pm–midnight.

Mesón de la Villa Plaza F. Ramirez de Madrid, 200m south of the Turismo. Inviting small restaurant with a terrace on this palm-fringed plaza. Serves a range of fish and meat dishes – *rabo de toro* (stewed bull's tail) is a special. Plus good tapas in its bar, and a reasonably priced wine list. *Menú* for around €10. Daily 12.30–4pm & 8–11pm.

Restaurante Pesetas C/Bóveda s/n, near the Alcázar. One of the best places in town for meat, fish and *mariscos* served on a superb terrace with stunning views. A varied menu includes *solomillo de cerdo* (pork loin) and *zarzuela de pescado* (fish stew). Main dishes €8–14. Tues–Sun noon–4pm & 7pm–midnight.

★ **Tres Hermanos** Paseo Marítimo s/n. This excellent *chiringuito* has a great beachfront terrace and friendly service. The *mariscos* and fish – *lubina a la sal* (sea bass) is recommended – are super-fresh and paella is a house special. Don't miss out on the outstanding salads. There's a *menú* for €9.

5

Almuñécar

Fifteen kilometres west of Salobreña, **ALMUÑÉCAR** is Granada's flagship seaside resort and, although marred by a number of towering holiday apartments, has made admirable attempts to preserve its *andaluz* character. Founded early in the first millennium BC by the Phoenicians as the wonderfully named Sexi, it possesses ruins both from this and its later Roman and Moorish periods. The town's pebble **beaches**, it has to be said, are rather cramped and not improved by the greyish sand, but the esplanade, **Paseo Puerta del Mar** (aka Paseo del Altillo), behind them, with palm-roofed bars (many offering free tapas) and restaurants, is fun, and the *casco antiguo*, or old town, atmospherically attractive.

The Castillo de San Miguel

Barrio de San Miguel • April–Sept Tues–Sat 10.30am–1.30pm & 6.30–9pm, Sun 10am–12.30pm; Oct–March Tues–Sat 10am–1.30pm & 5–7.30pm, Sun 10.30am–2pm • €2.30

Almuñécar's impressive sixteenth-century **Castillo de San Miguel**, sitting atop a headland – the Peñon del Santo – which bisects the resort's two bays, replaced the Moorish Alcazaba, itself built on top of an earlier Roman fort, in the time of Carlos V. Distinctive for its massive tower known as **La Mazmorra** ("the dungeon") this is where, in the Nasrid period, Granada's rulers imprisoned out-of-favour ministers or over-weening military commanders whom they saw as a threat. During the *Reconquista* it was taken by Fernando and Isabel in 1489, three years before the fall of Granada itself,

ALMUÑÉCAR

● **RESTAURANTS & BARS**
Bar-Taberna El Cortijillo	5
Bodega Francisco	4
El Chaleco	1
Horno de Candida	2
La Última Ola	6
Restaurante La Muralla	3

■ **ACCOMMODATION**
Hostal Plaza Damasco	2
Hostal Rocamar	1
Hotel Almuñécar Playa	5
Hotel Casablanca	7
Hotel Goya	6
Hotel Helios	4
Hotel La Najarra	3
Hotel Playa San Cristóbal	8

and given the name of Almuñécar's patron saint. Held by the French in the War of Independence, in 1808 it was bombarded by the British navy and largely ruined, after which it served as the town's graveyard. This was recently dug up – bones, coffins and all – and relocated to a new cemetery on the outskirts of town, and the castle restored. The interior now houses the town's **museum,** containing artefacts and information documenting Almuñécar's distinguished three-thousand-year history.

Museo Arqueológico

Plaza Eras Castillo • April–Sept Tues–Sat 10.30am–1.30pm & 6.30–9pm, Sun 10am–12.30pm; Oct–March Tues–Sat 10am–1.30pm & 5–7.30pm, Sun 10.30am–2pm • €2.30 or same ticket as Castillo de San Miguel

It's well worth stopping off at the small **Museo Arqueológico**, above and south of the elegant Plaza Ayuntamiento (officially the Plaza de la Constitución, a name nobody uses) in the Cueva de los Siete Palacios ("Cave of the Seven Palaces"), an ancient structure that may well have been a water reservoir. The exhibits – mostly discovered locally – are from the Phoenician, Roman and Moorish periods, including an inscribed seventeenth-century BC **Egyptian vase** which carries not only the oldest piece of written text discovered on the Iberian peninsula, but also the only known reference to the early sixteenth-century BC pharaoh Apophis I, a ruler during Egypt's hazy Hyksos period when foreign usurpers grasped the throne. If archeology is your thing, ask at the Turismo for directions to remains of a first-century two-level **Roman aqueduct** to the north of town.

Factoría de Salazones

Parque Botánico El Majuelo, Avda. de Europa • Free

Below the castle, to the west in the Parque Botanico El Majuelo, a remarkable **Factoría de Salazones** or Roman fish-curing factory has been excavated. The tanks in which the garum was prepared are well preserved, and the quality of the famous fish sauce is recorded in the writings of Pliny the Elder. The surrounding botanical garden (open site) is extremely peaceful with fine views towards the castle and walls.

Parque Ornitológico

Plaza Abderraman • Daily: April–Sept 11am–2pm & 6–9pm; Oct–March 11am–2pm & 5–7pm • €4

To the south of the Castillo de San Miguel, the **Parque Ornitológico** is an aviary filled with a squawking collection of 1500 birds representing 120 international species including macaws, peacocks, owls, toucans and ducks.

Aquarium Almuñécar

Plaza Kuwait s/n • July–Sept daily 10.30am–9pm, Oct–June Mon–Fri 10am–6.30pm, Sat & Sun 10.30am–7.30pm • €12

Almuñécar's **aquarium** is a fun experience especially if you've got kids to entertain. After various tanks containing fish and crustaceans from around the world, the highlight is the water tunnel where sharks, stingrays, turtles and multitudes of other fish glide effortlessly a few centimetres above your head.

The ship house

Avda. El Mediterráneo 34 near the N340 *autovía*

One remarkable but little-known sight is the astonishing **ship house** built by an ex-merchant sea captain, José-María Pérez Ruiz, in the northeastern suburb of the town close to the N340 *autovía*. After captaining his ship for thirty years, upon retirement Señor Pérez Ruiz decided to recreate his vessel on dry land – in concrete. When you approach the house you see nothing less than a 50m-long hull towering above the road complete with a bridge (now the captain's lounge and bedroom) sporting radar masts, radio antennae and all flags flying. The "deck" has all the paraphernalia of a real ship, and a swimming pool as well. It's not open to visitors but if you're a guest at Señor Pérez Ruiz's hotel (see p.540) you may just get a guided tour.

5

By bus The bus station – with frequent connections to Granada and Málaga – is at the junction of Avda. Juan Carlos I and Avenida Fenicia, northeast of the centre.

Turismo Avda. de Europa s/n (Daily: Sept–June 10am–2pm & 5–8pm; July & Aug 10am–2pm & 6–9pm; ☎ 958 631 125, ⓦ almunecar.info). Located in a striking nineteenth-century neo-Moorish garden mansion, Almuñécar's tourist office can provide copious information on the town and the Costa Tropical.

Internet Locutorio Africa-Ciber, Avda. de Andalucía 18 (daily 10am–2pm & 5pm–midnight), south of the bus station.

Festival There's an annual jazz festival – now one of the most important in Spain, and often attracting big names – held in July.

ACCOMMODATION

The pressure on **accommodation** in Almuñécar is not as acute as on the Costa del Sol and there are more than enough hotels to cope with the summer crush. Good-value *hostales* encircle the central Plaza de la Rosa in the old town and there are more to be found just east of here, in the streets off the Avda. de Andalucía. The nearest campsites lie10km west at La Herradura (see p.541). The prices quoted here are for July and August; outside those months they can fall by up to 50 percent.

Hostal Plaza Damasco C/Cerrajeros 8 ☎ 958 630 165. Cosy *hostal* just off the plaza it's named after, offering a/c en-suite rooms with TV. Can assist with parking. **€50**

Hostal Rocamar C/Córdoba 3, near the bus station ☎ 958 630 023. Welcoming, clean and tidy *hostal* with functional but perfectly acceptable a/c en-suite rooms. **€40**

Hotel Almuñécar Playa Paseo San Cristóbal s/n ☎ 958 639 450, ⓦ playasenator.com. The glaring terracotta exterior of this 225-room luxury hotel conceals a spectacular atrium lobby with waterfall and plants dangling from the glass roof. Not to everyone's taste, but you get all the frills associated with a four-star hotel, including minibar, internet access and a pool. B&B **€208**

★ **Hotel Casablanca** Plaza San Cristóbal 4 (aka Plaza Abderramán) ☎ 958 635 575, ⓦ hotelcasablanca almunecar.com. With a wonderfully flamboyant neo-Moorish facade and interior, this family-run establishment is a gem. The service is friendly and the rooms, most with sea-facing terrace balconies, are well equipped and come with free wi-fi. Own garage. **€65**

Hotel Goya Avda. Europa s/n ☎ 958 630 550 ⓦ hotel goyaalmunecar.com. Appealing hotel with comfortable, airy a/c rooms opposite the Turismo and 50m from the Playa de San Cristóbal. On-street parking nearby. **€65**

Hotel Helios Paseo San Cristóbal s/n ☎ 958 634 459, ⓦ heliosalmunecar.com. Long Almuñécar's leading hotel, the *Helios* offers tastefully furnished terrace balcony rooms with sea views, plus a pool and rooftop solarium. **€161**

Hotel La Najarra C/Guadix 12 ☎ 958 630 873, ⓦ hotelnajarra.com. Well-equipped three-star hotel with a/c rooms plus garden pool, tennis courts and easy parking a couple of minutes' walk from the Playa de San Cristóbal. Rates halve during the months outside July–Sept. **€78**

Hotel Playa San Cristóbal Plaza San Cristóbal 5 ☎ 958 633 612, ⓔ hotelplayasancristobal@hotmail .com. Old-fashioned place with a bar full of characters and a/c balcony rooms with TV above. The eccentric proprietor, an ex-sea captain, constructed the remarkable "ship house" in the north of the town (see p.539). Rates halve outside July & Aug. **€90**

EATING AND DRINKING

There are countless **places to eat** lined along the Paseo Puerta del Mar, many of them offering cheap if unspectacular *menús*. The town's more interesting possibilities lie away from the seafront hurly-burly in the *casco antiguo* and beyond: Almuñécar has become something of a gastronomic hotspot in recent years and has a number of outstanding restaurants.

Bar-Taberna El Cortijillo Plaza Kelibia 4. Lively *freiduría* and *raciónes* bar popular with young locals, in an attractive square with a lively scene on summer nights. *Costillitas con patatas* (spare ribs) is a special here. Daily noon–5pm & 7.30pm–midnight.

Bodega Francisco C/Real 15, north of Plaza Rosa. Wonderful old bar with barrels stacked up to the ceiling and walls covered with ageing *corrida* posters and mounted boars' heads. The fino and *montilla* are both excellent, and the bar offers a wide range of tapas and *platos combinados*. A dining area has recently been added and impromptu flamenco sometimes adds to the fun. Tues–Sun 1–4pm & 8–11.30pm.

★ **El Chaleco** Avda. Costa del Sol 37 ☎ 958 632 402. Slightly out of the way, this is a stunningly good-value Belgian-French restaurant with an outstanding kitchen. Among their signature dishes are *ensalada de mejillones* (mussel salad), *croquetas de pescado* (fish croquettes) and *conejo a la cerveza con ciruelas* (rabbit cooked in beer with prunes) and you can choose three courses off the menu for €21. Add in very reasonable wine prices and you have one of the best dining-out bargains in Andalucía (which is why it's advisable to book). Tues–Sat 12.30–3pm & 7.30–10.30pm, Sun 12.30–3pm.

★ **Horno de Candida** C/Orovia 3 ☎ 958 883 284. The restaurant of Almuñécar's hotel school is in an elegant mansion which itself incorporates a remarkable Moorish brick oven (*horno*), now a dining room. The food is excellent and there's a wonderful roof terrace, too. Main dishes €12–18 with a *menú de degustación* for €29. Tues–Sun 1–4pm & 8–11pm.

La Última Ola Paseo Puerta del Mar 4. This excellent mid-priced seafront fish restaurant also serves tapas and squeezes a few meat dishes onto its menu as well. One of

its noted dishes is *dorada a la gaditana* (sea bream) and they also offer paella and other rice dishes. Main dishes €10–20. Daily 1–5pm & 8pm–midnight.

Restaurante La Muralla C/Ángel Gamay s/n. Excellent bodega serving a range of outstanding tapas and *raciones* as well as meals in their interior room or alfresco in a tiny alley. Main dishes €12–20. Mon–Sat 1–4pm & 8–11pm, Sun 1–4pm.

NIGHTLIFE

Almuñecar's nightlife centres around the focal Plaza Kelibia and the revamped seafront Paseo del Altillo where a line of music **clubs** and **bars** – many with outdoor terraces – fill up on summer nights.

La Herradura

Beyond Almuñécar, the N340 passes tracks leading down to inviting coves with quiet **beaches**, a few of which have welcoming bars. After 8km the road descends into **LA HERRADURA**, a fishing village-resort with a long, sandy beach making it a good place to stop off for a swim.

ARRIVAL AND INFORMATION
LA HERRADURA

By bus A daily bus service connects La Herradura with Almuñécar and there are stops along the seafront Paseo Andrés Segovia.

Turismo municipal Paseo Segovia s/n at the extreme eastern end of the seafront (daily 10am–2pm & 5–8pm;

📞 958 827 984).

Windsurfing Windsurf La Herradura, Paseo Marítimo 34 (📞 958 640 143, 🌐 windsurflaherradura.com). Friendly and efficient windsurf, catamaran, kayak and dinghy sailing outfit who rent out gear and give courses.

ACCOMMODATION

Hostal La Caleta Paseo Andrés Segovia 11 📞 958 827 007. This friendly *hostal* at the eastern end of the seafront offers pleasant en-suite a/c rooms with TV, and some with seaview. **€50**

Hostal Peña Parda Paseo Andrés Segovia 65 📞 958 640 066, 🌐 pensionpenaparda.com. At the western end of the seafront, this is a decent *hostal* offering en-suite rooms with ceiling fans and TV; some have sea views. Free wi-fi and parking. **€60**

Hotel Almijara C/Acera del Pilar 6 📞 958 618 053,

🌐 hotelalmijara.com. The comfortable *Hotel Almijara*, slightly inland from the sea, is a good three-star hotel with light, well-equipped rooms with minibar and TV. However, it lacks a pool. Rates halve outside July & Aug. **€105**

Nuevo Camping Paseo Andrés Segovia s/n at the extreme western end of the seafront 📞 958 640 634, 🌐 nuevocamping.com. There are a couple of summer campsites with confusingly similar names; this is the best, with plenty of shade and good facilities. **€6** per person, **€6** per tent, **€5** per vehicle

EATING AND DRINKING

La Gaviota Paseo Andrés Segovia s/n 📞 958 827 550. Excellent fish restaurant on the other side of the road from the *Peña Parda* (see below) fronting the beach. The house specials are *ensalada de pulpo* (octopus salad) and an outstanding *gambas pil-pil* (prawns with garlic). There's a wonderful sea-view terrace. Tues–Sun 1–4.30pm & 8–11.30pm.

La Parilla Paseo Andrés Segovia 39 📞 958 640 619. A popular mid-priced seafront restaurant specializing in charcoal-grilled meat and fish dishes. There's also a *menú* for around €13. Main dishes €14–19. Tues–Sat 1–4.30pm & 8pm–midnight, Sun 1–4.30pm.

Mesón El Tinao Paseo Marítimo s/n, set back slightly

from the seafront 📞 958 827 488. Atmospheric little bar-restaurant serving good tapas and *raciones* and full meals. They offer a great value *menú de degustación* for two for €40 (including wine) or a fish and meat paella for two for €30. Daily noon–4pm & 8–11pm.

Restaurante El Rincón de Peña Parda Paseo Andrés Segovia 66 📞 958 827 354. Next door to the similarly named *hostal* (see above) this is a very good and economical option with an attractive sea-view terrace. House specials include paella and *codillo de cerdo* (pork) as well as tasty salads. There's also a *menú* for €12.50. Tues–Sat 1–4pm & 7.30–11.30pm, Sun 1–4pm.

5

The Costa de Almería

The **Costa de Almería**, east of Almería, has a somewhat wild air, with developments constrained by lack of water and roads and by the confines of the **Parque Natural de Cabo de Gata**, a protected zone since 1987. If you have transport, it's still possible to find deserted beaches without too much difficulty, while small inlets shelter relatively low-key resorts such as **San José**, **Los Escullos**, **Las Negras** and **Agua Amarga**.

Further north is **Mojácar**, a picturesque hill village, which has become a beach resort of quite some size over the past decade. It is easiest – and most speedily – approached on the inland routes via Níjar (the A7-E15) or the "desert" road (N340A) through Tabernas and Sorbas.

Almería to Mojácar

The coast between Almería and Mojácar is backed by the **Sierra del Cabo de Gata**, which gives it a bit of character and wilderness. **Buses** run from Almería to all the main resorts, though to do much exploring, or seek out deserted strands, transport of your own is invaluable. The heat is blistering here throughout the summer, and you should bear in mind that during July and particularly August accommodation in the park is at a premium – try and book ahead if possible.

El Cabo de Gata and around

Heading east from Almería along the main AL12, and following a turn-off to the right, 3km beyond the airport, will take you south to **EL CABO DE GATA** (aka El Cabo). This is the closest resort to the city with any appeal: a lovely expanse of coarse sand, best in the mornings before the sun and wind get up. In the village itself there are plentiful bars, cafés and shops, plus a fish market.

Arriving at El Cabo, you pass a lake, the **Laguna de Rosa**, a protected locale that is home to flamingos and other waders. Four kilometres south of El Cabo, just beyond Las Salinas, is **ALMADRABA DE MONTELVA**, more a continuation than a separate destination, but an altogether more appealing place to hang around.

CABO DE GATA NATURAL PARK

Protected since 1987, the 71,500 acres of the **Cabo de Gata Natural Park** stretch from Retamar to the east of Almería across the cape to the Barranco del Honda, just north of Agua Amarga. The Sierra de Gata is volcanic in origin and its adjacent dunes and saltings are some of the most important wetland areas in Spain for **breeding birds** and **migrants**. At Las Salinas alone more than eighty species can be sighted throughout the year, including the magnificent pink flamingos as well as avocet, storks and egrets during their migrations. And there have been rarer sightings of Andouin's gull, as well as Bonelli's eagle and eagle owls around the crags.

Other **fauna** include the rare Italian wall lizard (its only habitat in Spain), with its distinctive green back with three rows of black spots, as well as the more common fox (sporting its Iberian white tail tip), hare and grass snake. Among the **flora**, the stunted dwarf fan palm is mainland Europe's only native palm and the salt marshes are home to a strange parasitic plant, the striking yellow-flowering *Cistanche phelypaea*, which feeds on goosefoot.

The best times for sighting the fauna here are at **dawn and dusk** as, with temperatures among the highest in Europe and rainfall at 10cm a year the lowest, energy has to be conserved. There are three official **Puntos de Información** in the park: at the Cabo de Gata lighthouse (see p.544), Pozo de Frailes (near San José; p.545) and the main centre at Rodalquilar (see p.547). There is also a private information office in the resort of San José (p.545). The three official offices should have free copies of *Cuaderno de Senderos* (in Spanish) detailing eighteen walks in the park of between two and twelve kilometres. Any hiking in the park is greatly assisted by using the Editorial Alpina 1:50.000 *Cabo de Gata-Níjar* map which accurately marks trekking routes, tracks and campsites.

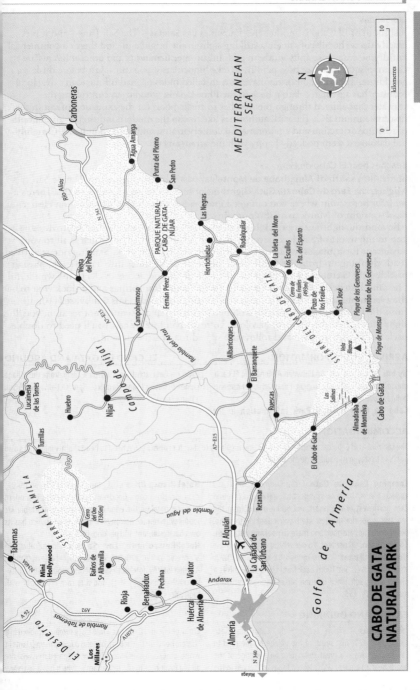

MEDITERRANEAN SEA

Carboneras

Agua Amarga

Punta del Plomo

San Pedro

Río Alías

N-341

PARQUE NATURAL CABO DE GATA-NÍJAR

Las Negras

Rodalquilar

Hortichuelas

La Isleta del Moro

Los Escullos

Pta. del Esparto

Cerro de los Frailes (493m)

Venta del Pobre

Campohermoso

Fernán Pérez

Pozo de los Frailes

San José

Playa de los Genoveses

Morrón de los Genoveses

A7-E15

Albaricoques

El Barranquete

Rambla del Agua

S I E R R A   D E L   C A B O   D E   G A T A

Vela Blanca

Playa de Mónsul

Lucainena de las Torres

Huebro

Níjar

C a m p o   d e   N í j a r

Ruescas

Las Salinas

Playa de los Genoveses

Turrillas

A-7

El Cabo de Gata

Almadraba de Montelva

Cabo de Gata

S I E R R A   A L H A M I L L A

Cerro del Oro (1365m)

A7-E15

Rambla del Agua

Retamar

Tabernas

N-340A

Mini Hollywood

Baños de Sª Alhamilla

Rioja

Benahadux

Pechina

Viator

Andarax

Huércal de Almería

El Alquián

La Cañada de Sª Urbano

G o l f o   d e   A l m e r í a

A-92

Rambla de Tabernas

A-1075

El Desierto

Los Millares

Almería

N-340

N-340

E-15

A l m e r í a

Málaga

CABO DE GATA NATURAL PARK

N

0   kilometres   10

5

Las Salinas

Just south of El Cabo is another area known as **Las Salinas** – The Salt Pans – and it is exactly that. The hills of salt are a striking sight in the bright sun, and there's a commercial salt-drying enterprise at its southern end. In summer **flamingos** and other migrants are a common sight here (see box, p.542), so take binoculars if you can – just before dusk is a good time. The park authorities have now installed **hides** (signed off the road). The local industry has a pedigree dating back to the Phoenicians, who began controlling the seawater that entered through the marshes to create pools for the extraction of salt in the first millennium BC. The park authorities like to cite the modern industry as an example of resource extraction and environmental conservation working hand in hand. Certainly the flamingos seem perfectly happy with the arrangement.

Beaches near El Cabo de Gata

Some 4km south of **Almadraba de Montelva**, past a hill known as the Pico de San Miguel, the **Faro de Cabo de Gata** (lighthouse) marks the cape's southern tip. There's a *mirador* here, from where you can get a great view of the rock cliffs and – on clearer days – a sight of Morocco's Rif mountains.

Beyond the lighthouse a track leads to two of the finest **beaches** in the province, and to the resort of San José beyond. This track is closed to cars, which is all to your advantage for it makes for a fine walk through the Natural Park. Starting out as a paved road, climbing up from the lighthouse, this soon degenerates into a dirt track, passing prickly pear cactus plantations grown for their fruit, and access tracks to the wonderful fine sand beaches of **Monsul** (6km out) – with freshwater springs and a track west to the even more secluded Media Luna cove – and further east, **Los Genoveses** (10km from the lighthouse). A couple of kilometres further, and beyond another spur, you'll sight the sea and the resort of San José. To reach San José **by car**, you'll need to double back to El Cabo de Gata and follow the signed road further inland.

ARRIVAL AND INFORMATION   EL CABO DE GATA AND AROUND

By bus Six buses a day run between Almería and El Cabo, making an intermediate stop at Retamar, a retirement/holiday development.
Cabo de Gata Natural Park information In the

Cabo de Gata lighthouse car park, 8km from the village (June–Oct daily 11am–3pm & 6–8pm; Oct–May Sat & Sun 11am–3pm).

ACCOMMODATION

The seafront at El Cabo has a rather listless air and no places to stay; for **rooms** you'll need to head slightly inland. It's also possible to stay in Almadraba de Montelva.

Camping Cabo de Gata Ctra. Cabo de Gata s/n ☏ 950 160 443, ⓦ campingcabodegata.com. Around 2km northwest of the resort and 800m inland from the sea, this is not the shadiest site if you're looking to camp. But the facilities are good and there's a pool and restaurant. €6 per person, €6 per tent, €6 per vehicle
Hostal Las Dunas C/Barrionuevo 58 ☏ 950 370 072, ⓦ lasdunas.net. Set 100m back from the beach, this is a pleasant enough place offering air-conditioned en-suite rooms with TV. €55

Hotel Blanca Brisa C/Las Joricas 49 ☏ 950 37 00 01, ⓦ blancabrisa.com. Good-value and welcoming modern two-star hotel on the edge of town with comfortable a/c rooms with terrace balcony, TV and free wi-fi. Also has its own bar-restaurant and parking. B&B €70
Hotel-Restaurante Las Salinas Almadraba de Montelva ☏ 950 370 103, ⓦ lasalinascabodegata.com. A rather kitschy hotel with some decent rooms (with a fifty-percent surcharge in Aug), and a terrace restaurant with high prices. €60

EATING AND DRINKING

★ **Chiri-Bus** Torreón (tower) de Cabo de Gata ☏ 639 888 421. Just south of the village on the road to Las Salinas, this is a great *chiringuito* on the edge of the beach near an ancient watchtower. Tapas are served in the

atmospheric and lively bar while tasty *sardinas* (cooked in a "barbie boat" on the beach), *almejas a la marinera* (clams in white wine) and *mejillones al vapor* (steamed mussels) are all big favourites in the restaurant – which has a sea-view

terrace. Daily noon–5pm & 8–11pm.
El Faro Cabo de Gata lighthouse. A friendly tapas bar serving tasty locally caught fried fish and paella.

La Almadraba Almadraba de Montelva. The friendlier and more down-to-earth of the restaurants in Almadraba, a seafront place with excellent fish and *mariscos*.

San José

The attractive little resort of **SAN JOSÉ** has a sandy beach in a small cove, with shallow water, while more fine beaches lie within walking distance. Only a few years ago it was almost completely undeveloped, though things are changing, with a rash of apartments and a new yacht harbour.

If you've followed the walk from the lighthouse to San José (see p.544) and want to continue along the coast there's another **track**, running 12km north to Los Escullos and La Isleta. To start the walk take the road north out of San José, along which you'll shortly come to a turn-off along a dirt track on the right that heads around a hill – Cerro del Enmedio – towards the coast. The track branches at various points and you'll have to decide whether to follow the coastal tracks (which can be impassable) or the surer inland route. The first track off to the coast provides access to a beautiful and secluded cove. Further on, the route skirts the 500m-high Cerro de los Frailes, beyond which lie the inlets of Los Escullos and La Isleta.

ARRIVAL AND INFORMATION   SAN JOSÉ

By bus San José is served by three daily buses from Almería.
Natural park information There's a privately run information centre for the natural park on Avda. de San José, near the centre of the village (daily 10am–2pm & 5.30–8.30pm; ☎ 950 380 299, ⊛ cabodegata-nijar.com). They have lots of information on activities such as guided walks and horse treks in the area and a complete list of accommodation and information on apartments to rent. At Pozo de los Frailes, 4km from San José, you'll find a Punto de Información kiosk (June–Sept daily 10am–2pm & 6–8pm), which also has information on the natural park.

Internet You can get online at the park information centre and, nearby, at Bla Bla Bla (daily 9am–midnight), Pasaje Curry.
Adventure activities Horses can be rented for exploring the park from the *Hotel Cortijo El Sotillo* (see below). Alpha (☎ 950 380 321, ⊛ alphabuceo.com) is a PADI-certificated diving centre located in the Puerto Deportivo (yacht harbour) for courses in snorkelling and scuba diving.
Shops Along Avda. de San José there's a bank with ATM cash machine, plus a couple of well-stocked supermarkets for picnic supplies.

ACCOMMODATION

The only time it's difficult to find a room is during **high season** (July & Aug), when some places want stays of at least five days (applying a surcharge for shorter durations). It's essential to ring ahead in high season and advisable at other times of the year, too. As with other seaside destinations, rates fall by up to fifty percent outside July and Aug (we quote the high-season rates here).

Albergue Juvenil C/Montemar s/n ☎ 950 380 353, ⊛ alberguesanjose.com. Reached by the same road that leads to the campsite (see below) this privately run youth hostel has 86 places in rooms sleeping from two to eight persons. Wi-fi zone. It is usually booked solid at Easter and in Aug. **€14** per person.
Camping Tau Camino de Cala Higuera s/n ☎ 950 380 166, ⊛ campingtau.com. San José's good campsite has modern facilities and plenty of shade. It's reached via a signed road on the left as you enter the village. Wi-fi zone. Closed Nov–March. **€7** per person, **€8** per tent, **€7** per vehicle
Cortijo El Sotillo Ctra. San José s/n ☎ 950 611 100, ⊛ cortijoelsotillo.es. To the left on the main road in, and 1km from the centre, this is a refurbished eighteenth-century ranch-house converted into a four-star country hotel with elegant rustically furnished rooms, decent

mid-priced restaurant, bar, pool, tennis courts, and stables with horses for hire. Free wi-fi and parking. **€150**
Hostal Aloha C/Cala Higuera s/n ☎ 950 380 461, ⊛ hostalaloha.com. Good *hostal* with excellent a/c en-suite balcony rooms and the bonus of a fine palm-fringed pool at the rear; they also have a very good tapas bar below. B&B **€80**
Hostal Brisa Mar C/Ancla s/n ☎ 950 380 431, ⊛ hostal brisamar.com. Over the road from *Las Gaviotas* (see below), with bright and airy a/c en-suite balcony rooms with TV and a pretty garden. **€70**
Hostal Las Gaviotas C/Córdoba s/n ☎ 950 380 010, ⊛ hlasgaviotas.com. Almost next door to *Hotel Agades Agidir* (see p.546) this is a more economical (outside high season) option for modern en-suite rooms with a/c and TV. **€84**

5

Hostal San José C/Las Olas s/n ☎950 611 080, ⓦservimar.net. An upmarket *hostal*, perched on a hill overlooking the harbour, with modern a/c en-suite rooms equipped with kitchenette and balcony terraces with fine sea views. €95

Hostal Sol Bahía C/Correos 5 ☎950 380 307, ⓦsol bahiasanjose.es. Near the main junction in the centre of the village, this is one of the better-value central places, offering spacious a/c en-suite balcony rooms with TV. €70

Hotel Agades Agidir C/Córdoba s/n ☎950 380 390, ⓦhotelagades.com. Very good option where a/c en-suite balcony rooms come with satellite TV and there's

a garden pool, bar and restaurant. It's on the right-hand side of the main road as you come in (a 5min walk from the village). €95

Hotel Doña Pakyta C/Correo s/n ☎950 611 175, ⓦhotelpakyta.es. One of the swishest places in town, at the western end of the bay, offering light and airy terrace balcony rooms with four-star frills and stunning sea views. B&B €175

Hotel La Posada de Paco C/Correo s/n ☎950 380 010, ⓦlaposadadepaco.com. On the main street and slightly east of the main junction, this is a stylish small hotel with pool and a/c terrace rooms with satellite TV. €97

EATING AND DRINKING

There are numerous **bars** and **restaurants** on the central Plaza de Génova and facing the nearby beach on C/del Puerto Deportivo, offering everything from fast food and pizzas to excellent fresh local fish.

Bar-Restaurante El Emigrante C/Correos s/n (opposite the *Hostal Sol Bahía*). Near the village's main junction, this is a friendly and good-value place for breakfasting or, later in the day, tapas and *raciones* or full meals. It prepares good fish and *platos combinados* and has a *menú* for €10. Wed–Mon 9am–4pm & 7–11pm.

La Cueva Paseo Marítimo 36. A reliable harbourfront restaurant serving predominantly seafood; house specials include *salmonetes* (red mullet fried with garlic), *ensalada de salmón marinado* and *conejo con caracoles* (rabbit with snails). Daily 1–5pm & 7.30–11pm.

La Gallineta Pozo de los Frailes ☎950 380 501, 4km back along the entry road. Set inside an elegantly furnished traditional house beside a restored Moorish water-wheel, this is the area's only place with any pretensions, serving up sophisticated Mediterranean meat and fish dishes. A very attractive dining room is complemented by some very good cooking and *cerdo ibérico* (black-pig pork), *arrozes* (rice dishes) and paellas

all feature, along with a "fish of the day" dish, too. Main dishes €10–25. Tues–Sun 1.30–3.30pm & 9–11pm.

Mediterráneo Puerto Deportivo s/n. This harbourfront seafood restaurant has an inviting terrace and offers a wide variety of fish and rice dishes as well as salads and couscous. Daily noon–4pm & 7.30–11.30pm.

Restaurante Casa Miguel Avda. de San José 43. On the main street near the tourist office, this is perhaps the best of the village centre places. It offers a range of well-prepared fish and meat dishes, and *arroz a la marinera* (seafood paella) is a house speciality. There's also a decent wine list. They have a sister restaurant on the harbour. Wed–Mon noon–5pm & 7–11pm.

Taberna del Puerto Puerto Deportivo s/n. Overlooking the Puerto Deportivo, which lies beyond the main harbour, this is an atmospheric little bar-restaurant serving *mariscos* and fish tapas in its bar or full meals in a cosy restaurant; *carpaccio de atún fresco* (fresh tuna) is a house special. Also has a small terrace. Thurs–Tues 9am–11pm.

Los Escullos

The next village beyond San José along this rugged coastline is the isolated and peaceful hamlet of **LOS ESCULLOS**, 8km north by road, with a good if rather pebbly beach and a formidable once-ruined – but recently refurbished – fort, the eighteenth-century **Castillo de San Felipe**.

ACCOMMODATION AND EATING	**LOS ESCULLOS**
Camping Los Escullos Paraje Los Escullos s/n ☎950 389 811, ⓦlosescullossanjose.com. Los Escullos's campsite is set back from the sea with limited shade, but has decent facilities including pool, restaurant and shop. €7 per person, €11 per tent.	**Casa Emilio** Paseo Marítimo s/n ☎950 389 761, ⓦhostalcasaemilio.com. This beachfront *hostal-restaurante*, offering a/c en-suite rooms with sea-view terrace balcony, is the best of a couple of options here with a good bar and restaurant below. €60

La Isleta

LA ISLETA, 2km beyond Los Escullos, is a slowly expanding fishing village that still manages to retain a sleepy atmosphere and has a rather scruffy pebble beach, although there's a better one – Playa la Ola – to the east backed by a car park.

ACCOMMODATION AND EATING LA ISLETA

★ **Bar-Restaurante La Ola** Off the village's main square and set back from the beach. The best tapas bar-restaurant in these parts, with a shady terrace. Wonderfully atmospheric, it serves up seafood tapas and *raciones* plus great fish and *mariscos*. House favourites here include a mouthwatering *arroz con bogavante* (lobster) and *parillada de pescado*

(fried seafood platter). Dec–Sept daily 9.30am–6pm & 8.30pm–midnight.

Isleta del Moro ☎ 950 389 713. This welcoming *hostal-restaurante*, overlooking the harbour, has reasonably priced en-suite sea-view balcony rooms plus a decent bar-restaurant serving tapas, seafood and a good-value *menú* for around €12. **€50**

Rodalquilar

The road north of La Isleta climbs over the cliffs above the village and heads inland before descending to a pleasant valley, passing after 4km the desert hamlet of **RODALQUILAR** surrounded by scrub, palms and cactuses. Once a centre of gold mining initiated by the Romans, its nineteenth-century workings scar the crags behind the village where a daunting edifice still bears the inscription in English "Guard Block B." You will also pass the lines of ruined miners' dwellings from this era along the entry road leading to a natural park information office (see below). Today the village has a vaguely "alternative" air about it and its desert location has attracted many artists and creative types who have houses in the village and around.

ARRIVAL AND INFORMATION RODALQUILAR

By bus Rodalquilar is served by a single daily bus from Almería.

Natural Park information office C/Fundición s/n,

opposite the church in the centre (June–Sept daily 10am–2pm & 4–8pm; Oct–March Sat & Sun 10am–2pm & 4–6pm; ☎ 950 389 820).

ACCOMMODATION AND EATING

El Cinto C/Santa Bárbara 13. In the heart of the village near the natural park information office, this is a popular little *taberna* cooking up a range of dishes including fried fish and *mariscos*. Daily noon–4pm & 8pm–midnight.

Hotel Rodalquilar Paraje de los Albacetes ☎ 950 389

838, ⊕ hotelrodalquilar.com. An attractive desert inn, on the village's eastern edge, with comfortable tile-floored rooms arranged around a sunken courtyard; a restaurant, pool, spa, sauna and gym plus free loan of mountain bikes are just a few of the facilities on offer. **€88**

Las Negras

LAS NEGRAS, an expanding beach settlement 5km further along the coast beyond Rodalquilar, is situated in the folds of a beautiful cove, with an *atalaya* (watchtower) sited on the edge of the village as you approach. There's a pebbly beach backed by a few **bars** and eating places and that's about it. On the seafront, the PADI certificated Buceo de Las Negras (☎ 950 388 217) offers **scuba-diving** courses (beginners and advanced) and also rents out kayaks and mountain bikes and offers **internet** access.

ACCOMMODATION LAS NEGRAS

Camping La Caleta La Playa s/n ☎ 950 525 237, ⊕ campinglacaleta.com. The village campsite, set in a tranquil location with its own bay, has reasonable shade and good facilities including a pool, supermarket and restaurant. It's reached via a 1km-long road signed on the right just outside the village on the way in. **€6** per person, **€7.50** per tent, **€6** per vehicle.

Estanco Piedra García C/Bahía s/n ☎ 950 388 075, ⊕ lasnegras.com. In summer plenty of places around the village post signs offering accommodation to let. Another

option for longer stays (five nights plus in high season) is the collection of apartments and chalets in coastal and country locations rented out by this main street tobacconist and information office whose proprietors speak good English. **€60**

Hostal Arrecife C/Bahía 6 ☎ 950 388 140. A friendly and very good value *hostal* close to the *estanco* (see above), with attractive a/c en-suite sea-view terrace balcony rooms with TV. **€45**

5

EATING

El Manteca Playa s/n. Appealing seafront restaurant with a great terrace fronting the beach and where paella, *arroz con bogavante* (lobster) and fresh *mariscos* are the main attractions. Daily 1–4pm & 8–11pm.

La Palma C/Bahía s/n. At the end of the main street fronting the beach with a sea-view terrace, this is a good place for fish and *mariscos*. *Sardinas a la plancha* (grilled sardines) is a house special. Tues–Sun noon–4.30pm & 8–11.30pm.

San Pedro

If you fancy a change of beach scene, ask at the *estanco* in Las Negras; they should be able to arrange for someone to row you up the coast to the ruined village of **SAN PEDRO**. If you can't find an oarsman, you'll have to walk – no bad hike when it's cool – to visit the village with its caves and ruined castle; it lies 4km north on a poor track. The place was inhabited until a few years ago when the mainly elderly residents upped sticks to Las Negras, which had acquired a road, leaving their houses – sometimes occupied by north European pseudo-hippies – to crumble. If you are feeling really energetic, you could walk 7km on from here along the coast to Agua Amarga, via another pleasant beach at **Cala del Plomo**. If you attempt these walks in summer remember to take along drinking water as there is none to be had en route or at San Pedro.

Agua Amarga

AGUA AMARGA, just short of the Cabo de Gata Natural Park's northern boundary, is a delightful little fishing village cut off from the surrounding world by a long road and limited accommodation. To reach it from Las Negras (a route not served by public transport) you'll need to head inland to the village of **Fernan Pérez**, from where a new road heads east for 11km to reach the small resort.

Many of the summer visitors here are Italians who rent a tasteful crop of villas. The excellent, fine sand **beach**, backed by a number of bars and restaurants, has outlets renting windsurf boards and canoes. The PADI-certificated Centro de Buceo, behind the beach at Calle Aguada s/n (☎950 138 213) offers **scuba-diving** courses for beginners and experienced divers.

ACCOMMODATION
AGUA AMARGA

Caparrós Apartamentos C/Aguada 13 ☎950 138 246, ⊛costamarga2002.es. For longer stays (2 nights plus) this reliable agency has a range of fully equipped sea-view apartments with terrace, some fronting the beach. **€90**

Hostal-Restaurante La Palmera Right behind the central beach ☎950 138 208, ⊛hostalrestaurante lapalmera.com. Bright and cool a/c en-suite rooms with sea-view terrace balconies above a bar-restaurant. **€80**

Hotel El Tío Kiko C/Embarque 12 ☎950 138 080, ⊛eltiokiko.com. On a rise behind *Pensión Family*, this is a luxury boutique hotel with stylishly furnished terrace

sea-view rooms arranged around a pool. It also has its own good mid-priced restaurant. B&B **€125**

Hotel Las Calas C/Desagüe 1 ☎950 138 016, ⊛hotel lascalas.com. Fronting the beach at the southern end of the village, this hotel offers pristine rooms with minibar, terrace and sea view. **€116**

Pensión Family C/La Lomilla ☎950 138 014, ⊛hotelfamily.es. Friendly and charming French-run *hostal* set back from the south end of the beach, where attractive en-suite rooms (some with sea view) are complemented by a small garden pool and a very good restaurant. **€92**

EATING

Restaurante Rene & Michél Pensión Family, C/La Lomilla ☎950 138 014, ⊛hotelfamily.es. The *hostal* has a very good kitchen that turns out a range of Moroccan-French influenced dishes including couscous, *canard à l'orange* and *jabalí al horno* (oven-baked wild boar) – and don't miss out on the lemon sorbet dessert with a dash of vodka. An excellent-value *menú* costs €23

(including wine). Mon–Sat 1–4pm & 8–10.30pm, Sun 1–4pm.

Rincón de las Cuevas Hotel Las Calas, C/Desagüe 1 ☎950 138 016, ⊛hotellascalas.com. With its inviting garden terrace, this is well worth a visit; the speciality is seafood – try the *arroz a banda* (fish and rice) or *lubina a la sal* (sea bass baked in salt). Daily 1–4pm & 8–11pm.

Mojácar and around

Beyond the Cabo de Gata Natural Park, **CARBONERAS**, 11km north of Agua Amarga, is a large but easy-going fishing port with an average beach slightly marred by the shadow of a massive cement factory around the bay. North of here lies a succession of small, isolated coves, backed by a characteristically arid Almerian landscape of scrub-covered hills and dried up *arroyos*, or watercourses. The **Carboneras–Mojácar road** itself winds perilously – and scenically – through the hills and offers access to some deserted grey-sand beaches before ascending to the Punta del Santo with fine views along the coast. The descent from here brings you to the **Playa de Macenas**, another attractive beach with wild-camping possibilities. There are a couple more beaches – **Costa del Pirulico** is a good one with a beach *chiringuito* – before the urban sprawl of Mojácar takes over.

Mojácar

MOJÁCAR, Almería's main and growing resort, is split between the ancient hilltop village – **Mojácar Pueblo** – sited a couple of kilometres back from the sea, a striking town of white cubist houses wrapped round a harsh outcrop of rock, and the resort area of **Mojácar Playa** which ribbons for a couple of miles along the seafront.

In the 1960s, when the main Spanish *costas* were being developed, this was virtually a ghost town, its inhabitants having long since taken the only logical step, and emigrated. The town's fortunes revived, however, when the local mayor, using the popularity of other equally barren spots on the Spanish islands and mainland as an example, offered free land to anyone willing to build within a year. The bid was a modest success, attracting one of the decade's multifarious "artist colonies", now long supplanted by package holiday companies and second-homers. These days something of a tourist trap, the hill village has a plush 150-room hotel as well as a *parador* in the beach resort below, both symbolic of the changing times.

Mojácar Pueblo

The hilltop settlement of **MOJÁCAR PUEBLO** goes back at least to prehistoric Iberian times, and became prominent during the Roman period when Pliny described it as one of the most important towns of Baetica – as the Roman province was called. Coins found from this era give the Roman name as Murgis, which the later Moors adapted to Muxacra. The village's **main fountain** (the Fuente Mora) – signed to the right off the road climbing towards the centre – has been newly restored with lots of marble and geraniums and was where forty years ago veiled women still used to do the family washing. A plaque nearby relates how keen the Moors were to hang on to their hilltop eyrie when challenged by the *Reconquista*. First declaring loyalty to the Reyes Católicos the Moorish mayor, Alabez, then stated that if the Catholic monarchs wouldn't accede to the request to be left in peace, "rather than live like a coward I shall die like a Spaniard. May Allah protect you!" The monarchs were impressed and, for a time at least, prudently granted Alabez's wish.

An ancient custom, no longer practised but parodied on every bangle and trinket sold in the tourist shops, was to paint an **indalo** on the doorways of the village to ward off evil. This symbol – a matchstick figure with arms outstretched, holding an arc – comes from the six-thousand-year-old Neolithic drawings in the caves at Vélez Blanco to the north, and anthropologists believe that it is a unique case of a prehistoric symbol being passed down in one location for numerous millennia.

Indalos apart, sights in the upper village are limited to strolling around the sinuous, white-walled streets, looking at the heavily restored fifteenth-century church of **Santa María**, and savouring the view over the strangely formed surrounding hills and coast to the north from the **mirador** in the main square, Plaza Nueva.

5

Mojácar Playa

Down below on the seafront, **Mojácar Playa** is refreshingly brash: an excellent beach with warm and brilliantly clear waters, flanked by lots of fine beach bars and *discotecas*, rooms for rent, several hotels and *hostales*, and a good campsite. The beach resort's focal point is an ugly Centro Comercial, at the intersection – known locally as El Cruce – of the seafront highway with the road climbing inland to Mojácar Pueblo.

ARRIVAL AND DEPARTURE   MOJÁCAR

By bus Hourly buses run between the beach and Mojácar Pueblo; you can pick them up from a stop (known as "El Cruce") outside the Centro Comercial on Mojácar Playa, or at various stops along the seafront.

INFORMATION

MOJÁCAR PUEBLO
Turismo Plaza Frontón s/n (Mon–Fri 10am–2pm & 5–7pm, Sat 10am–1.30pm; ☎ 950 615 025, ⓦ mojacar.es) is in the square to east side of the church. You'll need their free map to negotiate the maze of narrow streets here. It also covers the coastal strip and is a useful aid to getting your bearings.

MOJÁCAR PLAYA
Internet Indal-futur, Paseo del Mediterráneo 293, just south of El Cruce (Mon–Fri 9am–2pm & 5–10pm, Sat & Sun 11am–2pm & 6–11pm; ☎ 950 615 156).

ACCOMMODATION

MOJÁCAR PUEBLO
Camping El Quinto Ctra. AL151 Mojácar–Turre ☎ 950 478 704. Mojácar's campsite lies 2km below the village along the Turre road. It's a well-ordered site with ample shade, and good facilities including restaurant and pool. **€5.50** per person, **€5.50** per tent, **€5.50** per vehicle.

Hostal Arco Plaza Nueva, beneath the arch on the north side ☎ 950 472 777, ⓔ arcoplazam@yahoo.es. Just off the main square, this is a reliable option for a/c en-suite rooms with TV. **€45**

★ **Mamabel's** C/Embajadores 3 ☎ 950 472 448, ⓦ mamabels.com. Upmarket but good-value hotel, on the way into town, with beautiful, individually styled en-suite rooms (no. 1 is a dream), some with stunning view, and a good restaurant. **€70**

Pensión El Torreón C/Jazmín 4, 75m west of the church ☎ 950 475 259. A friendly *hostal* with charming – if slightly pricey – rooms sharing bath. **€40**

MOJÁCAR PLAYA
Camping El Cantal de Mojácar Ctra. Garrucha–Carboneras ☎ 950 478 204. A couple of kilometres south of El Cruce, the Mojácar Playa campsite has decent facilities, good shade, a restaurant and a supermarket. **€4.50** per person, **€6** per tent, **€4.50** per vehicle.

Hotel Apartamentos Marazul Paseo del Mediterráneo 279, 1km south of El Cruce ☎ 950 478 336, ⓦ mojacarmarazul.com. Fully equipped sea-view studio apartments, sleeping up to three, with a pool. Prices are almost halved outside high summer. **€117**

Hotel El Puntazo Paseo del Mediterráneo s/n, 1km south from El Cruce ☎ 950 478 229 ⓦ mojacarhoteles .com. This sprawling seafront hotel is one of the resort's top addresses and an obvious landmark. Attractive and well-equipped rooms come with sea views and lots of frills, and there's a pool. **€139**

Hotel Río Abajo Paseo del Mediterráneo s/n ☎ 950 478 928, ⓦ rioabajomojacar.com. Great little chalet hotel 2km north of El Cruce and actually on the beach. Leafy gardens surround each cosy en-suite chalet and facilities include a bar and pool – the sea is just 40m away. Easy parking. **€70**

Hotel Sal Marina Paseo del Mediterráneo s/n, close to the Hotel El Puntazo hotel (see above) ☎ 950 472 404. Attractive and well-equipped a/c balcony rooms with sea views. Rates fall by thirty percent outside August. B&B **€65**

Hotel Virgen del Mar Paseo del Mediterráneo 245, 1.5km south of El Cruce ☎ 950 472 222, ⓦ hotelvirgen delmar.com. Good-value two-star seafront hotel with a/c rooms with TV. Most of them have seaview terrace balconies. **€70**

Parador de Mojácar Paseo del Mediterráneo 339, just south of El Cruce ☎ 950 478 250, ⓦ parador.es. Mojácar's modern seafront *parador* is none too exciting, but has been completely refurbished and offers classically furnished rooms with strongbox, TV and minibar, and many have a sea view. Public areas include a garden pool and restaurant. **€138**

EATING AND DRINKING

MOJÁCAR PUEBLO
Casa Minguito Plaza Ayuntamiento s/n, on the west side of the church, next to the town hall. A good mid-priced restaurant for carefully prepared Spanish standards. Specials include fish and *mariscos*, and they do a two-person paella for €26. There's also a *menú* for €15 and a terrace on this leafy square. Daily 11am–4.30pm & 7pm–midnight.

★ **El Palacio** Plaza del Cano s/n, southwest of the church ☎ 950 472 846. Perhaps the *pueblo's* most creative restaurant, with a reasonably priced menu and wine list, and signature dishes such as *mero a la naranja* (grouper with orange sauce) and *magret de pato al oporto* (duck with port). There's also a wonderful roof terrace for alfresco dining or a charming white walled interior room for cooler days. Main dishes €10–20. Daily: June–Sept 8–11pm; Oct–May 1–4pm & 8–11pm.

Mamabel's C/Embajadores 3 ☎ 950 472 448, ⓦ mamabels.com. The restaurant of the hotel (see p.550) is excellent, offering a good-value €20 *menú* – often featuring couscous, paella, *solomillo al vino tinto* (pork loin in wine) or even *pollo al curry* – that can be enjoyed on their crow's nest terrace. With vertiginously spectacular views over the coast, this guarantees a memorable meal. Daily 8–10.30pm.

Rincón de Embrujo C/Iglesia s/n. With a terrace on the plazuela fronting the church, this small bar-restaurant does inexpensive tapas, *raciones* and *platos combinados* – *almejas* (clams), *pulpo gallego* (octopus) and paella are regular specials. Daily 9am–4pm & 8–11pm.

MOJÁCAR PLAYA

Food along the **seafront** is generally dismal and overpriced, with standards falling markedly in high season; we've selected a few of the safer places to try below. Most of the reasonable options lie to the south of El Cruce.

Albatros Paseo del Mediterraneo s/n. Close to the *Hotel El Puntazo* (see opposite) on the seaward side of the road, this is a beachfront *chiringuito* with a wide range of fish and shellfish on offer. *Lubina a la sal* (sea bass) and *sardinas asadas* (grilled sardines) are popular choices here. Tues–Sun 1–4.30pm & 7.30–11.30pm.

Casa Egea Paseo del Mediterráneo 127, 2km south of El Cruce on the seafront. Long-established and reliable fish restaurant specializing in *arrozes* (fish with rice dishes) and paella. Its next-door neighbour *Omega* is also good for salads and pasta dishes.

Parador de Mojácar Paseo del Mediterráneo 339, just south of El Cruce ☎ 950 478 250, ⓦ parador.es. The *parador's* restaurant is perhaps the best place to eat on the seafront, with a bright and modern main room with panoramic sea views and an outdoor terrace. The kitchen serves a variety of regional dishes including fresh fish from Garrucha and there's a good-value *menú* for €32. Main dishes €10–18. Daily 1–4pm & 8–11pm.

Sal Marina Paseo del Mediterráneo s/n ☎ 950 472 404. Attached to the hotel of the same name (see p.550), with a sea-view terrace, this is an economical place to eat for meat and fish dishes. Paella is a speciality. Main dishes €7–15. Daily 1.30–4pm & 8–10.30pm.

NIGHTLIFE

MOJÁCAR PUEBLO

There's not much nightlife in the hill village, though there are a couple of good bars.

El Loro Azul Off Plaza Frontón, on the east side of the church. An oddball place often featuring jazz on the music system.

La Luna C/Estación Nueva north of the church. A popular haunt for late-night drinking.

MOJÁCAR PLAYA

After dark you'll find plenty of **nightlife** in throbbing beach bars and seafront *discotecas*. Most of the action takes place along the coastal strip covering the 3km to the south of El Cruce.

North of Mojácar

North from Mojácar, there's a clutch of resorts – none of them much to write home about – and a few last sights of interest, before the road crosses Andalucía's border into Murcia.

Garrucha

A couple of kilometres north of Mojácar, and served by occasional buses, **GARRUCHA** is a lively, if undistinguished, town and fishing harbour with a sizeable fleet. When this comes home to port with its catch in mid-afternoon the ensuing auction at the port-side market is wonderfully entertaining. The fleet also lands a good supply of the seafood – the prawns are renowned – served at the numerous **fish restaurants** lining the seafront harbour promenade, El Malecón.

ACCOMMODATION AND EATING   GARRUCHA

★ **El Almejero** Explanada del Puerto s/n ☎ 950 460 405. The most celebrated place in town for seafood, this outstanding restaurant has a terrace fronting the Puerto Pesquero harbourside, where the fish is landed – if the catch doesn't meet their exacting standards they don't open. All the fish dishes are recommended, especially their renowned *arroz caldoso* (fish and rice soup) and the *paella de mariscos*. There's also an excellent tapas bar attached

5

– try the mouthwatering *calamares* and *boquerones fritos*. Main dishes €12–25. Daily 1–4pm & 8–11pm.
Hostal-Restaurante Cortés Paseo Marítimo 200

☎ 950 132 813, ✆ hostalcortes.net. Pleasant a/c en-suite rooms with TV, overlooking the seafront promenade and excellent beach. **€60**

Cuevas del Almanzora

From Garrucha, the road heads 9km inland, skirting the estuary of the Río Almanzora and the small farming town of Vera, to **CUEVAS DEL ALMANZORA**, 6km farther north. A town with a distinguished past, it has a number of sights, including a well-preserved sixteenth-century Gothic castle built to defend the settlement from piracy, and a handful of Guadix-style cave dwellings where evidence of habitation by Neanderthal and Cro-Magnon man was found. The castle – the splendidly restored **Castillo del Marqués de Los Vélez** – now houses an interesting archeological museum and the **Museo Campoy** displaying artworks by Goya, Picasso, Miró, Toral and Vásquez Díaz among others (both Tues–Sat 10am–1.30pm & 5–8pm, Sun 10am–1.30pm; €1).

Palomares

From Cuevas del Almanzora there's a road to the coast and the village of **PALOMARES**, of nuclear notoriety. The rather curious feature of this otherwise dull hamlet is a church

---

PALOMARES AND THE H-BOMBS

Palomares was once at the centre of one of the world's biggest nuclear scares. Here, on January 17, 1966, an American B-52 bomber collided with a tanker aircraft during a midair refuelling operation. Following the collision in which many of the crew of both aircraft perished, three ten-megaton **H-bombs** (each one hundred times more powerful than that used at Hiroshima) fell on land and a fourth into the sea, just off the village. Those that fell in the fields were recovered quickly, though one had been damaged, causing radioactive contamination nearby. Fifteen US warships and two submarines searched for many weeks before the fourth bomb was recovered. On March 19, thousands of barrels of plutonium-contaminated soil were transported by the USAF for disposal in South Carolina. Nobody has ever convincingly explained how the incident happened, nor is it known why the bombs didn't explode, for the damaged bomb had actually lost its safety catch.

The fourth bomb made a fortune for local fisherman Francisco Simó Orts (known ever after as **"Paco, él de la Bomba"**) who saw where the missile fell into the sea and aided the search to locate it. With the assistance of a lawyer he also – as the finder – claimed salvage rights under maritime law calculated at one or two percent of the value of the object salvaged. As each bomb was worth 2 billion dollars according to the Pentagon the sum claimed was twenty million dollars and Paco appeared at the New York Federal Court to make his case. The Pentagon duly settled out of court for an undisclosed sum. Palomares' world-famous fisherman died in 2003.

The story, however, is far from over. In 2004 when tests on plots designated for housing construction revealed significant **radioactive contamination**, the land was immediately expropriated by the Spanish government. In 2006 the Spanish and US governments agreed to sharing the cost of a further decontamination programme and a survey of the area to determine how this should be done revealed abnormal levels of radiation in snails and other wildlife indicating dangerous amounts of radioactive material still in the subsoil. In 2008 it was revealed that scientists had located two highly radioactive trenches – near where one of the bombs had fallen – used by the US Army to bury contaminated earth following the incident in 1966. The US government agreed to pay for the earth's removal and transportation to the US in addition to the decontamination of the surrounding area. Further tests by US scientists following this operation revealed that **significant contamination remains** and in a meeting between the Spanish foreign minister and US Secretary of State Hillary Clinton in July 2011 Spain requested that the US take full responsibility for ridding the area of contamination once and for all. Clinton gave an assurance that the US government is treating this question very seriously. In response to this the mayor of Palomares retorted that "Clinton's words are all very well, but we want action."

5

tower that resembles – with its rounded cone – an atom bomb. Near where you rejoin the coast, Vera's **Parque Aquático** (daily 10.30am–7.30pm; €19) is a fun place to kill a couple of hours, especially if you're towing kids; it's got all the usual water features, and they allow you to take your own picnic inside.

Vélez Rubio to Orce

In the north of Almería province, two small towns are worth an excursion: at **Vélez Rubio**, there's a cave with important **prehistoric paintings** depicting the *indalo* (see p.549), while at neighbouring **Vélez Blanco** there's a fine Renaissance **castle**. Although both are served by a single daily **bus** from Almería, transport of your own will make these detours much more rewarding.

Vélez Rubio

Inland from Cuevas del Almanzora, a rambling 60km drive along the A7-E15 and A327 will bring you out at the town of **VÉLEZ RUBIO**, surrounded by *sierras*, olive groves and fields of cereals. It's no great shakes as towns go (Vélez Blanco is a better proposition for an overnight stop), but has some diversions. A small town **museum**, Calle Carrera del Carmen 19 (April–Sept Tues–Sat 9am–2pm plus Sat 5–7.30pm; Oct–March Tues–Thurs 10am–2pm, Fri & Sat 10am–2pm & 4–7pm), inside the eighteenth-century Hospital Real, contains an interesting collection of artefacts and ceramics from prehistoric to Moorish times, with a section on the ancient cave paintings in this area.

La Encarnación

Plaza La Encarnación • Tues–Sun 10am–1pm • Free

The magnificent Baroque church (Almería province's biggest) of **La Encarnación**, constructed in the eighteenth century, has an imposing carved facade that includes, above the entrance, the arms of the marquises of Villafranca y Vélez, who built it. Inside, the main altar has a superbly detailed, 20m-high carved wood **retablo**, and there's a splendid Baroque organ constructed in 1796.

Cueva de los Letreros

4km north of Vélez Rubio • Guided tours Wed, Sat & Sun: April–Sept 6pm; Oct–March 4.30pm; the guide will meet you at the kiosk near the campsite on the opposite side of the road to the petrol station, but check first with the tourist offices in Vélez Rubio (see below) or Vélez Blanco (see p.555) or call the guide herself • €2 • ☎ 649 901 680 • Take the A317 north until you reach a petrol station on the left; the caves are signed from here

The main point of a trip to Vélez Rubio is to see the prehistoric cave paintings of the **Cueva de los Letreros**. The cave or *abrigo* (rock shelter) is beyond a secure fence on the side of the hill behind the petrol station, a good kilometre's walk. Once through the gate of the compound you will be able to see remarkably fresh-looking red and brown sketches of human figures, birds, animals, astronomical signs and not very well-preserved *indalos* (see p.549) which have been dated to around 4000 BC and are among the oldest representations of people and animals together. Unfortunately the local practice of touching the *indalos* and throwing water on the paintings in order to make them clearer has not helped their preservation, but what remains is still stunning.

INFORMATION VÉLEZ RUBIO

Turismo In the town museum, C/Carrera del Carmen 19 (April–Sept Tues–Fri 9am–2pm, Sat 9am–2pm & 5–7.30pm; Oct–March Tues–Thurs 10am–2pm, Fri & Sat 10am–2pm & 4–7pm; ☎ 950 412 560, ✇ aytovelezrubio.org).

Vélez Blanco

Nestling at the foot of a rocky outcrop, the whitewashed village of **VÉLEZ BLANCO**, 6km north of Vélez Rubio, is a smaller and more attractive conurbation. Its main attraction is its **castle**, which looms over the town from the top of the hill.

The castle

Tues–Sun May-Sept 10am–2pm & 5–8pm, Oct–April 10am–2pm & 4–6pm; if you can't get in during normal hours call, or contact the Ayuntamiento (☎ 950 614 800) on C/La Corredera • Free • ☎ 607 415 055

Atop the hill is an outstanding **Renaissance castle** – an extension of the original Moorish *alcazaba* – built by the marquises of Vélez Blanco in the early years of the sixteenth century. It is today something of a trompe-l'oeil, with an empty shell behind the crenellated battlements: a gutting that took place as recently as 1904, after the castle was sold off by the impecunious marquis for 80,000ptas (€500) to an American millionaire, George Blumenthal, who tore out the whole interior including the **Patio de Honor** – a fabulous courtyard carved in white marble by Italian craftsmen – and shipped it off to the United States. After service as this plutocrat's Xanadu, it has since been reconstructed inside the Metropolitan Museum of Art in New York. The castle's interior, much of it now supported by steel girders, has fragments of the original decoration. Given the Met's reluctance to return its dubiously acquired prize exhibit, a complete and exact reconstruction of the original using marble from the nearby quarries of Macael has begun (which may temporarily close off parts of the castle over the coming years). A book on sale in the small shop at the entrance – *El Castillo de Vélez Blanco* by Alfonso Ruiz García – has an image of the reconstituted patio in the New York Met, plus a watercolour of what it looked like *in situ*. Make sure to take in the fine **views** from the tower, the Torre del Homenaje.

INFORMATION   **VÉLEZ BLANCO**

Information office The Almacén del Trigo information office (Tues–Sat 10am–2pm & 4–6pm, Sun 10am–2pm; ☎ 950 415 354) at the far end of the town (follow the signs), has information on Vélez and the surrounding Parque Natural de la Sierra de María (see p.556).

ACCOMMODATION AND EATING

Camping Pinar del Rey Ctra. de Vélez Blanco s/n ☎ 649 901 680, ⓦ pinardelrey.es. The campsite lies on the edge of town towards Vélez Rubio, close to the Letreros cave, and has ample shade and good facilities including a pool and restaurant. €4 per person, €4 per tent, €4 per vehicle.

★ **Casa de los Arcos** C/San Francisco 2, near the information office ☎ 950 614 805, ⓦ hotelcasadelosarcos.com. Excellent-value option offering simple but elegantly furnished rooms in a beautifully restored eighteenth-century *casa señorial* overlooking a gorge. The hotel also organizes daily guided visits to the Letreros cave which are open to non-guests. **€63**

Hostal La Sociedad C/Corredera 14 ☎ 950 415 027. The *hostal* of the popular bar (see below) lies across the road in a separate building and has plain but functional budget en-suite rooms with heating and TV. **€35**

EATING

Bar Sociedad C/Corredera 14 ☎ 950 415 027. The busiest bar in town serves up good tapas and *raciones* inside or, in better weather, on a lively pavement terrace. Daily 8.30am–11pm.

Mesón Antonia C/Al'qua-sid s/n, near the castle entrance. A popular lunch stop with visitors to the castle, offering tapas and *raciones* as well as a *menú* for around €8. The nearby *Barbacoa María Fernández* (aka *Mavi*) at C/Al'qua-sid 10 is another good little place. Daily noon–4pm & 8–10.30pm.

Restaurante El Molino Curtidores s/n ☎ 950 415 070. The town's best restaurant lies a stone's throw from the *Bar Sociedad*, up some steps opposite a tiled fountain. With three rooms and a small terrace, it offers very good fish and meat dishes – (house specialities include *paletilla de cabrito* (kid) and *perdiz estofada* (partridge) as well as fresh trout. Main dishes €10–20. Tues–Sat 1–4pm & 8–11pm, Sun 1–4pm.

Sierra de María

Walkers – and those in need of greenery after endless desert landscapes – may be tempted to continue northwest from Vélez Blanco along the A317 to **María**, a small town set among pine woods and, incidentally, the highest settlement in Almería, which is also the jumping-off point for the **SIERRA DE MARÍA**, a recently declared natural park.

Beyond María the AL9101 soon enters an extensive plain covered with wheatfields and stretches arrow-straight and apparently endlessly to the distant mountains. In high summer this plain is a cauldron beneath vast cloudless skies and you'll be lucky to meet another vehicle. Apart from a couple of godforsaken hamlets and the occasional wheeling eagle overhead, there are few features to punctuate this desolate but beautiful panorama. The landscape takes on a doubly dramatic aspect when you realize that one and a half million years ago this plain was a great lake visited by elephants, hippos, rhinos, water buffaloes, musk oxen, giant bears and ferocious hyenas as well as lions, leopards and lynxes. Early humans were known to have been in the area as early as 500,000 years ago but recent finds seem to have pushed this back by an astonishing additional one million years which, if scientifically confirmed, would make it the earliest appearance of primitive humans on the continent of Europe by a long way. These Stone Age arrivals probably came from Africa and lived on a diet of wild plants and carrion supplemented by fracturing the craniums and bones of the dead beasts to extract the brains and marrow – they had not yet developed the technology to take on and hunt big game.

INFORMATION
SIERRA DE MARÍA

Visitor centre Information about walking trails, and on the park in general is available from a visitors' centre (Fri–Sun 10am–2pm & 6–8pm; ☎950 527 005), 2.5km beyond María on the Orce road.

Orce

When you finally reach it, the dusty and impoverished little settlement of **ORCE** hardly lives up to the self-styled billing – now proclaimed on all its literature – as the *Cuna de la Humanidad Europea* (Cradle of European Man). The heart of the village is a tree-lined main square, **Plaza Nueva**, with an eighteenth-century fountain fronted by the Ayuntamiento and, in one corner the village's main bar, *Bar Plaza*.

Other than the **prehistoric museum**, Orce's only other sights of note lie just off the main square. The first is the eleventh-century **Moorish alcazaba** (Sat, Sun & holidays noon–2pm & 4–6pm; free) with an impressive tower, and the other, opposite across a square, is the eighteenth-century **Iglesia de Santa María** (open service times 7–9pm) with some serious structural problems and a fine retablo.

Along the Galera road, 1km out of Orce, the green valley of the Río Galera contains the Manantial de Fuen Caliente, a beautiful natural pond filled with fish, which has become the local **swimming pool**, complete with *cafetería*.

Museo de la Prehistoria

C/Tiendas 18 • Tues–Sun: April–Sept 10am–2pm & 5–9pm; Oct–March 10am–2pm & 4–6pm • €2

Just behind Plaza Nueva (with a rear entrance onto it) is the **Casa Palacio de los Segura**, a sixteenth-century *casa señorial* with an elegant tower. Inside, the superbly presented **Museo de la Prehistoria** exhibits the Orce discoveries. As well as impressive animal remains from the periods of the finds there are displays (in Spanish) reconstructing the lifestyle of these early humans. The star exhibit is a copy (the original is under lock and key in the Ayuntamiento) of the small million-and-a-half-year-old **fragment of human skull** that has brought worldwide celebrity to the town. While the theory is not accepted conclusively by many experts (a point made in the museum presentation), its discoverers claim it belonged to a child of unknown sex who is thought to have been

5

devoured by a great hyena. Most archeologists and paleontologists working in the area are now fairly sure that the skull fragment is not human but the same experts are convinced that the dating *will* eventually be confirmed due to crucial evidence turned up in 1998–99 of remarkable **lithic artefacts** (stone tools; displayed in the museum) around 1.4 million years old; finding genuine human remains, they believe, is only a matter of time.

INFORMATION   ORCE

Turismo In the Museo de la Prehistoria, C/Tiendas 18 (Tues–Sun: April–Sept 10am–2pm & 5–9pm; Oct–March

10am–2pm & 4–6pm; ☎ 958 746 171, ⓦ orce.es)

ACCOMMODATION

★ **Cuevas de Orce** Ctra. de María s/n ☎ 958 746 281 ⓦ cuevasdeorce.com. A wonderful cave hotel, which you pass on the way into the village coming from María. Cosy en-suite cave dwellings come with kitchen and curious cave bathrooms. Ten percent discount for

Rough Guide readers with this guide. **€75**
Hotel La Morata Avda. Los Caños 1, next to the museum ☎ 958 065 172. A new and good value *hotel rural* with beamed and tiled-floor rooms with TV and free wi-fi. **€52**

EATING

Bar Plaza Plaza Nueva s/n. The village's main bar serves up good tapas and *raciones* and even pizzas, which can be eaten inside or on their terrace on the leafy square. Daily 8.30am–11pm.
Mesón La Mimbrera C/Chorreador s/n ☎ 958 746 148.

Just off the main square, this is the village's best place to eat, serving tasty game and regional dishes – *cordero asado* (roast lamb) is a speciality. There's also a lunchtime *menú* for €10. Daily 1–4pm & 8–11pm.

Inland Almería

One way of reaching the coast to the east of Almería is to take a trip through the weird lunar landscape of Almería's distinctive desert scenery. There are two possible routes: via **Níjar** along the A7–E15 *autovía* to Carboneras, or via the more interesting **Tabernas** and **Sorbas** route (along the N340) to Mojácar. The latter more northerly route, described below, passes by Almería's old western film set, **Mini Hollywood**, and a detour off this road can also be made to the pottery centre of **Níjar**. A visit to the underground caves of **Sorbas** is also a great adventure.

The road to Tabernas

The main road to Tabernas heads north out of Almería along the valley of the Río Andarax and forks right at Benhadux – along the A340 – passing the village of **Rioja** before it enters a dramatic brown-tinged-with-purple eroded landscape which looks as if it should be the backdrop for a Hollywood western. Some 10km past Rioja, in a particularly gulch-riven landscape, at **Mini Hollywood** you discover that someone else had the same idea first.

As well as the landscape and cheap labour costs, the film-makers were also drawn to the same unpolluted crystalline air which has lured astronomers here, and to the north of Tabernas, at Calar Alto in the Sierra de Filabres, a series of high-powered telescopes enables the **Hispano–German observatory** to study the heavens.

Mini Hollywood

Daily: June–Oct 10am–9pm; Nov–May 10am–7pm; daily shows noon, 5pm & 8pm • €20, kids €9.90 • ☎ 902 533 532 • Regular buses from Almería's Intermodal bus-train station

A visit to **MINI HOLLYWOOD** (aka Oasys Parque Temático) is hard to resist – especially if you're travelling with kids – although better value if timed with one of

5

the daily shows. The old film set's most famous production was a *Fistful of Dollars*, a connection that its publicity flyers never tire of repeating. Once inside, you'll see a main street overlooked by a water tower, which you may just recognize from the 1960s classic, or from *The Good, the Bad and the Ugly*, another film made here along with countless other spaghetti and paella westerns. You can wander into the *Tombstone Gulch* saloon for a drink, and in summer there are daily shows when actors in full cowboy rig and blasting off six-guns stage such epics as the capture, escape and final shooting of Jesse James, whilst in between the saloon stages shows of cancan girls flaunting their frillies. There's also a somewhat incongruous **zoo** – with birds, reptiles and big cats prowling depressingly small cages – plus a **pool** and numerous **fast food** outlets.

Texas Hollywood

April–Oct daily 9am–8pm; three shows morning and afternoon • €16.50, kids €9

Beyond Mini Hollywood and towards Tabernas, on the left, is **Texas Hollywood**, the location for *Once Upon a Time in the West* among other productions. Here you can see a couple of less commercialized film sets in a much more spectacular setting, including an Indian village complete with wigwams, a Mexican town and a US cavalry frontier fort as well as camels and buffaloes.

Tabernas

Some 8km along the N340 beyond Texas Hollywood, and surrounded by torrid desert scrubland, **TABERNAS** lies at the foot of a hill dominated by an impressive-looking **Moorish castle** where Fernando and Isabel ensconced themselves during the siege of Almería. Unfortunately, the castle is mainly ruined and there's little to hang around for – though you might want to stop for a drink in the searing summer heat. Just beyond the village a road on the left – followed after 1km by a right turn towards the hamlet of Senés – leads to the **Centro Solar**, one of Europe's biggest solar energy fields, where row upon row of mirrors reflect the powerful sunlight and generate energy. Still at the development stage, it's hoped that when the system is commercially viable it could power massive desalination plants to regenerate the desert.

ACCOMMODATION AND EATING   TABERNAS

Hospedería del Desierto Four kilometres beyond Tabernas on the right ☎950 369 444, ⊛hospederia deldesierto.es. A comfortable desert *hostal*-hotel with palms, yuccas and cactuses filling its gardens, and a pool. The restaurant has a *menú del día* for €10. Hotel €54, hostal €39

★ **Venta del Compadre** Ctra. N340 km7.4 ☎950 362 838. If you have your own transport, try this excellent *venta* just beyond Tabernas on the N340. There's a great-value €10 *menú* and they also serve up some of the tastiest *pollo asado* (roast chicken) in the region. The weekends often see flamenco performances (not to be missed). Daily noon–4pm & 7–11pm.

Across the Sierra Alhamilla

Beyond Tabernas there are more dramatic landscapes – badlands with naked ridges of pitted sandstone, cut through by twisted and dried-up riverbeds, all of which vary in colour from yellow to red and from green to lavender-blue depending on the time of day and the nature of the stone. After 9km a road on the right opens up the possibility of a wonderfully scenic trip south to Níjar **across the Sierra Alhamilla**. This road climbs through more Arizona-type landscape, first to the hamlet of **Turrillas**, and then turns east to **Lucainena de las Torres**, a cluster of white boxes surrounding its red-roofed church. Beyond Lucainena the road snakes over the rugged Sierra Alhamilla to descend into Níjar, 16km to the south.

Níjar

5

NÍJAR is a neat, white and typically Almerian little town, with – in its upper Moorish *barrio* – narrow streets designed to give maximum shade. Little remains of the Moorish fort here but a strong **pottery** tradition – dating back to when the Moors held sway and including attractive traditional patterns created with mineral dyes – lives on. The town is also known for its **jarapas**: bed-covers, curtains and rugs made from rags.

Now firmly on the tourist trail, due to the inexpensive handmade pottery manufactured in **workshops** around the town (especially along Avenida García Lorca – the broad main street – and the parallel Calle Real), it still retains a relaxed and tranquil air.

INFORMATION

NÍJAR

Turismo C/Real 1, at junction of C/Real with Avda. García Lorca (Mon–Sat 10am–2pm & 4–8pm; ☏ 950 612 243, ⓦ nijar.es). They can provide information on the town and the region as well as the Parque Natural de Cabo de Gata (p.542).

ACCOMMODATION

Hostal Montes Avda. García Lorca 26 ☏ 950 360 157. The best of the budget options, this welcoming place has clean and tidy en-suite rooms above a bar-restaurant. **€30**

Hostal-Restaurant Asensio C/Parque 2 ☏ 950 361 056, ⓦ hostalrestauranteasensionijar.com. A reasonable option for en-suite rooms with bath and TV. They also have a bar restaurant below. **€40**

EATING

There are plenty of **bars** and **restaurants** along the main street, Avda. García Lorca, but don't miss out on the **tapas bars** on the very appealing square beyond the church in the *barrio alto*, Plaza de la Glorieta.

Bar La Glorieta Plaza de la Glorieta s/n. Friendly little bar with an elevated terrace that offers decent tapas and *raciones* – paella is often on the menu here – as well as being a good place for a nightcap. Daily 9am–11pm.

Bar La Untá Avda. García Lorca 6. You can get tasty tapas – try the *morcilla al vino* (blood sausage) – and *raciones*, as well as *platos combinados* and a €10 *menú*, at this appealing bar-restaurant, which also has a small street terrace. Daily 8.30am–midnight.

El Pipa Plaza de la Glorieta s/n. A good terrace bar for tapas and *raciones* – *pinchos de lomo* (pork) and *morunos* (spicy kebab) are favourites. Daily 10am–11pm.

BLOOD WEDDING

An event at Níjar in 1928 inspired one of Lorca's most powerful plays, **Bodas de Sangre** (*Blood Wedding*). A young woman named Francisca was about to marry a man named Casimiro at a farmhouse near Níjar. She was an heiress with a modest dowry and a reluctant bride, he a labourer pressured by his scheming brother and sister-in-law to make this match and thus bring money into the family. A few hours prior to the wedding, Francisca eloped with her cousin, with whom she had been in love since childhood, but who had only realized his feelings when confronted with the reality of losing her. They were swiftly intercepted by Casimiro's brother, who shot her cousin dead. His brother was convicted of the murder, whilst Casimiro, the groom, was unable to overcome his humiliation and, it is said, never looked upon Francisca or even her photograph again. Francisca never married and lived as a recluse until her death in 1978.

Lorca avidly followed the story in the newspapers and had a knowledge of the area from time spent in Almería as a child. An interesting afterword is told by the writer Nina Epton, who, on a visit to San José in the 1960s, was dining at the house of a wealthy Spanish *señorón*, or landowner, while a group of farm labourers waited outside on a long bench, no doubt for payment. In her book *Andalusia* she describes what happened when eventually she accompanied Don José, her host, to speak to the men:

Among them was a wizened old man called Casimiro whom I would not have looked at twice before I was told that a dramatic incident in his youth had inspired Federico García Lorca to take Casimiro for his model of the novio in "Blood Wedding".

5

SHOPPING

Pottery Head to the shops along Avda. García Lorca – the broad main street – or, for more authentic work, the *barrio alfarero*, along Calle Real running parallel to García Lorca, where the *talleres* (workshops; 10am–2pm & 4–7pm) of Gongora, Granados, El Oficio and the friendly Angel y Loli (at no. 54) are located. Also here, off the bottom of the street in a studio-shop called La Tienda de los Milagros (☎ 950 360 359), is resident English ceramic artist Matthew Weir who has a more modernist approach. His *almeriense* wife Isabel is a skilled producer of *jarapas* and textiles in her own right.

Sorbas

As you head east along the N340 from Tabernas, 18km beyond the turn-off to Lucainena de las Torres, you will come to the extraordinary small town of **SORBAS**. Surrounded by moonscapes, its clifftop houses overhang an ashen gorge, it's best seen from the main road. Like Níjar, it is reputed for its **pottery** – although the designs are less original. You can buy at a trio of inconspicuous *alfarerías* (workshops, near one of which still stands a remarkable **Moorish kiln**) in the lower part of town, near a white-walled *ermita* (chapel) and signed from the main square, Plaza del Ayuntamiento. This tidy little place is also on the tourist trail, especially on Thursdays when trippers flock in from Mojácar for the weekly **market** in the same plaza.

Paraje Natural de Karst en Yesos

Just south of Sorbas, signed from the main N340 • April–Oct guided tours (English & Spanish), organized by the Turismo, daily on the hour 10am–8pm; check the website for details of more challenging explorations lasting 3–6hr • ⓦ cuevasdesorbas .com • €13

The main pull for visitors to Sorbas is the astonishing scenery in the surrounding **Paraje Natural de Karst en Yesos**, where around six million years ago water erosion carved out subterranean chasms full of stalagmites and stalactites. Guided visits to the caves are a two-hour adventure – with helmets and flashlights and not a little scrambling and squeezing. Above ground, the water's action has created flat-topped, volcano-like protrusions and deep gorges. These are visible from the main N340, but for a closer look take the minor A1102 towards Los Molinos del Río Aguas east of Sorbas. At the crest of a hill, a track to the left leads to a peak above the gorge, where sweeping circular views extend over the lunar landscape as far as the snowcapped peaks of the Sierra Nevada; it's a great place to watch the sunset. Alternatively, you could follow the track descending through the tumbledown but picturesque hamlet of **Los Molinos** to follow the course of the dried-up river gorge.

INFORMATION
SORBAS

Turismo C/Terraplén 9, just off the main N340 on the way into town (July & Aug Mon–Fri 10.30am–2.30pm & 5.30–8pm; Sept–June Tues–Fri 10.30am–2.30pm; ☎ 950 364 476, ⓦ sorbas.es).

Centro de Visitantes Fifty metres downhill from the Turismo, this is an interesting and informative information centre for the Karst en Yesos caves (April–Sept daily 11am–2pm & 4–7pm; ring for winter hours; ☎ 950 364 563).

ACCOMMODATION

Hostal Rural Montelés C/Calvo Sotelo 4 ☎ 950 364 635, ⓦ hostalmonteles.com. By far the nicest place to put up here is at this *hostal rural* in a striking nineteenth-century mansion just off the main square, Plaza del Ayuntamiento. The en-suite rooms are full of character with original tiled floors and wooden beams. Free wi-fi. They can assist with parking. €50

Hostal Sorbas Ctra. 340 s/n, on the right as you come in from Tabernas ☎ 950 364 160. Good *hostal* on the main road at the entrance to the town, offering comfortable a/c rooms with TV. B&B €50

EATING

Bar-Restaurante Sol de Andalucía Ctra. N340 km496 on the main road opposite Hostal Sorbas ☎950 364 193. Reliable bar and restaurant serving *platos combinados* and *raciones*; they also have a *menú* for €10. Daily 9am–11pm.

Café-Bar El Suave N340 s/n at the exit from the town going northeast. This is a handy roadside bar-restaurant for tapas and substantial *platos combinados*. There's also an outdoor terrace from where you'll get the best view of Sorbas's clifftop houses.

Cafetería Caymar Plaza del Ayuntamiento 8. Sited on the main square, the town's main bar offers breakfast standards as well as tapas and *raciones*. Daily 8.30am–10.30pm.

FLAMENCO

Contexts

History

As the southernmost region of the Iberian peninsula, Andalucía has manifested throughout its history a character essentially different from the rest of Spain. Due to the variety of peoples who settled here, the region has always had an enriching influence on the territories further north. This meeting place of seas and cultures, with Africa just 14km off the coast of its southern tip, brought Andalucía into early contact with the sophisticated civilizations of the eastern Mediterranean and a long period as part of the North African Moorish empire. The situation was later reversed when Andalucía sent out explorers to the New World and became the gateway to the Spanish American empire.

Prehistory

The first Europeans of whom we have knowledge lived in Andalucía. A recent series of spectacular discoveries at **Orce**, 113km northeast of Granada, rocked the archeological world as the date for the **arrival of early humans in Europe** was pushed back from c.700,000 years ago to perhaps a million years before this, making Orce – if the findings are scientifically confirmed – the earliest known site of human occupation in Europe by a long way. Arriving from Africa and crossing the straits by swimming or on rafts these Stone Age people colonized an area of now vanished lakeland near Orce. Here they hunted hippos, hyenas, mammoths and vultures and made tools from flint. Evidence of occupation by Stone Age societies stretching back some 400,000 years was already known about from discoveries at nearby **Venta Micena** where early inhabitants hunted elephant and rhino and left behind tools and camp fires. Some of the earliest **human fossils** found on the Iberian peninsula were unearthed inside the **Gibraltar** caves with evidence of **Neanderthals** dating from around 100,000 BC. In the Paleolithic period, the first **Homo sapiens** arrived on the Iberian peninsula from southern France, settling around the Bay of Biscay as well as in the south. They were cave dwellers and hunter-gatherers and at the Pileta and Nerja caves in Málaga have left behind remarkable **cave paintings** depicting the animals that they hunted. During the later Neolithic phase, a sophisticated material culture developed in southern Spain attested to by the finds of esparto sandals and baskets as well as jewellery in the **Cueva de los Murciélagos** in Granada.

Subsequent prehistory is more complex and confused. There does not appear to have been any great development in the cave cultures of the north. Instead the focus shifts south – where **Neolithic colonists** had arrived from North Africa – to Valencia and **Almería**. Cave paintings have been found in rock shelters such as those at **Vélez Blanco** dating from around 4000 BC. Here also, not long afterwards, **metalworking** began and the debate continues as to what led to this dramatic leap forward: a development by

1.5 million years ago	25,000 BC	12,000 BC
Early humans active at Orce, in today's Granada province, after arriving from Africa.	Cave dwellers occupying caves in Málaga province.	Dolmens constructed in Málaga and Catalunya.

the indigenous inhabitants, or the arrival of "technicians" – evidenced by many trading artefacts such as ivory and turquoise – from the eastern Mediterranean. The fortified site of **Los Millares** (c.2700 BC), in the centre of a rich mining area in Almería, with its Aegean-style "beehive" tombs is one of the most important remains from this era. In the same period, **dolmens** were being built such as those at **Antequera**, a building style that spread from here throughout the peninsula and into the rest of Europe. This dolmenic culture also influenced a ceramic style, typified by bell-shaped artefacts and giving rise to the name **Beaker folk**. More developments occurred in the same area of Almería about 1700 BC when the **El Argar** civilization started to produce bronze and worked silver and gold, trading across the Mediterranean. This culture fanned out across the south between 1700 and 1000 BC and, during the first millennium BC, the **Iberian civilization** fully established itself.

Tartessus and the Iberians

The **kingdom of Tartessus** appeared early in the first millennium BC and typifies the great strides forward being made by the Iberians of the south. Both the Bible (which names it Tarshish) and Greek and Latin texts refer to this important kingdom and trading centre. It was probably sited on the estuary of the Río Guadalquivir on the border of Huelva and Seville provinces; its precise location has yet to be identified, although its prowess as a producer and exporter of bronze, gold and silver as well as a creator of sophisticated **jewellery** is apparent from the finds displayed in Seville's archeological museum. The Tartessians were also a literate people, but nothing of their literature survives apart from scattered inscriptions that have thus far defied translation. In the mid-sixth century BC Tartessus incurred the wrath of the rising power of Carthage through its friendship with the Greeks and not long after that appears to have been destroyed by them.

The Iberians at other centres in the south also developed sophisticated cultures based upon agriculture, stockbreeding, fishing, mining and iron production. When the Romans came into contact with them in the third century BC they found a literate people with written laws, and a vibrant culture that included music and dance. Their skills in the plastic arts – an enduring flair throughout the peninsula's history – are displayed in artefacts such as the splendid **Dama de Baza**, a dramatic fourth-century-BC painted terracotta statue of a woman, discovered at Baza in Granada. The Iberian skill with masonry and stone sculpture can be seen at the necropolis at **Toya** in Jaén province, and other remarkable works from the fifth century BC are in the museum at Jaén itself.

The first colonists

The southern coast attracted colonists from different regions of the Mediterranean. The **Phoenicians** – founders of a powerful trading empire based in modern Lebanon – established the port of Gadir (Cádiz) about 1100 BC. This was obviously connected with their intensive **trading operations** in the metals of the Guadalquivir valley carried from Tartessus where they may even have had a factory. Their wealth and success gave rise to a Spanish "Atlantis" myth, based around Huelva. Besides metals, the Phoenicians

c.4000 BC	2500 BC	c.1100 BC	9th–4th century BC
Neolithic colonists arrive from north Africa. Esparto baskets and jewellery found in Cueva de Murciélagos, Granada.	Chalcolithic (copper age) sites flourish in Almería.	Phoenicians found Cádiz.	Kingdom of Tartessus flourishes around Guadalquivir estuary. Greeks establish trading posts along east coast.

also came for the rich fishing along the southern coast, which stimulated industries for salting and preserving the catch. The salt itself was gained from beds such as those at the **Cabo de Gata** – still commercially operating today – in Almería. Other operations, such as the **purple dyeing industry**, for which the Phoenicians were famous, exploited the large stocks of murex shellfish in coastal waters. The coastline of Andalucía is dotted with Phoenician **settlements** from this time such as those at Malaka (Málaga), Sexi (Almuñécar) and Abdera (Adra). Market rivalry also brought the **Greeks**, who established their trading colonies along the northeastern coast – the modern Costa Brava – before penetrating southwards into the Phoenician zone. They were encouraged by the Tartessians, no doubt in an attempt to break the Phoenician economic stranglehold on the region.

When the Phoenicians were incorporated into the Persian Empire in the sixth century BC, however, a former colony, **Carthage**, moved into the power vacuum, destroyed Tartessus and ejected the Greeks from the south. Carthage then turned the western Mediterranean into a jealously guarded trading monopoly, sinking ships of other states who attempted to trade there. This she tenaciously held on to, as the rising power of Rome forced her out of the central Mediterranean. In the course of the third century BC, Carthage built up Spain into a new base for her empire, from which to regain strength and strike back at her great rival. Although making little impact inland, the Carthaginians occupied most of Andalucía and expanded along the Mediterranean seaboard to establish a new capital at Cartagena ("New Carthage") in Murcia. The mineral wealth of Andalucía, particularly **silver**, was used to finance the military build-up as well as to recruit an enormous army of Iberian mercenaries. Under Hannibal they prepared to invade Italy and in 219 BC attacked Saguntum (modern Sagunto), a strategic ally of the growing Roman Empire. This precipitated the **Second Punic War**, bringing Roman legions to the Spanish peninsula for the first time. Heading south from modern Catalunya, they successively conquered the coastal towns; the **end of Carthaginian domination** of Spain was sealed in 206 BC at the battle of Ilipa (Alcalá del Río), just north of Seville. When Cádiz fell the following year, Rome became master of the southern peninsula and **Itálica** (near Seville) was founded as the first Roman city in Spain. A new and very different age had begun.

The Romans and Visigoths

The **Roman colonization** of the peninsula was far more intense than anything previously experienced and met with great resistance from the Celtiberian tribes of the north and centre, although much less so in Andalucía where the Turditanian people, tired of Carthaginian oppression, welcomed the invaders. In the final years of the Roman republic many of the crucial battles for control of the Roman state were fought out in Spain, ending with Julius Caesar's victory at Munda, south of Córdoba, in 45 BC. After Caesar's assassination, his successor Augustus reorganized Spain into three provinces, the southernmost of which became **Hispania Baetica**, roughly modern Andalucía, with **Corduba** (Córdoba) as its capital.

In this period Spain became one of the most important and wealthiest centres of the Roman Empire and Andalucía was its most urbane heartland. Unlike the rugged and fractious Celtiberians further north, the sophisticated Iberians of the south had their own

5th century BC	214 BC	210 BC	27 BC
Carthage colonizes southern Spain. Celto-Iberian culture develops, with Greek influence.	Second Punic War with Rome.	Roman colonization begins. Important Roman cities at Itálica, Córdoba, Cádiz, Carmona and Málaga.	Octavian-Augustus becomes first Roman Emperor and divides Spain into three parts: Lusitania, Baetica and Tarraconensis.

municipal traditions and took easily to Roman ideas of government. Indeed, their native languages and dialects had disappeared early in the first century AD as Latinization became complete. For four centuries Andalucía enjoyed a "**Golden Age**" with unprecedented prosperity based on the production of olive oil, wool, grain, wine and the highly prized *garum* fish sauce made at centres such as **Baelo Claudia** near Tarifa. Another important development was a massive expansion of mining at **Río Tinto** in Huelva. During this period, Baetica supplied **two Roman emperors**, Trajan (one of the greatest) and his adopted son Hadrian, along with the outstanding writers Seneca and Lucan. The finest monuments of the period were built in the provincial capital at Córdoba, and cities such as Cádiz, Itálica, Málaga and Carmona, linked by a network of superb roads and adorned with temples, baths, amphitheatres and aqueducts, were the equal of any in the empire. In the fourth and fifth centuries, however, the Roman political framework began to show signs of **decadence and corruption**. Although the actual structure didn't totally collapse until the Muslim invasions of the early eighth century, it became increasingly vulnerable to **barbarian invasions** from northern Europe. Early in the fifth century AD, the Suevi (Swabians), Alans and Vandals swept across the Pyrenees leaving much devastation in their wake. The Romans, preoccupied with attempts to stave off Gothic attacks on Italy, bought off the invaders by allowing them to settle within the imperial borders. The Suevi settled in Galicia, the Alans in Portugal and Murcia, whilst the **Vandals** put down roots in Baetica, providing the origin of Andalucía's name. The resulting wars between the invaders only served to further weaken Rome's grip on the peninsula as a burgeoning Christian Church – its first Spanish council was held at Iliberis (Granada) – gained more influence over the population.

The Visigoths

Internal strife was heightened by the arrival of the **Visigoths** from Gaul, allies of Rome and already Romanized to a large degree. The triumph of Visigothic strength in the fifth century resulted in a period of spurious unity, based upon an exclusive military rule from their capital at Toledo, but their numbers were never great and their order was often fragmentary and nominal, with the bulk of the subject people kept in a state of disconsolate servility and held ransom for their services in times of war. Above them in the ranks of the military elite there were constant plots and factions – exacerbated by the Visigothic system of elected monarchy and by their adherence to the heretical Arian philosophy. When **King Leovigild** attempted to impose this creed on Andalucía in the mid-sixth century, the region revolted with the king's son Hermenegild at its head, but the insurrection was brutally crushed. In 589 **King Recared** converted to Catholicism, which for a time stiffened Visigothic control, but religious strife was only multiplied: forced conversions, especially within the Jewish enclaves, maintained a constant simmering of discontent. The Visigoths precariously held on to their domain for a further century as plots and counterplots surrounded the throne. This infighting led indirectly to the Moorish invasions of Andalucía when **King Witiza**, who died in 710, was thwarted by a usurper, Roderic, duke of Baetica, from handing over the throne to his son, Achila. Once **King Roderic** had installed himself on the throne the embittered family of Witiza appealed to the Muslims in North Africa for assistance to overthrow him. The North Africans, who had long eyed the riches of Andalucía with envy, now saw their opportunity.

c.409–415 AD	5th–7th century	711	718
Vandals invade southern Spain.	Visigoths take control of most of Spain.	Moors under Tariq invade and defeat Visigothic King Roderic near Jerez. Peninsula conquered in seven years.	Pelayo defeats Moors at Covadonga in Asturias in northern Spain; the *Reconquista* begins.

The Moorish conquest

In contrast to the long-drawn-out Roman campaigns, the **Moorish conquest** of the peninsula was effected with extraordinary speed. This was a characteristic phenomenon of the spread of Islam – Muhammad left Mecca in 622 and by 705 his followers had established control over all of North Africa. Spain, with its political instability, wealth and fertile climate, was an inevitable extension of their aims. In 711 **Tariq**, governor of Tangier, led a force of seven thousand Berbers across the straits and routed the Visigoth army of King Roderic on the banks of the Río Guadalete close to Jerez. Two years later the Visigoths made a last desperate stand at Mérida and within a decade the Moors had conquered all but the wild mountains of Asturias. The land under their authority was dubbed **al-Andalus**, a fluid term which expanded and shrank with the intermittent gains and losses of the Reconquest. It was Andalucía, however, that was destined to become the heartland of the Moorish ascendancy and where the Moors were to remain in control for most of the next eight centuries.

The Moorish incursion was not simply a military conquest. The Moors (a collective term for the numerous waves of Arab, Syrian and Berber settlers from North Africa) were often content to grant a limited autonomy in exchange for payment of tribute; their administrative system was tolerant and easily absorbed both Spanish Jews and Christians, those who retained their religion being known as "Mozarabs". This **tolerant attitude** was illustrated when the Moorish army reached Córdoba where they found the large Visigothic church of St Vincent, now the fabulous Mezquita. Unlike previous invaders, they did not sack or burn the heathen temple but purchased half of it to use as a mosque whilst the Christians continued to use the other half for their own services. Al-Andalus was a distinctly Spanish state of Islam. Though at first politically subject to the eastern caliphate (or empire) of Baghdad, it was soon virtually independent. In the tenth century, at the peak of its power and expansion, Abd ar-Rahman III asserted total independence, proclaiming himself caliph of a new **western Islamic empire**. Its capital was **Córdoba** – the largest, most prosperous and most civilized city in Europe. This was the great age of Muslim Spain: its scholarship, philosophy, architecture and craftsmanship were without rival and there was an unparalleled growth in urban life, trade and agriculture, aided by magnificent irrigation projects. These and other engineering feats were not, on the whole, instigated by the Moors who instead took the basic Roman models and adapted them to a new level of sophistication. In **architecture** and the **decorative arts**, however, their contribution was original and unique – as may be seen in the astonishingly beautiful monuments of Seville, Córdoba and Granada.

The Cordoban caliphate (and the emirate that preceded it) created a remarkable degree of unity, despite a serious challenge to their authority by the rebel leader **Ibn Hafsun** from his Bobastro fortress (north of Málaga) in the latter years of the ninth century. But its rulers were to become decadent and out of touch, prompting the brilliant but dictatorial **al-Mansur** to usurp control. Under this extraordinary ruler Moorish power reached new heights, using a professional Berber army to push the Christian kingdom of Asturias-León back into the Cantabrian mountains and sacking its most holy shrine, Santiago de Compostela, in 997. However, after al-Mansur's death the caliphate quickly lost its authority and in 1031 disintegrated into a series of small independent kingdoms or **taifas**, the strongest of which was Seville.

756	928	967
Abd-ar-Rahman I proclaims Emirate of Córdoba. Great mosque of Córdoba (Mezquita) begun.	Abd-ar-Rahman III constructs palace of Medina Azahara near Córdoba and extends Mezquita.	Al-Mansur usurps Caliphal powers of Córdoba Caliphate and forces Christians back into Asturias.

ALMOHAD ARCHITECTURE

In the eleventh century, Andalucía fragmented into rival kingdoms or *taifas*, allowing successive waves of Moorish invaders to move into the power vacuum. One of these, the ultra-fundamentalist **Almohads**, left behind a number of remarkable buildings of which the foremost is the magnificent **Giralda** tower in Seville (see p.258), the surviving minaret of the Friday mosque demolished to construct the Gothic cathedral. At 100m high with elaborate *sebka* brickwork panels adorning its exterior walls, it was started in 1184 under architect Ahmed ibn Baso and completed twelve years later.

Internal divisions meant that the *taifas* offered less resistance to the Christian kingdoms that were rallying in the north, and twice North Africa had to be called upon for reinforcement. This resulted in two distinct new waves of Moorish invasion – first by the fanatically Islamic **Almoravids** (1086) and later by the **Almohads** (1147), who restored effective Muslim authority and left behind one of Moorish Spain's most elegant monuments, the **Giralda** tower in Seville. However, their crushing defeat by the Christian forces under Alfonso VIII in 1212, at the battle of **Las Navas de Tolosa** in Jaén, marked the beginning of the end for Moorish Spain.

The Christian Reconquest

The **Reconquest** of land and influence from the Moors – the *Reconquista* – was a slow and intermittent process. It began with a symbolic victory by a small force of Christians at Covadonga in the region of Asturias (722) in northern Spain and was not completed until 1492 with the conquest of Granada by Fernando and Isabel.

Covadonga resulted in the formation of the tiny Christian **kingdom of the Asturias**. Initially just 25km by 19km in area, it had by 914 reclaimed León and most of Galicia and northern Portugal. At this point, progress was temporarily halted by the devastating campaigns of al-Mansur. However, with the fall of the Cordoban caliphate and the divine aid of Spain's Moor-slaying patron saint, the avenging Santiago (St James the Apostle), the *Reconquista* moved into a new and powerful phase. The frontier castles built against Arab attack gave name to **Castile**, founded in the tenth century as a county of León-Asturias. Under Fernando I (1037–65) it achieved the status of a kingdom and became the main thrust and focus of the *Reconquista*. In 1085 this period of confident Christian expansion reached its zenith with the capture of the great Moorish city of Toledo. The following year, however, the Almoravids arrived by invitation from Seville, and military activity was effectively frozen – except, that is, for the exploits of the legendary **El Cid**, a Castilian nobleman who won considerable lands around Valencia in 1095, thus checking Muslim expansion up the eastern coast.

The next concerted phase of the *Reconquista* began as a response to the threat imposed by the Almohads. The kings of León, Castile, Aragón and Navarra united in a crusade that resulted in the great victory at Las Navas de Tolosa. Thereafter Muslim power was paralysed and the **Christian armies** moved on to take most of al-Andalus. Fernando III ("El Santo", the saint) led Castilian soldiers into Córdoba in 1236 and twelve years later into Seville. By the end of the thirteenth century only the Nasrid **kingdom of Granada** remained under Muslim authority and this was to provide a

1013	1037	1085	1086
Caliphate disintegrates into *taifas*, or petty kingdoms.	Fernando I unites kingdoms of Castile and León-Asturias.	Christians capture Toledo.	Almoravids invade Spain from north Africa.

brilliant sunset to Moorish rule in Andalucía. Its survival for a further two centuries whilst surrounded by its Christian enemies was due as much to skilful diplomacy as to payment of tribute to the monarchs of Castile.

Two factors should be stressed regarding the *Reconquista*. First, its unifying religious nature – the **spirit of crusade**, intensified by the religious zeal of the Almoravids and Almohads, and by the wider European climate (which in 1085 gave rise to the First Crusade). At the same time the *Reconquista* was a movement of **recolonization**. The fact that the country had been under arms for so long meant that the nobility had a major and clearly visible social role, a trend perpetuated by the redistribution of captured land in huge packages, or **latifundia**. Heirs to this tradition still remain as landlords of the great estates, most conspicuously in Andalucía where it has produced wretched conditions for the workers on the land ever since. Men from the ranks were also awarded land, forming a lower, larger stratum of nobility, the **hidalgos**. It was their particular social code that provided the material for Cervantes in *Don Quijote*.

Any spirit of mutual cooperation that had temporarily united the Christian kingdoms disintegrated during the fourteenth century, and independent lines of development were once again pursued. **Castile** emerged as the strongest over this period: self-sufficiency in agriculture and a flourishing wool trade with the Netherlands enabled the state to build upon the prominent military role under Fernando III.

Los Reyes Católicos

Los Reyes Católicos – the Catholic Monarchs – was the joint title given to **Fernando V of Aragón** and **Isabel I of Castile**, whose marriage in 1479 united the two largest kingdoms in Spain. Unity was in practice more symbolic than real: Castile had underlined its rights in the marriage vows and Aragón retained its old administrative structure. So, in the beginning at least, the growth of any national unity or Spanish – as opposed to local – sentiment was very much dependent on the head of state. Nevertheless, from this time on it begins to be realistic to consider Spain as a single political entity.

At the heart of Fernando and Isabel's popular appeal lay a **religious bigotry** that they shared with most of their Christian subjects. The **Inquisition** was instituted in Castile in 1480 and in Aragón seven years later. Aiming to establish the purity of the Catholic faith by rooting out heresy, it was directed mainly at Jews (despite Fernando's half-Jewish parentage) – resented for their enterprise in commerce and influence in high places, as well as for their faith. Expression had already been given to these feelings in a pogrom in 1391; it was reinforced by an edict issued in 1492 that forced up to 400,000 Jews to flee the country. A similar spirit was embodied in the reconquest of the Nasrid **kingdom of Granada**, also in 1492. During this long campaign Gonzalo Fernández de Córdoba, "El Gran Capitán", developed the Spanish army into a formidable force that was set to dominate the battlefields of Europe for the next century and a half. As Granada was the last stronghold of Muslim authority, the religious rights of its citizens were guaranteed under the treaty of surrender. Then the policy was reversed and forced mass conversions were introduced. The subsequent and predictable rebellions – particularly violent in **Las Alpujarras** – were brutally put down and within a decade those Muslims under Christian rule had been given the choice between conversion or expulsion.

1147	1212	1236–48
Invasion by Almohads from Morocco; Seville becomes Moorish capital in Spain.	Almohad advance halted by Christian victory at Las Navas de Tolosa (Jaén).	Fernando III conquers Córdoba and Seville.

COLUMBUS AND THE CATHOLIC MONARCHS

After many frustrating years trying to find backers for his plan **to reach the Indies by sailing west**, Columbus's luck turned in 1491 when he spent a period at the Franciscan monastery of **La Rábida** in the province of Huelva. The abbot of La Rábida, Juan Pérez, a former confessor to Queen Isabel, was moved to write to her on Columbus's behalf. It was a timely moment as Granada had just fallen, the treasury was empty, and the promise of gold and glory for a resurgent Spain now attracted Isabel and her husband King Fernando. On August 3, 1492, Columbus set out from Palos, a port in Huelva, with three small vessels and 120 men. On October 12, he made landfall on Watling Island (aka San Salvador) in the Bahamas. After leaving a colony of men on Hispaniola (modern Haiti) he returned to Palos on March 15, 1493, to enormous acclaim. The Spanish conquest of the Americas had begun.

The New World

The year 1492 was symbolic of a fresh start in another way: it was in this year that **Columbus** sailed from Huelva to make the **discovery of America**, and the papal bull that followed, entrusting Spain with the conversion of the American Indians, further entrenched Spain's sense of a mission to bring the world to the "True Faith". The next ten years saw the systematic conquest, colonization and exploitation of the **New World**, with new territory stretching from Labrador in modern Canada to Brazil, and new-found wealth pouring into the royal coffers. The control of trade with the New World was carried on through **Seville** where the Casa de Contratación (House of Trade) was established in 1503. The city rapidly grew into one of the great cities of Europe during which it enjoyed two centuries of commercial monopoly. Paradoxically, Andalucía as a whole benefited little from this wealth, which was appropriated by the crown for its foreign campaigns and by absentee landlords. Over the succeeding two centuries the region languished as a backwater and the poverty of the peasants led many to emigrate to the New World in order to better themselves, turning much of the region into a vast, unpopulated desert.

The Habsburg Age

Carlos I, a Habsburg, came to the throne in 1516 as a beneficiary of the marriage alliances of the Catholic monarchs. Five years later, he was elected emperor of the Holy Roman Empire as Carlos V (**Charles V**), inheriting not only Castile and Aragón, but also Flanders, the Netherlands, Artois, the Franche-Comté and all the American colonies to boot. With such responsibilities it was inevitable that attention would be diverted from Spain, whose chief function became to sustain the Holy Roman Empire with gold and silver from the Americas. It was only with the accession of **Felipe II** in 1556 that Spanish politics became more centralized and that the notion of an absentee king was reversed.

This was a period of unusual religious intensity: the **Inquisition** was enforced with renewed vigour, and a "final solution" to the problem of the Moriscos (subject Moors), who continued to adhere to their ancient traditions and practise Muslim worship in secret, resulted in a decree banning Arabic dress, books and speech. The result was another rising of Moriscos in Las Alpujarras that was fiercely suppressed, with Muslims

1238	1262–92	1469
Ibn al-Ahmar founds the Nasrid dynasty and starts construction of the Alhambra palace.	Cádiz falls to Alfonso X, Sancho IV takes Tarifa.	Castile and Aragón united by the marriage of Isabel and Fernando, los Reyes Católicos (the Catholic Monarchs).

being forcibly deported to other parts of the country. Felipe III later ordered the expulsion of half the total number of Moriscos in Spain – allowing only two families to remain in each Alpujarran village in order to maintain irrigation techniques. The **exodus** of both Muslim and Jews created a large gulf in the labour force and in the higher echelons of commercial life – and in trying to uphold the Catholic cause, an enormous strain was put upon resources without any clearcut victory. Despite being a golden literary and artistic age, politically and economically the seventeenth century was a disaster for Spain. Lurching progressively deeper into debt, she suffered heavy defeats on the battlefield as her possessions in the Netherlands and France were lost, and recurring financial crises and economic stagnation engendered a deepening mood of disillusionment. **Andalucía** shared in this decline, exacerbated by the tendency of the mercantile classes to involve themselves only in entrepôt trade which left most of the profits in the hands of other countries. There was also no stimulus given to industrial production by the custom of merchants retiring from commerce and investing their profits in land, which created a landed gentry weighed down by honours and titles whose lifestyle came to be looked upon as being incompatible with commerce.

The Bourbons

The **Bourbon dynasty** succeeded to the Spanish throne in the person of Felipe V (1700); with him began the **War of the Spanish Succession** against the rival claim of Archduke Charles of Austria, assisted by British forces. As a result of the Treaty of Utrecht that ended the war (1713), Spain was stripped of all territory in Belgium, Luxembourg, Italy and Sardinia, but Felipe V was recognized as king. **Gibraltar** was seized by the British in the course of the war. For the rest of the century Spain fell very much under the French sphere of influence, an influence that was given political definition by an alliance with the French Bourbons in 1762. This Gallic connection brought the ideas of Enlightenment Europe into the peninsula and during the reign of Carlos III (1759–88) a number of radically minded ministers attempted to deal with the nation's chronic problems. Along with a more tolerant attitude towards the **gypsies**, who had become victims of racial abuse and hostility, the king's minister, Pablo de Olavide, began an imaginative, if ultimately unsuccessful, scheme to **repopulate the Sierra Morena** in Andalucía with foreign immigrants.

Contact with France also made involvement in the **Napoleonic Wars** inevitable and led eventually to the defeat of the Spanish and French fleet at the **Battle of Trafalgar** off the coast of Cádiz in 1805. Popular outrage was such that the powerful prime minister, Godoy, was overthrown and King Carlos IV forced to abdicate (1808). Napoleon seized the opportunity to install his brother, Joseph, on the throne, whilst French armies and generals ransacked and stole much of the country's artistic heritage.

Fierce local resistance in the form of guerrilla warfare was accompanied by armies raised by the various local administrations. Thus it was that a militia put in the field by the junta of Seville inflicted a resounding defeat on a French army at **Bailén** in Jaén in 1808, which forced Joseph, the "intruder king", to flee back across the border. This resistance was eventually backed by the muscle of a British army, first under Sir John Moore, later under the Duke of Wellington, and the French were at last driven out in the course of the **War of Independence** (Peninsular War). Meanwhile, the **American**

1479	1492	1516
Spanish Inquisition begins in Seville.	Fall of Granada, the last Moorish kingdom. Discovery of America by Cristóbal Colón (Columbus).	Carlos V succeeds to the throne and (1520) becomes the Holy Roman Emperor, inaugurating the Golden Age.

colonies had been successfully asserting their independence from a preoccupied centre and with them went Spain's last real claim of significance on the world stage. The entire nineteenth century was dominated by the struggle between an often reactionary monarchy and the aspirations of liberal constitutional reformers.

The nineteenth century

Between 1810 and 1813, whilst the war raged on across the peninsula, an ad hoc Cortes (parliament) meeting in **Cádiz** had set up a **liberal constitution** which stipulated a strict curtailment of the powers of the crown with ministers responsible to a democratically elected chamber. The first act of the despotic Fernando VII on being returned to the throne was to abolish this, and until his death in 1833 he continued to stamp out the least hint of liberalism. But the Constitution of 1812 was to remain a "sacred text" for a future democratic Spain, besides introducing the word "liberal" to Europe's political vocabulary. On Fernando's death, the right of succession was contested between his brother, Don Carlos, backed by the Church, conservatives and Basques, and his infant daughter, Isabel, who looked to the Liberals and the army for support.

So began the **First Carlist War**, a civil war that divided Spanish emotions for six years. Isabel II was eventually declared of age in 1843, her reign a long record of scandal, political crisis and constitutional compromise. Liberal army generals under the leadership of General Prim effected a coup in 1868 and the queen was forced to abdicate, but attempts to maintain a Republican government foundered. The Cortes was again dissolved and the throne returned to Isabel's son, Alfonso XII. The military began increasingly to move into the power vacuum left by the weakened monarchy. The **pronunciamiento** – whereby an officer backed by military force "pronounced" what was in the best interests of a city or region – was born in this period and was to plague the country into modern times.

The **nineteenth century** in Andalucía mirrored Spain's national decline. The loss of the American colonies had badly hit the region's trade, and this was compounded by the phylloxera plague from the 1870s onwards which wiped out most of the vineyards, brought the sherry industry to its knees, and fuelled the growth of strikes in the cities and popular uprisings on the land as the economy deteriorated. Parodoxically, this century also did more than any other to bestow on Andalucía the image it has held ever since. Writers, artists and travellers of the **Romantic Age** saw in its bullfights, flamenco, bandits and beguiling women a world of gaiety and colour, epitomized in the operas *Carmen* and *The Barber of Seville*, both works from this period. The years preceding World War I merely heightened the discontent, which found expression in the growing **political movements** of the working class. The Socialist Workers' Party was founded in Madrid after the restoration of Alfonso XII, and spawned its own trade union, the UGT (1888). Its anarchist counterpart, the CNT (Confederación Nacional de Trabajo), was founded in 1911, gaining substantial support among the oppressed peasantry of Andalucía. The loss of **Cuba** in 1898 emphasized the growing isolation of Spain in international affairs and added to economic problems with the return of soldiers seeking employment where there was none. In Andalucía a regionalist movement known as **Andalucismo** was born demanding land reform and greater Andalucian autonomy.

1519	1556	1587	1588
Magellan starts global voyage from Sanlúcar de Barrameda; Cortés lands in Mexico.	Accession of Felipe II (d.1598)	Sir Francis Drake carries out raid on Cádiz.	The British defeat the Spanish Armada; Spain's demise as a sea power begins.

Into the twentieth century

A call-up for army reserves to fight in **Morocco** in 1909 provoked a general strike and the "Tragic Week" of rioting in Barcelona. Between 1914 and 1918, Spain was outwardly neutral but inwardly turbulent; inflated prices made the postwar recession harder to bear. The general disillusionment with parliamentary government, together with the fears of employers and businessmen for their own security, gave **General Primo de Rivera** sufficient support for a military coup in 1923. Coming himself from Jerez de la Frontera, the paternalistic general backed the great **Ibero-American Exhibition of 1929** at Seville which, it was hoped, would calm the agitation for radical change by promoting a "rose-coloured" image for the troubled region; its most immediate effect was to bankrupt the city. Dictatorship did result in an increase in material prosperity, heavily assisted by a massive public works policy, but serious political misjudgements and the collapse of the peseta in 1929 made Rivera's voluntary resignation and departure into exile inevitable. The legacy of this dictatorship was to reinforce a belief on the Right that only a firm military hand would be capable of holding society together, and many of those who served in Primo de Rivera's administration were to back the Franco regime in the next decade. The victory of anti-monarchist parties in the 1931 municipal elections forced the abdication of the hopelessly out of touch King Alfonso XIII, and the **Second Republic** was declared.

The Second Republic

The **Second Republic**, which lasted from 1931 to 1936, was ushered in on a wave of optimism that finally some of the nation's fundamental ills and injustices would be rectified. But the government – a coalition of radicals, socialists and leftist republicans – struggling to curb the power of vested interests such as the army, the Church and the landowning class, was soon failing to satisfy even the least of the expectations that it had raised. Moreover it lost support when it got involved in activities identified with earlier repressive regimes, as happened at the village of **Casas Viejas** (modern Benalup-Casas Viejas) in Cádiz, when it ordered the troops to open fire on a group of starving workers who had been the victims of a lockout by the local landowner and who were attempting to raise the area in an anarchist revolt.

Anarchism was gaining strength among the frustrated middle classes as well as among workers and peasantry. The **Communist Party** and left-wing **socialists**, driven into alliance by their mutual distrust of the "moderate" Socialists in government, were also forming a growing bloc. There was little real unity of purpose on either left or right, but their fear of each other and their own exaggerated boasts made each seem an imminent threat. On the right the **Falangists**, basically a youth party founded in 1923 by **José Antonio Primo de Rivera** (son of the dictator), made uneasy bedfellows with conservative traditionalists and dissident elements in the army upset by modernizing reforms.

In an atmosphere of growing confusion, with mobs fighting on the streets and churches and monasteries being torched whilst landed estates were taken over by those impatient for agrarian reform, the left-wing Popular Front alliance won the general election of **February 1936** by a narrow margin. Normal life, though, became increasingly impossible: the economy was crippled by strikes, the universities became

1609	1649	1700
Expulsion of Moriscos, last remaining Spanish Muslims.	Great plague in Seville wipes out one third of the population.	War of Spanish Succession brings Bourbon Felipe V to the throne. The British seize Gibraltar.

hotbeds for battles between Marxists and Falangists, and the government failed to exert its authority over anyone. Finally, on July 17, 1936, the military garrison in Morocco rebelled under **General Franco**'s leadership, to be followed by risings at military garrisons throughout the country. It was the culmination of years of scheming in the army, but in the event far from the overnight success its leaders almost certainly expected. Airlifting his troops into Seville by means of German transport planes, Franco ensured that the south and west quickly fell into Nationalist hands, but Madrid and the industrialized north and east remained loyal to the Republican government.

The Civil War

The ensuing **Civil War** was undoubtedly one of the most bitter and bloody the world has seen. Violent reprisals were taken on their enemies by both sides – the Republicans shooting priests and local landowners wholesale, the Nationalists carrying out mass slaughter of the population of almost every town they took. Contradictions were legion in the way the Spanish populations found themselves divided from each other. Perhaps the greatest irony was that Franco's troops, on their "holy" mission against a godless "anti-Spain", comprised a core of Moroccan troops from Spain's North African colony.

It was, too, the first **modern war** – Franco's German allies demonstrated their ability to wipe out entire civilian populations with their bombing raids on Gernika and Durango in the Basque country, and radio proved an important weapon, as Nationalist propagandists offered the starving Republicans "the white bread of Franco". Despite sporadic help from Russia and thousands of volunteers in the International Brigades, the Republic could never compete with the professional armies and the massive assistance from Fascist Italy and Nazi Germany enjoyed by the Nationalists. As hundreds of thousands of refugees flooded into France, **General Francisco Franco**, who had long before proclaimed himself head of state, took up the reins of power.

Franco's Spain

The early reprisals taken by the victors were on a massive and terrifying scale. Executions were commonplace in towns and villages, and upwards of two million people were put in concentration camps until "order" had been established by authoritarian means. Only one party was permitted and censorship was rigidly enforced. By the end of World War II, during which Spain was too weak to be anything but neutral, **Franco** was the only fascist head of state left in Europe, and responsible for sanctioning more deaths than any other in Spanish history. Spain was economically and politically isolated and, bereft of markets, suffering – almost half the population were still tilling the soil for little or no return. The misery of the peasantry was particularly acute in Andalucía and forced mass emigrations to Madrid and Barcelona and Europe beyond.

When General Eisenhower visited Madrid in 1953 with the offer of huge loans, it came as water to the desert, and the price, the **establishment of American nuclear bases** such as those at Rota near Cádiz and Morón de la Frontera, was one Franco was more than willing to pay. Once firmly in the US camp the Franco regime (administered by the so-called *tecnocratas* group of ministers) rapidly transformed Spain into a market

1759–88	1808	1812
Enlightenment ideas enter Spain; colonies of Germans, French and Swiss settle in the Sierra Morena.	French occupy Spain.	Liberal constitution declared in Cádiz.

THE LAW OF HISTORICAL MEMORY

In Spain as well as abroad the **legacy of Franco** remains controversial. In the years following the restoration of democracy there was no national debate about the dictator's 35-year rule and unlike other countries, such as Germany and Argentina, Spain has never fully come to terms with its former dictatorship. Instead politicians on both sides of the divide tacitly agreed not to mention the legacy of the Franco regime and no war crimes trials were held. But many others were angry at a pact that meant that crimes committed in the Franco years not only went unpunished, but weren't even recognized as having taken place. In 2007 the Spanish PSOE government – led by José Luís Rodrigo Zapatero, whose own grandfather was executed by Franco's forces – decided to address this issue and passed into law **La Ley de Memoria Histórica** (The Law of Historical Memory). This rules that sentences handed down by kangaroo courts during the regime – that led to the imprisonment or execution of thousands of Franco's opponents – were "illegitimate." It also decrees that local governments must locate, exhume from mass graves and identify the victims of the Franco regime. Historians claim that the remains of tens of thousands of Franco's opponents are buried in unmarked graves throughout the country.

The law also stipulates that all statues, plaques, street name plates and symbols relating to the regime must be removed from public buildings (however, church property was excluded). It deals, too, with the dictatorship's monumental legacy – the vast basilica of the **Valle de los Caídos** near Madrid where the remains of Franco and the founder of the fascist Falange party, José Antonio Prima de Rivera, are interred. The law prohibits all political events at the site, thus preventing the traditional "mass for the Caudillo" formerly celebrated every 20 November (the anniversary of Franco's death), and its celebration of the fascist cause.

economy and in the late Fifties the country joined the International Monetary Fund, the International Bank for Reconstruction and Development and the OECD in quick succession. However belated, economic development was incredibly rapid, with Spain enjoying a growth rate second only to that of Japan for much of the 1960s, a boom fuelled by the tourist industry, the remittances of Spanish workers abroad and the illegality of strikes and industrial action at home. Increased **prosperity**, however, only underlined the political bankruptcy of Franco's regime and its inability to cope with popular demands. Higher incomes, the need for better education, and a creeping invasion of Western culture made the anachronism of Franco ever clearer. His only reaction was to attempt to withdraw what few signs of increased liberalism had crept through, and his last years mirrored the repression of the postwar period. Franco finally died in November 1975, nominating **King Juan Carlos** as his successor.

The new Spain

On October 28, 1982, *sevillano* Felipe González's Socialist Workers' Party – the PSOE – was elected with massive support to rule a country that had been firmly in the hands of the right for 43 years. The **Socialists** captured the imagination and the votes of nearly ten million Spaniards with the simplest of appeals: "for change". It was a telling comment on just how far Spain had moved since Franco's death, for in the intervening years change seemed the one factor that could still threaten the new-found democracy.

1830–70	1835	1898
Romantic Age. Richard Ford's *Handbook for Travellers in Spain* (1845) puts Andalucía on the visitors' map.	First Carlist War. Peasant risings throughout Andalucía.	Loss of Cuba, Spain's last American colony.

Certainly, in the Spain of 1976 the thought of a freely elected left-wing government would have been incredible. **King Juan Carlos** was the hand-picked successor of Franco, groomed for the job and very much in with the army – of which he remains official commander-in-chief. His initial moves were cautious in the extreme, appointing a government dominated by loyal Francoists who had little sympathy for the growing opposition demands for "democracy without adjectives".

To his credit, however, Juan Carlos recognized that some real break with the past was now urgent and inevitable, and set in motion the process of **democratization**. He legitimized the Socialist Party and, controversially, the Communists. When elections were held in June 1977, the centre-right **UCD** Christian–Democrat party gained a 34 percent share of the vote, the **PSOE** (Spanish Socialist Workers' Party) coming in second with 28 percent, and the Communists and Francoist Alianza Popular both marginalized at nine percent and eight percent.

It was almost certainly a vote for democratic stability rather than for ideology. The king, perhaps recognizing that his own future depended on the maintenance of the new democracy, lent it his support – most notably in February 1981 when a tragicomic Civil Guard colonel named Tejero stormed the Cortes brandishing a revolver and, with other officers loyal to Franco's memory, attempted to institute an **army coup**. But the crisis, for a while, was real. Tanks were brought out onto the streets of Valencia, and only three of the army's ten regional commanders remained unreservedly loyal to the government. But as it became clear that the king would not support the plotters, most of the rest affirmed their support. Juan Carlos had taken the decision of his life and emerged with immensely enhanced prestige in the eyes of most Spaniards.

The new political system had successfully dealt with the first real challenge to its authority and following these events Spanish democracy – even in army circles where most of the old guard were gradually pensioned off – now became firmly institutionalized. And in the fourteen-year rule of the charismatic **Felipe González** (always known as "Felipe") and the PSOE the system found, at least until the Nineties' slide into the political mire and defeat, a party of enduring **stability** and to the left of exasperating **moderation**.

The swing to the right

The final years of González's and the PSOE's period in power were dogged by a series of **scandals**. The most serious of all, however, was the **GAL affair** (Grupo Antiterrorista de Liberación) when it was discovered that a state-sponsored anti-terrorist unit had been fighting a dirty war against ETA that included kidnappings and even assassinations of suspected terrorists. The press – and a later judicial investigation – exposed police participation in these crimes and a clear chain of command reaching up to the highest echelons of the PSOE government. González narrowly avoided being hauled before the courts, and the nation's progressive disillusion with his government saw the rise to prominence of **José-María Aznar** as leader of the **Partido Popular** conservatives (a merger of the UCD and Alianza Popular).

A former tax inspector with little charisma, Aznar's dogged criticism of the PSOE government's incompetence and corruption finally won the PP a narrow **victory** in the

1923–30	1931	1936
Primo de Rivera dictatorship. De Rivera resigns due to ill health and popular agitation urges a republic.	King Alfonso XIII is forced out; Second Republic is declared.	Spanish Civil War begins when army officers in Spanish Morocco under generals Mola and Francisco Franco lead a revolt.

1996 elections. Unable to make any significant impact on changing public opinion and with the PSOE in turmoil, early in 1998 González finally **resigned** from the leadership of the party he had led in government and opposition for 23 years.

A desperate PSOE then formed an alliance with the ex-communist Izquierda Unida party, believing that their combined votes could still prevent a likely Aznar victory in the forthcoming general election. However the outcome of the March 2000 **general election** was a stunning **triumph for Aznar** and the PP, and for the first time since the death of Franco the right was in power with an overall majority.

The PSOE leader, Joaquín Almunia, resigned and a relatively unknown young politician was elected leader: **José Luis Rodríguez Zapatero**, a member of the moderate socialist "Nueva Vía" (New Way) group within the PSOE. Zapatero admitted the PSOE's past mistakes, stating emphatically that any government led by him would be radically different. This seemed to go down well with the electorate, and the opinion polls began to move in the PSOE's favour.

The return of the PSOE

In 2001, José María Aznar – ever an enigma to those around him – announced that he would lead the PP up to the general election of 2004 but would then resign, and that it must seek a new leader. As leader designate (to take over after the poll) the party chose Aznar's nominee, the less prickly, cigar-puffing **Mariano Rajoy**, minister for the interior and deputy prime minister. Despite the highest level of **unemployment** in the EU and a **general strike** in June 2002, caused by opposition to labour law and social security reforms intended to free up the labour market and slash social security benefits, the opinion polls still showed solid public support for the Aznar administration. Throughout 2003 Aznar relentlessly urged the electorate to back the party that had brought steady economic growth and low inflation. This strategy appeared to work, and early in 2004 all the indicators suggested the following March general election would deliver a comfortable victory for the ruling PP and its new leader, Rajoy.

Then, on March 11, and three days before polling day, a series of **bombs exploded on rush-hour commuter trains** travelling into Madrid, killing 192 people and injuring almost two thousand others. The nation was thrown into shock at the most savage attack seen in Spain since the Civil War. Despite the discovery by police within hours of a van connected to the bombings containing detonators and a Koranic audiotape, the PP leadership decided that the Basque terrorist group ETA had to be the culprits. This was a high-risk tactic for the government but it seemed convinced that by pinning the responsibility on ETA it would deflect attention away from its support for the Iraq war (ninety percent of Spaniards had been against it) just long enough for the votes to be counted. No mention was to be made of any possible link with Islamic militant groups and at the same time the blaming of ETA would conveniently vindicate Aznar's hardline stance against Basque terrorism and separatism.

For the three days prior to the election the heavily state-influenced media and Spanish diplomats around the world attempted to peddle the "ETA is responsible" line. But soon doubts began to surface and in the hours before the polls opened the electorate seems to have become highly suspicious of the government's tactic of using

1936	1939	1953	1975
Blas Infante, "Father of Andalucían nationalism", executed by Franco's forces in Seville.	Civil War ends; Franco dictatorship begins.	US makes economic deal with Franco in return for military bases.	Death of Franco. Spain reverts to a constitutional monarchy.

ETA as a scapegoat to save its skin, believing that the attack – as was subsequently proved – was the work of **Islamic terrorists** and a retaliation for Spain's participation in the unpopular Iraq war.

The nation turned out in force (turnout went up by a crucial eight percent over the 2000 poll) to give its verdict and Zapatero and the PSOE an **unexpected victory**. Two million new young voters angered by Aznar's unwavering support for the Iraq war seem to have been pivotal to the final result. The lies and distortion accusations hurled at the Partido Popular following the election result only intensified when it was revealed that the outgoing government had hired a specialist company to destroy all computer records dealing with the bombings before leaving office.

Zapatero's first term

The first act carried out by Zapatero as government leader was to announce the immediate **withdrawal of Spanish troops from Iraq**, an election promise. This aligned him firmly with the German and French governments in Europe to whom Aznar had been hostile, but incurred the displeasure of US president George W. Bush, who shunned Zapatero for the rest of his presidency and turned down requests by the Spanish leader for a meeting at the White House or in Madrid.

In his first four years of office, leading up to the 2008 elections, Zapatero's record was competent if unspectacular. His government will probably be remembered for being Spain's first in which half the cabinet seats were occupied by women and for legalizing **gay marriages** rather than for any dramatic shifts of policy. He also enjoyed the benefit of favourable economic circumstances with consistently high economic growth figures and an economy producing more jobs than any other euro-zone member. International financial number-crunchers declared in 2007 that's Spain's GDP per head had overtaken that of Italy. But in the latter part of the same year the impact of the world **economic downturn** was also felt in Spain as one of the major drivers of the Spanish economy, the huge construction industry, went into meltdown. Unemployment figures started to rise as worried consumers put off making major purchases.

An uncertain future

The **general election** of March 2008 took place against a background of economic uncertainty, and although the result was another **PSOE victory**, they had scraped home seven seats short of the overall parliamentary majority that Zapatero had stated was the party's main campaign target. The fact that the PSOE had won at all was as much due to a lacklustre campaign fought by opposition leader Mariano Rajoy and the PP as the PSOE's rather tame appeal to the voters that offered few new ideas. The government's second term was dominated by the **world financial and economic crisis**. The recession caused unemployment to rise to alarming levels, while an austerity programme aimed at dealing with the government's massive debt lost it much support as civil service and teachers' salaries were cut, benefits and pensions were frozen and welfare programmes cancelled. In an effort to turn public support in the government's favour, in the autumn of 2010 Zapatero unveiled an extensive cabinet reshuffle and cut a deal with the Basque Nationalist Party that would guarantee that the government ran its full term. In return the Basques won further transfers of power and funds to the already highly devolved Basque regional government.

1980	1981	1982
Andalucía votes to become an autonomous region.	Attempted military coup fails; members of parliament are held hostage in the Spanish Parliament.	Sevillano and PSOE leader Felipe González elected prime minister. Elections for first Andalucían parliament.

Little changed, however, during the winter of 2010 as the economy foundered and the unemployment figure passed twenty percent – the highest in the EU. Political commentators observed that some government ministers – Zapatero in particular – appeared indecisive and weary. In early April 2011 the PSOE leader announced that he would not lead the party after the general election of 2012 and that it must seek a new leader. It appeared that while he had been a capable, if undistinguished, prime minister in times of plenty, he had little stomach for the long haul ahead to bring the Spanish economy out of deep recession.

The local and regional elections held in May 2011 produced a **resounding victory for the opposition Partido Popular**. The scale of the defeat was shocking – even the PSOE bastion of Castilla La Mancha fell to the PP for the first time since democracy was restored. The party then chose **Alfredo Pérez Rubalcaba**, a wily sexagenarian politician – and a minister in all the PSOE administrations since the 1990s – to succeed Zapatero and in June he assumed the title of leader designate (to take over at the start of the general election campaign). The party's clear intention was that Rubalcaba's "safe pair of hands" might be able to thwart a massacre, if not the seemingly inevitable defeat, at the approaching general election.

At end of July 2011 Zapatero announced that he would call an **early general election** for the following November. The heavy local election defeats and continuing financial crisis in which Spain was a target for speculators were given as the reason, with the PSOE leader stating that the country needed a strong government with a clear majority able to "project economic and political certainty" on the world stage. The election was held on November 20 and the PP swept to **a landslide victory** with a crushing 16 percentage point win over Rubalcaba's socialists – the PSOE's worst result since the return of democracy. In his victory speech the PP leader, and now prime minister, **Mariano Rajoy** gravely announced that "Difficult times are coming," as the financial crisis continued to wreak havoc across world markets.

It remains to be seen whether a Partido Popular government will succeed in carrying out the **vital reforms** necessary to restore prosperity to the peninsula. With the collapse of the construction and tourism sectors, which since the end of the Franco regime had accounted for close to 25 percent of GDP, many experts now believe that Spain has no alternative but to build an advanced export-based economy in order to survive. The cornerstone of any new export-based economy, however, has to be **education** – and here Spain will need to put in a Herculean effort if it is to become competitive in the knowledge-based economy of the twenty-first century.

In a 2011 report the IMF predicted that Spain's unemployment would remain the highest in the eurozone for at least five years and warned of the grave risk of a "lost generation" being excluded from the job market.

During and after the May local and regional elections of 2011 **multitudes of young people**, many of them unemployed with little chance of finding a job, gathered in protest in makeshift campsites in the central squares and parks of major towns and cities across Spain. Coordinated via Facebook and Twitter, these protests were against a political system they claimed is self-serving, inward-looking and oblivious to their plight. Their plight is real: unemployment in Spain averages nearly 45 percent among 16- to 29-year-olds. Whether the political establishment is capable of responding remains to be seen.

1985	1986	1992	1996
Spain-Gibraltar frontier opens after being closed by Franco in 1969 protesting the British presence.	Spain joins the European Union.	Expo '92 World Fair in Seville celebrates 500th anniversary of Columbus's discovery of America.	Felipe González and PSOE lose general election after fourteen years in power.

Modern Andalucía

Andalucía shared in the progressive decentralization of power in Spain throughout the post-Franco period and in 1980 became an **Autonomous Region** with a regional government (Junta de Andalucía) based in Seville. Largely because of its enduring social problems, Andalucía remained a socialist bulwark for the PSOE throughout the Eighties – the so-called *sartenilla* (frying pan) of the south that traditionally "fries" the right-wing votes further north. Throughout the 1990s this support enabled the discredited PSOE government of Felipe González to remain in power while denying Aznar's PP its longed-for majority when it finally did become the largest party.

In the **general election of 2000** there was a significant shift in voting patterns away from the left and towards Aznar and the PP that contributed significantly to the right's victory. In the **poll of 2004** Andalucía shared in the national fury at the PP government's attempts to shift the blame for the Madrid bombings onto ETA and they turned out once more to vote for Zapatero and the PSOE, increasing the number of votes for the Socialist Party by almost three million over the 2000 figure.

Despite a more fickle attitude to voting (or abstaining) in general elections that allowed the PP to win a majority in Andalucía, in the 2008 regional elections to Andalucía's **autonomous parliament** the region voted solidly to maintain this in the hands of the PSOE. This was the socialist party's eighth consecutive victory since regional elections were inaugurated in 1982, due in no small part to the PSOE's leader in Andalucía, **Manuel Chaves**. A canny and popular politician and president of the autonomous government since 1990, he presided over a revolution in Andalucía that saw rapid growth in tourism, a vast improvement in communications and the eradication of poverty in large parts of the region. It was inevitable that the Madrid government would wish to add such a proven winner to the cabinet and prime minister Zapatero persuaded him to join the PSOE administration as a minister in 2009.

Chaves was replaced as president of the Junta de Andalucía by **José Antonio Griñán**, his vice-president and number two. With an avuncular demeanour and designer stubble, Griñán has not found it easy to combat the growing **wave of anti-PSOE sentiment** across the region, despite its strongly left-leaning traditions. In the general election of November 2011 *andaluz* voters turned out to give the PP a stunning majority in seven out of Andalucía's eight provinces.

Times of crisis

Contradicting the sunny image presented to most of its visitors, chronic economic and social problems continue to plague the region, and not for nothing is Andalucía known as the "workhouse of Spain". The regional **unemployment** level is among the European Union's highest at an alarming thirty percent (compared with twenty percent for Spain as a whole), and earnings per head are a third lower than the national average. The region has also been severely affected by Spain's **economic recession**. The collapse of the building sector has led to construction companies going bust, estate agents filing for bankruptcy and tens of thousands of unemployed building workers swelling the dole queues. The position of Andalucía's 200,000 **agricultural workers**, who face nine months' unemployment each year and depend on

2000	2002	2003
Partido Popular election victory gives the right an overall majority for first time since Franco dictatorship.	Spain adopts the euro currency.	Picasso museum opens in Málaga, the artist's birthplace.

patronage from the great landowners for work during the other three, also remains unresolved. Industries such as fishing have also been affected by EU regulations limiting the size of catches to conserve dwindling fish stocks, with a consequent rise in unemployment in port towns throughout Andalucía. All this has compelled a greater dependence on **tourism**, a sector that now faces stiff competition from up-and-coming low-cost holiday destinations and the inevitable knock in the industry that comes during recession. In any case, tourism's decades of success has produced its own problems as many flocked to the coast in search of work leaving a mere twenty percent of the population in provinces such as Almería inhabiting the hinterland. The Junta de Andalucía regional government now mounts an annual "rural tourism" campaign to attract visitors inland in order to channel some of the tourist income away from the coast.

An area now receiving belated attention is the region's **educational system** where serious flaws have long been evident in both high schools and higher education. Other outstanding problems include the waves of **illegal immigrants** who arrive (if they do not perish en route) almost daily on Andalucía's beaches, packed into flimsy fishing boats, and the spread of **crime and corruption** on the Costa del Sol, where many foreign criminal syndicates are based.

The stringent **austerity measures** announced by the incoming PP government will inevitably squeeze the finances of autonomous regions like Andalucía even further and many work creation schemes provided by regional and local governments will now be cut. Town halls already in debt (Jerez city council alone has a billion euros of arrears) will struggle to pay back these huge sums while others like Granada with its two-thirds built – but now stalled due to a shortage of funds – new metro system will be unable to complete lavish trophy projects started in the boom years.

Andalucía made headlines across Europe in late 2011 when the EU announced the ten regions in the union with the highest unemployment, eight of which were in Spain. Andalucía was cited as the region with the worst jobless figure of the ten and the small town of **Benalup–Casas Viejas** in Cádiz the municipality with the **EU's highest level of unemployment**. With over a quarter of its adult population out of work, Benalup is a microcosm for what has happened across the region. In 2004 eighty percent of the town's labour force was employed in the construction industry, building holiday homes or new hotels on the nearby Costa de la Luz, and the average wage was €3000 a month. The number of banks doubled, and a lending war ensued as everyone bought new cars, houses and second homes. When the bubble burst in 2008 the number of unemployed soared, as did the mortgage repossessions. Now, as the situation becomes increasingly desperate, many of the unattached younger population are leaving to find jobs in other parts of Europe, as did their forebears in the 1950s and Sixties. The jobless and bewildered populace left behind have placed their hopes in the new PP government to get them out of the mess. Disturbingly for Benalup, and many hundreds of other Benalups across the region, new prime minister Mariano Rajoy's first message after his election victory was to declare that "There will be no miracles".

2004	2007–8	2010
Madrid train bombings kill 191 and injure 2050, influencing the outcome of the general election held three days later.	World economic downturn hits Andalucía; unemployment rises steeply.	Spain wins the FIFA World Cup for first time, in South Africa, following its victory in the European Nations Cup in 2008.

Flamenco

Flamenco is undoubtedly the most important musical-cultural phenomenon in Spain. Over the past couple of decades it has experienced a huge resurgence in popularity, and a profile that has reached out far beyond its Andalucian homeland. The sanitized kitsch flamenco, all frills and castanets, exploited as an image of tourist Spain during the Franco period, has been left far behind by a new age expressing the vitality and attitudes of a younger generation of flamenco clans. In line with this trend, in 2010 UNESCO added flamenco to its intangible cultural heritage list, as a world-class art form to be encouraged, protected and supported.

In Andalucía, the fact that the public are so knowledgeable and demanding about flamenco means that musicians, singers and dancers found even at the most humble local club or festival are usually very good indeed.

Origins

The **roots of flamenco** evolved in southern Spain from many sources: Morocco, Egypt, India, Pakistan, Greece and other parts of the Near and Far East. How exactly they came together as flamenco is a source of great debate and obscurity, though most authorities believe the roots of the music were brought by **gypsies** arriving in the fifteenth century. In the following century, it fused with elements of Arab and Jewish music in the Andalucian mountains, where Jews, Muslims and "pagan" gypsies had

---

NUEVO FLAMENCO: AN EVOLVING ART FORM

In the 1980s, the Spanish press hailed **Ketama** (named after a Moroccan village famed for its hashish) as creators of the music of the "New Spain" after the release of their eponymous first album, which fused flamenco with rock and Latin salsa. Later they pushed the frontiers of flamenco further still by recording *Songhai*, an album collaborating with Malian kora player Toumani Diabate and British bassist Danny Thompson, followed by *De Aki A Ketama* developing more rock-fusion themes. *Blues de la Frontera* (Frontier Blues), the first disc of **Pata Negra** ("black leg" – the highest quality of cured ham – and an everyday term used for anything good), caused an equal sensation. This flamenco revival of the 1980s and 1990s is no longer confined to the purists who kept old-time flamenco alive in their *peñas* or clubs. On radio and on CD-players blaring from market stalls right across the country you hear the typical high-pitched treble tones of commercial flamenco singers such as **Tijeritas**. The European success of the flamenco-rumba of the **Gipsy Kings**, a high-profile gypsy group from southern France, has further opened and prepared the ear of European popular audiences for something more powerful. Rumba, a Latin form, has come back to Spain from Latin America, and so is known as a music of *ida y vuelta* ("go and return"), one of the many fusions of the Spanish music taken to the New World with the *conquistadores* and their descendants, where it has mixed with African and other elements, before making its way back again. The impetus began at the end of the 1970s, with the innovations of guitarist **Paco de Lucía** and, especially, the late great singer, **El Camarón de la Isla**. These were musicians who had grown up learning from their flamenco families but whose own musical tastes have embraced international rock, jazz and blues. Paco de Lucía blended jazz and salsa with the flamenco sound. Camarón, simply, was an inspiration – and one whose own idols (and fans) included Chick Corea and Miles Davis, as well as flamenco artists. Latterly flamenco musicians are to be found playing in many different contexts, including rock and folk genres – the result is an exciting and dynamic scene.

taken refuge from the forced conversions and clearances effected by the Catholic monarchs and the Church. The main flamenco centres and families are to be found today in quarters and towns of gypsy and refugee origin, such as Alcalá del Río, Utrera, Jerez, Cádiz and the Triana *barrio* of Seville.

There are two theories about the origins of the name flamenco. One contends that Spanish Jews migrated through trade to Flanders, where they were allowed to sing their religious chants unmolested, and that these chants became referred to as flamenco by the Jews who stayed in Spain. The other is that the word is a mispronunciation of the Arabic words *felag* (fugitive) and *mengu* (peasant), a plausible idea, as Arabic was a common language in Spain at the time.

The gypsy inheritance

Flamenco aficionados enjoy heated debate about the purity of their art and whether it is more validly performed by a **gitano** (gypsy) or a **payo** (non-gypsy). Certainly, flamenco seems to have thrived enclosed, preserved and protected by the oral tradition of the gypsy clans. Its power, and the despair which its creation overcomes, has emerged from the precarious and vulnerable lives of a people surviving for centuries at the margins of society. Flamenco reflects a passionate need to preserve their self-esteem. These days, there are as many acclaimed *payo* as *gitano* flamenco artists. However, the concept of an **active inheritance** is crucial. The veteran singer **Fernanda de Utrera**, one of the great voices of "pure flamenco", was born in 1923 into a gypsy family in Utrera, one of the *cantaora* centres. She was the granddaughter of the legendary singer "Pinini", who had created her own individual flamenco forms, and with her younger sister Bernarda, also a notable singer, inherited their flamenco with their genes. Even the members of **Ketama**, the groundbreaking Madrid-based flamenco-rock group who split up in 2004, came from two gypsy clans – the Sotos and the Carmonas.

The Golden Age

Although flamenco's exact origins are obscure, it is generally agreed that its "laws" were established in the nineteenth century. Indeed, from the mid-nineteenth century into the early twentieth, flamenco enjoyed a legendary "**Golden Age**", the tail-end of which is preserved on some of the earliest 1930s recordings. The original musicians found a home in the *cafés cantantes*, traditional taverns which had their own group of performers (*cuadros*). One of the most famous was the *Café de Chinitas* in Málaga (see p.70), immortalized by the Granada-born poet García Lorca. In his poem *A las cinco de la tarde* (*At five in the afternoon*), Lorca claimed that flamenco is deeply related to bullfighting, not only sharing root emotions and passions, flashes of erratic genius, but because both are possible ways to break out of social and economic marginality. Just such a transformation happened in 1922 when the composer Manuel de Falla, the guitarist Andrés Segovia and the poet García Lorca were present for a legendary *Concurso de Cante Jondo*. A gypsy boy singer, **Manolo Caracol**, reportedly walked all the way from Jerez and won the competition with the voice and flamboyant personality that were to make him a legend throughout Spain and South America. The other key figure of this period, who can be heard on a few recently remastered recordings, was **Pastora Pavón**, known as *La Niña de Los Peines*, and popularly acclaimed as the greatest woman flamenco voice of the twentieth century. In addition to *cafés cantantes*, flamenco surfaced – as it does today – at fiestas, in bars or *tablaos*, and at *juergas*, informal, private parties.

The art of flamenco

It is essential for an artist to invoke a response, to know they are reaching deep into the emotional psyche of their audience. They may achieve the rare quality of **duende** – total emotional communication with their audience, and the mark of great flamenco

FLAMENCO DANCE

Most popular images of flamenco dance – twirling bodies in frilled dresses, rounded arms complete with castanets – are **sevillanas**, the folk dances performed at fiestas, and, in recent years, on the nightclub floor. "Real" flamenco dance is something rather different and, like the music, can reduce the onlooker to tears in an unexpected flash, a cathartic point after which the dance dissolves. What is so visually devastating about flamenco dance is the physical and emotional control the dancer has over the body: the way the head is held, the tension of the torso and the way it allows the shoulders to move, the shapes and angles of seemingly elongated arms, and the feet, which move from toe to heel, heel to toe, creating rhythms. These rhythms have a basic set of moves and timings but they are improvised as the piece develops and through interaction with the guitarist.

Flamenco dance dates back to about 1750 and, along with the music, moved from the streets and private parties into the *cafés cantantes* at the end of the nineteenth century. This was a great boost for the dancers' art, providing a home for professional performers, where they could inspire each other. It was here that legendary dancers like **El Raspao** and **El Estampio** began to develop the spellbinding footwork and extraordinary moves that characterize modern flamenco dance, while women adopted for the first time the flamboyant **hata de cola** – the glorious long-trained dresses, cut high at the front to expose their fast moving ankles and feet.

Around 1910, flamenco dance had moved into Spanish theatres, and dancers like **La Niña de los Peines** and **La Argentina** were major stars. They mixed flamenco into programmes with other dances and also made dramatic appearances at the end of comic plays and silent movie programmes. **Flamenco opera** was established, interlinking singing, dancing and guitar solos in comedies with a local flamenco flavour.

In 1915 the composer Manuel de Falla composed the first flamenco ballet, **El Amor Brujo** (Love, the Magician), for the dancer Pastora Imperio. The celebrated dancer, **La Argentina**, who had established the first Spanish dance company, took her version of the ballet abroad in the 1920s, and with her choreographic innovations flamenco dance came of age, working as a narrative in its own right. Another key figure in flamenco history was **Carmen Amaya**, who from the 1930s to the 1960s took flamenco dance on tour around the world, and into the movies. In the 1950s, dance found a new home in the **tablaos**, the aficionados' bars, which became enormously important as places to serve out a public apprenticeship. More recently the demanding audiences at local and national fiestas have played a part.

Artistic developments were forged in the 1960s by **Matilde Coral**, who updated the classic dance style, and in the 1970s by **Manuela Carrasco**, who had such impact with her fiery feet movement, continuing a rhythm for an intense and seemingly impossible period, that this new style was named after her (*manuelas*). Manuela Carrasco set the tone for the highly individual dancers of the 1980s and 1990s, such as **Mario Maya** and **Antonio Gades**. These two dancers and choreographers have provided a theatrically inspired staging for the dance, most significantly by extending the role of a dance dialogue and story – often reflecting on the potency of love and passion, their dangers and destructiveness.

Gades has led his own company on world tours but it is his influence on film that has been most important. He had appeared with Carmen Amaya in *Los Araños* in 1963 but in the 1980s began his own trilogy with filmmaker Carlos Saura: *Boda de Sangre* (Lorca's play, *Blood Wedding*), *Carmen* (a reinterpretation of the opera) and *El Amor Brujo*. The films featured Paco de Lucía and his band, and the dancers **Laura del Sol** and **Christina Hoyos** – the latter one of the great contemporary dancers. Hoyos herself created a superb ballet, *Sueños Flamencos* (*Flamenco Dreams*) and was also a force behind the founding of Seville's Museo del Baile Flamenco (p.276).

of whatever style or generation. *Duende* is an ethereal quality: moving, profound even when expressing happiness, mysterious but nevertheless felt, a quality that stops listeners in their tracks. And many of those listeners are intensely involved, for flamenco is not just a music, for many it is a way of life, a **philosophy** that influences daily activities. A flamenco is not only a performer but anyone who is actively and emotionally involved in the unique philosophy.

The music

For the musicians, this fullness of expression is integral to their art, which is why, for as many famous names as one can list, there are many, many other lesser-known musicians whose work is startlingly good. Not every superb flamenco musician gets to be famous, or even to record, for flamenco thrives most in **live performance**. Exhilarating, challenging and physically stimulating, it is an art form that allows its exponents huge scope to improvise while obeying certain rules. Flamenco guitarist Juan Martín has remarked that "in microcosm it imitates Spanish society – traditional on the outside but, within, incredible anarchy".

There is a **classical repertoire** of more than sixty flamenco songs (*cantes*) and dances (*danzas*) – some solos, some group numbers, some with instrumental accompaniment, others *a cappella*. These different forms of flamenco are grouped in "families" according to more or less common melodic themes. The most common beat cycle is twelve – like the blues. Each piece is executed by juxtaposing a number of complete musical units called *coplas*. Their number varies depending on the atmosphere the *cantaor* wishes to establish and the emotional tone they wish to convey. A song such as a *cante por solea* may take a familiar 3/4 rhythm, divide phrases into 4/8 measures, and then fragmentally subdivide again with voice ornamentation on top of that. The resulting complexity and the variations between similar phrases constantly undermine repetition, contributing greatly to the climactic and cathartic structure of each song.

Songs and singer

Flamenco **songs** often express pain, and with a fierceness that turns that emotion inside out. Generally, the voice closely interacts with improvising guitar (*toque*), the two inspiring each other, aided by the **jaleo**: the hand-clapping *palmas*, finger-snapping *palillos* and shouts from participants at certain points in the song. This *jaleo* sets the tone by creating the right atmosphere for the singer or dancer to begin, and bolsters and appreciates the talent of the artist as they develop the piece.

Aficionados will shout encouragement, most commonly "*¡Olé!*" – when an artist is getting deep into a song – but also a variety of stranger-sounding phrases. A stunning piece of dancing may, for example, be greeted with "*¡Viva la máquina escribir!*" (long live the typewriter), as the heels of the dancer move so fast they sound like a machine; or the cry may be "*¡Agua!*" (water), as the scarcity of water in Andalucía has given the word a kind of glory. An essential characteristic of flamenco is the singer or dancer taking certain risks, by putting into their performance feelings and emotions that arise directly from their own life experience, exposing their own **vulnerabilities**. Aficionados tend to acclaim more a voice that gains effect from surprise and startling moves than one governed by recognized musical logic. Vocal prowess or virtuosity can be deepened by sobs, gesticulation and an intensity of expression that can have a shattering effect on an audience. Thus pauses, breaths, body and facial gestures of anger and pain transform performance into **cathartic events**. *Siguiriyas*, which date from the Golden Age, and whose theme is usually death, have been described as cries of despair in the form of a funeral psalm. In contrast there are many songs and dances such as *tangos*, *sevillanas* and *fandangos* that capture great **joy**.

The **sevillana** originated in medieval Seville as a spring country dance, with verses improvised and sung to the accompaniment of guitar and castanets (which are rarely used in other forms of flamenco). **El Pali** (Francisco Palacios), who died in 1988, was the most well-known and prolific *sevillana* musician, his unusually gentle voice and accompanying strummed guitar combining an enviable musical pace with a talent for composing popular poetic lyrics. In the last few years dancing *sevillanas* has become popular in bars and clubs throughout Spain, but their great natural habitats are **Seville's April Feria** and the annual pilgrimage to **El Rocío**. It is during the Seville *feria* that most new recordings of *sevillanas* emerge.

Among the best contemporary singers are the aforementioned **Fernanda** and **Bernarda de Utrera**, **Enrique Morente**, **El Cabrero**, **Juan Peña El Lebrijano**, the **Sorderas**, **Fosforito**, **José Menese** and **Carmen Linares**. However, one of the most popular and commercially successful singers of modern flamenco was the extraordinary **El Camarón de la Isla** (the "Shrimp of the Isle" of León, near his Cádiz home), who died in 1992. Collaborating with the guitarists Paco and Pepe de Lucía, and latterly, Tomatito, Camarón raised **cante jondo**, the virtuoso "deep song", to a new art. His high-toned voice had a corrosive, rough-timbred edge, cracking at certain points to release a ravaged core sound. His incisive sense of rhythm, coupled with almost violent emotional intensity, made him the quintessential singer of the times.

Flamenco guitar

The flamenco performance is filled with pauses. The singer is free to insert phrases seemingly on the spur of the moment. The **guitar accompaniment**, while spontaneous, is precise and serves one single purpose – to mark the *compas* (measures) of a song and organize rhythmical lines. Instrumental interludes which are arranged to meet the needs of the *cantaor* (as the creative singer is called) not only catch the mood and intention of the song and mirror it, but allow the guitarist to extemporize what are called *falsetas* (short variations) at will. When singer and guitarist are in true rapport the intensity of a song develops rapidly, the one charging the other, until the effect can be overwhelming.

The flamenco **guitar** weighs less than most acoustic guitars and often has a pine table and pegs made of wood rather than machine heads. This is to produce the preferred bright responsive sound that does not sustain too long (as opposed to the mellow and longer sustaining sound of classical guitar). If the sound did sustain, particularly in fast pieces, chords would carry over into each other.

The guitar used to be simply an accompanying instrument – originally the singers themselves played – but at the end of the nineteenth century and in the early decades of the twentieth century it began developing as a **solo** form, absorbing influences from classical and Latin American traditions. The greatest of these early guitarists was **Ramón Montoya**, who revolutionized flamenco guitar with his harmonies and introduced tremolo and a whole variety of arpeggios – techniques of right-hand playing. After him the revolution was continued by Sabicas and Niño Ricardo and Carlos Montoya. The classical guitarist **Andrés Segovia** was another influential figure; he began his career playing flamenco in Granada. Then in the 1960s came the two major guitarists of modern times, **Paco de Lucía** (see p.587) and **Manolo Sanlúcar**. These days, solo guitarists have immediately identifiable sounds and rhythms: the highly emotive **Pepe Habichuela** and **Tomatito**, for example, or the unusual rhythms of younger players like **Ramón el Portugués**, **Enrique de Melchor** and **Rafael Riqueni**. Flamenco guitar has now consolidated its position on the world's great stages as one of the most successful forms of instrumental music.

Nuevo flamenco

One of flamenco's great achievements has been to sustain itself while providing much of the foundation and inspiration for new music emerging in Spain today. In the 1950s and 1960s, rock'n'roll displaced traditional Spanish music, as it did indigenous music in many parts of the world. In the 1980s, however, flamenco reinvented itself, gaining new meaning and a new public through the music of Paco de Lucía, who mixed in **jazz**, **blues** and **salsa**, and, later, groups like Pata Negra and Ketama, who brought in more **rock** influences. Purists hated these innovations but, as José "El Sordo" (Deaf One) Soto, Ketama's main singer, explained, they were based on "the classic flamenco that we'd been singing and listening to since birth. We just found new forms in jazz and salsa: there are basic similarities in the rhythms, the constantly changing harmonies and improvisations. Blacks and gypsies have suffered similar segregation so our music has a lot in common."

Paco de Lucía, who made the first moves, is the best known of all contemporary flamenco guitarists, and reached new audiences through his performance in Carlos Saura's films *Blood Wedding* and *Carmen*, along with the great flamenco dancers, Cristina Hoyos and Antonio Gades. Paco, who is a non-gypsy, won his first flamenco prize at the age of 14, and went on to accompany many of the great traditional singers, including a long partnership with Camarón de la Isla, one of the greatest collaborations of modern flamenco. He introduced new harmonies, chord structures, scales, open tunings and syncopation that initiated the most vital renaissance of *toque* since Ramón Montoya, a remarkable achievement considering the rigid and stylized nature of this most traditional of forms. He started forging new sounds and rhythms for flamenco following a trip to Brazil, where he fell in love with bossa nova, and in the 1970s he established a sextet with electric bass, Latin percussion, and, perhaps most shocking, flute and saxophone from Jorge Pardo. Paco has also introduced into Spanish flamenco the Peruvian **cajón**, a half-box resembling an empty drawer played by sitting straddled across the top; this reintroduced the sound of the foot of the dancer. Over the past twenty years he has worked with jazz-rock guitarists such as John McLaughlin and Chick Corea, while his own regular band, featuring singer Ramón de Algeciras, remains one of the most original and distinctive sounds on the flamenco scene.

Other artists experimented, too, throughout the 1980s. **Lolé y Manuel** updated the flamenco sound with original songs and huge success; **Jorge Pardo** followed Paco's jazz direction; **Salvador Tavora** and **Mario Maya** staged flamenco-based spectacles; and **Enrique Morente** and **Juan Peña El Lebrijano** both worked with Andalucian orchestras from Morocco, while **Amalgama** worked with southern Indian percussionists, revealing surprising stylistic unities. Another interesting crossover came with **Paco Peña**'s 1991 *Misa Flamenca* recording, a setting of the Catholic Mass to flamenco forms with the participation of established singers such as Rafael Montilla "El Chaparro" from Peña's native Córdoba, and a classical academy chorus. The more commercially successful crossover with rock and blues, pioneered by **Ketama** and **Pata Negra**, became known, in the 1990s, as **nuevo flamenco**. This "movement" is associated particularly with the label Nuevos Medios, and in Andalucía, and also Madrid, where many of the bands are based, is a challenging, versatile and musically incestuous new scene, with musicians guesting at each other's gigs and on one another's records. The music is now a regular sound at nightclubs, too, through the appeal of young singers like **Aurora**, one of the first to crack the pop charts, and **Martirio** (Isabel Quiñones Gutiérrez), a flamboyant personality who appears dressed in lace mantilla and shades, like a cameo from a Pedro Almodóvar film, and sings songs with ironical, contemporary lyrics about life in the cities.

In general, the new songs are more sensual and erotic than the traditional material, expressing a pain, suffering and love worth dying for. Martirio's producer, **Kiko Veneno**, who wrote Camarón's most popular song, *Volando voy*, is another artist who has brought a flamenco sensitivity to Spanish rock music, as has Rosario, one of Spain's top female singers. Other contemporary bands and singers to look out for on the scene include **La Barbería del Sur** (who add a dash of salsa), **Wili Giménez** and **Raimundo Amador**, and **José El Francés**. In the mid-1990s **Radio Tarifa** emerged as an exciting group who started out as a trio, expanded to include African musicians, and whose output mixes Arabic and traditional sounds onto a flamenco base.

Jan Fairley

Books

The listings on these pages represent a selective reading list on Andalucía and matters Spanish, especially in the sections on history. Most titles are in print, although we've included a few older classics. We have also included websites below for some publishers whose publications are not widely distributed and where it is possible to order from their website. Where the publisher has more than one entry the website appears in the details of the first publication listed.

A reliable specialist source in the UK for out-of-print books on all aspects of Spain is Paul Orssich, 2 St Stephens Terrace, London SW8 1DH (☏020 7787 0030, ⊛orssich .com). The ★ symbol indicates titles that are especially recommended.

GENERAL ACCOUNTS

INTRODUCTIONS

David Baird *Inside Andalusia; Back Roads of Southern Spain; East of Málaga* (Santana, Málaga; ⊛santanabooks.com). *Inside* is a book that grew out of the author's series of articles published in the now defunct *Lookout* magazine, giving an anecdotal yet perceptive overview of the region with plenty of interesting and offbeat observations and glossy illustrations. *Back Roads* is a drivers' guide to Andalucía, displaying the same erudition, while *East of Málaga* is an in-depth guide to the Axarquía and its coastline.

★ **John Hooper** *Spaniards: A Portrait of the New Spain*. This excellent, authoritative portrait of post-Franco Spain was originally written (by *The Guardian*'s then Spain correspondent) in the 1980s. The revised second edition (2006) has already become somewhat dated, but despite only passing references to Andalucía, along with Giles Tremlett's book (see below), this is still one of the best possible introductions to contemporary Spain.

★ **Michael Jacobs** *Andalusia*. Well-crafted, opinionated and wide-ranging introduction to Andalucía. It covers everything from prehistory to the Civil War and manages to cram in perceptive pieces on flamenco, gypsies and food and drink. A gazeteer at the back details major sights. One of the best introductions to the region.

★ **Giles Tremlett** *Ghosts of Spain*. Tremlett (the Madrid correspondent of *The Guardian*) digs into the untold story of Spain's Civil War dead and the collective conspiracy of silence surrounding the war's terrors, and goes on to peel away the layers of the post-Franco era to present an enthralling and often disturbing study of contemporary Spain.

RECENT TRAVELS AND ACCOUNTS

Alastair Boyd *The Sierras of the South: Travels in the Mountains of Andalusia*. A sensitively worked portrait of the Serranía de Ronda which describes one Englishman's continuing love affair with a region he knew as home for twenty years. His earlier *The Road from Ronda* (Collins, UK) is a Sixties' view of the same landscape – the *campesinos* are still struggling.

Adam Hopkins *Spanish Journeys: A Portrait of Spain*. Although researched a couple of decades ago, this is still an enjoyable and highly stimulating exploration of Spanish history and culture, weaving its considerable scholarship in an accessible and unforced travelogue form, and full of illuminating anecdotes.

Elizabeth Nash *Seville, Córdoba and Granada: a cultural and literary history*. An eloquent, themed and multilayered exploration of the literary and cultural history of Andalucía's three major cities by *The Independent*'s Madrid correspondent.

★ **Chris Stewart** *Driving Over Lemons*. Author and musician Stewart describes – often hilariously – his move with family to an Alpujarran farmhouse (El Valero) and the numerous adventures involved in setting up house there. The sequel, *A Parrot in the Pepper Tree*, has more stories

Spanish-speakers should look out for **Mercurio** (⊛revistamercurio.es), an excellent monthly literary review carrying articles on Andalucía's literary figures past and present as well as reviews of many new books (fiction and non-fiction) dealing with *andaluz* and broader Spanish themes. Best of all, it's free and available from most good bookshops in the region's major towns and provincial capitals. If you can't locate a copy, email them from their website for a list of stockists.

from El Valero interspersed with accounts of some of the author's earlier adventures as a sheep shearer in Sweden, drummer with rock band Genesis, and greenhorn flamenco guitarist in Seville. The saga's latest episode, *The Almond Blossom Appreciation Society*, delivers another cocktail of humorous, improbable and poignant tales.

EARLIER TWENTIETH-CENTURY WRITERS

★ **Gerald Brenan** *South From Granada; The Face of Spain*. *South From Granada* is an enduring classic. Brenan lived in a small village in Las Alpujarras in the 1920s, and records this and the visits of his Bloomsbury contemporaries Virginia Woolf, Lytton Strachey and Bertrand Russell. *The Face of Spain* is a later collection of highly readable travel writings gathered on a trip through Franco's Spain in 1949 with a substantial chunk devoted to Andalucía.

★ **Laurie Lee** *As I Walked Out One Midsummer Morning; A Rose For Winter; A Moment of War*. *Midsummer Morning* is the irresistibly romantic account of Lee's walk through Spain – from Vigo to Málaga – and his gradual awareness of the forces moving the country towards Civil War. As an autobiographical account, of living rough and busking his way from the Cotswolds with a violin, it's a delight; as a piece of social observation, painfully sharp. In *A Rose For Winter* Lee describes his return, twenty years later, to a very different Andalucía, while in *A Moment of War* he looks back again to describe a winter fighting with the International Brigade in the Civil War – an account by turns moving, comic and tragic.

James A. Michener *Iberia*. A bestselling, idiosyncratic and encyclopedic compendium of fascinating interviews and impressions of Spain in 1968 on the brink of the post-Franco years.

Jan Morris *Spain*. Morris wrote this in six months in 1960, on her (or, at the time, his) first visit to the country. It is an impressionistic account – good in its sweeping control of place and history, though prone to see everything as symbolic. The updated edition is plain bizarre in its ideas on Franco and dictatorship – a condition towards which Morris seems to believe Spaniards were naturally inclined.

Walter Starkie *Don Gypsy*. The tales of a Dublin professor who set out to walk the roads of Spain and Andalucía in the 1930s with only a fiddle for company. The pre-Civil War world – good and bad – is astutely observed and his adventures are frequently amusing. Like Borrow earlier (see below), he fell for the gypsies and became an expert on their culture.

CUSTOMS AND CULTURE

★ **Edward Lewine** *Death and the Sun: A matador's season in the heart of Spain*. Bullfight aficionado Lewine takes on the perilous task of trying to make this Spanish bloodsport comprehensible to non-believers. He spends a year on the road in the company of top *matador* Francisco

OLDER CLASSICS

George Borrow *The Bible in Spain; The Zincali*. On first publication in 1842, *The Bible in Spain* was subtitled by Borrow *Journeys, Adventures and Imprisonments of an English-man*; it is one of the most famous books on Spain – slow in places but with some very amusing stories. *Zincali* is an account of the Spanish gypsies, whom Borrow got to know pretty well and for whom he translated the Bible into *gitano*.

★ **Richard Ford** *A Handbook for Travellers in Spain; Readers at Home; Gatherings from Spain*. The *Handbook*, first published in 1845, must be the best guide ever written to any country and stayed in print as a Murray's Handbook (one of the earliest series of guides) well into the twentieth century. Massively opinionated, it is an extremely witty book and in its British, nineteenth-century manner, incredibly knowledgeable and worth flicking through for the proverbs alone. *Gatherings* is a filleted – but no less entertaining – abridgement of the *Handbook* produced "for the ladies" who were not expected to be able to digest the original. Also recommended is a recent biography *Richard Ford, Hispanophile, Connoisseur and Critic* by Ian Robertson (Michael Russell, UK): a fascinating read, it illuminates the creation of Ford's great work and places him in the context of the Victorian world of arts and letters.

★ **Washington Irving** *Tales of the Alhambra* (originally published 1832; abridged editions are on sale in Granada). Half of Irving's book consists of Oriental stories, set in the Alhambra; the rest of accounts of his own residence there and the local characters of his time. Irving also wrote *The Conquest of Granada* (1829; out of print), a description of the fall of the Nasrids.

ANTHOLOGIES

Jimmy Burns (ed) *Spain: A Literary Companion*. A good anthology, including worthwhile nuggets of most authors recommended in this bibliography, amid a whole host of others.

Lucy McCauley *Travellers' Tales: Spain*. A wide-ranging anthology slanted towards more recent writing on Spain; includes strong pieces on Andalucía by many of the authors mentioned in this bibliography.

David Mitchell *Travellers in Spain: an Illustrated Anthology* (Santana, Málaga). A well-told story of how four centuries of travellers – and most often travel writers – saw Spain. It's interesting to see Ford, Brenan, Laurie Lee and the rest set in context.

Rivera Ordóñez – whose great-grandfather was revered by Hemingway – and provides fascinating background on the gruelling routine of long road journeys between towns, often dingy hotels and the bitter recriminations when the "boss" has had a disastrous day in the ring.

Timothy Mitchell *Flamenco Deep Song*. Diametrically opposed to Woodall's work (see below), the author sets out to debunk the mystagogy of flamenco purists by arguing that they are shackling the form's development and ends up with an improbable defence of the Gipsy Kings. A well-researched and entertaining read whether or not you accept its iconoclastic premise.

Eamonn O'Neill *Matadors*. Subtitled "a journey into the heart of modern bullfighting", this is part autobiographical travelogue, part sociological study of the role of bullfighting in modern Spain, throwing light on a peculiarly Iberian industry worth a billion dollars annually.

Paul Richardson *Our Lady of the Sewers*. An articulate and kaleidoscopic series of insights into rural Spain's customs and cultures, fast disappearing.

★ **James Woodall** *In Search of the Firedance: Spain through Flamenco*. This is a terrific history and exploration of flamenco, and as the subtitle suggests it goes way beyond the music alone to get to the heart of the culture.

HISTORY

GENERAL HISTORY

Juan Lalaguna *A Traveller's History of Spain*. A lucid background history to the country, which spans the Phoenicians to Franco, Felipe González and the emergence of democratic Spain.

M. Vincent & R.A. Stradling *Cultural Atlas of Spain and Portugal*. The deceptive, coffee-table format belies a formidable historical, artistic and social survey of the Iberian peninsula from ancient times to the present; excellent colour maps and well-chosen photos amplify the text.

PREHISTORIC AND ROMAN PERIODS

James M. Anderson *Spain: 1001 Archaeological Sites*. A good guide and gazetteer of Spain's archeological sites with detailed instructions on how to get to them.

Henri Breuil *Rock Paintings of Southern Andalucía*. Published in 1929, this is still the definitive guide to the subject.

Roger Collins *Spain: An Archeological Guide*. Covering around 140 sites, temples, mosques and palaces dating from prehistory to the twelfth century, this book devotes more space per entry to maps, plans and data, making it a more useful *vade mecum* to the major sites than Anderson's work (see above).

Maria Cruz Fernández Castro *Iberia in Prehistory*. A major study of the Iberian peninsula prior to the arrival of the Romans, which includes extensive coverage of early Andalucian sites such as Los Millares as well as the later Iberian settlements encountered by the Phoenicians and Greeks. This is the first volume of the publisher's (Blackwells) important series on the history of Spain from the prehistoric era through to the Civil War.

S.J. Keay *Roman Spain* (British Museum Publications/ California UP). Definitive survey of a neglected subject, well illustrated and highly readable.

John S. Richardson *The Romans in Spain*. A new look at how Spain came to be a part of the Roman world, which also examines the influences that flowed from Spain to Rome as well as vice versa.

Chris Stringer & Robin McKie *African Exodus*. If you want to understand Spain's role in the Neanderthal story, this lively and accessible account by an expert in the field (aided by the science editor of *The Observer*) is the book. The story of the last of the Neanderthals hanging on in a cave above the Zaffaraya Pass in northern Málaga only adds to the drama of the landscape itself.

VISIGOTHIC SPAIN TO THE NINETEENTH CENTURY

J.M. Cohen *The Four Voyages of Christopher Columbus*. The man behind the myth; Columbus's astonishing voyages as described by the man himself in his log are interwoven with opinions of contemporaries on the great explorer, including his biographer son Hernando. A fascinating collection, superbly translated.

Roger Collins *The Arab Conquest of Spain 710–97*. Cogently argued and controversial study which documents the Moorish invasion and the significant influence that the conquered Visigoths had on the formative phase of Muslim rule by a scholar uniquely expert in both fields. Collins's *Visigothic Spain* is a significant companion volume, while his earlier *Early Medieval Spain 400–1000* takes a broader overview of the same subject.

★ **J.H. Elliott** *Imperial Spain 1469–1716*. Best introduction to "the Golden Age" – academically respected and a gripping tale.

★ **Richard Fletcher** *Moorish Spain*. A fascinating, provocative and highly readable narrative with a suitably iconoclastic conclusion to the history of Moorish Spain. The best introduction to the subject.

L.P. Harvey *Islamic Spain 1250–1500*. Comprehensive account of its period – both the Islamic kingdoms and the Muslims living beyond their protection.

Henry Kamen *The Spanish Inquisition: An Historical Revision; Philip of Spain; Spain's Road to Empire*. Kamen's 1965 *Inquisition* was a highly respected examination of the Inquisition and the long shadow it cast across Spanish history and development. *The Spanish Inquisition: An Historical Revision* returns to the subject in the light of more recent evidence, while *Philip of Spain* is the first full biography of Felipe II, the ruler most closely associated with the Inquisition. In *Empire*, Kamen skilfully dissects the conquest of the Americas and Philippines and concludes that the Spanish were ill-suited to the imperial role, displaying both organizational incompetence and little interest in the peoples they subjugated.

Elie Kedourie *Spain and the Jews: the Sephardi Experience, 1492 and after.* A collection of essays on the three-million-strong Spanish Jews of the Middle Ages and their expulsion by the Catholic monarchs.

John Lynch *Spain 1516–1598.* New interpretation of Spain's rise to empire with plenty of interesting detail on Andalucía's trading role – especially the cities of Seville and Cádiz – in the exploitation of the Americas. The same author's *Hispanic World in Crisis and Change 1598–1700* and *Bourbon Spain 1700–1808* carry the story forward to the critical crossroads that determined Spain's future for the ensuing century and a half.

Bernard F. Reilly *The Contest of Christian and Muslim Spain.* A fascinating and detailed study of the stresses and strains of the crucial tenth and eleventh centuries when Christians, Muslims and Jews were locked in a struggle for supremacy on one hand and survival on the other, by an acknowledged expert on the subject.

James Reston Jr *Dogs of God.* An alternative take on the Inquisition to Kamen's (see p.590) connecting it with the epic year 1492 and linking religious intolerance to the final defeat of the Moors in Spain and Columbus' sudden widening of the Spanish crown's sphere of influence.

THE TWENTIETH CENTURY

★ **Gerald Brenan** *The Spanish Labyrinth.* First published in 1943, Brenan's study of the social and political background to the Civil War is tinged by personal experience, yet still an impressively rounded account.

★ **Raymond Carr** *Modern Spain 1875–1980; The Spanish Tragedy: the Civil War in Perspective.* Two of the best books available on modern Spanish history – concise and well-told narratives.

★ **Ronald Fraser** *Blood of Spain; In Hiding; The Pueblo.* Subtitled *An Oral History of the Spanish Civil War, Blood* is an impressive – and brilliantly unorthodox – piece of research, constructed entirely of oral accounts. *In Hiding* is a fascinating individual account of a Republican mayor of Mijas (in Málaga) hidden by his family for thirty years until the Civil War amnesty of 1969. *Pueblo* is a penetrating and compelling study of the trials and struggles of one Costa del Sol mountain village seen through the eyes of its inhabitants which speaks for much of Andalucía today.

★ **Ian Gibson** *Federico García Lorca; The Assassination of Federico García Lorca; Lorca's Granada.* The biography is a gripping book and *The Assassination* a brilliant reconstruction of the events at the end of his life, with an examination of fascist corruption and of the shaping influences on Lorca, twentieth-century Spain and the Civil War. *Granada* explores Lorca's city by way of a collection of fascinating walks around the town.

★ **Paul Preston** *Concise History of the Spanish Civil War; Franco; The Spanish Holocaust.* A formidable expert on the period, Preston has succeeded in his attempt to provide a manageable guide to the Civil War labyrinth – with powerful illustrations. *Franco* is a penetrating – and monumental – biography of the dictator and his regime, which provides as clear a picture as any yet published of how he won the Civil War, survived in power so long, and what, to this day, was his significance. *Holocaust* relates the grisly story of the tens of thousands executed in the 1930s and 1940s during Franco's reign of terror, as well as the abuse of women and children.

★ **Hugh Thomas** *The Spanish Civil War.* This exhaustive 1000-page study is regarded (both in Spain and abroad) as the definitive history of the Civil War, but is not as accessible for the general reader as Preston's account (see above).

★ **Gamel Woolsey** *Málaga Burning* (Pythia Press, US); original title *Death's Other Kingdom* (Eland, UK). A long-ignored minor classic written in the late 1930s and recently reprinted (and retitled) by a US publisher in which the American poet and wife of Gerald Brenan vividly describes the horrors of the descent of their part of Andalucía into civil war. The Eland edition includes an interesting biographical afterword by Michael Jacobs.

ART AND ARCHITECTURE

Marianne Barrucand & Achim Bednoz *Moorish Architecture.* A beautifully illustrated guide to the major Moorish monuments.

Bernard Bevan *History of Spanish Architecture.* Classic study of Iberian and Ibero-American architecture which includes extensive coverage of the Mudéjar, Plateresque and Baroque periods.

★ **Titus Burckhardt** *Moorish Culture in Spain* (o/p). An outstanding book which opens up ways of looking at Spain's Islamic monuments, explaining their patterns and significance and the social environment in which, and for which, they were produced.

Godfrey Goodwin *Islamic Spain.* Architectural guide with descriptions of virtually every significant Islamic building in Spain, and a fair amount of background.

★ **Michael Jacobs** *Alhambra.* If you've fallen under the Alhambra's spell then this sumptuously produced volume with outstanding photographs and expert commentary is the perfect book. It authoritatively guides you through the history and architecture of Andalucía's emblematic monument, placing it in its Islamic context, and concludes with a fascinating essay on the hold that the palace has had on later artists, travellers and writers from Irving and Ford to de Falla and Lorca.

David Talbot Rice *Islamic Art.* A classic introduction to the whole subject.

FICTION AND POETRY

SPANISH FICTION

Pedro de Alarcón *The Three-Cornered Hat and Other Stories* (o/p). Ironic nineteenth-century tales of the previous century's corruption, bureaucracy and absolutism by a writer born in Guadix. He also wrote *Alpujarra* (o/p), a not very well-observed tour through the Sierra Nevada.

Arturo Barea *The Forging of a Rebel.* Superb autobiographical trilogy, taking in the Spanish war in Morocco in the 1920s, and Barea's own part in the Civil War in Andalucía and elsewhere. The books were published under the individual titles *The Forge, The Track* and *The Clash*.

★ **Miguel de Cervantes** *Don Quijote. Quijote* (or *Quixote*) is of course the classic of Spanish literature and remains an excellent and witty read, especially in J.M. Cohen's classic Penguin translation or a new version by Edith Grossman.

Juan Ramón Jiménez *Platero and I.* Andalucía's Nobel Prize-winning poet and writer from Moguer in Huelva paints a lyrically evocative picture of Andalucía and its people in conversations with his donkey, Platero.

Antonio Machado *Eighty Poems; Juan de Mairena* (o/p). The best-known works in English of this eminent *sevillano* poet and writer. The novel *Juan de Mairena* draws on his experience as a schoolteacher in Baeza.

★ **Arturo Pérez Reverte** *The Seville Communion.* An entertaining crime yarn by one of Spain's leading writers, involving a hacker in the pope's computer, a stubborn old local priest up against rapacious bankers eager to bulldoze his church, a number of corpses, and an investigator dispatched by the Vatican. All is played out against the colourfully described backdrop of Seville. *The Dumas Club,* an engrossing tale about a bibliophile's search for a book on black magic, *The Fencing Master,* a political thriller set in nineteenth-century Spain, and *The Nautical Chart,* a search for treasure in a galleon sunk off the coast of Andalucía, are other translated works by Pérez Reverte. His most recent novel in translation, *The Queen of the South,* relates the story of a female drug trafficker running narcotics between Morocco and Cádiz.

SPANISH PLAYS AND POETRY

A.J. Arberry (trans.) *Moorish Poetry.* Excellent collection of Hispano-Arab verse.

Cola Franzen (trans.) *Poems of Arab Andalusia.* Sensitively rendered collection of verse by some of the best poets of Moorish al-Andalus.

Federico García Lorca *Five Plays: Comedies and Tragicomedies; Selected Poems; Poem of the Deep Song.* Andalucía's great pre-Civil War playwright and poet. The first two volumes have his major theatrical works and poems, while the last is a moving poetic paean to *cante jondo,* flamenco's blues, inspired by his contact with *gitano* culture. Arturo Barea's *Lorca: the Poet and his People* is also of interest.

San Juan de la Cruz *The Poetry of Saint John of the Cross.* Excellent translation by South African poet Roy Campbell of the poems of this mystical confessor to Teresa of Ávila who died at Úbeda.

FOREIGN FICTION

★ **Douglas Day** *Journey of the Wolf.* Outstanding first novel by an American writer, given the seal of approval by Graham Greene ("gripping and poignant"). The subject is a Civil War fighter, "El Lobo", who returns as a fugitive to Poqueira, his village in the Alpujarras, forty years on.

Ernest Hemingway *Fiesta/The Sun Also Rises; For Whom the Bell Tolls.* Hemingway remains a major element in the American myth of Spain. *Fiesta* contains some lyrically beautiful writing while *For Whom the Bell Tolls* – set in Civil War Andalucía – is considerably more laboured. He also published an enthusiastic and not very good account of bullfighting, *Death in the Afternoon.*

Amin Maalouf *Leo the African.* A wonderful historical novel, recreating the life of Leo Africanus, the fifteenth-century Moorish geographer, in the last years of the kingdom of Granada, and on his subsequent exile in Morocco and world travels.

SPECIALIST GUIDES

★ **Phil Ball** *Morbo – The Story of Spanish Football.* Excellent account of Spanish football from its nineteenth-century beginnings with the British workers at the mines of Río Tinto to the golden years of Real Madrid and the dark days of Franco, with the ever-present backdrop of the ferocious *morbo* – political, historical, regional and linguistic rivalry – that has driven it since.

Christopher Turner *The Penguin Guide to Seville.* A set of interesting guided walks around Andalucía's capital city.

★ **Sandy Walker** *Campo – A Guide to the Spanish Countryside* (Santana, Málaga). On one level a how-to book on planting and cultivating trees, on another a guide to almost every kind of fruit tree grown in Andalucía (where

the author has her farm). All kinds of trees from almonds and olives to carobs and pomegranates are covered and there's fascinating detail on the history, local background, and the medicinal potential of each species – she even throws in the odd recipe.

HIKING AND CYCLING

David & Ros Brawn *Sierra de Aracena* (Discovery, UK; ⓦ www.walking.demon.co.uk). Excellent walking guide to this magnificent Sierra by two experienced walkers. Covers 27 walks (from 3–14km) with an accompanying map (sold separately) and all routes are GPS waypointed.

Matt Butler *Holiday Walks from the Costa del Sol* (Sigma,

UK; @ sigmapress.co.uk). Holiday walks within reach of a Costa del Sol base, covering the coast from Cádiz province in the west to Granada province in the east. Free internet updates available.

Chris Craggs *Andalusian Rock Climbs.* Introductory guide to one of Andalucía's fastest-growing sports. Has descriptions of all the major climbs plus details of how to get there.

Charles Davis *Costa del Sol Walks* (Santana, Málaga). Well-written guide to 34 walks – between 4km and 8km – along the Costa del Sol between Nerja and Estepona; each walk has its own map. The same author's *Walk! The Axarquía* (Discovery, UK) is a reliable guide to this picturesque region, describing thirty walks between 5km and 22km, all GPS-waypointed. Davis has also published *34 Alpujarras Walks* (Discovery, UK) with a similar format detailing 34 GPS-waypointed treks between 4km and 25km. In both, each walk has its own map; there are also waterproof 1:40,000 *Axarquía/ Alpujarras Tour and Trail* maps (sold separately) with all walks (and GPS points) marked.

Harry Dowdell *Cycle Touring in Spain.* Well-researched cycle touring guide which describes eight touring routes of varying difficulty in the north and south of Spain. Plenty of practical information on preparing your bike for the trip, transporting it, and what to take.

★ **Guy Hunter-Watts** *Walking in Andalucía* (Santana, Málaga). First-rate walking guide to the Natural Parks of Grazalema, Cazorla, Los Alcornocales, Aracena and La Axarquía as well as the Alpujarras and the Sierra Nevada, comprising 32 walks between 8km and 17km in length, each with its own colour map.

★ **John & Christine Oldfield** *Andalucía and the Costa del Sol.* This addition to the popular *Landscapes* walking guide series has 23 clearly described walks (with maps) ranging from 5km to 22km in Las Alpujarras, Sierra Nevada, Axarquía and Grazalema, as well as the areas bordering the Costa del Sol.

Jeremy Rabjohns *Holiday Walks in the Alpujarra* (Sigma, UK). Excellent walking guide by Alpujarras resident Rabjohns describing 24 walks between 3km and 22km in length with clear maps (including many village street maps) and background information. Free updates and corrections available onlines.

Kirstie Shirra & Michelle Lowe *Walking the GR7 in Andalucía.* A well-described guide to hiking the 700km-long GR7 from Tarifa to the fringes of the Cazorla Natural Park in Jaén. Both the northern (via Cazorla) and southern (via Las Alpujarras) routes are covered, and there's plenty of background detail. The route can easily be broken up into shorter walks of a day's duration, taking a bus or taxi back to the start point.

Andy Walmsley *Walking in the Sierra Nevada* (Cicerone, UK). Forty-five walks of varying distance and difficulty

from 3hr strolls to the seriously arduous *Tres Mils* (3000m-plus) peaks.

WILDLIFE

John R. Butler *Birdwatching on Spain's Southern Coast* (Santana, Málaga). A guide to the major – and many minor – birdwatching sites of Andalucía including the Costa de Almería, Costa de la Luz and the Doñana national park. The author – who lives in Málaga and leads birdwatching tours – includes maps and the usual bird calendars as well as the highly unusual (and laudable) information concerning sites accessible (the vast majority are) to wheelchair-using and disabled twitchers.

Teresa Farino & Mike Lockwood *Travellers' Nature Guides: Spain.* Excellent illustrated wildlife guide to the peninsula by two Spanish-based experts; conveniently divided into regional groupings with detailed maps, it covers many of Andalucía's major habitats for spotting flora and fauna.

Ernest García & Andrew Paterson *Where to Watch Birds in Southern Spain.* A well-planned guide to bird-watching sites throughout Andalucía with location maps and reports detailing species to be seen according to season.

Frederic Grunfeld and Teresa Farino *Wild Spain.* A knowledgeable and practical guide to Spain's national parks, ecology and wildlife with a section on Andalucía.

Oleg Polunin & Anthony Huxley *Flowers of the Mediterranean.* Useful if by no means exhaustive field guide.

Oleg Polunin & B. E. Smythies *Flowers of South-West Europe.* Covers all of Spain, Portugal and southwest France; the taxonomy is old, but still unsurpassed for its plates, line drawings and keys.

★ **Svensson, Grant, Mullarney & Zetterstrom** *The Collins Bird Guide.* The best bird field guide yet published covers (and illustrates) the birds of Europe including almost everything you're likely to encounter in Spain.

FOOD AND WINE

★ **Vicky Benninson** *A Taste of Place: Andalucía.* A cornucopia of a book covering all aspects of food and drink in Andalucía: what to buy, where to buy it, and what to do with it in the kitchen; plus – if you prefer to dine out – where to eat *andaluz* cuisine at its very best throughout the region.

Penelope Casas *The Foods and Wines of Spain; Tapas: the little dishes of Spain.* An excellent overview of classic Spanish and Andalucian cuisine, plus the same author's guide to the tapas labyrinth.

Jon Clarke *Dining Secrets of Andalucía* (Santana, Málaga). Excellent guide to many up-and-coming (as well as established) quality restaurants in Andalucía with selections from all eight of the region's provinces.

★ **Alan Davidson** *The Tío Pepe Guide to the Seafood of Spain and Portugal.* An indispensable book that details and illustrates every fish and crustacean you're likely to meet in Andalucía. His *Mediterranean Seafood* is another classic.

★ **Julian Jeffs** *Sherry.* The story of sherry – history, production, blending and brands. Rightly a classic and the best introduction to Andalucía's great wine. The same author's *Wines of Spain* is an erudite guide to traditional and emerging wine regions with details of vineyards, grape varieties and vintages.

Jean Claude Juston *The New Spain – Vegan and Vegetarian Restaurants* (copies available from ⓦ vegetarian guides.co.uk or ⓦ ivu.org/atelier). Very useful guide to vegetarian and vegan restaurants throughout Spain by the owner/chef of a vegetarian restaurant in the Alpujarras. Each listing has its own review and there's lots of background information on Spanish veggie websites and magazines plus details of animal-friendly organizations.

Elisabeth Luard *The La Ina Book of Tapas; Flavours of Andalucía.* The first is the bible for all classic tapas recipes, while the *Flavours of Andalucía* parades the major dishes of the region province by province.

John Radford *The New Spain; The Wines of Rioja.* The lavish coffee-table format disguises *New Spain*'s serious content: a detailed region-by-region guide to Spanish wine with colour maps, bodega and vintage evaluations and fine illustrations. *Wines of Rioja* is a comprehensive survey of the wines and producers in this emblematic Spanish wine region.

★ **Jan Read** *Guide to the Wines of Spain.* Regularly updated, encyclopedic guide to the classic and emerging wines of Spain by a leading authority. Includes maps, vintages and vineyards – and it fits in your pocket.

★ **Paul Richardson** *Late Dinner.* A joyous dissection of the food of Spain, region by region, season by season, nibble of ham by shoot of asparagus. A celebration of culture and cuisine, this is the best general introduction to what Spanish food – and life – is really all about.

LEARNING SPANISH

★ *Collins Spanish Dictionary* Recognized as the best single-volume bookshelf dictionary. Regularly revised and updated, so make sure you get the latest edition.

★ *Get by in Spanish* (BBC Publications, UK; ⓦ www .bbcactive.com/languages; book and CD). One of the BBC's excellent crash-course introductions (at a bargain price), which gets you to survival-level Spanish (bars, restaurants, asking the way, etc) in a couple of weeks. The CD content can be downloaded to an MP3 player to take on the trip.

Learn Spanish Now! (Transparent Language, UK/US; ⓦ transparent.com). CD-Rom-based (with facility for MP3 use) interactive course incorporating all kinds of gadgets enabling you to compare your pronunciation with a native speaker, access web-based additional learning resources and play skill-improving interactive games.

Rough Guide Spanish Dictionary. Good pocket-size dictionary that should help with most travel situations.

Michel Thomas Method *Foundation Course and Advanced Spanish.* The revolutionary "100 percent audio" CD-based learning system devised by the late polyglot Thomas has been praised by many learners (including Woody Allen and Emma Thompson) who have struggled with the more traditional "grammar grind" methods.

LIVING IN SPAIN

David Hampshire *Living and Working in Spain* (Survival Books, UK; ⓦ survivalbooks.net). An information-packed comprehensive guide to moving to, and setting up home or working in, Spain.

Guy Hobbs & Heleina Postings *Live and Work in Spain and Portugal* (Vacation Work, UK). Well-researched handbook full of useful information on moving to the peninsula, buying property, seeking work, starting a business, finding schools and lots more.

David Searl *You and the Law in Spain* (Santana, Málaga). Invaluable, lucid and comprehensive guide to the Spanish legal and tax system (now in its twenty-first updated edition) and an essential read if you are thinking of buying property, working or setting up a business in Spain.

Language

Once you get started, Spanish is among the easiest languages to get a grip on. English is spoken, but only in the main tourist areas to any extent, and wherever you are you'll get a far better reception if you at least try communicating with Spaniards in their own tongue. Being understood, of course, is only half the problem – getting the gist of the reply, often rattled out at a furious pace, may prove far more difficult.

The rules of **pronunciation** are pretty straightforward and, once you get to know them, strictly observed. Unless there's an **accent**, words ending in d, l, r, and z are stressed on the last syllable, all others on the second last. All **vowels** are pure and short; combinations have predictable results.

A somewhere between the "A" sound of back and that of father

E as in get

I as in police

O as in hot

U as in rule

C in Castilian (standard Spanish) is lisped before E and I, hard otherwise: *cerca* is pronounced "thairka". However, many parts of Andalucía pronounce as an "s" – "sairka" or even "Andalusia".

G works the same way, a guttural "H" sound (like the ch in loch) before E or I, a hard G elsewhere – *gigante* becomes "higante".

H is always silent

J the same sound as a guttural G: *jamón* is pronounced "hamon".

LL sounds like an English Y or LY: *tortilla* is pronounced torteeya/torteelya.

N is as in English unless it has a tilde (accent) over it, when it becomes NY: *mañana* sounds like "manyana".

QU is pronounced like an English K.

R is rolled, RR doubly so.

V sounds more like B, *vino* becoming "beano".

X has an S sound before consonants, normal X before vowels.

Z (in *castellano*) is the same as a soft C, so *cerveza* becomes "thairvaitha", but again much of Andalucía prefers the "s" sound – "sairvaisa".

The list of essential words and phrases that follows should be enough to get you started. If you're using a dictionary, bear in mind that in Spanish CH, LL, and Ñ count as separate letters and are listed after C, L, and N respectively. There is a list of recommended books and CDs on learning Spanish in the "Books" section of this guide (see p.594).

USEFUL WORDS AND PHRASES

BASICS

Yes, No, OK	Sí, No, Vale
Please, Thank you	Por favor, Gracias
Where, When?	¿Dónde, Cuando?
What, How much?	¿Qué, Cuánto?
Here, There	Aquí, Allí
This, That	Esto, Eso
Now, Later	Ahora, Más tarde
Open, Closed	Abierto/a, Cerrado/a
With, Without	Con, Sin
Good, Bad	Buen(o)/a, Mal(o)/a
Big, Small	Gran(de), Pequeño/a
Cheap, Expensive	Barato, Caro
Hot, Cold	Caliente, Frío
More, Less	Más, Menos
Today, Tomorrow	Hoy, Mañana
Yesterday	Ayer

GREETINGS AND RESPONSES

Hello, Goodbye	Hola, Adiós
Good morning	Buenos días
Good afternoon/night	Buenas tardes/noches
See you later	Hasta luego
Sorry	Lo siento/discúlpeme
Excuse me	Con permiso/perdón
How are you?	¿Como está (usted)?
I (don't) understand	(No) Entiendo
Not at all/You're welcome	De nada
Do you speak English?	¿Habla (usted) inglés?
I don't speak Spanish	No hablo español

My name is …	Me llamo …	What's that?	¿Qué es eso?
What's your name?	¿Como se llama usted?	What's this called in	¿Como se llama éste en
I am English	Soy inglés(a)	Spanish?	español?
…Australian	australiano(a)		
…Canadian	canadiense(a)	**NUMBERS AND DAYS**	
…American	americano(a)	**one**	un/uno/una
…Irish	irlandés(a)	**two**	dos
		three	tres

HOTELS AND TRANSPORT

I want	Quiero	**four**	cuatro
I'd like	Quisiera	**five**	cinco
Do you know …?	¿Sabe …?	**six**	seis
I don't know	No sé	**seven**	siete
There is (is there)?	(¿)Hay(?)	**eight**	ocho
Give me … (one like that)	Deme …(uno así)	**nine**	nueve
Do you have …?	¿Tiene …?	**ten**	diez
the time	la hora	**eleven**	once
a room	una habitación	**twelve**	doce
… with two beds/	… con dos camas/	**thirteen**	trece
double bed	cama matrimonial	**fourteen**	catorce
… with shower/bath	… con ducha/baño	**fifteen**	quince
It's for one person/	Es para una persona/	**sixteen**	diez y seis
two people	dos personas	**twenty**	veinte
It's for one night/	Es para una noche/	**twenty-one**	veintiuno
one week	una semana	**thirty**	treinta
It's fine, how much is it?	¿Está bien, cuánto es?	**forty**	cuarenta
It's too expensive	Es demasiado caro	**fifty**	cincuenta
Don't you have anything	¿No tiene algo más barato?	**sixty**	sesenta
cheaper?		**seventy**	setenta
		eighty	ochenta
Can one …?	¿Se puede …?	**ninety**	noventa
…camp (near) here?	…¿acampar aquí (cerca)?	**one hundred**	cien(to)
Is there a hostel nearby?	¿Hay un hostal aquí cerca?	**one hundred and one**	ciento uno
How do I get to …?	¿Por dónde se va a …?	**two hundred**	doscientos
Left, right, straight on	Izquierda, derecha,	**two hundred and one**	doscientos uno
	todo recto	**five hundred**	quinientos
Where is …?	¿Dónde está …?	**one thousand**	mil
… the bus station	… la estación de	**two thousand**	dos mil
	autobuses	**two thousand and one**	dos mil un
… the train station	… la estación de	**two thousand and two**	dos mil dos
	ferrocarril	**two thousand and three**	dos mil tres
… the nearest bank	… el banco más cercano	**first**	primero/a
… the post office	… el correos/la oficina	**second**	segundo/a
	de correos	**third**	tercero/a
…the toilet	…el baño/aseo/servicios	**fifth**	quinto/a
Where does the bus to …	¿De dónde sale el autobús	**tenth**	décimo/a
leave from?	para …?	**Monday**	lunes
Is this the train for	¿Es este el tren para	**Tuesday**	martes
Seville?	Sevilla?	**Wednesday**	miércoles
I'd like a (return)	Quisiera un billete	**Thursday**	jueves
ticket to …	(de ida y vuelta) para …	**Friday**	viernes
What time does it leave	¿A qué hora sale	**Saturday**	sábado
(arrive in …)?	(llega a …)?	**Sunday**	domingo
What is there to eat?	¿Qué hay para comer?		

FOOD AND DRINK

"Quisiera uno así" ("I'd like one like that") can be an amazingly useful phrase.

BASICS

Aceite	Oil
Ajo	Garlic
Arroz	Rice
Azúcar	Sugar
Fruta	Fruit
Huevos	Eggs
Mantequilla	Butter
Pan	Bread
Pimienta	Pepper
Queso	Cheese
Sal	Salt
Verduras/Legumbres	Vegetables
Vinagre	Vinegar

RESTAURANT TERMS

Almuerzo	Lunch
Botella	Bottle
Menú	Set meal
La carta	Menu
Cena	Dinner
Cubierto	Set of cutlery
Cuchara	Spoon
Cuchillo	Knife
La cuenta	The bill
Desayuno	Breakfast
Mesa	Table
Tenedor	Fork
Vaso	Glass

MENU TERMS

a la brasa	(charcoal) grilled
a la gallego/a	Galician style
a la navarra	stuffed with ham
a la parilla/plancha	grilled
a la romana	fried in batter
a la rondeña	Ronda style
a la sal	baked in a salt crust
al ajillo	in garlic
al horno	baked
alioli	with mayonnaise
asado	roast
cazuela, cocido	stew
cocina casera	home-made
en salsa	in (usually tomato) sauce
escabeche/escabechado	pickled or marinated
frito	fried
guisado	casserole
ibérico	superior meat from Spanish black pigs
rehogado	baked

SOUPS AND STARTERS (*SOPAS Y ENTREMESES*)

Ajo blanco	Creamy gazpacho with garlic and almonds
Caldillo	Clear fish soup
Caldo verde/gallego	Thick, cabbage-based broth
Gazpacho	Chilled tomato, peppers and garlic soup
Migas	Fried breadcrumbs
Sopa de cocido	Meat soup
Sopa de gallina	Chicken soup
Sopa de mariscos	Seafood soup
Sopa de pasta	Noodle soup (*fideos*)
Sopa de pescado	Fish soup
Sopa de picadillo	Chicken and vegetable broth garnished with egg

SALAD (*ENSALADA*)

Arroz a la cubana	Rice with fried egg and home-made tomato sauce
Ensalada (mixta/verde)	(Mixed/green) salad
Pimientos rellenos	Stuffed peppers
Verduras con patatas	Boiled potatoes with greens

FISH (*PESCADOS*)

Anchoas	Anchovies (tinned)
Anguila	Eel
Angulas	Elvers (baby eel)
Atún	Tuna
Bacalao	Cod (often salt)
Besugo/Pargo	Red bream
Bonito	Tuna
Boquerones	Anchovies (fresh)
Chanquetes	Whitebait
Dorada	Gilt head bream
Lenguado	Sole
Lubina	Sea bass
Merluza	Hake
Mero	Grouper
Mojama	Salted blue-fin tuna
Pescadilla	Small whiting
Pez espada	Swordfish
Pulpo	Octopus
Rape	Monkfish
Rodaballo	Turbot
Salmón	Salmon
Salmonete	Mullet
Sardinas	Sardines
Trucha	Trout
Urta	Member of the bream family

SHELLFISH (*MARISCOS*)

Almejas	Clams
Calamares	Squid
Cangrejo	Crab
Centollo	Spider crab
Chipirones	Small squid
Cigalas	King prawns
Conchas finas	Large scallops
Erizo de mar	Sea urchin
Gambas	Prawns/shrimps
Langosta	Lobster
Langostinos	Giant king prawns
Mejillones	Mussels
Ostras	Oysters
Percebes	Goose barnacles
Puntillitas	Baby squid
Sepia	Cuttlefish
Vieiras/Conchas	Scallops
Zamburiñas	Baby clams

MEAT (*CARNE*) AND POULTRY (*AVES*)

Albóndigas	Meatballs
Cabra	Goat
Callos	Tripe
Carne de vaca	Beef
Cerdo	Pork
Cerdo Ibérico	Black pig pork
Chorizo	Spicy sausage
Choto/Cabrito	Kid
Chuletas	Chops
Ciervo/Venado	Deer/Venison
Cochinillo	Suckling pig
Codorniz	Quail
Conejo	Rabbit
Cordero	Lamb
Criadillas	Testicles
Escalopa	Escalope
Faisán	Pheasant
Hamburguesa	Hamburger
Hígado	Liver
Jabalí	Wild boar
Lengua	Tongue
Lomo	Loin (of pork)
Mollejas	Sweetbreads
Morcilla	Blood sausage
Pato	Duck
Pavo	Turkey
Perdiz	Partridge
Pollo	Chicken
Rabo de toro	Stewed bull's tail
Riñones	Kidneys
Salchicha	Sausage
Salchichón	Cured salami-type sausage
Sesos	Brains

Solomillo	Pork tenderloin
Ternera	Veal

VEGETABLES (*LEGUMBRES*)

Aguacate	Avocado
Ajo	Garlic
Alcachofas	Artichokes
Berenjena	Aubergine/eggplant
Calabaza	Pumpkin
Cebollas	Onions
Champiñones/Setas	Mushrooms
Coliflor	Cauliflower
Espárragos	Asparagus
Espinacas	Spinach
Garbanzos	Chick-peas
Guisantes	Peas
Habas	Broad beans
Judías blancas	Haricot beans
Judías verdes, rojas, negras	Green, red, black beans
Lechuga	Lettuce
Lentejas	Lentils
Nabos	Turnips
Palmitos	Palm hearts
Patatas (fritas)	Potatoes (chips/french fries)
Pepino	Cucumber
Pimientos	Peppers
Puerros	Leeks
Repollo	Cabbage
Setas	Mushrooms
Tomate	Tomato
Zanahoria	Carrot

RICE DISHES

Arroz a banda	Rice with seafood, the rice served separately
Arroz a la marinera	Paella: rice with seafood and saffron
Arroz negro	"Black rice", cooked with squid ink
Paella a la catalana	Mixed meat and seafood sometimes distinguished from a seafood paella by being called paella *a la valenciana*

DESSERTS (*POSTRES*)

Alfajores	Honey and almond pastries
Arroz con leche	Rice pudding
Crema catalana	Crème brûlée
Dulces	Tarts or cakes
Flan	Crème caramel
Helado	Ice cream

Melocotón en almíbar	Peaches in syrup
Miel	Honey
Nata	Whipped cream (topping)
Natillas	Custard
Pastel	Cake or pudding
Peras al vino	Pears cooked in wine
Pestiños	Anís or wine fritters
Polvorones	Almond cakes
Pudín	Pudding
Tarta de Santiago	Pastry tart with almond filling
Tocino de cielo	Andalucía's rich crème caramel
Yemas	Egg-yolk cakes
Yogur	Yogurt

FRUIT (*FRUTAS*)

Albaricoques	Apricots
Almendras	Almonds
Castañas	Chestnuts
Cerezas	Cherries
Chirimoyas	Custard apples
Chumbo	Prickly pear
Ciruelas	Plums, prunes
Dátiles	Dates
Fresas	Strawberries
Granada	Pomegranate
Higos	Figs
Limón	Lemon
Manzanas	Apples
Melocotón	Peach
Melón	Melon
Membrillo	Quince
Naranjas	Oranges
Nectarinas	Nectarines
Pera	Pear
Piña	Pineapple
Plátanos	Bananas
Pomelo	Grapefruit
Sandía	Watermelon
Uvas	Grapes

TAPAS AND SNACKS

Aceitunas	Olives
Albóndigas	Meatballs, usually in sauce
Anchoas	Anchovies
Banderilla	*Tapa* on a cocktail stick
Berberechos	Cockles
Boquerones	Fresh anchovies
Calamares a la romana	Squid, deep fried in rings
Calamares en su tinta	Squid in ink
Callos	Tripe
Caracoles	Snails, often served in a spicy/curry sauce

Caracolas	Whelks
Carne en salsa	Meat in tomato sauce
Cazón en adobo	Marinated and deep-fried dogfish
Champiñones	Mushrooms, usually fried in garlic
Chipirones	Whole baby squid
Chorizo	Spicy sausage
Cocido	Stew
Costillas	Spare ribs
Croqueta	Fish or chicken croquette
Empanadilla	Fish/meat pasty
Ensalada malagueña	Málaga salad with salt-cod, oranges and potato
Ensaladilla	Russian salad (diced vegetables in mayonnaise)
Escalibada	Aubergine (eggplant) and pepper salad
Espinacas con garbanzos	Spinach with chick-peas
Flamenquines	Ham or veal in breadcrumbs, deep fried
Gambas (al ajillo)	Shrimps (fried with garlic)
Habas con jamón	Broad beans with ham
Hígado	Liver
Huevo cocido	Hard-boiled egg
Jamón ibérico	Top-quality black pig mountain cured ham
Jamón serrano	Mountain- (or factory-) cured ham from white pigs
Jamón York	Regular ham
Judias	Beans
Mejillones	Mussels (either steamed, or served with diced tomatoes and onion)
Montadito	*Tapa* served on bread
Morcilla	Blood sausage (black pudding)
Navajas	Razor clams
Pan con tomate	Bread, rubbed with tomato and oil
Patatas alioli	Potatoes in garlic mayonnaise
Patatas/Papas a lo pobre	Potatoes cooked with garlic and parsley
Patatas bravas	Fried potato cubes topped with spicy sauce and mayonnaise
Pimientos	Peppers
Pincho moruno	Kebab
Pulpo	Octopus
Puntillitas	Deep-fried baby squid
Revuelto	Scrambled eggs
Riñones al Jerez	Kidneys in sherry

Salchichón	Cured sausage	**... (con gas)**	... (sparkling)
Sardinas	Sardines	**...(sin gas)**	... (still)
Sepia	Cuttlefish	**Leche**	Milk
Tabla	*Tapa* served on a wooden board	**Limonada**	Lemonade
		Zumo	Juice
Tortilla de camarones	Fritters with small prawns	**Horchata**	Tiger-nut drink
Tortilla española	Potato omelette		
Tortilla francesa	Plain omelette	**ALCOHOL**	
		Anís	Aniseed liqueur
DRINKS		**Brandy**	Coñac/brandy
Café	Coffee	**Cerveza**	Beer
Café solo	Espresso coffee	**Champán**	Champagne
Café con leche	White coffee	**Fino (de Jerez)**	Sherry
Descafeinado	Decaff	**Manzanilla**	Fino from Sanlúcar
Té	Tea	**Pacharán**	Sloes-based liqueur
Chocolate	Drinking chocolate	**Ron**	Rum
Agua	Water	**Vino**	Wine
Agua mineral	Mineral water		

GLOSSARY

Acequia irrigation channel.

Alameda park or tree-lined promenade.

Albariza type of soil in wine-growing zones with high chalk content enabling retention of moisture.

Alcalde mayor of town or village.

Alcazaba Moorish castle.

Alcázar Moorish fortified palace.

Almohads Muslims originally of Berber stock, who toppled the Almoravids and ruled Spain in the late twelfth and early thirteenth centuries.

Almoravids fanatical Berber dynasty from the Sahara who ruled much of Spain in the eleventh and twelfth centuries.

Artesonado wooden coffered ceiling of Moorish origin or inspiration.

Atalaya watchtower.

Autovía/autopista dual carriageway or highway/ motorway or expressway.

Ayuntamiento town hall (also Casa Consistorial).

Azulejos glazed ceramic tiles (originally blue – hence the name).

Balneario spa.

Barrio suburb or quarter.

Bodega cellar, wine bar or warehouse.

Bracero landless agricultural worker.

Calle street.

Camarín shrine (inside a church) with a venerated image.

Campiña flat stretch of farmland or countryside.

Cante jondo deeply felt flamenco song.

Capilla mayor chapel containing the high altar.

Capilla real royal chapel.

Carmen Granadan villa with garden.

Carretera highway or main road.

Cartuja Carthusian monastery.

Casa forestal woodland hunters' house/hotel.

Casa rural rural guesthouse or villa for rent.

Casa señorial/palacio aristocratic mansion.

Casco antiguo the old part of a town or city.

Casino social and gaming club.

Castillo castle.

Centro comercial shopping centre/mall.

Chiringuito beachfront restaurant.

Churrigueresque extreme form of Baroque art named after José Churriguera (1665–1725) and his extended family, its main exponents.

Ciudad town or city.

Ciudadela citadel.

Colegiata collegiate (large parish) church.

Comunidad autónoma autonomous region with significant powers of self-government.

Convento monastery or convent.

Converso Jew who converted to Christianity.

Copa/copas alcoholic drink(s).

Coro central part of church built for the choir.

Coro alto raised choir, often above west door of a church.

Corral type of patio or yard.

Correos post office.

Corrida de toros bullfight.

Cortes Spanish parliament in Madrid.

Cortijo rural farmhouse in Andalucía.

Coto de caza hunting reserve.

Cuesta slope/hill.

Cueva cave.

Custodia large receptacle or monstrance for Eucharist wafers.

Desamortización (disentailment) nineteenth-century expropriation of church buildings and lands.

Duende to have soul (in flamenco).

Embalse artificial lake, reservoir or dam.

Ermita hermitage.

Esparto grass used for mats, window blinds and olive presses.

Feria annual fair.

Finca farm.

Fogón stove.

Gitano gypsy.

Huerta vegetable garden.

Isabelline ornamental form of late Gothic developed during the reign of Isabel and Fernando.

Jarra wine jug or pitcher.

Jornalero landless agricultural day-labourer.

Judería Jewish quarter.

Juerga (gypsy) shindig.

Junta de Andalucía government of the Autonomous Region of Andalucía.

Latifundio large estate.

Locutorio telephone office.

Lonja stock exchange building.

Marismas marshes.

Matanza pig slaughter.

Medina Moorish town.

Mercado market.

Mesón traditional restaurant or inn.

Mezquita mosque.

Mihrab prayer niche of Moorish mosque facing towards Mecca.

Mirador viewing point.

Monasterio monastery or convent.

Morisco Muslim Spaniard subject to medieval Christian rule – and nominally baptized.

Movida the (nightlife) scene; where the action is.

Mozárabe Christian subject to medieval Moorish rule; normally allowed freedom of worship.

Mozarabic the architectural style evolved by Christians under Arab domination.

Mudéjar Muslim Spaniard subject to medieval Christian rule, but retaining Islamic worship; most commonly a term applied to architecture which includes buildings built by Moorish craftsmen for the Christian rulers and later designs influenced by the Moors. The 1890s–1930s saw a Mudéjar revival, blended with Art Nouveau and Art Deco forms.

Palacio aristocratic mansion.

Panadería bakery.

Pantano reservoir held by a dam.

Parador luxury state-run hotel, often converted from minor monument.

Parroquia parish church.

Paseo promenade; also the evening stroll thereon.

Paso float bearing tableau carried in Semana Santa processions.

Patio inner courtyard.

Piscina swimming pool.

Plateresco/plateresque elaborately decorative Renaissance style, the sixteenth-century successor of Isabelline forms. Named for its resemblance to silversmiths' work (*platería*).

Playa beach.

Plaza square.

Plaza de toros bullring.

Plaza mayor a town or city's main square regardless of its name.

Posada old name for an inn.

Pueblo village or town.

Puerta gateway, also mountain pass.

Puerto port.

Rambla dry riverbed.

Reconquista the Christian reconquest of Moorish Spain.

Reja iron screen or grille, often fronting a window or guarding a chapel.

Retablo carved or painted altarpiece.

Río river.

Rociero adhering to the traditions of the El Rocío pilgrimage.

Rococo late-Baroque style with a profusion of rock-like forms, scrolls and crimped shells. From the French *rocaille* – "rock-work".

Romería religious procession to a rural shrine.

Sacristía, sagrario sacristy or sanctuary of a church.

Sacristía (ii) wine cellar in sherry bodega.

Sagrario tabernacle or side chapel.

Saeta passionate flamenco song in praise of the Virgin and Christ.

Sebka decorative brickwork developed by the Almohads (eg, Giralda).

Semana Santa Holy Week, celebrated throughout Andalucía with elaborate processions.

Señoritismo behaving in a condescending manner; generally applied to rich landowners.

Sevillana rhythmic flamenco dance.

Sierra mountain range.

Sillería choir stall.

Solar aristocratic town mansion.

Solera blending system for sherry and brandy.

Tablao flamenco show.

Taifa small Moorish kingdom, many of which emerged after the disintegration of the Córdoba caliphate.

Tajo gorge.

Tetería Arabic tearoom.

Trascoro end-wall of the choir.

Torno dumbwaiter used by convents to sell their cakes and pastries.

Urbanización residential housing estate.

Vega cultivated fertile plain.

Venta roadside inn.

Yeso/yesería plaster/plasterwork.

POLITICAL PARTIES AND ACRONYMS

ETA Basque terrorist organization.

Falange Franco's old fascist party; now officially defunct.

Fuerza Nueva Descendants of the above, also on the way out.

IR Izquierda Republicana, left-wing republican party.

IU Izquierda Unida, broad-left alliance of communists and others.

MC Movimiento Comunista (Communist Movement), small radical offshoot of the PCE.

OTAN NATO.

PA Partido Andalucista, the Andalucian Nationalist Party.

PASOC Partido de Acción Socialista, "traditional" socialist group to the left of the PSOE.

PCE Partido Comunista de España (Spanish Communist Party).

PP Partido Popular, the right-wing party led by Mariano Rajoy; currently the government party in the Cortes.

PSOE Partido Socialista Obrero Español (Spanish Socialist Workers' Party). Currently the main opposition party led by Alfredo Pérez Rubalcaba.

UGT Unión General de Trabajadores, Spain's most powerful trade union.

Small print and index

Rough Guide credits

Editors: Samantha Cook, Gavin Thomas
Layout: Nikhil Agarwal
Cartography: Swati Handoo
Picture editor: Emily Taylor
Proofreader: Stewart Wild
Managing editor: Keith Drew
Assistant editor: Madhavi Singh
Production: Rebecca Short
Cover design: Nicole Newman, Rhiannon Furbear,
Nikhil Agarwal

Editorial assistant: Eleanor Aldridge
Senior pre-press designer: Dan May
Design director: Scott Stickland
Travel publisher: Joanna Kirby
Digital travel publisher: Peter Buckley
Reference director: Andrew Lockett
Operations coordinator: Becky Doyle
Publishing director (Travel): Clare Currie
Commercial manager: Gino Magnotta
Managing director: John Duhigg

Publishing information

This seventh edition published May 2012 by
Rough Guides Ltd,
80 Strand, London WC2R 0RL
11, Community Centre, Panchsheel Park,
New Delhi 110017, India
Distributed by the Penguin Group
Penguin Books Ltd,
80 Strand, London WC2R 0RL
Penguin Group (USA)
375 Hudson Street, NY 10014, USA
Penguin Group (Australia)
250 Camberwell Road, Camberwell,
Victoria 3124, Australia
Penguin Group (NZ)
67 Apollo Drive, Mairangi Bay, Auckland 1310,
New Zealand
Penguin Group (South Africa)
Block D, Rosebank Office Park, 181 Jan Smuts Avenue,
Parktown North, Gauteng, South Africa 2193
Rough Guides is represented in Canada by Tourmaline
Editions Inc. 662 King Street West, Suite 304, Toronto,
Ontario M5V 1M7
Printed in Singapore by Toppan Security Printing Pte. Ltd.

Help us update

We've gone to a lot of effort to ensure that the seventh
edition of **The Rough Guide to Andalucía** is accurate
and up-to-date. However, things change – places get
"discovered", opening hours are notoriously fickle,
restaurants and rooms raise prices or lower standards. If
you feel we've got it wrong or left something out, we'd like
to know, and if you can remember the address, the price,
the hours, the phone number, so much the better.

Please send your comments with the subject line
"Rough Guide Andalucía Update" to ✉ mail@uk
.roughguides.com. We'll credit all contributions and send a
copy of the next edition (or any other Rough Guide if you
prefer) for the very best emails.

Find more travel information, connect with fellow
travellers and book your trip on ⊕ roughguides.com

ABOUT THE AUTHORS

Mark Ellingham founded Rough Guides in 1981 – and co-wrote the *Rough Guide to Spain*, the second title in the series, the following year. He has spent time in Andalucía most years since then and his small press, Sort Of Books, publishes Chris Stewart's bestselling stories set in the Alpujarras, south of Granada.

Geoff Garvey is a writer and journalist and lives in a mountain village in the province of Cádiz. Favourite activities when not blinking at a computer screen include hiking, long *venta* lunches, following political scandals in the papers and feeding neighbour's dog Tobi his daily *ración* of chorizo. He also co-authors the *Rough Guide to Crete*.

Acknowledgements

On our seventh edition grateful thanks must once again go to Angela García and Josefina del Castillo for help in Almería province. Many thanks also to Pau for her help in Seville and to Chris and Ana Stewart for the lowdown on the western Alpujarras. We'd also like to say *"muchísimas gracias"* to Pam for all her help in Granada and also to Cat Gaa for sterling work on covering Seville nightlife. We are also indebted to Pedro Martín and Ana Fernández at the Alhambra, Granada; Pepa Babot at the Museo Picasso Málaga; Cristina Botija at the Museo Carmen Thyssen, Málaga; and Manuel Roca Rodríguez at the Parque de las Ciencias, Granada. A "dank je wel, schat" also goes from Geoff to Han for unstinting help in getting the job done.

Valuable assistance on the ground was also rendered by Christine and Jean Hofer in El Chorro, Paco Moyano and Lola Maiztegui in Alhama de Granada, Bienvenido Luque in Málaga, Julie Hetherington in Andújar, James Stuart and Carmen Atkins García in Vejer, Vicente Sousa in Aracena,

Jean-Claude Juston in Mecina Fondales, Rosella Macchi Parmiter in Macharaviaya, Gina de los Santos in Seville, Juan Carlos Ábalos and Clive Jarman in Zuheros, Antonio Gallego in Alcalá de los Gazules, Elma Thompson in Nerja, Francisco Javier Redondo in Córdoba, Rosa González in Conil, Raquel Ahedo in La Linea, Juan Carlos Raths Aznar in Mojácar, Anton Peer in Segura de la Sierra, Beatriz Cuevas in Osuna, María Maldonado in Granada, Pepe Morales in Punta Úmbria and last but by no means least Pasqual Rovira and Quica Caballero Mata at the donkey sanctuary in Rute.

Special thanks are due to Tony Wailey for Civil War background, Bienvenido Martínez Navarro for updates on excavations at Orce, and Mark Honigsbaum for surfing tips. We were greatly helped with advice on birdspotting from Huw Morgan and Anthony Winchester. We would also like to thank Ignacio Vasallo and Charo Lapeyra Ahedo at the Spanish Tourist Office in London.

Readers' letters

Thanks to all readers who have taken the time to write with comments and suggestions (and apologies if we've inadvertently omitted or misspelt anyone's name):

Phil Andre, Louise Ansari, Helen Atkinson, Bill Bain, Samantha Barton, Peter Bennett, Tony Bishop, Frances Beresford, Jimena Blázquez, Tobias Boese, Nancy Brinton, Margaret Bullows, Ian Burrell, Nicholas Butcher, Iain Campbell Aird, Helena Carley, Mike Coleman, Noel Cooper, David Cox, Thomas Dougan, Jack Edwards, Huw Evans, Kay Farrell, Linda Fletcher, Michael Ford, Emma Fowler, Audrie & Barrie Gant, Bertrand García, Andy Gemmell, Edward Gold, Lisa Gordon, Sean Gostage, Katie Griffiths, Paul Guest, Dennis Hill, Tony Hodson, Peter Household, Sophia Hughes, Alice Kildsgaard, Linda Kimpe, Marjan Kuyken, David Lanfear,

Linda Lashford, Brian Lawson, Jenny Lunnon, Sheila MacDonald, Patricia McHugo, Isabel Martínez, Paul Mason, John & Rose Meech, Martin Menski, Alison Mudge, Joanna Mudie, Marie Murphy, Tim Murray-Walker, Caroline Nash, Vincent Nordell, Beatriz Pérez, Michael Pollit, Jordi Pons, Eliza Pozzi, Sue Reeves, Tim Renwick, Harry Shelton, Joanne V. Small, Vince Smeaton, Andy Smith, Marian Smith, Nick Spinks, John Stein, Kate Summers, Celia Taylor, Hilary Taylor, Rocío Martín-Górriz Trillo, Luís Velasco, Jan Voisey, Alison Waites, Elizabeth Washburn, John White, Mark Wilcox, Linda Woodhouse, Derek Workman.

Photo credits

All photos © Rough Guides except the following:
(Key: t-top; c-centre; b-bottom; l-left; r-right)

Index

Maps are marked in grey

Map symbols

The symbols below are used on maps throughout the book

✈	Airport	♦	Place of interest	⊠	Entrance gate	▦	Building
P	Parking	⊤	Fountain	▲	Mountain peak	✝	Church
✉	Post office	⍾	Lighthouse	◠	Cave	⬚	Park
ⓘ	Information office	⚅	Viewpoint	›‹	Pass	▢	Beach
⊞	Hospital	⊙	Statue	⛰	Cliff	⊟	Cemetery
☾	Telephone office	♖	Mosque	☽	Sand dunes		
@	Internet access	✡	Synagogue	∴	Ruins		

Listings key

■ Accommodation

● Restaurant/café/tapas bar

■ Nightlife/flamenco

ROUGH GUIDES

GET LOST

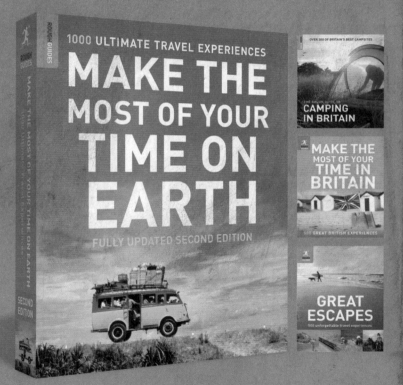

1000 ULTIMATE TRAVEL EXPERIENCES

MAKE THE MOST OF YOUR TIME ON EARTH

FULLY UPDATED SECOND EDITION

ROUGH GUIDES

SECOND EDITION

OVER 300 OF BRITAIN'S BEST CAMPSITES

THE ROUGH GUIDE TO
CAMPING IN BRITAIN

MAKE THE
MOST OF YOUR
TIME IN
BRITAIN

GREAT BRITISH EXPERIENCES

**GREAT
ESCAPES**
500 unforgettable travel experiences

ESCAPE THE EVERYDAY
WITH OVER 700 **BOOKS**, **EBOOKS** AND **APPS**
YOU'RE SURE TO BE INSPIRED

Start your journey at **roughguides.com**
MAKE THE MOST OF YOUR TIME ON EARTH™